YEARBOOK OF AMERICAN & CANADIAN CHURCHES 1990

Fifty-eighth issue

Annual

YEARBOOK OF AMERICAN & CANADIAN CHURCHES 1990

Constant H. Jacquet, Jr., Editor

Alice Jones, Editorial Associate

Prepared and edited in the Communication Unit
of the National Council of the Churches of Christ
in the U.S.A., 475 Riverside Drive, New York, NY 10115

**Published and Distributed
by Abingdon Press
Nashville**

Printed in the United States of America
ISBN 0-687-46645-8
ISSN 0195-9034
Library of Congress catalog card number: 16-5726

PREVIOUS ISSUES

INTRODUCTION

This edition of the **Yearbook of American and Canadian Churches** is the 58th in a series that began in 1916. A listing of years of publication, titles, and editors appears under the heading "Previous Issues." Although the title of the book refers to "churches," it should be stressed that the **Yearbook** contains information on many different faiths, not only Christian bodies, which the term *churches* implies.

Without the cooperation of many hundreds of people in the United States and Canada a reference volume of this complexity and scope could not be produced. The editor thanks all who have made this edition possible by supplying information about their organizations, correcting directory forms, filling out statistical reports, providing articles and other materials, and passing on innovative suggestions about how to improve the **Yearbook.**

The **Yearbook** has been a binational volume since 1972 and has a Canadian Advisory Committee which meets in Toronto annually to advise the editor on the Canadian sections of the book, in light of recent developments in organized religion in that country, and to make suggestions on deletions and additions. To these Canadian friends and advisors, the editor extends thanks.

Special recognition is due Alice Jones, editorial associate, who has worked on twenty editions of the **Yearbook.** She has made valuable contributions to this edition by her careful and patient work.

There being no established legal definitions of churches, clergy, or religion, these concepts are always subjective. The constitutional separation of church and state has left religious organizations basically free from guidance, classification, and regulation. Religious bodies, though incorporated legally in a state in the U.S. or in a province in Canada, determine their own institutions, doctrines, and standards of conduct.

Religious life in the United States and Canada is quite complex. The dynamic nature of these two nations, the patterns of immigration, the exchange of ideas and movements across the border, religious liberty, and the high degree of affluence provide conditions supporting the development of religious organizations. This has led to the formation of a bewildering diversity of sects and cults, primarily in the U.S. We do not attempt to list these bodies in the **Yearbook.** Many other small religious bodies, numbering in the hundreds, have, of necessity, also been excluded from the listings. Other sources of information exist on many of these groups.

What we do attempt to describe and record are those major religious bodies in the United States and Canada having the great majority of churches, clergy, and membership. The editor will be grateful for knowledge of any significant omissions that fall within the categories now covered in the various directory sections in this volume.

Which religious bodies are included in each edition of the **Yearbook of American and Canadian Churches** must, for reasons stated above, be an editorial matter based upon subjective criteria to some extent, and exclusion from the **Yearbook** should not necessarily be interpreted by readers as an adverse reflection on the nature, purpose, or reputation of any religious body.

Constant H. Jacquet, Jr.
Editor

A GUIDE FOR THE USER OF CHURCH STATISTICS

This guide is placed in a prominent position in each edition of the **Yearbook** to emphasize the fact that church statistics, like those of many other groups, vary greatly in quality and reliability. Therefore, necessary qualifications concerning them must be stated clearly and without reservation.

This year in Section III, the Statistical and Historical Section, the **Yearbook of American and Canadian Churches** reports data from 219 U. S. religious bodies. Of these, 106 report current data—that is, data for the years 1989 or 1988. Current data, comprising 48.4 percent of all reports, account for 74.0 percent of recorded membership. Concerning the denominations gathering statistics, some computerize data and have an accurate bank of information on cards or tape. Perhaps the largest group of denominations still gathers statistics by conventional hand-tabulation methods. Quite a few bodies are still operating on the basis of "educated guesses" in many statistical areas.

In addition to these general observations, four major qualifications should be made:

1) Church statistics are always incomplete, and they pass through many hands, some skilled and some not so skilled, and come up through many channels in church bureaucratic structures.

2) Church statistics are not always comparable. Definitions of membership, and of other important categories, vary from denomination to denomination. Jewish statistics are estimates of the number of individuals in households where one or more Jews reside and, therefore, include non-Jews living in these households as the result of intermarriage. The total number of persons in Jewish households is estimated to be 7 percent larger than the number of Jewish persons residing in these households. It should be noted that estimates of numbers of Jews have nothing to do with membership in synagogues. Roman Catholics and some Protestant bodies count all baptized persons, including children, as members. Other Protestant bodies include as members those who make a declaration of faith and become baptized. This can happen as early as age 9.

3) Church statistical data reported in the **Yearbook** are not for a single year. Not only do the reporting years differ from denomination to denomination, but some bodies do not report regularly. Therefore the reports based on data for the year 1987 or earlier are "non-current" reports. Attempts to combine current and non-current data for purposes of interpretation or projection will lead to difficulties.

4) Many of the more important types of statistical data are simply not available for a large group of denominations. Records of church attendance are not universally kept, and there are no socioeconomic data generally available. Statistics of members' participation in church activities and programs do not exist.

Statistics form an important part of church life and are necessary for the sound development of planning and program. Therefore strong efforts should be made in each denomination to upgrade the quality of its statistics. Interdenominational cooperation leading toward standardization of categories and sharing of techniques, it is hoped, will continue to grow. New ways of adapting to church needs and programs the data gathered by the U. S. Bureau of the Census must be discovered and utilized. The use of survey methods to obtain valuable socioreligious information about American religious life should be encouraged and expanded.

CONTENTS

I

A CALENDAR FOR CHURCH USE

1990–1993

This Calendar presents for a four-year period the major days of religious observance for Christians, Jews, and Muslims; and, within the Christian Community, major dates observed by Roman Catholic, Orthodox, Episcopal, and Lutheran Churches. Within each of these communions many other days of observance, such as saints' days, exist, but only those regarded major are listed. Thus, for example, for the Roman Catholic Church mainly the "solemnities" are listed. Dates of interest to many Protestant communions are also included.

Many days of observance, such as Christmas and Easter, do not carry the list of communions observing them since it is assumed that practically all Christian bodies do. In certain cases, a religious observance will be named differently by various communions and this is noted.

In the Orthodox dates, immovable observances are listed in accordance with the Gregorian calendar. Movable dates (those depending on the date of Easter) will differ often from Western dates, since Pascha (Easter) in the Orthodox communions does not always fall on the same day as in the Western churches. For Orthodox churches that use the old Julian calendar, observances are held thirteen days later than listed here.

Ecumenical dates, such as Week of Prayer for Christian Unity and World Communion Sunday, are also included.

For Jews and Muslims, who follow differing lunar calendars, the dates of major observances are translated into Gregorian dates. For Muslim observances, the festivals are dated according to astronomical calculations that have been published in Paris, not the United States, and this could lead to slight variations. Since the actual beginning of a new month in the Islamic calendar is determined by the appearance of the new moon, the corresponding dates given here on the Gregorian calendar may vary slightly. It is also possible for a festival to occur twice in the same Gregorian year. Only 'Id al-Fitr and the 'Id al-Adha are religious holidays that are prescribed by the texts of Islam. Other Islamic dates are nevertheless key moments in the lives of Muslim believers. Jewish observances begin at sundown of the day previous to those listed below and end at sundown of the last day.

(Note: In the Calendar, "RC" stands for Roman Catholic, "O" for Orthodox, "E" for Episcopal, "L" for Lutheran, "ECU" for Ecumenical.)

	1990	1991	1992	1993
1st Sunday of Advent......................................	Dec 2	Dec 1	Nov 29	Nov 28
Feast Day of St. Andrew the Apostle (RC, O, E, L)............	Nov 30	Nov 30	Nov 30	Nov 30
Immaculate Conception of the Blessed Virgin Mary (RC)......	Dec 8	Dec 8	Dec 8	Dec 8
1st Day of Hanukkah (Jewish, 8 days)............................	Dec 12	Dec 2	Dec 20	Dec 9
4th Sunday of Advent (Sunday before Christmas)................	Dec 23	Dec 22	Dec 20	Dec 19
Christmas...	Dec 25	Dec 25	Dec 25	Dec 25
New Year's Day (RC—Solemnity of Mary; O—Circumcision of Jesus Christ; E—Feast of the Holy Name; L—Name of Jesus)...	Jan 1	Jan 1	Jan 1	Jan 1
Epiphany (Armenian Christmas)...................................	Jan 6	Jan 6	Jan 6	Jan 6
Feast Day of St. John the Baptist (O).............................	Jan 7	Jan 7	Jan 7	Jan 7
1st Sunday After Epiphany (Feast of the Baptism of Our Lord)...	Jan 7	Jan 13	Jan 12	Jan 10
Transfiguration of the Lord (L)	Jan 7	Jan 13	Jan 12	Jan 10
Week of Prayer for Christian Unity (ECU)........................	Jan 18 to 25	Jan 18 to 25	Jan 18 to 25	Jan 18 to 25
Week of Prayer for Christian Unity, Canada (ECU).............	Jan 21 to 28	Jan 20 to 27	Jan 19 to 26	Jan 17 to 24
Ecumenical Sunday (ECU)...	Jan 28	Jan 20	Jan 19	Jan 24
Presentation of Jesus in the Temple (O—The Meeting of Our Lord and Savior Jesus Christ).......................................	Feb 2	Feb 2	Feb 2	Feb 2
Brotherhood Week (Interfaith).....................................	Feb 18 to 24	Feb 17 to 23	Feb 16 to 22	Feb 21 to 27
Last Sunday After Epiphany......................................	Feb 25	Feb 10	Mar 1	Feb 21
Ash Wednesday (Western churches).................................	Feb 28	Feb 13	Mar 4	Feb 24
Easter Lent Begins (Eastern Orthodox)............................	Feb 26	Feb 18	Mar 10	Mar 1
World Day of Prayer (ECU)...	Mar 2	Mar 1	Mar 6	Mar 5
Purim (Jewish)..	Mar 11	Feb 28	Mar 19	Mar 7
Joseph, Husband of Mary (RC, E, L)...............................	Mar 19	Mar 19	Mar 19	Mar 19
The Annunciation (RC, O, E, L)....................................	Mar 25	Mar 25	Mar 25	Mar 25
'Id al-Fitr (Festival of the End of Ramadan, celebrated on the first day of the month of Shawwal).....................................	Apr 28	Apr 17	Apr 5	Mar 25
First Day of the Month of Ramadan...............................	Mar 29	Mar 18	Mar 6	Feb 23
Holy Week (Western Churches)....................................	Apr 8 to 14	Mar 24 to 30	Apr 12 to 18	Apr 4 to 10
Holy Week (Eastern Orthodox).....................................	Apr 8 to 14	Mar 31 to 6	Apr 19 to 25	Apr 11 to 17
Sunday of the Passion (Palm Sunday) (Western churches)......	Apr 8	Mar 24	Apr 12	Apr 4
Palm Sunday (Eastern Orthodox)..................................	Apr 8	Mar 31	Apr 19	Apr 11
Holy Thursday (Western churches)................................	Apr 12	Mar 28	Apr 16	Apr 8
Holy Thursday (Eastern Orthodox)................................	Apr 12	Apr 4	Apr 23	Apr 15

1

	1990	1991	1992	1993
Good Friday (Friday of the Passion of Our Lord) (Western churches)	Apr 13	Mar 29	Apr 17	Apr 9
Holy (Good) Friday, Burial of Jesus Christ (Eastern Orthodox)	Apr 13	Apr 5	Apr 24	Apr 16
Easter (Western churches)	Apr 15	Mar 31	Apr 19	Apr 11
1st Day of Passover (Jewish, 8 days)	Apr 10 to 11	Mar 30 to 31	Apr 18 to 19	Apr 6 to 7
Pascha (Eastern Orthodox Easter)	Apr 15	Apr 7	Apr 26	Apr 18
National Day of Prayer	May 3	May 2	May 7	May 6
May Fellowship Day (ECU)	May 4	May 3	May 1	May 7
Rural Life Sunday (ECU)	May 13	May 12	May 10	May 9
Ascension Day (Western churches)	May 24	May 9	May 28	May 20
Ascension Day (Eastern Orthodox)	May 24	May 16	June 4	May 27
1st Day of Shavuot (Jewish, 2 days)	May 30 to 31	May 19 to 20	June 7 to 8	May 26 to 27
Pentecost (Whitsunday) (Western churches)	June 3	May 19	June 7	May 30
Pentecost (Eastern Orthodox)	June 3	May 26	June 14	June 6
Visitation of the Blessed Virgin Mary (RC, E, L)	May 31	May 31	May 31	May 31
Holy Trinity (RC, E, L)	June 10	May 26	June 14	June 6
Corpus Christi (RC)	June 17	June 2	June 21	June 13
Nativity of St. John the Baptist (RC, E, L)	June 24	June 24	June 24	June 24
Sacred Heart of Jesus (RC)	June 22	June 7	June 26	June 20
Saint Peter and Saint Paul, Apostles (RC, O, E, L)	June 29	June 29	June 29	June 29
Feast of the Twelve Apostles of Christ (O)	June 30	June 30	June 30	June 30
'Id al-Adha (Festival of Sacrifice at time of annual pilgrimage to Mecca)	July 5	July 5	June 12	June 1
First Day of the Month of Muharram (beginning of Muslim liturgical year)	July 24	July 13	July 2	June 21
Transfiguration of the Lord (RC, O, E)	Aug 6	Aug 6	Aug 6	Aug 6
Feast of the Blessed Virgin Mary (E; RC—Assumption of Blessed Mary, the Virgin; O—Falling Asleep (Dormition) of the Blessed Virgin Mary; L—Mary, Mother of Our Lord)	Aug 15	Aug 15	Aug 15	Aug 15
The Birth of the Blessed Virgin (RC, O)	Sept 8	Sept 8	Sept 8	Sept 8
1st Day of Rosh Hashanah (Jewish, 2 days)	Sept 20 to Oct 21	Sept 9 to 10	Sept 28 to 29	Sept 16 to 17
Holy Cross Day (O—The Adoration of the Holy Cross; RC—Triumph of the Cross)	Sept 14	Sept 14	Sept 14	Sept 14
Yom Kippur (Jewish)	Sept 29	Sept 18	Oct 7	Sept 25
1st Day of Sukkot (Jewish, 7 days)	Oct 4 to 5	Sept 23 to 24	Oct 12 to 13	Sept 30 to Oct 1
World Communion Sunday (ECU)	Oct 7	Oct 6	Oct 4	Oct 3
Mawlid al-Nabi (anniversary of Prophet Muhammad's birthday)	Oct 3	Sept 22	Sept 11	Aug 31
Laity Sunday (ECU)	Oct 14	Oct 13	Oct 11	Oct 10
Shemini Atzeret (Jewish)	Oct 11	Sept 30	Oct 19	Oct 7
Simhat Torah (Jewish)	Oct 12	Oct 1	Oct 20	Oct 8
Thanksgiving Day (Canada)	Oct 8	Oct 14	Oct 12	Oct 11
Reformation Sunday (L)	Oct 28	Oct 27	Oct 25	Oct 31
Reformation Day (L)	Oct 31	Oct 31	Oct 31	Oct 31
All Saints (RC, E, L)	Nov 1	Nov 1	Nov 1	Nov 1
World Community Day (ECU)	Nov 2	Nov 1	Nov 6	Nov 5
Stewardship Day (ECU)	Nov 11	Nov 10	Nov 8	Nov 14
Bible Sunday (ECU)	Nov 18	Nov 17	Nov 15	Nov 21
Last Sunday After Pentecost (RC, L—Feast of Christ the King)	Nov 25	Nov 24	Nov 22	Nov 21
Presentation of the Blessed Virgin Mary in the Temple (also Presentation of the Theotokos) (O)	Nov 21	Nov 21	Nov 21	Nov 21
Thanksgiving Sunday (U.S.)	Nov 18	Nov 24	Nov 22	Nov 21
Thanksgiving Day (U.S.)	Nov 22	Nov 28	Nov 26	Nov 25

A TABLE OF DATES AHEAD

The following table indicates the dates of Easter and other important festival days during the next few years. It also indicates the number of Sundays after Epiphany and after Pentecost for each year of the period. Easter may come as early as March 22 or as late as April 25, thus bringing a wide variation in the number of Sundays included in certain of the Christian seasons.

Year	Sundays After Epiphany	Ash Wednesday	Western Easter	Pascha (Orthodox Easter)	Pentecost	Sundays After Pentecost	First Sunday of Advent
1990	8	Feb 28	Apr 15	Apr 15	June 3	25	Dec 2
1991	5	Feb 13	Mar 31	Apr 7	May 19	27	Dec 1
1992	8	Mar 4	Apr 19	Apr 26	June 7	24	Nov 29
1993	7	Feb 24	Apr 11	Apr 18	May 30	25	Nov 28

II
DIRECTORIES

1. UNITED STATES COOPERATIVE ORGANIZATIONS, NATIONAL

NATIONAL COUNCIL OF THE CHURCHES OF CHRIST IN THE UNITED STATES OF AMERICA

The National Council of the Churches of Christ in the United States of America is a community of Christian communions which, in response to the gospel revealed in the Scriptures, confess Jesus Christ, the incarnate Word of God, as Savior and Lord. These communions covenant with one another to manifest ever more fully the unity of the Church. Relying upon the transforming power of the Holy Spirit, the Council brings these communions into common mission, serving in all creation to the glory of God.

Semiannual Meetings of the General Board
Pittsburgh, PA, May 16-18, 1990
Portland, OR, Nov. 14-16, 1990

Offices at 475 Riverside Dr., New York, NY 10115
except as stated below.
Tel. (212)870-2200

(Note: During 1990, the National Council of the Churches of Christ in the U.S.A. will be involved in a restructuring and related reorganization of personnel. It is expected that this process will be completed at the meeting of the NCC Governing Board in Portland, Oregon, Nov. 14-16, 1990. The following is the tentative structure of the Council as of February, 1990.)

GENERAL OFFICERS

President, Very Rev. Leonid Kishkovsky
President-Elect, Rev. Syngman Rhee
Vice-Presidents, Dr. I. Carleton Faulk; JoAnne Kagiwada; Dr. Jane Cary Peck; Dr. William G. Rusch; Dr. Reuben A. Sheares, II.
Secretary, Rt. Rev. David B. Reed
Treasurer, Joyce D. Sohl
Program Unit Chairpersons: Rev. Roland Pfile (Church and Society); Elaine M. Gasser (Education and Ministry); Rev. Syngman Rhee (Overseas Ministries); Bishop Philip R. Cousin (Church World Service); Dr. Beverly J. Chain (Communication Unit); Rev. Dr. Melanie May (Faith and Order); Rev. Jeanne Audrey Powers (Regional and Local Ecumenism); Rev. E. Wayne Antworth (Stewardship); Consuelo Urquiza (Justice and Liberation); Dr. Belle Miller McMaster (International Affairs)

ELECTED STAFF
OFFICE OF THE GENERAL SECRETARY

Gen. Sec., James A. Hamilton
Assoc. Gen. Sec. for Public Policy and Legal Affairs,

Dir. of the Washington Office, Mary Anderson Cooper, 110 Maryland Ave., NE, Washington, DC 20002. Tel. (202) 544-2350.CWS/LWR Rep. for Development Plng., Rev. Paul L. Minear
Assoc. Gen. Sec. for Unity and Relationships, Rev. Eileen W. Lindner
Asst. Gen. Sec. for Fincl. Develop., Sande Elinson

DISCIPLESHIP AND COMMUNICATION

Communication

Actg. Assoc. Gen. Sec. for Communication, Rev. J. Martin Bailey
Dir., for Media Resources, Rev. David W. Pomeroy
Assoc. Gen. Sec. for Media and Member Services, rev. J. Martin Bailey
Dir., News Services, Carol Fouke
Dir., Interpretation Resources, Sarah Vilankulu
Staff Assoc., Information Services and ed., *Yearbook of American and Canadian Churches,* Constant H. Jacquet, Jr.

Education and Ministry

Assoc. Gen. Sec. for Education and Ministry, Rev. Arthur O. Van Eck

EDUCATION FOR CHRISTIAN LIFE AND MISSION

Exec., Dorothy R. Savage
Staff Administrator, Cmte. on Uniform Lessons, Rev. Arthur O. Van Eck
Dir., Commission on Family Ministries and Human Sexuality, Dorothy R. Savage
Dir., Adult Ministries, Dorothy R. Savage

EDUCATION FOR MISSION

Exec. Dir., Edu. for Mission and Exec. Dir., Friendship Press, Audrey Miller; Ed., Friendship Press, Carol Ames; Audio-Visual Coord., Rev. David W. Pomeroy

ECUMENICAL MINISTRIES IN EDUCATION

Staff, Rev. John Cato
Dir. of Adult Literacy, Margaret Shafer

PROFESSIONAL CHURCH LEADERSHIP
Staff Assoc., Peggy L. Shriver
Women in Ministry, Elizabeth Verdesi

BIBLE TRANSLATION AND UTILIZATION
Staff: Rev. Arthur O. Van Eck

Evangelization

Staff, _____

Stewardship

Asst. Gen. Sec. for Stewardship, Rev. Ronald E. Vallet

Worship

Staff, _____

INTERNATIONAL MINISTRIES AND SERVICE

Church World Service

Actg. Assoc. Gen. Sec. and Actg. Exec. Dir. for Church World Service, Ann N. Beardslee
Actg. Assoc. Exec. Dir./Development Prog. Dir., Rev. Lowell H. Brown
Dir., Disaster Response, Kenlynn Schroeder
Dir., Overseas Personnel, Rev. Paul W. Yount, Jr.
Dir., Material Resources, Soon-Young Hahn
Dir. Immigration and Refugees, Dale Stuart DeHaan; Assoc. Dir. for Adm., John W. Backer
Exec. Dir., Global Education, Loretta Whalen, 2115 N. Charles St., Baltimore, MD 21218. Tel. (301)727-6106
CWS/Elkhart: mailing Address, CWS, P.O. Box 968, Elkhart, IN 46515. Tel. (219)364-3102, Actg. Dir., Educ. and Fund-Raising Prog., Douglas R. Beane; Dir., Ofc. of Cmty. Outreach, _____; Dir., Creative Services, Linda Robbins, 330 W. Lexington, Elkhart, IN 46515. Tel. (219)264-3102

Overseas Ministries

Actg. Assoc. Gen. Sec. For Overseas Ministries, Dr. L. Newton Thurber Financial Management Dir., Howard Yost

SPECIALIZED MINISTRIES

Agricultural Missions:
Dir., J. Benton Rhoads; Dir., Development Economics, Sinforoso A. Atienza; Dir., Agricultural/Technical Services, Lawrence W. Lewis
Human Rights, Interim Dir., Frederick Bronkema
Intermedia:
Dir., Rev. David W. Briddell; Dir. for Adult Basic Educ., Dorothy Ortner
Int'l. Cong. and Lay Ministry, Dir., Arthur Bauer
Leadership Development, Dir., John W. Backer
Overseas Personnel, Dir., Rev. Paul W. Yount, Jr.

GEOGRAPHIC OFFICES

Africa; Dir., Willis H. Logan
East Asia & the Pacific: Dir., Rev. Victor W. C. Hsu; China Program, Dir., Rev. Franklin J. Woo; Japan and Hong Kong Program: Dir., Ms. Patricia Patterson

Middle East: Dir., _____
Southern Asia: Dir., Rev. Robert L. Turnipseed
Europe/U.S.S.R.: Dir., Michael G. Roshak

International Affairs

Asst. Gen Sec. and Exec. Dir., Rev. Dwain C. Epps

PROPHETIC JUSTICE

Church and Society

Assoc. Gen. Sec. for Church and Society, Dr. Kenyon Burke
Dir., Religious and Civil Liberty, Rev. Dean M. Kelley
Dir., Racial Justice, _____
Dir., Environmental and Human Health, _____
Dir., Domestic Hunger and Poverty, Mary Ellen Lloyd
Dir., Child Advocacy Office, Karen Collins

RELATED MOVEMENTS OF CHURCH AND SOCIETY

Dir., Interfaith Center for Corporate Responsibility, Timothy Smith
Dir., National Farm Worker Ministry, Sr. Patricia Drydyk, O.S.F., 1337 W. Ohio, Chicago, IL 60622. Tel. (212)266-3334

UNITY AND RELATIONSHIPS

Faith and Order

Asst. Gen. Sec. for Faith and Order, Bro. Jeffrey Gros

The following is a Project of the Faith and Order unit in association with the Duncan Black Macdonald Center for the Study of Islam and Christian-Muslim Relations of the Hartford Seminary. Its staff is secunded to the National Council of Churches, not Elected Staff of the Council.

OFFICE FOR CHRISTIAN-MUSLIM RELATIONS

77 Sherman St., Hartford, CT 06105. Tel. (203)232-4451. Dir. Dr. R. Marston Speight

Justice and Liberation

Assoc. Gen. Sec. for Justice and Liberation, Lois M. Dauway

Regional and Local Ecumenism

Asst. Gen. Sec./Exec. Dir. for Regional and Local Ecumenism, Kathleen S. Hurty

The following are related programs. Staff members connected with these programs are not NCC Elected Staff but are employed under professional contract

OFFICE ON CHRISTIAN JEWISH RELATIONS

475 Riverside Dr., Room 870, New York, NY 10115. Tel. (212)870-2560. Dir., Dr. Jay T. Rock

PARTNERS IN ECUMENISM

475 Riverside Dr., Room 870, New York, NY 10115. Tel. (212)870-2175. Nat'l Dir., _____

ADMINISTRATION AND FINANCE

Actg. Assoc. Gen. Sec. for Administration and Finance, Rev. T. Donald Black

FINANCE AND SERVICES

Financial Management

Controller, Leo Lamb
Deputy Controller, Marian Perdiz
Asst. Controller, William B. Price

Business Services

Actg. Exec. Dir., Phyllis Sharpe

Publication Services

Dir., Terrence S. Taylor

Data Processing

Dir., Data Processing, Thomas McCloskey
Dir., Systems and Programming, Julio Devia

PERSONNEL

Office of Personnel

Asst. Gen. Sec. for Personnel, Emilio F. Carrillo, Jr.
Dir. of Compensation and Benefits, Michael W. Mazoki

Constituent Bodies of the National Council (with membership dates)

African Methodist Episcopal Church (1950)
African Methodist Episcopal Zion Church (1950)
American Baptist Churches in the U.S.A. (1950)
The Antiochian Orthodox Christian Archdiocese of North America (1966)
Armenian Church of America, Diocese of the (1957)
Christian Church (Disciples of Christ) (1950)
Christian Methodist Episcopal Church (1950)
Church of the Brethren (1950)
The Coptic Orthodox Church (1978)
The Episcopal Church (1950)
Evangelical Lutheran Church in America (1950)
Friends United Meeting (1950)
General Convention, the Swedenborgian Church (1966)
Greek Orthodox Archdiocese of North and South America (1952)
Hungarian Reformed Church in America (1957)
International Council of Community Churches (1977)
Korean Presbyterian Church in America, General Assembly of the (1986)
Moravian Church in America (1950)
National Baptist Convention of America (1950)
National Baptist Convention, U.S.A., Inc. (1950)
Orthodox Church in America (1950)
Philadelphia Yearly Meeting of the Religious Society of Friends (1950)
Polish National Catholic Church of America (1957)
Presbyterian Church (U.S.A.) (1950)
Progressive National Baptist Convention, Inc. (1966)
Reformed Church in America (1950)

Russian Orthodox Church in the U.S.A., Patriarchal Parishes of the (1966)
Serbian Orthodox Church for in U.S.A. and Canada (1957)
Syrian Orthodox Church of Antioch (1960)
Ukrainian Orthodox Church in America (1950)
United Church of Christ (1950)
The United Methodist Church (1950)

American Bible Society

More than 174 years ago, in 1816, pastors and laymen representing a variety of Christian denominations gathered in New York City to establish a truly interconfessional effort "to disseminate the Gospel of Christ throughout the habitable world." Since that time the American Bible Society (ABS) has continued to provide God's Word, without doctrinal note or comment, wherever it is needed and in the language and format the reader can most easily use and understand. The Society is, in effect, the servant of the denominations and local churches as it provides the Scriptures needed for their use at home and their worldwide outreach in mission and evangelism.

Today the ABS has the endorsement of more than 100 denominations and agencies, and its Board of managers is composed of distinguished clergy and laity drawn from these Christian groups.

Forty-four years ago the American Bible Society played a leading role in the founding of the United Bible Societies, whose members currently are involved in Scripture translation, publication, and distribution in 180 countries and territories around the world. The ABS contributes about 43 percent of the support provided by the UBS to those national Bible Societies financially unable to meet the total Scripture needs of people in their own countries.

The work of the ABS is supported through gifts from individuals, local churches, denominations and cooperating agencies. Their generosity made possible the distribution of 308,978,098 copies of the Scriptures during 1988, out of a total of 692,754,925 copies of the Scriptures distributed by all member societies of the UBS.

Offices: National Headquarters: 1865 Broadway, New York, NY 10023. Tel. (212)581-7400

OFFICERS

Pres., James Wood
Vice-Pres., Mrs. Norman Vincent Peale
Gen. Secs., Rev. John D. Erickson; Maria I. Martinez
Treas., Daniel K. Scarberry
Departmental Heads: Rev. Fred A. Allen, Dir., Church Relations; William P. Cedfeldt, Dir., Public Relations; Dr. Ernestine R. Galloway, Dir., Volunteer Activities; Rev. Robert S. House, Dir., National Distribution; Lorraine A. Kupper, Exec. Sec., Fund Raising; Philip Spina, Comptroller, Finance; Dr. Peter Wosh, Dir., Archives/Library Services

PERIODICAL

Bible Society Record (m), 1865 Broadway, New York, NY 10023, Clifford P. Macdonald, Managing Ed.

American Council of Christian Churches

Founded in 1941, The American Council of Christian Churches (ACCC) is comprised of major denominations—Bible Presbyterian Church, Evangelical Methodist Church, Fellowship of Fundamental Bible Churches (formerly Bible Protestant), Fellowship of Independent Methodists, Free Presbyterian Church of North America, Fundamental Methodist Church, General Association of

Regular Baptist Churches, Tioga River Christian Conference and Independent Churches Affiliated, along with hundreds of independent churches. The total membership nears 2 million. Each denomination retains its identity and full autonomy, but cannot be associated with the World Council of Churches, National Council of Churches, or NationalAssociation of Evangelicals.

The ACCC stands as an agency for fellowship and cooperation on the part of Bible-believing churches, for the maintenance of a pure testimony to the great fundamental truths of the Word of God: the inspiration and inerrancy of Scripture; the triune God—Father, Son, and Holy Spirit; the Virgin birth; substitutionary death and resurrection of Christ, and His second coming; total depravity of man; salvation by grace through faith; and the necessity of maintaining the purity of the Church in doctrine and life.

GENERAL ORGANIZATION

Headquarters: PO. Box 816, Valley Forge, PA 19482. Tel. (215)566-8154.
Annual Convention: October

OFFICERS

Pres., Senator Ray Taylor
Vice-Pres., Dr. James Fields
Sec., Rev. David Natale
Treas., Mr. William H. Worrilow, Jr.
Exec. Sec., Dr. B. Robert Biscoe

COMMISSIONS

Chaplaincy, Education; Laymen; Literature; Missions; Radio and Audio Visual; Relief; Youth

PERIODICALS

Fundamental News Service (bi-m).

American Tract Society

The American Tract Society is a nonprofit, nonsectarian, interdenominational organization, instituted in 1825 through the merger of most of the then-existing tract societies. As one of the earliest religious publishing bodies in the United States, ATS has pioneered in the publishing of Christian books, booklets, and leaflets. The volume of distribution has risen to more than 25 million pieces of literature annually.

Office: P. O. Box 462008, Garland (Dallas), TX 75046. Tel. (214)276-9408

OFFICERS

Chpsn., Stephen E. Slocum, Jr.
Vice Chpsns., Arthur J. Widman, Philip E. Worth
Sec., Edgar L. Bensen
Treas., Kent Bicknell

The Associated Church Press

The Associated Church Press was organized in 1916. Its member publications include major Protestant, Anglican, and Orthodox groups in the U.S. and Canada. Some Roman Catholic publications and major ecumenical journals are also members. It is a professional religious journalistic association seeking to promote better understanding among editors, raise standards, represent the interests of the religious press. It sponsors seminars, conventions, awards programs, workshops for editors, staff people, business managers.
Pres., Mary Lou Redding, Managing Ed., *The Upper Room*, 1908 Grand Ave., Nashville, TN 37202
Exec. Dir., Donald F. Hetzler, P.O. Box 306, Geneva, IL 60134. Tel. (312)232-1055
Treas., Kermon Thomasson, Ed., *Messenger*, 1451 Dundee Ave., Elgin, IL 60120

The Associated Gospel Churches

Organized in 1939, The Associated Gospel Churches is primarily a service agency for fundamental denominations, colleges, seminaries, and missions. It also provides fellowship for Bible-believing independent churches, various Christian workers, missionaries, chaplains, laymen, and students.

One of the chief functions of AGC is to endorse chaplain applicants from the various denominations it represents. It is recognized by the U.S. Department of Defense and espouses the cause of national defense.

AGC devotes considerable effort toward gaining proper recognition for fundamental colleges, seminaries, and Bible Institutes. It was one of the founders of The American Association of Christian Schools of Higher Learning.

Associated Gospel Churches believes in the sovereignty of the local church, believes in the doctrines of the historic Christian faith, and practices separation from the apostasy.

Office: 3209 Norfolk St., Hopewell, VA 23860. Tel. (804)541-2879

OFFICERS

Pres. and Chmn., Commission on Chaplains, Col H. P. Kissinger, USAR
Vice Pres., and Vice Chmn., Commission on Chaplains, Dr. George W. Baugham, AGC Admin. Office, P.O. Box 1605 Warrenton, VA 22186-1605. Tel. (703) 349-4508
Sec.-Treas., Mrs. Eva Baugham
Natl. Field Rep., Dr. Ev Thomas

Association of Regional Religious Communicators (ARRC)

ARRC is a professional association of regional, ecumenical and interfaith communicators who work with local, state and regional religious agencies to: Fulfill their needs by providing occasional syndicated TV and radio programs to members, and "ARRC Newsletter," a quarterly. ARRC also provides local representation on the Communication Commission of the National Council of Churches, before the Federal Communications Commission, and with the denominations. ARRC offers fellowship by participation at the annual convention of the North American Broadcast Section of the World Association for Christian Communication, by updating names and addresses of national and local communicators.

OFFICERS

Pres., Lydia Ann Talbot, Dir., Broadcast Communications, Church Federation of Greater Chicago, 18 S. Michigan, #900, Chicago, IL 60603
Exec. Sec., J. Graley Taylor, Exec. Dir., Religious Broadcasting Commission, 500 Wall St., Ste. 415, Seattle, WA 98101. Tel. (206)441-6110

Association of Statisticians of American Religious Bodies

This Association was organized in 1934 and grew out of personal consultations held by representatives from The Yearbook of American Churches, The National (now Official) Catholic Directory, the Jewish Statistical Bureau, The Methodist (now The United Methodist), the Lutheran, and the Presbyterian churches.

ASARB has a variety of purposes: to bring together those officially and professionally responsible for gathering, compiling, and publishing denominational statistics; to provide a forum for the exchange of ideas and sharing of problems in statistical methods and procedure; and to seek such standardization as may be possible in religious statistical data.

OFFICERS

Pres., James E. Horsch, Mennonite Church, 616 Walnut Ave., Scottdale, PA 15683

First Vice-Pres., Sheila Kelly, United Church of Christ, 132 W. 31st St., New York, NY 10001; Second Vice-Pres., Frank R. Helme, Christian Church (Disciples of Christ), P. O. Box 1986, Indianapolis, IN 46206

Sec.-Treas., Norman Green, Jr., American Baptist Churches in the U.S.A., P. O. Box 851, Valley Forge, PA 19482. Tel. (215)768-2480

Christian Holiness Association

The Association is a coordinating agency of those religious bodies that hold the Wesleyan-Arminian theological view. It was organized in 1867.

Central Office: CHA Center, S. Walnut St. Box 100, Wilmore, KY 40390.

122nd Annual Convention, Radisson Plaza Hotel, Lexington, KY, April 17-19, 1990.

OFFICERS

Pres., Jerald D. Johnson, Church of the Nazarene, 6401 The Paseo, Kansas City, MO 64131

Exec. Dir., Burnis H. Bushong, World Gospel Mission, Box WGM, Marion, IN 46952

COOPERATING ORGANIZATIONS

Methodist Protestant Church
Primitive Methodist Church
The Congregational Methodist Church
The Church of God (Anderson)
The Missionary Church

A Christian Ministry in the National Parks

The Ministry is an independent ecumenical movement providing interdenominational religious services in 65 National Parks, Monuments, and Recreation Areas. For 20 years it was administered in the National Council of Churches. On January 1, 1972, it became an independent movement representing over 40 denominations, 60 local park committees, over 300 theological seminaries, and 16 separate religious organizations. The program recruits and staffs 300 positions, winter and summer, in 65 areas. Office: 222½ E. 49th St., New York, NY 10017. Tel. (212) 758-3450

OFFICER

Dir., Dr. Warren W. Ost

PERIODICAL

Opportunities Alive (a), Warren W. Ost, Ed.

Church Women United in the U.S.A.

Church Women United in the U.S.A. is an ecumenical lay movement providing Protestant, Orthodox, and Roman Catholic and other Christian women with programs and channels of involvement in church, civic, and national affairs. CWU has some 1,750 units formally organized in communities located in all 50 states, Greater Washington, DC, and Puerto Rico. Office: 475 Riverside Dr., Room 812, New York, NY 10115. Tel. (212)870-2347. Other Offices: 777 United Nations Plz., New York, NY 10017. Tel. (212)661-3856; Rm. 108, CWU Washington Office, 110 Maryland Ave. NE, Washington, DC 20002. Tel. (202)544-8747

OFFICERS

Pres., Claire Randall, New York, NY
1st Vice-Pres., Fran Craddock, Indianapolis, IN

2nd Vice-Pres., Jo Walton, Tuskegee, AL, OH
3rd Vice-Pres., Doris Hanson, Frederick, MD
Sec., Helen Quirino, Portland, OR
Treas., Lois Holmes, Hot Springs, AR
Regional Coordinators: Kathleen Clark, Greenfield, IA (Central); Lillian Nunnelly, Frankfort, KY (East Central); Geraldine Glick, Broadway, VA (Mid-Atlantic); Roberta Grimm, Buffalo, NY (Northeast); Marilyn Bauman, Caldwell, ID (Northwest); Oouida Dorr, Houston, TX (South Central); Catharine Vick, Cary, NC (Southeast); Beverley Wolford, Phoenix, AZ (Southwest)

STAFF

Gen. Dir., Patricia J. Rumer
Assoc. Gen. Dir./Dir. of Prog. (Citizen Action and Constituency Development), Ada Maria Isasi-Diaz
Comptroller, Anne Martin
Dir. of Ecumenical Celebration/Global Rel., Mary Cline Detrick
Staff Assoc. for the Imperative, Frances Kennedy
Ed./Art Dir., Margaret Schiffert
Dir. of Media and Interpretation, Jane Burton
Dir. of Intercontinental Grants, Carol Barton
Dir. of Financial Dev. and Computer Services, Marcia Parker
Staff, UN and Global Aff., Carol Barton
Staff Washington Ofc., Sally Timmel

PERIODICAL

Churchwoman (4/yr.)

CODEL—Coordination in Development

CODEL is a consortium of Protestant and Roman Catholic mission-sending agencies, Communions and Christian organizations working together in international development. Founded in 1969, CODEL is committed to an ecumenical approach in the development process. The 40 U.S.-based member organizations combine expertise, funds, planning, project implementation and evaluation in a spirit of Christian unity working toward self-sufficiency of the poorest peoples and communities of the world.

Presently there are about 90 projects in 38 countries in health, agriculture, community development, and informal education. Other CODEL programs include seminars on current issues, development education activities, environment and development projects and workshops. CODEL's budget for 1989/90 is $2,343,000.

Headquarters: Rm. 1842, 475 Riverside Dr., New York NY. Tel. (212)870-3000.

OFFICERS

Pres., Dr. Norman Barth
Vice-Pres., Sr. Sheila McGinnis
Sec., Ms. Betty Jo Swyze
Treas., Dr. Lloyd Van Vactor

STAFF

Exec. Dir., Rev. Boyd Lowry
Coordinator for Africa, Ms. Caroline Njuki
Coordinator for Asia and the Pacific, Mr. Ellis Shenk
Coord. for Latin America and Caribbean, Ms. Joanne Fujimoto
Seminar Program/Environment and Development, Sr. Mary Ann Smith
Ecumenical Relations/Development Education, Rev. Nathan VanderWerf
Accountant, Robert Lopulisa

PERIODICAL

CODELnews (6/yr.), Suzanne Arden, Ed.

Consultation on Church Union

Officially constituted in 1962, the Consultation on Church Union is a venture in reconciliation of nine American communions. It has been authorized to explore the formation of a united church truly catholic, truly evangelical, and truly reformed. In 1988 the participating churches were African Methodist Episcopal Church, African Methodist Episcopal Zion Church, Christian Church (Disciples of Christ), Christian Methodist Episcopal Church, The Episcopal Church, International Council of Community Churches, Presbyterian Church (U.S.A.), United Church of Christ, The United Methodist Church

SECRETARIAT

Address: Research Park, 151 Wall St., Princeton, NJ 08540. Tel. (609)921-7866
Gen. Sec., Dr. David W. A. Taylor
Treas./Bus. Mgr., Christine V. Bilarczyk

GENERAL ORGANIZATION

The *Plenary Assembly,* which normally meets every two to four years, is composed of ten delegates and ten associate delegates from each of the participating churches. Included also are observer-consultants from over twenty other churches, other union negotiations, and conciliar bodies. The most recent Plenaries have been held in 1984 (Baltimore) and 1988 (New Orleans.)

The *Executive Committee* is composed of the president, two representatives from each of the participating churches, and the secretariat.

The *Secretariat* consists of the full-time executive staff of the Consultation, all of whom are based at the national office in Princeton, NJ.

Various *commissions* are convened to fulfill certain assignments. In 1988 there were five commisions: Church Order, Theology, Worship, Racism, Strategy/Interpretation. In addition there was a Women's Task Force, a Workgroup on Persons with Disabilities, and an Editorial Board for the annual *Lenten Booklet.*

OFFICERS

Pres., Dr. Vivian U. Robinson, 1256 Hernlen St., Augusta, GA 30901
Vice Pres., Bishop J. Clinton Hoggard, 1100 W. 42nd St., Indianapolis, IN 46208; Dr. Alice Cowan, St. Paul School of Theology, 5123 Truman Rd., Kansas City, MO 64127
Sec., Rev. Clyde Miller, Jr. 1370 Pennsylvania St., Denver, CO 80203

REPRESENTATIVES FROM PARTICIPATING CHURCHES

African Methodist Episcopal Church, Bishop Vinton R. Anderson, P O Box 6416, St. Louis, MO 63107; Bishop Frederick H. Talbot, P. O. Box 684, Frederikstead, St. Croix, U.S. Virgin Islands 00841
African Methodist Episcopal Zion Church, Bishop J. Clinton Hoggard, 1100 W. 42nd St., Indianapolis, IN 46206; Bishop Cecil Bishop, AME Zion Ch. 5401 Broadwater St., Temple Hill, MD 20031
Christian Church (Disciples of Christ), Rev. Dr. Paul A. Crow, Jr., P. O. Box 1986, Indianapolis, IN 46206; Rev. Dr. Albert M. Pennybacker, University Christian Church, 2720 University Dr., Ft. Worth, TX 76109
Christian Methodist Episcopal Church, Bishop Marshall Gilmore, 109 Holcomb Dr., Shreveport, LA 71103; Dr. Vivian U. Robinson, 1256 Hernlen St., Augusta, GA 30901
The Episcopal Church, Rt. Rev. William G. Burrill, 935 East Ave., Rochester, NY 14607; Dr. Alice Cowan, St. Paul School of Theology, 5123 Truman Rd., Kansas City, MO 64127
International Council of Community Churches, Rev. J. Ralph Shotwell, 900 Ridge Rd., Homewood, IL 60430; Mrs. Dorothy Bascom, 2101 Park Ave., Baltimore, MD 21217

Presbyterian Church (U.S.A.), Rev. Dr. Cynthia M. Campbell, P. O. Box 585, Salina, KS 67402; Rev. George H. Pike, 10086 Brookwood Ct., Louisville, KY 40223
United Church of Christ, Rev. Clyde Miller, 1370 Pennsylvania, Denver, CO 80203; Rev. Dr. Thomas E. Dipko, 4041 N. High St., Ste. 301, Columbus, OH 43214
The United Methodist Church, Bishop William B. Grove, 900 Washington St., E., Charleston, WV 25301; Mrs. Margaret Sonnenday, 7490 Teasdale St., St. Louis MO 63160

PUBLICATIONS

An Affirmation of the Baptismal Covenant (also Called Confirmation)
Word, Bread, Cup (Guidelines for Ecumenical Worship)
Digest of the Proceedings of the COCU Plenary (1984), (1988)
An Order of Thanksgiving for the Birth or Adoption of a Child
Congregations Uniting for Mission
Oneness in Christ: The Quest and the Questions (1981)
God's Power and Our Weakness
The Word and the Words
. . . Like Trees Walking: Biblical Meditations on Healing (1988)
In Common (Occ. Newsletter)
The COCU Consensus: In Quest of a Church of Christ Uniting (1985)
Churches in Covenant Communion: The Church of Christ Uniting (1988)
Sacrament of the Lord's Supper—A New Text (1984)
An Order for the Celebration of Holy Baptism, with Commentary

The Evangelical Church Alliance

The Evangelical Church Alliance was incorporated in 1928 in Missouri as The World's Faith Missionary Association and was later known as The Fundamental Ministerial Association. The title Evangelical Church Alliance was adopted in 1958.

ECA (1) licenses and ordains ministers who are qualified and provides them with credentials from a recognized ecclesiastical body; (2) provides through the Bible Extension Institute, courses of study to those who have not had seminary or Bible school training; (3) provides an organization for autonomous churches so they may have communion and association with one another; (4) provides an organization where members can find companionship through correspondence, Regional Conventions, and General Conventions; (5) cooperates with churches in finding new pastors when vacancies occur in their pulpits. ECA is an interdenominational, nonsectarian, Evangelical organization. Total ordained and licensed clergy members—1,720.

Headquarters: Rev. Glen E. Seaborg, Exec. Dir., 1273 Cardinal Dr., P.O. Box 9, Bradley, IL 60915. Tel. (815)937-0720
International Convention: Annual, next meeting, August 7-10, 1990, Williamson Christian Center, Carlinville, IL.

OFFICERS

Pres., Dr. Charles Wesley Ewing, 321 W. Harrison St., Royal Oak, MI 48067
1st Vice-Pres., Rev. John H. Bishop, 162 Grandview Ave., S., Newport, KY 41071
2nd Vice-Pres., Dr. Sterling L. Cauble, Sunman Bible Church, Box 216, Sunman, IN 47041
Exec. Dir., Rev. Glen E. Seaborg, P.O. Box 9, Bradley, IL 60915

PERIODICAL

Asst. Exec. Dir., Rev. George L. Miller, P. O. Box 9, Bradley, IL 60915
The Evangelical Church Alliance Evangel, (a), P.O. Box 9, Bradley, IL 60915

Evangelical Press Association

The Evangelical Press Association is an organization of editors and publishers of Christian periodicals which seeks to promote the cause of Evangelical Christianity and enhance the influence of Christian journalism.

OFFICERS

Pres., Mavis Sanders, Scripture Press, 1825 College Ave., Wheaton, IL 60187
Pres. Elect, Roger Palms, Decision Magazine, 1300 Harmon Pl., Minneapolis, MN 55403
Sec., Joel Belz, World Magazine, P.O. Box 2300, Asheville, NC 28802
Treas., Ramona Cass, Journal of Christian Nursing, P.O. Box 1650, Downers Grove, IL 60515
Exec. Dir., Gary Warner, P.O. Box 4550, Overland Park, KS 66204. Tel. (913)381-2017

Higher Education Ministries Team

The Higher Education Ministries Team has emerged out of United Ministries in Education. It embodies the covenant-based ministry coalition created more than thirty years ago and carried forward the work of United Campus Christian Fellowhship, United Ministries in Education and Ministires in Public Education (K-12). HEMT works with churches and educational institutions as they seek to express their concern about the ways in which educating forces affect quality of life. HEMT focuses on the goal to design, manage, facilitate, nurture and participate in partnerships with regional and denominational organizations in support of ministry in higher education. Current programs include mission and resource partnerships, campus ministry training for fundraising, AIDS prevention education, strategic conversations for developing models and planning strategies at the state and regional levels, training for new campus ministers and chaplains, personnel services, support and network for Christian student organizations including the World Student Christian Federation and the Council for Ecumenical Student Christian Ministry and promoting the informal networking of people, resources and experiences of "people in the field."

OFFICERS

Admn. Coord., Clyde O. Robinson, Jr., 7407 Steele Creek Rd., Charlotte, NC 28217. Tel. (704)588-2182.
Treas., Gary Harke, P. O. Box 386, Sun Prairie, WI 53590. Tel. (608)837-0537
Personnel Service, Lawrence S. Steinmetz, 11780 Borman Dr., Ste. 100, St.Louis, MO 63146. Tel. (314)991-3000
Resource Center, Linda Freeman, 7407 Steele Creek Rd., Charlotte, NC 28217. Tel. (704)588-2182

PERIODICALS

UME Connexion (q)

PARTICIPATING DENOMINATIONS

Christian Church (Disciples of Christ)
Church of the Brethren
The Episcopal Church
Moravian Church (Northern Province)
Presbyterian Church (U.S.A.)
United Church of Christ

Interfaith Action for Economic Justice

Interfaith Action for Economic Justice, recognized as one of the most effective forces for economic justice in the nation's capitol, has five priorities adopted by its membership: to support and advocate policies that would reduce poverty in the United States; to support and advocate international development policy that addresses the basic needs of poor people and helps them to improve the quality of their lives; to support and advocate policies that promote a just, sustainable, and secure farm and food system; to increase the participation of people who are poor and people of color in the electoral process; and to support and advocate moral U.S. budgetary policies.

Office: 110 Maryland Ave., NE, Ste. 509, Washington, DC 20002. TEl. (202) 543-2800. Exec. Dir., Rev. Arthur B. Keys, Jr.

OFFICERS

Pres., Jim McDaniel, United Church Board for Homeland Ministries
Chair, Melva Jimerson, Church of the Brethren
Sec., Rev. Thomas E. Hayden, Africa Faith and Justice Network
Treas. Neill Richards, United Church Board for World Ministries

PUBLICATIONS

Legislative Updates Tel. (800) 424-7290
Annual Report
Domestic Human Needs Networker, Family Farm Networker, International Development Networker, Voting Rights Networker
ACTION Newsletter
Various Reports and Study Materials
Publications list available upon request.

MEMBERS

African Methodist Episcopal Zion Church:
    Home Missions Department
American Baptist Churches, USA
Baptist Joint Committee on Public Affairs
Bread for the World
Center of Concern
Columban Fathers
Christian Church (Disciples of Christ)
Church of the Brethren
Church Women United
Episcopal Church
Evangelical Lutheran Church in America
Friends Committee on National Legislation
Jesuit Social Ministries
Maryknoll Fathers and Brothers
Mennonite Central Committee
Moravian Church in America
National Council of Churches of Christ:
    Church World Service
National Council of Jewish Women
NETWORK
Presbyterian Church (USA)
Progressive National Baptist Convention
Reformed Church in America
Society of African Missions
Southern Baptist Convention:
    Christian Life Commission
Union of American Hebrew Congregations
Unitarian Universalist Association
Unitarian Universalist Service Committee
United Church of Christ:
    Board for Homeland Ministries
    Board for World Ministries
    Office for Church in Society
United Methodist Church:
    General Board of Church and Society
    General Board of Global Ministries
        National Division
        Women's Division
        World Division

International Christian Youth Exchange (ICYE)

ICYE sponsors the exchange of young people between nations as a means of international and ecumenical education in order to further commitment to and responsibility for reconciliation, justice, and peace. Exchangees 16–30 years of age spend one year in another country and participate in family, school, church, voluntary service projects and community life. Short term, ecumenical, international workcamp experiences are also available for 18-35 year olds.

The U.S. Committee works in cooperation with national committees in thirty-two other countries and the Federation of National Committees for ICYE, which has headquarters in West Berlin, Federal Republic of Germany.

Exchanges for American youth going abroad and for overseas youth coming to the U.S. are frequently sponsored by local churches and/or community groups. Participation is open to all regardless of religious affiliation. Denominational agencies are sponsors of ICYE, including: American Baptist Churches in the U.S.A.; Christian Church (Disciples of Christ); Church of the Brethren; Episcopal Church; Evangelical Lutheran Church in America; Presbyterian Church (U.S.A.); Reformed Church in America; United Church of Christ; and The United Methodist Church. Collaborating organizations include the National Federation of Catholic Youth Ministry and the National Catholic Education Association. Scholarships are provided by most sponsoring denominations.

Office: 134 W. 26th St., New York, NY 10001. Tel. (212) 206-7307. Fax: (212)633-9085

OFFICER

Exec. Dir., Edwin H. Gragert

International Society of Christian Endeavor

Christian Endeavor is an international, interracial, and interdenominational youth movement in evangelical Protestant churches. It unites its members for greater Christian growth and service under the motto "For Christ and the Church." The first society was formed by Francis E. Clark in Portland, Maine, February 2, 1881.

The movement spread rapidly and, in 1885, the United Society of Christian Endeavor was organized. In 1927 the name was changed to the International Society of Christian Endeavor, to include Canada and Mexico. The World's Union was organized in 1895; in 1981 provision was made to include the territories of the United States. The movement has thousands of societies in local churches, for all age groups. Worldwide there are societies and unions in approximately 78 nations and island groups, with over two million members.

Office: 1221 E. Broad St., P.O. Box 1110, Columbus, OH 43216. Tel. (614)258-9545.
Convention: Lebanon University, Annville, PA, July 1991.

OFFICERS

Pres., Rev. Clarence A. Kopp, Jr.
Gen. Sec./Treas., Rev. David G. Jackson

PERIODICAL

The Christian Endeavor World (q) 1221 E. Broad St., P.O. Box 1110, Columbus, OH 43216, David G. Jackson, Ed.

Interreligious Foundation for Community Organization (IFCO)

IFCO is a national ecumenical agency created in 1966 by several Protestant, Roman Catholic, and Jewish organizations, to be an interreligious, interracial agency for support of community organization and education in pursuit of social justice. Through IFCO, national and regional religious bodies collaborate in development of social-justice strategies and provide financial support and technical assistance to local, national, and international social-justice projects.

IFCO serves as a bridge between the churches and communities, and acts as a resource for ministers and congregations wishing to better understand and do more to advance the struggles of the poor and oppressed. IFCO conducts training workshops for community organizers and uses its vast national and international network of organizers, clergy, and other professionals to crystallize, publicize, and act in the interest of justice.

National Office: 402 W. 145th St., New York, NY 10031. Tel. (212)926-5757.
Exec. Dir., Rev. Lucius Walker, Jr.

OFFICERS

Pres., Dr. Ernest Newborn, Christian Church (Disciples of Christ), Director, Reconciliation Committee
Vice-Pres., Dr. Benjamin Greene, Jr., American Baptist Churches in the U.S.A. Director, Community Development, National Ministries

PERIODICAL

IFCO NEWS (4/yr.)

Inter-Varsity Christian Fellowship of the U.S.A.

Inter-Varsity Christian Fellowship is a nonprofit, interdenominational student movement that ministers to college and university students in the United States. Inter-Varsity began in the United States when students at the University of Michigan invited C. Stacey Woods, then General Secretary of the Canadian movement, to help establish an Inter-Varsity chapter on their campus. InterVarsity Christian Fellowship-USA was incorporated two years later, in 1941. Inter-Varsity's uniqueness as a campus ministry lies in the fact that it is student-initiated and student-led. Inter-Varsity's strives to build collegiate fellowships that engage their campus with the gospel of Jesus Christ and develop disciples who live out biblical values. Inter-Varsity students are encouraged in evangelism, spiritual discipleship, serving the Church, human relationships, righteousness, vocational stewardship and world evangelization. Our triennial missions conference held in Urbana, IL, jointly sponsored with InterVarsity-Canada, has long been a launching point for missionary service.

National Office: 6400 Schroeder Rd., P.O.Box 7895, Madison, WI 53707. Tel. (608)274-9001

Pres. & CEO, Stephen A. Hayner
Vice Pres., C. Barney Ford
Vice Pres., Robert A. Fryling
Vice Pres., Samuel Barkat
Sec., H. Yvonne Vinkemulder
Treas., Thomas H. Witte
Bd.Chpsn., James W. Kay
Bd. Vice-Chpsn: James Gray

Joint Strategy and Action Committee

This is a national ecumenical agency created by several denominational home mission and program agencies.

Through the JSAC system, agencies collaborate with each other about issues, develop strategy options, screen project requests, and work on joint actions. JSAC has a series of national staff coalitions which work as Task Forces, Work Groups, or Networks. National Office: 475 Riverside Dr., Rm. 450, New York, NY 10115. Tel. (212)870-3105

OFFICERS

Pres., Rev. Dr. William A. Norgren, The Episcopal Church
Vice-Pres., Rev. J. Perry Grubbs, Church of God, Anderson,Ind.
Sec., Ms. Susan Thompson
Treas., Rev. Joe Marlock, Cumberland Presbyterian Church
Exec. Dir., Rev. Dr. Jeffrey C. Wood

MEMBER DENOMINATIONAL AGENCIES

American Baptist Churches
Church of God (Anderson)
Church of the Brethren
Cumberland Presbyterian Church
The Episcopal Church
Evangelical Lutheran Church in America
Presbyterian Church (U.S.A.)
Reformed Church in America
The United Church of Canada
United Methodist Church

COOPERATING DENOMINATIONAL AGENCIES

African Methodist Episcopal Church
African Methodist Episcopal Zion Church
American Friends Service Committee
American Jewish Committee
Associate Reformed Presbyterian Church
Christian Church (Disciples of Christ)
Christian Methodist Episcopal Church
Christian Reformed Church
Church Women United
Evangelical Lutheran Church in Canada
Leadership Conference of Women Religious
Mennonite Central Committee
Moravian Church in America
Presbyterian Church in Canada
Progressive National Baptist Convention
Unitarian-Universalist Church
United Church of Christ
United States Catholic Conference

PERIODICAL

Grapevine (10 times a year), James E. Solheim

The Liturgical Conference

Founded in 1940 by a group of Benedictines. The Liturgical Conference is an independent, interconfessional, international association of persons concerned about liturgical renewal and meaningful worship. The Liturgical Conference is known chiefly, for its periodicals, books, materials, and sponsorship of regional and local workshops on worship-related concerns in cooperation with various church groups.

Headquarters: 1017 12th St., NW, Washington, DC 20005. Tel. (202)898-0885

OFFICERS

Pres., James Schellman
Vice Pres., Ralph Van Loon
Sec., Winnie Crapson
Treas., Laurence Stookey
Exec. Dir., Rachel Reeder

PERIODICALS

Liturgy (q), Rachel Reeder, Ed.
Accent on Liturgy (4/yr.) Rachel Reeder, Ed.
Homily Service (m), Rachel Reeder, Ed.

The Lord's Day Alliance of the United States

The Lord's Day Alliance of the United States has served the church and nation for 100 years. It was founded in 1888 in Washington, D.C., and is the only national organization the sole purpose of which is the preservation and cultivation of Sunday, the Lord's Day, as a day of rest and worship. The Alliance also seeks to safeguard a Day of Common Rest for all people regardless of their faith. Its Board of Managers is composed of representatives from twenty-five denominations.

It serves as an information bureau, publishes a magazine Sunday, furnishes speakers and a variety of materials such as pamphlets, a book, The Lord's Day, videos, posters, radio spot announcements, decals, cassettes, news releases, articles for magazines and TV programs, and a new 15-minute motion picture.

Office: Ste. 107/2930 Flowers Road, South, Atlanta, GA 30341. Tel. (404)451-7315

OFFICERS

Exec. Dir. and Ed., Dr. James P. Wesberry
Pres., Dr. Paul Craven, Jr.
Vice-Pres., Donald R. Pepper, Roger A. Kvam, Timothy E. Bird, John H. Schall, Faith Willard, W. David Sepp.
Sec., Rev. Ernest A. Bergeson
Treas., Mr. E. Larry Eidson

PERIODICAL

Sunday (q), Dr. James P. Wesberry, Ed.

The Mennonite Central Committee

The Mennonite Central Committee is the relief and service agency of North American Mennonite and Brethren in Christ Churches. Representatives from Mennonite and Brethren in Christ groups make up the MCC, which meets annually in January to review its program and to approve policies and budget Founded in 1920, MCC administers and participates in programs of agricultural and economic development, education, medicine, self-help, relief, peace, and disaster service. MCC has over 1000 workers serving in 50 countries in Africa, Asia, Europe, Middle East, and South, Central, and North America.

MCC has service programs in North America that focus on both urban and rural poverty areas. Additionally there are North American programs focusing on such diverse matters as handicap concerns, community conciliation, employment creation and criminal justice issues. These programs are administered by two national bodies—MCC U.S. and MCC Canada.

Contributions from North American Mennonite and Brethren in Christ churches provide the largest part of MCC's support. Other sources of financial support include the contributed earnings of volunteers, grants from private and government agencies, and contributions from Mennonite churches abroad. The total income in 1988, including material aid contributions, amounted to $31,867,000.

In the projects it undertakes, MCC tries to strengthen local communities by working in cooperation with local churches. Many personnel are placed with other agencies, including missions. Programs are planned with sensitivity to locally felt needs.

International and U.S. headquarters: 21 S. 12th St., Akron, PA 17501. Tel. (717)859-1151
Canadian office: 134 Plaza Dr., Winnipeg, Manitoba R3T 5K9

OFFICER

Exec. Secs., John A. Lapp (International); Dan Zehr; (Canada) and Lynette Meck (U.S.)

National Association of Ecumenical Staff

This is the successor organization, to the Association of Council Secretaries, which was founded in 1940. The name change was made in 1971.

NAES is an association of professional staff in ecumenical services. It was established to provide creative relationships among them, and to encourage mutual support and personal and professional growth. This is accomplished through training programs, through exchange and discussion of common concerns at conferences, and through the publication of the journal.

Headquarters: Room 870, 475 Riverside Dr., New York, NY 10115. Tel. (212)870-2158
Annual Meeting: July 7-12. 1990, Tacoma, WA

OFFICERS

Pres., Sr. Sylvia Schmidt, Exec. Dir., Tulsa Metropolitan Ministry, 240 East Apache St., Tulsa, OK 74106. Tel. (918)582-3147
Vice-Pres., Rev. Bruce Theunissen, Exec. Dir., Houston Metropolitan Ministries, 3217 Montrose Blvd., Houston, TX 77006. Tel. (713) 522-3955
1990 Program Chair, Dr. Wallace Ford, Exec. Sec., New Mexico Conference of Churches, 124 Hermosa SE, Albuquerque, NM 87108. Tel. (505)255-1509
Sec., Ms. Mary Cooper, National Council of Churches, 110 Maryland Ave., NE, Washington, DC 20002. Tel. (202)544-2350.

PERIODICAL

Corletter (bi-m), Rm. 870, 475 Riverside Dr. New York, NY 10115.

The National Association of Evangelicals

The National Association of Evangelicals is a voluntary fellowship of evangelical denominations, churches, schools, organizations and individuals. Its purpose is not to eliminate denominations, but protect them; not to force individual churches into a mold of liberal or radical sameness, but provide a means of cooperation in evangelical witness; not to do the work of the churches, but stand for the right of churches to do their work as they feel called of God.

Based upon the affirmation of a common faith resting squarely in God's Word, the Bible, NAE provides evangelical identification for 50,000 churches from more than 77 denominations; with a service constituency of more than 15 million through its commissions, affiliates and subsidiary.

GENERAL ORGANIZATION

Headquarters: 450 Gundersen Dr., Carol Stream, IL 60188. Tel. (708)665-0500; Fax (708)665-8575
Office of Public Affairs: 1023 15th St., N.W., Ste. 500, Washington, DC 20005. Tel. (202)789-1011; Fax (202)842-0392

OFFICERS

Pres., Dr. John H. White, Geneva College, Beaver Falls, PA 15010
1st Vice Pres., Dr. B. Edgar Johnson, 6401 The Paseo, Kansas City, MO 64131

2nd Vice-Pres., Dr. Don Argue, 910 Elliott Ave., Minneapolis, MN 55404
Sec., Dr. Jack Estep, P. O. Box 828, Wheaton, IL 60189
Treas., Mr. Paul Steiner, 1825 Florida Dr. Ft. Wayne, IN 46805

STAFF

Exec. Dir., Dr. Billy A. Melvin
Assoc. to the Exec. Dir., Robert W. Patterson
Dir. of Field Services, Dr. R. Gordon Bacon
Dir. of Information, Rev. Donald R. Brown
Dir. of Business Adm., Mr. Darrell L. Fulton
National Field Representative, Rev. David L. Melvin
Dir. of Public Affairs, Dr. Robert P. Dugan, Jr.; Research, Richard Cizik; Counsel, Forest Montgomery, 1023 15th St., NW, Ste. 500 Washington, DC 20005. Tel. (202)789-1011.

COMMISSIONS, AFFILIATES, SERVICE AGENCIES

Commissions: Chaplains Commission, Christian Higher Education Commission, Churchmen Commission, Evangelism and Home Missions Association, Hispanic Commission, National Christian Education Association, Social Action Commission, Christian Stewardship Association, Women's Commission
Affiliates: Evangelical Child and Family Agency, Evangelical Foreign Missions Assn., National Religious Broadcasters
Subsidiary: World Relief Corporation
Service Agency: Evangelical Adoption and Family Services, Inc.

PERIODICAL

United Evangelical Action (bi-m), P. O. Box 28, Wheaton, IL 60189, Rev. Donald R. Brown, Ed.
NAE Washington Insight (m), 1023 15th St., NW, Ste. 500, Washington, DC 20005
National Evangelical Directory (biennial), P. O. Box 28, Wheaton, IL 60189. Donald Brown, Ed.

MEMBER DENOMINATIONS

Advent Christian General Conference
Assemblies of God
Baptist General Conference
Brethren Church (Ashland, Ohio)
Brethren in Christ Church
Christian Catholic Church (Evangelical Protestant)
Christian Church of North America
Christian and Missionary Alliance
Christian Reformed Church in N.A.
Christian Union
Church of God (Cleveland, Tenn.)
Church of God of the Mountain Assembly
Church of the Nazarene
Church of the United Brethren in Christ
Churches of Christ in Christian Union
Conservative Congregational Christian Conference
Conservative Lutheran Association
Elim Fellowship
Evangelical Christian Church
Evangelical Church of North America
Evangelical Congregational Church
Evangelical Free Church of America
Evangelical Friends Alliance
Evangelical Mennonite Brethren
Evangelical Mennonite Church
Evangelical Methodist Church
Evangelical Presbyterian Church
Evangelistic Missionary Fellowship
Fellowship of Evangelical Bible Churches
Fire-Baptized Holiness Church of God of the Americas
Free Methodist Church of North America
Full Gospel Pentecostal Assn.
General Association of General Baptists

International Church of the Foursquare Gospel
International Pentecostal Church of Christ
International Pentecostal Holiness Church
Mennonite Brethren Churches, USA
Midwest Congregational Christian Fellowship
Missionary Church
Oklahoma State Association of Free Will Baptists
Open Bible Standard Churches
Pentecostal Church of God
Pentecostal Free Will Baptist Church
Presbyterian Church in America
Primitive Methodist Church, USA
Reformed Presbyterian Church of North America
Wesleyan Church

National Conference of Christians and Jews

The National Conference of Christians and Jews (NCCJ) is a non-profit human relations organization engaged in a nationwide program of intergroup education so that people of different religious, racial, and ethnic backgrounds learn to live together without bigotry and discrimination and without compromising distinctive faiths or identities. Founded in 1928, the NCCJ promotes education for citizenship in a pluralistic democracy and attempts to help diverse groups discover their mutual self-interest. Primary program areas include interfaith and interracial dialogue, youth intercultural communications, training for the administration of justice, and the building of community coalitions. The NCCJ has 72 offices nationally, staffed by approximately 240 people. Nearly 300 members comprise the National Board of Trustees and members from that group form the 22-member Executive Board. Each regional office has its own local board of trustees with a total of about 2,000. The National Board of Trustees meets once annually; the Executive Board at least three times annually.

Headquarters: 71 Fifth Ave., New York, NY 10003. Tel. (212)206-0006

OFFICER

Pres., Jacqueline G. Wexler

National Conference on Ministry to the Armed Forces

The Conference is an incorporated civilian agency. Representation in the Conference with all privileges of the same is open to all endorsing or certifying agencies or groups authorized to provide chaplains for any branch of the Armed Forces.

The purpose of this organization is to provide a means of dialog to discuss concerns and objectives and, when agreed upon, to take action with the appropriate authority to support the spiritual ministry to and the moral welfare of Armed Forces personnel.

GENERAL ORGANIZATION

4141 N. Henderson Rd., Ste. 13, Arlington, VA 22203. Tel. (703)276-7905

STAFF

Coordinator, Clifford T. Weathers
Adm. Asst., Maureen Francis

OFFICERS

Chpsn., Rev. Ralph R. Monson; Vice Chpsn., Rev. Jearl C. Smith; Treas., A. Eugene Hall; Sec., Rev. Charles E. McMillan; Committee Members: Catholic Representative, Msgr. John P. Gilhooley; Protestant Representative, Chaplain C. E. Bracebridge; Jewish Representative, Rabbi David Lapp; Orthodox Representative, Gregory Pelesh; Member-at-Large, W. Robert Johnson, III

National Interfaith Coalition on Aging, Inc.

The National Interfaith Coalition on Aging (NICA) is composed of Protestant, Roman Catholic, Jewish, and Orthodox organizations and individuals concerned about the needs of older people and the religious community's response to problems facing our nation's aging population. NICA was organized in 1972 to address spiritual concerns of older adults through religious sector action.

Primary objectives of NICA: to enable religious organizations to serve older adults; to encourage religious communities to promote ministry by and with older adults; to support religious workers in aging in their many roles; to be a forum for religious dialogue about aging; and to be an advocate for older adults' concerns.

NICA supports development of programs and services for older people by religious organizations, agencies, judicatories and congregations; develops and distributes resources that help churchs and synagogues develop ministries that respond to the needs and improve the quality of life of older people; convenes national and regional conferenes for those who work with older adults; sponsors training and continuing education programs concerned with quality of life and religious programming for older people. Office: 298 South Hull St., P.O. Box 1924, Athens, GA 30603. Tel. (404)353-1331

Actg. Exec. Dir., Dr. Thomas B. Robb

OFFICERS

Pres., Rev. John F. Evans
Vice Pres., Mrs. Lillian Husted; Ms. Jane Stenson
Sec., Dr. Carol S. Pierskalla
Treas., Lt. Col. Beatrice Combs

PERIODICAL

NICA Inform (bi-m), Journal of Religion and Aging (q), P. O. Box 1924, Athens, GA 30603

National Interreligious Service Board for Conscientious Objectors

NISBCO, formed in 1940, is a nonprofit service organization sponsored by a broad coalition of national religious bodies. NISBCO responds to the needs of conscientious objectors by: providing information on how to register and document one's convictions as a conscientious objector; providing professional counseling for those who are working through convictions of conscientious objection and training religious CO counselors; alerting citizens to the latest developments in the drive to bring back the draft and the efforts to institute compulsory national service; aiding COs in the armed forces who seek noncombatant transfer or discharge; maintaining an extensive referral service to local counseling agencies in all areas of the country, and to attorneys who can aid those in need of legal counsel; acting as a national resource center for those interested in CO/peace witness of all religious bodies in the United States: encouraging citizens through articles, speaking engagements, and NISBCO publications, to decide for themselves what they believe about participation in war based upon the dictates of their own consciences.

Office: Ste. 750, 15011 Connecticut Ave., NW, Washington, DC 20009. Tel. (202)483-4510

OFFICERS

Chpsn., L. Robert McClean, UMC, 777 United Nations Plz., New York, NY 10017
Exec. Dir., Rev. L. William Yolton

PERIODICAL

The Reporter for Conscience' Sake (m)

13

National Religious Broadcasters

National Religious Broadcasters is an association of more than 1,400 organizations which produce religious programs for radio and television or operate stations carrying predominately religious programs. NRB member organizations are responsible for more than 75 percent of all religious radio and television in the United States, reaching an average weekly audience of millions by radio and television.

Dedicated to the communication of the Gospel, NRB was founded in 1944 to safeguard free and complete access to the broadcast media. By encouraging the development of Christian programs and stations, NRB helps make it possible for millions to hear the good news of Jesus Christ on the electronic media.

GENERAL ORGANIZATION

Executive Offices: P. O. Box 1926, Morristown, NJ 07962. Tel. (201)428-5400.
Exec. Dir., Ben Armstrong
Annual Meeting: 1990 National Convention, Washington, DC, Jan. 27-31, 1990

OFFICERS

Pres., Jerry Rose, WCFC-TV, Chicago
1st Vice Pres., David Clark, CBN, Virginia Beach, VA
2nd Vice Pres., Robert Ball, Salem Communications, Camarillo, CA
Sec., Kay Arthur, Precept Ministries, Chattanooga, TN
Treas., Robert Straton, Walter Bennett Co., Philadelphia, PA

PERIODICALS

Religious Broadcasting (11/yr.), P. O. Box 1926, Morristown, NJ 07962, Ben Armstrong, Exec. Ed.
Directory of Religious Broadcasting (Annual)

North American Academy of Ecumenists

Organized in 1967, the stated purpose of the NAAE is: "to inform, relate, and encourage men and women professionally engaged in the study, teaching, and other practice of ecumenism."
Mailing Address: c/o Prof. Eugene Zoeller, 2001 Newburg Rd., Louisville, KY 40205

OFFICERS

Pres., Prof. Margaret O'Gara, Fac. of Theol., Univ. of St. Michael's College, Toronto, ON M5S 1J4
Pres. Elect, Rev. J. Robert Wright, General Theol. Sem., New York, NY 10011
Sec., Walter Bildstein, Univ. of Waterloo, Waterloo, ON N2L 3G1
Membership Sec./Treas., Eugene Zoeller, Theol. Dept. Bellarmine College, Louisville, KY 40205

PERIODICAL

Journal of Ecumenical Studies (q), Temple University, Philadelphia, PA 19122, Leonard Swidler, Ed. (This periodical is affiliated with the Academy.)

North American Baptist Fellowship

Organized in 1964, the North American Baptist Fellowship is a voluntary organization of Baptist Conventions in Canada and the United States, functioning as a regional body within the Baptist World Alliance. Its objectives are: (a) to promote fellowship and cooperation among Baptists in North America, and (b) to further the aims and objectives of the Baptist World Alliance so far as these affect the life of the Baptist churches in North America. Its membership,

however, is not identical with the North American membership of the Baptist World Alliance.

Church membership of the Fellowship bodies is over 28 million.

The NABF assembles representatives of the member bodies once a year for exchange of information and views in such fields as evangelism and education, missions, stewardship promotion, laymen's activities, and theological education. It conducts occasional consultations for denominational leaders on such subjects as church extension. It encourages cooperation at the city and county level where churches of more than one member group are located.

Headquarters: 6733 Curran St., McLean VA 22101. Tel. (703)790-8980.

EXECUTIVE OFFICERS

Pres., Dr. V. Simpson Turner, Pastor, Mt. Carmel Baptist Ch., 714 Quincy St., Brooklyn, NY 11221
Vice-Pres., Dr. Richard Coffin, Canadian Baptist Federation, 7185 Millcreek Dr., Mississauga, ON, Canada
Sec. and Staff Exec., Dr. Archie R. Goldie, Dir., Div. of Bapt. World Aid, 6733 Curran St., McLean VA 22101
Representing the Baptist World Alliance: Dr. Noel Vose, BWA Pres., Baptist College, Hayman Rd., Bentley, Western Australia 6102; Dr. Denton Lotz, Gen. Sec./Treas., Baptist World Alliance, 6733 Curran St., McLean VA 22101

MEMBER BODIES

American Baptist Churches in the U.S.A.
Canadian Baptist Federation
General Association of General Baptists
National Baptist Convention of America
National Baptist Convention, USA, Inc.
Progressive National Baptist Convention, Inc.
Seventh Day Baptist General Conference
North American Baptist Conference
Southern Baptist Convention

North American Broadcast Section, World Association for Christian Communication

This group was created in 1970 to bring together those persons in Canada and the U.S.A. who have an interest in broadcasting from a Christian perspective.

An annual conference is held during the week after Thanksgiving in the U.S.A. that draws over 200 persons from at least 25 communions.

Office: 1300 Mutual Building, Detroit, MI 48226. Tel. (313)962-0340

STAFF

Business Mgr., Rev. Edward Willingham

Pentecostal Fellowship of North America

Organized at Des Moines, Iowa, in October, 1948 shortly after the first World Conference of Pentecostal Believers was held in Zurich, Switzerland, in May, 1947, the PFNA has the following objectives: 1) to provide a vehicle of expression and coordination of efforts in matters common to all member bodies including missionary and evangelistic effort; 2) to demonstrate to the world the essential unity of Spirit-baptized believers; 3) to provide services to its constituents to facilitate world evangelism; 4) to encourage the principles of comity for the nurture of the body of Christ, endeavoring to keep the unity of the Spirit until we all come to the unity of the faith.

The PFNA has local chapters in communities where churches of the member groups are located, and fellowship rallies are held. On the national level, representatives of the member bodies are assembled for studies and exchange of views in the fields of home missions, foreign missions, and youth.

EXECUTIVE OFFICERS

Chpsn., Rev. James M. MacKnight, 10 Overlea Blvd., Toronto, Ontario M4H 1A5
1st Vice-Chpsn., B. E. Underwood, P. O. Box 12609, Oklahoma City, OK 73157
2nd Vice-Chpsn., _____
Sec., Don Sauls, P. O. Box 1568, Dunn, NC 28334
Treas., J. Eugene Kurtz, 110 Glendale Blvd., Los Angeles, CA 90026

PERIODICAL

P.F.N.A. News (q), 10 Overlea Blvd., Toronto, Ontario M4H 1A5

MEMBER GROUPS

Anchor Bay Evangelistic Association
Apostolic Church of Canada
Assemblies of God
Christian Church of North America
Church of God
Church of God of Apostolic Faith
Church of God, Mountain Assembly
Congregational Holiness Church
Elim Fellowship
Free Gospel Church, Inc.
Garr Memorial Ch., Carolina Evangelistic Assn.
International Church of the Foursquare Gospel
International Pentecostal Church of Christ
International Pentecostal Holiness Church
Italian Pentecostal Church of Canada
Open Bible Standard Churches, Inc.
Pentecostal Asssemblies of Canada
Pentecostal Asssemblies of Newfoundland
Pentecostal Church of God
Pentecostal Free-Will Baptist Church
Pentecostal Holiness Church of Canada

Project Equality, Inc.

Project Equality is a non-profit national interfaith program for affirmative action and equal employment opportunity.

Project Equality serves as a central agency to receive and validate the equal employment commitment of suppliers of goods and services to sponsoring organizations and participating institutions, congregations, and individuals. Employers filing an accepted Annual Participation Report are included in the Project Equality *Buyer's Guide*.

Workshops, training events and consultant services in affirmative action and equal employment practices in recruitment, selection, placement, transfer, promotion, discipline and discharge are also available to sponsors and participants.

Office: Project Equality, Inc., 1020 E. 63rd St., Ste. 102, Kansas City, MO 64110. Tel. (816)361-92222

OFFICERS

Chpsn., Ms. Barbara Thompson, Gen. Sec., Comm. on Religion and Race, United Methodist Church
Vice-Chpsn., Emilio Carrillo, Asst. Gen. Sec. for Personnel, National Council of Churches
Sec., Kenneth Martin, Assoc. Exec. Sec., American Friends Service Cmte.
Treas., Howard Belton, National Education Association
Pres., Rev. Maurice E. Culver

PUBLICATIONS

Buyer's Guide; Update (q); EEO News (q); PE Action (q)

SPONSORS/ENDORSING ORGANIZATIONS

American Baptist Churches in the U.S.A.
American Friends Service Committee
American Jewish Committee
Christian Church (Disciples of christ)
Church of the Brethren
Church Women United
Consultation on Church Union
The Episcopal Church
Evangelical Lutheran Church in America
International Council of Community Churches
National Catholic Confernce for Interracial Justice
National Council of the Churches of Christ in the U.S.A.
National Education Association
National Federation of Priests Council
Presbyteian Church (U.S.A.)
Reformed Church in America
Roman Catholic Dioceses and Religious Orders
Unitarian Universalist Association
United Church of Christ
United Methodist Church
YWCA of the USA

Religion In American Life, Inc.

Religion In American Life (RIAL) is a unique cooperative program of some 50 major national religious groups (Catholic, Eastern Orthodox, Jewish, Protestant, etc.). It provides services for denominationally-supported, congregation-based outreach and growth programs. These programs are promoted through national advertising campaigns reaching the American public by the use of all media. The ad campaigns are produced by a volunteer agency (currently FCB/Leber Katz Partners), with production/distribution and administration costs funded by denominations and business groups, as well as by individuals. Since 1949, RIAL ad campaign project has been accepted under the aegis of The Advertising Council. This results in as much as $50 to $60 million worth of time and space in a single year, contributed by the media as a public service. Through RIAL, religious groups demonstrate respect for other traditions and the value of religious freedom. The RIAL program also includes seminars and symposia, research, leadership awards programs, and Worship Directories in hotels, motels, and public places throughout the nation. Project for the next 10 years: Invite a Friend/200 Million by the Year 2000.

Office: 2 Queenston Pl., Rm. 200, Princeton, NJ 08540. Tel. (609)921-3639

OFFICERS

Chpsn. of Bd., Rabbi Joseph B. Glaser (CCAR)
Vice-Chpsns.: Dr. Harold C. Bennett (SBC); Mr. Neal Gilliatt; Archbshp. Torkom Manoogian (Armen. Ch. Am.); John Cardinal O'Connor; Rabbi Ronald B. Sobel
Treas., Mr. Robert E. Gralley
Sec., Mr. Roy J. Adler

STAFF

Pres., Dr. Nicholas B. van Dvck
Worship Directory Mgr., Ms. Jane Kelly

PERIODICAL

RIAL News (q), 2 Queenston Pl., Rm 200, Princeton, NJ 08540. Tel. (609)921-3639.

Religion Newswriters Association

Founded in 1949, the RNA is a professional association of religion news editors and reporters on secular daily and weekly newspapers, news services, and news magazines. It sponsors four annual contests for excellence in religion news coverage in the secular press. Annual meetings during a major religious convocation.

OFFICERS

Pres., Ed Briggs, Richmond Times-Dispatch, Richmond, VA 23293
1st Vice-Pres., John Dart, Los Angeles Times, Los Angeles, CA 90053
2nd Vice-Pres., Jim Jones, Ft. Worth Star-Telegram, Ft. Worth, TX 76102
Sec., Cecile Holmes White, Houston Chronicle, Houston, TX 77210
Treas., Richard Dujardin, Providence Journal-Bulletin, Providence, RI 02902

PERIODICAL

News Letter, 634 Johnson Ct., Teaneck, NJ 07666, Charles M. Austin, ed.

Religious Conference Management Association, Inc.

The Religious Conference Management Association, Inc. (RCMA) is an interfaith nonprofit professional organization of men and women who have responsibility for planning and/or managing meetings, seminars, conferences, conventions, assemblies, or other gatherings for religious organizations.

Founded in 1972, RCMA is dedicated to promoting the highest professional performance by its members and associate members through the mutual exchange of ideas, techniques, and methods.

Today RCMA has more than 1,150 members and associate members.

The association conducts an annual conference which provides a forum for its membership to gain increased knowledge in the arts and sciences of religious meeting planning and management.

Office: One Hoosier Dome, Ste. 120, Indianapolis, IN 46225. Tel. (317)632-1888.

OFFICERS

Pres., Melvin L. Worthington, National Association of Free Will Baptists, P.O. Box 1088, Nashville, TN 37202
Vice Pres., Rainer B. Wilson, Sr., Church of Christ, Holiness, U.S.A., 819 Hampton Ave., Newport News, VA 23607
Sec.-Treas., Marvin C. Wilbur, 32 Windsor Rd., Tenafly, NJ 07670
Exec. Dir., DeWayne S. Woodring, Religious Conference Management Association, One Hoosier Dome, Suite 120, Indianapolis, IN 46225

PERIODICALS

RCMA Highlights (bi-m), One Hoosier Dome, Suite 120, Indianapolis, IN 46225
Who's Who In Religious Conference Management (Annual), One Hoosier Dome, Ste. 120, Indianapolis, IN 46225

The Religious Public Relations Council, Inc.

The Religious Public Relations Council, Inc., is an organization whose purposes are to establish, raise and maintain high standards of public relations and communication to the end that religious faith and life may be advanced; and to promote fellowship, counseling, and exchange of ideas among its members.

The Council is an interfaith non-profit professional association, founded as the Religious Publicity Council on November 27, 1929, in Washington, D.C. There were 29 charter members, representing seven denominations, the Federal Council of Churches, and four church-related agencies.

Today RPRC has over 700 members in 14 chapters, as well as over 150 members-at-large in 30 states and Canada and six nations overseas.

The Council conducts an annual convention, sponsors two awards programs: the Wilbur Awards for secular journalism and broadcasting; the other, the De Rose/Hinkhouse Memorial Awards of excellence in nine categories for its own members.

Office: 357 Righters Mill Rd., P.O. Box 315, Gladwyne, PA 19035. Tel. (215)642-8895

OFFICERS

Pres., Thomas S. McAnally, United Methodist Communications, 810 Twelfth Ave. S., Nashville, TN 37203
Vice Pres., Wesley M. Pattillo, Vice-Pres., Univ. Rel., Samford Univ., 800 Lakeshore Dr., Birmingham, AL 35229
Exec. Sec., Anne M. Reimel, Religious Public Relations Council, Inc. P.O. Box 315, Gladwyne, PA 19035

PERIODICALS

Counselor (q), P.O. Box 315, Gladwyne, PA 19035, Londia Darden, Ed.
Mediakit (q), P.O. Box 315, Gladwyne, PA 19035

Standing Conference of Canonical Orthodox Bishops in the Americas

This body was established in 1960 to achieve cooperation among the various Eastern Orthodox Churches in the U.S.A. The Conference is "a voluntary association of the Bishops in the Americas established . . . to serve as an agency to centralize and coordinate the mission of the Church. It acts as a clearing house to focus the efforts of the Church on common concerns and to avoid duplication and overlapping of services and agencies. Special departments are devoted to campus work, Christian education, military and other chaplaincies, regional clergy fellowships, and ecumenical relations."

Office: 8-10 East 79th St., New York, NY 10021. Tel. (212)570-3500

OFFICERS

Chpsn., Most Rev. Archbishop Iakovos
Vice Chpsn., Most Rev. Metropolitan Philip
Sec., V. Rev. R. W. Schneirla
Treas., Bishop Peter (L'hullier)

MEMBER CHURCHES

Albanian Orthodox Diocese of America
American Carpatho-Russian Orthodox Greek Catholic Church
Antiochian Orthodox Christian Archdiocese of All North America
Bulgarian Eastern Orthodox Church
Greek Orthodox Archdiocese of North and South America
Orthodox Church in America
Romanian Orthodox Church in America
Serbian Orthodox Church for the U.S.A. and Canada
Ukrainian Orthodox Church of America
Ukrainian Autocephalic Orthodox Church in Exile

YMCA of the USA

The Young Men's Christian Association (YMCA) is one of the largest private voluntary organizations in the world, serving about 25 million members in 97 countries. In the United States, some 2,000 local branches, units, camps, and centers annually serve almost 14 million people of all ages, religions, races, abilities, and incomes. About 46 percent of those served are female. The YMCA was begun in London, England, in 1844; the first YMCA in the U.S. was established at Boston, Mass., in 1851.

YMCAs actively promote a set of Judeo-Christian values for living. The YMCA believes that people are responsible for their own lives and actions and that they should join together in positive association with one another, serving the needs of all and preserving the key concepts of equality and justice. It operates on the principle that all people are children of God, worthy of respect.

YMCAs promote values through a diverse set of programs, including health and fitness, camping, youth sports, family events, aquatics, child care, juvenile justice, senior citizens' activities, international education and exchange, teen programs, programs for the homeless, youth employment, adult literacy and more. Some still offer residential and hotel facilities, through that number is decreasing. The kind of programs offered at each YMCA will vary; each is controlled by volunteer board members from the community who make their own program, policy, and financial decisions, based on the needs of that community.

While each YMCA is a separate non-profit organization, those in the U.S.A. are tied together by five basic goals which override the differences in programs, buildings, and leaders. These goals are to promote healthy life-styles, strengthen the modern family, develop leadership qualities in youth, increase international understanding, and assist in community development.

Corporate Name: YMCA of the USA
Office: 101 N. Wacker Dr., Chicago, IL 60606. Tel. (312) 977-0031

OFFICERS

Board Chpsn., Harold Davis
Exec. Dir., Solon B. Cousins

Young Women's Christian Association of the United States of America

The YWCA of the U.S.A. is an Association comprised of some 450 affiliates in communities and on college campuses across the United States and serving some 2 million members and program participants. It seeks to empower women and girls and to enable them, coming together across lines of age, race, religious belief, economic and occupational status to make a significant contribution to the elimination of racism and the achievement of peace, justice, freedom and dignity for all people. Its leadership is vested in a National Board, whose functions are to unite into an effective continuing organization the autonomous member Associations for furthering the purposes of the National Association and to participate in the work of the World YWCA.

NATIONAL BOARD

Office: 726 Broadway, New York, NY 10003. Tel. (212) 614-2700

OFFICERS

Pres., Glendora McIlwain Putnam
Sec., Olga Madrid
Exec. Dir., Gwendolyn Calvert Baker

Youth for Christ / USA

Founded in 1945, the mission of YFC is to communicate the life-changing message of Jesus Christ to every young person.

Locally controlled YFC programs serve in 220 cities and metropolitan areas of the U.S.

YFC's Campus Life Club program involves teens who attend approximately 1,365 high schools in the United States. YFC's highly trained staff now numbers over 1,000. In addition, approximately 8,800 part-time and volunteer staff supplement the full-time staff. Youth Guidance, a ministry for nonschool-oriented youth includes group homes, court referrals, institutional services, and neighborhood ministries. The year-round conference and camping program involves approximately 35,000 young people each year. A family oriented ministry designed to enrich individuals and church family education programs is carried on through Family Forum, a daily 5 minute radio program on over 300 stations. Independent, indigenous YFC organizations also work in 65 countries overseas.

GENERAL ORGANIZATION

Headquarters: 360 S. Main Place, Carol Stream, IL 60188.
  Pres., Dr. Richard Wynn
International Organization: Singapore, Pres., Rev. Jim Groen, Gen. Dir., James Wilson.
Canadian Organization: 220 Attwell Dr., Unit #1, Rexdale, Ontario M9W 5B2. Pres., Robert Simpson.

2. CANADIAN COOPERATIVE ORGANIZATIONS, NATIONAL

This directory of Canadian Cooperative Organizations attempts to list major organizations working interdenominationally on a national basis. The editor of the **Yearbook of American and Canadian Churches** would appreciate receiving information on any significant organizations not now included. Those directories not reviewed for this edition carry the symbol (+) in front of them

The Canadian Council of Churches

The Canadian Council of Churches was organized in 1944. Its basic purpose is to provide the churches with an agency for conference and consultation and for such common planning and common action as they desire to undertake. It encourages ecumenical understanding and action throughout Canada through local councils of churches. It also relates to the World Council of Churches and other agencies serving the worldwide ecumenical movement.

The Council has a Triennial Assembly, a General Board which meets semiannually, and an Executive Committee. Program is administered through three commissions— Faith and Witness, Justice and Peace, and Ecumenical Education and Communication.

40 St. Clair Ave. E., Toronto, Ontario M4T 1M9 Tel. (416)921-4152

OFFICERS AND STAFF

Pres., Rev. Dr. Donald W. Sjoberg
Vice-Pres., Rev. Alyson Barnett-Cowan; Most Rev. John M. Sherlock; Major Malcolm Webster
Treas., Mr. John Hart
Assoc. Secs., Dr. Nancy Cocks, Mr. James Hodgson, Rev. Tadashi Mitsui
Gen. Sec., Dr. Stuart E. Brown
Assoc. Sec., Rev. Tadashi Mitsui

AFFILIATED INSTITUTION

Ecumenical Forum of Canada, 11 Madison Ave., Toronto, Ontario M5R 2S2. Dir., Rev. Tim Ryan S.F.M. Tel. (416) 924-9351

MEMBERS

The Anglican Church of Canada
The Armenian Church of America—Diocese of Canada
Baptist Convention of Ontario and Quebec
Canadian Conference of Catholic Bishops*
Christian Church (Disciples of Christ)
Coptic Orthodox Church of Canada
Ethiopian Orthodox Church in Canada
Evangelical Lutheran Church in Canada
Greek Orthodox Diocese of Toronto (Canada)
Orthodox Church in America, Diocese of Canada
Polish National Catholic Church
Presbyterian Church in Canada
Ethiopian Orthodox Church in Canada
Reformed Church in America—Classis of Ontario
Religious Society of Friends—Canada Yearly Meeting
Salvation Army—Canada and Bermuda
The United Church of Canada
*Associate Member

Canadian Bible Society

For almost two centuries the Canadian Bible Society has had a distinguished presence in this country and a widening international role as a leading translator, publisher and distributor of God's Word.

Although formally chartered in 1906, the Canadian organization had already been active for almost a century as an early extension of the British and Foreign Bible Society, founded in 1804 in London, England.

As a member of the worldwide United Bible Societies, the non-denominational Canadian Bible Society helps to provide scriptures without doctrinal note or comment in 1,907 languages and dialects to believers worldwide.

From its national office and 17 district offices, Canadian Bible Society responds not only to the ministries and missions of its own country, but also to the frontiers of Christianity wherever need arises.

National Office: 10 Carnforth Road, Toronto, Ontario M4A 2S4. Tel. (416)757-4171; Fax: (416)757-3376

OFFICER

Gen. Sec., Rev. Floyd C. Babcock

Canadian Council of Christians and Jews

The Canadian Council of Christians and Jews is an organization which builds bridges of understanding between Canadians. Its techniques of effecting social change are dialogue and education. The CCCJ believes that there exist in any community in Canada the reservoirs of good will, the mediating skills, and the enlightened self-interest which make accommodation to change and the creation of social justice possible.

The CCCJ was established in Toronto in 1947 by a group of prominent business, civic and religious leaders.

Its mandate is: "to promote justice, friendship, cooperation and understanding among people differing in race, religion or nationality.

National Office: 49 Front St., E., Toronto, Ontario M5E 1B3. Tel. (416)364-3101.

STAFF

National Exec. Dir., Mrs. Elizabeth Loweth

Canadian Tract Society

The Canadian Tract Society was organized in 1970 as an independent distributor of gospel leaflets to provide Canadian churches and individual Christians with quality materials proclaiming the Gospel through the printed page. It is affiliated with the American Tract Society, which encouraged its formation and assisted in its founding, and for whom it serves as an exclusive Canadian distributor. The CTS is a nonprofit international service ministry.

Address: Box 203, Port Credit P.O., Mississauga, Ontario L5G 4L7

OFFICERS

Pres., Stanley D. Mackey
Exec. Sec., Robert J. Burns

Evangelical Fellowship of Canada

The Fellowship was formed in 1964. Presently there are 27 denominations, 88 organizations, and 756 local churches, and thousands of individual members.

Its purposes are threefold: "Fellowship in the gospel" (Phil. 1:5). "the defence and confirmation of the gospel" (Phil. 1:7), and "the furtherance of the gospel" (Phil. 1:12).

The Fellowship believes the Holy Scriptures, as originally given, are infallible and that salvation through the Lord Jesus Christ is by faith apart from works.

In national and regional conventions the Fellowship urges Christians to live exemplary lives and to openly challenge the evils and injustices of society. It encourages cooperation with various agencies in Canada and overseas that are sensitive to social and spiritual needs.

Office: 175 Riviera Dr., Markham, Ontario L3R 5J6. (416)479-5885; Fax (416)479-4742
Mailing Address: P.O. Box 8800, Sta. B, Willowdale, Ontario M2K 2R6

OFFICERS

Exec. Dir., Rev. Brian C. Stiller
Pres., Bishop Donald Bastian
Vice Pres., Rev. Douglas Moffat; Dr. John Redekop
Treas., Major Earl McInnes
Sec., Dr. Donald Jost
Committee Members at Large, Rev. Bernice Gerard, Dr. Ian Rennie, Rev. Mervin Sanders, Rev. William Wan
Chpsn., Social Action Commission, Dr. Paul Marshall
Chpsn., Task Force on Evangelism, Rev. Alan Andrews
Chpsn., Task Force on the Family, Dr. Mavis Oleson

Inter-Varsity Christian Fellowship of Canada

Inter-Varsity Christian Fellowship is a non-profit, interdenominational Canadian student movement centering on the witness to Jesus Christ in campus communities: universities, colleges, high schools, and through a Canada-wide Pioneer camping programme. IVCF was officially formed in 1928-29 through the enthusiastic efforts of the late Dr. Howard Guinness, whose arrival from Britain challenged students to follow the example of the Inter-Varsity Fellowship from which he came, in organising themselves in prayer and Bible Study fellowship groups. Inter-Varsity has always been a student-initiated movement, emphasizing and developing leadership on the campus to call Christians to outreach, challenging other students to a personal faith in Jesus Christ, and study of the Bible as God's revealed truth within a fellowship of believers. A strong stress has been placed on missionary activity, and the triennial conference held at Urbana, Ill. (jointly sponsored by US and Canadian IVCF) has been a means of challenging many young people to service in Christian vocation. Inter-Varsity works closely with, and is a strong believer in, the work of local and national churches.

Headquarters: 1840 Lawrence Ave., E., Scarborough, Ontario M1R 2Y4. Tel. (416)487-3431

OFFICERS

Gen. Dir., James E. Berney

Lutheran Council in Canada

The Lutheran Council in Canada was organized in 1967 and is a cooperative agency of the Evangelical Lutheran Church in Canada and the Lutheran Church-Canada.

The Council's activities include communications, coordinative service and national liaison in social ministry, chaplaincy, and scout activity.

Office: 25 Old York Mills Rd., Willowdale, Ontario M2P 1B5. Tel. (416)488-9430

OFFICERS

Exec. Dir., Lawrence R. Likness

Mennonite Central Committee Canada (MCCC)

Mennonite Central Committee Canada was organized in 1964 to continue the work which several regional Canadian inter-Mennonite agencies had been doing in relief, service, immigration, and peace. All but a few of the smaller Mennonite groups in Canada belong to MCC Canada.

MCCC is part of the binational Mennonite Central Committee (MCC) which has its headquarters in Akron, Pennsylvania, from where the overseas development and relief projects are administered. In 1988 MCCC's budget was $18,376,000, representing about 40 percent of the total MCC budget. There were 436 Canadians of a total of 992 MCC workers serving one to three year terms in North America and abroad during the same time period.

The MCC office in Winnipeg administers projects located in Canada. Domestic programs of Voluntary Service, Native Concerns, Peace and Social Concerns, Food Program, Employment Concerns, Ottawa Office, Victim/Offender Ministries, Mental Health, and immigration are all part of MCC's Canadian ministry. Whenever it undertakes a project, MCCC attempts to relate to the church or churches in the area, thus supporting the local church.

Office: 134 Plaza Dr., Winnipeg, Manitoba R3T 5K9. Tel. (204)261-6381

OFFICER

Exec. Dir., Daniel Zehr

People for Sunday Association of Canada

A secular organization devoted to achieving for Canada Sunday as a national common day of rest and leisure.

The Association produces its publications *Sound About Sunday* and *Update* and furnishes speakers when requested.

Office: P. O. Box 457, Islington, Ontario M9A 4X4, Tel. (416)625-8759

OFFICERS

Pres., Canon Thomas Rocke
Exec. Dir., Les Kingdon

Student Christian Movement of Canada

The Student Christian Movement of Canada was formed in 1921 from the student arm of the YMCA. It has its roots in the Social Gospel movements of the late nineteenth and early twentieth centuries. Throughout its intellectual history, the SCM in Canada has sought to relate the Christian faith to the living realities of the social and political context of each student generation.

The present priorities are built around the need to form more and stronger critical Christian communities on Canadian campuses within which individuals may develop their social and political analyses, experience spiritual growth and fellowship, and bring Christian ecumenical witness to the university.

The Student Christian Movement of Canada is affiliated with the World Student Christian Federation.

Office: 310 Danforth Ave., Ste. C3, Toronto, Ontario M4K 1N6. Tel. (416)463-4312
Gen. Sec., Frederick P. Dunleavy

Women's Interchurch Council of Canada

An ecumenical movement through which Christians may express their unity by prayer, fellowship, study, action. The purpose is: to enable Christian women across Canada to live in love and fellowship so that all people may find fullness of life in Christ. WICC sponsors the World Day of Prayer and the Fellowship of the Least Coin in Canada. Human rights projects are supported and ecumenical study kits produced. A newsletter is issued four times a year. Membership is composed of one appointment by each participating national denomination which confesses the Lord Jesus Christ as God and Saviour and members elected through the nominating process set out in the by-laws.

Office: 77 Charles St., W., Toronto, Ontario M5S 1K5 Tel. (416)922-6177

OFFICERS

Pres., Betty Turcott
Exec. Dir., Vivian Harrower

Young Men's Christian Association in Canada

The first YMCA in Canada was established in Montreal, November 25, 1851, the declared purpose being "the improvement of the spiritual and mental condition of young men." Toronto and Halifax followed in 1853. At the 125th anniversary of the Canadian movement (1976), YMCAs were found in 75 cities from St. John's, Newfoundland to Victoria, B.C., with programs for intellectual, spiritual, and physical development of all Canadians.

Originally forming a single movement with the YMCAs in the United States, the Canadian Associations formed their own National Council in 1912. However, the international outreach (assisting in the establishment of YMCA movements in Latin America, Asia, and Africa) was administered jointly with the YMCA in the U.S. through an International Committee until 1970, when an agreement recognized the Canadian YMCA's independent service abroad. Today many "partnership Programs" exist between the Canadian Associations and YMCAs in developing countries.

YMCA Canada: 2160 Yonge St., Toronto, Ontario M4S 2A9. Tel. (416)485-9447

OFFICERS

Chpsn., Donald S. McCreesh
Chief Exec. Officer, Richard R. Bailey
Dir., Int'l & Social Devel., Robert Vokey

Young Women's Christian Association of/du Canada

The YWCA of/du Canada is a national voluntary organization serving 46 YWCAs and YM-YWCAs across Canada. Dedicated to the development and improved status of women and their families, the YWCA is committed to service delivery, to being a source of public education on women's issues, and an advocate of social change. Services provided by YWCAs and YM-YWCAs include adult education programs, residences and shelters, childcare, fitness activities, wellness programs and international development education. As a member of the World YWCA, the YWCA of/du Canada is part of the largest women's organization in the world.

Office: 80 Gerrard St.E., Toronto, Ontario M5B 1G6. Tel (416)593-9886

OFFICERS

Exec. Dir., Rita S. Karakas

3. RELIGIOUS BODIES IN THE UNITED STATES

Introduction

The following is a series of directories of United States religious bodies arranged alphabetically by official name. Individual denominational directories have been corrected by the religious bodies themselves. Those directories which have not been updated for this edition of the **Yearbook** by denominational officials carry the symbol (†) in front of the title of denomination.

Generally speaking, each directory listing follows the following organization: a historical or doctrinal statement: a brief statement of current statistics (data for 1989 or 1988), if any; information on general organization; officers; other organizations; and major periodicals.

More complete statistics will be found in the Statistical and Historical Section of this **Yearbook** in the table on Current and Non-Current Statistics and also in the table entitled "Some Statistics of Church Finances."

A listing of religious bodies by family groups (e.g., Baptists, Lutheran) is found at the end of this directory.

A published work by Dr. J. Gordon Melton entitled *A Directory of Religious Bodies in the United States*, New York, Garland Publishing Co., 1977 lists 1,275 "primary" religious bodies currently functioning in the United States. The title, address and principal publication is supplied. There is a typology for classification of these primary religious bodies which are then listed by family groups.

Advent Christian Church

The Advent Christian Church is a conservative, evangelical denomination, which grew out of the Millerite movement of the 1830s and 1840s. Like most evangelicals, the members stress the authority of Scripture, justification by faith in Jesus Christ alone, the importance of evangelism and world missions, and the soon visible return of Jesus Christ.

Organized in 1860, the Advent Christian Church maintains headquarters in Charlotte, North Carolina, with regional offices in Rochester, New Hampshire; Augusta, Georgia; Fort Worth, Texas; Lewiston, Idaho; and Lenoir, NC. Missions are maintained in India, Nigeria, Japan, Malaysia, the Philippines, Mexico and Memphis, Tennessee.

While the Advent Christian Church is considered conservative and evangelical in theology, it maintains doctrinal distinctives in three areas: conditional immortality, the sleep of the dead until the return of Christ, and belief that the kingdom of God will be established on earth made new by Jesus Christ.

Churches: 251; Inclusive Membership: 19,900; Sunday or Sabbath School: 300; Total Enrollment: 18,472; Ordained Clergy: 560

GENERAL ORGANIZATION

General Conference: triennial
Office: P.O. Box 23152, Charlotte, NC 28212, David H. Northup, Exec. Vice-Pres. Tel. (704)545-6161
Organizations and periodicals are all at this address unless otherwise noted.

OFFICERS

Pres., Rev. Donald E. Wrigley, 219 Mt. Carmel Rd., Walterboro, SC 29488
Sec., Rev. Marshall Tidwell, 1002 Grove Ave., SW, Lenoir, NC 28645
Appalachian Vice-Pres., Rev. Orville Harvey, Rt. 9, Box 734, Princeton, WV 24740
Central Vice-Pres., Rev. Dwight Carpenter, 7919 Kandy Lane, N. Richland Hills, TX 76180
Eastern Vice-Pres., Rev. Irvin Verrill, 20 Highland Cliff Rd., Windham, ME 04062
Southern Vice-Pres., Rev. Larry Withrow, 318 Crescent Dr., Clayton, NC 27520
Western Vice-Pres., Mrs. Luella Johnson, Rt. 6, Box 292, Live Oak, FL 32060
The Woman's Home & Foreign Mission Society: Pres., Mrs. Bea Moore, Route 8, Box 274, Loudon, NH 03301

PERIODICALS

The Advent Christian Witness (m), Rev. Robert Mayer, P. O. Box 23152, Charlotte, NC 28212
Advent Christian News (m), Rev. Robert Mayer, Ed.
Maranatha (q), Rev. Robert Mayer, Ed.
Insight (q), Millie Griswold, Ed.

African Methodist Episcopal Church

This church began in 1787 in Philadelphia when persons in St. George's Methodist Episcopal Church withdrew as a protest against color segregation. In 1816 the denomination was started, led by Rev. Richard Allen, who had been ordained deacon by Bishop Asbury, and who was ordained elder and elected and consecrated bishop.

GENERAL ORGANIZATION

General Conference: quadrennial (Next meeting, 1992)
General Board, Annual Meeting 3rd Monday each year, June
Council of Bishops, Annually meeting 3rd Wednesday each year, June

OFFICERS

Senior Bishop, Bishop John H. Adams, 208 Auburn Ave., N.E., Atlanta, GA 30303. Tel.(404)524-8279
Gen. Sec., A.M.E. Church, Dr. O. Urcille Ifill, Sr., P. O. Box 19039, East Germantown Sta., Philadelphia, PA 19138. Tel. (215) 877-8330
Pres., Council of Bishops, Bishop J. Haskell Mayo, P. O. Box 53539, 400 E. 41st St., Ste. 114, Chicago, IL 60653. Tel. (312)373-6587
Sec. Council of Bishops, Bishop Harold B. Senatle, P. O. Box 12, Residensia, 1980 Republic of South Africa. Tel. 27-016-371929
Pres. General Board, Bishop John H. Adams, 208 Auburn Ave., N.E., Atlanta, GA 30303. Tel. (404)524-8279
Sec. General Board, Dr. O. Urcille Ifill, Sr., P. O. Box 19039, East Germantown Sta., Philadelphia, PA 19138. Tel. (215)877-8330
Treas., A.M.E. Church, Dr. Joseph C. McKinney, 2311 "M" St., N.W., Washington, DC 20037. Tel. (202)337-3930
Historiographer, Dr. Dennis Dickerson, P. O. Box 301, Williamstown, MA 02167
Pres. Judical Council, Atty, P. A. Townsend, 1010 Macvicar St., Topeka, KS 66604

DEPARTMENTS

Missions: Dr. Frederick C. Harrison, 475 Riverside Dr., Rm. 1926, New York, NY 10115. Tel. (212)870-2258
Church Extension: Dr. Hercules Miles, Sec.-Treas., 3526 Dodier, St. Louis, MO 63107. Tel. (314)534-4272
Christian Education: Dr. Edgar Mack, Sec., 500 8th Ave., S., Nashville, TN 37203. Tel. (615)242-1420
Sunday School Union: Dr. Lee Henderson, Sec-Treas., 500 Eighth Ave., S., Nashville, TN 37203. Tel. (615)256-5882
Evangelism: Yale B. Bruce, Dir., 5728 Major Blvd., Orlando, FL. Tel. (305)352-6515
Publications: Dr. A. Lee Henderson, Sec.-Treas., 500 8th Ave., S., Nashville, TN 37203. Tel. (615)256-5882

Pension: Dr. Floyd Alexander, Sec.-Treas., 500 8th Ave., S., Nashville, TN 37203. Tel. (615)256-7725

Finance Department: Dr. Joseph C. McKinney, 2311 "M" St., NW, Washington, DC 20037. Tel. (202)337-3930

Statistical Department: Dr. O. Ucille Ifill, Sr., P. O. Box 19039, East Germantown Sta., Philadelphia, PA 19138. Tel. (215)877-8330

Minimum Salary: Dr. Alonzo W. Holman, 280 Hernando St., Memphis, TN 38126. Tel. (901)526-4281

Religious Literature Department: Dr. Cyrus S. Keller, Sr., Editor-in-Chief, P.O. Box 5327, St. Louis, MO 63115. Tel. (314)535-8822

Women's Missionary Society: Mrs. Delores L. K. Williams, Pres., 2311 "M" St., N.W., Washington, DC 20037. Tel. (212)337-1335

Lay Organization: Dr. Kathryn M. Brown, Connectional Pres., 171 Ashby St., Atlanta, GA 30314

PERIODICALS

A.M.E. Christian Recorder: Dr. Robert H. Reid, Ed., 500 8th Ave., S., Nashville TN 37203. Tel. (615)256-8548

A.M.E. Review: Dr. Jamye Coleman Williams, 500 Eighth Ave., S., Nashville, TN 37203. Tel. (615)320-3500

Voice of Missions: Maeola Herring, Ed., 475 Riverside Dr., Rm. 1920, New York, NY 10115

Women's Missionary Magazine: Mrs. Bertha O. Fordham, 800 Risley Ave., Pleasantville, NJ, 08232

Secret Chamber: Dr. Yale B. Bruce, 5728 Major Blvd., Orlando, FL 82819. Tel. (305)352-6515

Journal of Christian Education: Dr. Edgar L. Mack, 500 Eighth Ave., S., Nashville, TN 37202. Tel. (615)242-1420

BISHOPS IN THE U.S.A.

First District: Frank C. Cummings, 5070 Parkside, Ste. 1410, Philadelphia, PA 19131. Tel. (215)877-3771

Second District: H. Hartford Brookins, 6209 Stoneham La., McLean, VA Tel. (703)442-0261

Third District: Richard Allen Hildebrand, 700 Bryden Rd., Ste. 135, Columbus, OH 43215. Tel. (614)461-6496

Fourth District: J. Haskell Mayo, Jr., P. O. Box 53539; 400 E. 41st St., Ste. 114, Chicago, IL 60653. Tel. (312)373-6587

Fifth District: Vinton R. Anderson, P. O. Box 6416, St. Louis, MO 63107. Tel. (314)534-4274

Sixth District: John H. Adams, 208 Auburn Ave. N.E., Atlanta, GA 30303. Tel (404)524-8279

Seventh District: Frederick C. James, 370 Forest Dr., Ste. 402, Columbia, SC 29204

Eighth District: Donald G. Ming, 2138 St. Bernard Ave., New Orleans, LA 70119. Tel. (504)948-4251

Ninth District: Cornelius E. Thomas, 2101 Magnolia, Birmingham, AL 35205. Tel. (205)252-2612

Tenth District: J. Robert L. Pruitt, Republic Bank Tower, Oak Cliff—Ste. 813, Dallas, TX 75208. Tel. (214)941-9323

Eleventh District: Philip R. Cousin, P.O. Box 2140, Jacksonville, FL 32203. Tel. (904)398-3797

Twelfth District: Henry A. Belin, Jr., 604 Locust St., North, Little Rock, AR 72114. Tel. (501)375-4310

Thirteenth District: Vernon R. Byrd, 500 8th Ave., So., Nashville, TN 37203. Tel. (615)242-6814

Fourteenth District: John R. Bryant, P. O. Box 4191, Monrovia, Liberia, West Africa. Tel. 221792

Fifteenth District: Robert Thomas, Jr., 28 Walmer Rd., Woodstock 7925, Capetown, Republic of South Africa. Tel. 27-021-475786

Sixteenth District: Henry A. Belin, Jr., 131 Ashford Rd., Cherry Hill, NJ 08003. Tel. (609)751-7288

Seventeenth District: Richard A. Chapelle, P. O. Box 183, St. Louis, MO 63166. Tel. (314)355-7371

Eighteenth District: Richard A. Chappelle, P. O. Box MS 223, Masery 100, Lesotho, South Africa. Tel. 226 16

Nineteenth District: Harold Ben Senatle, P. O. Box 12, Residensia, 1980 Republic, South Africa. Tel. 27-016-371929

Ecumenical Officer: Frederick H. Talbot, P. O. Box 684, Frederiksted, St. Croix, U. S. Virgin Islands 00840. Tel. (809)772-0723

Located: Rembert E. Stokes, 783 Hidden Circle, Dayton, OH 45459. Tel. (513)436-7347

Retired Bishops:

Henry W. Murph, 5940 Holt Ave., Los Angeles, CA 90056. Tel. (213)410-0266

D. Ward Nichols, 2295 Seventh Ave., New York, NY 10030. Tel. (516)427-0225

Ernest L. Hickman, 1320 Oakcrest Dr., S.W., Atlanta, GA 30311. Tel. (404)349-1336

Harrison J. Bryant, 4000 Bedford Rd., Baltimore, MD 21207. Tel. (301)484-7508

H. Thomas Primm, 2820 Monaco Parkway, Denver, CO 80207. Tel. (303)335-9545

Hubert N. Robinson, 357 Arden Park, Detroit, MI 48202. Tel. (313)875-4967

Bishop Harold I. Bearden, 644 Skipper Dr., Atlanta, GA 30314. Tel. (404)691-9642

African Methodist Episcopal Zion Church

The A.M.E. Zion Church is an independent body, having withdrawn from the John Street Methodist Church of New York City in 1796. The first bishop was James Varick.

GENERAL ORGANIZATION

General Conference: Quadrennial

OFFICERS

Senior Bishop, Bishop William Milton Smith, 3753 Springhill Ave., Mobile, AL 36608

Sec., Board of Bishops, Bishop John Henry Miller, Sr., 8605 Caswell Court, Raleigh, NC 27612

Asst. Sec., Bishop Clinton R. Coleman, 3513 Ellamont Rd., Baltimore, MD 21215

OTHER AGENCIES

Gen. Sec.-Aud., Rev. W. Robert Johnson, P.O. Box 32843, Charlotte, NC 28232. Tel. (704)332-3851

Fin. Sec., Ms. Madie L. Simpson, P.O. Box 31005, Charlotte, NC 28230. Tel. (704)333-4847

A.M.E. Zion Publishing House: Dr. Lem Long, Jr., General Mgr., P.O. Box 30714, Charlotte, NC 28230. Tel. (704)334-9596

Dept. of Overseas Missions: Rev. Dr. Kermit J. DeGraffenreidt. Sec.-Treas, 475 Riverside Dr., Ste. 1910, New York, NY 10115. Tel. (212)870-2952

Dept. of Home Missions, Pensions, and Relief: Rev. Dr. Jewett Walker, Sec.-Treas., P.O. Box 30846, Charlotte, NC 28231. Tel. (704)333-3779

Dept. of Christian Education: Rev. G. L. Blackwell, Sec., 128 E. 58th St., Chicago, IL 60637. Tel. (312)667-0183

Dept. of Church School Literature: Ms. Mary A. Love, Ed., P. O. Box 31005, Charlotte, NC 28230. Tel. (704)332-1034

Dept. of Church Extension: Dr. Lem Long, Jr., Sec.-Treas., P. O. Box 31005, Charlotte, NC 28231. Tel. (704)334-2519

Dept. of Evangelism: Dr. Norman H. Hicklin, Dir., P.O. Box 4, Asheville, NC 28802. Tel. (704)353-5108

Dept. of Public Relations: Gregory R. Smith, Dir., 344 Hawthorne Terr., Mt. Vernon, NY 10550. Tel. (212)234-1544

Woman's Home and Overseas Missionary Society: Gen Pres., Mrs. Grace L. Holmes, 2505 Linden Ave., Knoxville, TN. Tel. (615)525-1523; Exec. Sec., Ms. Barbara Shaw, 4002 Maine Ave., Baltimore, MD 21207. Tel. (301)578-8239; Treas., Mrs. Gwendolyn B. Johnson, 2011 Sterns Dr., Los Angeles, CA 90034. Tel. (213)939-9417

Connectional Lay Council, Pres., Mr. James E. Hewitt, Jr., 5718 Victoria Ave., Los Angeles, CA 90043

Star of Zion (w), Rev. Morgan Tann, Ed., P.O. Box 31005, Charlotte, NC 28230

Quarterly Review (q), Rev. James D. Armstrong, Ed., P. O. Box 31005, Charlotte, NC 28231

Missionary Seer. (m), Rev. Kermit J. DeGraffenreidt, Ed., 475 Riverside Dr., Ste. 1910, New York NY 10115. Tel. (212) 870-2952

Church School Herald (q), Ms. Mary A. Love, Ed., P. O. Box 31005, Charlotte, NC 28230

BISHOPS

First Episcopal District: Bishop William Milton Smith, 3753 Springhill Ave., Mobile, AL 36608. Tel. (205) 344-7769

Second Episcopal District: Bishop Alfred G. Dunston Jr., Presidential Commons, A 521, City Line and Presidential Blvd., Philadelphia, PA 19131. Tel. (215) 877-2659

Third Episcopal District: Bishop J. Clinton Hoggard, 1511 K St., NW Ste. 1100, Washington, DC 20005. Tel. (202)347-1419

Fourth Episcopal District: Bishop Clinton R. Coleman, 3513 Ellamont Rd., Baltimore, MD 21215. Tel. (301) 466-2220

Fifth Episcopal District: Bishop John H. Miller, Springdale Estates, 8605 Caswell Ave., Raleigh, NC 27612. Tel. (919)848-6915

Sixth Episcopal District: Bishop Ruben L. Speaks, 1238 Marshall St., P. O. Box 986, Salisbury, NC 28144. Tel. (704)637-1471

Seventh Episcopal District: Bishop Herman L. Anderson, 7031 Toby St., Charlotte, NC 28213. Tel. (704)598-7419

Eighth Episcopal District: Bishop Cecil Bishop, 5401 Broadwater St., Temple Hill, MD 20748. Tel. (301)894-2165

Ninth Episcopal District: Bishop Richard L. Fisher, 607 N. Grand Ave., Ste. 701, St. Louis, MO 63130. Tel. (314)727-4439

Tenth Episcopal District: Bishop Alfred E. White, 10 Hardin Lane, Glastonbury, CT 06033. Tel. (203)633-3089

Eleventh Episcopal District: Bishop George W. Walker, 3654 Poplar Road, Flossmoor, IL 60422. Tel. (312)799-5599

Twelfth Episcopal District: Bishop Milton A. Williams,1706 Lewellyn Dr., Greensboro, NC 27408. Tel. (919)288-3527

Albanian Orthodox Archdiocese in America

The Albanian Orthodox Church in America traces its origins to the groups of Albanian immigrants which first arrived in the United States in 1886, seeking religious, cultural, and economic freedoms denied them in the homeland.

In 1908 in Boston, the Rev. Fan Stylian Noli (later Archbishop) served the first liturgy in the Albanian language in 500 years, to which Orthodox Albanians rallied, later forming their own diocese in 1919. Parishes began to spring up through New England and the Mid-Atlantic and Great Lakes states.

In 1922, clergy from the U.S. traveled to Albania to proclaim the self-governance of the Orthodox Church in the homeland at the Congress of Berat.

By the 1950s newer generations witnessed a diocesan publication of nearly 42 liturgical and hymnographic volumes of Orthodox classic works in English.

In 1971 the Albanian Archdiocese sought and gained union with the Orthodox Church in America, expressing the desire to expand the Orthodox witness to America at large, giving it an indigenous character.

The Albanian Archdiocese remains vigilant for its brothers and sisters in the homeland who are denied the lifegiving mysteries of the faith, and serves as an important resource for human rights issues and Albanian affairs, in addition to its programs for youth, theological education, vocational interest programs, and retreats for young adults and women. A Lay Ministry program was recently formed to engage a more active witness among the laity.

OFFICERS

Metropolitan Theodosius, 529 E. Broadway Boston, MA 02127. Tel. (617)268-1275

Chancellor, Very Rev. Arthur E. Liolin, 60 Antwerp St., East Milton, MA 02186. Tel. (617)698-3366

Lay Chpsn., Thomas Sotir, 145 Highland St., Newton, MA 02102 Tel. (617)244-5670

Treas., Ronald Nasson, 26 Enfield St., Jamaica Plains, MA 02130. Tel. (617)522-7715

PERIODICAL

The Vineyard (Vreshta), (q), Rev. Stephen Siniari, 5490 Main St., Trumbull, CT 06611

Albanian Orthodox Diocese of America

This Diocese was organized in 1950 as a canonical body administering to the Albanian faithful. It is under the ecclesiastical jurisdiction of the Ecumenical Patriarchate of Constantinople (Istanbul).

Churches: 2; Inclusive Membership: 586; Sunday or Sabbath Schools: 2; Total Enrollment: 31; Ordained Clergy: 3

GENERAL ORGANIZATION

Headquarters: Mailing Address: 2100 S. Stockton Ave., Las Vegas, NV 89104. Tel. (702)457-6443

OFFICER

Vicar General, The Rev. Ik. Ilia Katre

Allegheny Wesleyan Methodist Connection (Original Allegheny Conference)

This body was formed in 1968 by members of the Allegheny Conference (located in eastern Ohio and western Pennsylvania) of the Wesleyan Methodist Church, which merged in 1966 with the Pilgrim Holiness Church to form The Wesleyan Church.

The Allegheny Wesleyan Methodist Church is composed of persons "having the form and seeking the power of godliness, united in order to pray together, to receive the word of exhortation, and to watch over one another in love, that they may help each other to work out their salvation." There is a strong commitment to congregational government and to holiness of heart and life. There is a strong thrust in church extension, developing churches throughout the U.S.

GENERAL ORGANIZATION

Annual Conference: next session, June 1990

General Conference: quadrennial (next session, June 1990).

Headquarters: 1827 Allen Dr., Salem, OH 44460. Tel. (216)337-9376.

OFFICERS

Pres., Rev. John B. Durfee, 1827 Allen Dr., Salem, OH 44460

Vice-Pres., Rev. John Englant, Pittsfield, PA 16340

Sec., Rev. W. H. Cornell, Box 266, Sagamore, PA 16250

Treas., Mr. Clair Taylor, 858 E. Philadelphia Ave., Youngstown, OH 44502

PERIODICAL

The Allegheny Wesleyan Methodist (m), 1827 Allen Dr., Salem, OH 44460, Rev. John B. Durfee, Ed.

Amana Church Society

The Amana Church Society was founded by a God-fearing, God-loving, and pioneering group not associated with any other church or organization. It had its beginning as the Community of True Inspiration in the year 1714 in the province of Hesse, Germany. The members were much persecuted in Germany because of their belief in the 'power of divine inspiration,' because they would not send their children to the ten established schools, and because they were pacifistic in their beliefs and aims.

The Community of True Inspiration, which had its humble beginning under the inspired leadership of Eberhard Ludwig Gruber and Johann Friedrich Rock, was more or less dormant during the early nineteenth century until renewal came under Christian Metz assumed the leadership. He, while divinely inspired, designated that their path lay to the West and the New World. This trek, begun in 1842, ended in the Ebenezer Community, which they established near Buffalo in New York state. Because of deterring and worldly influences, the Ebenezer lands were abandoned in 1854 and subsequently the Amana Colonies were founded in Iowa in 1855.

The Amana Church Society does no proselyting, does not do missionary work, and does not actively work to make converts to the faith. It believes in a peaceful, quiet, 'brotherly' way of life. Although many of the stricter church rules have been relaxed over the years, the Amana Church Society still maintains its simple, unostentatious churches and rituals; although there have been no divinely inspired leaders since the demise of Barbara Landman Heinemann in 1883, the faith is still paramount in divine revelation of the Word of God through his chosen representatives on earth, and the testimonies of the aforementioned religious leaders are still read in all the regular services. Although the Amana Church has no connection with any other church society, the permanency of this small group over the years attests to a faith in God that makes the term *Amana* truly meaningful—"as a rock" or "to remain faithful."

GENERAL ORGANIZATION
Board of Trustees

OFFICERS
Pres., Kirk Setzer, Amana, IA 52203. Tel. (319)622-3799
Vice-Pres., Steward Geiger, Cedar Rapids, IA 52203
Sec., Martin Roemig, Amana, IA 52203. Tel. (319)622-3262
Treas, Henry Schiff, Amana, IA 52203

The American Baptist Association

The American Baptist Association (ABA) is an international fellowship of independent Baptist churches voluntarily cooperating in missionary, evangelistic, benevolent, and Christian education activities throughout the world. Its beginnings can be traced to the landmark movement of the 1850s. Led by James R. Graves and J. M. Pendleton, a significant number of Baptist churches in the South, claiming a New Testament heritage, rejected as extrascriptural the policies of the newly formed Southern Baptist Convention (SBC). Because they strongly advocated church equality, many of these churches continued doing mission and benevolent work apart from the SBC, electing to work through local associations. Meeting in Texarkana, Texas, in 1924, messengers from the various churches effectively merged two of these major associations—the Baptist Missionary Association of Texas and the General Association—forming the American Baptist Association.

Since 1924, mission efforts have been supported in Canada, Mexico, Central and South America, Australia, Africa, Europe, Asia and India. An even more successful domestic mission effort has changed the ABA from a predominately rural southern organization to one with churches in 45 states.

Through its publishing arm in Texarkana, the ABA publishes literature and books numbering into the thousands. Major seminaries include the Missionary Baptist Seminary, founded by Dr. Ben M. Bogard in Little Rock, Arkansas, Texas Baptist Seminary, Henderson, Texas; Oklahoma Missionary Baptist College in Marlow, Oklahoma; and Florida Baptist Schools in Lakeland, Florida.

While no person may speak for the churches of the ABA, all accept the Bible as the inerrant Word of God. They believe Christ was the virgin-born Son of God, that God is a triune God, that the only church is the local congregation of scripturally baptized believers, and that the work of the church is to spread the gospel.

GENERAL ORGANIZATION
American Baptist Association Offices: 4605 N. State Line Ave., Texarkana, TX 75503. Tel. (214) 792-2783

OFFICERS
Pres., Dr. James B. Powers, 607 N. Aubrey Circle, Grenwood, MS 38930
Vice-Presidents, Dr. Don Price, 5300 Stagecoach Rd., Little Rock, AR 72204; Dr. James A. Krikland, P.O. Box 415, White Oak, TX 75693; Conan Doyle, Amory, MS
Rec. Clks., Larry Clements, P.O. Box 234, Monticello, AR 71655; Gene Smith, 1208 W. 35th St., Pine Bluff, AR 71601
Ed.-in-Chief Publications, Dr. Bill Johnson, P.O. Box 502, Texarkana, AR 75504
Bus. Mgr., Publications, Tom Sannes, Box 1828, Texarkana, AR 75501
Dir. Meeting Arrangements, Edgar N. Sutton, P.O. Box 240, Alexander, AR 72002
Sec.-Treas., D. S. Madden, P.O. Box 1050, Texarkana, AR-TX 75504

PERIODICALS
Missionary Baptist Searchlight (s-m), Box 663, Little Rock, AR 72203
Baptist Monitor (s-m), Box 591, Henderson, TX 75652
The Missionary (m), Box 5116, Nashville, TN 37206
The Baptist Anchor (s-m), Box 1641, Lakeland, FL 33802
The Missionary Baptist News, Box 123, Minden, LA 71055
Baptist Sentinel, Box 848, Bellflower, CA 90706
The Baptist Review, Box 287, Marlow, OK 23055
Christian Education Bulletin (q), P.O. Box 901, Texarkana, AR-TX 76605
A. B. A. Missions (q), P.O. Box 1050, Texarkana, AR-TX 75504

American Baptist Churches in the U.S.A.

Originally known as the Northern Baptist Convention, this body of Baptist churches changed the name to American Baptist Convention in 1950 with a commitment to "hold the name in trust for all Christians of like faith and mind who desire to bear witness to the historical Baptist convictions in a framework of cooperative Protestantism."

In 1972 American Baptist Churches in the U.S.A. was adopted as the new name. Although national missionary organizational developments began in 1814 with the

24

establishment of the American Baptist Foreign Mission Society and continued with the organization of the American Baptist Publication Society in 1824 and the American Baptist Home Mission Society in 1832, the general denominational body was not formed until 1907. American Baptist work at the local level dates back to the organization by Roger Williams of the First Baptist Church in Providence, R. I. in 1638.

Churches: 5,839; Inclusive Membership: 1,549,563; Sunday or Sabbath Schools: N.R.; Total Enrollment: 361,265; Ordained Clergy: 8,276

GENERAL ORGANIZATION

Convention: Biennial
Offices: P. O. Box 851, Valley Forge Pa. 19482 Tel. (215) 768-2000

OFFICERS

Pres., Beverly C. Davison
Vice-Pres., Richard E. Ice
Budget Review Officer: Dorothy J. Herrin
Gen. Sec., Daniel E. Weiss
Assoc. Gen. Sec./Treas.: Robert J. Allen
National Secs:, Jean B. Kim, Paul Nichols, John A., Sundquist, Dean R. Wright
Office of the General Secretary: Gen.Sec., Daniel E. Weiss; Assoc. Gen. Sec./Treas., Robert J. Allen; Assoc. Gen. Sec. for Adminstrative Services, Barbara A. Williams; Deputy Gen. Sec. for Communication, Philip E. Jenks; Deputy Gen. Sec. for Cooperative Christianity, Moley G. Familiaran; Assoc. Gen. Sec. for Regional Ministries, J. Ralph Beaty; Deputy Gen. Sec. Research and Planning, Richard K. Gladden; Assoc. Gen. Sec. for World Mission Support, Richard E. Rusbuldt

REGIONAL ORGANIZATIONS:

Central Region, American Baptist Churches of, Fred W. Thompson, Box 4105, Topeka, KS 66604 (Kansas and Oklahoma)
Chicago Baptist Associaton, William K. Cober, Interim, 59 E. Van Buren, Ste. 2517 Chicago 60605
Cleveland Baptist Association, Richard E. Johnson, 1737 Euclid Ave., Ste. 240, Cleveland 44115
Connecticut, American Baptist Churches of, Robert H. Roberts, 100 Bloomfield Ave., Hartford 06105
District of Columbia Baptist Convention, James A. Langley, 1628 16th St., NW, 20009
Great Rivers Region, American Baptist Churches of the, Daniel W. Holland, Interim, P.O. Box 3786, Springfield, IL 62708 (Illinois & Missouri)
Indiana, American Baptist Churches of, L. Eugene Ton, 1350 North Delaware St., Indianapolis 46202
Indianapolis, ABC of Greater, Larry D. Sayre, 1350 N. Delaware St., Indianapolis 46202
Los Angeles Baptist City Mission Society, Emory C. Campbell, 1212 Wilshire Blvd., Los Angeles, 90017
Maine, American Baptist Churches of, Calvin L. Moon, 107 Winthrop St., Augusta 04330
Massachusetts, American Baptist Churches of, Roscoe C. Robison, 88 Tremont St., Room 500, Boston 02108
Metropolitan New York, American Baptist Churches of Carl E. Flemister, 475 Riverside Dr., Rm. 432, New York, NY 10115
Michigan, American Baptist Churches of, Robert E. Shaw, 4578 S. Hagadorn Rd., East Lansing MI 48823
Mid-American Baptist Churches, Telfer L. Epp, Suites 15 & 16, 2400 86th St., Des Moines, IA 50322, (Iowa & Minnesota)
Nebraska, American Baptist Churches of, Dennis D. Hatfield, 6404 Maple St., Omaha 68104
New Jersey, American Baptist Churches of, George D. Younger, 161 Freeway Dr. E., East Orange, 07018

New York State, American Baptist Churches of, Sumner M. Grant, 3049 E. Genesee St., Syracuse 13224
Niagara Frontier, American Baptist Churches of the, Kathryn W. Baker, 1272 Delaware Ave., Buffalo, N.Y. 14209 (Buffalo & vicinity)
North Dakota Baptist State Convention, Richard L. Waltz, 1524 S. Summit Ave., Sioux Falls, SD 57105
Northwest, American Baptist Churches of, Gaylord Hasselblad, 321 First Ave. W., Seattle, 98119 (Idaho, Montana, Utah, Washington)
Ohio Baptist Convention, Rev Robert A. Fisher, P.O. Box 376, Granville 43023
Oregon, American Baptist Churches of, James T. Ledbetter, 0245 SW Bancroft St., Ste. G, Portland 97201
Pacific Southwest, American Baptist Churches of the, W. Lowell Fairley, 970 Village Oaks Dr., Covina, CA 91724 (Arizona, Baja, Southern California, So. Nevada & Hawaii)
Pennsylvania & Delaware, American Baptist Churches of, Edith M. Vanderbeck, Interim, American Baptist Churches USA, Room C-127, Valley Forge, PA 19481
Philadelphia Baptist Association, Larry K. Waltz, 1701 Arch St., Rm. 417, Philadelphia 19103
Pittsburgh Baptist Association, Clayton R. Woodbury, 1620 Allegheny Bldg., 429 Forbes Ave., Pittsburgh, PA 15219
Puerto Rico, Baptist Churches of, E. Yamina Apolinaris, Mayaguez #21, Hato Rey, PR 00917
Rhode Island, American Baptist Churches of, Donald H. Crosby, 734 Hope St., Providence, RI 02906
Rochester/Genessee Region, American Baptist Churches of, Carrol A. Turner, 175 Genesee St., Rochester, NY 14611
Rocky Mountains, American Baptist Churches of, O. Dean Nelson, 1344 Pennsylvania St., Denver 80203 (Colorado, Wyoming)
South Dakota Baptist Convention, Richard L. Waltz, 1524 South Summit Ave., Sioux Falls 57105
South, American Baptist Churches of the, Walter L. Parrish II, 525 Main St., Suite. 105, Laurel, MD 20707 (Alabama, Florida, Georgia, Kentucky, Louisiana, Maryland, Mississippi, North Carolina, Oklahoma, South Carolina, Tennessee, Texas, Virginia)
Vermont /New Hampshire, American Baptist Churches of, Robert W. Williams, P. O. Box 796, Concord, NH 03302
West, American Baptist Churches of, Robert D. Rasmussen, P.O. Box 23204, Oakland, CA 94623 (Northern California, Northern Nevada)
West Virginia Baptist Convention, Douglas W. Hill, P.O. Box 1019, Parkersburg 26101.
Wisconsin, American Baptist Churches of, William L. Wells, 15330 W. Watertown Plank Rd., Elm Grove, 53122

Board of Educational Ministries (incorporated as the American Baptist Board of Education and Publication) including Judson Press and Judson Mail Order. Office: P.O. Box 851, Valley Forge, PA 19482. Exec. Dir., Jean B. Kim; Treas., L. Dean Hurst; Department Dirs.: Church School, Linda R. Isham; Discipleship, Donald T-M Ng; Finance and Business, L. Dean Hurst; Judson Press, Kristy Arnesen Pullen; Leader Development, John L. Carroll; Marketing, Edward Hunter. Officers of the Board: Pres., Albert D. Matthews; Vice-Pres., Margaret C. Susman; Rec. Sec., Arthur J. Munson, Jr.
American Baptist Assembly (National Training Center) Green Lake, WI 54941. Exec. Dir., Paul W. LaDue; Dir. of Programming/Scheduling, Arlo R. Reichter; Dir. of Finance, L. B. Standifer III; Officers of the Board: Pres., Thomas O. Jones Vice-Pres., Ralph J. Beaty; Treas., Ina May Fakhoury; Sec., Gloria A. Marshall.
American Baptist Historical Society (Archives and History), 1106 S. Goodman St., Rochester, NY 14620; and P.O. Box 851, Valley Forge, PA 19482; Admn./Archivist,

Beverly C. Carlson; Dir. of Library, James R. Lynch; Pres., John F. Mandt.
American Baptist Men: Exec. Dir., Richard S. McPhee, P. O. Box 851, Valley Forge, PA 19482. Pres., Robert H. Swan, Sr.
American Baptist Women: Exec. Dir., Donna M. Anderson, P. O. Box 851, Valley Forge, PA 19482; Pres., Nita W. Myers
Commission on the Ministry: Exec. Dir., Linda C. Spoolstra, P. O. Box 851, Valley Forge, PA 19482.

Board of International Ministries (incorporated as American Baptist Foreign Mission Society). Office: Valley Forge, PA 19482. Pres., Mrs. Marjorie Erickson; Vice-Pres., Rev. Earl W. Lawson; Exec. Dir., Dr. John A. Sundquist; Amer. Baptist World Relief Officer, Rev. Charles W. Sydnor; Budget Dir., Charles H. Stuart.
Overseas Division: Miss Alice M. Findlay, Dir.; Africa (Zaire, Rwanda), Rev. Ivan E. George; East Asia (Japan, Okinawa, Philippines), Rev. Raymond W. Beaver; Middle East and Europe, Miss Alice M. Findlay; Latin America (Baja CA, Bolivia,Costa Rica, Cuba, El Salvador, Mexico, Nicaragua), Rev. Victor M. Mercado; Caribbean (Haiti, Dominican Republic, Barbados), Rev. P. Reidar Lindland; Southern Asia (Bangladesh, Burma, India, Nepal), Rev. Gladys M. Peterson; Southeast Asia (China, Hong Kong, Singapore, Thailand), Rev. Cecil E. Carder; Sec. for International Issues Dr. Russell E. Brown (Interim); Coord. for Bapt. Cncl. on World Missions, Mrs. Louise Paw (Interim); Sec. for Recruitment, Miss Betty L. Beaman; Sec. for Personnel Development, Rev. P. Reidar Lindland; **Public Relations Division:** Dir., Rev. Hugh W. Smith; Assoc. Directors: Mrs. Charlotte Gillespie (Mission Education, White Cross, Spec. Interest Missionaries); Rev. Alan Williams, (Resource Development); **Business and Finance Division:** Treas. & Dir., Mr. Cornelius C. Jones; Assoc. Treas. & Assoc. Dir., Austin B. Windle; Fund Accountant, Rev. William R. Bartlett

Board of National Ministries (incorporated as The American Baptist Home Mission Society and Woman's American Baptist Home Mission Society). Office: Valley Forge, PA 19482. Pres., J. Terry Wingate; Vice-Pres., Jo Ann Vredenburg; Exec. Dir., Paul Nichols; Rec. Sec., and Deputy Exec. Dir., Richard M. Jones; Interim Mgr.; Adm. Support Unit, and Treas., Harold B. Cooper; Mgr., Church & Community Development Unit, Roy L. Thompson; Interim Mgr., Direct & Contract Services Unit, Harold B. Cooper; Interim Natl. Dir., American Baptist Personnel Services, Edward H. Kaechele; Mgr. Individual & Corp. Responsibility Unit, Elizabeth J. Miller; Mgr., Personal & Public Witness Unit and Evangelism Dir., Emmett V. Johnson; Mgr., Program Support Unit, Richard M. Jones.
The Ministers and Missionaries Benefit Board: Office: 475 Riverside Dr., New York, NY 10115: Pres., John W. Reed; Vice-Pres., Hella Mears Hueg; Actuary: Hay/Huggins, 229 S. 18th St., Rittenhouse Sq., Philadelphia, PA 19103; Exec. Dir., Dean R. Wright; Deputy Exec. Dir. & Treas., Gordon E. Smith; Sec., Sara E. Hopkins; Assoc. Exec. Dir., Margaret Ann Cowden; Assoc. Exec. Dir., East, Richard Arnesman; Assoc. Exec. Dir., West, Terry L. Burch.
Minister Council: Exec. Dir., Harley D. Hunt; Pres., Wendell A. Johnson.

PERIODICALS

The American Baptist (bi-m), P.O. Box 851, Valley Forge, PA 19482. Philip Jenks, Ed.
The Baptist Leader (bi-m), P.O. Box 851, Valley Forge, PA 19482, Linda R. Isham, Ed.

The Secret Place (q), P.O. Box 851, Valley Forge, PA 19482. Michelle Esbenshade, Ed.,
American Baptist Quarterly (q), P.O. Box 851, Valley Forge, PA 19482, William R. Millar, Ed.

The American Carpatho-Russian Orthodox Greek Catholic Church

The American Carpatho-Russian Orthodox Greek Catholic Church is a self-governing diocese that is in communion with the Ecumenical Partriarchate of Constantinople. The late Patriarch Benjamin I, in an official Patriarchal Document listed as No. 1379 and dated September 19, 1938, canonized the Diocese in the name of the Orthodox Church of Christ.

GENERAL ORGANIZATION

Sobor: triennial (Next Sobor 1992, Johnstown, PA)
Headquarters: Johnstown, PA 15906. Tel. (814) 536-4207

OFFICERS

Bishop: Rt. Bishop Nicholas (Smisko), 312 Garfield St., Johnstown, PA 15906
Vicar General: Rt. Mitred Peter E. Molchany, 903 Ann St., Homestead, PA 15120
Chancellor: Very Rev. Msgr. John Yurcisin, 249 Butler Ave., Johnstown, PA 15906
Treas.: Very Rev. Msgr. Ronald A. Hazuda, 115 East Ave., Erie, PA 16503

PERIODICAL

Cerkovnyj Vistnik—Church Messenger (bi-w), 419 S. Main St., Homer City, PA 15748, Very Rev. James S. Dutko, Ed.

American Evangelical Christian Churches

Founded in 1944, the A.E.C.C. functions as a denominational body with interdoctrinal views incorporating into its ecclesiastical position both the Calvinistic and Arminian doctrines. The purpose of the organization is the propagation of the gospel through the establishment of churches, missions, and places of worship. It is not affiliated with any other religious body or organization but seeks fellowship with all who hold to the concepts set forth in the teachings of Jesus the Christ. Ministerial credentials are issued by the American Evangelical Christian Churches to men and women approved by the Credentials Committee and who subscribe to the following Articles of faith: the Bible as the written word of God; the Virgin birth; the Deity of Jesus the Christ; salvation through the atonement; the guidance of our life through prayer. Its churches operate under the name Community Churches, American Bible Churches, and Evangelical Christian Churches. Each group is an independent sovereign body. An affiliated body operates in the British Isles under the name Ministers of Evangelism by authority of the charter granted to it by the Crown. The AECC has its own Bible training school, the American Bible College. The school is interdenominational, specializing in off-campus theological studies, with numerous extension centers in various parts of the country.

National Headquarters: Chicago, IL
OFFICERS
Mod., Dr. G. W. Hyatt, Waterfront Dr., Pineland FL 33945
Sec., Dr. Ben Morgan, 64 South St., Southport, IN 46227
REGIONAL MODERATORS
Vernon Bucher, New Albany, OH
Alvin House, Bozeman, MT
Joseph Schwalb, East Northport, NY
Kenneth White, Hagerstown, MD

American Rescue Workers

Founded in 1884, as a national religious and charitable movement which operates on a quasimilitary basis. Membership includes officers (clergy); soldiers/adherents (laity); members of various activity groups; and volunteers who serve as advisors, associates, and committed participants in ARW service functions.

The American Rescue Workers is motivated by the love of God and a practical concern for the needs of humanity. Its purpose is to preach the gospel, disseminate Christian truths, supply basic personal necessities, provide personal counseling and undertake the spiritual and moral regeneration and physical rehabilitation of all persons in need who come within its sphere of influence regardless of race, color, creed, sex or age.

GENERAL ORGANIZATION

Council: annual
Headquarters: 2827 Frankford Ave., Philadelphia, PA 19134. Tel. (215) 739-6524; Washington DC Capital Area Office: 716 Ritchie Rd., Capitol Heights, MD 20743. Tel. (301)336-6200
Commander-In-Chief and Pres. of Corp., General Paul Martin; Pres., Lt. Col. Claude Astin, Jr. (Chief of Staff); Natl. Sec., Col. George Gossett; National Communication/Development Dir., Lt. Col. Robert N. Coles, Nat'l. Board Pres., Maj. Gen. Helen Gossett.

PERIODICAL

The Rescue Herald (q), Box 175, Hightstown, NJ 08520, Capt. Robert Turton III, Ed.

The Anglican Orthodox Church

This body was founded on November 16, 1963, in Statesville, North Carolina, by the Most Rev. James P. Dees who is the Presiding Bishop. The church holds to 39 Articles of Religion, the 1928 Prayerbook, the King James Version of the Bible, and basic Anglican traditions and church government.

The church upholds biblical morality and emphasizes the fundamental doctrines of the virgin birth, the incarnation, the atoning sacrifice of the cross, the Trinity, the resurrection, the second coming, salvation by faith alone, and the divinity of Christ.

GENERAL ORGANIZATION

General Convention: Annually (Next meeting, 1990)

OFFICER

Presiding Bishop, The Most Rev. James Parker Dees, 323 Walnut St., P. O. Box 128, Statesville, NC 28677. Tel. (704) 873-8365

PERIODICAL

The News (m)

The Antiochian Orthodox Christian Archdiocese of North America

Since the late nineteenth century through the present, Antiochian Christians have emigrated to other parts of the world from their homelands in the Middle East. The spiritual needs of Antiochian faithful in North America were first served through the Syro-Arabian Mission of the Russian Orthodox Church. This mission was established in 1892. In 1895 the Syrian Orthodox Benevolent Society was organized by Antiochian immigrants in New York City. Dr. Ibrahim Arbeeny, prominent Damascene physician, was the society's first president. Conscious of the needs of

his fellow countrymen and coreligionists, Dr. Arbeeny wrote to Raphael Hawaweeny, a young Damascene clergyman serving as professor of Arabic language at the Orthodox theological academy in Kazan, Russia, inviting him to come to New York to organize the first Arabic-language parish in North America. Father Raphael, a missionary at heart, went to the imperial capital of St. Petersburg to meet with His Grace Nicholas, the head of the Russian Church in North America, who happened to be visiting in Russia at that time. After being canonically received under the omophorion of Bishop Nicholas, Hawaweeny came to the United States in 1896.

Upon his arrival in New York City, Archimandrite Raphael established the first Syrian Greek Orthodox parish at 77 Washington St. in lower Manhattan, the center of the Syrian immigrant community. By 1900, approximately 3,000 Syrian immigrants had crossed the East River, establishing Brooklyn as the largest Syrian community in America at that time. Therefore, in 1902 Hawaweeny's parish purchased a larger church building in that borough. The church, placed under the heavenly patronage of Saint Nicholas the Wonderworker of Myra, was located at 301-303 Pacific St. Following renovation for Orthodox worship, the church was consecrated by Bishop Tikhon, who succeeded Nicholas as Bishop of North America on October 27, 1902. Saint Nicholas Cathedral, now located at 355 State St. in Brooklyn, is considered the "mother parish" of the Archdiocese.

At the request of Bishop Tikhon, Hawaweeny was elected his vicar bishop and head of the Syro-Arabian Mission. His consecration as Bishop of Brooklyn took place at Saint Nicholas Church on Pacific St. on March 12, 1904. Bishop Raphael thus became the first Orthodox bishop to be consecrated in North America. He traveled throughout the continent and established new parishes for his scattered flock. He also founded Al-Kalimat (The Word magazine) in 1905 and published many liturgical books for use in his parishes. After a brief but very fruitful ministry, Bishop Raphael Hawaweeny fell asleep in Christ on February 27, 1915, at the age of 54.

With the death of Bishop Raphael and the chaos in North American church administration occasioned by the Bolshevik revolution in Russia and the First World War, the unity of Orthodoxy in the New World was ruptured. Even the small Syrian Greek Orthodox community was split into factions, each founded on differing ecclesiastical loyalties. It was not until sixty years after the death of Bishop Raphael, in June 1975, that total jurisdictional and administrative unity was restored among the children of Antioch in North America. Some of the hierarchs who have led the Syrian Greek Orthodox community in North America are Germanos Shehadi, Aftimios Ofiesh, Victor Abo-Assaley, Emmanuel Abo-Hatab, Samuel David, and Antony Bashir.

On June 24, 1975, Metropolitan Philip Saliba, of the Antiochian Archdiocese of New York, and Metropolitan Michael Shaheen of the Antiochian archdiocese of Toledo, Ohio, signed the Articles of Reunification which restored administrative unity among all Antiochian Orthodox Christians in the United States and Canada. This document was presented to the Holy Synod of the Patriarchate, which ratified the contents on August 19, 1975, recognizing Saliba as the Metropolitan Primate and Shaheen as Auxiliary Archbishop. On January 9, 1983, a second auxiliary to the Metropolitan, Bishop Antoun Khouri, was consecrated at Brooklyn's Saint Nicholas Cathedral.

The Archdiocesan Board of Trustees (consisting of 50 elected and appointed clergy and lay members) and the Metropolitan's Advisory Council (consisting of clergy and lay representatives from each parish and mission) meet regularly to assist the Primate in the administration of the

Archdiocese. Each summer six regional Parish Life Conferences are convened (Canadian-American Region, New England Region, Eastern Region, Midwest Region, Southwest Region, and Western Region) which attract thousands of people of all ages from the parishes and missions.

Churches: 150; Inclusive Membership: 300,000; Sunday or Sabbath Schools: 150; Total Enrollment: 21,500; Ordained Clergy: 172

GENERAL ORGANIZATION

General Assembly: biennial.
Headquarters: 358 Mountain Rd., Englewood, NJ 07631. Tel. (201) 871-1355

OFFICERS

Metropolitan Philip (Saliba), Primate; Archbishop Michael (Shaheen), Auxiliary; Bishop Antoun (Khouri), Auxiliary

PERIODICAL

The Word (m), V. Rev. George S. Corey

Apostolic Catholic Assyrian Church of the East, North American Dioceses

This is the ancient Christian Church, and even though the official name of the Church is the Holy Apostolic Assyrian Church of the East, there are many variations of this combination of words. It is also known as Assyrian Church, Assyrian Orthodox, Persian (Babylonian) and the misnomer "Nestorian" Church, among others.

The Church was founded in 37 A.D., the year our Lord Jesus was crucified, by Sts. Peter, Thomas, Thaddaeus and Bartholomew of the Twelve and Mari and Aggai of the Seventy, in Edessa (Urhai), state of Oshroene in the Persian Region. Prior to the Great Persecution, at the hands of Tamerlane and others that followed, the Church was said to have been the largest Christian Church in the world.

The doctrine of the Church is that of the Apostles, stressing two natures and two "Qnume" in one person, perfect God and perfect man. The Church accepts the title "Mother of Christ" for the Blessed Virgin Mary, but rejects the appelation of "Mother of God", the original Nicene Creed, the Ecumenical Councils of Nicaea and Constantinople, and the Church Fathers of those periods. The Church has maintained a line of patriarchs from the time of the Holy Apostles until the present. The Church, is governed by the patriarch, His Holiness Mar Dinkha IV, Catholicos-Patriarch of the East, the 120th successor to the See, the metropolitans and the bishops, comprising the Synod.

Churches: 22; Inclusive Membership: 120,000; Sunday or Sabbath Schools: 22; Total Enrollment: 1,050; Ordained Clergy: 109

GENERAL ORGANIZATION

Diocesan Council of Clergy: Annual (Summer or Fall)
Diocesan Central Committee (Lay representatives of each parish): Annual
Bishops' main office as follows: Bishop Mar Aprim Khamis, Eastern USA & Canada, 8908 Birch Ave., Morton Grove, IL 60053. Tel. (312) 966-0009
Bishop Mar Bawai, c/o Archdeacon Nenos Michael, 1623-43rd Ave., San Francisco, CA 94122. Tel (415)564-9126

PERIODICAL

Qala Min Madinka (Voice from the East) (q), Mr. Akhitiar B. Moshi and Rev. Samuel Dinkha, Eds.

Apostolic Christian Church (Nazarene)

This body was formed in America by an immigration from various European nations, from a movement begun by Rev. S. H. Froehlich, a Swiss pastor, whose followers are still found in Switzerland and Central Europe.

OFFICERS

Apostolic Christian Church Foundation, P.O. Box 151, Tremont, IL 61568, Gen. Sec., Eugene R. Galat, P.O. Box 151, Tremont, IL 61568. Tel. (309) 925-5162

PERIODICAL

Newsletter (bi-m)

Apostolic Christian Churches of America

The Apostolic Christian Church of America consists of 11,000 members in 20 congregations in 18 states, one in Canada, and two in Japan. The church was founded in the early 1830's in Switzerland by Samuel Froehlich, a young divinity student who experienced a religious conversion based on the pattern found in the New Testament and founded a church known as Evangelical Baptist. His work resulted in the formation of 110 congregations in 35 years in various surrounding countries.

In 1847, Elder Benedict Weyeneth, an associate of Froehlich, came to America and the first church was established in upstate New York. Other churches were formed with the highest concentration today in the Midwest farm belt. In America, the church became known as Apostolic Christian.

Church doctrine is based on a literal interpretation of the Bible, the infallible Word of God. The church believes that a true faith in Christ's redemptive work at Calvary is manifested by a sincere repentance and conversion. Following baptism by immersion and the laying on of hands of the presbytery, members strive for sanctification and separation from worldliness. This is as a consequence of salvation, not a means to obtain it. Security in Christ is believed to be conditional based on faithfulness. Discipline is lovingly applied to erring members.

A high degree of brotherhood and closely knit fellowship exist throughout the denomination. The biblical ideals of likemindedness adn uniform observance of scriptural standards of holiness are stressed. Holy Communion is confined to members of the church. Members do not swear oaths, but affirm. Male members are willing to serve in the military, but do not bear arms. The holy kiss is practiced and women wear headcoverings during prayer and worship.

Doctrinal authority rests with a council of elders, each of whom also serves as a local elder (bishop). Both elders and ministers are chosen from local congregations, do not attend seminary, and serve without compensation. Sermons are delivered extemporaneously as led by the Holy Spirit, using the Bible as a text.

Churches: 80; Inclusive Membership: 11,390; Sunday or Sabbath Schools: 80; Total Enrollment: 7,000; Ordained Clergy: 329

SECRETARY

Elder (Bishop) Dale Eisenmann, 6913 Wilmette, Darien, IL 60559. Tel. (312)969-7021

Apostolic Faith Mission of Portland, Oregon

The Apostolic Faith Mission of Portland, Oregon, was founded in 1907. It had its beginning in the Latter Rain outpouring on Azusa street in Los Angeles, California, in 1906.

Some of the main doctrines are justification by faith; spiritual new birth, as Jesus told Nicodemus and as Martin Luther proclaimed in the Great Reformation; sanctification, a second definite work of grace, the Wesleyan teaching of holiness, which Jesus prayed for us to have in John 17; the baptism of the Holy Ghost as experienced on the Day of Pentecost, and again poured out at the beginning of the Latter Rain revival in Los Angeles.

Mrs. Florence L. Crawford, who had received the baptism of the Holy Ghost in Los Angeles, brought this Latter Rain message to Portland on Christmas Day 1906. It has spread to the world by means of literature which is still published and mailed everywhere without a subscription price. Collections are never taken in the meetings and the public is not asked for money.

Camp meetings have been held annually in Portland, Oregon, since 1907, with delegations coming from around the world.

Missionaries from the Portland headquarters have established churches in Korea, Japan, and the Philippines. In the early days, European churches were established by people of different nationalities reutrning with the Good News to their homelands. the message has always been that people can have their sins forgiven and go forth, as Jesus said, to "sin no more."

GENERAL ORGANIZATION

Convention: annual (July)
Headquarters: 6615 S.E. 52nd Ave., Portland, OR 97206
Tel. (503) 777-1741

OFFICER

Gen. Overseer, Rev. Loyce C. Carver; 6615 S.E. 52nd Ave., Portland, OR 97206

PERIODICAL

The Light of Hope (bi-m), 6615 S.E. 52nd Ave., Portland, OR 97206. Tel. (503) 777-1741. Rev. Loyce C. Carver, Ed.

Apostolic Faith Mission Church of God

The Apostolic Faith Mission Church of God was founded and organized July 10, 1906, by Bishop F. W. Williams in Mobile, Alabama.

Bishop Williams was saved and filled with the Holy Ghost at a revival in Los Angeles under Elder W. J. Seymour of The Divine Apostolic Faith Movement. After being called into the ministry, Bishop Williams went out to preach the gospel stopping in Mississippi, then moving on to Mobile, Alabama.

On October 9, 1915, the Apostolic Faith Mission Church of God was incorporated in Mobile, Alabama under Bishop Williams who was also the general overseer of this church.

Churches: 18; Inclusive Membership 6,200; Sunday or Sabbath Schools: 18; Total Enrollment: 1,570; Or dained Clergy: 32

GENERAL ORGANIZATION

General Assembly; annual in the third week in June, Birmingham, AL
Headquarters: 3344 Pearl Ave., N., Birmingham, AL 36101

OFFICERS

Board of Bishops: Presiding Bishop, Houston Ward, P. O. Box 551, Cantonment, FL 39533. Tel. (904) 587-2339; Billy Carter, J. L. Smiley, T. L. Frye, D. Brown, T. C. Tolbert, R. B. Hawthorne and N. M. Andrews.

NATIONAL DEPARTMENTS

Missionary Dept., Pres., Sr. Sarah Ward, Cantonment, FL
Youth Dept., Pres., W. J. Wills, Lincoln, AL
Sunday School Dept., Supt., Thomas Brooks, Decatur, GA
Mother Dept., Pres., Mother Juanita Phillips, Birmingham, AL

Apostolic Lutheran Church of America

Organized in 1872 as Solomon Korteniemi Lutheran Society, this Finnish body was incorporated in 1929 as the Finnish Apostolic Lutheran Church in America and changed its name to Apostolic Lutheran Church of America in 1962.

This body stresses preaching the Word of God and therefore there is an absence of liturgy and formalism in worship. A seminary education is not required of pastors. Being called by God to preach the Word is the chief requirement for clergy and laity. The church stresses personal absolution and forgiveness of sins, as practiced by Martin Luther, and the importance of bringing converts into God's kingdom.

Churches: 57; Inclusive Membership: 7,707; Sunday or Sabbath Schools: 44; Total Enrollment: 2,010; Ordained Clergy 34

GENERAL ORGANIZATION

Meets annually in June

OFFICERS

Pres., Richard E. Sakrisson, 7606 NE Vancouver Mall Dr. #14, Vancouver, WA 98662
Sec., James Johnson, Rt. 1, Box 462, Houghton, MI 49931
Treas., Rev. Richard Barney, Rt. 2, Box 210, Chassell, MI 49916

PERIODICAL

Christian Monthly (m), Apostolic Lutheran Book Concern, P.O. Box 537, Brush Prairie, WA 98606, Alvar Helmes, Ed.

Apostolic Overcoming Holy Church of God, Inc.

The late Right Reverend William Thomas Phillips (1893–1973), one of the greatest religious leaders of this Christian era, was thoroughly convinced in 1912 that Holiness was a system through which God wanted him to serve. In 1916 he was led to Mobile, Alabama, where he organized the Ethiopian Overcoming Holy Church of God on March 16. Realizing that God's message was to all people, on April 1, 1941, the church was incorporated in the state of Alabama under its present title. Upon his death on November 30, 1973, Bishop Phillips had successfully served for 57 years.

The disciples of the church have retained their congregational policy, with each congregation managing its own affairs, united under districts governed by overseers and diocesan bishops, and assisted by an executive board comprised of bishops, ministers, laymen, and the National Secretary. The General Assembly convenes annually (June 1–10). Our chief objective is to enlighten people of God's holy Word and to be a blessing to every nation on earth. The main purpose of this church is to ordain elders, appoint pastors, and send out divinely called misionaries and teachers. This church enforces all ordinances enacted by Jesus Christ. We believe in water baptism according to Acts 2:38, 8:12, and 10:47. We administer the Lord's Supper and observe the washing of

29

feet according to John 13:4-7. We believe and teach that Jesus Christ shed his blood to sanctify the people and cleanse them from all sin. Matrimonies are solemnized in accordance with Hebrews 13:4, and the burying of the dead is enacted according to Genesis 23:3-4. We believe in the resurrection of the dead and the second coming of Christ.

Churches: 177; Inclusive Membership: 12,479; Sunday or Sabbath Schools: N.R.; Total Enrollment: N.R.; Ordained Clergy: 130

OFFICERS

Senior Bishop and Exec. Head, Rt. Rev. Jasper Roby, 1120 N. 24th St., Birmingham, AL 35234
Associate Bishops: Bishop G. W. Ayers, 1717 Arlington Blvd., El Cerrito, CA 94530; Bishop L. M. Bell, 2000 Pio Nono Ave., Macon, GA 31206; Bishop Gabriel Crutcher, 526 E. Bethune St. Detroit, MI 48202; Bishop John Mathews, 12 College St., Dayton, OH 45407; Bishop Joe Bennett, 15718 Drexel Ave., Dalton, IL 60419
Exec. Sec., Mrs. Juanita R. Arrington, 1120 N. 24th St., Birmingham, Al 35234

PERIODICAL

The People's Mouthpiece(q); The Young Educator (a)

Armenian Apostolic Church of America

Widespread movement of the Armenian people over the centuries caused the development of two seats of religious jurisdiction of the Armenian Apostolic Church in the World: the See of Etchmiadzin, now in Soviet Armenia, and the See of Cilicia, in Lebanon.

In America, the Armenian Church functioned under the jurisdiction of the Etchmiadzin See from 1887 to 1933, when a division occurred within the American diocese over the condition of the church in Soviet Armenia. One group chose to remain independent until 1957, when the Holy See of Cilicia agreed to accept them under its jurisdiction.

Despite the existence of two dioceses in North America, the Armenian Church has always functioned as one church in dogma and liturgy.

GENERAL ORGANIZATION

National Representative Assembly: annual
Headquarters: 138 E. 39 St., New York, NY 10016. Tel. (212) 689-7810

OFFICERS

Prelate, Eastern Prelacy, Archbishop Mesrob Ashjian, 138 E. 39th St., New York, NY 10016. Tel. (212) 689-7810
Prelate, Western Prelacy, Archbishop Datev Sarkissian, 4401 Russell Ave., Los Angeles, CA 90026
Chpsn., Eastern Prelacy, Nerses Chitjian
Chpsn., Western Prelacy, Vatché Mandenlian

DEPARTMENTS

AREC, Armenian Religious Educational Council, Exec. Coord., Mrs. Joanna Baghsarian
ANEC, Armenian National Educational Council, Exec. Coord., Hourig Sahagian-Papazian

PERIODICAL

Outreach (m), 138 E. 39th St., New York, NY 10016

Armenian Church of America, Diocese of the

The Armenian Apostolic Church was founded at the foot of the biblical mountain of Ararat in the ancient land of Armenia. Saints Thaddeus and Bartholomew preached Christianity in this ancient land. In 301 the historic Mother Church of Etchmiadzin was built by Saint Gregory the Illuminator, the first Catholicos of All Armenians. This cathedral still stands and serves as the center of the Armenian Church. A branch of this Church was established in North America in 1889 by the then Catholicos of All Armenians, Khrimian Hairig. Armenian immigrants built the first Armenian church in the new world in Worcester, Massachusetts, under the jurisdiction of Holy Etchmiadzin.

In 1927, as a result of the growth of the communities in California, the churches and the parishes there were formed into a separate Western Diocese under the jurisdiction of Holy Etchmiadzin, Armenia. The parishes in Canada formed their own diocese in 1984, under the jurisdiction of the Mother See of Etchmiadzin. In 1933 a few parishes seceded from the Armenian Church Diocese of America and in 1958 were formed into an illicit diocese, keeping, however, its oneness in dogma and liturgy.

The Armenian Apostolic Church, under the jurisdiction of Holy Etchmiadzin, also includes the Armenian Patriarchate of Jerusalem and the Armenian Patriarchate of Constantinople.

GENERAL ORGANIZATION

Eastern Diocese
Diocesan Assembly: Annual
Diocesan offices: 630 Second Ave., New York, NY 10016. Tel. (212) 686-0710

Western Diocese
Diocesan Assembly: Annual
Diocesan offices: 1201 N. Vine St., Hollywood, CA 90038. Tel. (213) 466-5265

Canadian Diocese
Diocesan Assembly: Annual
Diocesan offices: 615 Stuart Ave., Outremont, Quebec, Canada H2V 3H2. Tel. (514) 276-9479

OFFICERS

Eastern Diocese
Primate, His Eminence the Most Rev. Archbishop Torkom Manoogian, 630 Second Ave., New York, NY 10016
Vicar Gen., V. Rev. Fr. Khajag Barsamian, 630 Second Ave., New York, NY 10016
Chpsn., Diocesan Council, Vincent Gurahian, Macauhay Rd., RFD 2, Katonah, NY 10536
Sec., Diocesan Council: Edward Onanian, 13010 Hathaway Dr., Wheaton, MD 20906
Western Diocese
Primate, His Eminence Archbishop Vatche Hovsepian, 1201 N. Vine St., Hollywood, CA 90038, Tel. (213) 466-5265
Chpsn., Diocesan Council: The Rev. Fr. Vartan Kasparian, St. Mary Armenian Church, P.O. Box 367, Yettem, CA 93670
Sec., Diocesan Council: Armen Hampar, 6134 Pat Ave., Woodland Hills, CA 91367

PERIODICALS FOR BOTH DIOCESES

The Armenian Church, (m), 630 Second Ave., New York, NY 10016
Dept. of Religious Education Bulletin (m), 630 Second Ave., New York, NY 10016
The Mother Church (m), 1201 No. Vine St., Hollywood, CA 90038, Rev. Fr. Sipan Mekhsian, Ed

Assemblies of God

From a few hundred delegates at its founding convention in 1914 at Hot Springs, Arkansas, the Assemblies of God has become the largest church group in the modern Pentecostal movement worldwide. Throughout its existence it has emphasized the power of the Holy Spirit to change lives and the participation of all members in the work of the church.

The revival that led to the formation of the Assemblies of God and numerous other church groups early in the twentieth century began during times of intense prayer and Bible study. Believers in the United States and around the world received spiritual experiences like those described in the Book of Acts. Accompanied by baptism in the Holy Spirit and its initial physical evidence of "speaking in tongues," or a language unknown to the person, their experiences were associated with the coming of the Holy Spirit at Pentecost (Acts 2), so participants were called Pentecostals.

Along with the baptism in the Holy Spirit, the church also believes that the Bible is God's infallible Word to man, that salvation is available only through Jesus Christ, that divine healing is made possible through Christ's suffering, and that Christ will return again for those who love him. In recent years, this Pentecostal revival has spilled over into almost every denomination in a new wave of revival sometimes called the charismatic renewal.

Assemblies of God leaders credit their church's rapid and continuing growth to its acceptance of the New Testament as a model for the present-day church. Aggressive evangelism, and missionary zeal at home and abroad characterize the denomination.

Assemblies of God believers observe two ordinances—water baptism by immersion and the Lord's Supper, or Holy Communion. The church is trinitarian, holding that God exists in three persons, Father, Son, and Holy Spirit.

Churches: 11,123; Inclusive Membership: 2,147,041; Sunday or Sabbath Schools: 10,792; Total Enrollment: 1,363,881; Ordained Clergy: 30,552

GENERAL ORGANIZATION

General Council: biennial, (August)
International Headquarters: 1445 Boonville Ave., Springfield, MO 65802. Tel. (417) 862-2781

EXECUTIVE PRESBYTERY

Gen. Supt: G. Raymond Carlson; Asst. Supt.: Everett R. Stenhouse
Gen. Sec.: Joseph R. Flower
Gen. Treas.: Thomas Trask
Exec. Dir., Foreign Missions: Loren O. Triplett; Great Lakes: Robert K. Schmidgall, P.O. Box 296-1155 Aurora Ave., Naperville, IL 69540; Gulf: Philip Wannenmacher, 1301 N. Boonville, Springfield, MO 65802; North Central: Herman H. Rohde, 1315 Portland Ave. S, Minneapolis, MN 55404; Northeast: Almon Bartholomew, P.O. Box 39, Liverpool, NY 13081; Northwest: R. L. Brandt, 1702 Colton Blvd., Billings, MT 59102; South Central: Paul Lowenberg, 6015 E. Ninth St., Wichita, KS 67208; Southeast: J. Foy Johnson, P.O. Drawer C, Lakeland, FL 33802; Southwest: Glen D. Cole, 9470 Micron Rd., Sacramento, CA 95827

INTERNATIONAL HEADQUARTERS

All departmental offices are at Assemblies of God International Headquarters, 1445 Boonville Ave., Springfield, MO 65802
General Superintendent's Office Administration: Gen. Supt., G. Raymond Carlson
Spiritual Life-Evangelism: Coord., C. W. Denton; MAPS Coord., Lamar Headley; MAPS Construction Rep. for Home Missions, Patrick J. Donadio; MAPS Construction Rep. for Foreign Missions, Gerald Jackson; MAPS Promotions Coord., Helen Braxton; Evangelists Field Rep., Robert M. Abbott, Conference and Convention Coord., John V. Ohlin
Personnel: Mgr., Arlyn Pember
General Services: Administrator, Jimmy Dunn
Buildings and Properties: Administrator, Melvin Sachs

Legal Counselor: Richard R. Hammar
Research: Sec., Norma Thomas
General Secretary's Office Administration: Gen. Sec., Joseph R. Flower; Secretariat Supervisor, Linda Reece, Statistician, Sherri Coussens
A/G Archives: Dir. of Archives, Wayne Warner; Archives Asst., Joyce Lee
Division of the Treasury: Gen. Treasurer, Thomas E. Trask; Adm., Clyde L. Hawkins
Stewardship Dept., Deferred Giving and Trusts Dept.: Sec., Mel DeVries; Deferred Giving and Trusts Regional Consultants, David Watson, Ray Loven, J. Don Ross; Troy Lyon; Promotion Coord., Freda Jackson
Finance Dept.: Administrator of Accounting Services, Kenneth Tripp
Benevolences Dept.: Sec., Stanley V. Michael; Field Representative and Church Relations Coord., Robert Bornert; Promotions Coord./Ed., Owen Wilkie
Church Loan Dept.: Sec., Glenn A. Renick, Jr.; Field Rep., Phil Illum.
Division of Christian Education, Actg. Natl. Dir., Everett R. Stenhouse
Church School Literature Dept.: Ed., Charles W. Ford; Assoc. Ed., Gary Leggett; Adult Ed., John Maempa; Youth Ed., Nick Knoth; Elementary Ed., Cathy Ketcher; Early Childhood Ed., Sharon Ellard; Children's Church Ed., Sinda Zinn; Christian School Bible Curriculum Ed., Lorraine Mastrorio; Spanish Ed. Camilo Hernandez
Education Dept.: Sec., David Bundrick; Promotions Coord./Ed., Jewell Ready
Division of Church Ministries: Natl. Dir., Silas Gaither; Men's Ministries Dept.: Sec., Ken Riemenschneider; Light-for-the-Lost Sec., Billy J. Strickland; Royal Rangers Nat'l. Cdr., _____; Royal Ranger Nat'l. Deputy Commander, Paul Stanek; Editor of Publications, Jim Erdmann
Music Dept.: Sec., L. B. Larsen; Music Ed./Promotions Coord., Carmen Wassam; Senior Ed./Composer/Arranger/Producer, Randy Wright
Sunday School Department: Sec., George Edgerly; Adult Ministries Consultant, William Campbell; Children's Ministries Consultant, Richard Gruber; Early Childhood Consultant/BGMC Coord., Sandra K. Askew; Growth and Admin. Consultant, _____; Publications Ed. and Trng. Coord., Sylvia Lee; Field Services & Promotion Coord., Efraim Espinoza
Women's Ministries Dept.: Sec., Sandra Clopine; Publications Coord., Aleda Swartzendruber; Auxiliaries Coord., Linda Upton; WM Representative, _____; Trng. Coord., Joanne Ohlin; Off. of Fin./Field Serv. Coord., Karlene Gannon
Youth Dept.: Sec., Terrell Raburn; AIM/High School Ministries Rep., James Wellborn; Discipleship/Fine Arts Festival/Bible Quiz Rep., Terry King; Speed-the Light Field Rep., Brenton Osgood; Speed-the-Light Adm. Clk., Gail Mitchell; Ed. of Youth Publications, Thomas Young
Division of Communications: Natl. Dir., Leland Shultz
Advance Magazine: Ed., Gwen Jones
Audiovisual Dept.: Sec., Melvin Snyder
Office of Information: Sec., Juleen Turnage; Coord. of District/Church Relations, Robert Michels; Promotions/ Productions Coord., Rick Griepp
Radio and Television Dept.: Broadcast Speaker, Dan Betzer; Sec., Don Upton; Publicity Dir., Stephen J. Vaudrey; Revivaltime Choir Dir., Cyril A. McLellan
Pentecostal Evangel Magazine: Ed., Richard G. Champion; Man. Ed., Harris Jansen; Technical and Research Ed., Ann Floyd; News Ed., Gary Speer
Division of Foreign Missions: Exec. Dir., Loren O. Triplett; Adm. Asst., Norman L. Correll
Foreign Field Dirs.: Africa, Donald R. Corbin; Eurasia, Jerry L. Parsley; Asia/Pacific, Robert W. Houlihan;

31

Latin America & Caribbean, _____; Sec. of Foreign Mission Finance, Jerry L. Burgess; Sec. of Publications, Joyce Wells Booze; Sec. of Foreign Missionary Personnel, Ronald Iwasko; Missionary Family Specialist, Robert G. Fricsen; Personnel Coord., Paul Sherman; Sec. of Foreign Missions Relations in U.S., Fred Cottriel; Spec. Service Coord., _____; Sec. of Foreign Missions Support, Paul Brannan; Promotion Coord., Rosalie McMain; Life Publishers International: Pres., Bob D. Hoskins, International Correspondence Institute: Pres., George M. Flattery; International Media Ministries Coord., David Lee; Center for Muslim Ministries, Coord., Delmar Kingsriter

Division of Home Missions: Natl. Dir., Robert W. Pirtle; Finance Supervisor, Carolyn Stalnaker; Ed. Promotion Coord., Jeffrey Champion

Chaplaincy Dept.: Chpsn., Comm. on Chaplains, G. Raymond Carlson; Sec. Lemuel McElyea

New Church Evangelism Dept.: Sec., Robert W. Pirtle

Intercultural Ministries Dept.: Sec., James Kessler; Blind and Handicapped Ministries Rep., Kay Marchand; Deaf Ministries Rep., Albert Linderman; Spec. Rep., American Indians, John McPherson Teen Challenge Dept., Sec., Snow Peabody

Division of Publication (Gospel Publishing House): Natl. Dir., William Eastlake

Production Dept.: Mgr., Merrell Cooper

Marketing and Distribution Dept.: Mgr., Thomas F. Sanders

PERIODICALS

All Assemblies of God periodicals are produced by the Gospel Publishing House, 1445 Boonville Ave., Springfield, MO 65802

Advance (m), Gwen Jones, Ed.
At Ease (bi-m), Lemuel McElyea, Ed.
Caring (8/yr.) Owen Wilkie, Ed.
Curriculum Publications (q), Charles W. Ford, Ed.
Dispatch (q), _____, Ed.
High Adventure (q), _____, Ed.
Missionettes Memos (q), Linda Upton, Ed.
Motif (q), L. B. Larsen, Ed.
Mountain Movers (m), Joyce Wells Booze, Ed.
Paraclete (q), David Bundrick, Ed.
Pentecostal Evangel (w), Richard G. Champion, Ed.
Sunday School Counselor (m), Sylvia Lee, Ed.
Today's Man (q), Jim Ederman, Ed.
Woman's Touch (bi-m), Sandra Clopine, Ed.
Youth Alive! (m), Terry King, Ed.
Youth Alive! (m), Thomas Young, Ed.

Assemblies of God International Fellowship (Independent/ Not affiliated)

April 9, 1906 is the date commonly accepted by Pentecostals as the twentieth century outpouring of God's Spirit in America, which began in a humble Gospel Mission at 312 Asusa Street in Los Angeles.

This Spirit Movement spread across the U.S. and gave birth to the Independent Assemblies of God (Scandanavian). Early pioneers instrumental in guiding and shaping the fellowship of ministers and churches into a nucleus of indepdendent churches included Pastor B. M. Johnson, founder of Lakeview Gospel Church in 1911; Rev. A. A. Holmgren, a Baptist minister who received his baptism of the Holy Spirit in the early Chicago outpourings and was publisher of *Sanningens Vittne*, a voice of the Scandanavian Independent Assemblies of God, and also served as secretary of the fellowship for many many years; Gunnar Wingren, missionary pioneer in Brazil; and Arthur F. Johnson, who served for many years as chairman of the Scandanavian Assemblies.

In 1935, the Scandanavian group dissolved its incorporation and united with the Independent Assemblies of God of the U.S. and Canada which is now known as Assemblies of God International Fellowship

GENERAL ORGANIZATION

Convention: annual
Headquarters: 8504 Commerce Ave., San Diego, CA 92121. Tel. (619)530-1727

OFFICERS

Exec. Dir., Rev. T. A. Lanes, 8504 Commerce Ave., San Diego, CA 92121
Sec., Canada: Harry Nunn, Sr., 15 White Crest Ct., St. Catherines, Ontario 62N 6Y1

PERIODICAL

The Fellowship Magazine, 8504 Commerce Ave., San Diego, CA 92121. Rev. T. A. Lanes, Ed.

Associate Reformed Presbyterian Church (General Synod)

Associate Reformed Presbyterian Church (General Synod) stems from the 1782 merger of Associate Presbyterians and Reformed Presbyterians. In 1822, the Synod of the Carolinas broke with the Associate Reformed Presbyterian Church (which eventually became part of the United Presbyterian Church of North America).

The story of the Synod of the Carolinas began with the Seceder Church, formed in Scotland in 1733 and representing a break from the established Church of Scotland. Seceders, in America called Associate Presbyterians, settled in South Carolina following the Revolutionary War. They were joined by a few Covenanter congregations, which, along with the Seceders, had protested Scotland's established church. The Covenanters took their name from the Solemn League and Covenant of 1643, the guiding document of Scotch Presbyterians. In 1790 some Seceders and Covenanters formed the Presbytery of the Carolinas and Georgia at Long Cane, South Carolina. Thomas Clark and John Boyse led in the formation of this presbytery, a unit within the Associate Reformed Presbyterian Church. The presbytery represented the southern segment of that church.

In 1822 the southern church became independent of the northern Associate Reformed Presbyterian Church and formed the Associate Reformed Presbyterian Church of the South. "Of the South" was dropped in 1858 when the northern group joined the United Presbyterian Church and "General Synod" was added in 1935. The General Synod is the denomination's highest court; it is composed of all the teaching elders and at least one ruling elder from each congregation.

Doctrinally, the church holds to the Westminster Confeson of Faith. In 1959 the presbyteries approved some 15 changes in the confessions, including the arrangement of existing material into new chapters on the Holy Spirit and the gospel. Liturgically, the synod has been distinguished by its exclusive use of psalmody; in 1946 this practice became optional.

Churches: 181; Inclusive Membership: 36,949; Sunday or Sabbath Schools: 164; Total Enrollment: 16,042; Ordained Clergy: 237

GENERAL ORGANIZATION

General Synod: Annual, June.

OFFICERS

Moderator, Rev. John L. Carson, P. O. Box 576, Due West, SC 269639
Principal Clk., Rev. C. Ronald Beard, 3132 Grace Hill Rd., Columbia, SC 29204

AGENCIES AND INSTITUTIONS

Associate Reformed Presbyterian Center, One Cleveland St., Greenville, SC 29601.Tel. 803-232-8297. Office of Administrative Services, Dir., Mr. Ed. Hogan. (Headquarters for the following):
Associate Reformed Presbyterian Foundation, Inc.
Associate Reformed Presbyterian Retirement Plan
Office of Christian Education, Dir., Rev. J. B. Hendrick
Office of Church Extension, Dir., Rev. W. C. Lauderdale
Office of Synod's Treasurer, Mr. W. Herman Lesslie
Office of Secretary of World Witness, Exec. Sec., John E. Mariner. Tel. (803)233-5226

PERIODICAL

The Associate Reformed Presbyterian, Mr. Ben Johnston, Ed.

Baha'i Faith

The Bahá'í Faith is an independent world religion with adherents in virtually every country. Within the continental United States approximately 110,000, Bahá'ís reside in more than 7,000 localities.

Baha'is are followers of Bahá'u'lláh (1817-1892). The religion upholds the basic principles of the oneness of God, the oneness of religion, and the oneness of mankind. The central aim of the Bahá'í Faith is the unification of mankind.

The Bahá'í administrative order consists of elected local Spiritual Assemblies, National Spiritual Assemblies and the Universal House of Justice. The Local and National Spiritual Assemblies are elected annually. The Universal House of Justice is elected every five years. There are 151 National Assemblies and over approximately 20,000 local Local Assemblies worldwide. In the United States there are over approximately 1,700 local Local Assemblies. Bahá'í literature of the Bahá'í Faith has been published in 800 languages.

GENERAL ORGANIZATION

National Spiritual Assembly, Headquarters: 536 Sheridan Rd., Wilmette, IL 60091. Tel. (708)869-9039

OFFICERS

Chpsn., Judge Dorothy Nelson; Sec. Gen., Robert Henderson, Sec. for External Affairs, Firuz Kazemzadeh

PERIODICALS

World Order (q)
US Bahá'í Report (q)

Baptist Bible Fellowship International

Organized on May 24, 1950 in Fort Worth, Texas, the Baptist Bible Fellowship was founded by about 100 pastors and lay people who had grown disenchanted with the policies and leadership of the World Fundamental Baptist Missionary Fellowship, an outgrowth of the Baptist Bible Union formed in Kansas City in 1923 by fundamentalist leaders from the Southern Baptist, Northern Baptist, and Canadian Baptist Conventions.

The BBF elected W. E. Dowell as its first president and established offices and a three-year (now four-year with a graduate school) Baptist Bible College for training pastors, missionaries, evangelists, and other Christian workers.

The BBF statement of faith was essentially that of the Baptist Bible Union, adopted in 1923, a variation of the New Hampshire Confession of Faith. It presents an infallible Bible, belief in the substitutionary death of Christ, his physical resurrection, and his premillennial return to earth. It advocates local church autonomy and strong pastoral leadership and maintains that the funda-

mental basis of fellowship is a missionary outreach. The BBF vigorously stresses evangelism and the international missions office reports 734 adult missionaries working on 80 fields throughout the world in 1989.

There are BBF-related churches in every state of the U.S., with special strength in the upper South, the Great Lakes region, southern states west of the Mississippi, Kansas, and California. There are 7 related colleges and 1 graduate school or seminary.

A Committee of Forty-Five, elected by pastors and churches within the states, sits as a representative body, meeting in three subcommittees, each chaired by one of the principal officers: an administration committee chaired by the president; a missions committee chaired by a vice-president; an education committee chaired by a vice-president. The latter reviews the work of 7 approved schools, receiving annual reports from each.

GENERAL ORGANIZATION

Annual Meetings 1990: third week of February, at First Coast Baptist Church, Jacksonville, FL; third week of May, at Baptist Bible College, Springfield, MO; fourth week of September, at Landmark Baptist Church, Cincinnati, OH
Offices: Baptist Bible Fellowship Missions Building, 720 E. Kearney St., Springfield, MO 65803. Mailing Address: P.O. Box 191, Springfield, MO 65801. Tel. (417) 862-5001.

OFFICERS

Pres., Bob Perryman, Parkcrest Baptist Church, 816 W. Republic Rd., Springfield, MO 65807
First Vice-Pres., Ben Sanders, Bethlehem Baptist Church, 4601 West Ox Rd., Fairfax, VA 22030
Second Vice-Pres., Don Elmore, Temple Baptist Church, P. O. Box 292, Springdale, AR 72764
Sec., K. B. Murray, Millington Street Baptist Church, Box 524, Winfield, KS 67156
Treas., Billy Hamm, Mtn. States Baptist Temple, 8333 Acoma Way, Denver CO 80221
Mission Dir., Dr. Bob Baird, P. O. Box 191, Springfield MO 65801

PERIODICAL

The Baptist Bible Tribune (tri-w), P.O. Box 309 HSJ, Springfield, MO 65801, James O. Combs, Ed. Tel. (417)831-3996

Baptist General Conference

The Baptist General Conference, rooted in the pietistic movement of Sweden during the nineteenth century, traces its history to August 13, 1852. On that day a small group of believers at Rock Island, Illinois, under the leadership of Gustaf Palmquist, organized the first Swedish Baptist Church in America. Swedish Baptist churches flourished in the upper Midwest and Northeast, and by 1879, when the first annual meeting was held in Village Creek, Iowa, 65 churches had been organized, stretching from Maine to the Dakotas and South to Kansas and Missouri.

Nearly a decade before, John Alexis Edgren, an immigrant sea captain and pastor in Chicago, had begun the first publication and a theological seminary. By 1902, the conference showed significant growth, with 324 churches and nearly 26,000 members. Succeeding years showed the membership growing from 34,000 in 1927 and 40,000 in 1945 to 135,000 in 1982.

Christian Education has played an important part. Many churches began as Sunday schools. The seminary evolved into Bethel, a four-year liberal arts college with 1,800 students and the theological seminary, with over 500 students, located in Arden Hills, Minnesota.

Missions, the planting of churches, has been a main objective both in America and overseas. Today churches have been established in the U.S., Canada, and Mexico, as well as a dozen countries overseas. In 1985 the churches of Canada founded an autonomous denomination, The Baptist General Conference of Canada.

The Baptist General Conference is a member of the Baptist World Alliance, the Baptist Joint Committee on Public Affairs, and the National Association of Evangelicals. It is characterized by the balancing of a conservative doctrine with an irenic and cooperative spirit. Its basic objective is to seek the fulfillment of the great commission and the Great Commandment.

Churches: 789; Inclusive Membership: 135,125; Sunday or Sabbath Schools: 789; Total Enrollment: 67,030; Ordained clergy: 1,700

GENERAL ORGANIZATION

General Conference: annual (June)
Headquarters: 2002 S. Arlington Heights Rd., Arlington Heights, IL 60005. Tel. (312) 228-0200

ORGANIZATION

Pres. & Chief Exec. Officer, Dr. Robert S. Ricker, 2002 S. Arlington Heights Rd., Arlington Heights, IL 60005

OTHER ORGANIZATIONS

Business & Planning: Vice-Pres., Dr. Clifford E. Anderson
Board of Home Missions: Exec. Dir.; Dr. John C. Dickau
Board of World Missions: Exec. Dir., Rev. Herbert Skoglund
Church & Pastoral Services: Exec. Dir., Dr. J. Daniel Baumann
Board of Regents: Pres. of Bethel College & Seminary, Dr. George Brushaber, 3900 Bethel Dr., St. Paul, MN 55112

PERIODICAL

The Standard (m), 2002 S. Arlington Heights Rd., Arlington Heights, IL 60005, Dr. Donald Anderson, Ed.

Baptist Missionary Association of America

A group of regular Baptist churches organized in associational capacity in May, 1950, in Little Rock, Ark. as North American Baptist Association. Name changed in 1969 to Baptist Missionary Association of America. There are several state and numerous local associations of cooperating churches. In theology these churches are evangelical, missionary, fundamental, and in the main premillennial.

Churches: 1,347; Inclusive Membership: 227,879; Sunday or Sabbath Schools: N.R.; Total Enrollment: 95,406; Ordained Clergy: 2,650

GENERAL ORGANIZATION

The Association meets annually (in April).

PRESIDING OFFICERS

Pres., Rev. Gary D. Divine, 155 Ninth Ave., Chickasaw, AL 36611
Vice-Pres.'s, Rev. Alan Henson, 1801 Highland Dr., Carrollton, TX 75006; Rev. J. Harold Hodges, 717 Eagle Dr., Moore, OK 73160
Rec. Secs.: Rev. Ralph Cottrell, P.O. Box 1203, Van, TX 75790; Rev. O. D. Christian Rt. 1, Box 267, Streetman, TX 75859 and G. H. Gordon, Rt. 1, Box 430-AA, Stringer, MS 39481

DEPARTMENTS

Missions: Gen. Sec., Rev. F. Donald Collins, 721 Main St., Little Rock, AR 72201
Publications: Ed.-in-Chief, Rev. James L. Silvey, 1319 Magnolia, Texarkana, TX 75501

Christian Education: Baptist Missionary Association Theological Seminary, Seminary Heights, 1410 E. Pine St., Jacksonville, TX 75766, Dr. Philip R. Bryan, Pres., Wilbur Benningfield, Dean.
Baptist News Service: Dir., Rev. James C. Blaylock, P. O. Box 97, Jacksonville, TX 75766; Asst., Rev. Douglas A. Wilson, P. O. Box 97, Jacksonville, TX 75766
LifeWord Broadcast Ministries: Rev. George Reddin, Dir., P.O. Box 6, Conway, AR 72032
Armed Forces Chaplaincy: Exec. Dir., William Charles Pruitt Jr., P.O. Box 912, Jacksonville, TX 75766
National Youth Department: Bobby Tucker, P. O. Box 3376, Texarkana, TX 75504
Daniel Springs Encampment: James Speer, P.O. Box 310, Gary, TX 75643
Ministers Benefit Dept., James A. Henry, 4001 Jefferson St., Texarkana, AR 75501

OTHER ORGANIZATIONS

Baptist Missionary Association Brotherhood: Pres., Randy Boyd, Rt. 2, Box 520, Warren, AR 71671
National Women's Missionary Auxiliary: Pres., Bill (Deborah) Goodwin, Rt. 3, Box 213-Fl, Cabot, AR 72023

PERIODICALS

The Advancer (m), P.O. Box 7270, Texarkana, TX 75502Larry Slivey, Ed.
The Gleaner (m), 721 Main St., Little Rock, AR 72201, F. Donald Collins, Ed.
Baptist Progress (w), P.O. Box 2085, Waxahachie, TX 85165, Danny Pope, Ed.
Baptist Trumpet (w), P.O. Box 19084, Little Rock, AR 72219, David Tidwell, Ed.
Mississippi Baptist (s-m), P. O. Box 8181, Laurel, MS 39440. Rev. D. J. Brown, Ed.
Missouri Missionary Baptist (s-m), 11229 Midland Blvd., St. Louis, MO 63114. James Hoffman, Ed.
Louisiana Baptist Builder (m), P. O. Box 1297, Denham Springs, LA 70727. Rev. Leroy Mayfield, Ed.
Oklahoma Baptist (m), 809 S.W. 4th St., Moore, OK 73160, Doug Brewer, Ed.
Baptist Herald (m), P.O. Box 218, Galena, KS 66739. Jerry Derfelt, Ed.
Alabama Baptist Banner (m) 306 Laurie Ln., Warner Robins, GA 31093. Edward Strawmier, Ed.
The Advocate, (m) 8101 Joffree Dr., Jacksonville, FL 32210, Ronald J. Beasley, Ed.
Illinois and Indiana Missionary Baptist (m), 5134 E. Wilson St., Batria, IL 60510, Leroy Franklin, Ed.
Midwest Missionary Baptist (m), 50865 CR 652, Mattawan, MI 49071, Dennis Aho, Ed.

Beachy Amish Mennonite Churches

This group originates mostly from the Old Order Amish Mennonite Church.

Two congregations had been formed as early as 1927, but the others have all been organized since 1938. Worship is held in meeting houses. Nearly all have Sunday schools, many have prayer meetings, and most of them either sponsor or have access to Christian day schools. They sponsor evangelical missions at home and abroad; a monthly magazine, Calvary Messenger, as an evangelical and doctrinal witness; and Calvary Bible School, nine weeks each winter, for an in-depth study of the Word of God to better equip their youth for Christian service.

Churches: 100; Inclusive Membership: 6,800; Sunday or Sabbath Schools: N.R.; Total Enrollment: N.R.; Ordained Clergy: 325

Ervin N. Hershberger, R. D. 1, Meyersdale, PA 15552. Tel. (814) 662-2483

Berean Fundamental Church

Founded 1932 in Denver, Colorado, this body emphasizes conservative Protestant doctrines.

GENERAL ORGANIZATION

Headquarters: Lincoln, NB 68506. Tel. (402)483-2647
Annual Conference: September

OFFICERS

Pres., Rev. Curt Lehman, 6400 South 70th St., Lincoln, NB 68516. Tel. (402)423-6512
Vice-Pres., Rev. Richard Cocker, 20th and East D, Torrington, WY 82240. Tel. (307)532-2497
Sec., Rev. Frank Van Campen, P. O. Box 1136, Chadron, NE 69337
Treas., Virgil Wiebe, P. O. Box 6130, Lincoln NB 68506
Founder Advisor to the Council, Dr. Ivan E. Olsen
Exec. Advisor, Rev. Carl M. Goltz, P.O. Box 397, North Platte, NB 69103. Tel. (308)532-6723

The Bible Church of Christ, Inc.

The Bible Church of Christ was founded on March 1, 1961 by Bishop Roy Bryant, Sr. Since that time, the Church has grown to include congregations in the U.S., Africa and India. The church is trinitarian and accepts the Bible as the divinely inspired Word of God. Its doctrine includes miracles of healing and the baptism of the Holy Ghost.

Churches: 6; Inclusive Membership: 6,405; Sunday or Sabbath Schools: 6; Total Enrollment: 684; Ordained Clergy: 47

GENERAL ORGANIZATION

General Meeting: annual
Headquarters: 1358 Morris Ave., Bronx, NY 10456. Tel. (212) 588-2284

OFFICERS

Pres., Bishop Roy Bryant, Sr., 3033 Gunther Ave., Bronx, NY 10469. Tel. (212) 379-8080
Vice-Pres., Bishop Roy Bryant, Jr., 34 Tuxedo Rd., Montclair, NJ 07042. Tel. (201) 746-0063
Sec., Sissieretta Bryant
Treas, Elder Artie Burney

EXECUTIVE TRUSTEE BOARD

Chpsn., Leon T. Mims, 1358 Morris Ave.,Bronx, NY 10456. Tel. (212) 588-2284
Vice-Chpsn., Peggy Rawls, 100 W. 2nd St., Mount Vernon, NY 10550. Tel. (914) 664-4602

OTHER ORGANIZATIONS

Foreign Missions: Pres., Elder Diane Cooper
Home Missions: Pres., Evangelist Elizabeth Price
Sunday Schools: Gen. Supt., Elder Diane Cooper
Evangelism: National Pres., Evangelist Gloria Gray
Youth: Pres., Deacon Tommy Robinson
Minister of Music: Leon T. Mims
Prison Ministry Team; Pres., Evangelist Marvin Lowe
Presiding Elders: (Delaware), Elder Roland Miflin, Diamond Acre, Dagsboro, DE 19939. (North Carolina), Elder Larry Bryant, West Johnson Rd., Clinton, NC 28328. (Monticello), Elder Jesse Alston, 104 Waverly Ave., Monticello, NY 12701. (Mount Vernon), Elder Artie Burney, Sr., 100 W. 2nd St., Mount Vernon, NY 10550. (Bronx), Elder Anita Robinson, 1358 Morris Ave., Bronx, NY 10456; Annex: Elder Betty Gilliard, 1069 Morris Ave., Bronx, NY 10456

Bible School: Pres., Dr. Roy Bryant, Sr., 1358 Morris Ave., Bronx, NY 10456. Tel. (212)588-2284.
Bookstore: Mgr., Elder Elizabeth Johnson, 1358 Morris Ave., Bronx, NY 10456. Tel. (212)293-1928

PERIODICAL

The Voice (q), 1358 Morris Ave., Bronx, NY 10456. Tel. (212) 588-2284. Montrose Bushrod, Ed.

Bible Way Church of Our Lord Jesus Christ World Wide, Inc.

This body was organized in 1957 in the Pentecostal tradition for the purpose of accelerating evangelistic and foreign missionary commitment and to effect a greater degree of collective leadership than was found in the body in which they had previously participated.

The doctrine is the same as that of the Church of Our Lord Jesus Christ of the Apostolic Faith, Inc. of which some of the churches and clergy were formerly members.

The growth of this organization has been very encouraging. There are approximately 300,000 members, with 300 churches and missions located in Africa, England, Guyana, Trinidad, and Jamaica, and churches in 25 states in America.

The Bible Way Church WW is involved in humanitarian, as well as evangelical outreach, with concerns for urban housing and education and economic development.

GENERAL ORGANIZATION

Headquarters: 1100 New Jersey Ave., N.W., Washington, DC 20001

OFFICERS

Presiding Bishop, Smallwood E. Williams, 4720 16th St., N.W., Washington, DC 20011
Gen. Sec., Bishop Edward William, 5118 Clarendon Rd., Brooklyn, NY 11226

PERIODICALS

The Bible Way News Voice (q), Washington, DC

Brethren Church (Ashland, Ohio)

It was organized by progressive-minded German Baptist Brethren in 1883. They reaffirmed the teaching of the original founder of the Brethren movement, Alexander Mack, and returned to congregational government.

Churches: 124; Inclusive Membership; 14,753; Sunday or Sabbath Schools: 124; Total Enrollment: 6,893; Ordained Clergy: 173

GENERAL ORGANIZATION

General Conference: annual (August)
Headquarters: 524 College Ave., Ashland, OH 44805. Tel. (419) 289-1708
Dir. of Pastoral Ministries, Rev. Dave Cooksey
Dir. of Brethren Church Ministries, Rev. Ronald W. Waters
Ed. of Publications, Rev. Richard C. Winfield
Conf. Mod. (1989-1990), Dr. Mary Ellen Drushal

BOARD

The Missionary Board, 524 College Ave., Ashland, OH 44805. Exec. Dir., James R. Black

Brethren in Christ Church

The Brethren in Christ Church was founded in Lancaster County, Pa. in about the year 1778 and was an outgrowth of the religious awakening which occurred in that area during the latter part of the eighteenth century. This group became known as "River Brethren" because of their original location near the Susquehanna River. The name "Brethren in Christ" was officially adopted in 1863. In theology they have accents of the Anabaptist, Armenian, and holiness movements.

GENERAL ORGANIZATION

General Conference: biennial

OFFICERS

Mod., Bishop John A. Byers, 501 E. Mulberry St., Lancaster, PA 17022
Gen. Sec., Dr. R. Donald Shafer, P.O. Box 245, Upland, CA 91785
Treas., Harold D. Chubb, P.O. Box 450, Mechanicsburg, PA 17055

OTHER ORGANIZATIONS

Board of Administration: Chpsn., John A. Byers, 501 E. Mulberry St., Lancaster, PA 17022;; Gen. Sec., Dr. R. Donald Shafer, P.O. Box 245, Upland, CA 91785; Treas., Harold D. Chubb, P.O. Box 450, Mechanicsburg, PA 17055

Board of Bishops: Chpsn., John A. Byers, 501 E. Mulberry St., Lancaster, PA 17022; Sec., Owen H. Alderfer, P.O. Box 57, West Milton, OH 45383

Board of Brotherhood Concerns: Chpsn, Lenora H. Stern, 345 Gettysburg Pike, Mechanicsburg, PA 17055; Sec., Paul A. Wengert, Jr., 10 Holly Dr., New Cumberland, PA 17070; Treas., Glenn Dalton, Jr., 201 S. 20th St., Harrisburg, PA 17104; Exec. Dir., David R. Brubaker, P.O. Box 246, Mt. Joy, PA 17552

Board for Congregational Life: Chpsn., Warren Hoffman; Sec., Mary J. Davis; Treas., Ronald L. Miller, Messiah College, Grantham, PA 17027; Exec. Dir., Ken Letner, 2134 Sherwal Ave., Lancaster, PA 17601

Board of Directors: Chpsn., John A. Byers, 501 E. Mulberry St., Lancaster, PA 17022; Gen. Sec., Dr. R. Shafer, P.O. Box 245, Upland, CA 91785; Treas., Harold D. Chubb, P.O. Box 450, Mechanicsburg, PA 17055

Board for Evangelism and Church Planting: Chpsn., Doublas P. Sider, 142 Streb Cresc., Saskatoon, Sask., Canada S7M 4T8; Sec., Dale H. Engle, R.D. 1, Box 464, Mt. Joy, PA 17552, Canadian Treas., Walter J. Kelly, 32 Canora Ct., Welland, Ontario, Canada L3C 6H7; U.S. Treas., Donald J. Winters, 1727 Lincoln Hwy. E., Lancaster, PA 17602; Exec. Dir., R. Dale Shaw, 4411 Bee Ridge Rd., Ste. 444, Sarasota, FL 34233

Board for Media Ministries: Chpsn., Emerson C. Frey, R.D. 1, Box 232A, Millersville, PA 17551; Sec., J. Wilmer Heisey, R. 2, Box 1711, Mt. Joy, PA 17552; Treas., Robert A. Leadley, 4497 Bowen Rd., Stevensville, Ontario LOS 1SO; Exec. Dir., Roger Williams, 301-305 N. Elm St., Nappanee, IN 46550

Board for Ministry and Doctrine: Chpsn., Luke L. Keefer, Jr., 1344 Twp. Rd. #523, Ashland, OH 44805; James Ernst, 1865 Fruitville Pk., Lancaster, PA 17601; Treas, Roy J. Peterman, 54 N. Penryn Rd., Manheim, PA 17545; Exec. Dir., Glenn A. Ginder, P.O. Box 9587, Wichita, KS 67277

Board for World Missions: Chpsn., Lowell D. Mann, 8 W. Bainbridge St., Elizabethtown, PA 17022; Sec., Harold H. Engle, 925 Messiah Village, Merchanicsburg, PA 17055; Canadian Treas., Harold Albrecht, R.R. 2, Petersburg, Ontario NOB 2HO; U.S. Treas., W. Edward Rickman, 63 Opal Dr., Chambersburg, PA 17201; Exec. Dir., Donald R. Zook, P.O. Box 390, Mt. Joy, PA 17552

Commission on Christian Education Literature: Chpsn., Dale W. Engle, 1067 Foxhaven Dr., Ashland, OH

44805; Sec., Glen A. Pierce, P.O. Box 166, Nappanee, IN 46550
Commission on Education Institutions: Chpsn., John A. Brubaker, Box 68, Refton, PA 17568; Sec., Harold K. Sider, 644 Vallejo Way, Upland, CA 91786
Jacob Engle Foundation Board of Directors: Chpsn., Dwight E. Bert, P.O. Box 216, Upland, CA 91785; Sec., Mark S. Hess, 135 N. School Lane, Lancaster, PA 17603; Treas., A. Graybill Brubaker, 465 Center St., Chambersburg, PA 17201; Exec. Dir., Donald R. Zook, P.O. Box 450, Mechanicsburg, PA 17055
Pension Fund Trustees: Chpsn., Donald R. Zook, P.O. Box 390, Mt. Joy, PA 17552; Sec., Elbert N. Smith, 309 Woodlawn Ln., Carlisle, PA 17013; Canadian Treas., Lester C. Fretz, Box 207, Vineland, Ontario LOR 2CO; U. S. Treas., Keith Heise, 2904 Dallas NE, Albuquerque, NM 87110
Chpsn., Harold Chubb, P. O. Box 450, Mechanicsburg, PA 17055
Board for Stewardship: Dir. of Finance, Charles F. Frey, P.O. Box 284, R.R. 2, Conestoga, PA 17516; Dir. of Stewardship, Canada, Robert Leadley, R.R. 1, Stevensville, Ontario LOS 1SO; Dir. of Stewardship, Merle Brubaker, P.O. Box 450, Mechanicsburg, PA 17055; Sec., Ivan E. Beachy, 648 Belvedere St., Carlisle, PA 17013

Publishing House: Evangel Press, 301 N. Elm, Nappanee, IN 46550; Exec. Dir., Roger Williams

PERIODICAL

Evangelical Visitor (m), Nappanee, IN 46550, Glen A. Pierce, Ed.

Buddhist Churches of America

Founded in 1899, organized in 1914 as the Buddhist Mission of North America, this body was incorporated in 1944 under the present name and represents the Jodo Shinshu Sect of Buddhism affiliated with the Hongwanji-ha Hongwanji denomination in the continental United States. It is a school of Buddhism which believes in becoming aware of the ignorant self and relying upon the Infinite Wisdom and Compassion of Amida Buddha, which is expressed in sincere gratitude through the recitation of the Nembutsh, Namu Amida Butsu.

GENERAL ORGANIZATION

Conference: annual (February)
Headquarters: 1710 Octavia St., San Francisco, CA 94109. Tel. (415)776-5600; TeleFAX: (415)771-6293

OFFICERS

Bishop Seigen H. Yamaoka
Exec. Asst. to the Bishop: Rev. Seikan Fukuma
Adm. Officer: Henry Shibata
Dir. of Buddhist Education: Rev. Carol Himaka

OTHER ORGANIZATIONS

Federation of Buddhist Women's Assoc
Federation of Dharma School Teachers' League
Institute of Buddhist Studies, a graduate school
Young Adult Buddhist Association
Western Young Buddhist League
Affiliated U.S. Organizational Jurisdiction: Honpa Hongwanji Mission of Hawaii, 1727 Pali Hwy., Honolulu, HI 96813
Affiliated Canadian Organizational Jurisdiction: Buddhist Churches of Canada, 220 Jackson Ave., Vancouver, B.C. V6A 3B3

Bulgarian Eastern Orthodox Church

Bulgarian immigration to the United States and Canada started around the turn of the century, and the first

36

Bulgarian Orthodox church was built in 1907 in Madison, Illinois. In 1938, the Holy Synod of the Bulgarian E. O. Church established the diocese in New York as an Episcopate, and Bishop Andrey was sent as diocesan Bishop. In 1947, the diocese was officially incorporated in New York State and Bishop Andrey became the first elected Metropolitan.

By a decision of the Holy Synod in 1969, the Bulgarian Eastern Orthodox Church was divided into the Diocese of New York (incorporated Diocese of New York) and the Diocese of Akron (incorporated American Bulgarian Diocese of N. & S. America and Australia, Akron, Ohio).

OFFICERS

New York Diocese, Metropolitan Ghelasiy, 550 A, West 50th St., New York, NY 10019. Tel. (212) 581-3756
Akron Diocese, Metropolitan Joseph, 1953 Stockbridge Rd., Akron, OH 44313. Tel. (216)836-8955

Christ Catholic Church

The church is a catholic communion established in 1968 to minister to the growing number of people seeking an experiential relationship with God, and who desire to make a total commitment of their lives to him. The church is catholic in faith and tradition and its orders are recognized as valid by catholics of every tradition.

Churches: 13; Inclusive Membership: 1,382; Sunday or Sabbath Schools: None; Total Enrollment: None; Ordained Clergy: 12

GENERAL ORGANIZATION

Synod: annual. Next meeting, June, 1990

OFFICERS

Presiding Bishop, The Most Reverend Karl Pruter, Cathedral Church, Highlandville, MO 65669. Tel. (417) 587-3951

PERIODICAL

St. Willibrord Journal, 701 W. Pine, Deming, NM 88030

Christadelphians

A body of people who believe the Bible to be the divinely inspired word of God, written by "Holy men who spoke as they were moved by the Holy Spirit" (II Peter 1:21); in the return of Christ to earth to establish the Kingdom of God; the resurrection of those dead, at the return of Christ, who come into relation to Christ in conformity with his instructions, to be judge as to worthiness of eternal life; in opposition to war; spiritual rebirth requiring belief and immersion in the name of Jesus; and in a godly walk in this life.

The denomination was organized in 1844 by a medical doctor, John Thomas, who came to the United States from England in 1832, having survived a near shipwreck in a violent storm. This experience affected him profoundly, and he vowed to devote his life to a search for the Truth of God and a future hope from the Bible.

NO GENERAL ORGANIZATION

Co-Ministers, Norman Fadelle, 815 Chippeewa Dr., Elgin, IL 60120; Norman D. Zilmer, 1000 Mohawk Dr., Elgin, IL 60120

The Christian and Missionary Alliance

An evangelical and evangelistic church begun in 1887 when Dr. Albert B. Simpson founded two organizations, The Christian Alliance (a fellowship of Christians dedicated to the experiencing of the deeper Christian life) and the Evangelical Missionary Alliance (a missionary sending organization). The two groups were merged in 1897 and became The Christian and Missionary Alliance. The denomination stresses the sufficiency of Jesus—Savior, Sanctifier, Healer, and Coming King—and has earned a worldwide reputation for its missionary accomplishments. The Canadian districts became autonomous in 1981 and formed The Christian and Missionary Alliance in Canada.

Churches: 1,793; Inclusive Membership: 259,612; Sunday or Sabbath Schools: 1,606; Total Enrollment: 189,424; Ordained Clergy: 2,241

GENERAL ORGANIZATION

Council: annual (May or June)
Headquarters: P O. Box 35000, Colorado Springs, CO 80935. Tel. (719)599-5999

OFFICERS

Pres., David L. Rambo
Vice-Pres., Paul F. Bubna
Sec., R. Harold Mangham
Vice Pres. for Fin./Treas., Duane Wheeland
Vice Pres. for Church Ministries, Richard W. Bailey
Vice Pres. for Overseas Ministries, David H. Moore
Vice Pres. for Gen. Services, James A. Davey

BOARD OF MANAGERS

David L. Rambo, Chairman

DIVISIONS OF ADMINISTRATION

Division of Finance: Adminis. Staff: Vice Pres./Treas., Duane Wheeland; Ass't. Vice Pres., Larry McCooey; Trust Accountant, _____; Dir. of Accounting, W. E. Stedman; Dir. of Alliance Development Fund, H. E. Maynard; Payroll Mgr., Larry Keeports; Sr. Acct. David Graf
Division of Church Ministries: Adminis. Staff: Vice Pres., R. W. Bailey; Ass't. Vice Pres., J. L. Ng; Dir. of Church Growth, F. C. King; Ass't. Dir. of Church Growth, _____; Dir. of Christian Education, D. D. Dale; Dir. of Intercultural Minis., E. A. Cline; Assoc. Dir. of Intercultural Minis., A. E. Hall; Dir. of Missionary Deputation, R. H. Pease; Dir. of Alternative Education, M. S. Winters;
Division of Overseas Ministries: Adminis. Staff: Vice Pres., D. H. Moore; Ass't. Vice Pres., Arni Shareski; Dir. for East Asia and Pacific Islands, P. N. Nanfelt; Dir. for Southeast Asia/Middle East/Europe/Australia and New Zealand, R. W. Reed; Dir. for Africa, D. L. Kennedy; Dir. for South America, D. K. Volstad; Dir. for Missionary Candidates, D. O. Young
Division of General Services: Adminis. Staff: Vice Pres., J. A. Davey; Alliance Life, M. R. Irvin; Dir. of Data Processing, R. N. Mapstone; Mgr. of Computer Operations, D. G. Ingram; Dir. of Stewardship, S. L. Bjornson; Dir. of Business Affairs, M. J. Reese; Dir. of Communications, G. McAlister; Dir. of Personnel, D. M. Johnson.
Christian Publications, Inc.: Pres., J. A. Davey; Vice Pres., B. S. King; Exec. Vice Pres./Treas., K. N. Foster; Sec., D. A. Wiggins

DISTRICTS

Central: Howard D. Bowers, Sup't., 1218 High St., Wadsworth, OH 44281, Tel. (216) 336-2911
Central Pacific: Richard C. Taylor, Sr., Sup't., 3824 Buell St., Suite A, Oakland, CA 94619, Tel. (415) 530-5410
Eastern: Rev. Leon W. Young, Sup't., 1 Sherwood Dr., Mechanicsburg, PA 17055, Tel. (717) 766-0261
Great Lakes: Dahl B. Seckinger, Sup't. 315 W. Huron St., Ste. 380-B, Ann Arbor, MI 48103. Tel. (313)662-6702.
Metropolitan: Rev. Paul Hazlett, Sup't., 349 Watchung Ave., N. Plainfield, NJ 07060, Tel. (201) 668-8421
Mid-Atlantic: C. E. Mock, Sup't., Shady Grove Professional Park, 9015 Shady Grove Ct., Gaithersburg, MD 20877, Tel. (301) 258-0035
Midwest: John W. Fogal, Sup't., 260 Glen Ellyn Rd., Bloomingdale, IL 60108, Tel. (312) 893-1355

New England: Cornelius W. Clark, Sup't., Box 288, S. Easton, MA 02375, Tel. (617) 238-3820

Northeastern: Woodford C. Stemple, Jr., Sup't., 6275 Pillmore Dr., Rome, NY 13440, Tel. (315) 336-4720

Northwestern: Gary M. Benedict, Sup't., 1813 N. Lexington Ave., St. Paul, MN 55113, Tel. (612) 489-1391

Ohio Valley: Keith M. Bailey, Sup't, 4051 Executive Park Dr., Ste. 402, Cincinnati, OH 45241. Tel. (513)733-4833

Pacific Northwest: R. Harold Mangham, Sup't., P. O. Box 640, Canby, OR 97013, Tel. (503) 226-2238

Puerto Rico: Jorge Cuevas, Sup't., P.O. Box 51394, Levittown, PR 00950. Tel. (809) 795-0101

Rocky Mountain: Harvey A. Town, Sup't., 1215 24th W., Ste. 210, Billings, MT 59102, Tel. (406) 656-4233

South Atlantic: Gerald G. Copeland, Sup't., 3421-B, St. Vardell Ln., Charlotte, NC 28217, Tel. (704) 523-9456

South Pacific: Francis N. McGeaughay, Sup't., 9055 Haven Ave., Rte. 107, Rnch., Cacamoga, CA 91730. Tel. (714)945-92441

Southeastern: Harry J. Arnold, Sup't., P.O. Box 580708, Orlando, FL 32858, Tel. (305) 298-5460

Southern: _____, Sup't., P. O. Box 4484, Birmingham, AL 35206, Tel. (205) 836-4048

Southwestern: Loren G. Calkins, Sup't., P. O. Box 120756, Arlington, TX 76012, Tel. (817) 261-9631

Western: Anthony G. Bollback, Sup't., 1301 S. 119th St., Omaha, NE 68144, Tel. (402) 330-1888

Western Pennsylvania: David K. Muir, Sup't., P. O. Box 429, Punxsutawney, PA 15767, Tel. (814) 939-6920

INTERCULTURAL MINISTRIES DISTRICTS

Cambodian: Joseph S. Kong, Dir., 1616 S. Palmetto Ave., Ontario, CA 91761. Tel. (714)988-9434

Dega: c/o Rev. A. E. Hall, P. O. Box 35000, Colorado Springs, CO 80935

Haitian: Mr. Jean Remy, P.O. Box 791, Nyack, NY 10960. Tel. (914)947-3462

Hmong: Yong Xeng Yang, Field Dir., P.O. Box 219, Brighton, CO 80601, Tel. (303) 659-1538

Jewish: Rev. Abraham Sandler, Admn. Asst., 9820 Woodfern Rd., Philadelphia, PA 19115. Tel. (215)698-9089

Native American: Craig Smith, Dir., 3075 Packmule Ct., Colorado Springs, CO 80922. Tel. (719)597-6591

Korean: Rev. John H. Pang, Dir., 3214 W. Lawrence Ave., #206, Chicago, IL 60625. Tel. (312)539-3222

Lao: Sisouphanah Ratthahao, Dir., 459 Addison St., Elgin, IL 60120. Tel. (312)741-3879

Spanish Central: Ken Brisco., Dir., 515 Ogden Ave., 3rd Fl., Downers Grove, IL 60515. Tel. (312)964-5592

Spanish Eastern: G. Rolando Pichardo, Dir., 700 North Dixie Hwy., Hollywood, FL 33021. Tel. (305)923-7278

Spanish Western: Angel Ortiz. Dir., 1904 Carmelina Dr., San Diego, CA 92116. Tel. (619)421-4422

Vietnamese: Tai Anh Nguyen, Dir., P.O. Box 2468, Fullerton, CA 92633. Tel. (714)870-0792

PERIODICAL

Alliance Life, P. O. Box 35000, Colorado Springs, CO 80935

Christian Brethren (also known as Plymouth Brethren)

An orthodox and evangelical movement which began in the British Isles in the 1820's and is now worldwide. Congregations are usually simply called "assemblies." The name Plymouth Brethren was given by others because this group in Plymouth, England, was a large congregation. In recent years the term Christian Brethren has replaced Plymouth Brethren for the "open" branch of the movement in Canada and British Commonwealth countries, and to some extent in the U.S.

The unwillingness to establish a denominational structure makes the autonomy of local congregations an important feature of the movement. Other features are weekly observance of the Lord's Supper and adherence to the doctrinal position of conservative, evangelical Christianity.

In the 1840's the movement divided. The "exclusive" branch, led by John Darby, stressed the interdependency of congregations. Since disciplinary decisions were held to be binding on all assemblies, exclusives had sub-divided into seven or eight main groups by the end of the century. Since 1925 a trend toward reunification has reduced that number to three or four. U.S. congregations number approximately 300, with an inclusive membership estimated at 19,000.

The "open" branch of the movement, stressing evangelism and foreign missions, is now the larger of the two. Following the leadership of George Muller in rejecting the "exclusive" principle of binding discipline, this branch has escaped large-scale division. U.S. congregations number approximately 850, with an inclusive membership estimated at 79,000. There are 400 "commended" full-time ministers, not including foreign missionaries.

NO GENERAL ORGANIZATION

Correspondent: Interest Ministries, Bruce R. McNicol, Pres., 218 W. Willow, Wheaton, IL 60187. Tel. (312) 653-6573.

OTHER ORGANIZATIONS

Christian Missions in Many Lands, Box 13, Spring Lake, NJ 07762

Stewards Foundation, 218 W. Willow, Wheaton, IL 60187

International Teams, Box 203, Prospect Heights, IL 60070

PERIODICALS

Interest Magazine (m), 218 W. Willow, Wheaton, IL 60187

Missions Magazine (m), Box 13, Spring Lake, NJ 07762

Food for the Flock (bi-m), 9257 Caprice Dr., Plymouth, MI 48170

Christian Catholic Church (Evangelical-Protestant)

This church was founded by the Rev. John Alexander Dowie on February 22, 1896 at Chicago, IL. In 1901 the church opened the city of Zion, Illinois as its home and headquarters. Theologically, the church is rooted in evangelical orthodoxy. The Scriptures are accepted as the rule of faith and practice. Other doctrines call for belief in the necessity of repentance for sin and personal trust in Christ for salvation, baptism by triune immersion, and tithing as a practical method of Christian stewardship. The church teaches the Second Coming of Christ.

As a small association, the Christian Catholic Church is a denominational member of The National Association of Evangelicals. It has work in ten other nations in addition to the United States. Branch ministries are found in Michigan City, IN; Phoenix, AZ; Tonalea, AZ; Russell, IL and Lindenhurst, IL

Churches: 6; Inclusive Membership: 2,500; Sunday or Sabbath Schools: 6; Total Enrollment: 1,000; Ordained Clergy: 19

GENERAL ORGANIZATION

Convocation: annual (last week of September) Headquarters: Dowie Memorial Dr., Zion, IL 60099. Tel. (312) 746-1411

OFFICER

Gen. Overseer, Roger W. Ottersen

PERIODICAL

Leaves of Healing (bi-m), Dowie Memorial Dr., Zion, IL 60099, Roger W. Ottersen, Ed.-in-Chief

Christian Church (Disciples of Christ)

Born on the American frontier in the early 1800s as a movement to unify Christians, this body drew its major inspiration from Thomas and Alexander Campbell in western Pennsylvania and Barton W. Stone in Kentucky. Developing separately for a quarter of a century, the "Disciples," under Alexander Campbell, and the "Christians," led by Stone, united in Lexington, Kentucky, in 1832.

The Christian Church (Disciples of Christ) is marked by informality, openness, individualism and diversity. The Disciples claim no official doctrine or dogma. Membership is granted after a simple statement of belief in Jesus Christ and baptism by immersion—although most congregations accept transfers baptized by other forms in other denominations. The Lord's Supper—generally called Communion—is open to Christians of all persuasions. The practice is weekly Communion, although no church law insists upon it.

Thoroughly ecumenical, the Disciples helped organize the National and World Councils of Churches. The church is a member of the Consultation on Church Union. The Disciples and the United Church of Christ have declared themselves to be in "full communion" through the General Assembly and General Synod of the two churches. Official theological conversations have been going on since 1967 directly with the Roman Catholic Church, and since 1987 with the Russian Orthodox Church.

Disciples have supported vigorously world and national programs of education, agricultural assistance, urban reconciliation, care of mentally retarded, family planning, and aid to victims of war and calamity. Operating ecumenically, Disciples personnel or funds work in more than 90 countries outside North America.

Three levels of church polity (general, regional, and congregational) operate as equals, managing their own finances, property, and program, with strong but voluntary ties to one another. Local congregations own their own property and have full control of their budgets and program. A General Assembly meets every two years and has voting representation direct from each congregation.

Churches: 4,159; Inclusive Membership: 1,073,119; Sunday or Sabbath Schools: 4,159; Total Enrollment: 327,354; Ordained Clergy: 6,849

GENERAL ORGANIZATION

General Assembly, biennial
General Office: 222 S. Downey Ave., Box 1986, Indianapolis, IN 46206. Tel. (317) 353-1491

OFFICERS

Gen. Minister and Pres., John O. Humbert
Mod., K. David Cole, 6140 Swope Parkway, Kansas City, MO 64130
1st Vice-Mod., Fran Craddock, 6439 Chapelwood Ct., Indianapolis, IN 46268
2nd Vice-Mod., C. William Bailey, 13526 Sherman Rd., NW, Seattle, WA 98177

GENERAL OFFICERS

Gen. Minister and Pres., John O. Humbert
Deputy Gen. Minister and Vice-Pres. for Communication, Claudia E. Grant
Deputy Gen. Minister and Vice-Pres. for Administration, Donald B. Manworren
Deputy Gen. Minister and Vice-Pres. for Inclusive Ministries, John R. Foulkes

ADMINISTRATIVE UNITS

Board of Church Extension: 110 S. Downey Ave., Box 7030, Indianapolis, IN 46207. Tel. (317) 356-6333. Pres., Harold R. Watkins
Christian Board of Publication (Bethany Press): Box 179, 1316 Convention Plaza Dr., St. Louis, MO 63166. Tel. (314) 231-8500. Pres., James C. Suggs
Christian Church Foundation: 222 S. Downey Ave., Box 1986, Indianapolis, IN 46206 Tel. (317) 353-1491, Pres., James R. Reed

Church Finance Council, Inc.: 222 S. Downey Ave., Box 1986 Indianapolis, IN 46206. Tel. (317) 353-1491. Pres., James P. Johnson
Council on Christian Unity: 222 S. Downey Ave., Box 1986, Indianapolis, IN 46206 Tel. (317) 353-1491. Pres., Paul A. Crow, Jr.
Disciples of Christ Historical Society: 1101 19th Ave. S., Nashville, TN 37212. Tel. (615) 327-1444. Pres., James M. Seale
Division of Higher Education: 11780 Borman Dr., Ste. 100, St. Louis, MO 63146. Tel. (314) 991-3000. Pres., James I. Spainhower
Division of Homeland Ministries: 222 S. Downey Ave., Box 1986, Indianapolis, IN 46206. Tel. (317) 353-1491. Pres., Ann Updegraff Spleth
Division of Overseas Ministries: 222 S. Downey Ave., Box 1986, Indianapolis, IN 46206. Tel. (317) 353-1491. Pres., William J. Nottingham
National Benevolent Association: 11780 Borman Dr., Ste. 200, St. Louis, MO 63146. Tel. (314) 993-9000. Pres. Richard R. Lance
Pension Fund: 200 Barrister Bldg., 155 E. Market St., Indianapolis, IN 46204. Tel. (317) 634-4504. Pres., Lester D. Palmer

REGIONAL UNITS OF THE CHURCH

Alabama-Northwest Florida: Christian Church (Disciples of Christ) in Alabama-Northwest Florida, 1336 Montgomery Hwy., S., Birmingham, AL 35216. Tel. (205) 823-5647. Carl R. Flock, Regional Minister
Arizona: Christian Church (Disciples of Christ) in Arizona., 4423 N. 24thSt., Phoenix, AZ 85016. Tel. (602)468-3815. Bruce L. Jones, Regional Minister
Arkansas: The Christian Church (Disciples of Christ) in Arkansas, 6100 Queensboro Dr., P.O. Box 9739, Little Rock 72219. Tel. (501)562-6053. W. Chris Hobgood, Exec. Minister
California North Nevada: The Christian Church (Disciples of Christ) of Northern California-Nevada, 111-A Fairmount Ave., Oakland, CA 94611. Tel. (415)839-3550, Richard Lauer, Regional Minister—President
Canada: Christian Church (Disciples of Christ) in Canada, 55 Cork St., E., Ste. 303, Guelph, Ontario N1H 2W7, Tel. (519)823-5190. Robert W. Steffer, Exec. Regional Minister
Capital Area: Christian Church (Disciples of Christ)—Capital Area, 8901 Connecticut Ave., Chevy Chase, MD 20815. Tel. (301)654-7794. Richard L. Taylor, Regional Minister
Central Rocky Mountain Region: Christian Church (Disciples of Christ) Central Rocky Mountain Region, ABS Building, 7000 N. Broadway, Ste. 400, Denver CO 80221. Tel. (303)427-1403. William E. Crowl, Exec. Regional Minister
Florida: Christian Church (Disciples of Christ) in Florida, 924 N. Magnolia, Ste. #248, Orlando, FL 32803. Tel. (407) 843-4652 Jimmie L. Gentle, Regional Minister
Georgia: Christian Church (Disciples of Christ) in Georgia, Inc., 2370 Vineville Ave., Macon 31204. Tel. (912) 743-8649. David L. Alexander, Regional Minister
Idaho-South: Christian Church (Disciples of Christ) of South Idaho, 4900 No. Five Mile Rd., Boise, ID 83704. Tel. (208) 322-0538. Larry Crist, Regional Minister
Illinois-Wisconsin: Christian Church (Disciples of Christ) in Illinois and Wisconsin, 1011 N. Main St., Bloomington, IL 61701. Tel. (309) 828-6293. Nathan S. Smith, Regional Minister and President
Indiana: Christian Church (Disciples of Christ) in Indiana, 1100 W. 42nd St., Indianapolis IN 46208. Tel. (317) 926-6051. Howard B. Goodrich, Jr., Regional Minister
Kansas: Christian Church in Kansas (Disciples of Christ), 2914 S.W. MacVicar, Topeka, KS 66611. Tel. (913) 266-9414. Ralph L. Smith, Regional Minister/President
Kansas City (Greater): The ChristianChurch (Disciples of

39

Christ) of Greater Kansas City, 7203 The Paseo, P.O. Box 17088, Kansas City, MO 64132. Tel. (816) 361-7771. David C. Downing, Regional Minister/President
Kentucky: Christian Church (Disciples of Christ) in Kentucky, 1125 Red Mile Rd., Lexington 40504. Tel. (606)233-1391. A. Guy Waldrop, General Minister
Louisiana: Christian Church (Disciples of Christ) in Louisiana, 3524 Holloway Prairie Rd., Pineville 71360. Tel. (318) 443-0304. Bill R. Boswell, Regional Minister
Michigan: Christian Church (Disciples of Christ) Michigan Region, 2820 Covington Ct., Lansing 48912. Tel. (517) 372-3220. Morris Finch, Jr., Regional Minister
Mid-America Region: Christian Church (Disciples of Christ) of Mid-America, Hwy. 54 W., Box 104298, Jefferson City, MO 65110. Tel. (314) 636-8149. Stephen V. Cranford, Regional Minister
Mississippi: Christian Church (Disciples of Christ), in Mississippi, 1619 N. West St., Jackson 39202. Tel. (601) 352-6774. William E. McKnight, Regional Minister
Montana: Christian Church (Disciples of Christ) in Montana, 1019 Central Ave., Great Falls 59401. Tel. (406) 452-7404. James E. Kimsey, Jr., Regional Minister
Nebraska: Christian Church (Disciples of Christ) in Nebraska, 1268 S. 20th St., Lincoln 68502. Tel. (402) 476-0359. N. Dwain Acker, Regional Minister
North Carolina: Christian Church (Disciples of Christ), in North Carolina, 509 NE Lee St., Box 1568, Wilson 27893. Tel. (919) 291-4047. Bernard C. Meece, Regional Minister
Northeastern Region: Christian Church (Disciples of Christ), Northeastern Region, Inc., 1272 Delaware Ave., Buffalo, NY 14209. Tel. (716) 886-2634. Charles F. Lamb, Regional Minister
Northwest Region: The Northwest Regional Christian Church (Disciples of Christ), 6558-35th Ave., SW, Seattle, WA 98126. Tel. (206)938-1008, Robert Clarke Brock, Regional Minister—Pres.
Ohio: The Christian Church in Ohio (Disciples of Christ) 38007 Butternut Ridge Rd., Elyria 44035. Tel. (216) 458-5112. Howard M. Ratcliff, Regional Pastor and Pres.
Oklahoma: Christian Church (Disciples of Christ) in Oklahoma, 301 N.W. 36th St., Oklahoma City 73118. Tel. (405) 528-3577. Eugene N. Frazier, Exec. Regional Minister
Oregon: Christian Church (Disciples of Christ) in Oregon, 0245 S.W. Bancroft St., Suite F, Portland 97201. Tel. (503) 226-7648, Mark K. Reid, Regional Minister
Pacific Southwest Region: Christian Church (Disciples of Christ) of the Pacific Southwest Region, 3126 Los Feliz Blvd., Los Angeles, CA 90039. Tel. (213)665-5126. Margaret Owen Clark, Regional Pastor.
Pennsylvania: Christian Church (Disciples of Christ) in Pennsylvania, 670 Rodi Rd., Pittsburgh 15235. Tel. (412) 731-7000. Dwight L. French, General Minister
South Carolina: Christian Church of South Carolina, (Disciples of Christ), 1098 E. Montague Ave., North Charleston, SC 29406. Tel (803) 554-6886. _____, Regional Minister
Southwest Region: Christian Church (Disciples of Christ) in the Southwest, 2909 Lubbock Ave., Fort Worth, TX 76109. Tel. (817) 926-4687. _____, Regional Minister
Tennessee: Christian Church (Disciples of Christ) in Tennessee, 3700 Richland Ave., Nashville 37205. Tel. (615) 269-3409. G. Bronson Netterville, Regional Minister and Pres.
Upper Midwest Region: Christian Church (Disciples of Christ) in the Upper Midwest, 3300 University Ave., Box 1024, Des Moines, IA 50311. Tel. (515) 255-3168. William L. Miller, Jr., Regional Minister
Utah: Christian Church of Utah (Disciples of Christ), 1370 Pennsylvania, Ste. 400, Denver, CO 80203. Tel. (303) 839-0075. William E. Crowl, Exec. Regional Minister

Virginia: The Christian Church (Disciples of Christ) in Virginia, 518 Brevard St., Lynchburg 24501. Tel. (804) 846-3400. Jack S. Austin, Regional Minister
West Virginia: Christian Church (Disciples of Christ) in West Virginia. Rt. 5, Box 167, Parkersburg 26101. Tel. (304) 428-1681. William B. Allen, Regional Minister

PERIODICALS

The Disciple (m), Box 179, St. Louis, MO 63166, James L. Merrell, Ed.
Vanguard (church planning), 222 S. Downey Ave., Box 1986, Indianapolis, IN 46206. Ann Updegraff Spleth, Ed.-in-Chief

Christian Church of North America, General Council

Originally known as the Italian Christian Church, its first General Council was held in 1927 at Niagara Falls, New York. This body was incorporated in 1948 at Pittsburgh, Pennsylvania, and is described as Pentecostal but does not engage in the "the excesses tolerated or practiced among some churches using the same name."
The movement recognizes two ordinances—baptism and the Lord's supper. Its moral code is conserative and its teaching is orthodox. Members are exhorted to pursue a dedicated life of personal holiness, setting an example to others. A conservative position is held in regard to marriage and divorce. The governmental form is, by and large, congregational in nature. District and National officiaries, however, are referred to as Presbyteries led by Overseers.
The group functions in cooperative fellowship with the Italian Pentecostal Church of Canada and the Evangelical Christian Churches—Assemblies of God in Italy—and is an affiliate member of the Pentecostal Fellowship of North America and of the National Association of Evangelicals.

GENERAL ORGANIZATION

General Council: meets annually (September).
Headquarters: Rt. 18 & Rutledge Rd., Box 141-A, R.D. #1, Transfer, PA 16154. Tel. (412) 962-3501

OFFICERS

Executive Board: Gen. Overseer, Rev. Guy BonGiovanni, 3740 Longview Rd., W. Middlesex, PA 16159
Asst. Gen. Overseers: Exec. Vice-Pres., Rev. David Farina, 41 Sherbrooke Rd., Trenton, NJ 08638; Rev. James Demola, P.O. Box 159, Mullica Hill, NJ 08072; Rev. Andrew Farina, 3 Alhambra Pl., Greenville, PA 16125; Rev. Joseph Ronisisvalle, 1031 Hermosa Dr., Rocklege, FL 32955; Rev. Charles Guy, 26 Delafield Dr., Albany, NY 12205; Rev. Anthony Freni, 10 Elkway Ave., Norwood, MA 02062
Gen. Sec.-Treas., Rev. R. Allen Noyd, Box 141-A R. D. #1, Transfer, PA 16154
Department Dirs.:
Publications & Promotion, Rev. Frank Bongiovanni, 6165 Baer Rd., Sanborn, NY 14132
Faith, Order, Credentials, Unity & Standard, Rev. David Farina, 41 Sherbrooke Rd., Trenton, NJ 08638
Church Growth & Media Ministries, _____
Youth, Sunday School & Education, Rev. Lou Fortunato, Jr., 248 Curry Pl., Youngstown, OH 44504
Foreign & Home Missions, Rev. John Del Turco, Box 141-A, R. D. #1, Transfer, PA 16154
Institutions, Benevolences & Fellowships, Rev. Eugene DeMarco, 155 Scott St., New Brighton, PA 15066
Finance, Rev. R. Allen Noyd, 390 Rexford Dr., Apt. 72, Hermitage, PA 16158

Honorary Personnel:
Gen. Overseer, Rev. Frank P. Fortunato, 3167 Welsh Rd., Philadelphia, PA 19136; Carmine Saginario, P.O. Box 1048, Hermitage, PA 16148
Missions, Rev. Richard L. Corsini, 921 6th Ave., Apt. #3, New Brighton, PA 15066

PERIODICALS
Il Faro (m), 708 Jeffrey Street, Herkimer, NY 13350, Rev. Guido Scalzi, Ed.
Vista (m) R.D. #4, West Middlesex, PA 16159, Mr. Joseph Zentis, Ed.

Christian Churches and Churches of Christ

The fellowship, whose churches were always strictly congregational in polity, has its origin in the American movement to "restore the New Testament church in doctrine, ordinances and life" initiated by Thomas and Alexander Campbell, Walter Scott and Barton W. Stone in the early years of the nineteenth century.

Churches: 5,579; Inclusive Membership: 1,070,616; Sunday or Sabbath Schools: N.R.: TotalEnrollment: N.R.; Ordained Clergy: 6,596

NO GENERAL ORGANIZATION

CONVENTIONS

North American Christian Convention (founded 1927), Dir., Rod Huron, 3533 Epley Rd., Cincinnati, OH 45239. NACC mailing address: Box 39456 Cincinnati, OH 45239. Tel. (513)385-2470
National Missionary Convention (founded 1947), Coord., Walter Birney, Box 11, Copeland, KS 67837. Tel. (513)668-5250
Eastern Christian Convention, 5300 Norbeck Rd., Rockville, MD 10853

PERIODICALS

Christian Standard (w), 8121 Hamilton Ave., Cincinnati, OH 45231, Sam E. Stone, Ed.
Restoration Herald (m), 5664 Cheviot Rd., Cincinnati, OH 45329. Tom Thurman, Ed.
Directory of the Ministry (a), 1525 Cherry Rd., Springfield, IL 62704. Ralph D. McLean, Ed. Tel. (217) 546-7338
Horizons (bi-w), Box 2427, Knoxville, TN 37901. Norman L. Weaver, Ed. Tel. (615)577-9740

The Christian Congregation, Inc.

The Christian Congregation is a denominational evangelistic association that originated in 1798 and was active on the frontier in areas adjacent to the Ohio River. The church was an unincorporated organization until 1887. At that time a group of ministers who desired closer cooperation formally constituted the church. The charter was revised in 1898 and again in 1970.

Governmental polity basically is congregational. Local units are semiautonomous. Doctrinal positions, strongly biblical, are essentially universalist in the sense that ethical principles, which motivate us to creative activism, transcend national boundaries and racial barriers. A central tenet, John 13:34-35, translates to such respect for sanctity of life that abortions on demand, capital punishment, and all warfare are vigorously opposed. No distinctions are made between so-called just wars and unjust ones. All are unjust. International strife of this type is obsolete as a means of resolving disputes.

Early leaders were John Chapman, John L. Puckett, and Isaac V. Smith. Bishop O. J. Read was chief administrative and ecclesiastic officer for 40 years until 1961. Rev. Dr. Ora Wilbert Eads has been general superintendent since 1961.

Ministerial affiliation for independent clergymen is provided.

Churches: 1,456; Inclusive Membership: 107,902; Sunday or Sabbath Schools: 1,310; Total Enrollment: 79,187; Ordained Clergy: 1,460

OFFICER

Gen. Supt., Rev. Ora Wilbert Eads, 804 W. Hemlock St., LaFollette, TN 37766

Christian Methodist Episcopal Church

In 1870 the General Conference of the M.E. Church, South, approved the request of its colored membership for the formation of their conferences into a separate ecclesiastical body, which became the Colored Methodist Episcopal Church.

At its General Conference in Memphis, Tenn., May 1954, it was overwhelmingly voted to change the name of the Colored Methodist Episcopal Church to the Christian Methodist Episcopal Church. This became the official name on January 3, 1956.

GENERAL ORGANIZATION

General Conference: quadrennial. (Next meeting in 1990)

OFFICERS

Exec. Sec., Dr. W. Clyde Williams, 2805 Shoreland Dr., Atlanta, GA 30331. Tel. (404)344-3886
Sec. Gen. Conf., Rev. Edgar L. Wade, P.O. Box 3403, Memphis, TN 38103

OTHER ORGANIZATIONS

Christian Education: Gen. Sec., Dr. Ronald M. Cunningham, 1474 Humber St., Memphis, TN 38106. Tel. (901)947-3144
Lay Ministry: Gen. Sec., Dr. I. Carlton Faulk, 1222 Rose St., Berkeley, CA 94702. Tel. (415)655-4106
Evangelism, Missions & Human Concerns: Gen Sec., Rev. Raymond F. Williams, P.O. Box 9067, Silver Spring, MD 20906. Tel. (301)598-2653
Finance: Sec., Mr.Joseph C. Neal, Jr., P.O. Box 75085, Los Angeles, CA 90030. Tel. (213)233-5050
Publications: Gen. Sec., Rev. Lonnie L. Napier, P.O. Box 2018, Memphis, TN 38101. Tel. (901)947-3135
Personnel Services: Gen. Sec., Dr. N. Charles Thomas, P.O. Box 74, Memphis, TN 39101. Tel. (901)947-3135
Women's Missionary Council: Pres., Dr. Sylvia M. Faulk, 623 San Fernando Ave., Berkeley, CA 94707. Tel. (415)526-5536

PERIODICALS

Christian Index, The (bi-m), P. O. Box 665, Memphis, TN 38101, Rev. L. L Reddick III, Ed.
Missionary Messenger, The (m), 2309 Bonnie Ave., Bastrop, LA 71220. Tel. (318)281-3044, Mrs. P. Ann Pegues, Ed.

BISHOPS

First District: Bishop William H. Graves, 564 Frank Ave., Memphis, TN 38101. Tel. (901) 947-6180
Second District: Bishop Othal H. Lakey, 6322 Elwynne Dr., Cincinnati, OH 45236. Tel. (513) 984-6825
Third District: Bishop Dotcy I. Isom, Jr., 11470 Northway Dr., St. Louis, MO 63136. Tel. (314)381-3111
Fourth District: Bishop Marshall Gilmore, 109 Holcomb Dr., Shreveport, LA 71103. Tel. (318) 222-6284
Fifth District: Bishop Richard O. Bass, 308 10th Ave. W., Birmingham, AL 35204. Tel. (205) 252-3541
Sixth District: Bishop Joseph C. Coles, Jr., 2780 Collier Dr., Atlanta, GA 30018. Tel. (404) 794-0096
Seventh District: Bishop Oree Broomfield, Sr., 6524 16th St., N.W., Washington, DC 20012. Tel. (202) 723-2660

Eighth District: Bishop C. D. Coleman, Sr., 2330 Sutter St., Dallas, TX 75216. Tel. (214) 942-5781
Ninth District: Bishop E. Lynn Brown, P.O. Box 11276, Los Angeles, CA 90011. Tel. (213)216-9278
Tenth District: Bishop Nathaniel L. Linsey, P.O. Box 170127, Atlanta, GA 30317
Retired: Bishop E. P. Murchison, 4094 Windsor Castle Way, Decatur, GA 30034; Bishop Henry C. Bunton, 853 East Dempster Ave., Memphis, TN 38106; Bishop Chester A. Kirkendoll, 10 Hurtland, Jackson, TN 38305; Bishop P. Randolph Shy, 894 Falcon Dr. S.W., Atlanta, GA 30311

Christian Nation Church U.S.A.

Organized in 1895, at Marion, Ohio, as a group of "equality evangelists," who later formed the Christian Nation Church. This church is Wesleyan and Arminian in doctrine, emphasizes the Pre-Millenial Coming of Christ, semi-congregational in government; and emphasizes evangelism. Reincorporated as Christian Nation Church U.S.A., 1961.

GENERAL ORGANIZATION

Congress: annual

OFFICERS

Gen. Overseer, Rev. Harvey Monjar, Box 513, Lebanon, OH 45036. Tel.(513)932-0360
Asst. Overseer, Rev. Ronald Justice, 11245 State Rt. 669 NE, Rosedale, OH 43777. Tel. (614)982-7827
Gen. Sec., Rev. Randy Lusk, P.O. Box 113, Fanrock, WV 24834. Tel. (304)732-7792

Christian Reformed Church in North America

The Christian Reformed Church represents the historic faith of Protestantism. Founded in the United States in 1857, it asserts its belief in the Bible as the inspired Word of God, and is creedally united in the Belgic Confession (1561), the Heidelberg Catechism (1563), and the Canons of Dort (1618-19). (Note: For total statistics for this body see also those listed under the Christian Reformed Church in North America in Directory 4, Religious Bodies in Canada, which follows.)

Churches: 699; Inclusive Membership: 222,408; Sunday or Sabbath Schools: N.R.; Total Enrollment: N.R.; Ordained Clergy: 1,075

GENERAL ORGANIZATION

Synod: annual (June)

OFFICERS

Stat. Clk., Rev. Leonard J. Hofman, Office Address: 2850 Kalamazoo Ave. S.E., Grand Rapids, MI 49560. Tel. (616)246-0744
Denominational Financial Coord., Harry Vander Meer, 2850 Kalamazoo Ave., SE Grand Rapids, MI 49560

OTHER ORGANIZATIONS

The Back to God Hour: Dir. of Ministries, Dr. Joel H. Nederhood; Exec. Dir., Mr. David Vander Ploeg; International Headquarters: 6555 W. College Dr., Palos Heights, IL 60463
Christian Reformed Board World Ministries: Exec. Sec. Dr. Roger S. Greenway, 2850 Kalamazoo Ave. S.E., Grand Rapids, MI 49560; Christian Reformed World Missions Cmte., Dir., Rev. William Van Tol, 2850 Kalamazoo Ave. S.E., Grand Rapids, MI 49560; Christian Reformed World Relief Committee: Exec. Dir., John De Haan, 2850 Kalamazoo Ave. S.E. Grand Rapids, MI 49560

Christian Reformed Board of Home Missions: Exec. Dir., Rev. John A. Rozeboom, 2850 Kalamazoo Ave. S.E., Grand Rapids, MI 49560
CRC Publications: Exec. Dir., Gary Mulder, 2850 Kalamazoo Ave., S.E., Grand Rapids, MI 49560
Ministers' Pension Fund, Adm., Dr. Ray Vander Weele, 2850 Kalamazoo Ave., S.E., Grand Rapids, MI 49560

PERIODICAL

The Banner (w), 2850 Kalamazoo Ave. S.E., Grand Rapids, MI 49560, Rev. Galen Meyer, Ed.

Christian Union

Organized in 1864 in Columbus, Ohio. It stresses the oneness of the Church with Christ as its only head. The Bible is the only rule of faith and practice and good fruits the only condition of fellowship. Each local church governs itself.

GENERAL ORGANIZATION

General Council: triennial. (Next meeting, June, 1992)
Home Office: P. O. Box 397, Excelsior Springs, MO 64024. Tel. (816) 637-5345.

OFFICERS

Pres., Dr. Joseph Harr, 73 Indianhead Dr., Heath OH 43056. Tel. (614)522-4973
Vice-Pres., Rev. Dan Williams, 2-4964-B, Delta, OH 43515 Tel. (419)822-4261
Sec., Rev. Joseph Cunningham, 1005 N. 5th St., Greenfield, OH 45123. Tel. (513)981-3476
Asst. Sec., Rev. Earl Mitchell, 175000 Hidden Valley Rd., Independence, MO 64057. Tel. (816)373-3416
Treas., Rev. Lawrence Rhoads, 902 N.E. Main St., West Union, OH 45693. Tel. (513)544-2950

PERIODICAL

Christian Union Witness (m), 106 W. Broadway, Excelsior Springs, MO 64024.

Church of Christ

Organized April 6, 1830, at Fayette, New York, by Joseph Smith and five others. In 1864 this body was directed by revelation through Granville Hedrick to return in 1867 to Independence, Mo. to the "consecrated land" dedicated by Joseph Smith. They did so and purchased the temple lot dedicated in 1831.

GENERAL ORGANIZATION

General Conference: annual
Headquarters: Temple Lot, Independence, MO

OFFICERS

Sec., Council of Apostles, Apostle William A. Sheldon, P. O. Box 472, Independence, MO 64051. Tel. (816) 833-3995
Gen. Bus. Mgr., Bishop Alvin Harris, P.O. Box 472, Independence, MO 64051
General Recorder, Isaac Brockman, P.O. Box 472, Independence, MO 64051

PERIODICAL

Zion's Advocate, P.O. Box 472, Independence, MO 64051, Gary Housknecht, Ed.

Church of Christ, Scientist

The Christian Science Church was founded by New England religious leader Mary Baker Eddy in 1879 "to commemorate the word and works of our Master (Christ Jesus), which should reinstate primitive Christianity and its lost element of healing." In 1892 the church was reorganized and established as The First Church of Christ, Scientist, in Boston, also called The Mother Church, with local branch churches around the world, of which there are nearly 2,700 in 66 countries today.

The church is administered by a five-member board of directors in Boston. Local churches govern themselves democratically. Since the church has no clergy, services are conducted by laypersons elected to serve as Readers. There are also about 3,000 Christian Science practitioners who devote their full time to healing through prayer.

GENERAL ORGANIZATION

Board of Directors, Headquarters: The First Church of Christ, Scientist, 175 Huntington Ave., Boston, MA 02115

OFFICERS

Bd. of Dirs., Harvey W. Wood, Ruth Elizabeth Jenks, Jill Gooding, Richard C. Bergenheim, John Lewis Selover
Pres., David E. Sleeper
Treas., Donald C. Bowersock
Clk., Mrs. Virginia S. Harris
First Reader, Horacio Omar Rivas
Second Reader, Marion Sheldon Pierpont

OTHER ORGANIZATIONS

Board of Education: Teaches a class of 30 pupils once in 3 years for the purpose of providing authorized teachers of Christian Science
Board of Lectureship: Made up of about 90 members, delivers free lectures worldwide
Committee on Publication: Source of public information on the denomination
Publishing Society: Publishes and/or sells the authorized literature of Christian Science

PERIODICALS

The Christian Science Monitor (d) (w), Boston, MA
The Christian Science Journal (m), Boston, MA
Christian Science Sentinel (w), Boston, MA
Christian Science Quarterly (q), Boston, MA
The Herald of Christian Science (m), in French, German, Portuguese, Spanish; (q), in Danish, Dutch, Greek, Indonesian, Italian, Japanese, Norwegian, Swedish, and Braille
World Monitor Mazagine (m), Boston, MA

Church of Daniel's Band

A body Methodistic in form and evangelistic in spirit, organized in Michigan in 1893.

GENERAL ORGANIZATION

Conference: annual

OFFICERS

Pres., Rev. Wesley Hoggard, 213 S. Five Mile Rd., Midland, MI 48640.
Vice-Pres., Rev. Jim Seaman, Adams St., Coleman, MI 48618. Tel. (517)465-6059
Sec./Treas., Rev. Marie Berry, Roehrs St., Beaverton, MI 48612.

The Church of God

Inaugurated by Bishop A. J. Tomlinson, who served as General Overseer, 1903 to 1943, and from which many groups of the Pentecostal and Holiness Movement stemmed. Bishop Homer A. Tomlinson served as General Overseer, 1943 to 1968. Episcopal in administration, evangelical in doctrines of justification by faith, sanctification as a second work of grace, and of the baptism of the Holy Ghost, speaking with other tongues, miracles of healing.

GENERAL ORGANIZATION

National Assembly, U.S.A.: annual, Chaffee, MO

National Headquarters: U.S.A. Box 13036, 1207 Willow Brook, Apt. #2, Huntsville, AL 35802. Tel. (205) 881-9629

OFFICERS

Gen. Overseer and Bishop, Voy M. Bullen; Gen. Sec., and Treas., Marie Powell
Church of God Publishing House, Box 13036, 1207 Willow Brook Apt. #2, Huntsville, AL 35802
Bus: Mgr., _____

CHURCH AUXILIARIES

Address: Box 13036, 1207 Willow Brook, Apt. #2, Huntsville AL 35802
Assembly Band Movement: Gen. Sec., Bishop Bill Kinslaw
Women's Missionary Band: Gen. Sec., Shirley Metcalf
Theocratic Bands: Gen. Sec., Rev. Ted Carr
Victory Leader's Band, Youth: Gen. Sec., Rev. Jan Benson
Administration for Highway and Hedge Campaign: Earnest Hoover

PERIODICALS

The Church of God (s-m), Box 13036, 1207 Willow Brook, Apt. #2, Huntsville, AL 35802
Forward With Christ (m), 144 Fifth Ave., New York, NY 10011. Christopher Economou, Ed.
The Church of God Quarterly (q), Box 13036, 1207 Willow Brook, Apt. #2, Huntsville, AL 35802; Voy M. Bullen, Ed.

Church of God (Anderson, Ind.)

The Church of God (Anderson, Ind.) began in 1881 when Daniel S. Warner and several associates in northern Indiana felt constrained to forsake all denominational hierarchies and formal creeds, trusting solely in the Holy Spirit as their overseer and the Bible as their statement of belief. Warner and those of similar persuasion saw themselves at the forefront of a movement to restore unity and holiness to the church. It was not their intention to establish yet another denomination, but to promote primary allegiance to Jesus Christ so as to transcend (and even obliterate) denominational loyalties.

Deeply influenced by Wesleyan theology and Pietism, the Church of God has emphasized conversion, holiness, and attention to the Bible. Worship services tend to be informal, accentuating expository preaching and robust singing. Although some are much larger, the typical Church of God congregation is small, with Sunday morning worship attendance averaging about 100.

Not only is the Church of God noncreedal. There is no formal membership. The contention is that "salvation makes you a member." Hence persons are assumed to be members on the basis of witness to a conversion experience and evidence that supports such witness. The basis for this is that only Christ may add members to the church. The absence of formal membership is also consistent with the church's understanding of how Christian unity is to be achieved—that is, by preferring the label Christian before all others.

As might be expected, the Church of God is congregational in its government. Each local congregation is autonomous and as such, may call any recognized Church of God minister to be its pastor and may retain him or her as long as is mutually pleasing. Ministers are ordained and disciplined by state or provincial assemblies made up predominantly (but not usually exclusively) of ministers. National program boards serve the church through coordination and resource materials. A growing trend is the development of state offices which perform similar functions.

The Church of God maintains a strong interest in evangelism in this country and in missions overseas. There are Church of God congregations in 78 foreign countries, most of which are resourced by one or more missionaries.

There are slightly more Church of God adherents overseas than in North America. Heaviest concentration is in the nation of Kenya.

Churches: 2,336; Inclusive Membership: 198,842; Sunday or Sabbath Schools: 2,226; Total Enrollment: 181,667; Ordained Clergy: 3,315

GENERAL ORGANIZATION

General Assembly: annual. Chpsn., Samuel G. Hines, 9553 Fort Foote Rd., Fort Washington, MD 20744

EXECUTIVE COUNCIL

Box 2420, Anderson, IN 46018. Tel. (317) 642-0256. Exec. Sec., Edward L. Foggs; Assoc. Sec., David L. Lawson; Exec. Dir. Church Service, Keith Huttenlocker; Exec. Dir. World Service, James Williams
Dir. of World Service, David L. Lawson
Dir. of Church Service, Keith Huttenlocker

OTHER ORGANIZATIONS

Board of Christian Education: Exec. Dir., Sherrill D. Hayes, Box 2458, Anderson, IN 46018
Board of Church Extension and Home Missions: Pres., J. Perry Grubbs, Box 2069, Anderson, IN 46018
Foreign Missionary Board: Pres., Norman S. Patton, Box 2498, Anderson, IN 46018
Women of the Church of God: Exec. Sec.-Treas., Doris Dale, Box 2328, Anderson, IN 46018
Board of Pensions: Exec. Sec.-Treas., Harold A. Conrad, Box 2299, Anderson, IN 46018
Mass Communications Board: Sec.-Tras., Dwight L. Dye, Box 2007, Anderson, IN 46018
Warner Press, Inc.: Pres., James L. Edwards, Box 2499, Anderson, IN 46018

PERIODICALS

Vital Christianity (bi-w), Box 2499, Anderson, IN 46018, Arlo F. Newell, Ed.
Church of God Missions (m), Box 2337, Anderson, IN 46018, Dondeena Caldwell, Ed.

Church of God by Faith, Inc.

Founded 1914, in Jacksonville Heights, Florida, by Elder John Bright. This body believes the word of God as interpreted by Jesus Christ to be the only hope of salvation, and Jesus Christ the only mediator for man.

GENERAL ORGANIZATION

General Assembly: meets twice yearly.
Headquarters: 3220 Haines St., Jacksonville, FL 32206. Tel. (904)353-5111

OFFICERS

Bishop Emeritus, W. W. Matthews, P.O. Box 907, Ozark, AL 36360
Bishop James E. McKnight, P.O. Box 121, Gainesville, FL 32601
Treas., Elder C. M. Fogle, 2710 North Fogle Dr., Avon Park, FL 33825
Ruling Elders: Elder John Robinson, 300 Essex Dr., Ft. Pierce, FL 33450; Elder Theodore Brown, 93 Girard Pl, Newark, NJ 07108
Exec. Sec., Elder George Matthews, 8834 Camphor Dr., Jacksonville, FL 32208

PERIODICAL

The Spiritual Guide (m), 3220 Haines St., Jacksonville, FL 32206

Church of God (Cleveland, Tenn.)

America's oldest Pentecostal Church began in 1886 as an outgrowth of the holiness revival under the name Christian Union. Reorganized in 1902 as the Holiness

Church and in 1907 the church adopted the name Church of God. Its doctrine is fundamental and Pentecostal; it maintains a centralized form of government and an evangelistic and missionary program.

Churches: 5,763; Inclusive Membership 582,203; Sunday or Sabbath Schools: 5,436; Total Enrollment: 509,250; Ordained Clergy: 7,544

GENERAL ORGANIZATION

General Assembly: biennial (Next meeting, San Antonio, Texas, August 1990)
International Offices, P.O. Box 2430, Cleveland, TN 37320. Tel. (615) 472-3361

EXECUTIVES

Gen. Overseer, Raymond Crowley
Asst. Gen. Overseers, Ray H. Hughes, R. Lamar Vest, John D. Nichols
Gen. Sec.-Treas., Robert E. Fisher

DEPARTMENTS

World Missions: Gen. Dir., Lovell Cary
Youth and C. E.: Gen. Dir., Junus Fulbright
Publishing House: Publisher, Floyd Carey
Public Relations: Dir., Lewis J. Willis
Media Ministries: Dir., _____
Television and Radio Minister: H. B. Thompson, Jr.
Evangelism & Home Missions: Dir., W. C. Ratchford, Sr.
Office of Ministerial Development: Exec. Dir., R. Lamar Vest
Ladies Ministries: Pres., Mrs. Raymond Crowley

PERIODICALS

Church of God Evangel (bi-w), Hoyt Stone, Ed.
Leadership (q), James Humbertson, Ed.
Sow (q), Christopher Moree, Ed.
Flame (q), W. C. Ratchford, Ed.
Unique (m), Mrs. Raymond Crowley, Ed.
Church School Literature, James Humbertson, Ed.

Church of God General Conference (Oregon, Ill.)

This church is the outgrowth of several independent local groups of similar faith. Some were in existence as early as 1800, and others date their beginnings to the arrival of British immigrants in this country around 1847. Many local churches carried the name Church of God of the Abrahamic Faith. The corporate name is Church of God General Conference, Oregon, Illinois.

State and district conferences of these groups were formed as an expression of mutual cooperation. A national organization was instituted at Philadelphia in 1888. However, because of strong convictions on the questions of congregational rights and authority, it ceased to function until 1921, when the present General Conference was formed at Waterloo, Iowa.

The Bible is accepted as the supreme standard of faith. Adventist in viewpoint, the second (premmillenial) coming of Christ is strongly emphasized. The church teaches that the kingdom of God will be literal, beginning in Jerusalem at the time of the return of Christ and extending to all nations. Emphasis is placed on the oneness of God and the Sonship of Christ, that Jesus did not preexist prior to his birth in Bethlehem, and that the Holy Spirit is the power and influence of God. It believes in the restoration of Israel, the times of restitution, the mortalityof man (asleep in death until the resurrection), the literal resurrection of the dead, the reward of the righteous on earth, and the complete destruction of the wicked in the second death. Membership is dependent on faith, repentance, and baptism (for the remission of sins) by immersion.

The work of the General Conference is carried on under the direction of the board of directors, which meets as necessary throughout the year. The executive officer is a president who administers the work as a whole. Because of the congregational nature of the church's government, the General Conference exists primarily as a means of mutual cooperation and for the development of yearly projects and enterprises.

Churches: 88; Inclusive Membership: 5,767; Sunday or Sabbath Schools: 88; Total Enrollment: 3,357; Ordained Clergy: 87

GENERAL ORGANIZATION

General Conference: annual (August)
Headquarters: Oregon, IL 61061. Tel. (815) 732-7991

OFFICERS

Chpsn., Pastor Scott Ross, 7606 Jaynes St., Omaha, NE 68134
Vice-Chpsn., Dr. William D. Lawrence, 32 E. Marhsall Phoenix, AZ 85012
Pres., David Krogh, Box 100, Oregon, IL 61061
Sec., Mrs. Brenda Wessel, RR 1 Box 100, Frederick, IL 62639
Treas., Mr. Elmo Gaspar, Box 517, Eden Valley, MN 55329

OTHER ORGANIZATIONS

(All located at Box 100, Oregon, IL 61061)
Business Adm., Wilbur Burnham
Publishing Dept., Russell Magaw
Oregon Bible College, Kent Ross

PERIODICALS

The Restitution Herald (bi-m), Box 100, Oregon, IL, Russell Magaw, Ed.
Church of God Progress Journal (bi-m) Box 100, Oregon, IL 61061, Russell Magaw, Ed.

The Church of God in Christ

The Church of God in Christ was founded in 1906 in Memphis, Tenn., and was organized by Bishop Charles Harrison Mason, a former Baptist minister who pioneered the embryonic stages of the Holiness movement beginning in 1895 in Mississippi.

The Church further developed when its founder organized four major departments between 1910–1916. These departments were (1) Womens' Department, (2) Sunday School, (3) Young Peoples Willing Workers (YPWW), (4) Home and Foreign Mission.

Doctrinally, the Church is basically trinitarian. It teaches the infallability of scripture, the need for regeneration and subsequent baptism of the Holy Ghost. It emphasizes holiness as God's standard for Christian conduct. It recognizes as ordinances Holy Communion, Water Baptism and Feet Washing. Its governmental structure is basically episcopal with the General Assembly being the Legislative body.

The Church is headquartered at Memphis, Tenn. The organization has experienced tremendous growth and expansion of its ministries under the leadership of the late Presiding Bishop, Bishop J. O. Patterson.

GENERAL ORGANIZATION

International Convocation: annual (November)
General Assembly: semi-annual (April and November)
National Headquarters: Mason Temple, 939 Mason St., Memphis, TN 38126
World Headquarters: 272 South Main St., Memphis, TN 38103. Tel. (901) 578-3800
The Mother Church: Pentecostal Institutional, 229 S. Danny Thomas Blvd., Memphis, TN 38126. Tel. (901) 527-9202

GENERAL OFFICES

All located at 272 S. Main St., Memphis, TN 38103. Mail: P. O. Box 320, Memphis, TN 38101
Office of the Presiding Bishop
Tel. (901) 578-3838

Interim Presiding Bishop, Rt. Rev. L. H. Ford.
Exec. Sec., Elder A. Z. Hall, Jr.
Sec., Mrs. Linda K. Wilkins
The General Board
Interim Presiding Bishop, Rt. Rev. L. H. Ford, 9401 M. L. King Drive, Chicago, IL 60619
Bishop J. D. Husband, P.O. Box 824, Atlanta, GA 30301
Bishop C. L. Anderson, Jr., 20485 Mendota, Detroit, MI 48221
Bishop L. R. Anderson, 265 Ranch Trail West, Amherst, NY 14221
Second Asst. Presiding Bishop C. D. Owens, 14 Van Velsor Pl., Newark, NJ 07112
Bishop O. T. Jones, Jr., 363 N. 60th St., Philadelphia, PA 19139
Bishop Jacob Cohen, 3120 N.W. 48th Terr., Miami, FL 33142
Bishop P. A. Brooks, 30945 Wendbrook Lane, Birmingham, MI 48010
Bishop S. L. Green, 2416 Orcutt Ave., Newport News, VA 23607
Bishop J. N. Haynes, 6743 Talbot, Dallas, TX 75216
Bishop C. E. Blake, 3045 S. Crenshaw, Los Angeles, CA 90016
Bishop Levi Willis, 645 Church St., Ste. 400, Norfolk, VA 23510
Bishop R.L.H. Winbush, 317 12th St., Lafayette, LA 70501
Office of the General Secretary
Tel. (901) 521-1163
General Secretary, Bishop G. R. Ross
Asst. Gen. Sec. for Registration, Bishop E. Harris Moore
Asst. Gen. Sec. for Records, Bishop Herbert J. Williams; Bishop A. LaDell Thomas, Coord.
Dir. of Research and Survey, Elder Ronald A. Blumburg
Office of the Financial Secretary
Tel. (901) 744-0710
Secretary, Dr. S. Y. Burnett
Gen. Treas., Bishop Theodore Davis
Chmn. of Finance, Bishop Benjamin Crouch
Office of the Board of Trustees
Chmn., Dr. Roger L. Jones
Sec., Elder Warren Miler
Office of the Clergy Bureau
Tel. (901) 523-7045
Dir., Elder Samuel Smith
Sec., Mrs. Dorothy Motley
Office of the Superintendent of National Properties
Tel. (901) 774-0710
Superintendent, Bishop W. L. Porter
Sec., Ms. Sandra Allen
Board of Publications
Tel. (901) 526-3644
Chmn., Bishop Norman Quick
Sec.-Treas., Ms. Sylvia H. Law
Headquarters Rep., Elder David Hall
Publishing House:
Tel. (901) 578-3842
Manager, Mr. Hugheau Terry
Department of Missions
Tel. (901) 578-3876
Pres., Bishop Carlis L. Moody
Exec. Sec., Elder Jesse W. Denny
Department of Women
Tel. (901) 578-3834
Pres.-Gen. Supervisor, Dr. Mattie McGlothen
Asst. Supervisor, Mrs. Emma Crouch
Exec. Sec., Mrs. Elizabeth C. Moore
Sec. of the Women's Convention, Mrs. Freddie J. Bell
Treas., Mrs. Mary L. Belvin
Fin. Sec., Mrs. Olive Brown

45

Department of Evangelism
Pres., Dr. Edward L. Battles, 4310 Steeplechase rail, Arlington, TX 76016. Tel. (817) 429-7166
Department of Music
Pres., Mrs. Mattie Moss Clark, 18203 Sorrento, Detroit MI 48235
Vice Pres., Mrs. Mattie Wigley, 1726 S. Wellington, Memphis, TN 38106
Department of Youth (Youth Congress)
Pres., Bishop C. H. Brewer, 260 Roydon Rd., New Haven, CT 06511
Department of Sunday Schools
Gen. Supt., Bishop Cleveland W. Williams, 270 Division St., Derby, CT 06418
United National Auxiliaries Convention
UNAC-5; Bishop F. E. Perry, Jr., Chmn.; Bishop G. R. Ross, Sec. of Exec. Committee
Church of God in Christ Book Store
Mgr., Mrs. Geraldine Miller, 272 S. Main St., Memphis, TN 38103. Tel. (901) 578-3803
Charles Harrison Mason Foundation
Exec. Dir., Elder O.T. Massey, 272 S. Main St., Memphis, TN 38103. Tel. (901)578-3803
Chmn., Bd. of Dir., Bishop P. A. Brooks
Department of Finance:
Chief Financial Officer, Mrs. Sylvia H. Law; Asst. to C.F.O., Elder A.Z. Hall, Jr.; Acntg. Clks., Gloria Hall, Carol Robinson
Fine Arts Department:
Dir., Mrs. Sara J. Powell; Dir. National Orchestra, Mrs. Luvonia Whittley; Dir. National Drama Department, Mrs. Brenda Rivette

PERIODICALS

Whole Truth, P.O. Box 2017, Memphis, TN 38101, Dr. David Hall, Ed.
Sunday School Literature, Publishing House, Church of God in Christ, 272 S. Main St., Memphis, TN 38103. Bishop Roy L. H. Winbush, Ed.
Y.P.W.W. Topics, 67 Tennyson, Highland Park, MI 48203. Elder James L. Whitehead, Jr., Ed.
Sunshine Band Topics, 648 Peart St., Benton Harbor, MI 29022. Mrs. Mildred Wells, Ed.
Purity Guide, P. O. Box 1526, Gary, IN 46407, Mrs. Pearl McCullom, Ed.
International Directory, 930 Mason St., Memphis, TN 38126.
The Pentecostal Interpreter, P. O. Box 320, Memphis, TN 38101. Bishop H. Jenkins Bell, Ed.
The Voice of Missions, 1932 Dewey Ave., Evanston, IL 60201. Ms. Jenifer James, Ed.

BISHOPS IN THE U.S.A.

(Address: Right Rev.)
Alabama: First, Chester A. Ashworth, 2901 Snavely Ave., Birmingham, AL 35211; Second, W. S. Harris, 3005 Melrose Pl., N.W., Huntsville, AL 35810
Alaska: Charles D. Williams, 2212 Vanderbilt Cir., Anchorage, AK 99504
Arizona: Felton King, P.O. Box 3791, Phoenix, AZ 84030
Arkansas: First, L. T. Walker, 2315 Chester St., Little Rock, AR 72206; Second, D. L. Lindsey, 401 W. 23rd St., North Little Rock, AR 72114
California: North-Central, G. R. Ross, 815 Calmar Ave., Oakland, CA 94610; Northern, B. R. Stewart, 734 12th Ave., San Francisco, CA 94118; Northeast, L. B. Johnson, 3121 Patridge Ave., Oakland, CA 94605; Evangel, E. E. Cleveland, 31313 Braeburn Ct.,

Haywood, CA 96045; Northwest, Bishop W. W. Hamilton, 14145 Mountain Quail Rd., Salinas, CA 93906; Southern #1, C. E. Blake, 1731 Wellington Rd., Los Angeles, CA 90019; Southern #2, George McKinney, 5848 Arboles, San Diego, CA 92120 ; Southern Metropolitan, Bishop B. J. Crouch, 12418 Gain St., Pacoima, CA 91331; Southwest, B. R. Benbow, 504 Rexford Dr., Beverly Hills, CA 90210; Valley, Warren S. Wilson, 1435 Modoc St., Fresno, CA 93706
Colorado: Frank Johnson, 12231 E. Arkansas Pl., Aurora, CO 80014
Connecticut: First, Charles H. Brewer, Jr., 180 Osborne St., New Haven, CT 06515; Second, H. Bordeaux, 135 Westwood Rd., New Haven, CT 06511
Delaware: Lieutenant T. Blackshear, Sr., 17 S. Booth Dr., Penn Acres, New Castle, DE 19720
District of Columbia: Bishop W. Crudup, 5101 Martin Dr., Oxon Hill, MD 20745
Florida: Central, Calvin D. Kensey, 9462 August Dr., Jacksonville, FL 32208; Eastern, Jacob Cohen, 3120 N.W. 48th Terr., Miami, FL 33142; Southwestern, W. E. Davis, 2008 33rd Ave., Tampa, FL 33610; Western, M. L. Sconiers, P.O. Box 5472, Orlando, FL 32805
Georgia: Central and Southeast, J. D. Husband, P. O. Box 824, Atlanta, GA 30301; Georgia Southeast, Andrew Hunter, Rt. 4, Box 328, St. Simons Island, GA 31502; Northern, J. Howard Dell, 1717 Havilon Dr., S.W., Atlanta, GA 30311; Southern, C. J. Hicks, 1894 Madden Ave., Macon, GA 31204
Hawaii: First, _____; Second, W. H. Reed, 1223 W. 80th St., Los Angeles, CA 90044
Idaho: Nathaniel Jones, 630 Chateau, Barstow, CA 92311
Illinois: First, L. H. Ford, 9401 M. L. King Dr., Chicago, IL 60619; Fifth, B. E. Goodwin, 286 E. 16th St., Chicago Heights, IL 60411; Sixth, W. Haven Bonner, 1039 Bonner Ave., Aurora, IL 60505; Central, T. T. Rose, 1000 Dr. Taylor Rose Sq., Springfield, IL 62703; Northern, Cody Marshall, 8836 Blackstone, Chicago, IL 60637; Southeast, L. E. Moore, 7840 Contour Dr., St. Louis, MO 63121; Southern, J. Cobb, 323-30th St., Cairo, IL 62914
Indiana: First, Milton L. Hall, 1404 Delphos, Kokomo, IN 46901; Second, Oscar Freeman, 1760 Taft St., Gary, IN 46404; Indiana Northern, J. T. Dupree, 1231 Hayden St., Fort Wayne, IN 40806
Iowa: Hurley Bassett, 1730 4th Ave., S.E., Cedar Rapids, IA 52403
Kansas: Central, I. B. Brown, 1635 Hudson Blvd., Topeka, KS 66607; East, William H. McDonald, 1627 N. 78th St., Kansas City, KS 66112; Southwest, J. L. Gilkey, 2403 Shadybrook, Wichita, KS 67214
Kentucky: First, Bishop M. Sykes, P. O. Box 682, Union City, TN 38621
Louisiana: Eastern, #1, Bishop J. E. Gordon, 6610 Chenault Dr., Marrero, LA 70072; Eastern #2, Bishop J. A. Thompson, 2180 Holiday, New Orleans, LA 70114; Estern #3, Bishop H. E. Quillen, 1913 Lasley St., Bogalusa, LA 70427; Western, Roy L. H. Winbush, 235 Diamond Dr., Lafayette, LA 70501
Maine: Bishop B. W. Grayson, 1237 Eastern Parkway, Brooklyn, NY 11213
Maryland: Central, S. L. Butts, P. O. Box 4504, Upper Marboro, MD 20775; Eastern Shore, James L. Eure, 635 West Main St., Salisbury, MD 21801; Greater, David Spann, 5023 Gwynn Oak Ave., Baltimore, MD 21207
Massachusetts: First, L. C. Young, 19 Almont St., Mattapan, MA 02126; Second and New Hampshire, C. W. Williams, 270 Division St., Derby, CT 06418; C. D. Williams, 2212 Vanderbilt Cir., Anchorage, AK 99504; West, Bryant Robinson, Sr., 1424 Plumtree Rd., Springfield, MA 01119

46

Michigan: *Great Lakes,* C. L. Anderson, 20485 Mendota, Detroit, MI 48221; *North Central,* Herbert J. Williams, 1600 Cedar St., Saginaw, MI 48601; *Northeast,* P. A. Brooks II, 30945 Wendbrook Lane, Birmingham, MI 48010; *Southwest, First,* W. L. Harris, 1834 Outer Dr., Detroit, MI 48234; *Second,* Earl J. Wright, 18655 Autumn Lane, Southfield, MI 48076; *Third,* Rodger L. Jones, 1118 River Forest, Flint, MI 48594; *Fourth,* N. W. Wells, 530 Sue Lane, Muskogon, MI 49442
Minnesota: Bishop S. N. Frazier, 4309 Park Ave. So., Minneapolis, MN 55409
Mississippi: *Northern,* T. T. Scott, 1066 Barnes Ave., Clarksdale, MS 38614; *Southern First,* Theodore Roosevelt Davis, 1704 Topp Ave., Jackson, MS 39204; *Southern #2,* Bishop R. Nance, 803 Fayard St., Biloxi, MS 39503
Missouri: Central, MO; *Eastern #1,* R. J. Ward, 4724 Palm Ave., St. Louis, MO 63115; *Eastern #2,* W. W. Sanders, 8167 Garner Lane, Berkeley, MO 63134; *Western,* E. Harris Moore, 405 E. 64th Terr., Kansas City, MO 64131
Montana: Bishop C. L. Moody, 2413 Lee St., Evanston, IL 60202
Nebraska: *Eastern,* Monte J. Bradford, 3901 Ramelle Dr., Council Bluff, IA 51501; *Northeastern,* B. T. McDaniels, 1106 N. 31st St., Omaha, NB 68103
Nevada: E. N. Webb, 1941 Goldhill, Las Vegas, NV 89106
New Jersey: *First,* Esau Courtney, 12 Clover Hill Cir., Trenton, NJ 08538; *Third,* Chandler David Owens, 14 Van Velsor Pl., Newark, NJ 07112
New Mexico: W. C. Griffin, 3322 Montclaire, Albuquerque, NM 87110
New York: *Eastern,* #1 Bishop Ithiel Clemmons, 190-08 104th Ave., Hollis, NY 11412; *Eastern #2,* Bishop Frank White, 67 The Boulevard, Amityville, NY 11701; *Eastern #3,* Bishop D. W. Grayson, 1233 Eastern Parkway, Brooklyn, NY 11213; *Eastern #4,* Bishop C. L. Sexton, 153 McDougal St., Brooklyn, NY 11233; *Western #1,* LeRoy R. Anderson, 265 Ranch Trail, W., Amherst, NY 14221; *Western #2,* Charles H. McCoy, 168 Brunswick Blvd., Buffalo, NY 14208
North Carolina: *Greater,* L. B. Davenport, P. O. Box 156, Plymouth, NC 28803; *Second,* J. Howard Sherman, Sr., P. O. Box 329, Charlotte, NC 28201
North Dakota: Carlis L. Moody (Mission Dept.), 272 S. Main St., Memphis, TN 38103
Ohio: *Northern,* Bishop William James, 3758 Chippendale Ct., Toledo, OH 44320; Robert S. Fields, 419 Crandell Ave., Youngstown, OH 44504; *Northwest,* Robert L. Chapman, 3194 E. 18th St., Cleveland, OH 44120; *Northern,* Bishop Warren Miller, 3618 Beacon Dr., Clelveland OH 44122; *Southern,* Floyde E. Perry, Jr., 3716 Rolliston Rd., Shaker Heights, OH 44120
Oklahoma: *Northwest,* J. A. Young, P.O. Box 844, Lawton, OK 73501; *Southeast,* Bishop F. D. Lawson, P.O. Box 581, Stillwater, OK 74076
Oregon: *First,* Bishop A. R. Hopkins, 1705 N.E. Dekum, Portland, OR 97211; *Second,* J. C. Foster, 2716 N.E. 9th Ave., Portland, OR 97212
Pennsylvania: *Commonwealth,* O. T. Jones, Jr., 363 N. 60th St., Philadelphia, PA 19139; *Eastern,* DeWitt A. Burton, 1400 Wistar Dr., Wyncote, PA 19095; *Western,* Gordon E. Vaughn, 6437 Stanton Ave., Pittsburgh, PA 15206
Rhode Island: Norman Quick, 1031 E. 215th St., Brooklyn, NY 11221
South Carolina: Johnnie Johnson, 649 Liberty Hall Rd., Goose Creek, SC 29445
South Dakota: Carlis L. Moody, 2413 Lee St., Evanston, IL 60202
Tennessee: *Headquarters,* F. Douglas Macklin, 1230 Tipton, Memphis, TN 38071 ; *Second,* H. J. Bell, P.O. Box 6118, Knoxville, TN 37914; ; *Central,* W. L. Porter, 1235 East Parkway, S., Memphis, TN 38114

Texas: *Eastern,* J. E. Lee, 742 Calcutta Dr., Dallas, TX 75241; *Northeast,* J. Neauell Haynes, 6743 Talbot, Dallas, TX 75216; *Northwest,* W. H. Watson, 1301 47th St., Lubbock, TX 79412; *South Central,* Nathan H. Henderson, 15622 Rockhouse Rd., Houston, TX 77060; *Southeast #1,* Robert E. Woodard, 2614 Wichita, Houston, TX 77004; *Southeast #2,* A. LaDell Thomas, 4401 McArthur Dr., Waco, TX 76708; *Southeast,* R. E. Ranger, 6604 Sabrosa Ct., W., Fort Worth, TX 76110; *Southwest,* T. D. Iglehart, 325 Terrell Rd., San Antonio, TX 78209
Utah: Nathaniel Jones, c/o Mission Dept., 630 Chateau Rd., Barstow, CA 92311
Vermont: Frank Clemons, Sr., 1323 Carroll St., Brooklyn, NY 11216
Virginia: *First,* Ted Thomas, Sr., 4145 Sunkist Rd., Chesapeake, VA 23321; *Second,* Samuel L. Green, Jr., 2416 Orcutt Ave., Newport News, VA 23607; *Third,* Levi E. Willis, 5110 Nichal Ct., Norfolk, VA 23508
Washington: T. L. Westbrook, 1256 176th St., Spanaway, WA 98402
West Virginia: *Northern,* Bishop G. F. Walker, P.O. Box 1467, Princeton, VA 24740; *Southern,* St. Claire Y. Burnett, P. O. Box 245, Altamonte Springs, FL 32715
Wisconsin: *First,* Dennis Flakes, 3420 N. 1st St., Milwaukee, WI 53212; *Northwest,* P. J. Henderson, 1312 W. Burleigh, Milwaukee, WI 53206; *Third,* J. C. Williams, 4232 N. 24th Pl., Milwaukee, WI 53209
Wyoming: A. W. Martin, 2453 N. Fountain St., Wichita, KS 67220

Church of God in Christ, International

Organized in 1969 in Kansas City, Missouri, by fourteen bishops of the Church of God in Christ of Memphis, Tennessee. The doctrine is the same, but the separation came because of disagreement over polity and governmental authority. The Church is Wesleyan in theology (two works of grace) but stresses the experience of full baptism of the Holy Ghost with the initial evidence of speaking with other tongues as the spirit gives utterance.

GENERAL ORGANIZATION

The General Assembly: annual
College of Bishops: April and August
Headquarters: 170 Adelphi St., Brooklyn, NY 11205 Tel. (718) 625-9175

OFFICERS

Presiding Bishop: The Most Rev. Carl E. Williams, Sr., 170 Adelphi St., Brooklyn, NY 11205
Vice-Presiding Bishop, Rt. Rev. J. P. Lucas, 90 Holland St., Newark, NJ 07103
Sec.-Gen. Treas., Rev. William Hines, 170 Adelphi St., Brooklyn, NY 11205
Nat. Supervisor-Womens' Dept., Dr. Louise Norris, 360 Colorado Ave., Bridgeport, CT 06605
Pres. Youth Department, Evangelist Joyce Taylor, 137-17 135th Ave., S., Ozone Park, NY 11420
Nat'l. Super., Sunday Schools, Rev. Ronald L. Figueroa, 433 Macon St., Brooklyn, NY 11233
Pres. Music Department, Beatrice Summerville, 210 Elmwood Ave., Bridgeport, CT 06605
Chpon., Duard ot Bishops, Bishop J. C. White, 360 Colorado Ave., Bridgeport, CT 06605
Nat'l. Dir. of Public Relations, Rev. Eric Dunn, GPO Box 710, Brooklyn NY 11202

Church of God in Christ (Mennonite)

A section of the Mennonite body organized in 1859, in Ohio, for the reestablishment of the order and discipline of the Church.

47

Churches: 70; Inclusive Membership: 9,256; Sunday or Sabbath Schools: N.R.; Total Enrollment: N.R.; Ordained Clergy: 347

GENERAL ORGANIZATION

Headquarters: 420 N. Wedel St., Moundridge, KS 67107. Tel. (316) 345-2532

OFFICER

Conf. Mod., Norman Koehn, 314 Crawford Dr., Victoria, TX 77904. Tel. (512)576-1057

PERIODICAL

Messenger of Truth (bi-w), Rt. 2, Box 264, Macon, MS 39341. Gladwin Koehn, Ed.

Church of God of Prophecy

The Church of God of Prophecy (the name it has borne since 1952) historically shares some of the early years of the Holiness classical pentecostal church, The Church of God (Cleveland). A. J. Tomlinson, a dynamic pentecostal pioneer, was the church's most prominent figure in the first half of this century. Having observed many prominent turn-of-the-century ministers, he came under the influence of holiness teaching, and, finally, classical pentecostal theology. During his leadership the Church of God became a national, then an international body, various educational, social, and ecclesiastical programs were developed.

At the death of A. J. Tomlinson in 1943, M. A. Tomlinson was duly designated as leader of the organization. His tenure as general overseer, which continues to this day, has been marked by its call for church unity and fellowship, not limited socially, racially, or nationally. The church is racially integrated on all levels and various leadership positions are occupied by women.

The official teachings include special emphasis on repentance and sanctification as well as the doctrine of Spirit-baptism, with speaking in holy unknown tongues as the initial evidence. Other prominent doctrinal commitments: an imminence-oriented eschatology involving a premillennial return of the risen Jesus, which will be preceded by a series of events; a call for the sanctity of the home which includes denial of a multiple marriage; practice of water baptism by immersion, the Lord's Supper, and washing of the saints' feet; total abstinence from intoxicating beverages and tobacco; a concern for modesty in all dimensions of life; an appreciation for various gifts of the Holy Spirit, with special attention to divine healing.

Churches: 2,111; Inclusive Membership: 73,977; Sunday or Sabbath Schools: 2,308; Total Enrollment: 88,432; Ordained Clergy: N.R.

GENERAL ORGANIZATION

General Assembly: Annual Conclave
Mailing Address: P.O. Box 2910, Cleveland, TN 37320. Tel. (615) 479-8511

OFFICERS

Gen. Overseer, Milton A. Tomlinson
Exec. Comm.: Gen. Overseer, Milton A. Tomlinson, Gen. Treas. Leonard Kendrick; Business Mgr., White Wing Publishing House (Printing/Publishing Div. of Church), Henry O'Neal; Field Sec. to Gen. Overseer, Hugh R. Edwards; Asst. Ed., White Wing Messenger, Robert J. Pruitt

GENERAL STAFF

Field Sec. to Gen. Overseer: Hugh R. Edwards, Jose Reyes, E. L. Jones
Department Directors:
Dept. of Pastoral Care: J. E. Brisson

Bible Training Institute: Ray C. Wynn, Supt.; Representatives: Jose Rivera, Benjamin Lawrence
Church of Prophecy Marker Association: D. Frank Hughes
Communication Business Manager: Thomas Duncan
Communication Minister (English) and Music Dept. Dir.: Elwood Matthews
Communication Minister (Spanish): Jose A. Reyes, Sr.
Evangelism and Home Mission Rep.: Verlin D. Thornton
Gen. Office Mgr., Leonard Kendrick
Military Service Rep.: Bobby R. Snow
Ministerial Aid: Roy D. Mixon
Public Relations: Perry Gillum
Sunday School: Harold Hunter
Tomlinson College Pres.: Perry Gillum
Victory Leaders (Youth): William M. Wilson
World Missions: Adrian Varlack; Representatives: Bobby R. Snow, E. E. Van Deventer, Paul Torres, Arthur C. Moss
Women's Missionary Auxiliary: Elva Howard
World Language: Felix R. Garcia

PERIODICALS

Sunday School Literature (q), Jessie Cagle, Ed.
White Wing Messenger, (bi-w), Robert J. Pruitt, Asst. Ed.
Happy Harvester (m), Robert J. Pruitt, Ed.

The Church of God of the Mountain Assembly, Inc.

Founded in 1906 by J. H. Parks, S. N. Bryant, Thomas Moses, and Andrew J. Silcox.

GENERAL ORGANIZATION

Headquarters and General Offices: Florence Ave., Jellico, TN 37762. Tel. (615) 784-8260. General Assembly, annually in August

OFFICERS

Gen. Overseer, Rev. Jasper Walden, Box 157, Jellico, TN 37762
First Asst. Gen. Overseer, Rev. Kenneth E. Massingell, Box 157, Jellico, TN 37762
Gen. Sec.-Treas., Rev. James L. Cox, Jr., Box 157, Jellico, TN 37762

PERIODICAL

The Gospel Herald (m), P.O. Box 157, Jellico, TN 37762, Rev. Bob J. Vance, Ed.

The Church of God (Seventh Day), Denver, Colo.

The Church of God (Seventh Day) began in southwestern Michigan in 1858, when a group of Sabbath-Keepers led by Gilbert Cranmer refused to give endorsement to the visions and writings of Mrs. Ellen G. White, a principal in the formation of the Seventh-Day Adventist Church. Another branch of Sabbath-keepers, which developed near Cedar Rapids, Iowa, in 1860, joined the Michigan church in 1863 to publish a paper called The Hope of Israel, the predecessor to the Bible Advocate, the church's present publication. As the church's membership grew and spread into Missouri and Nebraska, it organized the General Conference of the Church of God in 1884. The parenthized words (Seventh Day) were added to its name in 1923. The headquarters of the church was in Stanberry, Missouri, from 1888 until 1950, when it moved to Denver, Colorado.

The church observes the seventh day as the Sabbath; believes in the imminent, personal, and visible return of Jesus; that the dead are in an unconscious state awaiting to be resurrected, the righteous to immortality and the wicked to extinction by fire; and that the earth will be the eternal abode of the righteous. It observes two ordinances: baptism by immersion and an annual Communion service accompanied by foot washing.

48

GENERAL ORGANIZATION

General Conference: biennial (Next meeting, 1991)
Headquarters: 330 W. 152nd Ave., P.O. Box 33677, Denver, CO 80233. Tel. (303) 452-7973

OFFICERS

Chpsn., Calvin Burrell
Sec.-Treas., Jayne Kuryluk
Spring Vale Academy: Principal, Ken Durham
Youth Agency: Dir., Vernon Caswell
Bible Advocate Press: Dir., LeRoy Dais
Media Outreach Services: Dir., Jerry Moldenhauer
Women's Assoc., Pres., Mrs. Emogene Coulter
Summit School of Theology: Dir., Daniel Davila
Missions Abroad: Dir., Robert Coulter

PERIODICALS

Bible Advocate (m), Denver, CO 80233, Jerry Griffin, Ed.
Harvest Field Messenger (bi-m), Denver, CO 80233, Gina Tolbert, Ed.

Church of God (Which He Purchased with His Own Blood)

This body was organized in 1953 in Oklahoma City, Okla. by William Jordan Fizer after his excommunication from the Church of the Living God (C.W.F.F.) over doctrinal disagreements relating to the Lord's Supper. The first annual convention was held in Oklahoma City, November 19-21, 1954.

The Church of God (W.H.P.W.H.O.B.) believes that water is not the element to be used in the Lord's Supper but rather grape juice or wine and unleavened bread. The Lord's Supper is observed every Sunday.

This body is non-Pentecostal and does not practice speaking in tongues. Its doctrine holds that the Holy Ghost is given to those who obey the Lord. Feet washing is observed as an act of humility and not the condition of salvation. Baptism must be administered in the name of the Father, Son, and Holy Ghost. The Church of God believes it is the Body of Christ, and because of scriptural doctrine and practice, that it is the church organized by Jesus Christ. The Chief Bishop organized the people into the church by calling them into the true doctrine of Christ. The members are urged to lead consecrated lives unspotted from the world. Tobacco and strong drinks are condemned. Divine healing is an article of faith, but not to the exclusion of doctors.

GENERAL ORGANIZATION

Convention: Annual, ending on the second Sunday in October; Annual Sunday School and Training Union; ending on the fourth Sunday in July.
Headquarters: 1628 N.E. 50th, Oklahoma City, OK 73111. Tel. (405) 427-8264

OFFICERS

Chief Bishop, William J. Fizer, 1907 N.E. Grand Blvd., Oklahoma City, OK 73111. Tel. (405) 427-2166
Gen. Sec. and Treas., Alsie Mae Fizer
Overseers: J. W. Johnson, R.1, Box 214, Choctaw, OK 73020; M. Roberson, Rt. 2, Box 214, Mounds, OK 74047

PERODICAL

Gospel News (m), William J. Fizer, Ed.

The Church of Illumination

Organized in 1908 for the express purpose of establishing congregations at large, offering a spiritual, esoteric, philosophic interpretation of the vital biblical teachings, thereby satisfying the inner spiritual needs of those seeking spiritual truth, yet permitting them to remain in, or return to, their former church membership.

GENERAL ORGANIZATION

The Assemblage: annual
Headquarters: "Beverly Hall," Clymer Rd., Quakertown, PA 18951

OFFICERS

Dir., Gerald E. Poesnecker, P.O. Box 220, Quakertown, PA 18951

The Church of Jesus Christ (Bickertonites)

Organized 1862 at Green Oak, Pennsylvania, by William Bickerton, who obeyed the Restored Gospel under Sidney Rigdon's following in 1845.

Churches: 70; Inclusive Membership, 2,986; Sunday or Sabbath Schools: 68; Total Enrollment: 1,816; Ordained Clergy: 282

GENERAL ORGANIZATION

General Conference: annual (October)
Headquarters: Sixth & Lincoln Sts., Monongahela, PA 15063. Tel. (412)258-3066

OFFICERS

Pres., Dominic Thomas, 6010 Barrie, Dearborn, MI 48126
First Counselor, Nicholas Pietrangelo, 24106 Meadow Bridge Dr., Mt. Clemens, MI 48043
Second Counselor, V. James Lovalvo, 5769 Pleasant Ave., Fresno, CA 93711
Exec. Sec., Paul Palmieri, 319 Pine Dr., Aliquippa, PA 15001. Tel (412) 378-4264

PERIODICAL

The Gospel News (m), 15843 Manning, Detroit, MI 48205, Anthony Scolaro, Ed.

The Church of Jesus Christ of Latter-day Saints

Organized April 6, 1830, at Fayette, New York, by Joseph Smith. Members believe Joseph Smith was divinely directed to restore the gospel to the earth, and that through him the keys to the Aaronic and Melchizedek priesthoods and temple work also were restored. In addition to the Bible, members believe the Book of Mormon (a record of the Lord's dealings with His people on the American continent 600 B.C. - 421 A.D.) to be scripture. Membership is worldwide, approaching 7 million in 1989.

GENERAL ORGANIZATION

General Conference sessions, April and October, Salt Lake City, Utah
Headquarters: 50 East North Temple St., Salt Lake City, UT 84150

OFFICERS

Pres., Ezra Taft Benson
1st Presidency: Ezra Taft Benson, Gordon B. Hinckley, 1st Counselor; Thomas S. Monson, 2nd Counselor
The Quorum of the Twelve: Howard W. Hunter, Boyd K. Packer, Marvin J. Ashton, L. Tom Perry, David B. Haight, James E. Faust, Neal A. Maxwell, Russell M. Nelson, Dallin H. Oaks, M. Russell Ballard, Joseph B. Wirthlin, Richard G. Scott

49

The Presidency of the Seventy: (Comprised of seven brethren)
The First Quorum of the Seventy: (Currently comprised of twenty-eight brethren)
The Second Quorum of the Seventy: (Currently comprised of twenty-eight brethren)
The Presiding Bishopric: Robert D. Hales, Presiding Bishop; Henry B. Eyring, 1st Counselor; Glenn L. Pace, 2nd Counselor

AUXILIARY ORGANIZATIONS

Sunday Schools: Gen. Pres., Hugh W. Pinnock
Relief Society: Gen. Pres., Barbara Winder
Young Men: Pres., Vaughn J. Featherstone
Young Women: Gen. Pres., Ardith G. Kapp
Primary: Gen. Pres., Michaelene P. Grassli

PERIODICALS

Ensign magazine (adults)
New Era magazine (youth; young adults)
Friend magazine (children)

Church of Our Lord Jesus Christ of the Apostolic Faith, Inc.

This Church as an organized body was founded by Bishop R. C. Lawson in Columbus, Ohio, and moved to New York City in 1919. It is founded upon the teachings of the Apostles and Prophets, Jesus Christ being its chief cornerstone.

GENERAL ORGANIZATION

National Convocation: annual (August)
Headquarters: 2081 Adam Clayton Powell Jr. Blvd., New York, NY 10027. Tel. (212) 866-1700

OFFICERS

Board of Apostles: Pres., Bishop William L. Bonner; Bishop J. P. Steadman; Bishop Frank S. Solomon; Bishop Henry A. Ross, Sr.; Bishop Matthew A. Norwood; Bishop Wilbur L. Jones; Bishop Gentle L. Groover
Board of Bishops: Bishop Chris Dobbins, Chmn.
Board of Presbyters: District Elder Kenneth Bligen, Pres.
Exec. Secretariat: Sec., Bishop T. E. Woolfolk
Natl. Rec. Sec., Elder Fred Rubin, Sr
Natl. Fin. Sec., District Elder Clarence Groover
Natl. Corr. Sec., Elder Raymond J. Keith, Jr.
Natl. Treas., Bishop Thomas J. Richardson

PERIODICAL

The Contender for the Faith (semi-a)

Church of the Brethren

German pietists-anabaptists founded in 1708 under Alexander Mack, Schwarzenau, Germany, entered the colonies in 1719 and settled at Germantown, Pennsylvania. They have no other creed than the New Testament, hold to principles of nonviolence, temperance, and voluntarism, and emphasize religion in life.

Churches: 1,079; Inclusive Membership: 151,169; Sunday or Sabbath Schools: N.R.; Total Enrollment: N.R.; Ordained Clergy: 1,553

GENERAL ORGANIZATION

General Conference: annual
Headquarters: Church of the Brethren General Offices, 1451 Dundee Ave., Elgin, IL 60120. Tel. (708)742-5100
New Windsor Service Center: P.O. Box 188, New Windsor, MD 21776
Washington Office: 110 Maryland Ave., NE, Box 50, Washington, DC 20002

OFFICERS

Mod., Curtis Dubble
Mod.-Elect, Philip Stone
Sec., Anne Myers

GENERAL BOARD STAFF

Office of General Secretary: Gen. Sec., Donald E. Miller; Exec. of Committee on Interchurch Relations, Melanie May; Coord., Sue Snyder
Office of Human Resources: Exec., Melanie May; Admn. Asst., Barbara Greenwald; Consultant for Ministry, Robert E. Faus; Dir. of Admn. Services, NW, Eleanor Rowe; Dir. Personnel, David Leatherman; Recruitment, Karen Shallenberger; Dir. of Dist. Ministries, NW, Ronald Row
Treasurer's Office: Treas., Darryl Deardorff; Controller, Judy Keyser; Controller, NW, Karen Heckman; Dir. of Computer Operations, Perry Hudkins; Dir. Bldg. and Grounds, David Ingold
General Services Commission: Assoc. Gen. Sec./Exec. of Commission, Dale E. Minnich; Admn. Asst., Elsie Holderread; Archivist, Kenneth Shaffer; Congregational Support, Donald Michaelsen; Dir. of Interpretation; Howard E. Royer; Messenger, Ed., Kermon Thomasson; Messenger, Mgr. Ed./Dir. of New Services, Wendy C. McFadden; Dir. of Planned Giving, Donald Stern; Planned Giving Officer, SE, Ronald Wyrick; Planned Giving Officer, NE. Roy Johnson; Planned Giving Officer, W. Herbert Fisher; Dir. of Stewardship Education, Connie L. Burk; Brethren Press, Gen. Mgr., Robert Durnbaugh; Dir. Marketing, Gerald Peterson; Actg. Book Ed., Ralph McFadden
Parish Ministries Commission: Assoc. Gen. Sec./Exec. of Commission, Joan G. Deeter; Admn. Asst., Joan Pelletier; Congregational Nurture, June Gibble; Dir. of Ministry Training, Rick Gardner; Training in Ministry, East, Wayne Eberly; Training in Ministry, West, Karen Calderon; Ed of Study Resource, Karen Miller; Evangelism/Korean Ministries, Paul E. R. Mundey; Health & Welfare, Jay E. Gibble; New Church Development/Hispanic Ministries, Merle Crouse, Outdoor Ministries, Nancy Knepper; Program for Women, Judith Kipp; Youth and Young Adult Program/Urban Ministries, Christine Michael
World Ministries Commission: Assoc. Gen. Sec./Exec. of Commission, J. Robert Schrock; Admn. Asst., Barbara Ober; Africa & Middle East Rep., Kenneth Holderread; Dir. of Brethren Volunteer Service, Janeth Schorock; Dir. of BVS Orientation, Debra Eisenbise; Economic Justice/Rural Crisis, Shantilal Bhagat; Latin American & Caribbean Rep., Yvonne Dilling; Peace Consultant, David Radcliff; Peace & International Affairs/Europe & Asia Rep., H. Lamar Gibble; Dir. of Center Operations, NW, D. Miller Davis; Dir. On Earth Peace, NW, Harold Smith; Dir. of Refugee/Disaster Services, NW, Donna Derr; Dir. of SERV, NW, James Forbus; Wash. Rep., Leland Wilson.
Annual Conference: Mgr., Doris I. Lasley
Brethren Benefit Trust: Exec. and Treas., Wilfred E. Nolen; Admin. Asst., Sandra Pryde; Dir. Operations, Cheryl Ingold; Dir. Interpretation, Elizabeth Jamsa

PERIODICAL

Messenger (m), Church of the Brethren General Offices, Elgin, IL 60120. Kermon Thomasson, Ed.

Church of the Living God (Motto: Christian Workers for Fellowship)

William Christian was born a slave in Mississippi on November 10, 1856. He grew up uneducated and in 1875, united with the Missionary Baptist Church and began to preach. In 1888, he left the Baptist Church and began what was known as Christian Friendship Work. Believing himself to have been inspired by the Spirit of God, through divine revelation and close study of the Scriptures he was led to the truth that the Bible refers to the church as The Church of the Living God (I Tim. 3:15).

At Caine Creek, near Wrightsville, Arkansas, in April

1889, the Rev. William Christian became founder and organizer of The Church of the Living God, the first black church in America without Anglo-Saxon roots or not begun by white missionaries.

The church believes in the infallibility of the Scriptures, is Trinitarian, and believes there are three sacraments ordained by Christ: baptism (by immersion), the Lord's Supper (unleavened bread and water), and foot washing. The Church of the Living God, C.W.F.F., believes in holiness as a gift of God subsequent to the New Birth and manifested only by a changed life acceptable to the Lord.

GENERAL ORGANIZATION

General Assembly: every four years; Annual Assembly; Annual District Conventions.

Headquarters: 434 Forest Ave., Cincinnati, OH 45229

OFFICERS

Executive Board: Bishop W. E. Crumes, Chief Bishop, 434 Forest Ave., Cincinnati, OH 45229; Bishop I. C. Collins, Vice-Chief Bishop, 3824 - 13th Ave., Sacramento, CA 94820; Bishop C. A. Lewis, Exec. Sec., 1360 N. Boston, Tulsa, OK 73111; Gen. Sec., Elder Milton S. Herring, 6302 Blossom Park, Dayton, OH 45429. Tel. (513)268-6511; Bishop J. C. Hawkins, Gen. Treas., 3804 N. Temple Ave., Indianapolis, IN 46205; Bishop E. L. Bowie, 2037 N.E. 18th, Oklahoma City, OK 73111; Bishop L. H. Dixon, 8425 S. Damen Ave., Chicago, IL 60620; Bishop E. A. Morgan, Chaplain, 735 S. Oakland Dr., Decatur, IL 62525; Bishop L. A. Crawford, 3711 Biglow, Dallas, TX 74216; Bishop A. L. Ponder, 5609 N. Terry, Oklahoma City, OK 73111; Bishop A. R. Powell, 8557 S. Wabash, Chicago, IL 60619; Bishop Jeff Ruffin, 226 S. Catamaran Ct., Pittsburg, CA 94565; Bishop R. S. Morgan, Aux. Bishop, 4508 N. Indiana, Oklahoma City, OK 73118; Overseer S. E. Shannon, 1034 S. King Highway, St. Louis, MO 63110

NATIONAL DEPARTMENTS

Convention Planning Committee, Young Peoples Progressive Union, Christian Education Dept., Sunday School Dept., Nat'l Evangelist Board, Nat'l Nurses Guild, Nat'l Women's Work Department, Nat'l Music Department, Gen. Secretary's office.

PERIODICALS

The Gospel Truth (m)
Sunday School Quarterly (q)
Annual Convention Journal

Church of the Lutheran Brethren of America

The Church of the Lutheran Brethren of America was organized in December 1900. Five independent Lutheran congregations met together in Milwaukee, Wisconsin and adopted a constitution patterned very closely to that of the Lutheran Free Church of Norway.

The spiritual awakening in the mid-west during the 1890's brought new concerns to mind in the hearts of pastors and lay people concerning some of the practices in the local congregation. These concerns crystallized into convictions that led to the formation of a new church body. Chief among these concerns were church memberhsip practices, observance of Holy Communion, confirmation practices and local church government.

The Church of the Lutheran Brethren is non-liturgical in worship with the sermon as the primary part of the worship service. It believes that personal profession of faith is the primary criterion for membership in the congregation. The Communion service is reserved for those who profess faith in Christ as savior. Each congregation is autonomous and the synod serves the congregations in advisory and cooperative capacities.

The synod supports a very extensive world mission program in Cameroon, Chad, Japan and Taiwan. Approximately forty percent of the synodical budget is earmarked for world missions. A growing home mission ministry is planting new congregations in the United States and Canada. The educational mission of the synod has existed since the very beginning. A Bible School was founded in 1903. The Bible School expanded to become the Seminary and some years later a high school department was added. The three departments continue to serve the needs of many people to this day. The three schools are located on adjacent campuses in Fergus Falls, Minnesota. The Synod Administration Offices and Faith and Fellowship Press are located near the school campuses. Affiliate organizations operate sevearl retirement/nursing homes, conference and retreat centers.

Churches: 128; Inclusive Membership: 13,695; Sunday or Sabbath Schools: 122; Total Enrollment: 10,884; Ordained Clergy: 202

GENERAL ORGANIZATION

Convention: annual (June)
Headquarters: 1007 Westside Dr., Box 655, Fergus Falls, MN 56537. Tel. (218) 739-3336

OFFICERS

Pres., Rev. Robert M. Overgard, Sr., Box 655, Fergus Falls, MN 56537
Vice-Pres., Rev. Joel Egge, Rt 4, River Oaks Dr., Fergus Falls, MN 53537
Sec., Rev. Richard Vettrus, 707 Crestview Dr., West Union, IA 52175
Dir. of Finance, Mr. Ronald Egge, Box 655, Fergus Falls, MN 56538
Pres., Lutheran Brethren Schools, Rev. Oma Gjerness, Lutheran Brethren Schools, Box 317, Fergus Falls, MN 56537
Exec. Dir. of World Missions, Rev. Jarle Olson, Box 655, Fergus Falls, MN 56537
Exec. Dir. of Home Missons, Rev. John Westby, Box 655, Fergus Falls, MN 56537
Exec. Dir. of Church Services, Rev. David Rinden, Box 655, Fergus Falls, MN 56537

PERIODICAL

Faith and Fellowship (m), 704 Vernon Ave., W. Fergus Falls, MN 56537

Church of the Lutheran Confession

The Church of the Lutheran Confession held its constituting convention in Watertown, South Dakota, in August of 1960. The Church of the Lutheran Confession was born as a result of the people and congregations who came to their own individual convictions, based on Scripture, and were moved to withdraw from church bodies that made up what was then known as the Synodical Conference. The specific error in the Synodical Conference was the error of unionism. Following such passages as I Corinthians 1:10 and Romans 16:17-18, the Church of the Lutheran Confession holds the conviction that agreement with the doctrines of Scripture is essential and necessary before exercise of church fellowship is appropriate.

Members of the Church of the Lutheran Confession uncompromisingly believe the Holy Scriptures to be verbally inspired and therefore inerrant. It subscribes without reservation to the historic Lutheran Confessions as found in the Book of Concord of 1580, because they are a clear and correct exposition of Scripture.

The Church of the Lutheran Confession exists and holds its confessional position out of concern and appreciation for the gospel. It exists to proclaim, preserve, and spread the saving truth of the gospel of Jesus Christ, so that the redeemed of God, both here and elsewhere, may learn to know Jesus Christ as their Lord and Savior, and to follow him through this life to the life to come.

Churches: 67; Inclusive Membership: 8,655; Sunday or Sabbath Schools: 64; Total Enrollment: 1,379; Ordained Clergy: 72

GENERAL ORGANIZATION

Biennial Synodical Convention (Next meeting, 1990) Headquarters: 460 75th Ave., NE, Minneapolis, MN 55432. Tel. (612) 784-8784

OFFICERS

Pres., Rev. Daniel Fleischer, 460 75th Ave., NE, Minneapolis, MN 55432
Vice Pres., Rev. Rollin Reim, 994 Emerald Hill Rd., Redwood City, CA 94061
Mod., Prof. Ronald Roehl, 515 Ingram Dr. W., Eau Claire, WI 54701
Sec., Rev. Paul Nolting, 626 N. Indian Landing Rd., Rochester, NY 14625
Treas., Lowell Moen, 3455 Jill Ave., Eau Claire, WI 54701
Archivist-Historian, John Lau
Statistician, Harvey Callies

PERIODICALS

The Lutheran Spokesman (m), 11315 E. Broadway, Spokane, WA 99206, Rev. Paul Fleischer, Ed.
Ministry by Mail (w), 626 N. Indian Landing Rd., Rochester, NY 14625
C.L.C. Directory (a), 994 Emerald Hill Rd., Redwood City, CA 94061. Rollin Reim, Ed.
Journal of Theology (4/yr.), Immanuel Lutheran College, Eau Claire, WI 54701. Prof. John Lau, Ed.

Church of the Nazarene

The origins of the Church of the Nazarene are in the broader holiness movement which arose soon after the American Civil War. It is the result of the merging of three independent holiness groups already in existence in the United States. An eastern body, located principally in New York and New England and known as the Association of Pentecostal Churches in America, joined at Chicago in 1907 with a California body called the Church of the Nazarene; the two merging churches agreed on the name Pentecostal Church of the Nazarene. The southern group, known as the Holiness Church of Christ, united with this Pentecostal Church of the Nazarene at Pilot Point, Texas, in 1908. This is considered the birth date of the Church of the Nazarene. Principal leaders in the organization were Phineas Bresee, founder of the church in the West; William Howard Hoople and H. F. Reynolds from the East; and C. B. Jernigan in the southern group. The first Church of the Nazarene in Canada was organized in November 1902 by Dr. H. F. Reynolds, in Oxford, Nova Scotia. In 1919 the word Pentecostal was dropped from the name, leaving it as we know it today, Church of the Nazarene.

The Church of the Nazarene is distinctive in its emphasis on the doctrine of entire sanctification on the proclamation of Christian Holiness. It stresses the importance of a devout and holy life and a positive witness before the world by the power of the Holy Spirit. The church feels that caring is a way of life for its constituents.

Nazarene government is representative, a studied compromise between episcopacy and congregationalism. Quadrennially, the various districts elect delegates to a general assembly, at which 6 general superintendents are elected for a term of 4 years to supervise the work of the denomination.

The church, an international denomination, is comprised of over 257 districts, 8,615 local congregations, 10 liberal arts colleges, 2 graduate seminaries, 16 seminaries,

and 24 Bible colleges. The church maintains missionaries in 90 countries around the world. The world services include medical, education, and religious ministries. Books, periodicals, and other Christian literature are published at the Nazarene Publishing House. A radio program, "Master Plan," is heard each week on more than 500 stations around the world.

The Church of the Nazarene is a member of two interchurch organizations, Christian Holiness Association and the National Association of Evangelicals.

Churches: 5,129; Inclusive Membership: 552,264; Sunday or Sabbath Schools: 5,050; Total Enrollment: 861,761; Ordained Clergy: 8,988

GENERAL ORGANIZATION

General Assembly: quadrennial (Next meeting, Houston, TX, June 1993)
International Headquarters: 6401 The Paseo, Kansas City, MO 64131. Tel. (816) 333-7000

OFFICERS

Gen. Supts.: Eugene L. Stowe, Jerald Johnson, John A. Knight, Raymond Hurn, William J. Prince, and Donald D. Owens
Gen. Sec., _____
Gen. Treas., Norman O. Miller

OTHER ORGANIZATIONS

General Board: Sec., _____; Treas., Norman O. Miller
General Church Divisions and Ministry/Services: Church Growth Div. Dir., Bill Sullivan; Church Ext. Ministries, Dir., Mike Estep; Evangelism Ministries, Dir., M. V. Scutt; Pastoral Ministries, Dir. Wilbur Brannon: Communications Div., Dir. Cecil D. Paul; Media Services, Dir., Paul Skiles: Publications International, Dir., Bennette Dudney: Finance Div. Dir., D. Moody Gunter; Personnel and Physical Plant, Dir., Paul Spear; Life Income Gifts Services, Dir., Robert Hempel; Pensions & Benefits Services, Dir., Dean Wessels; Stewardship Services, Dir., D. Moody Gunter: Sunday School Ministries Div. Dir., Phil Riley; Adult Ministries, Dir., Tim Stearman; Children's Ministries, Dir., Miriam Hall; Youth Ministries, Dir., Bill Sullivan: World Mission Div. Dir., Robert H. Scott; Nazarene World Missionary Society, Dir., Nina Gunter: International Board of Education, Ed. Commissioner, Stephen Nease.

PERIODICALS

Herald of Holiness (m), Wesley Tracy, Ed.
World Missions (m), Robert H. Scott, Ed.
Preacher's Magazine (m) Randal Denney, Ed.
Bread (m), Karen DeSollar, Ed.
All published by the Nazarene Publishing House, Box 527, Kansas City, MO 64141

Churches of Christ

Churches of Christ are autonomous congregations, whose members appeal to the Bible alone to determine matters of faith and practice. There are no central offices or officers. Publications and institutions related to the churches are either under local congregational control or independent of any one congregation.

Churches of Christ shared a common fellowship in the 19th century with the Christian Churches/Churches of Christ and the Christian Church (Disciples of Christ). Fellowship was gradually estranged following the Civil War due to theistic evolution, higher critical theories, and centralization of church-wide activities through a missionary society.

Members of Churches of Christ believe in the inspiration of the Scriptures, the divinity of Jesus Christ, and immersion into Christ for the remission of sins. The New Testament pattern is followed in worship and church organization.

Churches: 13,375; Inclusive 1,626,000; Sunday or Sabbath Schools: N.R.; Total Enrollment: N.R.; Ordained Clergy: N.R.

NO GENERAL ORGANIZATION

PERIODICALS

Over 100 periodicals are published by members of Churches of Christ. Below are listed representative publications.

Christian Chronicle (m), Box 1100, Oklahoma City, OK 73136, Howard W. Norton, Ed.

The Christian Echo (m), Box 37266, Los Angeles, CA 90037, R. N. Hogan, Ed.

Firm Foundation (m), Box 17200, Pensacola, FL 32522, William Cline, Ed.

Gospel Advocate (sm), Box 150, Nashville, TN 37202, Furman Kearley, Ed.

Gospel Tidings (m), 7533 E. Easter Way, Edgewood, CO 80112, Travis Allen, Ed.

Guardian of Truth (m), Box 9670, Bowling Green, KY 42101, Mike Willis, Ed.

Image (m), 115 Warren Dr., Ste., D., West Monroe, LA 71291, Reuel Lemmons, Ed.

Old Paths Advocate (m), RR 1, Lebanon, MO 65536, Clovis T. Cook, and Edwin S. Morris, Eds.

Power for Today (q), Box 40536, Nashville, TN 37204, Steven S. and Emily Y. Lemley, Eds.

Restoration Quarterly (q), Box 8227, Abilene, TX 79699, Everett Ferguson.

Twentieth Century Christian (m), Box 40526, Nashville, TN 37204, M. Norval Young, Ed.

Up Reach, Box 2001, Abilene, TX 79604, Harold Hazelip, Ed.

Churches of Christ in Christian Union

Organized in 1909 at Washington Court House, Ohio, as the Churches of Christ in Christian Union. This body believes in the new birth and the baptism of the Holy Spirit for believers. It is Wesleyan with an evangelistic and missionary emphasis.

Reformed Methodist Church merged in September, 1952, with Churches of Christ in Christian Union.

Churches: 260; Inclusive Membership: 10,418; Sunday or Sabbath Schools: 260; Total Enrollment: 18,200; Ordained Clergy: 360

GENERAL ORGANIZATION

General Council: biennial (Next meeting 1990)
District Councils: annual
General Headquarters: 1426 Lancaster Pike. (Mailing address: Box 30), Circleville, OH 43113

OFFICERS

Gen. Supt., Rev. Robert Kline, Box 30, Circleville, OH 43113
Asst. Gen. Supt., Dr. Dan Tipton, Box 30, Circleville, OH 43113
Gen. Sec., Rev. Robert Barth, 641 S. Madriver, Bellefontaine, OH 43311
Gen. Treas., Bevery R. Salley, Box 30, Circleville, OH 43113
Gen. Board of Trustees: Chm., Rev. Robert Kline, Box 30, Circleville, OH 43113; Vice-Chpsn., Dr. Dan Tipton; Sec., Rev. Robert Barth, 641 S. Madriver, Bellefontaine, OH 43311
District Superintendents (all District Superintendents are also members of the Gen. Bd. of Trustees); West Central District, Rev. David Dean, P. O. Box 30, Circleville, OH 43113; South Central District, Rev. Daniel Tipton, P.O. Box 30, Circleville, OH 43113; Northeast Dist., Rev. Art Penird, Rt. 2, P.O. Box 790, Port Crane, NY 13833

PERIODICALS

Advocate (m), P. Lewis Brevard, Office, Ed.
Missionary Tidings (m), Betty Seymour, Ed.

Churches of God, General Conference

The Churches of God, General Conference had its beginnings in Harrisburg, Penna., in 1825.

John Winebrenner, recognized founder of the Church of God movement, was an ordained minister of the German Reformed Church. His experience-centered form of Christianity, particularly the "new measures" he used to promote it, his close connection with the local Methodists, his "experience and conference meetings" in the church, and his "social prayer meetings" in parishioners' homes resulted in differences of opinion and the establishment of new congregations. Some independent congregations also began to look to Winebrenner for leadership. Extensive revivals, camp meetings, and mission endeavors led to the organization of additional congregations across central Pennsylvania and westward through Ohio, Indiana, Illinois, and Iowa.

In 1830 the first system of cooperation between local churches was initiated as an "eldership" in eastern Pennsylvania. The organization of other elderships followed. In 1835 The Gospel Publisher was established as a Church of God paper; its successor since 1846 is The Church Advocate. A General Eldership was organized in 1845, and in 1974 the official name of the denomination was changed from General Eldership of the Churches of God in North America to its present name.

The Churches of God, General Conference, is composed of sixteen conferences in the United States. The polity of the church is presbyteial in form. The church has mission ministries in the southwest among native Americans and is extensively involved in church planting and whole life ministries in Bangladesh, Haiti, and India.

The General Conference convenes in business session triennially. An Administrative Council composed of 38 regional representatives serving on 7 commissions is responsible for the administration and ministries of the church between sessions of the General Conference.

Churches: 343; Inclusive Membership: 33,778; Sunday or Sabbath Schools: 343; Total Enrollment: 27,623; Ordained Clergy: 327

GENERAL ORGANIZATION

General Conference: meets triennially
Legal Headquarters: United Church Center, Rm. 200, 900 So. Arlington Ave., Harrisburg, PA 17109. Tel. (717) 652-0255
Administrative Offices: General Conference Administrator, Pastor William H. Reist, 700 E. Melrose Ave., P. O. Box 926, Findlay, OH 45839. Tel. (419) 424-1961
Assoc. in Ministry: Mrs. Linda M. Draper; Church Publications; Mr. Daniel A. Fortney, Cross-Cultural Ministries; Dr. Royal P. Kear, Computer Operations and Pensions; Rev. Marilyn Rayle Kern, Curriculum; Rev. Douglas E. Nolt, Campus Ministries; Rev. Frederick C. Quade, Development; Rev. R. Joe Roach, Education and Family Life; Mr. Earl E. Mills, Dir. of Youth Ministry; Mr. Robert E. Stephenson, Finance

OFFICERS

Pres., Pastor Stephen L. Dunn, 6012 S. Bend Dr., Ft. Wayne, IN 46804. Tel. Office: (219)432-3342; Home: (219)432-0417
Vice-Pres., Pastor George Reser, 701 S. Clay, Mt. Carroll, IL 61053. Tel. (815)244-4453
Journalizing Sec., Pastor David L. Meador, 28 N. Pendleton Ct., Federick, MD 21701 Tel. (301)663-0741
Treas., Mr. Robert E. Stephenson, 700 E. Melrose Ave., P.O. Box 926, Findlay, OH 45839. Tel. (419) 424-1961

COMMISSIONS

Church Development: Chpsn., Pastor Alvin D. Rockey, Box 221, Idaville, IN 47950; Sec., Pastor Conrad L. Chambers, 700 E. Melrose Ave., Findlay, OH 45839
Church Vocations: Chpsn., Pastor Dale R. Brougher, 1000 N. Main St., Findlay, OH 45840; Sec., Mrs. Rosamond E. Kear, 1718 Cherry Lane, Findlay, OH 45840
Education: Chpsn., Pastor Ronald E. Dull, 12 Dogwood Ct., Shippensburg, PA 17257; Sec., Mrs. Marilyn J. Dunn, 2211 Market St., Harrisburg, PA 17103
Evangelism: Chpsn., Pastor Glenn E. Beatty, 1114 Circle Dr., Latrobe, PA 15650; Sec., Dr. John A. Parthemore, Jr., 235 W. High St., Middletown, PA 17057
National Ministries: Chpsn., Howard L. Ruley, 100 W. Franklin, P. O. Box 247, Wharton, OH 43359; Sec., Pastor G. Gordon Jenkins, 3827 E. Court Dr., Decatur, IL 62526
Stewardship: Chpsn., Pastor David M. Larkin, RR 1 Box 103, Casey, IL 62420; Sec., Dr. A. Gail Dunn, 900 S. Arlington Ave., Rm. 200, Harrisburg, PA 17109
World Missions: Pastor Jim G. Martin, 339 Lincoln Way, E., Chambersburg, PA 17201; Sec., Pastor James L. Monticue, RR 1 Box 51, Markleton, PA 15551

PERIODICALS

The Church Advocate (m), P. O. Box 926, Findlay, OH 45839, Mrs. Linda Draper, Ed.
The Missionary Signal (bi-m), P.O. Box 926, Findlay, OH 45839, Dr. LaVonna Powell, Ed.
The Workman (q), P.O. Box 926, Findlay, OH 45839, Pastor Marilyn Rayle Kern, Ed.
The Gem (w), P.O. Box 926, Findlay, OH 45839, Pastor Marilyn Rayle Kern, Ed.

Community Churches, International Council of

This body is a fellowship of locally autonomous, ecumenically minded, congregationally governed, non-creedal Churches. The Council came into being in 1950 as the union of two former councils of community churches, one formed of black churches known as the Biennial Council of Community Churches, and the other of white churches known as the National Council of Community Churches.

Churches: 250; Inclusive Membership: 250,000; Sunday or Sabbath Schools: N.R.; Total Enrollment: N.R.; Ordained Clergy: 350

GENERAL ORGANIZATION

Conference: Annual
International Office: 900 Ridge Rd., LL1, Homewood, IL 60430. Tel. (312) 798-2264

OFFICERS

Pres., Paul Scott
Vice-Pres., Norman Towler & Orsey Malone
Sec., Carl Hargrave, Jr.
Treas., Robert Mingus
Exec. Dir., J. Ralph Shotwell

OTHER ORGANIZATIONS

(All may be contacted through the Central Office)
Commission on Church Relations
Commission on Ecumenical Relations
Commission on Clergy Relations
Commission on Laity Relations
Commission on Faith and Order
Commission on Social Concerns
Commission on Missions
Commission on Informational Services
Women's Christian Fellowship, Pres., Mozella Weston

Samaritans (Men's Fellowship), Pres., Abraham Wright
Young Adult Fellowship, Pres., Jacqueline Clinkscales
Youth Fellowship, Pres., Charmayne Little

PERIODICALS

The Christian Community (m), 900 Ridge Rd., LL1, Homewood, IL 60430. J. Ralph Shotwell, Ed.
The Pastor's Journal (q), 900 Ridge Rd., LL1 Homewood, IL 60430, Robert Puckett, Ed.

Congregational Christian Churches, National Association of

Organized 1955 in Detroit, Michigan by delegates from Congregational Christian Churches committed to continuing the Congregational way of faith and order in church life. Participation by member churches is voluntary.

Churches: 400; Inclusive Membership: 90,000; Sunday or Sabbath Schools: N.R.; Total Enrollment: N.R.; Ordained Clergy: 575

GENERAL ORGANIZATION

Annual Meeting: Beloit College, Beloit, WI, June 1990

OFFICERS

Mod., Harold Frentz; Exec. Sec., J. Fred Rennebohm; Assoc. Exec. Secs., Rev. Dr. Michael Halcomb, Rev. Harry W. Clark; Office, Mgr., Marilyn Beck, P.O. Box 1620, Oak Creek, WI 53154. Tel. (414) 764-1620

PERIODICAL

The Congregationalist, Rev. Dr. Louis Gerhardt, Ed.

Congregational Holiness Church

A body which was organized in 1921 and which embraces the doctrine of Holiness and Pentecost. It carries on mission work in Mexico, Honduras, Costa Rica, Cuba, Brazil, Guatemala, India, Nicaragua and El Salvador.

GENERAL ORGANIZATION

General Conference, meets every two years. General Committee, meets as called. Represents nine state districts.
General Headquarters: 3888 Fayetteville Hwy., Griffin, GA 30223. Tel. (404) 228-4833

EXECUTIVE BOARD

Gen. Supt., Bishop Cullen L. Hicks
1st Asst. Gen. Supt., Rev. William L. Lewis
2nd Asst. Gen. Supt., Rev. Kenneth Edenfield
Gen. Sec., Rev. Kenneth Law
Gen. Treas., Rev. Dennis Phillips
Supt. of World Missions, Rev. Hugh B. Skelton
Supt. of Church Ministries, Rev. Hayward Clark

PERIODICAL

The Gospel Messenger (m), 3888 Fayetteville Hwy., Griffin, GA 30223, Mrs. Donna Clark, Ed.

Conservative Baptist Association of America

Organized May 17, 1947, at Atlantic City, New Jersey. The Old and New Testaments are regarded as the divinely inspired Word of God and are therefore infallible and of supreme authority. Each local church is independent and autonomous, and free from ecclesiastical or political authority.

Churches: 1,121; Inclusive Membership: 204,496; Sunday or Sabbath Schools: N.R.; Total Enrollment: N.R.; Ordained Clergy: N.R.

GENERAL ORGANIZATION

Meets annually

Headquarters: 25W560 Geneva Rd., Box 66, Wheaton, IL 60189. Tel. (312) 653-5350
Gen. Dir., Dr. Tim Blanchard, Box 66, Wheaton, IL 60189. Tel. (312) 653-5350

OTHER ORGANIZATIONS

Conservative Baptist Foreign Mission Society: Box 5, Wheaton, IL 60189, Gen. Dir., Dr. Warren W. Webster
Conservative Baptist Home Mission Society: Box 828, Wheaton, IL 60189, Gen. Dir., Dr. Jack Estep
Conservative Baptist Higher Education Council: c/o Dr. Earl D. Radmacher, Pres., Western Conservative Baptist Seminary, 5511 SE Hawthorne Blvd., Portland, OR 97215

PERIODICAL

Conservative Baptist, P.O. Box 66, Wheaton, IL 60189

Conservative Congregational Christian Conference

In the 1930s, evangelicals within the Congregational Christian Churches felt a definite need for fellowship and service. By 1945, this loose association crystalized in the Conservative Congregational Christian Fellowship, concerned to maintain a faithful, biblical witness.

In 1948 in Chicago, the Conservative Congregational Christian Conference was established to provide a continuing fellowship for evangelical churches and ministers on the national level, and after several years, entered a period of healthy growth. There are now regional fellowships throughout the United States and one in Ontario, Canada. Scores of churches participate in these groups.

In recent years, many churches have joined the Conference from backgrounds other than Congregational. These Community or Bible Churches are truly congregational in polity and thoroughly evangelical in conviction, but in many cases have never enjoyed the values of inspiration and cooperation gained in the work that Christian churches must do together. The CCCC welcomes all evangelical churches that are, in fact, congregational. The CCCC believes in the necessity of a regenerate membership, the authority of the Holy Scriptures, the Lordship of Jesus Christ, the autonomy of the local church, and the universal fellowship of all Christians.

The Conservative Congregational Christian Conference is a member of the World Evangelical Congregational Fellowship (formed in 1986 in London, England) and the National Association of Evangelicals.

Churches: 176; Inclusive Membership: 29,015; Sunday or Sabbath Schools: 157; Total Enrollment: 11,692; Ordained Clergy: 457

GENERAL ORGANIZATION

General Conference
Headquarters: 7582 Currell Blvd., Ste. #108, St. Paul MN 55125

OFFICERS

Pres., Rev. Jay Warren, Rt. 3, Box 88, Highland, IL 62249
Vice-Pres., Mr. William V. Nygren, 583 Sterling, Maplewood, MN 55119
Conf. Min., Rev. Clifford R. Christensen 57 Kipling St., St. Paul, MN 55519
Controller, Mr. Orrin H. Bailey, 4260 Eastlake Rd., Muskegon, MI 49444
Treas., Mr. John D. Nygren, 579 Sterling St., Maplewood, MN 55119
Recording Sec., Rev. Doug Jones, 2620 E. Maple Rapids Rd., Eureka, MI 48833
Editor, Rev. Robert H. Wilber, 222 E. Second St., Perry, MI 48872
Historian, Rev. Daniel E. Wray, 17 Bromley Place, Scotia, NY 12302

Coptic Orthodox Church

This body is part of the ancient Coptic Orthodox Church of Egypt which is currently headed by His Holiness Pope Shenouda III. In the United States many parishes have been organized consisting of Egyptian immigrants to the United States. Copts exist outside of Egypt in Ethiopia, Europe, Asia, Australia, Canada, and the United States. In all, the world Coptic community is estimated at 9 million, the vast majority being located in Egypt, however.

Churches: 40; Inclusive Membership: 160,000; Sunday or Sabbath Schools: N.R.; Total Enrollment: N.R.; Ordained Clergy: 44

CORRESPONDENT

Archpriest Fr. Gabriel Abdelsayed, 427 West Side Ave., Jersey City, NJ 07304. Tel. (201) 333-0004; (516) 931-6242

Cumberland Presbyterian Church

The Cumberland Presbyterian Church was organized in Dickson County, Tennessee, on February 4, 1810. It was an outgrowth of the Great Revival of 1800 on the Kentucky and Tennessee frontier. The founders were Finis Ewing, Samuel King, and Samuel McAdow, ministers in the Presbyterian Church who rejected the doctrine of election and reprobation as taught in the Westminster Confession of Faith.

The Cumberland Presbytery, constituted at the time of the organization of the Church, originally consisted of only three ministers. By October 1813, it had grown to encompass three presbyteries which constituted a synod. This synod met at the Beech Church in Sumner County, Tennessee, and formulated a "Brief Statement," which set forth the points in which Cumberland Presbyterians dissented from the Westminster Confession:

1. That there are no eternal reprobates;
2. That Christ died not for a part only, but for all mankind;
3. That all those dying in infancy are saved through Christ and the sanctification of the Spirit;
4. That the Spirit of God operates on the world, or as coextensively as Christ has made atonement, in such a manner as to leave all men inexcusable.

From its birth in 1810, the Cumberland Presbyterian Church grew to a membership of 200,000 at the turn of the century. In 1906 the church voted to merge with the then Presbyterian Church. Those who dissented from the merger became the nucleus of the continuing Cumberland Presbyterian Church.

Churches: 752; Inclusive Membership: 91,491; Sunday or Sabbath Schools: 752; Total Enrollment: 42,536; Ordained Clergy: 725

GENERAL ORGANIZATION

General Assembly

OFFICERS

Mod., William Rustenhaven, 168 E. Parkway S., Memphis, TN 38104
Stated Clk., Robert Prosser, 1978 Union Ave., Memphis, TN 38104
Chpsn. of General Assembly's Executive Committee, Rev. Robert E. Shelton, 8525 Audelia, Dallas TX 75238

INSTITUTIONS

Cumberland Presbyterian Center, 1978 Union Ave., Memphis, TN 38104. (Headquarters for program boards, Frontier Press, and resource center.

BOARDS

Board of Christian Education: Exec. Dir., Rev. Harold Davis, 1978 Union Ave., Memphis TN 38104

Board of Missions: Exec. Dir., Rev. Joe E. Matlock, 1978 Union Ave., Memphis, TN 38104
Board of Finance: Exec. Sec., Rev. Richard Magrill, 1978 Union Ave., Memphis, TN 38104

PERIODICALS

The Cumberland Presbyterian (bi-w), 1978 Union Ave., Memphis, TN 38104, Rev. Mark Brown, Interim Ed.
The Missionary Messenger (m), 1978 Union Ave., Memphis, TN 38104, Rev. Dudley Condron, Ed.
Church School Literature (q). Bd. of Christian Ed., 1978 Union Ave., Memphis, TN 38104

Duck River (and Kindred) Associations of Baptists

A group of Baptist associations found in Tennessee, Alabama, Georgia, Kentucky, composed of the following associations: Duck River, Mt. Zion, Mt. Pleasant #1, Mt. Pleasant #2, New Liberty, East Union and Union Baptist.

GENERAL ORGANIZATION
Meets yearly, 4th week in October

OFFICERS
Duck River Association: Mod., Elder Wayne L. Smith, Rt. 1 Box 429, Lynchburg, TN 37352; Clk., Elder Marvin Davenport, Rt. 1, Auburntown, TN 37016
General Association: Mod., Elder Calvin Jenkins, 607 State Line Rd., Chattanooga, TN 37412. Tel. (615)867-2394; Clk., Rev. Randy Heart, Lexington, TN 38351

Elim Fellowship

The Elim Fellowship, a Pentecostal Body, established in 1947, is an outgrowth of the Elim Ministeral Fellowship, which was formed in 1933.

It is an association of churches, ministers and missionaries seeking to serve the whole Body of Christ. It is of Pentecostal conviction and charismatic orientation providing ministerial credentials and counsel and encouraging fellowship among local churches. Elim Fellowship sponsors leadership seminars at home and abroad, and serves as a transdenominational agency sending long-term, short-term, & tent-making missionaries to work with national movements.

GENERAL ORGANIZATION
Annual Representative Assemblies; Board of Administration meets semi-annually and Council of Elders meets bimonthly.

OFFICERS
Gen. Overseer, L. Dayton Reynolds, Elim Fellowship, Lima, NY 14485. Tel. (716) 582-2790
Asst. Gen. Overseer, Bernard J. Evans, 3727 Snowden Hill Rd., New Hartford, NY 13413. Tel. (315)736-0966
Gen. Sec., Chester Gretz, Elim Fellowship, Lima, NY 14485. Tel. (716) 582-2790.
Gen. Treas., Ronald Taylor, 451 Westfield Dr., Manlius, NY 13104. Tel. (315) 682-8282

The Episcopal Church

The Episcopal Church entered the colonies with the earliest settlers (Jamestown, Virginia, 1607) as the Church of England. After the American Revolution it became autonomous in 1789 as The Protestant Episcopal Church in the United States of America. (The Episcopal Church became the official alternate name in 1967.) Samuel Seabury of Connecticut was elected the first bishop and consecrated in Aberdeen by bishops of the Scottish Episcopal Church in 1784. In organizing as an independent body The Episcopal Church created a bicameral legislature, the General Convention, modeled after the new U.S. Congress. It comprises a House of Bishops and a House of Clerical and Lay Deputies and meets every three years. A 40-member Executive Council, which meets three times a year, is the interim governing body. An elected presiding bishop serves as Primate and Chief Pastor.

After severe setbacks in the years immediately following the Revolution because of its association with the British Crown and the fact that a number of its clergy and members were Loyalists, the church soon established its own identity and sense of mission. Spreading westward, it sent missionaries into the newly settled territories of the United States, establishing dioceses from coast to coast, and also undertook substantial missionary work in Africa, Latin America, and the Far East. Today the overseas dioceses are developing into independent provinces of the Anglican Communion, the worldwide fellowship of churches in communion with the Church of England the the Archbishop of Canterbury.

The beliefs and practices of The Episcopal Church, like those of other Anglican churches, are both Catholic and Reformed, with bishops in the apostolic succession and the historic creeds of Christendom regarded as essential elements of faith and order, along with the primary authority of Holy Scripture and the two chief sacraments of Baptism and Eucharist.

Churches: 7,360; Inclusive Membership: 2,455,422; Sunday or Sabbath Schools: N. R.; Total Enrollment: 556,168; Ordained Clergy: 14,694

GENERAL ORGANIZATION
General Convention: Triennial (Next meeting, July 11-20, 1991, Phoenix, AZ)
Headquarters: 815 Second Ave., New York, NY 10017. Tel. (212) 867-8400; 1-800-334-7626

OFFICERS OF THE GENERAL CONVENTION
Presiding Bishop and Primate, Most Rev. Edmond L. Browning; Sec., Ho. of Bishops, Rt. Rev. Herbert A. Donovan, Jr., Box 164668, Little Rock, AR 72216
Pres., Ho. of Deputies, V. Rev. David B. Collins, 815 Second Ave., New York, NY 10017; Vice-Pres., Ho. of Deputies, Mrs. Pamela P. Chinnis; Sec., Rev. Donald A. Nickerson, Jr.
Sec., of the Gen. Conv., Rev. Donald A. Nickerson, Jr.; Exec. Officer, Gen. Conv., Rev. Donald A. Nickerson, Jr.; Treas., Gen. Conv., Mrs. Ellen F. Cooke

THE EXECUTIVE COUNCIL
Pres. and Chpsn., Most Rev. Edmond L. Browning
Vice-Chpsn., V. Rev. David B. Collins
Vice-Pres., _____
Treas., Mrs. Ellen F. Cooke
Sec., Rev. Donald A. Nickerson, Jr.

The Domestic and Foreign Missionary Society of PECUSA:
Pres., Presiding Bishop, Most Rev. Edmond L. Browning
Treas., Mrs. Ellen F. Cooke
Sec., Rev. Donald A. Nickerson, Jr.
Board of Directors: Executive Council

EPISCOPAL CHURCH CENTER AND STAFF
Episcopal Church Center, 815 Second Ave., New York, NY 10017. Tel. (212)867-8400
Office of the Presiding Bishop: Presiding Bishop and Primate, Most Rev. Edmond L. Browning; Senior Exec. for Mission Operations, D. Barry Menuez; Exec. for Mission Support/Treas., Mrs. Ellen F. Cooke; Exec. for Mission Planning, Rt. Rev. Furman C. Stough; Deputy for Adm., Rev. Richard Chang; Deputy for Anglican Relationships, Rev. Patrick Mauney; Suffragan Bishop for Chaplaincies to Military, Prisons, and Hospitals, _____; Asst. Rev. Donald W. Beers; Suffragan Bishop for Europe and the Diaspora, Rt. Rev. Matthew P. Bigliardi; Exec. for Pastoral Development, The Rt. Rev. Harold A. Hopkins, Jr.; Exec. Officer, Gen. Conv., Rev. Donald A. Nickerson, Jr.

Stewardship/Development: Exec., _____; Staff Officer for Stewardship, Rev. Ronald Reed; Staff Officer for Planned Giving, Frederick H. Osborn III; Staff Officer for Congregational Development, Rev. Robert H. Bonner; Staff Officer for Stewardship Educ., Mrs. Laura E. Wright

Communication: Exec., Ms. Sonia J. Francis; News Dir., _____; Deputy News Dir., Dir. Publications, Frank Tedeschi; Asst. Dir. of Publications, Br. Tobias Haller; Video & Audiovisuals Producer, Whitney Smith; Electronic Media Dir., Clement W. K. Lee; Printing Production Dir., Robert Nangle; Art Dir., Ms. Rochelle Arthur; Eds., Ms. Julie Wortman, Bruce Campbell; Electronic Media Producer, _____

Education for Mission and Ministry: Exec., Rev. David Perry; Adm. Asst., Mrs. Ruby Miller; Field Officer for Educ. and Training, Dr. John D. Vogelsang; Coord. for Inst. of Higher Education, Dr. E. Nathaniel Porter; Youth Min. Coord., Rev. Sheryl Kujawa; Ministry Development Officer. Rev. John T. Docker; Evangelism Officer Rev. A. Wayne Schwab; Congreg. Devel., Rev. Arlin Rothauge; Prog. Resource Developer, Dr. Irene V. Jackson-Brown; Coord. for Children's Min., _____; Exec. Dir., Bd. for Theol. Educ., Rev. Preston T. Kelsey; Exec. Dir. Church Deployment Office, Mr. William A. Thompson; Exec. Dir., Office of Pastoral Development, Rt. Rev. Harold Hopkins; Suffragan Bishop for Chaplaincies to Military and Prisons, Rt. Rev. Charles Burgreen; Exec. Asst. Chaplain, Rev. Donald Beers

National Mission in Church and Society: Exec., Rev. Earl A. Neil; Staff Officer for Housing and Training, Howard Quander; Staff Officer for Coalition for Human Needs Commission, Ms. Gloria Brown; Staff Officer for Social and Specialized Min., Marcia L. Newcombe; Staff Officer for Black Min., Rev. Canon Harold T. Lewis; Staff Officer for Indian Min., Ms. Owanah B. Anderson; Staff Officer for Hispanic Min., Rev. Dr. Herbert Arrunategui; Staff Officer for Asiamerica Min., Rev. Winston W. Ching; Staff Officer for National Mission Development, Rev. Richard E. Gary; Women in Mission and Ministry, Ms. Ann Smith; Assoc. Ecumenical Officer for Washington Affairs, Rev. Robert Brooks; Staff Officer for Jubilee Min., Rev. Canon Peter P. Q. Golden; Public Issues Officer, Rev. Brian Grieves.

World Mission in Church and Society: Exec., Ms. Judith M. Gillespie; Adm. Asst., Br. James E. Treets, BSG; Deputy and Asia & Pacific Partnership Officer, Rev. J. Patrick Mauney; Africa Partnership Officer, Rev. Canon Burgess Carr; Latin America & Caribbean Partnership Officer, Rev. Ricardo T. Potter; Mission Information and Education Officer, Mrs. Margaret S. Larom; Coordinator Overseas Personnel, Rev. Mark Harris; Assoc. Overseas Leadership Training, Ms. Sonia Kelly; Assoc. Volunteers for Mission, Mrs. Dorothy Gist; Logistics Associate, Ms. Marcella Pambrun; Overseas Development Planning Officer, Mrs. Carolyn Rose-Avila; Ecumenical Relations Officer, Rev. William A. Norgren; Asst. Ecumenical Staff Officer, _____; United Thank Offering Staff Officer, Ms. Willeen V. Smith. Automations Supervisor, Ms. Rita M. Grant; Assistant for Program Adm. & Planning, Ms. Andrea L. Gerlin.

Presiding Bishops Fund for World Relief: Interim Exec. Dir., Ms. Bobbie Bevill; Asst. Dir. for Migration Affairs, Mrs. Marion M. Dawson; Asst. for Admin., Mrs. Nancy Marvel; Asst. for Interpretation and Network Development, Dr. David Crean; Communications/Information Officer Refugee/Migration, Rev. Gene T. White; Sponsorship Development Officer Refugee/Migration, Ms. Sarah Dresser.

Mission Support: Exec. and Treas., Mrs. Ellen F. Cooke; Asst. Treas., Louis H. Gill, Philippe Labbe; Dir. Mission Operation Support, Robert E. Brown; Controller, Clinton F. Best; Asst. Controller, Ms. Arlissa Salamone, Internal Auditor, Dr. Christopher Cabrera; Dir., MIS., Rev. Frederick J. Howard; Data Processing Super., Ms. Barbara Price; Clerical Super., Ms. Barbara Wilson

Administration: Service Manager, Terence Adair; Assist., Richard Corney; Human Resources Officer, Ms. Barbara Quinn; Asst. Human Resources Officer, James A. Lewis.

General Convention Executive Office: Exec. Officer, Rev. Donald A. Nickerson, Jr.; Sec. and Registrar, Rev. Donald A. Nickerson, Jr.; Deputy Registrar, Richard T. Biernacki, BSG; Treas., Mrs. Ellen F. Cooke; Asst., Ms. Cheryl J. Dawkins; Convention Mgr., Ms. Lori M. Arnold; Asst. Meeting Coord., Ms. Carolyn Sciortino; Ed., Rev. Charles Scott; Information Systems Mgr., Mrs. Diana Morris.

OFFICIAL AGENCIES

Church Pension Fund and Affiliates: Pres., Robert A. Robinson, 800 Second Ave., New York, NY 10017

Episcopal Church Building Fund: Exec., Rev. Sherrill Scales, Jr., 815 Second Ave., New York, NY 10017, Tel. (212) 697-6066

The Episcopal Church Foundation: Exec., Mr. Jeffrey H. Kittross, 815 Second Ave., New York, NY 10017. Tel. (212) 698-2858

Archives of The Episcopal Church: Dr. V.Nelle Bellamy, Archivist

PUBLICATIONS

Episcopal Life (m), 815 2nd Ave., New York, NY 10017. Jerrold Hames, Ed.

Forward Movement Publications: 412 Sycamore St., Cincinnati, OH 45202. Rev. Charles H. Long, Ed. Tel. (513)721-6659.

The Living Church (w), 407 E. Michigan St., Milwaukee, WI 53202, Rev. H. Boone Porter, Jr. Ed.

Historical Magazine (q), Box 2247, Austin, TX 78705, Rev. J. F. Woolverton, Ed.

The Churchman (m), 1074 23rd Ave., N., St. Petersburg, FL 33704, Edna Ruth Johnson

Anglican Theol. Review (q), 600 Haven St., Evanston, IL 60201, Rev. W. Taylor Stevenson, Seabury-Western Theological Seminary, 2122 Sheridan Rd., Evanston, IL 60201

Pan-Anglican (occ.), 1335 Asylum Ave., Hartford, CT 06105

Cathedral Age, Mt. St. Albans, Washington, DC, Nancy Montgomery, Ed.

The Episcopal Church Annual, 78 Danbury Rd., Wilton, CT 06897, E. Allen Kelly, Ed.

Episcopal Clerical Directory, Church Pension Fund, 800 Second Ave., New York, NY 10017

St. Luke's Journal of Theology, The School of Theology, University of South, Sewanee, TN 37375

ACTIVE BISHOPS IN THE U.S.A.

(Note: C, Coadjutor; S, Suffragan; A, Assistant)
(Address: Right Reverend)

Headquarters Staff: Presiding Bishop and Primate, The Most Rev. Edmond L. Browning; Field Officer, Rt. Rev. Harold Hopkins; Suffragan Bishop for Chaplaincies to Military, Prisons and Hospitals, _____

Alabama, Robert O. Miller, 521 N. 20th St., _____ Birmingham 35203

Alaska, George C. Harris, Box 441, Fairbanks 99707

Albany, Rt. Rev. David S. Ball, 62 S. Swan St., Albany, NY 12210

Arizona, Joseph T. Heistand, P.O. Box 13647, Phoenix 85002

Arkansas, Herbert Donovan, Jr., 300 W. 17th St., P.O. Box 6120, Little Rock 72206

Atlanta, Frank Kellog Allan, 2744 Peachtree Rd. N.W., Atlanta, GA 30305

Bethlehem, J. Mark Dyer, 333 Wyandotte St., Bethlehem, PA 18015

California, William E. Swing, 1055 Taylor St., San Francisco 94108

Central Florida, William H. Folwell, 324 N. Interlachen Ave., Box 790, Winter Park, 32789

Central Gulf Coast, Charles F. Duvall, P.O. Box 8547, Mobile, AL 36608

Central N.Y., O'Kelley Whitaker, 310 Montgomery St., Syracuse 13203

Central Pennsylvania, Charlie F. McNutt, 221 N. Front St., Harrisburg 17101, P.O. Box W, Harrisburg 17108

Chicago, Frank T. Griswold III, 65 E. Huron St., Chicago, IL 60611

Colorado, William C. Frey, William Harvey Wolfrum (S), P.O. Box M, Capitol Hill Sta., Denver 80218

Connecticut, Arthur E. Walmsley; Clarence N. Coleridge (S); Jeffrey William Rowthorn (S), 1335 Asylum Ave., Hartford 06105

Dallas, Donis D. Patterson; 1630 Garrett St., Dallas, TX 75206

Delaware, Calvin C. Tennis, 2020 Tatnall St., Wilmington 19802

East Carolina, B. Sidney Sanders, P.O. Box 1336, Kinston, NC 28501

East Tennessee, William E. Sanders, Box 3807, Knoxville, TN 37917

Eastern Oregon, Rustin R. Kimsey, P.O. Box 620, The Dalles, OR 97058

Easton, Elliott L. Sorge, P.O. Box 1027, Easton, MD 21601

Eau Claire, William C. Wantland, 510 S. Farwell St., Eau Claire, WI 54701

El Camino Real, C. Shannon Mallory, P.O. Box 1903, Monterey, CA 93940

Florida, Frank S. Cerveny, 325 Market St., Jacksonville 32202

Fond du Lac, William L. Stevens, P.O. Box 149, Fond du Lac, WI 54935

Fort Worth, Clarence Cullam Pope, Jr., 3572 Southwest Loop 820, Fort Worth, TX 76133

Georgia, Harry W. Shipps, 611 East Bay St., Savannah 31401

Hawaii, Donald P. Hart, Queen Emma Square, Honolulu 96813

Idaho, _____, IV, Box 936, Boise 83701

Indianapolis, Edward W. Jones, 1100 W. 42nd St., Indianapolis 46208

Iowa, C. Christopher Epling, 225 37th St., Des Moines 50312

Kansas, William E. Smalley, Bethany Place, Topeka 66612

Kentucky, David B. Reed, 421 S. 2nd St., Louisville 40202

Lexington, Don A. Wimberly, 530 Sayre Ave., Lexington, KY 40508

Long Island, Robert Campbell Witcher, Henry B. Hucles, III (S), 36 Cathedral Ave., Garden City, NY 11530

Los Angeles, Frederick H. Brosch, Oliver B. Garver, Jr. (S), 1220 W. 4th St., Los Angeles, CA 90017

Louisiana, James Barrow Brown, P.O. Box 15719, New Orleans 70175

Maine, Edward C. Chalfant, 143 State St., Portland 04101

Maryland, A. Theodore Eastman; Barry Valentine (A), 105 W. Monument St., Baltimore 21230

Massachusetts, David Elliott Johnson, Morris F. Arnold (S), Barbara Harris (S), 1 Joy St., Boston 02108

Michigan, H. Coleman McGehee, Jr., Harry Irving Mayson (S); William J. Gordon (A), 4800 Woodward Ave., Detroit 48201

Milwaukee, Roger J. White, 804 E. Juneau Ave., Milwaukee, WI 53202

Minnesota, Robert M. Anderson, 309 Clifton Ave., Minneapolis 55403

Mississippi, Duncan M. Gray, Jr., P.O. Box 1636, Jackson 39205

Missouri, William Augustus Jones, Jr., 1210 Locust St., St. Louis 63103

Montana, Charles I. Jones, 515 North Park Ave., Helena 59601

Nebraska, James Daniel Warner, 200 N. 62nd St., Omaha 68132

Nevada, Stewart C. Zabriskie, 2930 W. 7th St., Reno 89503

New Hampshire, Douglas E. Theuner, 63 Green St., Concord 03301

New Jersey, G. P. Mellick Belshaw, Vincent K. Pettit (S), 808 W. State St., Trenton 08618

New York, Richard F. Grein, Walter D. Dennis (S), 1047 Amsterdam Ave., New York 10025

Newark, John Shelby Spong, 24 Rector St., Newark, NJ 07102

North Carolina, Robert W. Estill; Frank Harris Vest, Jr. (S), 201 St. Alban's, P.O. Box 17025, Raleigh 27609

North Dakota, Harold A. Hopkins Jr., 809 8th Ave. S., Fargo 58102

Northern California, John L. Thompson, III, 1322 27th St., P.O. Box 161268, Sacramento 95816

Northern Indiana, Frank C. Gray, 117 N. Lafayette Blvd., South Bend 46601

Northern Michigan, Thomas K. Ray, 131 E. Ridge St., Marquette 49855

Northwest Texas, Sam Byron Hulsey, Texas Commerce Bank Bldg., Ste. 506, 1314 Ave. K, P.O. Box 1067, Lubbock 79408

Northwestern Pennsylvania, Donald J. Davis, 145 W. 6th St., Erie, PA 16501

Ohio, James R. Moodey, Arthur B. Williams (S), 2230 Euclid Ave., Cleveland, 44115

Oklahoma, Gerald N. McAllister P. O. Box 1098; William J. Cox (A)

Olympia, Robert H. Cochrane, 1551 Tenth Ave., East, Seattle, WA 98102

Oregon, Robert Louis Ladehoff, 11800 SW Military La., Portland 97219, P.O. Box 467, Portland, OR 97034

Pennsylvania, Allan C. Bartlett, Franklin D. Turner (S), 1700 Market St., Ste. 1600, Philadelphia 19103

Pittsburgh, Alden M. Hathaway, 325 Oliver Ave., Pittsburgh, PA 15222

Quincy, Edward H. MacBurney, 3601 N. North St., Peoria, IL 61604

Rhode Island, George Hunt, 275 N. Main St., Providence 02903

Rio Grande, Terence Kellshaw, 4304 Carlisle NE, Albuquerque, NM 87107

Rochester, William G. Burrill, Jr., 935 East Ave., Rochester, NY 14607

San Diego, C. Brinkley Morton, St. Paul's Church, 2728 6th Ave., San Diego, CA 92103

San Joaquin, David Schofield, 4159 East Dakota, Fresno, CA 93726

South Carolina, C. FitzSimons Allison, G. Edward Haynesworth (A), 1020 King St., Drawer 2127, Charleston 29403

South Dakota, Craig B. Anderson, 200 W. 18th St., P.O. Box 517, Sioux Falls 57101

Southeast Florida, Calvin O. Schofield, Jr., 525 NE 15 St., Miami 33132

Southern Ohio, William G. Black, Herbert Thompson, Jr. (C), 412 Sycamore St., Cincinnati 45202

Southern Virginia, Claude Charles Vaché, 600 Talbot Hill Rd., Norfolk 23505

Southwest Florida, Roger S. Harris; Box 20899, St. Petersburg 33742

Southwestern Virginia, A Heath Light, P.O. Box 2068, Roanoke 24009

Spokane, Leigh Allen Wallace, Jr., 245 E. 13th Ave., Spokane 99202

Springfield, Donald M. Hultstrand, 821 S. 2nd St., Springfield, IL 62704

Tennessee, George Lazenby Reynolds, Box 3807, Knoxville, TN 37917

Texas, Maurice M. Benitez, Gordon T. Charlton (S); Anselmo Carroll (A), 520 San Jacinto St., Houston 77002

Upper South Carolina, William A. Beckham; Rogers Sanders Harris, (S), P.O. Box 1789, Columbia 29202

Utah, George E. Bates, 231 E. First St. South, Salt Lake City 84111

Vermont, Daniel L. Swenson, Rock Point, Burlington 05401

Virginia, Peter J. Lee, David H. Lewis, Jr. (S), 110 W. Franklin St., Richmond 23220

Washington, Interim, Ronald Haines (S), Mt. St. Alban, Washington, DC 20016

West Missouri, Arthur Vogel, 415 W. 13th St., P.O. Box 23216, Kansas City 64141

West Tennessee, Alex D. Dickson, 692 Poplar Ave., Memphis, TN 38105

West Texas, John H. McNaughton, Earl N. MacArthur (S), P.O. Box 6885, San Antonio 78209

West Virginia, Robert P. Atkinson; William Franklin Carr (S), 1608 Virginia St. E., Charleston, 25311

Western Kansas, John F. Ashby, 142 S. 8th St., P.O. Box 1383, Salina 67401

Western Louisiana, Willis R. Henton, P. O. Box 4046, Alexandria, LA 71301

Western Massachusetts, Andrew F. Wissemann, 37 Chestnut St., Springfield 01103

Western Michigan, Howard S. Meeks, 2600 Vincent Ave., Kalamazoo 49001

Western New York, David C. Bowman, 1114 Delaware Ave., Buffalo 14209

Western North Carolina, William G. Weinhauer, P.O. Box 368, Black Mountain 28711

Wyoming, Bob Gordon Jones, 104 S. 4th St., Box 1007, Laramie 82070

American Churches in Europe—Jurisdiction, Matthew P. Bigliardi, The American Cathedral, 23 Avenue Georges V, 75008, Paris, France

Navajoland Area Mission, Steven Plummer, P.O. Box 720, Farmington, NM 47401

The Estonian Evangelical Lutheran Church

The Estonian Evangelical Lutheran Church (EELC) was founded in 1917 in Estonia and reorganized in Sweden in 1944. The teachings of the EELC are based on the Old and New Testaments, explained through the Apostolic, Nicean and Athanasian confessions, the unaltered Confession of Augsburg and other teachings found in the Book of Concord.

Churches: 24; Inclusive Membership: 7,399; Sunday or Sabbath Schools: N.R.; Total Enrollment: N.R.; Ordained Clergy: 19

GENERAL ORGANIZATION

Executive Board headed by the Archbishop, Consisterium, Auditing Committee and District Conference.
Headquarters: 383 Jarvis St., Toronto, Ontario, Canada M4A 2R3. Bishop Karl Raudsepp, Ed.

OFFICERS

Bishop in North America, Rev. Karl Raudsepp, 30 Sunrise Ave., Apt. 216, Toronto, Ontario, Canada M4A 2R3
Assts. to the Bishop: Dean U. Petersoo, 383 Jarvis St., Toronto, Ontario, Canada M5B 2C7, Rev. T. Nommik, 3 Mapleside Ave., Hamilton, Ont., Canada L8P 3Y4

PERIODICAL

Eesti Kirik (m), 383 Jarvis St., Toronto, Ontario, Canada M4A 2R3. Bishop Karl Raudsepp, Ed.

Ethical Culture Movement

A national federation of Ethical Humanist Societies—religious and educational fellowships based on ethics, believing in the worth, dignity, and fine potentialities of the individual, encouraging freedom of thought, committed to the democratic ideal and method, issuing in social action.

Churches: 21; Inclusive Membership: 3,212; Sunday or Sabbath Schools: 12; Total Enrollment: 357; Ordained Clergy: 43

AMERICAN ETHICAL UNION

Assembly: annual (June)
Headquarters: 2 West 64th St., New York, NY 10023. Tel. (212) 873-6500

OFFICERS

Pres., Ron Solomon
Vice-Pres., Paul Farbman
Treas., Sophie Meyer
Sec., Annabelle Glasser
Adm., Margaretha E. Jones
Dir. Rel. Education, Pat Hoertdoerfer
Washington Ethical Action Office, Herb Blinder

ORGANIZATIONS

National Leaders Council, Chpsn., Joseph Chuman
National Service Conference, Pres., Lotte Bernard
A.E.U. Weis Ecology Center, Dir., James Markstein
International Humanist & Ethical Union, Representative, Dr. Matthew Ies Spetter, Joseph Chuman

The Evangelical Church

The Evangelical Church was born June 4, 1968, in Portland, Oregon, when 46 congregations and about 80 ministers, under the leadership of V. A. Ballantyne and George Millen, met in an organizing session. Within two weeks a group of about twenty churches and thirty ministers from the Evangelical United Brethren and Methodist churches in Montana and North Dakota became a part of the new church. Richard Kienitz and Robert Strutz were the superintendents.

Under the leadership of Superintendent Robert Trosen, the former Holiness Methodist Church became a part of the Evangelical Church in 1969, bringing its membership and a flourishing mission field in Bolivia. The Wesleyan Covenant Church joined in 1977, with its missionary work in Mexico, in Brownsville, Texas, and among the Navajos in New Mexico.

The Evangelical Church in Canada, where T. J. Jesske was superintendent, became an autonomous organization on June 5, 1970. In 1982, after years of discussions with the Evangelical Church of North America, a founding General Convention was held at Billings, Montana, where the two churches united.

The following distinctive guide the life, program, and devotion of this church: faithful, biblical, and sensible preaching and teaching of those truths proclaimed by the scholars of the Wesleyan-Arminian viewpoint; an itinerant system which reckons with the rights of individuals and the desires of the congregations; local ownership of all local church properties and assets.

The church is affiliated with the Christian Holiness Association, the National Association of Evangelicals, World Gospel Mission, and OMS International. Through the two latter agencies and the mission in Bolivia, more than 55 of the denomination's more than 115 missionaries have been appointed. The Evangelical Church continues to grow as congregations join and new churches are planted.

GENERAL ORGANIZATION

Denominational Council: quadrennially

Executive Council: annually

OFFICERS

Gen. Supt., Dr. George K. Millen, 3223 S.E. Deswell, Portland, OR 97267.

Gen. Supt. Chmn. of Denominational and Exec. Councils, Dr. George K. Millen, 7525 SE Lake Rd., Ste. #7, Milwauie OR 97267. Tel. (503)652-1029

PERIODICAL

Overview (q), George Millen, Ed.

Evangelical Congregational Church

This denomination had its beginning in the movement known as the Evangelical Association, organized by Jacob Albright in the early nineteenth century. In 1891 a division occurred in the Evangelical Association, which resulted in the organization of the United Evangelical Church in 1894. An attempt to heal this division was made in 1922, but a portion of the United Evangelical Church was not satisfied with the plan of merger and remained apart, taking the above name in 1928. This denomination is Arminian in doctrine, evangelistic in spirit, and Methodistic in church government, with congregational ownership of local church property.

Congregations are located basically from New Jersey to Illinois. A denominational center is located in Myerstown, Penn., as well as a retirement village and a seminary, Evangelical School of Theology. Three summer youth camps and three camp meetings continue evangelistic outreach. A worldwide missions movement includes conferences in North East India, Liberia, Mexico, and Japan. The denomination is a member of National Association of Evangelicals.

Churches: 156; Inclusive Membership: 33,318; Sunday or Sabbath Schools: 153; Total Enrollment: 17,510; Ordained Clergy: 197

GENERAL ORGANIZATION

General Conference: quadrennial. (Next meeting, Sept. 1990)

Headquarters: Evangelical Congregational Church Center, 100 W. Park Ave., P. O. Box 186, Myerstown, PA 17067

Presiding Bishop, Dr. Richard A. Cattermole, Myerstown, PA 17067

Dir. of Church Ministries, Rev. Keith R. Miller, Myerstown, PA 17067

Dir. of Christian Education, Rev. Donald Metz, Myerstown, PA 17067

Dir. of Missions, Rev. David G. Hornberger, Myerstown, PA 17067

OFFICERS

1st Vice-Chpsn., Rev. David C. Greulich, 1717 W. Livingston St., Allentown, PA 18104

2nd Vice-Chpsn., Rev. Robert M. Daneker, Sr., 122 S. Emerson St., Allentown, PA 18104

Sec., Rev. E. J. Vondran, 130 Wyomissing Ave., Shillington, PA 19607

Asst. Sec's.: Rev. Robert Stahl, Lebanon, PA and Rev. Keigh Mong, Seneca, PA

Stat. Sec., Rev. Carl Fetterhoff, 750 N. Second St., Reading, PA 19601

Treas., Stanley Heimbach, Evangelical Congregational Church, Myerstown, PA 17067

Dir. of Missions, Rev. David G. Hornberger, P.O. Box 186, Myerstown, PA 17067

Supt., E. C. Church Retirement Village, Rev. Franklin H. Schock, Myerstown, PA 17067

Pres., Evangelical School of Theology, Dr. Ray A. Seilhamer, Myerstown, PA 17067

OTHER ORGANIZATIONS

Administrative Council: Chpsn., Bishop Richard A. Cattermole; Vice-Chpsn., Rev. Robert W. Zetterberg; Treas., Stanley Heimbach

Div. of Evangelism and Spiritual Care: Chpsn., Rev. Richard A. Cattermole, Myerstown, PA

Div. of Church Ministries: Chpsn., Rev. Keith R. Miller, Myerstown, PA 17067

Div. of Church Services: Chpsn., Keith M. Miller, Myerstown, PA 17067

Div. of Missions: Chpsn., Rev. David G. Hornberger, Myerstown, PA 17067

Board of Pensions: Pres., Mr. Homer Luckenbill, Jr., Pine Grove, PA; Sec., Dr. J. D. Yoder, Myerstown, PA

PERIODICALS

The United Evangelical (m), Rev. D. H. Reed, Ed. Pub., Church Center Press, Myerstown, PA

The Evangelical Covenant Church

The Evangelical Covenant Church has its roots in historical Christianity as it emerged in the Protestant Reformation, in the biblical instruction of the Lutheran State Church of Sweden, and in the great spiritual awakenings of the nineteenth century. These three influences have in large measure shaped its development and are to be borne in mind in seeking to understand its distinctive spirit.

The Covenant Church adheres to the affirmations of the Protestant Reformation regarding the Holy Scriptures, the Old and the New Testament, as the Word of God and the only perfect rule for faith, doctrine, and conduct. It has traditionally valued the historic confessions of the Christian church, particularly the Apostles' Creed, while at the same time it has emphasized the sovereignty of the Word over all creedal interpretations. It has especially cherished the pietistic restatement of the doctrine of justification by faith as basic to its dual task of evangelism and Christian nurture, the New Testament emphasis upon personal faith in Jesus Christ as Savior and Lord, the reality of a fellowship of believers which recognizes but transcends theological differences, and the belief in baptism and the Lord's Supper as divinely ordained sacraments of the church.

While the denomination has traditionally practiced the baptism of infants, in conformity with its principle of freedom it has given room to divergent views. The principle of personal freedom, so highly esteemed by the Covenant, is to be distinguished from the individualism that disregards the centrality of the Word of God and the mutual responsibilities and disciplines of the spiritual community.

Churches: 584; Inclusive Membership: 87,750; Sunday or Sabbath Schools: 532; Total Enrollment: 74,922; Ordained Clergy: 1,260

GENERAL ORGANIZATION

General Conference: annual (June 20-24, 1990)

Headquarters: 5101 N. Francisco Ave., Chicago, IL 60625. Tel. (312) 784-3000

OFFICERS

Pres., Dr. Paul E. Larsen, Chicago, IL

Vice-Pres., Rev. Timothy C. Ek, Chicago, IL

Sec., John R. Hunt, Chicago, IL

Treas., Robert T. Jackson, Naperville, IL

ADMINISTRATIVE BOARDS

Board of Christian Education and Discipleship: Chpsn., Dr. John C. Pearson; Sec., Rev. Stanley Olsen; Exec. Sec., Christian Education and Discipleship, Rev. Evelyn M. R. Johnson

Board of Church Growth and Evangelism: Chpsn., Rev. Steven W. Armfield; Sec., Rev. Philip K. Brockett; Exec. Sec., Dr. Robert C. Larson

Board of Covenant Women: Chpsn., Mrs. Ruth West; Sec., Mrs. Gwen Bagaas; Exec. Sec., Rev. Deirdre M. Bank

Board of Human Resources: Chpsn., Rev. Everett L. Wilson; Sec., Rev. William H. Liljegren

Board of the Ministry: Chpsn., Rev. Glen R. Palmberg; Sec., Rev. Wendell E. Danielson; Exec. Sec. of the Ministry, Rev. Donald A. Njaa

Board of Pensions: Chpsn., William J. Kelley; Sec. & Dir. of Pensions, Rev. Donald A. Njaa

Board of Publication: Chpsn., Rev. Donn W. Anderson; Sec., Rev. Carol J. Nordstrom; Exec. Sec. of Publications, Rev. James R. Hawkinson

Board of World Mission: Chpsn., Rev. Donald E. Logue; Sec., Rev. Neil E. White; Exec. Sec., World Mission, Rev. Raymond L. Dahlberg

Board of Benevolence: Chpsn., Robert H. Peterson; Sec., Lawrence P. Anderson; Pres. of Covenant Benevolent Institutions, Nils G. Axelson, 5145 N. California Ave., Chicago, IL 60625

Board of Directors of North Park College and Theological Seminary: Chpsn., Dean A. Lundgren; Sec., Dr. Kristine E. Strand; Pres., Dr. David G. Horner, 3225 W. Foster Ave., Chicago, IL 60625

PERIODICALS

Covenant Companion (m), Chicago, IL, Rev. James R. Hawkinson, Ed.

Covenant Quarterly (q), Chicago, IL, Dr. Wayne C. Weld, Ed.

Covenant Home Altar (q), Chicago, IL, Rev. James R. Hawkinson, Ed.

The Evangelical Free Church of America

In October 1884, 27 representatives from Swedish churches met in Boone, Iowa, to establish the Swedish Evangelical Free Church. In the fall of that same year, two Norwegian-Danish groups began worship and fellowship (in Boston and in Tacoma) and by 1912 had established the Norwegian-Danish Evangelical Free Church Association. These two denominations, representing 275 congregations, came together at a merger conference in 1950.

The Evangelical Free Church is an association of local, autonomous churches across the United States and Canada, blended together around common principles, policies, and practices. A 12-point statement addresses the major doctrines, but also provides for differences of understanding on minor issues of faith and practice.

Overseas outreach includes 324 career, 56 apprentice in missions (one to two years) and 8 short termers, serving on mission fields in 15 countries.

GENERAL ORGANIZATION

Conference: annual
Home Office: 1515 E. 66 St., Minneapolis, MN 55423. Tel. (612) 866-3343

OFFICERS

Pres., Dr. Thomas A. McDill, 1515 E. 66th St., Minneapolis, MN 55423
Pres. Emeritus, Dr. Arnold T. Olson, 6126 Park Ave., Minneapolis, MN 55417

Mod., Rev. Michael P. Andrus, 13172 Dougherty Ridge Ct., St. Louis, MO 63131
Vice-Mod., Kenneth R. Larson, 3060 Centerville Rd., Little Canada, MN 551117
Gen. Sec., Mr. Ronald O. Sollie, 4201 13th Ave. S., Minneapolis, MN 55407
Vice-Sec., Mr. Gene Hugoson, Rt. 2, Box 218, Granada, MN 56039
Fin. Sec., Mr. Gordon Johnson, 2114 Cedar Dr., Rapid City, SD 57702
Treas., Gordon Engdahl, 10455 N. Hadley Circle, White Bear lake, MN 551110
Exec. Dir. of Overseas Missions, Rev. Robert Dillon, 1515 E. 66th St., Minneapolis, MN 55423
Interim Exec. Dir. of Church Ministries, Dr. Milo Lundell, 1515 E. 66th St., Minneapolis, MN 55423

PERIODICAL

Evangelical Beacon (semi-m), 1515 E. 66 St., Minneapolis, MN 55423 George Keck, Ed.

Evangelical Friends Alliance

Formed in 1965 as an organization representing one corporate step of denominational unity, brought about as a result of several movements of spiritual renewal within the Society of Friends. These movements are: (1) the general evangelical renewal within Christianity, (2) the New scholarly recognition of the evangelical nature of seventeenth century Quakerism, and (3) the Association of Evangelical Friends, the predecessor to EFA.

The EFA is conservative in theology and makes use of local pastors. Sunday morning worship includes singing, Scripture reading, a period of open worship—usually—and a sermon by the pastor.

YEARLY MEETINGS

Evangelical Friends Church, Eastern Region, Ron Johnson, 1201 - 30th St. N.W., Canton, OH 44709
Rocky Mountain YM, John Brawner, P.O. Box 9629, Colorado Springs, CO 80932
Mid-America YM, Ed Key, 2018 Maple, Wichita, KS 67213
Northwest YM, Mark Ankeny, 600 E. Third St., Newberg, OR 97132

Evangelical Lutheran Church in America

The Evangelical Lutheran Church in America (ELCA) was organized April 20-May 3, 1987, in Columbus, Ohio, bringing together the 2.3 million-member American Lutheran Church, the 2.9 million-member Lutheran Church in America, and the 100,000-member Association of Evangelical Lutheran Churches.

The ELCA is both the youngest and at the same time, through its predecessor church bodies, the oldest of the major U.S. Lutheran churches. Its roots stretch back to the mid-17th century when a Dutch Lutheran congregation was formed in New Amsterdam (now New York). Most of the oldest congregations, however, were the result of early German and Scandinavian immigration, dating from the first part of the 18th century, to Delaware, Pennsylvania, the Hudson and Mohawk River Valleys in New York, and the Piedmont region of the Carolinas.

The first Lutheran association of congregations, the Pennsylvania Ministerium, was organized in 1748 under Henry Melchior Muhlenberg, known as the patriarch of American Lutheranism.

In 1820, a national federation of synods, the General Synod, was formed. A split in 1867 resulted in a second major body, the General Council. Earlier, as a result of the Civil War, southern synods had broken away from the

General Synod to form the United Synod in the South. These three bodies were reunited in 1918 as the United Lutheran Church in America.

In 1962, the Lutheran Church in America (LCA) was formed by a merger of the United Lutheran Church with the Augustana Lutheran Church, founded in 1860 by Swedish immigrants; the American Evangelical Lutheran Church, founded in 1872 by Danish immigrants; and the Finnish Lutheran Church or Suomi Synod, founded in 1891 by Finnish immigrants.

Two years before the LCA was formed, the American Lutheran Church (ALC) was created through a merger of an earlier American Lutheran Church, which was formed in 1930 by four synods that traced their roots primarily to German immigration; the Evangelical Lutheran Church, which dated from 1917 through a merger of churches chiefly of Norwegian ethnic heritage; and the United Evangelical Lutheran Church in America, which arose from Danish immigration. On February 1, 1963, the Lutheran Free Church merged with the ALC.

The Association of Evangelical Lutheran Churches arose in 1976 from a doctrinal split with the Lutheran Church—Missouri Synod.

The ELCA, through its predecessor church bodies, was a founding member of the Lutheran World Federation, the World Council of Churches, and the National Council of the Churches of Christ in the USA.

Churchwide office of the ELCA is in Chicago. The church is divided into 65 geographical areas, or synods. These 65 synods, in turn, are grouped into nine regional centers for mission, joint programs, and service.

Churches: 11,120; Inclusive Membership: 5,251,534; Sunday or Sabbath Schools: 10,125; Total Enrollment: 1,166,059; Ordained Clergy: 16,083

GENERAL ORGANIZATION

Churchwide Assembly meets biennially. Next meeting, 1991, in Orlando, FL
Churchwide Office: 8765 West Higgins Road, Chicago, IL 60631. Tel. (312)380-2700

OFFICERS

Bishop, The Rev. Dr. Herbert W. Chilstrom
Sec., The Rev. Dr. Lowell G. Almen
Treas., George E. Aker
Vice Pres., Christine H. Grumm
Office of the Bishop: Exec. for Adm., Rev. Dr. Robert N. Bacher; Exec. Asst. for Federal Chaplaincies, Rev. Lloyd W. Lyngdal; Exec. Assts., Lita B. Johnson and Rev. Dr. Morris A. Sorenson

OFFICES

Office for Ecumenical Affairs, Exec. Dir., Rev. Dr. William G. Rusch; Stnd. Comm. Chpsn., Rev. Dr. Edward D. Schneider
Office for Finance, Treas., George E. Aker; Stnd. Comm. Chpsn., Richard L. McAuliffe
Office for Personnel, Exec. Dir., A. C. Stein; Stnd. Comm. Chpsn., Patsy Gottschalk
Office for Research, Planning and Evaluation, Exec. Dir., Ruth Ann Killion; Stnd. Comm. Chpsn., Helen R. Harms

DIVISIONS

Division for Congregational Life, Exec. Dir., Rev. Eldon G. DeWeerth; Board Chpsn., Susan Hermodson; Lutheran Youth Organization, Pres., Brian King

Division for Education, Exec. Dir., Rev. Dr. W. Robert Sorensen; Board Chpsn., Rev. Dennis H. Dickman
Division for Global Missions, Exec. Dir., Rev. Dr. Mark W. Thomsen; Board Chpsn., Rev. Dr. William E. Lesher
Division for Ministry, Exec. Dir., Rev. Dr. Joseph M. Wagner; Board Chpsn., E. Marlene Wilson
Division for Outreach, Exec. Dir., Rev. Dr. Malcolm L. Minnick, Jr.; Board Chpsn., Nancy Lee Atkins
Division for Social Ministry Organizations, Exec. Dir., Rev. Charles S. Miller, Board Chpsn., Pamela J. Berven

COMMISSIONS

Commission for Church in Society, Exec. Dir., Rev. Dr. Jerald L. Folk; Board Chpsn., Kathleen L. Hurty
Commission for Communication, Exec. Dir., Carol Becker Smith, Board Chpsn., Robert E. A. Lee
Commission for Financial Support, Exec. Dir., Rev. Paul A. Johns; Board Chpsn., Rev. Donald J. Hillerich; Lutheran Laity Movement, Dir., James W. Pellot
Commission for Multicultural Ministries, Exec. Dir., Rev. Craig J. Lewis; Board Chpsn., Pelagie Snesrud
Commission for Women, Exec. Dir., Christine Myers Crist, Board Chpsn., Doris Pagelkopf

CHURCHWIDE UNITS

Conference of Bishops, Exec. Dir., Rev. Dr. Edwin Bersagel; Chpsn. Rev. Dr. Paul Werger
ELCA Foundation, Exec. Dir., Rev. Dr. Harvey A. Stegemoeller. ELCA Publishing House, Exec. Dir., Albert E. Anderson; Board Chpsn., Rev. Dr. H. George Anderson. Board of Pensions, Exec. Dir., John G. Kapanke; Board Chpsn., Mildred M. Berg. Women of the ELCA, Exec. Interim Dir., Doris E. Strieter, Board Chpsn., Jeanne W. Rapp

SYNODICAL BISHOPS

Region 1
Alaska, Rev. Donald D. Parsons, 4201 Tudor Centre Rd., Ste. 315, Anchorage, AK 99516, Tel. (907)561-8899
Northwestern Washington, Rev. Lowell E. Knutson, 5519 Pinney Ave., N. Seattle, WA 98103, Tel. (206)783-9292
Southwestern Washington, Rev. David C. Wold, 420 121st St., S., Tacoma, WA 98444, Tel. (206)535-8300
Eastern Washington-Idaho, Rev. Robert M. Keller, S. 314-A, Spokane, WA 99204, Tel. (509)838-7987
Oregon, Rev. Paul R. Swanson, 2801 N. Gantebein, Portland, OR 97227, Tel. (503)280-4191
Montana, Rev. Dr. Norman G. Wick, 2415 13th Ave. S., Great Falls, MT 59405, Tel. (406)453-1461
Regional Coordinator: Ronald Coen, Region 1 Center for Mission, 766-B John St., Seattle, WA 98109, Tel. (206)624-0093

Region 2
Northern California-Northern Nevada, Rev. Lyle G. Miller, 401 Roland Way, #240, Oakland, CA 94641, Tel. (415)430-0500
Southern California (West), Rev. J. Roger Anderson, 1340 S. Bonnie Brae St., Los Angeles, CA 90006, Tel. (213)387-8183
Southern California (East)-Hawaii, Rev. Robert L. Miller, 23655 Via Del Rio, Ste. B, Yorba Linda, CA 92686. Tel. (714)970-2791
Arizona-Southern Nevada, Rev. Dr. Howard E. Wennes, 4423 N. 24th St., Ste. 400, Phoenix, AZ 85016. Tel. (602)957-3223

Rocky Mountain, Rev. Dr. Wayne Weissenbuehler, ABS Bldg., #101, 7000 Broadway, Denver, CO 80211. Tel. (303)427-7554
Regional Coordinator: Patricia Robertson, Region 2 Center for Mission, 2700 Chandler, Ste. A6, Las Vegas, NV 89120. Tel. (702)798-3980

Region 3
Western North Dakota, Rev. Robert D. Lynne, 721 Memorial Way, P.O. Box 370, Bismarck, ND 58502, Tel. (701)223-5312
Eastern North Dakota, Rev. Dr. Wesley N. Haugen, 1703 32nd Ave., S., Fargo, ND 58107, Tel. (701)232-3381
South Dakota, Rev. Norman D. Eitrheim, Augustana College, Sioux Falls, SD 57197, Tel. (605)336-4011
Northwestern Minnesota, Rev. Dr. Harold R. Lohr, P.O. Box 678, Moorhead, MN 56560. Tel. (218)299-3019
Northwestern Minnesota, Rev. Roger L. Munson, 3900 London Rd., Duluth, MN 55804, Tel. (218)525-1947
Southwestern Minnesota, Rev. Dr. Darold H. Beekmann, P. O. Box 277, Redwood Falls, MN 56283, Tel. (507)637-3904
West Metropolitan Minnesota, Rev. David W. Olson, 122 W. Franklin Ave., Rm. 600, Minneapolis, MN 55404. Tel. (612)870-3610
East Metropolitan Minnesota, Rev. Lowell O. Erdahl, 105 W. University Ave., St. Paul, MN 55103, Tel. (612)224-4313
Southeastern Minnesota, Rev. Glenn W. Nycklemoe, Assisi Heights, P. O. Box 4900, 1001-14 St., NW, Rochester, MN 55903. Tel. (507)280-9457
Regional Coordinator: Ms. Shirley Teig, Region 3 Center for Mission, Brockman Hall, 2481 Como Ave., W. St. Paul, MN 55108. Tel. (612)649-0454

Region 4
Nebraska, Rev. Dr. Dennis A. Anderson, 124 S. 24th St., Ste. 204, Omaha, NE 68102, Tel. (402)341-4155
Missouri-Kansas, Rev. Dr. Charles H. Maahs, 6400 Glenwood, Ste. 210, Shawnee Mission, KS 66202. Tel. (913)362-0733
Arkansas-Oklahoma, Rev. Dr. Robert H. Studtmann, 4803 S. Lewis, Tulsa, OK 74105, Tel. (918)747-8517
Northern Texas-Northern Louisiana, Rev. Mark B. Hebener, PO Box 560587, Dallas, TX 75356, Tel. (214)637-6865
Southwestern Texas, Rev. Arthur B. Rode, 1800 Northeast Loop 410, PO Box 171270, San Antonio, TX 78217, Tel. (512)824-0068
Southeastern Texas-Southern Louisiana, Rev. Martin L. Yonts, 350 Glenborough Dr., Ste. 310, Houston, TX 77067, Tel. (713)873-5665
Regional Coordinator: Bruce R. Klitzky, Region 4 Center for Mission, 1210 River Bend Dr., Ste. 108, Dallas, TX 75247. Tel. (214)634-0518

Region 5
Metropolitan Chicago, Rev. Sherman Hicks, 18 S. Michigan Ave., Rm. 605, Chicago, IL 60603, Tel. (312)346-3150
Northern Illinois, Rev. Ronald K. Hasley, Luther Center, 103 W. State St., Rockford, IL 61101, Tel. (815)964-9934
Central/Southern Illinois, Rev. Dr. John P. Kaitschuk, 1201 Veterans Pkwy., Ste. D, Springfield, IL 62704, Tel. (217)546-7915
Southeastern Iowa, Rev. Dr. Paul M. Werger, Box 3167, Iowa City, IA 52244, Tel. (319)388-1273
Western Iowa, Rev. Curtis H. Miller, 1121 N. Lake Ave., Storm Lake, IA 50588, Tel (712)732-4968
Northeastern Iowa, Rev. Dr. L. David Brown, 2700 5th Ave., NW, Waverly, IA 50677, Tel. (319)353-1414
Northern Wisconsin-Upper Michigan, Rev. Harry S. Andersen, 1029 N. Third St., Marquette, MI 49855. Tel. (906)228-2300

West-Central Wisconsin, Rev. Gerhard I. Knutson, 12 W. Marshall St., Box 730, Rice Lake, WI 54868, Tel. (715)234-3373
East-Central Wisconsin, Rev. Dr. Robert H. Herder, 3003 N. Richmond St., Appleton, WI 54911, Tel. (414)734-5381
Southeastern Wisconsin, Rev. Peter Rogness, 1212 S. Layton Blvd., Milwaukee, WI 53215. Tel. (414)671-1212
South-Central Wisconsin, Rev. Dr. Lowell H. Mays, 2705 Packers Ave., Madison, WI 53704, Tel. (608)249-4848
Southwestern Wisconsin, Rev. Stefan T. Guttormsson, 2350 S. Ave., Ste. 106 LaCrosse, WI 54601, Tel. (608)788-5000
Regional Coordinator: Rev. Edward F. Weiskotten, Region 5 Center for Mission, 333 Wartburg, Pl., Dubuque, IA 52001. Tel. (319)589-0200

Region 6
Eastern Michigan, Rev. Milton R. Reisen 19711 Greenfield Rd., Detroit, MI 48235, Tel (313)837-3522
Western Michigan, Rev. Dr. Reginald H. Holle, 801 S. Waverly Rd. Ste. 201, Lansing, MI 48917 Tel. (517)321-5066
Indiana-Kentucky, Rev. Dr. Ralph A. Kempski, 9102 N. Meridian St., Ste. 405, Indianapolis, IN 46260, Tel. (317)846-4026
Northwestern Ohio, Rev. James A. Rave, 241 Stanford Pkwy., Ste. A, 45840. Tel. (419)423-3664
Northeastern Ohio, Rev. Dr. Robert W. Kelley, St. John Lutheran Church, 282 W. Bowery, 3rd Fl., Akron, OH 44307. Tel. (216)253-1500
Southern Ohio, Rev. Dr. Kenneth H. Sauer, 517 E. Main St., Columbus, OH 43215, Tel. (614)464-3532
Regional Coordinator: Ms. Charlotte Shafer, Region 6 Center for Mission, 6100 Channing Way Blvd., Ste. 503, Columbus, OH 43232. Tel. (614)759-9090

Region 7
New Jersey, Rev. Herluf M. Jensen, 1930 State Hgwy. 33, Trenton, NJ 08690, Tel. (609)586-6800
New England, Rev. Robert L. Isaksen, 90 Madison St., Ste. 303, Worcester, MA 01608. Tel. (508)791-1530
Metropolitan New York, Rev. Dr. William H. Lazareth, 360 Park Ave., S., New York, NY 10010. Tel. (212)532-6350
Upper New York, Rev. Dr. Edward K. Perry, 3049 E. Genesee St., Syracuse, NY 13224, Tel. (315)446-2502
Northeastern Pennsylvania, Rev. Dr. Harold S. Weiss, 4865 Hamilton Blvd., Wescosville, PA 18106, Tel. (215)395-6891
Southeastern Pennsylvania, Rev. Dr. Lawrence L. Hand, 2900 Queen Lane, Philadelphia, PA 19129, Tel. (215)438-0600
Slovak Zion, Rev. Dr. John Adam, 13 Kingswood Rd., Danbury, CT 06811, Tel. (203)746-5318
Regional Coordinator: Rev. George E. Handley, Region 7 Center for Mission, Hagan Hall, 7301, Germantown Ave., Philadelphia, PA 19119. Tel. (215)248-4616

Region 8
Northwestern Pennsylvania, Rev. Paull E. Spring, 308 Seneca St., Oil City, PA 16301. Tel. (814)677-5706
Southwestern Pennsylvania, Rev. Donald J. McCoid, 9625 Perry Hgwy., Pittsburgh, PA 15237, Tel. (412)367-8222
Allegheny, Rev. Gerald E. Miller, 701 Quail Ave., Altoona, PA 16602, Tel. (814)942-1042
Lower Susquehanna, Rev. Dr. Guy S. Edmiston Jr., 900 S. Arlington Ave., Rm. 208, Harrisburg, PA 17109, Tel. (717)652-1852
Upper Susquehanna, Rev. Dr. A. Donald Main, Box 36, 241 Fairgrown Rd., Lewisburg, PA 17837, Tel. (717)524-9778

Maryland, Rev. Dr. Morris Zumbrun, 7604 York Rd., Baltimore, MD 21204, Tel. (301)825-9520
Metropolitan Washington, D.C., Rev. Dr. E. Harold Jansen, 224 E. Capitol St., Washington, DC 20003. Tel. (202)543-8610
West Virginia, Rev. L. Alexander Black, Atrium Mall, 503 Morgantown Avenue, Fairmont, WV 26554. Tel. (304)363-4030
Regional Coordinator: Rev. Eugene Beutel, Region 8 Center for Mission, c/o United Church Center, 900 S. Arlington Ave., Rm. 210, Harrisburg, PA 17109

Region 9
Virginia, Rev. Richard F. Bansemer, Drawer 70, Salem, VA 24153, Tel. (703)389-1000
North Carolina, Rev. Dr. Michael C. D. McDaniel, 1988 Lutheran Synod Dr., Salisbury, NC 28144, Tel. (704)633-4861
South Carolina, Rev. Dr. James S. Aull, P.O. Box 43, Columbia, SC 29202, Tel. (803)765-0590
Southeastern, Rev. Dr. Harold C. Skillrud, 756 Peachtree St. N.W., Atlanta, GA 30308, Tel. (404)873-1977
Florida, Rev. Lavern G. Franzen, 3838 W. Cyprus St., Tampa, FL 33607, Tel. (813)876-7660
Caribbean, Rev. Rafael Malpica-Padilla, P.O. Box 14426, Bo-Obrero Station, Santurce, PR 00916, Tel. (809)727-6015
Regional Coordinator: Ms. Dorothy Jeffcoat, Region 9 Center for Mission, 756 W. Peachtree St., NW, Atlanta, GA 30308 (404)881-6145

PERIODICAL

The Lutheran (18/yr.), 8765 W. Higgins Road, Chicago, IL 60631, Editor and Exec. Dir., Rev. Dr. Edgar R. Trexler; Adv. Comm. Chpsn., William F. Chamberlin

Evangelical Lutheran Synod

The Evangelical Lutheran Synod had its beginning among the Norwegian settlers who brought with them their Lutheran heritage and established it in this country. It was organized in 1853. It was reorganized in 1917 by those who desired to adhere to these principles not only in word, but also in deed.
To carry out the above-mentioned objectives, the Synod owns and operates Bethany Lutheran College in Mankato, Minnesota. It also owns and operates Bethany Lutheran Theological Seminary for the training of pastors. The seminary is also at Mankato, MN

Churches: 123; Inclusive Membership: 21,378; Sunday or Sabbath Schools: 110; Total Enrollment: 3,900; Ordained Clergy: 141

GENERAL ORGANIZATION
Synod: annual (June)

OFFICERS
Pres., Rev. George Orvick, 447 Division St., Mankato, MN 56001
Sec., Rev. Alf Merseth, 106 13th St. S., Northwood, IA 50459
Treas., Mr. LeRoy W. Meyer, 1038 S. Lewis Ave., Lombard, IL 60148

OTHER ORGANIZATIONS
Lutheran Synod Book Co.: Office, Bethany Lutheran College, Mankato, MN 56001

PERIODICAL
Lutheran Sentinel, (m), Lake Mills, IA 50450. Rev. P. Madson, Ed., 813 S. Willow Ave., Sioux Falls, SD 57104
Lutheran Synod Quarterly, (q), W. W. Peterson, Ed., Bethany Lutheran College, 734 Marsh St., Mankato, MN 56001

Evangelical Mennonite Church, Inc.

The Evangelical Mennonite Church traces its heritage directly to the early reformation period of the 16th century to a group known as Swiss Brethren, who believed that salvation could come only by repentance for sin and faith in Jesus Christ; that baptism was only for believers; and, that the church should be separate from controls of the state. These Swiss Brethren became known as Anabaptists. As the Anabaptist movement spread to other countries, a Dutch priest; Menno Simons, left the Catholic priesthood and became one of its leaders. Much of the Anabaptist movement became identified with the name of Menno Simons, and in the course of time the group became known as Mennonites.
Around 1700 a Mennonite minister named Jacob Ammon lead a division which came to be known as the Amish. Both the Mennonites and the Amish were much persecuted in some areas of Europe. Migrations to America took place in the early 1700's and at later times. Out of these, in the middle 1800's, emerged a minister of an Amish congregation in Indiana by the name of Henry Egly. After a deep spiritual renewal in his own life, he strongly emphasized the need of being "born again" as a prerequisite to baptism and church membership. This led to his separation from the group in 1865 and the beginning of what is now the Evangelical Mennonite Church, with congregations in Michigan, Ohio, Indiana, Illinois and Kansas.

Churches: 26; Inclusive Membership: 3,888; Sunday or Sabbath Schools: 25; Total Enrollment: 4,018; Ordained Clergy: 62

GENERAL ORGANIZATION
Conference: annual (August)
Headquarters: 1420 Kerrway Ct., Fort Wayne, IN 46805. Tel. (219) 423-3649

OFFICERS
Pres., Rev. Gary Gates, 1420 Kerrway Ct., Ft. Wayne, IN 46805
Chpsn., Rev. Doug Habegger, 1033 Lee, Morton, IL 61550
Vice-Chpsn., Rev. Charles Rupp, Box 1, Lawton, MI 49065
Sec., Gene L. Rupp, Taylor Univ., Upland, IN 46989
Treas., Dennis Zimmerman, 5519 Albany Ct., Ft. Wayne, IN 46835

PERIODICALS
EMC Today (m), Fort Wayne, IN 46805. Gary Gates, Ed.

Evangelical Methodist Church

Organized 1946 at Memphis, Tennessee, largely as a movement of people who opposed modern liberalism and wished for a return to the historic Wesleyan position. In 1960 merged with the Evangel Church (formerly Evangelistic Tabernacles) and with the People's Methodist Church in 1962.

GENERAL ORGANIZATION
General Conference, District Conference, and Annual Church Conference
Headquarters: 3000 West Kellogg, Wichita, KS 67213. Tel. (316) 943-3278

OFFICERS
Gen. Supt., Clyde Zehr, Wichita, KS 67213
Gen. Conf. Sec., Rev. Ronald D. Driggers, Wichita, KS 67213

Evangelical Presbyterian Church

The Evangelical Presbyterian Church (EPC), established in March 1981, is a conservative denomination of eight geographic presbyteries in the U.S., and one in Argentina. From its inception, with 12 churches, the EPC has grown to over 155 churches with a membership of over 48,500. In 1987 the General Assembly approved the formation of St. Andrews Presbytery, currently consisting of six churches in Buenos Aires, Argentina. Newest U.S. presbytery is the Mid-Atlantic, which began operations January, 1989.

Planted firmly within the historic Reformed tradition, evangelical in spirit, the EPC places high priority on church planting and development along with world missions. Several missionary families serve at home and abroad. Fourth annual meeting of the Joint Committee on Mission between the EPC and the Presbyterian Church of Brazil (IPB) was held in the fall of 1989 in Sao Paulo, Brazil.

Based on the truth of Scripture and adhering to the Westminster Confession of Faith and the EPC *Book of Order*, the denomination is committed to the "essentials of the faith." Freedom is allowed in areas of nonessentials, issues secondary to the gospel of Jesus Christ. The motto "In essentials, unity; In nonessentials, liberty; In all things, charity" summarizes the life of EPC, along with Ephesians 4:15, "truth in love."

The Evangelical Presbyterian Church is a member of the World Alliance of Reformed Churches, National Association of Evangelicals, World Evangelical Fellowship, and Evangelical Council for Financial Accountability. Representatives also attend the annual convocation of the National Association of Presbyterian and Reformed Churches (NAPARC).

Churches: 155; Inclusive Membership: 50,300; Sunday or Sabbath Schools: 155; Total Enrollment: 25,000; Ordained Clergy: 225

GENERAL ORGANIZATION

Headquarters: Office of the General Assembly, 26049 Five Mile Rd., Detroit, MI 48239. Tel. (313) 532-9555.
General Assembly: Annual (next meeting, June 25-27, 1990, Fourth Presbyterian Church, Bethesda, MD

OFFICERS

Moderator, Dr. Andrew Jumper, Central Presbyterian, 7700 Davis Dr., St. Louis, MO 63105
Stated Clerk, Rev. L. Edward Davis, Office of the General Assembly

PERMANENT COMMITTEES

Committee on Administration: Chmn., Mr. Richard Heidtman, 12301 E. Stanley Rd., Columbiaville, MI 48421
Committee on Church Development: Chmn., Dr. W. Wallace Hostetter, Faith EPC, 1000 W. University Blvd. #108, Rochester, MI 48063
Committee on World Outreach: Chmn., Rev. Samuel Harris, Faith EPC, Box 7887, Roanoke, VA 42019
Committee on Ministerial Vocation: Chmn., Mr. Jerry Alpert, 9600 Clayton Rd., Ladue, MO 63124
Committee on Christian Education and Publication: Chmn., _____
Committee on Fraternal Relations: Chmn., Dr. Robert Norris, Fourth Presbyterian, 5500 River Rd., Bethesda, MD 20816
Committee on Women's Ministries: Chmn., _____
Permanent Judicial Commission: Moderator, Rev. Robert Ralston, Faith Presbyterian, 11373 E. Alameda Ave., Aurora, CO 80012
Committee on Theology: Chmn., Rev. Anthony DeOrio. Grace Chapel, 23233 Drake Rd. Farmington Hills, MI 48024
Committee on Youth Ministries: Chmn., Rhett Payne, EPC of Marshall, 403 E. Burleson, Marshall, TX 75670

PRESBYTERIES

Allegheny:
Rev. Daniel Lacich, Stated Clerk, North Park EPC, 600 Ingomar Rd., Wexford, PA 10590

Central South:
Mr. Paul Lawrence, Stated Clerk, 20 Cripple Shin Bluff Dr., Rogers, AR 72756
East:
Rev. L. Michael Winship, Christ Church, 6602 Degen Dr., Burke VA 22015
Far West:
Rev. James Brown, Jr., Stated Clerk, Santa Maria Community Church, 210 W. Fesler, Santa Maria, CA 93454
Mid-Atlantic:
Mr. Liew Fisher, 3164 Golf Colony, Salem, VA 24153
Midwest:
Mr. Robert Sanborn, 26049 FIve Mile Rd., Detroit, MI 48239
Southeast:
Mr. Robert Garment, Trinity EPC, 5150 Oleander, Ft. Pierce, FL 34982
St. Andrews:
Mr. Freddie Berk, Stated Clerk, Iglesia Presbyteriana San Andres, Peru 352, 1067 Buenos Aires, Argentina
West:
Mr. Claude Russell, Stated Clerk, c/o Faith Presbyterian, 11373 E. Alameda, Aurora, CO 80012

Fellowship of Evangelical Bible Churches

Formerly known as Evangelical Mennonite Brethren, this body emanates from the Russian immigration of Mennonites into the United States, 1873–74. Established with the emphasis on true repentance, conversion, and a committed life to our Savior and Lord, the conference was founded in 1889 under the leadership of Isaac Peters and Aaron Wall. The founding churches were located in Mountain Lake, Minnesota, and in Henderson and Janzen, Nebraska. The conference has since grown to a fellowship of 36 churches with approximately 4,400 members. The churches are located in four countries—Argentina, Canada, Paraguay, and United States.

From its earliest days, foreign missions have been a vital ingredient of the total ministry of the F.E.B.C. Today missions constitute about 75 percent of the total annual budget, with one missionary for every 30 members in the home churches. Since the conference does not develop and administer foreign mission fields of its own, it actively participates with existing evangelical "faith" mission societies. The conference has representation on several mission boards and has missionaries serving under approximately 32 different agencies around the world.

The F.E.B.C. has determined to maintain doctrinal purity in holding fast to the inerrency of Scripture, the Deity of Christ, the need for spiritual regeneration of man from his sinful natural state, by faith in the death, burial, and resurrection of Jesus Christ as payment for sin. They look forward to the imminent return of Jesus Christ and retain a sense of urgency to share the gospel with those who have never heard of God's redeeming love.

Churches: 14; inclusive membership: 1,925; Sunday or Sabbath schools: 14; Total Enrollment: 1,680; Ordained Clergy: 47

GENERAL ORGANIZATION

Convention: annual (July)
Headquarters: 5800 S. 14th St., Omaha, NE 68107. Tel. (402)731-4780

OFFICERS

Pres., Rev. Jerry Franz, 1175 Howe St., Dallas, OR 97338
Vice-Pres., Mr. Stan Seifert, 2732 Springhill St., Clearbrook, British Columbia, Canada V2T 3V9
Rec. Sec., Rev. Melvin Epp, RR 1, Wymark, Saskatchewan, S0N 2Y0
Adm. Sec., Robert L. Frey, 5800 So. 14th, Omaha, NE 68107

Commission on Churches, Chpsn., Dr. J. Paul Nyquist, 7820 Fort St., Omaha, NE 68134
Commission on Missions, Chpsn. Rev. Allan Wiebe, 1104 Day Dr., Omaha, NE 68005
Commission of Trustees, Chpsn., Mr. Neil C. J. DeRuiter, 298 Regal Ave., Winnipeg, Manitoba R2M 0P5
Commission on Education & Publication, Chpsn., Mr. Joel Penner, Rt. 1, Box 55, Butterfield, MN 56120
Commission on Church Planting, Chpsn., Rev. Randy Smart, Box 1446, Winkler, Manitoba R0G 2X0

PERIODICAL

Gospel Tidings, 5800 S. 14th St., Omaha, NE 68107. Robert L. Frey, Ed.

Fellowship of Fundamental Bible Churches

This body, until 1985, was called the Bible Protestant Church. The FFBC is a fellowship of fundamental Bible-believing local autonomous churches which believe in an inerrant and infallible Bible, is dispensational as related to the study of the Scriptures, espouses the pre-Tribulation Rapture, and is premillenial. The FFBC is evangelistic and missions-oriented. It regards itself as separatistic in areas of personal life and ecclesiastical association and believes that Baptism by immersion of believers most adequately reflects the symbolic truth of death and resurrection with Christ.

The Fellowship of Fundamental Bible Churches relates historically to the Eastern Conference of the Methodist Protestant Church, which changed its name to Bible Protestant Church at the 2nd Annual Session, held in Westville, New Jersey, September 26-30, 1940.

GENERAL ORGANIZATION

Mailing Address: P.O. Box 43, Glassboro NJ 08028

OFFICERS

Pres., Rev. Daniel Baker, RD 2 Box 378, Lake Aiel, PA 18436
Vice-Pres., Rev. Mark Franklin, RD 1 Box 415, Monroeville, NJ 08343
Sec., Rev. A. Glen Doughty, 134 Delsea Dr., Westville NJ 08093
Asst. Sec., Rev. William Williams, R.D. 5, Box 249, Moscow PA 18444
Treas., Mr. William Rainey, R.D. 1, Box 302, Monroeville, NJ 08343
National Rep., Rev. Howard E. Haines, P.O. Box 43, Glassboro, NJ 08028

The Fire Baptized Holiness Church (Wesleyan)

This church came into being about 1890 as the result of definite preaching on the doctrine of holiness in some Methodist churches in southeastern Kansas. It became known as The Southeast Kansas Fire Baptized Holiness Association, which name in 1945 was changed to The Fire Baptized Holiness Church. It is entirely Wesleyan in doctrine, episcopal in church organization, and intensive in evangelistic zeal.

GENERAL ORGANIZATION

Headquarters: 600 College Ave., Independence, KS 67301. Tel. (316) 331-3049

OFFICERS

Gen. Supt., Gerald Broadaway
Gen. Sec., Wayne Knipmeyer, 1203 N. Penn, Independence, KS 67301
Gen. Treas., Victor White, 709 N. 13th, Independence, KS 67301

PERIODICALS

The Flaming Sword (m), 10th St. & College Ave., Independence, KS 67301
John Three Sixteen (w), 10th St. & College Ave., Independence, KS 67301

Free Christian Zion Church of Christ

Organized 1905, at Redemption, Arkansas, by a company of Negro ministers associated with various denominations, with polity in general accord with that of Methodist bodies.

GENERAL ORGANIZATION

General Assembly: annual (November)
Headquarters: 1315 Hutchinson St., Nashville, AR 71852
Chief Pastor, Willie Benson, Jr.

Free Lutheran Congregations, The Association of

The Association of Free Lutheran Congregations (AFLC), rooted in the Scandinavian revival movements, was organized in 1962 by a Lutheran Free Church remnant which rejected merger with The American Lutheran Church. The original 42 congregations were joined by other like-minded conservative Lutherans, especially from the former Evangelical Lutheran Church and the Suomi Synod. There has been a fourfold increase in the number of congregations during the AFLC's first quarter century, and concern over the current Lutheran merger has led to a new surge of growth.

Congregations subscribe to the Apostles, Nicene, and Athanasian creeds; Luther's Small Catechism; and the Unaltered Augsburg Confession. A statement of polity and practice, the Fundamental Principles and Rules for Work (1897), declaring that the local congregation is the right form of the kingdom of God on earth, subject to no authority but the Word and the Spirit of God, is also central to the life of the church body.

Distinctive emphases: (1) the infallibility and inerrancy of Holy Scriptures as the Word of God; (2) congregational polity; (3) the spiritual unity of all believers, resulting in fellowship and cooperation transcending denominational lines; (4) evangelical outreach, calling all to enter a personal relationship with Jesus Christ; (5) a wholesome Lutheran pietism that proclaims the Lordship of Jesus Christ in all areas of life and results in believers becoming the salt and light in their communities; (6) a conservative stance on current social issues.

A two-year Bible school and a theological seminary are located on a campus in suburban Minneapolis, Minnesota. Support is channeled also to sister churches in Brazil, Mexico, and Canada.

Churches: 193; Inclusive Membership: 26,870; Sunday or Sabbath Schools: 180; Total Enrollment: 8,100; Ordained Clergy: 139

GENERAL ORGANIZATION

Conference: annual (June)
Headquarters: 3110 E. Medicine Lake Blvd., Minneapolis, MN 55441; Tel. (612) 545-5631

Pres., Rev. Richard Snipstead, 3110 E. Medicine Lake Blvd, Minneapolis, MN 55441
Vice Pres., Rev. Robert L. Lee, 3430 Georgia Ave., Minneapolis, MN 55427
Sec., Rev. Ronald Knutson, 402 W. 11th St., Canton, SD 57013

PERIODICAL

The Lutheran Ambassador (bi-w), 3110 East Medicine Lake Blvd., Minneapolis, MN 55441. Rev. Raynard Huglen, Ed.

Free Methodist Church of North America

The Free Methodist Church was organized in 1860 in Western New York by ministers and laymen who had called the Methodist Episcopal Church to return to what they considered the original doctrines and life style of Methodism. The issues included human freedom (anti-slavery), freedom and simplicity in worship, free seats so that the poor would not be discriminated against, and freedom from secret oaths (societies) so the truth might be spoken freely at all times. They emphasized the teaching of the entire sanctification of life by means of grace through faith.

The denomination continues to be true to its founding principles. It communicates the gospel and its power to all men without discrimination through strong missionary, evangelistic, and educational programs. Six colleges, a Bible college, and numerous overseas schools train the youth of the church to serve in lay and ministerial roles.

Its members covenant to maintain simplicity in life and worship, daily devotion to Christ, and responsible stewardship of time, talent, and finance.

Churches: 1,071; Inclusive Membership: 73,647; Sunday or Sabbath Schools: 1,088; Total Enrollment: 107,723; Ordained Clergy: 1,802

GENERAL ORGANIZATION

General Conference (next meeting, 1989 in Seattle WA)
Headquarters: 901 College Ave., Winona Lake, IN 46590. Tel. (219) 267-7656 Fax: (219)269-7431
Free Methodist Publishing House: 999 College Ave., Winona Lake, IN 46590. Tel. (219) 267-7161

OFFICERS

Bishops: Robert F. Andrews, Donald N. Bastian, Gerald E. Bates, David M. Foster, Bya'ene Akulu Ilangyi, Noah Nzeyimana, Clyde E. Van Valin, Daniel Ward
Gen. Conf. Sec., Melvin J. Spencer
Gen. Hdqtrs. Admin., T. Dan Wollam
Gen. Church Treas., Philip B. Nelson
Gen. Dir. of Christian Educ., Daniel L. Riemenschneider
Gen. Dir. of Evangelism and Church Growth, Raymond W. Ellis
Gen. Dir. of Higher Educ. and Ministry, Bruce L. Kline
Editor, Light and Life magazine, Robert B. Haslam
Exec. Dir., Light and Life Men Int'l, Lucien E. Behar
Free Methodist Foundation, Stanley B. Thompson
Pres., of Women's Ministries Inernational, Mrs. Carollyn Ellis
Gen. Dir. of World Missions, Elmore L. Clyde

PERIODICALS

Free Methodist Pastor (q), Wayne G. McCown, Ed.
Light and Life (m), Robert B. Haslam, Ed.
Missionary Tidings (m), Marian W. Groesbeck, Ed.
Yearbook (a, October), J. Marcos Gilmore, Ed.
901 Report/901 Review (m), _____, Ed.

Free Will Baptists, National Association of

This evangelical group of Arminian Baptists was organized by Paul Palmer in 1727 at Chowan, North Carolina. Another movement (teaching the same doctrines of free grace, free salvation, and free will) was organized June 30, 1780, in New Durham, New Hampshire, but there was no connection with the southern organization except for a fraternal relationship.

The northern line expanded more rapidly and extended into the West and Southwest. This body merged with the Northern Baptist Convention October 5, 1911, but a remnant of churches reorganized into the Cooperative General Association of Free Will Baptists December 28, 1916, at Pattonsburg, Missouri.

Churches in the southern line were organized into various conferences from the beginning and finally united in one General Conference in 1921.

Representatives of the Cooperative General Association and the General Conference joined November 5, 1935 to form the National Association of Free Will Baptists.

Churches: 2,496; Inclusive Membership: 204,382; Sunday or Sabbath Schools: 2,496; Total Enrollment: 155,666; Ordained Clergy: 2,895

GENERAL ORGANIZATION

National Association meets annually (July)
National Offices: 1134 Murfreesboro Rd., Nashville, TN 37217. Tel. (615) 361-1010
Mailing Address: P.O. Box 1088, Nashville, TN 37202

OFFICERS

Exec. Sec., Dr. Melvin Worthington, P. O. Box 1088, Nashville, TN 37202. Tel. (615) 361-1010
Mod., Rev. Ralph Hampton, P.O. Box 50117, Nashville, TN 37205

DENOMINATIONAL AGENCIES

Executive Office, P.O. Box 1088, Nashville, TN 37202
Free Will Baptist National Offices, P.O. Box 1088, Nashville, TN 37202
Free Will Baptist Foundation: Exec. Sec., Herman Hersey
Free Will Baptist Bible College: Pres., Dr Charles Thigpen
Foreign Missions Dept.: Dir., Rev. R. Eugene Waddell
Home Missions Dept.: Dir., Rev. Roy Thomas
Board of Retirement: Dir., Rev. Herman Hersey
Historical Commission: Chpsn., David Joslin
Commission for Theological Integrity: Chpsn., Rev. Leroy Forlines
Music Commission: Chpsn., Bill Gardner, 2518 Una-Antioch Pike, Antioch, TN 37013
Radio & Television Commission: Chpsn., Mr. Joseph Goodfellow, P.O. Box 50117, Nashville, TN 37205
Sunday School and Church Training Dept.: Dir., Dr. Roger Reeds
Woman's National Auxiliary Convention: Exec. Sec., Dr. Mary R. Wisehart
Master's Men Dept.:, Dir., Mr. James Vallance

PERIODICALS

Contact (m), P.O.Box 1088, Nashville, TN 37202, Jack Williams, Ed.
Free Will Baptist Gem (m), P. O. Box 991., Lebanon, MO 65536, Rev. Clarence Burton, Ed.
Bible College Bulletin (m), 3606 West End Ave., Nashville, TN 37205, Bert Tippett, Ed.
Heartbeat, Foreign Missions Office, P. O. Box 1088, Nashville, TN 37202, Don Robirds, Ed.
Mission Grams, Home Missions Office, P. O. Box 1088, Nashville, TN 37202, Pat Thomas, Ed.

Happenings (q), P.O. Box 1088, Nashville, TN 37202, Vernie Hersey, Ed.

Co-Laborer, Woman's National Auxiliary Convention (bi-m), P.O. Box 1088, Nashville, TN 37202, Lorene Miley, Ed.

Friends General Conference

Friends General Conference is an association of yearly meetings open to all Friends meetings which wish to be actively associated with its programs and services. It was organized in 1900 bringing together four associations, including the First-day School Conference (1868) and the Friends Union for Philanthropic Labor (1882).

Friends General Conference is primarily a service organization and has no authority over constituent meetings. A Central Committee, to which constituent yearly meetings name appointees approximately in proportion to membership, or its Executive Committee, is responsible for the direction of the FGC's program of year-round services. A staff of twelve administers the programs.

There are six standing program committees: Advancement & Outreach, Christian & Interfaith Relations, Long Range Conference Planning, Ministry & Nurture, Publications & Communication, and Religious Education. The Advancement & Outreach Committee actively promotes intervisitation among Friends, nurtures new worship groups, and distributes material to interpret the Religious Society of Friends and to attract seekers. The Christian & Interfaith Relations Committee fosters a dialogue with Friends United Meeting and other Quaker groups, participates in ecumenical activities, maintains an active relationship with the World Council of Churches, and is an informal participant in the Quaker Theological Discussion Group. The Long Range Conference Planning Committee is responsible for establishing the annual Gathering planning committees, and for overall Gathering policy and communication with host colleges.

The Ministry & Nurture Committee oversees the FGC Field Secretary program, and nurtures the life of the Spirit within monthly meetings, yearly meetings, and within the FGC Central Committee. It also sponsors visits by staff and Central Committee members to yearly meetings. The Publications & Communications Committee publishes and distributes a wide variety of First-day School curriculum and other Quaker materials, and publishes the *FGC Quarterly*, which contains inspirational and informational articles intended to strengthen monthly meeting life. It has a circulation of approximately 26,000 households. The Religious Education Committee creates curriculum for First-day School and home use, sponsors leadership training workshops, and supports religious education in junior yearly meeting programs and in monthly meetings.

GENERAL ORGANIZATION

Gathering of Friends: annual (July)
Headquarters: 1216 Arch St., 2B, Philadelphia, PA 19107. Tel. (215) 561-1700
Gen. Sec., Meredith Walton

OFFICERS

Gen. Sec., Meredith Walton
Clk., Elizabeth H. Muench
Treas., Tyla Ann Burger-Arroyo

PERIODICAL

FGC Quarterly (q), 1216 Arch St., 2B, Philadelphia, PA 19107, Liz Yeats, Ed.

YEARLY MEETINGS

(Note: * denotes Meetings which are also affiliated with Friends United Meeting)

Philadelphia YM, Samuel D. Caldwell, 1515 Cherry St., Philadelphia, PA 19102

Lake Erie YM, Clemence Mershon, RD 2, Box 159, Conneautville, PA 16406

*New England YM, William Kriebel, 19 Rufus Jones Lane, No. Easton, MA 02356

*New York YM, Mary Foster Cadbury, Bulls Head Rd., Clinton Corners, NY 12514

*Baltimore YM, Katherine Smith, 17100 Quaker Lane, Sandy Spring, MD 20860

*Canadian YM, Edward Bell, 2339 Briar Hill Dr., Ottawa, ON K1H 7A7, Canada

Illinois YM, Paul Buckley, RR1, Dewey St., Matteson, IL 60443

Ohio Valley YM, Barbarie Hill, 6921 Stonington Rd., Cincinnati, OH 45230

South Central YM, Gary Hicks, 2109 Prather Lane, Austin, TX 78704

*Southeastern YM, Virginia Redfield, 117 Brackenwood Rd., Palm Beach Gardens, FL 33418

Northern YM, Marian Van Dellen, 5312 11th Avenue, SW, Rochester, MN 55902

Piedmont FF, Peirce Hammond, 718 Lake Boone Trail, Raleigh, NC 27607

Southern Appalachian YM & Assoc., Steve Meredith, P.O. Box 125, Alvaton, KY 42122

Central Alaska F. C., Jim Cheydleur, P.O. 81177, Fairbanks, AK 99708

Friends United Meeting

Friends United Meeting was organized in 1902 (originally Five Years Meeting of Friends, the name was changed in 1963) as a loose confederation of North American yearly meetings to facilitate a united Quaker witness in missions, peace work, and Christian education.

Today Friends United Meeting is comprised of eighteen member yearly meetings (12 North American plus Cuba, East Africa, East Africa Yearly Meeting (South) Elgon Religious Society of Friends, Nairobi and Jamaica Yearly Meetings) representing about half the Friends in the world. FUM's current work includes programs of mission and service, peace education, leadership and stewardship development, and the publication of Christian education curriculum, books of Quaker history and religious thought, and a magazine, *Quaker Life.*

Churches: 545; Inclusive Membership: 54,501; Sunday or Sabbath Schools: 463; Total Enrollment: 24,000; Ordained Clergy: 601

GENERAL ORGANIZATION

Friends United Meeting: 1990 Trennial Sessions held at Indiana University, Bloomington, IN

OFFICERS

Presiding Clk., Paul Enyart, 101 Quaker Hill Dr., Richmond, IN 47374. Tel. (317)962-7573

Treas., John Norris, 101 Quaker Hill Dr., Richmond, IN 47374

Gen. Sec., Stephen Main, 101 Quaker Hill Dr., Richmond, IN 47374. Tel. (317)962-7573

DEPARTMENTS

(All located at 101 Quaker Hill Dr., Richmond, IN 47374). Tel. (317)962-7573

World Ministries Commission, Assoc. Sec., Bill Wagoner

Meeting Ministries Commission, Assoc. Sec., Mary Glenn Hadley

Communications Commission, _____

Quaker Hill Bookstore Mgr., Dick Talbot

Friends United Press, Ardith Talbot, Ed.

PERIODICALS

Quaker Life, 101 Quaker Hill Dr., Richmond, IN 47374, J. Stanley Banker, Ed.

YEARLY MEETINGS

(Note: * denotes Meetings which are also affiliated with the Friends General Conference)

Nebraska YM, Don Reeves, R.R. 1, Box 66, Central City, NV 68826

*New England YM, William Kriebel, 19 Rufus Jones Lane, North Easton, MA 02356

*New York YM, Mary Foster Cadbury, Bulls Head Rd., Clinton Corners, NY 12514

*Baltimore YM, Winifred Walker-Jones, 17100 Quaker La., Sandy Spring, MD 20860

Iowa YM, Louise Davis, 1644 140th St., Clemons, IA 50051

Western YM, Lester Paulsen, P.O. Box 235, Plainfield, IN 46168

North Carolina YM Carter Pike, 903 New Garden Rd., Greensboro, NC 27410

Indiana YM, Horace Smith, Rt. 2, Box 291, Hagerstown, IN 47346

Wilmington YM, Rudy Haag, P.O. Box 19, Cuba, OH 45114

Cuba YM, Maulio Ajo Berencen, Libertad 114, c/o Argamente and Garayalde, Holguin 80100, Holguin, Cuba

*Canadian YM, Edward Bell, 2339 Briar Hill Dr., Ottawa, Ontario K2H 7A7

Jamaica YM, Angela Johnson, 4 Worthington Ave., Kingston 5, Jamaica, W.I.

*Southeastern YM, Virginia Redfield, 117 Brackenwood Dr., Palm Beach, FL 33410

Southwest YM, Lind Coop, 15915 E. Russell St., Whittier, CA 90603

East Africa YM, James Ashihunde, P.O. Box 1510, Kakamega, Kenya, East Africa

East Africa YM (South), Joseph Kisia, P.O. Box 160, Vihiga, Kenya, East Africa

Nairobi YM, Stanley Ndezwa, P.O. Box 377, Nakuru, Kenya, East Africa

Elgon Religious Society of Friends, Elisha Wakube, P.O. Box 98, Kimilili, Kenya, East Africa

Full Gospel Assemblies International

This Pentecostal body had its beginning in 1972 as an adjunct to an established school of biblical studies known as Full Gospel Bible Institute under the leadership of Dr. Charles E. Strauser.

GENERAL ORGANIZATION

Headquarters: R.D. #2, Box 520, Parkesburg, PA 19365. Tel. (215)857-2357

OFFICERS

Pres.: Dr. Charles E. Strauser
Asst.: Dr. Annamae Strauser
Executive Board: Dr. C. E. Strauser, Dr. Annamae Strauser, Rev. Simeon Strauser, Miss Carol Ann Strauser
Bd. of Directors: Rev. Harold Oswold, 340 Rand St., Rochester, NY 14611; Rev. Harry E. Constein, III, 2235 Blossom Valley Rd., Lancaster, PA 17601; Simeon Strauser, Box 38, Sadsburyville, PA 19369; Dr. Samuel Strauser, Box 450, Delaware Water Gap, PA 18327; Dr. Annamae Strauser, P.O. Box 1230, Coatesville, PA 19320

PERIODICAL

The Charisma Courier, P. O. Box 1230, Coatesville, PA 19320. C. E. Strauser, Ed. Tel. (215)857-2357

Full Gospel Fellowship of Churches and Ministers International

In the early 1960s, a conviction grew in the hearts of many ministers that there ought to be closer fellowship between the people of God who believed in the apostolic ministry. Also, a great number of independent churches were experiencing serious difficulties in receiving authority from the IRS to give governmentally accepted tax-exempt receipts for donations.

In September 1962, a group of ministers met in Dallas, Texas, to form a Fellowship to give expression to the essential unity of the Body of Christ under the leadership of the Holy Spirit—a unity that goes beyond individuals, churches, or organizations. This was not a movement to build another denomination, but rather an effort to join ministers and churches of like feeling across denominational lines.

To provide opportunities for fellowship and to support the objectives and goals of local and national ministries, regional conventions and an annual international convention are held.

GENERAL ORGANIZATION

Annual Conference (next convention, July 11-13, 1989, Greenwood Inn, Beaverton (Portland), OR
Headquarters: FGFCMI General Conference, 1545 W. Mockingbird Lane, Ste. 1012, Dallas, TX 75235. Tel. (214) 630-1941. Office Mgr., Tracy L. Wagner

OFFICERS

Pres., James H. Helton, P.O. Box 2787, Muncie, IN 47302
1st Vice-Pres., Don Arnold, P. O. Box 324, Gasden, AL 35901
Treas., Dr. H. K. McKnight, 1857 Fenwick St., Augusta, GA 30904
Sec., Dr. Chester P. Jenkins, P.O. Box 309, Hamlin, PA 18427
Vice-Presidents at Large: R. Richard Edgar, 5937 Franconia Rd.; Alexandria, VA 22310; Maurice Hart, P. O. Box 4316, Omaha NE 68104; Don Westbrook, 4434 Talcott Dr., Durham, NC 27705
Regional Vice-Presidents: Southeast, Don Arnold, P. O. Box 324, Gadsden, AL 35901; South Central, Turner Scogin, 2601 Pecos, Ft. Worth, TX 76119; Southwest, Neil Glasse, P. O. Box 1380, Tracy CA 95378; Northeast, Dr. Ray L. Chamberlain, P.O. Box 986, Salisbury, MD 21801; North Central, Raymond Rothwell, P.O. Box 367, Eaton, OH 45320; Northwest, Ralph Trask, 3212 Hyacinth St. N.E., Salem, OR 97303

Fundamental Methodist Church, Inc.

This group traces its origin through the Methodist Protestant Church. It withdrew from The Methodist Church and organized on August 27, 1942.

GENERAL ORGANIZATION

Conference: Annual (at Conference Grounds, Lawrence Country, Ash Grove, MO)
Headquarters: 1028 N. Broadway, Springfield, MO 65802
Treas., Mr. Everett Etheridge, 3844 Dover, Springfield, MO 65802. Tel. (417)865-4438

Sec., Mrs. Betty Nicholson, Rt. 2, Box 397, Ash Grove, MO 65604. Tel. (417) 672-2268

Dist. Supt., Rev. Ronnie Fieker, Rt. 2, Ash Grove, MO 65604. Tel. (417)672-2076

General Association of Regular Baptist Churches

Founded in May, 1932, in Chicago, Illinois, by a group of churches which had withdrawn from the Northern Baptist Convention (now the American Baptist Churches in the U.S.A.) because of doctrinal differences. Its Confession of Faith, which it requires all churches to subscribe to, is essentially the old, historic New Hampshire Confession of Faith with a premillennial ending applied to the last article.

Churches: 1,585; Inclusive Membership: 260,000; Sunday or Sabbath Schools: 1,585; Total Enrollmen: 310,000; Ordained Clergy: 2,150

GENERAL ORGANIZATION

Meets annually

Home Office: 1300 N. Meacham Rd., Schaumburg, IL 60173. (708) 843-1600

OFFICERS

Chpsn., Dr. David Nettleton

Vice-Chpsn., Dr. Paul Dixon

Treas., Vernon Miller

Sec., Dr. John White

National Representative, Dr. Paul Tassell, 1300 N. Meacham Rd., Schaumburg, IL 60173

PERIODICAL

Baptist Bulletin (m), 1300 N. Meacham Rd., Schaumburg, IL 60173 Vernon Miller, Ed.

General Baptists (General Association of)

Similar in doctrine to those General Baptists organized in England in the early seventeenth century, the first General Baptist churches were organized on the Midwest frontier following the Second Great Awakening. The first church was established by the group's founding father, Rev. Benoni Stinson, in 1823 at Evansville, Ind.

Stinson's major theological emphasis was general atonement—"Christ tasted death for every man." The group also allows for the possibility of apostasy. It practices open Communion and believer's baptism by immersion.

Called "liberal" Baptists because of their emphasis on the freedom of man, General Baptists organized a General Association in 1870 and invited other "liberal" Baptists (e.g., "free will" and Separate Baptists) to participate. Only a few churches did so.

Today the policy-setting body is composed of delegates from local General Baptist associations. Each local church is autonomous but belongs to an association. The group currently consists of more than 60 associations in 16 states, as well as several associations in the Philippines, Guam, Saipan, Jamaica, and India. One unique aspect of General Baptist polity is that ministers and deacons are ordained by a presbytery.

A number of boards continue a variety of missions, schools, and other support ministries. General Baptists belong to the Baptist World Alliance and the North American Baptist Fellowship, and the National Association of Evangelicals.

Churches: 868; Inclusive Membership: 74,086; Sunday or Sabbath Schools: N.R.; Total Enrollment: N.R.; Ordained Clergy: 1,483

GENERAL ORGANIZATION

General Association: annual

Headquarters: 100 Stinson Dr., Poplar Bluff, MO 63901

OFFICERS

Mod., Rev. Ron Black, 100 Stinson Dr., Poplar Bluff, MO 63901

Clerk, Rev. Edwin Runyon, 801 Kendall, Poplar Bluff, MO 63901

Exec. Dir., Dr. Glen O. Spence, 100 Stinson Dr., Poplar Bluff, MO 63901

OTHER ORGANIZATIONS

General Board: Sec., Rev. Edwin Runyon, 801 Kendall, Poplar Bluff, MO 63901

Foreign Mission Board: Exec. Dir., Rev. Charles Carr, 100 Stinson Dr., Poplar Bluff, MO 63901

Board of Christian Education and Publications: Exec. Dir., Rev. Vyron Yount, 100 Stinson Dr., Poplar Bluff, MO 63901

Home Mission Board Exec. Dir., Dr. Leland Duncan, 100 Stinson Dr., Poplar Bluff, MO 63901

Ministers' Aid Board: Sec., Mr. Charles Weir, 7300 Oakdale Dr., Newburgh, IN 47630

Brotherhood Board: Exec. Dir., Mr. Austin Hearon, P.O. Box 452, Clay, KY 42404

Women's Mission Board: Exec. Dir., Mrs. Brenda Kennedy, 100 Stinson Dr., Poplar Bluff, MO 63901

Stewardship Dir., Rev. Ron D. Black, 100 Stinson Dr., Poplar Bluff, MO 63901

Nursing Home Adm., Ms. Wanda Britt, Rt. #2, Box 230, Campbell, MO 63933

College Board: Pres., Dr. James Murray, Oakland City College, P.O. Box 235, Oakland City, IN 47660

Publishing House, General Baptist Press, 400 Stinson Dr., Poplar Bluff, MO 63901. Rev. Wayne Foust

PERIODICALS

General Baptist Messenger (m), 100 Stinson Dr., Poplar Bluff, MO 63901, Rev. Wayne Foust, Ed.

Capsule, Rev. Charles Carr, Ed.

Voice, Dr. Leland Duncan, Ed.

WMS Newsletter, Mrs. Brenda Kennedy, Ed.

General Church of the New Jerusalem

The General Church of the New Jerusalem is the result of a reorganization in 1897 of the General Church of The Advent of the Lord. It stresses the full acceptance of the doctrines contained in the theological writings of Emanuel Swedenborg.

GENERAL ORGANIZATION

General Assembly (International), meets every three or four years

Headquarters: Bryn Athyn, PA 19009. Tel. (215) 947-4660

OFFICERS

Presiding Bishop, Rt. Rev. L. B. King

Sec., Mr. Boyd Asplundh

Treas., Neil M. Buss

PERIODICAL

New Church Life (m), Bryn Athyn, PA 19009 Rev. Donald L. Rose, Ed.

General Conference of Mennonite Brethren Churches

A small group, which had been requesting that closer attention be paid to prayer and Bible study, withdrew in 1860 from the Mennonite Church in the Ukraine. Pietistic in organization, the group adopted a Baptistic policy. In 1874, small bodies of German-speaking Mennonites left Russia, reached Kansas in 1876, then spread to the Pacific Coast and into Canada. In 1960, the Krimmer Mennonite Brethren Conference merged with this body. Today the General Conference of Mennonite Brethren Churches conducts services in many European languages as well as in

Vietnamese, Mandarin, and Hindi. It works with other denominations in missionary and development projects in 23 countries outside North America.

GENERAL ORGANIZATION

General Convention: triennial

OFFICERS

Chpsn., Herbert J. Brandt, 984 Monashee Pl., Kelowna, British Columbia V1V 1J8
Vice-Chpsn., Edmund Janzen, 1717 S. Chestnut Ave., Fresno, CA 93727
Sec., Roland Reimer, 1631 N. Callahan, Wichita, KS 67212

PERIODICALS

Christian Leader (bi-w), Hillsboro, KS 67063, Don Ratzlaff, ed.
Mennonite Brethren Herald, Winnipeg, Manitoba Canada, Ron Geddert, Ed.

General Conference of the Evangelical Baptist Church, Inc.

This denomination is an Arminian, Wesleyan, premillennial group whose form of government is congregational.

It was organized in 1935, and was formerly known as the Church of the Full Gospel, Inc.

GENERAL ORGANIZATION

General Conference: annual (Third Week in October)
Headquarters: 1601 E. Rose St., Goldsboro, NC 27530. Tel. (919) 734-2482

OFFICERS

Pres., Rev. David J. Crawford, 101 William Dr., Goldsboro, NC 27530. Tel. (919)734-2482
1st Vice-Pres., Dr. Harry E. Jones, 616 Chad Dr., Rocky Mount, NC 27801. Tel. (919)443-1239
2nd Vice-Pres., Rev. George C. Wallace, 909 W. Walnut St., Chanute, KS 66720. Tel. (316)431-0706
Sec./Treas., Mrs. Evelyn Crawford, 101 William Dr., Goldsboro, NC 27530. Tel. (919)734-2482
Dir. of Evangelism, Rev. B. L. Proctor, Rt. 3, Box 442, Nashville, NC 27856. Tel. (919)459-2063
Dir. of Women's Work, Mrs. Elizabeth Davis, Rt. 2 Box 222, Pikeville, NC 27865
Dir. of Youth Work, Rev. Ralph Jarrell, P.O. Box 1112, Burgaw, NC 28425. Tel. (919)259-9329

General Convention of The Swedenborgian Church

Founded in North America in 1792 as the Church of the New Jerusalem, the General Convention was organized as a national body in 1817 and incorporated in the state of Illinois in 1861.

Its biblically based theology is derived from the spiritual, or mystical, experiences and exhaustive biblical studies of the Swedish scientist and philosopher Emanuel Swedenborg (1688–1772).

The church centers its worship and teachings on the historical life and the risen and glorified present reality of the Lord Jesus Christ. It looks with an ecumenical vision toward the establishment of the kingdom of God in the form of a universal Church, active in the lives of all people of good will who desire and strive for freedom, peace, and justice for all. It is a member of the NCCC and active in many local councils of churches.

With churches and groups throughout the United States and Canada, the Convention's central administrative offices and its seminary—Swedenborg School of Religion—are located in Newton, Mass. Affiliated churches are found in Africa, Asia, Australia, Canada, Europe, the United Kingdom, Japan, and South America. Many internationally prominent philosphers and writers, past and present, have acknowledged their appreciation of the teachings of Emanuel Swedenborg, which form the basis of this global church.

Churches: 50; Inclusive Membership: 2,423; Sunday or Sabbath Schools: N.R.; Total Enrollment: N.R.; Ordained Clergy: 54

GENERAL ORGANIZATION

General Convention: annual (June)

OFFICERS

Pres., Rev. Richard H. Tafel, Jr., c/o General Convention, 48 Sargent St., Newton, MA 02158
Vice-Pres., Mrs. Elizabeth S. Young, 3715 Via Palomino, Palos Verdes Estates, CA 90274
Sec., Mrs. Dorothy deB. Young, 88 Turnpike St., South Easton, MA 02375
Treas., John C. Perry, RFD 2, Box 2341A, Brunswick, ME 04011
Office Dir., Miss Ethelwyn Worden, 48 Sargent St., Newton, MA 02158

PERIODICAL

The Messenger (m), 1592 N. 400 W., LaPorte, IN 46350, Mrs. Patt Levan, Ed.

General Six Principle Baptists

A Baptist Group, organized in Rhode Island in 1653, drawing its name from Heb. 6:1-2.

GENERAL ORGANIZATION

Conferences in Rhode Island and Pennsylvania: annually, in September

OFFICERS

Rhode Island Conference: Pres., Rev. Edgar S. Kirk, 350 Davisville Rd., North Kingstown, RI 02852. Tel. (401)884-2750
Clk., Miss Sylvia Stoner, RR #1, Box 170, Wyoming, RI 02898
Pennsylvania Association: Pres., Elder Daniel E. Carpenetti, Nicholson, PA 18446. Tel. (717)942-6578
Clk., Mrs. Eleanor Warner, Rt. 1, Nicholson, PA 18446

Grace Brethren Churches, Fellowship of

A division occurred in the Church of the Brethren in 1882 on the question of the legislative authority of the annual meeting. It resulted in the establishment of this body under a legal charter requiring congregational government.

OFFICERS

Mod., Roger Peugh, 401 Wood St., Winona Lake, IN 46590
Mod. Elect, Jerry Young, 414 S. Cape Hill Dr., Manheim, PA 17545
Conf. Coord., Charles Ashman, P.O. Box 386, Winona Lake IN 46590. Tel. (219)267-5566 or (219)267-6623
Sec., Rev. Kenneth Koontz, 855 Turmbull St., Delona FL 32725. Tel. (904)789-6512
Treas., Steve Poppenfoose, R. 1, Box 425A, Warsaw, IN 46580
Statistician, Rev. Sherwood Durkee, Rural Rt. 8, Box 49, Warsaw, IN 46580

Foreign Missionary Society: Exec. Dir., Rev. Tom Julien, P.O. Box 588, Winona Lake, IN 46590; Treas., Mr. Herman J. Schumacher, R1, Lakes Estate, Lot #65, Warsaw, IN 46580

Brethren Home Missions: Exec. Dir., Larry Chamberlain, P.O. Box 587, Winona Lake, IN 46590

Grace Schools, 200 Seminary Dr., Winona Lake, IN 46590. Tel. (210)372-5100. Pres., Dr. John Davis

Brethren Missionary Herald Co.: Publisher & Gen. Mgr., Charles Turner, P.O. Box 544, Winona Lake, IN 46590

Women's Missionary Council: Pres., Mrs. Betty Ogden, 8400 Good Luck Rd., Lanham, MD 20706

CE National: Exec. Dir., Rev. Ed Lewis, P.O. Box 365, Winona Lake, IN 46590

Grace Brethren Men & Boys: Exec. Dir., Rev. Ed Jackson, P.O. Box 416, Winona Lake, IN 46590

PERIODICAL

Brethren Missionary Herald, P.O. Box 544, Winona Lake, IN 46590 Ed., Rev. Charles Turner

Grace Gospel Fellowship

The Grace Gospel Fellowship was organized in 1944 by a group of pastors who held to a dispensational interpretation of Scripture. Most of these men had ministries in the Midwest (Ill., Ind., Wis., Ohio, Mo.). Two prominent leaders were J. C. O'Hair of Chicago and Charles Baker of Milwaukee.

Subsequent to 1945, a Bible Institute was founded (now Grace Bible College of Grand Rapids, Mich.), and a previously organized foreign mission (now Grace Ministries International of Grand Rapids) was affiliated with the group. Churches have now been established in most sections of the country.

The body has remained a fellowship, each church being autonomous in polity. All support for its college, mission, and headquarters is on a contributary basis.

The binding force of the Fellowship has been the members' doctrinal position. They believe in the Deity and Saviorship of Jesus Christ and subscribe to the inerrant authority of Scripture. Their method of biblical interpretation is dispensational, with emphasis on the distinctive revelation to and the ministry of the apostle Paul.

Churches: 52; Inclusive Membership: 4,500; Sunday or Sabbath School: N.R.; Total Enrollment: N.R.; Ordained Clergy: 125

GENERAL ORGANIZATION

National Cabinet which recommends policies and programs to the annual convention for approval. After approval it presents them to the constituent churches for voluntary united action.

OFFICERS

Pres., Charles E. O'Connor, 1011 Aldon St., SW, Grand Rapids, MI 49509. Tel. (616) 531-0046

OTHER ORGANIZATIONS

Grace Bible College, 1011 Aldon St., S.W., Grand Rapids, MI 49509. Pres., Dr. Samual Vinton

Grace Ministries International, 2125 Martindale Ave., SW, Grand Rapids, MI 49509. Exec. Dir., Wayne Schoonover

Missionary Literature Distributors, 7514 Humbert Rd., Godfrey, IL 62305. Dir., Mrs. Betty Strelow

Prison Mission Association, P.O. Box 3397, Riverside, CA 92509. Gen. Dir., Mr. Joe Mason

Grace Publications, Inc., 2125 Martindale Ave., SW, Grand Rapids, MI 49509. Exec. Dir., Timothy Conklin

Bible Doctrines to Live By, P.O. Box 2351, Grand Rapids, MI 49501. Exec. Dir., Lee Homoki

PERIODICAL

Truth (bi-m), 1011 Aldon, S.W., Grand Rapids, MI 49509

Greek Orthodox Archdiocese of North and South America

The Greek Orthodox Archdiocese of North and South America is under the jurisdiction of the Ecumenical Patriarchate of Constantinople, in Istanbul. It was chartered in 1922 by the State of New York and has parishes in the United States, Canada, Central and South America. The first Greek Orthodox Church was founded in New Orleans, Louisiana, in 1864.

GENERAL ORGANIZATION

His Eminence Archbishop Iakovos, Primate of the Greek Orthodox Church of North and South America and Exarch of the Ecumenical Patriarchate in the Western Hemisphere

Headquarters: 8-10 E. 79th St., New York, NY 10021. Tel. (212) 570-3500

ARCHDIOCESAN COUNCIL

Chpsn., Archbishop Iakovos

Vice-Chpsn., Metropolitan Silas of New Jersey

Officers:

Pres., Andrew A. Athens (Chicago, IL)

1st Vice-Pres., George Chimples, (Cleveland, OH)

2nd Vice-Pres., Michael Jaharias, (New York, NY)

Sec., Peter Kourides (New York, NY)

Treas., Peter Dion, Theodore Prounis, (New York, NY)

SYNOD OF BISHOPS

His Eminence Archbishop Iakovos, Chpsn.

His Excellency Metropolitan Silas of New Jersey, 8 East 79th St., New York, NY 10021

His Grace Bishop Iakovos of Chicago, Forty East Burton Pl., Chicago, IL 60610

His Grace Bishop Timothy of Detroit, 19504 Renfrew, Detroit, MI 48211

His Grace Bishop Sotirios of Toronto, 40 Donlands Ave., Toronto, Ontario M4J 3N6

His Grace Bishop Anthony of San Francisco, 372 Santa Clara Ave., San Francisco, CA 94127

His Grace Bishop Maximos of Pittsburgh, 5201 Ellsworth Ave., Pittsburgh, PA 15232

His Grace Bishop Gennadios of Buenos Aires, Avenida Figueroa Alcorta 3187, Buenos Aires, Argentina

His Grace Bishop Methodios of Boston, 162 Goddard Ave., Brookline, MA 02146

ASSISTANT BISHOPS TO ARCHBISHOP IAKOVOS

(Unless otherwise indicated, located at 8-10 E. 79th St., New York, NY 10021)

His Grace Bishop Philotheos of Meloa; His Grace Bishop Kallistos of Zelon, Patriarch Athenagoras Retreat Center, Cheyenne WY 82001; His Grace Bishop Philip of Daphnousia, St. Basil Academy, Rt. 9D, Garrison, NY 10524; His Grace Bishop Athenagoras of Dorylaion; His Grace Bishop Isaiah of Aspendos, Chancellor; His Grace Bishop Alexios of Troas, Chorepiscopos of Astoria, 27-09 Crescent St., Astoria, NY 11102

ARCHDIOCESAN DEPARTMENTS

(Unless otherwise indicated, located at 8-10 E. 79th St., New York, NY 10021)

Rel. Ed., 50 Goddard Ave., Brookline MA 02146; Youth Ministry and Camping, 39-10 Broadway, Astoria NY 11106; Church and Society; Economic Development; Ecumenical Office; Stewardship; Registry; Ionian Village; Communications, 27-09 Crescent St., Astoria, NY 11102; Archives; Logos, 36-10 Broadway, Mission Center, P.O. Box 4319, St. Augustine, FL 32085

ORGANIZATIONS

(Unless otherwise indicated, located at 8-10 E. 79th St., New York, NY 10021)

Ladies Philoptochos Society, 319 E. 74th St., New York, NY 10021

Greek Orthodox Young Adult League (GOYAL), 27-09 Crescent St., Astoria, NY 11102

Order of St. Andrew the Apostle

Archdiocesan Presbyters' Council

National Sisterhood of Presbyters

National Forum of Greek Orthodox Church Musicians, 1700 N. Walnut St., Bloomington, IN 47401

PERIODICAL

The Orthodox Observer (bi-w), 8 E. 79th St., New York, NY 10021

The Holiness Church of God, Inc.

Established at Madison, North Carolina, in 1920; incorporated in 1928 at Winston-Salem, North Carolina

GENERAL ORGANIZATION

General Assembly: annual

Headquarters: Winston-Salem, NC

OFFICERS

Pres., Bishop B. McKinney, 602 E. Elm St., Graham, NC 27253

Vice-Bishop, Melvin Charley, 140-39 172nd St., Springfield Gardens, NY 11434

Gen. Sec., Mrs. Nina B. Hash, Box 541, Galax, VA 24333

Overseer, Northern Area of N.E. Dist., Melvin Charley, 140-39 172nd St., Springfield Gardens, NY 11434

Overseer, So. Dist., Bishop T. R. Rice, 1439 Sedgefield Dr., Winston-Salem NC 27105. Tel. (919)227-4755

Overseer, Va. & W. Va., Area of N.W. Dist., Elder Arnie Joyce, Thorpe, WV 24888

Overseer, North Carolina Area of N.W. Dist., James Compton, 3661 Barkwood Dr., Winston-Salem, NC 27105

Holy Ukrainian Autocephalic Orthodox Church in Exile

Organized in a parish in New York in 1951. The laymen and clergy who organized it came from among the Ukrainians who settled in the Western Hemisphere after World War II. In 1954 two bishops, immigrants from Europe, met with clergy and laymen and formally organized the religious body.

GENERAL ORGANIZATION

Headquarters: 103 Evergreen St., W. Babylon, NY 11704

Administrator: Rt. Rev. Serhij K. Pastukhiv. Tel. (516) 669-7402

House of God, Which is the Church of the Living God, the Pillar and Ground of the Truth, Inc.

This body, founded by Mary L. Tate in 1919, is episcopally organized.

GENERAL ORGANIZATION

Meets annually, in October

OFFICER

Bishop Raymond W. White, 6107 Cobbs Creek Pkwy., Philadelphia, PA 19143. Tel. (215) 748-6338

PERIODICAL

Spirit of Truth Magazine (m), 3943 Fairmont Ave., Philadelphia, PA 19104. Bishop Raymond A. White, Ed.

Hungarian Reformed Church in America

A Hungarian Reformed Church was organized in New York in 1904 in connection with the Reformed Church of Hungary. In 1922 the Church in Hungary transferred most of her congregations in the U.S. to the Reformed Church in the U.S. Some, however, preferred to continue as an autonomous, self-supporting American denomination, and these formed the Free Magyar Reformed Church in America. This group changed its name in 1958 to Hungarian Reformed Church in America.

This Church is a member of the World Alliance of Reformed Churches, Presbyterian and Congregational, the WCC and the NCCC. It is deeply involved in the Roman Catholic, Presbyterian Reformed Consultation, of which for over 12 years Dr. Andrew Harsanyi has been co-chairman.

Churches: 31; Inclusive Membership: 12,500; Sunday or Sabbath Schools: 20; Total Enrollment: 600; Ordained Clergy: 26

OFFICERS

Bishop, Rt. Rev. Dr. Andrew Harsanyi, P.O. Box D, Hopatcong, NY 07843

Chief Lay-Curator, Anthony C. Beke, Box 335, Crosswick, NJ 08515

Gen. Sec., Rt. Rev. Dezso Trombitas, 751 Crenshaw Blvd., Los Angeles, CA 90005

Gen. Sec. (Lay), Prof. Stephen Szabo, 464 Forest Ave., Paramus, NJ 07652

Dean, New York Classis, The Very Rev. Alex Forro, 13 Grove St., Poughkeepsie, NY 12601

Dean, Western Classis, The Very Rev. Andor Demeter, 3921 W. Christy Dr., Phoenix, AZ 85029

Dean, Eastern Classis, The Very Rev. Stefan M. Torok, 331 Kirkland Pl., Perth Amboy, NJ 08861.

PERIODICAL

Magyar Egyhaz (Magyar Church) (6/yr.), Stefan Torok, Perth Amboy, NJ, Ed.

Hutterian Brethren

Small groups of Hutterites deriving their names from Jacob Hutter a 16-century Anabaptist who advocated communal ownership of property and was burned as a heretic in Austria in 1536.

Many believers are of German descent and still use their native tongue at home and in church. Much of the denominational literature is produced in German and English. "Colonies" share property, practice non-resistance, dress differently, refuse to participate in politics, and operate their own schools. There are 360 colonies with 37,000 members in North America.

Each congregation conducts its own youth work through Sunday school. Until age 15, children attend German school after attending public school. All youth, ages 15 to 20 must attend Sunday school. They are baptized upon confession of faith, around age 20.

CORRESPONDENT

Rev. Paul S. Gross, Rt. 1, Box 6E, Reardon WA 99029. Tel. (509)299-5400

Independent Fundamental Churches of America

Organized 1930 at Cicero, Illinois by representatives of the American Council of Undenominational Churches and representatives of various independent churches. The founding churches and members had separated themselves from various denominational affiliations.

The IFCA provides an advance movement among independent churches and ministers to unite in a close fellowship and cooperation, in defense of the fundamental teachings of Scripture and in the proclamation of the gospel of God's grace.

GENERAL ORGANIZATION

Headquarters: 3520 Fairlanes, Grandville, MI 49418. Tel. (616)531-1840
Mailing Address: PO. Box 810, Grandville, MI 49468

EXECUTIVE OFFICERS

National Exec. Dir., Dr. Richard Gregory, 2684 Meadow Ridge Dr., Byron Center, MI 49315. Tel. (616)878-1285
Pres., Dr. Richard Keltner, 1315 North Adams Dr., Colorado Springs, CO 80904
1st Vice-Pres., Dr. Richard Mercado, 1733 W. Devonshire, Phoenix, AZ 85015
2nd Vice-Pres., Dr. Elwood H. Chipchase, 3645 S. 57th Ct., Cicero, IL 70650

PERIODICAL

The Voice (m), P.O. Box 810, Grandville, MI 49468. Rev. Paul J. Dollaske, Ed.

International Church of the Foursquare Gospel

Founded by Aimee Semple McPherson in 1927, the InternationalChurch of the Foursquare Gospel proclaims the message of Jesus Christ the Savior, Healer, Baptizer with the Holy Spirit and Soon-coming King. Headquartered at Angelus Temple in Los Angeles, CA, this evangelistic missionary body of believers consists of nearly 1,300 churches in the United States and Canada.

The International Church of the Foursquare Gospel is incorporated in the State of California and governed by a Board of Directors who direct its corporate affairs. A Missionary Cabinet, consisting of the Board of Directors, District Supervisors of the various districts of Foursquare churches in the United States and other elected or appointed members, serves in an advisory capacity to the President and the Board of Directors.

Each local Foursquare church is a subordinate unit of the International Church of the Foursquare Gospel. The pastor of the church is appointed by the Board of Directors and is responsible for the spiritual and physical welfare of the church. To assist and advise the pastor, a church council is elected by the local church members.

Through a program entitled *2000 Before 2000*, the Foursquare church has envisioned 2,000 churches throughout the United States before the year 2000. Complementing this expansion, Foursquare churches seek to build strong believers through Christian education, Christian day schools, youth camping and ministry, United Foursquare Women who support and encourage Foursquare missionaries abroad, radio and television ministries, the Foursquare World ADVANCE magazine and 102 Bible Colleges worldwide.

Worldwide missions remains the focus of the Foursquare Gospel Church with nearly 20,913 churches, 15,319 national Foursquare pastors/leaders and 1,253,093 members and adherents in 68 countries around the globe.

Churches: 1,363; Inclusive Membership: 198,715; Sunday or Sabbath Schools: 1,014; Total Enrollment: 46,624; Ordained Clergy: 5,076

GENERAL ORGANIZATION

International Church of the Foursquare Gospel: 1910 W. Sunset Blvd., Ste. 610, Los Angeles, CA 90026. Tel. (213)484-2400
International Foursquare Convention: annual
Headquarters: Angelus Temple, 1100 Glendale Blvd., Los Angeles, CA 90026. Tel. (213) 484-1100

OFFICERS

Pres., Dr. John R. Holland

Vice-Pres., Dr. Roy Hicks, Jr.
Gen. Supervisor, Rev. J. Eugene Kurtz
Dir. of Missions International, Roy Hicks, Jr.
Sec., Rev. John W. Bowers
Treas., Rev. Virginia Cravans
Exec. Sec., Dr. Charles Duarte
Board of Directors: Dr. John R. Holland, Dr. Rolf K. McPherson, Dr. Roy Hicks, Jr., Dr. John W. Bowers, Dr. Harold Helms, Dr. Howard P. Courtney, Dr. Leland B. Edwards; Dr. J. Eugene Kurtz, Mr. John M. Boone, Rev. James Ritch, Rev. Ron Williams
District Supervisors:
Eastern, Rev. Dewey Morrow
Great Lakes, Dr. Fred Parker
Midwest, Rev. Glen Metzler
Northwest, Rev. Cliff Hanes
South Central, Dr. Sidney Westbrook
Southeast, Dr. Glenn Burris
Southern California, Rev. Don Long
Southwest, Rev. John Watson
Western, Dr. Fred Wymore
Missionary Cabinet: Composed of Board of Directors, District Supervisors, Dr. Charles Duarte, Dr. Jack Hamilton, Charles Aldridge, Rev. Tim Peterson, Dr. Colman Phillips, Rev. Dan Ussery, David Holland

SUPPORT MINISTRIES

National Department of Youth: National Youth Minister, Rev. Gregg Johnson
National Department of Christian Education and Publications: Dir., Rev. Rick Wulfestieg
United Foursquare Women: Pres., Shirley West

MEMBER OF OTHER ORGANIZATIONS

Pentecostal Fellowship of North America
National Association of Evangelicals
World Pentecostal Fellowship

PERIODICALS

(All published at 1100 Glendale Blvd., Los Angeles. CA 90026)
Foursquare World Advance (7/yr.) Rev. Ron Williams, Ed.
United Foursquare Women's Magazine, Shirley West

The International Pentecostal Church of Christ

At a General Conference held at London, Ohio, August 10, 1976, the International Pentecostal Assemblies and the Pentecostal Church of Christ, after a two-year trial period, by overwhelming majority votes from each group, consolidated into one body, taking the name International Pentecostal Church of Christ.

The International Pentecostal Assemblies was the successor of the Association of Pentecostal Assemblies and the International Pentecostal Missionary Union. The other body involved in the merger, the Pentecostal Church of Christ, was founded by John Stroup of Flatwoods, Kentucky, on May 10, 1917, and was incorporated at Portsmouth, Ohio, in 1927.

The International Pentecostal Church of Christ is an active member of the Pentecostal Fellowship of North America, as well as a member of the National Association of Evangelicals.

The priorities of the International Pentecostal Church of Christ are to be an agency of God for evangelizing the world, to be a corporate body in which man may worship God, and to be a channel of God's purpose to build a body of saints being perfected in the image of his Son.

The Annual Conference is held each year during the first full week of August on Route 42 in London, Ohio, which houses the Conference Center offices and national campgrounds.

Churches: 75; Inclusive Membership: 2,628; Sunday or Sabbath Schools: 75; Total Enrollment: 3,884; Ordained Clergy: 123

GENERAL ORGANIZATION

Headquarters: 2245 St. Rt. 42 SW; Mailing Address: P. O. Box 439, London, OH 43140. Tel. (614) 852-0348

EXECUTIVE COMMITTEE

Gen. Overseer, Tom G. Grinder, P. O. Box 439, London OH 43140. Tel. (614) 852-0348
Asst. Gen. Overseer, Clyde M. Hughes, P.O. Box 439, London OH 43140. Tel. (614)852-0448
Gen. Sec., Rev.Thomas Dooley, 3200 Dueber Ave. S.W., Canton OH 44706. Tel. (216)484-6053
Gen. Treas., Rev. Clifford A. Edwards, P. O. Box 18145, Atlanta, GA 30316. Tel. (404)627-2681
Dir. of Global Missions, Dr. James B. Keiller, P. O. Box 18145, Atlanta, GA 30316. Tel. (404) 627-2681

PERIODICAL

The Bridegroom's Messenger, 121 W. Hunters Trail, Elizabeth City, NC 27909

Israelite House of David

The Israelite House of David, commonly called House of David, was established in 1903 in Benton Harbor, Michigan, by Brother Benjamin, our founder and leader, after he had preached the Life of the Body without going to the grave, while traveling for seven years throughout a number of mid-American states.

We are a Christian Association following Jesus' teachings (I Tim. 1:16) and the first born among many brethren (Rom. 8:29). We believe Brother Benjamin to have been the voice of the seventh angel referred to in Revelation 10:7; Malachi 3:1; Job 33:23-25. In his writings he points out the way for the elect to receive the Life of the Body (Hosea 13:14; Isa. 38:18; I Thess. 5:23; Matt. 7:14; Titus 1:2; II Tim. 1:10; John 10:10, 27, 28).

Three classes are mainly referred to in the Bible—Jew, Gentile, and Israel. The Jew and the Gentile will receive the Soul Salvation, a free Gift (Eph. 2:8). The Elect of Israel—a few (Matt. 5:5), numbered in the seventh and fourteenth chapters of Revelation as 144,000 of all the tribes of the children of Israel—will receive the Life of the Body. In Zechariah 13:8 we read, "Two parts shall be cut off and die, but the third part shall be left therein." According to Isaiah 19:24, Israel will be the third.

In Brother Benjamin's writings are revealed many keys to the Scriptures, which bring harmony to many apparent contradictions sealed till the time of the end (Dan. 12:9; I Cor. 10:11). We expect to gather the 12 tribes of Israel (Jer. 31:1; Ezek. 20:34, 34:13, 14; Hosea 1:11), which will be carried over into the millennium day of rest, 1,000 years (Rev. 20:1, 2 and 21:2, 4; Isa. 11:6-9, 35:1, 55:13, 54:13). Israel will be gathered from both Jew and Gentile.

GENERAL ORGANIZATION

Headquarters: P.O. Box 1067, Benton Harbor, MI 49022. Tel. (616) 926-6695

OFFICERS

Chpsn. of Bd., Lloyd H. Dalager
Pillar & Sec., H. Thomas Dewhirst

Jehovah's Witnesses

The modern history of Jehovah's Witnesses began a little more than 100 years ago. In the early 1870s an inconspicuous Bible study began in Allegheny City, Pennsylvania, now a part of Pittsburgh. Charles Taze Russell was the prime mover of the group. In July 1879, the first issue of Zion's Watch Tower and Herald of Christ's Presence appeared. (Now called The Watchtower with a circulation of 13,045,000 in 104 languages.) By 1880 scores of congregations had spread from that one small Bible study into nearby states. In 1881 Zion's Watch Tower Tract Society was formed, and in 1884 was incorporated with Russell as president. The Society's name was later changed to Watch Tower Bible and Tract Society. Many witnessed from house to house, offering biblical literature.

By 1909 the work had become international, and the Society's headquarters was moved to its present location in Brooklyn, New York. Printed sermons were syndicted in newspapers, and by 1913 were in four languages in 3,000 newspapers in the United States, Canada, and Europe. Books, booklets, and tracts had been distributed by the hundreds of millions.

Russell died in 1916 and was succeeded the following year by Joseph F. Rutherford. Under his direction the magazine Golden Age was introduced (now called Awake! with a circulation of 11,350,000 in 54 languages). In 1931 the name Jehovah's Witnesses, based on Isaiah 43:10-12, was adopted.

During the 1930s and 1940s Jehovah's Witnesses fought many court cases in the interest of preserving freedom of speech, press, assembly, and worship. In the United States, appeals from lower courts resulted in the Witnesses winning 43 cases before the Supreme Court. Professor C. S. Braden stated, "In their struggle they have done much to secure those rights for every minority group in America."

When Rutherford died in 1942, he was succeeded by N. H. Knorr, who immediately instituted a concerted program of training for all Jehovah's Witnesses. The Watchtower Bible School of Gilead was established in 1943 for training missionaries. It has been primarily through the efforts of these missionaries that the word has expanded today to include 212 countries.

From that small beginning in Pennsylvania, the Witnesses have expanded to the far corners of the earth and now number more than 3½ million. The present president F. W. Franz and a small group of fellow administrators serve as a governing body, overseeing the work, organized under 93 branches.

From the beginning Jehovah's Witnesses have believed in one almighty God, Jehovah, creator of heaven and earth. They believe that Christ is God's Son, the first of God's creations and subject to Jehovah. Christ's human life was paid as a ransom for obedient humans. Jehovah has assigned him a Kingdom, a government for which all Christians pray and through which Christ will cleanse the earth of wickedness and rule it in righteousness and peace. The book of Revelation assigns 144,000 individuals "who have been bought from the earth," to rule with him. This Kingdom government will rule over the "meek who will inherit the earth" mentioned in the Sermon on the Mount. These people from all nations, along with the resurrected dead, will work to transform the earth into a global Edenic paradise. This is the "good news" Jehovah's Witnesses are commissioned to preach from house to house during these last days of the present system of things. When this has been accomplished Jesus says "the end will come" and will be followed by the righteous rule of his kingdom (Matt. 24:14).

Churches: 8,851; Inclusive Membership: 804,639; Sunday or Sabbath Schools: None; Total Enrollment: None; Ordained Clergy: None

GENERAL ORGANIZATION

Headquarters: 25 Columbia Heights, Brooklyn, NY 11201. Tel. (718) 625-3600

OFFICER

Pres. Frederick W. Franz

PERIODICALS

The Watchtower and Awake! 25 Columbia Heights, Brooklyn, NY 11201

Jewish Organizations

Jews arrived in the colonies before 1650. The first Congregation is recorded in 1654, in New York City, the Shearith Israel (Remnant of Israel).

Congregations: 3,416; Community: 5,935,000; Total Number of Rabbis: 6,500

CONGREGATIONAL AND RABBINICAL ORGANIZATIONS

Federation of Reconstructionist Congregations and Havurot: Church Road and Greenwood Ave., Wyncote, PA 19095. Tel. (215)576-0800; Pres., Roger Price; Exec. Dir., Rabbi Mordechai Liebling
*Union of American Hebrew Congregations (Reform): 838 Fifth Ave., New York, NY 10021. Tel. (212) 249-0100; Pres.,. Rabbi Alexander M. Schindler; Bd. Chpsn., Allan B. Goldman.
*United Synagogue of America (Conservative): 155 Fifth Ave.,NY 10010. Tel. (212) 533-7800; Pres., Franklin D. Kreutzer; Exec. Vice Pres., Rabbi Benjamin Z. Kreitman
*Union of Orthodox Jewish Congregations of America: 45 W. 36th St., New York, NY 10018. Tel (212)563-4000; Pres., Sidney Kwestel; Exec. Vice Pres., Rabbi Pinchas Stolper
*Central Conference of American Rabbis (Reform): 192 Lexington Ave., New York, NY 10016. Tel. (212) 684-4990; Pres., Rabbi Eugene J. Lipman; Exec. Vice-Pres., Rabbi Joseph B. Glaser
Rabbinical Alliance of America (Orthodox): 3 W. 16th St., 4th Fl., New York, NY 10011. Tel. (212)242-6420; Pres., Rabbi Abraham B. Hecht
*The Rabbinical Assembly (Conservative): 3080 Broadway, New York, NY 10027. Tel. (212) 678-8060; Pres., Rabbi Albert L. Lewis; Exec. Vice-Pres., Rabbi Wolfe Kelman
*Rabbinical Council of America, Inc. (Orthodox): 275 Seventh Ave., New York, NY 10001. Tel. (212) 807-7888; Pres., Rabbi Max N. Schreier; Exec. Vice-Pres., Rabbi Binyamin Walfish
Reconstructionist Rabbinical Association: Church Rd. and Greenwood Ave., Wyncote, PA 19095. Tel. (215) 576-0800. Pres., Rabbi Sandy Sasso; Adm., Michael Cohen
Union of Orthodox Rabbis of the United States and Canada: 235 E. Broadway, New York, NY 10002. Tel. (212) 964-6337; Dir., Rabbi Hersh M. Ginsberg
*Synagogue Council of America: 327 Lexington Ave., New York, NY 10016. Tel. (212) 686-8670; Pres., Rabbi Gilbert Klaperman; Exec. Vice-Pres., Rabbi Henry D. Michelman
*Synagogue Council of America is the coordinating body of the organizations starred above.

EDUCATIONAL AND SOCIAL SERVICE ORGANIZATIONS

American Council for Judaism, The: 298 Fifth Ave. New York, NY 10001. Tel. (212) 947-8878; Bd. Chpsn., Clarence L. Coleman, Jr.; Pres., Alan V. Stone
American Jewish Committee: 165 E. 56th St., New York, NY 10022. Tel. (212) 751-4000; Pres., Sholom D. Comay; Exec. Vice-Pres., Ira Silverman
American Jewish Congress: 15 E. 84th St., New York, NY 10028. Tel. (212) 879-4500; Pres., Robert L. Lifton; Exec. Dir., Henry Siegman
American Jewish Historical Society: 2 Thornton Rd., Waltham, MA 02154. Tel. (617) 891-8110; Pres., Phil David Fine; Dir., Bernard Wax
American Jewish Joint Distribution Committee: 711 Third Ave., New York, NY 10017. Tel. (212) 687-6200; Pres., Heinz Eppler; Exec. Vice-Chpsn., Michael Schneider

Anti-Defamation League of B'nai B'rith: 823 United Nations Plaza, New York, NY 10017, Tel. (212) 490-2525. Chpsn., Burton S. Levinson; Dir., Abraham H. Foxman
B'nai B'rith Hillel Foundations; Inc.: 1640 Rhode Island Ave. NW, Washington, DC 20036. Tel. (202) 857-6560; Chpsn., B'nai B'rith Hillel Cmte., Edwin Shapiro; Assoc. Intl. Dirs., Richard M. Joel; Assoc. Intl Dir., Rabbi William D. Rudolph
Conference of Presidents of Major American Jewish Organizations: 515 Park Ave., New York, NY 10022. Tel. (212) 752-1616; Chpsn., Seymour D. Reich; Exec. Dir., Malcolm Hoenlein
Council for Jewish Education: 426 W. 58th St., New York, NY 10019. Tel. (212) 713-0290. Pres., Rabbi Bernard Ducoff; Exec. Dir., Philip Gorodetzer
Council of Jewish Federations: 730 Broadway, New York, NY 10003. Tel. (212) 475-5000; Pres., Mandel O. Berman; Exec. Vice-Pres., Carmi Schwartz
Hadassah, The Women's Zionist Organization of America: 50 W. 58th St., New York, NY 10019. Tel. (212) 355-7900; Nat'l Pres., Carmela E. Kalmanson; Exec. Dir., Aileen Novick
HIAS, Inc. (Hebrew Immigrant Aid Society): 200 Park Ave., S., New York, NY 10003. Tel. (212) 674-6800; Pres., Ben Zion Leuchter; Exec. Vice-Pres., Karl D. Zukerman
Jewish Publication Society: 1930 Chestnut St., Philadelphia, PA 19103. Tel. (215) 564-5925; Pres., Edward E. Elson; Exec. Vice Pres., Richard Malina
Jewish Reconstructionist Foundation: Church Rd. and Greenwood Ave., Wycote, PA 19095. Tel. (215)887-1988. Pres., Lillian S. Kaplan; Exec. Dir., Rabbi Mordechai Liebling;
JWB (National Jewish Welfare Board): 15 E 26th St., New York, NY 10010. Tel. (212) 532-4949; Pres., Donald R. Mintz; Exec. Vice-Pres., Arthur Rotman
Jewish War Veterans of the United States of America, Inc.: 1811 R St., Washington, DC 20009. Tel. (202) 265-6280; Natl. Exec. Dir., Steven Shaw
National Federation of Temple Brotherhoods: 838 Fifth Ave., New York, NY 10021. Tel. (212) 570-0707; Pres., Richard D. Karfunkle; Exec. Dir., Lewis Eisenberg
National Federation of Temple Sisterhoods: 838 Fifth Ave., New York, NY 10021. Tel. (212) 249-0100; Pres., Delores Wilkenfeld; Exec. Dir., Eleanor R. Schwartz
National Jewish Community Relations Advisory Council: 443 Park Ave., S., 11th Fl., New York, NY 10016. Tel. (212) 684-6950; Chpsn., Michael A. Pelavin; Exec. Vice-Chpsn. Albert D. Chernin
United Jewish Appeal: 99 Park Ave., New York, NY 10016. Tel. (212) 818-9100; Natl. Chmn., Morton A. Kornreich; Pres., Stanley Horowitz; Chpsn. Board of Trustees, Martin F. Stein
Women's Branch of the Union of Orthodox Jewish Congregations of America: 156 Fifth Ave., New York, NY 10010. Tel. (212) 929-8857; Pres., Gitti Needleman
Women's League for Conservative Judaism: 48 E. 74th St., New York, NY 10021. Tel. (212) 628-1600; Pres. Evelyn Auerbach; Exec., Bernice Balter
Zionist Organization of America: 4 E. 34th St., New York, NY 10016. Tel. (212) 481-1500; Pres., Milton S. Shapiro; Natl. Exec. Dir., Paul Flacks

PERIODICALS

Orthodox
Jewish Action (q), 45 W.36th Ave., New York, NY 10018. Tel. (212) 244-2011; Heidi Tenzer, Ed.
Tradition (semi-a), 275 Seventh Ave., New York, NY 10001. Tel. (212) 807-7888; Rabbi Meyer Hager, Ed.
Conservative
United Synagogue Review (bi-a), 155 Fifth Ave., New York, NY 10010. Tel. (212) 533-7800; Rochel Berman, Ed.

Conservative Judaism (q), 3080 Broadway, New York, NY 10027. Tel. (212) 678-8049; Rabbi David Silverman, Ed.

Reform
Journal of Reform Judaism, (q), 192 Lexington Ave., New York 10016. Tel. (212) 684-4990; Samuel Stahl, Ed.

Reform Judaism (q), 838 5th Ave., New York, NY 10021. Tel. (212) 249-0100; Aron Hirt-Manheimer, Ed.

Reconstructionist
The Reconstructionist (6/yr.), Church Rd. and Greenwood Ave., Wycote, PA 19095. Jacob J. Staub, Ed. ____

Jewish Education (q), Council for Jewish Education, 426 W. 58th St., New York, NY 10019. Tel. (212) 245-8200; Alvin I. Schiff, Ed.

The Pedagogic Reporter (q), Jewish Education Service of North America, 730 Broadway, New York, NY 10003. Tel. (212) 529-2000; Mordecai H. Lewittes, Ed.

American Jewish History (q), American Jewish Historical Society, 2 Thornton Rd., Waltham, MA 02154. Tel. (617) 891-8110; Marc Lee Raphael, Ed.

Note: For details concerning many aspects of Jewish life and organization in the United States and throughout the world, consult *American Jewish Yearbook, 1989* prepared by the American Jewish Committee, New York, and the Jewish Publication Society of America, Philadelphia, David Singer, Ed.

Kodesh Church of Immanuel

Founded 1929 and incorporated in April 1930 by Rev. Frank Russell Killingsworth and 120 laymen, some of whom were former members of the African Methodist Episcopal Zion Church. On January 22, 1934, the Christian Tabernacle Union, a body of holy people with headquarters in Pittsburgh, merged with the Kodesh Church of Immanuel. This body is an interracial body of believers whose teachings are Wesleyan and Arminian.

GENERAL ORGANIZATION
Annual Assembly—convening once a year
General Assembly—meeting quadrennially

OFFICERS
Supervising Elder: Dr. Kenneth O. Barbour, 932 Logan Rd., Bethel Park, PA 15102. Tel. (412) 833-1351

OTHER ORGANIZATIONS
Church Extension Board: Chmn., Mrs. Thelma P. Homes, 6537 Deary St.,Pittsburgh, PA 15206
Foreign Mission Board: Pres., Mrs. E. Lucille Lockhart, 1934 N. Charles St., Pittsburgh, PA 15214
Young People's Societies: Gen. Pres., Mrs. Catherine B. Harris, 1428 Forrester Ave., Greenhill Park, Sharon Hill, PA 19079
Harty Bible School: Dr. Kenneth O. Barbour, 932 Logan Rd., Bethel Park, PA 15102
Sunday Schools: Gen. Supt., Mrs. Bernice Williams, 47 Mt. Vernon Dr., Aliquippa, PA 15001

Korean Presbyterian Church in America, General Assembly of the

This body came into official existence in the United States in 1976 and is currently an ethnic church, using the Korean language.

GENERAL ORGANIZATION
General Assembly meets annually.
Headquarters: 1251 Crenshaw Blvd., Los Angeles, CA 90019. Tel. (213)857-0361.

OFFICERS
Mod., Rev. Chang Sun Moon, 2237 W. Winnemac, Chicago, 60625. Tel. (312)561-9892
Vice-Mod., Rev. Chung Kuk Kim, 39-29 57 St., 2nd Fl., Woodside, NY 11377. Tel. (718)639-2536
Gen. Sec., Ruling Elder Nicholas C. Chun, 1251 Crenshaw Blvd., Los Angeles, CA 90019. Tel. (213)851-0361
Chpsn., Int'l Mission Cmte., Rev. Kwang Soo Choi, 249 S. Occidental Blvd., #306, Los Angeles, CA 90057
Stated Clerk, Rev. Moo Yeoul Rah, 2207 W. Woodley Ave., Anaheim, CA 92801. Tel. (714)772-7909

The Latvian Evangelical Lutheran Church in America

This body was organized into a denomination on August 22, 1975, after having existed as the Federation of Latvian Evangelical Lutheran Churches in America since 1955. This church is a regional constituent part of the Lutheran Church of Latvia in Exile, a member of the Lutheran World Federation and the World Council of Churches.

The Latvian Evangelical Lutheran Church in America works to foster religious life, traditions and customs in its congregations in harmony with the Holy Scriptures, the Apostles', Nicean and Athanasian Creeds, the unaltered Augsburg Confession, Martin Luther's Small and Large Catechisms and other documents of the Book of Concord.

The LELCA is ordered by its Synod (General Assembly), executive board, auditing committee, and district conferences.

Churches: 56; Inclusive Membership: 13,211; Sunday or Sabbath Schools: N.R.; Total Enrollment: N.R.; Ordained Clergy: 45

CORRESPONDENT
Pres., Rev. Vilis Varsbergs, 6551 W. Montrose Ave., Chicago, IL 60634. Tel. (312) 725-3820

The Liberal Catholic Church—Province of the United States of America

Founded February 13, 1916 as a reorganization of the Old Catholic Church in Great Britain, the Rt. Rev. James I. Wedgwood being the first Presiding Bishop. The first ordination of a Priest in the United States was Fr. Charles Hampton, later a Bishop. The first Regionary Bishop for the American Province was the Rt. Rev. Irving S. Cooper (1919-1935).

GENERAL ORGANIZATION
Board of Trustees, meets July 1, annually.
Provincial Episcopal Synod and Provincial Synod: Triennial
Provincial Headquarters: 1620 San Gabriel Rd., Ojai, CA 93023. Tel. (805) 646-2960

OFFICERS
Pres. and Regionary Bishop, The Rt. Rev. Lawrence J. Smith, 9740 S. Avers, Evergreen Park IL 60642. Tel. (312) 424-8329
Vice-Pres. and Vicar Gen., Very Rev. Alfred Strauss, 10606 Parrot Ave., Apt. A, Downey, CA 90241. Tel. (213)861-7569
Sec. (Provincial), The Rt. Rev. Dr. Hein VanBeusekom, 12 Krotona Hill, Ojai, CA 93023.
Provost, The Very Rev. Wm. Holme, P.O. Box 7042, Rochester, MN 55903
Treas., Pro Tem, Rt. Rev. Lawrence J. Smith, 9740 S. Avers, Evergreen Park, IL 60642. Tel. (312)424-8329
Chancellor, The Rt. Rev. Dr. Gerrit Munnik, 16 Krotona, Ojai CA 93023. Tel. (805) 646-2960 (AM only)

BISHOPS

Regionary Bishop for the American Province: The Rt. Rev. Lawrence J. Smith, 9740 S. Avers, Evergreen Park, IL 60642. Tel. (312) 424-8329.

Ep. Vicar Gen. for the Americas and Regionary Emeritus: The Rt. Rev. Dr. Gerrit Munnik, 16 Krotona, Ojai, CA 93023

Auxiliary Bishops of the American Province: (Address Rt. Rev.), Dr. Robert S. McGinnis, Jr., 2204 Armond Blvd., Destrehan, LA 70065; Joseph L. Tisch, PO. Box 1117, Melbourne, FL 23901; Dr. Hein VanBeusekom, 12 Krotona Hill, Ojai, CA 93023; Raja Watson, 7541 W. Forest Preserve Ave., Chicago, IL 60634

PERIODICAL

Ubique: American Province (q), P.O. Box 1117, Melbourne, FL 32901. Rt. Rev. Joseph Tisch, Ed.

Liberty Baptist Fellowship

The Liberty Baptist Fellowship consists of independent Baptist churches and pastors organized for the purpose of planting indigenous local New Testament churches in North America. The Fellowship is in general accord with the doctrines and philosophy of the Independent Baptist movement.

GENERAL ORGANIZATION

National Meeting: Annual
International Headquarters: Candler's Mountain Rd., Lynchburg, VA 24506. Tel. (804) 237-5961, ext. 325

OFFICERS

Exec. Comm: Chmn., Jerry Falwell; A. Pierre Guillermin; Exec. Dir., Elmer L. Towns; Exec. Sec., Dennis Fields, Sr.
Nat'l Comm: Pres., George Sweet; First Vice-Pres., Steve Reynolds; Second Vice-Pres., David Brown, John Cartwright, Bob Gass, Mike Grooms, Eddie Guy, Benny Hampton, Rudy Holland, Lindsay Howan, Danny Lovett, Ray Lyons, Allen MacFarland, Daren Ritchey, David Rhodenhizer

OTHER ORGANIZATIONS

Liberty Baptist Missions: Dir., Vernon Brewer

PERIODICALS

Liberty Journal (q), Elmer Towns, Ed.
Fundamentalist Journal (q), Jerry Falwell, Ed.

The Lutheran Church— Missouri Synod

The Lutheran Church—Missouri Synod, which began in the state of Missouri in 1847, has 9,000 groups of worshipers in 33 countries. Its 2.6 million North American membership forms the second-largest Lutheran denomination.

Christian education for all ages offers an array of weekday, Sunday school and Bible-class opportunities. The 6,000-plus North American congregations operate the largest elementary and secondary school systems of any Protestant denomination in the nation, and 12 colleges and seminaries in the U.S. enroll 9,100 students.

Traditional beliefs concerning the authority and interpretation of Scripture are important. In the late 1960s, a controversy developed, but following a decade of soul-searching that resulted in the walkout of most faculty members and students from one seminary and the eventual departure of slightly more than 100,000 members, little evidence of the controversy remains.

The synod is known for mass-media outreach through "The Lutheran Hour" on radio, "This Is The Life" dramas on television, and the products of Concordia Publishing House, the third-largest Protestant publisher, whose Arch Books children's series has sold 50 million copies.

An extensive Braille volunteer network makes devotional materials for the blind; 54 of the 85 deaf congregations affiliated with U.S. denominations are LCMS; and many denominations use the Bible lessons prepared for developmentally disabled persons.

The involvement of women is high, though they do not occupy clergy positions. Serving as teachers, deaconesses, and social workers, women comprise approximately 42 percent of total professional workers.

The members' responsibility for congregational leadership is a distinctive characteristic of the synod, a word that means *walking together*. Practice holds that the pastor is the equipper of the saints, but a pastor might find it difficult to locate the proper slot in a modern-day organizational chart. Power is vested in voters' assemblies, generally comprised of adults of voting age. Synod decision making is given to the delegates at national and regional conventions, where the franchise is equally divided between lay and pastoral representatives.

Churches: 5,939; Inclusive Membership: 2,604,278; Sunday or Sabbath Schools: 5,737; Total Enrollment: 652,332; Ordained Clergy: 8,193

GENERAL ORGANIZATION

General Convention: every three years, next meeting, 1992
Headquarters: The Lutheran Church—Missouri Synod, International Center, 1333 S. Kirkwood Rd., St. Louis, MO 63122

OFFICERS

Pres., Dr. Ralph A. Bohlmann
1st Vice-Pres., Dr. August T. Mennicke
2nd Vice-Pres., Dr. Robert King
3rd Vice-Pres., Dr. Robert C. Sauer
4th Vice-Pres., Dr. Eugene Bunkowske
5th Vice-Pres., Dr. Walter A. Maier
Sec., Dr. Walter L. Rosin
Treas., Dr. Norman Sell
Adm. Officer of Bd. of Dir., Dr. John P. Schuelke
Dir. of Personnel: Mr. William J. Barge
Board of Directors: Dr. Henry L. Koepchen, Setauket, NY; Rev. Arnold G. Kuntz, Cypress, CA; Rev. Victor H. Marxhausen, White Bear Lake, MN; Rev. Richard L. Thompson, Billings, MT; Mr. Clifford Dietrich, Ft. Wayne, IN; Mr. Donald J. Brosz, Laramie, WY; Mr. John L. Daniel, Emmaus, PA; Mr. Robert W. Hirsch, Yankton, SC; Dr. Florence Montz, Bismarck, ND; Dr. Harold M. Olsen, Springfield, IL; Mr. Lester W. Schultz, Russellville, AR, and Mr. Gilbert E. LaHaine, Lansing, MI, Mr. Donald Snyder, Henrietta, NY

BOARDS AND COMMISSIONS

(All at The Lutheran Church—Missouri Synod International Center, 1333 S. Kirkwood Rd., St. Louis, MO 63122, unless different address is given)
Board for Communication Services: Exec. Dir., Rev. Paul Devantier
Board for Evangelism Services: Exec. Dir., Dr. Erwin J. Kolb
Board for Mission Serivces: Exec. Dir., Dr. Edward A. Westcott
Board for Parish Services: Exec. Dir., Dr. H. James Boldt
Board for Higher Education Services: Exec. Dir., Dr. M. J. Stelmachowicz
Board for Youth Services: Exec. Dir., Mr. Richard W. Bimler
Board for Social Ministry Services: Exec. Dir., Dr. Eugene Linse
Board, Worker Benefit Plans: Administrator, Mr. Earl E. Haake

Lutheran Church Extension Fund-Missouri Synod: Pres., Mr. Arthur C. Haake
Ministry to the Armed Forces Standing Committee: Exec. Dir., Rev. James Shaw
Dept. of Stewardship and Financial Support: Dir., Mr. Richard L. Engdahl

AUXILIARY ORGANIZATIONS

Concordia Publishing House: 3558 S. Jefferson Ave., St. Louis, MO 63118. Pres./CEO, John Gerber
Concordia Historical Institute: Concordia Seminary, 801 De Mun Ave., St. Louis, MO 63105. Dir., Dr. August R. Suelflow
International Lutheran Laymen's League CEO: 2185 Hampton Ave., St. Louis, MO 63110. Exec. Dir., Mr. J. Schoedel
KFUO Radio: 801 De Mun Ave., St. Louis, MO 73105. Dir. of Broadcast Ministries, _____
International Lutheran Women's Missionary League: 3558 S. Jefferson Ave., St. Louis, MO 63118. Pres., Mrs. John L. (Betty) Duda

PERIODICALS

The Lutheran Witness (m), Rev. David Mahsman, News and Inf. Dir. and Ed.
Reporter/Alive (w), Rev. David Mahsman, Ed.

Lutheran Churches, The American Association of

This church body was constituted on November 7, 1987. The AALC was formed by laity and pastors of the former American Lutheran Church in America who held to a high view of Scripture (inerrancy and infallibility). This church body also emphasizes the primacy of evangelism and world missions and the authority and autonomy of the local congregation.

Congregations of the AALC are distributed throughout the continental United States from Long Island, New York to Los Angeles, California. The primary decision making body is the General Convention to which each congregation has proportionate representation.

Churches: 78; Inclusive Membership: 15,150; Sunday or Sabbath Schools: N.R.; Total Enrollment: N.R.; Ordained Clergy: 80

GENERAL ORGANIZATION

General Convention: annual (Next meeting, June, 20-23, 1990, Northwestern Bible College, Roseville, MN)
Headquarters: The AALC National Office, 10800 Lyndale Ave., S., Ste. 124, Minneapolis, MN 55420. Mailing Address: P.O. Box 17097, Minneapolis, MN 55417
The AALC Regional Office, 214 South St., Waterloo, IA 50701

OFFICERS

Presiding Pastor, Dr. Daune R. Lindberg, P.O. Box 416, Waterloo, IA 50701. Tel. (319)232-3971
Asst. Presiding Pastor, Rev. Donald C. Thorson, P.O. Box 775, Chippewa Falls, WI 54729
Sec., Rev. Thomas V. Aadland, 2415 Ensign St., Duluth MN 55811. Tel. (218)722-7931
Treas., Rev. James E. Minor, 341 S. Hamline Ave., St. Paul, MN 55105
Admn. Coord., Mr. Gene Quist, 11 Norman Ridge Dr., Bloomington, MN 55437

PERIODICAL

The Evangel (m), 214 South St., Waterloo, IA 50701. Dr. Christopher Barnekov, Ed.

Mennonite Church

The Mennonite Church in North America traces its beginnings back to 16th century Europe and the Protestant Reformation. Conrad Grebel, Georg Blaurock, and a small band of radical believers who felt that reformers Martin Luther and Ulrich Zwingli had not gone far enough in their break with Roman Catholic tradition and a return to New Testament discipleship Christianity, baptized one another in Zurich, Switzerland, on January 21, 1525. First nicknamed Anabaptists (Rebaptizers) by their opponents (they themselves preferred to use the term Brothers and Sisters in Christ), the Mennonites later took their name from the Dutch priest Menno Simons who joined the movement in 1536, and emerged as their leader.

The Mennonites' refusal to conform to majesterial decrees including bearing of arms and the swearing of oaths, attracted fierce animosity. Thousands were martyred for their beliefs in nearly a century of persecution. Eager to find freedom to live out their faith elsewhere, they moved to many places, including the United States and Canada where some arrived as early as 1683. Between four and five thousand Mennonites settled in southeastern Pennsylvania between 1717 and 1756 in the first major migration from Europe. Caught between the warring factions of America's struggle for independence, many moved west to Ohio, Indiana, Iowa, and especially north to upper Canada (now Ontario).

North American Mennonites began their first home mission program in Chicago, Ill., in 1893 and their first foreign mission program in India in 1899. Since the 1920s the church has established extensive emergency relief and development services in conjunction with its mission program.

Mennonites hold that the Word of God is central and that new life in Christ is available to all who believe. Adult "Believer's" baptism is practiced, symbolizing a conscious decision to follow Christ. Mennonites take seriously Christ's command to witness in word and deed. Concerned for both physical and spiritual aspects of life, they regard faith and works as two sides of the same coin. They stress that Christians need the support of a faith community for encouragement and growth. In times of crisis their "mutual aid" network makes time, money, and goods available to those in need. They view Jesus' teachings as directly applicable to their lives. Following the Prince of Peace, Mennonites generally refuse to serve in the military or to use violent resistance.

Currently the largest body of Mennonites in North America, the denomination has approximately 93,000 members in 42 states and the District of Columbia, and 9,600 members in six Canadian provinces (1987 statistics). The Mennonite Church is a member of the Mennonite and Brethren in Christ World Conference—a fellowship of 164 bodies in 60 countries around the world with a membership of 803,000. The denomination is also a member of Mennonite Central Committee, a world-wide relief and service agency representing 17 North American churches and bodies. While the denomination does not hold membership in any major ecumenical organizations in the United States and Canada, individuals and program agencies do participate in a variety of ecumenical activities at various levels of church life.

Churches: 1,023; Inclusive Membership: 92,682; Sunday or Sabbath Schools: N.R.; Total Enrollment: N.R.; Ordained Clergy: 2,469

GENERAL ORGANIZATION

General Assembly: biennial. Next meeting, 1991
General Office: 421 S. Second St., Ste. 600, Elkhart, IN 46516. Tel. (219)294-7131

OFFICERS

Mod., David W. Mann, 421 S. Second St., Ste. 600, Elkhart, IN 46516. Tel. (219)294-7131

OTHER ORGANIZATIONS

General Board: Exec. Sec. James M. Lapp, 421 S. Second Ste. 600, Elkhart, IN 46516

Historical Committee: Exec. Sec., Leonard Gross, 1700 S. Main, Goshen, IN. Tel. (219) 533-3161

Council on Faith, Life, and Strategy: Chpsn., Phyllis Pellman Good, 3513 Old Philadelphia Pike, Intercourse, PA 17534. Tel. (717)768-7171

Board of Congregational Ministries: Exec. Sec., Everett Thomas, Box 1245, Elkhart, IN 46515, Tel. (219) 294-7536

Board of Education: Exec. Sec., Albert Meyer, Box 1142, Elkhart, IN 46515. Tel. (219) 294-7531

Board of Missions: Pres., Paul M. Gingrich, Box 370, Elkhart, IN 46515. Tel. (219) 294-7523

Mutual Aid Board: Pres., James Kratz, 1110 North Main, P. O. Box 483, Goshen, IN 46526 Tel. (219) 533-9511

Mennonite Publication Board: Publisher, J. Robert Ramer, 616 Walnut Ave., Scottdale, PA 15683. Tel. (412) 887-8500

PERIODICALS

Gospel Herald (w), Scottdale, PA 15683 Daniel Hertzler, Ed.

Christian Living (m), Scottdale, PA 15683. David E. Hostetler, Ed.

Builder (m), Scottdale, PA 15683. David R. Hiebert, Ed.

Rejoice! (q) Scottdale, PA. Marjorie Waybill Assoc. Ed.

Mennonite Historical Bulletin (q), Goshen, IN 46526. Leonard Gross, Ed.

Mennonite Yearbook (biennial), Scottdale, PA 15683. James E. Horsch, Ed.

Mennonite Quarterly Review (q), Goshen, IN 46526 John S. Oyer Ed.

With (m), Scottdale, PA 15683. Lavon Welty, Assoc., Ed.

Purpose (w), Scottdale, PA 15683. James E. Horsch, Ed.

On the Line (w), Scottdale PA 15683. Virginia A. Hostetler, Ed.

Sent (q), Elkhart, IN 46515. James L. Derstine, Ed.

Sharing (q), Goshen, IN 46526. Maggie Glick, Ed.

Story Friends (w), Scottdale, PA 15683. Marjorie Waybill, Ed.

Ecos Menonitas (q), Elkhart, IN 46515. Arnoldo Casas, Ed.

United Action Newsletter (q), Elkhart, IN 46516.

Voice (11/yr), Elkhart, IN 46516. Eve MacMaster, Ed.

Information: James E. Horsch, Ed., Mennonite Yearbook, Scottdale, PA 15683

Mennonite Church, The General Conference

The General Conference Mennonite Church was formed in 1860, uniting Mennonites throughout the U.S. who were interested in doing missionary work together. Today 65,000 Christians in 372 congregations try to follow the way of Jesus in their daily lives.

The conference consists of people of many ethnic backgrounds—Swiss and German, Russian and Dutch, Black, Hispanic, Chinese, Vietnamese, Laotian. Some native Americans in both Canada and the U.S. also relate to the conference.

The basic belief and practice of the conference come from the life and teachings of Jesus Christ, the early church of the New Testament, and the Anabaptists of the 16th-century Reformation. Thus the conference seeks to be evangelical, guided by the Bible, led by the Holy Spirit, and supported by a praying, discerning community of believers in congregations and fellowships. Peace, or shalom, is at the very heart of members, who seek to be peacemakers in everyday life.

The goals of the conference for the next three to six years are to evangelize, teach and practice biblical principles, train and develop leaders, and work for Christian unity.

Churches: 224; Inclusive Membership: 34,693; Sunday or Sabbath Schools: 224 Total Enrollment: 16,179; Ordained Clergy: 379

GENERAL ORGANIZATION

General Conference: triennial. Next meeting, 1992 Central Office: 722 Main, Newton, KS 67114. Tel. (316) 283-5100

OFFICERS

Mod., Florence Driedger, 3833 Montague St., Regina, Saskatchewan S4S 3J6

Asst. Mod., Ronald Krehbiel, RR 2, Box 161, Freeman, SD 57029

Sec., Myron Schultz, Bloomfield, MT 59315

Gen. Sec., Vern Preheim, 722 Main, Newton, KS 67114

OTHER ORGANIZATIONS

(All at central office)

Commission on Home Ministries: Exec. Hubert Brown

Commission on Overseas Mission: Exec. Sec., Erwin Rempel

Women in Mission: Coordinator, Sara Regier

Commission on Education: Exec. Sec., Norma Johnson

Division of Administration: Exec. Secs., Ted Stuckey, Ray Frey, Gary Franz

PERIODICALS

The Mennonite (bi-w), Box 347, 722 Main St., Newton, KS 67114, Muriel Thiessen Stackley, Ed.

Builder (m), 722 Main St., Newton, KS 67114

Window to Mission (q), 722 Main St., Newton, KS 67114, Lois Deckert, Ed.

Der Bote (w) 600 Shaftesbury Blvd., Winnipeg, Manitoba, Canada R3P 0M4, Gerhard Ens, Ed.

The Metropolitan Church Association, Inc.

Organized as the result of a revival movement in Chicago in 1894, as the Metropolitan Holiness Church, and in 1899 chartered as the Metropolitan Church Association. It has Wesleyan theology.

GENERAL ORGANIZATION

General Assembly: annual

International Headquarters: 323 Broad St., Lake Geneva, WI 53147. Tel. (414)248-6786

OFFICERS

Pres., Rev. Warren W. Bitzer

Vice-Pres. & Sec., Elbert L. Ison

Treas., Gertrude J. Puckhaber

PERIODICAL

The Burning Bush (bi-m), Lake Geneva, WI, Rev. E. L. Adams, Ed. (Publishing House, The Metropolitan Church Association, Lake Geneva, WI 53147)

Metropolitan Community Churches, Universal Fellowship of

Founded October 6, 1968 by the Rev. Troy D. Perry in Los Angeles, California with a particular but not exclusive outreach to the gay community. Since that time, the Fellowship has grown to include congregations throughout the world.

The group is trinitarian and accepts the Bible as the

divinely inspired Word of God. The Fellowship has two sacraments, baptism and holy communion, as well as a number of traditionally recognized rites such as ordination.

"This Fellowship acknowledges the Holy Scriptures interpreted by the Holy Spirit in conscience and faith, as its guide in faith, discipline, and government. The government of this Fellowship is vested in its General Council (consisting of Elders and District Coordinators), Clergy and church delegates, who exert the right of control in all of its affairs, subject to the provisions of its Articles of Incorporation and By-Laws."

GENERAL ORGANIZATION

General Conference: 14th General Conference (biennial) Minneapolis, MN, July, 1991
Headquarters: 5300 Santa Monica Blvd., #304, Los Angeles, CA 90029. Tel. (213) 464-5100

OFFICERS

(All at headquarters unless otherwise noted)
Mod., Rev. Elder Troy D. Perry
Vice-Mod., Rev. Elder Freda Smith, POB 20125 Sacramento, CA 95820
Treas., Rev. Elder Donald Eastman (at headquarters)
Clk., Elder Larry Rodriguez, 5300 Santa Monica Blvd., #304, Los Angeles, CA 90029
Rev. Elder Nancy L. Wilson
Rev. Elder Dr. Charlie Arehart, c/o M.C.C. of Rockies, 980 Clarkson St., Denver, CO 80218
Rev. Elder Jean A. White, 2A Sistova Rd., Balham, SW12 9OT, England
Dir. of Admn., Mr. Ravi Verma

DISTRICT COORDINATORS

Great Lakes District: Rev. La Paula Turner, 305 W. Newby Ave., #C, San Gabriel, CA 91776
Gulf Lower Atlantic District: Mr. Jay Neely, P.O. Box 8356, Atlanta, GA 30306
Mid-Central District: Rev. Bonnie Daniel, 1364 Collins Ave., Topeka, KS 66604
Mid-Atlantic District: R. Adam DeBaugh, P.O. Box 7864, Gaithersburg, MD 20898
Northeast District: Rev. Jeff Pulling, P.O. Box 340529, Hartford, CT 06134
Northwest District: Rev. Edward Sherriff, P.O. Box 5795, Sacramento, CA 95817
South Central District: Clarke Friesen, P.O. Box 262822, Houston, TX 77207
Southeast District: Rev. Thomas Bigelow, 625 Jefferson Ave. N., Sarasota, FL 34237
Southwest District: Rev. Don Pederson, 10913 Fruitland Dr., #117, Studio City, CA 91604

OTHER COMMISSIONS & COMMITTEES

Excel International: Exec Dir., Brenda Blizzard, P.O. Box 20054, Ferndale, MI 48220
World Church Extension: Exec. Sec., Rev. Elder Jean White, 2A Sistova, Balham, London, England SW12 9QT
Faith Fellowship & Order: Chpsn., Rev. Steven Torrence, 1215 Petronia St., Key West, FL 33040
Dept. of People of Color: Dir., Rev. La Paula Turner, 305 W. Newby Ave., #C, San Gabriel, CA 91776
Commission on the Laity: Chpsn., JoNee Shelton, 917 Elysian Fields, New Orleans, LA 70117
Clergy Credentials & Concerns: Chpsn., Rev. James Lewey, 1136 W. Woodlawn Ave., San Antonio, TX 78201
Board of Pensions: Pres., Rev. Arthur R. Green, 13655 NE 10th Ave., Unit 112, N. Miami, FL 33161; Administrator: Lois Luneburg, P. O. Box 107, Arnold, CA 95223

Ecumenical Witness & Ministry: Chief Officer, Rev. Elder Nancy Wilson, 5879 Washington Blvd., Culver City, CA 90232; Dir., Rev. Sandi Robinson, 5930 Comey Ave., Los Angeles, CA 90034
UFMCC AIDS Ministry: Exec Dir., Rev. Elder Don Eastman, c/o UFMCC; Field Dir., Rev. Steve Pieters, c/o UFMCC

The Missionary Church

The Missionary Church was formed in 1969 through a merger of the United Missionary Church (organized in 1883) and the Missionary Church Association (founded in 1898). It is evangelical and conservative with a strong emphasis on missionary work and church planting

There are three levels of church government with local, district, and general conference. There are ten church districts in the United States. The general conference meets every two years. The denomination operates two colleges in the U. S.
Churches: 290; Inclusive Membership: 26,332; Sunday or Sabbath Schools: N.R.; Total Enrollment: N.R.; Ordained Clergy: 615

GENERAL ORGANIZATION

U.S. Headquarters: 3901 S. Wayne Ave., Ft. Wayne, IN 46807. Tel. (219) 456-4502
Publishing Headquarters: Bethel Publishing Co., 1819 S. Main St., Elkhart, IN 46516. Tel. (219) 293-8585

OFFICERS

Pres., Dr. John Moran
Vice-Pres., Rev. William Hossler
Sec., Rev. Paul DeMerchant
Treas., Mr. Edwin W. Crewson
Asst. to the Pres., Rev. Bob Ransom
Dir., Overseas Ministries, (World Partners), Rev. Charles Carpenter
Dir., Admin. Services, Mr. David von Gunten
Dir., Publications, Mr. Richard Oltz
Dir., Communication, Rev. Michael Reynolds
Dir., Stewardship, Rev. Ken Stucky
Youth Dir., _____
Children's Dir., Mr. Neil McFarlane
Adult Dir., Dr. Duane Beals
Missionary Men International: Pres., Mr. Herb Amstutz
Missionary Women International, Pres., Mrs. Opal Speicher
Investment Foundation, Mr. Bob Henschen

PERIODICAL

Emphasis on Faith and Living (m), 3901 S. Wayne Ave., Ft. Wayne, IN 46807. Rev. Michael Reynolds, Ed.

Moravian Church in America (Unitas Fratrum)

In 1735 German Moravian missionaries of the pre-Reformation faith of Jan Hus came to Georgia, in 1740 to Pennsylvania, and in 1753 to North Carolina. They established the American Moravian Church, which is broadly evangelical, ecumenical, liturgical, with an episcopacy as a spiritual office and in form of government "conferential."

GENERAL ORGANIZATION

Provincial Synods (Northern, Southern, and Alaska)

NORTHERN PROVINCE

Headquarters: 1021 Center St., P.O. Box 1245, Bethlehem, PA 18016. Tel. (215) 867-7566

Churches: 100; Inclusive Membership: 31,468; Sunday or Sabbath Schools: 99; Total Enrollment: 7,071; Ordained Clergy: 169

OFFICERS
Provincial Elders' Conference:
Pres., Dr. Gordon L. Sommers
Vice-Pres. (Eastern District) and Sec., Rev. Donald E. Fulton
Vice-Pres. (Western District), Rt. Rev. Wilbur Behrend, Sun Prairie, WI
Treas., John F. Ziegler, 1021 Center St., P.O. Box 1245, Bethlehem, PA 18016.

PERIODICAL
The Moravian (m), 1021 Center St., P.O. Box 1245, Bethlehem, PA 18016. Rev. Herman I. Weinlick, Ed.

SOUTHERN PROVINCE
Headquarters: 459 S. Church St., Winston-Salem, NC 27108. Tel. (919) 725-5811

Churches: 54; Inclusive Membership: 21,467; Sunday or Sabbath Schools: 54; Total Enrollment: 8,968; Ordained Clergy: 87

OFFICERS
Provincial Elders' Conference:
Pres., Rev. Graham H. Rights
Vice-Pres., Mrs. Becky K. Cook
Sec., Rev. Carl S. Southerland
Treas., Ronald R. Hendrix, 459 S. Church St., Winston-Salem, NC 27101 (Mailing Address: Drawer O. Salem Station, Winston-Salem, NC 27108)

ALASKA PROVINCE
Headquarters: P.O. Box 545, Bethel, AK 99559

Churches: 23; Inclusive Membership: 5,234; Sunday or Sabbath Schools: 23; Total Enrollment: 1,932; Ordained Clergy: 14

OFFICERS
Chpsn., Rt. Rev. Jacob Nelson, Sr.
Vice-Chpsn., Rev. David Paul
Sec., Rev. Joe Albrite, Jr.
Treas., James D. Lewis
Dir. of Theological Education, Rev. Kurt H. Vitt

PERIODICAL
The Moravian, 1021 Center St., P.O. Box 1245, Bethlehem, PA 18016, Rev. Herman I. Weinlick, Ed.

Muslims

Islam now claims approximately six million adherents in the U.S. Some of them are immigrants who represent almost every part of the world, or children of such immigrants. Others are Americans who converted to Islam or children of such converts. These are apart from those who come to America temporarily, such as Muslim diplomats, students, and those who work in international institutions such as the World Bank, the International Monetary Fund, and the United Nations.

Muslims are found in nearly every American town, and are engaged in all professions, including teaching, medicine, accounting, engineering, and business. Their number increases in large industrial and commercial cities in the East and Midwest, but there are also large numbers of Muslims in some areas on the West Coast such as Los Angeles and San Francisco.

Many Islamic organizations exist in the U.S. under such titles as Islamic Society, Islamic Center, or Muslim Mosque. The aim is to provide a group in a locality with a place of worship and of meeting for other religious, social, and educational purposes. These societies and organizations are not regarded as religious sects or divisions. Their multiplication arises from the needs of each group in a given area, long distances separating the groups, and the absence in Islam of organized hierarchy, a factor which gives liberty to ambitious personalities to start their own group. All the groups hold the same beliefs, aspire to practice the same rituals: namely, prayers, fasting, almsgiving, and pilgrimage to Makkah. The only difference that may exist between black organizations and other Muslim institutions may be that the former may mix civil rights aspirations with Islamic objectives and may, therefore, follow a rigid discipline for their members.

The main Islamic organizations are the Islamic centers which are found in all 300 large cities. Their objectives are cultural, religious, and educational; and each one has a mosque or a prayer hall.
Prominent among these is:
The Islamic Center of Washington, 2551 Massachusetts Ave. NW, Washington, DC 20008. Tel. (202) 332-8343. Dir., Dr. A. Khouj. Publication: Al-Nur (q).

REGIONAL AND NATIONAL GROUPS
Apart from the Islamic Centers, a number of regional and national groups were started with the objective of helping local groups coordinate their work, and promote closer unity among them. These include:
Council of Masajid (Mosques) in the U.S.A., 99 Woodview Dr., Old Bridge, NJ 08857. Sec. Gen., Dawud Assad. Tel. (201)679-8617. Publication: *Majallat Al-Masjid (newsletter)*
The Federation of Islamic Associations in the United States and Canada, 25351 Five Mile Rd., Redford Township, MI 48239. Sec. Gen. Nihad Hamid. Publication: *The Muslim Star,* 17514 Woodward Ave., Detroit, MI 48203.
Islamic Society of North America, P. O. Box 38, Plainfield, IN 46168, Tel. (317) 839-8157. Publications: *The Islamic Horizons* (m)
Council of Muslim Communities of Canada, 1250 Ramsey View Ct., Ste. 504, Sudbury Ontario P3E 2E7. Tel. (705)522-2948. Dir., Dr. Mir Iqbal Ali
Muslim World League, 134 W. 26th St., New York, NY 10001, P.O. Box 1674, New York, NY 10116-1674, Tel. (212)627-4330. Actg. Exec. Dir., Dawad Assad

National Baptist Convention of America

The National Baptist Convention of American, Incorporated was organized in 1880 following a dispute over control of the publishing board in which another Convention was organized. Membership of the churches is largely African-American.

GENERAL ORGANIZATION
Convention: annual (September)
Congress of Christian Workers: Annual (June)

OFFICERS
Pres., E. Edward Jones, 1450 Pierre Ave., Shreveport LA 71103
1st Vice Pres.: Dr. Albert Chew, 2823 N. Houston St., Ft. Worth TX 76106; 2nd Vice-Pres., Dr. Wallace S. Hartsfield, 3100 E. 31st St., Kansas City MO 64128
Aide to the Pres., Rev. Joe R. Gant, Jr., 5821 Ledbetter, Shreveport, LA 77108
Gen. Rec. Sec., Dr. Clarence C. Pennywell, 2016 Russell Rd., Shreveport LA 71107
1st Asst. Sec., Dr. Louis W. Smith, 1455 Granada St., New Orleans, LA 70122
2nd Asst. Sec., Rev. T. E. Gainous, 2020 W. Gore St., Orlando, FL 32805
3rd Asst. Sec., Dr. W. A. Johnson, 225 Wood St., Georgetown, SC 29440
4th Asst. Sec., Dr. L. Z. Blankenship, Rt. 3, Box 280, Foxworth, MS 39483

Corresponding Sec., Rev. Stephen J. Thurston, 740 E. 77th St., Chicago, IL 60619

Treas., Rev. Floyd N. Williams, 5902 Bealt St., Houston TX 77091

Hist., Rev. Marvin C. Griffin, 1010 E. Tenth St., Austin, TX 78702. Tel. (512) 478-1875

Statistician, Rev. E. E. Stafford, 6614 S. Western Ave., Los Angeles CA 90047

Auditor, Rev. J. Carlton Allen, 1639 Hays St., San Antonio, TX 78202. Tel. (512)225-7907

Youth Advisor, Dr. Benjamin J. Maxon, Jr., 2926 Jackson Ave., New Orleans, LA 70126

Organist, Rev. Andrew Berry, 2712 Ave. L, Galveston, TX 77550

Social Justice Commission, Rev. Mac Charles Jones, 1414 Truman Rd., Kansas City, MO

Transportation Commission, Rev. C. L. Royston, 1009 W. Chestnut, Louisville, KY 40203

Commission on Chaplaincy, Dr. Frank K. Sims, 4501 S. Vincennes Ave., Chicago, IL 60653

Commission on Orthodoxy, Rev. F. D. Sampson, 4812 Bennington, Houston, TX 77016

OTHER ORGANIZATIONS

Education Board: Chpsn., Dr. J. B. Adams, 602 S.W. 9th St., Belle Glade, FL 33430; Exec. Sec./Treas., Dr. W. M. Brent, 3639 Mt. Vernon Dr., Los Angeles, CA 90008

Baptist Training Union: Sec./Treas., Dr. Timothy J. Winters, 6126 Benson Ave., San Diego, CA 92114; Corr. Sec., Mrs. Joyce Sipsey, 5422 Golf Dr., Houston, 77091

Evangelical Board: Chpsn., Rev. Earl A. Pleasant, 601 E. 99 St., Inglewood, CA 90301; Sec./Treas., Dr. Hayward Wiggins, 1621 Pleasant Ville Dr., Houston, TX 77029

Foreign Mission Board: Chpsn., Rev. Asa W. Sampson, 149 Winkler, Houston, TX 77087; Exec. Sec./Treas., Rev. Isadore Edwards, Jr., 2600 Rosedale E., Fort Worth, TX 76105

Benevolent Board: Chpsn., Dr. C. B. T. Smith, 1101 E. Sabine St., Dallas, TX 75203; Sec/Treas., Rev. Joe Hargrett, 2603 Myakka Dr., Orlando, FL 32809

Publishing Board: Chpsn., Dr. Marvin C. Griffin, 1010 E. 10th St., Austin, TX 78702

Home Mission Board: Chpsn., Dr. Luke W. Mingo, 3993 S. King Dr., Chicago, IL 60653

Board of Christian Education: Chpsn., Dr. Timothy J. Winters, 6126 Benson Ave., San Diego, CA 92114

Women's Auxiliary: Pres., Mrs. Evelyn Reed, 4233 College St., Kansas City, MO 64130

Senior Women's Auxiliary #2: Pres., Mrs. Beulah M. Ward, 2727 Garfield Ave., Kansas City, MO 64109

Junior Women: Pres., Deborah Johnson, 2750 S. Jackson, Chicago, IL 60612

Nurses: Pres., Mrs. Della H. Bryson, 3040 Kings Lane, Nashville, TN 37216

Ushers: Pres., Mrs. Frankie A. Carter, 3013 E. 14th St., Austin, TX 78702

Brotherhood: Pres., Mr. Cornelius Lee, 2715 Park Row, Dallas, TX 75215

Young Brotherhood: Pres., Mr. Al Curtis Green, 2310 S. Pace St., Marion, IN 46953

National Baptist Convention, U.S.A., Inc.

The older and parent convention of black Baptists. This body is to be distinguished from the National Baptist Convention of America, usually referred to as the "unincorporated" body.

GENERAL ORGANIZATION

World Center Headquarters: 1720 Whites Creek Pike, Nashville, TEN 37201. Tel. (615)228-6292

Convention: annual

OFFICERS

Pres., Dr. T. J. Jemison, 915 Spain St., Baton Rouge, LA 70802. Tel. (504) 383-5401

Gen. Sec., Dr. W. Franklyn Richardson, 52 South 6th Ave., Mt. Vernon, NY 10550. Tel. (914) 664-2676

Vice-Pres.-at-large, Dr. C. A. Clark, 902 N. Good St., Dallas, TX 75204

Treas., Dr. Isaac Green, 3068 Iowa St., Pittsburgh, PA 15219. Tel. (412)556-1437

Vice-Pres.: Dr. David Matthews, P.O. Box 627, Indianola, MS; Dr. P. J. James, 1104 E. Cherry St., Blytheville, AR 72315; Dr. Henry L. Lyons; Dr. E. Victor Hill; Dr. Allen Stanley

Asst. Secs., Dr. B. J. Whipper, Sr., 15 Ninth St., Charleston, SC 29403; Rev. Otis B. Smith, P.O. Box 544, Tuscaloosa, AL 35404; Dr. Roger P. Derricotte, 539 Roseville Ave., Newark, NJ 07107; Dr. McKinley Dukes, 4223 S. Benton, Kansas City, MO 64130

Stat., Rev. H. L. Harvey, Jr., 3212 Reading Rd., Cincinnati, OH 45229

Hist., Dr. Clarence Wagner

OFFICERS OF BOARDS

Foreign Mission Board: 701 S. 19th St. Philadelphia, PA 19146. Sec., Dr. William J. Harvey, III

Home Mission Board: Exec. Sec., Dr. Jerry Moore, 1612 Buchanan St. N.W., Washington, DC 20011

Sunday School Publishing Board; 330 Charlotte Ave., Nashville, TN 37201. Exec. Dir., Mrs. C. N. Adkins

Education Board: 114 S. 22nd St., Saginaw, MI 48601. Chpsn., Dr. J. Parrish Wilson

Evangelism Board: Dr. Manuel Scott, 2600 S. Marsalis Ave., Dallas, TX 75216

Laymen's Movement: Pres., Mr. Walter Cade, 537 N. 82nd St., Kansas City, KS 66112

Woman's Auxiliary Convention: 584 Arden Pk., Detroit, MI 48202. Pres., Mrs. Mary O. Ross

Congress of Christian Education: 1014 East Pine St., Tulsa, OK 74106. Pres., Dr. T. Oscar Chappelle

PERIODICAL

National Baptist Voice (s-m), Dr. Roscoe Cooper, Ed. 2800 Third Ave., Richmond, VA 23222. Tel. (804)321-5115

National Primitive Baptist Convention, Inc.

Throughout the years of slavery and the Civil War, the Negro population of the South worshipped with the white population in their various churches. At the time of emancipation, their white brethren helped them to establish their own churches, granting them letters of fellowship, ordaining their deacons and ministers, and helped them in other ways.

The doctrine and polity of this body are quite similar to that of white Primitive Baptists, except that they are "opposed to all forms of church organization"; yet there are local associations and a national convention, organized in 1907.

Each church is independent and receives and controls its own membership. This body was formerly known as Colored Primitive Baptists.

GENERAL ORGANIZATION

Headquarters: P.O. Box 2355, Tallahassee, FL

CHIEF OFFICERS

National Convention: Pres., Elder F. L. Livingston, 1334 Carson St., Dallas, TX 75216. Tel. (214) 949-4650; Rec. Sec., Elder T. W. Samuels, 6433 Hidden Forest Dr., Charlotte, NC 28206, Tel. (704) 596-3153; Sec. Bd. of Dirs., Elder M. G. Miles, 1525 S. Bronough St.,

Tallahassee, FL 32301; Statistical Sec., Br. T. M. Batts, Jr., 4714 Walford Rd., Warrensville Heights, OH 44128
National Church School Training Union: Pres., Elder W.D. Judge, 1718 West Grand Ave., Orlando, FL 32805; Sec., Mrs. Icylene B. Horne, 2222 Metropolitan St., Dallas, TX 75215
National Ushers Congress: Pres., Sec., Bro. Carl Batts, 21213 Garden View Dr., Maples Heights, OH 44137; Mary Washington, 1500 Moretz Ave., Charlotte, NC 28206
Publishing Board: Chpsn., Elder T. W. Samuels, 6433 Hidden Forest Dr., Charlotte, NC 28206; Editorial Sec. and Chpsn. Bd. of Education, Elder J. L. Fitzgerald, 2703 Aspen Dr., Nashville, TN 37208
Women's Congress: Pres., Mrs. Lillian J. Brantley, 1795 N.W. 58th St., Miami, FL 33142; Sec., Mrs. F. B. Bell, 3412 E. 104th St., Cleveland, OH 44104
National Laymen's Council: Pres., George W. Brown, 405 E. 26th St., Patterson, NJ 07514; Sec., Bro. Ben Kelley, 765 Rilyland Pike, Huntsville, AL 35811
National Youth Congress: Pres., Levy Freeman, 3920 Gardenside Dr., NW, Huntsville, AL 35810; Sec. Mimberly Townes, 646 E. 36th St., Los Angeles, CA 90011

National Spiritualist Association of Churches

This organization is made up of believers that Spiritualism is a science, philosophy, and religion based upon the demonstrated facts of communication between this world and the next.

GENERAL ORGANIZATION

Convention: annual (October)
Pres., Joseph H. Merrill, 13 Cleveland Ave., Lily Dale, NY 14752
Vice-Pres., Evelyn Muse, 1104 Susan Dr., Edinburg, TX 78539
Sec., Elizabeth R. Edgar, P.O. Box 128, Cassadaga, FL 32706. Tel. (904) 228-2506
Treas., Rev. Alfred A. Conner, 293 Jersey St., San Francisco, CA 94114

OTHER ORGANIZATIONS

Bureau of Education: Supt., Rev. Joseph Sax, Morris Pratt Institute, 11811 Watertown Plank Rd., Milwaukee, WI 53226
Bureau of Public Relations: Rev. Anne Gehman, 9533 Jomar Dr., Fairfax, VA 22072
The Stow Memorial Foundation: Sec.-Treas., Rev. Elizabeth R. Edgar, P.O. Box 128, Cassadaga, FL 32706
Spiritualist Benevolent Society, Inc.: Cassadaga, FL 32706

PERIODICAL

The National Spiritualist Summit (m), P.O. Box 30172, Indianapolis, IN 46230. Herbert Ray Worth, Ed.

Netherlands Reformed Congregations

The Netherlands Reformed Congregations organized denominationally in 1907. In the Netherlands, the so-called Churches Under the Cross (established in 1839, after breaking away from the 1934 Secession congregations) and the so-called Ledeboerian churches (established in 1841 under the leadership of the Rev. Ledeboer, who seceded from the Reformed State Church), united in 1907 under the leadership of the then 25-year-old Rev. G. H. Kersten, to form the Netherlands Reformed Congregations. Many of the North American congregations left the Christian Reformed Church to join the Netherlands Reformed Congregations after the Kuyperian presup-

posed regeneration doctrine began making inroads into that denomination.

All Netherlands Reformed Congregations, officeholders, and members subscribe to three Reformed Forms of Unity: The Belgic Confession of Faith (by DeBres), the Heidelberg Catechism (by Ursinus and Olevianus), and the Canons of Dort. Both the Belgic Confession and the Canons of Dordt are read regularly at worship services, and the Heidelberg Catechism is preached weekly, except on church feast days.

GENERAL ORGANIZATION

Synod meets every two years (next meeting, 1990)

OFFICERS

Clk. of Synod: Dr. Joel R. Beeke, 2115 Romence Ave., N.E., Grand Rapids, MI 49503

OTHER ORGANIZATION

Netherlands Reformed Book and Publishing, 1020 N. Main Ave., Sioux Center, IA 51250

PERIODICALS

The Banner of Truth (m), 2115 Romence Ave., N.E., Grand Rapids, MI 29503. Dr. Joel R. Beeke, Ed.
Paul (bi/m). Dr. J. R. Beeke, Ed.
Insight Into (bi-m), 905 4th Ave., N.E., Sioux Center, IA 51250. Rev. H. Hofman, Ed.

New Apostolic Church of North America

This body is a variant of the Catholic Apostolic Church, which movement began in England in 1830. The New Apostolic Church distinguished itself from the parent body in 1863 by recognizing a succession of Apostles.

Churches: 491; Inclusive Membership: 36,972; Sunday or Sabbath Schools: N.R.; Total Enrollment: 2,203; Ordained Clergy: 823

GENERAL ORGANIZATION

Headquarters: 3753 N. Troy St., Chicago, IL 60618

OFFICERS

Pres., Rev. Michael Kraus, 267 Lincoln Rd., Waterloo, Ontario, Canada
First Vice-Pres., Rev. John W. Fendt, 36 Colony La., Manhasset, NY 11030
Second Vice-Pres., Rev. Erwin Wagner, 330 Arlene Pl., Waterloo, Ontario, Canada
Sec., Rev. William K. Schmeerbauch, 5516 Pine Wood Forest, St. Louis, MO 63128
Treas. and Asst. Sec., Ellen Eckhardt, 6380 N. Indian Rd., Chicago, IL 60646

PERIODICALS

(All published at 3753 N. Troy St., Chicago, IL 60618)
Word of Life (s-m)
Youth Guide (m)
New Apostolic Review (s-m)
The Good Shepherd (m)
Our Family (m)

North American Baptist Conference

The North American Baptist Conference had its beginning through immigrants from Germany in the middle of the 19th Century. The first church was organized by the Reverend Konrad Fleischmann in Philadelphia, Pennsylvania, in 1843. Actual organization of the North American Baptist Conference took place in 1865 when delegates of the churches met in Wilmot, Ontario. Today only a few churches still use the German language, mostly in a bilingual setting.

The Conference meets in general session once every three years for fellowship, inspiration and to conduct the business of the Conference through elected delegates from the local churches. The General Council, composed of representatives of the various Associations and Conference organizations and departments, meets annually to determine the annual budget and programs for the Conference and its departments and agencies. The General Council also makes recommendations to the Triennial Conference on policies, long-range plans and election of certain personnel, boards and committees. Conference departments and agencies make their recommendations for program and finances to the General Council.

Approximately 90 missionaries serve in Cameroon and Nigeria, West Africa, in Japan, in Brazil and in the Philippines, as well as among various ethnic groups throughout the United States and Canada. They are supported through the Conference Established and Expansion Ministries Budget.

NEW DAY, a youth music and drama group, is supported by the Conference in its evangelism and training ministry among North American Baptist churches.

Nine homes for the aged are affiliated with the Conference and ten camps are operated on the association level.

Churches: 259; Inclusive Membership: 42,629; Sunday or Sabbath Schools: 259; Total Enrollment: 23,485; Ordained Clergy: 445

GENERAL ORGANIZATION

Triennial Conference: Next meeting, 1991, Milwaukee, WI

Headquarters: 1 S. 210 Summit Ave., Oakbrook Terrace, IL 60181. Tel. (708) 495-2000

OFFICERS

Mod., Rev. Harvey Mehlhaff
Vice-Mod., Mr. Richard Russell
Exec. Dir., Dr. John Binder
Treas., Mr. Milton Hildebrandt

OTHER ORGANIZATIONS

Missions Dept.: Dir., Mr. Ron Salzman
Church Growth Min. Dept., Dir., Rev. David Sems
Development Dept., Dir., Rev. Lewis Petrie
Financial Services: Dir., Mr. Robert Mayforth
Area Ministries: Dir., Dr. Willis Potratz

PERIODICAL

The Baptist Herald (10/yr.), Barbara J. Binder, Ed., published by the North American Baptist Conference, 1 S. 210 Summit Ave., Oakbrook Terrace, IL 60181
Moments With God (4/yr.), Dorothy Ganoung, Ed.

North American Old Roman Catholic Church

The North American Old Roman Catholic Church can be traced back to the early 1700's to the Ultrajectine Tradition when the Church in Holland experienced a truly catholic reform. The Church came to the United States and Mexico in its present form in the early part of this century.

English and Latin pre-Vatican II masses are celebrated. The Baltimore Catechism is used in all CCD and adult classes. The Pontificale Romanum is used for consecration and other episcopal and liturgical functions. This Church recognizes the authority of the See of St. Peter.

Records of Succession may be found in the Vatican Library, as recorded by the Ecclesiastical Committee.

The sacraments and holy orders of the Old Roman Catholic Church are universally accepted as valid

OFFICERS

Archbishop, Most. Rev. Theodore J. Rematt, 4200 N. Kedvale Ave., Chicago, IL 60641. Tel. (312)286-5783

North American Old Roman Catholic Church (Archdiocese of New York)

This body is identical with the Roman Catholic Church in faith, but differs from it in discipline and worship. The Mass is offered with the appropriate rite either in Latin or in the venacular. All other sacraments are taken from the Roman Pontifical. This jurisdiction allows for married clergy.

Churches: 5; Inclusive Membership: 615; Sunday or Sabbath Schools: 3; Total Enrollment: 39; Ordained Clergy: 9

GENERAL ORGANIZATION

Synod: biennial; next meeting, May 1991, Brooklyn NY.
Chancery Address: Box 021647, G.P.O., Brooklyn, NY 11202. Tel. (718) 855-0600

OFFICERS

Primate Metropolitan, The Most Rev. Archbishop James H. Rogers, 118-09 Farmers Blvd., St. Albans, NY 11412
Vicar-Gen., Most Rev. Joseph M. Nevilloyd
Chancellor, Rev. Albert J. Berube

PERIODICAL

The Augustinian (occ), Box 021647, G.P.O., Brooklyn, NY 11202

Old German Baptist Brethren

A group which separated from the Church of the Brethren (formerly German Baptist Brethren) in 1881 as a protest against a liberalizing tendency.

Churches: 5; Inclusive Membership: 5,497; Sunday or Sabbath Schools: N.R.; Total Enrollment: N.R.; Ordained Clergy: 288

GENERAL ORGANIZATION

Conference, annual

OFFICERS

Foreman, Elder Clement Skiles, Rt. 1, Box 140, Bringhurst, IN 46913. Tel. (219) 967-3367
Reading Clk., Elder Herman Shuman, Rt. 4, Box 301, Pendleton, IN 46064
Writing Clk., Elder Carl Bowman, 4065 State Rt. 48, Covington, OH 45318. Tel. (513)473-2729

PERIODICAL

The Vindicator, 1876 Beamsville-Union City Rd., Union City, OH 45390, M. Keith Skiles, Ed.

Old Order Amish Church

The congregations of this Old Order Amish group have

no annual conference. They worship in private homes. They adhere to the older forms of worship and attire. This body has bishops, ministers, and deacons.

Churches: 756; Inclusive Membership: 68,040; Sunday or Sabbath Schools: N.R.; Total Enrollment: N.R.; Ordained Clergy: 3,049

NO GENERAL ORGANIZATION INFORMATION

Der Neue Amerikanische Calendar, c/o Raber's Book Store, 2467 C R 600, Baltic, OH 43804

Old Order (Wisler) Mennonite Church

This body arose from a separation of Mennonites dated 1870, under Jacob Wisler, in opposition to what were thought to be innovations.

At present, this group is located in the Eastern United States and Canada. There are approximately 9,850 members and 46 congregations, with 50 bishops, 110 ministers, and deacons.

Each state, or district, has its own organization or government and holds a yearly conference.

NO GENERAL ORGANIZATION INFORMATION

Arthur Van Pelt, 13550 Germantown Road, Columbiana, OH 44408. Tel. (216) 482-3691

Open Bible Standard Churches, Inc.

Open Bible Standard Churches originated from two revival movements: Bible Standard Conference, founded in Eugene, Oregon, under the leadership of Fred L. Hornshuh, in 1919, and Open Bible Evangelistic Association, founded in Des Moines, Iowa, under the leadership of John R. Richey, in 1932.

Basically similar in doctrine and government, the two groups amalgamated on July 26, 1935, taking the combined name, "Open Bible Standard Churches, Inc.," with headquarters in Des Moines, Iowa.

Two hundred ten ministers formed the original group which has enlarged to incorporate over 1,550 ministers and 680 churches in thirty countries.

Historical roots of the parent groups reach back to the outpouring of the Holy Spirit in 1906 at Azusa Street Mission in Los Angeles, California, and to the great full gospel movement in the Midwest. Both groups were organized under the impetus of pentecostal revival. Simple faith, freedom from fanaticism, emphasis on evangelism and missions, and free fellowship with other groups were characteristics of the growing organizations.

From its origin, Open Bible Standard Churches has emphasized world evangelism. The first missionary left Lodi, California, for India in 1926. Since that time, the program has grown to minister in China, Japan, Philippines, Papua New Guinea, Canada, Puerto Rico, Dominican Republic, Canary Islands, Cayman Islands, Cuba, Jamaica, St. Vincent, Grenada, Trinidad, Mexico, Guatemala, El Salvador, Argentina, Chile, Brazil, Spain, Uruguay, Paraguay, Peru, Guinea, Liberia, Ghana, Kenya and Uganda.

The highest governing body of Open Bible Standard Churches meets biennially and is composed of all ministers and one voting delegate per 100 members, or fraction thereof, from each church. A General Board of Directors, elected by the general and divisional conferences, conducts the business of the organization. The U. S. church serves through fourteen national departments, five geographical divisions and twenty-five districts.

Official Bible College is Eugene Bible College, Eugene, Oregon.

Open Bible Standard Churches is a member of the National Association of Evangelicals and is a charter member of the Pentecostal Fellowship of North America. It is also a member of the Pentecostal World Conference. Our officers serve on the governing bodies of these organizations.

Churches: 325; Inclusive Membership: 46,000; Sunday or Sabbath Schools: 285; Total Enrollment: 25,000; Ordained Clergy: 937

GENERAL ORGANIZATION

General Conference: biennial (June)
Headquarters: 2020 Bell Ave., Des Moines, IA 50315. Tel. (515) 288-6761.

OFFICERS

Gen. Supt., Ray E. Smith, Des Moines, IA
Asst. Gen. Supt., Milton J. Stewart, Eugene, OR
Sec.-Treas., Patrick L. Bowlin, Des Moines, IA
Dir. of World Missions, Paul V. Canfield, Des Moines, IA
Dir. of Christian Education, Randall A. Bach, Des Moines, IA

PERIODICALS

Address for periodicals: 2020 Bell Ave., Des Moines, IA 50315
Message of the Open Bible (m), Delores A. Winegar, Ed.
The Overcomer (q), Randall A. Bach, Ed.
World Vision (m), Paul V. Canfield, Ed.
Outreach Magazine (semi-a), Paul V. Canfield, Ed.

The (Original) Church of God, Inc.

This body was organized in 1886 as the first church in the U.S.A., to take the name "The Church of God." In 1917 a difference of opinion led this particular group to include the word (Original) in its name. It is a holiness body and believes in the whole Bible, rightly divided, using the New Testament as its rule and government.

GENERAL ORGANIZATION

General Convention: annual (October) at Chattanooga, TN
Headquarters: P.O. Box 3086, Chattanooga, TN 37404. Tel. (615)629-4505

OFFICERS

Gen. Overseer, Rev. W. D. Sawyer
Asst. Gen. Overseer, Rev. O. E. Lambeth
Sec.-Treas., Michael B. Mitchell
Supt. Y.P.C.U.W., Billy Perkins
Camp. Mgr., Roy Wm. Kyzer

PERIODICALS

The Messenger (m), 2214 E. 17th St., Chattanooga TN 37404, Rev. W. D. Sawyer, Ed. Tel. 615)629-4505
Youth Messenger (m), Billy Perkins, Ed. Tel. (615)866-2189

The Orthodox Church in America

The Russian Orthodox Greek Catholic Church of America entered Alaska in 1792 before its purchase by the U.S.A. in 1867. Its canonical status of independence (autocephaly) was granted by its Mother Church, the Russian Orthodox Church, on April 10, 1970, and it is now known as The Orthodox Church in America.

GENERAL ORGANIZATION

All-American Council (Triennial, next meeting, August 1989)
Primate: The Most Blessed Theodosius, Archbishop of Washington, Metropolitan of All America and Canada
Chancellor: V. Rev. Robert S. Kondratick, P. O. Box 675, Syosset, NY 11791. Tel. (516)922-0550

SYNOD

Chpsn. His Beatitude Theodosius, P.O. Box 675, Syosset NY 11791

The Rt. Rev. Kyrill, Bishop of Pittsburgh, P. O. Box R, Wexford, PA 15090

The Rt. Rev. Peter, Bishop of New York, 33 Hewitt Ave., Bronxville, NY 10708

The Rt. Rev. Dmitri, Bishop of Dallas, 4112 Throckmorton, Dallas, TX 75219

The Rt. Rev. Herman, Bishop of Philadelphia, St. Tikhon's Monastery, South Canaan, PA 18459

The Rt. Rev. Gregory, Bishop of Sitka, St. Michael's Cathedral, Box 697, Sitka, AK 99835

The Rt. Rev. Nathaniel, Bishop of Detroit, 2522 Grey Tower Rd., Jackson, MI 49201

The Rt. Rev. Job, Bishop of Hartford, 6 Clark Rd., Cumberland, RI 02864

The Rt. Rev. Tikhon, Bishop of San Francisco, 649 North Robinson St., Los Angeles, CA 90026

Auxiliary Bishops: The Rt. Rev. Mark, Bishop Fort Lauderdale, 9511 Sun Pointe Dr., Boynton Beach, FL 33437

The Rt. Rev. Seraphim, Bishop of Edmonton, RR 5 Spencerville, Ontario K0E 1X0

The Orthodox Presbyterian Church

On June 11, 1936, certain ministers, elders, and lay members of the Presbyterian Church in the U.S.A. withdrew from that body to form a new denomination. Under the leadership of the late Rev. J. Gresham Machen, noted conservative New Testament scholar, the new church determined to continue to uphold the Westminster Confession of Faith as traditionally understood by Presbyterians, and to engage in proclamation of the gospel at home and abroad.

The church has grown modestly over the years and suffered early defections, most notably one in 1937 that resulted in the formation of the Bible Presbyterian Church under the leadership of Dr. Carl McIntire. It now has congregations throughout the states of the continental United States.

The denomination is a member of the North American Presbyterian and Reformed Council.

GENERAL ORGANIZATION

General Assembly: annual
Headquarters: 7401 Old York Rd., Philadelphia, PA 19126. Tel. (215) 635-0700

OFFICERS

Mod., Rev. Donald J. Duff, 257 E. Scott St., Point Hueneme, CA 93041. Tel. (805)488-6692
Stated Clk., Rev. Richard A. Barker, 639 Shallowlawn Dr., Westfield, NJ 07090. Tel. (201)232-3311

Pentecostal Assemblies of the World, Inc.

An interracial Pentecostal holiness of the Apostolic Faith, believing in repentance, baptism in Jesus' Name, and being filled with the Holy Ghost, with the evidence of speaking in tongues. This organization, originating in the early part of the century in the Middle West has now spread throughout the country.

GENERAL ORGANIZATION

Convention: annual (August)
Headquarters; 3939 Meadows Dr., Indianapolis, IN 46205. Tel. (317) 547-9541

OFFICERS

Presiding Bishop, James A. Johnson, 12643 Conway Downs Dr., St. Louis, MO 63141; Asst. Presiding Bishop, Paul A. Bowers, 1201 Egan Hills, Cincinnati, OH 45225; Bishops, Arthur Brazier, 500 E. 33rd St., Chicago, IL 60616; David Braziel, 10 Pineridge Dr., Rt. 2, Silver Creek, GA; David Braziel, 112 Wilson Ave., Rome, GA 30161; George Brooks, 75 Brooklynlawn Circle, Westville, CT 06515; Ramsey Butler, 4627 Clay St., Washington, DC 20019; Morris E. Golder, 7474 Holliday W. Dr., Indianapolis, IN 46260; Francis L. Smith, 993 Kirkwall Dr., Akron, OH 44321; Brooker T. Jones, P.O. Box 1479, Princeton, WV 24740; C. R. Lee, 533 Oak St., Mansfield, OH 44707; Robert McMurray, 1639 Wellington Rd., Los Angeles, CA 90019; Ross P. Paddock, 818 Dwillare Dr., Kalamazoo, MI 49001; Philip L. Scott, 7133 Blue Spruce Dr., St. Louis, MO 63110; William L. Smith, 2460 Gramercy Pk., Los Angeles, CA 90019; A. J. Street 3906 N. 32nd St., Pine Bluff, AR 70601; Samuel A. Layne, 1240 N. Euclid St., St. Louis, MO 63113; Freeman M. Thomas, 436 Fielding Dr., Penn Hills Pk., VA 15235; James E. Tyson, 6431 N. Sunset La., Indianapolis, IN 64260
Gen. Sec., Dist., Elder Richard Young, Treas. Dist., Elder James Loving, Asst. Treas., Elder Willis Ellis

PERIODICAL

Christian Outlook (m), 3939 Meadow Dr., Indianapolis, IN 46208, Jane Sims, Ed.

Pentecostal Church of God

Growing out of the pentecostal revivals at the turn of the century, the Pentecostal Church of God was organized in Chicago, Illinois, on December 30, 1919, as the Pentecostal Assemblies of the U.S.A. The name was changed to Pentecostal Church of God on February 15, 1922, in 1934 was changed again to The Pentecostal Church of God of America, Inc., and finally to Pentecostal Church of God (Incorporated) in 1979.

The International Headquarters was moved from Chicago to Ottumwa, Iowa, in 1927, then to Kansas City, Missouri, in 1933, and finally to Joplin, Missouri, in 1951.

The denomination is evangelical and pentecostal in doctrine and practice. Active membership in the National Association of Evangelicals and the Pentecostal Fellowship of North America is maintained.

Doctrinally, the church is Trinitarian and teaches the absolute inerrancy of the Scripture from Genesis to Revelation. Among its cardinal beliefs are the doctrines of salvation, which includes regeneration; divine healing, as provided for in the atonement; the baptism in the Holy Ghost, with the initial physical evidence of speaking in tongues; and the premillennial second coming of Christ.

Churches: 1,157; Inclusive Membership: 86,000; Sunday or Sabbath Schools: N.R.; Total Enrollment: N.R.; Ordained Clergy: 1,584

GENERAL ORGANIZATION

Headquarters: 4901 Pennsylvania, P.O. Box 850, Joplin MO 64802
General Convention meets biennially. (Next Convention June 1991).

OFFICERS

Gen. Supt., Dr. James D. Gee
Gen. Sec.-Treas., Dr. Ronald R. Minor

OTHER GENERAL EXECUTIVES

Dir. of World Missions, Rev. Charles R. Mosier
Dir. of Indian Missions, Dr. C. Don Burke
Gen. PYPA Pres., Dr. Phil L. Redding
Dir. of Christian Ed., Dr. Aaron M. Wilson
Dir. of Home Missions/Evangelism, Dr. H. O. "Pat" Wilson

ASSISTANT GENERAL SUPERINTENDENTS

Northwestern Division, Dr. Lawrence D. Haddock
Southwestern Division, Dr. Norman D. Fortenberry
North Central Division, Dr. Denzel D. Parramore
South Central Division, Rev. E. Redding
Northeastern Division, Rev. Rick Farley
Southeastern Division, Rev. Melvin L. West

OTHER DEPARTMENTAL OFFICERS

Gen. PLA Pres., Mrs. Diana L. Gee
Ed., The Pentecostal Messenger, Rev. Donald K. Allen
Production Manager of MPH, Rev. Donald K. Allen
Sunday School Curriculum Ed., Ms. Billie Blevins
Messenger Publishing House, 4901 Pennsylvania, Joplin
Mo 64802

PERIODICALS

The Pentecostal Messenger (m), Donald K. Allen, Ed.
The Helper (q), Diana L. Gee, Ed.

Pentecostal Fire-Baptized Holiness Church

Organized in 1918, consolidated with Pentecostal Free
Will Baptists in 1919. Maintains rigid discipline over
members.

GENERAL ORGANIZATION

General Convention every two years. (Next meeting, 1991)
Headquarters: Dry Fork, VA 24549. Tel. (804)724-4879

OFFICERS

Gen. Treas., Kenwin (Bill) N. Johnson, P.O. Box 1528,
Laurinburg, NC 28352. Tel. (919)276-1295
Gen. Sec., W. H. Preskitt, Sr., Rt. 1 Box 169, Wetumpka,
AL 36092. Tel. (205)567-6565
Gen. Mod., Steve E. Johnson, Rt. 2 Box 204, Dry Fork,
VA 24549. Tel. (804)274-4879
Gen. Supt. Mission Bd., Harvey B. Johnson, Rt. 2, Box
204, Dry Fork, VA 24549

PERIODICAL

Faith and Truth (m), P.O. Box 212, Nicholson, GA 30565.
Edgar Vollrath, Rt. 5, Box 137, Commerce, GA 30529,
Ed.

The Pentecostal Free Will Baptist Church, Inc.

Organized 1855, as the Cape Fear Conference of Free
Will Baptists, merged in 1959 with The Wilmington
Conference and The New River Conference of Free Will
Baptists and renamed the Pentecostal Free Will Baptist
Church, Inc. The doctrines include regeneration, sancti-
fication, the Pentecostal baptism of the Holy Ghost, the
Second Coming of Christ, and divine healing.

GENERAL ORGANIZATION

General Meeting: Meets Semi-Annually.
General Headquarters: P.O. Box 1568, Dunn, NC 28334.
Tel. (919) 892-4161
Heritage Bible College, P.O. Box 1628, Dunn, NC 28334.
Tel. (919) 892-4268
Crusader Youth Camp, P.O. Box 1568, Dunn, NC 28334
Mutual Benevolent Fund, P.O. Box 1568, Dunn, NC 28334
Blessings Bookstore, 1006 Cumberland St., Dunn, NC
28334. Tel. (919)892-2401

OFFICERS

Gen. Supt., Rev. Don Sauls
Asst. Gen. Supt., Dr. W. L. Ellis
Gen. Sec., Rev. J. T. Hammond
Gen. Treas., Dr. W. L. Ellis
World Witness Dir., Dr. Herbert Carter
Christian Education Dir., Rev. J. T. Hammond
Gen Services Dir., Rev. Tim Crowder

Ministerial Council Dir., Rev. Preston Heath
Ladies' Auxiliary Dir., Mrs. Dolly Davis
Heritage Bible College: Pres., Dr. W. L. Ellis
Crusader Youth Camp Dir., Rev. J. T. Hammond

Pentecostal Holiness Church, International

This body grew out of the National Holiness Association
movement of the last century and has direct roots in
Methodism. Beginning in the South and Midwest, the
present church represents the merger of three different
holiness bodies: the Fire-Baptized Holiness Church
founded by B. H. Irwin in Iowa in 1895; the Pentecostal
Holiness Church founded by A. B. Crumpler in Goldsboro, North Carolina, in 1898; and the Tabernacle
Pentecostal Church founded by N. J. Holmes in 1898.

All three bodies joined the ranks of the pentecostal
movement as a result of the Azusa Street revival in Los
Angeles in 1906 and a 1907 pentecostal revival in Dunn,
North Carolina, conducted by G. B. Cashwell, who had
visited Azusa Street. In 1911 the Fire-Baptized and
Pentecostal Holiness bodies merged in Falcon, North
Carolina, to form the present church; the Tabernacle
Pentecostal Church was added in 1915 in Canon, Georgia.

The church stresses the new birth; the Wesleyan
experience of entire sanctification; the pentecostal baptism in the Holy Spirit, evidenced by speaking in tongues;
divine healing; and the premillennial second coming of
Christ.

Churches: 1,472; Inclusive Membership: 116,764; Sunday
or Sabbath Schools: 1,472; Total Enrollment: 146,776;
Ordained Clergy: 3,314

GENERAL ORGANIZATION

General Conference: quadrennial (Next meeting, 1993)
Headquarters: P.O. Box 12609, Oklahoma City, OK
73157 Tel. (405) 787-7110

OFFICERS

Gen. Supt., Bishop B. E. Underwood
Vice Chpsn./Asst. Gen. Supt.: Rev. Jesse Simmons
Asst. Gen. Supt., Rev. James Leggett
Gen. Sec./Treas., Rev. Jack Goodson

OTHER ORGANIZATIONS

The Publishing House (Advocate Press), Franklin Springs,
GA 30639. Charles Bradshaw, Gen. Administrator
Christian Education Dept.: Gen. Dir., Rev. Doyle
Marley, P. O. Box 12609, Oklahoma City, OK 73157
General Woman's Ministries: Pres., Mrs. Doris Moore, P.
O. Box 12609, Oklahoma City, OK 73157

PERIODICALS

Publications Editorial Office:
P.O. Box 12609, Oklahoma City, OK 73157
The Pentecostal Holiness Advocate (m), Mrs. Shirley
Spencer, Ed.
Helping Hand (m), Mrs. Doris Moore, Ed.
Sunday School Literature, Rev. Charles Bradshaw, Ed.
Witness (m), Rev. Joe Iaquinta, Ed.
Worldorama (m), Rev. Jesse Simmons, Ed.

Pillar of Fire

The Pillar of Fire was founded by Alma Bridwell White
in Denver, Colorado, December 29, 1901 as the Pentecostal Union. In 1917, the name was changed to Pillar of
Fire. Alma White was born in Kentucky in 1862 and taught
school in Montana where she met her husband, Kent
White, a Methodist minister, who was a University student
in Denver.

Because of Alma White's evangelistic endeavors, she
was frowned upon by her superiors, which eventually
necessitated in her withdrawing from Methodist Church
supervision. She was ordained as Bishop and her work
spread to many states, to England, and since her decease,

Liberia, West Africa; Malawi, East Africa; Yugoslavia; Spain; India; and the Philippines.

The Pillar of Fire organization is credited with being pioneers in Christian education, with a college and two seminaries stressing Biblical studies. The church continues to thrive throughout the United States under the present leadership of the granddaughter, Arlene White Lawrence, with the same goals and purposes in mind as the founder.

GENERAL ORGANIZATION

Headquarters: Zarephath, NJ 08890. Tel. (201) 356-0102
Western Headquarters: 1302 Sherman St., Denver, CO 80203

OFFICERS

Pres. and Gen. Supt., Bishop Donald J. Wolfram, 1st Vice-Pres., and Asst. Supt., Bishop Robert B. Dallenbach; 2nd Vice-Pres. Sec. and Treas., Lois R. Stewart; Trustees, Kenneth Cope; Ellworth N. Bradford, S. Rea Crawford, June Blue

PERIODICALS

Pillar of Fire (bi-m), Zarephath, NJ 08890, Bishop Donald J. Wolfram,Ed.

Plymouth Brethren
(See Christian Brethren)

Polish National Catholic Church of America

After a long period of dissatisfaction with Roman Catholic administration and ideology and, in addition, through the strong desire for religious freedom, this body was organized in 1897.

GENERAL ORGANIZATION

General Synod: every four years (Next General Synod, October 1990, Toronto, Ontario)
Headquarters: Office of Prime Bishop, 1002 Pittston Ave., Scranton, PA 18505. Tel. (717) 346-9131

OFFICERS

Prime Bishop, Most Rev. John F. Swantek, 115 Lake Scranton Rd., Scranton, PA 18505
Bishop of the Central Diocese, Rt. Rev. Anthony M. Rysz, 529 E. Locust St., Scranton, PA 18505
Bishop of the Eastern Diocese, Rt. Rev. Thomas J. Gnat, 635 Union St., Manchester, NH 03104
Bishop of the Buffalo-Pittsburgh Diocese, Rt. Rev. Francis G. Rowinski, 182 Sobieski St., Buffalo, NY 14212
Bishop of Western Diocese, Rt. Rev. Joseph K. Zawistowski, 2019 W. Charleston St., Chicago, IL 60647
Bishop of the Canadian Diocese, Rt. Rev. Joseph I. Nieminski, 186 Cowan Ave., Toronto, Ontario M6K 2N6
Ecumenical Officer, Very Rev. Stanley Skrzypek, 206 Main St., New York Mills, NY 13416. Tel. (315)736-9757

Presbyterian Church in America

The Presbyterian Church in America has a strong commitment to evangelism, missionary work at home and abroad and to Christian education.

Organized at a constitutional assembly in December 1973, this church was first known as the National Presbyterian Church but changed its name in 1974 to Presbyterian Church in America (PCA).

The PCA made a firm commitment on the doctrinal standards which had been significant in presbyterianism since 1645, namely the Westminster Confession of Faith and Catechisms. These doctrinal standards express the distinctives of the Calvinistic or Reformed tradition.

The PCA maintains the historic polity of Presbyterian governance, namely rule by presbyters (or elders) and the graded courts which are the session governing the local church, the presbytery for regional matters and the general assembly at the national level. It has taken seriously the position of the parity of elders, making a distinction between the two classes of elders, teaching and ruling.

In 1982 the Reformed Presbyterian Church, Evangelical Synod (RPCES) joined the PCA. It brought with it a tradition that had antecedents in Colonial America. It also included Covenant College in Lookout Mountain, Georgia and Covenant Theological Seminary in St. Louis, Missouri, both of which are the national denominational institutions of the PCA.

Churches: 1,067; Inclusive Membership: 208,394; Sunday or Sabbath Schools: N.R.; Total Enrollment: 101,543; Ordained Clergy: 1,905

GENERAL ORGANIZATION

General assembly: meets annually (Atlanta, GA, June 11-15, 1990)
Headquarters: 1852 Century Pl., Atlanta, GA 30345. Tel. (404)320-3366

OFFICERS

Mod., Rev. John B. White, Jr., Atlanta, GA
Stated Clk., Dr. Paul R. Gilchrist, 1852 Century Pl., Ste. 190, Atlanta, GA 30345. Tel. (404) 320-3366

PERMANENT COMMITTEES

Adm., Mr. Ross Cook, 1852 Century Pl., Ste. 190, Atlanta, GA 30345. Tel. (404)320-3366
Christian Education and Publications, Rev. Charles Dunahoo, 1852 Century Pl., Ste. 101, Atlanta, GA 30345. Tel. (404)320-3388
Mission to North America, Rev. Terry Gyger, 1852 Century Pl. Ste. 205, Atlanta, GA 30345
Mission to the World, Rev. John E. Kyle, 1852 Century Pl., Ste. 201, Atlanta, GA 30345

PERIODICAL

The PCA Messenger (m), 1852 Century Pl., Ste. 101, Atlanta, GA 30345, Charles Dunahoo, Ed.

Presbyterian Church (U.S.A.)

The Presbyterian Church (U.S.A.) was organized June 10, 1983, when the Presbyterian Church in the United States ("Southern Presbyterian Church") and the United Presbyterian Church in the United States of America merged in Atlanta, Georgia. Thus was healed the major division within American Presbyterianism, which had existed since the Civil War when the Presbyterian Church in the Confederate States of America withdrew from the Presbyterian Church in the United States of America.

The United Presbyterian Church in the United States of America had been created by the 1958 union of the Presbyterian Church in the United States of America and the United Presbyterian Church of North America. Of those two uniting bodies, the Presbyterian Church in the U.S.A. dated from the first Presbytery organized in Philadelphia about 1706. The United Presbyterian Church of North America was formed in 1858, when the Associate Reformed Presbyterian Church and the Associate Presbyterian Church united.

Strongly ecumenical in outlook, the Presbyterian Church (U.S.A.) is the result of at least ten different denominational mergers over the last two and a half centuries. A Structural Design for Mission, adopted by the General Assembly meeting in June 1986 has been implemented, and on October 29, 1988, the Presbyterian Church (U.S.A.) celebrated the dedication of its new headquarters facility which is now located in Louisville, Kentucky.

Churches: 11,505; Inclusive Membership: 2,929,608; Sunday or Sabbath Schools: N.R.; Total Enrollment: 1,097,095; Ordained Clergy: 19,746

GENERAL ASSEMBLY

Meets annually. Next meeting: June 6, 1990, Salt Lake City, UT

OFFICERS

Mod. (1989-90), Joan Salmon Campbell
Vice-Mod., Herb Meza
Stated Clerk, James E. Andrews
Assoc. Stated Clerks, Margrethe B. J. Brown, Catherine M. Phillippe
Headquarters: 100 Witherspoon St., Louisville, KY 40202. Tel. (502)569-5360; Fax: (502)569-5018

THE OFFICE OF THE GENERAL ASSEMBLY

100 Witherspoon St., Louisville, KY 40202. Tel. (502)569-5630
Stated Clerk, James E. Andrews;
Dir., Dept. of the Stated Clerk, Juanita H. Granady
Dir., Dept. of Administration, J. Scott Schaeffer; Mgr. Editing and Printing, Maggie Houston; Supervisor, Editing, Mary Henry: Mgr. Statistical Reports, Greta Lauria
Dir., Department of Constitutional Services, _____;
Mgr., Judicial Process, Gene Witherspoon; Marjorie Ward, Mgr. Comm. on Rep. Staff Services
Dir., Dept. of Governing Body, Ecumenical and Agency Relations, Margrethe B. J. Brown; Exec. Asst., Marian Liggins
Dir., Dept. of Assembly Services, Catherine M. Phillippe
Mgr. for Assembly Arrangements, Paul Thompson
Department of History Headquarters - Philadelphia, 425 Lombard St., Philadelphia, PA 19147. Tel. (215)627-1852; Fax (215)627-0509. Dir., Frederick J. Heuser, Jr.; Coordinator, Gen. Assembly Nominating Cmte., Jean Elliott; Mgr. of Research and Library Services, Gerald Gillette; Ed., *American Presbyterians and Journal of Presbyterian History,* James H. Smylie; Mgr. of Cataloguing Services, Barbara Schnur; Mgr. of Archives and Records Mgmt., _____; Jr., Mgr. of Information Services, Mary H. Plummer; Reference Librarian, Boyd T. Reese; Mgr. of Operations, John G. Peters
Department of History Branch - Montreat, P.O. Box 847, Montreat, NC 28757. Tel. (704)669-7061. Deputy Dir. of Prog., Robert Benedetto; Research Historian, William Bynum; Adm., Local Church History, Diana Sanderson; Technical Service Librarian, John Walker

GENERAL ASSEMBLY COUNCIL

Exec. Dir., S. David Stoner; Assoc. Dir., Wayne W. Allen; Assoc. for Admin., Marion L. Liebert; Coord., Finance & Budgets, Robb Gwaltney; Coord. Governing Body Relationships, Evelyn W. Fulton: Coord., Internal Audits, Sharon Adams; Coord. Policies and Spec. Proj., Frank Diaz; Coord., Resources and Plng., Ruth M. Creath; 100 Witherspoon St., Louisville, KY 40202. Tel. (502)569-5511.
New York Liaison Office, Coord., John B. Lindner, Rm. 420, Interchurch Center, 475 Riverside Dr., New York, NY 10115. Tel. (212)870-2101; Fax: (212)870-3229.

CHURCH VOCATIONS UNIT

Office of Director

Dir., Edgar W. Ward; Adm. Asst., Jewel McRae; Assoc. Dir., Enlistment, Preparation and Referral Services, Mary V. Atkinson; Assoc., Equal Employment, Lillian Anthony; Assoc. Dir., Management and Development Human Resources, _____

Section on Enlistment, Preparation and Referral Services

Office of Enlistment and Preparation for Ministry
Assoc., Preparation of Ministry, Charles Marks; Assoc., Enlistment Services, Judy Atwell

Office of Examinations, Certification and Accreditation
Assoc., Examination Services, _____; Assoc. Cert. & Accreditation, Donna Cook

Office for Services to Committees on Ministry Assoc., R. Howard McCuen

Office for Personnel Referral Services
Coord., Evelyn Hwang; Assoc. Operations, Agnes Holswade; Assoc., Matching, Margaret Willis; Assoc., Specialized Referral and Matching, JoRene Willis; Assoc., Specialized Personnel Services, Mary Serovy

Section on the Management and Development of Human Resources

Office of Human Resource Management
Employment Manager, Sharon Chaplain; Assoc. Salary Adm., Norman Folson; Assoc. for Benefits, Group Dir., Frances White

Office of Human Resources Development
Coord, Carlos Santin; Assoc., Professional Devel.; _____; Assoc. Support and Devel. of Governing Body Staff, Frances Perrin
Office of Monday Morning
Ed., Theodore A. Gill, Jr., Asst. Ed., Susan Ellison, Editorial Asst., Rosetta Holland

EDUCATION AND CONGREGATIONAL NURTURE

Director's Office

Dir., Donald Brown; Assoc., Communication, Promotion, and Planning, Ed Craxton; Assoc., Conferencing (Dir. Stony Point), Jim Palm, Crickettown Rd., Stony Point, NY 10980, Tel. (914)786-5674; Assoc., Conferencing (Dir., Ghost Ranch), Joe Keesecker, Abiquiu, NM 87510, Tel. (505)685-4333; Assoc. Conferencing (Dir. Montreat), William Peterson, P. O. Box 969, Montreat, NC 28757. Tel. (704)669-2911; Assoc. for Adm., Linda Knight

Leader Development Division

Assoc. Dir., _____; Assoc., Asian Leader Develop., C. W. Choi; Assoc. Leader Develop., Educ./Governing Bodies, Margaret Haney; Assoc. Leader Develop. Among Professional Educators/Pastors, Dottie Hedgepeth; Assoc. Leader Develop., Church Officer/Lay Leadership Resources, Ben Lane; Assoc., Leader Develop., Ministry with Men, Art Kamitsuka; Assoc. Leader Develop., Youth, Rodger Nishioka; Assoc. Leader Develop., Youth in Global Ministry, Janice Nessibou; Volunteer in Mission/Intern, Youth Leader Develop., Kirk Burdick; Assoc. for Aging, Tom Robb

Resourcing Division

Assoc. Dir., Donna Blackstock; Assoc. Ethnic Resource Develop./Hispanic, Ernestina Gutierrez; Assoc. Ethnic Resource Develop./Korean, Grace (Choon) Kim; Assoc. Curriculum Develop./Preschool Res., Martha Pillow; Assoc. Curriculum Develop./Children's Res., Kent Chrisman; Assoc. Curriculum Develop./Children's Res., Kent Chrisman; Assoc. Curriculum Develop./Children's Res., Faye Burdick; Assoc., Curriculum Develop/Youth Res., Beth Basham; Assoc., Curriculum Develop/Youth Res., James Clinesfelter; Assoc., Curriculum Res./Adult Res., Marvin Simmers; Assoc., Curriculum Res./Adult Res., Frank Hainer; Assoc., Family Res., Carol Rose Ikeler; Assoc., Men's Res., David Lewis; Assoc. Public/Social Education/Disability Concerns, Lew Merrick; Assoc., Resource Center Develop., Joe Bales Gallagher

Publications Service

Publisher/Director, Robert McIntyre; Publishing Assoc., Wanda Fuller; Ed., Denom. Res., Maureen O'Connor; Copy Ed., Susan Jackson; Dir., Trade Books, Davis Perkins; Assoc. Dir., Church/General, Walt Sutton; Assoc. Dir., Reference/Academic, Cynthis Thompson; Ed., Church/General, Alexa Smith; Dir., Copy Ed./Trade, Janet Baker; Copy Ed./Trade, Danielle Alexander; Copy Ed./Trade, Carl Helmich; Dir., Production, Joan Crawford; Assoc. Dir./Trade, Christopher Miller; Assoc, Dir./Curriculum, Jane James; Art Dir/Trade, Peter Gall; Art Dir/Curriculum, Peg Coots; Dir., Copy Editing/Curriculum, Nancy Roseberry; Copy Ed. /Curriculum, Carrie McCollough; Copy Ed./Curriculum, Shirley Murphey; Dir. Marketing, Robert Stratton; Mgr., Distribution/ Customer Serv., Vicki Miller; Marketing Dir., Curriculum/Retail Sales, Joe Paul Pruett; Assoc. Marketing Dir./General Materials, Paul Tuttle; Assoc. Marketing Dir., Curriculum, Nancy Combs; Marketing Assoc./ Curriculum, Brenda Hooks; Marketing Asst./Curriculum Res., Tracey Crockett; Marketing Asst./Curriculum Interpretation, Vicki Rucker; Bookstore Mgr., Pen Bogert; Dir., Sales Dept., Mina Grier; Sales Promotions Mgr., Ann McCannon; Dir., Publicity/Public Relations, Sally Telford; Dir., Subsidiary Rights & Permissions, Janine Bogert; Dir., Advertising, Bill Hendrick; Assoc. Advertising Dir., Curriculum, Tommy Larson; Copywriting/Curriculum, Debbie McCallister; Assoc. Advertising Dir./Trade, David Miller; Copywriting/Trade, Lina Bryant.

Survey

Ed./Publisher, Vic Jameson; Mgr. Ed., Catherine Cottingham; Assoc. Ed., Eva Stimson; Art Dir., Lee Jenkins; Dir., Advertising/Promotion, Ann Coffey

EVANGELISM AND CHURCH DEVELOPMENT MINISTRY UNIT

Dir., Evangelism & Church Development, Andrea Pfaff, Coord., for Admin., Communication, Research and Plng., Julianne Jens-Horton; Assoc. Dir., Presbyterian Evang., Gary Demarest; Assoc. Dir., Rural and Urban Ch. Develop., _____; Assoc. Dir., Mission Fncl. Res., Diana Stephen; Assoc. for Mission Program Grants, _____; Assoc. for Church Loan Services, Dan Park; Assoc. for Small Ch. Devel., James Cushman; Assoc. for Racial/Ethnic Res. Devel. & Trng., Mildred Brown; Assoc. for Redevelopment, Thomas Dietrich; Assoc. for Resource Develop. & Trng., Mary B. Love; Assoc. for Ch. Growth & New Ch. Develop., H. Stanley Wood; Assoc. for Int'l. Ch. Develop. and Evang., Morton Taylor

GLOBAL MISSION MINISTRY UNIT

Director, Clifton Kirkpatrick; Assoc. Dir., Unit Coord., Syngman Rhee; Assoc., Management and Budget, Mehdi Abhari

Ecumenical/Interfaith Office

Assoc., Ecumenical Coord., Lewis Lancaster; Assoc. Ecumenical Educ. & Facilitation, Robina Winbush; Assoc. Interfaith Relations, Margaret Thomas; Coord., New York Liaison Ofc., John B. Lindner

Health Ministries Office

Assoc. Dir., Health Ministries, Gwen Crawley; Assoc. for Program Development and Resourcing, Bob Ellis

Mutual Mission Office

Assoc. Dir., Internationalization of Mission, Elizabeth McAliley; Assoc., Mission to USA Personnel, Paul

Seto; Assoc. Ecumenical Exchange, Nancy Miller; Assoc. Synod/Presbytery Partnerships, Homer Rickabaugh

Partnership in Mission Office

Assoc. Dir., Partnership Coordination, Bruce Gannaway; Assoc., Southern Africa, Yenwith Whitney; Assoc., East/West Africa, John Pritchard; Assoc., East Asia/ Pacific, Insik Kim; Assoc. Middle East/South Asia, Byron Haines; Assoc., South America/Mexico, Benjamin Gutierrez; Assoc., Cent. Am./Caribbean, Julianne Junkin; Assoc., Europe, Robert Lodwick; Assoc., Intl. Evangelism, Morton Taylor

People in Mission Offices

Assoc. Dir., Mission Personnel, William Hopper; Assoc., Volunteers in Mission (USA), Linda Crawford; Assoc. Volunteers in Mission (International), Mike Stuart; Assoc. Missionary Recruitment, Morrisine Smith; Assoc. Missionary-Fraternal Worker Concerns, Marcia Borgeson;Assoc., Missionary Services/Pastoral Care, Harry Phillips

RACIAL ETHNIC UNIT

Dir., James Foster Reese; Assoc. Dir., Racial Justice Ministries, Jovelino Ramos; Coord., Asian Cong. Enhancement, Shun Chi Wang; Coord., Black Cong. Enhancement, Rita Dixon; Coord., Hispanic Cong. Enhancement, Jose Rodriguez; Coord., Korean Cong. Enhancement, Sun Bai Kim; Coord., Native Amer. Cong. Enhancement, Donald Eugene Wilson; Coord., Racial Justice Ministries, Wesley Woo; Coord., Racial Justice Policy Develop., Otis Turner; Coord., Racial Justice Ldrshp., Develop., Angela Abrego

SOCIAL JUSTICE AND PEACEMAKING UNIT

100 Witherspoon St., Louisville, KY 40202

Dir., Belle Miller McMaster; Assoc. Dir., Donald J. Wilson; Group Dir. - Human Devel. and Coord., Hunger Prog., Colleen Shannon; Assoc. Coord. PHP/ Assoc. for Int'l. Relief & Development, Lionel Derenoncourt; Assoc. for Hunger Educ., Rose C. Taul; Prog. Asst. for Resourcing, Hunger Prog., Diane Hockenberry; Assoc. for Cmty. Devel., Philip Newell; Coordinator—World Service, _____; Jinishian Memorial Prog., 475 Riverside Dr., Rm. 420, New York, NY 10115. Tel. (212)870-2465; William K. DuVal; Assoc. for Jinishian Field Service, Haig Tilbian; Assoc. for Disaster Response, Daniel O. Rift; Assoc. for Human Services, David Zuverink; Assoc. for Social Welfare Organizations, Presbyterian Health, Educ. & Welfare Assoc. (PHEWA), _____; Group Dir., Church and Public Issues, Vernon S. Broyles, III; Assoc. for Criminal Justice, Kathy Lancaster; Assoc. for Mission Responsibility Through Investments, William Somplatsky-Jarman; Assoc. for Intl. Justice, Harry F. J. Daniel; Group Dir., Peacemaking, Richard L. Killmer; Assoc. for Constituency Support, Richard Watts; Assoc. for Intl Peacemaking Personnel, Ollie Gannaway; Washington Office, 110 Maryland Ave., NE, Washington, DC 20002. Tel. (202)543-1126; Group Dir., Eleanor Ivory; Assoc. for International Issues, Walter L. Owensby; Assoc. for Peace Issues, Barbara G. Green; Jarvie Commonweal Service, 475 Riverside Dr., 4th Fl., New York, NY 10115, Tel. (212)870-2965, Coord., Ellsworth G. Stanton, III; Assoc. Coord. Ann Brownhill Gubernick; Social Caseworkers, Ann Bonnell, Adele Malhotra, Hazel Schuller, Patricia Charles; Helene Walker; Presbyterian Office, United Nations, Church Center for the UN, Tel. (212)697-4568, Assoc. for United Nations, Robert F. Smylie, 777 United Nations Plz., New York, NY 10017

STEWARDSHIP AND COMMUNICATION DEVELOPMENT MINISTRY UNIT

Dir., John Coffin; Assoc. Dir., Plan/Budget & Info/Coord., Vivian Johnson; Asst. for Adm., Clarisa Cuyler; Assoc. Dir., Comm. Develop., Lois Stover; Assoc. for Comm./Inf. Services, Nancy Heinze; Assoc. for Comm./Computer Systems, Mel Willard; Assoc. for Comm./Coord., Brenda Brooks; Asst. for Comm., Stanley Williams; Assoc. Dir., Media Services, Ann Gillies; Assoc. for Media Services, Bill Gee; Assoc. for Media Coord. and Marketing, Bill Huie; Asst. for Media Services, Lloyed Perkins; Assoc. Dir., Mission Fndg., Claude Godwin; Assoc for Spcl. Gifts, Kenneth Hollenbaugh, Special Gifts Office, 476 Spruce Lane, Nazareth, PA 18064. Tel. (215)837-8250; Assoc. for Selected Giving, Bill Amey; Assoc. for Selected Giving, Margaret Anderson; Asst. for Selected Giving, Guy Gauthier; Assoc. for Relationships with Foundations, Bruce Berry; Assoc. for CFCS Coord., Donald S. Myer, 11466 Ashley Woods Dr., Westchester, IL 60153. Tel. (312)409-0164; Asst. for CFCS, Ruth Anne Boklage (Louisville Ofc.).

Assoc. Dir. Mission Inter. & Prom., James T. Magruder; Assoc. for Interpretation/Marketing, Synod & Presby. Relations, Eileene Johnson MacFalls; Assoc. for Interpretation Resources/Publications, Ted Yaple; Assoc. for Interpretaion/Resources, David Eddy; Assoc. for Interpretaiton Resources/Coordinator, Sandra Woodcock; Assoc. for Interpretation/Speakers & Correspondence, Anne Howland; Assoc. for Intepretation/Spcl. Offerings, Alan Krome; Assoc. Dir., Research Services, Arthur Benjamin; Assoc. for Research Coord., Keith Wulff; Assoc. for Research/Information, Ida Smith; Assoc. for Research/Analyst, John Marcum; Asst. for Research/Adm., Betty Partenheimer Assoc. Dir. for Stewardship Educ., David McCreath; Assoc. for Stewardship Prom., Susan Rhoades; Assoc. for Stewardship Resources, Yvette Dalton; Assoc. for Stewardship Trng., Vene Atwell

THE BICENTENNIAL FUND

Dir., Richard M. Ferguson; Co-Dir., George N. Pike; Assoc. Dir., Rev. Earl Underwood; Dir. for Major and Special Gifts, Kenneth H. Hollenbaugh; Dir. for Public Rel., Dale M. Williams; Counselor at Large, Judy Schideler; Assoc. for Adm., Milly Mead

THEOLOGY AND WORSHIP MINISTRY UNIT

Director, George Telford, Jr.; Assoc. Dir., Joseph D. Small, III; Assoc., Theol. Studies, Jack B. Rogers; Assoc., Faith and Order, Aurelia Fule; Assoc. Liturgical Resources, Harold M. Daniels; Assoc., Worship and the Arts, Nalini (Marcia) Jayasuriya; Assoc., Discipleship and Spirituality, E. Dixon Junkin

WOMEN'S MINISTRY UNIT

Director, Mary Ann Lundy; Assoc. Dir., Annie Wu King; Assoc. Presbyterian Women, Gladys Strachan; Assoc., Women Employed by the Church, Ann DuBois; Assoc., Comte. of Women of Color, Patricia Gill Turner; Assoc., Justice for Women, Mary Kuhns; Assoc., Mission Participation, Marilyn Clark; *Horizons* Mag., Ed., Barbara Roche.
National Staff in the Regions:
Eastern Area Office, 475 Riverside Dr., New York, NY 10115, Yolanda Hernandez, Frances Unsell; *East Central Office*, 300 Sixth Ave., Ste. 1110, Pittsburgh, PA 15222, Margaret Hall, Glendora Paul; *West Central* Area Office, 7850 Holmes Rd., Kansas City, MO 64131, Judy Mead; *Western Area Office*, 330 Ellis St., Rm. 414, San Francisco, CA 94102, Joan Richardson, Lucille Rieben; *South Eastern Area Office*, 159 Ralph McGill Blvd., Rm. 411 Atlanta, GA 30365, Elizabeth Lunz, Vera Swann

SUPPORT SERVICES

Dir., Robert T. Mehrhoff; Mgr., Ofc. of News Services, Marj Carpenter; Mgr. Ofc. of Gen. Services, Susan D. Johns; Mgr., Ofc. of Inf. Services, John M. Mayberry; Gen. Counsel, PC (USA), Carolyn F. Shain

CENTRAL TREASURY CORPORATION

Pres./Treas., Delmar Byler; Vice Pres./Assoc. Treas., Arthur Clark, Sr.; Vice Pres., Controller, Nagy Tawfik; Assoc. Controller, Trisha Pitts; Payroll Mgr., Jerry Bradshaw; Payroll Specialist, Sue Schumuckie; A.V.P./Planning/Cap. Budget, Carmen Lopez; Mgr., Financial Resource Coordinator, Hope Bezold; Mgr. Central Receiving, William Partenheimer; Senior Financial Resource Coordinator, Robert Etheridge; Financial Resource Coordinators: Maria Alvarez, Hwa Ja Kim, Patricia Robbins, Jeanice Vazquez, Dean Duggins, Elsie Louden, Elias Sahiouny; Mgr. Accounts Payable, Thomas Abraham; Assoc. Mgr., Central Receiving, William Shumate; Accountant, Financial Reporting, Jennifer Yates; Supervisor, G/L Accounting, Robin Allen; Supervisor, A/R Loans, Sarah Zimmerman; Assoc. for Adm., Brenda Emerson; Assoc. Controller/Publications, Randy White; Supvr./Special Unit Accounting, John Moll; Accountants/Special Unit Accounting, Michael Agamemnonos, Agnes Hobson; Supvr./Sub. Ledger Accounting, Haesun Rhee; Accountant/Restricted Funds, Babu Gandhi; Mgr./Accounting (Publications), Erica Bowie; Mgr./Acquisitions (Publications), Ernesto Alvarez; Mgr./Credit & Collections (Publications) Teresa Keowa; Mgr./Risk Mgmt., Kas Vargo

COMMITTEE ON SOCIAL WITNESS POLICY

Dir., Dieter T. Hessel; Assoc. Dir., Policy Devel. and Interpretation, Ruth Duba; Assoc. for Resources & Admin., Sarah Stephens

COMMITTEE ON HIGHER EDUCATION

Dir., Duncan S. Ferguson; Assoc. Global Education and Leadership Devel., Haydn O. White; Assoc., Racial-Ethnic Schools and Colleges, George M. Conn, Jr.; Assoc., Higher Education Ministries, Clyde O. Robinson, Jr.

COMMITTEE ON THEOLOGICAL EDUCATION

Dir., Joyce Tucker; Assoc., Mission Cooperation, Roger Woods; Assoc., Funding Plan Implementation, Daniel L. Force; Fndg. Plan Coord., Patsy Godwin

PRESBYTERIAN CHURCH (U.S.A.) FOUNDATION

Offices: 200 E. Twelfth St., Jeffersonville, IN 47130
Chair of the Board, Paul B. Bell; Vice-Chair, Helen R. Walton; Pres., Geoffrey R. Cross; Sr. Vice-Pres. for Finance, Dennis J. Murphy; Vice-Pres. for Development, Robert F. Langwig

PERIODICALS

American Presbyterians: Journal of Presbyterian History (q), 425 Lombard St., Philadelphia, PA 19147. Rev. James H. Smylie, Ed.
Monday Morning (bi-m), 100 Witherspoon St., Louisville, KY 40202. Theodore A. Gill, Jr., Ed.
Church & Society Magazine (bi-m), 100 Witherspoon St., Louisville, KY 40202. Kathy Lancaster, Ed.
Horizons (semi-m), Presbyterian Women, Barbara Roche, Ed., 100 Witherspoon St., Louisville, KY 40202
These Days (bi-m), (jointly with the Cumberland Presbyterian Church, the Presbyterian Church in Canada, the Presbyterian Church (U.S.A.), The United Church of Canada, and the United Church of Christ), Arthur M. Field, Ed., Editorial Office, 100 Witherspoon St., Louisville, KY 40202
Presbyterian Survey, 100 Witherspoon St., Louisville, KY 40202

Alaska-Northwest, Rev. Elizabeth B. Knott, 2001 6th Ave., Ste. 2801, Seattle, WA 98121. Tel. (206) 448-6403
Covenant, Rev. George P. Morgan, 6172 Bush Blvd., Ste. 3000, Columbus, OH 43229. Tel. (614) 436-3310
Lakes & Prairies, Rev. Robert T. Cuthill, 8012 Cedar Ave., S., Bloomington, MN 55425. Tel. (612) 854-0144
Lincoln Trails, Rev. Verne E. Sindlinger, 1100 W. 42nd St., Indianapolis, IN 46208. Tel. (317) 923-3681
Living Waters, Rev. Harold J. Jackson, P.O. Box 290275, Nashville, TN 37229. Tel. (615)370-4008
Mid-America, Rev. John L. Williams, 6400 Glenwood, Ste. 111, Overland Park, KS 66202. Tel. (913) 384-3020
Mid-Atlantic, Carroll D. Jenkins, P. O. Box 27026, Richmond, VA 23261. Tel. (804)342-0016
Northeast, Rev. Eugene G. Turner, 3049 E. Genesee St., Syracuse, NY 13224. Tel. (315) 446-5990
Pacific, Rev. Philip H. Young, PO.Box 1810, San Anselmo, CA 94960. Tel. (415)258-0333
Puerto Rico, Rev. Harry Fred Del Valle, Medical Center Plaza, Oficina 216, Mayaguez, PR 00708. Tel. (809) 832-8375
Rocky Mountains, Rev. David T. Tomlinson, 1370 Pennsylvania Ave., Ste. 410, Denver CO 80203. Tel. (303) 830-6712
South Atlantic, Rev. John Niles Bartholomew, Interstate North Office Center, 435 Clark Rd., Ste. 404, Jacksonville, FL 32218. Tel. (904)764-5644
Southern Calif., Hawaii, Rev. Frederick J. Beebe; 1501, Wilshire Blvd., Los Angeles, CA 90017. Tel. (213) 483-3840
Southwest, Rev. Gary Skinner, 4423 N. 24th St., Ste. 800, Phoenix, AZ 85016. Tel. (602)468-3800
Sun, Rev. William J. Fogelman, 920 Stemmons Fwy., Denton, TX 76205. Tel. (817) 382-9656
Trinity, Rev. Thomas M. Johnston, Jr., 3040 Market St., Camp Hill, PA 17011. Tel. (717) 737-0421

Primitive Advent Christian Church

This body split from the Advent Christian Church. All its churches are located in West Virginia. the Primitive Advent Christian Church believes that the Bible is the only rule of faith and practice and that Christian character is the only test of fellowship and communion. The church agrees with Christian fidelity and meekness; exercises mutual watch and care; counsels, admonishes, or reproves as duty may require; and receives the same from each other as becomes the household of faith. Primitive Advent Christians do not believe in taking up arms against our fellow man in case of war.

The church believes that three ordinances are set forth by the Bible to be observed by the Christian church: (1) baptism by immersion; (2) the Lord's Supper, by partaking of unleavened bread and wine; (3) feet washing, to be observed by the saints' washing of one another's feet.

OFFICERS

Pres., Donald Young, 1640 Clay Ave., South Charleston, WV
Vice-Pres., Roger Hammons, 273 Frame Rd., Elkview, WV 25071. Tel. (304)965-6247
Sec. and Treas., Hugh W. Good, 395 Frame Rd., Elkview, WV 25071. Tel. (304) 965-1550

Primitive Baptists

A large group of Baptists, located throughout the United States, who are opposed to all centralization and to modern missionary societies. This body believes, and preaches Salvation by Grace alone.

GENERAL ORGANIZATION

Address: Cayce Publ. Co., S. Second St., P.O. Box 38, Thornton, AR 71766. Tel. (501) 352-3694

CORRESPONDENT

Elder W. H. Cayce, S. Second St., P.O. Box 38, Thornton, AR 71766. Tel. (501) 352-3694

PERIODICALS

Primitive Baptist (m), Thornton, AR 71766. W. H. Cayce, Ed.

For the Poor (m), Thornton, AR 71766. W. H. Cayce, Ed.
Baptist Witness, Box 17037, Cincinnati, OH 45217. L. Bradley, Jr., Ed.
Christian Baptist (m), P.O. Box 68, Atwood, TN 38220, S. T. Tolly, Ed.
Christian Pathway (m), Maryville, TN 37801, Elder Harold Hunt, Ed.

Primitive Methodist Church in the U.S.A.

Hugh Bourne and William Clowes, local preachers in the Wesleyan Church in England in the early 1800s, became interested in seeing their fellow workers converted and brought to Christ. Lorenzo Dow, a Methodist preacher from America, recounted with enthusiasm the story of the American camp meeting to Bourne and Clowes, and a whole day's meeting at Mow Cop in Staffordshire, England, on May 31, 1807, was arranged. Thousands were present and many were converted but, strange as it may seem, the church founded by that great open air preacher John Wesley refused to accept these converts and reprimanded the preachers for their evangelistic effort.

After waiting for a period of two years for a favorable action by the Wesleyan Society, Bourne and Clowes established The Society of the Primitive Methodists. The words of Bourne provide the evidence that this was not a schism, for "we did not take one from them . . . it now appeared to be the will of God that we, as a Camp Meeting Community, should form classes and take upon us the care of churches in the fear of God." The first Primitive Methodist missionaries were sent to New York in 1829, and a distinct conference in America was established on September 16, 1840.

Missionary efforts reach into Guatemala, Spain, and numerous other countries, with both Spanish and English work in the U.S.A. The denomination joins in federation with the Evangelical Congregational Church and the United Brethren in Christ Church, and is a member of the National Association of Evangelicals.

The Primitive Methodist Church believes the Bible to be the only true rule of faith and practice, the inspired Word of God, and holds its declarations final. It believes in the existence of one Triune God, the Deity of Jesus Christ, the Deity and personality of the Holy Spirit, the innocence of Adam and Eve, the Fall and corruption of the human race, the necessity of repentance, justification by faith of all who believe and regeneration witnessed by the Holy Spirit, sanctification by the Holy Spirit producing holiness of heart and life, the second coming of the Lord Jesus Christ, the resurrection of the dead and conscious future existence of all men, and future judgments and eternal rewards and punishments.

Churches: 85; Inclusive Membership: 8,244;Sunday or Sabbath Schools: 85; Total Enrollment. 4,898; Ordained Clergy: 84

GENERAL ORGANIZATION

The Conference, annual (Next Meeting, May 1990)

OFFICERS

Pres., Rev. J. William Reseigh, 3861 Laurel Run Rd., Wilkes-Barre, PA 18702
Vice-Pres., Gillard Evans, 92G Star Route, Gouldsboro, PA 18424

Exec. Dir., Rev. William H. Fudge, 1045 Laurel Run Rd., Wilkes-Barre, PA 18702
Gen. Sec., Rev. Reginald H. Thomas, 110 Pitston Blvd., Wilkes-Barre, PA 18702
Treas., Mr. Raymond C. Baldwin, 11012 Langton Arms Ct., Oakton, VA 22124

Progressive National Baptist Convention, Inc.

A body which held its organizational meeting at Cincinnati, November, 1961, and subsequent regional sessions, followed by the first annual session in Philadelphia in 1962

GENERAL ORGANIZATION

Annual Session: August.

OFFICERS

Pres., Dr. Fred C. Lofton, Metropolitan Baptist Church, 767 Walker Ave., Memphis, TN 38126
Gen. Sec., Rev. Tyrone S. Pitts, 601 50th St., N.E., Washington, DC 20019. Tel. (202) 396-0558

OTHER ORGANIZATIONS

Dept. of Christian Education: Sec., Rev. C. B. Lucas, 3815 W. Broadway, Louisville, KY 40211
Women's Auxiliary: Mrs. Goldie Hollie, 537 66th St., Oakland, CA 94609.
Home Mission Bd., Exec. Dir., Rev. Archie LeMone, 601 50th St., N.E., Washington, DC 20019.
Congress of Christian Education: Pres., Dr. Pauline C. Reeder, 788 E. 52nd St., Brooklyn, NY 11203
Baptist F. M. Bureau, Dr. Ronald K. Hill, 161-163 60th St., Philadelphia, PA 19139

PERIODICAL

Baptist Progress (q), Tabernacle Baptist Church, 1477 Copley Rd., Akron, OH 44320. Rev. Isaiah F. Paul, Ed.

The Protes'tant Conference (Lutheran), Inc.

The Conference came into being in 1927 as the result of expulsions of pastors and teachers from the Wisconsin Evangelical Lutheran Synod (WELS). The underlying cause which ignited the suspensions was a rebellion against what was labeled The Wauwatosa Theology, so named after the location of the Wisconsin Synod seminary at that time and the fresh approach to Scripture study there by the faculty. This approach sought to overcome the lazy and self-serving habits of dogmatism, which overtakes any group of Christians, particularly when they have been given a true and correct exposition of Christian doctrine, and is content to postulate formula to a given situation, but this rarely with the Gospel's or the faith's true interest at heart. Chiefly responsible for this renewal was Professor John Philipp Koehler.
The Conference was formed as the result of these suspensions, which were to be followed by other suspensions, and which continue to this day. To give testimony to the issues at operation in this controversy and in particular to bear witness to the grace of the Wauwatosa Theology, the Conference has published Faith-Life since 1928. Our roster of congregations, currently at six, is chiefly in Wisconsin. The Conference has no official officers as such. Our purpose has not been to build yet another church body interested chiefly in its survival among the many church bodies. Chief in influence on our history have been Professor J. P. Koehler (1859-1951), his son Karl Koehler (1885-1948) who was the chief architect of Faith-Life with its unique Policy and Purpose, and Paul

Hensel (1888-1977) who displayed the freshness of the Wauwatosa Theology in his writings and commentary.
A concise history of these things is to be found in Prof. Leigh Jordahl's Introduction to a reprinting of J. P. Koehler's "The History of the Wisconsin Synod," published by the Conference.

Churches: 7; Inclusive Membership: 1,035; Sunday or Sabbath Schools: 6; Total Enrollment: 136; Ordained Clergy: 7

GENERAL ORGANIZATION

Conference: meets 3 times annually

OFFICERS

Rec. Sec., Pastor Gerald Hinz, P.O. Box 86, Shiocton, WI 54170. Tel. (414)986-3918
Fin. Sec.-Treas., Michael Meler, 1023 Colan Blvd., Rice Lake, WI 54868

PERIODICAL

Faith-Life (bi-m), P.O. Box 2141, LaCrosse, WI 54601. Pastor Marcus Albrecht, Rt. 1, Mindoro, WI 54644, Ed.

Protestant Reformed Churches in America

The Protestant Reformed Churches in America were organized in 1926 as a result of doctrinal disagreement relating to such matters as world conformity, problems of higher criticism and God's grace that pervaded the Christian Reformed Church in the early 1920's.
After the passage of the formula on Three Points of Common Grace by the Synod of the Christian Reformed Church in 1924, and during the resulting storm of controversy, three clergy, and those in their congregations who agreed with them, were expelled from the Christian Reformed Church. These clergy were Herman Hoeksema of the Eastern Ave. Christian Reformed Church in Grand Rapids, Mich., George Ophoff, pastor of the Hope congregation in Riverbend, Mich., and Henry Danhof in Kalamazoo.
In March 1925, the consistories of these congregations signed an Act of Agreement and adopted the temporary name of "Protesting Christian Reformed Churches." Following the Synod of the Christian Reformed Church of 1926, when the break was made final, the three consistories participating in the Act of Agreement met, and in November, 1926, organized the Protestant Reformed Churches in America.
The Protestant Reformed Churches in America hold to the doctrinal tenets of Calvinism, the Belgic Confession, the Heidelberg Catechism and the Canons of Dordrecht.

GENERAL ORGANIZATION

General Synod: meets annually (June)
Headquarters: 16515 South Park Ave., South Holland, IL 60473. Tel. (708) 333-1314

OFFICER

Stat. Clk., Rev. M. Joostens, 2016 Tekonsha, S.E., Grand Rapids, MI 49506. Tel. (616) 247-0638

Reformed Church in America

The Reformed Church in America was established in 1628 by the earliest settlers of New York. It is the oldest Protestant denomination with a continuous ministry in North America. Until 1867 it was known as the Reformed Protestant Dutch Church.
The first ordained minister, Domine Jonas Michaelius, arrived in New Amsterdam from The Netherlands in 1628. Throughout the colonial period, the Reformed Church lived under the authority of the Classis of Amsterdam. Its churches were clustered in New York and New Jersey.

Under the leadership of Rev. John Livingston, it became a denomination independent of the authority of the Classis of Amsterdam in 1776. Its geographical base was broadened in the nineteenth century by the immigration of Reformed Dutch and German settlers in the midwestern United States. In the twentieth century, the Reformed Church spans the United States and Canada.

The Reformed Church accepts as its standards of faith the Heidelberg Catechism, Belgic Confession, and Canons of Dort. It has a rich heritage of world mission activity. It claims to be loyal to reformed traditions which emphasizes obedience to God in all aspects of life.

Although the Reformed Church in America has worked in close cooperation with other churches, it has never entered into merger with any other denomination. It is a member of the World Alliance of Reformed Churches, the World Council of Churches, and the National Council of the Churches of Christ in the United States of America.

Churches: 925; Inclusive Membership: 333,798; Sunday or Sabbath Schools: 900; Total Enrollment: 100,489; Ordained Clergy: 1,698

GENERAL ORGANIZATION

General Synod: annual (Next meeting, June 9-15, 1990,Orange City, IA)
Denominational Office: 475 Riverside Dr., New York, NY 10115. Tel. (212) 870-2841

OFFICERS AND STAFF OF GENERAL SYNOD

Pres., Sylvio J. Scorza, 475 Riverside Dr., Rm. 1811, New York NY 10115
Gen. Sec., Edwin G. Mulder

OTHER ORGANIZATIONS

Board of Direction: Pres., Jerrald Redeker, 475 Riverside Dr., Rm. 1811, New York NY 10115
Board of Pensions: Pres., Wilbur T. Washington, Sec., Edwin G. Mulder
General Program Council: Mod., Marlin A. Vander Wilt, 475 Riverside Dr., Rm. 1812, New York, NY 10115; Sec. for Program, Eugene P. Heideman
Office of Human Resources: Coord., Alvin J. Poppen
Office of Finance: Treas., Everett K. Hicks
Office of Promotion, Communications and Development: Dir., Wayne Antworth
Reformed Church Women: Exec Dir., Diana Paulsen
The Black Council: Exec. Dir., M. William Howard, Jr.
The Hispanic Council: Nat'l. Sec., Johnny Alicea-Baez
The American Indian Council: Sec., Roe B. Lewis
The Council for Pacific/Asian American Ministries: National Sec., Ella White

PERIODICAL

The Church Herald (m), 6157 - 28th St., SE, Grand Rapids, MI, John C. Stapert, Ed.

Reformed Church in the United States

Lacking pastors, early German Reformed immigrants to the American colonies were led in worship by "readers." One reader, schoolmaster John Philip Boehm, organized the first congregations near Philadelphia in 1725. A Swiss pastor, Michael Schlatter, was sent by the Dutch Reformed Church in 1746. Strong ties with the Netherlands existed until the formation of the Synod of the Reformed High German Church in 1793.

The "Mercersburg Theology" of the 1840s was a precursor to twentieth century liberalism, and to the merger of the Reformed Church with the Evangelical Synod of North America in 1934. Conservatives vigorously opposed the union, holding that it sacrificed the Reformed heritage. (The merged Evangelical and Reformed Church became part of the United Church of Christ in 1957.)

The Eureka Classis was organized in North and South Dakota in 1910 as one of fifty-eight classes (districts) in the church. These congregations were strongly influenced by the writings of H. Kohlbruegge, P. Geyser and J. Stark, who emphasized salvation by grace through faith, not by works. Under the leadership of pastors W. Grossmann and W. J. Krieger, the Eureka Classis refused to become part of the merger of 1934, and in 1942 incorporated as the continuing Reformed Church in the United States.

The growing Eureka Classis dissolved in 1986 to form a Synod with four regional classes. An heir to the Reformation theology of Zwingli and Calvin, the Heidelberg Catechism of 1563 is used as the confessional standard of the church. The Bible is strictly held to be the inerrant, infallible Word of God.

The RCUS has close relationships with other conservative Reformed and Presbyterian bodies. It supports Westminster Theological Seminary in Philadelphia and Escondido, CA; Dordt College and Mid-America Reformed Seminary in Iowa. The RCUS is the official sponsor to the Reformed Confessing Church of Zaire.

GENERAL ORGANIZATION

Synod: annual; Classis: semi-annual

OFFICERS

Pres., Rev. Robert Stuebbe, 401 Cherry Hill Dr., Bakersfield, CA 93309
Vice-Pres., Rev. Vernon Pollema, 235 James Street, Shafter, CA 93263
Clerk, Rev. Steven Work, 2340 Leigh Ave., San Jose, CA 95118. Tel. (408)377-2350
Treas., Mr. Dennis Carlson, Rte. 2, Box 99A; Hastings, NE 68901

PERIODICAL

The Reformed Herald (m), Box 362, Sutton, NE 68979, Rev. P. Grossmann, Ed.

Reformed Episcopal Church

The Reformed Episcopal Church was founded December 2, 1873, in New York City by Bishop George D. Cummins. Cummins was a major evangelical figure in the Protestant Episcopal church and from 1866 until 1873 was the assistant bishop of the diocese of Kentucky. However, Cummins and other evangelical Episcopalians viewed with alarm the influence of the Oxford Movement in the Protestant Episcopal Church, not only for the interest in Roman Catholic ritual and doctrine but also for the intolerance it bred toward evangelical Protestant doctrine both within and outside the Episcopal Church. Throughout the late 1860s, evangelicals and ritualists clashed over ceremonies and vestments, exchanges of pulpits with clergy of other denominations, and the proper meaning of critical passages in the Book of Common Prayer as well as the interpretation of the sacraments and validity of the so-called Apostolic Succession. These clashes culminated in October 1873, when other bishops publicly attacked Cummins in the church newspapers for participating in an ecumenical Communion service sponsored by the Evangelical Alliance. On November 10, 1873, Cummins resigned his office and, on November 13, drafted a call to Episcopalians to organize a new Episcopal Church for the "purpose of restoring the old paths of their fathers." At the organization of the new church on December 2 (known as the First General Council), a *Declaration of Principles* was adopted and the Rev. Charles E. Cheney was elected bishop to serve with Cummins. The Second General Council, meeting in May 1874 in New York City, approved a *Constitution and Canons* and a slightly amended version of the Book of

Common Prayer. In 1875, the Third General Council adopted a set of *Thirty-Five Articles* as a recast substitute to the Church of England's *Thirty-Nine Articles of Religion.*

Although Cummins died in 1876, the church had grown to nine jurisdictions in the U.S. and Canada at that time.

Although substantial growth ceased after 1900, the church now comprises three synods (New York-Philadelphia, Chicago, Charleston-Atlanta-Charlotte) and a missionary jurisdiction of the West. It maintains in its doctrine the founding principles of episcopacy (as an ancient and desirable form of church polity), a Biblical liturgy, Reformed doctrine, and evangelical zeal, and in its practice it continues to recognize the validity of nonepiscopal orders of evangelical ministry. The Reformed Episcopal Church is a member of the National Association of Evangelicals; it was a long-time member of the Federal Council of Churches but withdrew, and in 1938 it rejected remerger efforts with the Protestant Episcopal Church.

Churches: 78; Inclusive Membership: 6,274; Sunday or Sabbath Schools: 73; Total Enrollment: 3,877; Ordained Clergy: 122

GENERAL ORGANIZATION

General Council: triennial (Next meeting, May, 1990)

OFFICERS

Pres. and Presid. Bishop, Rev. William H. S. Jerdan, Jr., 414 W. Second South St., Summerville, SC 29483
Vice-Pres., Bishop Franklin H. Sellers, 1629 W. 99th St., Chicago, IL 60643
Sec., Rev. Roger F. Spence, 6300 Greenwood Pkwy., #203, Sagamore Hills, OH 44067
Treas., Mr. William B. Schimpf, 67 Westaway Lane, Warrington, PA 18976

OTHER ORGANIZATIONS

Board of Foreign Missions: Pres., Rev. William J. Holiman, Jr., 319 E. 50th St., New York, NY 10022; Sec., Mrs. Lyla Wildermuth, 22 Forest Ave., Willow Grove, PA 19090; Treas., Rev. Daniel Olsen, 11 S. Andover Ave., Margate, NJ 08402
Board of National Church Extension: Pres., Bishop Royal U. Grote, Jr., 19 Heather Ct., New Province, NJ 07974; Sec., Rev. Dale H. Crouthamel, 14 Culberson Rd., Basking Ridge, NJ 07920; Treas., Mrs. Joan Workowski, 1162 Beverly Rd., Jenkinton, PA 19046
Trustees Sustentation Fund: Pres., Mr. E. Earl Shisler, Jr., R.D. # 2, Perkasie, PA 18944. Treas., Mr. William B. Schimpf, 67 Westaway Lane, Warrington, PA 18976
Publication Society: Pres., Rev. Richard K. Barnard, 1314 Robincreek Cove, lewisville, TX 75067
The Reapers: Pres., Mrs. Nancy Fleischer, R.R. #1, Box 500, Pipersville, PA 18947; Treas., Mrs. Loralee Holiman, 319 E. 50th St., New York, NY 10022

BISHOPS

William H. S. Jerdan, 414 W. 2nd South St., Summerville, SC 29483
Sanco K. Rembert, P.O. Box 2068, Charleston, SC 29403
Franklin H. Sellers, 1629 W. 99th St., Chicago, IL 60643
Leonard W. Riches, R.D. 1, Box 501, Smithown Rd., Pipersville, PA 18947
Daniel G. Cox, 9 Hilltop Pl., Catonsville, MD 21228
Royal U. Grote, Jr., 19 Heather Ct., New Providence, NJ 07974
James C. West, 91 Anson St., Charleston, SC 29401

PERIODICALS

Episcopal Recorder (bi-m), 4225 Chestnut St., Philadelphia, PA 19104. Rev. George B. Fincke, Ed.
The Reformed Episcopalian, Board of National Church Extension, 4225 Chestnut St., Philadelphia, PA 19104. Bishop Royal U. Grote, Jr., Ed.

Reformed Mennonite Church

This group was reorganized in 1812 under John Herr because they did not know of any other organization that fully carried out New Testament teachings. They believe there can be only one true church, consisting of regenerated persons who are united in love and doctrine.

OFFICER

Bishop Earl Basinger, 1036 Lincoln Heights Ave., Ephrata, PA 17522

Reformed Methodist Union Episcopal Church

The Reformed Methodist Union Episcopal church was formed after a group of ministers withdrew from the African Methodist Episcopal Church following a dispute over the election of ministerial delegates to the General Conference.

These ministers held a meeting on January 22, 1885 at Hills Chapel (now known as Mt. Hermon RMUE church), on Fishburn St. in Charleston, S.C. This four-day meeting resulted in the organization of the Reformed Methodist Union church.

In this meeting the Rev. William E. Johnson was unanimously elected president of the new church. Following the death of Rev. Johnson in 1896 an extra session of the General Conference was called to elect a new leader for the church.

It was decided in this conference that the church would conform to regular American Methodism (the Episcopacy); the first Bishop, Edward Russell Middleton, was elected, and "Episcopal" was added to the name of the church.

Bishop Middleton was consecrated on Dec. 5, 1896, by Bishop P. F. Stephens of the Reformed Episcopal Church.

GENERAL ORGANIZATION

General Conference: annual Headquarters: Charleston, SC 29407

OFFICERS

Bishop: Rt. Rev. Leroy Gethers, 1136 Brody Ave., Charleston, SC 29407. Tel. (803) 766-3534
Asst. Bishop: Rt. Rev. Eugene Davies, Jr.
Gen. Sec., Rev. Fred H. Moore, 115 St. Margaret St., Charleston, SC 29403. Tel. (803)723-8857
Treas., Rev. Rufus German
Sec. of Education, Rev. William Polite
Sec. of Books Concerns, Rev. Earnest McKeever
Sec. of Pension Fund, Rev. Joseph Powell
Sec. of Church Extension, Rev. Joseph Gadsden
Sec. of Sunday School Union, Rev. Hercules Champaigne
Sec. of Mission, Rev. Jerry M. DeBoer

Reformed Presbyterian Church of North America

Also known as the Church of the Covenanters. Origin dates back to the Reformation days of Scotland when the Covenanters signed their "Covenants" in resistance to the king and the Roman Church in the enforcement of state church practices. The Church in America has signed two "Covenants" in particular, those of 1871 and 1954.

Churches: 68; Inclusive Membership: 5,174; Sunday or Sabbath Schools: 68; Total Enrollment: 2,925; Ordained Clergy: 127

GENERAL ORGANIZATION

Synod: annual

OFFICERS

Mod., Melville W. Martin, 107 Ridgewood Ave., Pittsbrug, PA 15229
Clk., Rev. Paul M. Martin, 1117 E. Devonshire, Phoenix, AZ 85014. Tel. (602) 277-3497

Asst. Clk., J. Bruce Martin, 813 Crawford, Clay Center, KS 67432

Stated Clk., Louis D. Hutmire, 7418 Penn Ave., Pittsburgh, PA 15208. Tel. (412) 731-1177

PERIODICALS

The Covenanter Witness (bi-w), 7418 Penn Ave., Pittsburgh, PA 15208. James Pennington, Ed.

Reformed Zion Union Apostolic Church

Organized in 1869, at Boydton, Va., by Elder James R. Howell of New York, a minister of the A.M.E. Zion Church; with doctrines of the Methodist Episcopal Church.

GENERAL ORGANIZATION

Annual Conferences (in August After the Third Sunday) General Conference: quadrennial (Next meeting, 1990)

OFFICER

Sec., Deacon, James C. Feggins, 416 South Hill Ave., South Hill, VA 23970. Tel. (804) 447-3374

Religious Society of Friends (Conservative)

These Friends mark their present identity from separations occurring by regions at different times from 1845 to 1904. They hold to a minimum of organizational structure. Their meetings for worship, which are unprogrammed and based on silent meditation, demonstrate the belief that all individuals may commune directly with God and may share equally in vocal ministry.

They continue to stress the importance of the Living Christ and the experience of the Holy Spirit working with power in the lives of individuals who obey it.

YEARLY MEETINGS

North Carolina YM, Ray Treadway, 710 E. Lake Dr., Greensboro, NC 27401

Iowa YM, John Griffith, 5745 Charlotte, Kansas City MO 64110

Ohio YM, Susan S. Smith, RD #4 Box 288, Harrisonburg, VA 22801

Religious Society of Friends (Unaffiliated Meetings)

Though all groups of Friends acknowledge the same historical roots, 19th-century divisions in theology and experience led to some of the current organizational groupings. Many newer yearly meetings, often marked by spontaneity, variety, and experimentation and hoping for renewed Quaker unity, have chosen not to identify with past divisions by affiliating in traditional ways with the larger organizations within the Society. Some of these unaffiliated groups have begun within the past 25 years.

UNAFFILIATED YEARLY MEETINGS

Alaska Yearly Meeting, Box 687, Kotzebue, AK 99752

Amigos Central de Bolivia, Casilla 11070, La Paz, Bolivia

Amigos de Santidad de Bolivia, Casilla 992, La Paz, Bolivia

Central Yearly Meeting of the Friends Church, Rt. 1, Box 226, Alexandria, IN 46001

Iglesia Evangelica Amigos, Apartado 235, Santa Rosa de Capan, Honduras

Iglesia Nacional Evangelica de Los Amigos-Bolivia, Calle Cochabamba No. 164, Casilla 9392, La Paz, Bolivia

Iglesia Nacional Evangelica de Los Amigos-Peru, Casilla 320, Puno, Peru

Intermountain Yearly Meeting, 2628 Granada SW, Albuquerque NM 87105

North Pacific Yearly Meeting, 20648 Novelty Hill Rd., Redmond, WA 98053

Pacific Yearly Meeting, 8885 Frontera Ave., Yucca Valley, CA 92284

Reunion General de Los Amigos en Mexico, Casa de los Amigos, Ignacio Mariscal 132, Mexico, D,F. 06030, Mexico

Yearly Meeting of Friends Church in Guatemala and El Salvador, Apartado 8, Chiquimula, Guatemala

Reorganized Church of Jesus Christ of Latter Day Saints

Founded April 6, 1830, by Joseph Smith, Jr., and reorganized under the leadership of the founder's son, Joseph Smith III, in 1860. The Church, with headquarters in Independence, MO, is established in 35 countries in addition to the United States and Canada. A biennial world conference is held in Independence, Missouri. The current president is Wallace B. Smith, great-grandson of the original founder.

The Church is currently engaged in a 60 million dollar Temple project, involving the construction of an administrative, educational and worship center in Independence, MO dedicated to peace and reconciliation.

Churches: 1,137; Inclusive Membership: 190,950; Sunday or Sabbath Schools: N.R.; Total Enrollment: N.R.; Ordained Clergy: 17,048

GENERAL ORGANIZATION

Conference: (World Conference: Biennial in April of even numbered years)

Headquarters: The Auditorium, P.O. Box 1059, Independence, MO 64051. Tel. (816) 833-1000

OFFICERS

First Presidency: Wallace B. Smith, Howard S. Sheehy, Jr., Counselor, Alan D. Tyree, Counselor

Pres. of Council of 12 Apostles: William T. Higdon

Presiding Bishopric: Gene M. Hummel, Presiding Bishop; Ray E. McClaran, Counselor; Norman E. Swails, Counselor

Presiding Patriarch: Duane E. Couey

World Church Sec.: W. Grant McMurray

Public Relations: Stephanie Kelley

PERIODICALS

Saints Herald (m), Independence, MO. Wallace B. Smith, Alan D. Tyree, Howard S. Sheehy, Jr., and Roger Yarrington, Eds.

Saints in Service (bi-m), Deam Ferris, Ed.

Restoration Witness (bi-m), Independence, MO, Barbara Howard, Ed.

The Roman Catholic Church

The largest single body of Christians in the U.S., the Roman Catholic Church, is under the spiritual leadership of His Holiness the Pope. Its establishment in America dates back to the priests who accompanied Columbus on his second voyage to the New World. A settlement, later discontinued, was made at St. Augustine, Florida. The continuous history of this Church in the Colonies began at St. Mary's in Maryland, in 1634.

Churches: 23,091; Inclusive Membership: 54,918,949; Sunday or Sabbath Schools: N.R.; Total Enrollment: 7,025,181; Ordained Clergy: 52,548

(The following information has been furnished by the editor of The Official Catholic Directory, published by P. J. Kenedy & Sons, 3004 Glenview Rd., Wilmette, IL 60091. Reference to this complete volume will provide more adequate information.)

INTERNATIONAL ORGANIZATION

His Holiness the Pope, Bishop of Rome, Vicar of Jesus Christ, Supreme Pontiff of the Catholic Church.
POPE JOHN PAUL II, Karol Wojtyla (born May 18, 1920; installed October 22, 1978)

APOSTOLIC PRO NUNCIO TO THE UNITED STATES

Archbishop Pio Laghi, 3339 Massachusetts Ave., N.W., Washington, DC 20008. Tel. (202) 333-7121

U.S. ORGANIZATION

National Conference of Catholic Bishops, 3211 Fourth St., 20017. Washington, DC 20017. Tel. (202) 541-3000

The National Conference of Catholic Bishops (NCCB) is a canonical entity operating in accordance with the Vatican II Decree, **Christus Dominus.** Its purpose is to foster the Church's mission to mankind by providing the Bishops of this country with an opportunity to exchange views and insights of prudence and experience and to exercise in a joint manner their pastoral office.

OFFICERS

Pres., Archbishop John L. May
Vice-Pres., Archbishop Daniel Pilarcyk
Treas., Archbishop Daniel Kucera
Sec., Bishop William E. Keeler

GENERAL SECRETARIAT

Gen. Sec., Rev. Robert N. Lynch
Assoc. Gen. Sec., Rev. Donald Heintschel, Mr. Francis X. Doyle
Sec. for Plng., Sr. Sharon A. Euart, R.S.M.
Sec. for Communication, Mr. Richard Daw

COMMITTEES

Ecumenical and Interreligious Affairs (Ecumenism): Chmn., Archbishop J. Francis Stafford
Secretariat: Exec. Dir., Rev. John Hotchkin
Assoc. Dir., Thaddeus Horgan
Liturgy:
Chmn., Bishop Joseph Delaney
Secretariat: Dir., Rev. Ronald Krisman, Assoc. Dir., Rev. Msgr. Alan Detscher; Rev. Kenneth F. Jenkins

Priestly Formation:
Chpsn., Bishop Howard J. Hubbard
Staff: Exec. Dir., Rev. Howard Bleichner, S.S.
Permanent Diaconate:
Chmn., Bishop William Skylstad
Secretariat: Exec. Dir., Deacon Constantino J. Ferriola, Jr.
Priestly Life and Ministry:
Chmn., Bishop Donald W. Wuerl
Secretariat: Exec. Dir., Rev. David E. Brinkmoeller
Pro-Life Activities:
Chmn., Joseph Cardinal Bernardin
Secretariat: Dir., Rev. John W. Gouldrick, C.M.

United States Catholic Conference, 3211 Fourth St., Washington, DC 20017, Tel. (202)541-3000

The United States Catholic Conference (USCC) is a civil entity of the American Catholic Bishops assisting them in their service to the Church in this country by uniting the people of God where voluntary, collective action on a broad diocesan level is needed. The USCC provides an organization structure and the resources needed to insure coordination, cooperation, and assistance in the public, educational, and social concerns of the Church at the national, regional, state, interdiocesan and, as appropriate, diocesan levels.

OFFICERS

Pres., Archbishop John L. May
Vice-Pres., Archbishop Daniel Pilarcyk
Treas., Archbishop Daniel Kucera
Sec., Bishop William E. Keeler

GENERAL SECRETARIAT

Gen. Sec., Rev. Robert Lynch
Assoc. Gen. Sec., Rev. Donald Heintschel, Mr. Francis X. Doyle, Jr.
Sec. for Planning, Sr. Sharon Euart, R.S.M.
Sec. for Communications, Mr. Richard W. Daw

STAFF OFFICES

Finance, Dir., Sister Frances A. Mlocek, I.H.M.
Accounting, Kenneth Korotky
Human Resources, Dir., Thomas Meehan
Office of Publishing and Promotion Services, Dir., Dan Juday
General Counsel, Mark E. Chopko
Government Liaison, Dir., Frank Monahan
Research, Dir., Rev. Eugene Hemrick

COMMITTEES AND DEPARTMENTS

Communication: Chmn., Edward J. O'Donnell; Sec., Mr. Richard W. Daw; National Catholic News Services Mr. Thomas N. Lorsung, Dir. & Ed.-in-Chief; Film and Broadcasting, Mr. Richard H. Hirsch
Education: Chpsn., Bishop Francis Shulte
Social Development and World Peace: Chmn., Bishop Joseph M. Sullivan; Sec., John Carr; Domestic Social Development, Sharon Daily; Health and Welfare Issues, Ronald M. White; Rural Energy and Food Issues, Walter Grazer; Urban and Economic Issues, Thomas Schellabarger; International Justice and Peace, _____; Latin American Affairs, Thomas Quigley; African and Western European Affairs, Robert A. Dumas, Sr.; Political and Military Affairs and Human Rights, Dr. Gerard F. Powers

RELATED ORGANIZATIONS

Campaign for Human Development: Nat'l. Chmn., Archbishop John L. May; Exec. Dir., Rev. Alfred LoPinto

Catholic Relief Services, 1011 First Ave., New York, NY 10022. Tel. (212) 838-4700. Exec. Dir., Mr. Lawrence Pezzulo

U.S.CATHOLIC BISHOPS' ADVISORY COUNCIL
Chmn., Mrs. Sheila Adams

NATIONAL ORGANIZATIONS
Catholic Charities,-USA Exec. Dir., Rev. Thomas J. Harvey, 1319 F St., N.W., Washington, DC 20004
Conference of Major Religious Superiors of Men, Exec. Dir., Rev. Ronald Faley, T.O.R., 8808 Cameron St., Silver Spring, MD 20910. Tel. (301) 588-4030
Leadership Conference of Women Religious, Exec. Dir., Sr. Janet Roesener, C.S.J., 8808 Cameron St., Silver Spring, MD 20910. Tel. (301)588-4955
National Catholic Educational Association, Pres., Sr. Catherine McNamee, 1077 30th St., N.W., Suite 100, Washington, DC 20007. Tel. (202) 337-6232
National Council of Catholic Laity, Pres., Mr. Thomas Simmons, 5664 Midforest Ln., Cincinnati, OH 45233. Tel. (513) 922-2495
National Council of Catholic Women, Pres., Mary Ann Kramer; Exec. Adm., Annette Kane, 1312 Massachusetts Ave. NW, Washington, DC 20005. Tel. (202)638-6050
National Office for Black Catholics, 3025 4th St., N.E., Washington,D.C. 20017.Tel (202)635-1778

CATHOLIC ORGANIZATIONS WITH INDIVIDUAL I.R.S. RULINGS
Canon Law Society of America, Exec. Coord., Rev. Edward Pfnausch, Catholic University, Washington, DC 20064. Tel. (202) 269-3491
Word of God Institute, Exec. Dir., Rev. John Burke, O. P., 487 Michigan Ave., NE, Washington, DC 20017. Tel. (202) 529-0001

ARCHDIOCESES AND DIOCESES
There follows an alphabetical listing of Archdioceses and Dioceses of The Roman Catholic Church. Each Archdiocese or Diocese contains the following information in sequence: Name of incumbent Bishop; name of Auxiliary Bishop or Bishops, and the Chancellor or Vicar General of the Archdiocese or Diocese, or just the address and telephone number of the chancery office.

Cardinals are addressed as "His Eminence" and Archbishops and Bishops as "Most Reverend."

Albany, Bishop Howard J. Hubbard. Chancellor, Rev. Michael A. Farano. Chancery Office, Pastoral Center, 40 N. Main Ave., Albany, NY 12203; Tel. (518) 453-6000
Alexandria-Shreveport, Bishop John C. Favolora; Chancellor, Rev. Msgr. Julius G. Walle. Office, 4400 Gardner Hwy., P.O. Box 7417, Alexandria, LA 71306. Tel. (318) 445-2401
Allentown, Bishop Thomas J. Welsh; Chancellor, Rev. Msgr. Anthony D. Muntone. Chancery Office, 202 N. 17th St., P.O. Box F, Allentown, PA 18104. Tel. (215) 437-0755
Altoona-Johnstown, Bishop Joseph V. Adamec; Chancellor, Rev. Msgr. George B. Flinn. Chancery Office, Box 126, Logan Blvd., Hollidaysburg, PA 16648. Tel. (814) 695-5579.
Amarillo, Bishop Leroy T. Mattiesen; Chancellor, Sr. Celine Thames, O.S.F., Chancery Office, 1800 N. Spring St., P.O. Box 5644, Amarillo, TX 79117. Tel. (806) 383-2243
Archdiocese of Anchorage, Archbishop Francis T. Hurley. Chancery Office, P.O. Box 2239, Anchorage, AK 99510. Tel. (907)258-7898.
Arlington, Bishop John Richard Keating, Chancellor, Rev. Msgr. William T. Reinecke. Chancery, Ste. 704, 200 N. Glebe Rd., Arlington, VA 22203. Tel. (703) 841-2500

Archdiocese of Atlanta, Archbishop Eugene Antones Marino; Chancellor, Rev. E. Peter Ludden. Chancery Office, 680 West Peachtree St., N.W., Atlanta, GA 30308. Tel. (404) 888-7802
Austin, Bishop John E. McCarthy; Vicar General, Rev. Msgr. Edward C. Matocha. Chancery Office, N. Congress and 16th, P.O. Box 13327 Capital Sta. Austin, TX 78711. Tel. (512) 476-4888
Baker, Bishop Thomas J. Connolly; Chancellor, Rev. Charles T. Grant. Chancery Office, 911 S.E. Armour, Bend, OR 97702; P.O. Box 5999 Bend, OR 97708. Tel. (503)388-4004.
Archdiocese of Baltimore, Archbishop William H. Keeler. Auxiliary Bishops of Baltimore: Bishop William C. Newman, Bishop P. Francis Murphy, Bishop John H. Ricard, Chancery Office, 320 Cathedral St., Baltimore, MD 21201. Tel. (301) 547-5446.
Baton Rouge, Bishop Stanley J. Ott; Chancellor, Rev. Msgr. Robert Berggreen. Chancery Office, P.O. Box 2028, Baton Rouge, LA 70821. Tel. (504) 387-0561
Beaumont, Bishop Bernard J. Ganter; Chancellor Rev. Bennie J. Patillo. Chancery Office, P.O. Box 3948, Beaumont, TX 77704, Tel. (409) 838-0451
Belleville, Bishop James P. Keleher; Chancellor, Rev. Msgr. Bernard O. Sullivan. Chancery Office, 222 S. Third St., Belleville IL 62220. Tel. (618)277-8181
Biloxi, Bishop Joseph Howze; Chancellor, Rev. Msgr. Andrew Murray. Chancery Office, P.O. Box 1189, Biloxi, MS 39533. Tel. (601) 374-0222
Birmingham, Bishop Raymond J. Boland; Chancellor, Rev. Paul L. Rohling. Chancery Office, P.O. Box 12047, Birmingham, AL 35202. Tel. (205) 833-0175
Bismarck, Bishop John F. Kinney, Chancellor, Sr. Joanne Graham, O.S.B. Chancery Office, 420 Raymond St., Box 1575, Bismarck, ND 58502. Tel. (701) 223-1347
Boise, Bishop Tod D. Brown; Chancellor, Rev. Mark R. Schumacher; Chancery Office, Box 769, 303 Federal Way, Boise, ID 83701. Tel. (208) 342-1311
Archdiocese of Boston, Bernard Cardinal Law; Auxiliary Bishops of Boston: Bishop Robert J. Banks, Daniel A. Hart, Bishop Alfred C. Hughes, Bishop John J. Mulcahy, Bishop Lawrence J. Riley, Bishop Roberto O. Gonzales, O.F.M. Chancellor, Mr. Paul Devlin. Chancery Office, 2121 Commonwealth Ave., Brighton, MA 02135. Tel. (617) 254-0100
Bridgeport, Bishop Edward M. Egan; Chancellor, Rev. Gregory Michael Smith. Chancery Office, 238 Jewett Ave., Bridgeport CT 06606. Tel. (203) 372-4301
Brooklyn, Bishop Thomas V. Daily. Auxiliary Bishops of Brooklyn: Bishop Joseph M. Sullivan, Bishop Rene A. Valero, Chancellor, Rev. Msgr. Otto L. Garcia. Chancery Office, 75 Greene Ave., Box C, Brooklyn, NY 11202. Tel. (718) 638-5500
Brownsville, Bishop John J. Fitzpatrick, Chancellor, Rev. Gustavo C. Barrera. Chancery Office, P.O. Box 2279, Brownsville, TX 78522. Tel. (512) 542-2501
Buffalo, Bishop Edward D. Head. Auxiliary Bishop of Buffalo: Bishop Donald M. Trautman, Chancellor, Rev. Msgr. Robert J. Cunningham. Chancery Office, 795 Main St., Buffalo, NY 14203. Tel. (716)847-5500
Burlington, Bishop John A. Marshall; Vicar General, Rev. Msgr. Edwin T. Buckley, Chancery Office, 351 North Ave., Burlington, VT 05401. Tel. (802) 658-6110
Camden, Bishop James T. McHugh; Auxiliary Bishop of Camden, Bishop James L. Schad. Chancellor, Rev. Msgr. Joseph W. Pokuska. Chancery Office, 1845 Haddon Ave., P.O. Box 709, Camden, NJ 08101. Tel. (609) 756-7900
Charleston, Bishop Ernest L. Unterkoefler; Vicar General, Rev. Msgr. Thomas R. Duffy. Chancery Office, 119 Broad St., P.O. Box 818, Charleston, SC 29402. Tel. (803) 723-3488
Charlotte, Bishop John F. Donoghue; Chancellor, Rev. John T. McSweeney, Chancery Office P.O. Box 36776, Charlotte, NC 28236. Tel. (704) 377-6871

Cheyenne, Bishop Joseph H. Hart; Chancellor, Rev. Lawrence Etchingham. Chancery Office, Box 426, Cheyenne, WY 82003. Tel. (307) 638-1530

Archdiocese of Chicago, Joseph Cardinal Bernardin, Auxiliary Bishops of Chicago: Bishop Alred L. Abramowicz, Bishop Wilton D. Gregory; Bishop Nevin W. Hayes, O. Carm; Bishop Timothy J. Lyne, Bishop Placido Rodriquez, C.M.F.; Bishop Thad J. Jakubowski; Bishop John R. Gorman. Chancellor, Rev. Robert L. Kealy, Chancery Office, P.O. Box 1979, Chicago, IL 60690. Chancery Office, 155 E. Superior Ave., Chicago, IL 60611. Tel. (312) 751-8200

Archdiocese of Cincinnati, Archbishop Daniel E. Pilarczyk. Auxiliary Bishop of Cincinnati: Bishop James H. Garland. Chancellor, Rev. R. Daniel Conlon. Chancery Office, 100 E. 8th St., Cincinnati, OH 45202. Tel. (513) 421-3131.

Cleveland, Bishop Anthony M. Pilla. Auxiliary Bishops of Cleveland: Bishop James P. Lyke, O.F.M., Bishop A. Edward Pevec, Bishop Gilbert I. Sheldon, Bishop A. James Quinn. Chancellor Rev. Ralph E. Wiatrowski. Chancery Office, 350 Chancery Bldg., Cathedral Square, 1027 Superior Ave., Cleveland, OH 44114. Tel. (216) 696-6525

Colorado Springs, Bishop Richard C. Hanifen; Chancellor, Sr. Patricia McGreevy, O.S.B. Chancery Office, 29 West Kiowa St., Colorado Springs, CO 80903. Tel. 303-636-2345

Columbus, Bishop James A. Griffin. Chancellor, Rev. Joseph M. Hendricks, Chancery Office, 198 E. Broad St., Columbus, OH 43215. Tel. (614) 224-2251

Corpus Christi, Bishop Rene H. Gracida; Chancellor, Rev. Msgr. Leonard Pivonka. Chancery Office, 620 Lipan St., Corpus Christi, TX 78401. Tel. (512) 882-6191

Covington, Bishop William A. Hughes; Chancellor, Rev. Roger L. Kriege. Chancery Office, P. O. Box 18548 Erlanger, KY 41018. Tel. (606)283-6210

Crookston, Bishop Victor Balke; Chancellor, Very Rev. Michael Patnode. Chancery Office, 1200 Memorial Dr., P.O. Box 610, Crookston, MN 56716. Tel. (218) 281-4533.

Dallas, Bishop Thomas Tschoepe; Chancellor, Rev. Msgr. Raphael Kamel. Chancery Office, 3915 Lemmon Ave., P.O. Box 190507, Dallas, TX 75219. Tel. (214) 528-2240

Davenport, Bishop Gerald Francis O'Keefe; Chancellor, Rev. Msgr. Leo Feeney. Chancery Office, 2706 Gaines St., Davenport, IA 52804. Tel. (319) 324-1911

Archdiocese of Denver. Archbishop J. Francis Stafford; Chancellor Very Rev. Edward M. Hoffman. Chancery Office, 200 Josephine St., Denver, CO 80206. Tel. (303) 388-4411

Des Moines, Bishop William H. Bullock; Chancellor, Rev. Frank E. Bognanno. Chancery Office, 818 5th Ave., P.O. Box 1816, Des Moines, IA 50306. Tel. (515) 243-7653.

Archdiocese of Detroit, Edmund Cardinal Szoka. Auxiliary Bishops of Detroit: Bishop Moses B. Anderson, S.S.E., Bishop Patrick R. Cooney, Bishop Thomas J. Gumbleton, Bishop Dale J. Melczek, Bishop Walter J. Schoenherr; Chancellor, Rev. John P. Zenz. Chancery Office, 1234 Washington Blvd., Detroit, MI 48226. Tel. (313) 237-5816

Dodge City, Bishop Stanley G. Schlarman; Chancellor, Rev. James E. Baker. Chancery Office, 910 Central Ave., P.O. Box 849, Dodge City, KS 67801.Tel. (316) 227-3131

Archdiocese of Dubuque, Archbishop Daniel W. Kucera; Auxiliary Bishop of Dubuque, Bishop Francis J. Dunn; Chancellor, Sr. Mary Kevin Gallagher, B.V.M., P.O. Box 479, Dubuque IA 52001. Tel. (319) 556-2580.

Duluth, Bishop Robert H. Brom; Chancellor, Very Rev. Patrick J. Moran. Chancery Office, 215 W. Fourth St., Duluth, MN 55806. Tel. (218) 727-6861

El Paso, Bishop Raymond J. Pena; Chancellor, Very Rev. David G. Fierro. Chancery Office, 499 St. Matthews, El Paso, TX 79907. Tel. (915) 595-5038

Erie, Bishop Michael J. Murphy; Chancellor, Rev. Msgr. Robert J. Smith, Chancery Office, P. O. Box 10397, Erie, PA 16514. Tel. (814) 825-3333

Evansville, Bishop Gerald A. Gettelfinger, Chancellor, Rev. Msgr. Kenneth R. Knapp. Chancery Office, 4200 N. Kentucky Ave., Evansville, IN 47711. Tel. (812) 424-5536

Fairbanks, Bishop Michael Kaniecki, S.J., Chancellor, Sr. Eileen Brown. Tel. (907) 456-6753. Chancery Office, 1316 Peger Rd., Fairbanks, AK 99709. Tel. (907) 474-0753

Fall River, Bishop Daniel A. Cronin; Chancellor, Rev. Msgr. John J. Oliveira. Chancery Office, 47 Underwood St., Box 2577, Fall River, MA 02722. Tel. (508) 675-1311.

Fargo, Bishop James S. Sullivan. Chancellor, Rev. T. William Coyle. Chancery Office, 1310 Broadway, P.O. Box 1750, Fargo, ND 58107. Tel. (701) 235-6429

Fort Wayne-South Bend, Bishop John M. D'Arcy; Auxiliary Bishop of Fort Wayne-South Bend, Bishop Joseph R. Crowley, Chancellor, James J. Wolf. Chancery Office, 1103 S. Calhoun St., P.O. Box 390. Fort Wayne, IN 46801. Tel. (219) 422-4611

Fort Worth, Bishop Joseph D. Delaney; Chancellor, Rev. Robert W. Wilson. Chancery Office, 800 W. Loop 820 South, Fort Worth TX 76108. Tel. (817) 560-3300

Fresno, Bishop Joseph J. Madera, M.Sp.S.; Chancellor, Rev. Msgr. J. Wayne Hayes. Chancery Office, P.O. Box 1668, 1550 N. Fresno St., Fresno, CA 93717. Tel. (209) 237-5125

Gallup, Bishop Jerome J. Hastrich; Coadjutor Bishop of Gallup, Bishop Donald Pelotte, S.S.S. Chancellor, Rev. Msgr. Arthur MacDonald. Chancery Office, 711 S. Puerco Dr., P.O. Box 1338, Gallup, NM 87301. Tel. (505) 863-4406

Galveston-Houston, Bishop Joseph A. Fiorenza; Auxilliary Bishops of Galveston-Houston: Bishop Enrique San Pedro, S. J.; Bishop Curtis J. Guillory, S.V.D. Chancellor, Rev. Msgr. Daniel Scheel. Chancery Office, 1700 San Jacinto St., Houston, TX 77002. Tel. (713) 659-5461

Gary, Bishop Norbert F. Gaughan; Chancellor, Sr. Helen Hayes, O.P. Chancery Office, 9292 Broadway, Merrillville, IN 46410 Tel. (219)769-9292

Gaylord, Bishop Robert J. Rose; Vicar General, Rev. James A. Suchocki. Chancery Office, 1665 West M-32, Seton Bldg., Gaylord, MI 49735. Tel. (517) 732-5147

Grand Island, Bishop Lawrence J. McNamara; Chancellor, Rev. Richard L. Pointkowski. Chancery Office, 311 W. 17th St., P.O. Box 996, Grand Island, NB 68802. Tel. (308) 382-6565

Grand Rapids, Bishop Joseph M. Breitenbeck, Auxiliary Bishop of Grand Rapids; Bishop Joseph McKinney, Chancellor, Rev. John Najdowski. Chancery Office, 660 Burton St. S.E., Grand Rapids, MI 49507. Tel. (616) 243-0491.

Great Falls-Billings, Bishop Anthony M. Milone; Chancellor, Rev. Martin J. Burke. Chancery Office, 121 23rd St. So., P.O. Box 1399, Great Falls, MT 59403. Tel. (406) 727-6683

Green Bay, Bishop Adam J. Maida; Auxiliary Bishop of Green Bay; Bishop Robert F. Morneau, Chancellor, Sr. Ann F. Rehrauer, O.S.F. Chancery Office, Box 66, Green Bay, WI 54305. Tel. (414) 435-4406

Greensburg, Bishop Anthony G. Bosco; Chancellor, Rev. Thomas L. Klinzing. Chancery Office, 723 E. Pittsburgh St., Greensburg, PA 15601. Tel. (412) 837-0901

Harrisburg, Adm. Msgr., Damian E. McGovern; Chancellor, Rev. Msgr. William M. Richardson. Chancery Office, P.O. Box 2153, 4800 Union Deposit Rd., Harrisburg, PA 17105. Tel. (717) 657-4804

Archdiocese of Hartford, Archbishop John F. Whealon. Auxiliary Bishop of Hartford: Bishop Peter A. Rosazza. Chancellor, Sr. Helen Margaret Feeney, C.S.J. Chancery Office, 134 Farmington Ave., Hartford, CT 06105. Tel. (203) 527-4201

100

Helena, Bishop Elden F. Curtiss. Chancellor, Rev. John W. Robertson. Chancery Office, 515 N. Ewing, P.O. Box 1729, Helena, MT 59624. Tel. (406) 442-5820

Honolulu, Bishop Joseph A. Ferrario; Chancellor, Sr. Grace Dorothy Lim, M.M. Chancery Office, 1184 Bishop St., Honolulu, HI 96813. Tel. (808) 533-1791

Houma-Thibodaux, Bishop Warren L. Boudreaux. Chancellor, Rev. Msgr. James B. Songy. Chancery Office, P.O. Box 9077, Houma, LA 70361. Tel. (504) 868-7720

Archdiocese of Indianapolis, Archbishop Edward T. O'Meara; Chancellor, Rev. David E. Coats. Chancery Office, 1400 N. Meridian St., P.O. Box 1410, Indianapolis, IN 46206. Tel. (317)236-1405

Jackson, Bishop William R. Houck; Vicar General, Rev. Francis J. Cosgrove. Chancery Office, 237 E. Amite St., P.O. Box 2248, Jackson, MS 39225. Tel. (601) 969-1880

Jefferson City, Bishop Michael F. McAuliffe; Chancellor, Rev. Michael J. Wilbers. Chancery Office, 605 Clark Ave., P.O. Box 417, Jefferson City, MO 65102. Tel. (314) 635-9127

Joliet, Bishop Joseph L. Imesch. Auxiliary Bishops of Joliet: Bishop Roger L. Kaffer; Bishop Raymond J. Vonesh. Chancellor, Rev. William E. Donnelly. Chancery Office, 425 Summit St., Joliet, IL 60435. Tel. (815) 722-6606

Juneau, Bishop Michael H. Kenny. Vicar General, Rev. Msgr. James F. Miller. Chancery Office, 419 6th St. Juneau, AK 99801. Tel. (907) 586-2227

Kalamazoo, Bishop Paul V. Donovan, Chancellor, Rev. Msgr. Dell F. Stewart. Chancery Office, P.O. Box 949, 215 N. Westnedge Ave., Kalamazoo, MI 49005. Tel. (616) 349-8714

Archdiocese of Kansas City in Kansas, Archbishop Ignatius J. Strecker, Auxiliary Bishop of Kansas City in Kansas, Bishop Marion F. Forst, Chancellor, Rev. Msgr. William T. Curtin. Chancery Office, 2220 Central Ave., P.O. Box 2328, Kansas City, KS 66110. Tel. (913) 621-4131

Kansas City-St. Joseph, Bishop John J. Sullivan; Chancellor, Rev. Richard F. Carney. Chancery Office, P.O. Box 419037, Kansas City, MO 64141. Tel. (816) 756-1850

Knoxville, Bishop Anthony J. O'Connell; Vicar General, Rev. Xavier Mankel. Chancery Office, 417 Erin Drive, Knoxville, TN 37919.

La Crosse, Bishop John J. Paul; Chancellor, Very Rev. John I. Nilles, Chancery Office, 3710 East Ave., La Crosse, WI 54602. Tel. (608) 788-7700

Lafayette in Indiana, Bishop William L. Higi; Chancellor, Rev. Msgr. Arthur A. Sego.Chancery Office, P. O. Box 260, 610 Lingle Ave., Lafayette, IN 47902. Tel. (317) 742-0275

Lafayette, Bishop Harry J. Flynn. Chancellor, Sr. Joanna Valoni, S.S.N.D., Chancery Office, Diocesan Office Bldg., P.O. Drawer 3387, Lafayette, LA 70501. Tel. (318) 261-5500

Lake Charles, Bishop Jude Speyrer; Chancellor Rev. Msgr. Harry Grieg. Chancery Office, 414 Iris St., P.O. Box 3223, Lake Charles, LA 70602. Tel. (318) 439-7404

Lansing, Bishop Kenneth J. Povish; Chancellor, Rev. James Murray. Chancery Office, 300 W. Ottawa, Lansing, MI 48933. Tel. (517) 372-8540

Las Cruces, Bishop Ricardo Ramirez; C.S.B.; Chancellor, Rev. Bob Getz. Chancery Office, P.O. Box 16318, Las Cruces, NM 88004. Tel. (505) 523-7577

Lexington, Bishop James K. Williams. Chancellor, Sr. Mary Kevan Stewart, S.N.D. Chancery Office, 947 P. O. Box 12350. Erlanger, KY 41018. (606)283-6200.

Lincoln, Bishop Glennon P. Flavin; Chancellor, Rev. Msgr. Thomas M. Kealy. Chancery Office, 3400 Sheridan Blvd., P.O. Box 80328, Lincoln, NE 68501. Tel. (402) 488-0921

Little Rock, Bishop Andrew J. McDonald; Chancellor, Rev. Msgr. Royce R. Thomas. Chancery Office, 2415 N. Tyler St., P.O. Box 7239, Little Rock, AR 72217. Tel. (501) 664-0340

Archdiocese of Los Angeles, Archbishop Roger M. Mahony. Auxiliary Bishops of Los Angeles: Bishop Juan Arzube, Bishop John J. Ward; Bishop Carol Fisher, S.S.J.; Bishop Armando Ochoa; Bishop Patrick Ziemann. Chancellor, Rev. Msgr. Stephen E. Blair. Chancery Office, 1531 W. Ninth St., Los Angeles, CA 90015. Tel. (213) 251-3200.

Archdiocese of Louisville, Archbishop Thomas C. Kelly, O.P.; Chancellor, Very Rev. Bernard J. Breen, P.O. Box 1073, Louisville, KY 40201. Chancery Office, 212 E. College St., Louisville, KY 40201. Tel. (502) 585-3291

Lubbock, Bishop Michael Sheehan; Chancellor, Sr. Elena Gonzalez, R.S.M. Chancery Office. P.O. Box 98700, Lubbock, TX 79499. Tel. (806) 792-3943

Madison, Bishop Cletus F. O'Donnell; Auxiliary Bishop of Madison, Bishop George O. Wirz, Chancellor, Rev. Joseph P. Higgins. Chancery Office, 15 E. Wilson St., Box 111, Madison, WI 53701. Tel. (608) 256-2677

Manchester, Bishop Odore J. Gendron. Auxillary Bishop of Manchester, Bishop Joseph Gerry, O.S.B. Chancellor Rev. Msgr. Francis J. Christian. Chancery Office, 153 Ash St., Manchester, NH 03105. Tel. (603) 669-3100

Marquette, Bishop Mark F. Schmitt. Chancellor, Rev. John J. Shiverski. Chancery Office, 444 S. Fourth St., P.O. Box 550, Marquette, MI 49855. Tel. (906) 225-1141

Memphis, Bishop Daniel Mark Buechlein, O.S.B.; Chancellor, Rev. J. Peter Sartain. Chancery Office, 1325 Jefferson Ave., P.O. Box 41679, Memphis, TN 38174. Tel. (901) 722-4737

Metuchen, Bishop Edward Hughes. Chancellor, Sr. M. Michaelita Wiechetek, C.S.S.F. Chancery Office, P.O. Box 191, Metuchen, NJ 08840. Tel. (201) 283-3800.

Archdiocese of Miami, Archbishop Edward A. McCarthy, Auxiliary Bishops of Miami, Bishop Agustin A. Roman; Bishop Norbert M. Dorsey. Chancellor, Very Rev. Gerard T. LaCerra. Chancery Office, 9401 Biscayne Blvd., Miami Shores, FL 33138. Tel. (305) 757-6241

Archdiocese for the Military Services, Bishop Joseph T. Ryan. Auxilliary Bishops: Bishop Joseph T. Dimino; Bishop Francis X. Roque; Bishop Lawrence J. Kenney; Bishop Angelo T. Acerra, O.S.B.; Bishop John G. Nolan. Chancellor Rev. Richard Saudis. Chancery Office, 962 Wayne Ave., Silver Spring, MD 20910. Tel. (301)495-4100.

Archdiocese of Milwaukee, Archbishop Rembert G. Weakland, O.S.B. Auxiliary Bishops of Milwaukee: Bishop Leo J. Brust, Bishop Richard J. Sklba, Chancellor, Rev. Ralph C. Gross. Chancery Office, 3501 S. Lake Dr., Milwaukee, WI 53207. Tel. (414)769-3340.

Archdiocese of Mobile, Archbishop Oscar H. Lipscomb; Chancellor, Very Rev. John R. Amos. Chancery Office, 400 Government St., P.O. Box 1966, Mobile, AL 36633. Tel. (205) 433-2241

Monterey, Bishop Thaddeus Shubsda; Chancellor, Rev. Msgr. Tod D. Brown. Chancery Office, 580 Fremont Blvd., P.O. Box 2048, Monterey, CA 93940. Tel. (408) 373-4345

Nashville, Bishop James D. Niedergeses; Chancellor, Rev. Stephen Klasek. Chancery Office, 2400 21st Ave., S., Nashville, TN 37212. Tel. (615) 383-6393

Archdiocese of Newark, Archbishop Theodore E. McCarrick; Auxiliary Bishops of Newark: Bishop David Arias, O.A.R., Bishop Joseph Francis, S.V.D, Bishop Robert F. Garner, Bishop Domonic A. Marconi, Bishop Jerome Pechillo, T.O.R., Bishop John M. Smith. Chancellor, Sr. Thomas Mary Salerno, S.C. Chancery Office, 31 Mulberry St., Newark, NJ 07102. Tel. (201) 596-4000

Archdiocese of New Orleans, Archbishop Francis B. Schulte. Auxiliary Bishops of New Orleans: Bishop Nicholas D'Antonio, O.F.M., Bishop Harold R. Perry, S.V.D., Chancellor, Rev. Msgr. Earl C. Woods. Chancery Office, 7887 Walmsley Ave., New Orleans, LA 70125. Tel. (504) 861-9521

Melkite Apostolic Exarchate of Newton, Bishop Joseph Tawil. auxiliary Bishop of Nwton: Bishop John A. Elya. Chancellor, Rev. George D. Gallaro. Chancery Office, 19 Dartmouth St., West Newton, MA 02165. Tel. (617) 969-8957

New Ulm, Bishop Raymond A. Lucker. Chancellor, Rev. Jerome Paulson. Chancery Office, 1400 Sixth North St., New Ulm, MN 56073. Tel. (507) 359-2966

Archdiocese of New York, Archbishop John Cardinal O'Connor, Auxiliary Bishops of New York: Bishop Patrick V. Ahern, Bishop Francis Garmendia, Bishop James P. Mahoney, Bishop Emerson J. Moore, Bishop Austin B. Vaughan, Bishop Anthony F. Mestice, Bishop William J. McCormack. Chancellor, Rev. Msgr. Raul Del'Valle. Chancery Office, 1011 First Ave., New York, NY 10022. Tel. (212) 371-1000

Norwich, Bishop Daniel P. Reilly; Chancellor, Rev. Msgr. Thomas R. Bride. Chancery Office, 201 Broadway, P.O. Box 587, Norwich, CT 06360. Tel. (203) 887-9294

Oakland, Bishop John S. Cummins, Chancellor, Rev. George E. Crespin. Chancery Office, 2900 Lakeshore Ave., Oakland, CA 94610. Tel. (415) 893-4711

Ogdensburg, Bishop Stanislaus J. Brzana. Chancellor, Rev. John R. Murphy. Chancery Office, Box 369, 622 Washington St., Ogdensburg, NY 13669. Tel. (315) 393-2920

Archdiocese of Oklahoma City, Archbishop Charles A. Salatka; Chancellor, Rev. John A. Steichen. Chancery Office, P.O. Box 32180, Oklahoma City, OK 73123. Tel. (405) 721-5651

Archdiocese of Omaha, Archbishop Daniel E. Sheehan; Chancellor, Rev. Eldon J. McKamy. Chancery Office, 100 N. 62nd St., Omaha, NB 68132. Tel. (402) 558-3100

Orange, Bishop Norman F. McFarland; Chancellor, Rev. John Urell. Chancery Office, 2811 Villa Real Dr., Orange, CA 92667. Tel. (714) 974-7120

Orlando, Bishop Thomas J. Grady; Chancellor, Rev. Art Bendixen. Chancery Office, 421 E. Robinson, P.O. Box 1800, Orlando, FL 32802. Tel. (305) 425-3556

Owensboro, Bishop John J. McRaith, Chancellor, Rev. Msgr. George Hancock. Chancery Office, c/o Chancellor's Residence, 4005 Frederica St., Owensboro, KY 42301. Tel. (502) 683-1545

Palm Beach, _____; Chancellor, Rev. James Murtagh. Chancery Office, 9995 N. Military Trail, Bldg. C #201, Palm Beach Gardens, FL 33418. Tel. (407) 627-8700.

Parma Eparchy, Bishop Andrew Pataki. Chancellor, Very Rev. Emil Masich Chancery Office, 1900 Carlton Rd., Parma, OH 44134. Tel. (216) 741-8773

Passaic (Greek Rite), Bishop Michael J. Dudick. auxillary Bishop of Passaic, Bishop George M. Kuzma; Chancellor, Rev. Msgr. Raymond Misulich. Chancery Office, 445 Lackawanna Ave., West Paterson, NJ 07424. Tel. (201)890-7777.

Paterson, Bishop Frank J. Rodimer. Chancellor, Rev. Msgr. Herbert K. Tillyer, Chancery Office, 777 Valley Rd., Clifton, NJ 07013. Tel. (201) 777-8818.

Pensacola-Tallahassee, Bishop J. Keith Symons, Chandellor, Rev. Msgr. John Amos. Chancery Office, 11 N. "B" St., Pensacola, FL 32501. Tel. (904) 432-1515

Peoria, Bishop Edward W. O'Rourke; Coadjutor Bishop of Peoria: Bishop John J. Myers. Chancellor, Rev. Terrance P. O'Brien. Chancery Office, P.O. Box 1406, 607 NE Madison Ave., Peoria, IL 61655. Tel. (309) 671-1550

Archdiocese of Philadelphia, Archbishop Anthony J.

Bevilacqua, Auxiliary Bishops of Philadelphia: Bishop John J. Graham, Bishop Louis A. DeSimone, Bishop Martin N. Lohmuller, Chancellor, Rev. Msgr. Samuel E. Shoemaker. Chancery Office, 222 N. 17th St. Philadelphia, PA 19103. Tel. (215) 587-3550

Ukrainian Rite—Philadelphia, Archbishop Stephen Sulyk. Chancellor, Sr. Thomas Hrynewich, S.S.M.I. Chancery Office, 827 N. Franklin St., Philadelphia, PA 19123. Tel. (215) 627-0143

Phoenix, Bishop Thomas J. O'Brien, Chancellor, Rev. Msgr. James E. McFadden. Chancery Office, 400 E. Monroe St., Phoenix, AZ 85004. Tel. (602) 257-0030

Pittsburgh, Bishop Donald W. Wuerl. Auxiliary Bishop of Pittsburgh: Bishop John B. McDowell, Chancellor, Rev. Lawrence A. DiNardo. Chancery Office, 111 Blvd. of Allies, Pittsburgh, PA 15222. Tel. (412) 456-3010

Metropolitan Archdiocese of Pittsburgh (Byzantine) Archbishop Stephen J. Kocisko. Auxiliary Bishop of Pittsburgh (Byzantine) & Chancellor. Bishop John M. Bilock. Chancery Office, 54 Riverview Ave., Pittsburgh, PA 15214. Tel. (412) 322-7300.

Portland, Bishop Joseph J. Gerry; Auxiliary Bishop of Portland: Bishop Amedee Proulx, Chancellor, Rev. J. Joseph Ford. Chancery Office, 510 Ocean Ave., Portland, ME 04101. Tel. (207) 773-6471

Archdiocese of Portland in Oregon, Archbishop William J. Levada; Archbishop Cornelius M. Power; Auxiliary Bishop of Portland in Oregon, Bishop Kenneth Steiner; Bishop Paul Waldschmidt, C.S.C., Chancellor, Very Rev. Gregory Moys. Chancery Office, 2838 E. Burnside St., Portland, OR 97214. Tel. (503) 234-5334

Providence, Bishop Louis E. Gelineau; Auxiliary Bishop of Providence, Bishop Kenneth A. Angell, Chancellor, Rev. Msgr. William I. Varsanyi. Chancery Office, 1 Cathedral Square, Providence, RI 02903. Tel. (401) 278-4500

Pueblo, Bishop Arthur N. Tafoya; Chancellor, Rev. Edward H. Nunez. Chancery Office, 1001 N. Grand Ave., Pueblo, CO 81003. Tel. (303) 544-9861

Raleigh, Bishop F. Joseph Gossman; Chancellor, Rev. Joseph G. Vetter. Chancery Office, 300 Cardinal Gibbons Dr., Raleigh, NC 27606. Tel. (919) 821-9700

Rapid City, Bishop Charles J. Chaput, O.F.M. Cap. Chancellor, Very Rev. Michael B. Woster. Chancery Office, 606 Cathedral Dr., P.O. Box 678, Rapid City, SD 57709. Tel. (605) 343-3541

Reno-Las Vegas, Bishop Daniel F. Walsh; Chancellor, Very Rev. Gilbert J. Canuel, Jr., Chancery Office, 515 Court St., Reno, NV 89501. Tel. (702) 329-9274

Richmond, Bishop Walter F. Sullivan. Auxiliary Bishop of Richmond, Bishop David E. Foley. Chancellor, Rev. Thomas F. Shreve. Chancery Office, 811 Cathedral Pl., Suite C, Richmond, VA 23220. Tel. (804) 359-5661

Rochester, Bishop Matthew H. Clark, Auxiliary Bishop of Rochester, Bishop Dennis W. Hickey, Chancery Office, 1150 Buffalo Rd., Rochester, NY 14624. Tel. (716) 328-3110

Rockford, Bishop Arthur J. O'Neill; chancellor, Very Rev. Charles W. McNamee. Chancery Office, 1245 N. Court St., Rockford, IL 61103 Tel. (815) 962-3709

Rockville Centre, Bishop John R. McGann, Auxiliary Bishop of Rockville Centre, Bishop James J. Daly, Bishop Alfred J. Markiewicz; Chancellor, Rev. Msgr. John A. Alesandro. Chancery Office, 50 N. Park Ave. Rockville Centre, NY 11570. Tel. (516) 678-5800

Sacramento, Bishop Francis A. Quinn; Auxiliary Bishop of Sacramento, Bishop Alphonse Gallegos, O.A.R., Chancellor, Sr. Bridget Mary Flynn, S.M. Chancery Office, 1119 K St., P.O. Box 1706, Sacramento, CA 95812. Tel. (916) 443-1996

Saginaw, Bishop Kenneth E. Untener. Chancellor, Rev. Msgr. Thomas P. Schroeder. Chancery Office, 5800 Weiss St., Saginaw, MI 48603. Tel. (517) 799-7910

St. Augustine, Bishop John J. Snyder, Chancellor, Rev. Msgr. Eugene C. Kohls, Chancery Office, P.O. Box 24000, Jacksonville, FL 32241. Tel. (904) 262-3200.

St. Cloud, Bishop Jerome Hanus, O.S.B.; Chancellor, Rev. Severin Schwieters. Chancery Office, P.O. Box 1248, St. Cloud, MN 56302. Tel. (612) 251-2340

St. Josaphat in Parma, Ukrainian Bishop Robert M. Moskal. Chancellor, Rev. Msgr. Thomas A. Sayuk. Chancery Office 5720 State Rd., Parma, OH 44134. Tel. (216) 888-1522.

Archdiocese of St. Louis, Archbishop John L. May. Auxiliary Bishops of St. Louis: Bishop Charles R. Koester, Bishop Edward J. O'Donnell, Bishop James Terry Steib, Chancellor, Rev. John R. Gaydos. Chancery Office, 4445 Lindell Blvd., St. Louis, MO 63108. Tel. (314) 533-1887

St. Maron of Brooklyn, Bishop Francis M. Zayek, Auxiliary Bishop of St. Maron, Bishop John G. Chedid. Chancelor, Rev. John D. Faris. Chancery Office, 8120 15th Ave., Brooklyn, NY 11228. Tel. (718) 259-9200

St. Nicholas in Chicago for the Ukrainians, Bishop Innocent Lotocky, O.S.B.M. Vicar General, Rev. Walter Klimchuk. Chancery Office, 2245 W. Rice St., Chicago, IL 60622. Tel. (312) 276-5080

Archdiocese of St. Paul and Minneapolis, Archbishop John R. Roach. Auxiliary Bishop of St. Paul-Minneapolis: Bishop Robert J. Carlson; Chancellor, Bishop J. Richard Ham, M.M. Chancery Office, 226 Summit Ave., St. Paul, MN 55102. Tel. (612) 291-4400.

St. Petersburg, Bishop W. Thomas Larkin; Chancellor, Very Rev. Brendan Muldoon. Chancery Office, 6363 9th Ave. N., P.O. Box 40200. St. Petersburg, FL 33743. Tel. (813) 344-1611

Salina, Bishop George K. Fitzsimons; Chancellor, Rev. Msgr. James E. Hake. Chancery Office, 7th & Iron, 8th Fl., P.O. Box 980 Salina, KS 67402. Tel. (913) 827-8746

Salt Lake City, Bishop William K. Weigand; Chancellor, Deacon Silvio Mayo. Chancery Office, 27 C. St., Salt Lake City, UT 84103. Tel. (801) 328-8641

San Angelo, Bishop Michael Pfeifer, O.M.I.; Chancellor, Very Rev. Larry J. Droll. Chancery Office, 804 Ford, (Mailing Address Box 1829) San Angelo, TX 76902. Tel. (915) 653-2466

Archdiocese of San Antonio, Archbishop Patrick F. Flores; Auxiliary Bishop of San Antonio: Bishop Bernard F. Popp. Chancellor, Rev. Msgr. Patrick J. Murray, Chancery Office, 2718 W. Woodlawn Ave., PO.Box 28410, San Antonio, TX 78228. Tel. (512) 734-2620

San Bernardino, Bishop Phillip F. Straling. Chancellor, Sr. Maura Feeley. Chancery Office, 1450 North D St., San Bernardino, CA 92405 Tel. (714) 889-8351

San Diego; Coadjutor, Robert Brom; Bishop Leo T. Maher, Auxiliary Bishop of San Diego; Bishop Gilbert E. Chavez. Chancery Office, P.O. Box 80428, San Diego, CA 92138. Tel. (619) 574-6300

Archdiocese of San Francisco, Archbishop John R. Quinn. Chancellor, Sr. Mary B. Flaherty, R.S.C.J. Chancery Office, 445 Church St., San Francisco, CA 94114. Tel. (415) 565-3600

San Jose, Bishop Pierre DuMaine. Chancellor, Sr. Patricia Marie Mulpeters, P.B.V.M. Chancery Office, 841 Lenzen Ave., San Jose, CA 95126. (408)925-0100.

Archdiocese of Santa Fe, Archbishop Robert F. Sanchez; Chancellor Rev. D. J. Starkey. Chancery Office, 4000 St. Joseph's Place, N.W. Albuquerque, NM 87120. Tel. (505) 831-8100

Santa Rosa, Bishop John T. Steinbock. Chancellor, Rev. Msgr. James E. Pulskamp. Chancery Office, 547 "B" St., P.O. Box 1297, Santa Rosa, CA 95402. Tel. (707) 545-7610

Savannah, Bishop Raymond W. Lessard. Chancellor, Rev. Jeremiah J. McCarthy. Chancery Office, 225 Abercorn St., P.O. Box 8789, Savannah, GA 31412. Tel. (912) 238-2320

Scranton, Bishop James C. Timlin, Auxiliary Bishop of Scranton: Bishop Francis X. Dilorenzo. Chancellor, Rev. Gerald F. Mullally. Chancery Office, 300 Wyoming Ave., Scranton, PA 18503. Tel. (717) 346-8910

Archdiocese of Seattle, Archbishop Raymond G. Hunthausen; Coadjutor Bishop of Seattle: Bishop Thomas J. Murphy. Chancellor, Very Rev. Michael G. Ryan. Chancery Office, 910 Marion St., Seattle, WA 98104. Tel. (206) 382-4560

Shreveport, Bishop William B. Friend. Chancellor, Sr. Margaret Daues, C.S.J., 2500 Line Ave., Shreveport, LA 71104. Tel. (318)222-2006

Sioux City, Bishop Lawrence D. Soens. Chancellor, Rev. Kevin C. McCoy. Chancery Office, P.O. Box 3379, Sioux City, IA 51102. Tel. (712) 255-7933

Sioux Falls, Bishop Paul V. Dudley; Chancellor, Rev. Gregory Tschakert. Chancery Office, 423 N. Duluth Ave., Box 5033, Sioux Falls, SD 57117. Tel. (605) 334-9861

Spokane, Bishop Lawrence H. Welsh, Chancellor, Rev. Mark Paulter. Chancery Office, P.O. Box 1453, Spokane, WA 99205. Tel. (509) 456-7100

Springfield-Cape Girardeau, Bishop John J. Leibrecht, Chancellor, Rev. Thomas E. Reidy, Chancery Office, 318 Park Central E., P.O. Box 50960, Springfield , MO 65805. Tel. (417)866-0841

Springfield in Illinois, Bishop Daniel L. Ryan; Chancellor Rev. John Renken, Chancery Office, P.O. Box 1667, Springfield, IL 62705. Tel. (217) 522-7781

Springfield, Bishop Joseph F. Maguire; Auxiliary Bishop of Springfield, Bishop Leo E. O'Neil, Chancellor, Rev. Thomas L. Dupre. Chancery Office, 76 Elliot St., P.O. Box 1730, Springfield, MA 01101. Tel. (413) 732-3175

Byzantine Ukrainian Rite—Stamford, Bishop Basil H. Losten. Chancellor, Rt. Rev. Matthew Berko. Chancery Office, 161 Glenbrook St., Stamford, CT 06902. Tel. (203) 324-7698

Steubenville, Bishop Albert H. Ottenweller. Chancellor, Mrs. Linda A. Nichols. Chancery Office, 422 Washington St., P.O. Box 969, Steubenville, OH 43952. Tel. (614) 282-3631

Stockton, Bishop Donald W. Montrose; Chancellor, Sr. Lorraine Pagendarm, O.P. Chancery Office, 1105 N. Lincoln St., Stockton, CA 95203, P.O. Box 4237, Stockton, CA 95204. Tel. (209) 466-0636

Superior, Bishop Raphael M. Fliss; Chancellor, Rev. James R. Horath. Chancery Office, 1201 Hughitt Ave., Box 969, Superior, WI 54880. Tel. (715) 392-2937

Syracuse, Bishop Joseph T. O'Keefe; Auxiliary Bishop of Syracuse; Bishop Thomas J. Costello, Chancellor, Rev. David W. Barry Chancery Office, P.O. Box 511, Syracuse, NY 13201. Tel. (315) 422-7203

Toledo, Bishop James R. Hoffman; Auxiliary Bishop of Toledo, Bishop Robert W. Donnelly. Chancery Office, 1933 Spielbush, Toledo, OH 43624. Tel. (419)244-6711

Trenton, Bishop John C. Reiss; Auxiliary Bishop of Trenton, Bishop Edward U. Kmiec, Chancellor, Rev. Msgr. William F. Fitzgerald. Chancery Office, P.O. Box 5309, Trenton NJ 08638. Tel. (609) 882-7125

Tucson, Bishop Manuel D. Moreno; Chancellor, Rev. John F. Allt. Chancery Office, 192 S. Stone Ave., Box 31, Tucson, AZ 85702. Tel. (602) 792-3410

Tulsa, Bishop Eusebius J. Beltran. Chancellor, Very Rev. Dennis C. Dorney. Chancery Office, 820 S. Boulder St., P.O. Box 2009, Tulsa, OK 74101. Tel. (918) 587-3115

Tyler, Bishop Charles E. Herzig. Vicar General, Rev. Msgr. Milam J. Joseph. Chancery Office, 1920 Sybil Lane, Tyler, TX 75703. Tel. (214)534-1077

Van Nuys Eparchy, Bishop Thomas V. Dolinay. Chancellor, Rev. Msgr. Michael Moran. Chancery Office, 18024 Parthenia St., Northridge, CA 91325. Tel. (818) 907-1051.

Venice, Bishop John J. Nevins, Chancellor, Very Rev. Jerome A. Carosella. Chancery Office, 1000 Pinebrook Rd., P.O. Box 2006, Venice, FL 34284. Tel. (813)484-9543.

Victoria, Bishop Charles V. Grahmann; Chancellor, Rev. Msgr. Thomas C. McLaughlin. Chancellor Office, P. O. Box 4708, Victoria, TX 77903. Tel. (512) 573-0828.

Archdiocese of Washington, James Cardinal Hickey. Auxiliary Bishop of Washington: Bishop Alvaro Corrada, S.J. Chancellor, Rev. William Kane. Chancery Office, 5001 Eastern Ave., P. O. Box 29260, NW, Washington, DC 20017. Tel. (301) 853-3800.

Wheeling-Charleston, _____; ;Auxiliary Bishop: Bishop Bernard W. Schmitt. Chancellor, Rev. Robert C. Nash. Chancery Office, 1300 Byron St., Wheeling, WV 26003. Tel. (304) 233-0880

Wichita, Bishop Eugene J. Gerber. Chancellor, Rev. Robert E. Hemberger. Chancery Office, 424 N. Broadway, Wichita, KS 67202. Tel. (316) 263-6262

Wilmington, Bishop Robert E. Mulvee; Auxiliary Bishop of Wilmington, Bishop James C. Burke, O.P., Chancellor, Rev. Msgr. Joseph F. Rebman. Chancery Office, P.O. Box 2030, 1925 Delaware Ave., Ste 1A, Wilmington, DE 19899. Tel. (302) 573-3100

Winona, Bishop John G. Vlazny; Chancellor, Rev. Donald P. Schmitz. Chancery Office, 55 W. Sanborn, P.O. Box 588, Winona, MN 55987. Tel. (507) 454-4643

Worcester, Bishop Timothy J. Harrington, Auxiliary Bishop of Worcester: Bishop George E. Rueger. Chancery Office, 49 Elm St., Worcester, MA 01609. Tel. (617) 791-7171

Yakima, Bishop William S. Skylstad; Vicar General, Very Rev. Perron J. Auve. Chancery Office, 5301-A Tieton Dr., Yakima, WA 98908. Tel. (509) 965-7117

Youngstown, Bishop James W. Malone, Auxiliary Bishop of Youngstown: Bishop Benedict C. Franzetta, Chancellor, Rev. James Clarke. Chancery Office, 144 W. Wood St., Youngstown, OH 44503. Tel. (216) 744-8451

The Romanian Orthodox Church in America

The Romanian Orthodox Church in America is an autonomous Archdiocese chartered under the name of "Romanian Orthodox Missionary Archdiocese in America."

Diocese was founded in 1929 and approved by the Holy Synod of the Romanian Orthodox Church in Romania in 1934. A decision of the Holy Synod of the Romanian Orthodox Church of July 12, 1950, granted it ecclesiastical autonomy in America, continuing to hold only dogmatical and canonical ties with the Holy Synod and the Romanian Orthodox Patriarchate of Romania.

In 1951, a group of approximately 40 parishes with their clergy from USA and Canada separated from this church and eventually joined in 1960 the Russian Orthodox Greek Catholic Metropolia now called the Orthodox Church in America which reordained for these parishes a bishop with the title "Bishop of Detroit and Michigan."

The Holy Synod of the Romanian Orthodox Church, in its session of June 11, 1973, elevated the Bishop of Romanian Orthodox Missionary Episcopate in America to the rank of Archbishop. Consequently the Annual Congress of the Romanian Orthodox Church in America, held on July 21, 1973, at Edmonton-Boian, Alberta, decided to change the title of the Diocese from "Episcopate" to that of "Archdiocese." This decision was approved by the Holy Synod of the Romanian Orthodox Church of Romania in its session of December 12, 1974, renewing at the same time the status as an Autonomous Archdiocese with the right to elect in addition to the Archbishop an Auxiliary Bishop for the Archdiocese.

GENERAL ORGANIZATION

Headquarters: 19959 Riopelle, Detroit, MI 48203. Tel. (313) 893-7191

Annual Congress in July, and biannual Archdiocesan Council

OFFICERS

Archbishop, His Eminence The Most Rev. Archbishop Victorin (Ursache), 19959 Riopelle, Detroit, MI 48203. Tel. (313) 893-7191

Vicar, Very Rev. Archim. Dr. Vasile Vasilachi, 40-03 48th Ave., Woodside, Queens NY 11377. Tel. (718) 784-4453

Dir., Inter-Church Relations, Rev. Fr. Nicholas Apostola, 14 Hammond St., Worcester, MA 01610. Tel. (617)799-0040

Sec., Very Archim, Rev. Felix Dubneae, 19959 Riopelle St., Detroit, MI 48203. Tel. (313) 892-2402

PERIODICALS

Credinta—The Faith (m), 19959 Riopelle, Detroit, MI 48203. Very Rev. Archim, Dr. Vasile Vasilachi, Ed.

Calendarul Credinta (yearbook), 19959 Riopelle, Detroit, MI 48203. Very Rev. Archim. Dr. Vasile Vasilachi, Ed.

The Romanian Orthodox Episcopate of America

This body of Eastern Orthodox Christians of Romanian descent was organized in 1929 as an autonomous Diocese under the jurisdiction of the Romanian Patriarchate. In 1951 it severed all relations with the Orthodox Church of Romania. Now under the canonical jurisdiction of the autocephalous Orthodox Church in America, it enjoys full administrative autonomy and is headed by its own Bishop.

Churches: 34; Inclusive Membership: 60,000; Sunday or Sabbath Schools: 30; Total Enrollment: 1,800; Ordained Clergy: 67

GENERAL ORGANIZATION

Church Congress: annual (July)

Headquarters: 2522 Grey Tower Road, Jackson, MI 49201. Tel. (517) 522-4800

OFFICERS

Ruling Bishop: His Grace Bishop Nathaniel (Popp)

The Council of the Episcopate: Sec., Rev. Fr. Laurence Lazar, 3355 Ridgewood Rd., Akron, OH 44313; Treas., Daniel Poroch, 21101 Winkel Dr., St. Clair Shores, MI 48081

OTHER ORGANIZATIONS

The American Romanian Orthodox Youth (AROY): Pres., Gary Danis, 24341 Ridgedale, Oak Park, MI 48237; Sec., Debra Cioca, 5110 Echo Valley St., N.W., North Canton, OH 44720; Spiritual Advisor, Rev. Fr. George Treff, 6075 Harrison St., Merrillville, IN 46410

Association of Romanian Orthodox Ladies' Auxiliaries (ARFORA): Pres. Mrs. Pauline Trutza, 1466 Waterbury Ave., Lakewood, OH 44107; Sec., Jean Dobrea, 3324 W. 159 St., Cleveland, OH 44111; SpiritualAdvisor, Rev. Fr. Romey Rosco, 625 Centralia; Ave., Dearborn Hts., MI 48127

Orthodox Brotherhood U.S.A.: Chpsn., Alexandra Carulea, 29 Rhoda, Youngstown, OH 44509

PERIODICALS

Solia-Herald News (m), Solia Calendar (a), 146 W. Courtland St., Jackson, MI 49201.

Russian Orthodox Church in the U.S.A., Patriarchal Parishes of the

This group of parishes is under the direct jurisdiction of the Patriarch of Moscow and All Russia, His Holiness Pimen, in the person of a Vicar Bishop, His Grace Clement, Bishop of Serpukhov.

GENERAL ORGANIZATION

Headquarters: St. Nicholas Cathedral, 15 E. 97th St., New York, NY 10029. Tel. (212) 831-6294

Archbishop: The Most Rev. Clement, Bishop of Serpukhov; Adm. of The Patriarchal Parishes of the Russian Orthodox Church in the United States of America

PERIODICALS
One Church (bi-m), 727 Miller Ave., Youngstown, OH 44502, Rt. Rev. Feodor Kovalchuk, Ed.
Journal of the Moscow Patriachate (Eng m), subscription list, St. Nicholas Cathedral, New York, NY 10029

The Russian Orthodox Church Outside of Russia

Organized in 1920 to unite in one body of dioceses the missions and parishes of the Russian Orthodox Church outside of Russia. The Governing body was set up in Constantinople sponsored by the Ecumenical Patriarchate. In November 1950, it came to the United States. The Russian Orthodox Church Outside of Russia lays emphasis on being true to the old traditions of the Russian Church, but it does not compromise with official church leaders in Moscow, "since that would amount to being under the influence and direction of a godless State."

GENERAL ORGANIZATION
Headquarters: 75 E. 93rd St., New York, NY 10128. Tel. (212) 534-1601
Council of Bishops, Synod, His Eminence Metropolitan Vitaly
Other Members: Sec., Archbishop Laurus of Syracuse and Trinity; Dep. Sec., Hilarion, Bishop of Manhattan
Sec. of the Synod of Bishops and Director of Public and Foreign Relations Dept., Archbishop Laurus of Syracuse & Trinity, 75 E. 93rd St., New York, NY 10128

PERIODICALS
Church Life (bi-m), (in Russian) by Synod of Bishops, 75 E. 93rd St., New York, NY 10128
Orthodox America, Box 2132, Redding, CA 96099
Orthodox Life, Holy Trinity Monastery, Jordanville, NY 13361
Pravoslavnaya Rus (2/mo.), in Russian, Holy Trinity Monastery, Jordanville, NY 13361
Living Orthodoxy (bi-m), St. John of Kronstadt Press., Rt. #1, Box 171, Liberty, TN 37095

The Salvation Army

The Salvation Army, founded in 1865 by William Booth (1829-1912) in London, England, and introduced into America in 1880, is an international religious and charitable movement organized and operated on a paramilitary pattern, and is a branch of the Christian church. To carry out its purposes, The Salvation Army has established a widely diversified program of religious and social welfare services which are designed to meet the needs of children, youth, and adults in all age groups.

Churches: 1,097; Inclusive Membership: 433,448; Sunday or Sabbath Schools: 1,121; Total Enrollment: 112,941; Ordained Clergy: 5,198

GENERAL ORGANIZATION
National Headquarters: 799 Bloomfield Ave., Verona, NJ 07044. Tel. (201) 239-0606

OFFICERS
Natl. Commander, Commissioner James Osborne
Natl. Chief Sec., Col. Kenneth Hood
Natl. Communications Dept., Dir., Lt. Colonel Leon Ferraez

TERRITORIAL ORGANIZATIONS
Eastern Territory, 120-130 W. 14th St., New York, NY 10011; Territorial Commander, Commissioner Robert E. Thomson; Chief Sec., Col. Robert A. Watson
Central Territory, 860 N. Dearborn St., Chicago, IL 60610; Territorial Commander, Commissioner Harold E. Shoults; Chief Sec., Col. Edward Johnson

Western Territory, 30840 Hawthorne Blvd., Rancho Palos Verdes, CA 90274. Territorial Commander, Commissioner Paul A. Rader; Chief Sec., Col. Ronald G. Irwin;
Southern Territory, 1424 Northeast Expressway, Atlanta, GA 30329. Territorial Commander, Commissioner Kenneth L. Hodder; Chief Sec., Col. Harold D. Hinson

PERIODICALS
The War Cry (w), Young Salvationist (m), The Young Soldier (m), National Publications Dept., 799 Bloomfield Ave, Verona, NJ 07044. Lt. Col. Henry Gariepy, Ed.-in-Chief

The Schwenkfelder Church

The Schwenkfelders are the spiritual descendants of the Silesian nobleman Caspar Schwenkfeld von Ossig (1489-1561), a scholar, reformer, preacher, and prolific writer who endeavored to aid in the cause of the Protestant Reformation. A contemporary of Martin Luther, John Calvin, Ulrich Zwingli, and Phillip Melancthon, Schwenkfeld sought no following, formulated no creed, and did not attempt to organize a church based on his beliefs. He labored for liberty of religious belief—a fellowship of all believers, for one united Christian church—the ecumenical Church.

He and his cobelievers supported a movement known as the Reformation by the Middle Way. Persecuted by state churches, ultimately 180 Schwenkfelders exiled from Silesia emigrated to Pennsylvania. They landed at Philadelphia Sept. 22, 1734, affirmed their allegiance to the crown of Great Britain on the 23rd and the following day, held a service of Thanksgiving for their deliverance and safe arrival in the New World.

In 1882, the Society of Schwenkfelders, the forerunner of the present Schwenkfelder Church, was formed. The church was incorporated in 1909.

The General Conference of the Schwenkfelder Church is a voluntary association for the Schwenkfelder Churches at Palm, Worcester, Lansdale, Norristown, and Philadelphia, Pennsylvania, with a total membership of approximately 2,900.

They practice adult baptism and dedication of children, and observe the Lord's Supper regularly with open Communion. In theology, they are Christo-centric; in polity, congregational; in missions, world-minded; in ecclesiastical organization, ecumenical.

The Schwenkfelder Church has no publishing house of its own. The ministry is recruited from graduates of colleges, universities, and accredited theological seminaries. In each community, the churches have been noted for leadership in ecumenical concerns through ministerial associations, community service and action groups, councils of Christian education, and other agencies.

Churches: 5; Inclusive Membership: 2,516; Sunday or Sabbath Schools: 5; Total Enrollment: 848; Ordained Clergy: 9

GENERAL ORGANIZATION
General Conference: semi-annual
Headquarters: Pennsburg, PA 18073

OFFICERS
Mod., Kenneth D. Slough, Jr., 197 N. Whitehall Rd., Norristown PA 19403
Sec., Miss Florence Schultz, P.O. Box 221, Palm, PA 18070
Treas., Ellis W. Kriebel, 523 Meetinghouse Rd., Harleysville, PA 19438

PERIODICAL
The Schwenkfeldian (q), Pennsburg, PA 18073. Nancy M. Byron, Ed.

Second Cumberland Presbyterian Church in U.S.

This church, originally known as the Colored Cumberland Presbyterian Church, was formed in May 1874. Prior to its founding, a convention was held on October 1868 in Henderson, Ky., at which Black ministers of the Cumberland Presbyterian Church began to speak openly about forming a new denomination.

In May 1869, at the General Assembly meeting in Murfreesboro, Tenn., Moses Weir, the spokesperson for the black delegation appealed for help in organizing a separate African church. Four reasons were cited: Blacks could learn self-reliance and independence; they could have more financial assistance; they could minister more effectively among Blacks if they existed as a separate denomination; they wanted to worship close to the altar, and not in the balconies, which symbolized restriction. Four requests were made: that the Cumberland Presbyterian Church organize Blacks into presbyteries and synods; develop schools to train Black clergy; grant loans to assist Blacks to secure hymnbooks, Bibles, and church buildings; establish a separate General Assembly. At the 1869 General Assembly, the Black churches of the Cumberland Presbyterian Church were set apart with their own ecclesiastical organization.

In 1874 the first General Assembly of the Colored Cumberland Presbyterian Church met in Nashville, Tenn. The moderator was Rev. P. Price and the stated clerk was Elder John Humphrey. At that time there were 46 ordained clergy, 20 licentiates, 30 candidates, and 3,000 communicants.

Currently, the denomination's General Assembly, the national governing body, is organized around its three program boards and agencies: Finance, Publication and Christian Education and Missons and Evangelism. Other agencies of the General Assembly are under these three program boards.

The church has four synods (Alabama, Kentucky, Tennessee, and Texas) a membership of 15,000, 15 presbyteries, 153 congregations, and 100 ordained clergy. The greatest strength of the SCPC is its Alabama synod which comprises nearly one-third of the denomination; East and Middle Tennessee areas also contain large numbers of members. The SCPC extends as far north as Cleveland, Ohio and Chicago; as far west as Marshalltown, Iowa, and Dallas, Texas; and as far south as Selma, Alabama.

GENERAL ORGANIZATION
General Assembly: annual 2nd Wed. in June

OFFICERS
Mod.: Rev. McKinley Jones, 2914 Broadview, Huntsville, AL 35810. Tel. (205)825-2235.
Stated Clk.: Rev. Dr. R. Stanley Wood, 226 Church St., Huntsville, AL 35801. Tel. (205)536-7481

SYNODS
Alabama, Stated Clk., Arthur Hinton, 511 10th Ave., N.W., Aliceville 35442
Kentucky, Stated Clk., Leroy Hunt, 1317 Monroe St., Paducah, Ky 42001
Tennessee, Stated Clk., Elder Clarence Norman, 145 Jones St., Huntington, TN 38334
Texas, Stated Clk., Arthur King, 2435 Kristen, Dallas, TX 75216

PERIODICAL
The Cumberland Flag, 226 Church St., Huntsville, AL 35801. Rev. Robert Stanley Wood, Interim Ed.

Separate Baptists in Christ

A group of Baptists found in Indiana, Ohio, Kentucky, Tennessee, Illinois, Virginia, West Virginia, Florida and North Carolina, dating back to an association formed in 1758 in North Carolina and Virginia.

Today this group consists of approximately 100 churches. They believe in the infallibility of the Bible, the divine ordinances of the Lord's Supper, feetwashing, baptism, and that he who endureth to the end shall be saved.

Churches: 101; Inclusive Membership: 10,000; Sunday or Sabbath Schools: N.R.; Total Enrollment: N.R.; Ordained Clergy: 165

GENERAL ORGANIZATION
General Association

OFFICERS
Mod., Rev. Jim Goff, 1020 Gagel Ave., Louisville, KY 40216
Asst. Mod., Rev. Pearl Cox, RR 1 Box 43, Oakland, IL 61943
Clk., Rev. Mark Polston, 316 Winter Park Dr., Somerset, KY 42501. Tel. (606)678-8753
Asst. Clk., Bro. Randy Polston, 1841 N. Hawthorne Lane, Indianapolis, IN 46218. Tel. (317)357-9898

Serbian Orthodox Church in the U.S.A. and Canada

The Serbian Orthodox Church is an organic part of the Eastern Orthodox Church. As a local church it received its autocephaly from Constantinople in 1219 A.D. The Patriarchal seat of the church today is in Belgrade, Yugoslavia. In 1921, a Serbian Orthodox Diocese in the United States of America and Canada was organized. In 1963, it was reorganized into three dioceses, and in 1983 a fourth diocese was created for the Canadian part of the church. The Serbian Orthodox Church in the USA and Canada received its administrative autonomy in 1982. The Serbian Orthodox Church is in absolute doctrinal unity with all other local Orthodox Churches.

Churches: 68; Inclusive Membership: 67,000; Sunday or Sabbath Schools: 56; Total Enrollment: 5,010; Ordained Clergy: 82

GENERAL ORGANIZATION
Episcopal Council
Central Church Council
Chancery: St. Sava Monastery, P.O. Box 519, Libertyville, IL 60048. Tel. (708) 362-2440

BISHOPS
Rt. Rev. Dr. Firmilian, Bishop of Midwestern America, P.O. Box 519 Libertyville, IL 60048. Tel. (708) 362-2440
Rt. Rev. Christopher, Bishop of Eastern America, P.O. Box 368, Sewickley, PA 15143. Tel. (412) 741-5686
Rt. Rev. George, Bishop of Canada, 5A Stockbridge Ave., Toronto, Ontario M8Z 4M6. Tel. (416) 231-4409
Rt. Rev. Chrysostom, Bishop of Western America, 2541 Crestline Terrace, Alhambra, CA 91803. Tel. (818)264-6825
Rt. Rev. Mitrofan, Vicar Bishop of Toplica, PO. Box 519, Libertyville, IL 60048. Tel. (312)367-0698.

OTHER ORGANIZATIONS
Brotherhood of Serbian Orthodox Clergy in the U.S.A. and Canada, Pres., V. Rev. Milan Savich, Schererville, IN
Federation of Circles of Serbian Sisters
Serbian Singing Federation

PERIODICAL
The Path of Orthodoxy, P.O. Box 36 Leetsdale, PA 15056. Tel. (412) 741-8660. Rev. Rade Merick, Eng. Ed.; V. Rev. Uros Ocokoljich and V. Rev. Nedeljko Lunich, Serbian Ed.

Seventh-day Adventist Church

The Seventh-day Adventist Church grew out of a worldwide religious revival in the mid-19th century.

People of many religious persuasions believed Bible prophecies indicated that the second coming or advent of Christ was imminent.

When Christ did not come in the 1840's, a group of these disappointed Adventists in the United States continued their Bible studies and concluded they had misinterpreted prophetic events and that the second coming of Christ was still in the future. This same group of Adventists later accepted the teaching of the seventh-day Sabbath and became known as Seventh-day Adventists. The denomination organized formally in 1863.

The church was largely confined to North America until 1874, when its first missionary was sent to Europe. Today 29,000 congregations meet in 184 countries. Membership exceeds 5.7 million and increases between six and seven percent each year.

In addition to a vigorous mission program, the church has the largest worldwide Protestant parochial school system with more than 5,200 schools with over 770,000 students on elementary through college and university levels.

The Adventist Development and Relief Agency (ADRA) helps victims of war and natural disasters, and many local congregations have Community Service facilities to help those in need close to home.

The church also has a worldwide publishing ministry with more than 50 printing facilities producing magazines and other publications in over 180 languages and dialects. In the United States and Canada, the church sponsors a variety of radio and television programs, including "Christian Lifestyle Magazine," "It Is Written," "Breath of Life," "Ayer, Hoy, y Mañana," "Voice of Prophecy," and "La Voz de la Esperanza."

Churches: 4,145; Inclusive Membership: 687,200; Sunday or Sabbath Schools: 4,193; Total Enrollment: 480,457; Ordained Clergy: 4,537

GENERAL ORGANIZATION

General Conference: quinquennial (next meeting, 1990) Headquarters: 12501 Old Columbia Pike, Silver Spring, MD 20904. 20012. Tel. (301)680-6000

OFFICERS

Pres., Neal C. Wilson
Sec., G. Ralph Thompson
Treas., Donald F. Gilbert

DEPARTMENTS

Church Ministries Dept.: Dir., George E. Knowles
Communication Dept.: Dir., Shirley Burton
Education Dept.: Dir., George H. Akers
Health and Temperance Dept.: Dir., G. Gordon Hadley
Ministerial Association: Sec., W. Floyd Bresee
Public Affairs and Religious Liberty Dept.: Dir., B. B. Beach
Publishing Dept.: Dir., Ronald E. Appenzeller

NORTH AMERICAN ORGANIZATIONS

The North American Division of Seventh-day Adventists, 12501 Old Columbia Pike, Silver Spring, MD 20904, Pres., Charles E. Bradford; Adm. Asst. to Pres., Gary B. Patterson; Secretaries, Robert L. Dale, Meade C. VAn Putten; Treasurers, George H. Crumley, Frank L. Jones. This Division includes the United States, Bermuda and Canada and is divided into 58 Conferences which are grouped together into 9 organized Union Conferences. The various Conferences work under the general direction of these Union Conferences.

Atlantic Union Conference, P.O. Box 1189, South Lancaster, MA 01561. Pres., Philip S. Follett; Sec., Alvin R. Goulbourne; Treas., Dale R. Beaulieu, (Territory: Connecticut, Maine, Massachusetts, New Hampshire, New York, Rhode Island, Vermont, and the Bermuda Islands)

Canada, Seventh-day Adventist Church in Canada (See Directory 4, **Religious Bodies in Canada**)

Columbia Union Conference, 5427 Twin Knolls Rd., Columbia, MD 21045. Pres., Ron M. Wisbey; Sec., Henry M. Wright; Treas., D. J. Russell (Territory: Delaware, Maryland, New Jersey, Ohio, Pennsylvania, Virginia, West Virginia, and District of Columbia)

Lake Union Conference, P.O. Box C, Berrien Springs, MI 49103, Pres., R. H. Carter; Sec., Herbert S. Larsen; Treas., Herbert Pritchard (Territory: Illinois, Indiana, Michigan, and Wisconsin)

Mid-America Union Conference, P.O. Box 6128, Lincoln, NE 68506. Pres., Joel O. Tompkins; Sec., George W. Timpson; Treas., Duane P. Huey (Territory: Colorado, Iowa, Kansas, Minnesota, Missouri, Nebraska, North Dakota, South Dakota, Wyoming, San Juan County in New Mexico)

North Pacific Union Conference, P.O. Box 16677, Portland, OR 97216. Pres., Bruce Johnston; Sec., Paul Nelson; Treas., Robert L. Rawson (Territory: Alaska, Idaho, Montana, Oregon, and Washington)

Pacific Union Conference, P. O. Box 5005, Westlake Village, CA 91359. Pres., Thomas J. Mostert, Jr.; Sec., Major C. White; Treas., S. D. Bietz (Territory: Arizona, California, Hawaii, Nevada, and Utah)

Southern Union Conference, P.O. Box 849, Decatur, GA 30031. Pres., A. C. McClure; Sec., W. D. Sumpter; Treas., Richard P. Center (Territory: Alabama, Florida, Georgia, Kentucky, Mississippi, North Carolina, South Carolina, and Tennessee)

Southwestern Union Conference, P. O. Box 4000, Burleson, TX 76028. Pres., Cyril Miller; Sec., Clayton R. Pritchett; Treas., Max A. Trevino (Territory: Arkansas, Louisiana, New Mexico [except San Juan County], Oklahoma, and Texas)

PERIODICALS

The Adventist Review (w), 12501 Old Columbia Pike, Silver Spring, MD 20904. W. G. Johnsson, Ed.

ASI News (bi-m), 12501 Old Columbia Pike, Silver Spring, MD 20904. W. C. Arnold, Ed.

Celebration! (m), 55 W. Oak Ridge Dr., Hagerstown, MD 21740. Jack Calkins, Ed.

Christian Record, (m), P. O. Box 6097, Lincoln NE 68506. R. J. Kaiser, Jr., Ed.

Church Ministries Worker (q), P.O. Box 7000, Boise, ID 83707. Graham Bingham, Ed.

Collegiate Quarterly (q), P.O. Box 7000, Boise, ID 83707. Graham Bingham, Ed.

Cornerstone Connections International (q), 55 W. Oak Ridge Dr., Hagerstown MD 21740. Mrs. Lyndelle Chiomenti, Ed.

Guide (w), 55 W. Oak Ridge Dr., Hagerstown, MD 21740. Jeannette R. Johnson, Ed.

Insight, (w), 55 W. Oak Ridge Dr., Hagerstown, MD 21740. J. Christopher Blake, Ed.

Journal of Adventist Education (5/yr.), 12501 Old Columbia Pike, Silver Springs, MD 20904. Victor S. Griffiths, Ed.

Liberty (bi-m), 55 W. Oak Ridge Dr., Hagerstown, MD 21740. R. R. Hegstad, Ed.

Listen (m), P. O. Box 7000, Nampa, ID 83707. Gary Swanson, Ed.

Message (8/yr), 55 W. Oak Ridge Dr., Hagerstown, MD 21740. D. W. Baker, Ed.

Ministry, The (m), 55 W. Oak Ridge Dr., Hagerstown, MD 21740. J. Robert Spangler, Ed.

Mission, Adult and Junior (q), 55 W. Oak Ridge Dr. Hagerstown, MD 21740. Janet Kangas, Ed.

Our Little Friend (w), P.O. Box 7000, Nampa, ID 83707. Aileen Andres Sox, Ed.

Primary Treasure (w), P.O. Box 7000, Nampa, ID 83707. Aileen Andres Sox, Ed.

Sabbath School Lesson Quarterlies, P.O. Box 7000, Nampa, ID 83707.

Shabat Shalom, (q), 55 W. Oak Ridge Dr., Hagerstown, MD 21740. Clifford Goldstein, Ed.

Signs of the Times (m), P.O. Box 7000, Nampa, ID 83707. K. J. Holland, Ed.

Vibrant Life (bi-m), 55 W. Oak Ridge Dr., Hagerstown, MD 21740. Raymond H. Woolsey, Ed.

The Winner (9/yr), 12501 Old Columbia Pike, Silver Spring, MD 20904. Barbara Wetherell, Ed.

Youth Ministry Accent (q), 12501 Old Columbia Pike, Silver Spring, MD 20904. James Joiner, Ed.

Seventh Day Baptist General Conference, USA and Canada

Seventh Day Baptists emerged during the English Reformation, organizing their first churches in England in the mid-1600's. The oldest of them all, the Millyard Seventh Day Baptist Church of London, continues to be active over 300 years later.

The first Seventh Day Baptist in America was Stephen Mumford, who emigrated from England in 1664. He became one of several Sabbathkeepers (observers of the seventh-day Sabbath, or Saturday) who fellowshipped with the First Baptist Church of Newport, R. I. In 1671 they withdrew to form the first Seventh Day Baptist Church in America at Newport.

Other Seventh Day Baptist churches were established early in New Jersey and Pennsylvania as well as New England. It was from these three centers that the denomination grew and expanded westward.

A desire to increase their fellowship and to organize for missionary efforts led to the founding of the Seventh Day Baptist General Conference in 1801.

The organized boards and agencies of the denomination reflect Seventh Day Baptist interest in missions, publishing and education. Women have always been encouraged to participate actively at local and denominational levels. From the earliest days religious freedom has been championed for all, and the separation of church and state advocated.

In the 20th century Seventh Day Baptists have been characterized by their ecumenical spirit, fellowshiping as in the early years with other Baptists in the Baptist World Alliance and affiliated organizations, and reaching out to other Sabbathkeeping groups. In 1965 the Seventh Day Baptist World Federation was organized with the S.D.B. General Conference in U.S.A. joining as one of 16 member conferences around the world.

GENERAL ORGANIZATION

General Conference: annual

Headquarters: Seventh Day Baptist Center, 3120 Kennedy Rd., P. O. Box 1678, Janesville, WI 53547. Tel. (608) 752-5055

OFFICERS

Pres., Rev. Joe A. Samuels, 511 Central Ave., Plainfield, NJ 07060

Exec. Sec., Rev. Dale D. Thorngate, 3120 Kennedy Rd., P. O. Box 1678, Janesville, WI 53547

Treas., Ron Ochs, Rt. 3, 4811 Brentwood Dr., Milton, WI 53563

OTHER ORGANIZATIONS

Seventh Day Baptist Missionary Society: Exec. Vice-Pres., Rev. Leon R. Lawton, 308 Washington Trust Bldg., Westerly, RI 02891

Seventh Day Baptist Board of Christian Education: Exec. Dir., Rev. Ernest K. Bee, Jr., P.O. Box 115, Alfred Station, NY 14803

Women's Society of the General Conference: Pres., Mrs.

Dorotha Shettel, 4290 Edgewood Pl., Riverside, CA 92506

Seventh Day Baptist Historical Society: Rev. Don A. Stanford, Historian; Mrs. Janet Thorngate, Librarian, 3120 Kennedy Rd., P. O. Box 1678, Janesville, WI 53547

Seventh Day Baptist Center on Ministry: Dir. of Pastoral Services, Rev. Rodney Henry, 3120 Kennedy Rd., P. O. Box 1678, Janesville, WI 53547

PERIODICAL

Sabbath Recorder (m), 3120 Kennedy Rd., P. O. Box 1678, Janesville, WI 53547. Rev. Kevin J. Butler, Ed.

Social Brethren

Organized 1867 among members of various bodies; confession of faith has nine articles; evangelical.

GENERAL ORGANIZATION

General Assembly: biennial

OFFICERS

Mod., of General Assembly, Rev. John Hancock, RR #3 Box 221, Harrisburg, IL 62946. Tel. (618)252-0802

Mod. (Union Association), James R. Hubbard, RR #1, Junction, IL 62954. Tel. (618)275-4492

Mod. (Illinois Association), Rev. Earl E. Vaughn, R.R. 2, Flora, IL 62839

Mod. (Midwestern Association), Rev. Edward Darnell, 53 E. Newport, Pontiac, MI 48055. Tel. (313)335-9125

Southern Baptist Convention

The Southern Baptist Convention was organized on May 10, 1845, in Augusta, Georgia.

Cooperating Baptist churches are located in all 50 states, the District of Columbia, Puerto Rico, American Samoa, and the Virgin Islands. The members of the churches work together through 1,207 district associations and 37 state conventions. The Southern Baptist Convention has an Executive Committee and 20 national agencies—four boards, six seminaries, seven commissions, a foundation and two associated organizations.

The purpose of the Southern Baptist Convention is "to provide a general organization for Baptists in the United States and its territories for the promotion of Christian missions at home and abroad and any other objects such as Christian education, benevolent enterprises, and social services which it may deem proper and advisable for the furtherance of the Kingdom of God" (Constitution, Article II).

The Convention exists in order to help the churches to lead people to God through Jesus Christ.

From the beginning, there has been a burning mission desire to share the Gospel with the peoples of the world. The Cooperative Program is the basic channel of mission support. In addition, the Lottie Moon Christmas Offering for Foreign Missions and the Annie Armstrong Easter Offering for Home Missions support Southern Baptists' world mission programs.

In 1988, there were 3,867 foreign missionaries serving in 114 foreign countries and 3,827 home missionaries serving within the United States.

In 1985, the Southern Baptist Convention adopted the continuation of the major denominational emphasis of Bold Mission Thrust for 1985-90. Bold Mission Thrust is an effort to enable every person in the world to have opportunity to hear and to respond to the Gospel of Christ by the year 2000.

Churches: 37,517; Inclusive Membership: 14,812,844; Sunday or Sabbath Schools: 36,211; Total Enrollment: 7,905,239; Ordained Clergy: 63,625

GENERAL ORGANIZATION

Convention: annual

Pres., C. Jerry Vines, First Baptist Church, 124 W. Ashley St., Jacksonville, FL 32202. Rec Sec., Martin B. Bradley, 127 9th Ave., N., Nashville, TN 37234.
Executive Committee: Offices, 901 Commerce, Nashville TN 37203. Tel. (615) 244-2355; Pres., Harold C. Bennett; Exec. Vice-Pres., Ernest E. Mosley; Vice-Pres., Business & Finance, Tim Hedquist; Vice-Pres., Public Relations, Alvin C. Shackleford.

GENERAL BOARDS AND COMMISSIONS

Foreign Mission Board: Box 6767, Richmond, VA 23230. Tel. (804) 353-0151. Pres., R. Keith Parks
Home Mission Board: 1350 Spring St., NW, Atlanta, Ga 30367. Tel. (404) 898-7701. Pres., Larry L. Lewis
Annuity Board: P.O. Box 2190, Dallas, TX 75221. Tel. (214) 720-0511. Pres., Darold H. Morgan; Exec. Vice Pres., Harold C. Richardson
Sunday School Board: 127 Ninth Ave., N., Nashville, TN 37234. Tel. (615) 251-2000. Pres., Lloyd Elder; Exec. Vice-Pres., James D. Williams.
Brotherhood Commission: 1548 Poplar Ave., Memphis, TN 38104. Tel. (901) 272-2461. Pres., James H. Smith
Southern Baptist Commission on the American Baptist Theological Seminary: Room 318, 901 Commerce St., Nashville, TN 37203. Tel. (615) 244-2362. Exec. Sec.-Treas., Arthur L. Walker, Jr.; Pres., of the Seminary, Odell McGlothian, Sr.
Christian Life Commission: 901 Commerce St., Nashville, TN 37203. Tel. (615) 244-2495. Exec. Dir., Richard Land
Education Commission; 901 Commerce St., Nashville, TN 37203. Tel. (615) 244-2362. Exec. Sec.-Treas., Arthur L. Walker, Jr.
Historical Commission: 901 Commerce St., Nashville, TN 37203. Tel. (615) 244-0344. Exec. Dir. Treas., Lynn E. May, Jr.; Asst. Exec. Dir., A. Ronald Tonks
The Radio and TV Commission: 6350 West Freeway, Ft. Worth, TX 76150. Tel. (817) 737-4011. Richard T. McCartney, Interim Pres.
Stewardship Commission: 901 Commerce St., Nashville, TN 37203. Tel. (615) 244-2303. Pres., A. R. Fagan; Exec. Vice-Pres., Harry S. Bonner

STATE CONVENTIONS

Alabama, Earl Potts, 2001 E. South Blvd., Montgomery 36198. Tel. (205) 288-2460
Alaska, Bill G. Duncan, 1750 O'Malley Rd., Anchorage 99516. Tel. (907) 344-9627
Arizona, Jack Johnson, 400 West Camelback Rd., Phoenix 85013. Tel. (602) 264-9421
Arkansas, Don Moore, P.O. Box 552, Little Rock 72203. Tel. (501) 376-4791
California, C.B. Hogue, 678 E. Shaw Ave., Fresno 93710. Tel. (Tel. (209) 229-9533
Colorado, Charles Sharp, 7393 So. Alton Way, Englewood 80112. Tel. (303) 771-2480
District of Columbia, James Langley, 1628 16th St. NW, Washington 20009. Tel. (202) 265-1526
Florida, John Sullivan, 1230 Hendricks Ave., Jacksonville 32207. Tel. (904) 396-2351
Georgia, James N. Griffith, 2930 Flowers Rd., S., Atlanta, GA 30341. Tel. (404) 455-0404
Hawaii, O. W. Efurd, 2042 Vancouver Dr., Honolulu 96822. Tel. (808) 946-9581
Illinois, Maurice Swinford, P.O. Box 19247 Springfield, 62794. Tel. (217) 786-2600
Indiana, Mark Coppenger, 900 N. High School Rd., Indianapolis 46224. Tel. (317) 241-9317
Kansas-Nebraska, R. Rex Lindsay, 5410 W. Seventh St., Topeka 66606. Tel. (913) 273-4880
Kentucky, William W. Marshall, P.O. Box 43433, Middletown 40243. Tel. (502) 245-4101
Louisiana, Mark Short, Box 311, Alexandria 71301. Tel. (318) 448-3402

Maryland/Delaware, Kenneth Lyle, 10255 S. Columbia Rd., Columbia 21064. Tel. (301)290-5290
Michigan, Robert Wilson, 15635 W. 12 Mile Rd., Southfield 48076. Tel. (313) 557-4200
Minnesota-Wisconsin, Otha Winningham, 519 16th St. SE, Rochester, MN 55904. Tel. (507) 282-3636
Mississippi, William W. Causey, P.O. Box 530, Jackson 39205. Tel. (601) 968-3800
Missouri, Donald V. Wideman, 400 E. High, Jefferson City 65101. Tel. (314) 635-7931
Nevada, Ernest B. Myers, 406 California Ave., Reno, NV 89509. Tel. (702)786-0406
New England, James H. Currin, Box 688, 5 Oak Ave., Northboro, MA 01532. Tel. (508) 393-6013
New Mexico, Claude Cone, P.O. Box 485, Albuquerque 87103. Tel. (505) 247-0586
New York, R. Quinn Pugh, 6538 Collamer Dr., East Syracuse, 13057. Tel. (315) 475-6173
North Carolina, Roy J. Smith, 205 Convention Dr., Cary, NC 27511, Tel. (919) 467-5100
Northwest Baptist Convention, Cecil Sims, 1033 N.E. 6th Ave., Portland, OR 97232. Tel. (503) 238-4545
Ohio, Tal Bonham, 1680 E. Broad St., Columbus 43203. Tel. (614) 258-8491
Oklahoma, William G. Tanner, 1141 N. Robinson, Oklahoma City 73103. (405) 236-4341
Pennsylvania-South Jersey, Wallace A. C. Williams, 4620 Fritchey St., Harrisburg 17109. Tel. (717) 652-5856
South Carolina, Ray Rust, 907 Richland St., Columbia 29201. Tel. (803) 765-0030
Tennessee, D. L. Lowrie, P.O. Box 728, Brentwood, 37024. Tel. (615) 373-2255
Texas, William M. Pinson, Jr., 333 N. Washington, Dallas 75246. Tel. (214) 828-5100
Utah-Idaho, C. Clyde Billingsley, Sec., P.O. Box 1039, Sandy, UT 84091. Tel. (801) 255-3565
Virginia, Reginald M. McDonough, P. O. Box 8568, Richmond 23226. Tel. (804)672-8731
West Virginia, Thomas A. Kinchen, 801 Sixth Ave., St. Albans 25177. Tel. (304) 727-2974
Wyoming, John W. Thomason, Box 3074, Casper, 82602. Tel. (307) 472-4087

FELLOWSHIPS

Dakota Southern Baptist Fellowship, Dewey W. Hickey, P.O. Box 7187, Bismarck, ND 58502. Tel. (701)255-3765
Iowa Southern Baptist Fellowship, O. Wyndell Jones, Westview #27, 2400 86th St., Des Moines, IA 50322. Tel. (515)278-1566
Montana Southern Baptist Fellowship, James Nelson, P.O. Box 99, Billings, MT 59103. Tel. (406)252-7537
Canadian Convention of Southern Baptists, Allen Schmidt, Postal Bag 300, Cochrane, Alberta T0L 0W0. Tel. (403)932-5688

PERIODICALS

Accent, P.O. Box 830010, Birmingham, AL 35283 Jan Turrentine, Ed.
Alabama Baptist (w), 3310 Independence Dr., Birmingham, AL 35259. Tel. (205) 870-4720. Hudson Baggett, Ed.
Alaska Baptist Messenger, 1750 O'Malley Rd., Anchorage, AK 99516. Bill G. Duncan, Ed. Tel. (907) 344-9627.
Ambassador Life, 1548 Poplar Ave., Memphis, TN 38104. Tel (901) 272-2461
Arkansas Baptist Newsmagazine (w), P. O. Box 552, Little Rock, AR 72203. Tel. (501) 376-4791. J. Everett Sneed, Ed.
Aware, P.O. Box 830010, Birmingham, AL 35283. Barbara Massey, Ed.

Baptist and Reflector (w), P.O. Box 728, Brentwood, TN 37024. Fletcher Allen, Ed. Tel. (615) 373-2255

Baptist Beacon (w), 400 W. Camelback Rd., Phoenix, AZ 85013. Elizabeth Young, Ed. Tel. (602) 264-9421

Baptist Courier (w), Box 2168, Greenville, SC 29602. John Roberts, Ed. Tel. (803) 232-8736

Baptist Digest (w), 5410 W. 7th, Topeka, KS 66606. John Hopkins, Ed. Tel. (913) 273-4880

Baptist Message (w), Box 311, Alexandria, LA 71309. Lynn Clayton, Ed. Tel. (318) 442-7728

Baptist Messenger (w), 1141, N. Robinson, Oklahoma City, OK 73103. Glenn A. Brown, Ed. Tel. (405) 236-4341

Baptist New Mexican (w), Box 485, Albuquerque, NM 87103. J. B. Fowler, Ed. Tel. (505) 247-0586

Baptist Program, SBC, 901 Commerce St., Nashville, TN 37203. Ernest E. Mosley, Ed. Tel. (615) 244-2355

Baptist Record (w), P.O. Box 530, Jackson, MS 39205. Don McGregor, Ed. Tel. (601) 968-3800

Baptist Standard (w), P.O. Box 660267, Dallas, TX 75266. Tel. (214) 630-4571. Presnall Wood, Ed.

Baptist True Union, 10255 S. Columbia Rd., Columbia, MD 21046. Robert Allen, Ed. Tel. (301)290-5290

Biblical Recorder (w), P.O. Box 26568, Raleigh, N. C. 27611. R. Eugene Puckett, Ed. Tel. (919) 847-2127

California Southern Baptist (w), 678 Shaw Ave., Fresno, CA 93710. Herb Hollinger, Ed. Tel. (209) 229-9533

Capital Baptist, 1628 16th St. NW, Washington, DC 20009. James Langley, Ed. Tel. (202) 265-1526

Christian Index (w), 2930 Flowers Rd., S., Atlanta, GA 30341. Richard Albert Mohler, Jr., Ed. Tel. (404) 455-0404

Commission, The, Box 6767, Richmond, VA 23230. Leland F. Webb, Ed.

Contempo, P.O. Box 830010, Birmingham, AL 35283. Diana Woodcock, Ed.

Discovery, P.O. 830010, Birmingham, AL 35283. Mrs. Barbara Massey, Ed.

Florida Baptist Witness (w), 1230 Hendricks Ave., Jacksonville, FL 32207. Jack Brymer, Ed. Tel. (904) 396-2351

Hawaii Baptist, 2042 Vancouver Dr., Honolulu 96822. O. W. Efurd, Ed. Tel. (808) 946-9581

Illinois Baptist (w), P.O. Box 19247, Springfield, 62794. Bill Webb, Ed. Tel. (217) 786-2600

Indiana Baptist (m), P.O. Box 24189, Indianapolis, IN 46224. Gary Ledbetter, Ed. Tel. (317) 241-9317

Michigan Baptist Advocate, 15635 W. Twelve Mile Rd., Southfield MI 48076. Robert Wilson, Ed. Tel. (313) 557-4200

Minnesota-Wisconsin Southern Baptist, 519 16th St. SE, Rochester, MN 55904 Mrs. Louise Winningham, Ed. Tel. (507)282-3636

Missions USA, 1350 Spring St. NW, Atlanta, GA 30367. William Junker, Ed. Tel. (404)873-4041.

New York Baptist, 6538 Collamer Rd., East Syracuse, NY 13057 Quentin Lockwood, Jr., Ed. Tel. (315) 433-1001

Northwest Baptist Witness, 1033 NE 6th Ave., Portland, OR 97232, James L. Watters, Ed. Tel. (503) 238-4545

Ohio Baptist Messenger (m), 1680 E. Broad, Columbus, OH 43203. Theo Sommerkamp Ed. Tel. (614) 258-8491

Penn.-Jersey Baptist, 4620 Fritchey St., Harrisburg, PA 17109. Ms. Peggy Masters, Ed. Tel. (717) 652-5856

Quarterly Review (q), 127 Ninth Ave. N., Nashville, TN 37234. Linda S. Barr, Ed. Tel. (615) 251-2000

Religious Herald (w), P.O. Box 8377, Richmond, VA 23226. Julian Pentecost, Ed. Tel. (804) 672-1973

Review and Expositor (q), 2825 Lexington Rd., Louisville, KY 40280. Tel. (502) 879-4011

Rocky Mountain Baptist, 7393 S. Alton Way, Englewood, CO 80112. Charles Sharp, Ed. Tel. (303) 771-2480

Royal Service, P.O. Box 830010, Birmingham, AL 35283. Edna M. Ellison, Ed.

Southwestern News, P.O. Box 22000, Seminary Hill, Fort Worth, TX 76122. John Seelig, Ed.

Start, P.O. Box 830010, Birmingham, AL 35283. Kathryn W. Kizer, Ed.

Utah-Idaho Southern Baptist Witness, P.O. Box 1039, Salt Lake City, UT 84091. C. Clyde Billingsley, Ed. Tel. (801) 255-3565

Western Recorder (w), Box 43401, Middletown, KY 40243. _____, Ed. Tel. (502) 245-4101

West Virginia Southern Baptist, 801 Sixth Ave., St. Albans, WV 25177. Jackson C. Walls, Ed. Tel. (304) 727-2974

Word and Way (w), 400 E. High, Jefferson City, MO 65101. Bob Terry, Ed. Tel. (314) 635-7931

Southern Methodist Church

Organized in 1939, this body is composed of congregations desirous of continuing in true Methodism and preserving the fundamental doctrines and beliefs of the Methodist Episcopal Church, South that declined to be a party to the merger of the Methodist Episcopal Church, The Methodist Episcopal Church, South, and the Methodist Protestant Church into The Methodist Church.

GENERAL ORGANIZATION

General Conference: quadrennial (next meeting, May 1990)

Annual Conferences: (1) The Carolinas-Virginia Conference; (2) Alabama-Florida-Georgia Conference; (3) Mid-South Conference (Mississippi, Tennessee); (4) South-Western Conference (Arkansas, Louisiana, Texas)

OFFICERS

Pres., Rev. W. Lynn Corbett, P.O. Drawer A, Orangeburg, SC 29116. Tel. (803) 536-1378

Vice-Presidents:

The Carolinas-Virginia Conf., Rev. Richard G. Blank, P. O. Box 233, Turbeville, SC 29162

Alabama-Florida-Georgia Conf., Rev. James H. O'Neal, 503 Sheffield Dr., Augusta, GA 30909

Mid-South Conf., Rev. Dr. Ronald R. Carrier, P. O. Box 150002, Nashville, TN 37215

Southwestern Conf., Rev. Arthur P. Meacham, 6011 Fairfield Ave., Shreveport, LA 71106

Treas., Gen. Conference, Rev. Patrick F. Endicott, P.O. Drawer A, Orangeburg, SC 29116

PERIODICAL

The Southern Methodist (m), P.O. Drawer A, Orangeburg, SC 29116

Sovereign Grace Baptists

The Sovereign Grace Baptists are a contemporary movement which began its stirrings in the mid-1950's when some pastors in traditional Baptist churches returned to a Calvinist theological perspective. But this upsurge of Calvinism among present-day Baptists is simply a return to what many Baptists used to believe.

The first "Sovereign Grace" conference was held in Ashland, KY in 1954 and since then conferences of this sort have been sponsored by various local churches on the West Coast, Southern and Northern states, and Canada.

This movement is a spontaneous phenomenon concerning reformation at the local church level. Consequently, there is no interest in establishing a Reformed Baptist "Convention" or "Denomination." Part of the oneness of doctrine of the Sovereign Grace Baptists is the conviction that each local church is to administer the keys to the kingdom. Thus any ecclesiastical structure above the local church is ruled out.

Most Sovereign Grace Baptists, formally or informally relate to the *First London* (1646), *Second London* (1689), or *Philadelphia* (1742) Confessions. Baptists who relate to these Confessions differ from other "Calvinistic" Baptists who either deny the necessity of preaching to all men (most Primitive Baptists and other hyper-Calvinists), or hold to a "Baptist succession" concept of the church (Landmark Baptists).

There is a wide variety of local church government in this movement. Many Calvinist Baptists have or desire a plurality of elders in each assembly. These elders are responsible for the spiritual oversight of the church. Deacons are primarily responsible to take care of the financial and physical needs of the flock. Other Sovereign Grace Baptists, however, prefer to function with one pastor and several deacons.

Membership procedures vary from church to church but all would require a credible profession of faith in Christ, and proper Baptism as a basis for membership.

Calvinistic Baptists financially support gospel efforts (missionaries, pastors of small churches at home and abroad, literature publication and distribution, radio programs, etc.) in various parts of the world. Some local churches have institutional training programs, advanced Bible studies, and Christian schools.

Churches: 275 Inclusive Membership: 2,600 Sunday or Sabbath Schools: 250; Total Enrollment: 1,900; Ordained Clergy: 275

GENERAL ORGANIZATION

Correspondent: Pastor Jon Zens, P. O. Box 548, St. Croix Falls, WI 54024

PERIODICALS

Searching Together, P.O. Box 548, St. Croix Falls, WI 54024.
Reformation Today (bi-m), 2817 Dashwood St., Lakewood, CA 90712. Erroll Hulse, Ed.

Syrian Orthodox Church of Antioch (Archdiocese of the United States and Canada)

An archdiocese in North America of the Syrian Orthodox Church of Antioch. The Syrian Orthodox Church, composed of several archdioceses, numerous parishes, schools and seminaries, professes the faith of the first three Ecumenical Councils of Nicaea, Constantinople, Ephesus, and numbers faithful in the Middle East, India, the Americas, Europe and Australia. The Church traces its origin to the Patriarchate established in Antioch by St. Peter the Apostle and is under the supreme ecclesiastical jurisdiction of His Holiness the Syrian Orthodox Patriarch of Antioch and All the East, now residing in Damascus, Syria.

The first Syrian Orthodox faithful came to North America during the late 1800's, and by 1907 the first Syrian Orthodox priest was ordained to tend to the community's spiritual needs. In 1949, His Eminence Archbishop Mar Athanasius Y. Samuel came to America and was soon appointed Patriarchal Vicar.

There are 21 official archdiocesan parishes in the United States located in California, Maryland, Georgia, Illinois, Massachusetts, Michigan, New Jersey, New York, Oklahoma, Oregon, Pennsylvania, Rhode Island and Texas. In Canada, there are 5 official parishes three in the Province of Ontario and two in the Province of Quebec.

Churches: 28; Inclusive Membership: 30,000; Sunday or Sabbath Schools: N.R.; Total Enrollment: N.R.; Ordained Clergy: 25

ORGANIZATION

Archdiocese of the U.S. and Canada, 49 Kipp Ave., Lodi, NJ 07644. Tel. (201)778-0638
Archdiocesan Convention: Annual

OFFICERS

Primate: Archbishop MarAthanasius Y. Samuel, 49 Kipp Ave., Lodi, NJ 07644. Tel. (201)778-0638

Archdiocesan Gen. Sec., Very Rev. Chorepiscopus John Meno, 45 Fairmount Ave., Hackensack, NJ 07601. Tel. (201)646-9443

Triumph the Church and Kingdom of God in Christ (International)

This church was given through the wisdom and knowledge of God himself to the Late Apostle Elias Dempsey Smith, on October 20, 1897, at 12:00 noon in Issaquena, County, Mississippi, while he was pastor of a Methodist church.

The Triumph Church, as this body is more commonly known, was founded in 1902, its doors opened in 1904, and confirmed in Birmingham, Alabama, with 225 members in 1915. It was incorporated in Washington, DC, 1918 and currently operates in 31 states and overseas. The General Church is divided into 18 districts including the Africa District.

Triumphant doctrine and philosophy is based on the following concepts and principles: Life, Truth and Knowledge; God in man, and being expressed through man; Manifested Wisdom; Complete and Full Understanding; Constant New Revelations. Its concepts and methods of teaching "the second coming of Christ" are based on these and all other attributes of goodness.

Triumphians put strong emphasis on the fact that God is the God of the living, and not the God of the dead.

GENERAL ORGANIZATION

Quarterly and Annual Conferences, International Religious Congress: quadrennial
Headquarters: 213 Farrington Ave., S.E., Atlanta,GA 30315

OFFICERS

Chief Bishop, Rt. Rev. A. J. Scott, 1323 N. 36th St., Savannah, GA 31404. Tel. (912)236-2877
Chspn. of Bd. of Trustees, Bishop C. W. Drumond, 7114 Idlewild, Pittsburgh, PA 15208. Tel. (412)731-2286
Nat. Gen. Rec. Sec., Bishop C. H. Whittaker, 9200 Miles Ave., Cleveland, OH 44105.

True (Old Calendar) Orthodox Church of Greece (Synod of Metropolitan Cyprian), American Exarchate

The American Exarchate of the True (Old Calendar) Orthodox Church of Greece adheres to the tenets of the Eastern Orthodox Church, which considers itself the legitimate heir of the historical Apostolic Church.

When the Orthodox Church of Greece, the official state Church, adopted the New or Gregorian Calendar in 1924, many felt that this breach with tradition compromised the Church's festal calendar, which is based on the Old or Julian calendar, and its unity with world Orthodoxy. A resistance movement to the reform culminated in 1935 when three State Church Bishops returned to the Old Calendar and established a Synod in Resistance, The True Orthodox Church of Greece. When the last of these Bishops died, the Russian Orthodox Church Abroad consecrated a new hierarchy for the Greek Old Calendarists and, in 1969, declared them a sister Church.

In the face of persecution by the state Church, some Old Calendarists denied the validity of the Mother Church of Greece and formed into two Synods, now under the direction of Archbishop Chrysostomos of Athens and Archbishop Andreas of Athens. A moderate faction under Metropolitan Cyprian of Oropos and Fili does not maintain communion with what it considers the ailing Mother Church of Greece, but recognizes its validity and seeks for a restoration of unity between the Old and New Calendarist factions by a return to the Julian Calendar and traditional ecclesiastical polity by the State Church. About two million Orthodox Greeks belong to the Old Calendar Church.

The first Old Calendarist communities in the U.S. were formed in the 1930s. There are about twenty thousand Old Calendarist Greeks in America, unevenly distributed among the Exarchates of the three Greek Synods. The Exarchate under Metropolitan Cyprian, headed by a Princeton-educated, former university professor, was established in 1986 and has attracted large numbers of the Faithful. Placing emphasis on clergy education, youth programs, and recognition of the Old Calendarist minority in American Orthodoxy, the Exarchate has encouraged the establishment of monastic communities and missions. Cordial contacts with the New Calendarist and other Orthodox communities are encouraged at the parish and administrative levels. A center for theological training and Patristic studies has been established at the Exarchate headquarters in Etna, California.

Churches: 7; Inclusive Membership: 1,100; Sunday or Sabbath Schools: None; Total Enrollment: None; Ordained Clergy: 13

GENERAL ORGANIZATION
Exarchate Headquarters: St. Gregory Palamas Monastery, P. O. Box 398, Etna, CA 96027. Tel. (916) 467-3228

OFFICERS
Synodal Exarch in America, His Grace Bishop Chrysostomos, P. O. Box 398, Etna, CA 96027
Dean of Exarchate, The Rev. James P. Thornton, P. O. Box 2833, Garden Grove, CA 92642

PERIODICALS
Orthodox Tradition (3/yr), Center for Traditionalist Orthodox Studies, Etna, CA 96027, Hieromonk Fr. Auxentios, Ed.
The Orthodox Path (bi-m), Convent of St. Elizabeth the Grand Dutchess, P. O. Box 126, Etna, CA. Mo. Elizabeth and Rev. James Thornton, Eds.

Ukrainian Orthodox Church of the U.S.A.
Formally organized in U.S.A. in 1919. Archbishop John Theodorovich arrived from Ukraine in 1924.

GENERAL ORGANIZATION
The Sobor, which elects a Council of Bishops, meets every three years. Next Sobor, 1991
Headquarters: P.O. Box 495, South Bound Brook, NJ 08880. Tel. (201) 356-0090

OFFICERS
Metropolitan: Most Rev. Mstyslav S. Skrypnyk, P.O. Box 495, South Bound Brook, NJ 08880; Archbishop Constantine Buggan, 15157 Waterman Dr., S., Holland IL 60473; Bishop Antony, 4 Von Steuben Lane, South Bound Brook, NJ 08880
Consistory: Pres., V. Rev. William Diakiw; Vice-Pres., V. Rev. Nestor Kowal; Sec., V. Rev. Mykola Haeta; Treas., V. Rev. Taras Chubenko

PERIODICAL
Ukrainian Orthodox Word, English and Ukrainian editions, P.O. Box 495, South Bound Brook, NJ 08880

Ukrainian Orthodox Church in America (Ecumenical Patriarchate)
This body was organized in America in 1928, when the first convention was held. In 1932 Dr. Joseph Zuk was consecrated as first Bishop. His successor was the Most Rev. Bishop Bohdan, Primate, who was consecrated by the order of the Ecumenical Patriarchate of Constantinople on February 28, 1937, in New York City. He was succeeded by the Most Rev. Metropolitan Andrei Kuschak, consecrated by the blessing of Ecumenical Patriarch by Archbishop Iakovos, Metropolitan Germanos and Bishop Silas of Greek-Orthodox Church, on January 26, 1967. His successor is Bishop Vsevolod, ordained on September 27, 1987 by Archbishop Iakovos, Metropolitan Silas and Bishops Philip and Athenagoras.

GENERAL ORGANIZATION
Sobor meets every 4 years.
Headquarters: St. Andrew's Ukrainian Orthodox Diocese, 90-34 139th St., Jamaica, NY 11435. Tel. (718) 297-2407

OFFICERS
Primate: Most Rev. Bishop Vsevolod
Administrator for Canada: Rt. Rev. Michael Pawlyskyn
Sec.: Rt. Rev. Ivan Tkaczuk
Members of Consistory: Rt. Rev. Michael Pawlyskyn, Dr. George Hordy, Ms. Dorothy Hordy, Mike Fedorak and Anatole Ohijenko

PERIODICAL
Ukrainian Orthodox Herald (q), Fr. Ivan Tkaczuk, Ed.

Unitarian Universalist Association
The Unitarian Universalist Association is the consolidated body of the former American Unitarian Association and the Universalist Church of America. The Unitarian movement arose in congregationalism in the 18th century, producing the American Unitarian Association in 1825. In 1865 a national conference was organized. The philosophy of Universalism originated with the doctrine of universal salvation in the first century, and was brought to America in the 18th century. Universalists were first formally organized in 1793. In May, 1961, the Unitarian and Universalist bodies were consolidated to become the Unitarian Universalist Association. The movement is noncreedal. The UUA has observer status with the National Council of Churches.

Churches: 956; Inclusive Membership: 178,623; Sunday or Sabbath Schools: 830; Total Enrollment: 46,242; Ordained Clergy: 1,140

GENERAL ORGANIZATION
General Assembly: annual
Headquarters: 25 Beacon St., Boston, MA 02108. Tel. (617) 742-2100. District offices, 23 in number

OFFICERS
Pres., Rev. William F. Schulz
Exec. Vice-Pres., Kathleen C. Montgomery
Mod., Natalie W. Gulbrandsen
Sec., Barry Johnson-Fay
Treas., David E. Provost
Financial Advisor, Arnold W. Bradburd

OTHER ORGANIZATIONS
(Address unless otherwise noted, 25 Beacon St., Boston, MA 02108)
Unitarian Universalist Ministers' Association: Pres., Rev. Carolyn Owen-Towle
Unitarian Universalist Women's Federation: Pres., Phyllis Rickter
Young Religious Unitarian Universalists (YRUU): Contact, Meg Riley
Unitarian Universalist Service Committee, Inc.: 78 Beacon St., Boston, MA 02108. Exec. Dir., Dr. Richard Scobie
Unitarian Universalist Historical Society, Pres., Rev. Janet Bowering
Church of the Larger Fellowship: Rev. O. Eugene Pickett
Beacon Press, Dir., Wendy Strothman

The World (6/yr), Ms. Linda C. Beyer, Ed., 25 Beacon St., Boston, MA 02108

United Brethren in Christ

The Church of the United Brethren in Christ had its beginning with Philip William Otterbein and Martin Boehm, who were leaders in the revivalistic movement in Pennsylvania and Maryland during the late 1760s and which continued into the early 1800s.

On September 25, 1800, they and others associated with them, formed a society under the name of United Brethren in Christ. Subsequent conferences adopted a Confession of Faith in 1815 and a constitution in 1841. The Church of the United Brethren in Christ adheres to the original constitution as amended in 1957, 1961 and 1977.

GENERAL ORGANIZATION

General Conference, quadrennial (next meeting, 1989) Headquarters: 302 Lake St., Huntington, IN 46750. Tel. (219) 356-2312

OFFICERS

Bishops: Chpsn., C. Ray Miller, Clarence A. Kopp, Jr., Jerry Datema
Gen. Treas./Office Mgr., Marda J. Hoffman
Dir., Dept. of Education, Dr. Eugene Habecker
Dir., Dept. of Church Services, Rev. Paul Hirschy

PERIODICAL

The United Brethren (m), Huntington, IN 46750, Steve Dennie, Ed.

United Christian Church

The United Christian Church originated during the period of the Civil War or shortly thereafter, about 1864 or 1865. There were some ministers and laymen in the United Brethren in Christ Church who were in disagreement with the position and practice of the church on issues such as infant baptism, voluntary bearing of arms and belonging to oath bound secret combinations. It was this group which formed a nucleus developing into United Christian Church, organized at a conference held in Campbelltown, Pa., on May 9, 1877, and given its name by a conference held January 1, 1878.

The principal founders of the denomination were George Hoffman, John Stamn, and Thomas Lesher. Hoffman appears to have been predominant because before they were organized, they were called Hoffmanites.

The United Christian Church has district conferences, a general conference held yearly, a general board of trustees, a mission board, a board of directors of the United Christian Church Home, a campmeeting board, a young peoples board, and has local organized congregations.

It believes in the Holy Trinity, the inspired Holy Scriptures with the doctrines they teach, and practices the ordinances of Baptism, Holy Communion, and Foot Washing.

It welcomes all into its fold who are born again, believe in Jesus Christ our Savior and Lord, and who have received the Holy Spirit and, therefore, are a part of the Church of Jesus Christ, or His Body.

GENERAL ORGANIZATION

General Conference: annual (3rd Saturday in March)

OFFICERS

Mod., Elder John Ludwig, Jr., 528 W. Walnut St., Cleona, PA 17042
Presiding Elder, Elder Henry C. Heagy, 2080 S. White Oak St., Lebanon, PA 17042
Conf. Sec., Elder David W. Heagy, 2080 S. White Oak St., Lebanon, PA 17042

OTHER ORGANIZATIONS

Mission Board: Pres., Elder John P. Ludwig, Jr., 528 W. Walnut St., Cleona, PA 17042; Sec., Elder Walter Knight, Jr., Rt. #1, Box 98, Palmyra, PA 17078; Treas., Elder Henry C. Heagy, Rt. 4, Box 100, Lebanon, PA 17042

United Church of Christ

The United Church of Christ was duly constituted on June 25, 1957 by the regularly chosen representatives of the Congregational Christian Churches and of the Evangelical and Reformed Church, in a Uniting General Synod held in Cleveland, Ohio.

The Preamble to the Constitution states the denomination's theological base in the following words: "The United Church of Christ acknowledges as its sole head, Jesus Christ, the Son of God and Saviour. It acknowledges as kindred in Christ all who share in this confession. It looks to the Word of God in the Scriptures, and to the presence and power of the Holy Spirit, to prosper its creative and redemptive work in the world. It claims as its own the faith of the historic Church expressed in the ancient creeds and reclaimed in the basic insights of the Protestant Reformers. It affirms the responsibility of the Church in each generation to make this faith its own in reality of worship, in honesty of thought and expression, and in purity of heart before God. In accordance with the teaching of our Lord and the practice prevailing among evangelical Christians, it recognizes two sacraments: Baptism and the Lord's Supper or Holy Communion."

The creation of the United Church of Christ brought together four unique traditions from the rich and diverse history of Christian experience:

(1) The Congregational Way first achieved prominence among English Protestants during the civil war of the 1640s, groundwork for the Congregational form having been laid by Calvinist Puritans and Separatists during the half-century preceding. Opposition to state control of their religious worship promoted followers of the Congregational form to emigrate to America, where an active part in colonizing New England occupied their energies throughout the 17th century. Since then, Congregationalists (self-consciously a denomination from the middle of the 19th century) have made strong contributions to the religious, civil, educational and secular dimensions of American institutions and culture.

(2) The Christian Churches originated as a restorationist movement in several parts of the U.S. late in the 18th century. Throughout their history the Christians emphasized Christ as the only head of the church, the New Testament as their only rule of faith, and "Christian" as their sole name. Unitive in spirit, this loosely organized denomination eventually found in the Congregational Churches a like disposition, and in 1931, the two bodies formally united as the Congregational Christian Churches.

(3) The German Reformed Church comprised an irenic aspect of the Protestant Reformation, as a second generation of Reformers drew on the insights of Zwingli, Luther and Calvin to formulate the Heidelberg Catechism of 1563. This confession of faith proved to be a unifying force, first in the German Palatinate, and then in other German lands. People of the German Reformed Church began immigrating to the New World early in the 18th century, and settlement in the middle Atlantic colonies saw the heaviest concentration locating in Pennsylvania. Independence from European supervision and the formal organization of the American denomination were completed in 1793. Succeeding years saw the church spreading across the country, and in the Mercersburg Movement, developing a strong emphasis on evangelical catholicity and Christian unity.

(4) By the opening of the 19th century in Germany,

Enlightenment criticism and Pietist inwardness had worked a marked decrease in long-standing conflicts between religious groups. The change was signalized in Prussia by a royal proclamation which merged Lutheran and Reformed people of the realm into one United Evangelical Church (1817). Members of this new church way migrated to America just as earlier German migrants were moving west. The Evangelicals settled in large numbers in Missouri and Illinois, there continuing their noncontroversial emphasis on pietistic devotion and unionism; in 1840 they formed the German Evangelical Church Society in the West. Union with other Evangelical church associations further expanded the movement's membership until in 1877 it took the name of the German Evangelical Synod of North America.

On June 25, 1934, this Synod and the Reformed Church in the U.S. (formerly the German Reformed Church) united to form the Evangelical and Reformed Church. In both groups the German ethnic traits had lost their influence as the Evangelical and Reformed Church entered the mainstream of American church life. In the formation of the Evangelical and Reformed Church there is a singular blend of the Reformed tradition's passion for the unity of the church and the Evangelical tradition's commitment to the liberty of conscience inherent in the gospel. These accents were critically important for the utilization of the spirit and ethos of the ecumenical movement of that time.

Churches: 6,362; Inclusive Membership: 1,644,787; Sunday or Sabbath Schools: 6,395; Total Enrollment: 437,-836; Ordained Clergy: 10,145

GENERAL ORGANIZATION

Synod: biennial
Headquarters: 700 Prospect Ave., E., Cleveland, OH 44115 Tel. (216)736-2100

OFFICERS

Pres., Rev. Paul H. Sherry
Sec., Rev. Carol Joyce Brun
Dir. of Finance & Treas., Rev. Doris R. Powell
Exec. Assoc. to the Pres., Ms. Bernice Powell
Asst. to Pres. for Planning & Correlation, _____.
Affirmative Action Officer, _____.
Chpsn. Exec. Council, Ms. Juanita J. Helphrey
V-Chpsn., Mr. Douglas S. Hatfield
Mod., Mrs. Charlotte P. Gosselink
Asst. Mod., Mr. Franklin W. Thomas
Asst. Mod., Mr. John Rogers

ORGANIZATIONS

UNITED CHURCH BOARD FOR WORLD MINISTRIES: Offices, 475 Riverside Dr., New York, NY 10115. Tel. (212) 870-2637; 14 Beacon St., Boston, MA 02108; 1400 N. 7th St., Ste. E, St., Louis, MO 63106; Exec. Vice Pres., Rev. Scott S. Libbey
Planning, Correlation, and Administration Unit: Gen. Sec., Rev. Scott S. Libbey; Assoc. for Planning and Admn., Rev. Bertrice Y. Wood; Personnel Mgr., Ms. Rita E. Maslanek
Mission Program Unit: Gen.Sec., Rev. Daniel F. Romero; Assoc. Gen. Sec., Rev. Lloyd Van Vactor; Regional Sec., Africa, Rev. Bonganvala Goba; Europe, Rev. Kenneth R. Ziebell; East Asia, Dr. Ching-fen Hsiao; Latin Amer./Carrib., Rev. David A. Vargas; Assoc. to Exec. Dir., Ms. Carmen A. Nebot; Middle East, Dr. Dale L. Bishop; Southern Asia Rev. Eric A. Gass; Southern Asia and Mission Assoc., _____; World Service Sec., Rev. Gustav H. Kuether; Overseas Pers. Sec., Rev. Elinor G. Galusha; Adm., Refugee Resettlement, Ms. Mary K. Kuenning; Adm. Child Sponsorship, Ms. Mercy Poulard ; Sec. for World Issues; Rev. Audrey C. Chapman; Assoc. for World Issues, Rev.

Kenneth R. Ziebell; Sec. for Mission Edu. and Interpretation, Ms. Sandra J. Rooney.
Support Services Unit: Treas. and Gen. Sec., Rev. Myles Walburn; Assoc. Treas., Mr. Bruce C. Foresman; Mngr. of Financial Services, Ms. Dorothy E. Teffeau; Mngr. Compr. Services, _____; Mngr. Bus. Services, Ms. Arlene Yellen.
UNITED CHURCH BOARD FOR HOMELAND MINISTRIES: 475 Riverside Dr., New York, NY 10115. Tel. (212)2100; Fax: (212)870-2106.
Office of Exec. Vice-Pres., Exec. Vice-Pres., Rev. Charles Shelby Rooks; Gen. Sec. Rev. Robert P. Noble, Jr.; Sec. for Admn., Mr. Nils E. Forstner; Sec. for Res. and Eval., Ms. Marjorie H. Royle; Sec. for Information Services, Ms. Sheila Kelly; Coord. Special Mission Emphases, Rev. Theodore H. Erickson; Communications Asst., Ms. Alberta Colbert; Clk. of the Bd. of Dirs., Ms. Amy Yoshinaga; Business Mgr., Ms. Mitzie Wang; Personnel Mgr., Ms. Angela McCray
Office of the Treasurer, Treas., Mr. Richard H. Dubie; Asst. Treas., Mr. Raymond J. Healy; Asst. Treas., Ms. Norma Robinson; Asst. Treas., Mr. Osborne Nichols; Asst. Treas., Ms. Patricia Rossi; Asst. Treas., Mr. Donald Hart; Corp. Social Responsibility Officer, Rev. Wayne Owens
Division of Education and Publication, Gen. Sec., Rev. Ansley Coe Throckmorton; Sec. Educ. in Parish Community, Rev. Thomas Carson; Sec. for Higher Ed. and Higher Prog. Resources, Rev. Verlyn L. Baker; Sec. for Youth Ed. and Ministries Resources, _____ _; Sec. for Childhood Ed. and Ministries Resources, Ms. Patricia J. Goldberg; Sec. for Publication, Rev. Larry E. Kalp; Sec. for Higher Ed. Relationships, Rev. James A. Smith, Jr.; Sec. Educ. in Local Church, Rev. Wilma Milagros Machin Vazquez; Sec. for Young Adult Ed. and Ministries Resources, Rev. Gordon J. Svoboda; Sec. for Curriculum Services, Rev. Morris D. Pike; Sec. for Racial and Ethnic Educational Ministries, Rev. Barbara J. Essex; Business Mgr., Publications Operations, Mr. Bill L. Shaw; Coord. of Church-College Relationships, Rev. Susan Newman Hopkins.
Division of Evangelism and Local Church Development, Gen. Sec., Rev. Robert L. Burt; Sec. for Evangelism & Membership Growth, Rev. Martha M. Swan; Sec. for Local Church Capital Development, Rev. Robert F. Haskins, Jr.; Sec. for Evangelism and Membership Growth, Rev. R. Alan Johnson; Sec. for Church Bldg., Mr. John R. Potts; Sec. for Ethnic and Minority Church Development, Rev. Henry T. Simmons; Sec. for Development, Rev. John W. Mingus; Sec. for Local Church Finance Advisory Services, Ms. Beatrice H. Starrett, Rev. P. William VanderWyden; Consultant, Rev. Gary L. Miller; Telecommunication Associates, Ms. Karin Stock-Whitson, Mr. Charles Whitson.
Division of American Missionary Association, Co-Gen. Sec., Rev. L. William Eichhorn; Co-Gen. Sec., Rev. B. Ann Eichhorn; Sec., Special Program and Services, Mr. Carl A. Bade; Sec., Local Churches and Community Mission, Rev. Paul R. Peters; Sec. AIDS Prog./Min., Rev. William R. Johnson; Sec., Human Devel. Programs and Concerns, Ms. Faith A. Johnson; Sec., Health and Welfare Program and Concerns, Mr. James A. McDaniel; Sec., Public Issues in Education, Ms. Nanette M. Roberts; Sec., Ministries to Special Groups, Rev. Alphonso A. Roman; Sec., Social and Racial Justice Programs, Rev. Marilyn A. Moore; Sec., Citizen Empowerment, _____; Dir. U.C.C. Hunger Prog., Rev. Steven Nunn-Miller
COMMISSION FOR RACIAL JUSTICE: 700 Prospect Ave., East, Cleveland, OH 44115; Office for Urban and National Racial Justice, 5113 Georgia Ave., NW, Washington, DC 20011. Tel. (202)291-1593; Office for Constituency Dev./Rural Racial Justice, P.O. Box 187,

Enfield, NC 27823, Tel. (919)437-1723; Office for Ecumenical/Int'l. Racial Justice, 475 Riverside Dr. NY, NY 10115, Tel. (212)870-2076; Exec. Dir., Rev. Benjamin F. Chavis, Jr. (OH); Exec. Asst., Ms. Pat DeLeon (OH) (216)736-2161; Dir. Washington DC Office, Ms. Toni A. Killings; Director, North Carolina Office, Rev. Vivian L. Lynn; Assoc. for Constituency Dev., Ms. Margaret Ellis (NC); Program Asst. (NC), Rev. Collins Kornegay; Assoc. for National Mission Interpretation, Rev. Leon White (OH); Assoc. for Research, Mr. Charles Lee (NY); Nat'l. Assoc. for Fiscal & Office Mgmt., Ms. Andrea Gibbs (OH); COUNCIL FOR AMERICAN INDIAN MINISTRY: 122 W. Franklin Ave., Rm. 300, Minneapolis, MN 55405. Interim Dir., Rev. Benjamin C. L. Crosby; Exec. Asst., Ms. Jackie Owen

COUNCIL FOR HEALTH AND HUMAN SERVICE MINISTRIES: 543 College Ave., Lancaster, PA 17603. Tel. (717)299-9945 (outside Penna., (800)844-4476). Exec. & Program Office: Exec. Dir., Rev. J. Robert Achtermann; Prog. Assoc., Ms. Cynthia S. Bumb; Prog. Consultant, Rev. Robert M. Glasgow; Assoc. Membership Recruitment, Rev. Paul P. Hass; Computer Services, Ms. Leslie J. Solove; Controller, Ms. Christine Gable

COORDINATING CENTER FOR WOMEN IN CHURCH AND SOCIETY: 700 Prospect Ave., East, Cleveland, OH 44115. Tel. (216)736-2150. Exec. Dir. Ms. Marilyn M. Brietling; Adm. Asst. to Exec. Dir., Ms. Deborah Walker; Assoc. for Constituency and Program Development, Rev. Leslie C. Taylor; Ed. Common Lot, Ms. Karen Roller (interim); Assoc. for Communication, Advocacy and Leadership Development, Rev. Mary Miller Brueggemann (interim)

OFFICE FOR CHURCH IN SOCIETY: 700 Prospect Ave., East, Cleveland, OH 44115; 110 Maryland Ave., N.E., Washington, DC 20002; Exec. Dir., _____ (OH); Assoc. for Church Empowerment, Rev. Charles McCollough (DC); Rev. Dale Edmunds (DC); Consultant, Black Ecu. Advocacy Network; Mr. Faith Evans (DC); Assoc. for Communications, _____, (DC); Dir., Washington, DC Office, Rev. James E. Lintner; Assoc. Policy Advocacy, Mr. James Wetekan, (DC); Rev. Patrick Conover (DC), Exec. Dir., Ms.Verna Rapp Uthman (OH); Consultant, ANIN/AIDS Ministry (DC), Rev. Ken South

OFFICE FOR CHURCH LIFE AND LEADERSHIP: 700 Prospect Ave., East, Cleveland, OH 44115. Exec. Dir., Rev. William A. Hulteen, Jr. (OH); Exec. Assoc., Rev. Thomas R. Tupper (OH); Assoc. Great Lakes Region, Rev. Charlotte H. Still (OH); Assoc., Middle Atlantic Region, Rev. Felix Carrion; Assoc. Southern Region, Rev. Ervin Milton, P. O. Box l658, Graham, NC 27253; Assoc. West Central Region, Peter Monkries; Assoc. Western Region, _____, 20 Woodside Ave., San Francisco, CA; Assoc. (Interim), New England Region, Rev. Ronald G. Kurtz, P. O. Box 915, Harwich, MA 02645; Assoc., Ms. Dorothy M. Lester, P.O. Box 684, Brookings, SD 57006. Assoc. for Media, _____.

OFFICE OF COMMUNICATION: 700 Prospect Ave., East, Cleveland, OH 44115. Tel. (216)736-2222; Fax (216)736-2223; 475 Riverside Dr., Rm. 852, New York, NY 10115. Tel. (212)870-2137. Adm. Asst., Mr. Lee Davenport (OH); Educ./Mkting. Coord., Rev. Eugene A. Schneider (OH); Ed. United Church News, Rev. Evan W. Golder (OH); Ed. Asst., Ms. Charlene Smith (OH); Pub. Rel. Coord., Mr. Hans Holznagel, (OH & NY); Pub. Rel. Asst. (Bios, photos), Ms. Sharon Jefferson (OH); Keeping You Posted, Ms. Martha R. Gotwals (NY); Video, Mr. William, C. Winslow (NY); Writer, Rev. Kathi D. Wolfe (OH); Assoc. for Communication Policy/ Advocacy (DC), Mr. Anthony L. Pharr. Tel. (202)331-4236; Asst. for Communication Policy/Advocacy (Telecommunications Consumer Coalition) (NY), Mr. Andrew Blalau

STEWARDSHIP COUNCIL: 700 Prospect Ave., East, Cleveland, OH 44115; 1400 N. Seventh St., St. Louis, MO 63106; 254 College St., Ste. 501, New Haven, CT 06510; 475 Riverside Dr., Rm. 1950, New York, NY 10115; Exec. Assoc., Rev. Dean O. Warburton; Assoc. for Stewardhsip Program & Admn., United Church Resources, Rev. Jack A. Batton (MO); Consultant for Financial Devl., Rev. Paul E. Baumer, 59 E. Mound St., Columbus, OH 43215. Tel. (615)224-8634; Assoc. for Stewardship Educ., Rev. David L. Beebe (MO); Adm. Assoc., Ms. Ethel M. Benish (CT); Consultant for Special Projects, Rev. Charles W. Cooper, Jr. (OH); Assoc. for Stewardship Communication, Rev. Christopher P. Goering (NY); Assoc. for Stewardship Devel., Ms. Veronica Jefferson (NY); Assoc. for Mission Educ., Mr. Alfred H. Jones (NY); Program Assoc., Rev. C. David Langerhans, 22 Longcourse Ln., Paoli, PA 19301; Managing Ed., Ms. Christina Villa (CT); Southern, Rev. Raymond W. Hargrove, P.O. Box 658, Graham, NC 27253

COMMISSION ON DEVELOPMENT: 475 Riverside Dr., Ste., 1950, New York, NY 10115, Rev. Donald G. Stoner, Dir. Planned Giving, Ms. Stella Schoen, Assoc.

HISTORICAL COUNCIL: 700 Prospect Ave., East, Cleveland, OH 44115. Office of Archivist, Philip Schaff Library, Lancaster Theological Seminary, 555 W. James St., Lancaster, PA 17603

PENSION BOARDS: 475 Riverside Dr., New York, NY 10115. Exec. Vice-Pres., Dr. John Ordway; Admn. Vice-Pres., Mrs. Joan F. Brannick; Treas., Mr. Richard H. Dubie; Sec. Treas., Sec. and Sec. Member Relations, Mr. Edmund G. Tortora; Sec., Benefits, Mr. Frank Patti; Insurance Benefits Mgr., Ms. Darlene Brown; Sec., Ministerial Asst., Rev. Donald E. Stumpf.

UNITED CHURCH FOUNDATION, Inc.: 475 Riverside Dr., New York, NY 10115. Financial Vice Pres. and Treas., Richard H. Dubic.

CONFERENCES

Western Region:
California, Northern, Rev. David J. Jamieson, 20 Woodside Ave.,San Francisco, CA 94127
California, Southern, Rev. Fred P. Register, 466 E. Walnut St., Pasadena, CA 91101
Hawaii, Rev. Norman Jackson, 15 Craigside Pl., Honolulu, HI 96817
Montana/Northern Wyoming, Rev. John M. Schaeffer, 1511 Poly Dr., Billings, MT 59102
Central Pacific, Rev. Donald J. Sevetson, 0245 SW Bancroft St., Portland, OR 97201
Rocky Mountain, Rev. Clyde H. Miller, Jr., 1370 Pennsylvania St., Ste. 420, Denver, CO 80203
Southwest, Rev. Carole G. Keim, 4423 N. 24th St., Ste. 600, Phoenix, AZ 85016
Washington-North Idaho, Rev. W. James Halfaker, 720 14th Ave. E., Seattle, WA 98102

West Central Region:
Iowa, Rev. Donald A. Gall, 600 42nd St., Des Moines, IA 50312
Kansas-Oklahoma, Rev. A. Gayle Engle, 1245 Fabrique, Wichita, KS 67218
Minnesota, Rev. Jeffrey N. Stinehelfer, 122 W. Franklin Ave., Rm. 323, Minneapolis, MN 55404
Missouri, Rev. Don R. Yungclas, (interim), 461 E. Lockwood, Ave., St. Louis, MO 63119
Nebraska, Rev. Clarence M. Higgins, Jr.,, 2055 "E" St., Lincoln, NE 68510
North Dakota, Rev. Jack J. Seville, Jr., 4007 State St., Ste., Bismarck, ND 58501
South Dakota, Rev. Ed Mehlhaff, Ste. B, 801 E. 41st St., Sioux Falls, SD 57105

Great Lakes Region:
Illinois, Rev. W. Sterling Cary, 1840 Westchester Blvd., P.O. Box 7208, Westchester, IL 60154
Illinois South, Rev. Martha Ann Baumer, Box 325 Broadway, Highland, IL 62249

Indiana-Kentucky, Rev. Ralph C. Quellhorst, 1100 W. 42nd St., Indianapolis, IN 46208

Michigan, Rev. Marwood E. Rettig, P.O. Box 1006, East Lansing, MI 48823

Ohio, Rev. Thomas E. Dipko, 41 Croswell Rd., Columbus, OH 43214

Wisconsin, Rev. Frederick R. Trost, 2719 Marshall Ct. Madison, WI 53705

Southern Region:

Florida, Rev. Charles L. Burns Jr., 222 E. Welbourne Ave., Winter Park, FL 32789

South Central, Rev. James Tomasek, Jr., 2704 Rio Grande #8, Austin TX 78705

Southeast, Rev. Rogers Knight, P.O. Box 29883, Atlanta, GA 30359

Southern, Rev. Rollin O. Russell, 2121 Edgewood Ave., P.O. Box 2410, Burlington, NC 27215

Middle Atlantic Region:

Central Atlantic, Rev. Curtis R. Clare, 620 Pershing Dr., Silver Spring, MD 20910

New York, Rev. William Briggs, The Church Center, Rm. 260, 3049 E. Genesee St., Syracuse, NY 13224

Penn Central, Rev. Lyle J. Weible, The United Church Center, Rm. 126, 900 South Arlington Ave., Harrisburg, PA 17109

Penn Northeast, Rev. Donald E. Overlock, 431 Delaware Ave., P.O. Box 177, Palmerton, PA 18071

Pennsylvania Southeast, Rev. Peter Doghramji, 620 Main St., Box G, Collegeville, PA 19426

Penn West, Rev. Paul L. Westcoat, Jr., 320 South Maple Ave., Greensburg, PA 15601

Puerto Rico, Rev. Jaime Rivera-Solero, Box 1013, Hato Rey, PR 00919

New England Region:

Connecticut, Rev. David Y. Hirano, 125 Sherman St., Hartford, CT 06105

Maine, Rev. Otto E. Sommer, 68 Main St., P.O. Box 730, Yarmouth, ME 04096

Massachusetts, Rev. Alfred E. Williams, Jr., P.O. Box 2246, Salem and Badger Rds., Farmingham, MA 01701

New Hampshire, Rev. Carole C. Carlson, Rev. Robert D. Witham, 85 N State St., P.O. Box 465, Concord, NH 03301

Rhode Island, Rev. H. Dahler Hayes, Interchurch Center, 734 Hope St., Providence, RI 02906

Vermont, Rev. D. Curtis Minter, 285 Maple St., Burlington, VT 05401

Nongeographic:

Calvin Synod, Rev. Zoltan D. Szucs, 3036 Glove Ave., Lorain, OH 44055

United Holy Church of America, Inc.

The United Holy Church of America, Inc. is an outgrowth of the great revival that began with the early outpouring of the Holy Ghost on the Day of Pentecost when 120 were filled. The church is built upon the foundation of the Apostles and Prophets, Jesus Christ himself being the chief cornerstone.

It was during this time of revival of repentence, regeneration and holiness of heart and life that swept through the South and West, that the United Holy Church was born. There was no desire on the part of the founding fathers to establish another denomination, but they were pushed out of organized churches because of this experience of holiness and testimony of the Spirit-filled life.

On the first Sunday in May 1886, in Method, NC, a meeting was held that gave birth to what is today known as the United Holy Church of America, Inc. The church was incorporated on September 25, 1918 and its work has steadily grown since that time into a great organization.

Ordinances of baptism by immersion, the Lord's Supper, and feet washing are observed. We accept the premillennial teaching of the Second Coming of Christ, Divine healing—not to the exclusion of medicine, justification by faith, sanctification as a second work of grace, and Spirit baptism.

GENERAL ORGANIZATION

Convocation: All Convocations and General Meetings held at Headquarters.

Headquarters: 5104 Dunstan Rd., Greensboro NC 27405. Tel. (919)621-0669

Mailing Address: 825 Fairoak Ave., Chillum, MD 20783

General Convocation, annually in May

Annual Worker's Conference: October, Greensboro, NC

OFFICERS

Gen. Pres., Bishop Joseph T. Bowens, 825 Fairoak Ave., Chillum, MD 20783. Tel. (301)559-0537

1st Vice-Pres., Bishop Thomas E. Talley, P. O. Box 1035, Portsmouth, VA 23705

2nd Vice-Pres., Bishop Odell McCollum, 3206 Blue Ridge Rd., Columbus, OH 43219

Gen. Rec. Sec., Rev. A. Thomas Godfrey, P.O. Box 7940, Chicago IL 60680

Gen. Fin. Sec., Mrs. Clarice L. Chambers, P.O. Box 3327, Harrisburg, PA 17104

Gen. Asst. Fin. Sec., Mrs. Vera Perkin Houghes, 1054 E. 145th St., Cleveland, OH 44110. Tel. (216)851-7448

Gen. Asst. Rec. Sec., Mrs. Beatrice S. Faison, 224 Wenz Rd., Toledo, OH 43615

Gen. Corresponding Sec., Mrs. Gloria Rainey, 825 Fairoak Ave., Chillum, MD 20783

Gen. Treas., Mrs. Bertha Williams, 4749 Shaw Dr., Wilmington, NC 28401

Gen. Pres., Missionary Dept., Rev. Mrs. Iris C. Fischer, 28 Cooper St., Brooklyn, NY 11207

Gen. Supt., Bible Church School, Mr. C. M. Corbett, 623 Belmont Ave., Youngstown, OH 44520

Gen. Pres., Y.P.H.A. Dept., Elder Dennis Ball, 409 N. Mountain Trail Ave., Sierra Madre, CA 91024

Gen. Education Dept., Dr. Chester Gregory, 1302 Lincoln Woods Dr., Baltimore, MD 21216

Gen. Ushers Dept., Mrs. Shirley Houghes, 1012 Prospect Ave., #401, Cleveland, OH 44115

PERIODICAL

The Holiness Union (m), 2907 Sprucewood Dr., Durham, NC 27707. Mrs. Annie H. Daye, Ed.

The United Methodist Church

The United Methodist Church was formed April 23, 1968 in Dallas, Texas, by the union of The Methodist Church and The Evangelical United Brethren Church. The two churches shared a common historical and spiritual heritage. The Methodist Church resulted in 1939 from the unification of three branches of Methodism—the Methodist Episcopal Church; the Methodist Episcopal Church, South; and the Methodist Protestant Church. The Methodist movement began in 18th-century England under the preaching of John Wesley, but the so-called Christmas Conference of 1784 in Baltimore is regarded as the date on which the organized Methodist Church was founded as an ecclesiastical organization. It was there that Francis Asbury was elected the first bishop in this country. The Evangelical United Brethren Church was formed in 1946 with the merger of the Evangelical Church and the Church of the United Brethren in Christ, both of which had their beginnings in Pennsylvania in the evangelistic movement of the 18th and early 19th centuries. Philip William Otterbein and Jacob Albright were early leaders of this movement among the German-speaking settlers of the Middle Colonies.

GENERAL ORGANIZATION

General Conference: quadrennial (next meeting May 5-15, 1992, Louisville, KY)

OFFICERS

Sec. of Gen. Conference, Carolyn M. Marshall, 204 N. Newlin St., Veedersburg, IN 47987

Council of Bishops: Pres., Bishop Leroy C. Hodapp, 1100 W. 42nd St., Indianapolis, IN 46208. Tel. (317)924-1341; Sec., Bishop Melvin G. Talbert, PO Box 467, San Francisco, CA 94101 Tel. (415)474-3101

ANNUAL CONFERENCES, BISHOPS AND CONFERENCE COUNCIL DIRECTORS (BY JURISDICTION)

North Central Jurisdiction

Central Illinois—Bishop Woodie W. White, Tel. (217) 544-4604; Donald Jones, PO Box 2050, Bloomington, IL 61701. Tel: (309) 828-5092.

Detroit—Bishop Judith Craig, Tel. (313) 961-8340; Alfred Bamsey, 155 W. Congress, Suite 200, Detroit, MI 48226. Tel: (313) 961-8340.

East Ohio—Bishop Edwin C. Bolton, Tel. (216) 499-8471; John I. E. Buchanan, 8800 Cleveland Ave. NW, North Canton, OH 44720. Tel: (216) 499-3972.

Iowa—Bishop Reuben P. Job, Tel. (515) 283-1991; Bruce Ough, 1019 Chestnut St., Des Moines, IA 50309. Tel: (515) 283-1991.

Minnesota—Bishop Sharon Brown Christopher, Tel. (612) 870-3648; Delton Kraueger, 122 W. Franklin Ave., Room 400, Minneapolis, MN 55404. Tel: (612) 870-3647.

North Dakota—Bishop William B. Lewis, Tel. (701) 232-2241; Ray Wagner, 2410 12th St. N., Fargo, ND 58102. Tel: (701) 232-2241

North Indiana—Bishop Leroy C. Hodapp, Tel. (317) 924-1321; John L. Shettle, PO Box 869, Marion, IN 46952. Tel: (317) 662-9444

Northern Illinois—Bishop R. Sheldon Duecker, Tel. (312) 782-1422; Carolyn H. Oehler, 77 W. Washington St., Suite 1806, Chicago, IL 60602. Tel: (312) 346-8752.

South Dakota—Bishop William B. Lewis, Tel. (701) 232-2241; Richard Fisher, P.O. Box 460, Mitchell, SD 57301. Tel: (605) 996-6552

South Indiana—Bishop Leroy C. Hodapp, Tel. (317) 924-1321; Robert Coleman, Box 5008, Bloomington, IN 47402. Tel: (812) 336-0186.

Southern Illinois—Bishop Woodie W. White, Tel. (217) 544-4604; William Frazier, 1919 Broadway, Mt. Vernon, IL 62864 Tel: (618) 242-4070.

West Michigan—Bishop Judith Craig, Tel. (313) 961-8340; Kenneth McCaw, PO Box 6247, Grand Rapids, MI 49506. Tel: (616) 459-4503.

West Ohio—Bishop Edsel A. Ammons, Tel. (614) 228-6784; Vance Summers, 471 E. Broad St., Suite 1106, Columbus, OH 43215. Tel: (614) 228-6784.

Wisconsin—Bishop David J. Lawson, Tel. (608) 837-8526; Frank Gaylord, , PO Box 220, Sun Prairie, WI 53590. Tel: (608) 837-7328.

Northeastern Jurisdiction

Baltimore—Bishop Joseph H. Yeakel, Tel. (301) 587-9226; Thomas Starnes, 5124 Greenwich Ave., Baltimore, MD 21229. Tel: (301) 233-7300.

Central Pennsylvania—Bishop Felton E. May, Tel. (717) 652-6705; Bruce Fisher, 900 S. Arlington Ave., Room 112, Harrisburg, PA 17109. Tel: (717) 652-0460.

Eastern Pennsylvania—Bishop Susan M. Morrison, Tel. (215) 666-9090; Robert Daughtery, PO Box 820, Valley Forge, PA 19482. Tel: (215) 666-9090.

Maine—Bishop F. Herbert Skeete, Tel. (617) 536-7764; Beverly Abbott, P.O. Box 277, Winthrop, ME 04364. Tel: (207) 377-2912.

New Hampshire—Bishop F. Herbert Skeete, Tel. (617) 536-7764; Philip M. Polhemus, 712A, Route 3A, Concord, NH 03301. Tel: (603) 225-6312.

New York—Bishop C. Dale White, Tel. (914) 997-1570; Wilson Boots, 252 Bryant Ave., White Plains, NY 10605. Tel: (914) 997-1570.

North Central New York—Bishop Forrest C. Stith, Tel. (315) 446-6731; James Pollard, 317 E. Jefferson St., Syracuse, NY 13202, Tel. (315) 479-5147

Northern New Jersey—Bishop Neil L. Irons, Tel. (609) 737-3940; Barrie T. Smith, P. O. Box 546, Madison, NJ 07940. Tel: (201) 377-3800.

Peninsula—Bishop Joseph H. Yeakel, Tel. (301) 587-9226; J. Gordon Stapleton, 139 N. State St., Dover, DE 19901. Tel: (302) 674-2626.

Puerto Rico—Bishop Susan M. Morrison, Tel. (215) 666-9090; Victor L. Bonilla, P.O. Box AP, UPR Station, San Juan, PR 00931. Tel. (809) 765-3195

Southern New England—Bishop F. Herbert Skeete, Tel. (617) 536-7764; Richard E. Wiborg, 566 Commonwealth Ave., Boston, MA 02115. Tel: (617) 266-3900

Southern New Jersey—Bishop Neil L. Irons. Tel. (609) 737-3940; George T. Wang, 1995 E. Marlton Pike, Cherry Hill, NJ 08003. Tel: (609) 424-1701

Troy—Bishop C. Dale White, Tel. (914) 997-1570; James M. Perry, P. O. Box 560, Saratoga Springs, NY 12866. Tel: (518) 584-8214

West Virginia—Bishop William B. Grove, Tel. (304) 344-8330; E. Wendell Eskew, PO Box 2313, Charleston, WV 25328. Tel: (304) 344-8330

Western New York—Bishop Forrest C. Stith, Tel. (315) 446-6731; J. Fay Cleveland, 8499 Main St., Buffalo, NY 14221. Tel: (716) 633-8558

Western Pennsylvania—Bishop George W. Bashore, Tel. (412) 776-2300; Paul E. Schrading, 1204 Freedom Rd., Mars, PA 16046. Tel. (412) 362-7162

Wyoming—Bishop Felton E. May, Tel. (717) 652-6705; Kenneth E. Wood, 3 Orchard Rd., Binghamton, NY 13905. Tel. (607) 772-8840

South Central Jurisdiction

Exec. Dir., Earl B. Carter, 6155 Samuel Blvd., Dallas, TX 75228. Tel. (214)321-7077

Central Texas—Bishop John W. Russell, Tel. (817)877-5222; Michael Patison, 464 Bailey, Ft. Worth, TX 76107. Tel: (817) 877-5222

Kansas East—Bishop Kenneth W. Hicks, Tel. (913) 272-0587; H. Sharon Howell, PO Box 4187, Topeka, KS 66604. Tel. (913) 272-9111

Kansas West—Bishop Kenneth W. Hicks, Tel. (913) 272-0587; Charles E. Winkler, 151 No. Volutsia, Wichita, KS 67214. Tel: (316) 684-0266

Little Rock—Bishop Richard B. Wilke, Tel. (501) 374-6679; Jay Lofton, 715 Center St., Suite 202, Little Rock, AR 72201. Tel: (501) 374-5027

Louisiana—Bishop William B. Oden, Tel. (504) 346-1646; Harvey G. Williamson, 527 North Blvd., Baton Rouge, LA 70802. Tel. (504) 346-1646.

Missouri East—Bishop W. T. Handy, Jr., Tel. (314) 367-5001; Duane Van Giesen, St. Louis, MO 63108. Tel: (314) 367-7422

Missouri West—Bishop W. T. Handy, Jr., Tel. (314) 367-5001; Cecil Neal, 1512 Van Brunt Blvd., Kansas City, MO 64127. Tel. (816) 241-7650

Nebraska—Bishop J. Woodrow Hearn, Tel. (402) 464-5994; Robert Folkers, PO Box 4553, Lincoln, NE 68504. Tel: (402) 464-5994

New Mexico—Bishop Louis W. Schowengerdt, Tel. (505) 883-5418; Mark Dorff, 8100 Mountain Rd., N.E., Albuquerque, NM 87110. Tel. (505) 255-8786

North Arkansas—Bishop Richard B. Wilke, Tel. (501) 374-6679; Jim Meadors, 723 Center St., Little Rock, AR 72201. Tel. (501) 374-1634

North Texas—Bishop Bruce Blake; Donald E. Barnes, P.O. Box 516069, Dallas, TX 75251. Tel. (214) 490-3438

Northwest Texas—Bishop Louis W. Schowengerdt, Tel. (505) 883-5418; Rex L. Mauldin, 1415 Ave. M, Lubbock, TX 79401. Tel: (806) 762-0201

Oklahoma—Bishop Dan E. Solomon, Tel. (405) 525-2252; Robert Montgomery, 2420 N. Blackwelder, Oklahoma City, OK 73130. Tel: (405) 525-2252

Oklahoma Indian Missionary—Bishop Dan E. Solomon, Tel. (405) 525-2252; Becky Thompson, PO Box 60427, Oklahoma City, OK 73146. Tel: (405) 521-1741

Rio Grande—Bishop Ernest T. Dixon, Tel. (512) 432-0401; Arturo Mariscal, Jr., PO Box 28098, San Antonio, TX 78284. Tel: (512) 432-7875

Southwest Texas—Bishop Ernest T. Dixon, Tel. (512) 432-0401; William J. Hughes, PO Box 28098, San Antonio, TX 78284. Tel: (512) 432-4680

Texas—Bishop Benjamin R. Oliphint, Tel. (713) 528-6881; Joe A. Wilson, 5215 S. Main St., Houston, TX 77002. Tel: (713) 521-9383

Southeastern Jurisdiction

Exec. Sec., Reginald Ponder, P.O. Box 237, Lake Junaluska, NC 28745. Tel. (704)452-1881

Alabama-West Florida—Bishop C. W. Hancock, Tel. (205) 277-1787; William Calhoun, PO Box 700, Andalusia, AL 36420. Tel: (205) 222-3127

Florida—Bishop H. Hasbrock Hughes, Jr., Tel. (813) 688-4427; Robert Bledsoe, PO Box 3767, Lakeland, FL 33802. Tel: (813) 688-5563

Holston—Bishop Clay F. Lee, Tel. (615) 525-1809; William J. Carter, PO Box 1178, Johnson City, TN 37601. Tel: (615) 928-2156

Kentucky—Bishop Robert H. Spain, Tel. (502) 893-6715; David L. Hilton, PO Box 5107, Lexington, KY 40555. Tel: (606) 254-7388

Louisville—Bishop Robert H. Spain, Tel. (502) 893-6715; W. Avril Allen, 1115 S. Fourth St., Louisville, KY 40203. Tel: (502) 584-3838.

Memphis—Bishop Ernest W. Newman, Tel. (615) 327-3462; Paul Douglass, Sr., 575 Lambuth Blvd., Jackson, TN 38301. Tel: (901) 427-8589

Mississippi—Bishop Robert C. Morgan, Tel. (601) 948-4561; Warren E. Pittman, P. O. Box 1147, Jackson, MS 39205. Tel: (601) 354-0515

North Alabama—Bishop J. Lloyd Knox, Tel. (205) 879-8665; George W. Hayes, 898 Arkadelphia Rd., Birmingham, AL 35204. Tel: (205) 251-9279

North Carolina—Bishop C. P. Minnick, Jr., Tel. (919) 832-9560; G. Robert McKenzie, Jr., PO Box 10955, Raleigh, NC 27605. Tel: (919) 832-9560

North Georgia—Bishop Ernest A. Fitzgerald, Tel. (404) 659-0002; Robert Bridges, 159 Ralph McGill Blvd. NE, Atlanta, GA 30365. Tel: (404) 659-0002

Red Bird Missionary—Bishop Robert H. Spain, Tel. (502) 893-6715; Charles Pinkston, Queendale Ctr., Box 3, Beverly, KY 40913. Tel: (606) 598-5915

South Carolina—Bishop Joseph B. Bethea, Tel. (803) 786-9486; Susan Henry-Crowe, 4908 Colonial Dr., Suite 101, Columbia, SC 29203. Tel: (803) 799-9627

South Georgia—Bishop Richard C. Looney, Tel. (404) 659-0002; William E. McTier, Jr., PO Box 408, St. Simons Island, GA 31522. Tel: (912) 638-8626.

Tennessee—Bishop Ernest W. Newman, Tel. (615) 327-3462; William Norris, PO Box 120607, Nashville, TN 37212. Tel: (615) 329-1177

Virginia—Bishop Thomas B. Stockton, Tel. (804) 359-9451; Joseph T. Carson, Jr., PO Box 11367, Richmond, VA 23230. Tel: (804) 359-9451

Western North Carolina—Bishop L. Bevel Jones, Tel. (704) 535-2260; Donald W. Maynes, PO Box 18005, Charlotte, NC 28218. Tel: (704) 535-2260

Western Jurisdiction

Alaska Missionary—Bishop William W. Dew, Jr., Tel. (503) 226-7931; Dennis Holway, 3402 Wesleyan Dr., Anchorage, AK 99508. Tel: (907) 274-1571

California-Nevada—Bishop Melvin G. Talbert, Tel. (415) 474-3101; James H. Corson, PO Box 467, San Francisco, CA 94101. Tel: (415) 474-3101.

California-Pacific—Bishop Jack M. Tuell, Tel. (818) 796-6607; J. Delton Pickering, 472 E. Colorado Blvd., P.O. Box 6006, Pasadena, CA 91109. Tel. (818) 796-6607

Desert Southwest—Bishop Elias Galvin, Tel. (602) 253-0847; Michael Nickerson, 1807 N. Central Ave., Ste. 100, Phoenix, AZ 85004. Tel. (602)253-0847

Oregon-Idaho—Bishop William A. Dew, Jr., Tel. (503) 226-7931; Bill McDonald, 1505 SW 18th Ave., Portland, OR 97201. Tel: (503) 226-7931.

Pacific Northwest—Bishop Calvin D. McConnell, Tel. (206) 728-7462; Edgar C. Hersh, 2112 Third Ave., Suite 300, Seattle, WA 98121. Tel: (206) 728-7462.

Rocky Mountain—Bishop Roy I. Sano, Tel. (303) 733-3736; John Blinn, 2200 S. University Blvd., Denver, CO 80210. Tel: (303) 733-3736.

Yellowstone—Bishop Roy I. Sano, Tel. (303) 733-3736; Carolyn Straub, 335 Broadwater Ave., Billings, MT 59101. Tel: (406) 256-1385.

OTHER ORGANIZATIONS

Judicial Council: Pres., Tom Matheny; Sec., Wayne Coffin, 2420 N. Blackwelder, Oklahoma City, OK 73106

Council on Finance and Administration: 1200 Davis St., Evanston, IL 60201. Tel. (708) 869-3345. Pres., Bishop John W. Russell; Vice-Pres., Bishop Forrest C. Stith; Rec. Sec., Ron Gilbert, Gen. Sec.and Treas., Clifford Droke; Section on Episcopal Matters: Asst. Gen Sec., Elizabeth Okayama; Section on Legal Services, Gen. Counsel, Craig R. Hoskins; Section on Mgmt. Information Systems: Asst. Gen. Sec., Al Fifhause; Dir., Computer Systems, Merna Johnson; Dir. of Council Operations, Mary Simmons.

Division of Financial Services: Assoc. Gen. Sec., Gary K. Bowen; Controller, Beth Taylor; Asst. Controller, Lesslie Keller; Payroll Dept., Dir., Phyllis Anderson; Service Centers: (Dayton) Asst. Gen. Treas., Lola Conrad; (Nashville) Comptroller, W. C. Hawkins; (Washington) Asst. Controller, Clarence Walddroff; (New York) Asst. Gen. Treas., Stephen F. Brimigion; Section on Investments, Gary K. Bowen

Division of Administrative Services: Asst. Gen. Sec., Geneva Dalton; Section on Records and Statistics: Asst. Gen. Sec., John L. Schreiber; Dir., Dept. of Records, Cynthia Haralson; Dir., Dept. of Statistics, Daniel A. Nielsen

Council on Ministries: 601 W. Riverview Ave., Dayton, OH 45406 Tel. (513) 227-9400. Pres., Bishop Felton E. May; Vice-Pres., Jean Dowell, Joel N. Martinez; Sec., J. Taylor Phillips; Treas., Donald L. Mayashi; Gen. Sec., C. David Lundquist; Assoc. Gen. Secs., Trudie Kibbe Preciphs, Royal Fishbeck, Jr., C. Leonard Miller, Mearle Griffith;

Commission on Communication/United Methodist Communications: P. O. Box 320 (810 12th Ave. S.), Nashville, TN 37202. Tel. (615) 742-5400. Pres., Bishop Rueben P. Job; Co-Vice Pres., Mary Silva; Sec., James Lane. Gen. Admn.: Gen. Sec., Roger L. Burgess; Assoc. Gen. Sec. Personnel and Admin., Newtonia Harris Coleman; Treas., Peggy Welshans; Dir., Conf. Serv. & Communication Ed., Shirley Whipple Struchen; Dir. of Public Relations, Roger L. Burgess

Division of Program and Benevolence Interpretation: Assoc. Gen. Sec., Donald E. Collier; Dir. Publications, Darrell R. Shamblin; Ed., *The Interpreter*, Laura Okumu; Ed., *El Interprete*, Edith LaFontaine; Editorial Dir., Barbara Dunlap-Berg, Dir., Mgmt. Info., Systems Dept., Susan Peek

Division of Production and Distribution: Assoc. Gen. Sec., Peggy J. West; Dir., AV/Media Production, Wilfred V. Bane, Jr.; Dir., Media Distribution and ECUFILM, Furman York; Mgr., Technical Services and Kingswood Productions, Dixie Parman; Dir. INFOSERV, Woodley McEachern

Division of Public Media: 475 Riverside Dr., Ste. 1901, New York, NY 10115. Tel. (212) 663-8900. Assoc. Gen. Sec., Nelson Price. Public Media Mktg: Dir., William R. Richards, TEl. (615)742-5405; United Methodist News Service: P. O. Box 320, Nashville, TN 37202. Tel. (615) 742-5470; Fax: (615)742-5469; Dir. of News Service, Thomas S. McAnally

Board of Church and Society: 100 Maryland Ave., NE, Washington, DC. 20002. Tel. (202) 488-5600. Pres. Bishop Robert C. Morgan; Vice-Pres., Edward Iwamoto; Rec. Sec., Helen G. Taylor; Treas., Andrea Allen; Gen. Sec.; Thom White Wolf Fassett; Assoc. Gen. Secs., Donna Morton-Stout, Ed. of Resources and *Christian Social Action,* Lee Ranck; U.N. Seminars on National and International Affairs: Designers, Jim Winkler, Andres Thomas, Christian Delardsa, Carol Barton, Debra Huntington, Cynthis Woods, David Wildman, Nan Won Kim; Business and Finance: Asst. Gen. Sec., Jean Robinson; Chpsn., Trustees, William Depp

Dept. of Human Welfare, Dir., Jane Hull Harvey
Dept. of Social and Economic Justice, Dir., George Ogle
Dept. of Political and Human Rights, Dir., Guillermo Chavez
Dept. of Peace and World Order, Dir., Robert McClean, 777 United Nations Plaza, New York, NY 10017. Tel. (212) 682-3633
Dept. of Environmental Justice and Survival, Dir., Jaydee Hanson
Dept. of Ethnic Minority Local Church, Dir., Manuel Espartero

Board of Discipleship: P. O. Box 840 (1908 Grand Ave. and 1001 19th Ave. S.), Nashville, TN 37202. Tel. (615) 340-7200. Pres., Bishop Woodie White; Vice-Pres., Bishop David Lawson; Sec., Evelyn Laycock, Treas., Isaac Brown; Gen Sec., Ezra Earl Jones; Assoc.Gen. Sec., Alan K. Waltz, Victor Perez-Silvestry, James H. Snead, Jr., Janice T. Grana, Duane A. Ewers, Office of Human Resources and Staff Services: Exec. Sec., Jean Suiter
Office of Financial Services: Exec. Sec., Isaac W. Brown; National Youth Ministry Org: Exec. Dir., Jack B. Harrison
Office of Publishing and Interpretation Service: Exec. Sec., David L. Hazlewood; Discipleship Resources Ed., Craig Galloway
Section on Ethnic Minority Local Church: Asst. Gen. Sec., David L. White
Section on Ministry of the Laity: Asst. Gen. Sec., David L. White
Section on Stewardship: Asst. Gen. Sec., Herbert Mather
Division on United Methodist Men: Assoc. Gen. Sec., James H. Snead, Jr.
Section on Evangelism: Actg. Asst. Gen. Sec., Joe A. Harding
Section on Worship: Asst. Gen. Sec., Thomas A. Langford, III
Section on Christian Education and Age Level Ministries: Asst. Gen. Sec., Marilyn W. Magee
The Upper Room: World Editor, Janice T. Grana
Division of Church School Publications: Ed., Church School Publications, Duane A. Ewers; Man. Ed., Church School Publications, Howard E. Walker. Curricuphone: 1-800-251-8591; Tenn. Call collect: Tel. (615) 749-6482

Board of Global Ministries: 475 Riverside Dr., New York, NY 10115. Tel. (212) 870-3600. Pres., Bishop Woodrow Hearn; Vice-Pres., Bishop F. Herbert Skeete; Gen. Sec., Randolph Nugent; Deputy Gen Secs., Brian Fetterman, Robert Harman, Theressa Hoover, Assoc. Gen. Secs.: Lorene F. Wilbur, Admn.; Sheila Fleming, Mission Resources; Cathie Lyons, Health & Welfare;

Norma Kehrberg, United Methodist Committee on Relief; Ombudsperson, Cherryetta Williams; Gen. Treas., Stephen F. Brimigion; Assoc. and Div. Treas., Brenda Norwood, Joyce Sohl, William Wyman; Gen. Comptroller, Lynette Davis Rice; Public Relations Dir., Betty Thompson.
National Division: Pres., Bishop F. Herbert Skeete; Deputy Gen. Sec., Brian Fetterman; Asst. Gen. Secs., Lula Garrett, Eli Rivera, Myong Gul Son; Treas., Brenda Norwood
Women's Division: Pres., Sally Ernst; Deputy Gen. Sec., Theressa Hoover; Asst. Gen. Secs., Barbara E. Campbell, Ellen Kirby, Elizabeth Calvin, Elaine Gasser
World Division: Pres., Bishop J. Lloyd Knox; Treas., William Wayman. Deputy Gen. Sec., Robert Harman; Asst. Gen. Secs., Sarla Lall, Doreen Tilghman, Jiro Mizuno, Nora O. Boots
Mission Education Cultivation Dept.: Chpsn., Carolyn H. Oehler; Assoc. Gen. Sec. Keith Muhleman; Asst. Gen. Secs., Susan Keirn Kester, William T. Carter
Health and Welfare Dept.: Chpsn., Martha Sanchez; Treas., Brenda Norwood; Assoc. Gen. Sec., Cathie Lyons
United Methodist Committee on Relief: Chpsn., Bishop C. P. Minnick, Jr; Assoc. Gen. Secs., Norman Kehrberg; Treas., William Wyman
Mission Resources Dept.: Chpsn., Bishop Edsel Ammons; Christopher; Assoc. Gen. Sec., Sheila Fleming; Treas., Stephen Brimigion

Board of Higher Education and Ministry: P.O. Box 871 (1001 Nineteenth Ave. S.), Nashville, TN 37202. Tel. (615)340-7000. Pres., Benjamin R. Oliphint; Gen. Sec., Roger Ireson; Assoc. Gen. Sec. for Administration, Clarke McClendon; Dir., Jennie Stockard; ; Office of Interpretation: Assoc. Gen.Sec., Judith E. Smith; Dir., Terri J. Hiers, Sharon J. Hels; Office of Loans and Scholarships: Asst. Gen. Sec., Angella Current
Division of Chaplains and Related Ministries: Assoc. Gen. Sec., James Townsend; Dirs., Patricia Barrett, Richard Stewart
Division of Diaconal Ministry: Assoc. Gen. Sec., Rosalie Bentzinger; Dirs., Joaquin Garcia, Paul Van Buren
Division of Higher Education: Assoc. Gen. Sec., Ken Yamada; Asst. Gen. Sec., Morris Wray, Alan Burry; Dirs., Robert Conn, Helen Neinast, Richard Hicks; Office of the Black College Fund: Exec. Dir., Shirley Lewis. National Methodist Foundation for Christian Higher Education: Pres., Alan Peer
Division of the Ordained Ministry: Assoc. Gen. Sec., Donald H. Treese; Dirs., Robert Kohler, Richard Yeager, Kil Sang Yoon, Kathy Nickerson

Board of Pensions: 1200 Davis St., Evanston, IL 60201. Tel. (708) 869-4550. Pres., Bishop Jack M. Tuell; Vice-Pres., Robert W. Stevens; Sec. Carrie L. Carter; Gen. Sec., James F. Parker; Sr. Assoc. Gen. Sec., Dir. of Corp. Rel., Allen M. Mayes; Chief Partic. Servcs., Gerald A. Beam; Chief, Oper. Servcs., Dale Knapp; Treasurer, Diane O. Pinney; Chief Fin. Officer, F. Gale Whiteson-Schmidt; Chief, Support Services, Kenneth Truman; Sr. Int. Audtr., Wilbert Blum; Asst. Treas., G. Warren Dare; Assoc. Gen. Sec. & Special Assistant, Joyce Gilman; Communications Dir., Cheryl Haack; Portfolio Dir., Mary Pat Kincaid; Offices Services Dir., John Lukasik; Human Resources Dir., V. Christyne Mackey; Sr. Actuary, Frank L. Markel; Assoc. Gen. Sec. & Benefits Dir., Thomas Marston; Assoc. Gen. Sec. & Operations Dir., Phillip Moulden; Assoc. Gen. Sec. & Management Informations Systems Dir., Bruce Slown; Gen. Counsel, James Walton-Myers; Actuary, Susan Wilson.

Board of Publication: Chpsn, _____; Vice-Chpsn., __ _____, Sec., _____.

The United Methodist Publishing House: P.O. Box 801, 201 Eighth Ave. So., Nashville, TN 37202. Tel. (615) 749-6000 or 1-800-672-1789. Pres. & Publisher, Robert

K. Feaster; Treas., Vice-Pres., Fin. and Admn., Larry L. Wallace; Vice-Pres., Retail Sales (Cokesbury) Division, Gary H. Vincent; Book Editor/Vice-Pres., Publishing Div., H. Claude Young, Jr.; Vice-Pres., Office of Planning & Research, Thomas K. Potter, Jr.; Vice-Pres., Public and Church Relations Division, Walter McKelvey; Vice-Pres., Human Resources Division, Stephen C. Tippens.

Commission on Archives and History: P.O. Box 127, Madison, NJ 07940. Tel. (201) 822-2787. Pres., Bishop Neil L. Irons; Vice-Pres., Mark Conrad; Rec. Sec., Marilyn Martin, Gen. Sec., Charles Yrigoyen, Jr.; Asst. Gen. Sec., Arthur Swarthout; Archivist and Records Adm., William C. Beal, Jr.; Dir., Women's and Ethnic History Project, Susan Eltsher; Asst. Dir., C. Jarrat Gray.

Commission on Christian Unity and Interreligious Concerns: 475 Riverside Dr., Rm. 1300, New York, NY 10115. Tel. (212) 749-3553. Pres., Bishop William Boyd Grove; Vice-Pres., Dorothy Mae Taylor; Sec., E. Dale Dunlap; Treas., Clifford Droke, Gen. Sec., Robert W. Huston; Assoc. Gen. Secs., Jeanne Audrey Powers, Nehemiah Thompson, Bruce W. Robbins

Commission on Religion and Race: 100 Maryland Ave., N.E., Washington, DC 20002. Tel. (202) 547-4270. Pres., Bishop Calvin D. McConnell; Vice-Pres., Bishop Joseph B. Bethea; Rec. Sec., Bradley Watkins; Gen. Sec., Barbara R. Thompson; Assoc. Gen. Secs., Kenneth Deere, Warren Hill, Esdras Rodriguez-Dias, Hidetoshi Tanaka, Evelyn Fitzgerald

Commission on the Status and Role of Women: 1200 Davis St., Evanston, IL 60201. Tel. (312) 869-7330. Pres., Linda Thomas; Vice-Pres., Joetta Rinehart, Rec. Sec., Winonah McGee; Secretariat, Nancy G. Self, Kiyoko Fujiu, Cecilia Long

Fellowship of United Methodists in Worship, Music, and Other Arts: 159 Ralph McGill Blvd., NE, Ste. 505, Atlanta, GA 30308. Tel. (404)577-7914. Exec. Sec., Jerry W. Henry; Pres., Sara Collins

PERIODICALS

Arkansas United Methodist (bi-w), P.O. Box 3547, Little Rock, AR 72203. Jane Dearing, Ed.

California-Nevada United Methodist Reporter (w), P.O. Box 467, San Francisco, CA 94101. Charles Lerrigo, Ed.

Central Illinois United Methodist Reporter (w), P.O. Box 515, Bloomington, IL 61702. Bettie W. Story, Ed.

Central Texas U.M. Reporter (w), 464 Bailey, Ste. 505, Ft. Worth, TX 76107. Wallace Bennett, Ed.

Christian Social Action (m), 100 Maryland Ave., NE, Washington, DC 20002. Lee Ranck, Ed.

Circuit Rider (m), P.O. Box 801, Nashville, TN 37202. Keith Pohl, Ed.

Circuit Rider U.M. Reporter (w), 5124 Greenwich Ave., Baltimore, MD 21229. Jan Lichtenwalter, Ed.

Circuit West (w), 4249 Cedar Ave., El Monte, CA 91732. Peg Parker, Ed.

Communicator, The (w), 139 N. State St., Dover, DE 19901. Constance Metzger, Ed.

Conference Connexion (m), 1919 Broadway, Mt. Vernon, IL. William Frazier,Ed.

Contact (w), 2420 N. Blackwelder, Oklahoma City, OK 73106. Boyce Bowdon, Ed.

Crossfire (bi-w), 151 N. Volutsia, Wichita, KS 67214. Kathy Kruger, Ed.

Desert Views (w), 6002 N. 43rd St., Paradise Valley, AZ 85253. Colleen Sanders-Hatfield, Ed.

East Ohio Today (w), P.O. Box 2800, N. Canton, OH 44720 Lawrence Moffett, Ed.

Eastern Pennsylvania United Methodist Reporter (w), P. O. Box 820, Valley Forge, PA 19482. _____, Ed.

El Interprete (q) (Spanish), P. O. Box 320, Nashville, TN 37202. Edith LaFontaine,Ed.

Florida United Methodist Reporter (w), P.O. Box 3767, Lakeland, FL 33802. Barbara Wilcox, Ed.

Hawkeye (m), 1019 Chestnut St., Des Moines, IA 50309. Karen J. Tisinger, Ed.

Holston United Methodist Reporter (w), P.O. Box 1178, Johnson City, TN 37605. Don Sluder, Ed.

Hoosier United Methodist (m), 1100 W. 42nd St., Indianapolis, IN 46208. James Steele, Ed.

Interchange (w), P.O. Box 4187, Topeka, KS 66604. Karen Robertson, Ed.

Interpreter, The (m), P. O. Box 320, Nashville, TN 37202. Laura Okumu, Ed.

Kentucky United Methodist Review (bi-w), P.O. Box 5107, Lexington, KY 40555. Raymond Gibson, Ed.

Link, The (m), 900 S. Arlington Ave., Rm. 112, Harrisburg, PA 17109. Gerald D. Wagner, Ed.

Louisiana United Methodist Reporter (w), P. O. Box 3057, Baton Rouge, LA 70802. Harvey G. Williamson, Ed.

Louisville U.M. Reporter, 1115 S. 4th St., Louisville, KY 40203. Tammy Harrod, Ed.

Maine United Methodist, The (bi-m), P.O. Box 277, Winthrop, ME 04364. Beverly J. Abbott, Ed.

Mature Years (q), 201 Eighth Ave. S., Nashville, TN 37202. Don Donnall, Ed.

Memphis Conference United Methodist Reporter (w), 575 Lambuth Blvd., Jackson, TN 38301. Cathy Farmer, Ed.

Methodist History (q), P.O. Box 127, Madison, NJ 07940. Charles Yrigoyen, Jr., Ed.

Michigan Christian Advocate (w), 316 Springbrook Ave., Adrian, MI 49221. Kay Lukins, Ed.

Minnesota United Methodist Reporter (w), 122 W. Franklin Ave., Rm. 400, Minneapolis, MN 55404. Jean Noren, Ed.

Mississippi United Methodist Advocate (bi-w), Box 1093, Jackson, MS 39205. Rayford Woodrick, Ed.

Missouri East United Methodist Reporter (w), 4625 Lindell Blvd., Suite 424, St. Louis, MO 63108. Dulcina R. McCoy, Ed.

Missouri West United Methodist Reporter (w), 1512 Van Brunt Blvd., Kansas City, MO 64127. Stephen Cox, Ed.

Nebraska Messenger (bi-w), P.O. Box 4553, Lincoln, NE 68504. Daniel R. Gangler, Ed.

New Mexico United Methodist Reporter (w), 209 San Pedro NE, Albuquerque, NM 87108. Mark L. Dorff, Ed.

New World Outlook (m), 475 Riverside Dr., Rm. 1351, New York, NY 10115. _____, Ed.

Newscope (w), P.O. Box 801, Nashville, TN 37202. Bette E. Prestwood, Ed.

North Carolina Christian Advocate (w), P.O. Box 508, Greensboro, NC 27402. C. A. Simonton, Jr., Ed.

North Central New York United Methodist Review (bi-w), R.D. 3 Delivery 121, Elmira, NY 14903. Carla Page, Ed.

North Texas U.M. Reporter (w), 1928 Ross Ave., Dallas, TX 75201. Lillian Sills, Ed.

Northern Illinois United Methodist Review (bi-w), 77 W. Washington St., Rm. 1806, Chicago, IL 60602. Dana Jones, Ed.

Northwest Texas United Methodist Reporter (w), 1415 Ave. M, Lubbock, TX 79401. Connie Nelson-Daniel, Ed.

Northwest United Methodist (m), 2112 Third Ave., #300 Seattle, WA 98121. June Click, Ed.

Pockets (m), P. O. Box 189, Nashville, TN 37202. Janet McNish Bugg, Ed.

Quarterly Review (q), P.O. Box 871, Nashville, TN 37202. Sharon Hels, Ed.

Reporter (w) (Spanish), P.O. Box 28098, San Antonio, TX 78284. Arturo Mariscal, Ed.

response (m), 475 Riverside Dr., Room 1344, New York, NY 10115. Carol M. Herb, Ed.

Rocky Mountain United Methodist Reporter (w), 2200 S. University Blvd., Denver, CO 80210. Suzanne Calvin, Ed.

South Carolina United Methodist Advocate (w), 4908 Colonial Dr., Rm. 207, Columbia, SC 29203. Willie Teague, Ed.

Southern New England U.M. Reporter (w), 566 Commonwealth Ave., Boston, MA 02215. Ann Whiting, Ed.

Southwest Texas U.M. Reporter, Box 28098, San Antonio, TX 78284. _____, Ed.

Tennessee United Methodist Reporter (w), P.O. Box 120607, Nashville, TN 37212. Ed Britt, Jr., Ed.

Texas U.M. Reporter (w), 5215 S. Main St., Houston, TX 77002. Mary L. Krause, Ed.

United Methodist (m), 1505 SW 18th Ave., Portland, OR 97201. Barbara Sawyer, Ed.

United Methodist Christian Advocate (bi-w), 909 Ninth Ave., W., Birmingham AL 35204. _____, Ed.

United Methodist Relay (m), 300 Ridge Rd., Fairhaven, NJ 07701. Robin E. Van Cleef, Ed.

United Methodist Reporter, The (w), P.O. Box 660275, Dallas, TX 75266. Spurgeon M. Dunnam III, Ed.

United Methodist Rural Fellowship Bulletin (q), P.O. Box 307, Louisville, TN 37777. James E. Hankins, Ed.

Update (bi-w), 252 Bryant Ave., White Plains, NY 10605. Roy Lloyd, Ed.

Upper Room (bi-m), P. O. Box 189, Nashville, TN 37202. Janice T. Grana, Ed.

Virginia Advocate (bi-w), P.O. Box 11367, Richmond, VA 23230. Alvan J. Horton, Ed.

Voice, The (m), 3 Orchard Rd., Binghamton, NY 13905. Wesley Rehberg, Ed.

Wesleyan Christian Advocate (w), P.O. Box 54455, Atlanta, GA 30308. G. Ross Freeman, Ed.

West Ohio News (bi-w), 471 Broad St., Suite 1106, Columbus, OH 43215. Tom Slack, Ed.

West Virginia United Methodist (m), P.O. Box 2313, Charleston, WV 25328. Tom Burger, Ed.

Western New York Communicator (bi-w), 8499 Main St., Buffalo, NY 14221. Marilyn Kasperak, Ed.

Western Pennsylvania United Methodist Reporter (w), 1204 Freedom Rd., Mars, PA 16046. Kevin Rippin, Ed.

World Parish (s-m), P.O. Box 518, Lake Junaluska, NC 28745. Joe Hale, Ed.

Zion's Herald (m), 566 Commonwealth Ave., Boston, MA 02215. Ann Whiting, Ed.

United Pentecostal Church International

The United Pentecostal Church International came into being through the merger of two oneness Pentecostal organizations—the Pentecostal Church, Inc., and the Pentecostal Assemblies of Jesus Christ. The first of these was known as the Pentecostal Ministerial Alliance from its inception in 1925 until 1932. The second was formed in 1931 by a merger of the Apostolic Church of Jesus Christ with the Pentecostal Assemblies of the World.

The United Pentecostal Church International contends that the Bible does not teach three separate, coequal and coeternal members of the Godhead, but rather one God who manifested himself as the Father in creation, in the Son in redemption, and as the Holy Spirit in regeneration. It is further believed that Jesus is the name of this absolute deity and that water baptism should be administered in his name, not in the titles Father, Son, and Holy Ghost. Scriptural basis for this teaching can be found in Acts 2:38, 8:16, and 19:6. This position should not be confused with the Unitarian view, which denies the deity of Jesus Christ.

The Fundamental Doctrine of the United Pentecostal Church International, as stated in its *Articles of Faith*, is "the Bible standard of full salvation, which is repentance, baptism in water by immersion in the name of the Lord Jesus Christ for the remission of sins, and the baptism of the Holy Ghost with the initial sign of speaking with other tongues as the Spirit gives utterance."

Further doctrinal teachings concern of a life of holiness and separation, the operation of the gifts of the Spirit within the church, the second coming of the Lord, and the church's obligation to take the gospel to the whole world. The traditional slogan of the United Pentecostal Church International is The Whole Gospel to the Whole World.

Churches: 3,592; Inclusive Membership: 500,000; Sunday or Sabbath Schools: N.R.; Total Enrollment: N.R.; Ordained Clergy: 7,279

GENERAL ORGANIZATION

Conference: annual
Headquarters: 8855 Dunn Rd., Hazelwood, MO 63042. Tel. (314) 837-7300

OFFICERS

Gen. Supt., Rev. Nathaniel A. Urshan, 8855 Dunn Rd., Hazelwood, MO 63042

Asst. Gen. Supts., Rev. James Kilgore, Box 15175, Houston, TX 77020; Jesse Williams, P. O. Box 64877, Fayetteville, NC 28306

Gen. Sec.-Treas., Rev. C. M. Becton, 8855 Dunn Rd., Hazelwood, MO 63042

Dir. of For. Miss., Rev. Harry Scism, 8855 Dunn Rd., Hazelwood, MO 63042

Gen. Dir. of Home Miss., Rev. Jack E. Yonts, 8855 Dunn Rd., Hazelwood, MO 63042

Editor-in-Chief, Rev. J. L. Hall, 8855 Dunn Rd., Hazelwood, MO 63042

Gen. Sunday School Dir., Rev. E. J. McClintock, 8855 Dunn Rd., Hazelwood, MO 63042

OTHER AUXILIARIES

The Pentecostal Publishing House, Rev. J. O. Wallace, Mgr.

Youth Division (Pentecostal Conquerors), Pres., Jerry Jones, Hazelwood, MO 63042

Ladies Auxiliary: Pres., Vera Kinzie, 4840 Elm Pl., Toledo, OH 43608

Harvestime Radio Broadcast: Dir., Rev. J. Hugh Rose, 698 Kerr Ave., Cadiz, OH 43907

Stewardship Dept.: Contact Church Division, Hazelwood, MO 63042

Education Division: Supt. Rev. Arless Glass, 4502 Aztec, Pasadena, TX 77504

Public Relations Division, Contact Church Division, Hazelwood, MO 63042

Historical Society & Archives: Calvin Rigdon, 8855 Dunn Rd., Hazelwood, MO 63042

PERIODICALS

The Pentecostal Herald, Hazelwood, Rev. J. L. Hall, Ed.
The Global Witness (Foreign Mission Div.), Rev. J. S. Leaman, Ed.
The Outreach (Home Mission Div.), J. L. Fiorino, Ed.
The Ephphatha (Deaf Ministry), Billie Savoie, Ed.
Homelife (Youth Div.), Rev. Mark Christian, Ed.
Conqueror (Youth Div.), Rev. Darrell Johns, Ed.
Reflections (Ladies Div.), Melissa Anderson, Ed.
Forward (for ministers only), Rev. J. L. Hall, Ed.

United Zion Church

A branch of the Brethren in Christ which settled in Lancaster County, Pennsylvania, and was organized under the leadership of Matthias Brinser in 1855.

GENERAL ORGANIZATION

Conference: annual

OFFICERS

Gen. Conf. Mod., Bishop J. Paul Martin, Box 212 D, RD #1, Annville, PA 17003. Tel. (717)867-4253

Asst. Mod., Rev. Leon Eberly, 615 N. Ridge Rd., Reinholds, PA 17569. Tel. (215)484-2614

Gen. Conf. Sec., Eugene Kreider, RD #2, Manheim, PA 17545. Tel. (717)653-8226

Gen. Conf.Treas., Carl Good, RD #1, Denver, PA 17517

121

Unity of the Brethren

Czech and Moravian immigrants in Texas (beginning about 1855) established congregations which grew into an Evangelical Union in 1903, and with the accession of other Brethren in Texas, into the Evangelical Unity of the Czech-Moravian Brethren in North America. In 1959, it shortened the name to the original name used in 1457, the Unity of the Brethren (Unitas Fratrum, or Jednota Bratrska).

Churches: 26; Inclusive Membership: 2,873; Sunday or Sabbath Schools: 22; Total Enrollment: 1,465; Ordained Clergy: 22GENERAL ORGANIZATIONSynod: Every two years.

OFFICERS

Pres., Mr. Marvin Chlapek, 2513 Revere Dr., Pasadena, TX 77502. Tel. (713)946-5027
1st Vice Pres., Rev. Rev. Robert Holaday, 1800 Peyton Ginn Rd., Austin, TX 78758
Sec., Dorothy Kocian, 107 S. Barbara, Waco, TX 76705. Tel. (817)799-5331
Fin. Sec., Mrs. Betsy Choate, 4608 Country Club View, Baytown, TX 77521
Treas., Roy Vajdak, 6424 S. Hudson, Littleton, CO 80121

ORGANIZATIONS

Sunday School Union: Chmn., Stanley F. Mrnustik, 205 N. Shaw St., Caldwell, TX 77836; Board of Christian Education: Chpsn., Rev. James Hejl, 700 Sloan St., Taylor, TX 76574
Christian Sisters Society: Pres., Mrs. Janet Pompkal
Brethren Youth Fellowship: Pres., Michele Diener
Young Adult Fellowship: Pres., Joyce Koslosky

PERIODICAL

Brethren Journal (m), Rev. Milton Maly, Ed. Rt. 3, Box 558N, Brenham, TX 77833

Vedanta Society

Followers of the Vedas, the scriptures of the Indo-Aryans, doctrines expounded by Swami Vivekananda at the Parliament of Religions, Chicago, 1893. There are altogether 13 such Centers in the U.S.A. All are under the spiritual guidance of the Ramakrishna Mission, organized by Swami Vivekananda in India.

Churches: 13 Inclusive Membership: 2,500 Sunday or Sabbath Schools: N.R. Total Enrollment: N.R. Ordained Clergy: 14

GENERAL ORGANIZATION

Correspondent: 34 W. 71st St., New York, NY 10023. Tel. (212) 877-9197

LEADER

Swami Tathagatananda

Volunteers of America

Volunteers of America, founded in 1896 by Ballington and Maud Booth, provides spiritual and material aid for those in need in more than 200 communities across the U.S. As one of the nation's largest multipurpose human-service agencies, VOA offers more than 400 programs for the elderly, families, youth, alcoholics, drug abusers, offenders, and the disabled.

GENERAL ORGANIZATION

National Headquarters: 3813 North Causeway Blvd., Metairie, LA 70002. Tel. (504) 837-2652

NATIONAL OFFICERS

Chpsn., Keven P. Reilly, Sr.
Pres., Raymond C. Tremont
Vice-Pres., Jack L. Dignum, David Bordenkircher, Robert E. Nolte, John A. Hood, J. Clint Cheveallier, Thomas J. Clark, J. Steven Tremont and Margaret Ratcliff

PERIODICAL

The Gazette (q), published at National Headquarters

The Wesleyan Church

The Wesleyan Church was formed on June 26, 1968, through the union of the Wesleyan Methodist Church of America (1843) and the Pilgrim Holiness Church (1897). Headquarters was established at Marion, Indiana and relocated in Indianapolis, Indiana in 1987.

The Wesleyan movement centers around the scriptural truth that the atonement in Christ provides for the regeneration of sinners and the entire sanctification of believers. A revival of these truths took place in the eighteenth century under John Wesley and continues until the present.

When a group of New England ministers led by Orange Scott began to crusade for the abolition of slavery, with which many Methodist ministers and members had become involved, the bishops and others sought to silence them. This led to a series of withdrawals from the Methodist Episcopal Church. In 1843 an organizing convention was held in Utica, New York, resulting in the organization of the Wesleyan Methodist Connection of America. Scott, Jotham Horton, LaRoy Sunderland, Luther Lee, and Lucius C. Matlack were prominent leaders in the new denomination. The crusade against slavery was carried to a successful conclusion with the Civil War.

As a result of the holiness revival which swept across many denominations in the last half of the nineteenth century, holiness replaced social reform as the major tenet of the Connection. In 1947 the name was changed from Connection to Church and a central supervisory authority was set up.

The Pilgrim Holiness Church was one of many independent holiness churches which came into existence as a result of the holiness revival. Under the leadership of Martin Wells Knapp and Seth C. Rees, the International Holiness Union and Prayer League was inaugurated in 1897 in Cincinnati, Ohio. Its purpose was to promote worldwide holiness evangelism and the Union had a strong missionary emphasis from the beginning. Membership was open to all who subscribed to its brief constitution, and it rapidly developed into a church by 1913.

The Wesleyan Church is now spread across most of the United States and Canada and 37 other countries. The Wesleyan World Fellowship was organized in 1972 to unite Wesleyan mission bodies developing into mature churches.

The Wesleyan Church is a member of the Christian Holiness Association, the National Association of Evangelicals, and the World Methodist Council.

GENERAL ORGANIZATION

General Conference: quadrennial (next session, 1992)
International Center: P.O. Box 50434, Indianapolis, IN 46250. Tel. (317) 842-0444

OFFICERS

Gen. Supts.: Dr. O. D. Emery, Dr. Earle L. Wilson, Dr. Lee M. Haines, Dr. H. C. Wilson
Gen. Sec., Dr. Ronald R. Brannon
Gen. Treas., Mr. Daniel D. Busby
Gen. Ed., Dr. Wayne E. Caldwell
Gen. Publisher, Rev. Nathan Birky
Gen. Sec. Evangelism and Church Growth, Rev. B. Marlin Mull
Gen. Sec. World Missions, Dr. Wayne W. Wright
Gen. Sec. Local Church Edu., Dr. David L. Keith
Gen. Sec. Youth, Rev. Thomas E. Armiger
Gen. Sec. Education and the Ministry, Dr. Kenneth Heer
Gen. Dir. Estate Planning, Rev. Howard B. Castle

Gen. Dir. Broadcast Ministries, Dr. Norman G. Wilson
Gen. Dir. Wesleyan Pension Fund, Mr. Leland K. Crist
Gen. Dir. Wesleyan Investment Foundation, Rev. John A. Dunn

PERIODICALS

The Wesleyan Advocate, Dr. Wayne E. Caldwell, Ed.
Wesleyan World, Rev. Stanley K. Hoover, Exec. Ed.

Wesleyan Holiness Association of Churches

This body was founded Aug. 4, 1959 near Muncie, Indiana by a group of ministers and laymen who were drawn together for the purpose of spreading and conserving sweet, radical, scriptural holiness. These men came from various church bodies. This group is Wesleyan in doctrine and standards.

GENERAL ORGANIZATION

General Conference meets every two years.
Headquarters: 108 Carter Ave., Dayton, OH 45405

OFFICERS

Gen. Supt., Rev. J. Stevan Manley, 108 Carter Ave., Dayton, OH 45405 Tel. (513) 278-3770
Asst. Gen. Supt., Rev. Leon Jackson, 7121 N. 43rd Ave., Phoenix, AZ 85021. Tel. (206) 535-0425
Gen. Sec.-Treas., Rev. Robert W. Wilson, 10880 State Rt. 170, Negley, OH. Tel. (216)385-0416
Gen. Youth Pres., Rev. Nadine Fetterman, P.O. Box 4, Summerhill, PA 15958. Tel. (814)495-9487

PERIODICAL

Eleventh Hour Messenger (bi-m), Rev. J. Stevan Manley, Ed.

Wisconsin Evangelical Lutheran Synod

Organized in 1850 at Milwaukee, Wisconsin by three pastors sent to America by a German mission society. The name Wisconsin Evangelical Lutheran Synod still reflects its origins, although it has lost its local character and presently has congregations in 50 states and 3 Canadian provinces.

The Wisconsin Synod federated with the Michigan and Minnesota Synods in 1892 in order to more effectively carry on education and mission enterprises. A merger of these three Synods followed in 1917 to give the Wisconsin Evangelical Lutheran Synod its present form.

Although at its organization in 1850 the Synod turned away from conservative Lutheran theology, today it is ranked as one of the most conservative Lutheran bodies in the U.S. The Synod confesses that the Bible is the verbally inspired, infallible Word of God and subscribes without reservation to the confessional writings of the Lutheran Church. Its interchurch relations are determined by a firm commitment to the principle that unity of doctrine and practice are the prerequisites of pulpit and altar fellowship and ecclesial cooperation. Consequently it does not hold membership in ecumenical organizations.

Churches: 1,191; Inclusive Membership: 418,691; Sunday or Sabbath Schools: 1,161; Total Enrollment: 49,713; Ordained Clergy: 1,538.

GENERAL ORGANIZATION

Convention: biennial (Next meeting, 1991)
National Offices: 2929 North Mayfair Rd., Wauwatosa, WI 53222. Tel. (414) 771-9357

OFFICERS

Pres., Rev. Carl H. Mischke, 2929 N. Mayfair Rd., Wauwatosa, WI 53222
1st Vice-Pres., Rev. Richard E. Lauersdorf, 105 Aztalan Ct., Jefferson, WI 53549
2nd Vice-Pres., Rev. Robert J. Zink, S66, WI4275 Janesville Rd., Muskego, WI 53150
Sec., Rev. David Worgull, 1201 W. Tulsa, Chandler, AZ 85224

OTHER ORGANIZATIONS

Bd. of Trustees: Admn., Rev. Robert C. Van Norstrand; Bd. for Worker Trng., Admn., Rev. Wayne Borgwardt; Bd. for Parish Education: Admn., Donald H. Zimmerman; Bd. for Home Missions: Admn., Rev. Harold J. Hagedorn; Bd. for World Missions: Admn., Rev. Duane K. Tomhave; Special Ministries Board: Admn., Alfons Woldt; Bd. for Evangelism: Admn., Rev. Robert C. Hartman; Public Relations: Dir., Rev. James P. Schaefer

PERIODICALS

Wisconsin Lutheran Quarterly (q), 11831 N. Seminary Dr., 65 W. Mequon, WI 53092. Prof. Wilbert R. Gawrisch, Mng. Ed.
Northwestern Lutheran (semi-m), 2929 N. Mayfair Rd., Wauwatosa, WI 53222. Rev. James P. Schaefer, Ed.
The Lutheran Educator, 2929 N. Mayfair Rd., Wauwatosa, WI 53222. Prof. John R. Isch, Ed.

World Confessional Lutheran Association

The World Confessional Lutheran Association (WCLA) was originally named Lutheran's Alert National (LAN) when it was founded in 1965 by a small group of conservative Lutheran pastors and laymen meeting in Cedar Rapids, Iowa. Its purpose was to help preserve from erosion the basic doctrines of Christian theology, including the inerrancy of Holy Scripture. The small group of ten grew to a worldwide constituency, similarly concerned over maintaining the doctrinal integrity of the Bible and the Lutheran Confessions.

The name World Confessional Lutheran Association was adopted by the board in 1984, to reflect the growing global outreach and involvement of our movement.

GENERAL ORGANIZATION

Board meets twice yearly (June and November).
Headquarters: 3504 N. Pearl St., P.O. Box 7186, Tacoma, WA 98407. Tel. (206) 759-1891

OFFICERS

Pres., Dr. Rueben H. Redal, 409 N. Tacoma Ave., Tacoma, WA 98403
Vice Pres., Dr. Arthur H. Braun, 341 S. Hamline Ave., St. Paul, MN 55105
Sec., Dr. Carl O. Pederson, 18284 Springdale Ct., Seattle, WA 98177. Tel. (206)542-3817
Treas., Mr. William A. Kunigk, 7902 52nd St. Ct. W., Tacoma, WA 98467
Dean, Faith Ev. Luth. Sem., Dr. John F. Falk, 7600 Juneau Ct., Port Orchard, WA 98366
Director of Ministries, Dr. Lloyd R. Nelson, 4611 N. 39th, Tacoma, WA 98407

PERIODICALS

Lutherans Alert National (m), P.O. Box 7186, Tacoma, WA 98407, Dr. Paul Vigness, Ed.
Lutheran World Concerns (q), P.O. Box 7186, Tacoma, WA 98407, Rev. Lloyd Nelson, Ed.

RELIGIOUS BODIES IN THE UNITED STATES ARRANGED BY FAMILIES

The following list of religious bodies appearing in the Directory Section of this **Yearbook** shows the "families," or related clusters into which American religious bodies can be grouped. For example, there are many communions that can be grouped under the heading "Baptist" for historical and theological reasons. It is not to be assumed, however, that all denominations under one family heading are similar in belief or practice. Often, any similarity is purely coincidental. The family clusters tend to represent historical factors more often than theological or practical ones. The family categories provided one of the major pitfalls of church statistics because of the tendency to combine the statistics by "families" for analytical and comparative purposes. Such combined totals are almost meaningless, although often used as variables for sociological analysis. **Religious bodies not grouped under family headings appear alphabetically and are not indented in the following list.**

ADVENTIST BODIES

Advent Christian Church
Church of God General Conference (Oregon, IL.)
Primitive Advent Christian Church
Seventh-day Adventists

Amana Church Society
American Evangelical Christian Churches
American Rescue Workers
Apostolic Christian Church (Nazarene)
Apostolic Christian Churches of America
The Anglican Orthodox Church
Baha'i Faith

BAPTIST BODIES

American Baptist Association
American Baptist Churches in the U.S.A.
Baptist Bible Fellowship, International
Baptist General Conference
Baptist Missionary Association of America
Bethel Ministerial Association, Inc.
Conservative Baptist Association of America
Duck River (and Kindred) Associations of Baptists
Free Will Baptists
General Association of Regular Baptist Churches
General Baptists, General Association of
General Conference of the Evangelical Baptist Church, Inc.
General Six-Principle Baptists
Liberty Baptist Fellowship
National Baptist Convention of America
National Baptist Convention, U.S.A., Inc.
National Primitive Baptist Convention, Inc.
North American Baptist General Conference
Primitive Baptists
Progressive National Baptist Convention, Inc.
Separate Baptists in Christ
Seventh Day Baptist General Conference
Southern Baptist Convention
Sovereign Grace Baptists

Berean Fundamental Church

BRETHREN (GERMAN BAPTISTS)

Brethren Church (Ashland, Ohio)
Church of the Brethren
Grace Brethren Churches, Fellowship of
Old German Baptist Brethren

BRETHREN, RIVER

Brethren in Christ Church
United Zion Church

Buddhist Churches of America,
Christadelphians
The Christian and Missionary Alliance
Christian Brethren
Christian Catholic Church

The Christian Congregation
Christian Nation Church U.S.A.
Christian Union
Church of Christ, Scientist
Church of Daniel's Band
The Church of Illumination
Church of the Living God (C.W.F.F.)
Church of the Nazarene
Churches of Christ in Christian Union

CHURCHES OF CHRIST-CHRISTIAN CHURCHES

Christian Church (Disciples of Christ)
Christian Churches and Churches of Christ
Churches of Christ

CHURCHES OF GOD

Church of God (Anderson, Ind.)
Church of God by Faith
The Church of God (Seventh Day), Denver, Colo.,
Church of God (Which He Purchased With His Own Blood)
Churches of God, General Conference

CHURCHES OF THE NEW JERUSALEM

General Church of the New Jerusalem
General Convention, The Swedenborgian Church

Community Churches, International Council of
Congregational Christian Churches, National Association of
Conservative Congregational Christian Conference

EASTERN CHURCHES

Albanian Orthodox Archdiocese in America
Albanian Orthodox Diocese of America
The American Carpatho-Russian Orthodox Greek Catholic Church
The Antiochian Orthodox Christian Archdiocese of N.A.
Apostolic Catholic Assyrian Church of the East, North American Diocese
Armenian Apostolic Church of America
Armenian Church of America, Diocese of the
Bulgarian Eastern Orthodox Church
Coptic Orthodox Church
Greek Orthodox Archdiocese of North and South America
Holy Ukrainian Autocephalic Orthodox Church in Exile
The Orthodox Church in America
Romanian Orthodox Church in America
The Romanian Orthodox Episcopate of America

Russian Orthodox Church in the U.S.A., Patriarchal
  Parishes of the
The Russian Orthodox Church Outside Russia
Serbian Orthodox Church in the U.S.A. and Canada
Syrian Orthodox Church of Antioch (Archdiocese of
  the U.S.A. and Canada)
True (Old Calendar) Orthodox Church of Greece
  (Synod of Metropolitan Cyprian), American Exar-
  chate
Ukrainian Orthodox Church of the U.S.A.
Ukrainian Orthodox Church in America (Ecumenical
  Patriarchate)

The Episcopal Church
Ethical Culture Movement
Evangelical Church of North America
Evangelical Congregational Church
The Evangelical Covenant Church
The Evangelical Free Church of America
Fellowship of Fundamental Bible Churches
The Fire-Baptized Holiness Church (Wesleyan)
Free Christian Zion Church of Christ

Friends

Evangelical Friends Alliance
Friends General Conference
Friends United Meeting
Religious Society of Friends (Conservative)
Religious Society of Friends (Unaffiliated Meetings)

Grace Gospel Fellowship
The Holiness Church of God, Inc.
House of God, Which is the Church of the Living God,
  the Pillar and Ground of the Truth, Inc.
Independent Fundamental Churches of America
Israelite House of David
Jehovah's Witnesses
Jews
Kodesh Church of Immanuel

Latter Day Saints

Church of Christ
The Church of Jesus Christ (Bickertonites)
The Church of Jesus Christ of Latter-day Saints
Reorganized Church of Jesus Christ of Latter Day
Saints

The Liberal Catholic Church-Province of the United States
of America

Lutherans

Apostolic Lutheran Church of America
Church of the Lutheran Brethren of America
Church of the Lutheran Confession
Estonian Evangelical Lutheran Church
Evangelical Lutheran Church in America
Evangelical Lutheran Synod
Free Lutheran Congregations, The Association of
Latvian Evangelical Lutheran Church in America
The Lutheran Church—Missouri Synod
Lutheran Churches, The American Association of
The Protestant Conference (Lutheran)
Wisconsin Evangelical Lutheran Synod
World Confessional Lutheran Association

Mennonite Bodies

Beachy Amish Mennonite Churches
Church of God in Christ (Mennonite)
Evangelical Mennonite Church
Fellowship of Evangelical Bible Churches

General Conference of Mennonite Brethren Churches
Hutterian Brethren
Mennonite Church
Mennonite Church, The General Conference
Old Order Amish Church
Old Order (Wisler) Mennonite Church
Reformed Mennonite Church

Methodist Bodies

African Methodist Episcopal Church
African Methodist Episcopal Zion Church
Allegheny Wesleyan Methodist Connection
  (Original Allegheny Conference)
Christian Methodist Episcopal Church
Evangelical Methodist Church
Free Methodist Church of North America
Fundamental Methodist Church, Inc.
Primitive Methodist Church in the U.S.A.
Reformed Methodist Union Episcopal Church
Reformed Zion Union Apostolic Church
Southern Methodist Church
The United Methodist Church
The Wesleyan Church

The Metropolitan Church Association
Metropolitan Community Churches, Universal Fellowship
of
The Missionary Church

Moravian Bodies

Moravian Church in America (Unitas Fratrum)
Unity of the Brethren

Muslims
National Spiritualist Association of Churches
New Apostolic Church of North America
North American Old Roman Catholic Church (Archdio-
  cese of New York)

Old Catholic Churches

Christ Catholic Church
North American Old Roman Catholic Church

Pentecostal Bodies

*Holiness-Pentecostal Denominations**
  The Apostolic Faith
  The Church of God
  Church of God (Cleveland, Tenn.)
  The Church of God in Christ
  Church of God in Christ, International
  The Church of God of Prophecy
  The Church of God of the Mountain Assembly
  Congregational Holiness Church
  International Pentecostal Church of Christ
  The (Original) Church of God
  Pentecostal Fire-Baptized Holiness Church
  Pentecostal Free-Will Baptist Church, Inc.
  Pentecostal Holiness Church, International
  United Holy Church of America
*Baptistic-Pentecostal Denominations**
  Assemblies of God
  Assemblies of God International Fellowship
    (Independent/Not Affiliated)
  The Bible Church of Christ, Inc.
  Christian Church of North America, General Council
  Elim Fellowship
  Full Gospel Assemblies, International
  Full Gospel Fellowship of Churches and Ministers,
    International
  International Church of the Foursquare Gospel

Open Bible Standard Churches
Pentecostal Church of God
Unitarian (Oneness)-Pentecostal Denominations*
Apostolic Faith Mission Church of God
Apostolic Overcoming Holy Church of God
Bible Way Church of Our Lord Jesus Christ, World
Wide, Inc.
Church of Our Lord Jesus Christ of the Apostolic Faith
Pentecostal Assemblies of the World
United Pentecostal Church, International
(*The above typology for Pentecostal Bodies was supplied
by Dr. H. Vinson Synan, Asst. Gen. Supt., International
Pentecostal Holiness Church, to whom the editor is
grateful. According to Dr. Synan, "Holiness-Pentecostal"
bodies are those that teach the three stages theory of
Christian experience [i.e., conversion, sanctification,
baptism of the Holy Spirit]. "Baptistic-Pentecostal"
denominations are those that teach a two-stage theory
[i.e., conversion and baptism of the Holy Spirit].
"Unitarian-Pentecostal" bodies deny the traditional concept of the Trinity and teach that Jesus Christ alone is
God.)

Pillar of Fire
Polish National Catholic Church of America

PRESBYTERIAN BODIES

Associate Reformed Presbyterian Church (General
Synod)
Cumberland Presbyterian Church
Evangelical Presbyterian Church
Korean Presbyterian Church in America,
General Assembly of the

The Orthodox Presbyterian Church
Presbyterian Church in America
Presbyterian Church in (U.S.A.)
Reformed Presbyterian Church of North America
Second Cumberland Presbyterian Church in U.S.

REFORMED BODIES

Christian Reformed Church in North America
Hungarian Reformed Church in America
Netherlands Reformed Congregations
Protestant Reformed Churches in America
Reformed Church in America
Reformed Church in the U.S.
United Church of Christ

Reformed Episcopal Church
The Roman Catholic Church
The Salvation Army
The Schwenkfelder Church
Social Brethren
Triumph the Church and Kingdom of God in Christ
Unitarian Universalist Association

UNITED BRETHREN BODIES

United Brethren in Christ
United Christian Church

Vedanta Society
Volunteers of America
Wesleyan Holiness Association of Churches

4. RELIGIOUS BODIES IN CANADA

A large number of Canadian religious bodies were organized by immigrants from Europe and elsewhere and a smaller number of them sprang up originally on Canadian soil. In the case of Canada, moreover, many denominations overlapping the U.S.-Canadian border have headquarters in the United States.

Over the years much effort has been made in developing this directory, and it is fairly complete in its listing of major denominations. The editor of the **Yearbook of American and Canadian Churches** would be grateful for information on any major Canadian religious body not now included.

What follows is, first, an alphabetical directory of religious bodies in Canada that have supplied information for this edition of the **Yearbook.** The second section is an alphabetical list, with addresses and other information, of bodies known to exist in Canada that have not yet supplied directory information. This second section is entitled "Other Religious Bodies in Canada."

Those denominations that have not checked and returned their directory for this edition carry the symbol (†) in front of the title.

A listing of Canadian religious bodies classified by family groups (e.g., Baptists) appears at the end of this directory.

Complete statistics for Canadian denominations will be found in the table "Canadian Current and Non-Current Statistics" in Section III of this **Yearbook.** Statistics appearing in the denominational directories which follow are Current only; that is, those gathered in 1988 and 1989:

The Anglican Church of Canada

Anglicanism came to Canada with the early explorers such as Martin Frobisher and Henry Hudson. Continuous services began in Newfoundland about 1700 and in Nova Scotia in 1710. The first Bishop, Charles Inglis, was appointed to Nova Scotia in 1787. The numerical strength of Anglicanism was increased by the coming of American Loyalists and by massive immigration both after the Napoleonic wars and in the later 19th and early 20th centuries.

The Anglican Church of Canada has enjoyed self-government for over a century and is an autonomous member of the worldwide Anglican Communion. The General Synod, which normally meets triennially, consists of the Archbishops, Bishops, and elected clerical and lay representatives of the 30 dioceses. Each of the Ecclesiastical Provinces—Canada, Ontario, Rupert's Land, and British Columbia—is organized under a Metropolitan and has its own Provincial Synod and Executive Council. Each diocese has its own Diocesan Synod.

Churches: 3,105; Inclusive Membership: 805,521; Sunday or Sabbath Schools: 1,907; Total Enrollment: 88,525; Ordained Clergy: 3,300

GENERAL SYNOD OFFICERS

Primate of the Anglican Church of Canada, Most Rev. M. G. Peers, 600 Jarvis St., Toronto, Ontario M4Y 2J6
Prolocutor, Ven. R. T. Pynn, 903-75th, Calgary, Alberta T2V 0S7
Gen. Sec., Ven. D. J. Woeller, 600 Jarvis St., Toronto, Ontario M4Y 2J6
Treas. of Gen. Synod and all Departments, John R. Ligertwood, 600 Jarvis St., Toronto, Ontario M4Y 2J6
Exec. Dir. of Program, Rev. L. C. Raymond, 600 Jarvis St., Toronto, Ontario M4Y 2J6.

DEPARTMENTS AND DIVISIONS

Offices: Church House, 600 Jarvis St., Toronto, Ontario M4Y 2J6. Tel. (416)924-9192
Dir. and Publ., Anglican Book Centre, Rev. M. J. Lloyd Missionary Society of the Anglican Church of Canada.
Exec. Sec., Rev. J. S. Barton
Dir. of World Mission: Rev. J. S. Barton
Dir. of Planning: Rev. W. E. Lowe
Division of Pensions: Dir., Mrs. J. Mason
Dir. of Administration and Finance: J. R. Ligertwood
Dir. of Communications, D. Tindal
Dir. of Resources and Ministry, Rev. D. Hodgkinson
Dir. of Social Action Ministries, Ms. J. Rowles

METROPOLITANS (ARCHBISHOPS)
(Address: The Most Reverend)

Ecclesiastical Province of:
Canada: _____
Rupert's Land: Walter Jones, 935 Nesbitt Bay, Winnipeg, Manitoba R3T 1W6. Tel. (204)453-6130
British Columbia: Douglas Hambidge, 302-814 Richards St.,Vancouver, British Columbia V6B 3A7, Tel. (604)684-6306
Ontario: John Bothwell, 67 Victoria Ave., S., Hamilton, Ontario L8N 2S8. Tel. (416)527-1117

DIOCESAN ARCHBISHOPS AND BISHOPS

(Address: The Most Reverend; The Right Reverend)
Algoma: L. Peterson, 619 Wellington St., E, Box 1168, Sault Ste. Marie, Ontario P6A 5N7. Tel. (705)256-5061
Arctic: J. R. Sperry, 1055 Avenue Rd., Toronto, Ontario M5N 2C8. Tel. (416)481-2263
Athabasca: G. Woolsey, Box 279, Peace River, Alberta T0H 2X0. Tel. (403)624-2767
Brandon: J. F. S. Conlin, 341-13th St., Brandon, Manitoba R7A 4P8. Tel. (204)727-7550
British Columbia: R. F. Shepherd, 912 Vancouver St., Victoria, British Columbia V8V 3V7. Tel. (604)386-7781
Caledonia: J. E. Hannen, Box 278, Prince Rupert, British Columbia V8J 3P6. Tel. (604)624-6013
Calgary: J. B. Curtis, 3015 Glencoe Rd. S. W., Calgary, Alberta T2S 2L9. Tel. (403)243-3673
Cariboo: J. S. P. Snowden, 1-440 Victoria St., Kamloops, British Columbia. V2C 2A7. Tel. (604)374-0237
Edmonton: K Genge, 10033 - 84 Ave., Edmonton, Alberta T6E 2G6. Tel. (403)439-7344
Fredericton: G. C. Lemmon, 115 Church St., Fredericton, New Brunswick E3B 4C8. Tel. (506)459-1801
Huron: Derwyn Jones, 4-220 Dundas St., London, Ontario N6A 1H3, Tel. (519)434-6893
Keewatin: H. J. P. Allan, Box 118, 217 Sixth Ave. S. Kenora, Ontario P9N 3X1. Tel. (807)468-7011
Kootenay: _____, Box 549, Kelowna, British Columbia V1Y 7P2 Tel. (604)762-3306
Montreal: R. Hollis, 1444 Union Ave., Montreal, Quebec H3B 2B8. Tel. (514)879-1722
Moosonee: C. J. Lawrence, Box 841, Schumacher, Ontario P0N 1G0. Tel. (705)267-1129
Eastern Newfoundland and Labrador: M. Mate, 19 King's Bridge Rd., St. John's, Newfoundland A1C 3K4. Tel. (709)576-6697
Central Newfoundland: M. Genge, 34 Fraser Rd., Gander, Newfoundland A1V 2E8 Tel. (709)256-2372
Western Newfoundland, S. S. Payne, 83 West St., Corner Brook, Newfoundland A2H 2Y6. Tel. (709)639-8712

New Westminster: D. W. Hambidge (Archbishop), 302-814 Richards St., Vancouver, British Columbia V6B 3A7. Tel. (604)684-6306
Niagara: J. C. Bothwell (Archbishop), 67 Victoria Ave. S., Hamilton, Ontario. L8N 2S8. Tel. (416) 527-1117
Nova Scotia: A. G. Peters, 5732 College St., Halifax, Nova Scotia B3H 1X3. Tel. (902) 420-0717
Ontario: A. A. Read, 90 Johnson St., Kingston, Ontario. K7L 1X7. Tel. (613) 544-4774
Ottawa: E. K. Lackey, 71 Bronson Ave., Ottawa, Ontario K1R 6G6. Tel. (613) 232-7124
Qu'Appelle: E. Bays, 1501 College Ave., Regina, Saskatchewan S4P 1B8. Tel. (306) 522-1608
Quebec: A. Goodings, 36 rue des Jardins, Quebec, Quebec G1R 4L5. Tel. (418) 692-3858
Rupert's Land: W. Jones, 935 Nesbitt Bay, Winnipeg, Manitoba R3T 1W6. Tel. (204) 453-6130
Saskatchewan: T. O. Morgan, Box 1088, Prince Albert, Saskatchewan S6V 5S6. Tel. (306) 763-2455
Saskatoon: R. A. Wood, Box 1965, Saskatoon, Saskatchewan S7K 3S5. Tel. (306) 244-5651
Toronto: T. Finlay, 135 Adelaide St., E., Toronto, Ontario M5C 1L8. Tel. (416) 363-6021
Yukon: R. C. Ferris, Box 4247, 41 Firth Rd., Whitehorse, Yukon Y1A 3T3. Tel. (403) 667-7746

The Antiochian Orthodox Christian Archdiocese of North America

There are approximately 100,000 members of the Antiochian Orthodox community living in Canada. They are under the jurisdiction of the Antiochian Orthodox Christian Archdiocese of North America with headquarters in Englewood, NJ. There are churches in Edmonton, Winnipeg, Halifax, London, Ottawa, Toronto, Windsor, Montreal, Borden, Saskatoon.

GENERAL ORGANIZATION

Metropolitan Philip Saliba, 358 Mountain Rd., Englewood, NJ 07631

Apostolic Christian Church (Nazarene)

This church was formed in Canada as a result of immigration from various European countries. The body began as a movement originated by the Rev. S. H. Froehlich, a Swiss pastor, whose followers are still found in Switzerland and Central Europe.

GENERAL ORGANIZATION

Headquarters: Apostolic Christian Church Foundation, P.O. Box 151, Tremont, IL 61568

OFFICER

Gen. Sec. Eugene R. Galat, P.O. Box 151, Tremont, IL 61568. Tel. (309) 925-5162

PERIODICAL

Newsletter (bi-m)

The Apostolic Church in Canada

The Apostolic Church in Canada is affiliated with the worldwide organization of the Apostolic Church with headquarters in Great Britain.

A product of the Welsh Revival (1904-1908), its Canadian beginnings originated in Nova Scotia in 1927. Today its main centers are in Nova Scotia, Ontario, and Quebec.

This church is evangelical, fundamental, and Pentecostal, with special emphasis on the ministry gifts listed in Ephesians 4:11-12.

Churches: 14 Inclusive Membership: 1,600; Sunday or Sabbath Schools: 14; Total Enrollment: 350; Ordained Clergy: 18

GENERAL ORGANIZATION

The Apostolic Church Council, twice yearly.

OFFICERS

Pres., Rev. D. S. Morris, 685 Park St. South, Peterborough, Ontario K9J 3S9
Natl. Sec., Rev. J. Kristensen, 388 Gerald St., Ville La Salle, Quebec H8P 2A5

Apostolic Church of Pentecost of Canada Inc.

This body was founded in 1921 at Winnipeg, Manitoba, by Pastor Frank Small. Doctrines include belief in eternal salvation by the grace of God, baptism of the Holy Spirit with the evidence of speaking in tongues, water baptism by emersion in the name of the Lord Jesus Christ.

Churches: 134; Inclusive Membership: 13,000; Sunday or Sabbath Schools: N.R.; Total Enrollment: N.R.; Ordained Clergy: 213

GENERAL ORGANIZATION

Annual Ministers Conference: Next meeting June 5-7, 1990, Prince George, British Columbia
Headquarters: 105, 807 Manning Rd. N.E., Calgary, Alberta T2E 7M9

OFFICERS

Moderator, Rev. W. S. Schindel, 105, 807 Manning Rd. N.E., Calgary, Alberta T2E 7M9
Clerk, Leonard K. Larsen, 105, 807 Manning Rd. N.E., Calgary, Alberta T2E 7M9
Missionary Council Chpsn., E. G. Bradley, Box 322, Maple Ridge, British Columbia V2X 7G2

PERIODICAL

End Times' Messenger (11/yr.), 105, 807 Manning Rd. N.E., Calgary, Alberta T2E 7M9. I. W. Ellis, Ed.

The Armenian Church of North America, Diocese of Canada

The Canadian branch of the ancient Church of Armenia founded in A.D. 301 by St. Gregory the Illuminator. It was established in Canada at St. Catherines, Ontario, in 1930. The diocesan organization is under the jurisdiction of the Holy See of Etchmiadzin, Armenia, U.S.S.R. The Diocese has churches in St. Catherine, Hamilton, Toronto, Scarborough, Ottawa, Vancouver, and Montreal.

GENERAL ORGANIZATION

Diocesan Offices: His Eminence Archbishop Vazken Keshishian Primate, Canadian Diocese, 615 Stuart Ave., Outremont, Quebec H2V 3H2. Tel. (514) 276-9479

PERIODICALS

Nor Serount (m) in Armenian and English, 20 Progress Ct., Scarborough, Ontario M1G 3T5.
Pourastan (m) in Armenian, 615 Stuart Ave., Montreal, Quebec H2V 3H2
Varaka Soorp Khatch (m), 225, Van Horne Ave., #1105, Willowdale, Ontario M2J 3T9
Avedaper (m) in Armenian and English, St. Mary Armenian Church, 8 Mayhurst Ave., Hamilton, Ontario L8K 3M8
Avarayr, in Armenian and English, St. Vartan Armenian Church, 1260 W. 67th Ave., Vancouver, British Columbia V6P 2T2

Armenian Evangelical Church

Founded in 1960 by immigrant Armenian evangelical families from the Middle East. This body is conservative doctrinally, with an evangelical, biblical emphasis. The polity of churches within the group differ with congregationalism being dominant, but there are Presbyterian Armenian Evangelical churches as well. Most of the local churches have joined main-line denominations. All of the Armenian Evangelical (Congregational or Presbyterian) local churches in the U.S. and Canada have joined with the Armenian Evangelical Union of North America.

GENERAL ORGANIZATION

Armenian Evangelical Union of North America. Meets every two years. Next convention, June 1990, Boston, MA

A.E.U.N.A. OFFICERS

Minister to the Union, Rev. Karl Avakian, 140 Forest Ave., Paramus, NJ 07652

OFFICERS

Minister, Rev. Yessayi Sarmazian, 42 Glenforest Rd., Toronto, Ontario M4N 1Z8. Tel. (416) 489-3188

PERIODICAL

Canada Armenian Press (q), 42 Glenforest Rd., Toronto, Ontario M4N 1Z8. Rev. Y. Sarmazian, Ed.

Associated Gospel Churches

The Associated Gospel Churches (A.G.C.) body traces its historical roots to the early years of the twentieth century, which were marked by the growth of liberal theology in many established denominations. Many individuals and, in many cases, whole congregations, seeking to uphold the final authority of the Scriptures in all matters of faith and conduct, withdrew from those denominations.

As a result, churches which fostered an evangelical ministry under the inspired Word of God were established. These churches defended the belief that "all Scripture is given by inspiration of God" and also declared that the Holy Spirit "gave the identical words of sacred writings of holy men of old, chosen by Him to be the channel of His revelation to man."

In 1922, four churches of similar background in Ontario banded together in fellowship for counsel and cooperation. Known as The Christian Workers' Church in Canada, the group consisted of the Gospel Tabernacle, Hamilton; the Winona Gospel Tabernacle; the Missionary Tabernacle, Toronto; and West Hamilton Gospel Mission. The principal organizers were Dr. P. W. Philpott of Hamilton and H. E. Irwin, K. C., of Toronto.

In 1925 the name was changed to Associated Gospel Churches under a new Dominion Charter. Since that time the A.G.C. has grown steadily.

Churchs: 120; Inclusive Membership: 17,000; Sunday or Sabbath Schools: N.R.; Total Enrollment: N.R.; Ordained Clergy: 223

GENERAL ORGANIZATION

Annual Conference. A 13-member Cabinet acts in the interim.

Headquarters: 280 Plains Rd. W., Burlington, Ontario L7T 1G4

OFFICERS

Pres., _____
Vice-Pres., _____
Mod., Rev. R. G. Gannett, 1500 Kerns Rd., Burlington, Ontario L7T 2M6. Tel. (416)639-8785

Sec.-Treas., Ritchie Penhall, 2 Bonnaventure Dr., Hamilton, Ontario L9C 4P3. Tel. (416)388-3672

PERIODICALS

Advance (q), 8 Silver St., Paris, Ontario N3L 1T6. Rev. W. Foster, Ed.

Association of Regular Baptist Churches (Canada)

Organized in 1957 by a group of churches for the purpose of mutual cooperation in missionary activities. The Association believes the Bible to be God's word, stands for historic Baptist principles, and opposes modern ecumenism.

Headquarters: 130 Gerrard St. E., Toronto, Ontario, M5A 3T4. Tel. (416) 925-3261

OFFICERS

Pres., Rev. Stephen Kring, 25 Sovereen St., Delhi, Ontario N4B 1L6
Field Sec., Rev. Tom Rush, Oromocto, New Brunswick
Sec., Rev. W. P. Bauman, 130 Gerrard St. E., Toronto, Ontario M5A 3T4

PERIODICAL

The Gospel Witness, 130 Gerrard St. E., Toronto, Ontario M5A 3T4. Rev. N. H. Street, Ed.

Baha'i Faith

(National Spiritual Assembly of the Bahá'ís of Canada).

Bahá'ís are followers of Bahá'u'lláh (1817-1892) whose religion teaches the essential oneness of all the great religions and promotes the oneness of mankind and racial unity.

The Bahá'í administrative order consists of nine-member elected institutions called spiritual assemblies, which function at the local and national level. The international administrative institution, the Universal House of Justice, is located in Haifa, Israel, at the Bahá'í World Centre, the spiritual headquarters of the Bahá'í community and the burial place of its founders.

In Canada, the Bahá'í Faith is administered by the National Spiritual Assembly. This body was incorporated by Act of Parliament in 1949. There are approximately 1500 Bahá'í centers in Canada, of which 350 elect local Spiritual Assemblies.

GENERAL ORGANIZATION

Bahá'í National Centre of Canada: 7200 Leslie St., Thornhill, Ontario L3T 6L8. Tel. (416)889-8168 Sec., Dr. H. B. Danesh

Baptist General Conference of Canada

Founded in Canada by missionaries from the United States. Originally a Swedish body, but no longer an ethnic body. The BGC-Canada includes people of many nationalities and is conservative and evangelical in doctrine and practice.

Head Office: #3,9833-44 Ave., Edmonton, Alberta T6E 5E3. Tel. (403) 438-9127

OFFICERS

Pres. John Harapiak, 816 Canford Crescent, S.W., Calary, Alberta T2W 1L2.
Exec. Dir., Rev. Abe Funk, 11635-51st Ave., Edmonton, Alberta T6H OM4. Tel. (403) 435-4403

1. The Central Canada Baptist Conference

Central Baptist Conference, originally a Scandinavian group, is one of three districts of the Baptist General Conference of Canada. In 1907, churches from Winnipeg—Grant Memorial, Teulon, Kenora, Port Arthur, Sprague, Erickson, and Midale—organized under the leadership of Fred Palmberg. Immigration from Sweden declined, and in 1947 only nine churches remained. In 1948 the group dropped the Swedish language, withdrew from the Baptist Union, city churches were started, and today CCBC has 37 functioning churches.

An evangelical Baptist association holding to the inerrancy of the Bible, CCBC seeks to reach Central Canada for Christ by establishing local gospel-preaching churches.

CCBC offers pastoral aid to new churches, loans for building, recommendations as to pastoral supply, counsel, and fellowship. It encourages contributions to the CCBC and BGC of Canada budgets, the purchase of CCBC Serial Notes, support of the Conference BATT program (contributions to special needs of churches), and other projects to assist needy churches and pastors.

The Annual Conference in May

Head Office: 1850 Ness Ave., Winnipeg, Manitoba R3J 3J9. Tel. (204) 837-2679

OFFICERS

Exec. Min., Dr. Dave Selness, Gen. Del., Stonewall, Manitoba R0C 2Z0

PERIODICAL

The Christian Link (m)

2. Baptist General Conference of Alberta

Annual Conference in May

Head Office: #4, 9825-44 Ave., Edmonton, Alberta T6E 5E3. Tel. (403) 438-9126

OFFICERS

Exec. Sec., Virgil Olson, 1843-104A St., Edmonton, Alberta. T6J 5C1

PERIODICAL

The Alberta Alert, # 4, 9825-44th Ave., Edmonton, Alberta T6E 5E3.

3. British Columbia Baptist Conference

British Columbia Baptist Conference is a district of the Baptist General Conference of Canada, with roots in Sweden, where Christians began to read the Bible in their homes. One convert, F. O. Nilsson, saw the significance of baptism subsequent to a personal commitment to Christ; he went to Hamburg, Germany, where he was baptized in the Elbe River by Rev. John Oncken. When Nilsson returned to Sweden five of his converts were baptized in the North Sea and, with him, formed the first Swedish Baptist Church. Nilsson was imprisoned by the local government for violation of state church regulations and later, when exiled from Sweden, went to the United States. As Swedish Baptists immigrated to the United States to escape persecution, they formed churches in Illinois, Iowa, Minnesota, and Wisconsin and carried on aggressive evangelism among other immigrating Swedes. In 1879 they formed the Swedish Baptist General Conference of America, later named The Baptist General Conference.

Columbia Baptist Conference, with churches in Washington, Oregon, Idaho, Montana, and Alaska, is a district of the Baptist General Conference. In 1910 Columbia Baptist Conference planted a new church in Matsqui, B.C., and by 1985 there were 20 Baptist General Conference churches in B.C. These 20 churches voted in June 1985 to become a new and separate district of the Baptist General Conference of Canada. There are strong ties of fellowship and involvement in special retreats and camping programs with the Columbia District, but the B.C. churches are a separate corporate entity of 23 churches, one of three districts in the Baptist General Conference of Canada, which has 75 churches, from Thunder Bay, Ontario, to Victoria, B.C.

The Swedish language is a cherished heritage of Baptist General Conference churches in the United States and Canada, but by 1935 the churches had become totally English-speaking. In recent years they have become multiethnic, ministering in Filipino, Hindi, Japanese, Chinese, and French, as well as English. A very low percentage of members have any Swedish connection.

The churches in British Columbia Baptist Conference are conservative in theology, evangelistic in activity, irenic in spirit, and pietistic in life-style. They participate with other Baptists and evangelical churches in cooperative ministries.

Annual Conference in May.

Head Office: 7600 Glover Rd., Langley,, British Columbia V3A 6H4.

OFFICERS

Interim Exec. Min., Rev. William Funk, 7600 Glover Rd., Langley, British Columbia V3A 6H4.

PERIODICAL

B.C. Conference Call, 7600 Glover Rd., Langley, British Columbia V3A 6H4. Rev. William Funk, Ed.

The Bible Holiness Movement

The Bible Holiness Movement, organized in 1949 as an outgrowth of the city mission work of the late Pastor William James Elijah Wakefield, an early-day Salvation Army officer, has been headed since its inception by his son, Evangelist Wesley H. Wakefield, its bishop-general.

It derives its emphasis on the original Methodist faith of salvation and scriptural holiness from the late Bishop R. C. Horner. It adheres to the common evangelical faith in the Bible, the Deity, and the atonement of Christ, and stresses a personal experience of salvation for the repentant sinner, of being wholly sanctified for the believer, and of the fullness of the Holy Spirit for effective witness.

Membership involves a life of Christian love, evangelistic and social activism, and the disciplines of simplicity and separation. This includes total abstinence from liquor and tobacco, nonattendance at popular amusements, and no membership in secret societies. Home permanency is affirmed by forbidding divorce and remarriage while there is a living spouse. Similar to Wesley's Methodism, members are, under some circumstances, allowed to retain membership in other evangelical church fellowships.

Government and ordination within the Movement is open to both men and women and is fully interracial and international. A number of interchurch affiliations are maintained with other Wesleyan-Arminian Holiness denominations.

The Movement is activist in both evangelism and social concern. Year-round evangelistic outreach is maintained through open-air meetings, visitation, literature, and other media. Noninstitutional welfare work, including addiction counseling, is conducted among minorities. There is direct overseas famine relief, as well as civil rights action, environment protection, and antinuclearism.

Sponsored organizations include a permanent committee on religious freedom and an active promotion of Christian racial equality.

Headquartered in Vancouver, Canada, the Movement has a world outreach with branches in the United States, India, Nigeria, Philippines, Ghana, Liberia, Cameroons, Kenya, Zambia, South Korea, and Haiti. It also ministers to 89 countries in 42 languages through literature, radio, and audio-cassetes.

Churches: 15; Inclusive Membership: 764; Sunday or Sabbath Schools: N.R.; Total Enrollment: N.R.; Ordained Clergy: 11 International Headquarters: Box 223 Postal Stn. A, Vancouver, British Columbia V6C 2M3. Tel. (604)498-3895

DIRECTORS

Evangelist Wesley H. Wakefield, Bishop-General. (International Leader)
Evangelist M. J. Wakefield, Oliver, British Columbia
Mrs. W. Sneed, #58, 5400 Dalhousie Rd., N.W., Calgary, Alberta
Mrs. E. A. Jamandre, Sagunto, Sison, Pangasinan, Philippines 0733
Pastor Vincente & Morasol Hernando, Urdaneta, Philippines
Pastor Daniel Stinnett, 1425 Mountain View W. Phoenix, AZ 85021
Pastor A. Sanon, Port-au-Prince, Haiti
Evangelist U. E. Udom, Ikona, Nigeria, West Africa
Pastor Augustus Theo Seongbae, Jr., Monrovia, Liberia
Pastor Choe Chong Dee, Cha Pa Puk, South Korea
Pastor E. Payako, Kenya, East Africa

PERIODICAL

Truth on Fire (bi-m), Box 223 Postal Stn. A., Vancouver, British Columbia V6C 2M3. Rev. Wesley H. Wakefield, Ed.

Brethren in Christ Church, Canadian Conference

The Brethren in Christ, formerly known as Tunkers in Canada, arose out of a religious awakening in Lancaster County, Pa., late in the eighteenth century. Representatives of the new denomination reached Ontario in 1788 and established the church in the southern part of the present province. Presently the conference has congregations in Ontario, Alberta, and Saskatchewan. In doctrine the body is evangelical, Arminian, holiness, and premillennial.

Churches: 36; Inclusive Membership: 3,587; Sunday or Sabbath Schools: 35; Total Enrollment: 2,254; Ordained Clergy: 51.
Headquarters: 301 N. Elm St., Nappanee, IN 46550. Tel. (219) 773-3164. Canadian Headquarters (Bishop's office): 1301 Niagara Pkwy., Ft. Erie, Ontario L2A 5M4. Tel. (416)382-3144

OFFICERS

Mod., Bishop Harvey Sider, 1301 Niagara Pkwy., Ft. Erie, Ontario L2A 5M4. Tel. (416)382-3144
Sec., Leonard J. Chester, 5384 Sherkston Rd., Sherkston, Ontario L0S 1RO

PERIODICAL

Evangelical Visitor (bi-w), Nappanee, IN 46550. Glen A. Pierce

British Methodist Episcopal Church of Canada

The British Methodist Episcopal Church was organized in 1856 in Chatham, Ontario and incorporated in 1913. It has congregations across the Province of Ontario.

GENERAL ORGANIZATION

Annual Conference: First week in July
Headquarters: 460 Shaw St., Toronto, Ontario M6G 3L3. Tel. (416)534-3831.

OFFICERS

Gen. Supt., Rev. Dr. D. D. Rupwate
Asst. Gen. Supt., Rev. M. A. Aylestock
Gen. Sec., Rev. Dr. W. Solomon
Gen. Treas., Mrs. A. Moore

Buddhist Churches of Canada

Founded at Vancouver, British Columbia in 1904. The first minister was the Rev. Senju Sasaki. This body is the Mahayana division of Buddhism, and its sectarian belief is the Pure Land School based on the Three Canonical Scriptures with emphasis on pure faith.

GENERAL ORGANIZATION

Administration Headquarters: 220 Jackson Ave., Vancouver, British Columbia V6A 3B3. Tel. (604)253-7033
Office of the Bishop: Bishop Toshio Murakami
B.C.C. Ministerial Association: Pres., Rev. Izumi

OFFICERS

Pres., Jitsoishi Oishi
Vice-Pres., Mitts Sakai
Sec., Mr. Roy Inouye
Treas., Mr. Jim Kitaura

Canadian and American Reformed Churches

The Canadian and American Reformed Churches accept the Bible as the infallible Word of God, as summarized in The Belgic Confession of Faith (1561), The Heidelberg Catechism (1563), and The Canons of Dordt (1618-1619). The denomination was founded in Canada in 1950 and American congregations have been formed since 1983.

Churches: 36; Inclusive Membership: 11,870; Sunday or Sabbath Schools: N.R. Total Enrollment: N.R.; Ordained Clergy: 42

GENERAL ORGANIZATION

Synod: Every three years. Next one in 1992. P. O. Box 124, Burlington, Ontario L7R 3X8
Canadian Reformed Churches: Contact Church is Ebenezer Canadian Reformed Church, P. O. Box 124, Burlington, Ontario L7R 3X8
American Reformed Churches: Contact Church is American Reformed Church, c/o Rev. P. Kingma, 3167-68th St., S.E., Caledonia, MI 49316.

PERIODICALS

Clarion: The Canadian Reformed Magazine, One Beghin Ave., Winnipeg, Manitoba R2J 3X5
CRTA Magazine, Immanuel Christian Highschool, 57 Suffolk St., W., Guelph, Ontario NIH 2J1
Diakonia: A Magazine for Office-Bearers, 3911 Mount Lehman Rd., Abbotsford, British Columbia V3S 4N9
Evangel: The Good News of Jesus Christ, The Reformed Evangelism Taskforce, Sta. A, P. O. Box 1008, Surrey, British Columbia V3S 4P5
In Holy Array. The Canadian Reformed Young Peoples' Societies, c/o Rev. E. Kampen, 21112 Thirty-fifth Ave. North-West, Edmonton Alberta T5P 4B7
Mission News, 10 Enola Ct., Hamilton, Ontario L8W 1S4
Reformed Perspective: A Magazine for the Christian Family, Box 12 Transcona Postal Sta., Winnipeg, Manitoba R2C 2Z5
Preach the Word, Rev. J. Visscher, 5734-191A St., Surrey, British Columbia V3S 4N9
Shield and Sword, Foundation for the Edification and Preservation of the Reformed Faith, P. O. Box 188, Smithville, Ontario LOR 2AO
Yearbook - Canadian and American Reformed Churches, One Beghin Ave., Winnipeg Manitoba R2J 3X5

Canadian Baptist Federation

The Canadian Baptist Federation has four federated member bodies: (1)Baptist Convention of Ontario and Quebec, (2)Baptist Union of Western Canada, (3)the United Baptist Convention of the Atlantic Provinces,

(4)Union d'Eglises Baptistes Françaises au Canada (French Baptist Union). Its main purpose is to act as a coordinating agency for the four groups.

Churches: 1,136; Inclusive Membership: 122,247; Sunday or Sabbath Schools: 935; Total Enrollment: 54,806; Ordained Clergy: 1,298

GENERAL ORGANIZATION

Office: 7185 Millcreek Dr., Mississauga, Ontario L5N 5R4 Tel. (416)826-0191

OFFICERS

Pres., Mr. Robert MacQuade, 54 Bessborough Ave., Moncton, New Brunswick E1E 4A2
Vice-Presidents, Rev. Nelson W. Hooper, 45 Applewood Cres., Cambridge, Ontario N1S 4K1; Mr. Carman Roberts, 48 Canyon Dr., N.W., Calgary, Alberta T2L OR3; Rev. Georges Rocher, 380 rue Deragon, Gramby, Quebec J2G 5J8
Gen. Sec.-Treas., Dr. Richard Coffin, 7185 Millcreek Dr., Mississauga, Ontario L5N 5R4
Gen. Sec., Canadian Baptist Overseas Mission Board, Rev. R. Berry, 7185 Millcreek Dr., Mississauga, Ontario L5N 5R4

1. *Baptist Convention of Ontario and Quebec*
The Baptist Convention of Ontario and Quebec was formally organized in 1888 as a convention of churches. McMaster University was founded in 1887.

The Convention has two educational institutions—the Baptist Leadership Education Centre at Whitby, for training lay leaders, and McMaster Divinity College in Hamilton, for training in pastoral/missionary leadership.

Overseas, the Convention works through the all-Canada missionary agency, the Canadian Baptist Overseas Mission Board. The churches also support the Sharing Way, the relief and development arm of the Canadian Baptist Federation.

Office: 217 St. George St., Toronto, Ontario M5R 2M2. Tel. (416)922-5163

Churches: 386; Inclusive Membership: 33,222; Sunday or Sabbath Schools: 319; Total Enrollment: 14,324; Ordained Clergy: 589

NOTE: *The above statistics are a subtotal for the Baptist Federation of Canada whose total statistics are reported initially.*

OFFICERS

Pres., Mrs. Catherine Stratton
1st Vice-Pres., Rev. Das Sydney
2nd Vice-Pres., Mr. Donald James
Treas./Bus. Adm., Mr. David Judd
Exec. Min., Dr. Byron Fenwick
Assoc. Exec. Min./Div. of Shared Mission, Rev. Robert G. Wilkins
Assoc. Exec. Min./Div. of Cong. Life, Rev. A. John Coutts
Assoc. Exec. Min./Div. of Pastoral Resources, Rev. George W. Scott

PERIODICAL

The Canadian Baptist, 217 St. George St., Toronto, Ontario M5R 2M2. Rev. Dr. William H. Jones, Islington, Ontario, Ed.

2. *Baptist Union of Western Canada, The*

Office: 202, 838-11th Ave. S.W., Calgary, Alberta T2R 0E5. Tel. (403) 234-9044

Churches: 167; Inclusive Membership: 21,310; Sunday or Sabbath Schools: 142; Total Enrollment: 12,865; Ordained Clergy: 232

Note: *The above statistics are a subtotal for the Baptist Federation of Canada whose total statistics are reported initially.*

OFFICERS

Pres., Dr. Rein Paasuke
Exec. Minister, Rev. William Cram
Assoc. Exec. Minister, Dr. C. Howard Bentall
Area Minister, Alberta, Rev. J. Dozois, 43 Strathbury Cir. SW, Calgary, Alberta T3H 1R9
Area Minister, British Columbia, _____, 201-7 St., New Westminster, British Columbia V3M 3K2
Area Minister, Manitoba, Saskatchewan, Rev. Ralph Orvis, 30 Eglinton Cr., Winnipeg, Manitoba R3Y 1E7
Dir. of Cong. Resources, Rev. Gerald Fisher, 14 Milford Cr., Sherwood Park, Alberta T8A 3V4
Principal, Carey Hall (Ministerial Education), Rev. Philip Collins, 5920 Iona Dr., Vancouver, British Columbia V6T 1J6; Field Edu. Dir., Rev. Philip Collins, 5920 Iona Dr., Vancouver, B.C., V6T 1J6
Principal, Baptist Leadership Training School (Lay), Rev. Ken Bellous, 4330-16 Street, SW, Calgary, Alberta T2T 4H9

3. *United Baptist Convention of the Atlantic Provinces*
The United Baptist Convention of the Atlantic Provinces is the largest Baptist Convention in Canada. Through the Canadian Baptist Federation, it is a member of the Baptist World Alliance.

Work in Canada began in the Atlantic Provinces in the 1700s when Baptists from New England began to migrate into the area. The Rev. Ebenezer Moulton organized a Baptist Church in Horton (now Wolfville, Nova Scotia) in 1763. The present church in Wolfville was formed in 1778 and is Canada's oldest continuing Baptist church. The United Baptist Convention was formed in 1905 when Calvinistic and Free Baptist churches merged; thus the name United Baptist is often used.

The first Baptist Association in Canada met in Nova Scotia in 1800. Today there are 21 Associations (usually comprised of one or two counties) within the convention. Through the Canadian Baptist Overseas Mission Board they support more than 100 missionaries in India, Kenya, Zaire, Brazil, Bolivia, Indonesia, and Sri Lanka. They have an active program of evangelism, Christian education, and church planting. They own and operate two colleges: Atlantic Baptist College in Moncton, New Brunswick, and Acadia Divinity College in Wolfville, Nova Scotia, which provides training for those entering the ministry and overseas missions. The convention operates six senior citizens' homes and a Christian bookstore.

Office: 1655 Manawagonish Rd., Saint John, New Brunswick, E2M 3Y2

Churches: 560; Inclusive Membership: 64,715; Sunday or Sabbath Schools: 450; Total Enrollment: 26,657; Ordained Clergy: 456
Note: *The above statistics are a subtotal for the Baptist Federation of Canada whose total statistics are reported initially.*

OFFICERS

Pres., Rev. James Cowan, 211 Main St., Saint John, New Brunswick E2K 1H7
Exec. Min., Dr. Eugene Thompson, 1655 Manawagonish Rd., Saint John, New Brunswick E2M 3Y2
Administrator-Treas., Rev. W. E. O'Grady, 1655 Manawagonish Rd., Saint John, New Brunswick E2M 3Y2
Dir. of Evangelism, Rev. Malcolm Beckett, 1655 Manawagonish Rd., Saint John, New Brunswick E2M 3Y2
Dir. of Christian Training, Rev. Harold Arbo, 1655 Manawagonish Rd., Saint John, New Brunswick E2M 3Y2

Note: *The above statistics are a subtotal for the Baptist Federation of Canada whose total statistics are reported initially.*

Dir. of Church Extension, Rev. Harry Gardner, 1665 Manawagonish Rd., St. John, New Brunswick E2M 2Y2

PERIODICAL

The Atlantic Baptist, Box 756, Kentville, Nova Scotia B4N 3X9. Rev. Michael Lipe, Ed.

4. **Union of French Baptist Churches in Canada** (Union d'Eglises Baptistes Françaises au Canada)

Baptist churches in French Canada first came into being through the labors of two missionaries from Switzerland, Rev. Louis Roussy and Mme. Henriette Feller, who arrived in Canada in 1835. The earliest church was organized in Grande Ligne (now St-Blaise), Québec, in 1838.

By 1900, there were 7 churches in the province of Quebec, together with 13 French-language Baptist churches in the New England states, where massive immigration from Quebec had taken place. The leadership was totally French Canadian.

By 1960, the process of Americanization had caused the disappearance of the French Baptist churches. A similar, but far less drastic process of Anglicization of all French Protestants took place in Quebec through the public (Protestant) school system, which was totally English-speaking. The school language situation changed very rapidly after 1960.

During the 1960s Quebec, as a society, entered into a very rapid change in all its facets: education, politics, social values, structures, etc. This has been called The Quiet Revolution. A veritable movement of mission, evangelism and church growth has once again become possible. In 1969, desiring to respond to the new conditions, the Grande Ligne Mission passed control of its work to the newly formed Union of French Baptist Churches in Canada, which at the time included 8 churches. By 1988, the French Canadian Baptist movement has grown to include 23 churches, plus a few nucleus congregations.

The Union d'Eglises Baptistes Françaises au Canada is a member body of the Canadian Baptist Federation and thus is affiliated with the Baptist World Alliance.

Headquarters: 2285 avenue Papineau, Montreal, Quebec H2K 4J5. Tel. (514)526-6643. Gen. Sec., Rev. John Gilmour

Churches: 23; Inclusive Membership: 3,000; Sunday or Sabbath Schools: 24; Total Enrollment: 960; Ordained Clergy: 21

Note: *The above statistics are a subtotal for the Baptist Federation of Canada whose total statistics are reported initially.*

Canadian Convention of Southern Baptists

The Canadian Convention of Southern Baptists was formed at the Annual Meeting, May 7-9, 1985, in Kelowna, British Columbia. It was formerly known as the Canadian Baptist Conference, founded in Kamloops, British Columbia, in 1959 by pastors of existing churches.

Churches: 98; Inclusive Membership: 122,247; Sunday or Sabbath Schools: 98; Total Enrollment: 6,257; Ordained Clergy: 101

Office: Postal Bag 300, Cochrane, Alberta T0L 0W0. Tel. (403)932-5688

OFFICERS

Exec. Dir.-Treas., Allen E. Schmidt, Box 7, Site 4, R. R. 1, Cochrane, Alberta T0L 0W0
Pres., Rev. Lewis Markwood, Cambrian Heights Baptist Church, 240 Cardiff Dr., N.W., Calgary, Alerta T2K 1S2.

The Canadian Yearly Meeting of the Religious Society of Friends

Founded in Canada as an offshoot of the Quaker movement in colonial America. Genesee Yearly Meeting, founded 1834, Canada Yearly Meeting (Orthodox), founded in 1867, and Canada Yearly Meeting, founded in 1881, united in 1955 to form the Canadian Yearly Meeting. The Canadian Yearly Meeting is affiliated with the Friends United Meeting and the Friends General Conference.

Churches: 25; Inclusive Membership: 1,156; Sunday or Sabbath Schools: 15; Total Enrollment: 124; Ordained Clergy: None

GENERAL ORGANIZATION

Meeting: annual
Headquarters: 91A Fourth Ave., Ottawa, Ontario K1S 1L1. Tel. (613)235-8553

CLERK

Edward S. Bell, 91 A Fourth Ave., Ottawa, Ontario K1S 1L1.

PERIODICAL

The Canadian Friend, Dorothy Parshall, Ed.

The Christian and Missionary Alliance in Canada

A Canadian movement, dedicated to the teaching of Jesus Christ the Saviour, Sanctifier, Healer and Coming King, commenced in Toronto in 1887 under the leadership of the Rev. John Salmon. Two years later the movement united with The Christian Alliance of New York, founded by Rev. A. B. Simpson, becoming the Dominion Auxiliary of the Christian Alliance, Toronto, under the presidency of the Hon. William H. Howland. Its four founding branches were Toronto, Hamilton, Montreal and Quebec.

In 1980 the Christian and Missionary Alliance in Canada became autonomous. Its General Assembly is held every two years.

NATIONAL LEADERSHIP

Pres., Rev. Melvin Sylvester, Box 7900, Postal Sta. B, Willowdale, Ontario M2K 2R6
Exec. Vice-Pres., _____
Vice Pres. of Pers. and Missions, Rev. Arnold L. Cook
Vice Pres. of Finance, Mr. Milton H. Quigg
Vice Pres. of Canadian Ministries, Rev. C. Stuart Lightbody
Vice Pres. of General Services, Mr. Kenneth Paton

DISTRICTS

Canadian Pacific: Rev. Gordon R. Fowler, Supt.
Western Canadian: Rev. Arnold Downey, Supt.
Canadian Midwest: _____
Eastern and Central: Rev. Robert J. Gould, Supt.
St. Lawrence: Rev. Jesse D. Jespersen, Supt.

Christian Brethren (Also known as Plymouth Brethren)

An orthodox and evangelical movement which began in the British Isles in the 1820's and is now worldwide. Congregations are usually simply called "assemblies." The name "Plymouth Brethren" was given by others because the group in Plymouth, England was a large congregation. In recent years the term Christian Brethren has replaced Plymouth Brethren for the "open" branch of the movement in Canada and British Commonwealth countries, and to some extent in the U.S.

Unwillingness to establish a denominational structure makes the autonomy of local congregations an important feature of the movement. Other features are weekly observance of the Lord's Supper and adherence to the doctrinal position of conservative, evangelical Christianity.

In the 1840's the movement divided. The "exclusive" branch, led by John Darby, stressed the interdependence of congregations. Since disciplinary decisions were held to be binding on all assemblies, exclusives had sub-divided into seven or eight main groups by the end of the century. Since 1925 a trend toward reunification has reduced that number to three or four. Canadian congregations number approximately 150, with an inclusive membership estimated at 11,000.

The "open" branch of the movement, stressing evangelism and foreign missions, is now the larger of the two. Following the leadership of George Muller in rejecting the "Exclusive" principle of binding discipline, this branch has escaped large-scale division. Canadian congregations number approximately 450, with an inclusive membership estimated at 41,000. There are 250 "commended" full-time ministers, not including foreign missionaries.

GENERAL ORGANIZATION

For Quebec: Christian Brethren Church in the Province of Quebec, 222 Alexander St., Sherbrooke, Quebec J1H 4S7, Norman R. Buchanan, Sec. (No General Organization for other provinces)Tel. (819)562-9198

Correspondent for North America: Interest Ministries, Bruce R. McNicol, Pres., 218 W. Willow, Wheaton, IL 60187. Tel. (708)653-6573

OTHER ORGANIZATIONS

Missionary Service Committee, Claude Loney, Exec. Dir., 1562A Danforth Ave., Toronto, Ontario M4J 1N4. Tel. (416)469-2012

PERIODICALS

Interest Magazine (m), 218 W. Willow, Wheaton, IL 60187

Missions Magazine (m), 1562A Danforth Ave., Toronto, Ontario M4J 1N4

News of Quebec (q), 222 Alexander St., Sherbrooke, Quebec J1H 4S7, Richard Strout, Ed.

Christian Church (Disciples of Christ) in Canada

Disciples have been in Canada since 1810 but were organized nationally in 1922 when the All-Canada Committee was formed. It seeks to serve the Canadian context as part of the whole Christian Church (Disciples of Christ)in the United States and Canada.

Churches: 36; Inclusive Membership: 4,006; Sunday or Sabbath Schools: 36; Total Enrollment: 806; Ordained Clergy: 52

Headquarters: 55 Cork St. E., Ste. 303, Guelph, Ontario N1H 2W7. Tel. (519)823-5190

OFFICERS

Moderator, Mrs. Marilyn Hodgson, 3228 Crosstree Ct., Mississauga, Ontario L5L 1G7

Vice-Moderator, Mr. Stan Litke, 255 Midvalley Dr., SE, Calgary, Alberta T2X 1K8

Exec. Min., Rev. Robert W. Steffer, 7 Lynwood Dr., Guelph, Ontario N1G 1P8

PERIODICAL

Canadian Disciple (4/yr.), 240 Home St., Winnipeg, Manitoba R3G 1X3. Rev. Raymond Cuthbert, Ed.

Christian Churches and Churches of Christ in Canada

This fellowship, dedicated to the "restoration of the New Testament Church in doctrine, ordinances and life,"

has been operating in Canada since 1820. There is no general organization. Each church within the fellowship is completely independent. For detailed information see: Directory of the Ministry, Christian Churches and Churches of Christ, 1525 Cherry Rd., Springfield, IL 62704, U.S.A.

Churches: 69; Inclusive Membership; 5,997; Sunday or Sabbath Schools: N.R.; Total Enrollment: N.R.; Ordained Clergy: 74

Christian Reformed Church in North America

The Christian Reformed Church in North America represents the historic faith of Protestantism and is creedally united in the Belgic Confession (1561), the Heidelberg Catechism (1563), and the Canons of Dort (1618-19). The denomination was founded in the U.S. in 1857. Canadian congregations have been formed since 1908.

Churches: 231; Inclusive Membership: 87,037; Sunday or Sabbath Schools: N.R.; Total Enrollment: N.R.; Ordained Clergy: 262

GENERAL ORGANIZATION

Synod: Annual (June)

United States Office: 2850 Kalamazoo Ave., S.E., Grand Rapids, MI 49560. Tel. (616)246-0744.

Canadian Office: 3475 Mainway P.O. Box 5070, Burlington, Ontario L7R 3Y8. Tel. (416)336-2920

OFFICERS

Stated Clerk, Rev. Leonard J. Hofman, 2850 Kalamazoo Ave., S.E., Grand Rapids, MI 49560

Denomination Financial Coordinator, Harry J. Vander Meer, 2850 Kalamazoo Ave. S.E., Grand Rapids, MI 49560

Council of Christian Reformed Churches in Canada: Exec. Sec., Arie G. Van Eek, 3475 Mainway PO Box 5070, Burlington, Ontario L7R 3Y8. Tel. (416)336-2920

Church of God (Anderson, Ind.)

This body is one of the largest of the groups which have taken the name "Church of God." Its headquarters are at Anderson, Indiana. It originated about 1880 and emphasizes Christian unity.

Churches: 54; Inclusive Membership 3,501; Sunday or Sabbath Schools: 48; Total Enrollment: 3,256; Ordained Clergy: 55

GENERAL ORGANIZATION

Ontario Assembly: Chpsn., Rev. John Campbell, 48 Leaside Dr., Welland, Ontario L3C 6B2

Western Canada Assembly: Exec. Sec., Lewis E. Hyslip, 4717 56th St., Camrose, Alberta T4V 2C4

PERIODICALS

Ontario Messenger (m), 85 Emmett Ave., #1109, Toronto, Ontario M6M 5A2. Paul Kilburn, Ed.

The Gospel Contact (m), 5014 48 St., Camrose, Alberta T4V 1M1. Lewis Hyslip, Ed.

Church of God (Cleveland, Tenn.)

This body began in the U.S. in 1886 as the outgrowth of the holiness revival under the name Christian Union, and in 1902 it was reorganized as the Holiness Church. In 1907, the church adopted the name Church of God. Its doctrine is fundamental and Pentecostal, it maintains a centralized form of government and an evangelistic and missionary program.

The first church in Canada was established in 1919 in Scotland Farm, Manitoba. Paul H. Walker became the first overseer of Canada in 1931.

GENERAL ORGANIZATION

General Assembly: biennial (Next Meeting, 1990) International Offices: Keith St. at 25th, N.W., Cleveland, TN 37311. Tel. (615) 472-3361
Exec. Office in Canada: Rev. S. A. Lankford, P.O. Box 2036, Bramalea, Ontario L6T 3S3. Tel. (416) 793-2213; Western Canada: Rev. Philip F. Siggelkow, 175 Rogers Rd., Regina; Saskatchewan S4R 6V1. Tel. (306) 545-5771

PERIODICAL

Church of God Beacon (m), P.O. Box 2036, Bramalea, Ontario L6T 3S3

The Church of God of Prophecy in Canada

In the late nineteenth century, men seeking God's eternal plan as they followed the Reformation spirit began to delve further for scriptural light concerning Christ and his church. On June 13, 1903, a small group gathered in Cherokee County, North Carolina, for prayer and further study of God's Word.

At that historic meeting the divine principles and purposes for the church as outlined in the Holy Scriptures began to shine through. Today that church is a visible, organized body, operating in all 50 states of the United States. In 1911 the first missionary effort was launched in the Bahamas; that outreach has continued, and today the church is represented in 91 countries and territories around the world.

In Canada, the first Church of God of Prophecy congregation was organized in Swan River, Manitoba, in 1937. Churches are now established in British Columbia, Manitoba, Alberta, Saskatchewan, Ontario, and Quebec.

The church accepts the whole Bible rightly divided, with the New Testament as the rule of faith and practice, government, and discipline. The membership upholds the Bible as the inspired Word of God and believes that its truths are known by illuminative revelation of the Holy Scriptures. The Trinity is recognized as one supreme Godhead in three persons—Father, Son, and Holy Ghost. Jesus Christ, the virgin-born Son of God, lived a sinless life, fulfilled his ministry on earth, was crucified, resurrected, and later ascended to the right hand of God.

Churches: 47; Inclusive Membership: 2,463; Sunday or Sabbath Schools: 48; Total Enrollment: 3,015; Ordained Clergy: 95

GENERAL ORGANIZATION

National headquarters for the Church of God of Prophecy in Canada is located at 1st Line East, R.R. 2, Brampton, Ontario L6V 1A1. Tel. (416) 843-2379
World Headquarters: Bible Place, Cleveland, TN U.S.A. 37311
General Meetings: National and Provincial (by district) annually

OFFICERS

Natl. Overseer, Canada East, Bishop Richard E. Davis, P.O. Box 457, Brampton, Ontario L6V 2L4. Tel. (416)843-2379
Natl. Overseer, Canada West, Bishop John Doroshuk, Box 952, Strathmore, Alberta T0J 3H0. Tel. (403) 934-4787

BOARD OF DIRECTORS

Pres., Bishop John Doroshuk
Vice Pres., Bishop Richard E. Davis
Sec., Bishop H. L. Martin
Member, Bishop M. A. Tomlinson
Member, Bishop Adrian Varlack
Member, Bishop T. James Bennett
Member, Bishop Leroy V. Greenaway

PERIODICALS

Canadian Trumpeter Canada-West, John Doroshuk, Ed.
Maple Leaf Communque Canada-East, Richard E. Davis, Ed.

The Church of Jesus Christ of Latter-day Saints in Canada

This body has no central headquarters in Canada, only stake and mission offices. Elders Rex. C. Reeve, Loren C. Dunn and John K. Carmack of the First Quorum of the Seventy oversee the Church's activities in Canada. They reside in Salt Lake City, Utah. All General Authorities may be reached at 50 East South Temple St., Salt Lake City, UT 84150. [See U. S. Directory, "Religious Bodies in the United States" in this edition for further details.]

In Canada, there are 34 stakes, 6 missions, 9 districts, 355 wards/branches (congregations).

For further information contact: Public Communications Director, The Church of Jesus Christ of Latter-day Saints, 7181 Woodbine Ave., #234, Markham, Ontario L3R 1A3

Church of the Lutheran Brethren

Organized in Milwaukee, Wis. in 1900. It adheres to the Lutheran Confessions and accepts into membership those who profess a personal faith in Jesus Christ. It practices congregational autonomy and conducts its services in a nonliturgical pattern. The synod has an advisory rather than ruling function on the congregational level, but in the cooperative efforts of all congregations (Education, American and World Missions, Publications, and Youth Ministries) it exercises a ruling function.

Churches: 7; Inclusive Membership: 458; Sunday or Sabbath Schools: 7 Total Enrollment: 532; Ordained Clergy: 5

GENERAL ORGANIZATION

Convention: annual in June
Headquarters: 1007 Westside Dr., Box 655, Fergus Falls, MN 56538. Tel. (218)739-3336

OFFICERS

Pres., Rev. Robert M. Overgaard, 1007 Westside Dr., Box 655, Fergus Falls, MN 56538
Vice Pres., Rev. Joel Egge, Rt. 4, River Oaks Dr., Fergus Falls, MN 53538
Sec., Rev. Richard Vettrus, 707 Crestview Dr., West Union, IA 52175
Dir., Fincl. Aff., Ronald Egge, 1007 Westside Dr., Box 655, Fergus Falls, MN 56538

Church of the Nazarene

The first Church of the Nazarene in Canada was organized in November, 1902, by Dr. H. F. Reynolds. It was in Oxford, Nova Scotia. The Church of the Nazarene is Wesleyan Arminian in theology, representative in church government, and warmly evangelistic.

Churches: 154; Inclusive Membership: 10,573; Sunday or Sabbath Schools: 150; Total Enrollment: 15,617; Ordained Clergy: 234

GENERAL ORGANIZATION

Executive Board: meets annually in January.
Exec. Adm., Neil Hightower, 107 Bryn Mawr Rd., Winnipeg, Manitoba R3T 3K8

OFFICERS

Chmn., Rev. William Stewart, 14 Hollywood Dr., Moncton, New Brunswick E1E 2R5

Vice Chmn., Charles Muxworthy, 5443 Meadedale Dr., Burnaby, British Columbia V5B 2E6
Sec., Dr. Robert Collier, 5710 Sherwood Blvd., Delta, British Columbia V4L 2C6
Treas., Robert Rimington, 6516 Lombardy Cres., S. W., Sta. B, Calgary, Alberta T3E 5R4

Churches of Christ in Canada

Churches of Christ are autonomous congregations, whose members appeal to the Bible alone to determine matters of faith and practice. There are no central offices or officers. Publications and institutions related to the churches are either under local congregational control or independent of any one congregation.

Churches of Christ shared a common fellowship in the 19th century with the Christian Churches/Churches of Christ and the Christian Church (Disciples of Christ). Fellowship was broken after the introduction of instrumental music in worship and centralization of church-wide activities through a missionary society. Churches of Christ began in Canada soon after 1800 largely in the middle provinces. The few pioneer congregations were greatly strengthened in the mid-1800s, growing in size and number.

Members of Churches of Christ believe in the inspiration of the Scriptures, the divinity of Jesus Christ, and immersion into Christ for the remission of sins. The New Testament pattern is followed in worship and church organization.

CORRESPONDENT
Mr. Eugene C. Perry, 4904 King St., Beamsville, Ontario L0R 1B6

Conference of Mennonites in Canada

The Conference of Mennonites in Canada began in 1902 as an organized fellowship of Mennonite immigrants from Russia in southern Manitoba and around Rosthern, Saskatchewan. The first annual sessions were held in July, 1903. Its members hold to traditional Christian beliefs, believer's baptism, and congregational polity. They emphasize practical Christianity: opposition to war, service to others, and personal ethics. Further immigration from Russia in the 1920s and 1940s increased the group which is now located in all provinces from New Brunswick to British Columbia. This conference is affiliated with the General Conference Mennonite Church whose offices are at Newton, Kansas.
Churches: 157; Inclusive Membership: 28,994; Sunday or Sabbath Schools: N.R.; Total Enrollment: N.R.; Ordained Clergy: 311

GENERAL ORGANIZATION
Conference of Mennonites in Canada meets annually in July.
Headquarters: 600 Shaftesbury Blvd., Winnipeg, Manitoba R3P 0M4. Tel. (204)888-6781

OFFICERS
Chpsn., Walter Franz, Box 90, Altona, Manitoba R0G 0B0
Vice-Chpsn., George Richert, 3504 Gordon Rd., Regina, Saskatchewan S4S 2V4
Sec., Ruth Enns, 2425 Haultain Ave., Saskatoon, Saskatchewan S7J 1R2
Gen. Sec., Larry Kehler, 600 Shaftesbury Blvd., Winnipeg, Manitoba R3P 0M4

Congregational Christian Churches in Ontario, The Conference of

This body originated in the early 19th century when devout Christians within several denominations in the northern and eastern United States, dissatisfied with sectarian controversy, broke away from their own denominations and took the simple title "Christians."

First organized in Canada at Keswick, Ontario, these churches became affiliated with the Conservative Congregational Christian Conference in the U.S.A.

In doctrine the body is evangelical, being governed by the Bible as the final authority in faith and practice; it believes that Christian character must be expressed in daily living; it aims at the unity of all true believers in Christ that others may believe in Him and be saved.

In church polity, the body is democratic and autonomous.
Churches: 5; Inclusive Membership: 270; Sunday or Sabbath Schools: 4; Total Enrollment: 125; Ordained Clergy: 13

GENERAL ORGANIZATION
Headquarters: Conservative Congregational Christian Conference, 7582 Currell Blvd., Ste. 108, St. Paul, MN 55125. Tel. (612)739-1474
Canadian Headquarters: Box 35, Keswick, Ontario L4P 3E1

OFFICERS
Pres., Mr. Keith McMinn, R. R. #1, Goodwood, Ontario L0C 1A0
1st Vice-Pres., Mr. Daniel Schut, R.R. #2, Stouffville, Ontario L4A 7X3
2nd Vice-Pres., Rev. John Rice, 928 Safari Dr., Kingston, Ontario K7M 6X7
Clerk, Mrs. Cathy Horlick, 301-74 Queensway S., Keswick, Ontario L4P 1Z3
Area Representative, Mr. Bill Bastedo, 45 Glenwood Ave., Toronto, Ontario M6P 3C7

PERIODICAL
Tidings, Mr. Clare Hart, Ed.

The Coptic Church in Canada

The Coptic Church in North America was begun in Canada in 1964 and was registered in the Province of Ontario in 1965. The Coptic Church has spread since then to a number of locations in North America.

The governing body of each local church is an elected Board of Deacons. The Diocesan Council is the national governing body and meets at least once a year.

OFFICER
Archpriest, Fr. M. A. Marcos, St. Mark's Coptic Orthodox Church, 41 Glendinning Ave., Agincourt, Ontario M1W 3E2. Tel. (416)494-4449, (416)470-8494

Elim Fellowship of Evangelical Churches and Ministers

The Elim Fellowship of Evangelical Churches and Ministers, a Pentecostal body, was established in 1984 as a sister organization of Elim Fellowship in the U.S.

This is an association of churches, ministers, and missionaries seeking to serve the whole body of Christ. It is Pentecostal and has a charismatic orientation.

GENERAL ORGANIZATION
Annual Representational Assemblies: Bd. of Dirs. meets quarterly; Council of Elders, quarterly

OFFICERS
Pres., Carlton Spencer, 7245 College St., Lima, NY 14485.
Vice Pres., Winston Nunes, 4 Palamino Cres., Willowdale, North York, Ontario M2K 1W1. Tel. (416)225-4824
Sec., Paul Heidt, 1303 Murphy Rd., Sarnia, Ontario N7S 2Y7. Tel. (519)542-8938
Treas. Errol Alchin, 43 Black Locust Way, Brantford, Ontario N3R 7C7

The Estonian Evangelical Lutheran Church

The Estonian Evangelical Lutheran Church (EELC) was founded in 1917 in Estonia and reorganized in Sweden in

1944. The teachings of the EELC are based on the Old and New Testaments, explained through the Apostolic, Nicean and Athanasian confessions, the unaltered Confession of Augsburg and other teachings found in the Book of Concord.

Churches: 13; Inclusive Membership: 7,009; Sunday or Sabbath Schools: N.R.; Total Enrollment: N.R.; Ordained Clergy: 15

GENERAL ORGANIZATION
Executive Board headed by the Archbishop, Consistorium, Auditing Committee and District Conference.
Headquarters: Wallingatan 32, Box 45074, 10430 Stockholm 45, Sweden.

OFFICERS
Bishop in North America, Rev. Karl Raudsepp, 30 Sunrise Ave., Apt. 216, Toronto, Ontario M4A 2R3.
Assts. to the Bishop: Dean Udo Petersoo, 583 Jarvis St., Toronto, Ontario M5B 2C7; Rev. Tonis Nommik, 3 Mapleside Ave., Hamilton, Ontario L8P 3Y4.

PERIODICAL
Eesti Kirik (m), Box 45074, S-104, 30 Stockholm 45, Sweden. Bishop K. Raudsepp, Ed.

Evangelical Baptist Churches in Canada, The Fellowship of
Formed in 1953 by the merging of the Union of Regular Baptist Churches of Ontario and Quebec with the Fellowship of Independent Baptist Churches of Canada.

Churches: 478; Inclusive Membership: 59,750; Sunday or Sabbath Schools: N.R.; Total Enrollment: N.R.; Ordained Clergy: N.R.

Headquarters: 3034 Bayview Ave., Willowdale, Ontario M2N 6J5. Tel. (416)223-8696

OFFICERS
Pres., Mr. Murray A. Pipe
Gen. Sec.-Treas., Dr. R. W. Lawson

PERIODICALS
Evangelical Baptist, 3034 Bayview Ave., Willowdale, Ontario, M2N 6J5, Dr. R. W. Lawson, Ed.
Intercom, Dr. R. W. Lawson, Ed.

The Evangelical Church in Canada
Founded early in the 19th century by Jacob Albright and William Otterbein in Pennsylvania as the Evangelical Church, this body became known later as the Evangelical United Brethren Church, which in the U.S. became a part of The United Methodist Church in 1968. This Canadian body is Methodist in organization and Arminian, Wesleyan, and Methodist in doctrine. It was incorporated in 1928 by Dominion Charter as The Northwest Canada Conference Evangelical Church. In 1970, this Canadian Conference was granted autonomy and became a separate denomination. In 1982 The Evangelical Church in Canada joined with The Evangelical Church of North America.

Churches: 50; Inclusive Membership: 3,741; Sunday or Sabbath Schools: 43; Total Enrollment: 3,823; Ordained Clergy: 76

GENERAL ORGANIZATION
Council of Administration: Meets 2 to 4 times each year. Annual Conference.

Headquarters: Evangelical Church Office Bldg., 2805 13th Ave., S.E., Medicine Hat, Alberta T1A 3R1. Tel. (403)527-4101

OFFICERS
General Supt., Dr. George K. Millen, 7525 S. E. Lake Rd., Ste. 7, Milwaukie, OR 97222

Conference Supt., Rev. Walter H. Erion, 30 Larkspur Ct., S.E., Medicine Hat, Alberta T1B 2J7
Conference Chpsn., Dr. G. K. Millen, 7525 Lake Rd., Ste. 7, Milwaukie, OR 97222
Conference Sec., Rev. Richard Kopanke, 11860 Montego St., Richmond, British Columbia V6X 1H4

PERIODICAL
Northwest Canada Echoes (m), c/o 2805-13th Ave., S.E., Medicine Hat, Alberta T1A 3R1. A.W. Riegel, Ed.

The Evangelical Covenant Church of Canada
A Canadian denomination organized in Canada at Winnipeg in 1904 which is affiliated with the Evangelical Covenant Church of America and with the International Federation of Free Evangelical Churches, which includes churches in eleven European countries.

This body believes in the one triune God as confessed in the Apostles' Creed, that salvation is received through faith in Christ as Saviour, that the Bible is the authoritative guide in all matters of faith and practice. Christian Baptism and the Lord's Supper are accepted as divinely ordained sacraments of the church. As descendants of the 19th century pietistic awakening, the group believes in the need of a personal experience of commitment to Christ, the development of a virtuous life, and the urgency of spreading the gospel to the "ends of the world."
Most of the members of this group came from Northern Europe originally, primarily from Scandinavia.

Churches: 23; Inclusive Membership: 1,250; Sunday or Sabbath Schools: 18; Total Enrollment: 1,573; Ordained Clergy: 34

GENERAL ORGANIZATION
Headquarters: 245 21st St. E., Prince Albert, Saskatchewan S6V 1L9
Mailing Address: same as above
Conference: annual.

OFFICERS
Supt. Rev. Jerome Johnson, 245 21st St. E., Prince Albert, Saskatchewan S6V 1L9
Chpsn., Les Doell, R.R. #2, Wetaskiwin, Alberta T9A 1W9
Sec., Melsie Waldner, 415 Perrault La., Saskatoon, Saskatchewan S7K 6B5
Treas., Mr. Al Prochnau, R.R. #2, Fort Saskatchewan, Alberta T8L 2N8

PERIODICAL
The Covenant Messenger (q), 245 21st St. E., Prince Albert, Saskatchewan S6V 1L9.

Evangelical Free Church of Canada
The Evangelical Free Churches in Canada celebrated 50 years of Free Church work under the American Evangelical Free Church by becoming incorporated as a Canadian organization on March 21, 1967. On July 8, 1984, the Evangelical Free Church of Canada was given its autonomy as a self-governing Canadian denomination.

Churches: 111; Inclusive Membership: 5,639; Sunday or Sabbath Schools: N.R.; Total Enrollment: N.R.; Ordained Clergy: 145

GENERAL ORGANIZATION
Board of Directors
Home Office: #4, 10008 - 29A Ave., Edmonton, Alberta T6N 1A8

OFFICERS
Pres., Rev. Ronald Swanson, # 4, 10008-29A Ave., Edmonton, Alberta T6N 1A8

Mod., Mr. Henry Wiebe, 14203 - 60 Ave., Edmonton, Alberta T6H 1J6
Vice-Mod., Rev. James Scobbie, Box 2354, Steinbach, Manitoba R0A 2A0
Fin. Chmn., Mr. Dave Smithers, Box 760, Three Hills, Alberta T0M 2A0

Evangelical Lutheran Church in Canada

The Evangelical Lutheran Church in Canada was organized in 1985 through a merger of The Evangelical-Lutheran Church of Canada (ELCC) and the Lutheran Church in America—Canada Section. The merger is a result of an invitation issued in 1972 by the ELCC to the Lutheran Church in America—Canada Section and the Lutheran Church—Canada (LC-MS). Three-way merger discussions took place until 1978 when it was decided that only a two-way merger was possible. The ELCC was the Canada District of the ALC until autonomy in 1967.

The Lutheran Church in Canada traces its history back more than 200 years. Congregations were organized by German Lutherans in Halifax and Lunenburg County in Nova Scotia in 1749. German Lutherans, including many United Empire Loyalists, also settled in large numbers along the St. Lawrence and in Upper Canada. In the late nineteenth century immigrants arrived from Scandinavia, Germany, and other central European countries, many via the U.S.A. The Lutheran synods in the U.S.A. have provided the pastoral support and needed help for the Canadian church.

Churches: 652; Inclusive Membership: 208,149; Sunday or Sabbath Schools: 540; Total Enrollment: 32,254; Ordained Clergy: 817

GENERAL ORGANIZATION
Convention: biennial. Next meeting, 1991

Headquarters: 1512 St. James St., Winnipeg, Manitoba R3H 0L2. Tel. (204)786-6707

OFFICERS
Bishop, Rev. Dr. Donald W. Sjoberg
Vice-Pres., Joan Meyer
Sec., Rev. Leon C. Gilbertson
Treas., Don Rosten

DIVISIONS AND OFFICES
Division for Canadian Missions, Exec. Dir., Rev. James A. Chell
Division for Church and Society, Exec. Dir., Rev. Ruth Blaser
Division for College and University Services, Exec. Dir., Rev. William Stauffer
Division for Parish Life, Exec. Dir., Rev. Dr. Lawrence Denef
Division for Theological Education and Leadership, Exec. Dir., Rev. William Stauffer
Division for World Mission, Exec. Dir., Rev. Paul G. Nostbakken
Office for Communication, _____
Office for Finance & Management and Committee of Pensions, Exec. Dir., Daniel A. Skaret
Office for Resource Development, Exec. Dir., Peter K. Schmidt
Evangelical Lutheran Women, Pres., Joyce Christensen; Exec. Dir. Diane Doth Rehbein

SYNODS
Alberta and the Territories: 10014-81 Ave., Edmonton, Alberta T6E 1W8. Tel. (403) 439-2636. Bishop: Rev. J. Robert Jacobson
Eastern: 50 Queen St. N., Kitchener, Ontario N2H 6P4. Tel. (519) 743-1461. Bishop: Rev. Dr. William D. Huras
British Columbia: 80-10th Ave., E., New Westminster, British Columbia V3L 4R5. Tel. (604) 524-1318. Bishop: Rev. Dr. Marlin Aadland
Manitoba/Northwestern Ontario:201-3657 Roblin Blvd., Winnipeg, Manitoba R3G 0E2. Tel. (204)889-3760. Bishop: Rev. G. W. Luetkehoelter

Saskatchewan: Rm. 707, Bessborough Towers, 601 Spadina Cres. E., Saskatoon, Saskatchewan S7K 3G8. Tel. (306)244-2474. Bishop: Rev. Telmor G. Sartison

PERIODICAL
Canada Lutheran (11/yr.), 1512 St. James St., Winnipeg, Manitoba R3H 0L2. Fergy E. Baglo, ed.

The Evangelical Mennonite Conference

The Evangelical Mennonite Conference (EMC) came about as the result of a renewal movement among a small group of Mennonites in Southern Russia in 1812. Their leader was Klaas Reimer, a Mennonite minister.

Mr. Reimer had become appalled at the lack of spiritual life in the church. The church had become lax in church discipline and condoned questionable practices such as card playing, smoking, drinking, etc. The church had also become too closely aligned with the Russian government as evidenced by their contributions to the Napoleonic War. Around 1812, Reimer and several others began separate worship services, and by 1814 they were organized as a separate group.

Increasing pressure from the Russian government in the area of military conscription, etc., finally led to a migration (1874-75) of the entire group to North America, with 158 families settling in Manitoba, Canada and 36 families settling in Jansen, Nebraska. The Nebraska group is no longer part of the EMC.

The name Evangelical Mennonite Conference, chosen in 1952 to replace the name *Kleine Gemeinde*, expresses the nature of the EMC. It is evangelical in that it stands for the truth of the gospel message of Jesus Christ. It is Mennonite in that it holds to the historic distinctives of the faith of the Mennonites. It is a Conference in that it works together as a group of churches in carrying on the ministry Jesus left to his followers.

The EMC has a strong missionary program, with some 150 workers (June 1987) on the roster of the Board of Missions. These workers are in some 23 countries of the world, both in its own missions program and in faith missions.

GENERAL ORGANIZATION
Annual Meeting
Headquarters: Box 1268, 440 Main St., Steinbach, Manitoba R0A 2A0. Tel. (204) 326-6401

OFFICERS
Conf. Mod., Harvey Plett, Box 3271, Steinbach, Manitoba R0A 2A0
Bd. of Missions, Exec. Sec., Henry Klassen, Box 1268, Steinbach, Manitoba R0A 2A0

PERIODICALS
The Messenger (bi-w), Box 1268, Steinbach, Manitoba R0A 2A0. Menno Hamm, Ed.

Evangelical Mennonite Mission Conference

Founded in 1936 as the Rudnerwelder Mennonite Church in Southern Manitoba and organized as the Evangelical Mennonite Mission Conference in 1959. It was incorporated in 1962.

GENERAL ORGANIZATION
Annual Conference meeting in July
Headquarters: 526 McMillan Ave., Winnipeg Manitoba R3L 0N5. Tel. (204) 477-1213

OFFICERS
Mod., Rev. Leonard Sawatzky, Box 2126, Steinbach, Manitoba R0A 2A0
Vice-Mod., Rev. Ron Adrian, Box 184, Winkler, Manitoba R0G 2X0

Sec., Mr. Bill Thiessen, Box 12, Randolph, Manitoba R0A 1L0

Exec. Sec., Henry Dueck. Tel. (204)489-2616

OTHER ORGANIZATIONS

Missions Dir., Mr. Lawrence Giesbrecht, Box 927, Altona, Manitoba R0G 0B0. Tel. (204)324-6179

The Gospel Message: Box 1622, Saskatoon, Saskatchewan S7K 3R8; 1712 Ave. E North, Saskatoon, Saskatchewan S7L 1V4. Tel. (306)242-5001; Radio Pastor, Rev. John D. Friesen, 1712 Ave. E North, Saskatoon, Saskatchewan S7L 1V4 Tel. (306)242-8842; Radio Administrator, Ernest Friesen, Tel. (306)384-7243

PERIODICAL

The Recorder (m), Box 126, Winnipeg, Manitoba R3C 2G1. Dave and Gladys Penner, Co-Eds.

Foursquare Gospel Church of Canada

The Western Canada District was formed in 1964 with the Rev. Roy Hicks as supervisor. Prior to 1964 it had been a part of the Northwest District of the International Church of the Foursquare Gospel with headquarters in Portland, Oregon.

A Provincial Society, The Church of the Foursquare Gospel of Western Canada, was formed in 1976; a Federal corporation, the Foursquare Gospel Church of Canada was incorporated in 1981, and a national church formed.

Churches: 37; Inclusive Membership: 2,483; Sunday or Sabbath Schools: 31; Total Enrollment: 1,355; Ordained Clergy: 86

GENERAL ORGANIZATION

National Convention, Annual.

Headquarters: #200 - 3965 Kingsway, Burnaby, British Columbia V5H 1Y7

OFFICER

Pres. and Gen. Supervisor, Victor F. Gardner, #200 - 3965 Kingsway, V5H 1Y7

PERIODICALS

Canadian Foursquare Challenge (1/yr.)

News & Views (3/yr.)

Free Methodist Church in Canada

The Free Methodist Church was founded in New York State in 1860 and expanded to Canada in 1880. It is Methodist in doctrine, evangelical in ministry, and emphasizes the teaching of holiness of life through faith in Jesus Christ.

The Free Methodist Church in Canada was incorporated in 1927 after the establishment of a Canadian Executive Board. In 1959 the Holiness Movement Church merged with the Free Methodist Church. Fuller autonomy was realized with the formation of a Canadian Jurisdictional Conference in 1974. Complete self-government for the Free Methodist Church in Canada will be achieved in 1989 when the Canadian General Conference is ratified.

Churches: 142; Inclusive Membership; 7,490; Sunday or Sabbath Schools: 142; Total Enrollment: 9,687; Ordained Clergy: 228

GENERAL ORGANIZATION

Canadian Jurisdictional Conference, meets annually in July. Three geographical conferences meet annually in June and July.

Headquarters: 4315 Village Centre Ct., Mississauga, Ontario L4Z 1S2. Tel. (416) 848-2600.

OFFICERS

Pres., Bishop Donald N. Bastian, 96 Elmbrook Crescent, Etobicoke, Ontario M9C 5E2. Tel. (416) 622-4157

Ex. Dir.-Treas., Rev. Paul G. Johnston, 3020 Oka Rd., Mississauga, Ontario L5N 3A5. Tel. (416) 824-0740.

Canada East Conference Supt.: Rev. Robert J. Buchanan, Box 670 Belleville. Ontario K8N 5B3. Tel. (613)968-8511

Canada Great Lakes Conference Supt.: Rev. Glen M. Buffam, 30 King St., Brantford, Ontario N3T 3C5. Tel. (519)753-7390

Canada West Conference Supt.: Rev. Joseph F. James, Box 268, Moose Jaw, Saskatchewan S6H 4N9. Tel. (306)693-4500

PERIODICAL

The Free Methodist Herald (m), 69 Browning Ave., Toronto, Ontario M4K 1W1. Donald Gregory Bastian, Ed. Tel. (416)463-4536.

Free Will Baptists

As revival fires burned throughout New England in the mid- and late 1700s, Benjamin Randall proclaimed his doctrine of Free Will to large crowds of seekers. In due time a number of Randall's converts moved to Nova Scotia. One such believer was Asa McGray, who was to become instrumental in the establishment of several Free Baptist churches. Local congregations were organized in New Brunswick, and for several years all went smoothly, with gains being made numerically and geographically.

However, disagreements surfaced over the question of music, Sunday school, church offerings, salaried clergy, and several other issues. When the situation remained irresolute, adherents of the more progressive element decided to form their own fellowship. Led by George Orser, they declared their intentions to become known as Free Christian Baptists. This the parent group strongly protested, arguing that the inclusion of the word Christian in the name had a negative connotation toward the original group.

Upon petitioning the province of New Brunswick for incorporation in 1898, a government official suggested the problem be resolved by employing the name Primitive Baptist Conference (to convey the idea of *first* by use of the term *Primitive*.)

Although the new group rejected some particular elements in the worship and practice of the Free Baptists, it faithfully adhered to the truths and doctrines which embodied the theological basis of Free Will Baptists. One may conclude that it has always been Free Will Baptist in doctrine and deportment, if not always in name.

Largely through the efforts of Archibald Hatfield, contact was made with Free Will Baptists in the United States, resulting in fellowship through visits of denominational leaders, the arranging of special services, and such. This contact began in the early 1960s and continues today.

Desiring to become more effective in missions, evangelism, and church growth, the association petitioned the National Association for affiliation and fellowship and was officially welcomed into the Free Will Baptist "family" in July 1981, when the National Association was in conference in Louisville, Kentucky.

Churches: 16; Inclusive Membership: 1,275; Sunday or Sabbath Schools: 14; Total Enrollment: 1,205; Ordained Clergy: 13

GENERAL ORGANIZATION

Annual Conference convenes in early July at Hartland, New Brunswick. Also quarterly meetings in October, January and April.

OFFICER

Conference moderator, Rev. Fred D. Hanson, Box 355, Hartland, New Brunswick E0J 1N0. Tel. (506) 375-6735

PERIODICAL

The Gospel Standard, Box 355, Hartland, New Brunswick E0J 1N0. Rev. Fred D. Hanson, Ed.

General Church of the New Jerusalem

The Church of the New Jerusalem is founded on the Writings of Emanuel Swedenborg (1688-1772). These were first brought to Ontario in 1835 by Christian Enslin.

Churches: 3; Inclusive Membership: 645; Sunday or Sabbath Schools: 3; Total Enrollment: 179; Ordained Clergy: 6

GENERAL ORGANIZATION

Annual Meeting General Church of the New Jerusalem in Canada each spring in Toronto or Kitchener.
Headquarters: 279 Burnhamthorpe Rd., Islington, Ontario M9B 1Z6. Tel. (416) 239-3054

OFFICERS

Pres., Rt. Rev. L. B. King Bryn Athyn, PA 19009
Exec. Vice-Pres., Rev. Louis D. Synnestvedt, 58 Chapel Hill Dr., Kitchener, Ontario N3G 3W5
Sec., Walter Bellinger, 110 Chapel Hill Dr., Kitchener, Ontario N2G 3W5
Treas., John Wyncoll, 19 Hampshire Heights, Islington, Ontario M9B 2J9

PERIODICAL

New Church Life (m), Bryn Athyn, PA 19009, Rev. Donald L. Rose, Ed.
New Church Canadian, 279 Burnhamthrope Rd., Islington, Ontario M9B 1Z6

The Gospel Missionary Association

Initially organized in 1951 under the chairmanship of Rev. W. J. Laing of the Bethel Baptist Church and a group of clergymen of independent missions and churches; then incorporated by the Province of Alberta in 1956. This Association consists of a body of affiliated churches, 10 in Alberta and 1 in the Yukon.
The doctrines of this body are fundamental and evangelical.

Annual Meeting: March

OFFICER

Pres., Rev. J.W. Sinclair, Bethany Baptist Ch., 3901-44 St., Red Deer, Alberta T4N 1G7. Tel. (403)347-7900

Greek Orthodox Diocese of Toronto (Canada)

Greek Orthodox Christians in Canada under the jurisdiction of the Ecumenical Patriarchate of Constantinople (Istanbul).

GENERAL ORGANIZATION

Headquarters: 40 Donlands Ave., Toronto, Ontario M4J 3N6. Tel. (416)462-0833

OFFICERS

Primate of the Archdiocese of North and South America: The Most Rev. Iakovos. (See U.S. listing.)
Bishop of the Diocese of Toronto: The Rt. Rev. Bishop Sotirios 40 Donlands Ave., Toronto, Ontario M4J 3N6. Tel. (416)462-0833

Independent Assemblies of God—Canada

This fellowship of churches has been operating in Canada for over twenty-five years. It is a branch of the Pentecostal Church in Sweden. Each church within the fellowship is completely independent.

GENERAL ORGANIZATION

General Convention, annual
Headquarters: 1920 Huron St., London, Ontario N5V 3A7. Tel. (519)452-3480

OFFICER

Gen. Sec., Rev. Harry Wuerch, 1211 Lancaster St., London, Ontario N5V 2L4.

PERIODICAL

The Mantle (m), 3840 5th Ave., San Diego, CA 92103. Rev. A. W. Rassmussen, Ed.

Independent Holiness Church

The former Holiness Movement of Canada merged with the Free Methodist Church in 1958. Some churches remained independent of this merger and they formed the Independent Holiness Church in 1960, in Kingston, Ontario. The doctrines are Methodist and Wesleyan.
Churches: 13; Inclusive Membership: 600; Sunday or Sabbath Schools: N.R.; Total Enrollment: N.R.; Ordained Clergy: 21

General Conference: every three years, next meeting, 1992

OFFICERS

Gen. Supt., Rev. R. E. Votary, Sydenham, Ontario K0H 2T0. Tel. (613) 376-3114
Dist., Supt., Rev. John Milligan, Box 43, D'Arcy Station, Saskatchewan S0N 0L0
Gen. Sec., Mr. Dwayne Reaney, Manotick, Ontario K0A 2N0.

PERIODICAL

Gospel Tidings (m)

The Italian Pentecostal Church of Canada

This body had its beginnings in Hamilton, Ontario, in 1912 when a few people of an Italian Presbyterian Church banded themselves together for prayer and received a Pentecostal experience of the Baptism in the Holy Spirit. Since 1912, there has been a close association with the teachings and practices of the Pentecostal Assemblies of Canada.
From Hamilton the work spread to Toronto, which became a center for all of Southern Ontario. The Church then spread to Montreal, where it also flourished.
In 1959, the Church was incorporated under its present name, in the Province of Quebec, Canada, and authorized by charter and Letters' Patent.
The early leaders of this body were the Rev. Luigi Ippolito and the Rev. Ferdinand Zaffuto. The churches have carried on active missionary work in Italy and among many thousands of immigrants recently arrived in Canada.

GENERAL ORGANIZATION

General Conference, annual, Oct.
Headquarters: 6724 Fabre St., Montreal, Quebec H2G 2Z6. Tel. (514) 721-5614

OFFICERS

Gen. Supt. Rev. Alberico DeVito, 7685 Tremblay St., Boussard, Quebec J4W 2W2
Gen. Sec., Rev. David DiStaulo, 6550 Maurice Duplesis, Montreal, Quebec H1G 6K9 Tel. (514) 323-3087
Gen. Treas., Mr. Joseph Manafo, 6730 Fabre St., Montreal, Quebec H1G 2Z6. Tel. (514) 721-5614
Overseers, Rev. Daniel Ippolito, 384 Sunnyside Ave., Toronto, Ontario M6R 2S1. Tel. (416) 766-6692; Rev. Elie DeVito, 643 Park Rd., N., P. O. Box 173, Brantford, Ontario N3T 5M8

Voce Evangelica (Evangel Voice) (q) Joseph Manafo, Daniel Ippolito, Eds.

Jehovah's Witnesses

For details on Jehovah's Witnesses see the directory in this edition "Religious Bodies in the United States."

Churches: 1,238; Inclusive Membership: 94,605; Sunday or Sabbath Schools: None; Total Enrollment: None; Ordained Clergy: None

GENERAL ORGANIZATION

Headquarters: 25 Columbia Heights, Brooklyn, NY 11201. Tel. (718) 625-3600
Canadian Branch Office: Box 4100, Halton Hills, Ontario L7G 4Y4

Jewish Organizations in Canada

The Jewish community of Canada numbered 296,425 persons in 1981 according to Statistics Canada. Jews are spread from coast to coast with organized communities ranging from Saint John's, Newfoundland, to Victoria, British Columbia. The largest concentration is in Montreal (some 95,000) and in Toronto (approximately 104,000).

The history of the Jewish Community began in 1760 with the conquest of Quebec by the British during the Seven Years War, although a few Jews had come north to Halifax from the Atlantic Colonies as early as 1752. The Colony of Lower Canada (new Quebec) had the first considerable settlement and it was there that, in 1768, a synagogue was organized, cemeteries established, rabbis were invited to officiate, and the community won its battles for official legal status and civic equality.

The first synagogue, Shearith Israel of Montreal, was affiliated with the Spanish-Portuguese Congregation in London and follows its rite to the present day. In 1846 the east European tradition was formally established by the issuance of a charter to the Congregation of Polish and German Jews (now Shaar Hashomayim) and in 1882 the Reform Temple Emanu-El was organized. In mid-19th century the Toronto community was formed with the establishment of a congregation (the present Holy Blossom Temple) and the consecration of a cemetery. At the same time the Hamilton community set up its facilities for worship and for the interment of its dead.

After 1880 a large number of immigrants from eastern Europe came to Canada and the present-day community took shape. Its social history parallels that of the United States, with its story of immigrant reception and settlement, industrial life in the garment industries of the large cities, the implantation of synagogues in the Russian tradition, and the slow integration and development of the community on every level.

In 1919 the Canadian Jewish community united in the Canadian Jewish Congress (CJC) which was only of short duration, but it was revived in 1934 in the face of the internal threat of anti-semitism and the world-wide problems of Jewry, which the Canadian community sought to ameliorate. In the years since, the Canadian Jewish Congress became a unique nation-wide institution which arranged for the reception of over 40,000 immigrants in the years following World War II. The Canadian Jewish Congress fought anti-semitism, coordinated the development of an admirable school system and voiced the concerns of the Jewish community of Canada in many areas. During the past decades the Jewish community developed a remarkable press and literature which bolstered civic pride among its members and ensured articulation and dignity for the entire community.

Among the CJC's important activities is the National Religious Department, which speaks for the varied and far-flung religious institutions of the community and participates in their behalf in the tripartite commission which unites Jews, Catholics and Protestants in a common program to make the voice of the community of faith heard in the councils of the nation, and also to strengthen the bonds of friendship between the adherents of the Judeao-Christian revelation.

In addition to the national interfaith program, a Committee of Dialogue, established on the initiative of the Archbishop of Montreal, brings together Jews, Protestants and Catholics for the purpose of closer understanding in the particular context of French Canada.

A census being compiled by the Religious Department of the Canadian Jewish Congress indicates 112 synagogues across the country, of which approximately 53 are Orthodox, 43 are Conservative, 14 are Reform and 2 are Reconstructionist.

Synagogues: 112; Inclusive Membership: 310,000; No. of Rabbis: N.R.

Note: *The Congregational and Rabbinical Organizations pertaining to Canada are the same as those for the United States and are listed in Directory 3, "Religious Bodies in the United States" under Jewish Organizations.*

EDUCATIONAL AND SOCIAL SERVICE ORGANIZATIONS

Canada-Israel Securities, Ltd., State of Israel Bonds: 1255 University St., #200, Montreal, Quebec H3B 3B2. Tel. (514)878-1871. Pres., Melvyn A. Dobrin; Nat'l Exec. Vice-Pres., Julius Briskin

Canadian Foundation for Jewish Culture: 4600 Bathurst St., Willowdale, Ontario M2R 3V2. Tel. (416) 635-2883. Pres., Mira Koschitzky; Exec. Sec., Edmond Y. Lipsitz

Canadian Jewish Congress: 1590 Ave. Docteur Penfield, Montreal, Quebec H3G 1C5. Tel. (514) 931-7531. Pres., Dorothy Reitman; Exec. Vice-Pres., Alan Rose

Canadian ORT Organization (Organization of Rehabilitation Through Training): 5165 Sherbrooke St., W., Ste. 208, Montreal, Quebec H4A 1T6. Tel. (514) 481-2787. Pres., Dr. Victor C. Goldbloom; Exec. Dir., Mac Silver

Canadian Sephardi Federation: 210 Wilson Ave., Toronto, Ontario M5M 3B1. Tel. (416)483-8968. Pres., Maurice Benzacar; Sec. Laeticia Benabou

Canadian Zionist Federation: 5250 Decarie Blvd., Ste. 550, Montreal, Quebec H3X 2H9. Tel. (514) 486-9526. Pres., David J. Azrieli; Exec. Vice-Pres., Rabbi Meyer Krentzman

Hadassah-WIZO Organization of Canada: 1310 Greene Ave., Ste. 900, Montreal, Quebec H3Z 2B8. Tel. (514) 937-9431. Nat'l. Pres., Naomi Frankenberg; Exec. Vice-Pres., Lily Frank

Jewish Immigrant Aid Services of Canada (JIAS): 5151 Cote St. Catherine Rd., Montreal, Quebec H3W 1M6. Tel. (514) 342-9351. Pres., Sheldon Sper; Exec. Vice-Pres., Herb Abrams

Jewish National Fund of Canada (Keren Kayemeth Le' Israel, Inc.): 1980 Sherbrooke, W., Ste. 500, Montreal, Quebec H3H 1E8. Tel. (514)934-0313. Pres., Neri J. Bloomfeld; Exec. Vice-Pres., Michael Goldstein

Labor Zionist Movement of Canada: 7005 Kildare Rd., Ste. 10, Cote St. Luc, Quebec H3W 1C1. Tel. (514) 484-1789. Chpsn., Nat'l. Coord. Cmte. Harry Simon; Adm. Vice-Pres., Abraham Shurem

National Council of Jewish Women of Canada: 1110 Finch Ave. W., #518, Downsview, Ontario M3J 2T2. Tel. (416) 665-8251. Pres., Penny Yellen; Exec. Dir., Eleanor Appleby

National Joint Community Relations Committee of Canadian Jewish Congress: 4600 Bathurst St., Willowdale, Ontario M2R 3V2. Tel. (416) 635-2883. Chpsn., Joseph L. Wilder; Nat'l. Exec. Dir., Manuel Prutschi

Zionist Organization of Canada: 788 Marlee Ave., Toronto, Ontario M6B 3K1. Tel. (416) 781-3571. Pres., Max Goody; Exec. Vice-Pres., George Liban

JEWISH WELFARE FUNDS,
COMMUNITY COUNCILS
Calgary, Alberta: Calgary Jewish Community Council,
1607 90th Ave., S.W. (T2V 4V7). Tel. (403) 253-8600.
Pres. Hal Joffe; Exec. Dir., Drew Stauffenberg
Edmonton, Alberta: Jewish Federation of Edmonton,
7200-156th St. (T5R 1X3). Tel. (403)487-5120. Pres.,
Shelly Maerov; Actg. Exec. Dir., Maxine Fischbein
Hamilton, Ontario: Jewish Federation of Hamilton Went-
worth & Area, Includes Jewish Welfare Fund, P.O. Box
7258, 1030 Lower Lion Club Rd., Ancaster, Ontario
(L9G 3N6). Tel. (416) 648-0605. Pres., Phillip Leon;
Exec. Dir., Sid Brail
London, Ontario: London Jewish Community Council,
536 Huron St. (N5Y 4J5). Tel. (519)673-3310. Pres.,
Gloria Gilbert; Exec. Dir., Gerald Enchin
Montreal, Quebec: Allied Jewish Community Services,
5151 Cote Ste. Catherine Rd. (H3W 1M6). Tel.
(514)735-3541. Pres., Peter Wolkove; Exec. Vice-Pres.,
John Fishel
Ottawa, Ontario: Jewish Community Council of Ottawa,
151 Chapel St. (K1N 7Y2). Tel. (613)232-7306. Pres.,
Steven Victor; Exec. Dir., Gerry Koffman
Toronto, Ontario: Toronto Jewish Congress, 4600 Bath-
urst St., Willowdale (M2R 3V2). Tel. (416)635-2883.
Pres., Herb Rosenthal; Exec. Dir., Steven Ain
Vancouver, British Columbia: Jewish Federation of
Greater Vancouver, 950 W. 41st Ave. (V5Z 2N7). Tel.
(604)266-8371. Pres., Daniel Pekarsky; Exec. Dir.,
Steve Drysdale
Windsor, Ontario: Jewish Community Council, 1641
Ouellette Ave. (N8X 1K9). Tel. (519)973-1772. Pres.,
Alan R. Orman; Exec. Dir., Joseph Eisenberg
Winnipeg, Manitoba: Winnipeg Jewish Community
Council, 370 Hargrave St. (R3B 2K1). Tel. (204)943-
0406. Pres., Evelyn Katz; Exec. Dir., Robert Freedman

PERIODICALS
Bulletin du Congres Juif Canadien (irregular), 1590 Ave.
Docteur Penfield, Montreal, Quebec H3G 1C5. Tel.
(514)931-7531. French Canadian Jewish Congress
Canadian Jewish Herald (Irregular), 17 Anselme Lavigne
Blvd., Dollard des Ormeaux, Quebec H9A 1N3. Tel.
(514)684-7667. Dan Nimrod, Ed.
Canadian Jewish News (w), 10 Gateway Blvd., Don Mills,
Ontario M3C 3A1. Tel. (416)422-2331. Maurice Lucow,
Ed.
Canadian Jewish Outlook (m), 6184 Ash St., #3,
Vancouver, British Columbia V5Z 3G9. Tel. (604)324-
5101. Ben Chud, Henry Rosenthal, Eds.
Canadian Zionist (5/yr.), 5250 Decarie Blvd., Ste. 550,
Montreal, Quebec H3X 2H9. Tel. (514)486-9526. Rabbi
Meyer Krentzman, Ed.
Jewish Eagle (w), 4180 De Courtrai, Rm. 218, Montreal,
Quebec H3S 1C3. Tel. (514)735-6577. B. Hirshtal, Ed.
Yiddish-Hebrew-French
Jewish Post and News (w), 117 Hutchings St., Winnipeg,
Manitoba R2X 2V4. Tel. (204)694-3332. Matt Bellan, Ed.
Jewish Standard (semi-m), 77 Mowat Ave., Ste. 319,
Toronto, Ontario M6K 3E3. Tel (416)537-2696. Julius
Hayman, Ed.
Jewish Western Bulletin (w), 3268 Heather St., Vancou-
ver, British Columbia V5Z 3K5. Tel. (604)879-6575.
Samuel Kaplan, Ed.
Journal of Psychology and Judaism (q.), 1747 Featherston
Dr., Ottawa, Ontario K1N 6P4. Tel (613)731-9119.
Reuven P. Bulka, Ed.
Ottawa Jewish Bulletin & Review (bi-w), 151 Chapel St.,
Ottawa, Ontario K1N 7Y2. Tel. (613)232-7306. Cynthia
Engel, Ed.
Undzer Veg (irregular), 272 Codsell Ave., Downsview,
Ontario M3H 3X2. Tel. (416)636-4024. Joseph Kage,
Ed. Yiddish-English

Windsor Jewish Community Council Bulletin (irregular),
1641 Ouellette Ave., Windsor, Ontario N8X 1K9. Tel.
(519)973-1772. Joseph Eisenberg, Ed.

Note: *For details concerning many aspects of Jewish life
and organization in Canada and throughout the world,
consult the American Jewish Year Book, 1989, edited by
David Singer and published by the American Jewish
Committee, New York, and the Jewish Publication Society
of America, Philadelphia.*

The Latvian Evangelical Lutheran Church in America

This body was organized into a denomination on August
22, 1975 after having existed as the Federation of Latvian
Evangelical Lutheran Churches since 1957. This church is
a regional constituent part of the Lutheran Church of
Latvia in Exile, a member of the Lutheran World
Federation and the World Council of Churches.

The Latvian Evangelical Lutheran Church in America
works to foster religious life, tradition and customs in its
congregations in harmony with the Holy Scriptures, the
Apostles', Nicaean, and Athanasian Creeds, the unaltered
Augsburg Confession, Martin Luther's Small and Large
Catechisms and other documents of the Book of Concord.

The LELCA is ordered by its Synod, executive board,
auditing committee, and district conferences.

Churches: 8; Inclusive Membership: 2,690; Sunday or
Sabbath Schools: N.R.; Total Enrollment N.R.; Ordained Clergy: 8

GENERAL ORGANIZATION
Synod: Meets every three years. Next meeting, 1990
Headquarters: 6551 West Montrose Ave., Chicago, IL
60634.

OFFICERS
Pres., Dean Vilis Varsbergs, 6551 West Montrose Ave.,
Chicago, IL 60634. Tel. (312)725-3820.
Vice-Pres., Rev. Juris Calitis, 8 Rolland Rd., Toronto,
Ontario M4G 1V5. Tel. (416)482-8403.
2nd Vice-Pres., Dr. Janis Robins, 11 Ludlow Ave., St.
Paul, MN 55108. Tel. (612)646-1980.
Sec., Dr. Ernests Reinbergs, 32 Hales Cres., Guelph,
Ontario N1G 1P6. Tel. (519)822-6842
Treas., Mr. Alfreds Trautmanis, 103 Rose St., Freeport,
NY 11520. Tel. (516)623-2646

PERIODICAL
Cela Biedrs (10/yr.), Dean Arturs Voitkus, 26 Chippewa
Ave., Ottawa, Ontario K2G 1X7

Lutheran Church—Canada

Establishd April 23, 1959 at Edmonton, Alberta, as a
federation of Canadian districts of the Lutheran Church,
Missouri Synod; constituted May 19, 1988, at Winnipeg,
Manitoba, as an autonomous church.

Churches: 354; Inclusive Membership: 90,944; Sunday or
Sabbath Schools: 296; Total Enrollment: 18,474;
Ordained Clergy: 341

GENERAL ORGANIZATION
Triennial Convention. Next meeting, 1993
Headquarters: 59 Academy Rd., Winnipeg, Manitoba
R3M 0E2. Tel. (204)452-2747
Pres., Edwin Lehman

OFFICERS
Pres., Rev. Edwin Lehman, 59 Academy Rd., Winnipeg,
Manitoba R3M 0E2.
Vice-Pres., Rev. Karl Koslowsky, 871 Cavalier Dr.,
Winnipeg, Manitoba R2Y 1C7; Rev. Orville Walz, 7128
Ada Blvd., Edmonton, Alberta T5B 4E4; _____

Sec., Rev. Rober Winger, 137 Queen St., S., Kitchener, Ontario N2G 1W2
Treas., Mr. Ken Werschler, 59 Academy Rd., Winnipeg, Manitoba R3M 0E2

Mennonite Brethren Churches, Canadian Conference of

Incorporated November 22, 1945

Churches: 173; Inclusive Membership: 26,034; Sunday or Sabbath Schools: 149; Total Enrollment: 16,344; Ordained Clergy: N.R.

GENERAL ORGANIZATION

Annual Conference: next meeting July
Headquarters: 3-169 Riverton Ave., Winnipeg, Manitoba R2L 2E5. Tel. (204) 669-6575

OFFICERS

Mod., Rev. Herb Neufeld, 1681 McCallum Rd., Abbotsford, British Columbia V2S 3M4. Te. (604)852-1001
Asst. Mod., Abe Konrad, 12404-40Ave., Edmonton, Alberta T6J 0S5. Tel. (403)435-1074
Menno Martens, 838-10th Ave. N.E., Swift Current, Saskatchewan S9H 2T2. Tel. (306)773-6262

PERIODICALS

Mennonite Brethren Herald (bi-w), 3-169 Riverton Ave., Winnipeg, Manitoba R2L 2E5. Herb Kopp, Ed.
Mennonitische Rundschau: 3-169 Riverton Ave., Manitoba R2L 1L4. Abe Schellenberg, Ed.

Mennonite Church (Canada)

(See: Conference of Mennonites in Canada)

Metropolitan Community Churches, Universal Fellowship of

The Universal Fellowship of Metropolitan Community Churches is a Christian church which directs a special ministry within, and on behalf of, the homosexual community.

Founded in 1968 in Los Angeles by the Rev. Troy Perry, the "U.F.M.C.C." has 250 member congregations worldwide. Ten congregations are in Canada, in Vancouver, Edmonton, Calgary, Toronto, London, Ottawa, Winnipeg, Kingston, and Victoria.

Theologically, the Metropolitan Community Churches stand within the mainstream of Christian doctrine, being "ecumenical" or "interdenominational" in stance (albeit a "denomination" in their own right).

The Metropolitan Community Churches are characterized by their belief that a) the love of God is a gift, freely offered to all people, regardless of "sexual orientation" and that b) no incompatability exists between human sexuality and the Christian faith.

The Metropolitan Community Churches in Canada were founded in Toronto in 1973 by the Rev. Robert Wolfe.

GENERAL ORGANIZATION

General Conference (International), biennial, next meeting, 1991, Phoenix, AZ.
District Conferences (Regional), semiannual.

OFFICERS

Western Canadian District, P. O. Box 245, Maple Rdge, British Columbia V2X 7G1. Tel. (604)534-9221. District Coordinator, Mr. Arthur Pearson.
Eastern Canadian District, Box 213, Sta. B, London, Ontario N6A 4V8. Tel. (519)438-9301. Rev. Rod McAvoy

The Missionary Church of Canada

This denomination in Canada is affiliated with the worldwide body of the Missionary Church. Historically part of the Anabaptist, Mennonite movement, it changed its name to the United Missionary Church in 1947 and in 1969 it merged with the Missionary Church Association of Fort Wayne, IN. It is an evangelical, missionary church and became an autonomous national church in Canada in 1987.

GENERAL ORGANIZATION

The Missionary Church of Canada meets biennially and the General Conference of the International Missionary Church meets biennially on alternate years. District Conferences meet annually.

OFFICERS

Missionary Church of Canada:
Pres., Rev. Alfred W. Rees, Banfield Memorial Church, 89 Centre Ave., North York, Ontario M2M 2L7
Canada East District: Dist. Supt., Rev. C. E. Prosser, 130 Fergus Ave., Kitchener, Ontario N2A 2H2
Canada West District: Dist. Supt., Rev. David Crouse, Box 640, Midnapore, Alberta T0L 1J0

Moravian Church in America, Northern Province, Canadian District of the

Note: The work in Canada is under the general oversight and rules of the Moravian Church, Northern Province, general offices for which are located at 1021 Center St., P.O. Box 1245, Bethlehem, PA 18016

Churches: 9; Inclusive Membership: 2,145; Sunday or Sabbath Schools: 9; Total Enrollment: 525; Ordained Clergy: 15

OFFICER

Pres., Mr. Elmer F. Kadatz, R.R. 1, Site 4, Box 8, Edmonton, Alberta T6H 4N6. Tel. (403)988-5096

Muslims

There are many thousands of Muslims in Canada, primarily in the larger cities. The Muslim community in Canada is gathered together by Islamic societies and Muslim Mosques. These societies and other organizations are not regarded as religious sects or divisions. Their multiplication arises from the needs of each group in a given area, long distances between groups, and the absence in Islam of organized hierarchy. All the groups hold the same beliefs, aspire to practice the same rituals; namely, prayers, fasting, almsgiving, and pilgrimage to Makkah Almukarramah (Mecca).

REGIONAL AND NATIONAL GROUPS

A number of regional and national groups exist which were started with the objective of helping local groups, coordinating their work, and promoting closer unity among them.
These include:

The Federation of Islamic Associations in the United States and Canada, 25351 Five Mile Rd., Redford Township, MI 48239.Sec. Gen., Nihad Hamid. Publication: The Muslim Star, 17514 Woodward Ave., Detroit, MI 48203

Islamic Society of North America P. O. Box 38, Plainfield, IN 46168. Tel. (317) 839-8157. Publications: The Islamic Horizons (m)

Council of Muslim Communities of Canada, 1250 Ramsey View Ct., Ste. 504, Sudbury, Ontario P3E 2E7. Tel. (705)522-2948. Dir., Dr. Mir Iqbal Ali

Council of Masajid (Mosques) in the U.S.A., 99 Woodview Dr., Old Bridge, NJ 08857. Sec. Gen., Dawud A. Assad. Tel. (201) 679-8617. Publication: Majallat Al-Masjid (newsletter)

Netherlands Reformed Congregations of North America

The Netherlands Reformed Congregations, presently numbering 162 congregations in the Netherlands (90,000 members), 25 congregations in North America (9,400 members), and a handful of congregations in various other countries, organized denominationally in 1907. The so-called Churches Under the Cross (established in 1839, after breaking away from the 1834 secession congregations) and the so-called Ledeboerian churches (established in 1841 under the leadership of Rev. Ledeboer who seceded from the Reformed state church), united in 1907 under the leadership of the then 25-year-old Rev. G. H. Kersten to form the Netherlands Reformed Congregations (*Gereformeerde Gemeenten*). Many of the North American congregations left the Christian Reformed Church to join the Netherlands Reformed Congregations after the Kuyperian presupposed regeneration doctrine began making serious inroads into that denomination.

All Netherlands Reformed congregations, office bearers, and members subscribe to three Reformed Forms of Unity: the *Belgic Confession of Faith* (by DeBres), the *Heidelberg Catechism* and the *Canons of Dordt*. The *Belgic Confession* and *Canons of Dordt* are read regularly at worship services, and the *Heidelberg Catechism* is preached weekly except on church feast days.

The NRC stresses the traditional Reformed doctrines of grace, such as the sovereignty of God, responsibility of humankind, the necessity of the new birth, and the experience of God's sanctifying grace.

Churches: 8; Inclusive Membership: 4,372; Sunday or Sabbath Schools: N.R.; Total Enrollment: N.R.; Ordained Clergy: 2

GENERAL ORGANIZATION

Clk. of Synod, Dr. J. R. Beeke, 2115 Romence St. N.E., Grand Rapids, MI 49503

North American Baptist Conference

Churches belonging to this conference emanated from German Baptist immigrants of more than a century ago. Although scattered across Canada and the U.S., they are bound together by a common heritage, a strong spiritual unity, a Bible-centered faith, and a deep interest in missions.

Note: The details of general organization, officers, and periodicals of this body will be found in the North American Baptist Conference directory in the United States section of this *Yearbook*. The international office at 1 S. 210 Summit Ave., Oakbrook Terrace, IL 60181, serves the Canadian and U.S. churches.

Churches: 112; Inclusive Membership: 17,374; Sunday or Sabbath Schools: 112; Total Enrollment: 9,109; Ordained Clergy: 182

The Old Catholic Church of Canada

Founded in 1948 in Hamilton, Ontario. The first bishop was the Rt. Rev. Georges Davis. The Old Catholic Church of Canada accepts all the doctrines of the Eastern Orthodox Churches and, therefore, not Papal Infallibility or the Immaculate Conception. The ritual is Western (Latin Rite) and is in the vernacular. Celibacy is optional. The Old Catholic Church of Canada is affiliated with the North American Old Roman Catholic Church, whose Presiding Bishop is Most Rev. Theodore Rematt of Chicago (see U.S. directory).

Churches: 2; Inclusive Membershi~ ~; Sunday or Sabbath Schools: None; Total lment: None; Ordained Clergy: 2

GENERAL ORGANIZATION

Headquarters: R. R. #1, Midland, Ontario L4R 4K3. Tel. (705)835-3526

OFFICER

Bishop, Most Rev. David Thomson, R. R. 1, Midland, Ontario L4R 4K3

Old Order Amish Church

This is the most conservative branch of the Mennonite Church and direct descendants of Swiss Brethren (Anabaptists) who emerged from the Reformation in Switzerland in 1525. The Amish, followers of Bishop Jacob Ammann, became a distinct group in 1693. They began migrating to America about 1720 where 95 percent of them still reside. They first migrated to Ontario in 1824 directly from Bavaria, Germany and also from Pennsylvania and Alsace-Lorraine. Since 1953 many Amish have migrated to Ontario from Ohio, Indiana, and Iowa.

In 1989, there were 17 congregations in Ontario, each being autonomous. No membership figures are kept by this group but membership has been estimated at 825. Being congregational in structure, there is no central headquarters. Each congregation is served by a bishop, two ministers, and a deacon, all of whom are chosen from among the male members by lot for life.

CORRESPONDENT

Mr. David Luthy, Pathway Publishers, Rte. 4, Aylmer, Ontario, N5H 2R3

PERIODICALS

Blackboard Bulletin; The Budget; The Diary; Die Botschaft; Family Life; Herold der Wahrheit; Young Companion

The Open Bible Standard Churches of Canada

This is the Canadian branch of the Open Bible Standard Churches, Inc., USA of Des Moines, Iowa. It is an evangelical, full gospel denomination emphasizing evangelism, missions, and the message of the Open Bible. The Canadian Branch was chartered January 7, 1982.

GENERAL ORGANIZATION

General Conference: Annual (April)
Headquarters: 82 Northline Rd., Toronto, Ontario M4B 3E5. Tel. (416)752-6481

OFFICERS

Supt. and Gen. Overseer, Rev. C. Russell Archer, P. O. Box 518, Vandalia, OH 45377
Prov. Supt., Rev. Richard Lewis, 82 Northline Rd., Toronto, Ontario M4B 3E5. Tel. (416)752-6481

The Pentecostal Assemblies of Canada

This body is incorporated under the Dominion Charter of 1919 and is also recognized in the Province of Quebec as an ecclesiastical corporation. Its beginnings are to be found in the revivals at the turn of the century, and most of the first Canadian Pentecostal leaders came from a religious background rooted in the Holiness movements.

The original incorporation of 1919 was implemented among churches of eastern Canada only. In the same year, a conference was called in Moose Jaw, Saskatchewan, to which the late Rev. J. M. Welch, gen. supt. of the then-organized Assemblies of God in the U.S., was invited. The churches of Manitoba and Saskatchewan were organized as the Western District Council of the Assemblies of God. They were joined later by Alberta and British Columbia. In 1921, a conference was held in Montreal, to which the general chairman of the Assemblies of God was invited.

Eastern Canada also became a district of the Assemblies of God, joining Eastern and Western Canada as two districts in a single organizational union.

In 1922, at Kitchener, Ontario, a special committee met with a delegation from both eastern and western churches, at which time it was agreed to dissolve the Canadian District of the Assemblies of God and unite under the name The Pentecostal Assemblies of Canada.

Today, The Pentecostal Assemblies of Canada operate throughout the nation, and religious services are conducted in more than 27 languages, in more than 200 ethnic churches. There are 109 native churches.

Churches: 1,168; Inclusive Membership: 191,607; Sunday or Sabbath Schools: N.R.; Total Enrollment: N.R.; Ordained Clergy: N.R.

OFFICERS

Gen. Supt., Rev. James M. MacKnight
Gen. Sec., Rev. Charles Yates
Gen. Treas., Rev. John Totafurno
Exec. Dir. Overseas Missions, Rev. W. C. Cornelius
Exec. Dir. Church Ministries, Rev. W. A. Griffin
Exec. Dir. Home Missions and Bible Colleges, Rev. Gordon R. Upton
Dir. Women's Ministries, Mrs. Eileen Stewart
Mgr. Full Gospel Publishing House, Mr. Harry E. Anderson

DISTRICT SUPERINTENDENTS

British Columbia, Rev. Lester E. Markham, 5641 176 A St., Surrey, British Columbia, V3S 4G8
Alberta, Rev. John A. Keys, 10585-111 St., #101, Edmonton, Alberta, T5H 3E8
Saskatchewan, Rev. L. Calvin King, 1223B Idylwyld Dr. N., Saskatoon, Saskatchewan S7L 1A1
Manitoba, Rev. Gordon V. Peters, 3081 Ness Ave., Winnipeg, Manitoba R2Y 2G3
Western Ontario, Rev. Earl K. Young, 3419 Mainway, Burlington, Ontario L7M 1A9
Eastern Ontario and Quebec, Rev. E. Stewart Hunter, Box 1600, Belleville, Ontario K8N 5J3
Maritime Provinces, Rev. David C. Slauenwhite, Box 1184, Truro, Nova Scotia B2N 5H1

CONFERENCES

German Conference, Rev. Horst Doberstein, P.O. Box 2310, St. Catharines, Ontario L2M 7M7
French Conference, Rev. Oscar Masseau, P. O. Box 2310, Sta. B, 1711 Henri-Bourassa Blvd., E., Montreal, Quebec H2C 1J5
Slavic Conferences: Eastern District, Rev. Walter Senko, R.R. 1, Wilsonville, Ontario N0E 1Z0; Western District, Rev. Michael Brandebura, Box 1149, Morinville, Alberta T0G 1P0
Finnish Conference, Rev. A. Wirkkala, 1920 Argyle Dr., Vancouver, British Columbia V5P 2A8

PERIODICAL

The Pentecostal Testimony, 10 Overlea Blvd., Toronto, Ontario M4H 1A5. Rev. Robert J. Skinner, Ed.

Pentecostal Assemblies of Newfoundland

This body began in 1910 and held its first assembly at the Bethesda Pentecostal Mission at St. John's. It was incorporated in 1925 as the Bethesda Pentecostal As-

semblies and changed its name in 1930 to the Pentecostal Assemblies of Newfoundland.

GENERAL ORGANIZATION

Headquarters: 57 Thorburn Rd., St. John's, Newfoundland A1B 3N4. Tel. (709)753-6314
General Conference: Bi-Annual, Next meeting, June, 1989

OFFICERS

Pres. and Gen. Supt., Roy D. King, 50 Brownsdale St., St. John's, Newfoundland A1E 4R2
First Asst. Supt.: B. Q. Grimes, 14 Chamberlain St., Grand Falls, Newfoundland A2A 2G4
Second Asst. Supt., H. E. Perry, P. O. Box 449, Lewisporte, Newfoundland A0G 3A0
Gen. Sec.-Treas., F. V. Rideout, 21 Dalhousie Crescent, Mount Pearl, Newfoundland A1N 2Y9

DEPARTMENTS

Youth and Sunday School, Dir., Robert H. Dewling, 26 Wicklow St., St. John's, Newfoundland A1B 3H2
Literature, Gen. Mgr., Calvin T. Andrews, 28 Royal Oak Dr., St. John's, Newfoundland, A1G 1S3
Women's Ministries, Dir., Mrs. Sylvia Purchase, Box 64, R.R. #3, Botwood, Newfoundland A1A 1W0
Missionettes, Dir., Mrs. Alma Clarke, Box 256, Clarke's Beach, Newfoundland A0A 1W0
Men's Fellowship, Dir., James F. Anthony, Box 82, Cox's Cove, Newfoundland, A0L 1C0

PERIODICALS

Good Tidings (m), 57 Thorburn Rd., St. John's Newfoundland A1B 3N4, Roy D. King, Ed.
The Ambassador (m), 57 Thorburn Rd., St. John's, Newfoundland A1B 3N4, R.H. Dewling, Ed.

Pentecostal Holiness Church of Canada

The first General Conference convened in May, 1971 in Toronto. Prior to this, the Canadian churches were under the leadership of the Pentecostal Holiness Church in the U.S.A.

GENERAL ORGANIZATION

General Conference every four years. Next meeting, 1990
Headquarters: Box 442, Waterloo, Ontario N2J 4A9. Tel. (519) 746-1310

OFFICERS

Gen. Supt., G. H. Nunn, Box 442, Waterloo, Ontario N2J 4A9
Asst. Supt., Walter Gamble, Vince Brufatto
Sec. Treas., Clarence Wood, R. R. # 1, Minden, Ontario K0M 2K0

PERIODICAL

Impact (q), Dept. of Publications, Box 442, Waterloo, Ontario N2J 4A9

Plymouth Brethren
(Also known as Christian Brethren, see above)

Polish National Catholic Church of Canada

This Diocese was created at the XII General Synod of the Polish National Catholic Church of America in October, 1967. Formerly, the Canadian parishes were a part of the Western Diocese and Buffalo-Pittsburgh Diocese of the Polish National Catholic Church in America.

GENERAL ORGANIZATION

Headquarters: 186 Cowan Ave., Toronto, Ontario M6K 2N6

The Rt. Rev. Joseph Nieminski, Bishop Ordinary, 186 Cowan Ave., Toronto, Ontario M6K 2N6. Tel. (416) 532-8249

Presbyterian Church in America (Canadian Section)

Canadian congregations of the Reformed Presbyterian Church, Evangelical Synod, became a part of the Presbyterian Church in America when the RPCES joined PCA in June 1982. Some of the churches were in predecessor bodies of the RPCES, which was the product of a 1965 merger of the Reformed Presbyterian Church in North America, General Synod, and the Evangelical Presbyterian Church. Others came into existence later as a part of the home missions work of RPCES. Congregations are located in six provinces, and the PCA is continuing church extension work in Canada. The denomination is committed to world evangelization and to a continuation of historic Presbyterianism. Its officers are required to subscribe, without reservation, to the Reformed faith as set forth in the Westminster Confession of Faith and Catechisms.

Churches: 16; Inclusive Membership: 782; Sunday or Sabbath Schools: N.R.; Total Enrollment: 327; Ordained Clergy: 19

CORRESPONDENT

Rev. Douglas Codling, 16292 Glenwood Cres., N., Surrey, British Columbia V3R 8M7. Tel. (604)589-4438

The Presbyterian Church in Canada

The nonconcurring portion of the Presbyterian Church in Canada that did not become a part of The United Church of Canada in 1925.

Churches: 1,035; Inclusive Membership: 213,690; Sunday or Sabbath Schools: 637; Total Enrollment: 34,629; Ordained Clergy: 1,168
Offices: 50 Wynford Dr., Don Mills, Ontario M3C 1J7. Tel. (416)441-1111

OFFICERS

Moderator, Dr. B. Miles
Clerks of Assembly: Principal Clerk, Dr. E. F. Roberts; Deputy Clerks, Dr. D. B. Lowry; Dr. T. Plomp Clerks Emeritus, Dr. E. H. Bean, Dr. D. C. MacDonald
Adm. Council: Sec., Dr. E. F. Roberts; Treas., Mr. G. Jones; Comp., Mr. D. A. Taylor

NATIONAL BOARDS

Board of World Missions: Gen. Sec., Rev. Peter Ruddell; Sec. for Africa, Adm. and Fin., Rev. C. R. Talbot; Sec., Edu. for Mission, Rev. M. L. Garvin; Sec., Canada Operations, Miss G. G. Kelly; Sec., Overseas Rel., Rev. H. G. Davis; Sec. for Mission Personnel Rev. Ian Morrison
Board of Congregational Life: Gen. Sec., Dr. L. E. Siverns; Sec. for Worship, Rev. E. M. MacNaughton; Sec. for Lay Ministries & Church Edu., Miss H. G. Tetley; Sec. for Church and Society, Dr. R. Hodgson; Sec. for Camping & Outdoor Min., Mrs. S. Ford; Sec. for Evangelism, Dr. R. van Auken
Communication Services: Consultant, Mr. Donald Stephens
Board of Ministry: Gen. Sec., Rev. T. Gemmell
Presbyterian World Service and Development: Dir., Miss Jean Davidson
Presbyterian Church Building Corp.: Dir., Rev. F. R. Kendall
Women's Missionary Society (WD): Pres., Mrs. G. Jess, Oshawa, Ontario
Women's Missionary Society (ED): Pres., Mrs. W. Wilson, Rexton, New Brunswick

PERIODICAL

The Presbyterian Record (m), 50 Wynford Ave., Don Mills, Ontario M3C 1J7. Rev. John Congram, Ed.

Reformed Church in Canada

The Canadian branch of the Reformed Church in America consists of 31 churches organized under the Council of the Reformed Church in Canada and within the classis of Ontario (19 churches), Cascades (11 churches), Lake Erie (1 church). The Reformed Church in America was established in 1628 by the earliest Dutch settlers in America as the Reformed Protestant Dutch Church. It is evangelical in theology and presbyterian in government.

Churches: 31; Inclusive Membership: 6,486; Sunday or Sabbath Schools: 29; Total Enrollment: 2,415; Ordained Clergy: 54

GENERAL ORGANIZATION

Gen. Sec., Rev. Edwin G. Mulder, 475 Riverside Dr., New York, NY 10115. Tel (212) 870-2841
Council of the Reformed Church in Canada; Exec. Sec., Rev. Dr. Jonathan N. Gerstrer, Reformed Church Center, R.R. #4, Cambridge, Ontario N1R 5S5. Tel. (519) 623-4860.

PERIODICAL

Pioneer Christian Monthly (m), Reformed Church Center, R.R. #4 Cambridge, Ontario N1R 5S5. Tel. (519) 623-4860. Mrs. Nellie S. From, Interim Ed.

Reformed Doukhobors, Christian Community and Brotherhood of

Doukhobors were founded in the late 17th century in Russia. Their doctrine is the "Living Book," which is based on traditional songs and chants and on contents of the Bible. The Living Book is memorized by each generation.

GENERAL ORGANIZATION

Headquarters: Site 8, Comp. 50, R.R. 1, Crescent Valley, British Columbia V0G 1H0

OFFICERS

Pastor, Stephan S. Sorokin (assisted by a 11-member Fraternal Council)

The Reformed Episcopal Church

The Canadian jurisdiction of the Reformed Episcopal Church (see U.S. listing in Directory 3, "Religious Bodies in the United States") maintains the founding principles of episcopacy (in historic succession from the apostles), Anglican liturgy, Reformed doctrine and evangelical zeal, and in its practice, continues to recognize the validity of certain nonepiscopal orders of evangelical ministry.

OFFICERS

Pres., Bishop W. W. Lyle, 1544 Broadview Ct., Coquitlam, British Columbia V3J 5X9
Vice Pres., Laurence Jackson, 600 Foul Bay Rd., Victoria, British Columbia V8S 4H3
Sec., Miss E. R. MacQueen, 736-13th St., New Westminster, British Columbia V3M 4M7. Tel. (604) 521-3580
Treas., J. A. Hill, 1209 Crown Cres., Victoria, British Columbia V8P 1M5

Reinlaender Mennonite Church

This group was founded in 1958 when ten ministers and approximately 600 members separated from the Sommerfelder Mennonite Church. In 1968, four ministers and about 200 members migrated to Bolivia. The church has work in Winkler, Altona, Blumenfeld, Austin, Grunthal and Stuartburn, Manitoba.

CORRESPONDENT

Bishop P. A. Rempel, 223 - 3rd St.,, Winkler, Manitoba R6W 2V9. Tel. (204)325-4595

Reorganized Church of Jesus Christ of Latter Day Saints

Founded April 6, 1830, by Joseph Smith, Jr., and reorganized under the leadership of the founder's son, Joseph Smith III, in 1860. The Church is established in 38 countries in addition to the United States and Canada. A biennial world conference is held in Independence, Mo. The current president is Wallace B. Smith, greatgrandson of the original founder.

Churches: 51; Inclusive Membership: 12,396; Sunday or Sabbath Schools: N.R.; Total Enrollment: N.R.; Ordained Clergy: 1,021

Headquarters: World Headquarters, The Auditorium, Independence, Mo.; Canadian Office, 390 Speedvale Ave., E., Guelph, Ontario N1E 1N5

CANADIAN REGIONS AND DISTRICTS

Northern Plains & Prairie Provinces Region, Canada and U.S.A., Regional Adm., Alvin Mogg, 41 Ranch Glen Dr., NW., Calgary Alberta T3G 1T2; *Alberta District,* G. Ivan Millar, #13, 20 Laval Blvd., Lethbridge, Alberta T1K 4E4; *Saskatchewan District,* Charles J. Lester, 635 Christopher Way, Saskatoon, Saskatchewan S7J 3S3

Pacific Northwest Region, Canada & U.S.A., Regional Adm., Robert Skoor, P.O. Box 18469, 4820 Morgan, Seattle, WA 98118: *British Columbia District,* Dennis L. McKelvie, 2594 Trillium Pl., Coquitlam, British Columbia V3E 2G8

Ontario Region; Regional Adm., Donald H. Comer, 390 Speedvale Ave., E., Guelph, Ontario N1E 1N5; *Chatham District,* John S. Scherer, 87 Glenwood Dr., Chatham, Ontario N7L 3X3; *Grand River District,* A. J. David Snell, 49-121 University Ave., E., Waterloo, Ontario N2J 4J1; *London District,* Larry Buchanan, Box 59, Straffordville, Ontario N0J 1Y0; *Northern Ontario District,* Donald Arrowsmith, 917 Woodbine Ave., Sudbury, Ontario P3A 2L8; *Ottawa District,* Roy A. Young, RR #4, Odessa, Ontario K0H 2H0; *Owen Sound District,* Grant Bennington, 3 Tatham Pl., Listowel, Ontario N4W 3C2; *Toronto District,* Larry D. Windland, 8142 Islington Ave., N., Woodridge, Ontario L7L 1B7

Eastern Canada Region (Includes New Brunswick, Newfoundland, Nova Scotia, Prince Edward Island and Quebec), Regional Adm., Paul Booth, RLDS Auditorium, P.O. Box 1059, Independence, MO 64051

Northern Canada Region (Includes Northern Canada, Northwest Territories and Yukon) Regional Adm., Kisuke Sekine, RLDS Auditorium, P.O. Box 1059, Independence, MO 64051

The Roman Catholic Church in Canada

The largest single body of Christians in Canada, the Roman Catholic Church is under the spiritual leadership of His Holiness the Pope. Catholicism in Canada dates back to 1534, when the first Mass was celebrated on the Gaspé Peninsula on July 7, by a priest accompanying Jacques Cartier. There seems little doubt that Catholicism had been implanted earlier by fishermen and sailors from Europe. Priests came to Acadia as early as 1604. Traces of a regular colony go back to 1608 when Champlain settled in Quebec City. The Recollets (1615), followed by the Jesuits (1625) and the Sulpicians (1657), began the missions among the native population. The first official Roman document relative to the Canadian missions dates from March 20, 1618. Bishop Francois de Montmorency-Laval, the first bishop, arrived in Quebec in 1659. The church developed in the East but not until 1818 did systematic missionary work begin in western Canada.

In the latter 1700s, English-speaking Roman Catholics, mainly from Ireland and Scotland, began to arrive in Canada's Atlantic provinces. After 1815 Irish Catholics settled in large numbers in what is now Ontario. The Irish potato famine of 1847 greatly increased that population in all parts of eastern Canada.

By the 1850s the Catholic Church in both English- and French-speaking Canada had begun to erect new dioceses and found many religious communities. These communities did educational, medical, and charitable work among their own people as well as among Canada's native peoples. By the 1890s large numbers of non-English and non-French-speaking Catholics had settled in Canada, especially in the Western provinces. In the 20th century the pastoral horizons have continued to expand to meet the needs of what has now become a very multiracial church.

INTERNATIONAL ORGANIZATION

His Holiness the Pope, Bishop of Rome, Vicar of Jesus Christ, Supreme Pontiff of the Catholic Church.

POPE JOHN PAUL II, Karol Wojtyla (born May 18, 1920; installed October 22, 1978)

Apostolic Pro Nuncio to Canada Archbishop Angelo Palmas, 724 Manor Ave., Rockcliffe Park, Ottawa, Ontario K1M 0E3. Tel. (613)746-4914

Churches: 5,878; Inclusive Membership: 11,375,914; Sunday or Sabbath Schools: N.R.; Total Enrollment: N.R.; Ordained Clergy: 11,838

CANADIAN ORGANIZATION

Canadian Conference of Catholic Bishops (Conférénce des évêques catholiques du Canada) 90 Parent Ave. Ottawa, Ontario, K1N 7B1. Tel. (613)236-9461. (All offices below are at this address and telephone number unless otherwise stated.)

The Canadian Conference of Catholic Bishops is an Association of Cardinals, Archbishops, and Bishops of Canada established to assure the progress of the Church and the Coordination of Catholic activities in Canada.

The Canadian Hierarchy is divided along linquistic lines between French and English.

OFFICERS

General Secretariat of the Episcopacy
Secrétaire général (French Sector) Père Alexandre TachéGeneral Secretary (English Sector) Rev. William J. Ryan
Assistant General Secretary (English Sector), Mr. Bernard Daly
Secrétaire général adjoint (French Sector), P. Roland Denis

EXECUTIVE COMMITTEE

National Level
Pres., Most Rev. James Hayes
Vice Pres., Mgr Robert Lebel
Co. Treas., Most Rev. Thomas Fulton; Mgr Charles Valois

EPISCOPAL COMMISSIONS

National Level
Social Affairs, Mgr Gilles Ouelett
Canon Law—Inter-rite, Mgr Louis-de-Gonzague Langevin
Ministries, Most Rev. Charles A. Halpin
Missions, Most Rev. John A. O'Mara
Ecumenism, Most Rev. Leonard Crowley
Theology, Mgr Bertrand Blanchet
Sector Level
Communications Sociales, Mgr Charles Valois
Social Communications, Most Rev. William E. Power
Education Chrétien, Mgr Donat Chiasson
Christian Education, Most Rev. Marcel Gervais
Liturgie, Mgr Maurice Couture
Liturgy, Most Rev. James L. Doyle

Secteur Francais

Office des Missions, Dir., Père Lucien Casterman, O.M.I.

Office des Communications Sociales, Dir., Abbé Lucien Labelle, 4005 rue de Bellechasse, Montreal, Québec. H1X 1J6. Tel. (514)729-6391

Office National de liturgie, coordonnateur: M. l'abbé Paul Boily, 3530 rue Adam, Montréal, Québec H1W 1Y8. Tel. (514)522-4930

Service Incroyance et Foi, Dir., Père Léopold de Reyès, ss.cc., 2930 Lacombe, Montréal, Québec H3T 1L4. Tel. (514)735-1565

Office National d'Oecumenisme, Rev. Thomas Ryan, C.S.P., 2065 ouest rue Sherbrooke, Montréal, Québec H3H 1G6. Tel. (514)937-9176

Services des Relations Publiques, Dir., M. Jacques Binet

Service des Editions, Dir., Mlle Claire Dubé.

English Sector

National Liturgical Office, Dir., Rev. Murray Kroetsch

National Office of Religious Education, Dir., Mrs. Bernadette Tourangeau

Office for Missions, Dir., Fr. Lucien Casterman, O.M.I.

Public Information Office, Dir., Miss Bonnie Brennan

Social Affairs, Dir., Mr. Tony Clarke

REGIONAL EPISCOPAL ASSEMBLIES

Atlantic Episcopal Assembly, Pres., Mgr Austin E. Burke; Vice-Pres., Most Rev. James MacDonald; Sec., Rev. Guy Léger, C.S.C., Site 1, Boîte 389, R.R. 1, St. Joseph, New Brunswick E0A 2Y0. Tel., (506)758-2531

Assemblée des Évêques du Quebec, Prés., Mgr Jean-Marie Fortier; Vice-Pres., Mgr Gilles Ouellet; Sécretaire général, L'abbé Michel Buron; Secrétariat: 1225 boulevard Saint Joseph est, Montréal, Québec H2J 1L7. Tél. (514)274-4323

Ontario Conference of Catholic Bishops, Pres., Most Rev. John O'Mara; Vice-Pres., Mgr Eugene LaRocque; Sec., Rev. Angus J. Macdougall, S.J.; Secretariat: 67 Bond St., Ste. 304, Toronto, Ontario M5B 1X5. Tel. (416)368-1804

Western Catholic Conference, Pres., Mgr Antoine Hacault; Vice-Pres., Most Rev. Maxim Hermaniuk; Sec., Mgr Peter Sutton, 108-1st St., West, P.O. Box 270, Le Pas, Manitoba R9A 1K4. (204)623-2503

MILITARY ORDINARIATE (ORDINARIAT MILITAIRE)

Ordinaire aux Forces canadiennes (Military Ordinary), Mgr André Vallée, p.m.é., National Defence Headquarters, Ottawa, Ontario K1A OK2. Tel. (613)992-2031

Canadian Religious Conference, 324 Laurier Ave., East, Ottawa, Ontario K1N 6P6. Tel. (613)236-0824. Sec. Gen., Fr. Albert Dumont, O.P.

ARCHDIOCESES AND DIOCESES

The Roman Catholic Church in Canada has 17 Archdioceses and 47 Dioceses of the Latin rite; 3 Archeparchies, 5 Eparchies and 1 Exarchate of the Oriental rite; 1 Abbacy Nullius; and the Military Ordinariate. Each of these ecclesiastical jurisdictions appears alphabetically in the following list and contains this information in sequence: Name of incumbent bishop, address of Chancery office (Evêché) or other headquarters, and telephone number.

Cardinals are addressed as "His Eminence" (in French as "Son Eminence") and Archbishops and Bishops as "Most Reverend" (in French as "Son Excellence").

LATIN RITE

Alexandria-Cornwall, Mgr Eugéne P. LaRocque. Centre diocésain, 220 Chemin Montréal, C. P. 1388 Cornwall, Ontario K6H 5V4. Tel. (613) 933-1138

Amos, Mgr Gérard Drainville. Evêché, 450, Principale Nord, Amos, Québec J9T 2M1. Tel. (819) 732-6515

Antigonish, Bishop Colin Campbell. Chancery Office, 155 Main St., P.O. Box 1330, Antigonish, Nova Scotia B2G 2L7. Tel. (902) 863-4818

Baie-Comeau, Mgr. Maurice Couture. Evêché, 639 Rue de Bretagne, Baie-Comeau, Québec G5C 1X2. Tel. (418) 589–5744

Bathurst, Mgr André Richard. Evêché, 645, avenue Murray, C. P. 460, Bathurst, New Brunswick E2A 3Z4. Tel. (506) 546-3493

Calgary, Bishop Paul J. O'Byrne. Bishop's Office, 1916 Second St. S.W., Calgary, Alberta T2S 1S3. Tel. (403) 228-4501

Charlottetown, Bishop James H. MacDonald. Bishop's Residence, P.O. Box 907, Charlottetown, Prince Edward Island C1A 7L9. Tel. (902) 892-1357

Chicoutimi, Mgr Jean-Guy Couture. Evêché, 602 est, rue Racine, C.P. 278, Chicoutimi,Québec G7H 6J6. Tel. (418) 543-0783

Churchill-Baie D'Hudson, Mgr Reynald Rouleau, O.M.I. Evêché, C.P. 10, Churchill, Manitoba, R0B 0E0. Tel. (204) 675-2541

Archdiocese of Edmonton, Archbishop Joseph N. MacNeil. Archdiocesan Office, 8421-101st Ave., Edmondton, Alberta T6A 0L1 Tel. (403) 469-1010

Edmundson, Mgr Gérard Dionne. Evêché, Centre diocesain, Edmundston, New Brunswick E3V 3K1. Tel. (506) 735-5578

Gaspé, Mgr Bertrand Blanchet. Evêché, C.P. 440, Gaspé, Québec G0C 1R0. Tel. (418) 368-2274

Gatineau-Hull, Mgr Roger Ebacher. Evêché, 119, rue Carillon, Hull, Québec J8X 2P8. Tel. (819) 771-8391

Grand Falls, Bishop Joseph Faber MacDonald. Chancery Office: P.O. Box 397, Grand Falls, Newfoundland, A2A 2J8. Tel. (709) 489-4019

Gravelbourg, Mgr Noel Delaquis. Secrétariat, C.P. 690, Gravelbourg, Saskatchewan S0H 1X0. Tel. (306) 648-2615

Archdiocése de Grouard-McLennan, Mgr Henri Légaré. Archevêché, C.P. 388, McLennan, Alberta T0H 2L0, Tel. (403) 324-3002

Archdiocese of Halifax, Archbishop James M. Hayes. Archbishop's Residence, 6541 Coburg Rd., P.O. Box 1527, Halifax, Nova Scotia B3J 2Y3. Tel. (902) 429-9388

Hamilton, Bishop Anthony Tonnos. Chancery Office, 700 King St. W., Hamilton, Ontario L8P 1C7. Tel. (416) 528-7988

Hearst, Mgr Roger A. Despatie. Evêché, C.P. 1330, Hearst, Ontario R0L 1N0. Tel. (705) 362-4903

Joliette, Mgr René Audet. Evêché, 2, rue St.-Charles Borromée, Nord. C.P. 470, Joliette, Québec J6E 6H6. Tel. (514) 753-7596

Kamloops, Bishop Lawrence Sabatini. Bishop's Residence, 635A Tranquille Rd., Kamloops, British Columbia V2B 3H5. Tel. (604) 376-3351

Archidiocése de Keewatin-LePas, Archbishop Peter-Alfred Sutton. Résidence, 108 1st St. W., C.P. 270, Le Pas, Manitoba R9A 1K4. Tel. (204) 623-3529

Archdiocese of Kingston, Archbishop Francis J. Spence. P. O. Box 997, 390 Palace Rd., Kingston, Ontario K7L 4X8. Tel. (613) 548-4461

Labrador City-Schefferville, Mgr Henri Goudreault. Evêché, 318 Ave. Elizabeth, Labrador City, Labrador A2V 2K7. Tel. (709) 944-2046

London, Bishop John M. Sherlock. Chancery Office, 1070 Waterloo St., London Ontario N6A 3Y2, Tel. (519) 433-0658

Mackenzie-Fort Smith (T.No.O.), Mgr Denis Croteau. Evêché, 5111, 53e rue, Bag 8900, Fort Smith, T.N.O. X1A 2R3. Tel. (403)872-2400

Archidiocèse de Moncton, Mgr Donat Chiasson. Archévêché, C.P. 248, Moncton, New Brunswick E1C 8K9. Tel. (506)857-9531

Mont-Laurier, Mgr Jean Gratton. Evêché, 435, rue de la Madone, C.P. 1290, Mont Laurier, Québec J9L 1S1. Tel. (819) 623-5530

Archidiocèse, de Montréal, M. le cardinal Paul Grégoire. Archévêché, 2000 ouest, rue Sherbrooke, Montréal, Québec H3H 1G4. Tel. (514) 931-7311

Moosonee, Mgr Jules LeGuerrier. Résidence, C.P. 40, Moosonee, Ontario P0L 1Y0. Tel. (705) 336-2908

Abbatia Nullius of Muenster, Abbot Ordinary Jerome Weber, OSB. Abbot's Residence, St. Peter's Abbey, Muenster, Saskatchewan S0K 2Y0. Tel. (306) 682-5521

Nelson, Bishop W. Emmett Doyle. Chancery Office, 813 Ward St., Nelson, British Columbia V1L 1T4. Tel. (604) 352-6921

Nicolet, Mgr J. Albertus Martin. Evêché, C.P. 820, Nicolet, Québec J0G 1E0. Tel. (819) 293-4234

Archidiocèse D'Ottawa, Mgr Joseph-Auréle Plourde. Chancellerie, 1247, avenue Kilborn, Ottawa, Ontario K1H 6K9 Tel. (613)738-5025

Pembroke, Bishop J. R. Windle. Bishop's Residence, 188 Renfrew St., P.O. Box 7, Pembroke, Ontario K8A 6X1. Tel. (613) 732-3895

Peterborough, Bishop James L. Doyle. Bishop's Residence, 350 Hunter St. W., Peterborough, Ontario K9J 6Y8. Tel. (705) 745-5123

Prince-Albert, Mgr Blaise Morand. Evêché, 1415-ouest, 4e Ave., Prince-Albert, Saskatchewan S6V 5H1. Tel. (306) 922-4747.

Prince-George, Bishop Hubert O'Connor. Chancery Office, 2935 Highway 16 West, P.O. Box 7000, Prince George, British Columbia V2N 3Z2. Tel. (604) 964-4424

Archidiocèse de Québec, M. le cardinal Louis-Albert Vachon. Archévêché, 2, rue Port Dauphin, C.P. 459, Québec, Québec G1R 4R6. Tel. (418) 692-3935

Archdiocese of Regina, Archbishop Charles A. Halpin. Chancery Office, 3225 13th Ave., Regina, Saskatchewan S4T 1P5. Tel. (306)352-1651

Archidiocèse de Rimouski, Mgr Gilles Ouellet. Archevêché, 34 ouest, rue de L'évêché, C.P. 730, Rimouski, Québec. G5L 7C7. Tel. (418) 723-3320

Rouyn-Noranda, Mgr Jean-Guy Hamelin, Evêché, 515, avenue Cuddihy, C.P. 1060, Rouyn-Noranda, Québec J9X 5W9. Tel. (819) 764-4660

Ste-Anne de la, Pocatière, Mgr André Gaumond. Evêché, C.P. 430 La Pocatière, Québec G0R 1Z0. Tel. (418) 856-1811

Archidiocèse de Saint-Boniface, Mgr Antoine Hacault. Archévêché, 151, ave de la Cathédrale, St-Boniface Manitoba R2H 0H6. Tel. (204) 237-9851

St. Catharine's, Bishop Thomas B. Fulton. Bishop's Residence, 122 Riverdale Ave., St. Catharines, Ontario L2R 4C2. Tel. (416) 684-0154

St. George's, Bishop Raymond J. Lahey. Bishop's Residence, 16 Hammond Dr., Corner Brook, Newfoundland A2H 2W2. Tel. (709) 639-7073

Saint Hyacinthe, Mgr Louis-de-Gonzague Langevin. Evêché 1900 ouest, Girouard, C. P. 190, Saint-Hyacinthe, Québec J2S 7B4. Tel. (514) 773-8581

Saint-Jean-de-Longueuil, Mgr Bernard Hubert. Evêché, 740 boul. Ste-Foy, C.P. 40, Longueuil, Québec J4K 4X8. Tel. (514) 679-1100

Saint-Jérôme, Mgr Charles Valois, Evêché, 355, rue St-Georges, C.P. 580, Saint-Jérôme, Québec J7Z 5V3. Tel. (514) 432-9741

Saint John, Bishop J. Edward Troy. Chancery Office, 1 Bayard Dr., Saint John, New Brunswick E2L 3L5. Tel. (506) 632-9222

Archdiocese of St. John's, Archbishop Alphonsus Penney. Archbishop's Residence, P.O. Box 37, Basilica Residence, St. John's, Newfoundland A1C 5H5. Tel. (709) 726-3660

Saint-Paul, Mgr Raymond Roy. Evêché, 4410 51e Ave., C.P. 339, St-Paul, Alberta T0A 3A0. Tel. (403) 645-3277

Saskatoon, Bishop James P. Mahoney. Chancery Office, 106-5th Ave., N., Saskatoon. Saskatchewan S7K 2N7. Tel. (306) 242-7831

Sault Ste. Marie, Bishop Marcel Gervais. Bishop's Residence, 480 McIntyre St., W., P.O. Box 510, North Bay, Ontario, P1B 8J1 Tel. (705) 476-1300

Archidiocèse de Sherbrooke, Mgr Jean-Marie Fortier, Archevêché, 130, rue de la Cathedrale, C.P. 430, Sherbrooke, Québec J1H 5K1. Tel. (819) 563-9934

Thunder Bay, Bishop John A. O'Mara. Bishop's Residence, 1306 Ridgeway St., Thunder Bay, Ontario P7C 4W6. Tel. (807) 623-6633

Timmins, Mgr Jacques Landriault. Centre diocésain, 65, avenue Jubilee est, Timmins, Ontario P4N 5W4. Tel. (705) 267-6224

Archdiocese of Toronto, His Eminence G. Emmett Cardinal Carter, Chancery Office, 355 Church St., Toronto, Ontario M5B 1Z8. Tel. (416) 977-1500

Trois-Rivièrés, Mgr Laurent Noël. Evêché, 362, rue Bonaventure, C.P. 879, Trois-Rivièrès, Québec G9A 5J9. Tel. (819) 374-9847

Valleyfield, Mgr Robert Lebel. Evêché, 31 rue Fabrique, C.P. 338, Valleyfield, Québec J6T 4G9. Tel. (514) 373-8122

Archdiocese of Vancouver, Archbishop James F. Carney, Chancery Office, 150 Robson St., Vancouver, British Columbia, V6B 2A7. Tel. (604) 683-0281

Victoria, Bishop Remi J. De Roo. Bishop's Office, 1-4044 Nelthorpe St., Victoria, British-Columbia V8X 2A1. Tel. (604) 479-1331

Whitehorse (Yukon), Bishop Thomas Lobsinger, O.M.I. Bishop's Residence, 5119 5th Ave., Whitehorse, Yukon Y1A 1L5. Tel. (403) 667-2052

Archdiocese of Winnipeg, Archbishop Adam Exner. Chancery Office 1-A, 1495 Pembina Hwy., Winnipeg, Manitoba R3T 2C6. Tel. (204) 452-2227

Yarmouth, Mgr Austin-Emile Burke. Evêché, 53, rue Park, Yarmouth, Nova Scotia B5A 4B2. Tel. (902) 742-7163

EASTERN RITES

The Hierarchy for Ukrainian Catholics of the Byzantine Rite in All of Canada

Eparchy of Edmonton, Eparch: Most Rev. Martin Greschuk. Eparch's Residence, 6240 Ada Blvd., Edmonton, Alberta T5W 4P1. Tel. (403) 479-0381

Eparchy of New Westminster, Eparch: Most Rev. Jerome I. Chimy. Eparch's Residence, 502 5th Ave., New Westminster, British Columbia V3L 1S2. Tel. (604) 521-8015

Eparchy of Saskatoon, Eparch: Most Rev. Basil Filevich. Eparch's Residence, 866 Saskatchewan. Crescent East, Saskatoon, Saskatchewan S7N 0L4. Tel. (306) 653-0138

Eparchy of Toronto, Eparch: Most Rev. Isidore Borecky. Eparch's Residence, 61 Glen Edyth Dr., Toronto, Ontario M4V 2V8. Tel. (416) 924-2381

Archeparchy of Winnipeg, Archeparch: Most Rev. Maxim Hermaniuk. Archeparch's Residence, 235 Scotia St., Winnipeg, Manitoba R2V 1V7. Tel. (204) 339-7457

The Eparchy for Slovak Catholics of the Byzantine Rite in All of Canada

Toronto, Ontario Eparchy, Eparch: Most Rev. Michael Rusnak. Chancery Office, Box 70, Unionville, Ontario L3R 2L8. Tel. (416) 477-4867.

The Melkite Archeparchy for All of Canada

Montréal (Qué) Archéparchie, Archéparque, Mgr Michel Hakim; Chancelier: Mgr Georges Coriaty. Chancellerie: 34 Maplewood, Montréal, Québec H2V 2M1. Tél. (514) 272-6430

The Maronite Archeparchy for All of Canada
Archéparchie de Montréal, Archéparque, Mgr Elias
Shaheen. Chancellerie, 12475 rue Grenet, Montréal,
Québec H4J 2K4. Tél. (514) 336-4220

Romanian Orthodox Church in America (Canadian Parishes)

The first Romanian Orthodox immigrants in Canada
called for Orthodox priests from their native country of
Romania. Between 1902-1914, they organized the first
Romanian parish communities and built Orthodox
churches in different cities and farming regions of western
Canada (Alberta, Saskatchewan, Manitoba) as well as in
the eastern part (Ontario and Quebec).

In 1929, the Romanian Orthodox parishes from Canada
joined with those of the U.S. in a Congress held in Detroit,
Mich., and asked the Holy Synod of the Romanian
Orthodox Church of Romania to establish a Romanian
Orthodox Missionary Episcopate in America (which was
the legal title of this body). The first Bishop, Policarp
(Morushca), was elected and consecrated by the Holy
Synod of the Romanian Orthodox Church and came to the
U.S. in 1935. He established his headquarters in Detroit
with jurisdiction over all the Romanian Orthodox parishes
in the U.S. and Canada.

In 1950, the Romanian Orthodox Church in America
(i.e. the Romanian Orthodox Missionary Episcopate in
America) was granted administrative autonomy by the
Holy Synod of the Romanian Orthodox Church of
Romania, and only doctrinal and canonical ties remain
with this latter body.

The Holy Synod of the Romanian Orthodox Church of
Romania, in its session of Dec. 12, 1974, recognized and
approved the Decision taken by the Annual Congress of
the Romanian Church in America, held on July 21, 1973,
at Edmonton-Boian, Alberta, relating to the elevation of
the Episcopate to the rank of "Archdiocese" with the
official title **The Romanian Orthodox Missionary Archdiocese in America,** renewing at the same time its status of
Ecclesiastical Autonomy.

The 46th Annual Church Congress of the Archdiocese
approved the amendment that the Archdiocese will be
known as The Romanian Orthodox Missionary Archdiocese in America and Canada.

GENERAL ORGANIZATION

Archbishop assisted by his Vicar and the Canadian
Diocesan Council. Annual Congress for both U.S. and
Canada.
Canadian Office: St. Demetrios Romanian Orthodox
Church, 103 Furby St., Winnipeg, Manitoba R3C 2A4.
Tel. (204) 775-3701

OFFICERS

Archbishop: Most Rev. Archbishop Victorin, 19959
Riopelle St., Detroit, MI 48203. Tel. (313) 893-7191
Vicar, V. Rev. Archim, Dr. Vasile Vasilachi 19959
Riopelle St., Detroit, MI 48203. Tel. (313) 893-7191
Cultural Councilor, V. Rev. Fr. Nicolae Ciurea, 19
Murray St., W., Hamilton, Ontario L8L 1B1. Tel. (416)
523-8268
Administrative Councilor, V. Rev. Fr. Mircea Panciuk,
11024-165th Ave., Edmonton, Alberta T5X 1X9
Sec., V. Rev. Arhim Felix Dubneac, 19959 Riopelle St.,
Detroit, MI 48203. Tel. (313) 893-7191

PERIODICALS

Credinta—The Faith (m), and Calendarul Credinta
(Yearbook with the Church Directory of the Archdio-
cese) (a). 19959 Riopelle St., Detroit, MI 48203. V.
Rev. Archim., Dr. Vasile Vasilachi, Ed.

The Romanian Orthodox Episcopate of America (Jackson, Michigan)

This body of Eastern Orthodox Christians of Romanian
descent was organized in 1929 as an autonomous Diocese
under the jurisdiction of the Romanian Patriarchate. In
1951, it severed all relations with the Orthodox Church of
Romania. Now under the canonical jurisdiction of the
autocephalous Orthodox Church in America, it enjoys full
administrative autonomy and is headed by its own Bishop.

Churches: 13; Inclusive Membership: 8,600; Sunday or
Sabbath Schools: 10; Total Enrollment: 663; Ordained
Clergy: 11

GENERAL ORGANIZATION

Church Congress, held annually in July
Headquarters: 2522 Grey Tower Rd., Jackson, MI 49201.
Tel. (517) 522-4800

OFFICERS

Ruling Bishop: Rt. Rev. Nathaniel (Popp).
Dean of all Canada: Very Rev. Archim. Martinian
Ivanovici, 1400 Rothwell St., Regina, Saskatchewan
S4N 2B3. Tel. (306)359-0370

OTHER ORGANIZATIONS

The American Romanian Orthodox Youth (AROY),
Teva Regule, 783 Washington St., Apt. #1, Brookline,
MA 02146
Association of Romanian Orthodox Ladies Auxiliaries
(ARFORA), Pauline Trutza, 1446 Waterbury Ave.,
Lakewood, OH 44107
Orthodox Brotherhood of Canada, Pres., John Bujea,
Box 1341, Regina, Saskatchewan S4P 3B8
Orthodox Brotherhood, USA, Sandra Caruleaa, 29
Rhoda Ave., Youngstown, OH 44509

PERIODICAL

Solia, Romanian News (m), 146 W. Cortland St., Jackson,
MI 49201. Tel. (517)789-9088
Solia Calendar (a)

Russian Orthodox Church in Canada, Patriarchal Parishes of the

Diocese of Canada of the former Exarchate of North
and South America of the Russian Orthodox Church.
Originally founded in 1897 by the Russian Orthodox
Archdiocese in North America.

GENERAL ORGANIZATION

General Conference: Meets annually at call from Bishop,
St. Barbara's Russian Orthodox Cathedral, 10105—
96th St., Edmonton, Alberta T5H 2G3.

OFFICERS

Administrator: Most Rev. Archbishop Nicholas, St.
Barbara's Complex, #303, 9566 - 101 Ave., Edmonton,
Alberta T5H 0B4

The Salvation Army in Canada

The Salvation Army is an international religious
movement whose members are motivated by love for God
and people. An evangelical branch of the Christian
church, its membership includes officers (clergy) and laity.
Its spiritual ministry comes from commitment to Jesus
Christ and reveals itself in practical service, regardless of
race, color, creed, sex, or age.

The goals of The Salvation Army are to preach the gospel, disseminate Christian truths, instill Christian values, enrich family life, and improve the quality of all life.

The organization provides personal counseling, supplies basic human necessities, and undertakes the spiritual and moral rehabilitation of all in need who come within its sphere of influence.

An evangelistic organization with a military government, it was first set up by General William Booth (1829-1912) in England in 1865. Converts from England started Salvation Army work in London, Ontario, in 1882. In 1884, Canada became a separate command which also has included Bermuda since 1933. An act to incorporate the Governing Council of The Salvation Army in Canada received royal assent on May 19, 1909.

Headquarters for Canada and Bermuda: Salvation Sq., Toronto, Ontario; P. O. Box 4021 Postal Sta. A, Toronto, Ontario M5W 2B1 Tel. (416) 598-2071

Churches: 398; Inclusive Membership: 88,899; Sunday or Sabbath Schools: 390; Total Enrollment: 27,321; Ordained Clergy: 2,008

OFFICERS

Territorial Commander, Commissioner Will Pratt
Territorial Pres., Women's Organizations, Mrs. Commissioner, Will Pratt
Chief Sec., Col. Arthur E. Waters
Field Sec. for Personnel, Col. Roy Calvert
Program Sec., Lt. Col. Joyce Ellery
Bus. Adm. Sec., Lt. Col. Ivor Rich
Fin. Sec., Maj. Douglas Kerr
Pub. Relations Sec., Lt. Col. Howard Moore
Property Sec., Lt. Col. Edwin Brown
Information Services Sec., Major Lloyd Eason

PERIODICAL

War Cry, Maj. Maxwell Ryan, Ed-in-Chief.

Serbian Orthodox Church in the U.S.A. and Canada, Diocese of Canada

The Serbian Orthodox Church is an organic part of the Eastern Orthodox Church. As a local church it received its autocephaly from Constantinople in 1219 A.D. The Patriarchal seat of the church today is in Belgrade, Yugoslavia. In 1921, a Serbian Orthodox Diocese in the United States of America and Canada was organized. In 1963, it was reorganized into three dioceses and in 1983 a fourth diocese was created for the Canadian part of the church. The Serbian Orthodox Church is in absolute doctrinal unity with all other local Orthodox Churches.

GENERAL ORGANIZATION

The Serbian Orthodox Diocese of Canada, 5a Stockbridge Ave., Toronto, Ontario M8Z 4M6. Tel. (416) 231-4409.

OFFICERS

Rt. Rev. Georgije, Serbian Orthodox Bishop of Canada, 5a Stockbridge Ave., Toronto, Ontario H8Z 4M6. Tel. (416) 231-4409
Dean of Western Deanery. Rev. Miroslav Dejanov, 620 E. 63rd Ave., Vancouver, British Columbia V5X 2K4. Tel. (604) 321-9750.
Dean of Eastern Deanery, V. Rev. Stevo Stojsavljevich, 143 Nash Rd., S., Hamilton, Ontario L8K 4J9. Tel. (416) 560-9424

PERIODICALS

The Path of Orthodoxy, P. O. Box 36, Leetsdale, PA 15056. Tel (412) 741-8660. Rev. Rade Merick, Eng. Ed.; V. Rev. Uros Ocokoljic, V. Rev. Nedeljko Lunich, Serbian Eds.

"Istoonik," Official Publication of the Serbian Orthodox Diocese of Canada, 5A Stockbridge Ave., Toronto, Ontario M8Z 4M6. Tel. (416) 231-4409. Rev. Vasilije Tomic; V. Rev. Mihajlo Doder, Ed. Eng. Sect.

Seventh-day Adventist Church in Canada

The Seventh-day Adventist Church in Canada is part of the worldwide Seventh-day Adventist Church with headquarters in Washington, D.C. The Seventh-day Adventist Church in Canada was organized in 1901 and reorganized in 1932.

Churches: 295; Inclusive Membership: 37,140; Sunday or Sabbath Schools: 314; Total Enrollment: 18,562; Ordained Clergy: 276

GENERAL ORGANIZATION

Headquarters: 1148 King St., E., Oshawa, Ontario L1H 1H8. Tel. (416) 433-0011

OFFICERS

Pres., D. D. Devnich
Vice Pres., L. G. Lowe
Treas., G. B. DeBoer
Sec., O. D. Parchment

DEPARTMENTS

A.S.I.: L. G. Lowe
Education: J. Saliba
Personal Ministries: _____
Communication Dept.: G. Karst
Public Affairs: G. Karst
Publishing: G. Dronen
Consultant to Health Care Institutions: A. G. Rodgers

PERIODICAL

Canadian Adventist Messenger, (m), Maracle Press, 1148 King St. E.,Oshawa, Ontario L1H 1H8. J. Polishuk, Ed.

Sikh

Sikhism was born in the northwestern part of the Indo-Pakistan sub-continent in Punjab province about five hundred years ago. Guru Nanak, founder of the religion, was born in 1469. He was followed by nine successor Gurus. The Guruship was then bestowed on the Sikh Holy Book, popularly known as the Guru Granth. The Granth contains writings of the Sikh Gurus and some Hindu and Muslim saints and was compiled by the fifth Guru, Arjan Dev. For the Sikhs, the Granth is the only object of worship. It contains, mostly, hymns of praise of God, the Formless One.

Sikhs started migrating from India more than a half century ago. A number of them settled on the West coast of North America, in British Columbia and California. More recently, a sizeable group has settled in the Eastern part of the Continent as well, particularly in Ontario, New York and Michigan. Sikhs are found in all major cities of the U.S. and Canada.

When Sikhs settle, they soon establish a Gurdwara, or Sikh temple, for worship and social gathering. Gurdwaras are found, among other places, in Toronto, Vancouver, Victoria, and Yuba City, California. At other places, they meet for worship in schools and community centers.

The First Sikh Conference was held on March 24-25, 1979 in Toronto. This is the first step in establishing a federation of all the Sikh Associations in Canada, and, if possible, in USA as well. A Sikh Heritage Conference was held September 19-21, 1981 in Toronto.
There are approximately 200,000 Sikhs in North America.

CORRESPONDENT

The Sikh Foundation, 1 Younge St., Ste. 1801, Toronto, Ontario M5E 5E1. Mr. Kawad Kohli. Tel. (416)299-1397

Syrian Orthodox Church of Antioch (Archdiocese of the United States and Canada)

An archdiocese of the Syrian Orthodox Church of Antioch in North America, the Syrian Orthodox Church professes the faith of the first three ecumenical councils of Nicaea, Constantinople, and Ephesus and numbers faithful in the Middle East, India, the Americas, Europe, and Australia. It traces its origin to the Patriarchate established in Antioch by St. Peter the Apostle and is under the supreme ecclesiastical jurisdiction of His Holiness the Syrian Orthodox Patriarch of Antioch and All the East, now residing in Damascus, Syria.
The Archdiocese of the Syrian Orthodox Church in the U.S. and Canada was formally established in 1957. The first Syrian Orthodox faithful came to Canada in the 1890s and formed the first Canadian parish in Sherbrooke, Quebec. Today five official parishes of the Archdiocese exist in Canada—two in the Province of Quebec and three in the Province of Ontario.

ORGANIZATION

Archdiocese of the U.S. and Canada, 49 Kipp Ave., Lodi, NJ 07644. Tel. (201)778-0638
Archdiocesan Convention: Annual

OFFICERS

Primate: Archbishop Mar Athanasius Y. Samuel, 49 Kipp Ave., Lodi, NJ 07644. Tel. (201)778-0638
Archdiocesan Gen. Sec., Very Rev. Chorepiscopus John Meno, 45 Fairmount Ave., Hackensack, NJ 07601. Tel. (201)646-9443

Ukrainian Greek-Orthodox Church of Canada

Toward the end of the 19th century the Ukrainian people began leaving their homeland, and many immigrated to Canada, which has been their homeland for 90 years. At Saskatoon, in 1918, the Ukrainian pioneers organized this Church. The Ukrainian Orthodox Church of Canada has grown rapidly in the past 67 years so that today it is the largest Ukrainian Orthodox Church beyond the borders of the Ukraine.

Churches: 258; Inclusive Membership: 120,000: Sunday or Sabbath Schools: N.R.; Total Enrollment: N.R.; Ordained Clergy: 91

GENERAL ORGANIZATION

General Organization: Sobor (General Council) meets every five years, Presidium meets monthly, Full Consistory, semi-annually
Headquarters: Consistory of the Ukrainian Orthodox Church of Canada, 9 St. John's Ave., Winnipeg, Manitoba R2W 1G8. Tel. (204) 586-3093

OFFICERS

Presidium, Chpsn., V. Rev. Dr. S. Jarmus, 9 St. John's Ave., Winnipeg, Manitoba R2W 1G8
Primate, Mt. Rev. Metropolitan Wasyly, 174 Seven Oaks Ave., Winnipeg, Manitoba R2V 0K8

PERIODICALS

Visnyk (s-m), 9 St. John's Ave., Winnipeg, Manitoba, R2W 1G8.

Union of Spiritual Communities of Christ (Orthodox Doukhobors in Canada)

Groups of Canadians of Russian origin living in the western provinces of Canada whose beginnings in Russia are unknown. The name "Doukhobors," or "Spirit Wrestlers," was given in derision by the Russian Orthodox clergy in Russia as far back as 1785. Victims of decades of persecution in Russia, about 7,500 Doukhobors finally arrived in Canada in 1899.
The whole teaching of the Doukhobors is penetrated with the Gospel spirit of love; worshiping God in the spirit they affirm that the outward Church and all that is performed in it and concerns it has no importance for them; the Church is where two or three are gathered together, united in the name of Christ. Their teaching is founded on tradition, which is called among them the "Book of Life," because it lives in their memory and hearts. In this book are recorded sacred songs or chants, partly composed independently, partly formed out of the contents of the Bible, and these are committed to memory by each succeeding generation. Doukhobors observe complete pacifism and non-violence.
The Doukhobors were reorganized in 1938 by their leader, Peter P. Verigin, shortly before his death, into the Union of Spiritual Communities of Christ, commonly called Orthodox Doukhobors. It is headed by a democratically elected Executive Committee which executes the will and protects the interests of the people.
In the present day at least 99 percent of the Doukhobors are law-abiding, pay taxes, and definitely "do not burn or bomb or parade in the nude" as they say a fanatical offshoot called the "Sons of Freedom" does.

GENERAL ORGANIZATION

General Meeting: Annual in February
Headquarters: USCC Central Office, Box 760, Grand Forks, British Columbia V0H 1H0. Tel. (604) 442-8252

OFFICERS

Honorary Chpsn. of the Exec. Comm., John J. Verigin, Box 760, Grand Forks, British Columbia V0H 1H0
Chpsn., Andrew Evin
Adm., S. W. Babakaiff

PERIODICAL

Iskra (bi-w) in Russian with part of Youth Section in English, Box 760, Grand Forks, British Columbia, V0H 1H0. D. E. (Jim) Popoff, Ed.

Unitarian Universalist Association

The headquarters of the Unitarian Universalist Association is located at 25 Beacon St., Boston, MA 02108. Tel. (617) 742-2100. Three of the twenty-three districts of the UUA are located partly or wholly in Canada, as are 43 of the 1,005 congregations. There is a Canadian Unitarian Council—Conseil Unitaire Canadien which handles matters of particular concern to Canadian churches and fellowships. Its office is located at 175 St. Clair Ave. W. Toronto, Ontario M4V 1P7

Churches: 42; Inclusive Membership: 6,061; Sunday or Sabbath Schools: 36; Total Enrollment: 1,250; Ordained Clergy: 37

DISTRICTS AND OFFICERS

Pacific Northwest, Rev. Alan Deale, 1011 S.W. 12th Ave., Portland OR 97205
St. Lawrence, Suzanne McNamara, 5 Sandpiper La., Pittsford, NY 14534
PrairieStar/Western Canada, Erv Miller, 921 Third Ave., SE, Rochester, MN 55901
Trustee-at-Large from Canada, Dr. Sheilah Thompson, 930 Whitchurch St., North Vancouver, British Columbia V7L 2A6

United Brethren in Christ, Ontario Conference

Founded in 1767 in Lancaster County, PA, missionaries came to Canada about 1850. The first class was held in Kitchener in 1855, and the first building was erected in Port Elgin in 1867.

The Church of the United Brethren in Christ had its beginning with Philip William Otterbein and Martin Boehm who were leaders in the revivalistic movement in Pennsylvania and Maryland during the late 1760s.

GENERAL ORGANIZATION

Ontario conference, Annual. Quadrennial conference: Next meeting, June 1993
Headquarters: 302 Lake St., Huntington, IN 46750
Conf. Supt., Rev. Martin Magnus, 118 Ross Ave., Kitchener, Ontario N2A 1V4. Tel. (519)576-7647
Treas., Mr. Brian Winger, 2233 Hurontario St., Apt. 916, Mississauga, Ontario L5A 2E9

PERIODICAL

The United Brethren (m), 302 Lake St., Huntington, IN 46750. Steve Dennie, Ed.

The United Church of Canada

The United Church of Canada was formed on June 10, 1925, through the union of the Methodist Church, Canada; the congregational Union of Canada; the Council of Local Union Churches; and 70 percent of the Presbyterian Church in Canada. The union culminated years of negotiation between the churches, all of which had integral associations with the development and history of the nation. In fulfillment of its mandate to be a uniting as well as a United Church, the denomination has been enriched by other unions during its history. The Wesleyan Methodist Church of Bermuda joined in 1930. On January 1, 1968, the Canada Conference of the Evangelical United Brethren became part of The United Church of Canada. At various times, congregations of other christian communions have also become congregations of the United Church. The United Church of Canada is a full member of the World Methodist Council, the World Alliance of Reformed Churches (Presbyterian and Congregational), and the Canadian and World Councils of Churches. The United Church is the largest Protestant denomination in Canada.

Churches: 4,138; Inclusive Membership: 2,052,342; Sunday or Sabbath Schools: 3,505; Total Enrollment: 207,768; Ordained Clergy: 3,795

GENERAL ORGANIZATION

National Offices: The United Church House, 85 St. Clair Ave. E., Toronto, Ontario M4T 1M8, Tel. (416) 925-5931; Fax: (416)925-3394
General Council, meets every two years. Next meeting, August, 1990 in London, Ontario.

THE GENERAL COUNCIL

The General Council is the highest legislative body of The United Church of Canada. The Moderator is elected at each meeting of the General Council to hold office until the following Council.
Mod., Rev. Dr. Sang Chul Lee
Sec., Rev. Dr. Howard M. Mills
Deputy Sec., (Management and Personnel), Barbara M. Copp, (Theology, Faith, and Ecumenism), Rev. Hallett E. Llewellyn
Personnel Director, Margaret C. Scriven
Archivist, Jean E. Dryden, 73 Queen's Park Cr., E., Toronto, Ontario M5C 1K7. Tel. (416) 585-4563
Dir., Dept. of Educ. and Information, Douglas L. Flanders

ADMINISTRATIVE DIVISIONS

Communication: Gen. Sec., Rev. Randolph L. Naylor; Dir. of Fin. and Admn., Alice E. Foster; Dir. Dept. of Media Resources, Rev. Rodney M. Booth
Productions (Berkeley Studo): Media Services: 315 Queen St. E., Toronto, Ontario M5A 1S7, Tel. (416) 366-9221; Fax: (416)368-9774
The United Church Publishing House: Gen. Mgr., Jitu T. Somani

Finance: Gen. Sec., William R. Davis
Dept. of the Treasury: Treas., Kenneth H. Ward
Dept. of Pensions and Group Insurance: Sec., Janet E. Petrie
Dept. of Stewardship Services: Sec., Rev. Vincent D. Alfano

Ministry Personnel and Education: Gen. Sec., Rev. Richard H. Moffatt
Theological Educ., Rev. Howard M. Pentland
Student Services: Rev. Ronald K. Coughlin
Diaconal Ministry and Continuing Educ., K. Virginia Coleman
Women in Ministry, J. Ann Naylor
Administrator, S. George Shehata

Mission in Canada: Gen. Sec., Dr. Gerald Hopkirk; Dir., (Ofc. of Christian Dev.), S. Ruth Evans; Dir., (Ofc. of Church in Society), Bonnie M. Greene; Dir., (Ofc. of Adm.), Lang Moffat.
Adult Prog. (Women), Deborah S. Marshall; Adult Resources, Lynda L. Newmarch; Children, Jean Olthius, Rev. Robin D. Wardlaw
Cong. & Mission Support, Rev. Roland Kawano, Richard Chambers; Evangelism, Rev. Gordon B. Turner.
Human Rights and Justice: (Economic Policy and Coalitions), Philippe LeBlanc; (Human Rights, International Affairs, and Peace), Philippe Le Blanc; (Native Concerns, Immigration, Refugees, Racism), Helga Kutz-Harder; (Energy and Environment, Persons with Special Needs); David G. Hallman; (French/English Rel., Criminal Justice), Claire Doran.
Program and Leadership Dev., Rev. Mary Ellen Grieve; Sexuality, Marriage and Family Life, Rev. A. Jean Ward; Planning, Dixie Kee; Resources, Betty Smythe; Senior Adults, Social Services, _____; Worship, Rev. Fred K. Graham; Youth & Recreational Ministries, Rev. R. Gordon Webber, Raymond D. McGinnis

World Outreach: Gen. Sec., Rev. Frederick M. Bayliss; Africa, Rev. James A. Kirkwood; Africa, Paula J. Butler; Caribbean and Latin America, Rev. Thomas C. Edmonds; Asia and Pacific, Rhea M. Whitehead, Personnel, Rev. George H. Lavery
Development, Lee R. Holland; Finance and Administration, Johanna M. Jamieson

CONFERENCE EXECUTIVE SECRETARIES

Alberta and Northwest: Rev. William F. A. Phipps, 9911 48 Ave., Edmonton, Alberta T6E 5V6, Tel. (403) 435-3995

All Native Circle: Rev. Alfred A. Dumont, Speaker, 366 McGregor St., Winnipeg, Manitoba R2W 4K3. Tel. (204)586-8023

Bay of Quinte: Rev. Peter M. McKellar, 218 Barrie St., Kingston, Ontario K7L 3K3, Tel. (613) 549-2503

British Columbia: Rev. Gordon C. How, 1955 W. 4th Ave., Vancouver, British Columbia V6J 1M7, Tel. (604) 734-0434

Hamilton: Rev. D. Bruce MacDougall, Box 100, Carlisle, Ontario L0R 1H0 (416) 659-3343

London: Rev. Douglas H. Ross, 359 Windermere Rd., London, Ontario N6G 2K3, Tel. (519) 672-1930

Manitoba and Northwestern Ontario: Mrs. H. Dianne Cooper, 120 Maryland St., Winnipeg, Manitoba R3G 1L1, Tel. (204) 786-8911

Manitou: Rev. J. Stewart Bell, 366 McIntyre St. W., North Bay, Ontario P1B 2Z1, Tel. (705) 474-3350

Maritime: Rev. Robert H. Mills, Box 1560, Sackville, Nova Scotia E0A 3C0, Tel. (506) 536-1334

Montreal and Ottawa: Rev. Guy A. Deschamps, 225-50 Ave., Lachine, Quebec H8T 2T7, Tel. (514) 613-8594

Newfoundland and Labrador: Rev. Boyd L. Hiscock, 320 Elizabeth Ave., St. John's, Newfoundland, A1B 1T9, Tel. (709) 754-0386

Saskatchewan: Rev. Wilbert R. Wall, 418 B McDonald St., Regina, Saskatchewan S4N 6E1, Tel. (306) 721-3311

Toronto: Rev. Lorne H. Taylor-Walsh, Rm. 404, 85 St. Clair Ave. E., Toronto, Ontario M4T 1L8, Tel. (416) 967-1880

PERIODICAL

United Church Observer, 85 St. Clair Ave. E., Toronto, Ontario M4T 1M8. _____, Ed. and Publ. Tel. (416)960-8500; Fax: (416)960-8477

United Pentecostal Church in Canada

This body, which is affiliated with the United Pentecostal Church, International with headquarters in Hazelwood, Missouri, accepts the Bible standard of full salvation, which is repentance, baptism by immersion in the Name of the Lord Jesus Christ for the remission of sins, and the baptism of the Holy Ghost with the initial signs of speaking in tongues as the Spirit gives utterance. Other tenets of faith include the Oneness of God in Christ, holiness, divine healing and the second coming of Jesus Christ.

Churches: 197; Inclusive Membership: 23,000; Sunday or Sabbath Schools: N.R.; Total Enrollment: N.R.; Ordained Clergy: N.R.

ORGANIZATION

Atlantic District, Dist. Supt., Rev. R. A. Beesley, Box 965, Sussex, New Brunswick E0E 1P0

British Columbia District, Dist. Supt., Rev. Paul V. Reynolds, 13447-112th Ave., Surrey, British Columbia V3R 2E7

Canadian Plains District, Dist. Supt., Rev. Johnny King, 1840 38th St., SE, Calgary, Alberta T2B 0Z3

Central Canadian District, Dist. Supt., Rev. J. E. Yonts, 8855 Dunn Rd., Hazelwood, MO 63042 (Home Missions Director)

Nova Scotia-Newfoundland District, Dist. Supt., Rev. John D. Mean, P.O. Box 2183, D.E.P.S., Dartmouth, Nova Scotia B2W 3Y2

Ontario District, Dist. Supt., Rev. William V. Cooling, Box 1638, Brighton, Ontario K0K 1H0

The Wesleyan Church of Canada

The Canadian portion of The Wesleyan Church which consists of the Atlantic and Central Canada districts. The Central Canada District of the former Wesleyan Methodist Church of America was organized at Winchester, Ontario, in 1889 and the Atlantic District was founded in 1888 as the Alliance of the Reformed Baptist Church which merged with the Wesleyan Methodist Church in July, 1966. In 1984 a Canada West District with pioneer status was inaugurated under the direction of the Department of Extension and Growth.

The Wesleyan Methodist Church and the Pilgrim Holiness Church merged in June, 1968, to become The Wesleyan Church. The doctrine is evangelical and Arminian and stresses holiness beliefs. For more details, consult the U.S. listing under The Wesleyan Church.

GENERAL ORGANIZATION

Central Canada District Conference: meets the third week in July at Silver Lake Campgrounds, Maberly, Ontario, (613) 268-2770. Office and Mailing Address: Ste. 102, 3 Applewood Dr., Belleville, Ontario K8P 4E3. Tel. (613) 966-7527

Atlantic District Conference: meets the first week in July. Office: 41 Summit Ave., Sussex, New Brunswick. Mailing Address: Box 20, Sussex, New Brunswick E0E 1PO. Tel: (506) 433-1007.

OFFICERS

District Supt. (Central Canada District), Rev. W. W. Jewell, Ste. 102, 3 Applewood Dr., Belleville, Ontario K8P 4E3. Tel. (613)966-7527

District Supt. (Atlantic District), Rev. Ray Barnwall, P.O. Box 20, Sussex, New Brunswick E0E 1P0

Western Canada Pioneer District: Dist. Supt., Rev. Martin Mull, Dist. Sec., Extension and Church Growth, The Wesleyan Ch. Liaison: Rev. Walter W. Jewell, Ste. 102, 3 Applewood Dr., Belleville, Ontario K8P 4E3. Tel. (613)966-7527

PERIODICALS

Wesleyan Advocate (s-m), P. O. Box 2000, Marion, IN 46952. Dr. Wayne F. Caldwell, Ed.

Central Canada Clarion (bi-m), Ste. 102, 3 Applewood Dr., Belleville, Ontario K8P 4E3. Rev. W. W. Jewell, Ed.

Atlantic Wesleyan (m), Box 20, Sussex, New Brunswick E0E 1P0. Rev. H. R. Ingersoll, Ed.

Wisconsin Evangelical Lutheran Synod

The W.E.L.S. was founded in Milwaukee, WI, in 1850. The Synod believes in a verbally inspired, inerrant Bible and embraces without reservation the Lutheran Confessions as found in the Book of Concord.

Churches: 9; Inclusive Membership: 1,059; Sunday or Sabbath Schools: 10; Total Enrollment: 236; Ordained Clergy: 9

GENERAL ORGANIZATION

No separate Canadian organization. National Convention meets biennially. Next meeting in 1991. For additional details, consult Wisconsin Evangelical Lutheran Synod listing in Directory 3, "Religious Bodies in the U.S."

OTHER RELIGIOUS BODIES IN CANADA

Although a sizable majority of Canadian religious bodies, having most of the Canadian church membership, is accounted for by denominations providing directory materials in the sectin immediately preceding, a number of important groups have not yet provided directory information.

For the sake of completeness, an alphabetical listing of these religious bodies not yet supplying directory information appears below.

The editor of the **Yearbook of American and Canadian Churches** would be grateful for any information concerning significant omissions from this listing of Religious Bodies in Canada as well as for any other information concerning this section.

African Methodist Episcopal Church in Canada, 765 Lawrence Ave. W., Toronto, Ontario M6A 1B7. Rev. L. O. Jenkins (9 churches)

Beachy Amish Mennonite Churches, 9675 Iams Rd., Plain City, OH 43064. Tel. (614) 873-8140 (3 congregations, 378 members)

Bergthaler (Mennonite) Congregations, John Neudorf, LaCrete, Alberta T0H 2H0.

Chortitzer (Mennonite) Conference, Bishop Wilhelm Hildebrandt Box 452, Steinbach, Manitoba R0A 2A0 (11 Congregations, 2,000 members)

Christadelphians in Canada, P.O. Box 221, Weston, Ontario M9N 3M7

Christian Science in Canada, Mr. J. Donald Fulton, 696 Yonge St., Ste. 403. Toronto, Ontario M4Y 2A7. Tel. (416) 922-7473

Church of God in Christ, Mennonite (Holdeman), P. O. Box 313, Moundridge, KS 67107. Tel. (316) 345-2533 (30 congregations, 3,004 members)

Fellowship of Evangelical Bible Churches, P.O. Box 456, Steinbach, Manitoba R0A 2A0. Tel. (204) 326-2108 (20 congregations, 1,987 members)

Hutterian Brethren, Elder Jacob Kleinsasser, Crystal Sprint Colony, Ste. Agatha, Manitoba R0G 1Y0 (246 congregations, 9,213 members)

New Apostolic Church of North America in Canada, c/o Rev. Michael Kraus, President, 267 Lincoln Rd., Waterloo, Ontario N2J 2P6

Old Colony Mennonite Church in Canada, Alberta, Deacon Herman Geisbrecht, La Crete, Alberta T0H 2H0 (650 members); British Columbia, Deacon Jacob Giesbrecht, Ft. St. John, British Columbia V0C P20 (320 members); Manitoba, Deacon Abram Driedger, Box 601, Winkler, Manitoba R0G 2X0 (930 members); Ontario, Bishop Henry Reimer, R. R. 3, Wheatley, Ontario N0P 2P0 (260 members); Saskatchewan, Deacon Klass Dyck, R. R. 4, Saskatoon, Saskatchewan (1,087 members)

Old Order Mennonite Church, R. 1, Fergus, Ontario N1M 2W3 (26 congregations, 3,280 members)

Ontario Old Roman Catholic Church (Christ Catholic Church in Canada). The Most Rev. Frederick P. Dunleavy, 1062 Woodbine Ave., Toronto, Ontario M4C 4C5 (1 congregation, 153 members)

Orthodox Church in America (Canada Section), Archbishop Metropolitan Theodosius, The Rt. Rev. Seraphim, Bishop of Edmonton, 55 Clarey Ave., Ottawa, Ontario K1F 2R6

Reformed Presbyterian Church of North America, Louis D. Hutmire, 7418 Penn Ave., Pittsburg, PA 15208. Tel. (412)731-1177

Sommerfelder (Mennonite) Church, Bishop John A. Friesen, Lowe Farm, Manitoba R0G 1E0 (13 congregations, 3,650 members)

Standard Church of America (Canadian Section), 243 Perth St., Brockville, Ontario K6V 5E7

RELIGIOUS BODIES IN CANADA ARRANGED BY FAMILIES

The following list of religious bodies appearing in Directory 4, "Religious Bodies in Canada," including "Other Religious Bodies in Canada," shows the "families" or related clusters into which Canadian religious bodies can be grouped. For example, there are many bodies that can be grouped under the heading "Baptist" for historical and theological reasons. It is not to be assumed, however, that all denominations under one family heading are necessarily similar in belief or practice. Often any similarity is purely coincidental since ethnicity, theological divergence, and even political and personality factors have shaped the directions denominational groups have taken.

Family categories provide one of the major pitfalls of church statistics because of the tendency to combine statistics by "families" for analytical and comparative purposes. Such combined totals are almost meaningless, although often used as variables for sociological analysis.

The editor would be grateful for any additions or corrections in the family table below. **Religious bodies not grouped under family headings appear alphabetically and are not indented in the following list.**

The Anglican Church of Canada
Apostolic Christian Church (Nazarene)
Armenian Evangelical Church
Associated Gospel Churches
Bahá'í Faith

BAPTIST BODIES

The Association of Regular Baptist Churches (Canada)
Baptist General Conference of Canada
  The Central Canada Baptist Conference
  Baptist General Conference of Alberta
  British Columbia Baptist Conference
Canadian Baptist Federation
  Baptist Convention of Ontario and Quebec
  Baptist Union of Western Canada
  Union of French Baptist Churches in Canada
  United Baptist Convention of the Atlantic Provinces
Canadian Convention of Southern Baptists
Evangelical Baptist Churches in Canada, The Fellowship of

Free Will Baptists
North American Baptist Conference

Bible Holiness Movement
Brethren in Christ Church, Canadian Conference
Buddhist Churches of Canada
The Canadian Yearly Meeting of the Religious Society of Friends
Christadelphians in Canada
The Christian and Missionary Alliance in Canada
Christian Brethren (aka Plymouth Brethren)
Christian Science in Canada
Church of God, (Anderson, Ind.)
Church of the Nazarene

CHURCHES of CHRIST—
CHRISTIAN CHURCHES

Christian Church (Disciples of Christ) in Canada
Christian Churches and Churches of Christ in Canada
Churches of Christ in Canada

Congregational Christian Churches in Ontario, The Conference of

Doukhobors

Reformed Doukhobors, Christian Community and
Brotherhood of
Union of Spiritual Communities of Christ (Orthodox
Doukhobors in Canada)

Eastern Churches

The Antiochian Orthodox Christian Archdiocese of
North America
The Armenian Church of North America, Diocese of
Canada
The Coptic Church in Canada
Greek Orthodox Diocese of Toronto, Canada
Orthodox Church in America (Canada Section)
Romanian Orthodox Church in America (Canadian
Parishes)
The Romanian Orthodox Episcopate of America (Jack-
son, Michigan)
Russian Orthodox Church in Canada, Patriarchal
Parishes of the
Serbian Orthodox Church in the U.S.A. and Canada,
Diocese of Canada
Syrian Orthodox Church of Antioch (Archdiocese of the
United States and Canada)
Ukrainian Greek-Orthodox Church of Canada

The Evangelical Covenant Church of Canada
Evangelical Free Church of Canada
General Church of the New Jerusalem
Gospel Missionary Association
Independent Holiness Church
Jehovah's Witnesses
Jewish Organizations in Canada

Latter Day Saints

The Church of Jesus Christ of Latter-day Saints
Reorganized Church of Jesus Christ of Latter Day Saints

Lutherans

Church of the Lutheran Brethren
The Estonian Evangelical Lutheran Church
The Evangelical Lutheran Church in Canada
The Latvian Evangelical Lutheran Church in America
Lutheran Church—Canada
Wisconsin Evangelical Lutheran Synod

Mennonite Bodies

Beachy Amish Mennonite Churches
Bergthaler Congregations
Chortitzer Mennonite Conference
Church of God in Christ, Mennonite (Holdeman)
Conference of Mennonites in Canada
The Evangelical Mennonite Conference
Evangelical Mennonite Mission Conference
Hutterian Brethren
Fellowship of Evangelical Bible Churches
Mennonite Brethren Churches, Canadian
Conference of

Old Colony Mennonite Church in Canada
Old Order Amish Church
Old Order Mennonite Church
Reinlaender Mennonite Church
Sommerfelder (Mennonite) Church

Methodist Bodies

African Methodist Episcopal Church in Canada
British Methodist Episcopal Church of Canada
The Evangelical Church in Canada
Free Methodist Church in Canada
The Wesleyan Church of Canada

Metropolitan Community Churches, Universal Fellowship
of
The Missionary Church of Canada
Moravian Church in America, Northern Province
Muslims
New Apostolic Church of North America in Canada
The Old Catholic Church of Canada
Ontario Old Roman Catholic Church

Pentecostal Bodies

The Apostolic Church in Canada
Apostolic Church of Pentecost of Canada
Church of God (Cleveland, Tenn.)
The Church of God of Prophecy in Canada
Elim Felowship of Evangelical Churches and Ministers
Foursquare Gospel Church of Canada
Independent Assemblies of God—Canada
The Italian Pentecostal Church of Canada
The Open Bible Standard Churches of Canada
The Pentecostal Assemblies of Canada
Pentecostal Assemblies of Newfoundland
Pentecostal Holiness Church of Canada
United Pentecostal Church in Canada

Polish National Catholic Church of Canada

Presbyterian Bodies

Presbyterian Church in America (Canadian Section)
The Presbyterian Church in Canada
Reformed Presbyterian Church of North America

Reformed Bodies

Canadian and American Reformed Churches
Christian Reformed Church in North America
Netherlands Reformed Congregations of North America
Reformed Church in Canada
The United Church of Canada

The Reformed Episcopal Church
The Roman Catholic Church in Canada
The Salvation Army in Canada
Seventh-day Adventist Church in Canada
Sikhs
Standard Church of America (Canadian Section)
Unitarian Universalist Association
United Brethren in Christ, Ontario Conference

5. INTERNATIONAL AGENCIES: CONFESSIONAL, INTERDENOMINATIONAL, COOPERATIVE

A listing of major confessional, interdenominational, and cooperative international agencies follows. The editor of the **Yearbook of American and Canadian Churches** would be grateful for details on major groups omitted from this listing.

WORLD COUNCIL OF CHURCHES

The World Council of Churches is a fellowship of more than 300 churches of the Protestant, Anglican, Orthodox, and Old Catholic traditions banded together for study, witness, service, and the advancement of unity. It includes in its membership churches in more than 100 countries with various forms of government, and its life reflects the immense richness and variety of Christian faith and practice. The World Council of Churches came into being after many years of preparation on August 23, 1948, when its First Assembly was held in Amsterdam, The Netherlands.

The basis for World Council membership is: "The World Council of Churches is a fellowship of Churches which confess the Lord Jesus Christ as God and Saviour according to the Scriptures and therefore seek to fulfill together their common calling to the glory of the one God, Father, Son, and Holy Spirit."

Membership is open to churches which express their agreement with this basis and satisfy such criteria as the Assembly or Central Committee may prescribe.

Headquarters: 150 route de Ferney (P.O. Box 2100), 1211 Geneva, 2, Switzerland. Tel. (022) 791 61 11; Telex: 415 730 OIK Ch; Fax: (022) 791 03 61
U.S. Office: 475 Riverside Dr., Rm. 915, New York, NY 10115. Tel. (212) 870-2533
New York Office, CCIA: 777 United Nations Plz., New York, NY 10017. Tel. (212) 867-5890

PRESIDENTS

Most Rev. W. P. K. Makhulu, Botswana
Metropolitan Dr. Paulos Mar Gregorios, India
Dame R. Nita Barrow, Barbados
Bishop Dr. Johannes Hempel, GDR
Dr. Marga Buehrig, Switzerland
Very Rev. Dr. Lois Wilson, Canada
His Beatitude Patriarch Ignatios IV, Syria

CENTRAL COMMITTEE

Moderator, Rev. Dr. Heinz Joachim Held, FRG
Vice-moderators, Metropolitan Chrysostomos of Myra, Turkey; Dr. Sylvia Talbot, USA

GENERAL SECRETARIAT

Gen. Sec., Rev. Dr. Emilio Castro.
Deputy Gen. Secs. Ms. Mercy Oduyoye; Prof. Todor Sabev; Ms. Ruth Sovik; Asst. Gen. Sec. for Finance and Administration, _____; Asst. to Gen. Sec., Ms. Jean Stromberg.
Income Coordination and Development, Dir., Ms. M. Béguin-Austin
Librarian, Mr. Pierre Beffa
Office for Resource Sharing, Mr. Huibert van Beek
Personnel Dir., Rev. Carlos Sintado
Ecumenical Institute: Dir., Rev. Dr. Samuel Amirtham,
Communication: Mr. Jan Kok
U. S. Office, Exec. Dir.: Rev. Joan Campbell

PROGRAM UNIT I—
FAITH AND WITNESS

Staff Moderator: Prof. Todor Sabev
Commission on Faith and Order: Dir., Rev. Dr. Günther Gassman.

Commission on World Mission and Evangelism: Dir., Rev. Dr. Christopher Duraisingh.
Sub-Unit on Church and Society: Dir., Rev. Wesley Grandberg-Michaelson Sub-Unit on Dialogue with People of Living Faiths: Dir., Rev. Dr. Wesley Ariarajah

PROGRAM UNIT II—
JUSTICE AND SERVICE

Staff Moderator: Ms. Ruth Sovik
Commission on Inter-Church Aid, Refugee and World Service: Dir., Dr. Klaus Poser
Commission of the Churches on International Affairs: Dir.: Mr. Ninan Koshy; Exec. Sec., New York Office,

Human Rights Resources Officer for Latin America: Rev. Charles Harper
Commission on the Churches' Participation in Development: Dir.: Mr. Oh Jae Shik
Program to Combat Racism: Dir., Rev. Barney Pityana;
Christian Medical Commission: Dir., Dr. Dan Kaseje

PROGRAM UNIT III—
EDUCATION AND RENEWAL

Staff Moderator: Ms. Mercy Oduyoye
Sub-Unit on Women in Church and Society: Dir.,

Sub-Unit on Renewal & Congregational Life: Dir., Prof. Ion Bria
Sub-Unit on Education: Dir., Rev. Clifford Payne;
Portfolio on Biblical Studies, Dr. Willie Riekkinen
Sub-Unit on Youth: Dir., Mr. Peter Brock
Program on Theological Education Dir., Rev. Dr. Samuel Amirtham

PERIODICALS

The Ecumenical Review (q), Rev. Emilio Castro.
The Ecumenical Press Service (w), Mr. Thomas H. Dorris, Ed., English edition.
International Review of Mission (q), Rev. Dr. Christopher Duraisingh.
One World, Mr. Marlin VanElderen, Ed.

Constituent Bodies of the World Council of Churches and Associate Member Churches

MEMBER CHURCHES

Angola
Evangelical Congregational Church in Angola

Argentina
Iglesia Evangélica del Río de la Plata (Evangelical Church of the River Plata)
Iglesia Evangélica Metodista Argentina (Evangelical Methodist Church of Argentina)

Australia
The Anglican Church of Australia
Churches of Christ in Australia
The Uniting Church in Australia

Austria
Alt-katholische Kirche Österreichs (Old Catholic Church of Austria)
Evangelische Kirche Augsburgischen u. Helvetischen Bekenntnisses (A.u.H.B.) (Evangelical Church of the Augsburg and Helvetic Confession)

Bahamas
Church in the Province of the West Indies (see under *West Indies*)
Methodist Church in the Caribbean and the Americas (see under *West Indies*)

Bangladesh
Bangladesh Baptist Sangha

Barbados
Church in the Province of the West Indies (see under *West Indies*)
Methodist Church in the Caribbean and the Americas (see under *West Indies*)
Moravian Church, Eastern West Indies Province (see under *West Indies*)

Belgium
Eglise protestante unie de Belgique (United Protestant Church of Belgium)

Benin (People's Republic of)
Eglise protestante méthodiste en République populaire du Bénin (Protestant Methodist Church in the People's Republic of Benin)

Botswana
Church of the Province of Central Africa
(see under *Central Africa*)

Brazil
Igreja Episcopal do Brasil (Episcopal Church of Brazil)
Igreja Evangélica de Confissão Luterana no Brasil (Evangelical Church of Lutheran Confession in Brazil)
Igreja Metodista do Brasil (Methodist Church in Brazil)
Igreja Reformada Latino Americana (The Latin American Reformed Church)

Bulgaria
Bulgarian Orthodox Church

Burma
Burma Baptist Convention
Church of the Province of Burma
Methodist Church, Upper Burma

Burundi
Church of the Province of Burundi, Rwanda and Zaire

Cameroon
Eglise évangélique du Cameroun (Evangelical Church of Cameroon)
Eglise presbytérienne camérounaise (Presbyterian Church of Cameroon)
Presbyterian Church in Cameroon
Union des Eglises baptistes du Cameroun (Union of Baptist Churches of Cameroon)

Canada
The Anglican Church of Canada
Canadian Yearly Meeting of the Society of Friends
Christian Church (Disciples of Christ)
The Evangelical Lutheran Church of Canada
The Presbyterian Church in Canada
The United Church of Canada

Central Africa
Church of the Province of Central Africa
(covers Botswana, Malawi, Zambia, Zimbabwe)

Chile
Iglesia Evangélica Luterana en Chile (Evangelical Lutheran Church in Chile)
Iglesia Pentecostal de Chile (Pentecostal Church of Chile)
Misión Iglesia Pentecosta (Pentecostal Mission Church)

Congo (People's Republic of the)
Eglise évangélique du Congo (Evangelical Church of the Congo)

Cook Islands
Cook Islands Christian Church

Costa Rica
Methodist Church in the Caribbean and the Americas (see under *West Indies*)

Cyprus
Church of Cyprus
Episcopal Church in Jerusalem and the Middle East (see under *Jerusalem*)

Czechoslovakia
Ceskobratrská církev evangelická (Evangelical Church of Czech Brethren)
Ceskoslovenská církev husitská (Czechoslovak Hussite Church)
Pravoslavná církev v CSSR (Orthodox Church of Czechoslovakia)
Ref. krest. církev na Slovensku (Reformed Christian Church in Slovakia)
Slezská církev evangelická a.v. (Silesian Evangelical Church of the Augsburg Confession)
Slovenská evanjelická církev a.v. v CSSR (Slovak Evangelical Church of the Augsburg Confession in the CSSR)

Denmark
Det danske Baptistsamfund (The Baptist Union of Denmark)
Den evangelisk-lutherske Folkekirke i Danmark (The Church of Denmark)

East Africa
Presbyterian Church of East Africa
(covers Kenya, Tanzania, Uganda)

Egypt
Coptic Orthodox Church
Coptic Evangelical Church—The Synod of the Nile

Episcopal Church in Jerusalem and the Middle East
(see under *Jerusalem*)
Greek Orthodox Patriarchate of Alexandria and All
Africa
Ethiopia
Ethiopian Orthodox Church
The Ethiopian Evangelical Church Mekane Yesus
Europe
Europaïsch-Festländische Brüder-Unität, Distrikt Bad
Boll (European Continental Province of the Mora-
vian Church—Western District)
Fiji
Methodist Church in Fiji
Finland
Suomen evankelis-luterilainen kirkko (Evangelical-Lu-
theran Church of Finland)
Orthodox Church of Finland
France
Eglise de la Confession d'Augsbourg d'Alsace et de
Lorraine (Evangelical Church of the Augsburg
Confession of Alsace and Lorraine)
Eglise évangélique luthérienne de France (Evangelical
Lutheran Church of France)
Eglise réformée d'Alsace et de Lorraine (Reformed
Church of Alsace and Lorraine)
Eglise réformée de France (Reformed Church of
France)
French Polynesia (formerly Tahiti)
Eglise évangélique de Polynésie française (Evangelical
Church of French Polynesia)
Gabonese Republic
Eglise évangélique du Gabon (Evangelical Church of
Gabon)
The Gambia
Church of the Province of West Africa
(see under *West Africa*)
German Churches
Federal Republic of Germany
Katholisches Bistum der Alt-Katholiken in Deutschland
(Catholic Diocese of the Old Catholics in Germany)
Europaïsch-Festländische Brüder-Unität, Distrikt Bad
Boll (see under *Europe*)
Evangelische Kirche in Deutschland (Evangelical Church
in Germany)
Evangelische Landeskirche in Baden
Evangelisch-Lutherische Kirche in Bayern*
Evangelische Kirche in Berlin-Brandenburg (Berlin
West)
Evangelisch-Lutherische Landeskirche in Braunsch-
weig*
Bremische Evangelische Kirche
Evangelisch-Lutherische Landeskirche Hannovers*
Evangelische Kirche in Hessen und Nassau
Evangelische Kirche von Kurhessen-Waldeck
Lippische Landeskirche
Nordelbische Evangelisch-Lutherische Kirche*
Evangelisch-Reformierte Kirche in Nordwestdeutsch-
land
Evangelisch-Lutherische Kirche in Oldenburg
Evangelische Christliche Kirche der Pfalz
Evangelische Kirche im Rheinland
Evangelisch-Lutherische Landeskirche Schaumburg-
Lippe*
Evangelische Kirche von Westfalen
Evangelische Landeskirche in Württemberg
Vereiningung der Deutschen Mennonitengemeinden
(Mennonite Church)

*This church is directly a member of the World Council of
Churches in accordance with the resolution of the General

Synod of the United Evangelical Lutheran Church of
Germany, dated 27 January, 1949, which recommended
that the member churches of the United Evangelical
Lutheran Church should make the following declaration to
the Council of the Evangelical Church in Germany
concerning their relation to the World Council of
Churches:

"The Evangelical Church in Germany has made it clear
through its constitution that it is a federation (Bund) of
confessionally determined churches. Moreover, the
conditions of membership of the World Council of
Churches have been determined at the Assembly at
Amsterdam. Therefore, this Evangelical Lutheran
Church declares concerning its membership in the
World Council of Churches:
   i) It is represented in the World Council as a church
      of the Evangelical Lutheran confession.
  ii) Representatives which it sends to the World
      Council are to be identified as Evangelical
      Lutherans.
 iii) Within the limits of the competence of the
      Evangelical Church in Germany it is represented
      in the World Council through the intermediary of
      the Council of the Evangelical Church in Ger-
      many."

German Democratic Republic
Bund der Evangelischen Kirchen in der Deutschen
Demokratischen Republik (Federation of the
Evangelical Churches in the GDR)
Evangelische Landeskirche Anhalts†
Evangelische Kirche in Berlin-Brandenburg†
Evangelische Kirche des Görlitzer Kirchengebietes†
Evangelische Landeskirche Greifswald†
Evangelisch-Lutherische Landeskirche Mecklen-
burgs†
Evangelische Kirche der Kirchenprovinz Sachsen†
Evangelisch-Lutherische Landeskirche Sachsens†
Evangelisch-Lutherische Kirche in Thüringen†
Evangelische Brüder-Unität (Distrikt Herrnhut)
(Moravian Church)
Gemeindeverband der Alt-Katholischen Kirche in der
Deutschen Demokratischen Republik (Federation
of the Old Catholic Church in the GDR)
United in a fellowship of Christian witness and service in
the Federation of Evangelical Churches in the GDR, these
churches are represented in the Council through agencies
of the Federation of Evangelical Churches in the GDR.
Ghana
Church of the Province of West Africa
(see under *West Africa*)
Evangelical Presbyterian Church
The Methodist Church, Ghana
Presbyterian Church of Ghana
Greece
Ekklesia tes Ellados (Church of Greece)
Helleniki Evangeliki Ekklesia (Greek Evangelical
Church)
Guyana
Church in the Province of the West Indies
(see under *West Indies*)
Methodist Church in the Caribbean and the Americas
(see under *West Indies*)
Haiti
Methodist Church in the Caribbean and the Americas
(see under *West Indies*)
Honduras
Methodist Church in the Caribbean and the Americas
(see under *West Indies*)
Hong Kong
The Church of Christ in China, The Hong Kong Council

159

Hungary

Magyarországi Baptista Egyház
(Baptist Church of Hungary)
Magyarországi Evangélikus Egyház
(Lutheran Church in Hungary)
Magyarországi Reformatus Egyház
(Reformed Church in Hungary)

Iceland

Evangelical Lutheran Church of Iceland

India

Church of North India
Church of South India
United Evangelical Lutheran Churches in India
Mar Thoma Syrian Church of Malabar
Malankara Orthodox Syrian Church
Methodist Church in India
The Samavesam of Telugu Baptist Churches

Indian Ocean

Church of the Province of the Indian Ocean
(covers Mauritius, Madagascar, Seychelles)

Indonesia

Gereja Batak Karo Protestan (Karo Batak Protestant Church)
Huria Kristen Batak Protestan (Batak Protestant Christian Church)
Gereja Kristen Protestan Indonesia (G.K.P.I.) (Christian Protestant Church in Indonesia)
The Evangelical Christian Church in Halmahera
Huria Kristen Indonesia (H.K.I.) (The Indonesian Christian Church)
Gereja Kristen Indonesia (Indonesian Christian Church)
Gereja Protestan di Indonesia (Protestant Church in Indonesia)
Gereja Kristen Injili di Irian Jaya (Evangelical Christian Church in West Irian)
Gereja Kristen Jawi Wetan (Christian Church of East Java)
Gereja-Gereja Kristen Java (Javanese Christian Churches)
Gereja Kalimantan Evangelis (Kalimantan Evangelical Church)
Gereja Protestan Maluku (Protestant Church in the Moluccas)
Gereja Masehi Injili Minahasa (Christian Evangelical Church in Minahasa)
Banua Niha Keriso Protestan (Nias Protestant Christian Church)
Gereja Kristen Pasundan (Pasundan Christian Church)
Gereja Masehi Injili Sangihe Talaud (GMIST) (Evangelical Church of Sangir Talaud)
Gereja Kristen Protestan Simalungun (Simalungun Protestant Christian Church)
Gereja Kristen Sulawesi Tengah (Christian Church in Central Sulawesi)
Gereja Masehi Injili di Timor (Protestant Evangelical Church in Timor)
Gereja Toraja (Toraja Church)

Iran

Apostolic Catholic Assyrian Church of the East
(see under *U.S.A.*)
Episcopal Church in Jerusalem and the Middle East
(see under *Jerusalem*)
Synod of the Evangelical Church of Iran

Italy

Chiesa Evangelica Metodista d'Italia (Evangelical Methodist Church of Italy)
Chiesa Evangelica Valdese (Waldensian Church)

Ivory Coast

Methodist Church, Ivory Coast

Jamaica

Church in the Province of the West Indies
(see under *West Indies*)
Methodist Church in the Caribbean and the Americas
(see under *West Indies*)
The Moravian Church in Jamaica
The United Church of Jamaica and Grand Cayman

Japan

Japanese Orthodox Church
Nippon Kirisuto Kyodan (The United Church of Christ in Japan)
Nippon Sei Ko Kai (Anglican-Episcopal Church in Japan)

Jerusalem

Episcopal Church in Jerusalem and the Middle East
(covers Jerusalem, Egypt, Iran, Cyprus, the Gulf)
Greek Orthodox Patriarchate of Jerusalem

Kenya

African Christian Church and Schools
African Israel Church, Nineveh
Church of the Province of Kenya
The Methodist Church in Kenya
Presbyterian Church of East Africa
(see under *East Africa*)

Kiribati (Pacific)

Kiribati Protestant Church

Korea

The Korean Methodist Church
The Presbyterian Church in the Republic of Korea
The Presbyterian Church of Korea

Lebanon

Armenian Apostolic Church
National Evangelical Synod of Syria and Lebanon
Greek Orthodox Patriarchate of Antioch and All the East
(see under *Syria*)
Union of the Armenian Evangelical Churches in the Near East

Lesotho

Lesotho Evangelical Church

Liberia

The Church of the Province of West Africa
(see under *West Africa*)
Lutheran Church in Liberia

Madagascar

Church of the Province of the Indian Ocean
(see under *Indian Ocean*)
Eglise de Jésus Christ à Madagascar (Church of Jesus Christ in Madagascar)
Eglise luthérienne malgache (Malagasy Lutheran Church)

Malawi

Church of the Province of Central Africa
(see under *Central Africa*)

Malaysia

The Methodist Church in Malaysia

Mauritius

Church of the Province of the Indian Ocean
(see under *Indian Ocean*)

Melanesia

Church of Melanesia
(see under *Solomon Islands*)

Mexico

Iglesia Metodista de México (Methodist Church of Mexico)

Netherlands

Algemene Doopsgezinde Sociëteit (General Mennonite Society)
Evangelisch Lutherse Kerk (Evangelical Lutheran Church)

De Gereformeerde Kerken in Nederland (The Reformed Churches in the Netherlands)
Nederlandse Hervormde Kerk (Netherlands Reformed Church)
Oud-Katholieke Kerk van Nederland (Old Catholic Church of the Netherlands)
Remonstrantse Broederschap (Remonstrant Brotherhood)

New Caledonia
Eglise évangélique en Nouvelle Calédonie et aux Iles Loyauté (Evangelical Church in New Caledonia and the Loyalty Isles)

New Zealand
Associated Churches of Christ in New Zealand
The Baptist Union of New Zealand
Church of the Province of New Zealand
The Methodist Church of New Zealand
The Presbyterian Church of Aotearoa New Zealand

Nicaragua
Convención Bautista de Nicaragua (Baptist Convention of Nicaragua)
Iglesia Morava en Nicaragua (Moravian Church in Nicaragua)

Nigeria
Church of the Lord Aladura
Church of the Province of Nigeria
Methodist Church, Nigeria
Nigerian Baptist Convention
The Presbyterian Church of Nigeria
Brethren Church of Nigeria

Norway
Den Norske Kirke (Church of Norway)

Pakistan
The Church of Pakistan
United Presbyterian Church of Pakistan

Papua New Guinea
The United Church in Papua New Guinea and the Solomon Islands

Philippines
Iglesia Filipina Independiente (Philippine Independent Church)
United Church of Christ in the Philippines
Iglesia Evangelica Metodista en las Islas Filipinas (The Evangelical Methodist Church in the Philippines)

Poland
Autocephalic Orthodox Church in Poland
Kosciola Ewangelicko-Augsburskiego w PRL (Evangelical Church of the Augsburg Confession in Poland)
Kosciola Polskokatolickiego w PRL (Polish Catholic Church in Poland)
Staro-Katolickiego Kosciola Mariatowitow w PRL (Old Catholic Mariavite Church in Poland)

Romania
Evangelische Kirche A.B. in der Sozialistischen Republik Rumänien (Evangelical Church of the Augsburg Confession in the Socialist Republic of Romania)
Biserica Ortodoxa Romana (Romanian Orthodox Church)
Reformed Church of Romania
Evangelical Synodal Presbyterial Church of the Augsburg Confession in the Socialist Republic of Romania

Rwanda
Church of the Province of Burundi, Rwanda and Zaïre (see under *Burundi*)
Eglise presbytérienne au Rwanda (Presbyterian Church of Rwanda)

Samoa
Congregational Christian Church in American Samoa
The Congregational Christian Church in Samoa
The Methodist Church in Samoa

Seychelles
Church of the Province of the Indian Ocean (see under *Indian Ocean*)

Sierra Leone
Church of the Province of West Africa (see under *West Africa*)
The Methodist Church of Sierra Leone

Solomon Islands
Church of Melanesia

South Africa (Republic of)
Church of the Province of Southern Africa
Evangelical Lutheran Church in Southern Africa
Evangelical Presbyterian Church in South Africa
The Methodist Church of Southern Africa
Moravian Church in South Africa
Presbyterian Church of Africa
The Presbyterian Church of Southern Africa
The Reformed Presbyterian Church of Southern Africa
The United Congregational Church of Southern Africa

Spain
Iglesia Evangélica Española (Spanish Evangelical Church)

Sri Lanka
The Church of Ceylon
Methodist Church

Sudan
Presbyterian Church in the Sudan
Province of the Episcopal Church of the Sudan

Surinam
Moravian Church in Surinam

Sweden
Estonian Evangelical Lutheran Church (see under *Other Churches*)
Svenska Kyrkan (Church of Sweden)
Svenska Missionsförbundet (The Mission Covenant Church of Sweden)

Switzerland
Christkatholische Kirche der Schweiz (Old Catholic Church of Switzerland)
Schweizerischer Evangelischer Kirchenbund, Fédération des Eglises protestantes de la Suisse (Swiss Protestant Church Federation)

Syria
The National Evangelical Synod of Syria and Lebanon (see under *Lebanon*)
Patriarcat Grec-Orthodoxe d'Antioche et de tout l'Orient (Greek Orthodox Patriarchate of Antioch and All the East)
Syrian Orthodox Patriarchate of Antioch and All the East

Taiwan
The Presbyterian Church in Taiwan

Tanzania
Church of the Province of Tanzania
Evangelical Lutheran Church in Tanzania
Joint Board of the Moravian Church in Tanzania
Presbyterian Church of East Africa (see under *East Africa*)

Thailand
The Church of Christ in Thailand

Togo
Eglise évangélique du Togo (Evangelical Church of Togo)

Tonga
Methodist Church in Tonga (Free Wesleyan Church of Tonga)

Trinidad
Church in the Province of the West Indies
(see under *West Indies*)
Methodist Church in the Caribbean and the Americas
(see under *West Indies*)
Moravian Church, Eastern West Indies Province
(see under *West Indies*)
The Presbyterian Church in Trinidad and Grenada

Turkey
Ecumenical Patriarchate of Constantinople

Tuvalu
Church of Tuvalu

Uganda
The Church of Uganda
Presbyterian Church of East Africa
(see under *East Africa*)

Union of Soviet Socialist Republics
Russian Orthodox Church
The Union of Evangelical Christian Baptists of USSR
Eglise apostolique arménienne (Armenian Apostolic Church)
Eesti Evangeelne Luterlik Kirik (Estonian Evangelical Lutheran Church)
Georgian Orthodox Church
Latvijas Evangeliska-Luteriski Baznica (Evangelical Lutheran Church of Latvia)

United Kingdom (of Great Britain and Northern Ireland) and Republic of Ireland

Churches with headquarters in England
The Baptist Union of Great Britain and Ireland
The Church of England
The Methodist Church
The Moravian Church in Great Britain and Ireland
The United Reformed Church in the United Kingdom

Churches with headquarters in Ireland
The Church of Ireland
The Methodist Church in Ireland

Churches with headquarters in Scotland
The Church of Scotland
The Congregational Union of Scotland
The Scottish Episcopal Church
United Free Church of Scotland

Churches with headquarters in Wales
The Church in Wales
The Presbyterian Church of Wales
Union of Welsh Independents

United States of America
African Methodist Episcopal Church
African Methodist Episcopal Zion Church
American Baptist Churches in the U.S.A.
Apostolic Catholic Assyrian Church of the East
Christian Church (Disciples of Christ)
Christian Methodist Episcopal Church
Church of the Brethren
The Episcopal Church
Evangelical Lutheran Church in America
Hungarian Reformed Church in America
International Council of Community Churches
International Evangelical Church
Moravian Church in America (Northern Province)
Moravian Church in America (Southern Province)
National Baptist Convention of America
National Baptist Convention, U.S.A., Inc.
The Orthodox Church in America
Polish National Catholic Church of America
Presbyterian Church (U.S.A.)

Progressive National Baptist Convention
Reformed Church in America
Religious Society of Friends
Friends General Conference
Friends United Meeting
United Church of Christ
The United Methodist Church

Uruguay
Iglesia Evangélica Valdense del Rio de la Plata
(part of the Waldensian Church—see under *Italy*)

Vanuatu
Presbyterian Church of Vanuatu

Venezuela
Church of the Province of the West Indies
(see under *West Indies*)

West Africa
The Church of the Province of West Africa
(covers The Gambia, Ghana, Liberia, Sierra Leone)

West Indies
The Church in the Province of the West Indies
The Methodist Church in the Caribbean and the Americas
Moravian Church, Eastern West Indies Province

Yugoslavia
Reformatska Crkve u SFRJ (The Reformed Church in Yugoslavia)
Serbian Orthodox Church
Slovenska ev.-kr. a.v. cirkev v. Juhuslavii (Slovak Evangelical Church of the Augsburg Confession in Yugoslavia)

Zaïre (Republic of)
Church of the Province of Burundi, Rwanda and Zaïre
(see under *Burundi*)
Eglise du Christ au Zaïre (Communauté baptiste du Zaïre Ouest [CBZO]) (Church of Christ in Zaïre—Baptist Community of Western Zaïre)
Eglise du Christ au Zaïre (Communauté épiscopale baptiste en Afrique [CEBA]) (Church of Christ in Zaire—Episcopal Baptist Community)
Eglise du Christ au Zaïre (Communauté des Disciples) (Church of Christ in Zaïre—Community of Disciples)
Eglise du Christ au Zaire (Commauté évangélique) (Church of Christ in Zaïre—Evangelical Community)
Eglise du Christ au Zaïre (Communauté lumière) (Church of Christ in Zaïre—Community of Light)
Eglise du Christ au Zaïre (Communauté mennonite au Zaïre) (Church of Christ in Zaïre-Mennonite Community)
Eglise du Christ au Zaïre (Communauté presbytériènne) (Church of Christ in Zaïre—Presbyterian Community)
Eglise du Jésus Christ sur la Terre par le Prophète Simon Kimbangu (Church of Jesus Christ on Earth by the Prophet Simon Kimbangu)

Zambia
Church of the Province of Central Africa
(see under *Central Africa*)
United Church of Zambia

Zimbabwe
Church of the Province of Central Africa
(see under *Central Africa*)
Methodist Church in Zimbabwe

Other Churches
Eesti Evangeeliumi Luteri Usu Kirik
(Estonian Evangelical Lutheran Church)
Latvijas Evangeliski Luteriska baznica eklisa
(Evangelical Lutheran Church of Latvia in Exile)

Algeria
Eglise protestante d'Algérie (Protestant Church of Algeria)

Angola
United Evangelical Church of Angola
Evangelical Pentecostal Church of Angola

Argentina
La Iglesia de Dios (Church of God)
Iglesia Evangélica Luterana Unida (United Evangelical Lutheran Church)
Iglesia de los Discípulos de Cristo (Church of the Disciples of Christ)

Bangladesh
Church of Bangladesh

Bolivia
Iglesia Evangélica Metodista en Bolivie (Evangelical Methodist Church in Bolivia)

Brazil
Igreja Presbiteriana Unida do Brasil (United Presbyterian Church of Brazil)

Cameroon
Eglise Protestante Africaine (African Protestant Church)

Chile
Iglesia Metodista de Chile (The Methodist Church of Chile)

Costa Rica
Iglesia Evangélica Metodista de Costa Rica (Evangelical Methodist Church of Costa Rica)

Cuba
Iglesia Metodista en Cuba (Methodist Church in Cuba)
Iglesia Presbiteriana-Reformada en Cuba (Presbyterian-Reformed Church in Cuba)

Equatorial Guinea
Iglesia Reformada de Guinea Ecuatorial (Reformed Church of Equatorial Guinea)

India
Bengal-Orissa-Bihar Baptist Convention

Indonesia
Gereja Kristen Protestan di Bali (Protestant Christian Church in Bali)
Gereja Punguan Kristen Batak (GPKB) (Batak Christian Community Church)

Italy
Baptist Union of Italy

Japan
The Korean Christian Church in Japan

Kenya
African Church of the Holy Spirit

Liberia
Presbytery of Liberia

Malaysia
Protestant Church in Sabah

Mozambique
Igreja Presbiteriana de Moçambique (Presbyterian Church of Mozambique)

Netherlands Antilles
Iglesia Protestant Uni (United Protestant Church)

Peru
Iglesia Metodista del Peru (The Methodist Church of Peru)

Portugal
Igreja Evangélica Presbiteriana de Portugal (Evangelical Presbyterian Church of Portugal)
Igreja Lusitana Catolica Apostolica Evangélica (Lusitanian Catholic-Apostolic Evangelical Church)

Singapore
Methodist Church in Singapore

Spain
Iglesia Española Reformada Episcopal (Spanish Reformed Episcopal Church)

Uruguay
Iglesia Evangélica Metodista en el Uruguay (The Evangelical Methodist Church in Uruguay)

Alliance World Fellowship

The Alliance World Fellowship, founded in 1975, at Nyack, New York, is a nonlegislative body whose members are the national churches raised up through the ministry of The Christian and Missionary Alliance and found under a variety of names in 53 nations of the world.

The purpose of the Fellowship is to provide a means of fellowship, consultation, cooperation and encouragement in the task of missions and evangelism which we understand to be the special calling of the church.

The AWF has a plenary convocation quadrennially. The first was in Nyack, NY, in 1975; the second in Hong Kong in 1979; the third in Lima, Peru, in 1983; the fourth in St. Paul, MN in 1987; and the fifth to be held in Abidjan, Ivory Coast in 1991.

Headquarters: P. O. Box 35000, Colorado Springs, CO 80935. Tel. (719)599-5999

OFFICERS

Pres., Dr. Benjamin de Jesus, Box 649, Manila, Republic of the Philippines 2800; Vice-Pres., Dr. Melvin P. Sylvester, Box 7900, Postal Sta. B, Willowdale, Ontario M2K 2R6; Sec., Rev. Arni Shareski, P. O. Box 35000, Colorado Springs, CO 80935; Treas., Rev. Roger Lang, P. O. Box 120, French's Forest, New South Wales, Australia 2686

Anglican Consultative Council

The Anglican Consultative Council is the central council for the worldwide Anglican Communion. Its creation was proposed by the Lambeth Conference of Bishops of the Anglican Communion in 1968, and came into being by the end of 1969 with the consent of all the Provinces (or member Churches). Council meetings are held in different parts of the world. Its first meeting was held in Limuru, Kenya, in 1971; the second in Dublin, Ireland, in July 1973; the third in Trinidad, April 1976; the fourth in Canada May 1979; the fifth in Newcastle, England, September 1981; the sixth meeting in Badagry, Nigeria, July, 1984. The seventh meeting was held in Singapore, April 25 - May 7, 1987. Its report is titled "Many Gifts, One Spirit." The eighth meeting will be held in Wales, July 21-August 4, 1990.

The membership includes bishops, priests, and lay people. Each Province (or member Church) is represented by up to three members and meetings are held every second or third year; the Standing Committee meets every year.

True to the Anglican Communion's style of working, the Council has no legislative powers. It fills a liaison role, consulting and recommending, and at times representing the Anglican Communion. Among its functions are "to share information about developments in one or more provinces with the other parts of the Communion and to serve as needed as an instrument of common action"; "to develop as far as possible agreed Anglican policies in the world mission of the Church and to encourage national and regional Churches to engage together in developing and implementing such policies by sharing their resources of manpower, money, and experience to the best advantage of all"; "to encourage and guide Anglican participation in the Ecumenical Movement and the ecumenical organizations." It is responsible for international dialogues with other world communions.

OFFICERS

Pres., The Archbishop of Canterbury, Most Rev. Robert Runcie, Lambeth Palace, London, SE1 7JU., England.
Chpsn., The Ven. Yong Ping Chung, P.O. Box 17, Sandakan, Sabah, Malaysia.
Sec. Gen., Rev., Canon Samuel Van Culin, Partnership House, 157 Waterloo Rd., London SE1 8UT. Tel. 01-620-1110; Telex: 8950907 ANGCOMG: Fax: 01-620-1070; Telecom Gold: 81:CELOOZ

Baptist World Alliance

The Baptist World Alliance is a voluntary association of Baptist conventions and unions which was formed at the first world gathering of Baptists in Exeter Hall, London, England, July 11-18, 1905. There have been fifteen meetings of the Alliance's Baptist World Congress, the most recent of which was held in Los Angeles, California, July 1985.

One hundred forty-one national bodies around the world participate in the Alliance, and these bodies represent approximately 36 million church members baptized upon their personal, conscient profession of faith in Jesus Christ. Along with children in member families, sympathizers and others considered under pastoral care, the Alliance world community would number more than 65 million persons.

BWA functions as: 1) A means of contact among world Baptists through publications, news, representational visits, correspondence and other communications; 2) A forum for study and fraternal discussion of doctrines, practice and ways of witness to the world; 3) A channel of world aid to the hungry and victims of disaster, for development projects and fraternal assistance to those in need; 4) An agency for monitoring and safeguarding religious liberty and other God-given rights; 5) a sponsor of regional and worldwide gatherings for the furtherance of the gospel; 6) an agency for consultation and cooperation among Baptists worldwide; 7) an agency for encouraging of evangelism and education; and 8) a sponsor of programs for lay development including conferences for Christian women, men and youth.

International Office: 6733 Curran St., McLean, VA 22101. Tel. (703) 790-8980; Fax: (703)893-5160. Next Congress: Seoul, Korea, Aug. 14-19, 1990.

OFFICERS

Pres., Dr. G. Noel Vose, Baptist Theological College, Hayman Rd.,Bentley 6102, Western Australia
Gen. Sec.-Treas., Rev. Dr. Denton Lotz.
Division Dirs., Dr. Archibald R. Goldie, Baptist World Aid; Dr. J. Ralph McIntyre, Evangelism and Education; Ms. Wendy Ryan, Communications; Rev. Elizabeth MacClaren, Women's Department; Dr. W. J. Isbell, Men's Department. 6733 Curran St., McLean, VA 22101. Tel. (703) 790-8980
Secretaries of Regional Fellowships: Africa, Dr. Samuel T. Ola, Akande, Nigeria; Asia, Rev. Edwin I. Lopez, Philippines; Caribbean, Rev. Azariah McKenzie, Jamaica; Rev. Karl-Heinz Walter, West Germany; North America, Dr. Archibald R. Goldie, U.S.A.; South America, Rev. Jose Missena, Paraguay

Disciples Ecumenical Consultative Council (DECC)

The Disciples Ecumenical Consultative Council is an international body of Disciples of Christ Churches, established in 1975, which has four major objectives: 1) to deepen the fellowship of Disciples with each other and with other Churches on the way to the visible unity God wills for his people; 2) to encourage participation in the ecumenical movement through joint theological study, church union conversations and other forms of dialogue, and programs of joint action and witness; 3) to gather, share and evaluate information about Disciples ecumenical activities in local, national and regional situations around the world; 4) to appoint fraternal representatives of Disciples to the assemblies of ecumenical bodies such as the World Council of Churches, and of other world families of churches, including the Roman Catholic Church.

OFFICERS

Moderator, Dr. Trevor A. Banks, 13 Eton Rd., Belmont 3216, Victoria, Australia
Gen. Sec., Dr. Paul A. Crow, Jr., P.O. Box 1986, Indianapolis, IN 46206. Tel. (317) 353-1491

ADVISORY COMMITTEE

Dr. Trevor Banks (Australia), Ms. Hazel Byfield (Jamaica), Rev. Carmelo Alvarez (Puerto Rico), Dr. Paul A. Crow, Jr. (U.S.A.)

MEMBERSHIP

Disciples of Christ Churches in Argentina, Australia, Canada, Great Britain/Ireland, Jamaica, Mexico, New Zealand, Paraguay, Puerto Rico, Southern Africa, United States of America, Vanuatu and Zaire.

Friends World Committee for Consultation Section of the Americas

The Friends World Committee for Consultation (FWCC) was formed in 1937. There has been an American Section as well as a European Section from the early days and an African Section was organized in 1971. In 1974 the name Section of the Americas was adopted by that part of the FWCC with constituency in North, Central and South America and in the Caribbean area. In 1985 the Asia-West Pacific Section was organized. The purposes of the Section of the Americas can be summarized as follows:

1) To encourage and strengthen the spiritual life within the Society of Friends through such measures as the promotion of intervisitation, study, conferences, and a wide sharing of experience on the deepest spiritual level.
2) To help Friends to gain a better understanding of the worldwide character of the Society of Friends and its vocation in the world today.

3) To promote consultation amongst Friends of all cultures, countries, and languages. The Committee seeks to bring the different groups of Friends into intimate touch with one another on the basis of their common Quaker heritage, with a view to sharing experience and coming to some measure of agreement in regard to their attitude to modern world problems.

4) To promote understanding between Friends of all countries and members of other branches of the Christian Church and members of other religious faiths, and to interpret the specific Quaker message to those who seek for further religious experience.

5) To keep under review the Quaker contribution in world affairs and to facilitate both the examination and presentation of Quaker thinking and concern.

Headquarters: 1506 Race St., Philadelphia, PA 19102. Tel. (215) 241-7250.

Other Officers: P.O. Box 1797, Richmond IN 47375. Tel. (317) 935-1967; P.O. Box 11715, Denver, CO 80211. Tel. (303)433-0509; P.O. Box 923, Oregon City, OR 97045. Tel. (503)635-3779.

Latin American Office: Casa de los Amigos, Ignacio Mariscal 132, Mexico. Tel. (905)705-0521.

Heads of Orthodox Churches

Among the churches that are referred to as "Orthodox" there are three distinct groups defined by the recognition of different ecumenical councils. Divisions of this family of churches stem from seven ecumenical councils held from the fourth to the eighth centuries. The Apostolic and Catholic Assyrian Church of the East accepts the first two ecumenical councils. The Oriental Orthodox Churches, The Armenian Apostolic Church, the Coptic Orthodox Church of Alexandria (Egypt), the Ethiopian Orthodox Church and the Syrian Orthodox Church, accept the first three ecumenical councils. The eighteen local churches referred to as "Eastern Orthodox" embody the teachings of all the seven ecumenical councils. The Ecumenical Patriarch of Constantinople is regarded by all as "first among equals," the first in honor and distinction without direct authority over churches other than his own.

ASSYRIAN CHURCH OF THE EAST

Patriarchate of the Apostolic and Catholic Assyrian Church of the East: His Holiness Mar Dinkha IV, Darya Now, Third Avenue No. 32, Tehran 14, Iran. (Presently residing at 7444 North Kildare, Chicago, Illinois 60076).

ORIENTAL ORTHODOX CHURCHES

Catholicossate of the Armenian Apostolic Church: His Holiness Vazken I, Supreme Patriarch and Catholicos of All Armenians, Etchmiadzin, Armenia, USSR.

Catholicossate of the Armenian Apostolic Church, See of Cilicia: His Holiness Karekin II, Catholicos of Cilicia Antelias, Lebanon.

Patriarchate of the Coptic Orthodox Church: His Holiness Pope Shenouda III, Pope of Alexandria and Patriarch of the See of St. Mark, Anba Rueiss Building, Ramses Street, Abbasyia, Cairo, Arab Republic of Egypt.

Patriarchate of the Ethiopian Orthodox Church: His Holiness Abuna Tekle Haimanot, Patriarch of the Ethiopian Orthodox Church, Post Office Box 1283, Addis Ababa, Ethiopia.

Patriarchate of Antioch and All the East of the Syrian Orthodox Church: His Holiness Moran Mor Ignatius Zakka I, Patriarch of Antioch and All the East, Supreme Head of the Universal Syrian Orthodox Church, Bab Tooma, Damascus, Syria.

EASTERN ORTHODOX CHURCHES

Ecumenical Patriarchate: His All-Holiness Demetrios I, Archbishop of Constantinople, and Ecumenical Patriarch, Rum Patrikhanesi, Fener, Istanbul, Turkey

Patriarchate of Alexandria: His Beatitude Parthenios, Patriarch of Alexandria, Greek Orthodox Patriarchate, P. O. Box 2006, Alexandria, Egypt

Patriarchate of Antioch: His Beatitude Ignatius IV, Patriarch of Antioch, Greek Orthodox Patriarchate, P. O. Box 9, Damascus, Syria

Patriarchate of Jerusalem: His Beatitude Diodoros, Patriarch of Jerusalem, P. O. Box 19, Jerusalem, Old City, Israel

Patriarchate of Russia: _____, Patriarch of Moscow and All Russia, 5 Tchisty Pereulok, Moscow 34, U.S.S.R.

Patriarchate of Serbia: His Holiness German, Patriarch of the Serbian Orthodox Church, 7 Juli 5, Belgrade, Yugoslavia

Patriarchate of Romania: His Holiness Teoctist, Patriarch of Romania, 29 Strada Antim, Bucharest, Romania

Patriarchate of Bulgaria: His Holiness Maxim, Patriarch of the Bulgarian Orthodox Church, The Orthodox Patriarchate, Sofia, Bulgaria

Church of Georgia: His Holiness Ilya II, Catholicos Patriarch of Georgia, Tiflis, Georgia, U.S.S.R.

Church of Cyprus: His Beatitude Chrysostomos, Archbishop of Cyprus, Nicosia, Cyprus

Church of Greece: His Beatitude Seraphim, Archbishop of Athens and All Greece, Athens, Greece

Church of Albania: _____, Tirana, Albania

Church of Poland: His Beatitude Vasilios, Metropolitan of Warsaw and All Poland, Aleja Generala K, Swiercewskiego 52, Warsaw 4, Poland

Church of Czechoslovakia: His Beatitude Dorotheos, Metropolitan of Prague and All Czechoslovakia V Jame 6, Prague 1, Czechoslovakia

Orthodox Church in America: His Beatitude Metropolitan Theodosius, Metropolitan of All America and Canada, P.O. Box 675, Syosset, NY 11791, U.S.A.

Church of Sinai: The Archbishop-Abbott Damian, Mt. Sinai, Egypt

Church of Finland: Most Rev. Archbishop John, Archbishop of Karelia and All Finland, Kupio, Finland

Church of Japan: His Eminence Metropolitan Theodosius, Metropolitan of All Japan, 3-1-4 Surugadai Kanda, Chiyoda Ku, Tokyo, Japan

Hierarchy of the Roman Catholic Church

The Hierarchy of the Roman Catholic Church consists of His Holiness, the Pope, Supreme Pastor of the Roman Catholic Church and the various bishops from around the world joined with the Pope in one apostolic body to care for the Church. Cardinals, now always bishops, number about one hundred and fifty. They serve as the chief counselors to the Pope.

The Supreme Pastor is further assisted by the Roman Curia, which consists of the Secretariat of State or the Papal Secretariat, and the Council for the Public Affairs of the Church, various Sacred Congregations, Secretariats, Tribunals, and Offices. The bishops, some bearing the title of Patriarch or Archbishop, are united with the Supreme Pastor in the government of the whole Church. The bishops, when assigned to particular sees, are individually responsible for the teaching, sanctification and governance of their particular jurisdictions of the Church.

The Papal territorial possessions are called the State of Vatican City situated within the city of Rome and occupying 108.7 acres. It is the smallest sovereign state in the world. Papal authority is recognized as supreme by virtue of a Concordat reached with the Italian state and ratified June 7, 1929. Included in Vatican City are the Vatican Palace, various museums, art galleries, libraries, apartments, officers, a radio station, post office and St. Peter's Basilica.

HIS HOLINESS THE POPE

John Paul II, Karol Wojtyla, Supreme Pastor of the Roman Catholic Church (born May 18, 1920, installed, October 22, 1978.)

THE ROMAN CURIA

(A few sections of the Roman Curia relevant to ecclesiastical bodies outside the Roman Catholic Church and to other groups and individuals are listed below.)

Pontifical Council for Christian Unity. This Council has responsibility for relations with non–Roman Catholic Christian religious bodies, is concerned with the observance of the principles of ecumenism, promotes bilateral conversations on Christian unity both on national and international levels; institutes colloquies on ecumenical questions and activities with churches and ecclesiastical communities separated from the Holy See; deputes Catholic observers for Christian congresses; invites to Catholic gatherings observers of the separated churches and orders into practice conciliar degrees on ecumenical matters. The Pontifical Council for Promoting Christian Unity deals with all questions concerning religious relations with Judaism. Cardinal Praeses: Jan Cardinal Willebrands; Sec., Most Rev. Pierre Duprey. Office: 1 via dell'Erba, Rome, Italy.

Pontifical Council For Inter-Religious Dialog. This Council deals with those who are outside the Christian religion, profess some religion, or have a religious sense. It fosters studies and promotes relations with non-Christians to bring about an increase in mutual respect and seeks ways to establish a dialogue with them. President: Francis Cardinal Arinze; Sec., Most Rev. Michael Louis Fitzgerald, Office: 1 via dell'Erba, Rome, Italy.

Pontifical Council For Dialog with Non-Believers. This Council studies atheism in order to expore more fully its nature and to establish a dialogue with non-believers who sincerely wish to collaborate. President: Paul Cardinal Poupard; Sec., Rev. Franc Rode, C.M. Office: 16 Palazza S. Calisto, Vatican City State.

(Note: For a complete description and listing of the Hierarchy of the Roman Catholic Church see: the Official Catholic *Directory, 1989*, P. J. Kenedy & Sons, 3004 Glenview Rd., Wilmette IL 60091, pp. xiii-xxii. For a description of the Roman Catholic Church in the United States and in Canada, see under Directory 3, "Religious Bodies in the United States," and Directory 4, "Religious Bodies in Canada," appearing in this **Yearbook**.)

International Bible Society

International Bible Society was founded in 1809 in New York City by a small group of evangelism-minded Christians who wanted to "extend the knowledge of th Holy Scriptures in which God has revealed . . . salvation." At that time it was the New York Bible Society and its ministry centered on that city—distributing Bibles in hotels, hospitals, and jails, aboard ships and to immigrants. Over the years it has expanded into an international ministry. To date International Bible Society has published God's Word in more than 430 languages on six continents. Overseas, the majority of its Scriptures are provided free of charge through gifts from Christians in America. These Scriptures are distributed by workers from dozens of evangelical organizations. In the United States most of the Bible Society's Scriptures are sold at cost for use in local evangelism.

As part of its efforts to make God's Word as clear as possible, International Bible Society sponsored the translation of the *New International Version*. Over 100 evangelical scholars worked to produce this highly accurate version of the Bible in modern English.

Throughout its history, International Bible Society's purpose has remained the same: To serve the Church in evangelism by translating, publishing and distributing God's Word so that all people everywhere may come to a saving faith in Jesus Christ. In keeping with this purpose, the Bible Society's main functions are:

Assisting in the translating and publishing of new Scripture translations, in partnership with Wycliffe Bible Translators, New Tribes Mission and others.

Providing Scriptures for areas where God's Word is restricted but evangelism is taking place, such as Eastern Europe and Asia.

Supporting evangelism projects and opportunities around the world with Scriptures. Examples include: Supplying Scriptures for Billy Graham and Luis Palau crusades and U.S. campus ministries, and placing Bibles in Africa's public schools.

Selling Bibles, New Testaments and portions at or below cost to individuals, churches and organizations such as the military for use in evangelism and worship. Helping believers use God's Word more effectively through the sponsorship of evangelism/church growth seminars.

International Bible Society is an independent, non-profit organization with membership in the Evangelical Council for Financial Accountability, the National Association of Evangelicals and the Evangelical Foreign Missions Association.

Headquarters: 1820 Jet Stream Dr., Colorado Springs, CO 80921, Tel. (719)488-9200
New York Bible Society, an affiliate of International Bible Society: 172 Lexington Ave., New York, NY 10016. Tel. (212)213-5454

OFFICERS

Chmn., Board of Directors, R. Stanley Ottoson
Pres., James R. Powell
Vice Pres./Treas., Kenneth S. Jacobsen
Vice Pres. and Publisher, John Cruz
Vice Pres./Ministries, Dr. Eugene F. Rubingh
Dir., of Development, Robert Horan
Dir., New York Bible Society, Charles S. Rigby

PERIODICAL

Faith Magazine, Annual Scripture Catalog

International Congregational Fellowship

ICF is a voluntary association, first formed at a world gathering of Congregationalists in Chrislehurst, England, in 1975. It is a successor to the International Congregational Council (formed in London, England, in 1891 and merged into the World Alliance of Reformed Churches in 1966, during which time it held 10 international meetings). The ICF has held additional meetings, the most recent at Leeuwen Horst Congres Center, Noordwijkerhout, The Netherlands. It is in contact with Congregational-related bodies and individuals, each autonomous, in 52 countries.

ICF functions as: 1) an agency of communication between Congregationalists through publications, dissemination of news, personal visits, and correspondence; 2) a forum for study and fraternal discussion of doctrines, practice, and ways of witnessing to the world; 3) a channel of cooperation in extending help to one another and those in need; 4) a vigilant force for safeguarding religious liberty and other God-given rights; 5) a sponsor of regional and worldwide gatherings for the furtherance of the gospel; 6) an agency for promotion, consultation, and cooperation among Congregationalists.

GENERAL ORGANIZATION

Headquarters: Correspondence to: 58 Donnersfield Lane, Harrow HA1 2LE, United Kingdom
Next meeting: Southern California, 1993.

OFFICERS

Co-Chpsns., Rev. John Travell, 44 Cornwall Rd., Dorchester, DT1 1RY, United Kingdom; Dr. Donald Ward, First Congregational Ch., 560 S. Commonwealth Ave., Los Angeles, CA 90020.
Regional Secretaries: United Kingdom, Rev. D. Gwylfa Evans, 58 Bonnersfield La., Harrow HA1 2LE; North America: Paul Miller, 6407 East Bayley, Wichita, KS 67207; Pacific and Australia: Rev. Jim Chambers, P.O. Box 2047, Raumati Beach, New Zealand; Central and Southern America, Pastor Teodoro Stricker, Primera Junta 286, 3315 Leandro N. Alem, Misiones, Republica Argentina; Africa and Central Europe, Rev. Phaedon Cambouropoulos, 82 Amissou St., New Smyrna, Athens, Greece.

International Council of Christian Churches

Founded in 1948 and consisting of denominations of Bible-believing churches throughout the world, the ICCC promotes worldwide fellowship of evangelical churches and councils, encourages member bodies to foster a loyal and aggressive revival of Bible Christianity, seeks to awaken Christians to the dangers of modernism and to call them to unity of mind and effort against unbelief and compromise with modernism.

GENERAL ORGANIZATION

Headquarters: 756 Haddon Ave., Collingswood, NJ 08108. Tel. (609) 854-8464.
Triennial Plenary Congress, Aug. 8-17, 1990. Vancouver, Canada.

OFFICER

Sec., Suzanne L. DiCanio

ORGANIZATIONS

Commissions: Christian Education; Evangelism; Information and Publication; International Affairs; International Christian Youth; Justice and Freedom; Missions; New Contacts; Radio; Social and Relief

PUBLICATIONS

Getrouw (m, in Dutch)   The Reformation Review (q)

Lambeth Conference of Bishops of the Anglican Communion

The Lambeth Conference consists of all the diocesan bishops and a limited number of other members of the Anglican Communion, and is called together by the personal invitation of the Archbishop of Canterbury.

The first Lambeth Conference was held in 1867 at the request of the bishops in Canada and the United States, and it became a recurring event at approximately ten-year intervals.

The Anglican Communion has no central legislative body but in 1968 the Lambeth Conference agreed to the formation of the Anglican Consultative Council, a body with a permanent office in London. It brings together clergy, lay, and episcopal representatives once every two or three years. This practice of consultation and acknowledged interdependence ensures the validity of the Anglican Communion as a worldwide family of autonomous churches and provinces in communion with the See of Canterbury.

After the Lambeth Conference of 1958, a full-time officer, who became known as the Anglican Executive Officer, was appointed "to collect and disseminate information, keep open lines of communication, and make contact when necessary with responsible authority." The next Lambeth Conference in 1968 proposed the setting up of an Anglican Consultative Council, which, with the consent of all the provinces (or member churches), came into being at the end of 1969. The appointment of Secretary General of the Council replaced that of Anglican Executive Officer. The Lambeth Conference of 1978 proposed regular meetings of the Primates of the Anglican Communion. These have taken place in England in 1979, in America in 1981, in Kenya 1983, in Canada in 1986, and in Cyprus in 1989. The next meeting is scheduled to be held in Ireland in 1991.

Pres., The Archbishop of Canterbury, Most Rev. Robert Runcie, Lambeth Palace, London, SE1 7JU., England.
Sec. Gen., Rev. Cannon Samuel Van Culin, 157 Waterloo Rd., London SE1 8UT England. Tel. (01)620-1110.

Lutheran World Federation

The Lutheran World Federation is the successor to an earlier organization of Lutheran churches named the Lutheran World Convention and organized at Eisenach, Germany, in 1923. World War II inflicted such tremendous damage upon the spiritual and welfare activities of Lutheran and other churches in western Europe and elsewhere in the world that it was felt necessary to establish a more functional organization. Thus, the Lutheran World Federation was organized on July 1, 1947, at Lund, Sweden, and plunged immediately into programs of emergency relief, interchurch aid, and studies. Currently it functions between assemblies through major departments of Communication, Studies, Church Cooperation, and World Service. The 1987 membership consists of 105 member churches from all parts of the world with constituencies approaching 55 million persons.

The LWF is incorporated under Swiss law and has its headquarters in Geneva. Its constitution stipulates that "the Lutheran World Federation shall be a free association of Lutheran Churches. It shall act as their agent in such matters as they assign to it. It shall not exercise churchly functions on its own authority, nor shall it have power to legislate for the Churches belonging to it or to limit the autonomy of any Member Church.

"In accord with the preceding paragraphs, the Lutheran World Federation shall:
(a) Further a united witness before the world to the Gospel of Jesus Christ as the power of God for salvation.
(b) Cultivate unity of faith and confession among the Lutheran Churches of the world.
(c) Develop fellowship and cooperation in study among Lutherans.
(d) Foster Lutheran interest in, concern for, and participation in ecumenical movements.
(e) Support Lutheran Churches and groups as they endeavor to extend the gospel and carry out the church's mission.
(f) Help Lutheran churches and groups, as a sharing community, to serve human need and to promote social and economic justice and human rights."

Headquarters: 150 Route de Ferney, 1211 Geneva 2, Switzerland. Meets every 5-7 years. Last meeting July 22-Aug. 5, 1984, Budapest, Hungary. Next Assembly: Jan. 30-Feb. 8, 1990, Curitiba, Brazil.

OFFICERS

Interim Pres: Rt. Rev.Dr. Johannes Hanselman, Evangelical Lutheran Church in Bavaria, Munich, Federal Republic of Germany.
Vice-Presidents: Rev. Dr. Augusto Ernesto Kunert, Evangelical Church of the Lutheran Confession in Brazil, Porto Alegre, Brazil; Rev. Dr. Soritua Nababan, Protestant Christian Batak Church, Jakarta, Indonesia; Ms. Susannah B. Telewoda, Lutheran Church in Liberia, Monrovia, Liberia; Rev. Dr. David Parus, Evangelical Lutheran Church in America, Chicago, IL.
Treas., Mr. Carl-Gustav Von Ehrenheim, Sweden
Gen. Sec., Rev. Dr. Gunnar Staalsett, Geneva, Switzerland.
Gen. Sec., U.S. National Committee, Rev. Dr. William G. Rusch, Office for Ecumenical Affairs, Evangelical Lutheran Church in America, 8765 W. Higgins Rd., Chicago, IL 60631. Tel. (312)380-2700

PERIODICALS

Lutheran Reports and Documentation.   LWF Information (news service in English, German, French)

Mennonite World Conference

Mennonite World Conference (MWC) began with a small meeting in Basel, Switzerland, in 1925. Today, all the major Mennonite and related church conferences around the world participate in the program of the MWC. These bodies represent approximately 800,000 baptized members. The three-fold purpose of the organization is communication, fellowship, and facilitation. MWC normally sponsors an Assembly (worldwide people's meeting) every six years. Assembly 12 is planned for July 24-29, 1990, in Winnipeg, Manitoba.

OFFICERS

Pres., Ross T. Bender, AMBS, 3003 Benham Ave., Elkhart, IN 45617
Exec. Sec., Paul N. Kraybill, 465 Gundersen Dr., Ste. 200, Carol Stream, IL 60188.
Exec. Sec.-Elect, Larry Miller, 27, rue des Jardiniers, F-67000, Strasbourg, France

Pentecostal World Conference

The Pentecostal World Conference was organized in 1947 at Zurich, Switzerland, where Pentecostal leaders met in conference seeking ways to help bring about greater understanding and cooperation among their churches.
Formed and continuing as a nonlegislative body, the conference provides a forum for exchanging ideas, sharing information, and participating in fellowship together.
The main event of the organization is the triennial worldwide convention. Past conventions have been in Paris, France; London, England; Stockholm, Sweden; Toronto, Canada; Jerusalem, Israel; Helsinki, Finland; Rio de Janeiro, Brazil; Dallas, Texas; Seoul, Korea; London, England; Vancouver, Canada; Nairobi, Kenya; Zurich, Switzerland and Singapore. The 1992 conference will be held in Brazil.
Between conventions the World Conference Advisory Committee supervises the work of the conference and plans the next convention. The 25-member committee is elected at each Pentecostal World Conference convention and has members from around the world.

OFFICERS

Chpsn., Dr. Ray H. Hughes, P.O. Box 2430, Cleveland, TN 37320
Sec., Rev. Jakob Zopfi, Heimstatte SPM, 6376 Emmetten NW, Switzerland

PERIODICAL

World Pentecost, (q), Rev. Jacob Zopfi, Ed.

United Bible Societies

The United Bible Societies is a world fellowship of 78 national Bible Societies and 32 Bible Society national offices which, through its national, regional, and global organization, coordinates the efforts of Bible Societies and their staff in over 180 countries, territories, and colonies.
The UBS was founded in 1946 to facilitate consultation and mutual support between its then 16 member Societies, thus helping them to carry out the translation, production and distribution of the Scriptures with ever-increasing effectiveness. In fulfilling this purpose the UBS has evolved over the years, and is now a single partnership of Societies—some old-established, some very recently formed—responsible corporately through national and regional representation in the operation of a World Service Budget (now totaling some $37 million annually), for planning, policy making, financing, and carrying out the worldwide work.
The UBS has functional subcommittees (on translation, production, personnel, etc.) and a team of technical consultants working in the four Regions of Africa, Americas, Asia/Pacific, and Europe. The UBS organizes training institutes and publishes technical helps for translators; coordinates and advises on the most efficient and economical production of the Scriptures; makes known and stimulates new methods of Scripture distribution, especially by church members, for whom training courses are organized; undergirds work on the New Readers Project, a graded series of Scriptures for the millions who study in the worldwide literacy campaigns and have no reading material at the end of their courses; represents Bible Society interests at world and regional interdenominational conferences and committees; and when necessary coordinates arrangements to provide Scriptures in emergency situations.

Office of the Gen. Sec.: 7th Fl., Reading Bridge House, Reading RG1 8PJ, England
Council meeting at least once every eight years.

Pres., The Rt. Rev. Dr. Edward E. Lohse
Gen. Sec., The Rev. Cinlo Rigos.

PERIODICALS
United Bible Societies Bulletin (semi-a); The Bible Translator (q)—Technical Papers (1 & 3), Practical Papers (2 & 4); The Bible Distributor (tri-a); World Report (m); Nouvelles Bibliques (m); Noticiero Mundial (m); Prayer Booklet

World Alliance of Reformed Churches (Presbyterian and Congregational)

The World Alliance of Reformed Churches (Presbyterian and Congregational) was formed in 1970 at Nairobi, Kenya, with the union of the former World Alliance of Reformed Churches and the former International Congregational Council. Both organizations were composed of member churches whose origins lie mainly in the Reformation with which the names of Calvin and Zwingli are linked.

Member churches constituent to WARC number 169 in more than 76 different countries with a total estimated 70 million people as members.

The constitution provides that *ordinarily* once in five years delegates from member churches will meet in General Council (Assembly). Only this Assembly has the authority to make and administer policies and plans, and to speak as the Alliance. Between Assemblies, the Executive Committee exercises general oversight of the Alliance work; it meets annually. The next General Council will be held in 1989.

The Executive Committee consists of the president, three vice-presidents, department heads, and fifteen members. WARC headquarters are in the ecumenical center in Geneva, Switzerland, and its staff members maintain close contact with departments and agencies of the World Council of Churches and with the executives of other world confessional organizations.

Regional needs and growing membership in all parts of the world have produced area organizations within the Alliance. Two areas are fully organized: the European and the Caribbean and North American; and an informal consultative group is at work in Latin America. The major object of such area organizations is to provide means of cooperation, fellowship, and study in specific regions of the world.

THE ALLIANCE OFFICERS
Pres., Rev. Dr. Allan A. Boesak, 6 Hoex St., Glenhaven, Capetown, Box 182, 7530, Republic of South Africa
Vice Presidents: Dr. Chung Hyun Ro, Korea; Dr. Jane Dempsey Douglass, U.S.A.; Rev. Abival Pieres da Silveira, Brazil
Gen. Sec., Dr. Milan Opocensky, 150 route de Ferney, 1121, Geneva, 2, Switzerland.
North American Actg. Sec., Rev. Margrethe B. J. Brown, 100 Witherspoon St., Louisville, KY 40202
Gen. Treas., Mr. Jean Francois Rochette, 11, Corraterie, 1204 Geneva, Switzerland

CARIBBEAN AND NORTH AMERICAN AREA COUNCIL OFFICERS
Chpsn., Mrs. Sally Mackey, 2127 S.W. 162nd St., Seattle, WA 98166
Vice Chpsn., Rev. Carlos M. Campos, Box 205, Matanzas, Cuba
North American Actg. Sec., Rev. Margrethe B. J. Brown, 100 Witherspoon St. Louisville, KY 40202
Sec., Rev. Robert D. Prossor, 1978 Union Ave., Memphis, TN 38104
Treas., John MacFarlane, 99 Acacia Ave., Ottawa, Ontario KIM 0P8

World Alliance of Young Men's Christian Associations

The World Alliance of YMCAs was constituted at the First World Conference of Young Men's Christian Associations, held in Paris in 1855. Geneva, Switzerland, was designated as its headquarters, and in the early years the work was largely undertaken by lay and honorary officers, using the professional assistance of the staff of some National Movements. In 1878 a permanent office was acquired and the first General Secretary, with related staff, was appointed.

The World Alliance is basically a confederation, its members being the National YMCAs around the world. At present 74 National YMCA Movements maintain membership in the Alliance, and in addition to these, the World Alliance cooperates with YMCAs in 23 other countries where National Movements have not yet been organized. Thus the World Alliance provides the coordination and service functions for National Movements which National Movements in turn provide for the Member Associations in their own countries.

The basis of the World Alliance, popularly known as the Paris Basis, because it was at the 1855 Conference in Paris that it was formulated, is as follows:

"The Young Men's Christian Association seek to unite those young men who, regarding Jesus Christ as their God and Saviour according to the Holy Scriptures, desire to be His disciples in their faith and in their life, and to associate their efforts for the extension of His Kingdom amongst young men.

"Any differences of opinion on other subjects, however important in themselves, shall not interfere with the harmonious relations of the Constituent Members and Associates of the World Alliance."

The World Alliance is governed by a World Council of YMCAs, which is held every three years to decide the future policy of the Alliance, determine its programs and elect an Executive Committee. The World Alliance helps to coordinate intermovement cooperation, particularly to extend the movement into new fields. It represents the YMCA at the United Nations and its agencies, and cooperates with churches and other world Christian bodies.

Headquarters: 37 Quai Wilson, 1201 Geneva, Switzerland. Tel. (022) 732-31-00

OFFICERS
Pres., Alejandro Vassilaqui
Sec. Gen., Lee Soo-Min, 37 Quai Wilson, 1201 Geneva, Switzerland.

World Association for Christian Communication

The World Association for Christian Communication (WACC) is a professional service organization working with churches and other groups in more than 50 countries to use media for the proclamation of the Christian values in their relevance to all of life.

WACC channels nearly $3 million yearly to more than 100 communication projects mainly in developing nations as well as providing professional services for management, planning and coordination. Funds come from churches and development agencies.

WACC also helps communicators improve skills through training, consultations, research and information exchange.

WACC's 240 corporate members include Protestant, Catholic and Orthodox churches and related groups as well as secular organizations. (WACC also has more than 300 personal members.) Members are divided into regional associations: Africa, Asia, Europe, Latin America-Caribbean, Middle East, Pacific and North America.

Headquarters: 357 Kennington Lane, London SE11 5QY, England. Tel. (01) 582-9139

OFFICERS

Pres., Dr. William F. Fore (USA)
Vice Pres., Nancy Mwendameke (Tanzania)
Sec., Dr. Judo Poerwowidagdo (Indonesia)
Treas., Ian McNeil (U.K.)
Chpsns. of Regional Associations, Africa, Rev. Daniel Ako'o (Cameroun); Asia, Judo Poerwowidagdo (Indonesia); Europe, Dr. Hans Wolfgang Hessler (W. Ger.); Latin America-Caribbean, Rev. Hilmar Kannenberg (Brazil); Middle East, Gabriel Habib (Lebanon); Pacific, Seru Verebalavu (Fiji); North America, Rev. Randy Naylor (Canada).

STAFF

Gen. Sec., Rev. Carlos Valle (Argentina)
Dir., Studies & Planning, Mr. Neville D. Jayaweera (Sri Lanka)
Dir. Project Evaluation, Dr. Albert D. Manuel (India)
Dir., Funding, Rev. Don Roper (USA)
Dir., Publications, Dr. Michael Traber (Switzerland)
Dir., Communication Education, Teresita Hermano (Philippines)
Information Coordinator, Editor of *Action,* Ann Shakespeare (U.K.)

PERIODICALS

Media Development (q), Philip Lee, Ed.
Action Newsletter (10/yr.), Ann Shakespeare, Ed.

World Convention of Churches of Christ

The World Convention of Churches of Christ was organized in 1930 in Washington, D.C. It normally meets every four years and is an international confessional grouping including churches and work in 60 countries of the world. It uses the name "Churches of Christ" because it is the name used by many of its churches in various parts of the world. The World Convention is aligned with the Christian Church (Disciples of Christ), Christian Churches/Churches of Christ.

This organization, according to its constitution, "may in no way interfere with the independence of the churches or assume the administrative functions of existing ongoing organizations among us." It exists "in order, more fully to show the essential oneness of the churches in the Lord Jesus Christ; impart inspiration to the world brotherhood; cultivate the spirit of fellowship; provide unity among the churches; and to cooperate with Christians everywhere toward the unity of the Church upon the basis of the New Testament."

Headquarters: First City Bank Center, 100 N. Central Expressway, Ste. 804, Richardson TX 75080
Next Convention: Long Beach, California, August 5-9, 1992.

OFFICERS

Pres., Harold R. Watkins, Indianapolis, Indiana
First Vice-Pres., Mrs. Donald I. Black, Guelph, Ontario
Gen. Sec., Dr. Allan W. Lee, Richardson, Texas, USA.

World Council of Synagogues (Conservative)

The World Council of Synagogues (Conservative) was organized in 1957 as an alliance of Conservative synagogues and synagogue organizations throughout the world. Its purpose is to extend fellowship and mutual aid to each other and to foster the growth and development of Conservative Judaism abroad.

OFFICERS

Pres., Rabbi Zachary I. Heller, 744 Avenue A, Bayonne, NJ 07002. Tel. (201)436-4499
Exec. Dir., Bernard Barsky, 155 Fifth Ave., New York, NY 10010, Tel. (212)533-7693

World Evangelical Fellowship

Founded in 1951 in the Netherlands, the World Evangelical Fellowship traces its roots to the Evangelical Alliance founded in 1846 in Britain. It is an international alliance of autonomous national and regional bodies serving as a resource and catalyst through these bodies to encourage, motivate, and help the local church fulfill its scriptural mandate.

International Headquarters: 141 Middle Rd., #05-05 GSM Bldg., Singapore 0718
European Office: Dreve de Nivelles, 53, B-1150 Bruxelles, Belgium. Tel. 2/771-14-37.
North American Office: P. O. Box WEF, Wheaton, IL 60189. Tel. (708) 668-0440

OFFICERS

Int'l. Dir., Dr. David M. Howard
Executive Council: Chpsn., Dr. Tokunboh Adeyemo, Nigeria; Pres., Dr. Theodore Williams, India; Sec., Rev. Alfred C. H. Yeo, Singapore; Treas., Mr. John E. Langlois, Channel Islands; Rev. David Ho, Jamaica; Dr. Emilio A. Nunez C., Guatemala; Pfarrer Hans-Winrich Scheffbuch, Fed. Rep. of Germany; Rev. Brian C. Stiller, Canada; Rev. Agustin B. Vencer, Jr., Philippines; Dr. Raymond V. J. Windsor, New Zealand.

Association of Evangelicals of Africa and Madagascar
Evangelical Association of the Caribbean
Evangelical Fellowship of Asia
European Evangelical Alliance

PERIODICALS

Evangelical World (m), P. O. Box WEF, Wheaton, IL 60189
Evangelical Review of Theology (q), P.O. Box 1943, Birmingham, AL 35201

WORLD EVANGELICAL FELLOWSHIP MEMBER BODIES

Association of Evangelicals of Angola
Argentine Alliance of Christian Churches
Australian Evangelical Alliance
National Christian Fellowship of Bangladesh
Evangelical Fellowship of Botswana
Federation of Evangelical Churches and Missions in Burkina Faso
Burma Evangelical Christian Fellowship
Evangelical Fellowship of Canada
Association of Central African Evangelical Churches
China Evangelical Fellowship (Taiwan)
Evangelical Alliance of Denmark
Dutch Evangelical Alliance
Fellowship of Evangelicals in Egypt
French Evangelical Alliance
German Evangelical Alliance
National Association of Evangelicals of Ghana
Evangelical Alliance of the United Kingdom
Evangelical Alliance of Guatemala
Evangelical Protestant Church of Guinea
Guyana Evangelical Fellowship
Council of Evangelical Churches of Haiti
Pan-Hellenic Evangelical Alliance
Evangelical Fellowship of India
Indonesia Evangelical Fellowship
United Christian Council in Israel
Italian Evangelical Alliance
Evangelical Federation of the Ivory Coast
Jamaica Association of Evangelicals
Japan Evangelical Association

Evangelical Fellowship of Kenya
Korea Evangelical Fellowship
Liberia Evangelical Fellowship
Evangelical Fellowship of Malawi
National Evangelical Christian Fellowship, Malaysia
Association of Evangelical Protestants of Mali
Evangelical Fellowship of South West Africa/Namibia
Nepal Christian Fellowship
Evangelical Fellowship of New Zealand
Nigeria Evangelical Fellowship
Evangelical Fellowship of Pakistan
Philippine Council of Evangelical Churches
Portugese Evangelical Alliance
Evangelical Fraternity of Senegal
Evangelical Fellowship of Singapore
Evangelical Fellowship, Sierra Leone
Evangelical Fellowship of South Africa
Evangelical Alliance of the South Pacific Islands
Spanish Evangelical Alliance
Evangelical Alliance of Sri Lanka
Swaziland Conference of Churches
Swiss Evangelical Alliance
Evangelical Fellowship of Thailand
Trinidad and Tobago Council of Evangelical Churches
National Association of Evangelicals (U.S.A.)
Evangelical Fellowship of Vietnam
Evangelical Fellowship of Zambia
Evangelical Fellowship of Zimbabwe

World Jewish Congress

The World Jewish Congress was organized in 1936 and, in the United States, in 1939. The WJC seeks to intensify bonds of world Jewry with Israel as a cultural force in Jewish life; to strengthen solidarity among Jews everywhere and secure their rights, status, and interests as individuals and communities; to encourage development of Jewish social, religious and cultural life throughout the world and coordinate efforts by Jewish communities and organizations to cope with any Jewish problems; to work for human rights generally.

Headquarters: 501 Madison Ave., 17th Fl., New York, NY 10022. Tel. (212)755-5770.

OFFICERS

Pres., Edgar M. Bronfman
Chmn., American Sect., Rabbi Wolfe Kelman

Sec.-Gen., Israel Singer
Dir., American Sect., Elan Steinberg

World Methodist Council

The World Methodist Council is an association of 64 different Methodist, or Methodist-related groups at work in 90 countries of the world. According to its constitution, "it does not seek to legislate for them nor to invade their autonomy. Rather it exists to serve them and to give unity to their witness and enterprise."

Although the name World Methodist Council was adopted in 1951 at Oxford, England, the Council dates from 1881, when the first Ecumenical Methodist Conference met in London, England. As the Ecumenical Methodist Conference, this world organization convened at ensuing ten-year intervals with the exception of the 1941 Conference, which because of World War II was not held until 1947. Since 1951, meetings have been held every five years.

The membership of the Council is composed of autonomous churches or such units of international church organizations as have attained a significant degree of autonomy.

The World Methodist Council seeks: to deepen the fellowship of the Methodist peoples over the barriers of race, nationality, color, and language; to foster Methodist participation in the ecumenical movement and to promote the unity of Methodist witness and service in that movement; to advance unity of theological and moral standards in the Methodist churches of the world; to suggest priorities in Methodist activity; to promote the most effective use of Methodist resources in the Christian mission throughout the world; to encourage evangelism in every land; to promote Christian education and the church's care for youth; to uphold and relieve persecuted or needy Christian minorities; to provide a means of consultation and cooperation between world Methodism and the other world communions of the Christian Church; to study union and reunion proposals which affect Methodist member churches and to offer advice and help as needed; to arrange the exchange of ministers, youth and laity through a program of world exchange; to train and equip men and women from the nations of the world as evangelists in their own culture through the Council's new Institute for World Evangelism.

World Methodists number 25,141,663 with the sphere of church influence reaching a community of more than 54 million.

OFFICERS

Chpsn., Exec. Cmte., Bishop Lawi Imathiu, Kenya; Vice-Chpsn., Dr. Donald English, U.K.; Treas., Mr. John R. Harper, U.S.A.; Asst. Treas., Mrs. Edna Alsdurf, U.S.A.
Presidium: Mr. Baltron A. Archer, Bahamas; Mr. Charles Boayue, Liberia; Dr. Phyllis Guthardt, New Zealand; Bishop Isaias Gutierrez, Chile; Bishop Ben R. Oliphant, UM, U.S.A.
Mrs. Sinta Sitorus, Indonesia; Bishop William M. Smith, AMEZ, U.S.A.; Dr. Melitta Tenner, German Democratic Republic; Mrs. Edith W. Ming, WFMW, U.S.A.;
Gen. Sec., Dr. Joe Hale, P.O. Box 518, Lake Junaluska, NC 28745, Tel.(704)456-9432; Geneva Sec., Mr. Ralph C. Young, 150 Route de Ferney, 1211 Geneva 20, Switzerland, Tel. 91-61-11; Asst. Treas. (Hdq. Operation), Mrs. Edna Alsdurf; Hon. Pres., Bishop William R. Cannon; Past Chpsns., Dr. Kenneth G. Greet, Bishop Prince A. Taylor, Jr.; Gen. Sec. Emeritus, Dr. Lee F. Tuttle.

World Student Christian Federation

The World Student Christian Association was founded in 1895 by a group of Student Christian Movement leaders, John R. Mott prominent among them.

WSCF now has movements in more than 90 countries with constituency at all levels of education: secondary schools, university and graduate institutions and the wider academic community. For many years, WSCF published the quarterly *Student World*, which has been replaced by regional publications, the *WSCF Journal*, and the quarterly *Federation News*. Information and subscriptions can be obtained by contacting the WSCF interregional office in Geneva, Switzerland.

At the General Assembly in Helsinki, Finland, in 1968, a decision was made to regionalize the WSCF. Now, six regional, continental offices serve to coordinate regional and interregional programs which seek to promote Christian community and a just world.

At the General Assembly, in San Francisco, California in August 1981, the WSCF adopted four major foci for the next quadrennium: education, human rights and solidarity, theology and ecumenism, and women. These program areas are a further development of WSCF's previous commitment to provide Christian witness in the struggle for liberation. Further development of these four program areas occurred at the XXIX WSCF General Assembly in Mexico City, March 1986, under the theme "That They May Have Life in All Its Fullness: Our Commitment to Peace with Justice." Continued and vigorous commitment to theological reflection and involvement in the church universal undergirds the programs. The next General Assembly is planned for 1990.

Interregional Office: 5, Route des Morillons, 1218 Grand-Saconnex, Switzerland. Tel. (022) 798 89 53

OFFICERS

Co-Gen. Secs., Manuel Quintero, Christine Ledger
Chpsn., Bishop Poulose mar Poulose

World Union for Progressive Judaism

The World Union for Progressive Judaism was established in London, England, in 1926, by representatives of Liberal, Progressive, and Reform congregational associations and individual synagogues from six nations. The movement has grown, and today the World Union stimulates the development of a worldwide movement and its congregations in 25 countries. The membership of these congregations totals approximately 1.1 million Jewish men, women, and children.

The World Union operates a secondary school in Haifa, Israel, and a college for training rabbis in London. It extends organizational and financial assistance to new congregations in many countries, assigns and employs rabbis wherever Jews are in search of their religious heritage, operates religious and social youth programs in Israel and Europe, publishes prayer books and other texts in many languages, holds biennial conferences for Jewish leaders and scholars from all corners of the world.

Offices: 838 5th Ave., New York, NY 10021. Tel. (212)249-0100; 13 King David St., Jerusalem, Israel. Tel. 02-234-748

OFFICERS

Pres., Mr. Donald Day
Exec. Dir., Rabbi Richard G. Hirsch.
North American Dir., Mr. Martin Strelzer
Dir., Int'l. Aff. & Devel., Rabbi Clifford Kulwin

World Young Women's Christian Association

The World YWCA was founded in 1894 by four of the existing National YWCAs: the Associations of Great Britain, Norway, Sweden, and the United States. During the first years of its history the world movement, reflecting the patterns of its national affiliates, was primarily made up of members of various Protestant denominations. However, as the work spread around the world, Roman Catholic and Orthodox Christians joined the Association and the World YWCA became consciously ecumenical. Today it includes large numbers of women from all confessions and serves women and girls of many faiths. The latest World YWCA constitution was adopted in 1955 and expressed the functions of the World Association as follows:

"The World YWCA provides a channel for the sharing of resources and the exchange of experience among its affiliated associations.

It helps its affiliated associations with the development of their leadership and programme.

It surveys new fields and promotes work to meet the needs therein.

It acts in cooperation with world voluntary movements and with intergovernmental organizations in matters of common concern.

It works for international understanding for improved social and economic conditions and for basic human rights for all people.

In times of emergency it undertakes and sponsors international humanitarian, welfare, and relief work, in accordance with Christian principles, irrespective of religious, social, political, national or racial differences."

The YWCA is now at work in 88 countries with programs including a variety of development projects with emphasis on self-reliance and appropriate technology, educational activities, vocational training programs for women and girls, hostels, rural projects, and programs of study and action in relation to social and economic issues. A wide network of sharing of financial resources and personnel between Associations and of financial aid from other sources forms the World YWCA program of development aid. The World YWCA also carries on refugee services in cooperation with other international agencies bodies and with its own member associations.

The World YWCA has a legislative Council which brings together representatives of its national affiliates every four years and an Executive Committee made up of twenty members from all parts of the world which meets annually. An international staff works at the headquarters in Geneva.

Headquarters: 37 Quai Wilson, 1201 Geneva, Switzerland. Tel. (022) 732-31-00.

OFFICERS

Pres., Jewel Graham
Gen. Sec., Elaine Hesse Steel

World's Christian Endeavor Union

Christian Endeavor is a movement composed of committed followers of Jesus Christ, organized in groups usually called societies, for the purpose of: leading young people (also children and adults) to accept Jesus Christ as Saviour and Lord; bringing them into the life of the church; sustaining and training them for the service of Christ and his cause; releasing them through all channels of human activity in the service of God and man.

Christian Endeavor societies are generally sponsored by a local church, which determines theology, program, activities, and relationships. In most countries it is a graded program including organizational pattern and materials for various age groups.

The first society was organized February 2, 1881, in Portland, Maine. The idea spread rapidly, and by 1895 Christian Endeavor had become a worldwide movement and the World's Christian Endeavor Union was organized in Boston, Mass. As the movement spread to other lands, many national unions were formed. Presently, Christian Endeavor operates in 78 nations and islands and is used by 93 different Christian groups; there are approximately 2 million members worldwide. World conventions are held quadrennially and conferences in the intervening years. The union is incorporated and is governed by a Council which meets every four years, a Board of Trustees which meets annually, and an Executive Committee which meets on call. There are no full-time paid employees. Most of the work is carried on by volunteer service.

Headquarters: 1221 E. Broad St., P.O. Box 1110. Columbus, OH 43216. Tel. (614) 258-9545
Next convention: 1990, Warwick Univ., Coventry, England, July 31-Aug. 4

OFFICERS

Pres., Rev. Konrad Brandt
Treas., Mrs. Phyllis Meadows
Gen. Sec., Rev. David G. Jackson

6. NATIONAL CHRISTIAN COUNCILS AND REGIONAL AND INTER-REGIONAL CONFERENCES

The following directory material is taken from the *Directory of Christian Councils, Fourth Edition, 1985*, published by the World Council of Churches, 150 route de Ferney, 1211 Geneva 2, Switzerland. Supplementary material supplied by the WCC was also used. This directory is produced in this abridged form by permission of the World Council of Churches. Listings below follow a geographical arrangement and within geographical area alphabetically by country. Each listing gives the name and address of the Christian Council or Interregional Conference, telephone number, cable and/or Telex, name of chief executive officer, President or other responsible person.

NATIONAL CHRISTIAN COUNCILS

AFRICA

Angola—Conselho Angolano de Igrejas Evangelicas (Angolan Council of Evangelical Churches), Caixa Postal 1659, Rua Amilcar Cabral No. 182, 1 andar 11, Luanda, People's Republic of Angola. Cable: CAIE, Luanda. Gen. Sec., Rev. Augusto Chipesse.

Botswana—Botswana Christian Council, P. O. Box 355, Gaborone, Botswana. Tel 51981, Cable: KOPANYO. Acting Gen. Sec., Churchill Grape.

Burundi—Conseil National des Eglises du Burundi (National Council of Churches of Burundi), B.P. 17, Bujumbura, Burundi. Tel.: 24216. Gen. Sec., Rev. Jean-Claude Kabeera.

Cameroun—Fédération des Eglises et Missions Evangéliques du Cameroun (Federation of Protestant Churches and Missions in Cameroun), B.P. 491, Yaoundé, Cameroun. Tel.: 22 30 78, Cable: FEMEC B.P. 491 Yaoundé. Gen. Sec., Rev. Grégoire Ambadiang.

The Gambia—Christian Council of The Gambia, P. O. Box 27, Banjul, The Gambia, West Africa. Gen. Sec., J. Tunde Taylor-Thomas.

Ghana—Christian Council of Ghana, P. O. Box 919, Accra, Ghana. Tel.: 76678/76725; Cable: CHRIST-CON. Gen. Sec., Rev. David A. Dartey.

Kenya—National Council of Churches of Kenya, P. O. Box 45009, Nairobi, Kenya, East Africa. Tel.: 338211/336763, Cable: OIKOUMENE. Gen. Sec., Rev. Samuel Kobia.

Lesotho—Christian Council of Lesotho, P. O. Box 547, 100 Maseru, Lesotho. Tel.: 323639, Cable: CHRIST-COL Maseru. Gen. Sec., Fr. Ramolulela Michael Taole.

Liberia—Liberian Council of Churches, 182 Tubman Blvd., P.O. Box 2191, Monrovia, Liberia. Tel. 262820. Gen. Sec., Mrs. Imogene M. Collins.

Madagascar—Fiombonan'ny Fiangonana Protestanta eto Madagascar, Fédération des Eglises Protestantes à Madagascar (Federation of the Protestant Churches in Madagascar), Vohipiraisana Ambohijatovo-Sud, 101-Antananarivo, Madagascar. Tel.: 201.44. Gen. Sec., Pasteur Charles Rakotoson. Fiombonan'ny Fiangonana Kristiana eto Madagasikara (Christian Council of Churches in Madagascar), B.P. 798, 101-Antananarivo, Madagascar. Tel. 290.52. Exec. Sec., Rev. Lala Andriamiharisoa.

Malawi—Christian Council of Malawi, P. O. Box 30068, Capital City, Lilongwe 3, Malawi, Tel.: 730499, Cable: EKLESIAS. Gen. Sec., _____

Mozambique—Christian Council of Mozambique, Av. Afonso de Albuquerque No. 1822, P. O. Box 108, Maputo, Mozambique. Tel.: 25103-3,22836, Cable: COCRIMO, Maputo, Telex: 6-199 cocri mo. Maputo. Gen. Sec., Rev. Filipe Sique Banze.

Namibia—Council of Churches of Namibia, P. O. Box 41, Windhoek 9000, Namibia. Tel. 37510/36511/37512/32976, Telex: 56834 wk. Gen. Sec., Dr. Abisai Shejavali.

Nigeria—Christian Council of Nigeria, 139 Ogunlana Dr., Surulere, P. O. Box 2838, Marina, Lagos, Nigeria. Tel. Lagos 836019, Cable: CHURCHCON, Lagos. Gen. Sec., Mr. C. O. Williams.

Rwanda—Conseil Protestant du Rwanda (Protestant Council of Rwanda) B.P. 79, Kigali, Rwanda. Tel.: 5825. Gen. Sec., Mr. Jean Utumabahutu.

Sierra Leone—The United Christian Council of Sierra Leone, 4 A Kingharman Rd., Brookfields, P. O. Box 404, Freetown, Sierra Leone. Tel.: 40568, Cable: UNCED, Freetown. Gen. Sec., Rev. Dr. Eustace L. Renner.

South Africa—South African Council of Churches, P. O. Box 4921, Johannesburg, 2000, South Africa. Tel.: (011) 28 22 51/8, Cable: Ecunews, Johannesburg, Telex: 4-86519 sa. Gen Sec., Rev. Frank Chikane.

Sudan—Sudan Council of Churches, P. O. Box 469 Khartoum, Sudan. Tel.: 42859/42855/41137, Cable: SUDCHURCH, Khartoum, Telex: 24099 scc, sd. Khartoum. Gen. Sec., Rev. Ezekiel Kutjok.

Swaziland—Council of Swaziland Churches, P. O. Box 1095, Manzini, Swaziland. Gen. Sec., Mrs. Eunice Nokuthula Sowazi.

Tanzania—Christian Council of Tanzania, P.O. Box 372, Dodoma, Tanzania. Tel:20445, Cable: UNITAS. Sec., Rev. Canon Stanford A. Shauri.

Zambia—Christian Council of Zambia, P. O. Box 30315, Lusaka, Zambia. Tel.: 214308/219379/219380, Telex: 45160 christ 2a. Gen. Sec., Rev. E. K. Lumbama.

Zimbabwe—Zimbabwe Christian Council, 128 Victoria St., P.O. Box 3566, Harare, Zimbabwe. Tel.: 791208; Cable: OIKOUMENE; Telex: 4752 C CARE ZW. Gen. Sec., Rev. M. C. Kuchera.

ASIA

Bangladesh—Jatiya Church Parishad, Bangladesh (National Council of Churches, Bangladesh), 395 New Eskaton Rd., P. O. Box 220, Moghbazar, Dhaka-2, Bangladesh. Tel.: 402869, Cable: CHURCHSERV Dhaka. Gen Sec., Mr. Subodh Adhikary.

Burma—(see: Union of Myanmar)

China—China Christian Council, 169 Yuen Ming Yuan Rd., Shanghai, China. Tel: 213396 and 13 Da Jian Yin Xiang, Nanjing, China. Tel: 41439/49053; Cable: 4377

Nanjing; Telex: 34136 glynj cn ccc. Assoc. Gen. Sec., (contact) Mr. Han Wenzao (Nanjing address).

Hong Kong—Hong Kong Christian Council, 33 Granville Rd., Tsim Sha Tsui, Kowloon, Hong Kong. Tel.: 3-670071. Gen. Sec., Dr. Heyward Wong.

India—National Council of Churches in India, Christian Council Lodge, Civil Lines, Nagpur 440 001, India. Tel.: 31312, Cable: AIKYA. Gen. Sec., Mr. Mathai Zachariah.

Indonesia—Communion of Churches in Indonesia, Jalan Salemba Raya 10, Jakarta 10430, Indonesia. Tel.: 884321, Cable.: OIKOUMENE Jakarta. Gen. Sec., Rev. Dr. Fridolin Ukur.

Japan—National Christian Council of Japan, Japan Christian Center, 2-3-18-24 Nishiwaseda, Shinjuku-ku, Tokyo, Japan 160. Tel. (03) 203-0372 to 4, Cable: JAPACONCIL Tokyo; Telex: 27890 ccrai-j. Gen. Sec., Rev. Maejima Munetoshi.

Korea—National Council of Churches in Korea, Rm. 706 Christian Building, 136-46 Yunchi Dong, Chrongro-Ku, Seoul 110, Korea. Tel.: 763-8427, 763-7323, Cable: KOCOUNCIL, Telex: Korencc K 26840. Gen. Sec., Rev. Kwon Ho Kyung.

Malaysia—Majlis Gereja-Gereja Malaysia (Council of Churches of Malaysia), 26 Jalan University, Petaling Jaya, Selangor, Malaysia. Tel.: 03.567092, Cable: ECUMENICAL PETALING JAYA. Hon. Gen. Sec., Mr. Varghese George.

Pakistan—National Council of Churches in Pakistan, P. O. Box 357, 32-B Shar-e-Fatima Jinna, Lahore-4, Pakistan. Tel.: 57307, Cable: ECUMENICAL, Lahore. Exec. Sec., Mr. Yousaf Saroia.

Philippines—National Council of Churches in the Philippines (Sangguniang Pambansa ng mga Simbahan sa Pilipinas) 879 Epifanio de los Santos Ave., Quezon City (P. O. Box 1767, Manila D-406), Republic of the Philippines. Tel.: 99-86-73, Cable: OIKOUMENE, Manila. Gen. Sec., Dr. Feliciano Carino.

Singapore—National Council of Churches, Singapore, Paza Lebar, P. O. Box 80, Singapore 9154. Tel.: 7322631. Hon. Gen. Sec., Rev. V. E. Thomas.

Sri Lanka—National Christian Council of Sri Lanka, 490/2 Havelock Rd., Colombo 6, Sri Lanka. Tel. 587285. Gen. Sec., Mr. Shirley J. S. Peiris.

Union of Myanmar—Burma Council of Churches, 263 Maha Bandoola St., GPO Box 1400, Yangon, Union of Myanmar. Tel.: 73290, Cable: OIKOUMENE, Yangon. Gen. Sec., U Win Tin; Yangon, Pres., Rev. Canon A. Mya Han.

AUSTRALASIA

Australia—Australian Council of Churches, 379 Kent St., Sydney, N.S.W. 2000, P. O. Box C 199 Clarence St., Sydney, N.S.W.2000. Tel.: (02) 29.2215, Cable: ECUMENICAL, Sydney, Telex: aa 171715 Sydacc, Sydney. Fax: (02)262-4514 Gen. Sec., Rev. David Gill.

New Zealand—Conference of Churches in Aotearoa New Zealand, Box 27-264, Wellington, New Zealand, 175 Victoria St., Wellington, New Zealand. Tel. (04)858-438; Fax: 64-4 828-496. Exec. Sec., Coordinator: Mrs. Jocelyn A. Armstrong. **Te Runanga Whakawhanaunga I Nga Haahi O Aotearoa** (Maori Council of Churches), P.O. Box 9573, Newmarket, Auckland, New Zealand. Gen. Sec., Rev. Rua Rakena.

CARIBBEAN, CENTRAL AMERICA & MEXICO

Antigua—Antigua Christian Council, P. O. Box 863, St. John's, Antigua, West Indies. Tel.: 20261. Exec. Sec., Rev. Lloyd Kitson.

Bahamas—The Bahamas Christian Council, P. O. Box SS-5863, The Shirley Street Post Office, Nassau, Bahamas. Tel. 32153/31441 Sec., Rev. Charles A. Sweeting.

Belize—Belize Christian Council, P. O. Box 508, 149 Allenby St., Belize City, Belize, C.A. Tel.: 02-7077. Exec. Sec., Ms. J. A. Jeffries.

Cuba—Consejo Ecuménico de Cuba (Ecumenical Council of Cuba), Calle 6, No. 273, entre 12 y 13, Vedado, La Habana 4, Cuba. Tel.: 3-7404, Cable: IGLEPICUBA. Gen. Sec., Rev. Raul Suarez Ramos.

Curaçao—Curaçao Council of Churches, Fortkerk, Fort Amsterdam, Curaçao, Netherlands Antilles. Tel. 611139. Exec. Sec. Rev. E. G. Stockmann

Jamaica—The Jamaica Council of Churches, 14 South Avenue, P. O. Box 30, Kingston 10, Jamaica, West Indies. Tel.: 092-60974; Cable: CILCHURCH. Gen. Sec., Mrs. Rubye Gayle.

Mexico—Federacion Evangélica de Mexico (Evangelical Federation of Mexico) Apartado 1830, Motolinia No. 8-107, Mexico 06001, D.F., Mexico. Tel.: 585-0594. Exec. Sec., Rev. Israel Ortiz Murrieta.

Puerto Rico—(See under Directory 7, "United States Regional and Local Ecumenical Agencies" in this **Yearbook.**)

St. Vincent—St. Vincent Christian Council, P. O. Box 445, Kingstown, St. Vincent, W.I. Tel.: 71809. Exec. Sec., Mr. Liley Cato.

Trinidad & Tobago—Christian Council of Trinidad & Tobago, Hayes Court, Hayes St., Port-of-Spain, Trinidad and Tobago. Tel. 809-622-2863. Exec. Sec., Mrs. Grace Steele.

EUROPE

Austria—Oekumenischer Rat der Kirchen in Österreich (Ecumenical Council of Churches in Austria), Lannerstr. 30, 1191 Vienna, Austria. Tel. 52 83 93. Mod., Rev. Dr. Ernst Kreuzeder.

Czechoslovakia— Czechoslovak Ecumenical Council of Churches, 18600 Prague 8—Karlin, Vitkova 13. Tel. 227581. Sec., Rev. Prof. Anezka Ebertova.

Denmark—Ecumenical Council of Denmark, Norregade 11, DK-1165 Copenhagen K. Tel.: 01-15 59 27. Sec., Mr. Peter Lodberg.

Federal Republic of Germany—Arbeitsgemeinschaft christlicher Kirchen in der Bundesrepublik Deutschland und Berlin (West) e. V. (Council of Christian Churches in the Federal Republic of Germany and West Berlin), Neue Schlesingergasse 22-24 Postfach 1017 62, 6000 Frankfurt/Main #1, FRG. Tel.: (069)7159.237. Gen. Sec., Dr. Athanasios Basdekis.

Finland—Ecumenical Council of Finland, Luotsikatu la, PL 185, SF-00161 Helsinki 16, Finland. Tel.: 3580-18021; Telex: infic 122357. Gen. Sec., Rev. Jaakko Rusama.

France—Fédération Protestante de France (French Protestant Federation), 47 rue de Clichy, Paris F-75009, France. Tel.: 1/4874. Telex: 642 380 f paribip., Gen. Sec., Rev. Louis Schweitzer

German Democratic Republic—Arbeitsgemeinschaft christlicher Kirchen in der Deutschen Demokratischen Republik (Council of Churches in the German Democratic Republic), Auguststrasse 80, 104 Berlin, GDR. Tel.: Berlin (GDR) 28660. Gen. Sec., Rev. Martin Lange.

Hungary—Ecumenical Council of Churches in Hungary, Szabadsag tér 2, H-1054 Budapest V, Hungary. Tel.: (36-1) 114-862, Cable: OIKOUMENE Budapest. Gen. Sec., Rev. Laszlo Lehel.

Ireland—The Irish Council of Churches, Inter-Church Centre, 48 Elmwood Ave., Belfast, BT9 6AZ, Northern Ireland. Tel.: Belfast 663145. Gen. Sec., Rt. Hon. David W. Bleakley.

175

Italy—Federazione delle Chiese Evangeliche in Italia (Federation of Protestant Churches in Italy), via Firenze 38, 00184 Rome, Italy. Tel.: 47 55 120. Pres., Rev. Aurelio Sbaffi

Netherlands, Raad van Kerken in Nederland (Council of Churches in The Netherlands), Kon. Wilhelminalaan 5, 3818 HN Amersfoort, The Netherlands. Tel. (3133) 633844, Gen. Sec., Rev. W. R. van der Zee.

Poland—Polska Rada Ekumeniczna (Polish Ecumenical Council), ul. Willowa 1, 00-790 Warszawa Poland. Tel.: 49 96 79/49 73 43, Cable: OIKUMENE Warsaw, Telex: 817 875 pec pl, Warszawa. Gen. Sec., Rev. Zdzislaw Pawlik.

Portugal—Conselho Portugués de Igrejas Christas (Portuguese Council of Christian Churches), Rua de Lapa 9, Sala I, 3080 Figueira da Foz, Portugal. Tel. 033-28279. Gen. Sec., Rev. Manuel Pedro Cardoso.

Sweden—Swedish Ecumenical Council, Stortorget 3, 11129 Stockholm, Sweden. Tel.: 08/10.12.35. Sec., Rev. Rune Forsbeck

United Kingdom—British Council of Churches, Inter-Church House, 35/41, Lower Marsh, Waterloo, London SE1 7RL, Tel.: 01-620-4444, Cable: KOINONIA London SWI, Telex: 916504 CHRAID G. Gen. Sec., Rev. Dr. Philip Morgan. Isle of Man Council of Churches—Sec., Rev. Douglas V. Brown, The Homestead, Bay View Rd., Port Erin, Isle of Man, U.K. Scottish Churches' Council—Scottish Churches' House, Dunblane, Perthshire, FK15 OAJ, Scotland, UK. Tel. Dunblane 823588. Gen. Sec., Rev. Canon Kenyon E. Wright. Cyngor Eglwysi Cymru (Council of Churches for Wales)—First Floor, 21 St. Helen's Rd., Swansea, West Glamorgan SA1 4AP, Wales, UK. Tel. (0792)460876. Gen. Sec., Rev. Noel A. Davies.

Yugoslavia—Ecumenical Council of Churches in Yugoslavia, Secretariat, Fah 182, 1101 Belgrade, Yugoslavia. Gen. Sec., Deacon Radomir Rakic.

MIDDLE EAST

Israel—International Christian Committee in Israel, P.O.B. 304, Nazareth 16102, Israel; Chpsn., Dr. Sami Geraisy, United Christian Council in Israel; Gen. Sec.: Mr. Charles Kopp, Box 546, Jerusalem 91004.

Jerusalem—International Christian Committee and Jerusalem Inter-Church Aid Committee, Sec., Mr. Elias Khouri, P. O. Box 19195, Jerusalem.

NORTH AMERICA

Canada—(See Canadian Council of Churches in Directory 2—"Canadian Cooperative Organizations, National" in this Yearbook for complete details.)

United States—(See National Council of the Churches of Christ in the U.S.A. in Directory 1—"United States Cooperative Organizations, National" in this Yearbook for complete details.)

PACIFIC

American Samoa—American Samoa Council of Christian Churches, c/o CCCAS Offices, P.O. Box 1537, Pago Pago, American Samoa 96799. Gen. Sec., Rev. Enoka L. Alesana

Cook Islands—Religious Advisory Council of the Cook Islands, P.O. Box 93, Takamoa Rarotonga, Cook Islands. Tel. 22851. Gen. Sec., Bishop Robin Leamy.

Fiji—Fiji Council of Churches, Actg. Gen. Sec., Mrs. Davila Walker, P.O. Box 2300, Government Buildings, Suva.

Papua New Guinea—Melanesian Council of Churches, P. O. Box 1015, Boroko, Port Moresby, Papua New Guinea. Tel.; 256410; Cable: Melcon Boroko; Telex: c/o 22213 Wantok. Gen. Sec., Rev. Leva Kila Pat.

Samoa—Samoa Council of Churches, P.O. Box 574, Apia, Western Samoa. Sec., Rev. Oka Fau'olo.

Solomon Islands—Solomon Islands Christian Association, P.O. Box 556, Honiara, Solomon Islands. Tel. 22898; Cable: SICA Honiara. Actg. Sec., Mr. P. Bochaligana.

Tonga—Tonga National Council of Churches, P.O. Box 1205, Nuku'alofa, Tonga. Tel. 21177; Cable: UNICIL Nuku'alofa; Telex: 66237 lipons ts. Exec. Sec., Mr. Laitia Fifita.

Vanuatu—Vanuatu Christian Council, P.O. Box 379, Port Vila, Vanuatu. Tel.: 2161. Sec., Rev. Allen Nafuki.

SOUTH AMERICA

Argentina—Federacion Argentina de Iglesias Evangélicas (Argentine Federation of Evangelical Churches) José Maria Moreno 873, 1424 Buenos Aires, Argentina. Tel.: 922-5356. Pres., Rev. Juan van der Velde.

Brazil—The National Council of Christian Churches in Brazil, C.P. 2876, 90.000 Porto Alegre, R.S., Brazil. Sec., Rev. Godofredo G. Boll. Tel. (0512) 24.50.10-1, Cable: ECLESIA; Telex: 512332

Guyana—The Guyana Council of Churches, 71 Murray St., Georgetown, Guyana. Tel. 66610. Sec., Mr. Michael McCormack

Uruguay—Federacion de Iglesias Evangélicas del Uruguay (Federation of Evangelical Churches of Uruguay), Av. 8 de Octubre 3324, Montevideo, Uruguay. Tel.: 81.33.16; Cable: OIKOUMENE, Montevideo. Exec. Sec., Mr. Lothar J. Driedger.

REGIONAL AND INTER-REGIONAL CONFERENCES

Africa—All Africa Conference of Churches (Conférence des Eglises de Toute l'Afrique), Waiyaki Way, P. O. Box 14205, Westlands, Nairobi, Kenya. Tel.: 62601/62602/62603, Cable: CHURCHCON, Nairobi, Telex: 22175 AACC Nairobi. Gen. Sec., Rev. José Chipenda

Asia—Christian Conference of Asia, Korean Christian Center, 2-6-10 Nakagama Nishi, Ikumo-ku, Osaka 544, Japan. Tel. (06) 712-2719; Telex: 65433 CCAJ. Gen. Sec., Rev. Park Sang Jung.

Caribbean—Caribbean Conference of Churches, P. O. Box 616, Bridgetown, Barbados. Tel.: (809) 42-72681, Cable: CHRISTOS, Telex: 2335 CADEC WB. Gen. Sec., Rev. Allan F. Kirton.

Europe—Conference of European Churches, P. O. Box 2100, 150 route de Ferney, 1211 Geneva 2, Switzerland. Tel.: 791 61 11, Cable: OIKOUMENE Geneva, Telex: 415 730 OIK CH; Fax: (022)791-03-61. Gen. Sec., Mr. Jean Fischer.

Latin America—Consejo Latinoamericano de Iglesias (CLAI), Latin American Council of Churches, Casilla, 85-22, Quito, Ecuador, South America. Tel.: 238.220; Telex: clai 2316 ietel ed. Gen. Sec., Rev. Felipe Adolf.

Middle East—The Middle East Council of Churches, Mail to: c/o P.O. Box 4259, Limassol, Cyprus. Tel.: (51) 26 022, Telex: 5378 oik cy; Telex West Beirut Office: 22662 oik le; East Beirut Office: 22054 telesco le for mecc. Gen. Sec., Mr. Gabriel Gergi Habib.

Pacific—Pacific Conference of Churches, P. O. Box 208, 4 Thurston St., Suva, Fiji, South Pacific. Tel.: 302-332, Cable: PACFICONS, Suva. Gen. Sec., Mr. S. K. Motu'ahala.

7. UNITED STATES REGIONAL AND LOCAL ECUMENICAL AGENCIES

One of the many ways Christians and Christian churches relate to one another locally and regionally is through ecumenical agencies. The membership in these ecumenical organizations is diverse. Historically, councils of churches were formed primarily by Protestants, but many local and regional organizations now include Orthodox and Roman Catholics. Many are made up of congregations or judicatory units of churches. Some have a membership-base of individuals. Others foster cooperation between ministerial groups, community ministries, coalitions, or church agencies. While Councils of Churches is a term still commonly used to describe this form of cooperation, other terms such as "conference of churches," "ecumenical councils," "churches united," "metropolitan ministries," are coming into use.

An increasing number of ecumenical agencies have been exploring ways to strengthen the interreligious aspect of life in the context of religious pluralism in the U.S. today. Some organizations in this listing are interfaith agencies primarily through the inclusion of Jewish congregations in their membership. Other organizations are considering ways to nurture partnership with a broader base of religious groups in their communities, especially in the areas of public policy and interreligious dialogue.

The interactive network embodied in these pages demonstrates the essential interrelatedness of the one ecumenical movement in its local and global dimensions, lifts up programs of study and action, and calls attention to the witness and experience of local and regional ecumenical and interreligious organizations.

This list does not include all local and regional ecumenical and interfaith instrumentalities in existence today. No such compilation currently exists. However, the Commission on Regional and Local Ecumenism of the National Council of Churches of Christ in the U.S.A. (CORLE) and the National Association of Ecumenical Staff (NAES), are cooperating on the compilation of such data.

The terms *regional* and *local* are sometimes relative, making identification somewhat ambiguous. Regional councils may cover sections of large states or cross state borders. Local councils may be made up of several counties, towns, or clusters of congregations. State councils or state-level ecumenical contacts exits in 45 of the 50 states. One of these, at the state level, is an interfaith council—the Arkansas Council of Churches and Synagogues.

In this listing, the organizations that work primarily across state borders are listed under the "regional" heading. Others are grouped by state and listed alphabetically, with state-wide ecumenical agencies listed first; then follow metropolitan, city, or area agencies with paid staff, listed alphabetically by name of agency, using significant geographical words in the title. For councils or agencies with paid staff, the name, address, and telephone number of the agency are given, and the names of professional staff are listed, as well as officers and major activities as reported by the agency. When the name of the city is omitted from an address, the city is the same as that of the headquarters of the organization.

For additional information about community ministries, ecumenical agencies with voluntary leadership, covenant congregations, or new developments within a specific area, consult the state or local councils.

For information concerning this listing or to report changes in staff, officers, mailing addresses, and program emphases for the agencies listed here, contact: Commission on Regional and Local Ecumenism, National Council of the Churches of Christ in the USA, 475 Riverside Dr., Rm. 870, New York, NY 10115. Tel. (212)870-2158.

Information concerning NAES, a professional association for persons engaged in ecumenical service—local, state, regional, national—may be obtained through CORLE at the address and phone listed above.

Listing includes information available through January 1990.

†Indicates information repeated from a previous Yearbook, since no more recent report has been received.

REGIONAL

Appalachian Ministries Educational Resource Center (AMERC)

Berea College , CPO Box 2341, Berea KY 40404
Tel (606)986-8789
Exec. Dir.: Rev. Dr.Mary Lee Daughtery
  (Aug.-May: 730 Amity Dr., Charleston, W.Va. 25302)
Chair, AMERC Bd.: Dr. Vincent Cushing, O.F.M.
Dir. Media Relations: Nina M. George. Tel. (212)316-3782
Endowment Campaign Dir.: Neil Eskelin
Field Placement Dir.: Helen Harms
AMERC Staff Associate: Dr. Judy Matheney
Summer Sec'y.: Dorothy Freeman

An ecumenical program providing critically needed specialized education and training for seminarians preparing to minister in small-town and rural churches in Appalachia. Classroom and on-site learning through January Travel Seminar and intensive Appalachian Summer Term. Largest consortium of interdenominational theological schools in the U.S., co-sponsored by The Commission on Religion in Appalachia and Berea College, associated with 9 major Christian denominations. Scholarships available.

The Commission on Religion in Appalachia, Inc.

864 Weisgarber Rd., NW, P.O. Box 19867, Knoxville, TN 37939
Tel. (615) 584-6133
Coordinator, Jim Sessions
Adm. Sec., Lee Mynatt
Resource Coord., Jim Rugh,
Financial Sec., Pearl Jones
Chpsn., Suzanne Tumblin, 4202 Barbara Dr., 37918
Appalachian Development Projects Cmte., Coord., Gaye Evans; Asst. Coord., Linda Selfridge; Co-Chpsns., Maureen Sullivan and Teri Vautrin
Coop. Congregational Devel. Prog. Unit, Coord., Tena Willemsma, Chpsn, Gladys Campbell
Coord., Volunteer Prog. Unit, John MacLean; Chapsn., Adv. Cmte., Helen Harms
Coord., Northern Prog. Cmte., Joyce Dukes, Chpsn., Charles Lady
Coord., Communications, Jamie Harris
Coord., Cmty Based Econ. Dev., J. William Troy
  A 13-state regional ecumenical agency composed of 18 communions and 10 state councils of churches.

IMPACT

100 Maryland Ave., NE, Washington, DC 20002
Tel. (202) 544-8636

National Director, Gretchen Eick
Publications Ed., Richard Houston
Producer of "Making an IMPACT" TV show, Kent Ward
Field Organizer, Tina Clarke
Finance and Administration, Barbara Edmundson
An interreligious legislative information and action coalition of 24 national religious organizations. Congregations and individuals join issue networks choosing from peace, economic justice, civil rights, immigration, the environment, and issues effecting women and families. Publications written by national staff of religious groups alert members to votes in Congress and provide background data and voting records. Monthly TV show features religious staff discussing these issues and why and how congregations are involved in them. Field organizing program in 30 congressional districts. Organizes annual 4-day legislative briefing on Capitol Hill. 24 state IMPACT affiliates work on state legislation.

National Farm Worker Ministry

1337 W. Ohio, Chicago, IL 60622
Tel. (312)266-3334
Exec. Dir., Sr. Patricia Drydyk
Assoc. Dir., Dr. Jon Lacy, Midwest Office, P. O. Box 4897, East Lansing, MI 48226. Tel. (517)332-0861
Continuing the National Migrant Ministry. Related to the National Council of the Churches of Christ in the U.S.A.
Major Activities: Ministry Among Pesticide Victims; Pesticide Seminars; UFW Table Grape Boycott; Farm Worker Week; Farm Labor Organizing Committee Support; Witness for Farm Worker Justice Delegations

North America Interfaith Network (NAIN)

c/o Wainwright House, 260 Stuyvesant Ave., Rye, NY 10580
Co-Chairs: Drs. Charles R. White, Mohammad Mehdi
Major Activities: Interfaith Directory; Interfaith Conferences: Networking between Interfaith Organizations

ALABAMA

Greater Birmingham Ministries

1205 North 25th St., Birmingham 35234.
Tel. (205)326-6821
Exec. Dir.: Doug Mitchell
Co-Chairs, Eco. Justice: Hattie Belle Lester, Rick Ambrose
Chair, Direct Services: Ronee Hawkins
Chair, Shelter: Vicki Ingham
Chair, Church and Community: Sandy Schrohenloher
Chair, Finance and Fund-Raising, Ed Senter
Pres., Debra McCallam
Sec., Charles Moore
Treas., Lillian Ford
Major Activities: Direct Service Ministries (Food and Nutrition Education, Shelter); Economic Justice Issues (Low Income Housing and Advocacy, Health Care, Community Development Block Grants, Jobs Creation); Church and Community Ministries (Interchurch Forum, Interpreting and Organizing, Bible Study).

Interfaith Mission Service

411-B Holmes Ave., Huntsville 35801.
Tel. (205)536-2401
Exec. Min., Rev. Robert Loshuertos
Pres., Richard C. Titus
Major Activities: Food Pantry and Emergency Funds; Sharing Families; Ecumenical Dialogue; Halloween

Harvest of Food; Ministry Development; Clergy Luncheon; Workshops; Evaluation of Member Ministries; Response to Community Needs; Information and Referral

ALASKA

Alaska Christian Conference

1316 Peger Rd., Fairbanks 99709
Pres., Rev. Francis E. Mueller, S. J. 1316 Peger Rd., Fairbanks 99709
Vice-Pres., Bishop Jacob Nelson, Sr., P.O. Box 9, Bethel 99559
Sec., Mrs. Betty Taylor, 1307 Grenac Rd., Fairbanks 99709
Treas., Barbara Shaffer, 303 Kimsham, Sitka 99835
Newsletter Ed., John Shaffer, 1104 Edgecumbe Dr., Sitka 99835
Major Activities: Legislative & Social Concerns, Resources and Continuing Education; New Ecumenical Ministries; Communication; Alcoholism, Education & Prevention; Family Violence, Education & Prevention; Native Issues; Ecumenical, Theological Dialogue; Criminal Justice.

ARIZONA

Arizona Ecumenical Council

4423 N. 24th St., Ste. 750, Phoenix 85016
Tel. (602)468-3818
Adm., Dr. Arlo Nau
Pres., Dr. Carl Wallen, 525 E. Alameda Dr., Tempe 85282
Major Activities: Donohoe Ecumenical Forum Series; Affordable Housing Documentary; Disaster Response Network; Political Action Team; Resident Alien Registration Assistance Taskforce; Hopi/Navajo Relocation Taskforce; State IMPACT; Arizona Ecumenical Indian Concerns Committee

ARKANSAS

Arkansas Council of Churches and Synagogues

415 N. Maple St., P.O. Box 5292, North Little Rock 72119.
Tel. (501) 375-1553
Conf. Exec.,, Rev. Dale E. Bard
Pres., Rev. W. S. Jones, 613 Cedar, 72114
Sec., Mrs. Frances Bing, 5009 Burrow Dr., Little Rock 72114
Treas., Mr. Jim Davis, Box 7239, 72217
Major Activities: Task Forces on Hunger, Aging, Energy & Disasters; Institutional Ministry; Church World Service; Heifer Project; Ecumenical Worship Seminar; Week of Prayer for Christian Unity; Interfaith Executives' Advisory Council; Theological Studies; Mt. Sequoyah Ecumenical Mission Conference; T.V. Awareness; Drug Abuse, Interfaith Relations; Church Women United; IMPACT; Ecumenical Lectures

CALIFORNIA

California Council of Churches, Office for State Affairs

1300 N. St., Sacramento 95814
Tel. (916) 442-5447
Exec. Dir., Patti Whitney-Wise

Major Activities: Monitoring State Legislation; Calif. IMPACT Network; Legislative Principles Food Policy Advocacy; Family Welfare Issues; Environment

Northern California Ecumenical Council

942 Market St., No. 702, San Francisco 94102
Tel. (415) 434-0670
Exec. Dir., _____
Dir., Nicaragua Interfaith Committee for Action, Janine Chagoya
Dir., Refugee Community Programs, Rod Miller
Dir., Human Rights in El Salvdor, Jesus Campos
Dir. of Finance, Mila Thomas
Dir. of Development, Janice Toohey
Pres., Rev. Michael Cooper White
Vice-Pres., _____
Sec., Rev. Phil Lawson
Treas., Mr. James Faulk
Major Activities: Peace with Justice; Faith and Witness; Ministry; Communications

Southern California Ecumenical Council

1010 S. Flower, Ste. 500, Los Angeles, 90015
Tel. (213) 746-7677
Exec. Dir., Mr. Charles ("Chuck") L. Jones
Admin. Coord., Gil Olmstead
Adm. Asst., Megaly Servillano
Pres., Rev. Dr. Margaret (Peggy) Owen Clark
Dir., ECUMEDIA, Diane Jacobs; Dir., El Rescate _____; Ed., Hope Publishing, Faith Sand; Dir., Interfaith Hunger Coalition, Rev. Kathy Cooper-Ledesma; Dir. Interfaith Taskforce on Cent. Am., Mary Brent Wehrli; Dir., Witness for Peace, _____; Dir., Peace with Justice, Lynn Halpin; Dir., Life and Work, Ignacio Castuera; Dir., Faith and Order, Randi Walker
Major Activities: Communications Div. (ECUMEDIA, Hope Publ. House, ECUNEWS newsletter); Faith and Order (Faith and Order Comm. Celebrations Cmte.); Life and Work (Clergy and Laity Concerned, Disaster Response, Econ. Devel., Ecology Task Force, LUZ); Peace with Justice (Southern Calif Interfaith Task Force on Central Am.; Southern Calif. Ecumenical Task Force on South AFrica; Witness for Peace; El Refugio; El Rescate; Interfaith Hunger Cmte.)

Pacific and Asian American Center for Theology and Strategies (PACTS)

1798 Scenic Ave. Berkeley 94709
Tel. (415) 849-0653
Dir., Julia K. Estrella
Pres., Rev. Katie Choy-Wong
Fin. Sec., Rev. Benjamin Wu
Major Activities: Collect and Disseminate Resource Materials; Training Conferences; Public Seminars, Communication, Network and Advocacy Center for Women in Ministry; Human Rights; Migration Issues; Lay Ministry; Continuing Educations; Racial and Ethnic Minority Concerns; Journal and Newsletter.

Council of Churches of Contra Costa County

1543 Sunnyvale Ave., Walnut Creek 94596
Tel. (415) 933-6030
Adm. Dir., Rev. Machrina L. Blaidsell
Chaplains: Rev. Keith Spooner; Rev. Norman Behrmann; Rev. J. Richard Flowers; Mr. Stan Klop

Pres., Rev. Shirley Sherrill
Treas., Mr. Bertram Sturm
Major Activities: Institutional Ministries; Social Education and Action

Fresno Metropolitan Ministry

1055 N. Van Ness, Ste. H., Fresno 93728
Tel. (209) 252-1889
Exec. Dir., Rev. Walter P. Parry
Adm. Asst., Jackie Church
Pres., Rev. Frank Baldwin
Major Activities: Hunger Relief Advocacy; Human Relations; Urban Education; Biblical & Theological Education for Laity; County Hospital Advocacy; Cross Cultural Mental Health; Homelessness; Child Care: Video

South Coast Ecumenical Council

3326 Magnolia Ave., Long Beach 90806
Tel. (213) 595-0268
Exec. Dir., Rev. Don E. Lindblom
Dir. of Aging, Mrs. Roberta Stabbert
Dir. of Cmty. Action, Rev. Grace Moore
Dir. of Counseling, Dr. Lester Kim
Pres., Dr. Ralph J. Mosby, Jr.
Major Activities: Weekday Christian Education; Immigration and Refugee Support Services; Interfaith Action for Aging; Farmers' Markets; Hunger Projects; Shelters for the Homeless; Lay Academy of Religion; Church Athletic Leagues

Marin Interfaith Council

35 Mitchell Blvd., Ste. 13
San Rafael 94903
Tel. (415)492-1052
Exec. Dir., Rev. Linda Compton
Major Activities: Basic Human Needs—Homelessness; Interfaith Dialogue; Religious Leadership and Values

The Ecumenical Council of the Pasadena Area Churches

444 E. Washington Blvd., Pasadena 91104
Tel. (818) 797-2402
Exec. Dir., Rev. Charles B. Milburn
Pres., Rev. Floyd Lawson
Major Activities: Christian Education; Community Worship; Community Concerns; Christian Unity; Youth; Ethnic Ministries; Hunger; Peace; Friends in Deed; Emergency Shelter Line; Alternative Christmas Markets

Pomona Valley Council of Churches

1753 N. Park Ave., Pomona 91768
Tel. (714) 622-3806
Pres. Ms. Gean Halliday
Exec. Dir., Ms. Pat Irish
Sec., Hazel Kennedy
Treas., Dorothy Becker
Major Activities: Advocacy and Education for Social Justice; Ecumenical Celebrations; Interfaith Legislative Action; Hunger Advocacy; Emergency Food and Shelter Assistance; Farmer's Market; Affordable Housing; Hospital Chaplaincy; Pastoral Counseling; Coalition to Combat Racism

San Fernando Valley Interfaith Council

10824 Topanga Canyon Blvd., No. 7, Chatsworth 91311
Tel. (818) 718-6460
Exec. Dir., Barry Smedberg
Pres., Rev. Dr. G. Nelson Stringer

Major Activities: Seniors' Multi-Purpose Centers; Nutrition & Services; Meals to the Homebound and Meals on Wheels; "Interfaith Reporter"; Interfaith Relations; Interfaith AIDS Committee; Social Adult Day Care; Hunger/Homelessness; Volunteer Care-Givers; Clergy Gatherings; Food Pantries and Outreach; Peace and Justice, Aging, Hunger; Human Relations

Interfaith Service Bureau

3720 Folsom Blvd., Sacramento 95816
Tel. (916) 456-3815
Exec. Dir., Mary Deuel
Pres., Marsha Vacca
Major Activities: Chaplaincy; Food Closet Coalition; Mass Media; Credit Union; Interfaith *Voice;* Indo-Chinese Assistance Center; Clergy Concerns Committee; Religious Cable Television; Project Home; Faith in Crisis

San Diego County Ecumenical Conference

4075 Park Blvd., P. O. Box 3628, San Diego 92103
Tel. (619) 296-4557
Exec. Dir., Rev. E. Vaughan Lyons
Dir. of Communication, Rev. Bernard Filmyer, S.J.
Administrator, Patricia R. Munley
Pres., Rev. Dennis L. Mikulanis
Treas., Mr. Joseph Ramsey
Major Activities: Interfaith Shelter Network for the Homeless: Emerging Issues; Communications; Faith Order & Witness; Worship & Celebration; Ecumenical Tribute Dinner; Advent Prayer Breakfast; AIDS Chaplaincy Program; Third World Opportunities Seafarer's Mission; *Sunday Focus* TV News; *Religion in the News* Radio Program; Seminars and Workshops

The Council of Churches of Santa Clara County

1229 Naglee Ave., San Jose 95126
Tel. (408) 297-2660
Exec. Dir., Rev. Hugh Wire
Sec. Mary Jo Cloe
Affordable Housing, Gertrude Welsh
Prog. Dev., George Felicetta
Pres., Darlene Krause
Major Activities: Social Education/Action; Hunger and Emergency Services; Ecumenical and Interfaith Witness; Affordable Housing

Westside Ecumenical Conference

P.O. Box 1402, Santa Monica 90406
Tel. (213) 394-1518
Exec. Dir., Rev. Gregory Garland
Major Activities: Convalescent Hospital Visiting; Meals on Wheels; Community Religious Services; Convalescent Hospital Chaplaincy; Shelter Coordinator

COLORADO

Colorado Council of Churches

1370 Pennsylvania Ste. 100, Denver 80203
Tel. (303)861-1884
Pres., Rev. Dr. O. Dean Nelson
Exec. Dir., Rev. Gilbert Horn
Major Activities: Ecumenical Witness and Religious Dialogue; Institutional Ministries; Human Needs and Economic Issues (Includes Homelessness, Rural Crisis, Justice in the Workplace); World Peace and Global Affairs; Communication, Media and the Arts; Child Care Network

Interfaith Council of Boulder

2650 Table Mesa Dr., Boulder 80303
Tel. (303) 499-5611
Exec. Dir., Marsha Caplan
Major Activities: Interfaith Dialogue and Programs; Thanksgiving Worship Services; Food for the Hungry; Share-A-Gift; Monthly Newsletter

CONNECTICUT

Christian Conference of Connecticut (CHRISCON)

60 Lorraine St., Hartford 06105
Tel. (203) 236-4281
Exec. Dir., Rev. Stephen J. Sidorak, Jr.
Exec. Asst., Sharon Anderson
Adm. Asst., Mildred Robinson
Pres., Rev. Walter M. Elwood
Vice-Pres., Rt. Rev. Arthur E. Walmsley
Sec., Most Rev. John F. Whealon
Treas., Gerald Lamb
Major Activities: Communications; Institutional Ministries; Conn. Bible Society; Conn. Council on Alcohol Problems; Ecumenical Forum; Faith & Order; Social Concerns

Council of Churches of Greater Bridgeport, Inc.

126 Washington Ave., Bridgeport 06604
Tel. (203) 334-1121
Exec. Dir., Rev. John S. Kidd
Pres., Frank Ober
Sec., Mrs. Dorothy Allsop
Treas., Thomas Holloway
Major Activities: Runaway and Homeless Youth; Nursing Home, Hospital, and Prison Ministries; Feeding Programs and Food Bank; Tutoring; Ecumenical Activities

Association of Religious Communities

213 Main St., Danbury 06810
Tel. (203) 792-9450
Exec. Dir., Samuel E. Deibler, Jr.
Pres., Lee Hawes

The Capitol Region Conference of Churches

30 Arbor St., Hartford 06106
Tel. (203) 236-1295
Exec. Dir., Rev. Roger W. Floyd
Dir. Pastoral Care & Training and Anna M. Fulling Chaplain, Rev. John Swift
Dir. Social Concerns, Rev. William Watson
Dir., B.T.A., Rev. Robert Feldmann
Community Organizer, Mr. Joseph Wasserman
Housing Advocate, Ms. Annette Carter
Hartford Correctional Center Chaplain, Rev. John Melendez, Rev. Raymond Sailor
Broadcast Ministry Consultant, Ivor T. Hugh
Pres., Sr. M. T. Winter
Major Activities: Organizing for Peace and Justice; Chaplaincy; Aging; Legislative Action; Cooperative Broadcast Ministry. Ecumenical Cooperation; Interfaith Reconciliation; Chaplaincies; Affordable Housing; Low-Income Senior Empowerment

Center City Churches

170 Main St., Hartford 06106
Tel. (203) 728-3201

Exec. Dir., Paul C. Christie
Pres., Rev. Pamela Haller
Sec., Sabrina Saunders
Treas., Jeff Stouppe
Major Activities: Aging; Youth and Community Resources; Tutorial Program; Food Pantry; Outreach Ministry; Community Mental Health; Indigent; Advocacy; AIDS Residency

Manchester Area Conference of Churches

736 East Middle Tpke., Box 773, Manchester 06040
Tel. (203) 649-2093
Exec. Dir., Nancy P. Carr
Dir., Dept. of Sheltering Ministries, Denise Cabrara
Dir., Dept. of Human Needs, Elizabeth Harlow
Dir., Project Reentry, Chara Roubeau
Pres., Harry Reinhorn
Treas., Florence Noyes
Major Activities: Provision of Basic Needs (Food, Fuel, Clothing, Furniture); Emergency Aid Assistance; Emergency Shelter; Soup Kitchen; Reentry Assistance to Ex-Offenders; Pastoral Care in Local Institutions; Interfaith Day Camp; Advocacy for the Poor; Ecumenical Education and Worship

New Britain Area Conference of Churches (NEWBRACC)

19 Chestnut St. New Britain 06051
Tel. (203) 229-3751
Exec. Minister, Rev. Dr. David D. Mellon
Pastoral Care/Chaplaincy, Rev. Hudson R. Richard; Rev. Susan Gregory-Davis
Pres., Rev. Marie Pina
Treas., Margaret Fletcher
Major Activities: Worship; Social Concerns; Emergency Food Bank; Communications-Mass Media; Hospital and Nursing Home Chaplaincy; Teacher Training; Elderly Programming; Homelessness and Hunger Programs

The Downtown Cooperative Ministry in New Haven

57 Olive St., New Haven 06511
Tel. (203) 776-9526
Coord., Rev. Samuel N. Slie
Pres., Dr. Martha Leonard, 20 Dorr St., Branford, 06405
Treas., Richard Snyder, P.O. Box 1721, New Haven 06507
Major Activities: Mission to Poor and Dispossessed; Criminal Justice; Elderly; Sheltering Homeless; Soup Kitchen; Low Income Housing; AIDS Residence

Christian Community Action

98 South Main St., South Norwalk 06854
Tel. (203) 854-1811
Coord., Eleanor Crystal
Major Activities: Emergency Food Program; Used Furniture & Clothing; Loans for Rent, Security, and Fuel

Council of Churches and Synagogues of Lower Fairfield County

628 Main St., Stamford 06901
Tel. (203) 348-2800
Exec. Dir., Rev. Brenda J. Stiers
Assoc. Dir., Mrs. Nancy Bowen Martell
Administrator, Marjorie Conine
Ofc. Mgr., Sally Bassler
Hospital Chaplain, Rev. William Scrivener
Pres., Rev. Dr. M. Lawrence Snow
Treas., P. Wardham Collyer

Major Activities: Prison Visitation; Counseling, Senior Neighborhood Support Services; Ecumenical Services; Interfaith Dialogues; Food Bank and Salvage Program; Media Commission/Cable/TV; Fuel Assistance; Interfaith AIDS Ministry; Elderly Visitation Programs; Adopt-A-House; Friendship House; Affordable Housing

Waterbury Area Council of Churches

24 Central Ave., Waterbury 06702
Tel. (203) 756-7831
Coordinator, Mrs. Virginia B. Tillson
Adm. Asst., Deirde Cornell
Pres., Rev. Larry Green
Major Activities: Emergency Food Program; Emergency Fuel Program; Soup Kitchens; Ecumenical Worship; Christmas Toy Sale

DELAWARE

Delmarva Ecumenical Agency

1626 N. Union St., Wilmington 19806,
Tel. (302) 655-6151
Exec. Dir., Dr. George F. Cora
Ofc. Mgr., Mrs. Judith G. Berry
sec., Roderica Curtis
Resource Centers Dir., Mrs. Elaine B. Stout
Pres., Rev. Carl W. Gittings, P.O. Box 851, Valey Forge, PA 19482. Tel. (215)768-2225
Major Activities: Facilitates and coordinates the work of churches and public and private agencies in urban, rural, social concerns, education, and worship ministries

DISTRICT OF COLUMBIA

Interfaith Conference of Metropolitan Washington

1419 V St., N.W. 20009
Tel. (202) 234-6300
Exec. Dir., Rev. Clark Lobenstine
Ofc. Mgr., Kadija Cloyd
Staff Assoc. for Issues and Advocacy, Kathleen Baumann
Staff Associate, Molly Ward
Sec., Roderica Curtis
Pres., Rev. Carl Nissen
1st Vice Pres., Rabbi Andrew Baker
Vice Pres., Bp. Harold E. Jansen
Vice Pres., Dr. Ibrahim M. Fofanah
Vice Pres., James Cardinal Hickey; Dr. Amrit Kaur
Sec., Rabbi Morris Gordon
Treas., Rev. John V. O'Connor
Major Activities: Interfaith Dialogue; Health; AIDS; Drugs; Hate Violence-Group Hatred; Interfaith Concert

The Council of Churches of Greater Washington

411 Rittenhouse St., N.W., Washington 20011
Tel. (202)722-9240
Interim Exec. Dir., Rev. Rodney L. Young
Asst. Dir. for Prog., City, Mr. Daniel Thompson
D.C. Communities Ministries, Rev. George N. Bolden
Prog. Coord., Hope Valley Camp, Mr. Daniel Thompson
Pres., Rev. Frank D. Tucker
Major Activities: Development of Group and Community Ministries; Church Development and Redevelopment; Liaison with Public Agencies; In-school Youth Employment; Summer Youth Employment; Hope Valley Camp; Institutional Ministry; Hunger Relief; Vision to

Action—Community Revitalization; Health Ministries; Cluster of Store Front Churches

FLORIDA

Florida Council of Churches

924 N. Magnolia Ave., Ste. 236, Orlando 32803
Tel. (407)839-3454
Exec. Dir., Walter F. Horlander
Admin., Asst., Mrs. Kay Schmaus
Dir. of Special Ministries, Joyce L. Voorhees
Major Activities: Faith and Order; Education and Renewal; Evangelism and Mission; Justice and Peace

Christian Service Center for Central Florida, Inc.

808 West Central Blvd., Orlando 32805
Tel. (407)425-2523
Exec. Dir., Dr. Patrick J. Powers
Adm. Asst., Shirley Swint
Family Emergency Services, Dir., Andrea Evans
Family Life Counseling, Dir., Dr. Gloria Lobnitz
Daily Bread, Dir., Rev. James Blount
Respite, Dir., Mary Ellen Ort
Fresh Start, Dir., Rev. William Carter
Dir. of Public Rel., Karen Leonard
Pres., Flossie Hellinger
1st Vice-Pres., James Hunt
2nd Vice-Pres., Mrs. Donald Skinner
Treas., Ms. Sally Mayer
Sec., Mrs. Alice Huhn
Major Activities: Provision of Basic Needs (food, clothing, shelter); Emergency Assistance; Professional Counseling. Noon-time Meals; Sunday Church Services at Walt Disney World; Collection and Distribution of Used Clothing; Shelter for Homeless; Training for Homeless

GEORGIA

Georgia Christian Council

P.O. Box 7193, Macon 31209
Tel. (912) 474-3906
Exec. Dir., Rev. Donald E. Leiter
Pres., Most Rev. Raymond W. Leonard, 601 E. Liberty St., Savannah 31401
Treas., Rev. Gordon Reinersten, 3264 Northside Pkwy., N.W. Atlanta 30327
Major Activities: Local Ecumenical Support and Resourcing; Legislation (GRAIN); Rural Development; Racial Justice; Networking for Migrant Coalition and Aging Coalition

Christian Council of Metropolitan Atlanta

465 Boulevard, S.E., Atlanta 30312
Tel. (404) 622-2235
Exec. Dir., Dr. Perry Ginn
Deputy Dir., Mrs. Margaret Koehler
Assoc. Dir., Mr. Neal P. Ponder, Jr.
Pres., Mr. Joseph H. Beasley
Treas., Ms. June B. Debatin
Major Activities: Refugee Services; Emergency Assistance; Hunger Programs; Chronically Mentally Ill; Voluntary Service; Employment; Racism; Homeless; Ecumenical and Interreligious Events; Computerized Action-Information Ministry and Human Needs Network; AIDS Education; Interchurch Ministry Planning; Persons with Handicapping Conditions: Womens Concerns; Seminary Student Placement

HAWAII

Hawaii Council of Churches

1300 Kailua Rd., Kailua 96734
Tel. (808)263-9788
Exec. Dir., Ms. Patricia Mumford
Major Activities: Laity and Clergy Education; Ecumenical Worship; Religious Art, Music, Drama; Legislative Concerns; Interfaith TV and Radio Ministry; Social Action; AIDS Education; Advocacy for Peace with Justice

IDAHO

The Regional Council for Christian Ministry, Inc.

P.O. Box 2236, Rm. 10 Trinity United Methodist Church, Idaho Falls 83403
Tel. (208) 522-7921
Exec. Sec., Phyllis Fjeld
Major Activities: Island Park Ministry; Community Food Bank; Community Observances; Community Information and Referral Service; F.I.S.H.

ILLINOIS

Illinois Conference of Churches

615 S. 5th St., Springfield 62703
Tel. (217) 544-3423
Interim Gen. Sec., Rev. John Hendrickson
Dir. IMPACT, Rev. _____
Dir. Farm Worker Ministry, Ms. Olgha Sandman, 935 Curtiss, Rm. 8, Downers Grove 60515, Tel. (312) 964-7474
Dir., Refugee and Immigration Prog., Ms. Mary Caroline Dana
Supervisor Chicago Refugee Services Ofc., Ms. May Campbell, 2320 W. Peterson, Ste. 505, Chicago 60659, Tel. (312) 764-0008
Dir., Community Care Toll Free Telephone Prog. for Aging, Barbara Manning
Dir., Domestic Violence Prog., Mrs. Jacqueline Clingan
Dir., Human Services Ministry, Mr. Richard Brumleve
Pres., Rev. J. Robert Sandman, 1840 Westchester Blvd., Box 7208, Westchester 60153
Treas., Rev. Donald Lowe, 501 E. Capitol Ave., Ste. 230, Springfield 62701
Major Activities: Poverty & Race; Migrant & Farm Worker Ministry; Chaplaincy in Institutions; Governmental Concerns and Illinois Impact; Ecumenical Courier; Ministry to Mentally Handicapped; Ministry with Aging; Church-Community Development; Hunger and Welfare Reform; Immigration and Refugee Resettlement; Peace Action; Domestic Violence

The Church Federation of Greater Chicago

18 S. Michigan Ave., Ste 900, 60603
Tel. (312) 977-9929
Exec. Dir., Rev. David M. Whitermore
Adm. Asst., Darlene M. Sawatzky
Broadcasting Dir., Lydia Talbot
Hunger Dir., Beverly Decker
Pres., Rev. Nathaniel Jarrett, Jr.
Treas., Rev. LeRoy Cronkite II
Major Activities: Radio, Television, Cable, Inter-faith/Ecumenical Development; Social/Justice Concerns; Christian Education; Hunger Ministry/Community Organization; Literacy Program; Chaplaincy

The Hyde Park & Kenwood Interfaith Council

1448 East 53rd St., Chicago 60615
Tel. (312) 363-1620
Exec. Dir., Mr. Werner H. Heymann
Pres., Rev. John Boyle
Treas., Ms. Barbara Krell

Evanston Ecumenical Action Council

P. O. Box 1414, Evanston 60204
Tel. (312) 475-1150
Exec. Dir., Tecla Sund Reklau
Dir. Hospitality Cntr. for the Homeless, Patricia Johnson
Pres., Rev. Paul Christensen
Treas., Charles Underwood, 1229 Fowler, 60202
Major Activities: Interchurch Communication and Education; Peace and Justice Ministries; Coordinated Social Action; Soup Kitchen; Multi-Purpose Hospitality Center for the Homeless; Worship and Renewal

Oak Park-River Forest Community of Churches

324 N. Oak Park Ave., Oak Park 60302
Exec. Sec. for the Council, Miss Ruth E. McNutt
Pres., Rev. Donald H. McCord
Major Activities: Community Affairs; Ecumenical Affairs; Youth; Education; Food Pantry; Senior Citizens Worship Services; Laity; Interfaith Thanksgiving Services; Good Friday Services, UNICEF; ASSIST; Workshops on Pornography; Sexual Exploitation of Youth; Christian Unity Week Pulpit Exchange; Peace and Justice; Hunger Walkathon

Churches United of the Quad Cities Area

630 9th St., Rock Island 61201
Tel. (309) 786-6494
Exec. Dir., Thomas N. Kalshoven
Assoc. Exec. Dir., Sheila D. Fitts
Pres., Dean Sutton
Treas., G. Pierson Brauch
Major Activities: Jail Ministry; Hunger Projects; Minority Enablement; Criminal Justice; Migrant Ministry; Radio-TV; Peace; Aging; Local Church Development

Contact Ministries of Springfield

401 E. Washington, Springfield 62701
Tel. (217) 753-3939
Dir., Ethel Butcher
Major Activities: Information; Referral and Advocacy; Ecumenical Coordination; Low Income Housing Referral; Food Pantry Coordination; Low Income Budget Counseling; Police Dept. Social Services

INDIANA

Indiana Council of Churches

1100 W. 42nd St. Rm. 225, Indianapolis 46208
Tel. (317) 923-3674
Exec. Dir., Rev. Scott J. Schliesswohl
Legislative Assoc., Mrs. Nancy Smith
Farm Worker Ministry Coord., Rev. Pamela Mason
Refugee Resettlement Facilitator, Ms. Sylvia Robles
Peace and Justice Facilitator, Rev. John Gaus
Pres., Bishop Edward W. Jones
Sec., Rev. Robert Stauffer
Treas., Mr. David F. Rees
Major Activities: Educational Ministries; Communications and Public Media; Social Ministries; Peace and Justice; Farmworker Ministries; Institutional Ministries; Ecumenical Concerns; Indiana Rural Justice Network; Refugee Resettlement; NAESNET; IMPACT

Ecumenical Assembly of Bartholomew County Churches

Love Chapel, 311 Center St.,
P.O. Box 1421, Columbus 47202
Tel. (812) 372-9421
Exec. Dir., Marjorie Wilson
Major Activities: Emergency Assistance Fund: FISH (Food and Prescriptions)

Christian Ministries of Delaware County

806 W. White River Blvd., Muncie 47303
Tel. (317) 288-0601
Exec. Sec., Donna Watson
Pres., David Cartwright
Treas., Billy Shepherd
Major Activities: Migrant Ministry, Christian Education, Feed-the-Baby Program; Youth Ministry at Detention Center; Community Church Festivals; Community Pantry; Community Assistance Fund

Church Community Services

1703 Benham Ave., Elkhart 46516
Tel. (219)295-3673
Exec. Dir., Mary Jane Carpenter

Evansville Area Council of Churches, Inc.

103 N.W. Tenth St., Evansville 47708
Tel. (812) 425-3524
Exec. Dir. Rev. Joseph N. Peacock
Weekday Supervisor, Mrs. Walter Foster
Pres., Rev. Conrad Grosenick
Sec., Alan Winslow
Fin. Chpsn., Rev. Will Jewsbury
Major Activities: Christian Education; Community Responsibility & Service; Public Relations; Interpretation; Church Women United; Institutional Ministries; Interchurch Foundation; Hunger Program; Housing Program; Jail Ministry; Emergency Shelter; Interfaith Dialogue

The Associated Churches of Fort Wayne & Allen County, Inc.

227 E. Washington Blvd., Ste. 102, Fort Wayne 46802
Tel. (219) 422-3528
Exec. Pastor, Rev. Vernon R. Graham
Adm. Asst., Sally L. Pickering
WRE Coord., Ruth Proctor
Prog. Devel.; Ellen Graham
Pres., John Cantrell, 10512 Morning Mist Trail 46804
Treas., Melvin McFall, 1300 S. Clinton 46802
Major Activities: Weekday Religious Education; Radio & TV; Church Clusters; Church and Society Commission; Education for Christian Life Division; Clergy United for Action; Faith and Order Commission; Christian Education; Widowed-to-Widowed; CROP; Campus Ministry; Food Bank System; Peace Education; Welfare Reform; Endowment Development; Habitat for Humanity; Child Care Advocacy; Project 25; Ecumenical Dialogue

The Church Federation of Greater Indianapolis, Inc.

1100 W. 42nd St., Indianapolis 46208
Tel. (317) 926-5371
Exec. Dir., Rev. C. Bruce Naylor
Ofc. Mgr., Marilyn V. Wilkes
Dir., Social Service, Rev. Roger Heimer
Dir. Development, Ms. Robin Andres
Dir., Communications, Mr. Don Frick
Pres., Dr. Philip Amerson
Treas., Mr. Thomas Evans
Major Activities: Celebrations and Unity; Ministries in Media; Ministries in Specialized Settings; Ministries in Society; Education and Training

Indiana Interreligious Commission on Human Equality

1100 W. 42nd St., Ste. 320, Indianapolis 46208
Tel. (317) 924-4226
Exec. Dir., Rev. James E. Taylor
Pres., Rev. E. Anne Henning Byfield
Treas., Dr. Ralph Quellhorst
Major Activities: Human Rights; Anti-Racism Training; Racism/Sexism Inventory; Cultural and Religious Intolerance; South Africa Consultations; Interfaith Dialogue

Indiana Office for Campus Ministries

1100 W. 42nd St., Indianapolis 46208
Tel. (317)923-4839
Exec. Dir., Dr. E. Max Case
Major Activities: In-Service Training and On-Site Consultation to Campus Ministers

Lafayette Urban Ministry

12 North 8th St., Lafayette 47901
Tel. (317) 423-2691
Dir. Rev. Jud Dolphin
Advocate Coord., Sara Bowling
Public Policy Coord., Joe Micon
Pres., Connie Smith
Treas., Bob Nulph
Major Activities: Social Justice Ministries With and Among the Poor

Interfaith Community Council, Inc.

702 E. Market St., New Albany 47150
Tel. (812) 948-9248
Exec. Dir., Rev. Dr. George Venable Beury
Dir. of Finance, Mary Ann Sodrel
Dir., Child Dev. Center, Susan Nguyen
Dir., Deaf Relay, Susan Wagner
Dir. RSVP, Matie Watts
Chpsn., Mr. David Hottel
Treas., Robert Craig, Sr., 1624 Hedden Ct. 47150
Major Activities: Child Development Center; Deaf Relay Teletype Center; Emergency Assistance; Hedden House (Half Way Home for Recovering Alcoholic Women); Retired Senior Volunteer Program; New Clothing and Toy Drives; Job Training; Convalescent Sitter & Mother's Aides; Senior Day College; Emergency Food Distribution

United Religious Community of St. Joseph County

2015 Western Ave., South Bend 46629
Tel. (219) 282-2397
Exec. Dir., Dr. James J. Fisko
Coord., State Prison Visitation, Sr. Susan Kintzele, CSC
Coord., Victim Offender Reconciliation Prog. (VORP), Rev. Daniel Stoltzfus

Coord., Shelter for the Homeless, Eugene Foust
Coord., Services to the Homeless, Tammy Oehm
Coord., Volunteer Advocacy Project, Sara Goetz
Coord. Peace Is Possible Prog., Phyllis Wezeman
Dir., Refugee Day Care, Carol McDonnell
Pres., Rev. Philip Sorensen
Major Activities: Religious Understanding; Social and Pastoral Ministries; Congregational Ministries

IOWA

Iowa Inter-Church Forum

3816 36th St., Des Moines 50310
Tel. (515) 255-5905
Ch. and Cmty Rel. Coord., Wendy E. Hanson Wagner
Major Activities: A forum dialogue related to theological faith issues and social concerns; opportunity to develop responses to discern needs and join in common mission

Iowa Inter-Church Agency for Peace and Justice

3816 36th St., Des Moines 50310
Tel. (515)255-5905
Prog. Coordinators: Roz Ostendorf, Suzanne Peterson
Major Activities: International Peace; Human Needs; Governmental Concerns; Chaplaincy

Churches United, Inc.

222 29th St. Drive, SE, Cedar Rapids 52403
Tel. (319) 366-7163
Adm. Sec., Mrs. Marcey Luxa
Pres., Maryana Dickinson
Treas., Gary VAnder Plaats, 1015 MNB Bldg. 52401
Major Activities: Community Food Bank; L.E.A.F. (Local Emergency Assistance Fund; CROP; Cooperative Low Income Store (O.N.E. Store); Community Information and Referral; Jail Chaplaincy; World Hunger; Nursing Home Ministry; Radio and TV Ministry; Ecumenical City-Wide Celebrations

Des Moines Area Religious Council

3816 36th St., Des Moines 50310
Tel. (515) 277-6969
Exec. Dir., Forrest Harms
Pres., Frances Bates
Treas., William Hines
Major Activities: Outreach and Nurture; Education; Social Concerns; Mission; Worship; Emergency Food Pantry; Ministry to Widowed; Child Care Assistance

KANSAS

Kansas Ecumenical Ministries

3615 S.W. 29th St., Topeka 66614
Tel. (913) 272-9531
Exec. Dir., Dorothy G. Berry
Pres., Rev. John Williams
Vice Pres., Jeanne Goddard
Sec., Rev. George Harvey
Treas., Tom Redman
Major Activities: Legislative Activities; Program Facilitation and Coordination; World Hunger; Lakes Ministry; Higher Education Concerns; Interfaith Rural Life Committee; Education; Mother-to-Mother Program; Peacemaking

Cross-Lines Cooperative Council

1620 S. 37th St., Kansas City 66106
Tel. (913)432-5497
Exec. Dir., Rev. Donald C. Bakely
Program Dir., Rev. Robert Moore
Pres., Charlotte Withrow
Treas., Larry Leighton
Major Activities: Emergency Assistance; Housing Repair;
Wood Shop; Adult School; Work Camps; Christmas
Store; Clothing Store; Education; Homeless Assistance;
Volunteer Services

Inter-Faith Ministries—Wichita

2020 Est Central, Wichita 67214
Tel. (316) 264-9303
Exec. Dir., Rev. James M. Bell
Assoc. Dir., Rev. Sylvia D. Farmer
Ofc. Administrator, Carolyn A. Bell
Dir., Communications, Robert Greenwood
Coord. Operation Holiday, Robert Greenwood
Dir., Indian Ministries, Mrs. Irene Heinze
Dir. Cmty. Min., Patrick Cameron
Dir., Homeless Shelter, Hem Sharma
Pres., Rev. John Billings
Major Activities: Communications; Urban Education;
Inter-religious Understanding; Community Needs and
Issues; Theology and Worship; Hunger; Advocacy

KENTUCKY

Kentucky Council of Churches

1039 Goodwin Dr., Lexington 40505
Tel. (606) 253-3027
Exec. Dir., Dr. John C. Bush
Coord., Kentucky Hunger Task Force, Ms. Anne Joseph
Coord., Disaster Recovery Prog., C. Nelson Hostetter
Ed., INTERCOM, Dr. David Berg
Pres., Rt. Rev. David B. Reed, 600 East Main St.
Louisville 40202. Tel. (502) 584-7148
Major Activities: Hunger, Church and Government;
Disaster Response; Christian Unity; Peace Issues;
Racism; Church Property Taxation; Health Care Issues;
Local Ecumenism; Rural Land/Farm Issues

Highlands Community Ministries

1140 Cherokee Rd., Louisville 40204
Tel. (502) 451-3695
Exec. Dir., Stan Esterle
Pres., Peter Glauber
Vice Pres., Jean Goff
Sec., Joyce Wynn
Treas., Rev. Richard Teaford
Major Activities: Welfare Assistance; Day Care; Coun-
seling with Youth, Parents and Adults; Adult Day Care;
Social Services for Elderly; Housing for Elderly and
Handicapped; Ecumenical Programs; Community
Classes; Activities for Children; Neighborhood and
Business

Kentuckiana Interfaith Community

P.O. Box 4671, Louisville 40204
Tel. (502) 458-4076
Exec. Dir., Rev. Kenneth D. MacHarg
Pres., Rabbi Stanley Miles
Vice Pres., Rev. Steve Hampton
Sec., _____

Treas., Rev. Brian Cope
Major Activities: Religious Workers Insurance Plan;
Radio and TV; Interfaith Dialogue; Religion and Race;
Ecumenical Newspaper; Civil Rights Comm.; Annual
Clergy-Funeral Dirs. Conf.; Heating Assistance Pro-
gram; Ecumenical Cable TV Channel; Inter-Christian
Dialgue; Justice Concerns; Educational Events

South East Associated Ministries (SEAM)

3728 Taylorsville Rd., Louisville 40220
Tel. (502)454-0380
Exec. Dir., Rev. Robert F. Owens
Dir., Life Skills Center, Martha Hinson
Dir., Volunteers, Marian Ziefell
Dir., Youth Services, Jackie Town
Pres., Rev. Rick White
Treas., Joe Hays
Major Activities: Emergency Food and Financial Assist-
ance; Life Skills Center (Programs of Prevention and
Self-Sufficiency Through Education, Empowerment,
Support Groups, etc.); Juvenile Court Diversion
Program; Bloodmobile; Ecumenical Education and
Worship; Family Counseling; Substance Abuse Coun-
seling

South Louisville Community Ministries

801 Camden Ave., Louisville 40215
Tel.(502)367-6445
Exec. Dir., J. Michael Jupin
Bd. Chair, George Buck
Bd. Vice Chair, Rev. Ernie Gross
Bd. Treas., Eugene Wells
Major Activities: Food, Clothing & Financial Assistance;
Home Delivered Meals, Transportation, Homemakers
for Elderly; Ecumenical Worship; Juvenile Diversion
Program; Affordable Housing

Northern Kentucky Interfaith Commission, Inc.

601 Greenup St. Covington 41011
Tel. (606) 581-2237
Exec. Dir., Rev. William C. Neuroth
Major Activities: Spiritual; Disaster Ministries; Interracial
and Intercultural Awareness; Peace & Justice

St. Matthews Area Ministries

4006 Shelbyville Rd., Louisville 40207
Tel. (502) 893-0205
Exec. Dir., A. David Bos
Dir., Youth Services, Patricia Fleet
Dir., Emergency Finc'l Assis., Linda Leeser
Dir. After-School Care Centers, Janet Hennessey
Major Activities: After-School Care; Youth Services;
Interchurch Worship and Education; Emergency Finan-
cial Assistance

Paducah Cooperative Ministry

1359 South Sixth St. Paducah 42001
Tel. (502) 442-6795
Dir., JoAnn Ross
Chpsn., Rev. John Andrews
Major Activities: The P.C.M. is a cooperative venture of
32 local churches and six denominational judicatories,
serving the community's hungry, elderly, poor, prison-
ers, homeless, handicapped and mentally retarded

LOUISIANA

Louisiana Interchurch Conference

440 North Foster Dr., Ste. 106, Baton Rouge 70806
Tel. (504)924-0213
Exec. Dir., Rev. James L. Stovall
Pres., Bishop William B. Friend, 2500 Line Ave.,
Shreveport 71104
Treas., Mr. Emile Reggie, Sr., P. O. Box 576, Crowley
70526
Major Activities: Ministries to Aging; Prison Reform;
Liaison with State Agencies; Ecumenical Dialogue;
Institutional Chaplains

Greater New Orleans Federation of Churches

4545 Magnolia St. #206, New Orleans 70115
Tel. (504) 897-4488
Pres./Exec. Dir., Dr. Tom S. Roote, Jr.
Coord. of Social Min., Rev. Cromwell C. Cleveland, Jr.
Admin. Sec., Mrs. Lucille Francis
REACH (Cable TV Channel), Actg. Dir./Prod. Mgr.,
Mr. Kerry Townson.
Police Chaplain, Rev. Sam Allen
Fire Chaplancy Coord., Rev. Cromwell C. Cleveland, Jr.
Fin. Sec., Mr. George Egan
Newsletter Editor, Dr. Tom S. Roote
Operation Mainstream-Literacy, Dir. Jackie Abreu
Chpsn. of Bd., Rev. Samuel Walker
Treas., Mr. Carlos Zervigon
Major Activities: Radio-TV Programs; Central Business
District Ministries; Regional Suburban Network; Lead-
ership Training; Senior Citizens; Social Action; Public
Information; Religious Census and Survey; Literacy;
Counseling Coordination; Cable T.V. Channel; Emer-
gency Food and Shelter; Community Awareness;
Evangelism; Hunger; Public Events: Crime Prevention;
Ministry to Nursing Homes; Church Growth; Coordi-
nate with Judicatories; Interfaith Conference; Coordi-
nate Special Services (Easter, Thanksgiving)

MAINE

Maine Council of Churches

15 Pleasant Ave., Portland 04103
Tel. (207)772-1918
Pres., Rev. Jean Bass
Exec. Dir., Thomas C. Ewell

MARYLAND

Central Maryland Ecumenical Council

Cathedral House, 4 East University Pkwy., Baltimore
21218
Tel. (301) 467-6194
Adm. Dir., Lynn A. Bopp
Pres., Dr. Fred H. Spigler, Jr.
AIRS Dir., _____
Major Activities: Interchurch Communications and Col-
laboration; Information Systems; Ecumenical Rela-
tions; Urban Mission and Advocacy; Staff Judicatory
Leadership Council; Interfaith Residential Services for
Persons with AIDS; Annual Ecumenical Choral Con-
cert; Annual Ecumenical Service

MASSACHUSETTS

Massachusetts Council of Churches

14 Beacon St., Boston 02108
Tel. (617) 523-2771

Exec. Dir., Rev. Diane C. Kessler
Assoc. Dir. for Public Policy, Dr. Roy Costa
Assoc. Dir., Ecumenical Development, Rev. David A.
Anderson

Attleboro Area Council of Churches, Inc.

505 N. Main St., Attleboro 02703
Tel. (508) 222-2933
Exec. Dir., Carolyn L. Bronkar
Admin. Sec., Joan H. Lindstrom
Program Aide, Patricia J. Hune
Hosp. Chpln., Rev. Linnea Prefontaine
Pres., Rev. Lowell Drotts, Ev. Cov. Ch., P. O. Box 208,
20703
Treas., David Quinlan, 20 Everett St., Plainville 02762
Major Activities: Hospital Chaplaincy; Radio Ministry;
Personal Growth/Skill Workshops; Ecumenical Worship;
Media Resource Center; Referral Center; Communica-
tions/Publications; Community Social Action; Food'n
Friends Kitchens; Emergency Food and Shelter Fund;
Nursing Home Volunteer Visitation Program

The Cape Cod Council of Churches, Inc.

142 Corporation Rd., Hyannis 02601
Tel. (508) 775-5073
Interim Exec. Dir., Alexandra MacCallum Clark
Adm. Asst., Muriel L. Eggers
Pres., Rev. John Williams
Chaplain, Cape Cod Hospital, Rev. William Wilcox
Chaplain, Barnstable County Hospital, Elizabeth Stommel
Chaplain, Falmouth Hospital, Allen Page
Chaplain, House of Correction & Jail, Rev. Thomas
Shepherd
Dir., Service Center and Thrift Shop, Joan McCurdy, Box
981 W. Dennis 02670. Tel. (508)394-6361; Asst to Dir.,
Merilyn Lansin
Major Activities: Pastoral Care; Social Concerns; Religious
Education; Emergency Distribution of Food, Clothing,
Furniture; Referral and Information; Church World
Service; Interfaith Relations

Massachusetts Commission on Christian Unity

82 Luce St., Lowell 01852
Tel. (508)453-5423
Exec. Sec., Rev. K. Gordon White
Major Activity: Faith and Order Dialogue with Church
Judicatories.

Inter-Church Council of Greater New Bedford

412 County St., New Bedford 02740
Tel. (617) 993-6242
Exec. Min., Dr. Lawrence van Heerden
Adm. Asst., Andrea Lentz
Pres., Rev. Christopher Drew
Treas., William Reed
Major Activities: Pastoral Counseling; Chaplaincy; Hous-
ing for Elderly; Urban Affairs; Parent-Child Center;
Social Rehabilitation Club

Cooperative Metropolitan Ministries

474 Centre St., Newton 02158
Tel. (617) 244-3650
Exec. Dir., Claire Kashuck
Cncl. Chpsn., Libby Titlebaum
Board Pres., Carolyn Panasevich
Treas. Gary Hicks
Sec., Mary Morrison

Major Activities: Low Income, Elderly, Affordable Housing; Emergency Food Program; Nursing Home Information; Legislative Advocacy; Hunger

Council of Churches of Greater Springfield

152 Sumner Ave. Springfield 01108
Tel. (413) 733-2149
Exec. Dir., Rev. Ann Geer
Dir. of Community Min., Rev. Jonathan Tetherly
Dir. Nursing Home Min., Patrick McMahon
Pres., V. Rev. Earl Wepley
Treas., Mr. Jerre Hoffman
Major Activities: Christian Education Resource Center; Advocacy; Emergency Fuel Fund; World Peace and Justice Division; Community Ministry; Visitor Ombudspersons to Nursing Homes; Task Force on Aging; Hospital and Jail Chaplaincies; Pastoral Service; Christian Social Relations; Crisis Counseling; Relief Collections; Ecumenical and Interfaith Relations; Ecumenical Dialogue with Roman Catholic Diocese; Mass Media; Church/Community Projects and Dialog

Worcester County Ecumenical Council

25 Crescent St., Worcester 01605
Tel. (508) 757-8385
Exec. Dir., Rev. Richard A. Hennigar
Asst. to Dir., D. Frizelle Mason-Jones
Pres., Rev. Donald Whitcomb
Major Activities: Clusters of Churches; Electronic Media; Economic Justice; Youth Ministries; Ecumenical Worship and Dialog; Interfaith Activities; Nursing Home Chaplaincies, Assistance to Churches; Peace; Hunger Ministries; AIDS Pastoral Care Network

MICHIGAN

Michigan Ecumenical Forum

P.O. Box 10206, Lansing 48901
Tel. (517) 485-4395
Interim Ecumenical Coordinator/Exec. Dir., Rev. Carroll E. Keegstra
Major Activities: Communication and Coordination; Studies and Fellowship; Church and Society Issues; Continuing Education

ACCORD—Area Churches Together . . . Serving

124 E. Michigan Ave, Battle Creek 49017
Tel. (616) 963-2280
Exec. Dir., _____
Pres., Rev. David Morton
Vice-Pres./Church, Rev. Michael Fedewa
Vice Pres/Admin., _____
Vice-Pres./Community, Rev. Erick Johnson
Major Activities: CROP Walk; Thanksgiving International Student Homestay; Food Closet; Christian Sports; Week of Prayer for Christian Unity; Nursing Home Vesper Services; Ecumenical Worship

Christian Communication Council of Metropolitan Detroit Churches

1300 Mutual Building, 28 W. Adams, Detroit 48226
Tel. (313) 962-0340
Exec. Dir., Rev. Edward Willingham
Assoc. Dir., Mrs. Angie Willingham
Media Assoc., Mrs. Tawnya Bender

Prog. Dir., Meals for Shut-Ins, Mr. John Simpson
Services Dir., Meals for Shut-ins, Mr. Clark Churchill
Coord., Summer Feeding Prog., Ms. Michelle Harper
Major Activities: Theological and Social Concerns; Ecumenical Worship; Educational Services; Electronic Media; Print Media; Meals for Shut-Ins; Summer Feeding Program

Greater Flint Council of Churches

927 Church St., Flint 48502
Tel. (313) 238-3691
Exec. Dir., Ms. Laurie Shaeffer
Council Adm., Ms. Shirley A. Stevens
Pres., Rev. Charles G. Robertson, Jr.
Treas., Ms. Joyce B. Best
Major Activities: Christian Education; Christian Unity; Christian Missions; Hospital and Nursing Home Visitors; Church in Society; American Bible Society Materials; Interfaith Dialogue; Church Visitor Exchange Sunday; Directory of Area Faiths and Clergy; Adopt A House Community Outreach Project; World of Difference Programs

Grand Rapids Area Center for Ecumenism (GRACE)

38 West Fulton, Grand Rapids 49503
Tel. (616) 774-2042
Exec. Dir., Rev. David P. Baak
Prog. Dir., Ms. Betty Zylstra
Major Activities: Hunger Walk; November Hunger and Shelter Awareness Week; Shelter Forum; Aging Committee; AIDS Pastoral Care Network; Clergy Interracial Forum; Annual Week of Prayer for Christian Unity; Ecumenical Eucharist and Pentecost Services, Educational Forums. Affiliates: ACCESS (All County Churches Emergency Support System); FISH for My People (Transportation); Habitat for Humanity/GR; *Grace Notes*

MINNESOTA

Minnesota Council of Churches

122 W. Franklin Avenue, #100, Minneapolis 55404.
Tel. (612) 870-3600
Exec. Dir., Rev. Margaret J. Thomas
Dir. of Life and Work and Hispanic Ministry, Carlos Mariani-Rosa
Dir. of Faith and Order, Rev. Rebecca J. Tollefson
Dir. Refugee Services, Shannon Bevans; Caseworker, Ge Cheuthang Yang
Dir., of Indian Concerns, Mary Ann Walt
Dir. of Facilities, Gus Margellos
Dir. Twin Cities Metropolitan Church Commission, Rev. Sally L. Hill
Dir. Joint Religious Legislative Coalition, Brian A. Rusche
Pres., Rev. Gregrey Renstrom
Major Activities: Minnesota Church Center; Local Ecumenism; Life and Work: Black Ministries, Hispanic Ministries, Indian Concerns, Youth Ministry, State Fair Ministry, Legislative Advocacy, Refugee Services, Regional Life Transformation, Violence in Significant Relationships; Faith and Order: Ecumenical Dialogue, Jewish Christian Relations, Consultation on Church Union; Spirituality; Communications

Community Emergency Assistance Program (CEAP)

7231 Brooklyn Blvd., Brooklyn Center 55429
Tel. (612 566-9600
Exec. Dir., Edward T. Eide

Major Activities: Provision of Basic Needs (Food, Clothing, Furniture); Emergency Financial Assistance for Shelter; Home Delivered Meals; Chore Services and Homemaking Assistance; Single Parent Loan Program; Volunteer Services

Arrowhead Council of Churches

230 E Skyline Pkwy., Duluth 55811
Tel. (218) 727-5020
Exec. Dir., Joel Huenemann
Pres., Tab Baumgartner
Major Activities: Inter-Church Evangelism; Community Concerns; Joint Religious Legislative Coalition; Downtown Ecumenical Good Friday Service; Corrections Chaplaincy; CROP Hunger Walk; Forum for Interfaith Dialogue; Church Women United; Community Seminars

Greater Minneapolis Council of Churches

122 W. Franklin Ave., Rm. 218 Minneapolis 55404
Tel. (612) 870-3660
Exec. Dir., Rev. Dr. Gary B. Reierson
Assoc. Exec. Dir., Indian Work, Mary Ellen Dumas
Dir., Twin Cities Metropolitan Church Commission, Rev. Sally Hill
Dir., Meals on Wheels, Barbara Green
Dir., Minnesota FoodShare, Rev. Peg Chemberlin
Correctional Chaplains: Rev. Norman Menke, Rev. Susan Allers Hatlie, Rev. Thomas Van Leer
Dir., Congregations Concerned for Children, Carolyn Henrixson
Dir., Dr. Richard Green Tutoring Program, Hallie Hendrieth-Smith
Dir., Metro Paint-A-Thon, Jodi Young
Dir., Chore/Housekeeping Services, DeLaine Brown
Pres., Rev. Kathi Austin Mahle
Treas., Roger Heegaard
Major Activities: Indian Work; Minnesota FoodShare; Metro Paint-A-Thon; Meals on Wheels; Dr. Richard Green Tutoring Program; Congregations Concerned for Children; Correctional Chaplaincy Program; Chore/Housekeeping Services; Education and Celebration; Church Women United; and Special Programs on Unemployment, Homelessness, and Adolescent Pregnancy.

The Joint Religious Legislative Coalition

122 West Franklin Ave., Minneapolis 55404
Tel. (612)870-3670
Exec. Dir., Brian Rusche
Resch. Dir., Jim Casebolt
Major Activities: Lobbying at State Legislature; Researching Social Justice Issues and Preparing Position Statements; Organizing Grassroots Citizen's Lobby

Twin Cities Metropolitan Church Commission

122 West Franklin, Rm. 218, Minneapolis 55404
Tel. (612) 870-3662
Exec. Dir., Rev. Sally L. Hill
Pres., Rev. Glenn Leaf, 4917 Elliot Ave., So. 55417
Major Activities: Education; Criminal Justice Coordinating Committee; Nursing Homes Project; Peacemaking Education; Peace Education Project; Interreligious Committee on Central America; Faith in Dialogue Seminars; Child Care Ecumenical Network

St. Paul Area Council of Churches

1671 Summit Ave., St. Paul 55105
Tel. (612)646-8805
Exec. Dir., Rev. Thomas Duke
Chaplaincy, Dr. Fred A. Hueners
Ecumenical Relations, Rev. Sally Hill
Congregations Concerned for Children, Ms. Peg Wangensteen, Ms. Karen O'Connell
Coop. Ministries for Children/Youth, Ms. Joel Young, Ms. Pat Watkins
Dept. of Indian Work, Ms. Sheila White Eagle
Pres., Rev. John Lohre
Treas., Arthur Sternberg
Major Activities: Chaplaincy at Detention and Corrections Authority Institutions; Police Chaplaincy; Education and Advocacy Regarding Children and Poverty; Assistance to Churches Developing Child Care Services; Ecumenical Encounters and Activities; Indian Ministries; Leadership in Forming Cooperative Ministries for Children and Youth

MISSISSIPPI

Mississippi Religious Leadership Conference

P. O. Box 68123, Jackson, 39286
Tel. (601)352-6752
Exec. Dir., Rev. Thomas E. Tiller, Jr.
Chair, Rev. Dr. Henry C. Clay, Jr.
Treas., Mrs. Lisa Hall
Major Activities: Foster trust, understanding and cooperation among religious leaders; Lay/Clergy Retreats; Social Concerns Seminars; Disaster Task Force; Advocacy for Disadvantaged

MISSOURI

Springfield Area Council of Churches

Box 3947, Springfield 65808
Tel. (417) 862-3586
Exec. Dir., Rev. Dorsey E. Levell
Assoc. Dir., Rosanna Bradshaw
Major Activities: Poverty Program; Community Treatment Program for Ex-Public Offenders; Legislative Affairs; Ministerial Alliance; Hospital Chaplains' Fellowship; Retired Senior Volunteer Program; Treatment Center for Alcoholics and Drug Abuse; Helping Elderly Live More Productively; Daybreak Adult Day Care Services; Ombudsman for Nursing Homes; Family Day Care Homes; USDA Food Program; Youth Ministry; Disaster Aid and Counseling; Homebound Shoppers; Community Service Program as an Alternative to Incarceration; Food and Clothing Pantry; Ozarks Food Harvest; Homesharing; Spiritual Care Chaplains Service

Interfaith Community Services

200 Cherokee, St. Joseph 64504
Tel. (816) 238-4511
Exec. Dir., David G. Berger
Major Activities: Child Development; Neighborhood Family Services; Group Home for Girls; Retired Senior Volunteer Program; Nutrition Program; Mobile Meals; Southside Youth Program; Church and Community; Housing Development

MONTANA

Montana Association of Churches
1511 Poly Dr. Billings 59102
Tel. (406) 252-7279
Exec. Dir., Rev. Dr. Lawrence F. Small
Adm. Asst., Mrs. Claris Peterson
Pres., Rev. Donald A. Guthrie, 130 S. 6th St., E. Missoula 59801
Treas., Mr. Gordon Bernhart, 3404 Racquet Dr., 59102
Rural Ministry Coord., Mrs. Mary Lou Heiken, 935 S. 72nd St., W., Billings 59106
Legislative Liaison, Mrs. Mignon Waterman, 530 Hazelgreen, Helena 59601

Major Activities: Christian Education; Montana Religious Legislative Coalition; Christian Unity; Junior Citizen Camp; Public Information; Ministries Development; Social Ministry; Rural Ministry

NEBRASKA

Interchurch Ministries of Nebraska
215 Centennial Mall S., Room 411, Lincoln 68508
Tel. (402) 476-3391
Exec. Sec., Dr. Mel H. Luetchens
Admin. Asst., Sharon K. Kalcik
Pres., Rev. Samuel R. Boman
Treas., Rev. "Clip" Higgins
Major Activities: Interchurch Planning and Development; Comity; Indian Ministry; Television Ministry; Teacher Training; Audio-Visual Center; Rural Church Strategy; World Hunger; CWS Refugee Coordination; United Ministries in Higher Education; Small Church Leadership Development; Disaster Response; Christian in Society Forum; Clergy Consultations; Farm Families Crisis Response Network; Video Technology; Visioning Ministry; Interim Ministry Network; Pantry Network; Rural Theological Education Network; Farm Mediation Services; Hispanic Ministry

Lincoln Interfaith Council
215 Centennial Mall South, Room 411, Lincoln 68508
Tel. (402) 474-3017
Exec. Dir., Rev. Dr. Norman E. Leach
Pres., Prof. John Comer
Treas., Mrs. Velma Struthers
Media Specialist, Laura Hayes
Major Activities: Media Ministry; Emergency Food Pantries; Police and Fire Chaplaincies; Center for Spiritual Growth; Lincoln-Lancaster County Jail Worship; Lincoln Clergy Fellowship; New Clergy Orientation; Clergy and Congregational Directory; Clergy Connection for Non-Lincoln Hospital Patients; Anti-Drug and Anti-Gang Programs; Boy Scouts/Girl Scouts/Campfire Religious Awards Program Coordination;; High School Baccalaureate; U.N.I.C.F. Drive; CROP Walk; Week of Prayer for Christian Unity; Rev. Dr. Martin Luther King, Jr. Birthday Observance; Holocaust Memorial Observance; Interfaith Passover Seder; Mayor's Interfaith Prayer Breakfast; Indian Concerns; Crime and Community Issues; Lincoln Housing Coalition; Emergency Services Seminar; Festival of Faith; Advocacy; Workshops and Seminars

Interchurch Ministries of Nebraska: Farm Hotline Response
Box 383, Walthill, 68067
Tel. (402)846-5578

Coord., Kathleen Severens
Staff, Joy Johnson
Chpsn. of I.M.N. Cncl., Norma Hall
Dir. of I.M.N., Dr. Melvin Leutchens, Ste 411, Lincoln Center Bldg., 215 Centennial Mall South Lincoln, 68508
Tel. (402)476-3391
Major Activities: Financial, Legal and Emotional Counseling for Farm Families in Economic Distress.

Interchurch Ministries of Nebraska: Nebraska Mediation Service
Box 37, Walthill 68067
Tel. (402)846-5105
Coord., Kathleen Severens
Staff, Rita Dunn
Chpsn. of I.M.N. Cncl., Norma Hall
Dir. of I.M.N., Dr. Melvin Luetchens, Ste. 411, Lincoln Cntr. Bldg., 214 Centennial Mall S., Lincoln 68508. Tel. (402)476-3393, in-state (800)446-4071
Major Activities: The program offers mediation services in the areas of farmer/creditor, interpersonal, and community disputes, as well as public education and training in mediation

NEVADA

(No current information)

NEW HAMPSHIRE

New Hampshire Council of Churches
24 Warren St., P.O. Box 1107, Concord 03302
Tel. (603) 224-1352
Exec. Sec., Rev. Frank H. Gross
Pres., Rev. Robert Williams, P. O. Box 796, 003302
Treas., Timothy Woodman, 63 Green St. 03301
Major Activities: Facilitating cooperative work of member denominations

NEW JERSEY

New Jersey Council of Churches
116 N. Oraton Pkwy., East Orange 07017
Tel. (201) 675-8600
176 W. State St., Trenton 08608
Tel. (609) 396-9546
Exec. Dir., Rev. Charles W. Rawlings
Commission on Impact and Public Witness, Ms. Marge Christie
Commission on Mission Planning and Strategy, Mrs. Christine Trigg
Commission on Theology and Interreligious Relations, Rev. Betty Jane Bailey
Dir., IMPACT, Ms. Joan Diefenbach
Pres., Rev. Peter Paulsen
Treas., Rev. William Jewett
Major Activities: Housing; Welfare Reform; Farm Workers and Farm Issues; Public Education; Chaplaincy; Tax Policy; Advocacy; Community Ethics

Bergen County Council of Churches
165 Burton Ave., Hasbrouck Heights 07604
Tel. (201) 288-3784
Exec. Sec., Neila Vander Vliet

Council of Churches of Greater Camden

Box 1208, Merchantville 08109
Tel. (609) 665-1919
Exec. Sec., Dr. Samuel A. Jeanes
Pres., Rev. Lawrence L. Dunn
Treas., Mr. William G. Mason
Major Activities: Radio & TV; Hospital Chaplaincy; United Services; Good Friday Breakfast; Mayors' Prayer Breakfast; Public Affairs; Easter Sunrise Service

Metropolitan Ecumenical Ministry

404 University Ave., Newark 07102
Tel. (201) 623-9259
Exec. Dir., David S. Burgess
Dir., Proj. Schools, Mr. Stephen Jones
Dir., Project YERN, Mr. Brian Crawford
Dir., Project Read, Ms. Claudia Connor
Chair, Housing Task Force, Ms. Nancy Zak and Mr. Frank Hutchins
Chair, Toxic Waste Task Force, Ms. Madelyn Hoffman
Chpsn. of Board, Beatrice Slaten
Sec., Gerald Meaker
Treas., Lin Powell
Major Activities: Project Read; Project Schools; Project Yern; Task Forces: Housing; Toxic Waste

Trenton Ecumenical Area Ministry (TEAM)

2 Prospect St., 08618
Tel. (609) 396-9166 or 393-3636
Exec. Dir., Rev. Angelique Walker-Smith
Hospital Chaplains: Rev. Leo Forgsberg, Rev. Fred Mechowski, Rev. Beverley Johnson
Campus Chaplains: Rev. Wayne Griffith, Rev. Nancy Schulter
Youth Prog. Coord., Mrs. Harrietta Walker, Ms. Kathy Barlow
Sec., Ms. Tina Swan
Chpsn., Rev. Frederick Wilkes
Major Activities: Racial Justice; Children & Youth Ministries; Advocacy; CROP Walk; Ecumenical Worship; Hospital Chaplains; Church Women United; Campus Chaplaincy; TV Program; Congregational Empowernment

NEW MEXICO

New Mexico Conference of Churches

124 Hermosa SE, Albuquerque 87108
Tel. (505) 255-1509
Exec. Sec., Dr. Wallace Ford
Pres., Rev. Jim Smith, Christian Church (Disciples of Christ), 10453 Springwood Dr., El Paso, TX 79925
Treas., Mr. Roy Nials, 3901 Indian School Rd., NE, A-401, Albuquerque 87110
Major Activities: State Task Forces: Peace With Justice; Poverty; Caring Inclusive Congregations; Legislative Concerns/Impact; Faith and Order; AIDS; Correctional Ministries; Public Education; Eco-Justice; Ecumenical Continuing Education. Church's Solidarity with Women; Marriage and Family Life. Regional Task Forces: Aging; Ecumenical Worship; Refugees; Emergency Care; Alcoholism

Inter-Faith Council of Santa Fe, New Mexico

P.O. Box 4637, Santa Fe 87502
Pres., Barbara Robinson
Chpsn. Peace with Justice Task Force, Hib Sabin

Chpsn. Hunger/Shelter Task Force, Jeanette Woodward
Major Activities: Faith Community Assistance Center; Hunger Walk, Interfaith Dialogues/Celebrations/Visitations; Peace Projects; Understanding Hispanic Heritage; Newsletter

NEW YORK

New York State Council of Churches, Inc.

362 State St., Albany 12210
Tel. (518) 436-9319
3049 E. Genesee St., Syracuse 13224
Tel. (315) 446-6151
Exec. Dir., Dr. Arleon L. Kelley
Assoc. for Adm. Services. Ms. Sylvenia Cochran
New York State IMPACT Coord., Edward Bloch
Pres., Dr. Judith E. Hjorth
1st Vice Pres., Rev. Carl E. Flemister
2nd Vice Pres., Rev. James H. Miller
Sec., Ms. Mary Lu Bowen
Treas., Dr. George H. DeHority
Major Activities: Public Policy and Ecumenical Ministries; Rural Poor and Migrants; Homeless; AIDS; U.S.-Canadian Border Concerns; Single Parent Families; Chaplaincy in State Institutions; Faith and Order; Environmental Issues; The Public and Its Issues

Christians United in Mission, Inc.

40 N. Main Ave., Albany, 12203
Tel. (518) 453-6795
Prog. Dir., Mr. Ronald K. Willis
Communications Dir., Mr. Stephen Esker
Major Activities: To promote cooperation/coordination among member judicatories in the areas of urban ministries, media communications, social action, criminal justice; emergency food and program development. AIDS and homelessness have been established as priorities for 1990.

Broome County Council of Churches, Inc.

81 Main St., Binghamton 13905
Tel. (607) 724-9130
Exec. Dir., Mr. Kenneth A. Cable
Admin. Asst., Mrs. Marilyn F. Sweet
Hospital Chaplains, Rev. LeRoy Flohr, Mrs. Betty Pomeroy
Jail Chaplain, Rev. Philip Singer
CREW (Youth Project) Dir., Mr. Barry Foster
Aging Ministry Coord., Mrs. Dorothy Myers
CHOW Prog. Coord., Ms. Pamela Brodsky
Pres., Rev. Dr. Wesley Hamlin, Jr.
Treas., Mr. Hayden Myers
Major Activities: Hospital and Jail Chaplains; Youth and Aging Ministries; CHOW (Emergency Hunger Program; Christian Education; Ecumenical Worship and Fellowship; Media; Community Affairs; Peace

Buffalo Area Council of Churches

1272 Delaware Ave., Buffalo 14209
Tel. (716) 882-4793
Exec. Dir., Rev. Dr. G. Stanford Bratton
Admin. Sec., Church Women United, Mrs. Norma Roscover
Chpsn, Radio-TV Ministry, Rev. Robert Hutchison
Pres., Mrs. Elizabeth Winters
Treas., Rev. Kenneth Neal
Major Activities: Radio-TV; Social Services; Hospital Chaplains; Church Women United; Ecumenical Relations

Buffalo Area Metropolitan Ministries, Inc.

775 Main St., Ste. 405, Buffalo 14203
Tel. (716) 854-0822
Exec. Dir., Rev. Charles R. White
Pres., Rabbi Eliot Marrus
Vice Pres., for Plng. and Prog., Rev. Craig French
Vice Pres. for Adm. and Fin., Rev. David A. Zwifka
Sec., Mark T. Kenmore
Treas., Richard McFail
Chair Food for All Prog., Rev. Kay Woike
Major Activities: Shelter; Hunger; Economic Issues; Interreligious Dialogue; Interfaith AIDS Network

Capital Area Council of Churches, Inc.

901 Madison Ave., Albany 12208
Tel. (518) 489-8441
Interim Exec. Dir., Rev. James Snedeker
Dir., Fncl. Dev., Ms. Laura Parker
Adm. Ms. Elaine Berg
Pres., Ms. Evelyn Stone
Treas., Mr. Alan Spencer
Major Activities: Hospital Chaplaincy; Food Pantries; CROP Walk; Jail and Nursing Home Ministries; Martin Luther King Memorial Service and Scholarship Fund; Emergency Shelter for the Homeless; Campus Relations; Forums on Social Concerns; Community Worship; Peace and Justice Education; Inter-Faith Programs; Legislative Concerns; Half-Way House for Ex-Offenders; Annual Ecumenical Musical Celebration

Council of Churches of Chemung County Inc.

330 W. Church St., Elmira 14901
Exec. Dir., Mrs. Joan Geldmacher
Pres., Rev. M. Russell Lee
Major Activities: CWS Clothing Collection; CROP Walk; UNICEF; Institutional Chaplaincies; Radio, Easter Dawn Service; Communications Network; Representation on Community Boards and Agencies; Meals on Wheels; Campus Ministry; Food Cupboards; Ecumenical Services

The Cortland County Council of Churches, Inc.

7 Calvert St., Cortland 13045
Tel. (607) 753-1002
Exec. Dir., Rev. Donald M. Wilcox
Major Activities: College Campus Ministry; Jail Ministry; Hospital Chaplaincy; Nursing Home Ministry; Newspaper Column; Interfaith Relationships; Hunger Relief; Family Life (Sexuality Education, Adoption, Child Abuse Prevention); UNICEF; CWS; Leadership Education; Community Issues; Peace Task Force; Criminal Justice; Mental Health Chaplaincy

Dutchess Interfaith Council, Inc.

9 Vassar St., Poughkeepsie 12601
Tel. (914) 471-7333
Exec. Dir., Mrs. Martha S. Miller

Protestant Chaplain, Rev. Dr. James E. Hunt
Roman Catholic Chaplain, Rev. Ernest D'Onofrio
Pres., Roberta E. Sheehan
Treas., Rev. Michael B. Webber
Major Activities: County Jail Chaplaincy; Radio; CROP Hunger Walk; Interfaith Music Festival; Public Worship Events; Indochinese Refugee Sponsorship; Interfaith Dialog; Christian Unity; Interfaith Forum; Oil Purchase Group; Volunteer Caregiver Program

Genesee Ecumenical Ministries

17 South Fitzhugh St., Rochester 14614
Tel. (716) 232-6530
Exec. Dir., Rev. Lawrence E. Witmer
Adm. Asst., Marie E. Gibson
Fin. Adm., Ilse Kearney
Pres., Ms. Margery Nurnberg
Treas., Rev. Donald Roth
Major Activities: Criminal Justice (Alternatives to Incarceration); Legislative IMPACT Network; Mission Education & Training; Refugee Resettlement; Hospital Chaplaincies; Hunger and Food Policies; Habitat for Humanity; Wellspring; Church Resource Service; One World Goods (Craft Sales)

The Long Island Council of Churches

Nassau County: 249 Merrick Rd. Box 105, Rockville Centre 11571. Tel. (516) 536-8707
Suffolk County: 235 Sweezy Ave., Riverhead 11901. Tel. (516) 727-2210
Exec. Dir., Rev. Robert L. Pierce
Exec. Dir., Rev. Ruth Phillips-Huyck
Adm. Asst., Ms. Barbara McLaughlin
Interim Dir., Pastoral Care Rev. Walter Baepler
Dir., Clinical Pastoral Educ., Rev. Kai Borner
Dir., Social Services, Mrs. Lillian Sharik
Pastor for Hispanic Ministries, Project Jericho Road, Rev. Rodolfo Saborio
Dir., Project REAL, Mr. Stephen Gervais
Dir., Counseling Services, Rev. S. Bruce Wagner
Nassau County Office: Social Services Sec., Ms. Paula Wankel
Suffolk County Office: Family Support, Mrs. Deborah Scott; Food Prog., Mrs. Carolyn Gumbs
Blood Prog. Coord., Ms. Marcie Agee, Ms. Leila Truman
Volunteer Consultant, Mr. Carey Smith
Major Activities: Pastoral Care in Hospitals and Jails; Clinical Pastoral Education; Emergency Aid and Food; Advocacy for Domestic and International Peace & Justice; Blood Donor Coordination; Church World Service; Central American Refugee Ministry Worship; Inter-faith Cooperation; Radio Program; Church Directory; Newsletter; Counseling Service; Community Residences for Adults with Psychiatric Disabilities; AIDS Advisory Board and AIDS Forum for Pastors, Project REAL; Special Projects

Council of Churches of the Mohawk Valley Area, Inc.

1644 Genesee St., Utica 13502
Tel. (315) 733-4661
Actg. Dir., Dr. Robert A. Hansen
Pres., David Mathis
Treas., Mr. James Turnbull IV
Major Activities: Christian Education; Social Action; Urban Ministry; Interfaith Relations; Ministry in Higher Education; Church Women United; Radio and TV; Teen Centers; Summer Day Camping; CROP; Clothing Collections; Multi-Cultural Coalitions

The Council of Churches of the City of New York

490 Riverside Dr., 10th Fl. Twr., New York 10027
Tel. (212) 749-1214
Exec. Dir., _____
Div. Dir., Dept. Pastoral Care, Dr. Lars J. Silverness
Div. Dir., Dept. Communications, _____
Chaplain, Protestant Ecumenical Chapel, Kennedy Airport, Dr. Lars J. Silverness
Ministries in Higher Education, _____
Pres., Bishop Norman N. Quick
Treas., _____
Major Activities: Radio & TV; Pastoral Care; Protestant Chapel, Kennedy International Airport; Family of Man

Bronx Division of the Council of Churches of the City of New York

39 W. 190th St., Bronx 10468
Tel. (212)367-0612
Pres., Rev. Robert L. Foley, Sr.
Exec, Dir., Joyce Thomas
Major Activities: Pastoral Care; Christian Education & Youth Ministry; Welfare & Advocacy; Substance Abuse

Brooklyn Division of the Council of Churches of the City of New York

125 Ft. Greene Pl. 11217
Tel. (718) 625-5851
Dir., Mr. Charles Henze
Pres., Rev. Franklin G. Sherrill
Treas., Rev. Albert J. Berube
Major Activities: Education Ministry; Justice Ministry; Hunger Ministry; Local Ecumenism; Pastoral Care; Community Issues; Youth Ministry

Staten Island Council of Churches

2187 Victory Blvd., Staten Island 10314
Tel. (718) 761-6782
Ofc. Mgr., Mrs. Marjorie R. Bergendale
Pres., Rev. John E. Covington
Vice-Pres., Rev. James A. Martin
Sec., Mrs. Mildred J. Saderholm
Major Activities: Support; Christian Education; Pastoral Care; Congregational Concerns; Urban Affairs

Queens Federation of Churches

86-17 105th St., Richmond Hill 11418
Tel. (718) 847-6764
Exec. Dir., Rev. N. J. L'Heureux, Jr.
Exec. Asst., Kevin Murphy
York College Chaplain, Rev. Hortense Merritt
Pres., Rev. Irvine A. Bryer, Jr.
Treas., Lloyd W. Patterson, Jr.
Major Activities: Emergency Food Service; York College Campus Ministry; Blood Bank; Scouting; Christian Education Workshops; Planning and Strategy; Church Women United; Community Consultations; Seminars for Church Leaders; Directory of Churches and Synagogues; Christian Relations (Prot/RC), Chaplaincies; Public Policy Issues; N.Y.S. Interfaith Commission on Landmarking of Religious Property; Queens Interfaith Hunger Network

East Harlem Interfaith

2050 2nd Ave., New York 10029
Tel. (212) 427-1500
Dir., Rev. John Vaughn
Bd. Chmn., Rev. Reginal Williams

Major Activities: Ecumenical Worship; Welfare and Hunger Advocacy; Health Advocacy; Community Organizing; Economic Development (Community Reinvestment)

The Niagara Council of Churches

228 Second St.
Niagara Falls 14303
Tel. (716) 285-7505
Exec. Dir., Ms. Claudia L. MacDonald
Pres., Rev. Knight Washburn, Bacon Memorial Presby. Ch., 166 - 59th St. 14304
Treas., Mr. Edward Weber, 1306 Maple Ave. 14305Major Activities: Ecumenical Worship; Bible Study; Christian Education and Social Concerns; Church Women United; Evangelism and Mission; Institutional Ministries Youth Activities; Hymn Festival; Week of Prayer for Christian Unity; Church World Service Projects; Store for Church Supplies and Audio-Visual Library; UNICEF Items

Rochester: see Genesee Ecumenical Ministries

Schenectady Inner City Ministry

5 Catherine St., Schenectady 12307
Tel. (518)374-2683
Exec. Dir., Rev. Phillip N. Grigsby
Adm. Asst., Ms. Karen Rembert
Emergency Food Liaison, Ms. Patricia Obrecht
Nutrition Dir., Donald VanDenbergh
Project SAFE Dir., Ms. Delores Edmonds-McIntosh
Pres., Mrs. Andrea Bailey
Major Activities: Emergency Food; Advocacy; Housing; Child Care; Alternatives to Prostitution for Runaway and At-Risk Youth; Neighborhood and Economic Issues; Ecumenical Worship and Fellowship; Community Research; Education in Churches on Faith Responses to Social Concerns; Legislative Advocacy; Nutrition Outreach Program; Hispanic Community Ministry

Syracuse Area Interreligious Council

910 Madison St., Syracuse 13210
Tel. (315)476-2001
Exec. Dir., Dorothy F. Rose
Pres., Rev. Nelson W. Gaetz
Assoc. Dir. Dale Hindmarsh
Assoc. Dir., Rev. Robert Stoppert
Dir. of Refugee Resettlement, Ms. Nona Stewart
Dir., Senior Companion Prog., Ms. Diane Rogers
Dir., Hunger Outreach Services, Ken Klein
Prog. Assoc., Ms. Virginia Frey
Bus. Mgr., Patricia McFall
Other Activities: Education and Dialogue; Worship; Institutional Pastoral Care; Covenant Housing Program; Youth Ministry; Project Exodus-Community Re-entry from Incarceration; Research; Public Advocacy and Planning

NORTH CAROLINA

North Carolina Council of Churches

Methodist Bldg., Ste. 162, Raleigh 27605
Tel. (919)828-6501
Exec. Dir., Rev. S. Collins Kilburn
Prg. Assoc., Evelyn Mattern, S.F.C.C.
Pres., Rt. Rev. Robert W. Estill, P. O. Box 17025, 17619
Treas., Dr. James W. Ferree, P. O. Box 11772, Winston-Salem 27116

Major Activities: Christian Nurture; Christian Unity; Christian Social Ministries; Legislative Program; Criminal Justice; Farmworker Ministry; Peace; Hunger; Rural Crisis; Racism; Disaster Response

Asheville-Buncombe Community Christian Ministry (ABCCM)

24 Cumberland AVe., Ashville 28801
Tel. (704)252-2752
Exec. Dir., Rev. Scott Rogers
Pres., Dr. John Hewett

Greensboro Urban Ministry

407 N. Eugene St., Greensboro 27401
Tel. (919)271-5959
Exec. Dir., Rev. Mike Aiken
Major Activities: Emergency Financial Assistance; Housing, Hunger Relief; Inter-Faith and Inter-Racial Understanding; Justice Ministry

Urban Ministry Center of Raleigh

310 W. Edenton St., Raleigh 27603
Tel. (919)834-4707
Exec. Dir., Anne M. Burke
Dir., Ark Shelters, Dorothy Lane Ellis
Dir., Open Door Clinic, Anne Sales
Dir., Crisis Intervention Prog., Jill Spooner
Employment Counselor, Rev. Wadih Antoun
Admin. Asst., Nancy K. Evans
Major Activities: Provision of Basic Needs (Financial Assistance for Fuel, Utilities, Rent, Medications, Food); Emergency Shelter for Homeless Men and Women; Free Medical and Dental Clinic for Medically Indigent Population

NORTH DAKOTA

North Dakota Conference of Churches

227 West Broadway, Bismarck 58501
Tel. (701)255-0604
Pres., Bishop John F. Kinney
Treas., Paula Rinquette, PBVM
Ofc. Mgr., Eunice Brinckerhoff
Major Activities: Prison Chaplaincy; Rural Life Crisis Ministry; Peace and Justice; Interfaith Dialogue; BEM Study; Faith and Order

OHIO

Ohio Council of Churches, Inc.

89 E. Wilson Bridge Rd., Columbus 43085
Tel. (614)885-9590
Exec. Dir., Rev. Carlton N. Weber
Assoc. Dir., Rev. Keene R. Lebold
Legislative Representative, Rev. David O. McCoy
Min. of Black Church and Cmty. Rel., _____
Dir. of Refugee Services, Ms. Grace Johnson
Sponsorship Developer, Ms. Carol Fisher
Sponsorship Coord., Ms. Thi Tuyet Nga Nguyen
Pres., Ms. Nancy Lee
Treas., Ms. Dolores Eyerman
Major Activities: Economic Justice; Minority Church Empowerment; Ecumenical Development; Public Policy Issues; Criminal Justice Issues; World Peace and Justice; Refugee Resettlement

Akron Area Association of Churches

750 Work Dr., Akron 44320
Tel. (216)535-3112

Exec. Sec., Rev. Lloyd F. O'Keefe
Pres. Bd. of Trustees, Dr. Arthur Kemp
Vice-Pres., Mr. Stan Michelich
Sec., Rev. Forrest Nees
Treas., Dr. Stephen Laning
Telecommunications, Rev. Bart Huizenga
Community Concerns, Janet Powell
Worship and Celebration, _____
Chr. Ed. Dir., Mrs. Kimberly Porter
Major Activities: Messiah Sing; Interfaith Council; Newsletters; S. E. Asian Refugee Resettlement; Resource Center; Community Worship; Training of Local Church Leadership; Hunger; Radio Programs; Adult Learning Fairs; Cable TV; Clergy Forum; Assistance to Elderly

Alliance of Churches

470 E. Broadway, Alliance 44601
Tel. (216)821-6648
Dir., Richard A. Duro
Pres., Rev. Robert Stewart
Treas., Betty Rush
Major Activities: Christian Education; Community Relations & Service; Ecumenical Worship; Community Ministry; Peacemaking; Medical Transportation for Elderly

Council of Christian Communions of Greater Cincinnati

2439 Auburn Ave., Cincinnati 45219
Tel. (513)579-0099
Exec. Dir., Dr. Richard P. Jameson
Assoc. Dir., for Justice Chaplaincy, Rev. Jack Marsh
Assoc. Dir., for Educ., Sharon D. Jones
Asst. Dir., Communication, John H. Gassett
Chaplain, Rollman Psychiatric Inst., Rev. Dwight Wilkins
Pres., Rev. James Lewis
Major Activities: Christian Unity & Interfaith Cooperation; Justice Chaplaincies; Police-Clergy Team; Adult and Juvenile Jail Chaplains; Religious Education; Broadcasting and Communications; Information Service; Social Concerns

Metropolitan Area Religious Coalition of Cincinnati (MARCC)

1035 Enquirer Bldg., 617 Vine St., Cincinnati 45202
Tel. (513)721-4843
Dir., Rev. Duane Holm
Pres., Rev. James Milton
Major Activities: Housing; Human Services; Public Education

Interchurch Council of Greater Cleveland

2230 Euclid Ave., Cleveland 44115
Tel. (216)621-5925
Exec. Dir., Rev. Thomas Olcott
Assoc. Dir. and Dir., Church and Society, Ms. Mylion Waite
Assoc. Dir. and Dir., Communications, Ms. Janice Giering
Pres., Rev. Valentino Lassiter
Chmn. of the Assembly, Gladys Howson
Major Activities: Church and Society; Communications; Hunger; Project Learn; Christian Education; Legislation; Faith and Order; Urban Crisis; Public Education; Interchurch News; Tutoring; Parent-Child Books Program; Books for People; Anti-Apartheid; Adult Literacy; Teen Pregnancy Prevention; Shelter for Homeless Women and Children; Radio and TV; Interracial Cooperation; Interfaith Cooperation

Inner City Renewal Society

2230 Euclid Ave., Cleveland 44115
Tel. (216)781-3913
Exec. Dir., Myrtle L. Mitchell
Coord. Friendly Town, Abigail Oberst
Dir., J.O.I.N. Prog., Rev. James Hughley
Dir., Chore Prog., (Mrs.) Maggie Robinson
Urban Ministries Trng. and Cmty. Dev. Center, Instructor, Dr. Edward Andrews
Dir., Alcoholism Prog., Rev. Thomas Chapman
Pres., Rev. Dr. Marvin McMickle
Treas., Rev. Kenneth Jones
Major Activities: To serve as the "Extended Arm of the Church in reaching humankind (especially poor & oppressed, wounded of spirit, and afflicted).

West Side Ecumenical Ministry

4315 Bridge Ave, Cleveland 44113
Tel. (216)651-2037
Exec. Dir., Robert T. Begin
Major Activities: Emergency Food Distribution Centers; Senior Meals Programs; Youth Services; Community Organization; Advocacy; Church Clusters; Drug Rehabilitation Program; Head Start Centers Theatre

Metropolitan Area Church Board

760 E. Broad St., Columbus 43205
Tel. (614)461-7103
Exec. Dir., Dr. Robert Lee Erickson
Ch. and Cmty. Coord., Interfaith Just Housing Proj., Fredericka Wallace
Support Service Coord., Kathryn Walls
Chmn. Bd., Rev. John Edgar
Vice Chmn., Mrs. Marilyn Shreffler
Sec., Rev. Mitchell McGuire
Treas., Mrs. Dolores Eyerman
Major Activities: Weekly Radio and Cable TV Programs; Newsletter; Liaison with Other Community Organizations; Annual Congregational Assembly; Week of Prayer for Christian Unity; Support for Ministerial Associations and Church Councils; Enrichment Seminars; Prayer Groups; "Emerging Social Issues Forums"; CROP Walk; Habitat for Humanity; Black Business Expo

Greater Dayton Council of Churches

212 Belmonte Park E., Dayton 45405
Tel. (513)222-8654
Exec. Dir., Dr. Richard C. Duncan
Coord., Montgomery County Voluntary Jail Prog., Sr. Mary Jean Foppe, R.S.M.
Pres., Dr. Charles Brown
Major Activities: Communications: Service to the Churches and Community; Housing Advocacy; Race Relations Advocacy; Substance Abuse Prevention

Churchpeople for Change and Reconciliation

221 W. North St., Lima 45801
Tel. (419) 229-6949
Exec. Dir., Betsy Bouska
Major Activities: New programs for minorities, poor, alienated, and despairing and spinning them off as independent agencies

Mahoning Valley Association of Churches

631 Wick Ave., Youngstown 44502
Tel. (216) 744-8946

Exec. Dir., Elsie L. Dursi
Pres., Rev. William Brewster, St. John's Epis. Ch., 323 Wick Ave. 44503
Treas., Mr. Paul Fryman, 42 Venloe Dr., Poland 44514
Major Activities: Communications; Christian Education; Ecumenism; Social Action; Advocacy

Pike County Outreach Council

122 East Second St., Waverly 45690
Tel. (614) 947-7151
Dir., Joy A. DeCamp

Metro-Toledo Churches United

444 Floyd St. Toledo 43620
Tel. (419) 242-7401
Adm., Ms. Nancy Lee Atkins
Prog. Dir., Ms. Polly White
Ecumenical Liaison, Rev. John McKissick
Exec. Dir., Toledo Campus Ministry, Rev. Glenn B. Hosman, Jr.
Exec. Dir., Toledo Metropolitan Mission, Ms. Nancy Atkins
Pres., Rev. C. Eugene Pearson
Treas., Fred Plassman
Major Activities: Social Service; Christian Education; Hunger; Interfaith Relations; Campus Ministry; Social Action (Public Education; Mental Retardation; Voter Registration/Education; Health Care; Community Economic Development; Urban Ministry; Employment; Community Organization; Welfare Rights; Housing; Refugee Assistance.)

Ecumenical Communication Commission of N.W. Ohio (Toledo)

P. O. Box 351, 1011 Sandusky, Ste. M., Perrysburg 43551
Tel. (419) 874-3932
Dir. Ms. Margaret Hoepfl
Major Activities: Ecumenical/Cooperative Communication; TV Production

Tuscarawas County Council for Church and Community

120 First Dr. SE, New Philadelphia 44663
Tel. (216) 343-6012
Exec. Dir., Barbara E. Lauer
Pres., Mr. Thomas L. Kane, Jr., 1221 Crater Ave., Dover 44622
Treas., Mr. James Barnhouse, 120 N. Broadway, New Philadelphia 44663
Major Activities: Human Services; Health; Family Life; Child Abuse; Housing; Educational Programs; Emergency Assistance; Legislative Concerns; Juvenile Prevention Program; Teen Pregnancy Prevention Program; Prevention Program for High Risk Children (The Council acts as a facilitator of the above.)

Youngstown: see Mahoning Valley

OKLAHOMA

Oklahoma Conference of Churches

P. O. Box 60288, Oklahoma City 73146
Tel. (405) 525-2928

Exec. Dir., Dr. William Moorer
Pres., Mrs. Rebecca Markham, 1912 S. 69th East Ave., Tulsa 74112
Treas., Dr. Charles Wells
Major Activities: Priority is Church and Unity Concerns with "BEM" Studies; Community Building Among Denominations; Church and Society; IMPACT; Disaster Response; Minority Affairs; Rural Farm Crisis; Refugee Resettlement; Concern for Poverty

Tulsa Metropolitan Ministry

240 East Apache, Tulsa 74106
Tel. (918) 582-3147
Exec. Dir., Sr. Sylvia Schmidt, S.C.C.
Assoc. Dir., Rev. Gerald L. Davis
Dir., Jail Ministry, Rev. Gerald L. Davis
Tenant Service Coordinators, Setlah Raha, Donnie Hamman
Dir., Homeless Programs, Marcia Sharp
Dir., Mentally Ill Homeless, Rev. Charles Boyle
Justice and Peace Prog. Advocate, Rev. Larry Cowan
Pres., Jessie F. Manering
Sec., Joyce Chapman
Treas., Joyce Unger
Major Activities: Corrections Ministry; Jewish-Christian Understanding; Police-Community Relations; Shelter for the Homeless; Women's Issues; Shelter for Mentally Ill; Outreach and Advocacy for Public Housing; Spirituality and Aging; Legislative Issues; Interfaith Dialogue TV Series; Christian Issues/Justice and Peace Issues

OREGON

Ecumenical Ministries of Oregon

0245 S. W. Bancroft St., Ste. B, Portland 97201
Tel. (503) 221-1054
Exec. Dir., Rev. Rodney I. Page
Assoc. Dir., Barbara J. George
Dir. of Center for Urban Education, Rodney I. Page
Dir., Legislative and Governmental Ofc., Ellen C. Lowe
Fin. Dev., Norene Goplen
Alcohol and Drugs Ministries, Nancy Anderson
Police Chaplain, Rev. Greg Kammann
Sponsors Organized to Assist Refugees, Ellen Martin
Dir. Emergency Food, Sheri Hawley
Dir., Folk-Time (Socialization Program for Chronically Mentally Ill), Susan Alperin
Dir., Job Opportunity Bank, _____
Pres., Fr. Bertram Griffin
Pres.-Elect, Catherine Lingas
Treas., David Teeter
Major Activities: Educational Ministries; Legislation; Urban Ministries; Refugees; Chaplaincy; Social Concerns; Direct Services; Jewish-Christian Relations; Farm Ministry; Alcohol and Drug Ministry; Welfare Advocacy; Faith & Order; Peace Ministries; IMPACT; Communications; AIDS Ministry; Prostitution Ministry; Farm and Rural Ministires; Racism

PENNSYLVANIA

The Pennsylvania Council of Churches

900 S. Arlington Ave., Rm. 100, Harrisburg 17109
Tel. (717) 545-4761
Exec. Dir., Rev. Albert E. Myers
Asst. to the Exec. Dir. for Ethnic Cooperation and Institutional Ministries, Rev. Debra L. Moody
Asst. to the Exec. Dir. for Special Min., Rev. Charles E. Dorsey

Asst. to the Exec. Dir., for Soc. Min., Rev. Paul D. Gehris
Ed. of Newscript, Rev. Kendall Link, 921 Wallace Ave., Chambersburg 17201
Pres., Rev. Paul L. Westcoat, Jr., 320 S. Maple Ave., Greensburg 15601
Vice Pres., Hon Gorham L. Black, Jr.
Sec., Mrs. Pearl Veronis
Treas., James R. Reeser
Bus. Mgr., Richard E. Lutz
Major Activities: Institutional Ministry; Migrant Ministry; Truck Stop Chaplaincy; Social Ministry; Park Ministry; Inter-Church Planning and Dialog; Conferences; Disaster Response; Trade Association Activities; Church Education; Radio Newscript Service; Ethnic Cooperation

Pennsylvania Conference on Interchurch Cooperation

P. O. Box 2835, Harrisburg 17105
Tel. (717) 545-4761
Co-Staff: Dr. Howard Fetterhoff, Rev. Albert E. Myers
Co-Chairpersons: Bishop Nicolas Patillo and Bishop Charlie F. McNutt, Jr.
Major Activities: Theological Consultation; Social Concerns; Inter-Church Planning; Conferences and Seminars; Disaster Response Preparedness

Allentown; see Lehigh County Conference

Ecumenical Conference of Greater Altoona

1208 Thirteenth St., P. O. Box 305, Altoona 16603
Tel. (814)942-0512
Exec. Dir., Mrs. Eileen Becker
Major Activities: Religious Education; Workshops; Ecumenical Activities; Religious Christmas Parade; Campus Ministry; Community Concerns; Peace Forum; Religious Education for Mentally Handicapped

Christians United in Beaver County

1098 Third Street, Beaver 15009
Tel. (412) 774-1446
Exec. Sec., Mrs. Lois L. Smith
Chaplains, Rev. Samuel Ward, Mrs. Erika Bruner, Rev. Edward O. Poole, Rev. Frank Churchill, Mr. Jack Kirkpatrick, Rev. Elaine Solomon
Pres., Rev. Edward Heist, 301 Adams St., Rochester 15074
Treas., Mr. Eugene Wilson, 162 Wm. Penn Way, New Brighton 15066
Major Activities: Christian Education; Evangelism; Radio; Social Action; Church Women United; United Church Men; Ecumenism; Hospital, Detention Home, and Jail Ministry

Greater Bethlehem Area Council of Churches

520 E. Broad St., Bethlehem 18018
Tel. (215) 867-8671
Coord., Mrs. Audrey Bertsch
Pres., Mr. Larry Kisslinger, 1015 Rockland Rd. 18017
Treas., Mrs. Polly McClure, 7 W. Washington Ave. 18018
Major Activities: Support Ministry; Institutional Ministry to Elderly and Infirm; Community-Wide Christian Education; Christian Concerts; World-Local Hunger Projects; Media Ministries; Elderly Ministry

Delaware Valley Media Ministry

1501 Cherry St., Philadelphia 19102
Tel (215) 563-7854
Exec. Dir., Ms. Nancy Nolde
Major Activities: Interfaith Communication and Television Production Agency

Easton Area Interfaith Council

330 Ferry St., Easton 18042
Tel. (215) 258-4955
Admin. Sec., Mirian Fretzo
Major Activities: Food Bank; Hospital and Nursing Home Chaplaincy; Center for Mentally Handicapped; Homeless

Inter-Church Ministries of Northwestern Pennsylvania

252 W. 7th St., Erie 16501
Tel. (814) 454-2411
Exec. Dir., Rev. Willis J. Merriman
Assoc. Dir., Rev. Deborah R. Dockstader
Adjunct Staff: Dr. David J. Sullivan, Pastoral Counseling; James A. Dimperio, Aging Prog.
Pres., Rev. Richard K. Schultz, 3108 Sterrettania Rd. 16506
Treas., Rev. Richard E. Kneller, 1249 W. 10th St. 16502
Major Activities: Local Ecumenism; Ministry with Aging; Social Ministry; Interchurch TV; Pastoral Counseling; Continuing Education; N.W. Pa. Conf. of Bishops and Judicatory Execs.; Institute of Pastoral Care; Theological Dialogue

Christian Churches United of the Tri-County Area

900 S. Arlington Ave., Rm. 128, Harrisburg 17109
Tel. (717) 652-2771
Interim Exec. Dir., Patrick Rooney
Pres., Rev. Jay Wesley House
Treas., Michael Harvey
Major Activities: Volunteer Ministries to Prisons, Hospitals, Institutionalized Aged, AIDS and for Christian Education; Harrisburg Area Emergency Life Survival Project (Housing, Rent, Food, Medication, Transportation, Home Heating, Clothing); La Casa de Amistad (The House of Friendship) same services as above but in the Hispanic area.

Lancaster County Council of Churches

447 E. King St., Lancaster 17602
Tel. (717) 291-2261
Interim Exec. Dir., Rev. William Brown
Prison Chaplain, Rev. David F. Myer
Dir. Prescott House, Casey Jones
Child Abuse, Ursula Wanner
Dir. CONTACT, Janet Sandham
Pres., Rev. Brad Wallace, 700 Pleasure Rd., 17601
Major Activities: Hospital Chaplaincy, Christian Social Ministry; Residential Ministry to Youthful Offenders; Prison Ministry; Housing; CONTACT; Widow Support; Advocacy; Child Abuse Prevention

Lebanon County Christian Ministries

818 Water St., P.O.Box 654, Lebanon 17042
Tel. (717)274-2601
Exec. Dir., Mrs. Elizabeth F. Greer
Food & Clothing Bank Dir., Sherry A. Wallis
H.O.P.E. Services Dir., Phyllis A. Holtry

Noon Meals Coord., Mrs. Glenda Wenger
Major Activities: H.O.P.E. (Helping Our People in Emergencies—Emergency Material Needs Services and Clearinghouse); Food & Clothing Bank; Free Noon Meal Program; Surplus Federal Commodity Distribution Program; Ecumenical Events; Chaplaincy and Support Services

Lehigh County Conference of Churches

36 S. 6th St., Allentown 18101
Tel. (215) 433-6421
Exec. Dir., Rev. William A. Seaman
Pres., Mr. Henry Messinger
Treas., Mr. James Hottenstein, 152 E. South St. 18103
Major Activities: Chaplaincy Program; Migrant Ministry; Social Concerns and Action; Clergy Dialogues; Drop-In-Center for De-Institutionalized Adults; Ecumenical Food Kitchen; Housing Advocacy Program; Pahways (Reference to Social Services)

Metropolitan Christian Council of Philadelphia

1501 Cherry St., Philadelphia 19102
Tel. (215) 563-7854
Exec. Dir., Rev. C. Edward Geiger
Assoc., Communications, Ms. Nancy L. Nolde
Adm. Asst., Mrs. Joan G. Shipman
Chairperson: Dr. Lawrence L. Hand
Pres., Dr. William J. Shaw
Treas., John A. Clark, 1 Franklin Plz. 19102
Major Activities: Congregational Clusters; Public Policy Advocacy; Communication; Interfaith Dialogue

Northwest Interfaith Movement

Greene Street at Westview, Philadelphia 19119
Tel. (215) 843-5600
Dir., Rev. Richard R. Fernandez
Coord. Nursing Home Prog., Mary Fallon
Chairperson, Eddilera E. Kinzer
Major Activities: Community Development & Community Reinvestment; Older Adult Concerns; Nursing Home Program; Unemployment; Economic Issues; Public Education; Peace; Racism; Poverty Issues

Christian Associates of Southwest Pennsylvania

239 Fourth Ave., Pittsburgh 15222
Tel. (412) 281-1515
Exec. Dir., Rev. John Wagner, Jr.
Assoc. Exec. Dir. Rev. Bruce H. Swenson
Cable TV Co-ordinator, Mr. Ron Bocchi
Adm. Asst., Mrs. Barbara Kovach
Pres., Canon Richard W. Davies

Treas., Sr. Ursula Kelly
Major Activities: Communications; Planning; Church and Community; Leadership Development; Theological Dialogue; Evangelism/Church Growth; Racism Committee

East End Cooperative Ministry

250 N. Highland Ave., Pittsburgh 15206
Tel. (412) 361-5549
Exec. Dir., Mrs. Judith Marker
Major Activities: Food Pantry; Soup Kitchen; Men's Emergency Shelter; Meals on Wheels; Casework and Supportive Services for Elderly; Information and Referral; Program for Children and Youth; Bridge Housing Program

Ecumenical Urban Ministries

100 N. Bellefield at Fifth Ave., Pittsburgh 15213
Tel. (412)682-2751
Interim Exec. Dir., Rev. Martha Orphe
Pres. of EUM Bd., Dr. Betty Jane McWilliams
Major Activities: Revitalization of Local Urban Churches; Ethics Panels; Advocacy Networks; Learning Opportunities

North Hills Youth Ministry

1566 Northway Mall, Pittsburgh 15237
Tel. (412) 366-1300
Exec. Dir., Ronald B. Barnes
Major Activities: Junior and Senior High School Family and Individual Counseling; Pre-Adolescent Youth Early Intervention Counseling; Educational Programming for Churches and Schools; Youth Advocacy

South Hills Interfaith Ministries

5171 Park Ave., Bethel Park 15102
Tel. (412) 833-6177
Exec. Dir., Robert Laird Brashear
Psychological Services, Mr. Don Zandier, Ms. Hilda Schorr-Ribera; Ms. Carol Loadman-Copeland
Cmty. Services, Mr. Thomas Tompkins, Mrs. Mary Ethel Patterson; Sr. Charlene M. Fregeolle
Adm. Asst., Ms. Jackie Riebel
Interfaith Reemployment Job Advocate, Mr. David Bates
Pres., Mr. Arthur Tombucci
Treas., Mr. Jerry Sherman
Major Activities: Basic Human Needs; Unemployment; Community Organization and Development Inter-Faith Cooperation; Family Hospice; Personal Growth

The Greater Reading Council of Churches

54 N. 8th St., Reading 19601
Tel. (215) 375-6108
Exec. Dir., Rev. Warren P. Wilfert, Jr.
Adm. Asst., Constance B. Reinholz
Pres., Rev. Steven Belinski
Rec. Sec., Mrs. Virginia Chudgar
Treas., Mr. Lee M. LeVan
Major Activities: Institutional Ministry; CWU; Social Action; Migrant Ministry; CWS; CROP Walk for Hunger; Emergency Assistance; Furniture Bank; Person Chaplaincy; AIDS Hospice Development

Reading Urban Ministry

230 N. Fifth St., Rm. 300,Reading 19601
Tel. (215) 374-6917
Exec. Dir., Rev. Douglas L. Shaffer

Pres., Mary Ann Cope
Vice Pres., _____
Sec., Jean Moylan
Treas., Raymond Drain
Major Activities: Community Clothing Center; Friendly Visitor Program to Elderly; Caring When It Counts (Emergency Intervention with Elderly); Summer Youth Program; Berks AIDS Health Crisis

United Churches of Williamsport and Lycoming County

202 E. Third St., Williamsport 17701
Tel. (717) 322-1110
Exec. Dir., Rev. Dr. Alton M. Motter
Ofc. Sec., Mrs. Linda Winter
Pres., Rev. Robert M. Logan, 369 Broad St., Montoursville 17754
Treas., Mr. Howard R. Baldwin, Jr., 1725 McConnell Dr., 17701
Dir., Ecumenism, Rev. Robert L. Dreisen, 324 Howard St., South Williamsport 17701
Dir., Educ. Ministries, Rev. Bruce R. Druckenmiller, 202 E. Third St. 17701
Dir., Institutional Ministry, Rev. David W. Schmuck, 1427 Memorial Ave.
Dir., Radio-TV, Rev. Michael D. Gingerich, Box 366, Picture Rocks 11762
Dir., Social Concerns, Rev. Mark A. Santucci, 426 Mulberry St.
Dir., Prison Ministry, Rev. John N. Mostoller, 1200 Almond St. 17701
Major Activities: Ecumenism; Educational Ministries; Church Women United; Church World Service and CROP; Prison Ministry; Radio-TV; Nursing Homes; Fuel Bank; Food Pantry; UNICEF; Family Life; Shepherd of the Streets Urban Ministry; Peace Concerns

Willkinsburg Community Ministry

710 Mulberry St., Pittsburgh 15221
Tel. (412)241-8072
Dir., Betty Dorsey Judson
Youth Prog. Coord., Beverly Burnett
Pres. of Bd., Marty Mills
Major Activities: Hunger and Clothing Ministry; After School Youth Programs, Including Child Care for Working Parents; Summer Bible School; Teen-Moms Infant Care; Support Programs for Single Parents and Pregnant Teens; Meals on Wheels; Telecare; Community Activities and Events; Fundraising

Wyoming Valley Council of Churches

35 S. Franklin St., Wilkes-Barre 18701
Tel. (717); 825-8543
Exec. Dir., Rev. Anita J. Ambrose
Ofc. Sec., Mrs. Sandra Karrott
Pres., Rev. Dr. Charles Johns
Treas., Miss Marjorie Trethaway
Major Activities: Hospital and Nursing Home Chaplaincy; Church Women United; High Rise Apartment Ministry; Hospital Referral Service; Emergency Response; Food Bank; Migrant Ministry; Meals on Wheels; Dial-A-Driver; Radio and TV; Leadership Schools; Interfaith Programs; Shepherd of the Streets Ministry; Night Chaplain Ministry, Area Hospitals; CROP Hunger Walks; Pastoral Care Ministries

York County Council of Churches

145 S. Duke St., York 17403
Tel. (717) 854-9504

Exec. Dir., Rev. Robert B. Ketcham
CONTACT-York Teleministry Dir., Mrs. Lois Wetzler
Pres., Rev. Edward Yarnell
Treas., Mr. William Anderson
Major Activities: Educational Development; Spiritual Growth and Renewal; Worship and Witness; Congregational Resourcing; Outreach and Mission

RHODE ISLAND

Rhode Island State Council of Churches

743 Hope St., Providence 02906
Tel. (401) 861-1700
Exec. Minister, Rev. Dr. Richard C. Brown
Adm. Asst., Peggy Macnie
Pres., Rev. Kate Penfield
Treas., Mr. Robert A. Mitchell
Major Activities: Urban Ministries; Radio-TV; Institutional Chaplaincy; Advocacy/Justice & Service: Legislative Liaison; Faith & Order; CWS; Leadership Development; Campus Ministries

SOUTH CAROLINA

South Carolina Christian Action Council, Inc.

P.O. Box 3663, Columbia 29230
Tel. (803) 786-7115
Exec. Minister, _____
Pres., Rev. Dr. Marion Aldridge
Major Activities: Advocacy and Ecumenism; Continuing Education; Interfaith Dialogue; Citizenship and Public Affairs; Publications

United Ministries

606 Pendleton St., Greenville 29601
Tel. (803) 232-6463
Exec. Dir., Rev. Beth Templeton
Pres., Barry Edwards
Vice-Pres., Fleming Markel
Sec., Helen Broadhead
Treas., Marion Beacham
Major Activities: Caring Volunteers; H.E.A.T. (Heat for Elderly and Toddlers); Caring for Unemployed People (C.U.P.); M.E.D. (Medication, Education; Dedication); Emergency Assistance; Hunger Pantry; Day Care Center for Homeless; Adopt-A-House

SOUTH DAKOTA

Association of Christian Churches

200 W. 18th St., Sioux Falls 57104
Tel. (605) 334-1980
Exec. Dir., Dr. Bruce Gray
Pres., Fr. Donald Kettler
Sec., Ms. Sally Miller
Major Activities: Ecumenical Forums; Continuing Education for Clergy; Church and Community Relations; Legislative Information; Resourcing Local Ecumenism; Native American Issues; Yoked Fields Ministries; Rural Economic Development

TENNESSEE

Tennessee Association of Churches

1785 Hayden Rd., Germantown 38138
Tel. (901)754-1716
Exec. Dir., Dr. C. Ray Dobbins, 1785 Hayden, Germantown 38118. Tel. (901)754-1716
Pres., Rev. Jude D. Weisenbeck
Major Activities: Faith and Order; Christian Unity; Social Concern Ministries; Legislative Concerns

Metropolitan Inter Faith Association (MIFA)

P.O. Box 3130, Memphis, 38173
Tel. (901) 527-0208
Exec. Dir., Mr. Allie Prescott
Major Activities: Emergency Housing; Emergency Services (Rent Assistance); Home-Delivered Meals

TEXAS

Texas Conference of Churches

2704 Rio Grande #9, Austin 78705
Tel. (512) 478-7491
Exec. Dir., Rev. Dr. Frank H. Dietz
Cons., Alcohol and Drug Abuse, Ms. Trish Merrill
Pres., Bishop Charles Grahmann
Major Activities: Church and Society; Ecumenism; Christian-Jewish Relations; Domestic Violence; Peace: Disaster Response; BARCA; Texas Church World Service/CROP; Alcoholism-Addiction Education; Church Woman United In Texas; Central American Issues; Texas IMPACT

Austin Metropolitan Ministries

44 East Ave., Ste. 302, Austin 78701
Tel. (512)472-7627
Exec. Dir., Patrick Flood
Pres., Rt. Rev. Anselmo Carral
Treas., Shaun P. O'Brien
Chaplain, Rev. H. Rex Lewis (Brackenridge Hospital)
Chaplain, Rev. Charles I. Fay (Travis Co. Jails)
Major Activities: Pastoral Care in Hospital and Jails; Broadcast Ministry; Emergency Assistance; Older Persons Task Force; Housing Task Force; Peace and Justice Commission; Economy and Jobs Issues

Corpus Christi Metro Ministries

1919 Leopard, Corpus Christi 78408
Tel. (512)887-0151
Exec. Dir., Rev. Edward B. Seeger
Dir., Adm., Daniel D. Scott
Dir., Volunteers, Ann Schiro
Fin. Coord., Sue McCown
Dir., Loaves and Fishes, Joe Jaimes
Dir., Counseling, Amie Harrell
Dir., Employment, James Hamby
Dir., Bethany House, James Shipley
Dir., Rainbow House, _____
Dir., Child Abuse Prevention, _____
Major Activities: Food Center; Shelters; Counseling; Job Readiness; Job Placement; Abuse Prevention and Intervention; Adult Day Care; Primary Health Care

Greater Dallas Community of Churches

2800 Swiss Ave., Dallas 75204
Tel. (214) 824-8680
Exec. Dir., Rev. Thomas H. Quigley
Dir., Hospital Chaplaincy, Dr. Benjamin H. E. Breitkreuz
Dir., County Jail Chaplaincy, Rev. Holsey Hickman
Dir., Community College Ministry, Rev. Chauncey Nealy
Dir., Church and Community Dept., Dr. Charles A. Hunter
Prog. Assoc., John Stoesz
Devel. Dir., Carole Rylander
Pres., Dr. Zan Holmes, Jr.
Treas., Ralph Cousins
Major Activities: Hospital Chaplaincy; Community College Ministry; Jail Chaplaincy; Housing; Hunger; Peacemaking; Faith and Life; Jewish-Christian Relations; Racial Ethnic Justice; Child Advocacy

Border Association for Refugees from Central America (BARCA)

P.O. Box 715, Edinburg 78540
Tel. (512)631-7447
Exec. Dir., Ninfa Ochoa-Krueger
Dir., Refugee Children Serv., Kathleen Grace
Major Activities: Food, Shelter, Clothing, to Central Americans; Medical and Other Emergency Aid; Legal Advocacy; Special Services to Children; Speakers on Refugee Concerns for Church Groups.

Tarrant Area Community of Churches

807 Texas St., Ste. 101, Fort Worth 76102
Tel. (817) 335-9341
Interim Dir., Mary Smith
Adm. Asst., Verna Deene Keene
Pres., Msgr. Charles King
Treas., George Scott
Major Activities: Developing Community Resources; Workshops and Seminars; Ecumenical Celebrations; Airport Chaplaincy; Ministry and Aging; Hunger; Faith & Life; Jewish-Christian Relations; Teenage Pregnancy Prevention Program; Jail Ministry

Northside Inter-Church Agency (NICA)

506 NW 15th St., Fort Worth 76106
Tel. (817) 626-1102
Dir., Francine Esposito Pratt

Southeast Area Churches (SEARCH)

P.O. Box 51256, Fort Worth 76105
Tel. (817) 531-2211
Dir., Ms. Dorothy Anderson

Southside Area Ministries (SAM)

305 W. Broadway, Fort Worth 76104
Tel. (817) 332-3778
Exec. Dir., Diane Smiley
Major Activities: Refugee Assistance; Community Development; Language Development; Tutoring

Houston Metropolitan Ministries

3217 Montrose Blvd., Houston 77006
Tel. (713) 522-3955
Exec. Dir., Rev. Bruce Theunissen
Assoc. Exec. Dir., Richard E. Clinton
Dir., Adm. and Fin., Douglas Simmons
Dir. of Develop., Lisa Estes
Dir. of Comm., Jane Brandenberger
Dir. RSVP, Candice Twyman
Dir., Senior Health and Meals on Wheels, Evelyn Velasquez
Dir., Youth Victim/Witness, Pamela R. Hobbs
Dir., Family Connection, Vincent Manning
Dir., EDGE for Youth, John O. Holmes
Dir., Interfaith Hunger Coalition, Ellen Mitchell
Dir., Refugee Resettlement, _____
Dir., Jail Chaplaincy, Rev. Rebecca Lewis
Pres., Rev. H. Richard Siciliano
Treas., Collyn Peddie
Major Activities: Urban Concerns; Combating Hunger; Youth; Aging; Refugee Services; Jail Chaplaincy; Congregational Relations; Interfaith Relations

United Board of Missions

1701 Bluebonnet Ave., P. O. Box 3856, Port Arthur 77643
Exec. Dir., Clark Moore
Pres., Claude Pinell
Major Activities: Emergency Assistance, i.e., Food and Clothing, Rent and Utility, Medical, Dental, Transportation; Share a Toy at Christmas; Counseling; Back to School Clothing Assistance; Information and Referral; Hearing Aid Bank; Meals on Wheels; Scholarships; Energy Conservation Programs

San Antonio Community of Churches

1101 W. Woodlawn, San Antonio 78201
Tel. (512)733-9159
Exec. Dir., Rev. Dr. C. Don Baugh
Instit. Chaplain, Dr. David Jester
Pres., Rev. Royce Makin
Vice Pres., Fr. Thomas Flanagan
Sec., _____
Treas., Mr. Dick Halter
Major Activities: Christian Educ.; Missions; Social Relations; Radio-TV; Continuing Education; Resource Center Infant Formula and Medical Prescriptions for Children of Indigent Families

San Antonio Urban Council

1602-A Goliad Rd., San Antonio 78223
Tel. (512)337-8550
Exec. Dir., Sue Kelly
Pres., Mr. Chris McDaniel
Major Activities: Homes for Discharged Mental Patients; After School Care for Latch Key Children; Christian Base Community Ministry; San Antonio Legalization Education Coalition

VERMONT

Vermont Ecumenical Council and Bible Society

285 Maple St., Burlington 05401
Tel. (802) 864-7723
Exec. Sec., Rev. John E. Nutting
Pres., Rt. Rev. Daniel E. Swenson
Treas., Jeanne Plo
Major Activities: Legislative Liaison; Christian Unity; Bible Distribution; Social Justice; Committees on Peace, Life and Work, Faith and Order, Bible

VIRGINIA

Virginia Council of Churches, Inc.

2321 Westwood Ave., Richmond 23230
Tel. (804) 353-5587
Gen. Min., Rev. James McDonald
Prog. Assoc., Rev. Judith Bennett
Coord., Weekday Rel. Ed., Miss Olive Clark, 137 Robin Rd., Waynesboro 22980
Dir., Refugee Resettlement, Rev. Dorothy D. France
Dir., Migrant Head Start, Rev. Myron Miller
Coord., Campus Ministry Forum, Rev. Robert Thomason, 5000 Echols Ave., Alexandria 22304
Major Activities: Educational Development; Church and Society; Direct Ministries; Ecumenical Affairs; Communications; Refugee Resettlement; Legislative Concerns and Public Witness; Park Ministries; Migrant Ministries; Day Care; Disaster Coordination; Rural Concerns

Community Ministry of Fairfax County

1920 Association Dr., Rm. 505, Reston 22091
Tel. (703)620-5014
Exec. Dir., Rev. Frederick S. Lowry
Newsletter Ed., James Vining
Chpsn., Bill Johnson
Sec., Debra Haraldson
Treas., John Wells
Major Activities: Ecumenical Social Ministry; Elderly; Criminal Justice; Housing; Public Education

Virginia Interfaith Center for Public Policy

6 North 6th St., Richmond 23219
Tel. (804) 780-2703
Exec. Dir., Rev. James A. Payne
Chpsn., Rev. Robert G. Hetherington
Sec.-Treas., Catherine Johnson
Major Activities: Interfaith Dialogue and Legislative Witness in Virginia; Legis-Link (Legislative Bulletin); Interact (Newsletter); Legislative Agenda (Annual Publication); Interfaith Legislative Education; State-Wide Conferences and Seminars; Cooperative Legislative Advocacy Prog. with Va. Cncl. of Chs.

WASHINGTON

Washington Association of Churches

4759 15th Ave., NE, Seattle 98105
Tel. (206) 525-1988
Exec., Min., Rev. John C. Boonstra
Dir., Immigration and Refugee Prog., Ms. Sally Mackey, 233 Sixth Ave., N., Ste. 110, 98103. Tel. (206)443-9219
Dir., Cent. Am. Refugee Prog., Mrs. Hermalinda Gonzales, 225 N. 70th 98103. Tel. (206) 789-7297
Pres., Ms. Trudy Thorleifson, 911 Stewart St. 98101. Tel. (206)682-3620
Treas., Rev. Dr. Robert C. Brock, 6558 35th Ave., S.W., Seattle 98126 Tel. (206) 938-1008
Major Activities: Faith and Order; Poverty and Justice Advocacy; Hunger Action; Legislation; Denominational Ecumenical Coordination; Theological Formation; Leadership Development; Refugee Resettlement; Immigration; International Solidarity

Center for the Prevention of Sexual and Domestic Violence

1914 N. 34th St., Ste. 105, Seattle 98103
Tel. (206)634-1903
Exec. Dir., Rev. Marie M. Fortune
Program Dir., Frances E. Wood
Admin. Dir., Jean Anton
Admin. Assoc., Sandra Barone
Clerical Asst., Lorna Newgent
Devel. Assoc., Lennie Ziontz
Major Activities: Educational Ministry; Clergy and Lay Training; Social Action.

Church Council of Greater Seattle

4759 15th Ave., NE, Seattle 98105
Tel. (206) 525-1213
Pres.-Dir., Rev. Dr. William B. Cate
Assoc. Dir.-Urban Min., Rev. David C. Bloom
Assoc. Dir.-Adm., Alice M. Woldt
Develop. Coord., Rev. Dr. David Aasen
Exec. Asst., Angela W. Ford
Dir., Central Amer. Peace Campaign, Beth Brunton
Dir., Emerg. Feeding Prog., Rev. Dr. O. J. Moore
Dir., Friend-to-Friend, Joe Rust
Dir., Bethany Proj. for Women Ex-Offenders, Ethel Ford
Dir., Youth Service Chaplaincy, Terri Ward
Dir., Mental Health Chaplaincy, Rev. Craig Rennebohm
Staff, Native Am. Task Force, Ron Adams
Staff, Leningrad-Seattle Sister Church, Karin Frankenburger
Staff, Mission for Music and Healing, Esther "Little Dove" John
Staff, Seattle Displacement Coalition, John Fox
Staff, Task Force on Aging, Mary Liz Chaffee
Staff, ACTfra, Gloria Yamote
Staff, Public Education, Rev. Joyce Manson
Housing and Homelessness Task Force, Josephine Archuleta
Vice-Pres., Laura Bailey
Treas., Dorothy Eley
Major Activities: Racial Justice; Peace Action; Pastoral Ministry; Hunger; Public Education; Housing; Employment; Mental Health; Gay Rights; Aging, Family; Central America; South Africa; Native Americans; Pacific Rim; Jewish-Christian Relations; Ecology; Homelessness; Farm Workers Support; Economic Justice

Ecumenical Metropolitan Ministry

P.O. Box 12272, Seattle 98102
Tel. (206) 625-0755
Exec. Dir., Ruth M. Velozo
Chpsn., Rev. Henry F. Seaman
Major Activities: Northwest Harvest (Hunger Response); Northwest Infants Corner (Special Nutrititional Products for Infants and Babies); Northwest Caring Ministry (Individuals and Family Crisis Intervention and Advocacy); Northwest Senior Nutrition (Special Food Needs for the Elderly); E.M.M. (Advocacy, Education, Communications Relative to Programs and Economic Justice).

Spokane Christian Coalition

E. 245-13th Ave., Spokane 99202
Tel. (509) 624-5156
Exec. Dir., Rev. John A. Olson
Pres., Fr. Michael Hatcher
Treas., Lula Hage, N. 1413 Superior 99202
Major Activities: Forums on Issues; Friend to Friend Visitation with Nursing Home Patients; "Fig Tree" Newspaper; Interstate Task Force on Human Relations; AIDS Task Force; Greater Spokane Coalition Against Poverty Task Force; Building Inter-racial Bridges Task Force

Associated Ministries of Tacoma-Pierce County

1224 South "I" St., Tacoma 98405
Tel. (206) 383-3056
Exec. Dir., Rev. David T. Alger, 650 N. Hawthorne 98406
Assoc. Dir., Janet E. Leng, 1809 N. Lexington 98406
Pres., Mr. Dennis Fulton
Sec., Mrs. Ruth Manter
Treas., Mr. Dennis Paul
Major Activities: FISH/Food Banks; Hunger Awareness; Economic Justice; Christian Education; Shalom (Peacemaking) Resource Center; Social Service Program Advocacy; Communication and Networking of Churches; Emergency Housing

Associated Ministries of Thurston County

Box 895, Olympia 98507
Tel. (206) 357-7224
Exec. Dir., Keturah Brown
Pres., Rev. James Blundell
Treas., Steve Davis
Major Activities: Church Information and Referral; Interfaith Worship; Workshops; Social and Health Concerns; Legislation

WEST VIRGINIA

West Virginia Council of Churches

1608 Virginia St. E., Charleston 25311
Tel. (304) 344-3141

Interim Exec. Dir., Rev. Harold A. LaParl
Dir., Support Services Network, Janet Harmon
Pres., Rev. James M. Kerr, 1511 Pleasant Valley Rd., Fairmont 26554
Vice Pres., Bishop L. Alexander Black, ELCA Synod of WV, 502 Morgantown Ave. - Atrium Mall, Fairmont 26554
Treas., Mrs. Phyllis Ringham, 306 Delaware Ave., 25302
Major Activities: Leisure Ministry; Disaster Response; Faith and Order; Family Concerns; Inter-Faith Relations; Peace and Justice; Government Concerns; Support Sevices Network

The Greater Wheeling Council of Churches

110 Methodist Bldg., Wheeling 26003
Tel. (304) 232-5315
Exec. Sec., Mrs. Mabel Griffith
Hospital Notification Sec., Mrs. Ruth Fletcher
Pres., Rev. Charles Ellwood
Treas., Dr. Beryl Hart
Major Activities: Christian Education; Evangelism; Vespers; Television; Institutional Ministry; Religious Film Library; Church Women United; Volunteer Pastor Care at OVMC Hospital; School of Religion; Hospital Notification; Hymn Sing in the Park; Free Lunch Program

WISCONSIN

Wisconsin Conference of Churches

1955 West Broadway, Ste. 104, Madison 53713
Tel. (608) 222-9779
Exec. Dir., Rev. John D. Fischer
Adm. Asst. and Asst. Treas., Mrs. Phyllis Brinkman
Public Policy Dir. and IMPACT Dir., Ms. Bonnee Voss
Dir. Broadcasting Ministry Commission, Rev. Robert P. Seater, 4240 N. 78th St., Milwaukee 53222. Tel. (414) 461-1774
Peace and Justice Ecumenical Partnership, Co-Dirs., Jane Hammatt-Kavaloski and Vincent Kavaloski, Rt. #3, Box 228 E, Dodgeville 53533
Pres., Rev. William Wells
Treas., Mr. Chester Spangler, 625 Crandall, Madison 53711
Major Activities: Church and Society; Religion and Leisure; Migrant Ministry; Pastoral Services; Broadcasting Ministry; Aging; IMPACT; Institutional Chaplaincy; Peace and Justice; Faith and Order; Rural Concerns Forum

Christian Youth Council

1715—52nd St., Kenosha 53140
Tel. (414) 652-9543
Exec. Dir., Ron Stevens
Sports Dir., Krisp Jensen
Outreach Dir., Krisp Jensen
Pres., Barry Wojtak
Major Activities: Leisure Time Ministry; Institutional Ministries; Ecumenical Committee; Social Concerns

Interfaith Conference of Greater Milwaukee

1442 N. Farwell Ave., Ste. 200, 53202
Tel. (414) 276-9050

Exec. Dir., Mr. Jack Murtaugh
Prog. Coord. on Poverty Issues, Mrs. Mary Strecker
Prog. Coord. for Cmty. Devel., Mr. Steve Holt
Ofc. Adm. Ms. Patricia Koppenhoefer
Prog. Coord. for Public Educ., Mrs. Charlotte Holloman
Consultant in Communications, Rev. Robert Seater
Chpsn., Rev. Dr. Carl R. Simon
Treas., Mrs. Ruth Olsen
Major Activities: Economic Issues - Unemployment; Emergency Assistance - Public Policy; Religion and Labor Committee; Economic Concerns - Private Sector Committee; Public Education Committee; TV Programming; Peace and International Issues Committee; Annual Membership Luncheon

Center for Community Concerns

1501 Villa St. Racine 53403
Tel. (414) 637-9176
Exec. Dir., Mrs. Jean Mandli
Skillbank Coord., Eleanor Sorenson
Volunteer Prog. Coord., Chris Udell-Solberg

VIPS (Volunteers for Intergenerational Programs in Schools) Coord., Chris Udell-Solberg
Adm. Asst., Bonnie Wrixton
Major Activities: Advocacy; Direct Services; Research; Community Consultant; Criminal Justice; Volunteerism; Senior Citizen Services

WYOMING

Wyoming Church Coalition

1215 Gibbon, Laramie 82070
Tel. (307)745-6000
Adm. Coord., Anne Ludlow
Chair, Rev. Warren Murphy, P.O. Box 1718, Cody 82414
Penitentiary Chaplain, Rev. Lynn Schumacher, P.O. Box 400, Rawlins 82301
Major Activities: M. L. King Holiday; Welfare; Prisons; Peace and Justice

8. CANADIAN REGIONAL AND LOCAL ECUMENICAL AGENCIES

Most of the organizations listed below are councils of churches in which churches participate officially, whether at the parish or judicatory level. They operate at either the city, metropolitan area, or county level. Parish clusters within urban areas are not included.

Canadian local ecumenical bodies operate without paid staff, with the exception a few which have part-time staff. In most cases the name and address of the president or chairperson is listed. As these offices change from year to year, some of this information may be out of date by the time the **Yearbook of American and Canadian Churches** is published. However, a letter to the address listed will be forwarded. Up-to-date information may be secured from the Canadian Council of Churches, 40 St. Clair Ave., E., Toronto, Ontario M4T 1M9.

ALBERTA

Calgary Inter-Faith Community Association
Rev. V. Hennig, 7515 7th St., Calgary, Alberta T2V 1G1

Calgary Inter-Faith Sawdap:
Mrs. Caroline Brown, #106-1916-2 St., S.W., Calgary, Alberta T2S 1S3

Calgary Council of Churches
Box 7550, Stn. E., Calgary, Alberta T3C 3M3

Edmonton & District Council of Churches
Rev. John Bergman, 13340-96th St., Edmonton, Alberta T5E 4B3

ATLANTIC PROVINCES

Atlantic Ecumenical Council of Churches
Pres., Rev. John E. Boyd, Box 637, 90 Victoria St., Box 637, Amherst, Nova Scotia B4H 4B4

BRITISH COLUMBIA

Canadian Ecumenical Action
Coordinator, 1410 West 12th Ave., Vancouver, British Columbia V6H 1M8

Greater Victoria Council of Churches
Pres., Mr. H. De Zwager, 1457 Clifford St., Victoria, British Columbia V8S 1M1

MANITOBA

Association of Christian Churches in Manitoba
240 Home St., Winnipeg, Manitoba R3G 1X3

Manitoba Provincial Interfaith Council
Rev. Canon W. J. G. Ayers, #8 - 400 Carpathia St., Winnipeg, Manitoba R3N 1Y4

NEW BRUNSWICK

Moncton Area Council of Churches

Ms. Faye L. MacKay, Site 9. Comp. 7, R.R. #1, Hillsborough, New Brunswick E0A 1X0

First Miramichi Inter-Church Council
Mrs. Victor Ross, Boiestown, New Brunswick E0H 1A0

NOVA SCOTIA

Amherst and Area Council of Churches
Mr. Ron Esta Brooks, RR#6, Amherst, Nova Scotia B3H 3Y4

Annapolis Royal Council of Churches
Rev. David Stokes, P. O. Box 7, Annapolis Royal, Nova Scotia B0S 1A0

Atlantic Baptist Fellowship
Rev. Donald Jackson, Tideways, Apt. 207, Wolfville, Nova Scotia B0P 1X0

Bedford and Sackville Church Association
Ms. Dianne Swineman, P. O. Box 585, Lower Sackville, Nova Scotia B4C 3J1

Bridgewater Inter-Church Council
Pres., Ms. Carroll Young, 159 High St., Bridgewater, Nova Scotia B4V 1W2

Cornwallis District Inter-Church Council
Pres., Mr. Tom Regan, Centreville, R.R. #2, Kings County, Nova Scotia B0T 1J0

Halifax-Dartmouth Council of Churches
Rev. Robert L. Johnson, 2021 Oxford St., Halifax, Nova Scotia B3L 2T3

Industrial Cape Breton Council of Churches
Mr. J. Redmond O'Keefe, 56 Rosewood Dr., Sydney, Nova Scotia B1P 1P4

Kentville Council of Churches
Rev. Canon S.J.P. Davies, 325 Main St., Kentville, Nova Scotia B4N 1C5

Mahone Bay Inter-Church Council
Mrs. Phyllis Smeltzer, R. R. 1, Mahone Bay, Nova Scotia B0J 2E0

Queen's County Council of Churches

Rev. Robert L. Johnson, P.O. Box 394, Milton, Nova Scotia B0T 1P0

Wolfville Inter-Church Council

Rev. Douglass Hergett, Box 786, Wolfville, Nova Scotia B0P 1X0

ONTARIO

Brockville & District Inter-Church Council

Rev. George Clifford, 5 Wall St., Brockville, Ontario K6V 4R8

Burlington Inter-Church Council

Mr. Fred Townsend, 425 Breckenwood, Burlington, Ontario L7L 2J6

Ottawa Christian Council of the Capital Area

1247 Kilborn Ave., Ottawa, Ontario K1H 6K9

Glengarry-Prescott-Russell Christian Council

Pres., Rev. G. Labrosse, St.-Eugene, Prescott, Ontario K0B 1P0

Hamilton and District Christian Churches Association

Chpsn., Rev. Dr. John A. Johnston, 147 Chedoke Ave., Hamilton, Ontario L8P 4P2

Ignace Council of Churches

Box 5, 205 Pine St., St. Ignace, Ontario P0T 1H0

Kitchener-Waterloo Council of Churches

Rev. Clarence Hauser, CR, 53 Allen St. E., Waterloo, Ontario N2J 1J3

London Inter-Church Council

Rev. R. Breitwieser, 172 High St., London, Ontario N6C 4K6

London Inter-City Faith Team

c/o United Church, 711 Colfourne St., London, Ontario N6A 3Z4

Manitoulin West Inter-Church Council

Mr. Douglas Wismer, Silver Water, Ontario P0P 1Y0

Massey Inter-Church Council

Rev. Hope Jackson, Box 248, Massey, Ontario P0P 1P0

Oshawa Ecumenical Group

Rev. James A. McKay, 333 Rossland Rd., N., Oshawa, Ontario L1J 3G4

Ecumenical Committee

Rev. William B. Kidd, 76 Eastern Ave., Sault Ste., Marie, Ontario P6A 4R2

Stratford District Council of Churches

Rev. N. S. Gibson, 20 Manning Ave., Stratford, Ontario N5A 5M9

Thorold Inter-Faith Council

1 Dunn St., St. Catharines, Ontario L2T 1P3

Thunder Bay Council of Churches

Rev. Richard Darling, 1800 Moodie St., E., Thunder Bay, Ontario P7E 4Z2

Waterloo Clergy Fellowship

50 Erb St., W., Waterloo, Ontario N2L 1T1

PRINCE EDWARD ISLAND

Charlottetown Christian Council

Rev. H. M. D. Westin, 21 Fitzroy St., Charlottetown, Prince Edward Island C1A 3K9

Summerside Christian Council

Mr. Paul H. Scherman, 181 Green St., Summerside, Prince Edward Island C1N 1Y8

West Prince Christian Council

Rev. Kenneth C. Jones, Box S, Ellerslie, Prince Edward Island C0B 1J0

QUEBEC

Hemmingford Ecumenical Committee

c/o Catherine Priest, Box 300, Hemmingford, Quebec J0L 1H0

Montreal Council of Churches

Rev. Stéphane Valiquette, 2065 Sherbrooke St., W., Montréal, Québec H3H 1G6

Montreal Ecumenical Association

Rev. William Derby, Box 158, Sta. B, Montreal, Quebec H3B 3J5

Centre for Ecumenism/Centre d'oecuménisme

Rev. Tom Ryan, 2065 Sherbrooke St., West, Montreal, Quebec H3H 1G6

Ecumenical Council of Churches/Downtown Montreal

Rev. Vernon Wishart, 3407 Avenue de Musee, Montréal, Québec H3G 2C6

The Ecumenical Group

c/o Mrs. C. Haten, 1185 Ste. Foy, St. Bruno, Quebec J3V 3C3

SASKATCHEWAN

Humboldt Clergy Council

Fr. Leo Hinz, O. S. B., Box 1989, Humboldt, Saskatchewan S0K 2A0

Melville Association of Churches

Attn., Catherine Gaw, Box 1078, Melville, Saskatchewan S0K 2A0

Inter-City Church Council

James Tait, 805 7th Ave., Saskatoon, Saskatchewan S7K 2V5

Saskatoon Council of Churches

816 Spadina Cres., E., Saskatoon, Saskatchewan S7K 3H4

Centre for Ecumenism—Saskatoon

Rev. Bernard de Margerie, 1006 Broadway Ave., Saskatoon, Saskatchewan S7N 1B9

9. THEOLOGICAL SEMINARIES AND BIBLE COLLEGES IN THE UNITED STATES

The following list of theological seminaries also includes certain departments of colleges and universities in which ministerial training is given. This list has been checked with the *Education Directory* published by the U. S. Office of Education, and with other directories. The compilation is fairly complete for Protestant and Jewish institutions and for the larger Roman Catholic seminaries. The listing of accredited Bible Colleges comes from the American Association of Bible Colleges.

The listings follow this order: Institution, affiliation, location, head, telephone number.

Abilene Christian University, Chs. of Chr. Abilene TX 79699. William J. Teague. Tel. (915)674-2000.

Academy of the New Church (Theol. Sch.), Gen. Ch. of the New Jerusalem. 2815 Huntingdon Pike, Bryn Athyn PA 19009. R. S. Junge. Tel. (215)947-4200

Alabama Christian School of Religion, Chs. of Chr. 7500 Taylor Rd., P.O. Box 17096, Montgomery AL 36117. Rex A. Turner, Jr. Tel. (205)277-2277; 1-800-351-3939.

Alaska Bible College, interdenom. P.O. Box 289, Glennallen, AK 99588. Gary J. Ridley, Sr., Tel. (907)822-3201.

Alliance Theological Seminary, Nyack College, Chr. and Miss. All. Nyack NY 10960. Rexford A. Boda. Tel. (914)358-1710

American Baptist College, Natl. Bapt., U.S.A., Inc.; So. Bapt. Conv. 1800 White's Creek Pike, Nashville TN 37207. Odell McGlothian, Sr. Tel. (615)262-1369.

American Baptist Seminary of the West, Am. Bapt. Chs., 2606 Dwight Way, Berkeley CA 94704. Theodore Keaton, actg. Tel. (415)841-1905.

Anderson University School of Theology, Ch. of God. Anderson IN 46012. Barry L. Callen. (317)641-4032

Andover Newton Theol. Sch., Amer. Bapt.; U. Ch. of Christ. 210 Herrick Rd., Newton Centre MA 02159. George Peck. Tel. (617)964-1100

Appalachian Bible College, indep. Bradley WV 25818. Daniel L. Anderson. Tel. (304)877-6428

Aquinas Institute of Theology, 3642 Lindell Blvd., St. Louis MO 63108. Charles E. Bruchard. Tel. (314)658-3882

Arizona College of the Bible, nondenom. 2045 W. Northern Ave., Phoenix AZ 85021. John L. Mitchell, Interim. Tel. (602)995-2670

Arlington Baptist College. 3001 W. Division, Arlington TX 76012. Wayne Martin. Tel. (817)461-8741

Asbury Theol. Sem., interdenom. Wilmore KY 40390. David McKenna. Tel. (606)858-3581

Ashland Theol. Sem., Breth. Ch. Ashland OH 44805. Joseph R. Shultz. Tel. (419)289-4142

Assemblies of God Theological Seminary, Assemblies of God. 1445 Boonville Ave., Springfield MO 65802. H. Glynn Hall. Tel. (417)862-3344

Atlanta Christian College, Ch. of Christ. 2605 Ben Hill Rd., East Point GA 30344. James C. Donovan. Tel. (404)761-8861

Austin Presbyterian Theol. Sem., PCUSA. 100 E. 27th St., Austin TX 78705. Jack L. Stotts. Tel. (512)472-6736

Azusa Pacific University, interdenom. P.O. Box APU, Azusa CA 91702. Paul E. Sago. Tel. (818)969-3434

Bangor Theol. Sem., U. Ch. of Christ. 300 Union St., Bangor ME 04401. Malcolm Warford. Tel. (207)942-6781

Baptist Bible College, Bapt. 628 E. Kearney, Springfield MO 65803. Leland Kennedy. Tel. (417)869-9811

Baptist Bible College and Seminary, Bapt. 538 Venard Rd., Clarks Summit PA 18411. Milo Thompson, Jr. Tel. (717)587-1172

Baptist Missionary Association Theol. Sem., Bapt. Missionary Assoc. of Amer. 1410 E. Pine, Jacksonville TX 75766. Philip R. Bryan. Tel. (214)586-2501

Bay Ridge Christian College, Ch. of God (And.). P.O. Box 726, Kendleton, TX 77451. Robert Williams. Tel. (409)532-3982

Berean Christian College, interdenom. 6801 Millmark Ave., Long Beach CA 90805. A. A. Bachman. Tel. (213)438-9302

Berkeley Divinity Sch. at Yale, Epis. 363 St. Ronan St., New Haven CT 06511. James E. Annand. Tel. (203)432-6106

Bethany Bible College, Assem. of God. 800 Bethany Dr., Santa Cruz, CA 95066. Richard Foth. Tel. (408)438-3800

Bethany Lutheran Theol. Sem., Evang. Luth. Synod. 447 N. Division St., Mankato MN 56001. W. W. Petersen. Tel. (507)625-2977

Bethany Theol. Sem., Ch. of Breth. Butterfield and Meyers Rd., Oak Brook IL 60521. Wayne L. Miller. Tel. (312)620-2200

Bethel Theol. Sem., Bapt. Gen. Conf. St. Paul MN 55112. George K. Brushaber. Tel. (612)638-6230

Beulah Heights Bible College, Pentecostal. 892-906 Berne St. S.E., Atlanta GA 30316. James B. Keiller. Tel. (404)627-2681

Biblical Theological Seminary, interdenom. 200 N. Main St., Hatfield PA 19440. David G. Dunbar. Tel. (215)368-5000

Boise Bible College, Indep., 8695 Marigold St., Boise, ID 83714. J. Richard Ewing. Tel. (208)376-7731

Boston University (Sch. of Theol.), U. Meth. 745 Commonwealth Ave., Boston MA 02215. Richard Nesmith. Tel. (617)353-3051

Brite Divinity Sch., Texas Christian University, Christian Ch. (Disc.). P.O. Box 32923, Fort Worth TX 76129. Leo G. Perdue. Tel. (817)921-7575

Calvary Bible College, nondenom. 15800 Calvary Rd. Kansas City MO 64147. Leslie Madison. Tel. (816)322-0110

Calvin Theol. Sem., Christian Ref. Grand Rapids MI 49546. J. A. DeJong. Tel. (616)957-6036

Catholic Theological Union, Cath. 5401 S. Cornell Ave., Chicago IL 60615. Donald Senior. Tel. (312)324-8000

Catholic University of America (Theol. College), 401 Michigan Ave. N.E., Washington DC 20017. Lawrence B. Terrien Tel. (202)635-5900

Central Baptist College, Bapt. CBC Station, Conway AR 72032. James R. Raines. Tel. (501)329-6872

Central Baptist Theol. Sem. in Indiana, Natl. Bapt., U.S.A., Inc.; Natl. Bapt. Conv. of Am. Prog. Natl. Bapt. Conv. of Am.; Natl. Missy. Bapt. Conv. of Am., 1535 Dr. A. J. Brown Ave., N., Indianapolis IN 46202. F. Benjamin Davis. Tel. (317)636-6622

Central Baptist Theol. Sem., Amer. Bapt. Kansas City KS 66102. John R. Landgraf. Tel. (913)371-5313

Central Bible College, Assem. of God. 3000 N. Grant Ave., Springfield MO 65803. H. Maurice Lednicky. Tel. (417)833-2551

Central Christian Col. of the Bible, Chr. Chs. 911 E. Urbandale, Moberly MO 65270. Lloyd M. Pelfrey. Tel. (816)263-3900

Central Indian Bible College, Assemb. of God, P.O. Box 550, Mobridge, SD 57601. Tel. (605)845-7801

Central Wesleyan College, Wesleyan Ch. Wesleyan Dr., Central SC 29630. John Newby. Tel. (803)639-2453

Chicago Theol. Sem., U. Ch. of Christ. 5757 University Ave., Chicago IL 60637. Kenneth B. Smith. Tel. (312)752-5757

Christ the King Sem., Cath. 711 Knox Rd., P.O. Box 607, East Aurora NY 14052. Daniel McLellan. Tel. (716)652-8900

Christ Church Sem., Am. Carpatho-Russ. Orth. Greek Cath. Diocese. 225 Chandler Ave., Johnstown PA 15906. Bishop Nicholas Smisko. Tel. (814)539-8086

Christian Theol. Sem., Christian Ch. (Disc.). 1000 W. 42nd St., Indianapolis IN 46208. Richard D. N. Dickinson. Tel. (317)924-1331

Church Divinity Sch. of the Pacific, Epis. 2451 Ridge Rd., Berkeley CA 94709. Donn F. Morgan, Actg. Tel. (415)848-3282

Cincinnati Bible College and Seminary, CC/CC. 2700 Glenway Ave., Cincinnati OH 45204. C. Barry McCarty. Tel. (513)244-8100

Circleville Bible College, Chs. of Chr. in Christian Union. P.O. Box 458, Circleville OH 43113. David Van Hoose. Tel. (614)474-8896

Clear Creek Baptist Bible College, So. Bapt., 300 Clear Creek Rd., Pineville, KY 40977. Bill Whittaker. Tel. (606)337-3196.

Colegio Biblico Pentecostal de Puerto Rico Ch. of God (Cleveland), P.O. Box 901, Saint Just, PR 00750. Roberto Rivera. Tel. (809)761-0640

Colgate Rochester Divinity School/Bexley Hall/Crozer Theological Seminary, multidenom. 1100 S. Goodman St., Rochester NY 14620. Shirley M. Jones. Tel. (716)271-1320

Colorado Christian University, interdenom. 180 S. Garrison St., Lakewood, CO 80226. Joe L. Wall. Tel. (303)238-5386

Columbia Bible College, interdenom. P.O. Box 3122, Columbia SC 29230. J. Robertson McQuilkin. Tel. (803)754-4100

Columbia Theol. Sem., PCUSA. P. O. Box 520, Decatur GA 30031. Douglas Oldenburg. Tel. (404)378-8821

Concordia Sem., Luth. Ch.—Mo. Synod. St. Louis (Clayton) MO 63105. Karl L. Barth. Tel. (314)721-5934

Concordia Theol. Sem., Luth. Ch.—Mo. Synod. Ft. Wayne IN 46825. Robert Preus. Tel. (219)481-2100

Covenant Theol. Sem., Presb. Ch. in Amer. 12330 Conway Rd., St. Louis MO 63141. Paul Kooistra. Tel. (314)434-4044

Cranmer Seminary, Ang. Orth. Ch., P.O. Box 329, Statesville, NC 28677. James P. Dees. Tel. (704)873-8365

Crichton College, Indep., 6655 Winchester St., Memphis, TN 38175. James Latimer. Tel. (901)367-9800

Criswell Center for Biblical Studies, 525 North Ervay, Dallas, TX 75201. W. A. Criswell. Tel. (214)954-0012

The Criswell College, Bapt. 525 N. Ervay, Dallas TX 75201. Paige Patterson. Tel. (214)855-7854

Dallas Christian College, Chr. Chs. 2700 Christian Pky., Dallas TX 75234. Gene Shepherd. Tel. (214)241-3371

Dallas Theol. Sem., interdenom. 3909 Swiss Ave., Dallas TX 75204. Donald K. Campbell. Tel. (214)824-3094

De Sales School of Theology, Cath. 721 Lawrence St. N.E., Washington DC 20017. John W. Crossin. Tel. (202)269-9412

Denver Conservative Bapt. Sem., Cons. Bapt. Box 10,000, Denver CO 80210. Haddon Robinson. Tel. (303)761-2482

Disciples Divinity House, Univ. of Chicago, Chr. Ch. (Disc. of Christ). 1156 E. 57th St., Chicago IL 60637. W. Clark Gilpin. Tel. (312)643-4411

Dominican House of Studies (Pontifical Faculty of the Immaculate Conception). 487 Michigan Ave. N.E., Washington DC 20017. William C. Dettling. Tel. (202)529-5300

Drew University (Theol. School), U. Meth. Madison NJ 07940. Thomas W. Ogletree. Tel. (201)408-3258

Dubuque, Univ. of (Theol. Sem.), PCUSA. 2000 University, Dubuque IA 52001. Walter F. Peterson. Tel. (319)589-3222

Duke University (Divinity Sch.), U. Meth. Durham NC 27706. Dennis M. Campbell. Tel. (919)684-3234

Earlham School of Religion, Friends (Quakers). Richmond IN 47374. Tom Mullen. Tel. (317)983-1423

East Coast Bible College, Ch. of God, 6900 Wilkinson Blvd., Charlotte, NC 28214. Ronald Martin. Tel. (704)394-2307

Eastern Baptist Theol. Sem., Amer. Bapt. City Line and Lancaster Ave., Philadelphia PA 19151. Manfred T. Brauch, Actg. Tel. (215)896-5000

Eastern Mennonite Seminary, Menn. Ch. Harrisonburg VA 22801. George E. Brunk, Ill. Tel. (703)433-2771

Eden Theol. Sem., U. Ch. of Christ. 475 E. Lockwood Ave., St. Louis MO 63119. Dr. Eugene S. Wehrli. Tel. (314)961-3627

Emmanuel Col. Sch. of Chr. Ministries, Pent. Holiness. P.O. Box 129, Franklin Springs GA 30639. David Hopkins. Tel. (404)245-7226

Emmanuel School of Religion, Chr. Chs. and Chs. of Christ, One Walker Dr., Johnson City, TN 37601. Calvin L. Phillips. Tel. (615)926-1186

Emmaus Bible College, Indep., 2570 Asbury Rd., Dubuque, IA. 52001. Daniel Smith. Tel. (319)588-8000

Emory University (The Candler Sch. of Theol.), U. Meth. Atlanta GA 30322. Jim L. Waits. Tel. (404)727-6324

Episcopal Divinity Sch., Epis. 99 Brattle St., Cambridge MA 02138. Otis Charles. Tel. (617)868-3450

Episcopal Theol. Sem. of the Southwest, Epis. P.O. Box 2247, Austin TX 78768. Durstan R. McDonald. Tel. (512)472-4133

Erskine Theol. Sem., Assoc. Ref. Presb. P.O. Box 171, Due West SC 29639. R. T. Ruble. Tel. (803)379-8885

Eugene Bible College. 2155 Bailey Hill Rd., Eugene OR 97405. Jeffrey E. Farmer. Tel. (503)485-1780

Evangelical Sch. of Theol., Evangel. Congreg. Ch. 121 S. College St., Myerstown PA 17067. Ray A. Seilhamer. Tel. (717)866-5775

Evangelical Theol. Sem., Inc., 2302-2400 E. Ash St., Goldsboro NC 27530. William Ralph Painter. Tel. (919) 735-0831

Faith Baptist Bible College and Seminary, Bapt. 1900 N.W. 4th St., Ankeny IA 50021. Robert Domokos. Tel. (515)964-0601

Florida Bible College, Indep. Fund. Chs. of Am. 1701 N. Poinciana Blvd., Kissimmee, FL 32758. Ron Von Behren. Tel. (407) 933-4500

Florida Christian College, Chr. Ch. 1011 Osceola Blvd., Kissimmee, FL 34744. A. Wayne Lowen. Tel. (407) 847-8966

Franciscan Sch. of Theol., Cath. 1712 Euclid Ave., Berkeley CA 94709. William J. Short. Tel. (415)848-5232

Free Will Baptist Bible College, Free Will Bapt. 3606 West End Ave., Nashville TN 37205. Charles A. Thigpen. Tel. (615)383-1340

Friends Bible College, Friends. P.O. Box 288, Haviland KS 67059. Robin W. Johnston. Tel. (316)862-5252

Fuller Theol. Sem., multidenom. 135 N. Oakland Ave., Pasadena CA 91182. David A. Hubbard. Tel. (818)584-5200

Garrett-Evangelical Theol. Sem., U. Meth. 2121 Sheridan Rd., Evanston IL 60201. Neal F. Fisher. Tel. (312)866-3900

General Theol. Sem., Epis. 175 Ninth Ave., New York NY 10011. James C. Fenhagen. Tel. (212)243-5150

George Mercer, Jr., Memorial Sch. of Theol., Epis. 65 Fourth St., Garden City NY 11530. George Hill. Tel. (516)248-4800

God's Bible School and College, Indep., 1810 Young St., Cincinnati, OH 45210. Bence Miller. Tel. (513)721-7944

Golden Gate Bapt. Theol. Sem., S. Bapt. Strawberry Point, Mill Valley CA 94941. William O. Crews. Tel. (415)388-8080

Gordon-Conwell Theological Seminary, interdenom. South Hamilton MA 01982. Robert E. Cooley. Tel. (508)468-7111

Goshen Biblical Sem., Menn. 3003 Benham Ave., Elkhart IN 46517. Marlin E. Miller. Tel. (219)295-3726

Grace Bible College, Grace Gospel Fell. P.O. Box 910, Grand Rapids MI 49509. Samuel R. Vinton, Jr. Tel. (616)538-2330

Grace College of the Bible, indep. 1515 S. 10th St., Omaha, NE 68108. Warren E. Bathke. Tel. (402)449-2800

Grand Rapids School of the Bible and Music, Indep., 1331 Franklin SE, Grand Rapids, MI 49506. John Montague. Tel. (616)452-9713

Grace Theol. Sem., Fellowship of Grace Breth. 200 Seminary Dr., Winona Lake IN 46590. John J. Davis. Tel. (219)372-5100

Graduate Theol. Union, nondenom. 2400 Ridge Rd., Berkeley CA 94709. Robert Barr. Tel. (415)647-2412

Great Lakes Bible College, Ch. of Christ/Chr. Ch. P.O. Box 40060, Lansing MI 48901. Philip H. Schlaegel. Tel. (517)321-0242

Greenville College, Free Meth. 315 E. College Ave., Greenville IL 62246. W. Richard Stephens. Tel. (618)664-1840; 1-800-345-4440

Harding University Graduate School of Religion, Chs. of Chr. 1000 Cherry Rd., Memphis TN 38117. C. Philip Slate. Tel. (901)761-1352.

Hartford Seminary, interdenom. Hartford CT 06105. Jackson W. Carroll. Tel. (203)232-4451

Harvard Divinity School, nondenom. 45 Francis Ave., Cambridge MA 02138. Ronald F. Thiemann. Tel. (617)495-5761

Hebrew Union College—Jewish Inst. of Religion, Jewish. 3101 Clifton Ave., Cincinnati OH 45220, Tel. (513)221-1875; 1 W. 4th St., New York NY 10012, Tel. (212)674-5300; 3077 University, Los Angeles CA 90007, Tel. (213)749-3424; 13 King David St., Jerusalem, Israel, Tel. 02-232444. Alfred Gottschalk

Hobe Sound Bible College, Indep., P. O. Box 1065, Hobe Sound, FL 33475. Robert Whitaker. Tel. (407)546-5534

Holy Cross Greek Orthodox School of Theology (Hellenic College), Greek Orthodox. 50 Goddard Ave., Brookline MA 02146. Alkiviadis Calivas. Tel. (617)731-3500

Holy Trinity Orthodox Seminary, Russian Orthodox. P. O. Box 36, Jordanville NY 13361. Archbishop Laurus (Skurla). Tel. (315)858-0940

Hood Theological Seminary, A.M.E. Zion. Salisbury NC 28144. Bernard W. Franklin. Tel. (704)638-5500

Howard University Divinity School, interdenom. 1400 Shepherd St., N.E., Washington DC 20017. Lawrence N. Jones. Tel. (202)269-1122

Huntington College, Graduate School of Christian Ministries, U. B. in Christ. Huntington IN 46750. Paul R. Fetters. Tel. (219)356-6000

Iliff School of Theol., The, U. Meth. 2201 S. University Blvd., Denver CO 80210. Donald Edward Messer. Tel. (303)744-1287

Indiana Wesleyan University, Wesleyan Ch. 4201 S. Washington, Marion IN 46953. Joseph W. Seaborn. Tel. (317)674-6901

Immaculate Conception Sem. Sch. of Theol. of Seton Hall Univ., Cath. South Orange NJ 07079. Richard M. Liddy. Tel. (201)761-9575

Interdenominational Theol. Center. 671 Beckwith St. S.W., Atlanta GA 30314. James H. Costen. Tel. (404)527-7702

International Bible College, Chs. of Christ, P. O. Box IBC, Florence, AL 35630. Charles Coil. Tel. (205) 766-6610

Jesuit School of Theology at Berkeley, Cath. 1735 LeRoy Ave., Berkeley CA 94709. Thomas F. Gleeson, Tel. (415)841-8804

Jewish Theol. Sem. of America, Jewish. 3080 Broadway, New York NY 10027. Ismar Schorsch. Tel. (212)678-8000

John Wesley College. 2314 N. Centennial St., High Point NC 27260. Brian C. Donley. Tel. (919)889-2262

Johnson Bible College, Christian Chs. 7900 Johnson Dr., Knoxville TN 37998. David L. Eubanks. Tel. (615)573-4517

Kansas City College and Bible School, Ch. of God-Holiness, 7401 Metcalf, Overland Park, KS 66204. John Page. Tel. (913) 722-0272

Kenrick-Glennon Seminary, Cath. 5200 Glennon Dr., St. Louis MO 63119. Ronald W. Ramson. Tel. (314)644-0266

Kentucky Christian College, Chr. Ch. Grayson KY 41143. Keith P. Keeran. Tel. (606)474-6613

Kentucky Mountain Bible Institute, Ky. Mtn. Holiness Assn., Box 10, Vancleve, KY 41385. J. Eldon Neihof. Tel. (606) 666-5000

Lancaster Bible College, Nondenom., 901 Eden Rd., Lancaster PA 17601. Gilbert A. Peterson. Tel. (717)569-7071

Lancaster Theol. Sem. of the U. Ch. of Christ. Lancaster PA 17603. Peter M. Schmiechen. Tel. (717)393-0654

Lexington Theol. Sem. Chr. Ch. (Disc.). 631 S. Limestone, Lexington KY 40508. William O. Paulsell. Tel. (606)252-0361

L.I.F.E. Bible College, Intl. Ch. Foursquare Gospel. 1100 Glendale Blvd., Los Angeles CA 90026. Jack E. Hamilton. Tel. (213)413-1234

Lincoln Christian College and Seminary, CC/CC. Box 178, Lincoln IL 62656. Charles A. McNeely. Tel. (217)732-3168

Loma Linda University, Seventh-day Adv. Loma Linda Campus, Loma Linda CA 92350, Tel. (714)824-4300; La Sierra Campus, Riverside CA 92515. Norman J. Woods. Tel. (714)785-2022

Louisville Presbyterian Theol. Sem., PCUSA. 1044 Alta Vista Rd., Louisville KY 40205. John M. Mulder. Tel. (502)895-3411

Luther Northwestern Theological Sem., Ev. Luth. Ch. in Am., 2481 Como Ave. W., St. Paul MN 55108. David L. Tiede. Tel. (612)641-3456

Lutheran Bible Institute in California, Luth., 641 S. Western Ave., Anaheim, CA 92804. Clifton Pederson. Tel. (714)827-1940

Lutheran Bible Institute of Seattle, Luth. Providence Heights, Issaquah WA 98027. A. G. Fjellman, Interim. Tel. (206)392-0400

Lutheran Brethren Seminary, Ch. of the Luth. Breth. Fergus Falls MN 56537. Rev. O. Gjerness. Tel. (218)739-3375

Lutheran Sch. of Theol. at Chicago, Ev. Luth. Ch. in Amer. 1100 E. 55th St., Chicago IL 60615. William E. Lesher. Tel. (312)753-0700

Lutheran Theol. Sem., Ev. Luth. Ch. in Amer. Gettysburg PA 17325. J. Russell Hale, Actg. Tel. (717)334-6286

Lutheran Theol. Sem. at Philadelphia, Ev. Luth. Ch. in Amer. 7301 Germantown Ave., Philadelphia PA 19119. John W. Vannorsdall. Tel. (215)248-4616

Lutheran Theol. Southern Sem., Ev. Luth. Ch. in Amer. Columbia SC 29203. Mack C. Branham, Jr. Tel. (803)786-5150

Magnolia Bible College, Chs. of Christ, P. O. Box 1109, Kosciusko, MS 39090. Cecil May, Jr. Tel. (601) 289-2896

Manhattan Christian College, Christian Churches. 1415 Anderson, Manhattan KS 66502. Kenneth Cable. Tel. (913)539-3571

Manna Bible Institute, Indep., 700 E. Church La., Philadelphia, PA 19144. Raymond Thomas. Tel. (215) 843-3600

Mary Immaculate Sem., Cath. 300 Cherryville Rd., Box 27, Northampton PA 18067. Richard J. Kehoe. Tel. (215)262-7866

Maryknoll School of Theology (Cath. For. Miss. Soc. of Amer., Inc.). Maryknoll NY 10545. John K. Halbert. Tel. (914)941-7590

McCormick Theol. Sem., PCUSA. 5555 S. Woodlawn Ave., Chicago IL 60637. David Ramage, Jr. Tel. (312)241-7800

Meadville/Lombard Theol. Sch., Unit. Univ. 5701 S. Woodlawn Ave., Chicago IL 60637. Spencer Lavan. Tel. (312)753-3195

Memphis Theol. Sem. of the Cumberland Presbyterian Church, 168 E. Parkway S., Memphis TN 38104. J. David Hester. Tel. (901)458-8232

Mennonite Biblical Sem., Gen. Conf. Menn. 3003 Benham Ave., Elkhart IN 46517. Henry Poettcker. Tel. (219)295-3726

Mennonite Brethren Biblical Sem., Menn. Breth. Ch. 4824 E. Butler at Chestnut Ave., Fresno CA 93727. Larry D. Martens. Tel. (209)251-8628

Meth. Theol. Sch. in Ohio, U. Meth. 3081 Columbus Pike, Delaware OH 43015. Norman E. DeWire. Tel. (614)363-1146

Miami Christian College, interdenom. 2300 N.W. 135th St., Miami FL 33167. Vacant. Tel. (305)953-1122

Mid-America Bible College, Ch. of God, 3500 SW 119th St., Oklahoma City, OK 73170. John Conley. Tel. (405)691-3800

Midwestern Bapt. Theol. Sem., S. Bapt. 5001 N. Oak Trafficway, Kansas City MO 64118. Milton Ferguson. Tel. (816)453-4600

Minnesota Bible College, Ch. of Christ. 920 Mayowood Rd. S.W., Rochester MN 55902. Donald Lloyd. Tel. (507)288-4563

Moody Bible Institute, interdenom. 820 N. La Salle Dr., Chicago IL 60610. Joseph M. Stowell, III. Tel. (312)329-4000

Moravian Theol. Sem., Morav. Bethlehem PA 18018. David A. Schattschneider. Tel. (215)861-1516

Moreau Sem. (Holy Cross Fathers), Cath. Notre Dame IN 46556. John C. Gerber. Tel. (219)283-7735

Morehouse School of Religion, Amer. Bapt.; Prog. Natl. Bapt.; Natl. Bapt. Conv. of Amer.; Natl. Bapt. Conv., U.S.A., Inc.; So. Bapt. Conv. 645 Beckwith St. S.W., Atlanta GA 30314. Charles S. Hamilton. Tel. (404)527-7777

Mt. Angel Sem., Cath. St. Benedict OR 97373. J. Terrence Fitzgerald. Tel. (503)845-3951

Mt. St. Mary's Sem., Cath. Emmitsburg MD 21727. Kenneth W. Roeltgen. Tel. (301)447-5295

Mt. St. Mary's Sem. of the West, Cath. 6616 Beechmont Ave., Cincinnati OH 45230. James J. Walsh. Tel. (513)231-2223

Multnomah School of the Bible, interdenom. 8435 N.E. Glisan St., Portland OR 97220. Joseph C. Aldrich. Tel. (503)255-0332

Mundelein Seminary of the Univ. of St. Mary-of-the-Lake, Cath. Mundelein IL 60060. Gerald F. Kicanas. Tel. (312)566-6401

Nashotah House (Theol. Sem.), Epis. 2777 Mission Rd. Nashotah WI 53058. Jack C. Knight. Tel. (414)646-3371

Nazarene Bible College, Naz. Box 15749, Colorado Springs CO 80935. Jerry Lambert. Tel. (719)596-5110

Nazarene Theol. Sem., Naz. 1700 E. Meyer Blvd., Kansas City MO 64131. Terrell C. Sanders, Jr. Tel. (816)333-6254

Nebraska Christian College, Chr. Ch. 1800 Syracuse Ave., Norfolk, NE 68701. Richard Wamsley. Tel. (402)371-5960

New Brunswick Theol. Sem., Ref. Amer. 17 Seminary Pl., New Brunswick NJ 08901. Robert A. White. Tel.(201)247-5241

New Orleans Baptist Theol. Sem., S. Bapt. New Orleans LA 70126. Landrum P. Leavell II. Tel. (504)282-4455

New York Theol. Sem., interdenom. 5 W. 29th St., New York NY 10001. Keith A. Russell. Tel. (212)532-4012

North American Baptist Sem., N. Amer. Bapt. Conf. 1321 W. 22nd St., Sioux Falls SD 57105. Charles M. Hiatt. Tel. (605)336-6588

North Central Bible College, Assem. of God. 910 Elliot Ave. S., Minneapolis MN 55404. Don Argue. Tel. (612)332-3491

North Park Theol. Sem., Ev. Cov. Ch. 3225 W. Foster Ave., Chicago IL 60625. David G. Horner. Tel. (312)583-2700

Northeastern Bible College, indep., 12 Oak La., Essex Fells NJ 07021. James Bjornstad. Tel. (201)226-1074

Northern Bapt. Theol. Sem., Amer. Bapt. 660 E. Butterfield Rd., Lombard IL 60148. Ian M. Chapman. Tel. (312)620-2100

Northwest Col. of the Assemb. of God, Assem. of God. P.O. Box 579, Kirkland WA 98083. D. V. Hurst. Tel. (206)822-8266

Notre Dame Sem., Cath. 2901 S. Carrollton Ave., New Orleans LA 70118. Gregory M. Aymond. Tel. (504)866-7426

Oak Hills Bible College, Indep., 1600 Oak Hills Rd., SW, Bemidji, MN 56601. Mark Hovestol. Tel. (218) 751-8670

Oblate College, Cath. 391 Michigan Ave. N.E., Washington DC 20017. Joseph C. Schwab. Tel. (202)529-6544

Oblate School of Theology, Cath. 285 Oblate Dr., San Antonio TX 78216. Patrick Guidon. Tel. (512)341-1366

Ozark Christian College, CC/CC. 1111 N. Main St., Joplin MO 64801. Ken Idleman. Tel. (417)624-2518

Pacific Christian College, nondenom. 2500 E. Nutwood Ave., Fullerton CA 92631. Knofel L. Staton. Tel. (714)879-3901

Pacific Lutheran Theol. Sem., Ev. Luth. Ch. in Am., 2770 Marin Ave., Berkeley CA 94708. Jerry L. Schmalenberger. Tel. (415)524-5264

Pacific Sch. of Religion, interdenom. 1798 Berkeley CA 94709. Neely D. McCarter. Tel. (415)848-0528

Payne Theol. Sem., A.M.E. P.O. Box 474, Wilberforce OH 45384. Louis-Charles Harvey. Tel. (513)376-2946

Pepperdine Univ., Chs. of Chr. Malibu CA 90265. David Davenport. Tel. (213)456-4357

Perkins Sch. of Theol. (Southern Methodist Univ.), U. Meth. Dallas TX 75275. James E. Kirby, Jr. Tel. (214)692-2138

Philadelphia College of Bible, interdenom. Langhorne Manor, Langhorne PA 19047. W. Sherrill Babb. Tel. (215)752-5800

Phillips Graduate Seminary, Chr. Chs. (Disc.). Box 2335, University Sta., Enid OK 73702. Roger Sizemore. Tel. (405)237-4433

Piedmont Bible College, Bapt. 716 Franklin St., Winston-Salem NC 27101. Howard L. Wilburn. Tel. (919)725-8344

Pittsburgh Theol. Sem., PCUSA. Pittsburgh PA 15206. Carnegie Samuel Calian. Tel. (412)362-5610

Point Loma Nazarene College, Naz. San Diego CA 92106. Jim Bond. Tel. (619)221-2200

Pontifical College Josephinum, Cath. 7625 N. High St., Columbus OH 43085. Dennis F. Sheehan. Tel. (614)885-5585

Pope John XXIII National Seminary, Cath. 558 South Ave., Weston MA 02193. Cornelius M. McRae. Tel. (617)899-5500

Practical Bible Training School, Independent Bapt. Drawer A, Bible School Park, NY 13737. Woodrow Kroll. Tel. (607)729-1581

Presbyterian School of Christian Education, PCUSA. 1205 Palmyra Ave., Richmond VA 23227. Heath K. Rada. Tel. (804)359-5031

Princeton Theol. Sem., PCUSA. CN821, Princeton NJ 08542. Thomas W. Gillespie. Tel. (609)921-8300

Protestant Episcopal Theol. Sem. in Virginia, Epis. Alexandria VA 22304. Richard Reid. Tel. (703)370-6600

Puget Sound Christian College, Chr. Chs. 410 Fourth Ave. N., Edmonds WA 98020. Glen R. Basey. Tel. (206)775-8686

Rabbi Isaac Elchanan Theol. Sem. (affil. of Yeshiva Univ.), Orth. Jewish. 2540 Amsterdam Ave., New York NY 10033. Zevulun Charlop. Tel. (212)960-5344

Reconstructionist Rabbinical College, Jewish. Church Rd. and Greenwood Ave., Wyncote PA 19095. Arthur Green. Tel. (215)576-0800

Reformed Bible College, Interdenom., 1869 Robinson Rd. S.E., Grand Rapids MI 49506. Edwin D. Roels. Tel. (616)458-0404

Reformed Presbyterian Theol. Sem., Ref. Presb. Ch. of N. Amer. 7418 Penn Ave., Pittsburgh PA 15208. Bruce C. Stewart. Tel. (412)731-8690

Reformed Theol. Sem., indep. 5422 Clinton Blvd., Jackson MS 39209. Luder G. Whitlock, Jr. Tel. (601)922-4988

Roanoke Bible College, Chs. of Ch. P.O. Box 387, Elizabeth City NC 27907. William A. Griffin. Tel. (919)338-5191

Saint Bernard's Institute, Cath. 1100 S. Goodman St., Rochester NY 14620. Sebastian A. Falcone. Tel. (716)271-1320

St. Charles Borromeo Sem., Cath. 100 East Wynnewood Rd., Overbrook, PA 19096. Daniel A. Murray. Tel. (215)667-3394

St. Francis Seminary, Cath. 3257 S. Lake Dr., Milwaukee WI 53207. Daniel J. Packenham. Tel. (414)747-6400

St. John's Sem., Cath. Brighton MA 02135. Thomas J. Daly. Tel. (617)254-2610

St. John's Sem., Cath. 5118 E. Seminary Rd., Camarillo CA 93010. Sylvester Ryan. Tel. (805)482-2755

St. John's University, School of Theology, Cath. Collegeville MN 56321. Dale Launderville, Actg. Tel. (612)363-2011

St. Joseph's Sem., Cath. 201 Seminary Ave., (Dunwoodie), Yonkers NY 10704. Edwin F. O'Brien. Tel. (914)968-6200

St. Louis Christian College, Chr. Chs. 1360 Grandview Dr., Florissant MO 63033. Thomas W. McGee. Tel. (314)837-6777

St. Mary Sem., Cath. 1227 Ansel Rd., Cleveland OH 44108, Allan R. Laubenthal. Tel. (216)721-2100

St. Mary's Sem., Cath. 9845 Memorial Dr., Houston TX 77024. Chester L. Borski. Tel. (713)686-4345

St. Mary's Sem. and Univ., Cath. 5400 Roland Ave., Baltimore MD 21210. Robert F. Leavitt. Tel. (301)323-3200

St. Meinrad School of Theology, Cath. St. Meinrad IN 47577. Eugene Hensell. Tel. (812)357-6611

St. Patrick's Sem., Cath. 320 Middlefield Rd., Menlo Park CA 94025. Gerald D. Coleman. Tel. (415)325-5621

St. Paul Bible College, Chr. and Miss. All., 6425 County Rd., 30, St. Bonifacius, MN 55375. Bill W. Lanpher. Tel. (612)446-4100

Saint Paul Sch. of Theol., U. Meth. 5123 Truman Rd., Kansas City MO 64127. Lovett H. Weems, Jr. Tel. (816)483-9600

St. Paul Sem. School of Divinity, Cath. 2260 Summit Ave., St. Paul MN 55105. Charles Froehle. Tel. (612)647-5715

Saint Thomas Theological Seminary, 1300 S. Steele St., Cath. Denver CO 80210. John E. Rybolt. Tel. (303)722-4687

St. Tikhon's Orthodox Theol. Sem., Russian Orth. South Canaan PA 18459. Bishop Herman. Tel. (717)937-4686

St. Vincent de Paul Regional Seminary, Cath. 10701 S. Military Trail, Box 460, Boynton Beach FL 33436. Joseph L. Cunningham. Tel. (305)732-4424

St. Vincent Sem., Cath., Latrobe PA 15650. Thomas Acklin. Tel. (412)539-9761

St. Vladimir's Orth. Theol. Sem., Eastern Orth. 575 Scarsdale Rd., Crestwood NY 10707. Metropolitan Theodosius. Tel. (914)961-8313

SS. Cyril and Methodius Sem., Cath. Orchard Lake MI 48033. Stanley E. Milewski. Tel. (313)682-1885

San Francisco Theol. Sem., PCUSA. San Anselmo CA 94960. J. Randolph Taylor. Tel. (415)258-6500

San Jose Christian College, nondenom. 790 South 12th St., P.O. Box 1090, San Jose CA 95108. Bryce L. Jessup. Tel. (408)293-9058

Savonarola Theol. Sem., Pol. Natl. Cath. 1031 Cedar Ave., Scranton PA 18505. John F. Swantek. Tel. (717)343-0100

Sch. of Theol. at Claremont, U. Meth. 1325 N. College Ave., Claremont CA 91711. Richard W. Cain. Tel. (714)626-3521

Seabury-Western Theol. Sem., Epis. 2122 Sheridan Rd., Evanston IL 60201. M. S. Sisk. Tel. (312)328-9300

Seminario Evangelico de Puerto Rico, interdenom., 776 Ponce de Leon Ave., Hato Rey, PR 00918. Luis Fidel Mercado. Tel. (809)751-6483

Seminary of the Immaculate Conception, Cath. 440 West Neck Rd., Huntington NY 11743. John J. Strynkowski. Tel. (516)423-0483

Seventh-day Adventist Theol. Sem., Andrews Univ., Seventh-day Adv. Berrien Springs MI 49104. Raoul Dederen. Tel. (616)471-3536

Seventh Day Bapt. Center on Ministry, Seventh Day Bapt. Gen. Conf. 3120 Kennedy Rd., P.O. Box 1678, Janesville WI 53547. Rodney Henry. Tel. (608)752-5055

Shaw Divinity School, Natl. Bapt. Raleigh NC 27611. James Z. Alexander. Tel. (919)755-4846

Simpson College, Chr. and Miss. All. 2211 College View Dr., Redding, CA 96003. Francis Grubbs. Tel. (916)243-1991

Southeastern Baptist College, Bapt. Missy. Assn. of Mississippi. P. O. Box 8276, Laurel, MS 39941. A. M. Wilson. Tel. (601)426-6346

Southeastern Baptist Theol. Sem., S. Bapt. Box 1889, Wake Forest NC 27587. Louis A. Drummond. Tel. (919)556-3101

Southeastern Bible College, interdenom. 3001 Highway 280 E, Birmingham AL 35243. John D. Talley, Jr. Tel. (205)969-0880

Southeastern College of the A/G, Assem. of God. 1000 Longfellow Blvd., Lakeland FL 33801. James L. Hennesy. Tel. (813)665-4404

Southern Baptist Theol. Sem., S. Bapt. 2825 Lexington Rd., Louisville KY 40280. Roy Lee Honeycutt, Jr. Tel. (502)897-4011

Southwestern Assemblies of God College, Assemb. of God. 1200 Sycamore St., Waxahachie TX 75165. Paul Savell. Tel. (214)937-4010

Southwestern Baptist Theol. Sem., S. Bapt. P.O.Box 22000, Fort Worth TX 76122. Russell H. Dilday. Tel. (817)923-1921

Southwestern College, Bapt. 2625 East Cactus Rd., Phoenix AZ 85032. Wesley A. Olsen. Tel. (602)992-6101

Starr King Sch. for the Ministry, Unit. Berkeley CA 94709. Til Evans, interim. Tel. (415)845-6232

Summit Christian College, Miss. Ch. 1025 W. Rudisill Blvd., Fort Wayne IN 46807. Donald D. Gerig. Tel. (219)456-2111

Swedenborg Sch. of Religion (formerly New Church Theol. Sch.), Genl. Conv., Swedenborgian Ch. 48 Sargent St., Newton MA 02158. Mary Kay Klein. Tel. (617)244-0504

Talbot School of Theology, interdenom. 13800 Biola Ave., La Mirada CA 90639. W. Bingham Hunter. Tel. (213)944-0351

Tennessee Temple Univ., Bapt. 1815 Union Ave., Chattanooga TN 37404. J. Don Jennings. Tel. (615)698-4100

Theol. Sem. of the Ref. Epis. Ch., Ref. Epis. 4225 Chestnut St., Philadelphia PA 19104. Leonard W. Riches. Tel. (215)222-5158

Toccoa Falls College, Chr. and Miss. All. Toccoa Falls GA 30598. Paul L. Alford. Tel. (404)886-6831

Trevecca Nazarene College (Relig. Dept.), Naz. 333 Murfreesboro Rd., Nashville TN 37203. H. Ray Dunning. Tel. (615)248-1387

Trinity Bible College, Assem. of God. Ellendale ND 58436. Lowell Lundstrom. Tel. (701)349-3621 (ND); 1-800-523-1603

Trinity College of Florida, Indep., P. O. Box 9000, Holiday, FL 34690. Barry Banther. Tel. (813)376-6911

Trinity Evangel. Divinity Sch., Evangel. Free Ch. of Amer. 2065 Half Day Rd., Deerfield IL 60015. Kenneth M. Meyer. Tel. (312)945-8800

Trinity Lutheran Seminary, Ev. Luth. Ch. in Am. 2199 East Main St., Columbus OH 43209. James M. Childs, Jr., Interim. Tel. (614)235-4136

Union Theol. Sem., interdenom. 3041 Broadway, New York NY 10027. Donald W. Shriver, Jr. Tel. (212)662-7100

Union Theol. Sem. in Va., PCUSA. 3401 Brook Rd., Richmond VA 23227. T. Hartley Hall IV. Tel. (804)355-0671

United Theol. Sem., U. Meth. 1810 Harvard Blvd., Dayton OH 45406. Leonard I. Sweet. Tel. (513)278-5817

United Theol. Sem. of the Twin Cities, U. Ch. of Christ. 3000 Fifth St. N.W., New Brighton MN 55112. Benjamin Griffin. Tel. (612)633-4311

United Wesleyan College, Wes. Ch. 1414 East Cedar St., Allentown PA 18103. John P. Ragsdale. Tel. (215)439-8709

University of Chicago (Divinity Sch.), interdenom. Swift Hall, Chicago IL 60637. Franklin I. Gamwell. Tel. (312)702-8221

University of Notre Dame, Dept. of Theology, Cath. Notre Dame IN 46556. Richard P. McBrien. Tel. (219)239-7811

University of the South (Sch. of Theol.), Epis. Sewanee TN 37375. Robert Giannini. Tel. (615)598-5931

Valley Forge Christian College, Assem. of God. Charlestown Rd., Phoenixville PA 19460, Wesley W. Smith. Tel. (215)935-0450

Vanderbilt University (Divinity Sch.), interdenom. Nashville TN 37240. Joseph C. Hough, Jr. Tel. (615)322-2776

Vennard College, interdenom. University Park IA 52595. Warthen T. Israel. Tel. (515)673-8391

Virginia Union University (Sch. of Theol.), Bapt. 1601 W. Leigh St., Richmond VA 23220. Allix B. James, Actg. Tel. (804)257-5715

Walla Walla College (Sch. of Theol.), Seventh-day Adv. College Pl., Walla Walla WA 99324. John Brunt. Tel. (509)527-2195

Wartburg Theol. Sem., Ev. Luth. Ch. in Am., 333 Wartburg Pl., Dubuque IA 52001. Roger Fjeld. Tel. (319)589-0200

Washington Bible College/Capital Bible Seminary, interdenom. 6511 Princess Garden Pkwy., Lanham MD 20706. Harry E. Fletcher. Tel. (301)552-1400

Washington Theological Consortium and Washington Institute of Ecumenics, 487 Michigan Ave. N.E., Washington DC 20017. David Trickett. Tel. (202)832-2675.

Washington Theological Union, Cath. 9001 New Hampshire Ave., Silver Spring MD 20903. Vincent D. Cushing. Tel. (301)439-0551

Wesley College, Cong. Meth. P.O. Box 70, Florence MS 39073. David Coker. Tel. (601)845-2265

Wesley Theol. Sem., U. Meth. 4500 Massachusetts Ave. N.W., Washington DC 20016. Douglass Lewis. Tel. (202)885-8600

West Coast Christian College, Ch. of God. 6901 N. Maple Ave., Fresno CA 93710. H. B. Thompson, Jr. Tel. (209)299-7201

Western Baptist College. 5000 Deer Park Dr. S.E., Salem OR 97301. John G. Balyo. Tel. (503)581-8600

Western Conservative Baptist Sem., Cons. Bapt. 5511 S.E. Hawthorne Blvd., Portland OR 97215. Earl D. Radmacher. Tel. (503)233-8561

Western Evangelical Seminary, interdenom. 4200 S.E. Jennings Ave., Portland OR 97267. Duane J. Beals. Tel. (503)654-5466

Western Theol. Sem., Ref. Ch. in Amer. Holland MI 49423. Marvin D. Hoff. Tel. (616)392-8555

Westminster Theol. Sem., Presb. Chestnut Hill, Philadelphia PA 19118. George C. Fuller. Tel. (215)887-5511

Weston School of Theol., Cath. 3 Phillips Pl., Cambridge MA 02138. Edward M. O'Flaherty. Tel. (617)492-1960

William Tyndale College, interdenom. 35700 W. Twelve Mile Rd., Farmington Hills MI 48331. Herbert Cocking. Tel. (313)553-7200

Winebrenner Theol. Sem., Churches of God, Gen. Conf. 701 E. Melrose Ave., P.O. Box 478, Findlay OH 45839. David E. Draper. Tel. (419)422-4824

Wisconsin Lutheran Sem., Luth. (Wis.). 11831 N. Seminary Dr., 65W, Mequon WI 53092. Armin Panning. Tel. (414)242-7200

Yale University (Divinity Sch.), nondenom. 409 Prospect St., New Haven CT 06511. Aidan Kavanagh, Actg. Tel. (203)432-5307

10. CANADIAN THEOLOGICAL SEMINARIES AND FACULTIES, AND BIBLE SCHOOLS

The following list has been developed by direct correspondence with the institutions involved and is, therefore, a current and reasonably comprehensive list of the major Canadian theological seminaries and faculties, and Bible schools. The editor of the **Yearbook** would be grateful for knowledge of any significant omissions from this compilation.

Listings are alphabetical by name of institution and generally have the following order: Institution, affiliation, location, head, telephone number.

Acadia Divinity College, Un. Bapt. Conv. of the Atlantic Provinces. Wolfville, Nova Scotia B0P 1X0. Andrew D. MacRae. Tel. (902)542-2285

Alberta Bible College, CC/CC. 599 Northmount Dr. N.W., Calgary, Alberta T2K 3J6. Tel. (403)282-2994

Aldersgate College, Free Meth. Ch. Box 460, Moose Jaw, Saskatchewan S6H 4P1. Joseph F. James. Tel. (306)693-7773

Arthur Turner Training School, Ang. Ch. of Canada. Pangnirtung, Northwest Territories X0A 0R0. Tel. (819)473-8768

Atlantic Baptist College, Un. Bapt. Conv. of the Atlantic Provinces. Box 1004, Moncton, New Brunswick E1C 9L7. W. Ralph Richardson. Tel. (506)858-8970

Atlantic School of Theology, ecumenical (Ang. Ch. of Canada; Cath.; Un. Ch. of Canada). 640 Francklyn St., Halifax, Nova Scotia B3H 3B5. G. Russell Hatton. Tel. (902)423-6801

Baptist Leadership Training School, Bapt. Un. of Western Canada. 4330 16th St. S.W., Calgary, Alberta T2T 4H9. Kenneth W. Bellous. Tel. (403)243-3770

Bethany Bible College—Canada. 26 Western St., Sussex, New Brunswick E0E 1P0. Ronald E. Mitchell. Tel. (506)433-3668

Bethany Bible Institute, Menn. Br. Chs. Box 160, Hepburn, Saskatchewan S0K 1Z0. Cliff Jantzen. Tel. (306)947-2175

Briercrest Bible College, interdenom. Caronport, Saskatchewan S0H 0S0. Henry H. Budd. Tel. (306)756-3200

Brockville Bible College, Stand. Ch. of Am. Box 1900, Brockville, Ontario K6V 6N4. Tel. (613)345-5001

Canadian Bible College, Chr. and Miss. All. 4400-4th Ave., Regina, Saskatchewan S4T 0H8. Robert A. Rose. Tel. (306)545-1515

Canadian Lutheran Bible Institute, Luth. 4837 52A St., Camrose, Alberta T4V 1W5. Tel. (403)672-4454

Canadian Mennonite Bible College. 600 Shaftesbury Blvd., Winnipeg, Manitoba R3P 0M4. John H. Neufeld. Tel. (204)888-6781

Canadian Nazarene College, Ch. of the Naz. 1301 Lee Blvd., Winnipeg, Manitoba R3T 2P7. Neil E. Hightower. Tel. (204)269-2120

Canadian Reformed Churches, Theol. College of the, Can. Ref. Chs. 110 West 27th St., Hamilton, Ontario L9C 5A1. J. Faber.

Canadian Theological Seminary, Chr. and Miss. All. 4400-4th Ave., Regina, Saskatchewan S4T 0H8. Robert A. Rose. Tel. (306)545-1515

Catherine Booth Bible College, Salv. Army. 447 Webb Pl., Winnipeg, Manitoba R3B 2P2. Major Earl Robinson. Tel. (204)947-6701

Central Baptist Seminary and Bible College, Fell. of Evan. Bapt. Chs.in Canada. 95 Jonesville Cres., Toronto, Ontario M4A 1H3. Jack A. Hannah. Tel. (416)752-1976

Central Pentecostal College, Pent. Assem. of Canada. 1303 Jackson Ave., Saskatoon, Saskatchewan S7H 2M9. J. Harry Faught. Tel. (306)374-6655

Centre d'Etudes Théologiques Evangéliques, Un. d' Eglises Bapt. Françaises au Canada. 2285, avenue Papineau, Montréal, Québec H2K 4J5. W. N. Thomson. Tél. (514)526-6643

Centre for Christian Studies, Ang. Ch. of Canada; Un. Ch. of Canada. 77 Charles St. W., Toronto, Ontario M5S 1K5. Gwyneth Griffith. Tel. (416)923-1168

Christianview Bible College, Pent. Holiness Chs. of Canada. 164 George St., Ailsa Craig, Ontario N0M 1A0. Tel. (519)293-3506

Church Army Training College, Ang. Ch. of Canada. 397 Brunswick Ave., Toronto, Ontario M5R 2Z2. Capt. Walter Marshall. Tel. (416)924-9279

College Dominicain de Philosophie et de Théologie, Cath. 96 avenue Empress, Ottawa, Ontario K1R 7G3. Michel Gourgues. Tel. (613)233-5696

College of Emmanuel and St. Chad, Ang. Ch. of Canada. 1337 College Dr., Saskatoon, Saskatchewan S7N 0W6. J. Russell Brown. Tel. (306)343-3753

Columbia Bible College, Menn. Breth.; Gen. Conf. Menn. 2940 Clearbrook Rd., Clearbrook, British Columbia V2T 2Z8. Walter Unger. Tel. (604)853-3358

Concordia Lutheran Seminary, Luth. Ch.-Canada. 7040 Ada Blvd., Edmonton, Alberta T5B 4E3. Milton L. Rudnick. Tel. (403)474-1468

Concordia Lutheran Theological Seminary, Luth. Ch.-Canada. 470 Glenridge Ave., Box 1117, St. Catharines, Ontario L2R 7A3. Howard Kramer. Tel. (416)688-2362

Covenant Bible College, Ev. Cov. Ch. of Canada. 245-21st St. E., Prince Albert, Saskatchewan S6V 1L9. W. B. Anderson. Tel. (306)922-3443

Eastern Pentecostal Bible College, Pent. Assem. of Canada. 780 Argyle St., Peterborough, Ontario K9H 5T2. R. W. Taitinger. Tel. (705)748-9111

Elim Bible Institute, Conf. of Menn. in Manitoba. Box 120 Altona, Manitoba R0G 0B0. Victor Kliewer. Tel. (204)324-8631

Emmanuel Bible College, Miss. Ch. 100 Fergus Ave., Kitchener, Ontario N2A 2H2. Thomas E. Dow. Tel. (519)742-3572

Emmanuel College (see Toronto School of Theology)

Ewart College, Presby. Ch. in Canada. 156 St. George St., Toronto, Ontario M5S 2G1. Irene Dickson. Tel. (416)979-2501.

Full Gospel Bible Institute, Apost. Ch. of Pent. Box 579, Eston, Saskatchewan S0L 1A0. A. B. Mortensen. Tel. (306)962-3621

Gardner Bible College, Ch. of God (And.). 4704 55th St., Camrose, Alberta T4V 2B6. Bruce Kelly. Tel. (403)672-0171

Great Lakes Bible College, Chs. of Christ. 4875 King St. E., Box 399, Beamsville, Ontario L0R 1B0. Harold H. Parker. Tel. (416)563-5374

Hillcrest Christian College, Ev. Ch. 2801-13th Ave. S.E., Medicine Hat, Alberta T1A 3R1. Kervin Raugust. Tel. (403)526-6951

Huron College, Ang. Ch. of Canada. Faculty of Theology, London, Ontario N6G 1H3. Charles Jago. Tel. (519)438-7224

Institut Biblique Béthel, Interdenom. C.P. 1600, Sherbrooke, Québec J1H 5M4. Tel. (819)569-3257

Institut Biblique Laval, Menn. Breth. 1775, boul. Edouard-Laurin, Ville Saint-Laurent, Québec H4L 2B9. Tél. (514)332-9326

International Bible College, Ch. of God (Cleveland, TN). 401 Trinity La., Moose Jaw, Saskatchewan S6H 0E3. Tel. (306)692-4041

Knox College (see Toronto School of Theology)

London Baptist Bible College, Indep. Bapt., 30 Grand Ave., London, Ontario NGC 1K8. David Barker. Tel. (519)434-6801

Lutheran Theological Seminary, Ev. Luth. Ch. in Canada. Saskatoon, Saskatchewan S7N 0X3. Roger Nostbakken. Tel. (306)975-7004

Lutheran Theological Seminary, Ev. Luth. Ch. in Canada. Saskatoon, Saskatchewan S7N 0X3. Roger Nostbakken. Tel. (306)975-7004

Maritime Christian College, CC/CC. Box 1145, 223 Kent St., Charlottetown, Prince Edward Island C1A 7M8. Stewart J. Lewis. Tel. (902)894-3828

McMaster Divinity College, Bapt. Conv. of Ontario and Quebec. Hamilton, Ontario L8S 4K1. William H. Brackney. Tel. (416)525-9140

Mennonite Brethren Bible College, Menn. Br. 1-169 Riverton Ave., Winnipeg, Manitoba R2L 2E5. James N. Pankratz. Tel. (204)669-6575

Montreal Diocesan Theological College, Ang. Ch. of Canada. 3473 University St., Montreal, Quebec H3A 2A8. A. C. Capon. Tel. (514)849-3004

Mountain View Bible College, Missy. Ch. of Can., Box 190, Didsbury, Alberta T0M 0W0. Virgil Stauffer. Tel. (403)335-3337

Newman Theological College, Cath. RR 8, Edmonton, Alberta T5L 4H8. W. Murchland. Tel. (403)447-2993

Nipawin Bible Institute, interdenom. Box 1986, Nipawin, Saskatchewan S0E 1E0. Jake Rempel. Tel. (306)862-3651

North American Baptist College and Divinity School, N. Amer. Bapt. Conf. 11525 - 23rd Ave., Edmonton, Alberta T6J 4T3. Paul Siewert. Tel. (403)437-1960

Northwest Baptist Theological College and Seminary, Fell. Bapt. 7600 Glover Rd., Langley, British Columbia V3A 6H4. Doug Harris.

Northwest Bible College, Pent. Assem. of Canada. 11617-106 Ave., Edmonton, Alberta T5H 0S1. G. K. Franklin. Tel. (403)452-0808

Okanagan Bible College, interdenom. Box 407, Kelowna, British Columbia V1Y 7N8. Dan Kelly. Tel. (604)860-8080

Ontario Christian Seminary, CC/CC. 260 High Park Ave., Box 324, Sta. D, Toronto, Ontario M6P 3J9. Donald Stevenson. Tel. (416)769-7115

Ontario Theological Seminary, multidenom. 25 Ballyconnor Ct., Willowdale, Ontario M2M 4B3. Wm. J. McRae. Tel. (416)226-6380

Peace River Bible Institute. Box 99, Sexsmith, Alberta T0H 3C0. Harold Peters. Tel. (403)568-3962

Prairie Bible Institute, interdenom. Three Hills, Alberta T0M 2A0. Ted S. Rendall. Tel. (403)443-5511

Presbyterian College. 3495 University St., Montreal, Quebec H3A 2A8. W. J. Klempa. Tel. (514)288-5256

Queen's College, Ang. Ch. of Can., St. John's Newfoundland A1B 3R6. F. Cluett. Tel. (709)753-0640

Queen's Theological College, Un. Ch. of Canada. Kingston, Ontario K7L 3N6. Tel. (613)545-2110

Regent College, transdenom. 2130 Wesbrook Mall, Vancouver, British Columbia V6T 1W6. Walter C. Wright, Jr. Tel. (604)224-3245

Regis College (see Toronto School of Theology).

St. Andrew's College, United Ch. of Canada. 1121 College Dr., Saskatoon, Saskatchewan S7N 0W3. Tel. (306)966-8970

St. Augustine Seminary (see Toronto School of Theology)

St. John's College, Univ. of Manitoba, Faculty of Theology, Ang. Ch. of Canada. Winnipeg, Manitoba R3T 2M5. Canon Tom Collings. Tel. (204)474-8518

St. Michael's College, Faculty of Theology (see Toronto School of Theology)

St. Peter's Seminary, Cath. 1040 Waterloo St., London, Ontario N6A 3Y1. P. W. Fuerth. Tel. (519)432-1824

St. Stephen's College, Graduate and Continuing Theological Education for Clergy and Laity, Un. Ch. of Canada. University of Alberta Campus, Edmonton, Alberta T6G 2J6. Garth I. Mundle. Tel. (403)439-7311

Salvation Army College for Officer Traning, The, Salv. Army. 2130 Bayview Ave., Toronto, Ontario M4N 3K6. Donald Kerr. Tel (416)481-6131

Steinbach Bible College, Menn.-Anabapt., Box 1420, Steinbach, Manitoba R0A 2A0. Gordon Daman. Tel. (204)326-6451

Swift Current Bible Institute, Menn. Box 1268, Swift Current, Saskatchewan S9H 3X4. David Hall. Tel. (306)773-0604

Toronto Baptist Seminary and Bible College, Bapt. 130 Gerrard St., E., Toronto, Ontario M5A 3T4. Norman Street, G. A. Adams. Tel. (416)925-3263

Toronto School of Theology (a federation of 7 theological colleges: 3 Roman Catholic, 2 Anglican, 1 Presbyterian, and 1 United Church of Canada. Affiliated with the University of Toronto. McMaster Divinity College is an associate member.). 47 Queen's Park Crescent E., Toronto, Ontario M5S 2C3. E. James Reed. Tel. (416)978-4039

Emmanuel College, Un. Ch. of Canada. 75 Queen's Park Crescent, Toronto, Ontario M5S 1K7. C. Douglas Jay. Tel. (416)585-4539

Knox College, Presb. Ch. in Canada. 59 St. George St., Toronto, Ontario M5S 2E6. Donald J. M. Corbett. Tel. (416)978-4500

Regis College, Cath. 15 St. Mary St., Toronto, Ontario M4Y 2R5. John E. Costello. Tel. (416)922-5474

St. Augustine's Seminary of Toronto, Cath. 2661 Kingston Rd., Scarborough, Ontario M1M 1M3. James Wingle. Tel. (416)261-7207.

Trinity College, Faculty of Divinity, Ang. Ch. of Canada. 6 Hoskin Ave., Toronto, Ontario M5S 1H8. R. H. Painter. Tel. (416)978-2525

University of St. Michael's College, Faculty of Theology, Cath. 81 St. Mary St., Toronto, Ontario M5S 1J4. Michael A. Fahey. Tel. (416)926-7140

Wycliffe College, Ang. Ch. of Canada. 5 Hoskin Ave., Toronto, Ontario M5S 1H7. P. R. Mason. Tel. (416)979-2870

Trinity College (see Toronto School of Theology)

United Theological College, Un. Ch. of Can. 3521 University St., Montreal, Quebec H3A 2A9

Université de Montréal, Faculté de théologie, Cath. C. P. 6128, Montréal Québec H3C 3J7. André Charron. Tel. (514)343-7167

Université de Sherbrooke, Faculté de théologie, Cath. Cité Universitaire, 2500 Boulevard de l' Université, Sherbrooke, Quebec J1K 2R1. Lucien Vachon. Tél. (819)821-7600

Université Laval, Faculté de théologie, Cath. Cité Universitaire Ste-Foy, Québec G1K 7P4. Jean-Claude Filteau. Tel. (418)656-7823

University of Winnipeg, Faculty of Theology, Un. Ch. of Canada. Winnipeg, Manitoba R3B 2E9. H. J. King. Tel. (204)786-9390

Université Saint-Paul, Faculté de théologie, Cath. 223 rue Main, Ottawa, Ontario K1S 1C4. M. Achiel Peelman. Tél. (613)236-1393

Vancouver School of Theology, Interdenom., 6000 Iona Dr., Vancouver, British Columbia V6T 1L4. Arthur Van Seters. Tel. (604)228-9031

Waterloo Lutheran Seminary, Ev. Luth. Ch. in Canada. Waterloo, Ontario N2L 3C5. Richard C. Crossman. Tel. (519)884-1970

Western Christian College, Chs. of Christ. North Weyburn, Saskatchewan S0C 1X0. E. Dan Wieb.

Western Pentecostal Bible College, Pent. Assem. of Canada. Box 1000, Clayburn, British Columbia V0X 1E0. James G. Richards. Tel. (604)853-7491

Winkler Bible Institute, Menn. Breth. 121 7th St., South, Winkler, Manitoba R6W 2N4. Eldon DeFehr. Tel. (204)325-4242

Winnipeg Bible College. Otterburne, Manitoba R0A 1G0. William R. Eichhorst. Tel. (204)284-2923

Wycliffe College (see Toronto School of Theology)

11. CHURCH-RELATED AND ACCREDITED COLLEGES AND UNIVERSITIES IN THE UNITED STATES

The following 684 alphabetically listed Protestant, Catholic, Jewish, and other religious colleges and universities have been identified as four-year, church-related, accredited institutions offering a bachelor's degree. The list does not include junior colleges, teachers' or other professional schools, or bible colleges. A listing of Bible Colleges is found in Directory 9, Theological Seminaries and Bible Colleges in the United States, in this **Yearbook.**

Although there are no up-to-date statistics, it was discovered by the U. S. Office of Education in 1981 that there were 1,978 four-year institutions of higher learning in the U. S. and that 1,420 of these were private. About 51 percent of these private colleges and universities were church-related, and most of the church-related institutions were identified as Protestant, outnumbering the Roman Catholic by roughly two to one.

The term *church-related* is difficult to define since it can mean many different things: church-owned and controlled; colleges and universities with independent boards of trustees, having a relationship to individual denominations through such forms as covenants; denominational representation on boards of trustees, and so on. For a detailed examination of the concept of church-relatedness, see *Church-Related Higher Education: Perceptions and Perspectives,* edited by Robert Rue Parsonage (Valley Forge, Pa.: Judson Press, 1978).

A majority of church-related colleges and universities identify themselves in various directories of higher education as church-controlled or affiliated. Many colleges and universities not so identified nevertheless maintain a degree of church-relatedness to a specific denomination or group of denominations. These institutions can be identified only by consulting denominational records or other private sources. This was done in the preparation of the list that follows.

Abbreviations for nationally recognized regional Accrediting Associations are as follows:

- MS   Middle States Association of Colleges and Schools
- NC   North Central Association of Colleges and Schools
- NE   New England Association of Schools and Colleges
- NW   Northwest Association of Schools and Colleges
- S   Southern Association of Schools and Colleges
- West   Western Association of Schools and Colleges

Other abbreviations are as follows:

C	Coeducational	W	Women
M	Men	Co-Ord.	Coordinate

Each item in the listing below has the following order: Name of institution, address, telephone number, head of institution, nature of student body, accrediting, denominational relationship, enrollment.

Abilene Christian University, Abilene TX 97699. Tel. (915) 674-2000. John C. Stevens, C S, Chs. of Christ, 4,181

Academy of the New Church, Byrn Athyn, PA 19009, Tel. (215) 947-4200. Geoffrey S. Childs, C MS, Ch. of New Jerusalem, 156

Adrian College, Adrian, MI 49221, Tel. (517) 265-5161. Stanley P. Caine, C NC, Un. Meth., 1,229

Agnes Scott College, Decatur, GA 30030, Tel. (404) 371-6000. Ruth A. Schmidt, W S, PCUSA, 526

Alaska Pacific University, Anchorage, AK 99508, Tel. (907) 561-1266. F. Thomas Trotter, C NW, Un. Meth., 625

Albertus Magnus College, New Haven, CT 06511, Tel. (203) 773-8550. Sr. Julia McNamara, C NE, Cath., 635

Albion College, Albion, MI 49224, Tel. (517) 629-5511. Melvin L. Vulgamore, C NC, Un. Meth., 1,721

Albright College, Reading, PA 19612, Tel. (215) 921-2381. David G. Ruffer, C MS, Un. Meth., 2,041

Alderson-Broaddus College, Philippi, WV 26416, Tel. (304) 457-1700. W. Christian Sizemore, C NC, Am. Bapt., 742

Allegheny College, Meadville, PA 16335, Tel. (814) 724-3100. Daniel F. Sullivan, C MS, Un. Meth., 1,992

Allentown College of Saint Francis de Sales, Center Valley, PA 18034, Tel. (215) 282-1100. Daniel G. Gambet, C MS, Cath., 1,386

Alma College, Alma, MI 48801, Tel. (517) 463-7111. Alan J. Stone, C NC, PCUSA, 1,086

Alvernia College, Reading, PA 19607, Tel. (215) 777-5411. Sr. M. Dolorey, C MS, Cath., 1,076

Alverno College, Milwaukee, WI 53215, Tel. (414) 382-6000. Sr. M. Joel Read, W NC, Cath., 2,191

Amber University, 1700 Eastgate Dr., Garland, TX 75041. Tel. (214) 279-6511. Douglas W. Warner, C S, Chs. of Christ, 1,130

American University, The, Washington, DC 20016, Tel. (202) 885-1000. Richard Berendzen, C MS, Un. Meth., 10,183

Anderson University, Anderson, IN 46012, Tel. (317) 649-9071. Robert A. Nicholson, C NC, Ch. of God, (And.), 2,050

Andrews University, Berrien Springs, MI 49104, Tel. (616) 471-7771. W. Richard Lescher, C NC, S.D.A., 2,858

Anna Maria College, Paxton, MA 01612, Tel. (617) 757-4586. Sr. Bernadette Madore, C NE, Cath., 1,166

Antillian College, Mayaguez, PR 00709, Tel. (809) 834-9595. Moises Velasquez,, C MS, S.D.A., 817

Aquinas College, Grand Rapids, MI 49506, Tel. (616) 459-8281. Peter D. O'Connor, C NC, Cath., 2,051

Arkansas Baptist College, Little Rock, AR 72202, Tel(501)374-7856. William T. Keaton, C NC, Bapt., 268

Arkansas College, Batesville, AR 72503, Tel. (501) 793-9813. Graham Holloway, C NC, PCUSA, 756

Ashland University, Ashland, OH 44805, Tel. (419) 289-4142. Joseph R. Schultz, C NC, Breth. Ch., 4,073

Assumption College, Worcester, MA 01615, Tel. (508) 752-5615. Joseph H. Hagan, C NE, Cath., 2,470

Atlantic Christian College, Wilson, NC 27893, Tel. (919) 237-3161. James B. Hemby, Jr., C S, Christian Church (Disc.), 1,384

Atlantic Union College, South Lancaster, MA 01561, Tel. (617) 365-4561. Lawrence T. Geraty, C NE, S.D.A., 725

Augsburg College, Minneapolis, MN 55454, Tel. (612) 330-1000. Charles S. Anderson, C NC, ELCA, 2,629

215

Augustana College, Rock Island, IL 61201, Tel. (309) 794-7000. J. Thomas Tredway, C NC, ELCA, 2,241

Augustana College, Sioux Falls, SD 57197, Tel. (605) 336-0770. Lloyd Svendsbye, C NC, ELCA, 2,048

Aurora University, Aurora, IL 60506, Tel. (312) 892-6431. Thomas H. Zarle, C NC, Adv. Chr. Ch., 2,061

Austin College, Sherman, TX 75091, Tel. (214) 813-2000. Harry E. Smith, C S, PCUSA, 1,269

Averett College, Danville, VA 24541, Tel. (804) 791-5600. Frank R. Campbell, C S, Bapt., 1,010

Avila College, Kansas City, MO 64145, Tel. (816) 942-8400. Larry Kramer, C NC, Cath., 1,585

Baker University, Baldwin City, KS 66006, Tel. (913) 594-6451. Daniel M. Lambert, C NC, Un. Meth., 878

Baldwin-Wallace College, Berea, OH 44017, Tel. (216) 826-2900. Neal Malicky, C NC, Un. Meth., 4,564

Baltimore Hebrew University, Baltimore, MD 21215, Tel. (301) 578-6900. Leivy Smolar, C MS, Jewish, 230

Baptist College at Charleston, Charleston, SC 29411, Tel. (803) 797-4011. Jairy C. Hunter, C S, So. Bapt., 1,928

Barat College, Lake Forest, IL 60045, Tel. (312) 234-3000. Lucy Morros, C NC, Cath., 707

Barber-Scotia College, Concord, NC 28025, Tel. (704) 786-5171. Tyrone Burkette, C S, PCUSA, 378

Bard College, Annandale-on-Hudson, NY 12504, Tel. (914) 758-6822. Leon Botstein, C MS, Epis., 915

Barry University, Miami, FL 33161, Tel. (305) 758-3392. Sr. Jeanne O'Laughlin, C S, Cath., 5,238

Bartlesville Wesleyan College, Bartlesville, OK 74006, Tel. (918) 333-6151. Paul R. Mills, C NC, Wesleyan Ch., 541

Bayamon Central University, Bayamon, PR 00621, Tel. (809) 786-3030. Vincent A. M. Van Rooij, C MS, Cath., 2,796

Baylor University, Waco, TX 76798, Tel. (817) 755-1011. Herbert H. Reynolds, C S, So. Bapt., 11,772

Beaver College, Glenside, PA 19038, Tel. (215) 572-2900. Bette E. Landman, C MS, PCUSA, 2,199

Belhaven College, Jackson, MS 39202, Tel. (601) 968-5919. Newton Wilson, C S, PCUSA, 693

Bellarmine College, Louisville, KY 40205, Tel. (502) 452-8211. Eugene V. Petrik, C S, Cath., 2,584

Belmont Abbey College, Belmont, NC 28012, Tel. (704) 825-6700. Edward L. Henry, Interim, C S, Cath., 1,029

Belmont College, Nashville, TN 37203, Tel. (615) 383-7001. William E. Troutt, C S, So. Bapt., 2,688

Beloit College, Beloit, WI 53511, Tel. (608) 365-3391. Roger Hull, C NC, U. Ch. of Christ, 1,136

Benedict College, Columbia, SC 29204, Tel. (803) 256-4220. Marshall C. Grigsby, C S, Am. Bapt., 1,488

Benedictine College, Atchison, KS 66002. Tel. (913) 367-6110. Thomas O. James, C NC, Cath., 750

Bennett College, Greensboro, NC 27401, Tel. (919) 273-4431. Gloria R. Scott, W S, Un. Meth. 632

Bethany College, Bethany, WV 26032, Tel. (304) 829-7000. D. Duane H. Cummins, C NC, Christian Church (Disc.), 844

Bethany College, Lindsborg, KS 67456, Tel. (913) 227-3311. Peter J. Ristuben, C NC, ELCA, 724

Bethel College, McKenzie, TN 38201, Tel. (901) 352-5321. William L. Odom, C S, Cumb. Presb., 596

Bethel College, North Newton, KS 67117, Tel. (316) 283-2500. Harold J. Schultz, C NC, Gen. Conf. Menn. Ch., 621

Bethel College, Mishawaka, IN 46545, Tel. (219) 259-8511. Norman V. Bridges, C NC, Miss. Ch., 540

Bethel College, St. Paul, MN, 55112, Tel. (612) 638-6400. George K. Brushaber, C NC, Bapt. Gen'l Conf., 1,800

Bethune-Cookman College, Daytona Beach, FL 32015, Tel. (904) 255-1401. Oswald P. Bronson, C S, Un. Meth., 1,860

Birmingham-Southern College, Birmingham, AL 35254, Tel. (205) 266-4600. Neil R. Berte, C S, Un. Meth., 1,828

Blackburn College, Carlinville, IL 62626, Tel. (217) 854-3231. David W. Brown, C NC, PCUSA, 521

Bloomfield College, Bloomfield, NJ 07003, Tel. (201) 748-9000. John F. Noonan, C MS, PCUSA, 1,484

Blue Mountain College, Blue Mountain, MS 38610, Tel. (601) 685-4771. E. Harold Fisher, W S, So. Bapt., 374

Bluefield College, Bluefield, WV 24605, Tel. (703) 326-3682. Roy A. Dobyns, C S, So. Bapt., 366

Bluffton College, Bluffton, OH 45817, Tel. (419) 358-8015. Elmer Neufeld, C NC, Menn. Ch., 608

Borromeo College of Ohio, Wickliffe, OH 44092, Tel. (216) 585-5900. James L. Caddy, M NC, Cath., 44

Boston College, Chestnut Hill, MA 02167, Tel. (617) 552-8000. J. Donald Monan, C NE, Cath., 14,561

Brescia College, Owensboro, KY 42301, Tel. (502) 685-3131. Sr. Ruth Gehres, C S, Cath., 666

Brewton-Parker College, Mount Vernon, GA 30445, Tel. (912)583-2241. Y. Lynn Holmes, C S, Bapt., 1,470

Briar Cliff College, Sioux City, IA 51104, Tel. (712) 279-5321. Sr. Margaret Wick, C NC, Cath., 1,103

Bridgewater College, Bridgewater, VA 22812, Tel. (703) 828-2501. Wayne F. Geisert, C S, Ch. Breth., 969

Brigham Young University, Provo, UT 84602 Tel. (801) 378-1211. Rex E. Lee, C NW, L.D.S., 26,986

Brigham Young University, Hawaii Campus, Laie Oahu, HI 96762, Tel. (808) 293-3211. Alton L. Wade, L.D.S., 2,088

Buena Vista College, Storm Lake, IA 50588, Tel. (712) 749-2351. Keith G. Briscoe, C NC PCUSA, 1,100

Cabrini College, Radnor, PA 19087, Tel. (215) 971-8100. Sr. Eileen Currie, C MS, Cath., 1,090

Caldwell College, Caldwell, NJ 07006, Tel. (201) 228-4424. Sr. Vivien Jennings, C MS, Cath., 961

California Baptist College, Riverside, CA 92504, Tel. (714) 689-5771. Russell R. Tuck, C West, So. Bapt., 666

California Lutheran University, Thousand Oaks, CA 91360, Tel. (805) 492-2411. Jerry H. Miller, C West, ELCA, 2,749

Calumet College of St. Joseph, Whiting, IN 46394, Tel. (219) 473-7770. Dennis C. Rittenmeyer, C NC, Cath., 1,059

Calvin College, Grand Rapids, MI 49506, Tel. (616) 957-6000. Anthony J. Diekema, C NC, Christ. Ref., 4,505

Campbell University, Buies Creek, NC 27506, Tel. (919) 893-4111. Norman A. Wiggins, C S, So. Bapt., 4,195

Campbellsville College, Campbellsville, KY 42718, Tel. (502) 465-8158. Kenneth W. Winters, C S, So. Bapt., 732

Canisius College, Buffalo, NY 14208, Tel. (716) 883-7000. James M. Demske, C MS, Cath., 5,000

Capital University, Columbus, OH 43209, Tel. (614) 236-6011. Josiah H. Blackmore, C NC, ELCA, 3,016

Cardinal Stritch College, Milwaukee, WI 53217, Tel. (414) 352-5400. Sr. M. Camille Kliebhan, C NC, Cath., 3,218

Carleton College, Northfield, MN 55057, Tel. (507) 663-4000. Stephen R. Lewis, Jr., C NC, U. Ch. of Christ, 1,880

Carlow College, Pittsburgh, PA 15213. Tel. (412) 578-6000. Sr. Grace Ann Geibel, W MS, Cath., 962

Carroll College, Helena, MT 59625, Tel. (406) 442-3450. Matthew J. Quinn, C NW, Cath., 1,418

Carroll College, Waukesha, WI 53186, Tel. (414) 547-1211. Daniel C. West, C NC, PCUSA, 2,202

Carson-Newman College, Jefferson City, TN 37760, Tel. (615) 475-9061. J. Cordell Maddox, C S, So. Bapt., 2,000

Carthage College, Kenosha, WI 53141, Tel. (414) 551-8500. F. Gregory Campbell, C NC, ELCA, 1,842

Catawba College, Salisbury, NC 28144, Tel. (704) 637-4111. Stephen H. Wurster, C S, U. Ch. of Christ, 984

Catholic University of America, Washington, DC 20064, Tel. (202) 635-5000. William J. Byron, C MS, Cath., 7,005

Catholic University of Puerto Rico, Ponce, PR 00732, Tel. (809) 841-2000. Fremiot Torres-Oliver, C MS, Cath., 11,551

Cedar Crest College, Allentown, PA 18104, Tel. (215) 437-4471. Dorothy G. Blaney, W MS, U. Ch. of Christ, 1,039

Cedarville College, Cedarville, OH 45314, Tel. (513) 766-2211. Paul H. Dixon, C NC, Bapt., 1,879

Centenary College of Louisiana, Shreveport, LA 71134, Tel. (318) 869-5011. Donald A. Webb, C S, Un. Meth., 1,081

Centenary College, Hackettstown, NJ 07840. Tel. (201) 852-1400. Stephanie M. Bennett, C MS, Un. Meth., 807

Central College, McPherson, KS 67460, Tel. (316)241-0723. Harvey L. Ludwick, C NC, Free Meth. Ch., 265

Central Methodist College, Fayette, MO 65248, Tel. (816) 248-3391. Joseph A. Howell, C NC, Un. Meth., 720

Central University of Iowa, Pella, IA 50219, Tel. (515) 628-9000 Kenneth J. Weller, C NC, Ref. in Am., 1,658

Central Wesleyan College, Central, SC 29630, Tel. (803) 639-2453. John M. Newby, C S, Wesleyan Ch., 679

Centre College of Kentucky, Danville, KY 40422, Tel. (606) 236-5211. Michael F. Adams, C S, PCUSA, 861

Chaminade University of Honolulu, Honolulu, HI 96816, Tel. (808) 735-4870. Kent M. Keith, C West, Cath., 1,243

Chapman College, Orange, CA 92666, Tel. (714) 997-6815. James Doti, Actg.; C West, Christian Church (Disc.), 2,185

Chestnut Hill College, Philadelphia, PA 19118, Tel. (215) 248-7000. Sr. Matthew Anita MacDonald, W MS, Cath., 1,022

Christ College Irvine, Irvine, CA 92715. Tel. (714) 854-8002. D. Ray Halm, C West, Luth. (Mo.), 542

Christendom College, Front Royal, VA. Tel. (701)636-2900. Damian P. Fedoryka, C S, Cath., 160

Christian Brothers College, Memphis, TN 38104, Tel. (901) 722-0200. Bro. Theodore Drahmann, C S, Cath., 1,791

Claflin College, Orangeburg, SC 29115, Tel. (803) 534-2710. Oscar A. Rogers, Jr., C S, Un. Meth., 750

Clark Atlanta University, Atlanta, GA 30314, Tel. (404) 880-8000 Thomas Cole, Jr., C S, Un. Meth., 3,144

Clarke College, Dubuque, IA 52001, Tel. (319) 588-6300. Catherine Dunn, C NC, Cath., 802

Coe College, Cedar Rapids, IA 52402, Tel. (319) 399-8000. John Brown, C NC, PCUSA, 1,242

College Misericordia, Dallas, PA 18612, Tel. (717) 675-2181. Pasquale Di Pasquale, Jr., C MS, Cath., 1,114

College of Great Falls, Great Falls, MT 59405, Tel. (406) 761-8210. William A. Shields, C NW, Cath., 1,200

College of Idaho, Caldwell, ID 83605, Tel. (208) 459-5011. Robert L. Hendren, Jr. C NW, PCUSA, 1,050

College of Mt. St. Joseph, Mt. St. Joseph, OH 45051, Tel. (513) 244-4200. Sr. Francis M. Thrailkill, W NC, Cath., 2,566

College of Mt. St. Vincent, Riverdale, NY 10471, Tel. (212) 549-8000. Sr. Doris Smith, C MS, Cath., 950

College of New Rochelle, New Rochelle, NY 10801, Tel. (914) 632-5300. Sr. Dorothy A. Kelly, C MS, Cath., 4,492

College of Notre Dame, Belmont, CA 94002, Tel. (415) 593-1601. Sr. Veronica Skillin, C West, Cath., 1,052

College of Notre Dame of Md., Baltimore, MD 21210. Tel. (301) 435-0100. Sr. Kathleen Feeley, W MS, Cath., 2,466

College of Our Lady of the Elms, Chicopee, MA 01013, Tel. (413) 594-2761. Sr. Mary A. Dooley, W NE, Cath., 1,088

College of St. Benedict, St. Joseph, MN 56374, Tel. (612) 363-5011. Sr. Colman O'Connell, Co-Ord. NC, Cath., 1,959

College of St. Catherine, St. Paul, MN 55105, Tel. (612) 690-6000. Sr. Anita Pompusch, W NC, Cath., 2,729

College of St. Elizabeth, Convent Sta., NJ 07961, Tel. (201) 292-6300. Sr. Jacqueline Burns, W MS, Cath., 1,040

College of St. Francis, Joliet, IL 60435, Tel. (815) 740-3360. John C. Orr, C NC, Cath., 4,040

College of St. Joseph, Rutland, VT 05701, Tel. (802) 773-5900. Frank J. Miglorie, Jr., C NE, Cath., 440

College of St. Mary, Omaha, NE 68124, Tel. (402) 399-2400. Kenneth Nielsen, W NC, Cath., 1,133

College of St. Rose, Albany, NY 12203, Tel. (518) 454-5111. Louis Vaccaro, C MS, Cath., 3,231

College of St. Scholastica, Duluth, MN 55811, Tel. (218) 723-6000. Daniel H. Pilon, C NC, Cath., 1,849

College of St. Thomas, St. Paul, MN 55105, Tel. (612) 647-5000. Terrence J. Murphy, C NC, Cath., 8,790

College of Santa Fe, Santa Fe, NM 87501, Tel. (505) 473-6011. James Fries, C NC, Cath., 1,602

College of the Holy Cross, Worcester, MA 01610, Tel. (617) 793-2011. John E. Brooks, C NE, Cath., 2,601

College of Wooster, Wooster, OH 44691, Tel. (216) 263-2000. Henry J. Copeland, C NC, PCUSA, 1,917

Columbia College, Columbia, SC 29203, Tel. (803) 786-3012. Peter T. Mitchell, W S, Un. Meth., 1,218

Columbia College, Columbia, MO 65216. Tel. (314) 875-8700, Donald B. Ruthenberg, C NC, Christian Ch. (Disc.), 714

Columbia Christian College, Portland, OR 97216, Tel. (503) 255-7060. Gary D. Elliott, C NW, Chs. of Christ, 279

Columbia Union College, Takoma Park, MD 20912, Tel. (301) 270-9200, William A. Loveless, C MS, S.D.A., 1,236

Conception Seminary College, Conception, MO 64433, Tel. (816) 944-2218. Gregory Polan, M NC, Cath., 85

Concordia College, River Forest, IL 60305, Tel. (312) 771-8300. Eugene L. Krentz, C NC, Luth. (Mo.) 1,369

Concordia College, Bronxville, NY 10708, Tel. (914) 337-9300. Ralph C. Schultz, C MS, Luth. (Mo.), 526

Concordia College, Ann Arbor, MI 48105, Tel. (313) 995-7300. David G. Schmiel, C NC, Luth. (Mo.), 544

Concordia College, Portland, OR 97211, Tel. (503) 288-9371. Charles E. Schlimpert, C NW, Luth. (Mo.), 460

Concordia College—Moorhead, Moorhead, MN 56560, Tel. (218) 299-3000. Paul J. Dovre, C NC, ELCA, 2,880

Concordia College—St. Paul, St. Paul, MN 55104, Tel. (612) 641-8278. John F. Johnson, C NC, Luth. (Mo.), 1,133

Concordia University Wisconsin, Mequon, WI 53092, Tel. (414) 243-5700. R. John Buuck, C NC, Luth. (Mo.), 1,276

Concordia Lutheran College, Austin, TX 78705, Tel. (512) 452-7661. Ray F. Martens, C S, Luth. (Mo.), 507

Cornell College, Mt. Vernon, IA 52314, Tel. (319) 895-4000. David G. Marker, C NC, Un. Meth., 1,129

Covenant College, Lookout Mountain, TN 30750, Tel. (404) 820-1560. Frank A. Brock, C S, Presby. Ch. in Am., 540

Creighton University, Omaha, NE 68178, Tel. (402) 280-2700. Michael G. Morrison, C NC, Cath., 5,958

Culver-Stockton College, Canton, MO 63435, Tel. (314) 288-5221. Robert W. Brown, C NC, Christian Church (Disc.), 1,037

Cumberland College, Williamsburg, KY 40769, Tel. (606) 549-2200. James Taylor, C S, So. Bapt., 1,904

Dakota Wesleyan University, Mitchell, SD 57301, Tel. (605) 995-2600. James B. Beddow, C NC, Un. Meth., 667

Dallas Baptist University, Dallas, TX 75211, Tel. (214) 331-8311. Gary R. Cook, C S, So. Bapt., 2,018

Dallas, University of, Irving, TX 75061, Tel. (214) 721-5000. Robert F. Sasseen, C S, Cath., 2,662

Dana College, Blair, NE 68008, Tel. (402) 426-9000. Myrvin F. Christopherson, C NC, ELCA, 500

David Lipscomb University, Nashville, TN 37204, Tel. (615) 269-1000. Harold Hazelip, C S, Chs. of Christ, 2,337

Davidson College, Davidson, NC 28036, Tel. (704) 892-2000. John W. Kuykendall, , C S, PCUSA, 1,415

Davis and Elkins College, Elkins, WV 26241, Tel. (304) 636-1900. Dorothy I. MacConkey, C NC, PCUSA, 811

Dayton, University of, Dayton, OH 45469, Tel. (513) 229-1000. Bro. Raymond L. Fitz, C NC, Cath., 11,090

Defiance College, The, Defiance, OH 43512, Tel. (419) 784-4010. Marvin Ludwig, C NC, U. Ch. of Christ, 1,030

Denver, University of, Denver, CO 80208, Tel. (303) 871-2000. Daniel Ritchie, C NC, Un. Meth., 6,824

DePaul University, Chicago, IL 60604, Tel. (312) 341-8000. John R. Cortelyou, C NC, Cath., 9,198

DePauw University, Greencastle, IN 46135, Tel. (317) 658-4800. Robert G. Bottoms, C NC, Un. Meth., 2,256

Detroit, University of, Detroit, MI 48221, Tel. (313) 927-1000. Robert A. Mitchell, C NC, Cath., 6,021

Dickinson College, Carlisle, PA 17013, Tel. (717) 243-5121. A. Lee Fritschler, C MS, Un. Meth. 2,054

Dillard University, New Orleans, LA 70122, Tel. (504) 283-8822. Samuel Dubois Cook, C S, U. Ch. of Christ, Un. Meth., 1,400

Divine Word College, Epworth, IA 52045, Tel. (319) 876-3353. Joseph D. Simon, M NC, Cath., 75

Doane College, Crete, NE 68333, Tel. (402) 826-2161. Frederic D. Brown, C NC, U. Ch. of Christ, 910

Dominican College of Blauvelt, Orangeburg, NY 10962, Tel. (914) 359-7800. Sr. Kathleen Sullivan, C MS, Cath., 1,443

Dominican College of San Rafael, San Rafael, CA 94901, Tel. (415) 457-4440. Joseph Fink, C West, Cath., 665

Dordt College, Sioux Center, IA 51250, Tel. (712) 722-3771. John B. Hulst, C NC, Christ. Ref. Ch., 987

Dr. Martin Luther College, New Ulm, MN 56073, Tel. (507) 354-8221. Lloyd C. Huebner, C NC, Wis. Ev. Luth. Synod., 447

Drew University, Madison, NJ 07940, Tel. (201) 408-3000. W. Scott McDonald, Jr., Interim, C MS, Un. Meth., 2,364

Drury College, Springfield, MO 65802, Tel. (417) 865-8731. John E. Moore,, Jr., C NC, U. Ch. of Christ, 1,442

Dubuque, University of, Dubuque, IA 52001, Tel. (319) 589-3000. Walter F. Peterson, C NC, PCUSA, 1,082

Duke University, Durham, NC 27706, Tel. (919) 684-8111. Keith H. Brodie, C S, Un. Meth., 9,828

Duquesne University, Pittsburgh, PA 15282, Tel. (412) 434-6000. John E. Murray, Jr., C MS, Cath., 6,453

D'Youville College, Buffalo, NY 14201, Tel. (716) 881-3200. Sr. Denise Roche, C MS, Cath., 1,200

Earlham College, Richmond, IN 47374. Tel. (317) 983-1200. Richard Wood, C NC, Friends, 1,173

East Texas Baptist University, Marshall, TX 75670, Tel. (214) 935-7963. Robert E. Craig, C S. So. Bapt., 809

Eastern College, St. Davids, PA 19087, Tel. (215) 341-5810. Roberta Hestenes, C MS, Am. Bapt., 1,155

Eastern Mennonite College, Harrisonburg, VA 22801, Tel. (703) 433-2771. Joseph L. Lapp, C S, Menn. Ch., 967

Eastern Nazarene College, Wollaston, MA 02170, Tel. (617) 773-6350. Stephen W. Nease, C NE, Nazarene, 979

Eckerd College, St. Petersburg, FL 33733, Tel. (813) 867-1166. Peter H. Armacost, C S, PCUSA, 1,326

Edgewood College, Madison, WI 53711, Tel. (608) 257-4861. James A. Ebben, C NC, Cath., 1,085

Edward Waters College, Jacksonville, Fl 32209, Tel. (904) 355-3030. Robert L. Mitchell, C S, A.M.E., 618.

Elizabethtown College, Elizabethtown, PA 17022, Tel. (717) 367-1151. Gerhard E. Spiegler, C MS, Ch. Breth., 1,773

Elmhurst College, Elmhurst, IL 60126, Tel. (312) 279-4100. Ivan Frick, C NC, U. Ch. of Christ, 3,135

Elon College, Elon College, NC 27244, Tel. (919) 584-9711. J. Fred Young, C S, U. Ch. of Christ, 3,305

Emmanuel College, Boston, MA 02115, Tel. (617) 277-9340. Sr. Janet Eisner, W NE, Cath., 973

Emory and Henry College, Emory, VA 24327, Tel. (703) 944-3121. Charles W. Sydnor, Jr. C S, Un. Meth., 788

Emory University, Atlanta, GA 30322, Tel. (404) 727-6123. James T. Laney, C S, Un. Meth., 9,285

Erskine College, Due West, SC 29639, Tel. (803) 379-2131. Henry G. Hollingsworth, C S, Asso. Ref. Presb., 497

Eureka College, Eureka, IL 61530, Tel. (309) 467-3721. George A. Hearne, C NC, Christian Church (Disc.), 447

Evangel College, Springfield, MO 65802, Tel. (417) 865-2811. Robert H. Spence, C NC, Assem. of God, 1,564

Evansville, University of, Evansville, IN 47722, Tel. (812) 477-6241, James S. Vinson, C NC, Un. Meth., 3,512

Fairfield University, Fairfield, CT 06430, Tel. (203) 254-4000. Aloysius P. Kelley, C NE, Cath., 4,878

Faulkner University, Montgomery, AL 36193. Billy D. Hiyler, CS, Chs. of Christ, 1,355

Felician College, Lodi, NJ 07644, Tel. (201) 778-1190, Sr. Theresa M. Martin, C MS, Cath., 650

Ferrum College, Ferrum, VA 24088, Tel. (703) 365-2121. Jerry M. Boone, C S, Un. Meth., 1,206

Findlay, The University of, Findlay, OH 45840, Tel. (419) 422-8313. Kenneth E. Zirkle, C NC, Ch. of God, Gen. Eldership, 2,075

Fisk University, Nashville, TN 37208, Tel. (615) 329-8500. Harry Ponder, C S, U. Ch. of Christ, 774

Florida Memorial College, Miami, FL 33054, Tel. (305) 625-4141. Willie C. Robinson, C S, Am. Bapt., 1,929

Florida Southern College, Lakeland, FL 33801, Tel. (813) 680-4111. Robert A. Davis, C S, Un. Meth., 2,593

Fontbonne College, St. Louis, MO 63105, Tel. (314) 862-3456. Maneve Dunham, C NC, Cath., 1,100

Fordham University, Bronx, NY 10458, Tel. (212) 579-2000. Joseph A. O'Hare, C MS, Cath., 13,036

Franciscan University of Steubenville, Steubenville, OH 43952, Tel. (614) 283-3771. Michael Scanlan, C NC, Cath., 1,369

Franklin College of Indiana, Franklin, IN 46131, Tel. (317) 736-8441. William B. Martin, C NC, Am. Bapt., 812

Franklin & Marshall College, Lancaster, PA 17604, Tel. (717) 291-3911. Richard Kneedler, C MS, U. Ch. of Christ, 1,850

Freed-Hardeman College, Henderson, TN 38340, Tel. (901) 989-6000. E. C. Gardner, C S, Chs. of Christ, 1,127

Fresno Pacific College, Fresno, CA 93702, Tel. (209) 453-2000. Richard Kriegbaum, C West., Menn. Breth. Ch., 1,200

Friends University, Wichita, KS 67213, Tel. (316) 261-5800. Richard E. Felix, C NC, Friends, 1,260

Furman University, Greenville, SC 29613, Tel. (803) 294-2000. John E. Johns, C S, So. Bapt., 2,794

Gannon University, Erie, PA 16541, Tel. (814) 871-7000. M. Daniel Henry, C MS, Cath., 4,500

Gardner-Webb College, Boiling Springs, NC 28017, Tel. (704) 434-2361. M. Christopher White, C S, So. Bapt., 2,183

Geneva College, Beaver Falls, PA 15010, Tel. (412) 846-5100. Joe McFarland, C MS, Ref. Presby. Ch., 1,230

George Fox College, Newberg, OR 97132, Tel. (503) 538-8383. Edward F. Stevens, C NW, Friends, 820

Georgetown College, Georgetown, KY 40324, Tel. (502) 863-8011. W. Morgan Patterson, C S, So. Bapt., 1,471

Georgetown University, Washington, DC 20057, Tel. (202) 687-0100. Leo J. O'Donnovan, C MS, Cath., 11,516

Georgian Court College, Lakewood, NJ 08701, Tel. (201) 364-2200. Sr. Barbara Williams, W MS, Cath., 2,054

Gettysburg College, Gettysburg, PA 17325, Tel. (717) 337-6000. Charles E. Anderson, Interim, C MS, ELCA, 2,001

Gonzaga University, Spokane, WA 99258, Tel. (509) 328-4220. Bernard J. Coughlin, C NW, Cath., 3,913

Gordon College, Wenham, MA 01984, Tel. (508) 927-2300. Richard F. Gross, C NE, Interdenom, 1,172

Goshen College, Goshen, IN 46526, Tel. (219) 535-7000. J. Victor Stoltzfus, C NC, Menn. Ch., 1,082

Grace College, Winona Lake, IN 46590, Tel. (219) 372-5100. John J. Davis, C NC, Fell. of Grace Br. Chs., 769

Graceland College, Lamoni, IA 50140, Tel. (515) 784-5000. Barbara J. Higdon, C NC, Reorg. L.D.S., 909

Grand Canyon University, Phoenix, AZ 85017, Tel. (602) 249-3300. Bill Williams, C NC, So. Bapt., 1,813

Grand Rapids Baptist College and Seminary, Grand Rapids, MI 49505, Tel. (616) 949-5300. Charles U. Wagner, C NC, Bapt, 885

Grand View College, Des Moines, IA 50316, Tel. (515) 263-2800. Arthur E. Puotinen, C NC, ELCA, 1,160

Greensboro College, Greensboro, NC 27401 Tel. (919) 272-7102. William H. Likins, C S, Un. Meth., 967

Greenville College, Greenville, IL 62246, Tel. (618) 664-1840. W. Richard Stephens, C NC, Free Meth., 753

Grinnell College, Grinnell, IA 50112, Tel. (515) 269-4000. George A. Drake, C NC, U. Ch. of Christ, 1,276

Grove City College, Grove City, PA 16127, Tel. (412) 458-2000, Charles S. MacKenzie, C MS, PCUSA, 2,133

Guilford College, Greensboro, NC 27410, Tel. (919) 292-5511. William R. Rogers, C S, Friends, 1,233

Gustavus Adolphus College, St. Peter, MN 56082, Tel. (507) 931-8000. John Kendall, C NC, ELCA, 2,413

Gwynedd-Mercy College, Gwynedd Valley, PA 19437, Tel. (215) 646-7300. Sr. Isabelle Keiss, C MS, Cath., 1,732

Hamline University, St. Paul, MN 55104, Tel. (612) 641-2800. Larry G. Osnes, C NC, Un. Meth., 2,425

Hampden-Sydney College, Hampden-Sydney, VA 23943. Tel. (804) 223-4381. James R. Leutze, III, M S, PCUSA, 937

Hannibal-La Grange College, Hannibal, MO 63401, Tel. (314) 221-3675. Paul E. Brown, C NC, So. Bapt., 813

Hanover College, Hanover, IN 47243, Tel. (812) 866-7000. Russell L. Nichols, C NC, PCUSA, 1,079

Hardin-Simmons University, Abilene, TX 79698, Tel. (915) 670-1000. Jesse C. Fletcher, C S, So. Bapt., 1,928

Harding University, Searcy, AR 72143, Tel. (501) 279-4000. David B. Burks, C NC, Chs. of Christ., 3,204

Hastings College, Hastings, NE 68901, Tel. (402) 463-2402. Thomas J. Reeves, C NC, PCUSA, 960

Haverford College, Haverford, PA 19041, Tel. (215) 896-1000. Tom G. Kessinger, C MS, Friends, 1,102

Hawaii Loa College, Kaneohe, HI 96744. Tel. (808) 235-3641. John Marvel, C West., Interdenom., 500

Hebrew College, Brookline, MA 02146. Tel. (617) 232-8710. Samuel Schafler, C NE, Jewish, 203

Hebrew Union College, New York Branch, New York, NY 10012, Tel. (212) 674-5300. Alfred Gottschalk, C MS, Jewish, 110

Heidelberg College, Tiffin, OH 44883, Tel. (419) 448-2000. William C. Cassell, C NC, U. Ch. of Christ, 960

Hellenic College, Brookline, MA 02146, Tel. (617) 731-3500. Alkiviades Calivas, C NE, Greek Orth., 140

Hendrix College, Conway, AR 72032, Tel. (501) 329-6811. Joe B. Hatcher, C NC, Un. Meth., 1,029

High Point College, High Point, NC 27262, Tel. (919) 841-9000. Jacob C. Martinson, C S, Un. Meth., 1,860

Hiram College, Hiram, OH 44234, Tel. (216) 569-3211. G. Benjamin Oliver, C NC, Christian Church (Disc.), 1,108

Hobart and William Smith Colleges, Geneva, NY 14456, Tel. (315) 789-5500. Carroll W. Brewster, Co. Ord. MS, Epis., 1,860

Holy Apostles College, Cromwell, CT 06416, Tel. (203) 635-5311. Ronald D. Lawler, C NE, Cath., 205

Holy Family College, Philadelphia, PA 19114, Tel. (215) 637-7700. Sr. M. Francesca Onley, C MS, Cath., 1,685

Holy Names College, Oakland, CA 94619. Tel. (415) 436-0111. Sr. Lois MacGillivray, C West, Cath., 718

Hood College, Frederick, MD 21701, Tel. (301) 663-3131. Martha E. Church, C MS, U. Ch. of Christ, 1,874

Hope College, Holland, MI 49423, Tel. (616) 392-5111. John H. Jacobson, C NC, Ref. Am., 2,781

Houghton College, Houghton, NY 14744, Tel. (716) 567-2211. Daniel R. Chamberlain, C MS, Wes. Ch., 1,164

Houston Baptist University, Houston, TX 77074, Tel. (713) 774-7661. William H. Hinton, C S, So. Bapt., 2,845

Howard Payne University, Brownwood, TX 76801, Tel. (915) 646-2502. Don Newbury, C S, So. Bapt., 1,247

Huntingdon College, Montgomery, AL 36194, Tel. (205) 265-0511. Allen Keith Jackson, C S, Un. Meth., 866

Huntington College, Huntington, IN 46750, Tel. (219) 356-6000. Eugene B. Habecker, C NC, U. Breth., 587

Huston-Tillotson College, Austin, TX 78702, Tel. (512) 476-7421. Joseph T. McMillan, C S, Un. Meth. and U. Ch. of Christ, 506

Illinois Benedictine College, Lisle, IL 60532, Tel. (312) 960-1500. Hugh Anderson, C NC, Cath., 2,515

Illinois College, Jacksonville, IL 62650. Tel. (217) 245-3000. Donald C. Mundinger, C NC, PCUSA, 842

Illinois Wesleyan University, Bloomington, IL 61702 Tel. (309) 556-3131. Minor C. Myers, Jr., C NC, Un. Meth. 1,750

Immaculata College, Immaculata, PA 19345, Tel. (215) 647-4400. Sr. Marian William, W MS, Cath., 2,095

Incarnate Word College, San Antonio, TX 78209. Tel. (512) 828-1261. Sr. Margaret P. Slattery, C S, Cath., 2,240

Indiana Wesleyan University, Marion, IN 46953, Tel. (317)674-6901. James Barnes, C NC, Wesleyan Ch., 2,032

Indianapolis, The University of, Indianapolis, IN 46227. Tel. (317) 788-3368. G. Benjamin Lantz, C NC, Un. Meth., 3,283

Iona College, New Rochelle, NY 10801. Tel. (914) 633-2000. Br. John G. Driscoll, C MS, Cath., 6,049

Iowa Wesleyan College, Mt. Pleasant, IA 52641, Tel. (319) 385-8021. Robert J. Prins, C NC, Un. Meth., 679

Jamestown College, Jamestown, ND 58401, Tel. (701) 252-3467. James S. Walker, C NC, PCUSA, 796

Jarvis Christian College, Hawkins, TX 75765, Tel. (214) 769-2174. Julius Nimmons, C S, Christian Ch. (Disc.), 542

John B. Stetson University, Deland, FL 32720, Tel. (901)734-4121. Pope A. Duncan, C S, So. Bapt., 2,844

John Carroll University, Cleveland, OH 44118, Tel. (216) 397-1886. Michael J. Lavelle, C NC, Cath., 4,082

Johnson C. Smith University, Charlotte, NC 28216, Tel. (704) 378-1000. Robert L. Albright, C S, PCUSA, 1,174

Judaism, University of, Los Angeles, CA 90077, Tel. (213) 476-9777. David L. Lieber, C West, Jewish, 162

Judson College, Elgin, IL 60123, Tel. (312) 695-2500. Harm A. Weber, C NC, Am. Bapt., 534

Judson College, Marion, AL 36756, Tel. (205) 683-6161. Norman H. McCrummen, W S, So. Bapt., 664

Juniata College, Huntingdon, PA 16652, Tel. (814) 643-4310. Robert W. Neff, C MS, Ch. Breth., 1,137

Kalamazoo College, Kalamazoo, MI 49007, Tel. (616) 383-8400, Timothy Light, Actg., C NC, Am. Bapt., 1,255

Kansas Newman College, Wichita, KS 67213, Tel. (316) 942-4291. Timothy J. Duszynski, C NC, Cath., 691

Kansas Wesleyan University, Salina, KS 67401, Tel. (913) 827-5541. Marshall P. Stanton, C NC, Un. Meth., 528

Kendall College, Evanston, IL 60201, Tel. (312) 866-1300. Andrew N. Cothran, C NC. Un. Meth., 384

Kentucky Christian College, Grayson, KY 41143, Tel. (606) 474-6613. Keith P. Keeran, C S, Chr. Chs./Chs. of Christ, 491

Kentucky Wesleyan College, Owensboro, KY 42301, Tel. (502) 926-3111. Paul W. Hartman, C S, Un. Meth., 765

Kenyon College, Gambier, OH 43022, Tel. (614) 427-5000. Philip H. Jordan, Jr., C NC, Epis., 1,576

Keuka College, Keuka Park, NY 14478, Tel. (315) 536-4411. Arthur F. Kirk, Jr., C MS, Am. Bapt., 600

King College, Bristol, TN 37620, Tel. (615) 968-1187. Don R. Mitchell, C S, PCUSA, 589

King's College, Briarcliff Manor, NY 10510, TEl. (914)941-7000. Friedhaim K. Radandt, C MS, Evangelical, 508

King's College, Wilkes-Barre, PA 18711, Tel. (717) 826-5900. James Lackenmier, C MS Cath., 2,304

Knoxville College, Knoxville, TN 37921, Tel. (615)524-6500. Hardy Liston, Jr., C S, PCUSA, 1,310

Lafayette College, Easton, PA 18042, Tel. (215) 250-5000. David W. Ellis, C MS, PCUSA, 2,030

LaGrange College, LaGrange, GA 30240, Tel. (404) 882-2911. Walter Y. Murphy, C S, Un. Meth., 967

Lake Forest College, Lake Forest, IL 60045, Tel. (312) 234-3100. Eugene Hotchkiss, III, C NC, PCUSA, 1,106

Lakeland College, Sheboygan, WI 530821, Tel. (414) 565-2111. David R. Black, C NC, U. Ch. of Christ, 1,535

Lambuth College, Jackson, TN 38301, Tel. (901) 425-2500, Thomas F. Boyd, C S, Un. Meth., 767

Lane College, Jackson, TN 38301, Tel. (901) 424-4600 Alex Chambers, C S, Chr. M.E., 541

La Roche College, Pittsburgh, PA 15237, Tel. (412) 367-9300. Sr. Margaret Huber, C MS, Cath., 1,852

La Salle University, Philadelphia, PA 19141, Tel. (215) 951-1000. Br. F. Patrick Ellis, C MS, Cath., 6,550

La Verne University of, La Verne, CA 91750, Tel. (714) 593-3511. Stephen C. Morgan, C West. Ch. of Breth., 5,876

Lebanon Valley College, Annville, PA 17003, Tel. (717) 867-6100. John A. Synodinos, C MS, Un. Meth., 1,331

Lee College, Cleveland, TN 37311, Tel. (615) 472-2111. Paul Conn, C S, Ch. of God, 1,532

Le Moyne College, Syracuse, N.Y. 13214, Tel. (315) 445-4100. Kevin G. O'Connell, C MS, Cath., 2,274

LeMoyne-Owen College, Memphis, TN 38126, Tel. (901) 774-9090. Irving P. McPhail, C S, interdenom., 1,130

Lenoir-Rhyne College, Hickory, NC 28603, Tel. (704) 328-1741. John E. Trainer, Jr., C S, ELCA, 1,596

Lewis University, Romeoville, Il 60441, Tel. (815) 838-0500. Br. James Gaffney, C NC, Cath., 3,390

Lewis & Clark College, Portland, OR 97219, Tel. (503) 293-2651. Michael Mooney, C NW, PCUSA, 3,197

Liberty University, Lynchburg, VA 24506, Tel. (804) 582-2000. A. Pierre Guillermin, C S, Bapt. 7,327

Lindenwood College, St. Charles, MO 63301, Tel. (314) 949-2000. Vacant, C NC, PCUSA, 1,563

Lindsey Wilson College, Columbia, KY 42748, Tel. (502)384-2126. John B. Begley, C S, Un. Meth., 1,060

Linfield College, McMinnville, OR 97128, Tel. (503) 472-4121. Charles U. Walker, C NW, Amer. Bapt. 1,501

Livingstone College, Salisbury, NC 28144, Tel. (704) 638-5500. Bernard W. Franklin, C S, A.M.E. Zion, 530

Loma Linda University, Loma Linda, CA 92350, Tel. (714) 824-4300. Norman J. Woods, C West, S.D.A., 4,392

Loras College, Dubuque, IA 52004, Tel. (319) 588-7100 James Barta, C NC, Cath., 1,751

Louisiana College, Pineville, LA 71359, Tel. (318) 487-7011. Robert L. Lynn, C S, So. Bapt., 1,017

Lourdes College, Sylvania, OH 43560, Tel. (419) 885-3211. Sr. Ann Francis Klimkowski, C NC, Cath., 773

Loyola College in Maryland, Baltimore, MD 21210, Tel. (301) 323-1010. Joseph A. Sellinger, C MS, Cath., 5,821

Loyola University of Chicago, Chicago, IL 60611, Tel. (312) 670-3000. Raymond C. Baumhart, C NC, Cath., 14,046

Loyola University, New Orleans, LA 70118, Tel. (504) 865-2011. James C. Carter, C S, Cath., 4,952

Loyola Marymount University, Los Angeles, CA 90045, Tel. (213) 642-2700. James N. Loughran, C West, Cath., 6,479

Lubbock Christian University, Lubbock, TX 79407, Tel. (806) 792-3221. Steven S. Lemley, C S, Chs. of Christ, 1,073

Luther College, Decorah, IA 52101, Tel. (319) 387-2000. H. George Anderson, C NC, ELCA, 2,214

Lycoming College, Williamsport, PA 17701, Tel. (717) 321-4000. James E. Douthat, C MS, Un. Meth. 1,163

Lynchburg College, Lynchburg, VA 24501, Tel. (804) 522-8100. George N. Rainsford, C S, Christian Church (Disc.), 2,447

Macalester College, St. Paul, MN 55105, Tel. (612) 696-6000. Robert M. Gavin, Jr., C NC, PCUSA, 1,847

MacMurray College, Jacksonville, IL 62650, Tel. (217) 245-6151. Edward J. Mitchell, C NC, Un. Meth., 603

Madonna College, Livonia, MI 48150, Tel. (313) 591-5000. Sr. Mary Francilene, C NC, Cath., 3,980

Mallinkrodt College Of The North Shore, Wilmette, IL 60091, Tel. (312) 256-1094. Sr. M. Patrice Noterman, C NC, Cath., 273

Malone College, Canton, OH 44709, Tel. (216) 489-0800. E. Arthur Self, C NC, Friends, 1,325

Manchester College, North Manchester, IN 46962, Tel. (219) 982-5000. William P. Robinson, C NC, Ch. Breth., 1,028

Manhattan College, Bronx, NY 10471, Tel. (212) 920-0100. Br. Thomas J. Scanlan, C MS, Cath., 4,016

Manhattanville College, Purchase, NY 10577, Tel. (914) 694-2200. Marcia A. Savage, C MS, Cath., 1,500

Marian College, Indianapolis, IN 46222, Tel. (317) 929-0123. Daniel A. Felicette, C NC, Cath., 1,215

Marian College of Fond du Lac, Fond du Lac, WI 54935, Tel. (414) 923-7600. Mathew G. Flanigan, C NC, Cath., 692

Marist College, Poughkeepsie, NY 12601, Tel. (914) 471-3240. Dennis J. Murray, C MS, Cath., 4,450

Marquette University, Milwaukee, WI 53233, Tel. (414) 288-7700. John P. Raynor, C NC, Cath., 12,184

Mars Hill College, Mars Hill, NC 28754, Tel. (704) 689-1111. Fred B. Bentley, C S, So. Bapt., 1,345

Mary Baldwin College, Staunton, VA 24401, Tel. (703) 887-7000. Cynthia H. Tyson, W S, PCUSA, 1,186

Mary University of, Bismarck, ND 58504, Tel. (701) 255-7500. Sr. Thomas Welder, C NC, Cath., 1,352

Mary Hardin-Baylor, University of, Belton, TX 76513, Tel. (817) 939-8642. Bobby E. Parker, C S, So. Bapt., 1,503

Marycrest College, Davenport, IA 52804, Tel. (319) 326-9512. Wanda D. Bigham, C NC, Cath., 2,569

Marygrove College, Detroit, MI 48221, Tel. (313) 862-8000. John E. Shay, Jr., C NC, Cath., 1,235

Marylhurst College for Lifelong Learning, Marylhurst, OR 97036, Tel. (503) 636-8141. Nancy Wilgenbusch, C NW, Cath, 1,005

Marymount College, Tarrytown, NY 10591, Tel. (914) 631-3200. Sr. Brigid Driscoll, W MS, Cath., 1,247

Marymount University, Arlington, VA 22207, Tel. (703) 522-5600. Sr. M. Majella Berg, C S, Cath., 2,977

Marymount Manhattan College, New York, NY 10021, Tel. (212) 517-0400. Sr. Raymonde McKay, W MS, Cath., 1,306

Maryville College, Maryville, TN 37801, Tel. (615) 981-8000. Richard I. Ferrin, C S, PCUSA, 647

Maryville College, St. Louis, MO 63141, Tel. (314) 576-9300. Claudius X. Pritchard, C NC, Cath., 2,934

Marywood College, Scranton, PA 18509, Tel. (717) 348-6211. Sr. Mary Reap, W MS, Cath., 3,006

Master's College, The, Newhall, CA 91322, Tel. (805) 259-3540. John MacArthur, Jr., C West, Bapt., 840

McKendree College, Lebanon, IL 62254, Tel. (618) 537-4481. Gerrit Tenbrink, C NC, Un. Meth., 1,012

McMurry College, Abilene, TX 79697, Tel. (915) 691-6200. Thomas K. Kim, C S, Un. Meth., 1,689

McPherson College, McPherson, KS 67460, Tel. (316) 241-0731. Paul W. Hoffman, C NC, Ch. Breth., 486

Medaille College, Buffalo, NY 14214, Tel. (716) 884-3281. Kevin I. Sullivan, C MS, Cath., 1,053

Mercer University Atlanta, Atlanta, GA 30341, Tel. (404) 451-0331, R. Kirby Godsey, C S, So. Bapt., 1,990

Mercer University Macon, Macon, GA 31207, Tel. (912) 744-2700. R. Kirby Godsey, C S, So. Bapt. 3,093

Mercy College, Dobbs Ferry, NY 10522, Tel. (914) 693-4500, Wilbert J. Lemelle, C MS, Cath., 6,117

Mercy College of Detroit, Detroit, MI 48219, Tel. (313) 592-6000. Sr. Maureen A. Fay, C NC, Cath., 2,302

Mercyhurst College, Erie, PA 16546, Tel. (814) 825-0200 William P. Garvey, C MS, Cath., 1,044

Meredith College, Raleigh, NC 27607, Tel. (919) 829-8600. John E. Weems, W S, So. Bapt., 2,168

Merrimack College, North Andover, MA 01845, Tel. (508) 683-7111. John E. Deegan, C NE, Cath., 3,580

Messiah College, Grantham, PA 17027, Tel. (717) 766-2511. D. Ray Hostetter, C MS, Breth. in Christ, 2,179

Methodist College, Fayetteville, NC 28311, Tel. (919) 488-7110 M. Elton Hendricks, C S, Un. Meth., 1,499

Mid-America Nazarene College, Olathe, KS 66061, Tel. (913) 782-3750. Vacant, C NC, Nazarene, 1,121

Midland Lutheran College, Fremont, NE 68025, Tel. (402) 721-5480. Carl. L. Hansen, C NC, ELCA, 910

Miles College, Birmingham, AL 35208, Tel. (205) 923-2771. Albert J. Sloan, II, Actg., C S, CME, 614

Milligan College, Milligan College, TN 37682, Tel. (615) 929-0116. Marshall J. Leggett, C S, CC/CC, 628

Millikin University, Decatur, IL 62522, Tel. (217) 424-6211. J. Roger Miller, C NC, PCUSA, 1,736

Millsaps College, Jackson, MS 39210, Tel. (601) 354-5201. George M. Harmon, C S, Un. Meth., 1,445

Mississippi College, Clinton, MS 39058, Tel. (601) 925-3000. Lewis Nobles, C S, So. Bapt. 3,540

Missouri Baptist College, St. Louis, MO 63141, Tel. (314) 434-1115. Patrick O. Copley, C NC, So. Bapt., 951

Missouri Valley College, Marshall, MO 65340, Tel. (816) 886-6924. Earl J. Reeves, C NC, PCUSA, 935

Mobile College, Mobile, AL 36613, Tel. (205) 675-3404. Michael A. Magnoli, C S, So. Bapt., 1,069

Molloy College, Rockville Centre, NY 11570, Tel. (516) 678-5000. Sr. Janet A. Fitzgerald, C MS, Cath., 1,384

Monmouth College, Monmouth, IL 61462, Tel. (309) 457-2311. Bruce Haywood, C NC, PCUSA, 676

Montreat-Anderson College, Montreat, NC 28757. Tel (704)669-8011. Silas M. Vaughn, C S, PCUSA, 386

Moravian College, Bethlehem, PA 18018, Tel. (215) 861-1300. Roger H. Martin, C MS, Morav, 1,807

Morningside College, Sioux City, IA 51106, Tel. (712) 274-5000. Miles Tommeraasen, C NC, Un. Meth., 1,219

Morris College, Sumter, SC 29150, Tel. (803) 775-9371. Luns C. Richardson, C S, Bapt., 744

Morris Brown College, Atlanta, GA 30314, Tel. (404) 525-7831. Calvert H. Smith, C S, A.M.E., 1,773

Mt. Angel Seminary, Saint Benedict, OR 97373, Tel. (503) 845-3951. J. Terrence Fitzgerald, M NW, Cath., 130

Mt. Marty College, Yankton, SD 57078, Tel. (605) 668-1011. Sr. Jacquelyn Ernster, C NC, Cath., 596

Mt. Mary College, Milwaukee, WI 53222, Tel. (414) 258-4810. Sr. Ruth Hollenbach, W NC, Cath., 1,367

Mt. Mercy College, Cedar Rapids, IA 52402, Tel. (319) 363-8213. Thomas R. Feld, C NC, Cath., 1,568

Mt. St. Mary College, Newburgh, NY 12550, Tel. (914) 561-0800. Sr. Ann V. Sakac, C MS, Cath., 1,226

Mt. St. Mary's College, and Seminary, Emmitsburg, MD 21727, Tel. (301) 447-6122. Robert J. Wickenheiser, C MS, Cath., 1,398

Mt. St. Mary's College, Los Angeles, CA 90049, Tel. (213) 476-2237. Sr. Karen Kennelly, W West, Cath., 1,203

Mount Olive College, Mount Olive, NC 28365, Tel. (919)658-2502. W. Burkette Raper, CS, Free Will Bapt. Ch., 944

Mount Saint Claire College, Clinton, IA 52732, Tel. (319) 242-4023. Charles E. Lang, C NC, Cath., 335

Mount Union College, Alliance, OH 44601, Tel. (216) 861-5320. Harold M. Kolenbrander, C NC, Un. Meth., 1,268

Mount Vernon, Nazarene College, Mount Vernon, OH 43050. Tel. (614) 397-1244. E. LeBron Fairbanks, C NC, Nazarene 1,087

Muhlenberg College, Allentown, PA 18104, Tel. (215) 821-3000. Johnathan C. Messerli, C MS, ELCA 1,620

Mundelein College, Chicago, IL 60660, Tel. (312) 262-8100. Sr. Mary Breslin, W NC, Cath., 1,010

Muskingum College, New Concord, OH 43762, Tel. (614) 826-8211. Samuel W. Speck, C NC, PCUSA, 1,169

Nazareth College, Nazareth, MI 49001, Tel. (616) 349-4200. Patrick Smith, C NC, Cath., 730

Nazareth College of Rochester, Rochester, NY 14610, Tel. (716) 586-2525. Rose Marie Beston, C MS, Cath., 2,935

Nebraska Wesleyan University, Lincoln, NE 68504, Tel. (402) 466-2371. John W. White, C NC, Un. Meth., 1,576

Neumann College, Aston, PA 19014, Tel. (215) 459-0905. Nan B. Hechenberger, C MS, Cath., 1,053

Newberry College, Newberry, SC 29108, Tel. (803) 276-5010. Hubert H. Setzler, Jr., C S, ELCA, 689

New England, University of, Biddleford, ME 04005, Tel. (207) 283-0171. Charles W. Ford, C NC, Cath., 1,071

Niagara University, Niagara University, NY 14109, Tel. (716) 285-1212. Brian J. O'Connell, C MS, Cath., 3,049

North Carolina Wesleyan College, Rocky Mount, NC 27804, Tel. (919) 977-7171. Leslie H. Garner, Jr., C S, Un. Meth., 1,524

North Central College, Naperville, IL 60566, Tel. (312) 420-3400. Gael D. Swing, C NC, Un. Meth., 2,343

North Park College, Chicago IL 60625, Tel. (312) 583-2700. David G. Horner, C NC, Evan. Cov. Ch. of Amer., 1,209

Northland College, Ashland, WI 54806, Tel. (715) 682-1669. Robert Parsonage, C NC, U. Ch. of Christ, 618

Northwest Christian College, Eugene, OR 97401, Tel. (503) 343-1641. James E. Womack, C NW, Christian Church (Disc.), 219

Northwest College of the Assemblies of God, Kirkland, WA 98083, Tel. (206) 822-8266, D. V. Hurst, C NW, Assem. of God, 687

Northwest Nazarene College, Nampa, ID 83651, Tel. (208) 467-8011. A. Gordon Wetmore, C NW, Nazarene, 1,148

Northwestern College, Orange City, IA 51041, Tel. (712) 737-4821. James E. Bultman C NC, Ref. Am., 953

Northwestern College, Watertown, WI 53094, Tel. (414) 261-4352. Robert J. Voss, M NC, ELCA, 203

Notre Dame College, Manchester, NH 03104, Tel. (603) 669-4298 Sr. Carol Descoteaux, C NE, Cath., 854

Notre Dame College, Cleveland, OH 44121, Tel. (216) 381-1680. Sr. Marcia Loehr, W NC, Cath., 748

Notre Dame, University of, Notre Dame, IN 46556, Tel. (219) 239-5000. Edward A. Malloy, C NC, Cath., 9,880

Nyack College, Nyack, NY 10960. Tel. (914) 358-1710. Rexford A. Boda, C MS, Chr. and Miss. All., 814

Oakland City College, Oakland City, IN 47660. Tel. (812) 749-4781. James W. Murray, C NC, Baptist, 626

Oakwood College, Huntsville, AL 35896, Tel. (205) 837-1630 Benjamin F. Reaves, C S, S.D.A., 1,236

Occidental College, Los Angeles, CA 90041, Tel. (213) 259-2500. John B. Slaughter, C West, PCUSA, 1,677

Ohio Dominican College, Columbus, OH 43219, Tel. (614) 253-2741, Sr. Mary Andrew Matesich, C NC, Cath., 1,331

Ohio Northern University, Ada, OH 45810, Tel. (419) 772-2000. De Bow Freed, C NC, Un. Meth., 2,540

Ohio Wesleyan University, Delaware, OH 43015, Tel. (614) 369-4431. David L. Warren, C NC, Un. Meth., 1,835

Oklahoma Baptist University, Shawnee, OK 74801, Tel. (405) 275-2850. Bob R. Agee, C NC, So. Bapt., 1,967

Oklahoma Christian College, Oklahoma City, OK 73136, Tel. (405) 425-5000. Terry Johnson, C NC, Chs. of Christ 1,657

Oklahoma City University, Oklahoma City, OK 73106, Tel. (405) 521-5000. Jerald C. Walker, C NC, Un. Meth., 3,535

Olivet College, Olivet, MI 49076, Tel. (616) 749-7000. Donald A. Morris, C NC, U. Ch. of Christ, 784

Olivet Nazarene University, Kankakee, IL 60901, Tel. (815) 939-5011. Leslie W. Parrott, C NC, Nazarene, 1,875

Oral Roberts University, Tulsa, OK 74171, Tel. (918) 495-6161. G. Oral Roberts, C NC, interdenom, 4,259

Ottawa University, Ottawa, KS 66067, Tel. (913) 242-5200. Wilbur D. Wheaton, C NC, Amer. Bapt., 528

Otterbein College, Westerville, OH 43081, Tel. (614) 890-3000. C. Brent Devore, C NC, Un. Meth., 2,209

Ouachita Baptist University, Arkadelphia, AR 71923 Tel. (501) 246-4531. Ben M. Elrod, C NC, So. Bapt., 1,352

Our Lady of the Holy Cross College, New Orleans, LA 70131, Tel. (504) 394-7744, Thomas E. Chambers, C S, Cath., 729

Our Lady of the Lake University of San Antonio, San Antonio, TX 78207, Tel. (512) 434-6711. Sr. Elizabeth A. Sueltenfuss, C S, Cath., 2,295

Ozarks, University of the, Clarksville, AR 72830, Tel. (501) 754-3839. Fritz H. Ehren, C NC, PCUSA, 802

Ozarks, School of the, Point Lookout, MO 65726, Tel. (417) 334-6411. Jerry C. Davis, C NC, PCUSA, 1,278

Pacific Christian College, Fullerton, CA 92631. Tel. (714) 879-3901. Knofel Staton, C West, Ch. of Christ, 557

Pacific Lutheran University, Tacoma, WA 98447, Tel. (206) 531-6900. William O. Rieke, C NW, ELCA, 3,975

Pacific Union College, Angwin, CA 94508, Tel. (707) 965-6311. D. Malcolm Maxwell, C West, S.D.A., 1,404

Pacific, University of the, Stockton, CA 95211. Tel. (209) 946-2011. Bill L. Atchley, C West, Un. Meth., 3,978

Pacific University, Forest Grove, OR 97116, Tel. (503) 357-6151. Robert F. Duvall, C NW, U. Ch. of Christ, 1,398

Paine College, Augusta, GA 30910, Tel. (404) 722-4471. Julius S. Scott, Jr., C S, Protestant Denoms., 606

Palm Beach Atlantic College, West Palm Beach, FL 33401, Tel. (407) 650-7700. Claude H. Rhea, C S, Bapt., 1,153

Park College, Parkville, MO 64152, Tel. (816) 741-2000. Donald J. Breckon, C NC, Reorg. L.D.S., 693

Paul Quinn College, Waco, TX 76704, Tel. (817) 753-6415. Warren W. Morgan, C S, A.M.E., 517

Pepperdine University, Malibu, CA 90265, Tel. (213) 456-4000. David Davenport, C West, Chs. of Christ, 7,119

Pfeiffer College, Misenheimer, NC 28109, Tel. (704) 463-7343. Zane E. Eargle, C S, Un. Meth., 874

Philander Smith College, Little Rock, AR 72202, Tel. (501) 375-9845. Myer L. Titus, C NC, Un. Meth., 604

Phillips University, Enid, OK 73701, Tel. (405) 237-4433. Robert D. Peck, C NC, Christian Church (Disc.), 945

Pikeville College, Pikeville, KY 41501, Tel. (606) 432-9200. William H. Owens, C S, PCUSA, 915

Point Loma Nazarene College, San Diego CA 92106, Tel. (619) 221-2200. Jim L. Bond, C West, Nazarene, 2,165

Pontifical College Josephinum, Columbus, OH 43235, Tel. (614) 885-5585. Dennis F. Sheehan, M NC, Cath., 200

Portland, University of, Portland, OR 97203. Tel. (503) 283-7911, Thomas C. Oddo, C NW, Cath., 2,400

Presbyterian College, Clinton, SC 29325, Tel. (803) 833-2820. Kenneth B. Orr, C S, PCUSA, 1,112

Providence College, Providence, RI 02918, Tel. (401) 865-1000. John F. Cunningham, C NE, Cath., 5,753

Puget Sound, University of, Tacoma, WA 98416, Tel. (206) 756-3100. Philip M. Phibbs, C NW, Un. Meth. 3,344

Queens College, Charlotte, NC 28274, Tel. (704) 337-2200. Billy O. Wireman, C S, PCUSA, 1,411

Quincy College, Quincy, IL 62301, Tel. (217) 222-8020. James Toal, C NC, Cath., 1,527

Randolph-Macon College, Ashland, VA 23005, Tel. (804) 798-8372. Ladell Payne, C S, Un. Meth., 1,117

Randolph-Macon Woman's College, Lynchburg, VA 24503, Tel. (804) 846-7392. Linda K. Lorimer, W S, Un. Meth., 746

Redlands, University of, Redlands, CA 92373, Tel. (714) 793-2121. James R. Appleton, C West, Am. Bapt., 1,350

Regis College, Denver, CO 80221, Tel. (303) 458-4100. David M. Clarke, C NC Cath., 4,085

Regis College, Weston, MA 02193, Tel. (617) 893-1820. Sr. Therese Higgins, W NE, Cath., 1,005

Rhodes College, Memphis, TN 38112, Tel. (901) 726-3000. James H. Daughdrill, Jr., C S, PCUSA, 1,308

Richmond, University of, Richmond, VA 23173, Tel. (804) 289-8000. Richard L. Morrill, Co. Ord., C S, So. Bapt. 4,956

Ripon College, Ripon, WI 54971, Tel. (414) 748-8115. William R. Stott, Jr., C NC, U. Ch. of Christ, 857

Rivier College, Nashua, NH 03060, Tel. (603) 888-1311 Sr. Jeanne Perreault, W NE, Cath., 2,399

Roanoke College, Salem, VA 24153, Tel. (703) 375-2500. David M. Gring, C S, ELCA, 1,594

Roberts Wesleyan College, Rochester, NY 14624, Tel. (716) 594-9471. William C. Crothers, C MS, Free Meth., 744

Rockhurst College, Kansas City, MO 64110, Tel. (816) 926-4000. Thomas J. Savage, C NC, Cath., 3,125

Rocky Mountain College, Billings, MT 59102, Tel. (406) 657-1000. Arthur H. Derosier, Jr., C NW, Un. Meth., U. Ch. of Christ, PCUSA, 705

Rosary College, River Forest, IL 60305, Tel. (312) 366-2490. Sr. Jean Murray, C NC, Cath., 1,625

Rosemont College, Rosemont, PA 19010, Tel. (215) 527-0200. Dorothy Brown, W MS, Cath., 651

Rust College, Holly Springs, MS 38635, Tel. (601) 252-4661. William A. McMillan, C S, Un. Meth., 925

Sacred Heart Major Seminary College, Detroit, MI 48206, Tel. (313) 868-8500. John C. Nienstedt, NC, Cath., 350

Sacred Heart University, Fairfield, CT 06432, Tel. (203) 371-7999. Anthony J. Cernera, C NE, Cath., 4,341

Sacred Heart, University of the, Santurce, PR 00914, Tel. (809) 728-1515. Jose A. Morales, C MS, Cath., 7,399

St. Alphonsus College, Suffield, CT 06078, Tel. (203) 668-7393. Patrick McGarrity, M NE, Cath., 35

St. Ambrose University, Davenport, IA 52803, Tel. (319) 383-8800. Edward J. Rogalski, C NC, Cath., 2,110

St. Andrews Presbyterian College, Laurinburg, NC 28352, Tel. (919) 276-3652. Thomas L. Reuschling, C S, PCUSA, 802

St. Anselm College, Manchester, NH 03102, Tel. (603) 641-7000. Br. Johnathan De Felice, C NE, Cath., 1,833

St. Augustine's College, Raleigh, NC 27610, Tel. (919) 828-4451. Prezell R. Robinson, C S, Epis., 1,665

St. Bonaventure University, St. Bonaventure, NY 14778, Tel. (716) 375-2000. Mathias Doyle, C MS, Cath., 2,852

St. Charles Borromeo Seminary, Philadelphia, PA 19096 Tel. (215) 667-3394. Daniel A. Murray, M MS Cath., 359

St. Edward's University, Austin, TX 78704, Tel. (512) 448-8400. Patricia A. Hayes, C S, Cath., 2,824

St. Francis College, Brooklyn, NY 11201, Tel. (212) 522-2300. Br. Donald Sullivan, C MS, Cath., 1,929

St. Francis College, Fort Wayne, IN 46808, Tel. (219) 432-3551. Sr. JoEllen Scheetz, C NC, Cath., 1,031

St. Francis College, Loretto, PA 15940, Tel. (814) 472-3000. Christian R. Oravec, C MS, Cath., 1,791

St. Hyacinth College, Granby, MA 01033, Tel. (413) 467-7191. Jude Surowiec, M NE, Cath., 36

St. John Fisher College, Rochester, NY 14618, Tel. (716) 385-8000. William L. Pickett, C NC, Cath., 2,359

St. John Vianney College Seminary, Miami, FL 33165, Tel. (305) 223-4561. Thomas O'Dwyer, M S, Cath. 45

St. John's Seminary College, Camarillo, CA 93010, Tel. (805) 482-2755. Sylvester Ryan, M West, Cath., 100

St. John's Seminary, Brighton, MA 02135. Tel. (617) 254-2610. Thomas J. Daly, M NE, Cath., 73

St. John's University, Collegeville, MN 56321, Tel. (612) 363-2011, Hilary Thimmesh, Coord. NC, Cath., 1,998

St. John's University, Jamaica, NY 11439, Tel. (718) 990-6161. Donald J. Harrington, C MS, Cath. 19,143

St. Joseph College, W. Hartford, CT 06117, Tel. (203) 232-4571. M. Payton Ryan, W NE, Cath., 1,634

St. Joseph's College, Rensselaer, IN 47978, Tel. (219) 866-7111. Charles H. Banet, C NC, Cath., 1,001

St. Joseph's College, North Windham, ME 04062, Tel. (207) 892-6766. Loring E. Hart, C NE, Cath., 614

St. Joseph's College, New York, Brooklyn, NY 11205, Tel. (718) 636-6800. Sr. George A. O'Connor, C MS, Cath., 794

St. Joseph's College, Mountain View, CA 94039, Tel. (415) 964-1400. Cale J. Crowley, M West, Cath., 64

St. Joseph's University, Philadelphia, PA 19131, Tel. (215) 660-1000. Nicholas S. Rashford, C MS, Cath., 5,787

St. Joseph Seminary College, Saint Benedict, LA 70457, Tel. (504) 892-1800. Ambrose G. Wathen, M Cath., 80

St. Leo College, St. Leo, FL 33574, Tel. (904) 588-8200. Frank M. Mouch C S, Cath., 6,500

St. Louis University, St. Louis, MO 63103, Tel. (314) 658-2222. Lawrence Boindi, C NC, Cath., 11,148

St. Louis University-Parks College, Cahokia, IL 62206, Tel. (618) 337-7500. Paul A. Whelan, C NC, Cath., 1,000

St. Martin's College, Lacey, WA 98503, Tel. (206) 491-4700. Conrad Rausch, C NW, Cath., 1,100

St. Mary College, Leavenworth, KS 66048, Tel. (913) 682-5151. Br. Peter Clifford, C NC, Cath., 1,066

St. Mary of the Plains College, Dodge City, KS 67801. Tel. (316) 225-4171. Michael J. McCarthy, C NC, Cath., 914

St. Mary-Of-the-Woods College, St. Mary-Of-the-Woods, IN 47876, Tel. (812) 535-5151. Sr. Barbara Doherty, W NC, Cath., 910

St. Mary's College, Notre Dame, IN 46556, Tel. (219) 284-4000. William A. Hickey, W NC, Cath., 1,821

St. Mary's College, Winona, MN 55987, Tel. (507) 452-4430. Br. Louis Dethomasis, C NC, Cath., 1,865

St. Mary's College, Orchard Lake, MI 48033, Tel. (313) 683-5123. Edward D. Meyer, C NC, Cath., 260

St. Mary's College of California, Moraga, CA 94575, Tel. (415) 631-4000. Br. Mel Anderson, C West, Cath., 3,658

St. Mary's Seminary and University, Baltimore, MD 21210. Tel. (301) 323-3200. Robert F. Leavitt, C MS, Cath., 340

St. Mary's University, San Antonio, TX 78284, Tel. (512) 436-3722. John J. Moder, C S, Cath., 3,654

St. Meinrad College, St. Meinrad, IN 47577, Tel. (812) 357-6611. Eugene Hensell, M NC, Cath., 127

St. Michael's College, Colchester, VT 05446, Tel. (802) 655-2000. Paul T. Reiss, C NE, Cath., 2,287

St. Norbert College, De Pere, WI 54115, Tel. (414) 337-3181. Thomas A. Manion, C NC, Cath., 1,851

St. Olaf College, Northfield, MN 55057, Tel. (507) 663-2222. Melvin D. George, C NC, ELCA, 3,162

St. Paul's College, Lawrenceville, VA 23868, Tel. (804) 848-3111. Thomas M. Law, C S, Epis., 592

St. Peter's College, Jersey City, NJ 07306, Tel. (201) 915-9000. Edward R. Glynn, C MS, Cath., 3,346

St. Thomas, University of, Houston, TX 77006, Tel. (713) 522-7911. William J. Young, C S, Cath., 1,661

St. Thomas Aquinas College, Sparkhill, NY 10976. Tel. (914) 359-9500. Donald T. McNelis, C MS, Cath., 1,983

St. Thomas University, Miami, FL 33054, Tel. (305) 625-6000. Richard E. Greene, C S, Cath., 1,530

St. Vincent College and Seminary, Latrobe, PA 15650, Tel. (412) 539-9761. John F. Murtha, C MS, Cath., 1,193

St. Xavier College, Chicago, IL 60655, Tel. (312) 779-3300. Ronald O. Champagne, C NC, Cath., 2,641

Salem-Teikyo University, Salem, WV 26426, Tel. (304) 782-5011. Ronald E. Ohl, C NC, 7th Day Bapt., 801

Salem College, Winston-Salem, NC 27108, Tel. (919) 721-2600. Thomas V. Litzenburg, Jr., W S, Morav, 842

Salve Regina-The Newport College, Newport, RI 02840, Tel. (401) 847-6650, Sr. M. Lucille McKillop, C NE, Cath., 2,252

Samford University, Birmingham, AL 35229, Tel. (205) 870-2011. Thomas E. Corts, C S, So. Bapt., 4,089

San Diego, University of, San Diego, CA 92110, Tel. (619) 260-4600. Author E. Hughes, C West, Cath., 5,858

San Francisco, University of, San Francisco, CA 94117, Tel. (415) 666-6886. John J. LoSchiavo, C West, Cath., 4,826

Santa Clara University Santa Clara, CA 95053, Tel. (408) 544-4764. Paul L. Locatelli, C West, Cath., 7,802

Scranton, University of, Scranton, PA 18510, Tel. (717) 961-7400. J. A. Panuska, C MS, Cath., 4,929

Schreiner College, Kerrville, TX 78028, Tel. (512) 896-5411. Sam M. Junkin, C S, PCUSA, 602

Seattle Pacific University, Seattle, WA 98119, Tel. (206) 281-2000. David C. LeShana, C NW, Free Meth., 3,356

Seattle University, Seattle, WA 98122, Tel. (206) 296-6000. William J. Sullivan, C NW, Cath., 4,416

Seton Hall University, South Orange, NJ 07079, Tel. (201) 761-9000. John J. Petillo, C MS, Cath., 8,066

Seton Hill College, Greensburg, PA 15601, Tel. (412) 834-2200. JoAnne W. Boyle, W MS, Cath., 870

Shaw University, Raleigh, NC 27611, Tel. (919) 755-4800. Talbert O. Shaw, C S, Am. Bapt., 1,402

Shenandoah College, Winchester, VA 22601, Tel. (703) 665-4500. James A. Davis, C S, Un. Meth., 1,007

Shorter College, Rome, GA 30161, Tel. (404) 291-2121. James D. Jordan, C S, So. Bapt., 831

Siena College, Loudonville, NY 12211, Tel. (518) 783-2300. William E. McConville, C MS, Cath., 3,481

Siena Heights College, Adrian, MI 49221, Tel. (517) 263-0731. Sr. Cathleen C. Real, C NC, Cath., 1,599

Silver Lake College, Manitowoc, WI 54220, Tel. (414) 684-6691. Sr. Barbara Belinske, C NC, Cath., 830

Simpson College, Redding, CA 96003. Tel. (415) (916)243-1991. Francis Grubbs, C West, Chr. and Miss. All., 202

Simpson College, Indianola, IA 50125, Tel. (515) 961-6251. Stephen G. Jennings, C NC, Un. Meth., 1,710

Sioux Falls College, Sioux Falls, SD 57105, Tel. (605) 331-5000. Thomas F. Johnson, C NC, Am. Bapt., 909

South, The University of The, Sewanee, TN 37375, Tel. (615) 598-5931, Samuel R. Williamson, C S, Epis., 1,142

Southeastern College of The Assemblies of God, Lakeland, FL 33801, Tel. (813) 665-4404. James L. Hennesy, C S, Assemb. of God, 1,155

Southern Baptist College, Walnut Ridge, AR 72476, Tel. (501) 886-6741. D. Jack Nicholas, C NC, So. Bapt., 517

Southern California College, Costa Mesa, CA 92626, Tel. (714) 556-3610. Wayne E. Kraiss, C West, Assem. of God., 923

Southern College of Seventh-Day Adventists, Collegedale, TN 37315, Tel. (615) 238-2111. Donald R. Sahly C S, S.D.A., 1,443

Southern Methodist University, Dallas, TX 75275, Tel. (214) 692-2000. A. Kenneth Pye, C S, Un. Meth., 8,944

Southern Nazarene University, Bethany, OK 73008, Tel. (405) 789-6400. Loren P. Gresham, C NC, Nazarene, 1,358

Southwest Baptist University, Bolivar, MO 65613, Tel. (417) 326-5281. James L. Sells, C NC, So. Bapt., 2,498

Southwestern College, Winfield, KS 67156, Tel. (316) 221-4150. Carl Martin, C NC, Un. Meth., 663

Southwestern Adventist College, Keene, TX 76059, Tel. (817) 645-3921. Marvin Anderson, C S, S.D.A., 778

Southwestern Assemblies of God College, Waxahachie, TX 75165, Tel. (214) 937-4010. Paul Savell, C S, Assemb. of God, 622

Southwestern Christian College, Terrell, TX 75160, Tel. (214) 563-3341. Jack Evans, C NC. Chs. of Christ, 276

Southwestern University, Georgetown, TX 78627. Tel. (512) 863-6511. Roy B. Shilling, Jr., C S, Un. Meth., 1,134

Spalding University, Louisville, KY 40203, Tel. (502) 585-9911, Eileen M. Egan, C S, Cath., 1,250

Spelman College, Atlanta, Ga 30314, Tel. (404) 681-3643. Johnneta B. Cole, Bapt., 1,730

Spertus College of Judaica, Chicago, IL 60605. Tel. (312) 922-9012. Howard A. Sulkin, C NC, Jewish, 153

Spring Arbor College, Spring Arbor, MI 49283, Tel. (517) 750-1200. Dorsey W. Brause, C NC, Free Meth., 782

Spring Hill College, Mobile, AL 36608, Tel. (205) 460-2121. Donald I. McLean, C S, Cath., 932

Sterling College, Sterling, KS 67579, Tel. (316) 278-2173. Roger Parrott, C NC PCUSA, 503

Stillman College, Tuscaloosa, AL 35403, Tel. (205) 349-4240. Cordell Wynn, C S, PCUSA, 771

Stonehill College, North Easton, MA 02357, Tel. (617) 238-1081. Bartley Mac Phaidin, C NE, Cath., 1,964

Susquehanna University, Selinsgrove, PA 17870, Tel. (717) 374-0101, Joel L. Cunningham, C MS, ELCA, 1,461

Swarthmore College, Swarthmore, PA 19081, Tel. (215) 328-8000. David W. Fraser C MS, Friends, 1,331

Tabor College, Hillsboro, KS 67063, Tel. (316) 947-3121. LeVon Balzer, C NC, Menn. Breth., 476

Talladega College, Talladega, AL 35160, Tel. (205) 362-0206. Joseph E. Thompson. Actg., C S, U. Ch. of Christ, 611

Tarkio College, Tarkio, MO 64491, Tel. (816) 736-4131. Roy McIntosh, C NC, PCUSA, 760

Tennessee Wesleyan College, Athens, TN 37303, Tel. (615) 745-7504. James E. Cheek II, C S, Un. Meth., 601

Texas Christian University, Fort Worth, TX 76129, Tel. (817) 921-7000. William E. Tucker, C S, Christian Church (Disc.), 6,993

Texas College, Tyler, TX 75702, Tel. (214) 593-8311. David H. Johnson, C S, Chr. Meth. Epis., 450

Texas Lutheran College, Seguin, TX 78155, Tel. (512) 379-4161. Charles H. Oestreich, C S, ELCA, 1,009

Texas Wesleyan College, Fort Worth, TX 76105, Tel. (817) 531-4444. Jerry Bawcom, C S, Un. Meth., 1,560

Thiel College, Greenville, PA 16125, Tel. (412) 589-2000. Louis T. Almen, C MS, ELCA, 941

Thomas More College, Fort Mitchell, Ky 41017, Tel. (606) 341-5800. Charles J. Bensman, C S, Cath., 1,100

Tougaloo College, Tougaloo, MS 39174, Tel. (601) 956-4941. Adib A. Shakir, C S, U. Ch. of Christ, 848

Transylvania University, Lexington, KY 40508, Tel. (606) 233-8300. Charles L. Shearer, C S, Christian Church (Disc.), 1,041

Trevecca Nazarene College, Nashville, TN 37210. Tel. (615) 248-1200. Homer J. Adams, C S, Nazarene, 1,977

Trinity College, Washington, DC 20017. Tel. (202) 939-5000. Patricia A. McGuire, W MS, Cath., 1,125

Trinity College, Deerfield, IL 60015, Tel. (312) 948-8980. Kenneth M. Meyer, C NC, Evan. Free Ch. of Am., 622

Trinity College, Burlington, VT 05401, Tel. (802) 658-0337. Sr. Janice E. Ryan, W NE, Cath., 1,063

Trinity University, San Antonio TX 78212, Tel. (512)

736-7011. Ronald Calgaard, C S, PCUSA, 2,512

Tusculum College, Greeneville, TN 37743, Tel. (615) 638-1111. Robert E. Knott, C S, PCUSA, 953

Union College, Barbourville, KY 40906, Tel. (606) 546-4151. Jack C. Phillips, C S, Un. Meth., 1,275

Union College, Lincoln, NE 68506, Tel. (402) 488-2331. John H. Wagner, C NC, S.D.A., 645

Union University, Jackson, TN 38305, Tel. (901) 668-1818. Hyran E. Barefoot, C S, So. Bapt., 2,017

United Wesleyan College, Allentown, PA 18103, Tel (215)439-8709, John P. Ragsdale, C MS, Wesleyan Ch., 163

Upsala College, E. Orange, NJ 07019, Tel. (201) 266-7000. Robert E. Karsten, ELCA, 1,130

Ursinus College, Collegeville, PA 19426, Tel. (215) 489-4111. Richard P. Richter, C MS, U. Ch. of Christ, 1,211

Ursuline College, Cleveland, OH 44124, Tel. (216) 449-4200. Sr. Anne Marie Diederich, C NC, Cath., 1,298

Valparaiso University, Valparaiso, IN 46383, Tel. (219) 464-5000. Alan F. Harre, C NC, Luth. (Mo.), 3,952

Villanova University, Villanova, PA 19085, Tel. (215) 645-4500. Edmond Dobbin, C MS, Cath., 12,000

Virginia Intermont College, Bristol, VA 24201, Tel. (703) 669-6101. Gary M. Poulton, C S, So. Bapt., 450

Virginia Union University, Richmond, VA 23220, Tel. (804) 257-5600. S. Dallas Simmons, C S, Am. Bapt., 1,248

Virginia Wesleyan College, Norfolk, VA 23502, Tel. (804) 461-3232. Lambuth M. Clarke, C S, Un. Meth., 1,261

Viterbo College, La Crosse, WI 54601, Tel. (608) 784-0040. Robert E. Gibbons, C NC, Cath., 1,022

Voorhees College, Denmark, SC 29042, Tel. (803) 793-3351. Leonard E. Dawson, C S, Epis., 592

Wadham's Hall Seminary and College, Ogdensburg, NY 13669, Tel. (315) 393-4231. Thomas J. Thottumkal, M MS, Cath. 38

Wake Forest University, Winston-Salem, NC 27109, Tel. (919) 761-5000. Thomas K. Hearn, C S, So. Bapt., 5,337

Walla Walla College, College Place, WA 99324, Tel. (509) 527-2615. H. J. Bergman, C NW, S.D.A., 1,515

Walsh College, Canton, OH 44720, Tel. (216) 499-7090. Br. Francis Blouin, C NC, Cath., 1,381

Warner Southern College, Lake Wales, FL 33853, Tel. (813) 638-1426. Leroy M. Fulton, C S, Church of God, 364

Warner Pacific College, Portland, OR 97215. Tel. (503) 775-4366. Marshall K. Christensen, C NW, Ch. of God, 383

Warren Wilson College, Swannanoa, NC 28778, Tel. (704) 298-3325. Alfred O. Canon, C S, PCUSA, 523

Wartburg College, Waverly, IA 50677, Tel. (319) 352-8200. Robert Vogel, C NC, ELCA, 1,358

Wayland Baptist University, Plainview, TX 79072, Tel. (806) 296-5521. Lanny Hall, C S, So. Bapt., 1,756

Waynesburg College, Waynesburg, PA 15370, Tel. (412) 627-8191. John P. Strange, C MS, PCUSA, 1,031

Wesley College, Dover, DE 19901, Tel. (302) 736-2300. Reed M. Stewart, C MS, Un. Meth., 1,187

Wesleyan College, Macon, GA 31297, Tel. (912) 477-1110. Robert K. Ackerman, W S, Un. Meth., 536

West Virginia Wesleyan College, Buckhannon, WV, 26201, Tel. (304) 473-8000, Thomas B. Courtice, C NC, Un. Meth., 1,488

Western Baptist College, Salem, OR 97301, Tel. (503) 581-8600. John G. Balyo, C NC, Bapt., 328

Westmar College, Le Mars, IA 51031, Tel. (712) 546-7081. Arthur W. Richardson, C NC, Un. Meth., 570

Westminster College, Fulton, MO 65251, Tel. (314) 642-3361. J. Harvey Saunders, C NC, PCUSA, 689

Westminster College, New Wilmington, PA 16172, Tel. (412) 946-8761. Oscar E. Remick, C MS, PCUSA, 1,475

Westminster College, of Salt Lake City, Salt Lake City, UT 84105, Tel. (801) 484-7651. Charles H. Dick, C NW, Interdenom., 1,856

Westmont College, Santa Barbara, CA 93108, Tel. (805)969-5051. David K. Winter, C West., Evang., 1,290

Wheaton College, Wheaton, IL 60187. Tel. (312) 260-5000. J. Richard Chase, C NC, Interdenom., 2,528

Wheeling Jesuit College, Wheeling, WV 26003, Tel. (304) 243-2000. Thomas S. Acker, C NC, Cath., 1,206

Whittier College, Whittier, CA 90608, Tel. (213) 693-0771. James L. Ash, Sr., C. West, Friends 1,572

Whitworth College, Spokane, WA 99251, Tel. (509) 466-1000. Arthur J. DeLong, C NW, PCUSA, 1,840

Wilberforce University, Wilberforce, OH 45384, Tel. (513) 376-2911. John L. Henderson, C NC, A.M.E., 720

Wiley College, Marshall, TX 75670. Tel. (214) 938-8341. David L. Beckley, C S, Un. Meth., 371

Willamette University, Salem, OR 97301, Tel. (503) 370-6300. Jerry E. Hudson, C NW, Un. Meth., 2,094

William Carey College, Hattiesburg, MS 39401, Tel. (601) 582-5051. James W. Edwards, Interim, C S, So. Bapt., 1,931

William Jewell College, Liberty, MO 64068, Tel. (816) 781-7700. J. Gordon Kingsley, C NC, Am. Bapt. and So. Bapt., 1,426

William Penn College, Oskaloosa, IA 52577, Tel. (515) 673-8311. John Wagoner, C NC, Friends, 675

William Woods College, Fulton, MO 65251, Tel. (314) 642-2251. John M. Bartholomy, W NC, Christian Church (Disc.), 708

Wilmington College, Wilmington, OH 45177, Tel. (513) 382-6661. Neil Thorburn, C NC, Friends Un. Mtg., 825

Wilson College, Chambersburg, PA 17201, Tel. (717) 264-4141. Mary-Linda Merriam, W MS, PCUSA, 665

Wingate College, Wingate, NC 28174, Tel. (704) 233-8000. Paul R. Corts, C S, So. Bapt., 1,729

Wisconsin Lutheran College, Milwaukee, WI 53226, Tel. (414)774-8620. Gary Greenfield, C NC, Luth., 229

Wittenberg University, Springfield, OH 45501, Tel. (513) 327-6231. William A. Kinnison, C NC, ELCA, 2,228

Wofford College, Spartanburg, SC 29303, Tel. (803) 585-4821. Joab M. Lesesne C S, Un. Meth., 1,135

Xavier University, Cincinnati, OH 45207, Tel. (513) 745-3000. Albert J. Diulio, C NC, Cath., 6,412

Xavier University of Louisiana, New Orleans, LA 70125, Tel. (504) 486-7411, Norman C. Francis, C S, Cath., 2,528

Yeshiva University, New York, NY 10033, Tel. (212) 960-5400. Norman Lamm, Co. Ord. MS, Jewish, 4,444

12. CHURCH-RELATED COLLEGES AND UNIVERSITIES IN CANADA

The majority of the colleges and universities established in Canada in the 19th century were church-related. In subsequent reorganizations of higher education, especially after World War II, a number of these institutions were secularized and a large number of new, entirely non-denominational institutions of higher learning were established.

A uniquely Canadian solution to church-state problems over educational jurisdiction has evolved which permits denominational colleges to affiliate with larger provincial universities. The former thereby obtain some government grants while retaining some independence of action. Also, the advantages of smallness and largeness are combined; that is, the old religious traditions are maintained while students are also exposed to the new trends from the outside world in a larger setting.

In Canada education is a provincial responsibility and each of the ten provinces has worked out its own particular solution as to how the state will support educational endeavors that have denominational sponsorship. The provincial governments by establishing and funding all colleges and universities within their jurisdiction thereby accredit them.

Despite the recent secularization of some formerly religiously oriented colleges and universities, there is often a pronounced residue of religious atmosphere remaining in them, especially in the French Canadian universities. There individual students can choose between a Roman Catholic or secular humanist approach to their studies. Even in the large non-denominational provincial universities, the major denominations in the area usually provide chaplaincy services for those students who wish them.

Following is a list of those Canadian colleges and universities which still claim to offer a religious atmosphere for their students, spiritually, intellectually and socially, even if it is only by providing denominationally operated residences for them. Canadian universities are either English or French speaking and a few are bilingual. In the listing below the English or French title of each university indicates the language used therein. All French universities are Roman Catholic and secular.

This list was drawn mainly from the 27th edition (1988-89) of the *Directory of Canadian Universities*, published by the Association of Universities and Colleges of Canada, 151 Slater St., Ottawa, Ontario K1P 5N1. Enrollment figures are for full-time undergraduates only. The colleges and universities are listed geographically from east to west with affiliated institutions listed under the major provincial university with which they are associated.

Abbreviations used are as follows: C-Coeducational, M-Men, W-Women. Each item in the listing below has the following order: Name of institution, address, telephone number, head of institution, nature of student body, denominational relationship, enrollment.

NEWFOUNDLAND

Memorial University of Newfoundland, Elizabeth Ave., St. John's Newfoundland A1C 5S7, Tel. (709) 737-8000. L. Harris, secular, C. Queen's, St. John's, Newfoundland A1B 3R6. Tel (709)753-0640. D. N. Oliver, C, Anglican Church of Canada, 20. (Has residences operated by the Anglican Church of Canada, the Roman Catholic Church, and United Church of Canada) 10,072

NOVA SCOTIA

Acadia University, Wolfville, Nova Scotia, B0P 1X0, Tel. (902) 542-2201. J. R. C. Perkin, C, nondenominational, formerly Baptist, 3,189.

Dalhousie University, Halifax, Nova Scotia B3H 3J5, Tel. (902) 424-2211. Howard C. Clark, C, nondenominational, 7,055. Associated universities: **The University of King's College,** Halifax, Nova Scotia B3H 2A1, Tel. (902) 422-1271. Marion G. Fry, C, Anglican Church of Canada, 530.

Mount Saint Vincent University, Halifax, Nova Scotia B3M 2J6, Tel. (902) 443-4450. Naomi Hersom, mostly W, Roman Catholic, 2,011. (Associated with Dalhousie U. but grants its own degrees).

Saint Francis Xavier University, Antigonish, Nova Scotia B2G 1C0, Tel. (902) 863-3300. Rev. G.A. MacKinnon, C, Roman Catholic, 2,547. Constituent college: **Mount Saint Bernard College,** Antigonish, Nova Scotia B2G 1C0, Roman Catholic. Residential accommodation for women.

St. Mary's University, Halifax, Nova Scotia B3H 3C3, Tel. (902) 420-5400. K. L. Ozmon, C, nondenominational, 3,543.

Université Sainte-Anne, Church Point, Nova Scotia B0W 1M0, Tel. (902) 769-2114. Harley D'Entremont, C, 222.

University College of Cape Breton, P.O. Box 5300, Sydney, Nova Scotia B1P 6L2, Tel. (902) 539-5300. W. M. Reid, C, Roman Catholic, and Protestant, 1,288.

NEW BRUNSWICK

Mount Allison University, Sackville, New Brunswick E0A 3C0. Tel. (506) 364-2200. Donald O. Wells, C, United Church of Canada, 1,748.

Saint Thomas University, Fredericton, New Brunswick, E3B 5G3, Tel. (506) 452-7700. Rev. G.W. Martin, C, Roman Catholic, 1,235. (Shares facilities with the Fredericton campus of the University of New Brunswick.)

St. Stephen's University, St. Stephen, New Brunswick, C, Interdenominational.

QUEBEC

Concordia University—Loyola Campus, 7141 Sherbrooke St., W., Montréal, Québec H4B 1R6, Tel. (514) 848-2424. P. J. Kenniff, C, nondenominational, formerly Roman Catholic, 11,599.

Université Laval, Cité Universitaire, Québec, Québec G1K 7P4. Tél. (418) 656-2131. Michel Gervais, non-confessional, (formerly Roman Catholic), C, 17,561.

Université de Montréal, Case Postale 6128, Succursale A, Montréal, Québec H3C 3J7, Tel. (514) 343-6111. Gilles G. Cloutier, C, 19,184.

Université de Sherbrooke, Cité Universitaire, boulevard de l'Université, Sherbrooke, Québec J1K 2R1, Tél. (819) 821-7680. Aldée Cabana, C, Roman Catholic, 7,248.

ONTARIO

Laurentian University of Sudbury, Ramsey Lake Road, Sudbury, Ontario P3E 2C6, Tel. (705) 675-1151. John Daniel, C, secular 4,706. Three federated universities: **Huntington University,** Sudbury, Ontario P3E 2C6, Tel. (705) 675-1151, ext. 1051, L.J. Winckel, C, United Church of Canada. **L'Université de Sudbury/The University of Sudbury,** Chemin du Lac Ramsey, Sudbury, Ontario P3E 2C6, Tel. (705) 673-5661. Rev. L. Larouche, C, Roman Catholic. **Thorneloe University,** Sudbury, Ontario P3E 2C6, Tel. (705) 675-1151, ext. 1052, J. W. K. Sandys-Wunsch, C, Anglican Church of Canada

Redeemer Reformed Christian College, Ancaster, Ontario L9G 3N6, Tel (416)648-2131. Henry R. DeBolter, C, Reformed tradition, 275.

Université d'Ottawa/University of Ottawa, Ottawa, Ontario K1N 6N5, Tel. (613) 564-3311. A. D'Iorio, C, secular, 11,526. Federated University: St. Paul's University, 223 Main St., Ottawa, Ontario K1S 1C4, Tel. (613)236-1393. P. Hurtubise, C, Roman Catholic, 256.

The University of Toronto, Toronto, Ontario M5S 1A1, Tel. (416) 978-2011. G. E. Connell, C, secular, 29,808. Three federated universities: The University of St. Michael's College, 81 St. Mary St., Toronto, Ontario M5S 1J4, Tel. (416) 926-1300. Rev. J. McConica, C, Roman Catholic, 2,779. Two constituent residential colleges for women: Loretto College, 70 St. Mary St., Toronto, Ontario M5S 1J3, Tel. (416) 925-2833. Sr. J. D'Agostino, W, Roman Catholic. St. Joseph's College, 90 Wellesley St., West, Toronto, Ontario M5S 1C5, Tel. (416) 924-2121. Sr. Mary Anne McCarthy, W, Roman Catholic. The University of Trinity College, Toronto, Ontario M5S 1H8, Tel. (416) 978-2522. R.H. Painter, C, Anglican Church of Canada, 1,009. Constituent residential college for women; St. Hilda's College, 44 Devonshire Pl., Toronto, Ontario M5S 2E2, Tel. (416) 978-3562. E.M. Rowlinson, W, Anglican Church of Canada. Victoria University, 73 Queen's Park, Toronto, Ontario M5S 1K7, Tel. (416) 585-4508. E. Kushner, C, United Church of Canada, 2,254. Residences for men and women.

The University of Waterloo, Waterloo, Ontario N2L 3G1, Tel. (519) 885-1211. D. T. Wright, C, secular, 14,541. Three affiliated colleges: Renison College, Waterloo, Ontario N2L 3G4, Tel. (519) 884-4400. Ian L. Campbell, C, Anglican Church of Canada. St. Paul's College, Westmount Rd., N., Waterloo, Ontario N2L 3G5, Tel. (519) 885-1460. F.C. Gérard, C, sponsored by United Church of Canada. Conrad Grebel College, Waterloo, Ontario N2L 3G6, Tel. (519) 885-0220. R. Sawatsky, C, Mennonite. Federated with the University of Waterloo: University of St. Jerome's College, Waterloo, Ontario N2L 3G3, Tel. (519) 884-8110. N. L. Choate, C, Roman Catholic, 545. Attached to St. Jerome's is Notre Dame College, a women's residence run by the School Sisters of Notre Dame.

The University of Western Ontario, London, Ontario N6A 3K7, Tel. (519) 679-2111. K. George Pedersen, C, nondenominational, 18,812. Three affiliated colleges: Brescia College, 1285 Western Rd., London, Ontario N6G 1H2, Tel. (519) 432-8353. Sr. Dolores Kuntz, W, Roman Catholic, 589. Huron College, London, Ontario N6G 1H3, Tel. (519) 438-7224. Charles Joseph Jago, C, Anglican Church of Canada, 579. King's College, 266 Epworth Ave., London, Ontario N6A 2M3, Tel. (519) 433-3491. P. J. Meuller, C, Roman Catholic, 1,295.

The University of Windsor, Windsor, Ontario N9B 3P4, Tel. (519) 253-4232. Ronald Ianni, C, nondenominational, 7,943. Two affiliated colleges: Holy Redeemer College, Windsor, Ontario N9B 3P4, Tel. (519)969-2840. A. Thomas, M, Roman Catholic. Iona College, 208 Sunset Ave., Windsor, Ontario N9B 3P4, Tel. (519)253-7257. Dr. J. Murray MacInnes, C, United Church of Canada. Federated university: Assumption University, Windsor, Ontario N9B 3P4, Tel. (519) 254-3783. Rev. David Gordon Heath, C, Roman Catholic.

MANITOBA

The University of Winnipeg, 515 Portage Ave., Winnipeg, Manitoba R3B 2E9, Tel. (204) 786-7811. R.H. Farquhar, C, United Church of Canada, 2,960. Associated institution: Mennonite Brethren College of Arts, 1-169 Riverton Ave., Winnipeg, Manitoba R2L 2E5, Tel. (204) 669-6575. J. Pankratz, C, Canadian Mennonite Brethren Conference.

The University of Manitoba, Winnipeg, Manitoba R3T 2N2, Tel. (204) 474-8880. Arnold Naimark, C, secular, 13,067. Four affiliated colleges: Collège universitaire de Saint Boniface, 200 avenue Cathédrale, Saint-Boniface, Mani-

toba R2H 0H7, Tel. (204) 233-0210. P. Ruest, C, Roman Catholic, St. John's College, 400 Dysart Rd., Winnipeg, Manitoba R3T 2M5, Tel. (204) 474-8531. Rev. M. McLean, C, Anglican Church of Canada. St. Paul's College, 430 Dysart Rd., Winnipeg, Manitoba R3T 2M6, Tel. (204) 474-8575. D. J. Lawless, C, Roman Catholic. St. Andrew's College, 475 Dysart Rd., Winnipeg, Manitoba R3T 2M7, Tel. (204) 269-3565. Rev. O. A. Krawchenko, C, Ukrainian Greek Orthodox Church of Canada.

Two approved teaching centers: Canadian Mennonite Bible College, 600 Shaftesbury Blvd., Winnipeg, Manitoba R3P 0M4, Tel. (204) 888-6781. Rev. J. Neufeld, C, Mennonite. Canadian Nazarene College, 1301 Lee Blvd., Winnipeg, Manitoba R3T 2P7, Tel. (204) 269-2120. N. Hightower, C, Church of the Nazarene.

SASKATCHEWAN

The University of Regina, Regina, Saskatchewan S4S 0A2, Tel. (306) 584-4111. L.I. Barber, C, secular, 5,551. Two federated colleges: Campion College, c/o University of Regina, Regina, Saskatchewan S4S 0A2, Tel. (306) 586-4242. Rev. Joseph Schner, sj, C, Roman Catholic, 505. Luther College, University of Regina, Regina, Saskatchewan S4S 0A2, Tel. (306) 584-0255. Donald G. Lee, C, Lutheran, 521.

The University of Saskatchewan, Saskatoon, Saskatchewan S7N 0W0, Tel. (306) 244-4343. L. F. Kristjanson, C, nondenominational, 12,451. Federated college: Saint Thomas More College, 1437 College Dr., Saskatoon, Saskatchewan S7N 0W6, Tel. (306) 966-8900. Rev. J. Hanrahan, csb, C, Roman Catholic, 1,058. Affiliated college: St. Peter's College, Muenster, Saskatchewan S0K 2Y0, Tel. (306) 682-5431. Rev. M. R. Weber, C, Roman Catholic.

ALBERTA

Camrose Lutheran College, Camrose, Alberta T4V 2R3, Tel. (403) 679-1100. K.G. Johnson, C, Ev. Luth. Ch. in Canada.

The University of Alberta, Edmonton, Alberta T6G 2E5, Tel. (403) 432-3111. M. Horowitz, C, secular, 22,407. Five affiliated colleges: Canadian Union College, Lacombe, Alberta T0C 0Z0, Tel. (403) 782-3381. R. E. Granson, C, Seventh-Day Adventist. Concordia Lutheran College, 7128 Ada Blvd., Edmonton, Alberta T5B 4E4, Tel. (403) 479-8481. O. Walz, C, Lutheran. The King's College, 10766 - 97 St., Edmonton, Alberta T5H 2M1, Tel. (403) 428-0727. H. W. H. Van Andel, C, Nondenom. St. Joseph's College, 11325 89 Ave., Edmonton, Alberta T6G 2M7, Tel. (403) 433-1569. Rev. P. W. Platt, C, Roman Catholic. St. Stephen's College, Edmonton, Alberta T6G 2M7, Tel. (403) 439-7311. G. I. Mundle, C, United Church of Canada.

BRITISH COLUMBIA

Trinity Western University, 7600 Glover Rd., Langley, British Columbia V3A 4R9, Tel. (604) 888-7511, Neil Snider, C, Ev. Free Ch., 982. Affiliated College: Northwest Baptist College, 3358 S.E. Marine Dr., Vancouver, British Columbia V5S 3W3, Tel. (604)433-2475.

The University of British Columbia, 2075 Westbrook Mall, Vancouver, British Columbia V6T 1W5, Tel. (604) 228-2211. David Strongway, C, secular, 18,211. Three residences for men: Carey Hall, 5920 Iona Ave., Vancouver, British Columbia, V6T 1J6, Tel. (604) 224-4308. Philip Collins, M, Baptist. St. Andrew's Hall, 6040 Iona, Vancouver, British Columbia, V6T 1J6, Tel. (604) 224-7720. Rev. B. J. Fraser, M, Presbyterian. St. Mark's College, 5935 Iona, Vancouver, British Columbia V6T 1J7, Tel. (604) 224-3311. Rev. Paul C. Burns, M, Roman Catholic. Also Affiliated: Regent College and Vancouver School of Theology.

228

13. RELIGIOUS PERIODICALS IN THE UNITED STATES

This list has been compiled for those who may wish to utilize a relatively large, representative group of religious periodicals. Many additional titles appear in the directories of religious bodies presented in this book. Probably the most inclusive list of religious periodicals published in the United States can be found in the *Gale Directory of Publications, and Broadcast Media, 1990*, (Gale Reserach, Inc., 835 Penobscot Bldg., Detroit, MI 48226).

Each entry lists, in this order: Title of periodical, frequency of publication, religious affiliation, editor's name, address, and telephone number.

ADRIS Newsletter (q), non-sect., Richard F. Smith, 3601 Lindell Blvd., St. Louis, MO 63108. Tel. (314)658-2588

Adventist Review (w), Seventh-day Adv., W. G. Johnsson, 12501 Old Columbia Pike, Silver Spring, MD 20904. Tel. (301)680-6561

Alliance Life (bi-w), The Christian and Missionary Alliance, Maurice Irvin, P. O. Box 35000 Colorado Springs, CO 80935. Tel. (719)599-5999

America (w), Cath., George W. Hunt, 106 W. 56th St., New York, NY 10019. Tel. (212)581-4640

American Baptist, The (bi-m), Am. Bapt., P.O. Box 851, Philip E. Jenks, American Baptist Churches, U.S.A., Valley Forge, PA 19482. Tel. (215)768-2216

American Bible Society Record (10/yr.), nondenom., Amer. Bible Society, Clifford P. Macdonald, 1865 Broadway, New York, NY. 10023,. Tel. (212)581-7400

American Journal of Theology & Philosophy (3/yr), Creighton Peden, Dept. of Philosophy, Augusta College, Augusta, GA 30910. Tel. (404)737-1710

American Presbyterians: Journal of Presbyterian History (q), PCUSA, James H. Smylie, 425 Lombard St., Philadelphia, PA 19147. Tel. (215)627-1852

Anglican and Episcopal History (q), Epis., John F. Woolverton, Historical Society of the Episcopal Church, P. O. Box 261, Center Sandwich, NH 03227.

Arkansas United Methodist, (semi-m), U. Meth., Jane Dearing, P.O. Box 3547, Little Rock, AR 72203. Tel. (501)374-4831

Banner, The (w), Chr. Ref., Galen H. Meyer, 2850 Kalamazoo Ave., S.E., Grand Rapids, MI 49560. Tel. (616)246-0732

Baptist and Reflector (w), S. Bapt., W. Fletcher Allen, P.O. Box 728, Brentwood, TN 37024. Tel. (615)371-2003

Baptist Bulletin (m), Gen. Assoc. Reg. Bapt. Chs., Vernon D. Miller, 1300 N. Meacham Rd., Schaumburg, IL 60173

Baptist Courier (w), S. Bapt., John E. Roberts, P.O. Box 2168, Greenville, SC 29602. Tel. (803)232-8736

Baptist Herald (m), N. A. Bapt. Conf., Barbara J. Binder, 1 S. 210 Summit Ave., Oakbrook Terrace, IL 60181

Baptist History and Heritage (q), S. Bapt., Lynn E. May, Jr., 901 Commerce St., Ste. 400, Nashville, TN 37203. Tel. (615)244-0344

Baptist Leader (m), Am. Bapt., Linda Isham, Valley Forge, PA 19482. Tel. (215)768-2153

Baptist Messenger (w), S. Bapt., Glenn A. Brown, Box 25816, Oklahoma City, OK 73125. Tel. (405)236-4341

Baptist Record (w), S. Bapt., Donald T. McGregor, Box 530, Jackson, MS 39205. Tel. (601)968-3800

Baptist Standard (w), S. Bapt., Presnall H. Wood, 2343 Lone Star Dr., P.O. Box 660267, Dallas TX 75266. Tel. (214)630-4571

Biblical Recorder (w), S. Bapt., R. Gene Puckett, P.O. Box 26568, Raleigh, NC 27611. Tel. (919)847-2127

Brethren Journal, The (m), Unity of Brethren, Milton Maly Rt. 3, Box 766, Brenham, TX 77833

Campus Life, Indepdt., Roy Coffman, 465 Gunderson Dr., Carol Stream, IL 60188. Tel. (312)260-6200

Catholic Chronicle (bi-w), Cath., Daniel J. McCarthy, 2130 Madison Ave., P.O. Box 1866, Toledo, OH 43603. Tel. (419)243-4178

Catholic Digest (m), Cath., Henry Lexau, P. O. Box 64090, St. Paul, MN 55164. Tel. (612)647-5296

Catholic Herald (w), Cath., Ethel M. Gintoft, 3501 S. Lake Dr., Milwaukee, WI 53207. Tel. (414)769-3500

Catholic Light (bi-w), Cath., Arthur F. Perry, The Chancery Bldg., 300 Wyoming Ave., Scranton, PA 18503

Catholic Review, The (w), Cath., Martin J. Cone, 320 Cathedral St., Baltimore, MD 21203. Tel. (301)547-5327

Catholic Standard and Times (w), Cath., David W. Givey, 222 N. 17th St., Philadelphia, PA 19103. Tel. (215)587-3660

Catholic Transcript, The (w), Cath., David M. Fortier, 785 Asylum Ave., Hartford, CT 06105. Tel. (203)527-1175

Catholic Worker (8/yr.), Cath., Meg Hyre, 36 E. First St., New York, NY 10003. Tel. (212)254-1640

Catholic World, The (bi-m), Cath., Laurie Felknor, 997 Macarthur Blvd., Mahwah, NJ 07430

Catholic Universe Bulletin (w), Cath., Michael G. Dimengo, 1027 Superior Ave., N.E., Cleveland, OH 44114. Tel. (216)696-6525

Celebration: A Creative Worship Service (m), Cath., William Freburger, P.O. Box 419493, Kansas City, MO 64141. Tel. (816)531-0538

Chicago Catholic, The, (See: New World, The,)

Childlife (q), nondenom., Terry Madison, 919 W. Huntington Dr., Monrovia, CA 91016. Tel. (818)357-7979

Christian Century, The (42/yr.), ecumen., James M. Wall, 407 S. Dearborn St., Chicago, IL 60605. Tel. (312) 427-5380

Christian Community, The (m, except Feb., June, Aug., and Sept.), International Council of Community Churches, J. Ralph Shotwell, 900 Ridge Rd., Homewood, IL 60430. Tel. (312)798-2264

Christian Endeavor World, The (q), interdenom., David G. Jackson, 1221 E. Broad St., P.O. Box 1110, Columbus, OH 43216. Tel. (614)258-9545

Christian Herald (bi-m), interdenom., Bob Chuvala, 40 Overlook Dr., Chappaqua, NY 10514 Tel. (914) 769-9000

Christian Index, The (w), S. Bapt., R. Albert Mohler, Jr., 2930 Flowers Rd., S., Atlanta, GA 30341.Tel. (404)455-0404

Christian Index, The (bi-m), Chr. Meth. Epis., Lawrence L. Reddick, III, P. O. Box 665, Memphis, TN 38101. Tel. (901)785-0222

Christian Life Magazine (m), undenom., Robert Walker, 396 East St. Charles Rd., Wheaton, IL 60188. Tel. (312)653-4200

Christian Ministry, The (6/yr.), ecumen., James M. Wall, 407 S. Dearborn St., Chicago, IL 60605. Tel. (312)427-5380

Christian Reader, The (bi-m), non-denom., Dwight Hooten, P.O. Box 220, Wheaton, IL 60189. Tel. (312)668-8300

Christian Science Journal, The (m), Chr. Sc., A. W. Phinney, Jr., One Norway St., Boston, MA 02115. Tel. (617)450-2701

Christian Science Quarterly-Bible Lessons, Chr. Sc., (English, Danish, Dutch, French, German, Greek, Indonesian, available in Indonesia only), Italian, Japanese, Norwegian, Polish, Portuguese, Spanish, Swedish, and English Braille editions (q), One Norway St., Boston, MA 02115. Tel. (617)262-2300

Christian Science Sentinel (w), Chr. Sc., A. W. Phinney, Jr., One Norway St., Boston, MA 02115. Tel. (617)450-2701

Christian Social Action (m), U. Meth., Lee Ranck, 100 Maryland Ave., N. E., Washington, DC 20002. Tel. (202)488-5632

Christian Standard (w), Christian Churches/Churches of Christ, Sam E. Stone, 8121 Hamilton Ave., Cincinnati, OH 45231

Christianity and Crisis (bi-w), ecumen., Leon Howell,537 W. 121st St., New York, NY 10027. Tel. (212)662-5907

Church Advocate, The (m), Chs. of God, Gen. Conf., Linda M. Draper, 700 E. Melrose Ave., P. O. Box 926, Findlay, OH 45839. Tel. (419)424-1961

Church and Society (bi-m), PCUSA, Kathy Lancaster, 100 Witherspoon St., Louisville, KY 40202

Church Herald, The (12/yr.), Ref. Ch. in Am., John Stapert, 6157-28th St., SE, Grand Rapids, MI 49546 Tel. (616)957-1351

Church History (q), undenom., Martin E. Marty, and Jerald C. Brauer, Swift Hall, The Univ. of Chicago, Chicago, IL 60637. Tel. (312)702-8215

Church Management: The Clergy Journal (10/yr), nondenom., Manfred Holck, Jr. P.O. Box 162527, Austin, TX 78716. Tel. (512)327-8501

Churchman's Human Quest, The (m), interdenom., Edna Ruth Johnson, 1074 23rd Ave., N., St. Petersburg, FL 33704. Tel. (813)894-0097

Churchwoman, (q), ecumen., Church Women United, Margaret Schiffert, 475 Riverside Dr., New York, NY 10115. Tel. (212)870-2344

Clarion Herald (w), Cath., Emile M. Comar, Jr., 523 Natchez St. P. O. Box 53247, New Orleans, 70153. Tel. (504)596-3030

Columban Mission (10/yr.), Cath., Richard Steinhilber, St. Columbans, NE 68056

Columbia (m), Cath., Richard McMunn, One Columbus Plz., P. O. Drawer 1670, New Haven, CT 06507

Commonweal (bi-w), Cath., Margaret O'Brien Steinfels, 15 Dutch St., New York, NY 10038. Tel. (212)732-0800

Congregationalist, The (bi-m), Congr. Chr. Chs., Natl. Assn. of, Louis B. Gerhardt, P. O. Box 9397, Fresno, CA 93792. Tel (209)227-6936

Congregational Journal, (3/yr.), Congr. Chr. Chs., Am. Cong. Cntr., Henry David Gray, 298 Fairfax Ave., Ventura, CA 93003. Tel. (805)644-3397

Conservative Judaism (q), Jewish, David Wolf Silverman, 3080 Broadway, New York, NY 10027. Tel. (212)678-8049

Courage in the Struggle for Justice and Peace (10/yr), Office for Church in Society, UCC, Russell, G. Claussen, 105 Madison Ave., New York, NY 10016. Tel. (212)683-5656

Criterion, The (w), Cath., John F. Fink, 1400 N. Meridian, P. O. Box 1717, Indianapolis, IN 46206. Tel. (317)236-1570

Cumberland Presbyterian, The (m, ex. July and Aug., when combined), Cumb. Presb., Mark Brown, 1978 Union Ave., Memphis, TN 38104. Tel. (901)276-4572

Currents in Theology and Mission (6/yr.), Luth. Sch. of Theol., Ralph W. Klein, 1100 E. 55th St., Chicago, Il 60615. Tel. (312)753-0763.

Decision (11/yr.), Billy Graham Evangelistic Assn., Roger C. Palms, 1300 Harmon Pl., Minneapolis, MN 55403 Tel. (612)338-0500.

Disciple, The (m), Chr. Ch. (Disc.), James L. Merrell, Box 179, St. Louis, MO 63166. Tel. (314)231-8500

Ecumenical Courier (2-4/yr), U.S. Conference for the World Council of Churches, Andrea R. Cano, Rm. 915, 475 Riverside Dr., New York, NY 10115. Tel. (212)870-2533

Ecumenical Review, The (q), interdenom., Emilio Castro, World Council of Churches, 150 Route de Ferney, CH-1211 Geneva 2, Switzerland

Ecumenical Trends (m), ecum., Patrick J. Cogan, Graymoor Ecumenical Institute, 475 Riverside Dr., Rm. 528, New York, NY 10115. Tel. (212)870-2330

Emphasis on Faith and Living (m), Missionary Ch. Michael Reynolds, 3901 S. Wayne Ave., Fort Wayne, IN 46807

Episcopal Life (m), Epis., Jerrold Hames, 815 Second Ave., New York, NY 10017. Tel. (212)867-8400

Episcopal Recorder (m), Ref. Epis., George B. Fincke, 4225 Chestnut St., Philadelphia, PA 19104. Tel. (215)222-5158

Eternity (m), interdenom., Donald J. McCrory, 1716 Spruce St., Philadelphia, PA 19103. Tel. (215)546-3696

Evangelist, The (w), Cath., James Breig, 40 N. Main Ave., Albany, NY 12203. Tel. (518)453-6688

Extension (10/yr), Cath., Bradley Collins, 35 East Wacker Dr., Chicago, IL 60601. Tel. (312)236-7240

Firm Foundation (semi-m), Chs. of Christ, William S. Cline, Box 17200, Pensacola, FL 32522

First Things: A Monthly Journal of Religion and Public Life, Richard J. Neuhaus, Inst. of Religion and Public Life, 156 Fifth Ave., Ste. 400, New York, NY 10010. Tel. (212)627-2278

Forum Letter (m), Luth., Richard J. Neuhaus, The Wartburg, Bradley Ave., Mt. Vernon, NY 10552. Tel. (914)699-1226

Free Will Baptist, The (w), Original Free Will Bapt., Janie Jones Sowers, Free Will Baptist Press, P. O. Box 159, Ayden, NC 28513. Tel. (919)746-6128

Friends Journal (m), Friends (Quakers), Vinton Deming, 1501 Cherry St., Philadelphia, PA 19102. Tel. (215)241-7277

Gospel Advocate (m), Chs. of Christ, Furman Kearley, Box 150, Nashville, TN 37202

Gospel Herald (w), Menn., Daniel Hertzler, Scottdale, PA 15683. Tel. (412)887-8500

Grapevine (10/yr.), Joint Strategy and Action Committee, James E. Solheim, 475 Riverside Dr., Rm. 450, New York, NY 10115. Tel. (212)870-3105

Herald of Christian Science, The, Chr. Sc., French, German, Portugese, and Spanish editions (m); Danish, Dutch, Greek, Indonesian, Italian, Japanese, Norwegian, Swedish editions (q), A. W. Phinney, One Norway St., Boston, MA 02115. Tel. (617)450-2701

Herald of Holiness (semi-m), Nazarene, Wesley D. Tracy, 6401 The Paseo, Kansas City, MO 64131. Tel. (816)333-7000.

Heritage (q), Assem. of God, Wayne E. Warner, 1445 Boonville Ave., Springfield, MO 65802. Tel. (417)862-2781.

Homiletic and Pastoral Review (m), Cath., Kenneth Baker, 86 Riverside Dr., New York, NY 10024. Tel. (212)799-2600

Horizons (7/yr.) PCUSA, Presby. Women, Barbara A. Roche, 100 Witherspoon St., Louisville, KY. Tel. (502)569-5367.

Image (m), Chs. of Chr., Denny Boultinghouse, 115 Warren Dr., Ste. D., West Monroe, LA 71291. Tel. (318)396-4366.

Interest (m), Christian Breth., William W. Conard, 218 W. Willow, Wheaton, IL 60187. Tel. (312)653-6573

International Bulletin of Missionary Research (q), nondenom., Gerald H. Anderson, 490 Prospect St., New Haven, CT 06511. Tel. (203)624-6672.

International Review of Mission (q), Commission on World Mission and Evangelism, World Council of Churches, Christopher Duraisingh, 150 Route de Ferney, P. O. Box 2100, CH-1211 Geneva 2, Switzerland

Interpretation (q), Union Theol. Sem. in Va., Paul J. Achtemeier, 3401 Brook Rd., Richmond, VA 23227. Tel. (804)355-0671

Interpreter, The (m), U. Meth., Laura J. Okumu, 810 Twelfth Ave. S., Nashville, TN 37202. Tel. (615)742-5400

Jewish Action (q), Jewish, Heidi Tenzer, 45 W. 36 St., New York, NY 10018. Tel. (212)244-2011

Journal of Christian Education of the African Methodist Episcopal Church, A.M.E. Edgar L. Mack, 500-8th Ave., S., Nashville, TN 37203. Tel. (615)242-1420

Journal of Ecumenical Studies (q), Leonard Swidler, Temple Univ. (022-38), Philadelphia, PA 19122. Tel. (215)787-7714

Journal of Pastoral Care, The (q), nondenom., Orlo Strunk, Jr., 1549 Clairemont Rd., Ste. 103, Decatur, GA 30030.

Journal of Religion (q), undenom., 1025 E. 58th St., Chicago, IL 60637. Tel. (312)702-8216

Journal of the American Academy of Religion (q), undenom., William Scott Green, Univ. of Rochester, Rochester, NY 14627. Tel. (716)275-5378

Judaism (q), Jewish, Robert Gordis, 15 E. 84th St., New York, NY 10028. Tel. (212)879-4500

Leadership: A Practical Journal for Church Leaders (q), indepdt. Marshall Shelley, 465 Gundersen Dr., Carol Stream, IL 60188. Tel. (312)260-6200

Liguorian (m), Cath., Allen J. Weinert, 1 Liguori Dr., Liguori, MO 63057. Tel. (314)464-2500

Living Church, The (w), Epis., H. Boone Porter, 816 E. Juneau Ave., Milwaukee, WI 53202. Tel. (414)276-5420

Long Island Catholic, The (51/yr.), Cath., Francis J. Maniscalco, 115 Greenwich St., P. O. Box 700, Hempstead, NY 11551. Tel. (516)538-8800

Lookout, The (w), Christian Churches/Churches of Christ, Mark Taylor, 8121 Hamilton Ave., Cincinnati, OH 45231. Tel. (513)931-4050

Louisiana United Methodist, The (w), U. Meth., Harvey G. Williamson, P. O. Box 3057, Baton Rouge, LA 70802

Lutheran, The (s-m), Ev. Luth. Ch. in Am., Edgar R. Trexler, 8765 W. Higgins Rd., Chicago, IL 60631. Tel. (312)380-2540

Lutheran Forum (q), Luth., Paul R. Hinlicky, The Wartburg, Bradley Ave., Mt. Vernon, NY 10552. Tel. (914)699-1226

Lutheran Witness (m), David L. Mahsman, Luth., Mo, Synod, 1333 S. Kirkwood Rd., St. Louis, MO 63122. Tel. (314)965-9000

Maryknoll (m), Cath., Ronald R. Saucci, Maryknoll Fathers and Brothers, Maryknoll, NY 10545. Tel. (914)941-7590

Marriage Partnership (q), indepdt., Harold Smith, 465 Gundersen Dr., Carol Stream, IL 60188. Tel. (312)260-6200.

Media & Values (q), nondenom., Elizabeth Thoman, 1962 S. Shenandoah St., Los Angeles, CA 90034. Tel. (213)559-2944

Mennonite, The, (semi-m), Gen. Conf. Menn., Muriel T. Stackley, Box 347, Newton, KS 67114. Tel. (316)283-5100

Message Magazine, The (bi-m), Seventh-day Adv., Delbert W. Baker, 55 West Oak Ridge Dr., Hagerstown, MD 21740. Tel. (301)791-7000

Messenger (m), Ch. Breth., Kermon Thomasson, Ch. Breth., 1451 Dundee Ave., Elgin, IL 60120. Tel. (312)742-5100

Messenger, The (m), Swedenborgian, James Lawrence, 48 Sargent St., Newton, MA 02158.

Mid-Stream: An Ecumenical Journal, (q), Chr. Ch. (Disc.), Paul A. Crow, Jr., P. O. Box 1986 Indianapolis, IN 46206. Tel. (317)353-1491

Mission Herald (bi-m), Natl. Bapt., Wm. J. Harvey, III, 701 S. 19th St., Philadelphia, PA 19146

Missionary Monthly (m), Chr. Ref. and Ref. Chs. Dick L. Van Halsema, (P.O. Box 6181), Grand Rapids, MI 49506. Tel. (616)957-4673

Missionary Seer, The (m), A.M.E. Zion, Kermit J. DeGraffenreidt, 475 Riverside Dr., Ste. 1910 New York, NY 10115. Tel. (212)870-2952

Missions USA, (m), S. Bapt., William Junker, 1350 Spring St., N.W., Atlanta, GA 30367. Tel. (404)873-4041

Mississippi United Methodist Advocate (bi-w), U. Meth., J. Rayford Woodrick, P. O. Box 1093, Jackson, MS 39215. Tel. (601)354-0515

Moody Monthly (m), interdenom., Dennis Shere, 820 N. LaSalle Dr., Chicago, IL 60610. Tel. (312)329-2163

Moravian, The (m), Morav., Hermann I. Weinlick, 1021 Center St., P.O. Box 1245, Bethlehem, PA 18016. Tel. (215)867-0594

Muslim World, The (q), undenom., Willem A. Bijlefeld, Duncan Black Macdonald Center, Hartford Seminary, 77 Sherman St., Hartford, CT 06105. Tel. (203)232-4451

National Catholic Reporter (w, Sept.-May; bi-w, June-Aug.), Cath., Thomas C. Fox, P.O. Box 419281, Kansas City, MO 64141. Tel. (816)531-0538

National Christian Reporter, The, (w), interdenom., Spurgeon M. Dunnam, III, P. O. Box 222198, Dallas, TX 75222. Tel. (214)630-6495.

(New Catholic World: (See The Catholic World)

New World, The, (w), Cath., Cathy Campbell, 1144 W. Jackson Blvd., Chicago, IL 60607. Tel. (312)243-1300

New Oxford Review (10/yr.), Cath., Dale Vree, 1069 Kains Ave., Berkeley, CA 94706. Tel. (415)526-5374

New World Outlook (m), U. Meth., Sherrie Boyens, 475 Riverside Dr., New York, NY 10115. Tel. (212)870-3758

North Carolina Christian Advocate (w), U. Meth., C. A. Simonton, Jr., P. O. Box 508, Greensboro, NC 27402. Tel. (919)272-1196

Orthodox Observer, The (bi-w), Greek Orth., P. J. Gazouleas, 8 E. 79th St., New York, NY 10021. Tel. (212)628-2590

Our Sunday Visitor (w), Cath., Robert Lockwood, 200 Noll Plaza, Huntington, IN 46750. Tel. (219)356-8400

Pastoral Life (m), Cath., Anthony Chenevey, Rte. 224, Canfield, OH 44406. Tel. (216)533-5503

PCA Messenger The (m), PCA, Robert G. Sweet, 1852 Century Pl., Ste. 101, Atlanta, GA 30345. Tel. (404)320-3388.

Pentecostal Evangel (w), Assem. of God, Richard G. Champion, 1445 Boonville Ave., Springfield, MO 65802. Tel. (417)862-2781

Perspectives on Science and Christian Faith (Journal of the American Scientific Affiliation) (q), Interdenom., J. W. Haas, Jr., P. O. Box 668, Ipswich, MA 01938

Pilot, The (w), Cath. Leila H. Little, Actg., 49 Franklin St., Boston, MA 02110. Tel. (617)482-4316

Praying (bi-m), Cath., Art Winter, 115 E. Armour Blvd., Kansas City, MO 64111. Tel. (816)531-0538

Presbyterian Layman, The (6/yr.), Presbyterian Lay Committee, Parker Williamson, 1489 Baltimore Pike, Ste. 301, Springfield, PA 19064. Tel. (215)543-0227

Presbyterian Outlook (w), PCUSA, Robert H. Bullock, Jr., Box C-32071, Richmond, VA 23261. Tel. (804)359-8442

Presbyterian Survey (m), PCUSA, Vic Jameson, 100 Witherspoon St., Louisville, KY 40202

Providence Visitor (w), Cath., John W. Hunt, 184 Broad St., Providence, RI 02903. Tel. (401)272-1010

Pulpit Digest, The (bi-m), interdenom., David A. Farmer, % Harper & Row, 151 Union St., Ste. 401., San Francisco, CA 94111

Quaker Life (m), Friends United Mtg., J. Stanley Banker, 101 Quaker Hill Dr., Richmond, IN 47374. Tel. (317)962-7573

Quarterly Review, U. Meth., Sharon Hels, Box 871, Nashville, TN 37202

Reform Judaism (4/yr.), Ref. Jewish, Aron Hirt-Manheimer, 838 Fifth Ave., New York, NY 10021. Tel. (212)249-0100

Religion Index One: Periodicals (formerly Index to Religious Periodical Literature) and Religion Index Two: Multi-Author Works. American Theological Library Association, Index Board. Albert E. Hurd, Exec. Dir., 820 Church St., Evanston, IL 60201

Religious Broadcasting (11/yr.), National Religious Broadcasters, Ben Armstrong, Box 1926, Morristown, NJ 07960. Tel. (201)428-5400

Religious Education (q), multi-faith, Jack D. Spiro, Virginia Commonwealth Univ., Richmond, VA 23284. Tel. (804)257-1224

Reporter (36/yr), Luth. Mo. Synod, David Mahsman, 1333 S. Kirkwood Rd., St. Louis, MO 63122. Tel. (314)965-9000

Research in Ministry, an index to Doctor of Ministry Projects and Reports—, 1981, American Theological Library Association Index Board, Albert E. Hurd, Exec. Dir., 820 Church St., Evanston, IL 60201

Resources for Youth Ministry (See: Youth Ministry Quarterly)

Response (11/yr.), U. Meth., Carol Marie Herb, 475 Riverside Dr., Rm. 1344, New York, NY 10115. Tel. (212)870-3755

Restoration Herald (m), Christian Chs., Ch. of Christ, Thomas D. Thurman, 5664 Cheviot Rd., Cincinnati, OH 45247. Tel. (513)385-0461

Restoration Quarterly (q), Chs. of Christ, Everett Ferguson, Box 8227, Abilene, TX 79699

Review for Religious (bi-m), Cath., David L. Fleming, 3601 Lindell Blvd., St. Louis, MO 63108. Tel. (314)535-3048

Review of Religious Research (4/yr.), The Religious Research Assoc., D. Paul Johnson, Dept. of Sociology, Univ. of South Florida, Tampa, FL 33620. Tel. (813)949-7524

Sabbath Recorder, The (m), Seventh Day Bapt., Kevin J. Butler, P.O. Box 1678, Janesville, WI 53547. Tel. (608)752-5055

Saint Anthony Messenger (m), Cath., Norman Perry, 1615 Republic St., Cincinnati, OH 45210. Tel. (513)241-5616

Saints' Herald (m), Reorg. Ch. of Jesus Christ of, L.D.S., Roger Yarrington, P.O. Box HH, Independence, MO 64055

Salt (m), Cath., Mark J. Brummel, 205 W. Monroe St., Chicago, IL 60606. Tel. (312)236-7782

Second Century, The (q), W. Everett Ferguson, Box 8227, Abilene, TX 79699.

Signs of the Times (m), Seventh-day Adv., K. J. Holland, Box 7000, Boise, ID 83707.

Social Questions Bulletin (bi-m), Methodist Fed. for Social Action (independent), Rev. George McClain, Shalom House, 76 Clinton Ave., Staten Island, NY 10301. Tel. (718)273-4941

Sojourners (11/yr.), nondemom., Jim Wallis, Box 29272, Washington, DC 20017. Tel. (202)636-3637

South Carolina United Methodist Advocate (w), U. Meth., Willie S. Teague, 4908 Colonial Dr., Ste. 207, Columbia, SC 29203. Tel. (803)786-9483

Southern New England United Methodist Reporter (w), U. Meth.; Ann Whiting, The United Methodist Center, 566 Commonwealth Ave., Boston, MA 02215. Tel. (617)266-9038

Southwestern News (m, except Aug.), S. Bapt., John Earl Seelig, Southwestern Bapt. Theol. Sem., Box 22,000-3E, Fort Worth, TX 76122

Spirituality Today (q), Cath., Richard Woods, 7200 W. Division St., River Forest, IL 60305. Tel. (312)771-4270

Standard, The (m), Bapt. Gen. Conf., Donald E. Anderson, 2002 S. Arlington Heights Rd., Arlington Heights, IL 60005. Tel. (312)228-0200, (1-800)323-4215

Star of Zion (w), A.M.E. Zion, Morgan W. Tann, P.O. Box 31005, Charlotte, NC 28230. Tel. (704)377-4329

Stewardship USA, Raymond Barnett Knudsen II, P. O. Box 1040, Westwood, NJ 07675. Tel. (201)664-8890

Sunday (q), interdenom., James P. Wesberry, 2930 Flowers Rd., S., Atlanta, GA 30341. Tel. (404)451-7315

Tablet, The (w), Cath., Ed Wilkinson, 1 Hanson Pl., Brooklyn, NY 11243. Tel. (718)789-1500

Theological Education (semi-a), undenom., Leon Pacala, Association of Theological Schools in the United States and Canada, P. O. Box 130, Vandalia, OH 45377

Theology Digest (q), Cath., Bernhard A. Asen, Rosemary Jermann, 3634 Lindell Blvd., St. Louis, MO 63108, Tel. (314)658-2857

Theology Today (q), undenom., Hugh T. Kerr, P. O. Box 29, Princeton, NJ 08542

Thought (q), Cath., G. Richard Dimler, Fordham Univ., Bronx, NY 10458. Tel. (212)579-2322

Tidings, The (w), Cath., Alphonse J. Antczak, 1530 W. Ninth St., Los Angeles, CA 90015. Tel. (213)251-3360

Today's Christian Woman (6/yr.), indepdt., Rebecca Grosenbach, 465 Gunderson Dr., Carol Stream, IL 60188. Tel. (312)260-6200

Tradition (semi-a) Jewish (Rabbinical Council of America), Meyer Hager, 275 7th Ave., New York, NY 10001. Tel. (212)807-7888

United Evangelical Action (bi-m), interdenom., Donald R. Brown, 450 E. Gundersen Drive, Carol Stream, IL 60188; P. O. Box 28, Wheaton, IL 60189. Tel. (312)665-0500

United Methodist Christian Advocate, The (bi-w), U. Meth., 909 9th Ave. W., Birmingham, AL 35204. Tel. (205)251-9279

United Methodist Reporter, The (w), U. Meth., Spurgeon, M. Dunnam, III, P. O. Box 660275, Dallas, TX 75266. Tel. (214)630-6495

Upreach (sm), Chs. of Christ, Phillip Morrison, Box 2001, Abilene, TX 79604

U.S. Catholic (m), Cath., Mark J. Brummel, 205 W. Monroe St., Chicago, IL 60606. Tel. (312)236-7782

Virginia United Methodist Advocate (bi-m), U. Meth., Alvin J. Horton, 4016 W. Broad St., Rm. 208, P. O. Box 11367, Richmond, VA 23230. Tel. (804)359-9451, Ext. 65

Vital Christianity (12/yr.), Ch. of God (Anderson, Ind.), Arlo F. Newell, Box 2499, Anderson, IN 46018. Tel. (317)644-7721

Voice of Missions (bi-m), Afr. Meth. Epis., Maeola Herring, 475 Riverside Dr., Rm. 1926, New York, NY 10115. Tel. (212)870-2258

War Cry, The (w), Salv. Army, Lt. Col. Henry Gariepy, 799 Bloomfield Ave., Verona, NJ 07044. Tel. (201)239-0606

Wesleyan Christian Advocate (w), U. Meth., G. Ross Freeman, 410-411 Methodist Center, 159 Ralph McGill Blvd., N. E., Atlanta, GA 30308. Tel. (404)659-0002

Western Recorder (w), S. Bapt., Jack D. Sanford, Box 43969, Middletown, KY 40243. Tel. (502)245-4101

White Wing Messenger, The (bi-w), Ch. of God of Prophecy, M. A. Tomlinson, Bible Pl., Cleveland, TN 37311

Word and Work (m), undenom., Alex V. Wilson, 2518 Portland Ave., Louisville, KY 40212

The World (6/yr.), Linda C. Beyer, 25 Beacon St., Boston, MA 02108

World Vision (bi-m), nondenom., Terry Madison, 919 W. Huntington Dr., Monrovia, CA 91016. Tel. (818)357-7979

Worship (6/yr.) Cath., R. Kevin Seasoltz, St. John's Abbey, Collegeville, MN 56321. Tel. (612) 363-2011

Your Church (bi-m), undenom., Phyllis Mather Rice, SMS Publications, Inc. 1418 Lake St., Evanston, IL 60201

Youth Ministry Quarterly (q), Luth., Mo. Synod, LeRoy Wilke, 1333 S. Kirkwood Rd., St. Louis, MO 63122. Tel. (314)965-9000

Zion's Herald (m), U. Meth., Ann Whiting, The United Methodist Center, 566 Commonwealth Ave., Boston, MA 02215. Tel. (617) 266-9038

14. RELIGIOUS PERIODICALS IN CANADA

The religious periodicals below constitute a basic core of important newspapers, journals, and periodicals circulated in Canada. For additional publications treating religion and religious affairs in Canada, the reader should check the denominational directories in this **Yearbook** in Directory 4, "Religious Bodies in Canada." Details on other religious periodicals circulating in Canada can also be found in Directory 3, "Religious Bodies in the United States" in this **Yearbook.**

Each entry generally appears in this order: title of periodical, frequency of publication, religious affiliation, editor's name, address, and telephone number.

Action (m), Pent. Assem. of Canada, The Overseas Mission Dept., 10 Overlea Blvd., Toronto, Ontario M4H 1A5. Tel. (416) 425-1010

Advance (q), Assoc. Gospel Chs., Wayne Foster, 8 Silver St., Paris, Ontario N3L 1T6. Tel. (519)442-6220

ALbERTa, The, Bapt. Gen. Conf., Rev. Virgil Olson, #4, 9825-44 Ave, Edmonton, Alberta T6E 5E3. Tel. (403) 438-9126

Anglican, The (10/yr.), Debbie Dimmick, 135 Adelaide St., E., Toronto, Ontario M5C 1L8. Tel. (416)363-6021

Anglican Journal/Journal Anglican (m), Ang. Ch. of Canada, Vianney Carrière, 600 Jarvis St., Toronto, Ontario M4Y 2J6. Tel. (416) 924-9192

Anglican Magazine: Living Message (7/yr.), Ang. Ch. of Can., John Bird, 600 Jarvis St., Toronto, Ontario M4Y 2J6. Tel. (416) 924-9192

ARC (2/yr), Fac. of Rel. Stud., McGill Univ., 3520 University St., Montreal, Quebec H3A 2A7. Tel. (514) 398-4121

Atlantic Baptist, The (m), Un. Bapt. Conv. of the Atlantic Provinces, Michael Lipe, Box 756, Kentville, Nova Scotia B4N 3X9. Tel. (902)678-6868

Atlantic Wesleyan (m), Wes. Ch., Rev. Ray E. Barnwell, Sr., Box 20, Sussex, New Brunswick E0E 1P0. Tel. (506) 433-1007

B. C. Fellowship Baptist (m), Fellowship of Reg. Bapt. Chs. of B. C., Gordon Reeve, 1420 E. 2nd Ave., Vancouver, British Columbia V5N 5L9. Tel. (604) 255-5471

Bible Tidings (q), Canadian Luth. Bible Inst., 4837-52A, Camrose, Alberta T4V 1W5. Tel. (403)672-4454

Briarcrest Echo, The, (q), Larry Hamm, Briarcrest Bible College, Caronport, Saskatchewan S0H 0S0. Tel. (306)756-3200

British Columbia Catholic, The (w), Cath., Vincent J. Hawkswell, 150 Robson St., Vancouver, British Columbia V6B 2A7. Tel. (604) 683-0281

Bulletin national de liturgie (See: Liturgie, Foi et Culture)

Cahiers de Josephologie (2/yr), Cath., Roland Gauthier, Centre de recherche, 3800 Ch. Reine-Marie, Montréal, Québec H3V 1H6. Tel. (514)733-8211

Cahiers de Spiritualité Ignatienne (q), Cath., Centre de Spiritualité Ignatienne, 2370 Rue Nicolas-Pinel, Ste. Foy, Québec G1V 4L6. Tel. (418)653-6353

Caledonia Times (10/yr.) Bill Graham, Ang. Ch. of Canada, Box 339, Burns Lake, British Columbia V0J 1E0

Calvinist-Contact (w), Ref., Bert Witvoet, 261 Martindale Rd., Unit 4, St. Catharines, Ontario L2W 1A1. Tel. (416) 682-8311

Campus News: Western Pentecostal Bible College (4/yr), West. Pent. Bible College, Box 1000, Clayburn, British Columbia V0X 1E0

Canada Armenian Press (q), Y. Sarmazian, 42 Glenforest Rd., Toronto, Ontario M4N 1Z8. Tel. (416) 485-4336

Canada Lutheran, The (11/yr), Ev. Luth. Ch. in Canada, Ferdy Baglo, 1512 St. James St., Winnipeg, Manitoba R3H 0L2. Tel. (204)786-6707

Canadian Adventist Messenger (12/yr), Seventh-day Adv. Ch. in Canada, Maracle Press, 1156 King St. E., Oshawa, Ontario L1H 7N4. Tel. (416)723-3438

Canadian Baptist, The (m), Bapt. Conv. of Ontario and Quebec, Bapt. Un. of West. Canada and Canadian Bapt. Fed., Larry Matthews, 217 St. George St., Toronto, Ontario M5R 2M2. Tel. (416)922-5163

Canadian Bible Society Quarterly Newsletter (q), Floyd Babcock, 10 Carnforth, Toronto, Ontario M4A 2S4. Tel. (416)757-4171

Canadian Buddhist (m), Buddhist Chs. of Canada, 220 Jackson Ave., Vancouver, British Columbia V6A 3B3. Tel. (603) 253-7033

Canadian Challenge (a), Foursquare Gospel Church of Canada, #200-3965 Kingsway, Burnaby, British Columbia V5H 1Y7

Canadian Council of Churches News Bulletin/Bulletin de nouvelles du Conseil canadien des Eglises (q), Canadian Council of Churches, 40 St. Clair Ave. E., Toronto, Ontario M4T 1M9. Tel. (416)921-4152

Canadian Disciple (q), Chr. Ch. (Disc. of Chr.) Raymond A. Cuthbert, 240 Home St., Winnipeg, Manitoba R3G 1X3. Tel. (204)783-5881

Canadian Ecumenical News (5/yr.), Jim Pence, 1410 W. 12th Ave., Vancouver, British Columbia V6H 1M8. Tel. (604)736-1613

Canadian Foursquare Challenge, Foursquare Gospel Ch. of Can., #200-3965 Kingsway, Burnaby, British Columbia V5H 1Y7

Canadian Friend, The, The Canadian Yearly Mtg. of the Rel. Soc. of Friends, Dorothy Parshall, Gen. Del., Bancroft, Ontario K0L 1CO.

Canadian Lutheran (bi-m), Frances A. Wershler, Luth Ch. Canada, Box 163, Stn. A., Winnipeg, Manitoba R3K 2A1. Tel. (204)832-0123

Canadian Trumpeter Canada-West, Ch. of God of Prophecy in Canada, John and Ruth Doroshuk, Box 952, Strathmore, Alberta T0J 3H0

Candle, The (m), Cath., Velma Brown, 2-B John St., Dartmouth, Nova Scotia B3A 1L4

Caravan (q), CCCB, Joanne Chafe, 90 Parent Ave., Ottawa, Ontario K1N 7B1. Tel. (613)236-9461

Catalyst (8/yr.), Citizens for Public Justice, Virginia

234

Smith, 229 College St., #311, Toronto, Ontario M5T 1R4. Tel. (416) 979-2443

Catholic New Times (bi-w), Cath., Frances Ryan, 80 Sackville St., Toronto, Ontario M5A 3E5. Tel. (416) 361-0761

Catholic Register, The (w), Cath., Rosemary McCracken, 67 Bond St., Toronto, Ontario M5B 1X6. Tel. (416) 362-6822

Catholic Times, The, (10/yr), Cath., Leo MacGillivray, 2005 St. Marc St., Montreal, Quebec H3H 2G8. Tel. (514)937-2301

Central Canada Clarion (bi-m), Wes. Ch., W. W. Jewell, 3 Applewood Dr., Ste. 102, Belleville, Ontario K8P 4E3

Channels (q), Renewal Fellowship, Presby. Ch. in Canada, J. H. (Hans) Kouwenberg, 2130 Wesbrook Mall, Vancouver, British Columbia V6T 1W6. Tel. (604)224-3245

China and Ourselves (q), Ecum., Canada China Prog., 40 St. Clair Ave. E., Toronto, Ontario M4T 1M9. Tel. (416)921-4152

Church of God Beacon (m), Ch. of God (Cleveland, Tenn.), P.O. Box 2036, Bramalea, Ontario L6T 3S3. Tel. (416)793-2213

Clarion (bi-w), Can. and Amer. Ref. Chs., One Beghin Ave., Winnipeg, Manitoba R2J 3X5

College Bulletin (q), Menn. Breth. Bible College, 1-169 Riverton Ave., Winnipeg, Manitoba R2L 2E5. Tel. (204)669-6575.

Communauté Chrétienne (6/yr), unaffil., Gilles Thibault, Institut de pastorale, 2715, chemin de la Côte Sainte-Catherine, Montréal, Québec H3T 1B6. Tel. (514) 739-9797

Companion Magazine (m), Conv. Franciscan Friars, Fr. Philip Kelly, P. O. Box 535, Stn.F, Toronto, Ontario M4Y 2L8. Tel. (416)924-6349

Communicator, The (4/yr) Assoc. of R.C. Communicators of Can., Ron Pickersgill, Box 2400, London, Ontario N6A 4G3. Tel. (519)439-7211

Connexions (4/yr), Ulli Dremer, 427 Bloor St. W., Toronto, Ontario M5S 1X7. Tel. (416)960-3903

Consensus: A Canadian Lutheran Journal of Theology (bi-a), Luth., Saskatoon Luth. Theol. Sem. and Waterloo Luth. Sem., 75 University Ave. W., Waterloo, Ontario N2L 3C5

Contact, The, Menn. Breth., Bethany Bible Institute, Box 160, Hepburn, Saskatchewan S0K 1Z0. Tel. (306)947-2175

Continental Reflections (bi-m), Continental Mission Inc., Box 98, Thompson, Manitoba R8N 1M9

Covenant Messenger, The (m), Evan. Cov. Ch. of Canada, Donna Wilson, 245 21st St. E., Prince Albert, Saskatchewan S6V 6Z1

Credo (French m), Église unie du Canada (United Church of Canada), Gérard Gautier, 3480 Boul. Décarie, Montréal, Québec H4A 3J5. Tél. (514)486-9213

Crosstalk (10/yr), Ang. Ch. of Can., W. A. Gilbert, 71 Bronson Ave., Ottawa, Ontario K1R 6G6. Tel. (613)233-6271

Crusader, The (2/yr), Ang. Ch. of Canada, Capt. W. Marshall, 397 Brunswick Ave., Toronto, Ontario M5R 2Z2. Tel. (416)924-9279

Crux (q), Donald Lewis, Regent College, 2130 Wesbrook Mall, Vancouver, British Columbia V6T 1W6

Currents (q), Canada Asia Working Group, 11 Madison Ave., Toronto, Ontario M5R 2S2. Tel. (416)921-5626

Dimanche et fête (6/yr), Cath., 1073 boul. St-Cyrille ouest, Sillery, Québec G1S 4R5. Tél. (418)688-1211

Discover the Bible (w), Cath., Walter Bedard, Archdiocese of Montreal Bible Center, 2065 Sherbrooke St. W., Montreal, Quebec H3H 1G6. Tel. (514)931-7311

Ecumenism/Oecuménisme, (q), Thomas Ryan, Canadian Centre for Ecumenism, 2065 Sherbrooke St. W., Montreal, Quebec H3H 1G6. Tel. (514)937-9176

Educational Ideabank (q), Menn. Br., Christian Education Coord., Christian Education Office of Mennonite Brethren Churches, 3-169 Riverton Ave., Winnipeg, Manitoba R2L 2E5

L'Eglise Canadienne (bi-m), Cath., Rolande Parrot, 1073, boulevard Saint-Cyrille ouest, Québec, Québec G1S 4R5. Tél. (418)681-8109

Eglise et Théologie: A Review of the Faculty of Theology, St. Paul University, (3/yr bilingual), Cath., Léo Laberge, 223 Main St. Ottawa, Ontario K1S 1C4

EMMC Recorder (m), Menn., Gladys Penner, Evangelical Mennonite Mission Conference, Box 126, Winnipeg, Manitoba R3C 2G1

End Times' Messenger (11/yr), Apost. Ch. of Pent. of Canada, 1. W. Ellis, 105, 807 Manning Rd. N.E., Calgary, Alberta T2E 7M9

Enterprise (q), Bapt., Frank Byrne, Canadian Baptist Overseas Mission Board, 7185 Millcreek Dr., Mississauga, Ontario L5N 5R4. Tel. (416)922-5163

Esprit (bi-m), Év. Luth. Women, Gwen Hawkins, Box 19, R.R. #1, Madeira Park, British Columbia VON 2H0. Tel. (604)883-2778

Evangelical Baptist (m), Bapt., R. W. Lawson, Fell. of Evang. Bapt. Churches in Canada, 3034 Bayview Ave., Willowdale, Ontario M2N 6J5. Tel. (416)223-8696

Exchange (3/yr), Un. Ch. of Canada, Lynda Newmarch, Div. of Mission in Canada, 85 St. Clair Ave. E., Toronto, Ontario M4T 1M8. Tel. (416)925-5931

Faith Today (bi-m), Evan. Fell. of Canada, Brian C. Stiller, Box 8800, Sta. B, Willowdale, Ontario M2K 2R6. Tel. (416)479-5885

Fish Eye Lens (4/yr), The Ecumenical Forum of Canada, 11 Madison Ave., Toronto, Ontario M5R 2S2. Tel. (416)924-9351

Focus on Social Justice (4/yr), Cath., Canadian Religious Conference-Ontario, 101-146 Laird Dr., Toronto, Ontario M4G 3V7. Tel. (416) 424-4664

For the Record, Luth., John M. Cobb, Canadian Luth. Hist. Assn., Box 86, Gen. Del., Wildwood, Alberta T0E 2M0

Free Methodist Herald, The (m), Free Meth., D. G. Bastian, 69 Browning Ave., Toronto, Ontario M4K 1W1. Tel. (416)463-4536

Gardner Insights and Alumni News (q), Ch. of God in West. Canada, 4704 55th St., Camrose, Alberta T4V 2B6

Glad Tidings (10/yr), Women's Miss. Soc., Presby. Ch. in Can., L. June Stevenson, 50 Wynford Dr., Rm. 100, Don Mills, Ontario M3C 1J7. Tel. (416)441-2840

Global Village Voice (q), Cath., Canadian Catholic

Organization for Development and Peace, Jack J. Panozzo, 3028 Dan forth Ave., Toronto, Ontario M4C 1N2. Tel. (416) 698-7770

Good Tidings (m), Pent. Assemb. of Nfld., Roy D. King, 57 Thorburn Rd., P.O. Box 8895, Stn.A., St. John's, Newfoundland A1B 3T2

Gospel Contact, The (10/yr), Ch. of God in West. Canada, Gospel Contact Press, 5005-49th St., Camrose, Alberta T4V 1N5

Gospel Herald (m), Chs. of Christ, Eugene C. Perry, Box 94, Beamsville, Ontario L0R 1B0

Gospel Standard, The (m), Fundamental, Perry F. Rockwood, Box 1660, Halifax, Nova Scotia B3J 3A1. Tel. (902)423-5540

Gospel Witness, The (22/yr.), Reg. Bapt., Jarvis St. Baptist Church, 130 Gerrard St. E., Toronto, Ontario M5A 3T4

Grail (q), Ecum., Univ. of St. Jerome's Col., Michael Higgins, Waterloo, Ontario N2L 3G3. Tel. (519)884-8110

Guide, The (9/yr.), Edward Vanderkloet, Christian Labour Association of Canada, 5920 Atlantic Dr., Mississauga, Ontario L4W 1N6. Tel. (416)670-7383

His Dominion (4/yr), Chr. & Miss. All., Franklin Pyles, Faculty of Canadian Theological Seminary, 4400 4th Ave., Regina Saskatchewan S4T 0H8. Tel. (306) 545-1515

Huron Church News (10/yr). Ang. Ch. of Canada, Geoffrey Dibbs, 4-220 Dundas St., London, Ontario N6A 1H3. Tel. (519)434-6893

Intercom (q), Fell. of Evang. Bapt. Churches in Canada, R. W. Lawson, 3034 Bayview Ave., Willowdale, Ontario M2N 6J5. Tel. (416)223-8696

Insight: A Resource for Adult Religious Education, CCCB, Joanne Chafe, 90 Parent Ave., Ottawa, Ontario K1N 7B1. Tel. (613) 236-9461

Insight●Insound●Intouch, (6/yr, q,q), John Milton Soc., Muriel Israel, 40 St. Clair Ave., E. Ste. 202, Toronto, Ontario M4T 1M9. Tel. (416)960-3953

Iskra (bi-w), Un. of Spiritual Communities in Christ (Orth. Doukhobors in Canada), D.E. (Jim) Popoff, Box 760, Grand Forks, British Columbia V0H 1H0

Journal of the Canadian Church Historical Society (2/yr), Ang., c/o The General Synod Archives, Anglican Church of Canada, 600 Jarvis St., Toronto, Ontario M4Y 2J6. Tel. (416)924-9192

Kerigma (2/yr), Cath., (bilingual) Martin Roberge, Institute of Mission Studies, Saint Paul Univ., 223 Main, Ottawa, Ontario K1S 1C4

Laval Théologique et Philosophique (3/yr), Cath., René-Michel Roberge, Pavillon Félix-Antoine Savard, Université Laval, Québec, Québec G1K 7P4 Tel. (418) 656-3576

Liberation (formerly Encounter) (bi-m), Ken Campbell, Box 100, Milton, Ontario L9T 2Y3. Tel. (416)878-8461

Liturgie, Foi et Culture (Bulletin national de liturgie), (3/yr.), Cath., Office national de liturgie, 3530, rue Adam, Montréal, Québec H1W 1Y8

Mandate (6/yr), Un. Ch. of Canada, Rebekah Chevalier, Division of Communication, The United Church of Canada, 85 St. Clair Ave. E., Toronto, Ontario M4T 1M8 Tel. (416) 925-5931

Maple Leaf Communique Canada-East, Ch. of God of Prophecy, Richard E. Davis, P.O. Box 457, Brampton, Ontario L6V 2L4. Tel. (416)843-2379

Marketplace, The: A Magazine for Christians in Business (m), Menn., Wally Kroeker, 402-280 Smith St., Winnipeg, Manitoba R3C 1K2. Tel. (204)944-1995

Martyrs' Shrine Message (m), Cath., Martyrs' Shrine, Midland, Ontario L4R 4K5. Tel. (416)526-3788

MCC Contact (m), Mennonite Central Committee Canada, 134 Plaza Dr., Winnipeg, Manitoba R3T 5K9. Tel. (204)261-6381

Mennonite, The, (bi-w), Gen. Conf. Menn., Muriel T. Stackley Box 347, 722 Main, Newton, KS 67114. Tel. (316)283-5100

Mennonite Brethren Communications Expression (q), Dan Block, Mennonite Brethren Communications, Box 2, Sta. F, Winnipeg, Manitoba R2L 2A5. Tel. (214) 667-9576

Mennonite Brethren Herald (bi-w), Menn. Breth. Ch., Ron Geddert, 3-169 Riverton Ave., Winnipeg, Manitoba R2L 2E5. Tel. (204)669-6575

Mennonite Historian (q) Menn. Breth. Hist. Soc. and Menn. Heritage Centre, Conf. of Menn. in Canada, Kenneth Reddig, Center for Mennonite Brethren Studies in Canada, 169 Riverton Ave., Winnipeg, Manitoba R2L 2E5

Mennonite Mirror (10/yr), Inter-Menn., Ruth Vogt, Mennonite Literary Society, 207-1317A Portage Ave., Winnipeg, Manitoba R3G 0V3. Tel. (204)786-2289

Mennonite Reporter (bi-w), Inter-Menn., Ron Rempel, 3 - 312 Marsland Dr., Waterloo, Ontario N2J 3Z1. Tel. (519)884-3810

Die Mennonitische Post (bi-m), Inter-Menn., Abe Warkentin, Box 1120, Steinbach, Manitoba R0A 2A0. Tel. (204)326-6790

Mennonitische Rundschau (German bi-w), Mennonite Brethren, Lorina Marsch, 159 Henderson Hwy., Winnipeg, Manitoba R2L 1L4

Messenger, The (bi-w), Evang. Menn. Conf., Menno Hamm, Board of Education and Publication, Box 1268, Steinbach, Manitoba R0A 2A0

Messenger (Of the Sacred Heart) (m), Cath., F. J. Power, Apostleship of Prayer, 661 Greenwood Ave., Toronto, Ontario M4J 4B3. Tel. (416)466-1195

Missions Magazine (m), Ply. Br., 27 Charles St. E., Toronto, Ontario M4Y 1R9. Tel. (416)920-4391

Missions Today (bi-m), Cath., Prop. of Faith, Bernard Prince, 3329 Danforth Ave., Scarborough, Ontario M1L 1C5. Tel. (416)699-7077

Monitor, The (m), Cath., Patrick J. Kennedy, P.O. Box 986, St. John's, Newfoundland A1C 5M3. Tel. (709)739-6553

Montreal Churchman (m), Ang. Ch. of Can., David Yarrow, Cathedral Pl., 1444 Union Ave., Montréal, Québec H3B 2B8. Tel. (514)879-1722

MPE News (2/yr.), Un. Ch. of Can., Jim Taylor, Div of Ministry Personnel and Edu., 85 St. Clair Ave. E., Toronto, Ontario M4T 1M8. Tel. (416)925-5931

Music Maker, The (q), Menn. Br., Chr. Edu. Coordinator, Christian Education Office, Canadian Conference of Mennonite Brethren Churches, 3-169 Riverton Ave., Winnipeg, Manitoba R2L 2E5

National Bulletin on Liturgy (4/yr), Cath., J. Frank Henderson, Canadian Conference of Catholic Bishops (Concacan) Publications Service, 90 Parent Ave., Ottawa, Ontario K1N 7B1. Tel. (613)236-9461

Newfoundland Churchmen (m), Ang. Ch. of Canada, Hollis Hiscock, 26 Empire Ave., St. John's, Newfoundland A1C 3E6. Tel. (709)579-0614

New Freeman, The (w), Cath., Robert G. Merzetti, One Bayard Dr., Saint John, New Brunswick E2L 3L5. Tel. (506)632-9226

Newsletter of the Diocese of London (q), Cath., Ron Pickersgill, P. O. Box 2400, London, Ontario N6A 4G3. Tel. (519)439-7211

News & Views (3/yr), Foursquare Gospel Ch. of Canada, #200-3965 Kingsway, V5H 1Y7. Burnaby, British Columbia V5H 1Y7

News of Quebec (q), Breth., Richard Strout, P.O. Box 1054, Sherbrooke, Quebec. Tel. (819)837-2725

Nor Serount (m, in Armenian and English), Holy Trinity Armenian Church of Toronto, Diocese of Canada, 20 Progress Ct., Scarborough, Ontario M1G 3T5

Northland, The (q), Ang. Ch. of Can., Mrs. M. Lawrence, P. O. Box 830 Schumacher, Ontario P0N 1G0. Tel. (705)267-4833

Northwest Canada Echoes (m), Evang. Ch. in Canada, A. W. Riegel, 2805 - 13th Ave., S.E., Medicine Hat, Alberta T1A 3R1. Tel. (403)527-4101

Ontario Messenger (m), Ch. of God (Anderson, Ind.), Paul Kilburn, 85 Emmett Ave., #1109, Toronto, Ontario M6M 5A2

Our Diocese, Cath., Magdalene O'Brien, 8 A Church Rd., Grand Falls, Newfoundland A2A 2J8. Tel. (709)489-4019

Pastoral Studies/Etudes pastoral (1/yr.) bilingual, Cath. Maureen Slattery, Inst. of Pastoral Studies, Saint Paul Univ., 223 Main, Ottawa, Ontario K1S 1C4

Pentecostal Testimony (m), Pent. Assemblies of Canada, R. J. Skinner, 10 Overlea Blvd., Toronto, Ontario M4H 1A5. Tel. (416)425-1010

Peoples' Magazine, The, People's Church, Paul B. Smith, 374 Sheppard Ave. E., Toronto, Ontario M2N 3B6. Tel. (416)222-3341

Pioneer Christian Monthly (m), Ref. Ch. in Am., Reformed Church Center, R. R. #4, Cambridge, Ontario N1R 5S5. Tel. (519)623-4860

PMC: The Practice of Ministry in Canada (5/yr.), Jim Taylor, PMC Board, 60 St. Clair Ave. E., Ste. 500, Toronto, Ontario M4T IN5. Tel. (416)928-3223

Prairie Messenger (w), Cath., Art B. Babych, Box 190, Muenster, Saskatchewan S0K 2Y0. Tel. (306)682-5215

Presbyterian Message, The (10/yr), Atlantic Miss. Soc., Mrs. Floyd Carter, Kouchibouguac, New Brunswick EOA 2AO. Tel. (506)876-4379

Presbyterian Record (m), John Congram, Presby. Ch. in Canada, 50 Wynford Dr., Don Mills, Ontario M3C 1J7. Tel. (416)441-1111

Reach (bi-m), Pent. Assemb. of Nfld., R. H. Dewling, 57 Thorburn Rd., St. John's, Newfoundland A1B 3N4

Regent College Bulletin (q), Regent College, 2130 Wesbrook Mall, Vancouver, British Columbia V6T 1W6

Relations (m), Cath., Compagnie de Jésus, Giselle Turcot, 8100 boul. St. Laurent, Montréal, Québec H2P 2L9. Tel. (514) 387-2541

Religious Studies amd Theology (3/yr), P. Joseph Cahill, University of Alberta, Religious Studies, Edmonton, Alberta T6G 2E5. Tel. (403)432-2173.

Revival Fellowship (m), interdenom., Canadian Revival Fellowship, Box 584, Regina, Saskatchewan S4P 3A3. Tel. (306)522-3685

Rivers of Living Water (q), interdenom., Nipawin Bible Institute, Box 1986, Nipawin, Saskatchewan S0E 1E0. Tel. (306)862-3651

Rupert's Land News (10/yr), Ang. Ch. of Can., Anita Schmidt, 935 Nesbitt Bay, Winnipeg, Manitoba R3T 1W6. Tel. (214)453-6130

Saskatchewan Anglican (10/yr), Ang. Ch. of Can., W. Patrick Tomalin, 1501 College Ave., Regina, Saskatchewan S4P 1B8. Tel. (316)522-1608

Scarboro Missions (11/yr), Scarboro For. Miss. Soc., G. Curry, 2685 Kingston Rd., Scarborough, Ontario M1M 1M4. Tel. (416)261-7135

Science et Esprit (3/yr), Cath., Science et Esprit, 5605 avenue Decelles, Montréal, Québec H3T 1W4

Servant, The (bi-m), Inter-Menn., Gordon Daman, Steinbach Bible College, Box 1420, Steinbach, Manitoba R0A 2A0

Servant Magazine, Interdenom., Phil Callaway, Prairie Bible Inst., Three Hills, Alberta TOM 2AO. Tel. (403)443-5511

Shantyman, The (bi-m), Non-denom., Arthur C. Dixon, 2110 Argentia Rd., Ste. 301, Mississauga, Ontario L5N 2K7. Tel. (416)821-1175

Shield and Sword, Fndn. for the Edification of the Reformed Faith, P. O. Box 188, Smithville, Ontario LOR 2AO

Small Voice, The (q), indep., The United Church Renewal Fellowship, 240 Bayview Dr., Unit 5, Barrie, Ontario L4N 4Y8

Solidarités (5/yr), Cath., Francois-A. Thuot, 2111 rue Centre, Montréal, Québec H3K 1J5. Tel. (514) 932-5136

Stevite, The (q), Un. Ch. of Canada, St. Stephen's College, Graduate and Continuing Theological Education for Clergy and Laity, University of Alberta Campus, Edmonton, Alberta T6G 2J6. Tel. (403) 439-7311

Studia Canonica (semi-a), Cath., Francis G. Morrisey, Faculty of Canon Law, Saint Paul Univ., 223 Main St., Ottawa, Ontario K1S 1C4. Tel. (613)236-1393

SR: Studies in Religion: Sciences religieuses (q), Tom Sinclair-Faulkner, c/o Wilfrid Laurier University Press, Waterloo, Ontario N2L 3C5

Theodolite: A Journal of Christian Thought and Practice (2/yr), Bapt., John T. Rook, McMaster Divinity College, Hamilton, Ontario L8S 4K1. Tel. (416)525-9140, x4401

Tidings, Cong. Chr. Chrs. in Ontario. Claire Hart, 44 Virginia Beach Blvd., Gen. Del., Sutton West, Ontario LOE 1RO

Tidings (10/yr), Un. Bapt. Woman's Missy. Un. of the Atlantic Prov., H. May Bartlett, 225 Massey St., Fredericton, New Brunswick E3B 2Z5. Tel. (506)455-9674

Topic (m), Ang. Dioc. of New Westminster, Lorie Chortyk, #302-814 Richards St., Vancouver, British Columbia V6B 3A7. Tel. (604)684-6306

Touchstone (3/yr), A. M. Watts, Faculty of Theology, University of Winnipeg, Winnipeg, Manitoba R3B 2E9. Tel. (204)786-9390

Truth on Fire (bi-m), Bible Holiness Movement, W. H. Wakefield, Box 223, Sta. A, Vancouver, British Columbia V6C 2M3. Tel. (604)498-3895

United Church Observer (m), Un. Ch. of Canada, 85 St. Clair Ave. E., Toronto, Ontario M4T 1M8. Tel. (416)960-8500

Update (q), multidenom., Wm. J. McRae, Ontario Bible College and Theological Seminary, 25 Ballyconnor Ct., Willowdale, Ontario M2M 4B3. Tel. (416)226-6380

Update/A Jour (2/yr). Ch. Cncl. on Justice and Corrections, Vern Redekop, 507 Bank St., Ottawa, Ontario K2P 1Z5. Tel. (613)563-1688

La Vie Chrétienne (French, m), Presby. Ch. in Canada, Jean Porret, 2302 Goyer, Montréal, Québec H3S 1G9. Tel. (514)737-4168

La Vie des Communautés religieuses (5/yr), Cath., Laurent Boisvert, 5750 boulevard Rosemont, Montréal, Québec H1T 2H2

La Vie Liturgique (10/yr), Cath., 1073 boul. Saint-Cyrille ouest, Sillery, Québec G1S 4R5. Tél. (418)688-1211

Visnyk (semi-m), Ukrainian Orthodox Ch. of Canada, 9 St. John's Ave., Winnipeg, Manitoba R2W 1G8

Voce Evangelica (q), Italian Pent. Ch. of Canada, Joseph Manafo and Daniel Ippolito, P.O. Box 599, Station Beaubien, Montreal, Quebec H2G 3E2. Tel. (514) 593-1944 or (416)766-6692.

War Cry, The (w), Salv. Army in Canada and Bermuda, Maj. Maxwell Ryan, 455 N. Service Rd. E., Oakville, Ontario L6H 1A5. Tel. (416)845-9235

Way, The (q), Faith at Work, (Canada) 29 Albion St., Belleville, Ontario K8N 3R7. Tel. (613)968-7409.

Wesleyan Advocate (m), Wes. Ch., Wayne Caldwell, P.O. Box 50434, Indianapolis, IN 46950

Western Catholic Reporter (w), Cath., Marjorie Bentley, Great Western Press, 10562 - 109 St., Edmonton, Alberta T5H 3B2. Tel. (403) 420-1330

Western Tract News (bi-m), interdenom. Western Tract Mission, 401 - 33rd St. W., Saskatoon, Saskatchewan S7L 0V5

Word Alive (5/yr), Interdenon., Wycliffe Bible Translators of Canada, Box 3068, Stn. B., Calgary, Alberta T2M 4L6. Tel. (403) 250-5411

World Wind/World View (3/yr), Un. Ch. of Can., Rebekah Chevalier, 85 St. Clair Ave., E., Toronto, Ontario M4T 1M8. Tel. (416)925-5931

Worth Reading (bi-m), Ch. of God in Can., 4704 - 55th St., Camrose, Alberta T4V 2B6

Youth Incites (q), Menn. Br., A. Ben Thiessen, Christian Education Coord., Chr. Edu. Ofc., Canadian Conference of Mennonite Brethren Churches, 3-169 Riverton Ave., Winnipeg, Manitoba R2L 2E5

15. UNITED STATES SERVICE AGENCIES: SOCIAL, CIVIC, RELIGIOUS

The Yearbook of American and Canadian Churches offers the following selected list of Service Agencies for two purposes. The first purpose is to direct attention to a number of major agencies which can provide resources of information and service to the churches. No attempt is made to produce a complete listing of such agencies. The second purpose is to illustrate the types of resources that are available. There are many agencies providing services which can be of assistance to local, regional or national church groups. It is suggested that a valuable tool in locating such service agencies is *The Encyclopedia of Associations*, Vol. I, *National Organizations of the United States*. The organizations are listed in Parts 1 and 2, and Part 3 is a name and keyword index. It is published by Gale Research Co., Book Tower, Detroit, Michigan 48226.

ADRIS (Association for the Development of Religious Information Systems): Dept. of Social & Cultural Sciences, Marquette Univ., Milwaukee, WI 53233. Tel. (414)288-6838. Coordinator, Dr. David O. Moberg; Ed., Rev. Richard F. Smith, Dept. of Theology, Fordham Univ., Bronx, NY 10458. Tel. (212)579-2400
Periodical: ADRIS Newsletter.

Alban Institute: 4125 Nebraska Ave. N.W., Washington, DC 20016. Tel. (202)244-7320. Exec. Dir., Loren B. Mead.
Periodical: Action Information (6/yr)

American Academy of Political and Social Science, The: 3937 Chestnut St., Philadelphia, PA 19104. Tel. (215)386-4594. Pres., Marvin E. Wolfgang
Periodical: The Annals of the American Academy of Political and Social Science (bi-m)

American Association for Adult and Continuing Education: 1112 Sixteenth St., N.W., Ste. 420, Washington, DC 20036. Tel. (202)463-6333. Exec. Dir., Judith Ann Koloski
Periodicals: Adult Education (4/yr); Lifelong Learning: an Omnibus of Practice and Research (8/yr)

American Association of Bible Colleges: P. O. Box 1523, Fayetteville, AR 72702. Tel. (501)521-8164. Exec. Dir., Randall E. Bell

American Association of Retired Persons: 1909 K St. N.W., Washington, DC 20049. Tel. (202)872-4700. Exec. Dir., Horace Deets
Periodicals: AARP News Bulletin (11/yr.); Modern Maturity (bi-m)

American Civil Liberties Union: 132 West 43rd St., New York, NY 10036. Tel. (212)944-9800. Pres., Norman Dorsen; Exec. Dir., Ira Glasser
Periodical: Civil Liberties (m).

American Council on Alcohol Problems: 3426 Bridgeland Dr., Bridgeton, MO 63044. Tel. (314)739-5944. Curt Scarborough

American Farm Bureau Federation: 225 Touhy Ave., Park Ridge, IL 60068. Washington office, 600 Maryland Ave., S.W., Washington, DC 20024. Pres. and Admin., Dean R. Kleckner; Sec. and Dir., Washington Ofc., John C. Datt.
Periodical: Farm Bureau News(w)

American Federation of Labor and Congress of Industrial Organizations: AFL-CIO Bldg., 815 16th St. N.W., Washington, DC 20006. Pres., Lane Kirkland
Periodicals: News (w)

American Friends Service Committee: 1501 Cherry St., Philadelphia, PA 19102. Tel. (215)241-7000. Clerk, Stephen G. Cary; Exec. Sec., Asia Alderson Bennett.
Periodical: Quaker Service Bulletin (3/yr.)

American Guild of Religious Historiographers: 3500 Fuller, N.E., Grand Rapids, MI 49505. Tel. (616)361-0694. Correspondent, Ms. Jean Heibel.

American Library Association: 50 E. Huron St., Chicago, IL 60611. Tel. (312)944-6780. Exec Dir., Linda Crismond

Periodicals: American Libraries (m except July-Aug. bi-m); Booklist (semi-m); Choice (11/yr.); College and Research Libraries (bi-m); ALA Washington Newsletter (m); Information Technology and Libraries (q); Library Resources and Technical Services (q); RQ: School Library Media Quarterly (q); Journal of Youth Services in Libraries (q)

American Medical Association: 535 N. Dearborn St., Chicago, IL 60610. Tel. (312)645-5000. Exec. Vice-Pres., James H. Sammons, M.D.
Periodicals: The Journal of the American Medical Association (w); The Citation (bi-w); American Medical News (w); Specialty Scientific Journals (m); Legislative Roundup (w); Facets (q)

American Protestant Health Association: 1701 E. Woodfield Rd., Ste. 311, Schaumburg, IL 60173. Tel. (312)240-1010. Pres., David A. Johnson.

American Public Health Association: 1015 15th St., N.W., Washington, DC 20005. Tel. (202)789-5600. Exec. Dir., William H. McBeath, M.D.
Periodical: American Journal of Public Health (m); The Nation's Health (10/yr.)

American Public Welfare Association: 810 First St., N.E. Ste. 500, Washington, DC 20002. Tel. (202)682-0100. Exec. Dir., A. Sidney Johnson, III
Periodicals: Public Welfare (q); This Week in Washington (50/yr); W-Memo. (30-40/yr); Public Welfare Directory (a)

American Red Cross, The: 17th & D Sts., N.W., Washington, DC 20006. Pres., Richard F. Schubert
Periodical: Red Cross News (m)

American Theological Library Association: Office of the Exec. Sec., St. Meinrad School of Theology, St. Meinrad, IN 47577. Pres., H. Eugene McLead; ATLA Exec. Sec., Rev. Simeon Daly, O.S.B.; Preservation Bd. Chair, Rev. John Bollier; Religion Index Board Chair, Sarah Lyons Miller; Dir., Albert Hurd, 820 Church St., 3rd Fl., Evanston, IL 60201

American Waldensian Society, The: Rm. 1850, 475 Riverside Dr., New York, NY 10115. Tel. (212)870-2671. Exec. Dir., Rev. Frank G. Gibson, Jr.
Periodical: Newsletter

Americans United for Separation of Church and State: 8120 Fenton St., Silver Spring, MD 20910. Tel. (301)589-3707. Exec. Dir., Robert L. Maddox; Ed., Joseph L. Conn
Periodical: Church & State (m)

Association of Catholic Diocesan Archivists, The: Diocese of San Diego, P.O. Box 80428. San Diego, CA 92138. Pres., Rev. Edmund Hussy, Archdiocese of Cincinnati, St. Paul Parish, 308 Phillips St., Yellow Spring, OH 45387. Tel. (513)767-7450; Sec.-Treas., Sr. Catherine Louise LaCoste, CSJ, Diocese of San Diego, P. O. Box 80428, San Diego, CA 92138. Tel. (619)574-6383.

Association for Clinical Pastoral Education: 1549 Clairmont Rd., Ste. 103, Decatur, GA 30030. Exec. Dir., Duane F. Parker. Tel. (404)320-1472
Periodical: APCE News (q)

Association of Jewish Chaplains of the Armed Forces: 15 E. 26th St., New York, NY 10010. Tel. (212)532-4949. Pres., Rabbi Jacob J. Greenberg

Association of Theological Schools in the United States and Canada: P.O. Box 130, Vandalia, OH 45377. Tel. (513)898-4654. Pres., Russell H. Dilday, Jr., Southwestern Baptist Theol. Sem., Box 22000, Fort Worth, TX 76122; Exec. Dir., Leon Pacala; Asso. Dirs., David S. Schuller, William L. Baumgaertner and Gail Buchwalter King

Baptist Joint Committee: 200 Maryland Ave., N.E., Washington, DC 20002. Tel. (202)544-4226. Exec. Dir., James M. Dunn
Periodical: Report from the Capital (10/yr.)

Bible Sabbath Association: Fairview, RD 1, Box 222, OK 73737. Tel. (405)227-3200 Exec. Dir., Richard A. Wiedenheft; Sec.-Treas., Lawrence Burrell.
Periodical: The Sabbath Sentinel (m), Richard A. Wiedenheft

B'nai B'rith International: B'nai B'rith Bldg., 1640 Rhode Island Ave., N. W., Washington, DC 20036. Tel. (202)857-6600. Pres., Seymour D. Reich; Exec. Vice-Pres., Thomas Neumann
Periodical: B'nai B'rith International Jewish Monthly

Boy Scouts of America: 1325 Walnut Hill Lane, P. O. Box 152079 Irving TX 75015. Tel. (214)580-2000. Pres., Harold S. Hook, Chief Scout Exec., Ben. H. Love
Periodicals: Scouting Magazine (6/year); Boys' Life (m); Exploring (4/year); BSA Today (q); NCCS Newsletter (Catholic) (q); Hatsofe (Jewish) (q); Scouting Ministry (Protestant) (q); New Trails (Baptist) (q); Scouting Notes (LDS) (q)

Boys Clubs of America: 771 First Ave., New York, NY 10017. Tel. (212)351-5900. Chmn. of Bd., Jeremiah Milbank; Pres., _____.: Nat'l. Dir., Tom Garth
Periodicals: Connections Magazine (q); Annual Report; Bulletin (bi-a)

Bread for the World: 802 Rhode Island Ave. N.E., Washington, DC 20018. Tel. (202)269-0200. Pres., Arthur Simon.
Periodicals: Action Alert Newsletter (m); Bread (q); Leaven (q); Background Papers on Hunger Related Issues (occ.)

Camp Fire Inc.: 4601 Madison Ave., Kansas City, MO 64112, Tel. (816)756-1950. Natl. Exec. Dir., David W. Bahlmann.
Periodical: Camp Fire Leadership (3/yr)

Campus Crusade for Christ International: Arrowhead Springs, San Bernardino, CA 92414. Tel. (714)886-5224. Pres., William R. Bright.
Periodical: Worldwide Challenge (bi-m)

CARE: 660 First Ave., New York, NY 10016, Tel. (212)686-3110. Exec. Dir., Philip Johnston

Carnegie Council on Ethics and International Affairs: 170 E. 64th St., New York, NY 10021. Tel. (212)838-4120. Chpsn., Maurice Spanbach; Vice Chpsn., Mrs. Helen Maguire Muller; Pres., Robert J. Myers
Periodicals: Ethics and International Affairs

Center for Applied Research in the Apostolate (CARA): 3700 Oakview Terr., NE, Washington, DC 20017. Tel. (202)832-2300. Pres., Francis Gillespie

Center for Parish Development: 5407 S. University Ave., Chicago, IL 60615. Tel. (312)752-1596; Genesis Division, 207 E. Buffalo, Ste. 326, Milwaukee, WI 53202. Tel. (414)224-1050. Dir., Paul Dietterich
Periodical: The Center Letter (m)

Christian Camping International (USA): P.O. Box 646, 2100 Manchester, Ste. 605, Wheaton, IL 60189. Tel. (312)462-0300. Dir., John Pearson.
Periodicals: Journal of Christian Camping (bi-m); Official Guide to Christian Camps and Conference Centers

Christian Children's Fund, Inc.: P.O. Box 26511, Richmond, VA 23261. Tel. (804)644-4654. Exec. Dir., Dr. Paul McCleary
Periodicals: Childworld (m); Field Notes (m)

Christian Ministries Management Association: P.O. Box 4638, Diamond Bar, CA 91765. Tel. (714)861-8861. Exec. Dir., Sylvia Nash.
Periodical: Christian Management Report (m)

Church Growth Center: Corunna, IN 46730. Tel. (219)281-2452. Dir., Dr. Kent R. Hunter

Churches' Center for Theology and Public Policy, 4500 Massachusetts Ave., N.W., Washington, DC 20016. Tel. (202)885-9100. Exec. Dir., James A. Nash; Pres., Walter J. Sullivan.
Periodicals: Theology and Public Policy

Committee, The—Witness to Reconciliation, Box 140215, Nashville, TN 37214. Tel. (615)754-8170. Exec. Dir. Will D. Campbell

Congress of National Black Churches: 600 New Hampshire Ave., N.W., Ste. 650, Washington, DC 20037. Tel. (202)333-3060. Chpsn., Dr. Charles William Butler

CONTACT Teleministries USA, Inc.: Pouch A, Harrisburg, PA 17105. Tel. (717)232-3501.

Council for Health and Human Service Ministries, The: 543 College Ave., Lancaster, PA 17603. Tel. (717)299-9945; outside PA 1-800-822-4476. Exec. Dir., J. Robert Achtermann.
Periodicals: Directory of Services (a); The Link (q); President's Newsetter (q); Shoptalk (m); Employment Opportunities (m); CHHSM Report: Papers on Public Policy Issues (2-3 a).

Periodical: Mountain Life and Work (m)

Counselor Association, Inc., The: P. O. Box 1040, Westwood, NJ 07675. Tel. (201)664-8890. Pres., Raymond Barnett Knudsen II.

Credit Union National Association: P.O. Box 431, Madison, WI 53701. Tel. (608)231-4000
Periodicals: Credit Union Magazine (m); Everybody's Money (q); Credit Union Executive (q); Credit Union Manager Newsletter (bi-w); Credit Union Newsletter for Directors (m); Credit Union Newswatch (w).

Evangelical Council for Financial Accountability (ECFA): P.O. Box 17456, Washington, DC 20041. Tel. (703)435-8888. Pres., Arthur C. Borden.

Fellowship of Reconciliation, The: Box 271, Nyack, NY 10960. Tel. (914)358-4601. Exec. Sec., Doug Hostetter.
Periodicals: Fellowship

Foreign Policy Association: 729 Seventh Ave., New York, NY 10019. Tel. (212)764-4050. Pres. and C.E.O., John W. Kiermaier
Periodicals: Headline Series (4/yr.); Great Decisions Book (a)

Friends Committee on National Legislation: 245 Second St., N.E., Washington, DC 20002. Tel. (202)547-6000. Exec. Sec., Edward F. Snyder
Periodical: FCNL Washington Newsletter (11/yr.)

General Federation of Women's Clubs: 1734 N St. N.W., Washington, DC 20036. Tel. (202)347-3168. Pres., Alice C. Donohue
Periodical: GFWC Clubwomen Magazine (bi-m)

Girl Scouts of the U.S.A.: 830 Third Ave., New York, NY 10022. Tel. (212)940-7500. Pres., Mrs. Betty F. Pilsbury; Nat'l. Exec. Dir., Mrs. Frances R. Hesselbein
Periodicals: Girl Scout Leader (4/yr)

Glenmary Research Center: 750 Piedmont Ave., N.E., Atlanta, GA 30308. Tel. (404)876-6518. Dir., Lou McNeil

Healing Community: 521 Harrison Ave., Claremont, CA 91711. Dir., Dr. Harold Wilke.
Periodical: The Caring Congregation.

Institute of International Education: 809 United Nations Plaza, New York, NY 10017. Tel. (212)883-8200. Pres., Richard M. Krasno

Institutes of Religion and Health: 3 W. 29th St., New York, NY 10001. Tel. (212)725-7850. Pres., Roger W. Plantikow
Periodical: Journal of Religion and Health (q)

Interfaith Forum on Religion, Art and Architecture: 1913 Architects Bldg., Philadelphia, PA 19103, Tel. (215)568-0960. Dir., Henry Jung.
Periodicals: Newsletter (q.), Faith and Forum (semi-a)

Japan International Christian University Foundation, Inc., The: 475 Riverside Dr., Rm. 1848, New York, NY 10115. Tel. (212)870-2893. Pres., David H. C. Read; Chmn, Exec. Comm., Raymond W. Beaver; Exec. Dir., Betty Gray

John Milton Society for the Blind: A Worldwide Ministry, 475 Riverside Dr., Rm. 455, New York, NY 10115. Tel. (212)870-3335. Exec. Dir., Richard R. Preston; Ed., Pam Toplisky
Periodicals: (Braille); John Milton Magazine, for Adults (m); Discovery magazine for youth, (m); John Milton Adult Lessons Quarterly (q)
Periodicals (recorded): Talking Book Magazine (bi-m, 8rpm); Adult Lessons (q, 8rpm).
Periodicals (large type): John Milton Magazine-Large Type Edition (m); Supplements in Feb. and Oct. for World Day of Prayer, and World Community Day (a)
All publications free on request to persons who cannot see to read ordinary printed matter

LAOS/Partners for Global Justice: 1109 E. Cherokee Ave., Ocean Springs, MS 39564. Exec. Dir., Kathy Penrose; Educ. Dir., Jean Martensen
Periodicals: Conversations (4/yr.); Newsletter

Laymen's National Bible Association: 475 Riverside Dr., Ste. 439, New York, NY 10115. Tel., (212)870-3387. Pres., Victor W. Eimicke; Exec. Dir., Reuben Gums
Periodical: Newsletter (q); Annual Report

League of Women Voters of the U.S.: 1730 M St., N.W., Washington, DC 20036. Tel. (202)429-1965. Pres., Nancy M. Neuman
Periodical: The National Voter (bi-m); Report From the Hill (bi-m)

Lutheran Church Library Association: 122 West Franklin Ave., Minneapolis, MN 55404. Tel. (612)870-3623. Exec. Dir., Wilma W. Jensen.
Periodicals: Lutheran Libraries (q)

Lutheran Educational Conference of North America: 122 C St., NW, Ste. 300, Washington, DC 20001. Tel. (202)783-7501. Exec. Dir., Don Stoike
Periodical: Lutheran Higher Education Directory (a)

Lutheran Immigration and Refugee Service: 360 Park Ave. S., New York, NY 10010. Tel. (212)532-6350. Exec. Dir., Donald H. Larsen.
Periodical: LIRS Bulletin (2/yr.)

Lutheran Resources Commission: 5 Thomas Circle, N.W., Washington, DC 20005. Tel. (202)667-9844. Chpsn., Charles Miller ELCA; Vice-Chpsn., Eugene Linse, LC-MS; Sec., Art Lewis ELCA; Treas., Floyd E. Anderson; Exec. Dir., Lloyd Foerster.
(A grants consultation agency serving units of the Lutheran Church bodies, the Presbyterian Church (U.S.A.), and The United Methodist Church.)

Lutheran World Relief: 360 Park Ave., S., New York, NY 10010. Tel. (212)532-6350. Pres., Robert J. Marshall; Exec. Dir., Norman E. Barth

National Association for the Advancement of Colored People: 4805 Mt. Hope Dr., Baltimore, MD 21215. Tel. (301)358-8900. Exec. Dir., Benjamin L. Hooks
Periodical: Crisis (10/yr.)

National Association of Church Business Administration, Inc.: 7001 Grapevine Hwy. #324, Fort Worth, TX 76180. Tel. (817)284-1732. Exec. Dir., F. Marvin Myers

National Association of Human Rights Workers (NAHRW): Pres., Dir., Gloria J. Battle; Human Relations, 115 S. Andrews Ave., Rm. 116, Fort Lauderdale, FL 33301. Tel. (305)357-6047

National Assoc. of Pastoral Musicians: 225 Sheridan St., N.W., Washington, DC 20011. Tel. (202)723-5800. Pres., Rev. Virgil C. Funk.
Periodical: Pastoral Music (6/yr); Pastoral Musicians' Notebook (Newsletter, bi-a)

National Association of Social Workers, Inc.: 7981 Eastern Ave., Silver Spring, MD 20910 . Pres., Richard L. Edwards; Exec. Dir., Mark G. Battle.

National Catholic Educational Association: 1077 30th St., N.W., Ste., 100, Washington, DC 20007. Tel. (202)337-6232. Pres., Catherine T. McNamee
Periodical: Momentum

National Consultation on Financial Development, P. O. Box 1040, Westwood, NJ 07675. Tel. (201)664-8890. Pres., Raymond Barnett Knudsen II

National Consumers League: 815 15th St., N.W., Ste. 516, Washington, DC 20005. Tel. (202)639-8140. Pres., Jack A. Blum; Exec. Dir., Linda F. Golodner
Periodicals: NCL Bulletin (bi-m); Alliance Against Telemarketing Fraud Update (q)

National Cooperative Business Associaton: Pres., Robert D. Scherer, 1401 New York Ave. NW, Ste. 1100, Washington, DC 20005. Tel. (202)638-6222.

National Council on Alcoholism: 12 W. 21st St., New York, NY 10010. Tel. (212)206-6770, Pres. and Exec. Dir., Hamilton Beazley; Chmn. of Bd.: Dr. Robert Sparks
Periodicals: Currents (5/yr); Bulletins, Alerts, Fact Sheets, Educational Brochures

National Council on Crime and Delinquency: 77 Maiden Lane, 4th Fl., San Francisco, CA 94180. Tel. (415)956-5651. Pres., Barry Krisberg
Periodicals: Crime and Delinquency (q); Journal of Research in Crime and Delinquency (semi-a)

National Education Association: 1201 16th St., N.W., Washington, DC 20036. Exec. Dir., Don Cameron
Periodical: Today's Education (a); NEA Today (8/yr.)

National Farmers Union: 10065 E. Harvard Ave., Denver, CO 80251. Tel. (303)337-5500. Pres., Leland H. Swenson
Periodical: Washington Newsletter (m)

National Federation of Business and Professional Women's Clubs, Inc.: 2012 Massachusetts Ave., N.W., Washington, DC 20036. Tel. (202)293-1100. Exec. Dir., Linda Colvard Dorian
Periodical: National Business Woman (6/yr)

National Grange: 1616 H Street, N.W., Washington, DC 20006. Tel. (202)628-3507. Robert E. Barrow, Master

National Housing Conference: 1126 16th St., N.W. Ste. 211 Washington, DC 20036. Tel. (202)223-4844. Exec. Dir., Juliette B. Madison

National Interreligious Task Force: 1307 South Wabash Ave., #221, Chicago, IL 60605. Tel. (312)922-1983. Exec. Dir., Sr. Ann Gillen

National Mental Health Association, The: 1021 Prince St., Alexandria, VA 22314. Tel. (703)684-7722. Exec. Dir., Preston J. Garrison
Periodical: NMHA Focus (q)

National Planning Association: 1616 P St. N.W., Ste. 400, Washington, DC 20036. Tel. (202)265-7685. Pres., Edward E. Masters
Periodicals: Looking Ahead (q)

National PTA, The (National Congress of Parents and Teachers): 700 N. Rush St., Chicago, IL 60611. Tel. (312)787-0997. Pres., Mrs. Manya S. Ungar
Periodicals: PTA Today (7/yr.); What's Happening in Washington (3/yr.)

National Urban League, Inc.: 500 E. 62nd St., New York, NY 10021. Tel. (212)310-9000 Chmn. of Bd., David T. Kearns; Pres., John E. Jacob.

OXFAM—America, 115 Broadway, Boston, MA 02116. Tel. (617)482-1211. Exec., John Hammock

Planned Parenthood Federation of America, Inc.: 810 Seventh Ave., New York, NY 10019. Tel. (212)541-7800. Pres. Faye Wattleton; Chpsn., Dr. Kenneth Edelin

Protestant Health and Welfare Assembly: 1701 E. Woodfield Rd., Ste. 311, Schaumburg, IL 60173. Tel. (312)240-1010. Exec. Sec., David A. Johnson

Protestant Radio and TV Center: 1727 Clifton Rd., N.E., Atlanta, GA 30329. Tel. (404)634-3324. Pres., William Horlock

Religious Education Association, The: 409 Prospect St., New Haven, CT 06511. Tel. (203)865-6141. Pres., Joanne Chafe; Exec. Sec., Dr. Donald T. Russo; Chpsn. of Bd., William B. Kennedy

Religious News Service: P. O. Box 1015, Radio City Sta., New York, NY 10101. Tel. (212)315-0870. Ed. and Dir., Judith L. Weidman; News Ed., Tom Roberts.

Religious Research Association, Inc.: Marist Hall, Rm. 108, Catholic Univ. of Am., Washington, DC 20064. Tel. (202)635-5447. Pres., Wade Clark Roof; Treas., David Roozen; Sec., William Swatos
Periodical: Review of Religious Research (4/yr.)

Society for Values in Higher Education: Georgetown Univ., P. O. Box B-2814, Washington, DC 20057. Exec. Dir., Charles Courtney
Periodicals: Newsletter (q.); Soundings: An Interdisplinary Journal (q)

Southern Christian Leadership Conference: 334 Auburn Ave., N.E., Atlanta, GA 30312. Tel. (404)522-1420. Pres. Joseph E. Lowery
Periodical: Newsletter (m)

Southern Regional Council: 2nd Fl., 60 Walton St., NW, Atlanta, GA 30303. Tel. (404)522-8764. Pres., Lottie Shackelford. Exec. Dir., Steve Suitts

Theos Foundation: 1301 Clark Bldg., 717 Liberty Ave., Pittsburgh, PA 15222. Tel. (412)471-7779. Contact: Lisa Torsop.
Periodical: Survivors Outreach (8/yr.)

United Nations Association of the U.S.A.: 485 Fifth Ave., New York, NY 10017. Tel. (212)697-3232. Chpsn. of the Assn., John C. Whitehead.
Periodicals: The Inter Dependent (6/yr); Issues before the General Assembly (a); Fact Sheets on Issues.

United Way of America.: 701 North Fairfax St., Alexandria, VA 22314. Tel. (703)836-7100. Pres., William Aramony
Periodical: Community (10/yr.)

USO World Headquarters: 601 Indiana Ave., NW, Washington, DC 20004. Tel. (202)783-8121. Pres. Hon. Charles T. Hogel.

Vellore Christian Medical College Board Inc.: 475 Riverside Dr., Rm. 243, New York, NY 10115. Tel. (212)870-2640; Exec. Dir., Linda L. Pierce.

Woman's Christian Temperance Union (National): 1730 Chicago Ave., Evanston, IL 60201. Tel. (312)864-1396. Pres., Mrs. Rachel Bubar Kelly
Periodicals: The Union Signal (m); The Young Crusader (m); Legislative Update

Women's International League for Peace and Freedom: 1213 Race St., Philadelphia, PA 19107. Tel. (215)563-7110. Pres., Anne Ivey
Periodicals: Peace and Freedom (8/yr.); Program and Action/Legislative Bulletin (bi-m); Newsletter (8/yr.)

World Conference on Religion and Peace: 777 United Nations Plaza, New York, NY 10017. Tel. (212)687-2163.
Periodical: Religion for Peace (occ.); WCRP/USA Newsletter (occ.)

World Education, Inc.: 210 Lincoln St., Boston, MA 02111. Tel. (617)482-9485. Pres., Joel H. Lamstein;
Periodical: World Education Reports (semi-a)

World Peace Foundation: 22 Batterymarch St., Boston, MA 02109. Tel. (617)482-3875. Exec. Dir., Richard J. Bloomfield.
Periodical: International Organization (q)

World Vision, Inc.: 919 W. Huntington Dr., Monrovia, CA 91016. Tel. (818)357-7979. Pres. and Chief Exec., Officer, Dr. Robert A. Seiple.
Periodicals: World Vision Magazine (bi-m)

16. CANADIAN SERVICE AGENCIES: SOCIAL, CIVIC, RELIGIOUS

The following list of Canadian service agencies is offered for purposes of directing the reader's attention to a number of major Canadian agencies that can provide resources of information and service to the churches. No attempt is made to produce a complete listing of such agencies, and the reader is referred to the *Canadian Almanac and Directory for 1989* and The *1990 Corpus Almanac and Canadian Source Book*, Vols. 1 & 2, for comprehensive listings of Canadian organizations.

Listings are alphabetical by name of institution and generally have the following order: Name of institution, address, telephone number, principal officers, periodical.

Aboriginal Rights Coalition (Project North): 151 Laurier, East, Ottawa, Ontario K1N 6N8. Tel. (613)235-9956. Staff Contact: Lorna Schwartzentruber
Periodical: Newsletter (q)

Alcohol and Drug Concerns: 11 Progress Ave., Ste. 200, Scarborough, Ontario M1P 4S7, Exec. Dir., Rev. Karl Burden. Tel. (416)293-3400
Periodical: Concerns (q)

Alcoholics Anonymous: 234 Eglinton Ave., E., Ste. 502, Toronto, Ontario M4P 1K5. Tel. (416)487-5591 (there are approx. 4,000 A.A. Groups in Canada). Correspondence to: Exec. Sec., Carole Blais

Alliance for Life: B1 - 90 Garry St., Winnipeg, Manitoba R3C 4H1. Tel. (204)942-4772

L'Association canadienne des périodiques catholiques: 9795, boul. Ste-Anne-de-Beaupré, C.P. 1000, Ste-Anne-de-Beaupré, Québec, Québec G0A 3C0. Tél. (418)827-4538. Prés., Jérôme Martineau.
Périodique: Annuaire

Association of Canadian Bible Colleges, The: 100 Fergus Ave., Kitchener, Ontario N2A 2H2. Sec.-Treas., Thomas Dow. Tel. (519)742-3572
Periodical: Directory and Informational Survey of Member Schools (a)

Association of Universities and Colleges of Canada: 151 Slater, Ottawa, Ontario K1P 5N1. Tel. (613)563-1236. Pres., Claude Lajeunesse.
Periodicals: University Affairs (10/yr.); Directory of Canadian Universities (bi-a); Canadian Directory of Awards for Graduate Study (bi-a); Academic and Administrative Officers at Canadian Universities (a); Compendium of University Statistics (a); Canadian University Resources for International Development (tri-a); Canadian Universities in International Development (4/yr.)

B'nai B'rith Canada, The League for Human Rights of: 15 Hove St., Downsview, Ontario M3H 4Y8. Tel (416)633-6224. Exec. Vice-Pres., Frank Dimant
Periodical: The Review of Anti-Semitism in Canada (a)

Boy Scouts of Canada, National Council: 1345 Baseline Rd., P.O. Box 5151, Sta. F., Ottawa, Ontario K2C 3G7. Tel. (613)224-5131. Chief Exec., J. Blain
Periodicals: The Canadian Leader (m)

Boys' Brigade in Canada, The: 115 St. Andrews Rd., Scarborough, Ontario M1P 4N2. Tel. (416)431-6052. Pres., Don Moore
Periodicals: Hotline (q);

Boys and Girls Clubs of Canada: 250 Consumers Rd., Ste. 505, Willowdale, Ontario M2J 4V6. Tel. (416)494-1212. Natl. Exec. Dir., Robert T. Duck
Periodical: National Newsletter

Canada China Programme: 40 St. Clair Ave. E. Ste. 201, Toronto, Ontario M4T 1M9. Tel. (416)921-4152. Dir., Theresa Chu

Canadian Alliance in Solidarity with the Native Peoples (CASNP); P.O. Box 574, Stn. P, Toronto, Ontario M5S 2T1. Tel. (416)588-2712
Periodical: Phoenix (newsletter)

Canadian Association for Adult Education: 29 Prince Arthur Ave., Toronto, Ontario M5R 1B2. Exec. Dir., Ian Morrison, Tel. (416)964-0559
Periodicals: Learning (occ.), Learning Resources Kit

Canadian Association for Community Living: Kinsmen Bldg., York Univ. Campus, 4700 Keele St., Downsview, Ontario M3J 1P3. Tel. (416)661-9611
Periodical: Entourage (q)

Canadian Association for Pastoral Education: P.O. Box 96, Roxboro, Quebec H8Y 3E8. Mrs. Verda Rochon. Tel. (514)624-0382

Canadian Association of Social Workers: 55 Parkdale Ave., Ottawa, Ontario, K1Y 1E5. Tel. (613)729-6668.
Periodicals: The Social Worker (q.)

Canadian Book Publishers' Council: 45 Charles St. E., 7th Floor Toronto, Ontario M4Y 1S2. Tel. (416)964-7231. Exec. Dir., Jacqueline Hushion

Canadian Catholic Organization for Development and Peace/Organisation Catholique Canadienne pour le Développement et la Paix: 5633, Sherbrooke est, Montreal, Quebec H1N 1A3. Exec. Dir., Gabrielle Lachance; Assoc. Exec. Dir., Tom Johnston. English Sector Offices: 3028 Danforth Ave., Toronto, Ontario M4C 1N2. Tel. (416)698-7770.
Periodicals (French Sector): Solidarités (newspaper)
Periodicals (English Sector): Education Notes (m), The Global Village Voice (bi-m)

Canadian Center for Ecumenism: 2065 Sherbrooke St. W., Montreal, Quebec H3H 1G6. Dir., Thomas Ryan. Tel. (514)937-9176
Periodical: Ecumenism (q); Oecuménisme (q)

Canadian Chamber of Commerce, The: 55 Metcalfe St., Ste. 1160, Ottawa, Ontario K1P 6N4. Tel. (613)238-4000. Pres., Timothy Reid.

Canadian Civil Liberties Association: 229 Yonge St., Ste. 403, Toronto, Ontario M5B 1N9. Tel. (416)363-0321. Gen. Counsel., A. Alan Borovoy

Canadian Co-operative Credit Society Limited: 300 The East Mall, Islington, Ontario M9B 6B7. Tel. (416)232-1262. National Credit Union Organization, Chief Exec. Off., Brian F. Downey
Periodicals: Briefs (bi-w)

Canadian Council of Crisis Centres: c/o Distress Centre, Inc. Box 393, Postal Sta. K, Toronto, Ontario M4P 2G7. Tel. (416)486-6766. Exec. Dir., Patricia Harnisch

Canadian Council on Social Development, The: 55 Parkdale Ave., Box 3505, Sta. C, Ottawa, Ontario K1Y 4G1. Tel (613)728-1865. Exec. Dir., Terrance M. Hunsley
Periodicals: Perception (4/yr.); Overview (4/yr.); Initiative (4/yr); Vis-à-Vis (q); Catalogue of Publications

Canadian Ecumenical Action: 1410 W. 12th Ave., Vancouver, British Columbia V6H 1M8. Tel.(604)736-1613. Pres. Dr. Bryan Colwell.
Periodical: Ecumenical News

Canadian Education Association/Association canadienne d' éducation: Ste. 8-200, 252 Bloor St. W., Toronto, Ontario M5S 1V5. Exec. Dir., Robert Blair. Tel. (416)924-7721
Periodicals: CEA Newsletter (9/yr.) Education Canada (q); Bulletin (9/année)

Canadian Girls in Training: Rm. 200, 40 St. Clair Ave., E., Toronto, Ontario M4T 1M9. Tel. (416)961-2036. Exec. Dir., Jean M. Day

Canadian Institute of Planners: 404-126 York St., Ottawa, Ontario K1N 5T5. Tel. (613)233-2105. Exec. Dir., David Sherwood.
Periodical: Plan Canada (6/yr)

Canadian Institute of Religion and Gerontology: 40 St. Clair Ave., East, Ste. 203, Toronto, Ontario M4T 1M9. Dir., Rev. Donald H. Powell. Tel. (416)924-5865.

Canadian Labour Congress: 2841 Riverside Dr., Ottawa, Ontario, K1V 8X7. Tel. (613)521-3400. Pres., Shirley G. E. Carr
Periodical: Canadian Labour (m)

Canadian Medical Association, The: 1867 Alta Vista Dr., Box 8650, Ottawa, Ontario K1G 0G8. Tel. (613)731-9331. Sec. Gen., Leo Paul Landry, M.D.

Canadian Mental Health Association: 2160 Yonge St., Toronto, Ontario M4S 2Z3. Tel. (416)484-7750. Gen. Dir., Edward J. Pennington

Canadian Prisoner's Aid Societies:
Elizabeth Fry Society of Toronto, 215 Wellesley St. E., Toronto, Ontario M4X 1G1. Tel. (416)924-3708. Exec. Dir., Ms. Darlene Lawson

John Howard Society of Ontario, 46 St. Clair Ave., E., 3rd Fl., Toronto, Ontario M4T 1M9. Tel. (416)925-2205. Exec. Dir. Gordon C. MacFarlane
Periodicals: Newsletter (4/yr.); Reform Bulletin (4/yr.)

The St. Leonard's Society of Canada, 3 Robert Speck Pkwy, Ste. 900, Mississauga, Ontario L4Z G5. Interim Exec. Dir. E. T. Gurney
Periodical: Annual Report; Report on Objectives

Canadian Red Cross Society: 1800 Alta Vista Dr., Ottawa, Ontario K1G 4J5. Tel. (613)739-3000. Sec. Gen., George Weber

Canadian Society of Biblical Studies: Exec. Sec., Wayne O. McCready,. Dept. of Religious Studies, Univ . of Calgary, Calgary, Alberta T2N 1N4. Pres., Sean McEvenue, Assoc. Vice-Rector Academic, Concordia Univ., Montreal, Quebec H4B 1R6
Periodicals: The Bulletin of the Canadian Society of Biblical Studies (a); Newsletter for Ugaritic Studies (3/yr); Newsletter for Targumic and Cognate Studies (3/yr.)

Canadian Society of Church History: c/o John Brian Scott, Dept. of Religious Studies, Univ. of Ottawa, 177 Waller St., Ottawa, Ontario K1N 6N5

Canadian UNICEF Committee: 443 Mount Pleasant Rd., Toronto, Ontario M4S 2L8. Tel. (416)482-4444. Exec. Dir., Harry S. Black
Periodicals: Communiqué Unicef Canada (q);

Canadian Unitarian Council, 175 St. Clair Ave. W., Toronto, Ontario M4V 1P7. Tel. (416)921-4506. Pres., Herman Boerma; Exec. Dir., Kathleen D. Hunter

Canadian Woman's Christian Temperance Union: #302 - 30 Gloucester St., Toronto, Ontario M4Y 1L6. Tel. (416)922-0757. Natl. Pres., Mrs. Brig. A. Rawlings, 875 Sunset Blvd., Woodstock, Ontario N4S 4A5
Periodical: Canadian White Ribbon Tidings (q)

CARE Canada: 1550 Carling Ave., P. O. Box 9000, Ottawa, Ontario K1G 4X6. Tel. (613)724-1122. Exec. Dir., A. John Watson.

Publication: CARE Donor Newsletter (q); Annual Report

Catholic Women's League of Canada, The: 3081 Ness Ave., Winnipeg, Manitoba R2Y 2G3. Tel. (204)885-4856. Exec. Dir., Miss Valerie J. Fall
Periodical: The Canadian League (q)

Christian Service Brigade of Canada: 1254 Plains Rd. E., Burlington, Ontario L7S 1W6. Tel. (416)634-1841. Gen. Dir., Robert A. Clayton
Periodical: The Torch Runner (q)

Church Army in Canada, The: 397 Brunswick Ave., Toronto, Ontario M5R 2Z2. Canadian Dir., Capt. Walter Marshall. Tel. (416)924-9279.
Periodical: The Crusader (q).

Church Council on Justice and Corrections, The: 507 Bank St., 2nd Fl., Ottawa, Ontario K2P 1Z5. Tel. (613)563-1688.

Churches and Corporate Responsibility, Taskforce on The: 129 St. Clair Ave. W., Toronto, Ontario M4V 1N5. Tel. (416)923-1758. Coordinator, Moira Hutchinson

Churches' Council on Theological Education in Canada, The 60 St. Clair Ave., Ste. 500, Toronto, Ontario M4T 1N5. Tel. (416)928-3223. Chpsn., Rev. Jean Armstrong; Exec. Dir., Lloyd Gesner

Consumers' Association of Canada: 49 Auriga Dr., Nepean, Ontario K2E 8A1. Tel. (613)723-0187. Pres., Ruth Robinson

Couchiching Institute on Public Affairs: 2000 Lawrence Ave., Toronto, Ontario M1R 2Z1. Tel., (416)252-1652. Exec. Sec., Lee Walsh

CUSO: 135 Rideau St. Ottawa, Ontario K1N 9K7. Tel. (613)563-1242.
Periodicals: CUSO Forum (5/yr); CUSO Journal (a)

Evangelical Theological Society of Canada: McMaster Divinity College, Hamilton, Ontario L8S 4K1. Tel. (416)525-9140. Pres., Clark H. Pinnock

Frontiers Foundation/Operation Beaver: 2615 Danforth Ave., Ste. 203, Toronto, Ontario M4C 1L6. Tel. (416)690-3930. Exec. Dir., Charles R. Catto
Periodical: Annual Report

GATT-Fly, A Project of Canadian Churches for Global Economic Justice: 11 Madison Ave., Toronto, Ontario M5R 2S2. Tel. (416)921-4615. Co-ordinator, John Dillon
Periodical: GATT-Fly Report (4/yr.)

Gideons International in Canada: 501 Imperial Rd. N., Guelph, Ontario N1H 7A2. Tel. (519)823-1140. Exec. Dir., H. Braun
Periodical: Canadian Gideon Magazine (6/yr.)

Girl Guides of Canada—Guides du Canada: 50 Merton St., Toronto, Ontario M4S 1A3. Tel. (416)487-5281. Exec. Dir., Mrs. Margaret Ringland.
Periodical: Canadian Guider (5/yr.)

Health League of Canada, The: P. O. Box 4000, Postal Sta. B, Scarborough, Ontario M1N 4C6. Tel. (416)261-3636. Exec. Dir., S. G. May
Periodical: Health News Digest

Institute for Christian Studies: 229 College St., Toronto, Ontario M5T 1R4. Tel. (416)979-2331. Pres., Dr. Harry Fernhout
Periodical: Perspective Newsletter (bi-m);

Inter-Church Committee on Human Rights in Latin America: 40 St. Clair Ave. E., Ste. 201. Toronto, Ontario M4T 1M9. Tel. (416)921-4152. Exec. Dir., Bill Fairbairn
Periodical: Newsletter

Inter-Church Committee for Refugees: 40 St. Clair Ave. E., Toronto, Ontario M4T 1M9. Tel. (416)921-4152. Officer: Dr. Tom Clark.

Interchurch Committee for World Development Education (Ten Days for World Development): 85 St. Clair Ave. E., Toronto, Ontario M4T 1M8, Nat'l Co-Ord., Jeanne Moffat

Inter-Church Communication: Berkeley Studio, The United Church of Canada, 315 Queen St., E., Toronto, Ontario M5A 1S7. Tel. (416)925-5931. Chmn. Donald Stephens

Inter-Church Fund for International Development (ICFID): 85 St. Clair Ave. E., Ste. 204, Toronto, Ontario M4T 1M8. Tel. (416)968-1411. Exec. Sec., Dr. Robert Fugere

John Milton Society for the Blind in Canada: 40 St. Clair Ave., E., Ste. 202, Toronto, Ontario M4T 1M9. Tel. (416)960-3953.
Periodicals: Insight (Large Print magazine bi-m); Insound (cassette magazine); In Touch (Braille magazine for Adults); National Library in Sound (Bible series, commentary and music); Meeting Place

Organisation Catholique Canadienne pour le Developpement et la Paix (see: Canadian Catholic Organization for Development and Peace)

OXFAM-Canada/National Office: 251 Laurier W., Ste. 301, Ottawa, Ontario K1P 5J6. Tel. (613)237-5236

Pioneer Clubs Canada, Inc.: Box 447, Burlington, Ontario L7R 3Y3. Tel. (416)681-2883. Nat'l. Dir., Richard G. Beurling
Periodicals: Perspective; In Touch (q)

Planned Parenthood Federation of Canada: 1 Nicholas St., Ste. 430, Ottawa, Ontario K1N 7B7. Tel. (613)238-4474. Exec. Dir., Sharon Coleman; Pres., B. Norman Borwin, M.D.

PLURA (Inter-Church Association to Promote Social Justice in Canada): Box 1023, New Hamburg, Ontario N0B 2G0. Tel. (519)662-3450. Sec., Roy Shepherd

Project North: See: Aboriginal Rights Coalition (Project North)

Project Ploughshares: Conrad Grebel College, Waterloo, Ontario N2L 3G6. Res. Coord., Ernie Regehr, Tel. (519)888-6541
Periodical: Ploughshares Monitor (q)

Religious Television Associates: Berkeley Studio, 315 Queen St. East, Toronto, Ontario M5A 1S7. Tel. (416)366-9221. Dir., Rev. Rod Booth

Save the Children Canada/Aide à l'enfance Canada: 3080 Yonge St., Ste. 6020, Toronto, Ontario M4N 3P4. Tel. (416)488-0306. Natl. Dir., Frank Folz
Periodical: Hotline

Scripture Union: 300 Steelcase Rd. W., #19, Markham, Ontario L3R 2W2. Tel. (416)475-0890. Gen. Dir., John F. Booker
Periodicals: S.U. News (q); Daily Bible Readng Guides

Shantymen International: 2110 Argentia Rd., Ste. 301, Mississauga, Ontario L5N 2K7. Tel. (416)821-1175. Pres., W. D. Morrison; Gen. Dir., Arthur C. Dixon
Periodical: The Shantyman (bi-m)

Social Science Federation of Canada and Canadian Federation for the Humanities: 151 Slater St., Ste. 415, Ottawa, Ontario K1P 5H3. Tel. (613)238-6112. Exec. Dir., Dr. Steen B. Esbensen (Social Science Fed. of Canada); Exec. Dir., Viviane Launay (Canadian Federation for the Humanities)

TELECARE Teleministries of Canada, Inc.: P.O. Box 695, Midland, Ontario L4R 4P4. Tel. (705)526-8058. Exec. Dir., Rev. James Manuel

Unitarian Service Committee of Canada: 56 Sparks St., Ottawa, Ontario K1P 5B1. Tel. (613)234-6827. Founder, Dir., Lotta Hitschmanova

United Nations Association in Canada: 63 Sparks St., Ste., 808 Ottawa, Ontario K1P 5A6. Tel. (613)232-5751. Pres., David Cadman; Exec. Dir., Angus Archer

Vanier Institute of the Family, Institut Vanier de la famille: 120 Holland Ave., Ste. 300, Ottawa, Ontario K1Y 0X6. Tel. (613)722-4007. Coord. of Adm. and Communication/Inf., Alan Mirabelli; Coord. of Prog. and Rsch., Dr. Robert Glossop
Periodical: Transition (q)

Voice of Women for Peace/La Voix des Femmes pour la Paix—Canada: 736 Bathurst St., Toronto, Ontario M5S 2R4. Tel. (416)537-9343. Natl. Staff: Carolyn Langdon
Periodical: Voice of Women Newsletter (q)

World Relief Canada: 201 Consumers Rd., Ste. 206; Box 874, Sta. B, Willowdale, Ontario M2K 2R1. Tel. (416)494-9930. Pres., Reg Reimer
Periodical: World Relief Today! (q)

World University Service of Canada: P. O. Box 3000, Stn. C. Ottawa, Ontario K1Y 4M8. Tel. (613)725-3121. Exec. Dir., William W. McNeill

World Vision Canada: 6630 Turner Valley Rd., Mississauga, Ontario L5N 2S4. Exec. Dir., J. Don Scott
Periodicals: Childview (bi-m)—English Sector; Vision Mondiale (4/yr)—French Sector; International Intercessors (m); Communique (bi-m)

Youth for Christ/Canada: 200 Attwell Dr., Rexdale, Ontario M9W 6H4. Tel. (416)674-0404. Pres., Robert E. Simpson

III
STATISTICAL AND HISTORICAL SECTION

This section of the **Yearbook** provides various types of statistical data and information on depositories of church history material for the U.S. and Canada. It is hoped that these materials will be useful in describing some major dimensions of religious life.

Much of the data presented here are unique, at least in form of presentation, and can be used judiciously to interpret developments in the religious life of the U.S. and Canada. Whenever necessary, qualifying statements have been made to warn the user of some of the pitfalls in the data.

Information in this section of the **Yearbook,** when compared with that of previous editions, suggests a number of interesting subjects for students, journalists, and church researchers to analyze and interpret. For the most part, generalizations on trends reflected in the data are left up to the reader.

The following information is contained in this Statistical and Historical Section.

1. **Current and Non-Current Statistical Data.** This section contains nine tables, numbered 1-A through 1-I, as follows: 1-A, United States Current and Non-Current Statistics, arranged alphabetically for 219 United States religious bodies. Included is information on Number of Churches, Inclusive Membership, Full, Communicant or Confirmed Members (current data only), Number of Pastors Serving Parishes, Total Number of Clergy, Number of Sunday or Sabbath Schools (current data only), and Total Enrollment (current data only). Table 1-B, Summary of United States Current and Non-Current Statistics, provides totals for 219 bodies in the above categories and compares these totals with those in the previous **Yearbook** for 1989. Table 1-C, Some Comparative United States Church Statistics, compares data mainly for 1988 with those mainly for 1987 with regard to Church Membership as a Percent of U.S. Population, Membership Gain and Percentage of Gain over Previous Year. Table 1-D, Current and Non-Current Canadian Statistics provides the same data for Canadian bodies as those described above for Table 1-A. Table 1-E provides a Summary of Canadian Current and Non-Current Statistics. Table 1-F, Number of United States Churches, and of Members, by Religious Groups, is continued from the previous year with all the necessary qualifications. Table 1-G, Constituency of the National Council of the Churches of Christ in the U.S.A., is followed by Table 1-H, Church Membership Statistics, 1940-1988, for Selected U.S. Denominations. Table 1-I, Inclusive Membership, 60 Compilations, concludes this section.

2. **Church Financial Statistics and Related Data.** Complete data on contributions of members of 69 United States and Canadian religious bodies are supplied in the following categories: Total Contributions, Total Congregational Finances, and Benevolences. Per-capita contributions based on both Inclusive and Full or Confirmed Membership are supplemented by some related data.

3. **Some Trends and Developments.** This section of the **Yearbook** begins with "A Study of Women in Ministry," by Juanne N. Clark and Grace Anderson of Wilfred Laurier University, Waterloo, Ontario relates to Canadian women clergy. Data from *The 1989 Official Catholic Directory,* providing statistical trends for the Roman Catholic Church, follow. "Trends in Seminary Enrollment, 1980-1989" supplied by The Association of Theological Schools in the United States and Canada, concludes this section.

4. **Surveys of Religion in American Life.** Three survey articles comprise this section. The first, "Return of the Baby Boomers to Organized Religion," by Wade Clark Roof, J. F. Rowny Professor of Religion and Society, University of California, Santa Barbara, is followed by a roundup of selected Church Attendance and Other Polls. "Value of New Construction of Religious Buildings" concludes this section.

5. **Main Depositories of Church History Material and Sources.** This is a listing, by denomination, of various major depositories of historical and archival materials in the United States and Canada, including a bibliographical guide to information on church archives.

1. CURRENT AND NON-CURRENT STATISTICAL DATA, UNITED STATES AND CANADA

Tables 1-A through 1-I in this section, containing current and non-current data, have been compiled from questionnaires returned to the **Yearbook of American and Canadian Churches** by statisticians and other officials of religious bodies. These statistics have been checked carefully, but in no case have they been "adjusted" by the editor in any way for any purpose. What is reported here are official reports.

In keeping with the bi-national organization of the **Yearbook**, statistical totals are given in separate tables for the United States and Canada for the 306 denominations or parts of denominations reporting. In some cases, therefore, statistical tables for a denomination with headquarters in the U.S., and which has a Canadian section, will vary slightly from officially reported statistics of that denomination, and it will be necessary to add the two parts together. For example, the Brethren in Christ Church had an official membership in 1988 of 20,668, of which 17,081 was in the United States and 3,587 in the Brethren in Christ Church, Canadian Conference.

In Table 1-A, the religious bodies in the U.S. are listed alphabetically and current data appear in **bold face** type. Non-current data appear in the light face type. Current data are those compiled and reported in 1989 or 1988. Non-current data are those for 1987 or earlier. Table 1-A contains 106 current and 113 non-current reports, making a total of 219. Current reports, comprising 48.4 percent of all reports, account for 74.0 percent of reported membership.

Statistics appearing in Table 1-G, Constituency of the National Council of Churches of Christ in the U.S.A., do not show the distinction between current and non-current data, although the date of the last statistical report received is noted for each religious body. This year Table 1-D, Canadian Current and Non-Current Statistics, contains statistical reports from 87 Canadian bodies, the same as the previous edition of the **Yearbook**.

Caution should be exercised in interpreting Table 1-B, Summary of United States Current and Non-Current Statistics, which indicates the general trends shown by the data in the 1990 and 1989 **Yearbooks**. Since current and non-current statistics are combined for this comparison, the dangers of elaborate generalizations are obvious. The same is true for Table 1-C, Some Comparative United States Church Statistics.

Users of church statistics are referred to "A Guide for the User of Church Statistics," found at the front of this **Yearbook**. It is essential reading for all who intend to work with and interpret statistics contained in this volume. The Guide is placed in this prominent position to highlight its importance, and its chief function is to state candidly the many qualifications that must be taken into account when using church statistics.

TABLE 1-A: UNITED STATES CURRENT AND NON-CURRENT STATISTICS

The following table provides current and non-current statistics for United States religious bodies listed alphabetically. Current statistics are defined as those gathered and reported for 1989 and 1988. Those bodies having current statistics, and the statistics themselves, are shown in **bold face** type. Non-current statistics are those for 1987 or earlier. They appear in light face type. No statistics for "Full, Communicant, or Confirmed members," "Number of Sunday or Sabbath Schools," and "Total Enrollment" are reported for bodies having non-current statistics.

Religious Body	Year Reported	No. of Churches	Inclusive Membership	Full, Communicant or Confirmed Members	No. of Pastors Serving Parishes	Total No. of Clergy	No. of Sunday or Sabbath Schools	Total Enrollment
ADVENT CHRISTIAN CHURCH.....**1988**		**251**	**19,900**	**19,900**	**300**	**560**	**300**	**18,472**
African Methodist Episcopal Church.....1981		6,200	2,210,000		6,050	6,550		
African Methodist Episcopal Zion Church.....1987		6,060	1,220,260		6,300	6,698		
Alaska Moravian Church.....1987		23	5,159		11	15		
Albanian Orthodox Archdiocese in America.....1978		16	40,000		18	25		
ALBANIAN ORTHODOX DIOCESE OF AMERICA.....**1989**		**2**	**586**	**586**	**1**	**3**	**2**	**31**
Allegheny Wesleyan Methodist Connection (Original Allegheny Conference).....1987		122	2,434		102	199		
Amana Church Society.....1987		7	810		12	13		
American Baptist Association.....1987		1,705	250,000		1,740	1,760		
AMERICAN BAPTIST CHURCHES IN THE U.S.A......**1988**		**5,839**	**1,549,563**	**1,549,563**	**5,250**	**8,276**	**N.R.**	**361,265**
American Carpatho-Russian Orthodox Greek Catholic Church.....1976		70	100,000		61	66		
American Rescue Workers.....1984		20	2,700		35	53		
The Anglican Orthodox Church.....1983		40	6,000		8	8		
THE ANTIOCHIAN ORTHODOX CHRISTIAN ARCHDIOCESE OF NORTH AMERICA.....**1988**		**150**	**300,000**	**300,000**	**138**	**172**	**150**	**21,500**
APOSTOLIC CATHOLIC ASSYRIAN CHURCH OF THE EAST, NORTH AMERICAN DIOCESE.....**1989**		**22**	**120,000**	**120,000**	**92**	**109**	**22**	**1,050**
Apostolic Christian Church (Nazarene).....1985		48	2,799		178	178		
APOSTOLIC CHRISTIAN CHURCHES OF AMERICA.....**1988**		**80**	**11,300**	**11,240**	**290**	**329**	**80**	**7,000**
Apostolic Faith Mission of Portland Oregon.....1987		45	4,100		74	84		
APOSTOLIC FAITH MISSION CHURCH OF GOD.....**1989**		**18**	**6,200**	**4,700**	**27**	**32**	**18**	**1,570**
APOSTOLIC LUTHERAN CHURCH OF AMERICA.....**1988**		**57**	**7,707**	**2,995**	**25**	**34**	**44**	**2,010**
APOSTOLIC OVERCOMING HOLY CHURCH OF GOD.....**1988**		**177**	**12,479**	**12,479**	**127**	**130**	**N.R.**	**N.R.**
Armenian Apostolic Church of America.....1986		18	29,070		16	19		
Armenian Church of America, Diocese of.....1979		66	450,000		45	61		
ASSEMBLIES OF GOD.....**1988**		**11,123**	**2,147,041**	**1,275,148**	**15,617**	**30,552**	**10,692**	**1,363,881**
Assemblies of God, International Fellowship (Independent/Not Affiliated).....1962		136	N.R.		136	367		
ASSOCIATE REFORMED PRESBYTERIAN CHURCH, GENERAL SYNOD.....**1988**		**181**	**36,949**	**31,922**	**157**	**237**	**164**	**16,042**

TABLE 1-A: UNITED STATES CURRENT AND NON-CURRENT STATISTICS—Continued

Religious Body	Year Reported	No. of Churches	Inclusive Membership	Full, Communicant or Confirmed Members	No. of Pastors Serving Parishes	Total No. of Clergy	No. of Sunday or Sabbath Schools	Total Enrollment
Baptist Bible Fellowship, International.	1986	3,449	1,405,900		3,400	4,500		
BAPTIST GENERAL CONFERENCE.	1989	789	135,125	135,125	1,200	1,700	789	67,030
BAPTIST MISSIONARY ASSOCIATION OF AMERICA	1988	1,347	227,897	227,379	1,500	2,650	N.R.	95,406
BEACHY AMISH MENNONITE CHURCH.	1989	100	6,800	6,800	86	325	N.R.	N.R.
Berean Fundamental Church.	1981	49	3,350		51	53		
THE BIBLE CHURCH OF CHRIST.	1988	6	6,405	4,800	8	47	6	684
Bible Way Church of Our Lord Jesus Christ, World Wide, Inc.	1970	350	30,000		350	350		
BRETHREN CHURCH (ASHLAND, OHIO).	1988	124	14,753	14,753	97	173	124	6,893
BRETHREN IN CHRIST CHURCH.	1988	193	17,081	16,580	185	233	185	9,365
Buddhist Churches of America.	1984	100	100,000		70	115	0	0
Bulgarian Eastern Orthodox Church (Diocese of N. & S. America and Australia)	1971	13	86,000		N.R.	11		
CHRIST CATHOLIC CHURCH.	1988	13	1,382	1,137	12	12		
Christadelphians.	1964	850	15,800		None	None	0	
THE CHRISTIAN AND MISSIONARY ALLIANCE	1988	1,793	259,612	133,575	1,669	2,261	1,606	189,424
Christian Brethren (a.k.a. (Plymouth Brethren).	1984	1,150	98,000		N.R.	500		
CHRISTIAN CATHOLIC CHURCH (EVANGELICAL PROTESTANT).	1988	6	2,500	2,500	10	19	6	1,000
CHRISTIAN CHURCH (DISCIPLES OF CHRIST).	1988	4,159	1,073,119	707,985	3,963	6,849	4,159	327,354
Christian Church of North America, General Council.	1985	104	13,500		107	169	N.R.	N.R.
CHRISTIAN CHURCHES AND CHURCHES OF CHRIST	1988	5,579	1,070,616	1,070,616	5,525	6,596	1,310	79,187
THE CHRISTIAN CONGREGATION.	1988	1,456	107,902	107,902	1,454	1,460		
Christian Methodist Episcopal Church.	1993	2,340	718,922		2,340	2,650		
Christian Nation Church, U.S.A.	1936	5	200		5	23		
CHRISTIAN REFORMED CHURCH IN NORTH AMERICA.	1988	699	222,408	143,424	609	1,075	N.R.	N.R.
Christian Union.	1934	114	6,000		80	114		
Church of Christ.	1972	32	2,400		169	188		
Church of Daniel's Band.	1951	4	200		4	10		
The Church of God.	1978	2,035	75,890		1,910	2,737		
CHURCH OF GOD (ANDERSON, IND.).	1938	2,336	198,842	198,842	1,989	3,315	2,226	181,667
Church of God by Faith.	1973	106	4,500		125	150		
CHURCH OF GOD (CLEVELAND, TENN.).	1989	5,763	582,203	582,203	6,207	7,544	5,436	509,250
CHURCH OF GOD GENERAL CONFERENCE (OREGON, ILL.).	1989	88	5,767	4,415	67	87	88	3,357
The Church of God in Christ	1982	9,982	3,709,661		9,204	10,426		

TABLE 1-A: UNITED STATES CURRENT AND NON-CURRENT STATISTICS—Continued

Religious Body	Year Reported	No. of Churches	Inclusive Membership	Full, Communicant or Confirmed Members	No. of Pastors Serving Parishes	Total No. of Clergy	No. of Sunday or Sabbath Schools	Total Enrollment
The Church of God in Christ, International	1982	300	200,000		700	1,600	N.R.	N.R.
CHURCH OF GOD IN CHRIST (MENNONITE)	1989	70	9,256	9,256	347	347	N.R.	N.R.
THE CHURCH OF GOD OF PROPHECY	1989	2,111	73,977	73,977	N.R.	N.R.	2,308	88,432
The Church of God of the Mountain Assembly	1977	105	3,125		162	162	124	10,884
Church of God (Seventh Day) Denver, Colo.	1987	135	6,498		73	100		
Church of God (Which He Purchased with His Own Blood)	1986	7	800		10	10		
Church of Illumination	1983	4	9,000		60	60		
THE CHURCH OF JESUS CHRIST (BICKERTONITES)	1988	70	2,986	2,657	272	282	68	1,816
The Church of Jesus Christ of Latter-Day Saints	1987	8,682	4,000,000		26,046	29,714		
Church of Our Lord Jesus Christ of the Apostolic Faith	1954	155	45,000		150	185	N.R.	N.R.
CHURCH OF THE BRETHREN	1988	1,079	151,169	151,169	975	1,553	N.R.	N.R.
Church of the Living God (C.W.F.)	1985	170	42,000		N.R.	170		
CHURCH OF THE LUTHERAN BRETHREN OF AMERICA	1988	128	13,695	7,827	115	202	124	10,884
CHURCH OF THE LUTHERAN CONFESSION	1988	67	8,655	6,304	52	72	64	1,379
CHURCH OF THE NAZARENE	1988	5,129	552,264	550,711	4,171	8,988	5,054	861,761
CHURCHES OF CHRIST	1989	13,375	1,626,000	1,278,000	N.R.	N.R.	N.R.	N.R.
CHURCHES OF CHRIST IN CHRISTIAN UNION	1988	260	10,418	10,418	167	360	260	18,200
CHURCHES OF GOD, GENERAL CONFERENCE	1988	343	33,778	33,778	237	327	343	27,623
COMMUNITY CHURCHES, INTERNATIONAL COUNCIL OF	1989	200	250,000	250,000	N.R.	350	N.R.	N.R.
CONGREGATIONAL CHRISTIAN CHURCHES, NATIONAL ASSOCIATION OF	1989	400	90,000	90,000	375	575	N.R.	N.R.
Congregational Holiness Church	1981	174	8,347		176	488	N.R.	N.R.
CONSERVATIVE BAPTIST ASSOCIATION OF AMERICA	1988	1,121	204,496	204,496	N.R.	N.R.	N.R.	N.R.
CONSERVATIVE CONGREGATIONAL CHRISTIAN CONFERENCE	1988	176	29,015	29,015	271	457	157	11,692
COPTIC ORTHODOX CHURCH	1989	40	160,000	160,000	44	44	N.R.	N.R.
CUMBERLAND PRESBYTERIAN CHURCH	1988	752	91,491	85,304	440	725	752	42,536
Duck River (and Kindred) Association of Baptists	1975	85	8,632		148	148		
Elim Fellowship	1983	36	N.R.		144	185		
THE EPISCOPAL CHURCH	1988	7,360	2,455,422	1,725,581	8,131	14,694	N.R.	556,168
THE ESTONIAN EVANGELICAL LUTHERAN CHURCH	1988	24	7,399	N.R.	19	N.R.	N.R.	N.R.
ETHICAL CULTURE MOVEMENT	1988	21	3,212	3,212	19	43	12	357
Evangelical Church	1987	155	17,417		160	288		
EVANGELICAL CONGREGATIONAL CHURCH	1988	156	33,318	24,980	113	197	153	17,510
THE EVANGELICAL COVENANT CHURCH	1988	584	87,750	87,750	836	1,260	532	74,922
Evangelical Free Church of America	1986	880	95,722		N.R.	1,484		

TABLE 1-A: UNITED STATES CURRENT AND NON-CURRENT STATISTICS—Continued

Religious Body	Year Reported	No. of Churches	Inclusive Membership	Full, Communicant or Confirmed Members	No. of Pastors Serving Parishes	Total No. of Clergy	No. of Sunday or Sabbath Schools	Total Enrollment
Evangelical Friends Alliance	1982	217	24,095		192	483		
EVANGELICAL LUTHERAN CHURCH IN AMERICA	1988	11,120	5,251,534	3,931,878	10,083	16,083	10,125	1,166,059
EVANGELICAL LUTHERAN SYNOD	1989	123	21,378	15,518	98	141	110	3,900
EVANGELICAL MENNONITE CHURCH	1989	26	3,888	3,888	43	62	25	4,018
Evangelical Methodist Church	1987	130	8,282		151	238		
EVANGELICAL PRESBYTERIAN CHURCH	1989	155	50,300	48,500	181	225	155	25,000
FELLOWSHIP OF EVANGELICAL BIBLE CHURCHES	1988	14	1,925	1,450	18	47	14	1,680
Fellowship of Fundamental Bible Churches	1984	31	1,840		31	52		
The Fire Baptized Holiness Church (Wesleyan)	1958	53	988		N.R.	N.R.		
Free Christian Zion Church of Christ	1956	742	22,260		321	420		
FREE LUTHERAN CONGREGATIONS, THE ASSOCIATION OF	1987	193	26,870	20,485	114	139	180	8,100
FREE METHODIST CHURCH OF NORTH AMERICA	1988	1,071	73,647	54,432	1,133	1,802	1,088	107,723
FREE WILL BAPTISTS, NATIONAL ASSOCIATION OF	1988	2,496	204,382	204,382	2,800	2,895	2,496	155,666
Friends General Conference	1987	505	31,690		None	None		
FRIENDS UNITED MEETING	1988	545	54,501	48,325	341	601	463	24,000
Full Gospel Assemblies, International	1984	150	3,800		122	399		
Full Gospel Fellowship of Churches and Ministers, International	1985	450	65,000		850	850		
Fundamental Methodist Church, Inc.	1987	13	733		14	21		
GENERAL ASSOCIATION OF REGULAR BAPTIST CHURCHES	1989	1,585	260,000	260,000	2,000	2,050	1,585	310,000
GENERAL BAPTISTS (GENERAL ASSOCIATION OF)	1988	868	74,086	74,086	N.R.	1,483	N.R.	N.R.
General Church of the New Jerusalem	1971	33	2,143		17	31		
General Conference of Mennonite Brethren Churches	1986	128	17,065		N.R.	N.R.		
General Conference of the Evangelical Baptist Church, Inc.	1952	31	2,200		22	37		
GENERAL CONVENTION, THE SWEDENBORGIAN CHURCH	1988	50	2,423	2,423	45	54	N.R.	N.R.
General Six Principle Baptists	1970	7	175		4	7		
Grace Brethren Churches, Fellowship of	1985	312	41,767		424	519		
GRACE GOSPEL FELLOWSHIP	1988	52	4,500	2,500	68	125	N.R.	N.R.
Greek Orthodox Archdiocese of North and South America	1977	535	1,950,000		610	655		
The Holiness Church of God, Inc.	1968	28	927		25	36		
Holy Ukrainian Autocephalic Church in Exile	1965	10	4,800		15	24		
House of God, Which is the Church of the Living God, the Pillar and Ground of the Truth, Inc.	1956	107	2,350		80	120		
HUNGARIAN REFORMED CHURCH IN AMERICA	1988	31	12,500	10,500	24	26	20	600
Hutterian Brethren	1987	77	3,988		N.R.	N.R.		
Independent Fundamental Churches of America	1980	1,019	120,446		782	1,366		

TABLE 1-A: UNITED STATES CURRENT AND NON-CURRENT STATISTICS—Continued

Religious Body	Year Reported	No. of Churches	Inclusive Membership	Full, Communicant or Confirmed Members	No. of Pastors Serving Parishes	Total No. of Clergy	No. of Sunday or Sabbath Schools	Total Enrollment
INTERNATIONAL CHURCH OF THE FOURSQUARE GOSPEL......1988		1,363	198,715	193,619	N.R.	5,076	1,014	46,624
INTERNATIONAL PENTECOSTAL CHURCH OF CHRIST......1989		75	2,628	2,628	123	123	75	3,884
JEHOVAH'S WITNESSES......1989		8,851	804,639	804,639	None	None	None	None
JEWS*......1988		3,416	5,935,700	3,750,000	N.R.	6,500	N.R.	N.R.
Kodesh Church of Immanuel......1980		5	326		2	28		
Korean Presbyterian Church in America, General Assembly of the......1986		180	24,000		200	225		
LATVIAN EVANGELICAL LUTHERAN CHURCH IN AMERICA, THE......1988		56	13,211	11,914	29	45	N.R.	N.R.
Liberal Catholic Church—Province of the United States of America......1987		34	2,800		64	127		
Liberty Baptist Fellowship......1987		510	200,000		150	N.R.		
THE LUTHERAN CHURCH—MISSOURI SYNOD......1988		5,939	2,604,278	1,962,674	5,238	8,193	5,737	652,332
LUTHERAN CHURCHES, THE AMERICAN ASSOCIATION OF......1988		78	15,150	11,210	63	80	N.R.	N.R.
MENNONITE CHURCH......1988		1,023	92,682	92,682	1,448	2,469	N.R.	N.R.
MENNONITE CHURCH, THE GENERAL CONFERENCE......1988		224	34,693	34,693	212	379	224	16,179
Metropolitan Church Association, Inc......1958		15	443		13	62		
Metropolitan Community Churches, Universal Fellowship of......1985		230	34,000		240	266		
THE MISSIONARY CHURCH......1988		290	26,332	26,332	317	615	N.R.	N.R.
MORAVIAN CHURCH—NORTHERN PROVINCE......1988		100	31,468	24,092	92	169	99	7,071
MORAVIAN CHURCH—SOUTHERN PROVINCE......1988		54	21,467	17,518	53	87	54	8,968
National Baptist Convention of America......1956		11,398	2,668,799		7,598	28,574		
National Baptist Convention, U.S.A., Inc......1958		26,000	5,500,000		26,000	27,500		
National Primitive Baptist Convention, Inc......1975		616	250,000		460	636		
National Spiritualist Association of Churches......1984		142	5,558		128	142		
Netherlands Reformed Congregations......1984		14	5,520		3	4		
NEW APOSTOLIC CHURCH OF NORTH AMERICA......1988		491	36,972	36,972	734	823	N.R.	2,203
NORTH AMERICAN BAPTIST CONFERENCE......1988		259	42,629	42,269	286	445	259	23,485
North American Old Roman Catholic Church......1986		133	62,611		109	150		
NORTH AMERICAN OLD ROMAN CATHOLIC CHURCH (ARCHDIOCESE OF NEW YORK)......1988		5	615	615	6	9	3	39
OLD GERMAN BAPTIST BRETHREN......1988		55	5,497	5,497	288	288	N.R.	N.R.
OLD ORDER AMISH CHURCH......1988		756	68,040	68,040	3,024	3,049	N.R.	N.R.
Old Order (Wisler) Mennonite Church......1980		36	9,731		N.R.	N.R.		
OPEN BIBLE STANDARD CHURCHES, INC......1989		325	46,000	42,000	587	937	285	25,000
The (Original) Church of God......1971		70	20,000		50	124		
Orthodox Church in America......1978		440	1,000,000		457	531		

TABLE 1-A: UNITED STATES CURRENT AND NON-CURRENT STATISTICS—Continued

Religious Body	Year Reported	No. of Churches	Inclusive Membership	Full, Communicant or Confirmed Members	No. of Pastors Serving Parishes	Total No. of Clergy	No. of Sunday or Sabbath Schools	Total Enrollment
The Orthodox Presbyterian Church	1987	188	19,094		160	334		
Pentecostal Assemblies of the World, Inc.	1960	550	4,500		450	600		
PENTECOSTAL CHURCH OF GOD, INC.	1988	1,157	86,000	40,000	N.R.	1,584	N.R.	N.R.
Pentecostal Fire-Baptized Holiness Church	1969	41	545		80	80		
The Pentecostal Free Will Baptist Church, Inc.	1985	130	10,700		118	171		
PENTECOSTAL HOLINESS CHURCH, INTERNATIONAL	1988	1,472	116,764	116,764	2,046	3,314	1,472	146,776
Pillar of Fire	1949	61	5,100		N.R.	N.R.	N.R.	
Polish National Catholic Church of America	1960	162	282,411		141	141		
PRESBYTERIAN CHURCH IN AMERICA	1988	1,067	208,394	169,846	1,139	1,905	N.R.	101,543
PRESBYTERIAN CHURCH (U.S.A.)	1988	11,505	2,929,608	2,929,608	10,549	19,746	N.R.	1,097,095
Primitive Advent Christian Church	1984	10	546		11	11		
Primitive Baptists	196C	1,000	72,000		N.R.	N.R.		
PRIMITIVE METHODIST CHURCH, U.S.A.	1989	85	8,244	5,779	54	84	85	4,898
Progressive National Baptist Convention, Inc.	1967	655	521,692		N.R.	863		
THE PROTESTANT CONFERENCE (LUTHERAN)	1988	7	1,035	768	7	7	6	136
Protestant Reformed Churches in America	1980	21	4,544		19	31		
REFORMED CHURCH IN AMERICA	1988	925	333,798	200,631	853	1,698	900	100,489
Reformed Church in the United States	1985	34	3,778		28	34		
REFORMED EPISCOPAL CHURCH	1988	78	6,274	6,274	66	122	73	3,877
Reformed Mennonite Church	1970	12	500		18	21		
Reformed Methodist Union Episcopal Church	1983	18	3,800		24	33		
REFORMED PRESBYTERIAN CHURCH OF NORTH AMERICA	1983	68	5,174	3,737	59	127	68	2,925
Reformed Zion Union Apostolic Church	1965	50	16,000		28	N.R.		
Religious Society of Friends (Conservative)	1984	28	1,744		N.R.	17		
Religious Society of Friends (Unaffiliated Meetings)	1980	112	6,386		N.R.	N.R.		
REORGANIZED CHURCH OF JESUS CHRIST OF LATTER DAY SAINTS	1988	1,137	190,950	190,950	17,048	17,048	N.R.	N.R.
THE ROMAN CATHOLIC CHURCH	1988	23,091	54,918,949	N.R.	34,390	52,948	N.R.	7,025,181
THE ROMANIAN ORTHODOX EPISCOPATE OF AMERICA	1988	34	60,000	60,000	28	67	30	1,800
Russian Orthodox Church in the U.S.A., Patriarchal Parishes	1965	38	9,780		37	45		
The Russian Orthodox Church Outside of Russia	1955	81	55,000		92	168		
THE SALVATION ARMY	1988	1,097	433,448	129,165	2,630	5,198	1,121	112,941
THE SCHWENKFELDER CHURCH	1988	5	2,516	2,516	7	9	5	848

TABLE 1-A: UNITED STATES CURRENT AND NON-CURRENT STATISTICS—Continued

Religious Body	Year Reported	No. of Churches	Inclusive Membership	Full, Communicant or Confirmed Members	No. of Pastors Serving Parishes	Total No. of Clergy	No. of Sunday or Sabbath Schools	Total Enrollment
Second Cumberland Presbyterian Church in the U.S.	1959	121	30,000		121	125		
SEPARATE BAPTISTS IN CHRIST	1988	101	10,000	10,000	101	165	N.R.	N.R.
Serbian Eastern Orthodox Church in the U.S.A. and Canada	1986	68	67,000		60	82		
SEVENTH-DAY ADVENTIST CHURCH	1988	4,145	687,200	687,200	2,265	4,537	4,193	480,457
Seventh Day Baptist General Conference	1987	81	5,149		39	92		
Social Brethren	1975	40	1,784		47	47		
SOUTHERN BAPTIST CONVENTION	1988	37,517	14,812,844	14,812,844	37,300	63,625	36,211	7,905,239
The Southern Methodist Church	1985	150	7,231		80	94		
SOVEREIGN GRACE BAPTISTS	1988	275	2,600	2,600	260	275	250	1,900
SYRIAN ORTHODOX CHURCH OF ANTIOCH (ARCHDIOCESE OF THE U.S.A. AND CANADA)	1988	28	30,000	N.R.	20	25	N.R.	N.R.
Triumph The Church and Kingdom of God in Christ (International)	1972	475	54,307		860	1,375		
TRUE (OLD CALENDAR) ORTHODOX CHURCH OF GREECE (SYNOD OF METROPOLITAN CYPRIAN), AMERICAN EXARCHATE	1989	7	1,100	1,100	5	13	N.R.	N.R.
Ukrainian Orthodox Church in the U.S.A.	1966	107	87,745		107	131		
Ukrainian Orthodox Church of America (Ecumenical Patriarchate)	1986	27	5,000		36	37		
UNITARIAN UNIVERSALIST ASSOCIATION	1988	956	178,623	N.R.	600	1,140	830	46,242
United Brethren in Christ	1982	256	26,869		320	382		
United Christian Church	1987	12	420		8	11		
UNITED CHURCH OF CHRIST	1988	6,362	1,644,787	1,644,787	5,096	10,145	6,395	437,836
United Holy Church of America	1960	470	28,890		379	400		
The United Methodist Church	1987	37,641	9,055,575		20,927	38,177		
UNITED PENTECOSTAL CHURCH, INTERNATIONAL	1989	3,592	500,000	500,000	N.R.	7,279	N.R.	N.R.
UNITED ZION CHURCH	1987	13	850		19	20		
Unity of the Brethren	1988	26	2,873	2,873	19	22	22	1,465
VEDANTA SOCIETY	1988	13	2,500	2,500	14	14	N.R.	N.R.
Volunteers of America	1978	607	36,634		704	704		
The Wesleyan Church	1987	3,217	185,861		2,662	3,783		
WISCONSIN EVANGELICAL LUTHERAN SYNOD	1988	1,191	418,691	316,987	1,111	1,538	1,161	49,713
World Confessional Lutheran Association	1987	12	1,530		18	27		

*Inclusive membership represents estimates of the total number of Jews seen as an ethnic, social, and religious community. Full membership is the number of Jews estimated to be associated with synagogues and temples of the Orthodox, Conservative, and Reform branches by officials of the congregational organizations of these three groups.

Table 1-B: SUMMARY OF UNITED STATES CURRENT AND NON-CURRENT STATISTICS

Current statistics are those reported for the years 1989 or 1988. Non-current statistics are those for the years 1987 and earlier. Only current totals are provided in the categories: Full, Communicant, or Confirmed Members; Number of Sunday or Sabbath Schools; Total Enrollment.

	No. of Bodies	No. of Churches	Inclusive Membership	Full, Communicant or Confirmed Members	No. of Pastors Serving Parishes	Total No. of Clergy	No. of Sunday or Sabbath Schools	Total Enrollment
1990 Yearbook								
Current...............	106	213,447	107,652,670	45,118,194	208,232	353,030	114,161	25,090,610
Non-Current...............	113	137,034	37,731,068	N.R.	127,157	184,349	N.R.	N.R.
Totals...............	219	350,481	145,383,738		335,389	537,379		
1989 Yearbook								
Current...............	106	219,384	110,066,003	48,286,383	229,557	381,085	112,197	27,210,060
Non-Current...............	113	129,997	33,764,803	N.R.	103,540	162,067	N.R.	N.R.
Totals...............	219	349,381	143,830,806		333,097	543,152		

TABLE 1-C: SOME COMPARATIVE UNITED STATES CHURCH STATISTICS

	1988	1989
Church Membership as a Percent of U.S. Population..................	58.6	58.7
Membership Gain or Loss over Previous Year..................	1,031,144	1,552,932
Percentage of Gain or Loss over Previous Year..................	0.72	1.1

TABLE 1-D: CANADIAN CURRENT AND NON-CURRENT STATISTICS

The following table provides current and non-current statistics for Canadian denominations listed alphabetically. Current statistics, defined as those gathered and reported for 1989 and 1988 are shown in **bold face** type. Non-current statistics are those for 1987 and earlier, and appear in light face.

Religious Body	Year Reported	No. of Churches	Inclusive Membership	Full, Communicant or Confirmed Members	No. of Pastors Serving Parishes	Total No. of Clergy	No. of Sunday or Sabbath Schools	Total Enrollment
THE ANGLICAN CHURCH OF CANADA	**1988**	**3,105**	**805,521**	**522,762**	**1,914**	**3,300**	**1,907**	**88,525**
The Antiochian Orthodox Christian Archdiocese of North America	1985	10	20,000		12	15		
Apostolic Christian Church (Nazarene)	1985	14	830		49	49		
APOSTOLIC CHURCH IN CANADA	**1989**	**14**	**1,600**	**1,200**	**14**	**18**	**14**	**350**
APOSTOLIC CHURCH OF PENTECOST OF CANADA	**1988**	**134**	**13,000**	**13,000**	**138**	**213**	**N.R.**	**N.R.**
Armenian Church of North America, Diocese of Canada	1979	7	25,000		3	3		
ASSOCIATED GOSPEL CHURCHES	**1989**	**120**	**17,000**	**17,000**	**135**	**223**	**N.R.**	**N.R.**
Baptist General Conference of Canada	1987	70	6,066		80	84		
BIBLE HOLINESS MOVEMENT	**1989**	**15**	**764**	**508**	**7**	**11**	**N.R.**	**N.R.**
BRETHREN IN CHRIST CHURCH, CANADIAN CONFERENCE	**1988**	**36**	**3,587**	**2,848**	**36**	**51**	**35**	**2,254**
British Methodist Episcopal Church	1978	13	2,000		9	9		
Buddhist Churches of Canada	1979	15	2,543		10	10		
THE CANADIAN AND AMERICAN REFORMED CHURCHES	**1988**	**36**	**11,870**	**6,008**	**28**	**42**	**N.R.**	**N.R.**
CANADIAN BAPTIST FEDERATION	**1988**	**1,136**	**122,247**	**114,647**	**720**	**1,298**	**935**	**54,806**
CANADIAN CONVENTION OF SOUTHERN BAPTISTS	**1988**	**98**	**5,779**	**4,602**	**88**	**101**	**98**	**6,257**
CANADIAN YEARLY MEETING OF THE RELIGIOUS SOCIETY OF FRIENDS	**1988**	**25**	**1,156**	**1,156**	**None**	**None**	**15**	**124**
The Christian and Missionary Alliance in Canada	1987	296	63,277		N.R.	N.R.		
Christian Brethren (a.k.a. Plymouth Brethren)	1985	600	52,000		N.R.	250		
CHRISTIAN CHURCH (DISCIPLES OF CHRIST) IN CANADA	**1988**	**36**	**4,006**	**2,454**	**28**	**52**	**36**	**806**
CHRISTIAN CHURCHES AND CHURCHES OF CHRIST	**1988**	**69**	**5,997**	**5,997**	**74**	**74**	**N.R.**	**N.R.**
CHRISTIAN REFORMED CHURCH IN NORTH AMERICA	**1988**	**231**	**87,037**	**49,759**	**199**	**262**	**N.R.**	**N.R.**
CHURCH OF GOD (ANDERSON, IND.)	**1988**	**54**	**3,501**	**3,501**	**35**	**55**	**48**	**3,256**
Church of God (Cleveland, Tenn.)	1987	86	4,996		86	198		
THE CHURCH OF GOD OF PROPHECY OF CANADA	**1989**	**47**	**2,463**	**2,463**	**47**	**95**	**48**	**3,015**
The Church of Jesus Christ of Latter-Day Saints in Canada	1987	370	118,000		1,100	1,263		
CHURCH OF THE LUTHERAN BRETHREN	**1988**	**7**	**458**	**259**	**5**	**5**	**7**	**532**
CHURCH OF THE NAZARENE	**1988**	**154**	**10,573**	**10,482**	**115**	**234**	**150**	**15,617**
Churches of Christ in Canada	1985	149	9,962		103	113		
CONFERENCE OF MENNONITES IN CANADA	**1988**	**157**	**28,994**	**28,994**	**203**	**311**	**N.R.**	**N.R.**
CONGREGATIONAL CHRISTIAN CHURCHES IN ONTARIO, THE CONFERENCE OF	**1988**	**5**	**270**	**270**	**4**	**13**	**4**	**25**

TABLE 1-D: CANADIAN CURRENT AND NON-CURRENT STATISTICS—Continued

Religious Body	Year Reported	No. of Churches	Inclusive Membership	Full, Communicant or Confirmed Members	No. of Pastors Serving Parishes	Total No. of Clergy	No. of Sunday or Sabbath Schools	Total Enrollment
The Coptic Church in Canada...1987		7	40,000		7	7		
THE ESTONIAN EVANGELICAL LUTHERAN CHURCH...1986		13	7,009	N.R.	13	15	N.R.	N.R.
EVANGELICAL BAPTIST CHURCHES IN CANADA, THE FELLOWSHIP OF...1988		478	59,750	59,750	N.R.	N.R.	N.R.	N.R.
THE EVANGELICAL CHURCH IN CANADA...1988		50	3,741	3,741	41	76	43	3,823
THE EVANGELICAL COVENANT CHURCH OF CANADA...1988		23	1,250	1,250	22	34	18	1,573
EVANGELICAL FREE CHURCH OF CANADA...1988		111	5,639	3,639	120	145	N.R.	N.R.
THE EVANGELICAL LUTHERAN CHURCH OF CANADA...1988		652	208,149	150,189	485	817	540	32,254
Evangelical Mennonite Conference...1987		48	5,724		108	109		
Evangelical Mennonite Mission Conference...1986		32	3,131		N.R.	N.R.		
FOURSQUARE GOSPEL CHURCH OF CANADA...1988		37	2,483	2,483	75	86	31	1,355
FREE METHODIST CHURCH IN CANADA...1988		142	7,490	5,282	172	228	142	9,687
FREE WILL BAPTISTS...1989		16	1,275	572	10	13	14	1,205
GENERAL CHURCH OF THE NEW JERUSALEM...1989		3	645	267	4	6	3	179
The Gospel Missionary Association...1981		13	N.R.		10	44		
Greek Orthodox Diocese of Toronto (Canada)...1984		58	230,000		45	49		
Independent Assemblies of God—Canada...1977		45	4,500		125	166		
Independent Holiness Church...1987		13	600		13	21		
The Italian Pentecostal Church of Canada...1985		17	3,800		24	26		
JEHOVAH'S WITNESSES...1989		1,238	94,605	94,605	None	None	None	None
Jews...1981		112	296,425		N.R.	N.R.		
THE LATVIAN EVANGELICAL LUTHERAN CHURCH IN AMERICA...1968		8	2,690	2,400	6	8	N.R.	N.R.
LUTHERAN CHURCH—CANADA...1968		354	90,944	67,576	231	341	296	18,474
MENNONITE BRETHREN CHURCHES, CANADIAN CONFERENCE OF...1988		173	26,034	26,034	222	N.R.	149	16,344
MENNONITE CHURCH (CANADA)...1988		114	9,448	9,448	98	155	N.R.	N.R.
Metropolitan Community Churches, Universal Fellowship of...1984		11	1,600		10	10		
The Missionary Church of Canada...1984		92	6,431		73	129		
MORAVIAN CHURCH IN AMERICA—NORTHERN PROVINCE, CANADIAN DISTRICT OF THE...1988		9	2,125	1,457	12	15	9	525
NETHERLANDS REFORMED CONGREGATIONS OF NORTH AMERICA...1938		8	4,372	2,002	1	2	N.R.	N.R.
NORTH AMERICAN BAPTIST CONFERENCE...1938		112	17,374	17,374	107	182	112	9,109
THE OLD CATHOLIC CHURCH OF CANADA...1988		2	55	25	2	2	None	None
Old Order Amish Church...1937		16	775		N.R.	N.R.		
The Open Bible Standard Churches of Canada...1987		4	1,000		5	6		

TABLE 1-D: CANADIAN CURRENT AND NON-CURRENT STATISTICS—Continued

Religious Body	Year Reported	No. of Churches	Inclusive Membership	Full, Communicant or Confirmed Members	No. of Pastors Serving Parishes	Total No. of Clergy	No. of Sunday or Sabbath Schools	Total Enrollment
THE PENTECOSTAL ASSEMBLIES OF CANADA	1988	1,068	191,607	191,607	N.R.	N.R.	N.R.	N.R.
Pentecostal Assemblies of Newfoundland	1982	163	34,000		128	188		
Polish National Catholic Church	1982	13	6,000		11	14		
PRESBYTERIAN CHURCH IN AMERICA (CANADIAN SECTION)	1988	16	782	498	17	19	N.R.	327
THE PRESBYTERIAN CHURCH IN CANADA	1988	1,035	213,690	156,912	1,168	1,168	637	34,629
REFORMED CHURCH IN CANADA	1988	31	6,486	3,914	33	54	29	2,415
Reformed Doukhobors, Christian Community and Brotherhood of	1986	1	2,108		None	None		
Reformed Episcopal Church, the First Synod in the Dominion of Canada	1986	2	386		4	6		
Reinlaender Mennonite Church	1987	7	800		10	10		
REORGANIZED CHURCH OF JESUS CHRIST OF LATTER DAY SAINTS	1988	51	12,396	12,396	1,021	1,021	N.R.	N.R.
THE ROMAN CATHOLIC CHURCH IN CANADA	1988	5,878	11,375,914	N.R.	7,075	11,838	N.R.	N.R.
The Romanian Orthodox Church in America (Canadian Parishes)	1972	19	16,000		19	19		
THE ROMANIAN ORTHODOX EPISCOPATE OF AMERICA (JACKSON, MICH.)	1988	13	8,600	8,600	11	11	10	663
Russian Orthodox Church in Canada, Patriarchal Parishes of the	1986	25	8,000		6	7		
THE SALVATION ARMY IN CANADA	1988	398	88,899	25,937	732	2,008	390	27,321
Serbian Orthodox Church in the U.S.A. and Canada, Diocese of Canada	1983	17	18,494		11	13		
SEVENTH-DAY ADVENTIST CHURCH IN CANADA	1988	297	37,865	37,865	175	385	330	18,059
UKRAINIAN GREEK-ORTHODOX CHURCH OF CANADA	1988	258	120,000	120,000	75	91	N.R.	N.R.
Union of Spiritual Communities of Christ (Orthodox Doukhobors in Canada)	1972	25	21,300		None	None		
UNITARIAN UNIVERSALIST ASSOCIATION	1988	42	6,061	60,061	17	37	36	1,250
United Brethren in Christ, Ontario Conference	1983	10	910		10	13		
THE UNITED CHURCH OF CANADA	1988	4,138	2,052,342	849,401	2,078	3,795	3,505	207,768
UNITED PENTECOSTAL CHURCH IN CANADA	1989	197	23,000	23,000	N.R.	N.R.	N.R.	N.R.
The Wesleyan Church	1986	75	4,961		67	183		
WISCONSIN EVANGELICAL LUTHERAN SYNOD	1988	9	1,059	753	9	9	10	236

TABLE 1-E: SUMMARY OF CANADIAN CURRENT AND NON-CURRENT STATISTICS

Current statistics are those reported for the year 1989 or 1988. Non-current statistics are those for the years 1987 and earlier. Only current totals are provided in the categories: Full, Communicant or Confirmed Members; Number of Sunday or Sabbath Schools; Total Enrollment.

	No. of Bodies	No. of Churches	Inclusive Membership	Full, Communicant or Confirmed Members	No. of Pastors Serving Parishes	Total No. of Clergy	No. of Sunday or Sabbath Schools	Total Enrollment
1990 Yearbook								
Current..........	52	22,453	15,809,602	2,662,948	17,822	28,926	9,601	562,863
Non-Current..........	35	2,455	1,011,619	N.R.	2,138	2,831	N.R.	N.R.
Totals..........	87	24,908	16,821,221		19,960	31,757		
1989 Yearbook								
Current..........	54	21,784	15,824,881	2,587,429	19,092	29,358	9,662	715,032
Non-Current..........	33	2,649	1,149,404	N.R.	1,480	2,654	N.R.	N.R.
Totals..........	87	24,433	16,974,285		20,572	32,012		

TABLE 1-F: NUMBER OF UNITED STATES CHURCHES, AND OF MEMBERS, BY RELIGIOUS GROUPS

The 219 U.S. religious bodies reporting in this edition of the **Yearbook** may be classified somewhat arbitrarily, into seven major categories.

It should be reiterated that comparisons of statistics of the various religious groups tabulated below are not meaningful because definitions of membership vary greatly from one religious body to another. For example, Roman Catholics count all baptized individuals, including infant members, as do many Protestant bodies. Some Protestant bodies, however, count as members those who have been received into the church at baptism, which can take place as early as age 9, thereby leaving out of official counts of membership many millions of children. Jewish statistics are estimates of the number of individuals in households in which one or more Jews reside and, therefore, include non-Jews living in such households as the result of intermarriage. The total number of persons in Jewish households is estimated to be 7 percent larger than the number of Jewish persons residing in these households.

The definition of membership in each case is of necessity left up to the religious body itself, and the statistics reported by various religious bodies are not adjusted by the editor of the **Yearbook.**

	Number Bodies Reporting	Number of Churches	Number of Members
Buddhists..	1	100	100,000
Eastern Churches.................................	18	1,689	4,077,011
Jews*..	1	3,416	5,935,000
Old Catholic, Polish National Catholic, Armenian Churches.......................	7	431	826,889
Protestants**......................................	186	320,624	79,328,686
Roman Catholics..................................	1	23,091	54,918,949
Miscellaneous***.................................	5	1,130	197,203
Totals..	219	350,481	145,383,738

*Including Orthodox, Conservative, and Reformed branches.

**Some bodies included here such as various Latter-Day Saints groups and Jehovah's Witnesses, are, strictly speaking, not "Protestant" in the usual sense.

***This is a grouping of bodies officially non-Christian, including those such as Spiritualists, Ethical Culture Movement, and Unitarian-Universalists.

TABLE 1-G: CONSTITUENCY OF THE NATIONAL COUNCIL OF THE CHURCHES OF CHRIST IN THE U.S.A.

A separate tabulation has been made of the constituent bodies of the National Council of Churches of Christ in the U.S.A. and is given below:

Religious Body	Year	Number of Churches	Inclusive Membership	Pastors Serving Parishes
African Methodist Episcopal Church	1981	6,200	2,210,000	6,050
African Methodist Episcopal Zion Church	1987	6,060	1,220,260	6,300
American Baptist Churches in the U.S.A.	1988	5,839	1,549,563	5,250
The Antiochian Orthodox Christian Archdiocese of North America	1988	150	300,000	138
Armenian Church of America, Diocese of the	1979	66	450,000	45
Christian Church (Disciples of Christ)	1988	4,159	1,073,119	3,963
Christian Methodist Episcopal Church	1983	2,340	718,922	2,340
Church of the Brethren	1988	1,079	151,169	975
Community Churches, International Council of	1988	200	250,000	N.R.
Coptic Orthodox Church	1989	40	160,000	44
The Episcopal Church	1988	7,360	2,455,422	8,131
Evangelical Lutheran Church in America	1988	11,120	5,251,534	10,030
Friends United Meeting	1988	545	54,501	341
General Convention, the Swedenborgian Church	1988	50	2,423	45
Greek Orthodox Archdiocese of North and South America	1977	535	1,950,000	610
Hungarian Reformed Church in America	1988	31	12,500	24
Korean Presbyterian Church in America, General Assembly of the	1986	180	24,000	200
Moravian Church in America				
Northern Province	1988	100	31,468	92
Southern Province	1988	54	21,467	53
National Baptist Convention of America	1956	11,398	2,668,799	7,598
National Baptist Convention, U.S.A., Inc.	1958	26,000	5,500,000	26,000
Orthodox Church in America	1978	440	1,000,000	457
Philadelphia Yearly Meeting of the Religious Society of Friends	1967	202	(1965) 16,965	(1965) 23
Polish National Catholic Church of America	1960	162	282,411	141
Presbyterian Church (U.S.A.)	1988	11,505	2,929,608	10,549
Progressive National Baptist Convention, Inc.	1967	655	521,692	N.R.
Reformed Church in America	1988	925	333,798	853
Russian Orthodox Church in the U.S.A., Patriarchal Parishes of the	1985	38	9,780	37
Serbian Orthodox Church for the U.S.A. and Canada	1986	68	67,000	60
Syrian Orthodox Church of Antioch (Archdiocese of the U.S.A. and Canada)	1987	28	30,000	20
Ukrainian Orthodox Church in America (Ecumenical Patriarchate)	1986	27	5,000	35
United Church of Christ	1988	6,362	1,644,787	5,096
The United Methodist Church	1987	37,641	9,055,145	20,927
Total (32) bodies		141,559	41,951,333	116,427

TABLE 1-H: CHURCH MEMBERSHIP STATISTICS, 1940–1988

Compiled by Constant H. Jacquet Jr., Editor,

The following statistical time series for 28 U.S. denominations is presented in this edition of the **Yearbook of American and Canadian Churches** as a response to a number of requests for such a tabulation. The denominations selected represent a cross-section of theological orientations, ecclesiastical structures, and geographical foci. Reliability and completeness in statistical reporting were the criteria used in selecting the bodies. Many conclusions can be drawn from the material presented below but interpretations are left to the user of the statistics. The reader is referred to the qualifications relating to statistical data stated throughout this statistical and historical section and in "A Guide for the User of Church Statistics."

Denomination	1940	1947*	1950	1955
Assemblies of God(b)	198,834	241,782	318,478	400,047
Baptist General Conference	N.A.	N.A.	48,647(c)	54,000
Christian and Missionary Alliance**	22,832(d)	N.A.	58,347	57,109(e)
Christian Church (Disciples of Christ)	1,658,966	1,889,066	1,767,964	1,897,736
Church of God (Anderson, Ind.)	74,497	95,325	107,094	123,523
Church of God (Cleveland, Tenn.)	63,216	N.A.	121,706(f)	142,668
Church of Jesus Christ of Latter-day Saints	724,401(d)	911,279	1,111,314	1,230,021
Church of the Brethren	176,908	182,497	186,201	195,609
Church of the Nazarene	165,532	201,487(g)	226,684	270,576
Cumberland Presbyterian Church	73,357	75,427	81,806	84,990
Episcopal Church	1,996,434	2,155,514	2,417,464	2,852,965(h)
Evangelical Covenant Church of America	45,634	N.A.	51,850	55,311
Evangelical Lutheran Church in America(m)	(3,117,626)	N.A.	(3,982,508)	(4,672,083)
Free Methodist Church of North America	45,890	46,783(g)	48,574	51,437
Jehovah's Witnesses	N.A.	N.A.	N.A.	187,120
Lutheran Church—Missouri Synod	1,277,097	1,422,513	1,674,901	2,004,110
Mennonite Church	51,304	52,596	56,480	70,283
North American Baptist Conference	N.A.	N.A.	41,560	47,319
Presbyterian Church (U.S.A.)	(2,690,969)	(2,969,382)	(3,210,635)	(3,701,635)
Reformed Church in America	255,107	274,455	284,504	319,593
Reorganized Church of Jesus Christ of Latter-Day Saints	106,554	116,888	124,925	137,856
Roman Catholic Church	21,284,455	24,402,124	28,634,878	33,396,647
Salvation Army	238,357	205,881	209,341	249,641
Seventh-day Adventist Church	176,218	208,030	237,168	277,162
Southern Baptist Convention	4,949,174	6,079,305	7,079,889	8,467,439
United Church of Christ	(1,708,146)	(1,835,853)	(1,977,418)	(2,116,322)
United Methodist Church	(8,043,454)	(9,135,248)	(9,653,178)	(10,029,535)
Wisconsin Evangelical Lutheran Synod	256,007(d)	259,097	307,216	328,969

*Reported in the **Christian Herald,** June 1947. Only bodies of 50,000 or more reported.
(a) Data for 1966
(b) Assemblies of God statistics for 1971 and later are full membership statistics.
(c) Data for 1952
(d) Data for 1939
(e) Data for 1954
(f) Data for 1951
(g) Data for 1945
(h) Data for 1956
(j) Data for 1961
(k) Adjusted downward to eliminate Canadian membership previously reported.
(m) Data in parentheses for 1985 and earlier are composite totals for Lutheran denominations merged together at various years that currently comprise the Evangelical Lutheran Church in America.
(n) Data for 1987
**A change in the basis of reporting occurred in this body; statistics from 1970 are inclusive statistics, as opposed to those reported earlier.

FOR SELECTED U.S. DENOMINATIONS

Yearbook of American and Canadian Churches

Note: Statistics contained in parentheses are composite totals for the denominations listed prior to merger of the several component bodies. The symbol NA means "Not Available." Most recent titles are used in the case of denominations listed. For information concerning dates and circumstances of merger, see the historical sketches for these denominations in Directory 3, "Religious Bodies in the United States" in this edition.

1960	1965	1970	1975	1980	1985	1988
508,602	572,123	625,027	785,348	1,064,490	2,082,878	2,147,041
72,056	86,719	103,955	115,340	133,385	132,546	135,125
59,657	64,586	112,519	145,833	189,710	227,846	259,612
1,801,821	1,918,471	1,424,479	1,302,164	1,177,984	1,116,326	1,073,119
142,796	143,231	150,198	166,257	176,429	185,593	198,842
−170,261	205,465	272,278	343,249	435,012	N.A.	582,203
1,486,887	1,789,175	2,073,146	2,336,715	2,811,000	3,860,000	N.A.
199,947	194,815	182,614	179,336	170,839	159,184	151,169
307,629	343,380	383,284	441,093	484,276	522,082	552,264
88,452	78,917	92,095	94,050	96,553	98,037	91,491
3,269,325	3,429,153(a)	3,285,826	2,857,513	2,786,004	2,739,422	2,455,422
60,090	65,780	67,441	71,808	77,737	84,150	87,750
(5,295,502)	(5,684,298)	(5,650,137)	(5,401,765)	(5,384,271)	(5,341,452)	5,251,534
55,338	59,415	64,901	67,043	68,477	72,223	73,647
250,000	330,358	388,920	560,897	565,309	730,441	804,639
2,391,195	2,692,889	2,788,536	2,763,545	2,625,650	2,628,164	2,604,278
73,125	80,087	88,522	94,209	99,511	91,167	92,682
50,646	53,711	55,080	42,150(k)	43,041	42,863	42,429
(4,161,860)	(4,254,460)	(4,045,408)	(3,535,825)	(3,362,086)	3,048,235	2,929,608
354,621	385,754	367,606	355,052	345,532	342,375	333,798
155,291	168,355	152,670	157,762	190,087	192,082	190,950
42,104,900	46,246,175	48,214,729	48,881,872	50,449,842	52,654,908	54,918,949
254,141	287,991	326,934	384,817	417,359	427,825	433,448
317,852	364,666	420,419	495,699	571,141	651,954	687,200
9,731,591	10,770,573	11,628,032	12,733,124	13,600,126	14,477,364	14,812,844
(2,241,134)	2,070,413	1,960,608	1,818,762	1,736,244	1,683,777	1,644,787
(10,641,310)	(11,067,497)	10,509,198	9,861,028	9,519,407	9,192,172	9,055,145(n)
348,184(j)	358,466	381,321	395,440	407,043	415,389	418,691

TABLE 1-I: INCLUSIVE MEMBERSHIP, 60 COMPILATIONS

The following are the figures reported on inclusive membership in religious bodies in the U.S. in 60 compilations, between 1890 and 1987 as reported in the Census of Religious Bodies, as indicated, and by private publications. For years omitted, no compilations were made.

Year	Membership	Source	Year	Membership	Source
1890	41,699,342	(CRB)[1]	1960	114,449,217	(YBAC)
1906	35,068,058	(CRB)	1961	116,109,929	(YBAC)
1916	41,926,852	(CRB)	1962	117,946,002	(YBAC)
1926	54,576,346	(CRB)	1963	120,965,238	(YBAC)
1931	59,268,764	(CH)[2]	1964	123,307,449	(YBAC)
1932	60,157,392	(CH)	1965	124,682,422	(YBAC)
1933	60,812,624	(CH)	1966	125,778,656	(YBAC)
1934	62,007,376	(CH)	1967	126,445,110	(YBAC)
1935	62,678,177	(CH)	1968	128,469,636	(YBAC)
1936	55,807,366	(CRB)	1969	128,505,084	(YBAC)
1936	63,221,996	(CH)	1970	131,045,053	(YBAC)
1937	63,848,094	(CH)[3]	1971	131,389,642	(YBAC)
1938	64,156,895	(YBAC)[3]	1972	131,424,564	(YBAC)
1940	64,501,594	(YBAC)	1973	131,245,139	(YBAC)
1942	68,501,186	(YBAC)	1974	131,871,743	(YBAC)
1944	72,492,699	(YBAC)	1975	131,012,953	(YBACC)[4]
1945	71,700,142*	(CH)	1976	131,897,539	(YBACC)
1946	73,673,182*	(CH)	1977	131,812,470	(YBACC)
1947	77,386,188	(CH)	1978	133,388,776	(YBACC)
1948	79,435,605	(CH)	1979	133,469,690	(YBACC)
1949	81,862,328	(CH)	1980	134,816,943	(YBACC)
1950	86,830,490	(YBAC)	1981	138,452,614	(YBACC)
1951	88,673,005	(YBAC)	1982	139,603,059	(YBACC)
1952	92,277,129	(YBAC)	1983	140,816,385	(YBACC)
1953	94,842,845	(YBAC)	1984	142,172,138	(YBACC)
1954	97,482,611	(YBAC)	1985	142,926,363	(YBACC)
1955	100,162,529	(YBAC)	1986	142,799,662	(YBACC)
1956	103,224,954	(YBAC)	1987	143,830,806	(YBACC)
1957	104,189,678	(YBAC)	1988	145,383,739	(YBACC)
1958	109,557,741	(YBAC)			
1959	112,226,905	(YBAC)			

Note: For certain other years *Christian Herald*, New York, published compilations of "communicant" or adult membership only. These totals are not included in the table because they are not comparable with the inclusive figures here noted.

[1] CRB—*Census of Religious Bodies*, Bureau of the Census, Washington.
[2] CH—*The Christian Herald*, New York.
[3] YBAC—*Yearbook of American Churches*, New York.
[4] YBACC—*Yearbook of American and Canadian Churches*, New York.
*Including only bodies with over 50,000 members.

As a general record of the trends in church membership since 1890, the above table is very useful since it presents the results of fifty-six compilations made by various statisticians. It is the only record existing on church membership. Although the table follows a logical progression upwards over time, it is by no means without its faults.

There are certain qualifications relating to the above data that should be kept in mind. First of all, aggregate data on inclusive membership, while accounting for the bulk of church membership, is always incomplete. A small number of religious bodies do not have membership statistics. Further, some religious groups, but not many major ones, are excluded from these totals by virtue of the definitions used for a "religious body" by the various compilers of these data.

Second, the totals here reported are additions of both current and non-current data which is made necessary because not all religious bodies gather and report statistics each year yet all bodies in the total must be aggregated each year for sake of completeness.

Third, definitions of inclusive membership vary from one religious body to another. Some count only full members and exclude probational members, children, and those nominally related while other religious bodies include this wider grouping. Occasionally an individual body will go from the more restrictive to the more inclusive definition over time. A third category of religious bodies has no actual statistical records and only make estimates of inclusive membership which roughly parallel the ethnic and cultural community to which they relate.

Last, these compilations were made by three different organizations from data derived from the religious bodies themselves; the U.S. Bureau of the Census made five compilations, *The Christian Herald* made twelve, and the **Yearbook of American and Canadian Churches** (formerly Yearbook of American Churches), made forty-three. Criteria for defining inclusive membership has not been completely standard over the 98-year period of these compilations.

2. CHURCH FINANCIAL STATISTICS AND RELATED DATA, UNITED STATES AND CANADA

For this edition of the **Yearbook of American and Canadian Churches,** complete financial data were supplied by 42 United States communions. The results are presented in the table entitled "Some Statistics of Church Finances—United States Churches." The data are complete for each communion in the three major categories of reporting. It will be noted that Total Contributions are the sum total of Total Congregational Finances and Total Benevolences.

Similarly, data were supplied by 27 Canadian church bodies. The information is included in the table "Some Statistics of Church Finances—Canadian Churches." Both the U.S. and Canadian data are current, and incomplete information submitted by denominations has been excluded from the tables.

A third table, "Summary Statistics of Church Finances," provides totals for the U.S. and Canadian bodies. The 42 U.S. bodies report total contributions of $15,765,112,942 and the 27 Canadian groups $776,108,251 (Canadian). It must be remembered however, that some of the Canadian groups are not wholly Canadian denominations but, rather, sections of denominations existing and headquartered in the U.S. A majority of the 27 bodies listed in the table "Some Statistics of Church Finances—Canadian Churches" are strictly Canadian denominations. Per capita contributions for full membership of U.S. communions amounted to $376.04 and for the Canadian bodies, $390.48 (Canadian). Benevolences as a percentage of total contributions amounted to 18.96 percent for the U.S. bodies and 21.90 percent for the Canadian.

Readers of the tables should be aware that the Canadian and U.S. financial data appearing in this section are only a significant part of total contributions from members of all communions. Not all bodies in the U.S. and Canada gather church financial data centrally, and some have information but do not reveal it publicly. Additionally, little is known about other major segments of church financial income such as earned income, interest from investments, and bequests.

Comparisons between this year's aggregate financial data and those in previous editions of the **Yearbook** should not be made, since the same bodies do not report financial data each year. However, for an individual denomination or groups of denominations reporting annually over time, comparisons can be made.

Comparative data for nine major Protestant denominations in the U.S. among the 42 listed in this section show a total 1988 full membership of 38,320,065, or 161,852 fewer members than the same churches' total for 1987. These members increased total giving in the nine denominations by 3.5 percent. When this is compared with a 4.4 percent inflation in the U.S. in 1988, the total effect is decreased real income for these denominations. For Canada, comparative statistics for nine communions indicate a decrease in membership from 1987 to 1988 to a total of 1,757,399, and an increase in giving of $24,203,963 (Canadian) to a total of $662,975,352 (Canadian). Assuming an inflation rate in Canada of 4.1 percent for 1988, the total contributions of these nine communions show a decrease, after inflation, of $1,985,664 (Canadian).

SOME STATISTICS OF CHURCH FINANCE:

COMMUNION	Year	Full or* Confirmed Membership	Inclusive** Membership	Total Contributions	Per Capita Full or Confirmed Membership	Per Capita Inclusive Membership
				TOTAL CONTRIBUTIONS		
American Baptist Churches in the U.S.A.	1988	1,549,563	1,549,563	$347,483,189	$224.25	$224.25
Apostolic Christian Churches of America	1989	11,240	11,390	6,457,000	574.47	566.90
Associate Reformed Presbyterian Church (General Synod)	1988	31,922	36,949	18,720,812	586.45	506.67
Baptist General Conference	1989	135,125	135,125	106,633,730	789.15	789.15
Christian and Missionary Alliance	1988	133,575	259,612	153,854,876	1,151.82	592.64
Christian Church (Disciples of Christ)	1988	707,985	1,073,119	339,414,124	479.41	316.29
Church of God (Anderson, Ind.)	1988	198,842	198,842	152,166,173	765.27	765.27
Church of God General Conference (Oregon, Ill.)	1989	4,415	5,767	4,053,000	918.01	702.79
Church of the Brethren	1988	151,169	151,169	61,378,873	406.03	406.03
Church of the Nazarene	1988	550,700	552,264	357,255,803	648.73	646.89
Churches of God General Conference	1988	33,778	33,778	17,472,191	517.26	517.26
Conservative Congregational Christian Conference	1988	29,015	29,015	17,974,521	619.49	619.49
Cumberland Presbyterian Church	1988	85,304	91,491	27,089,518	317.57	296.09
The Episcopal Church	1988	1,725,581	2,455,422	1,209,378,098	700.85	492.54
Ethical Culture Movement	1988	3,212	3,212	1,950,000	607.10	607.10
Evangelical Congregational Church	1988	24,980	33,318	14,858,635	594.82	445.96
Evangelical Covenant Church	1988	87,750	87,750	79,391,637	904.75	904.75
Evangelical Lutheran Church in America	1988	3,931,878	5,251,534	1,320,063,506	335.73	251.37
Evangelical Lutheran Synod	1989	15,518	21,378	6,757,385	435.45	316.09
Evangelical Mennonite Church	1989	3,888	3,888	4,280,571	1,100.97	1,100.97
Evangelical Presbyterian Church	1989	48,500	50,300	32,090,496	661.66	637.99
Free Methodist Church of North America	1988	57,432	73,647	58,740,144	1,022.77	797.59
Friends United Meeting	1988	48,325	54,501	17,846,616	369.30	327.46
General Association of General Baptists	1988	74,086	74,086	22,949,350	309.77	309.77
General Association of Regular Baptist Churches	1989	260,000	260,000	149,852,332	576.35	576.35
International Pentecostal Church of Christ	1989	2,628	2,628	2,648,470	1,007.79	1,007.79
The Latvian Evangelical Lutheran Church in America	1988	11,914	13,211	2,681,000	240.14	216.56
Lutheran Church–Missouri Synod	1988	1,962,674	2,604,278	771,983,173	393.33	296.43
Mennonite Church	1988	92,682	92,682	74,815,100	807.22	807.22
Mennonite Church—The General Conference	1988	34,693	34,693	21,038,412	606.42	606,42
Moravian Church in America, Northern Province	1988	23,526	31,468	10,432,122	443.43	331.52
Missionary Church	1988	26,332	26,332	31,188,183	1,184.42	1,184.42
North American Baptist Conference	1988	42,629	42,629	31,209,128	732.11	732.11
Presbyterian Church in America	1988	169,846	208,394	185,489,902	1,092.11	890.08
Presbyterian Church (U.S.A.)	1988	2,929,608	2,929,608	1,724,644,355	558.69	558.69
Reformed Church in America	1988	200,631	333,798	152,911,999	762.15	458.10
Reformed Episcopal Church	1988	6,274	6,274	7,562,728	1,205.41	1,205.41
Seventh-day Adventist Church	1988	687,200	687,200	574,618,190	836.17	836.17
Southern Baptist Convention	1988	14,812,844	14,812,844	4,396,019,065	296.77	296.77
United Church of Christ	1988	1,644,787	1,644,787	536,482,088	326.17	326.17
The United Methodist Church	1987	9,055,145	9,055,145	2,573,748,234	284.23	284.23
Wisconsin Evangelical Lutheran Synod	1988	316,987	418,691	139,348,213	439.61	332.81

*Full or Confirmed Membership refers to those with full, communicant, or confirmed members.
**Inclusive Membership refers to those who are full, communicant, or confirmed members, plus other members listed as baptized, nonconfirmed, or noncommunicant.

—UNITED STATES CHURCHES

	CONGREGATIONAL FINANCES			BENEVOLENCES		
Total Congregational Contributions	Per Capita Full or Confirmed Membership	Per Capita Inclusive Membership	Total Benevolences	Per Capita Full or Confirmed Membership	Per Capita Inclusive Membership	Benevolences As a Percentage of Total Contributions
$291,606,418	$188.19	$188.19	$55,876,771	$ 36.06	$ 36.06	16.08%
4,500,000	400.36	395.08	1,957,000	174.11	171.82	30.31
13,590,006	425.73	367.80	5,130,806	160.73	138.87	27.41
88,247,512	653.08	653.08	18,386,218	136.07	136.07	17.24
124,054,373	928.72	477.85	29,800,503	223.10	114.79	19.37
297,187,996	419.77	276.94	42.226,128	59.64	39.35	12.44
132,384,232	665.78	665.78	19,781,941	99.49	99.49	13.00
3,367,000	762.63	583.84	686,000	155,38	118.95	16.93
48,008,657	317.58	317.58	13,370,216	88.45	88.45	21.78
309,478,442	561.97	560.38	47,777,361	86.76	86.51	13.37
14,577,987	431.58	431.58	2.894,204	85.68	85.68	16.56
13,853,547	447.46	447.46	4,120,974	142.03	142.03	22.93
23,355,911	273.93	255.40	3,722,607	43.64	40.69	13.74
1,001,560,929	580.42	407.90	207,817,169	120.43	84.64	17.18
1,875,000	583.75	583.75	75,000	23.35	23.35	3.85
12,115,762	485.02	363.64	2,742,873	109.80	83.32	18.46
64,920,459	739,83	739.83	14,471,178	164.92	164.92	18.23
1,150,483,034	292.60	219.08	169,580,472	43.13	32.29	12.85
5,713,773	368.20	267.27	1,043,612	67.25	48.82	15.44
2,712,843	697.75	697.75	1,567,728	403.22	403.22	36.62
28,504,785	587.73	566.70	3,585,711	73.93	71.29	11.17
48,788,041	849.49	662.46	9,952,103	173.28	135.13	16.94
14,127,491	292.34	259.22	3,719,125	76.96	68.24	20.84
21,218,051	286.40	286.40	1,731,299	23.37	23.37	7.54
99,136,079	381.29	381.29	50,716,253	195.06	195.06	33.84
1,878,838	714.93	714.93	769,632	292.86	292.86	29.06
2,482,000	208.33	187.87	379,000	31.81	28.69	13.25
659,288,332	335.91	253.16	112,694,841	57.42	43.27	14.60
47,771,200	515.43	515.43	27,043,900	291.79	291.79	36.15
11,399,995	328.60	328.60	9,638,417	277.82	277.82	45.81
9,221,646	391.98	293.05	1,210,476	51.45	38.47	11.60
25,661,180	974.52	974.52	5,527,003	209.90	209.90	17.72
24,597,288	577.01	577.01	6,611,840	155.10	155.10	21.19
135,840,288	799.79	651.84	49,649,614	292.32	238.24	26.77
1,439,655,217	491.42	491.42	284,989,138	97.28	97.28	16.52
127,409,263	635.04	381.70	25,502,736	127.11	76.40	16.68
6,202,976	988.68	988.68	1,359,752	216.73	216.73	17.98
178,768,967	260.14	260.14	395,849,223	576.03	576.03	68.89
3,706,652,161	250.23	250.23	689,366,904	46.54	46.54	15.68
470,747,740	286.21	286.21	65,734,348	39.97	39.97	12.25
1,966,048,424	220.43	220.43	577,699,810	63.80	63.80	22.45
116,941,975	368.92	279.30	22,406,238	70.69	53.51	16.08

SOME STATISTICS OF CHURCH FINANCES

COMMUNION	Year	Full or* Confirmed Membership	Inclusive** Membership	TOTAL CONTRIBUTIONS(a)		
				Total Contributions	Per Capita Full or Confirmed Membership	Per Capita Inclusive Membership
The Anglican Church of Canada	1988	522,762	805,521	$179,037,647	$342.48	$222.26
Apostolic Church in Canada	1988	1,200	1,600	1,076,600	897.17	672.88
Baptist Convention of Ontario and Quebec	1988	33,222	33,222	33,778,000	1,016.74	1,016.74
Baptist Union of Western Canada	1988	15,498	21,310	19,826,579	1,279.30	930.39
Bible Holiness Movement	1989	508	764	179,860	354.06	235.41
Christian Church (Disciples of Christ) in Canada	1988	2,454	4,006	1,899,296	773.96	474.11
Church of the Nazarene	1988	10,482	10,513	8,599,981	820.45	818.03
Conference of Mennonites in Canada	1988	28,994	28,994	19,709,081	679.77	679.77
Congregational Christian Churches in Ontario, The Conference of	1988	270	270	232,929	862.70	862.70
Evangelical Church in Canada	1988	3,741	3,741	3,747,458	1,001.72	1,001.72
The Evangelical Covenant Church of Canada	1988	1,250	1,250	1,538,227	1,230.58	1,230.58
The Evangelical Lutheran Church in Canada	1988	150,189	208,149	47,467,397	316.05	228.04
Foursquare Gospel Church of Canada	1988	2,483	2,483	3,482,849	1,402.68	1,402.68
Free Will Baptists	1989	575	1,275	676,700	1,176.87	530.75
Latvian Evangelical Lutheran Church in America	1988	2,400	2,690	309,000	128.75	114.87
Lutheran Church–Canada	1988	67,576	90,944	26,023,950	385.11	286.15
Mennonite Church (Canada)	1988	9,448	9,448	10,371,071	1,097.70	1,097.70
Moravian Church in America, Northern Province, Canadian District	1988	1,457	2,125	1,365,282	937.05	642.48
North American Baptist Conference	1988	17,734	17,734	17,433,965	983.08	983.08
Presbyterian Church in America (Canadian Section)	1988	498	782	807,428	1,621.34	1,032.51
The Presbyterian Church in Canada	1988	156,912	213,690	62,229,340	396.59	291.22
Reformed Church in Canada	1988	3,914	6,486	3,297,539	842.50	508.41
Seventh-day Adventist Church in Canada	1988	37,865	37,865	41,969,432	1,108.40	1,108.40
Union d'Églises Baptistes Françaises au Canada	1988	1,222	3,000	712,067	582.71	237.36
United Baptist Convention of the Atlantic Provinces	1988	64,715	64,715	27,302,943	421.90	421.90
The United Church of Canada	1988	849,401	2,052,342	262,436,380	308.97	127.87
Wisconsin Evangelical Lutheran Synod	1988	753	1,059	597,250	793.16	563.97

(a) Although most denominations reported Canadian dollars for this table, certain denominations reported U.S. dollars. In order to standardize these amounts, U.S. dollars were multiplied by 1.2309, a factor which represents the average differential in exchange rates in 1988; thus all totals are expressed in Canadian dollars.

SUMMARY STATISTICS

	Total Bodies	Full or* Confirmed Membership	Inclusive** Membership	TOTAL CONTRIBUTIONS		
				Total Contributions	Per Capita Full or Confirmed Membership	Per Capita Inclusive Membership
United States Communions	42	41,924,183	45,441,782	$15,765,112,942	$376.04	$346.91
Canadian Communions(b)	27	1,987,523	3,625,978	776,108,251	390.48	214.03

*Full or Confirmed Membership refers to those with full, communicant, or confirmed status.
**Inclusive Membership refers to those who are full, communicant, or confirmed members, plus other members baptized, nonconfirmed, or noncommunicant.
(a)Shown in Canadian dollars.

—CANADIAN CHURCHES

	CONGREGATIONAL FINANCES			BENEVOLENCES			
Total Congregational Contributions	Per Capita Full or Confirmed Membership	Per Capita Inclusive Membership	Total Benevolences	Per Capita Full or Confirmed Membership	Per Capita Inclusive Membership	Benevolences As a Percentage of Total Contributions
$137,786,344	$263.57	$171.05	$41,251,303	$ 78.91	$ 51.21	23.04%
968,000	806.67	605.00	108,600	90.50	67.88	10.09
29,841,000	898.23	898.23	3,937,000	118.51	118.51	11.66
15,835,168	1,021.76	743.09	3,991,411	257.54	187.30	20.13
27,355	53.85	35.80	152,505	300.21	199.61	84.79
1,668,140	679.76	416.41	231,156	94.20	57.70	12.17
7,620,959	727.05	724.91	979,022	93.40	93.12	11.38
11,508,829	396.94	396.94	8,200,252	282.83	282.83	41.61
187,681	695.11	695.11	45,248	167.59	167.59	19.43
2,920,644	780.71	780.71	826,814	221.01	221.01	22.06
1,246,491	997.19	997.19	291,736	233.39	233.39	18.97
38,462,058	256.09	184.78	9,005,339	59.96	43.26	18.97
3,362,665	1,354.28	1,354.28	120,184	48.40	48.40	3.45
607,000	1,055.65	476.08	69,700	121.22	54.67	10.30
264,000	110.00	98.14	45,000	18.75	16.73	14.56
19,608,876	290.18	215.61	6,415,074	94.93	70.54	24.65
6,651,537	704.02	704.02	3,719,534	383.68	383.68	36.05
12,869,003	725.67	725.67	4,564,962	257.41	257.41	26.18
1,226,813	842.01	577.32	138,469	94.05	65.16	10.14
690,304	1386.15	882.74	117,124	235.19	149.77	14.51
51,914,129	330.85	242.94	10,315,211	65.74	48.27	16.58
2,707,690	691.80	417.47	589,849	150.70	90.94	17.89
11,625,916	307.04	307.04	30,343,516	801.36	801.36	72.30
592,142	484.57	197.38	119.925	98.14	39.98	16.84
21,927,124	338.83	338.83	5,375,819	83.07	83.07	19.69
223,528,463	263.16	108.91	38,907,917	45.81	18.96	14.83
501,768	666.36	473.81	95,482	126.80	90.16	15.99

OF CHURCH FINANCES

	CONGREGATIONAL FINANCES			BENEVOLENCES			
Total Congregational Contributions	Per Capita Full or Confirmed Membership	Per Capita Inclusive Membership	Total Benevolences	Per Capita Full or Confirmed Membership	Per Capita Inclusive Membership	Benevolences As a Percentage of Total Contributions
$12,775,946,818	$304.74	$281.11	$2,989,166,124	$71.30	$65.80	18.96%
606,150,099	304.97	167.16	169,958,152	85.51	46.87	21.90

EFFECTS OF INFLATION ON PER CAPITA GIVING
1961–1988

Constant H. Jacquet, Jr.
Communication Unit
National Council of Churches

Somewhere between 38 and 52 religious bodies have been able to supply annually complete financial data on total contributions received. Total contributions are the sum of all benevolences, plus all congregational finances. Representing roughly 20 percent of the total number of U.S. denominations and 30 percent of total U.S. membership reported to the *Yearbook of American and Canadian Churches,* giving to these bodies is approximately 40 percent of total church contributions in the U.S. in any given year.

At least four reasons why more denominations do not supply statistical data on church finanes are: 1) the desire to keep the information confidential, 2) a belief that there are biblical restrictions against this type of accounting, 3) a lack of adequate statistical programs in denominations to report accurate membership and financial data, and 4) denominational polities that do not require full reporting to a central office.

The fragmentary information currently received, however, provides a good sample that helps to determine what is happening in the area of U.S. church contributions. It should be remembered that these are aggregate data, and the experiences of individual denominations may vary from those presented here.

Organized religion, like other privately financed agencies, is, on the whole, struggling with powerful forces of inflation in the U.S. Although the dollar amounts of giving have increased from $69.00 per capita full member in 1961 to $376.04 in 1988, an increase of 445 percent, in constant 1967 dollars, the increase is only from $77.01 in 1961 to $106.14 in 1988, an increase in real terms of only 37.8 percent, or slightly less than 1.4 percent a year on average. Therefore much education and action in the area of stewardship has been necessary to defend the financial structure of organized religion.

DENOMINATIONAL PER CAPITA
FULL MEMBER CONTRIBUTIONS
AND ADJUSTED TO 1967 DOLLARS, 1961–1988

Year	No. of Denoms.	Per Capita Full Member	Constant 1967 Dollars	Year	No. of Denoms.	Per Capita Full Member	Constant 1967 Dollars
1961	46	$69.00	$77.01	1975	43	138.54	85.94
1962	42	68.76	75.89	1976	43	149.07	87.43
1963	41	69.87	76.19	1977	45	159.33	87.78
1964	41	72.04	77.55	1978	42	176.37	90.26
1965	38	77.75	82.38	1979	44	197.44	90.82
1966		(Not Reported)		1980	40	213.41	86.47
1967		(Not Reported)		1981	45	239.71	88.00
1968	52	95.31	91.47	1982	40	261.95	90.60
1969	48	99.68	90.78	1983	40	278.67	93.39
1970	45	96.84	83.27	1984	39	300.40	96.56
1971	42	103.94	85.69	1985	42	321.77	99.87
1972	39	110.29	88.02	1986	44	344.42	104.88
1973	40	118.16	88.77	1987	42	356.67	104.78
1974	44	$127.16	$86.09	1988	42	376.04	106.14

3. SOME TRENDS AND DEVELOPMENTS

A STUDY OF WOMEN IN MINISTRY: GOD CALLS, MAN CHOOSES

Juanne N. Clark, Ph.D.
and Grace Anderson, Ph.D.
Department of Sociology & Anthropology
Wilfred Laurier University, Waterloo, Ontario

Introduction

What happens in the secular world has an impact on the churches. Women are breaking into secular professions such as law and medicine, and into the business professions, in unprecedented numbers. This trend is also occurring within the churches as ever-larger numbers of women are entering the ordained ministry of the mainline Protestant denominations. More women are becoming theologians, church historians, Biblical and Classical archaeologists, pastors and chaplains, and are heading church-related social agencies and organizations than ever before. These women are looking at the old source of religious inspiration from new perspectives: they are bringing a new dynamism and creativity to their tasks, for the benefit of both men and women. Nowhere is faith being challenged more deeply than in the debates surrounding the ordination of marginalized groups such as women and homosexuals. In some churches the ordination of women is becoming commonplace, at least in the more densely populated urban areas. In other denominations, such as the federation Baptists, every ordination of a woman candidate tends to be a test case for women in ministry. In the Anglican Church in Canada, the views of the lcoal bishop may influence policy in the diocese whereas in the Presbyterian Church some progress is being made in the largest urban centres, but much yet remains to be done.

This paper is based on a study of women in four major Protestant denominations in Canada: the Anglican, Baptist, Presbyterian and United Churches, who have trained for church ministries. It reports on their attitudes to and their experiences within training and practice of their chosen occu-pations. It includes both women who were trained in 1950-1960 (Time I) as deaconnesses or in the case of Anglican women, Bishops messengers and women who were trained as ordained clergywomen in the years 1975-1985 (Time II).

Sample

The population from which this sample is drawn consists of all women graduates of the training institutions and seminaries affiliated with the major Canadian theological training centres of the four denominations enumerated above and/or the two time periods listed on the next page in Table 1. A total of 252 questionnaires was mailed at each time period.

The response rate from Time I graduates was 60.7%; 4.4% did not respond because of known sampling problems such as address change or lack of eligibility; 34.9% did not respond for unknown reasons. The response rate at Time II was 55.67%; 6.7% did not respond because of known sampling problems; 37.7% did not respond for unknown reasons: (i) a number of the respondents were located in remote areas in countries outside of Canada and even third world countries where the mail systems are frequently unreliable; (ii) several follow-up letters were sent to try to increase sample size; (iii) financial resources were limited so that further telephone calls and mailings were not possible.

Description of the Sample

We divided age into seven categories. None of the respondents was 20 years or under, 14% were between 21-30, 21.5% were between 31-40, 9.2% were between 41-50, 34.8% were between 51-60, 17.4% were between 61-70 and 2.7% were over 70 years of age. The majority of the respond-

TABLE 1: Population and Sample Sizes***

Time I 1950-1960 Graduates

College	Number of Graduating Women to whom questionnaires were sent
Ewart (Presbyterian)	65
Trinity** (Anglican)	3
Centre for Christian Studies (Anglican+ United)	184

Population n = 252
Final Sample n = 153

Time II 1975-1985 Graduates

College	Number of Graduating Women to whom Questionnaires were sent
Ewart (Presbyterian)	61
Knox (Presbyterian)	38
Trinity (Anglican)	50
McMaster* (Baptist)	28
Centre for Christian Studies (Anglican+ United)	75

Population n = 252
Final Sample n = 140

* McMaster was included in Time II only because the graduates of the earlier time period had recently been surveyed.

** Trinity College numbers are small because there were so few graduates.

*** The figures are the number of actual graduates with the exception of CCS in Time I when every second name was drawn because of the disproportionately large population size.

ents (58.4%) were married. Almost a third (32.4%) were single. Fewer than 5% were separated and divorced and 4.4% were widowed. Approximately one-third of the women are, or were, married to men who work for the church (33.8%). Slightly more than one-half (50.9%) had children, 40.6% were affiliated with the United Church, 32.1% with the Presbyterian Church, 20.8% with the Anglican Church, 4.4% with the (Federation) Baptist Church, and 0.3% with the Lutheran. More than a fifth (21.1%) had switched denominations from the denominations in which they were raised. Most (81.6%) of the women had parents who were either very active or at least moderately active in the church as they were growing up. Approximately one-third (33.1%) were employed full-time in, or by, the church at the time of the study. Thirteen per cent were in parttime employ of the church. Many were involved in one of several aspects of voluntary church work.

Thirty-one percent taught Church or Sunday School, 23.5% were involved in church music, 60.1% did "other" church work.

Data Collection Methods

Building on the revisions resulting from a pretest of twenty women who had graduated from either Waterloo Lutheran Seminary in Waterloo, Ontario, or from Lutheran Theological Seminary in Saskatoon, Saskatchewan, the data were collected by means of a mailed questionnaire. A letter accompanying the questionnaire explained our purposes, and stated that the researchers were asking for information about the following issues:

(a) the respondent's ideas about their own occupational role and the role of the contemporary church;

(b) the theological and general education of the respondent;

(c) the current church position of the respondent;

(d) the respondent's assessment of her position in the church; and

(e) basic background information.

The use to which the information would be put was explained and respondents were assured that their answers would remain confidential and that they themselves would not be identified. Each respondent was informed that the respective colleges from which their names had been solicited would receive a brief statistical report. Approximately three weeks after the first mailing, and after receiving more than 100 responses, a letter of reminder was mailed out to non-respondents.

Data Collection Instrument

The data collection instrument included 95 questions and included items concerning all of the following topics:

(a) basic demographic information such as age, marital status, the presence of children in the home;

(b) nature of current employment;

(c) job history, including paid and unpaid church labor;

(d) characteristics of the present church position, including "professional" personnel and the parishioners;

(e) satisfaction with current employment;

(f) satisfaction with career path options for women clergy;

(g) relationships, and levels of satisfaction with colleagues in the denomination and in the inter-church context;

(h) financial situation and degree of satisfaction with same;

(i) satisfaction with work in the church and with opportunities available to women;

(j) perceived support for the respondent in her current church position;

(k) self-assessment with respect to contribution to work in the church;

(l) theological position on various issues;

(m) reasons for decision to enter ministry.

A brief summary of some of the highlights of the finds of the study follows.

Findings

The sample description has indicated the socio-demographic characteristics of who have trained for church ministry. This next section will describe where the women are currently placed in church work, why they say they entered church work, and what they believe their particular strengths are.

First, Table 2 describes the present occupations of the women in the sample. As the table indicates, women are concentrated in the assistant or associate levels, among the ranks of Christian education directors, as chaplains, in the head offices of the denominations as staff, executive assistants and secretary. Only a minority, less than one third of those in church-related work, have achieved the position of sole pastor, senior pastor or co-minister. And less than one-sixth of all who have graduated from the theological training centre are among the ranks of pastors or co-pastors.

Since the study was conducted many months after graduation, it is of some concern that nine persons were still looking for work. Those who were not employed and not searching were usually married and looking after a home and children, or they were married to a minister and contributing to the work of the church on a voluntary basis. In some cases the spouse is employed in a location where no positions are vacant and so the wives are no longer looking for work. This category tends to mask the serious amount of underemployment of the women graduates. The relatively large numbers of retired persons is accounted for by the fact that a number of the graduates were already middle aged when they entered ministerial training, either ordained or diaconal, and are now of retirement age.

The numbers who have left salaried ministry for secular employment, also includes within its ranks persons who had looked for church employment for a considerable period without success before leaving. Furthermore, when they were asked about the difficulties that they expected that men and women would confront in the next five years, twice as many thought that women would have more difficulty finding a church-related position than men. Almost twice as many thought that ordination would be more difficult for women than men in the next five years. Considerable thought needs to be given to the matter of wasted or underutilized resources within the churches.

When asked why they had entered training for the ministry and what they saw as their major concerns and objectives as

TABLE 2: Present Positions of Women Graduates

CHURCH-RELATED

Sole pastor, senior pastor, co-minister	47
Assistant, associate pastor/minister	34
Christian Education minister/director	27
Chaplain	13
Denominational executive, staff member	11
Executive assistant, secretary	9
Diaconal minister, deaconess	5
Professor	3
Organist, music or choir director	2
Nurse	2
Administrative assistant	1
Total	**154**

NOT CURRENTLY IN LABOUR FORCE

Not employed, not looking	54
Retired	23
Looking for work	9

SECULAR EMPLOYMENT

Teacher, librarian, school consultant	13
Social work, community service	12
Nurse, nursing instructor, administrator	8
Professional, managerial	8
Secretary, clerical	8
Other secular	5
Total	**54**
Employed part-time	(1)

women trained in ministry they focused on the following:

(A) a full-range of occupational opportunities in church-related ministries to respond to God's call

(B) a return to New Testament and early church models of service for women, plus an updating of these to allow for cultural differences between the Judeo-Greco-Roman world and modern society

(C) redefining the traditional roles of women and men

(D) opportunities to use women's special strengths

(E) real participation and not tokenism.

(A) Opportunities to Respond to God's Call

Over half (51.8%) of the women in the sample manifested a profound sense of responding to God's call to enter ministry. They recognized God's claim upon their lives. They expressed an enormous reservoir of dedication in response to the request: *"Please explain in your own words why you chose a church vocation"* These were among the comments: "I felt a call or need to be working with people in the name of Christ and 'to be God's presence in their midst.' " "I felt that God was leading me toward a Church vocation," and, "I felt God calling me into this area of ministry." "I felt called and left my lucrative teaching job to join the ministry," and "I entered because of a call I received—that God had this purpose for my life." Several indicated that this confirmation of a sense of call remained with them and 18.2% expressed an overwhelming sense that they were drafted, that they had no choice but to respond to God's imperative. They commented, "I never felt that I had a choice . . . I was just called." "God persisted and would not accept a refusal." "Following conversion I could do no other." "I felt dissatisfied with the helping profession I had chosen, and felt called to ministry. I kept feeling this until I gave up and entered seminary."

(B) A Return to the New Testament and early church models, and
(C) Redefining the traditional roles of men and women

What these women were asking for was not a "new deal", but rather a return to the New Testament Church, the church of the first and second centuries (Howe, 1982). Misapprehensions abound regarding the nature of the early church. Recent research has uncovered the very central roles of women as abbesses, elders, deacons, and other sometimes powerful positions held by women in the early church. Recent linguistic analysis has also shown that some of the early translations of the Bible, interpreted through the eyes and minds of patriarchal cultures, limited and constrained the roles of women. For instance, the Greek word *diakonos* is translated in the King James Version (1611) of the Bible, when applied to a woman as "a servant of the church" and when applied to a man as a "minister." Jesus was, Himself, notably respectful of the women with whom he related.

Yet women in this sample continued to feel frustrations in their work in the church, frustrations due to what they felt were the outmoded limitations on the work that they could perform. Table 3, following, briefly lists some of the major areas of frustration experienced by women in ministry. As can be seen in the table most women in ministry (63.7%) say that, in spite of their personal sense of calling, they feel inner doubts and uncertainties. The sensitivity of women to the expectations and ambivalences of others is clearly evident in the high percentage with continual self-questioning. Many women express difficulties with male colleagues (55.6%). A sizeable percentage (40.7%) noted frustration at the restrictions and limitations placed upon their roles in the church.

In another question in which the women were asked which of the following qualities would you like in a future position they ranked their preferences as follows:

More potential for growth	70.5%
A different location	65.3%
Better or different working conditions	59.5%
More salary	57.3%

TABLE 3: Areas in Which Women in Ministry Experienced Difficulties

Areas of ministry in which participation is permitted	40.7%
Salary differences between female and male colleagues performing similar duties	28.5%
Personal relations with male colleagues	55.6%
Personal relations with female colleagues	24.0%
Relations with other members of church staff	27.6%
Response from the congregation	36.4%
Inner doubts, uncertainties, fears	63.7%

In spite of these frustrations that the women felt, they thought that as women they were very effective in a number of areas of ministry.

As Table 4 indicates, the rank order of the areas of church ministry in which women feel very effective is as follows: 1) planning and leading worship; 2) teaching children; 3) visitations; 4) teaching adults and; 5) preaching sermons.

As one woman explained, the opportunity to redefine the traditional roles of men and women was a central concern of the modern church:

I believe women in the ministry constitute the possibility of the experience of wholeness especially working in conjunction with male priests! . . . I sense the recovery of "the feminine" carried on by both women and men, is "the work" of our era—if we are to survive. The feminine concern for relationship is needed too because of the competitive attitude of the masculine mind.

(D) Opportunities to use the strengths of women in ministry

The women in the sample recognized themselves, and each other, as possessing special strengths or gifts which they bring to their work. A list of their strengths gleaned both from available socio-psychological literature and their own perspective follows:

WOMEN'S SPECIAL STRENGTHS

Emphasis on affect or emotion (a)
Caring and nurturing (b)
Openness and vulnerability (c)
Counselling skills (d)
Healing ministries (e)
Accentuating the feminine symbols in the church (f)
Inclusivity (g)
Humanizing Influence on Theology (h)
Renewed Emphasis on the Inner Journey (i)
Changing the Nature and Style of Leadership (j)

Of course, women in ministry do not have these gifts or strengths exclusively. Rather it is a matter of the degree of emphasis, extent of usage and style of ministry.

In keeping with such a list women in the sample made comments such as the following:

(a) (b) "women are more in tune with feelings and not so afraid to show feelings in pastoral situations"
(c) "women appear to be more approachable which allows for open sharing"
(d) "women often (but not always) excel in counselling situations"
(e) "women are often more suitable in any situation which requires sensitivity to marginalization"
(f) "the very presence of women in leadership positions in the church serves to emphasize the feminine symbols in the church"
(g) "I strongly agree with inclusiveness but not without education and patience and sensitivity to the average layperson"
(h) (i) _____
(j) "we must encourage 'the enabling involvement of laity and collegiality,' . . . affirming lay ministries"

(E) Real participation and not tokenism

Women said that they wanted to be included in the decision making processes of the church. They do not want *only* to serve at the lower ranks, in the least prestigious job, but they long for challenging positions which will enable them to contribute a full battery of their strengths to the work to which they feel called by God to perform. However, it must also be made clear that women tend not to think of their vocation as a career. They are more likely to view it as a "calling" from God and therefore, instead of speaking of "planning a career," they talk of "following where God leads," and of "being faithful disciples," and of "presenting the authenticity of the gospel." Therefore success is defined as "doing God's will," not as building up a church into ever-larger numbers of parishioners, but rather of "teaching discipleship." Many women in our sample insisted they were not after a career where they chase ever-larger church congregations or constantly search for ever-more-responsible positions. Nevertheless, they continued to feel frustration resulting from their restriction to certain limited spheres within the church.

Sexism and Sexual Harassment

A large (71%) majority of this group spoke of discrimination against them because of their gender. A smaller group (23%) indicated that they sometimes experienced sexism and discrimination but that they were often pleased by the fair way that they were treated. Clearly the norm is that women in ministry expect to experience sexism from their congregations and colleagues. Only 5% said that this was never a problem for them. Comments such as the following illustrate the experiential component of sexism on discrimination.

People can still be heard saying, "not bad for a woman."

It was interesting and frustrating to be the only clergyperson on staff while the congregation searched for a new senior minister and to hear folks say, "we are without a minister now."

I was one of several students who were unreasonably yelled at and wrongly accused. The professor felt threatened by competent women.

Sexism sometimes took a more agressive and sexually-focused form. A large minority of women (over one-quarter) said that they had been subject to sexual harassment of various forms within the church. This

TABLE 4: Perceived Effectiveness of Self as a Woman in Ministry

	Very Effective	Somewhat Effective	Somewhat Ineffective	Very Ineffective	Do not do this
Administration	28.9%	47.7%	8.6%	10.2%	4.7%
Counselling	23.4%	51.6%	3.9%	16.4%	4.7%
Preaching sermons	34.1%	43.7%	1.6%	15.9%	4.8
Planning and leading worship	48.1%	34.9%	0.8%	11.6%	4.7%
Managing the church budget	8.0%	17.0%	8.8%	0.8%	60.0%
Teaching adults	35.9%	52.3%	0.8%	7.0%	3.9%
Teaching children	43.2%	34.4%	2.4%	16.0%	4.0%
Presiding over a large meeting	24.2%	43.8%	3.9%	23.4%	4.7%
Pastoral counselling	27.3%	51.6%	4.7%	11.7%	4.7%
Visitations	36.7%	39.1%	8.6%	10.9%	4.7%
Organizing and motivating others	30.5%	49.2%	11.7%	0.8%	3.9%
Stimulating parishioners to engage in service	12.5%	52.3%	22.7%	0.8%	7.8%
Recruiting new members for the church	5.6%	40.3%	23.4%	2.4%	23.4%

ranged from flirtation to sexual assault. A few quotations will serve to illustrate:

> During the chaplaincy course I was the only female and was subjected to verbal abuse. Pictures from "soft porn" magazines were handed to me to see my reaction.

> I have been sexually approached many times.

> I was sexually harassed by the male ordained clergy that I teamed with during my first position. Although I called in the church officials and received some help, I was forced to leave this position.

Of the 49 women who chose to answer the specific question about sexual harassment, 48 or 98% answered that they had experienced it. While many of the incidents may seem relatively minor, the continual possibility hinders good relationships among men and women in the church. It causes women to be afraid to be alone in the church, to be the first in or the last out.

Conclusions

Clearly women in the ministry are experiencing pervasive sexism and sexual harassment. They explained many frustrations because their roles and rewards are severely truncated when compared with those of men. Yet they continue to hope, to feel called, to have faith in their calling and in their own, and in the future positions of their daughters in the church. They believe that they have important gifts to offer. It may be that they would hope for what Carroll, Hargrove and Lummis postulate:

> "that . . . a new cultural image of the ordained ministry will emerge, one that is androgynous, neither male nor female, but incorporating the strengths and gifts of both" (1983:213-4).

Bibliography

Jackson W. Carroll, Barbara Hargrove and Adair Lummis
1983
Women of the Cloth: A New Opportunity for the Churches. San Francisco: Harper & Row.

Margaret E. Howe
1982
Women and Church Leadership. Grand Rapids, Mich.: Zondervan Publishing Co.

THE 1989 OFFICIAL CATHOLIC DATA

As of January 1, 1989, U.S. Catholics numbered 54,918,989, an increase of 1,422,147 over the previous year, according to *The Official Catholic Directory* for 1989 published by P. J. Kenedy and Sons, 3004 Glenview Rd., Wilmette, IL 60091. These statistics are for 34 Archdioceses and 152 Dioceses, including the new Diocese in Knoxville, Tenn.

Catholic Population

The following statistics compare the number of Catholics to the total population of an archdiocese or diocese in the United States:

Archdiocese/Diocese	Total Catholics	Total Population	% Catholic
Baltimore	434,971	2,265,900	17
Boston	1,851,379	3,728,900	50
Chicago	2,350,000	5,789,800	41
Detroit	1,493,159	4,253,100	35
Hartford	881,998	1,814,180	49
Louisville	193,191	1,146,868	17
Los Angeles	3,394,462	9,538,300	36
Miami	614,920	3,074,600	20
Milwaukee	587,539	2,011,900	29
New Orleans	549,977	1,433,355	38
New York	2,205,298	5,076,532	43
Omaha	200,162	750,259	27
Philadelphia	1,271,015	3,769,100	34
San Antonio	584,847	1,611,700	36
St. Louis	533,982	1,989,500	27
St. Paul-Mnpls.	641,511	2,173,572	30

Religious Personnel

The following trends exist for various religious personnel over the thirty-year period 1959-1989:

	1959	1969	1979	1989
Priests	52,689	59,620	58,430	52,948
Deacons	. . .	. . .	3,296*	9,065
Brothers	9,709	11,755	7,965	6,977
Sisters	164,922	167,167	128,378	104,419

* Permanent Deacons first appeared statistically in the 1977 edition of *The Official Catholic Directory*, listing 1,900 Permanent Deacons for the United States.

Newly-ordained Diocesan priests totalled 482 in 1989 and approximately 255 Religious Order priests were ordained.

Converts and Infant Baptisms

According to church records there were 82,409 converts in 1989, and incrase of 670 from 1988.

In 1989, 946,303 infant baptisms were recorded, an increase over 1988 of 8,356.

Religious Instruction in Public Schools (C.C.D.)

In 1989, 3,833,596 pupils were receiving religious instruction in public schools. Of these, 759,856 were high school students, reflecting a decreased enrollment of 44,919 and 3,073,740 were elementary students, indicating an increase of 28,908.

Catholic School Attendance

"A gradual and significant decline in Catholic School attendance has continued over the last decade," according to *The Official Catholic Directory*. The figures reported for Catholic Education Institutions as of January 1, 1989 are as follows:

Number of	1989	1988
Diocesan Parochial High Schools	822	840
Total Students	390,473	424,729
Private High Schools	542	551
Total Students	270,811	283,460
Diocesan & Parochial Elementary Schools	7,268	7,387
Total Students	1,904,463	1,933,915
Private Elementary Schools	281	272
Total Students	74,372	55,551

Decline of Catholic Institutions Recorded, 1980-1989

	Diocesan and Parochial Schools	Private Catholic High Schools	Diocesan and Parochial Elementary Schools	Private Elementary Schools
1980	894	633	7,847	302
1981	881	623	7,802	315
1982	882	588	7,761	318
1983	889	581	7,657	312
1984	880	576	7,696	313
1985	870	555	7,658	299
1986	857	561	7,564	301
1987	850	558	7,485	287
1988	840	551	7,387	272
1989	822	542	7,268	281

Other Statistics on Religious Institutions

In 1989, there were 232 Catholic Colleges and Universities reporting an enrollment of 551,466.

There were 42,077,483 patients in 640 Catholic hospitals and 206 dispensaries. In Catholic hospitals alone, 40,485,316 patients were treated.

Diocesan seminaries, numbering 69, enrolled 3,576 seminarians and 166 religious seminaries contained 2,068 students. Both diocesan and religious seminaries noted a decrease in the number of students from the previous year.

TRENDS IN SEMINARY ENROLLMENT 1980–1989

The following tables offer an update for fall 1988 and 1989 enrollment in ATS member schools, the two years since the previous tables were published. In 1988 three schools ceased operations and five new schools were admitted to membership. Total enrollment of the schools which closed was 243 (206 FTE), whereas enrollment at the five new schools was 607 (403 FTE). Three of the new schools were Canadian with 292 students (210 FTE) whose presence is reflected in the growth in Canadian enrollment in 1988.

In 1988 the ATS issued a revised and somewhat expanded set of Annual Report Forms to member schools with more refined data and which also measured new areas such as age and admission data. This information will be available. The 1989 data reflect firmer figures as schools accommodated to the new Report Forms.

Opening fall 1989 enrollment in ATS member schools was 56,082. This represented an increase of 5.1% over the previous year (1988) and an increase of 0.6% over the 1987 figures. The 1987 figure of 55,405 was the low point in a steady slow decline since 1984. The sharp increase this year may well reflect the success of school efforts to serve a broader constituency with a variety of graduate level programs

TABLE 1: Autumn Enrollments in ATS Member Schools

	1980	1982	1984	1986	1987	1988	1989
Number of Schools	194	196	197	201	201	203	203
Total Enrollment	49,611	52,620	56,466	56,335	53,766	55,405	56,082
By Nation							
Canada	2,731	2,961	3,352	3,696	3,572	4,024	4,057
United States	46,880	49,659	53,114	52,639	52,194	51,381	52,025
By Membership							
Accredited	45,952	48,887	52,091	52,864	52,464	52,129	52,913
Not Accredited	3,659	3,733	4,375	3,471	3,302	3,276	3,169

The fall of 1989 saw a further decline in the full-time equivalent (FTE) enrollment of 3.5% since 1987. This represents a decline of 11% over the past decade from 76% to 65% of full-time equivalent enrollment in relation to head count (HC). Schools have been focusing their energies on increasing endowment for student financial aid in order to reverse this trend and to permit more applicants to become full-time students. It is obvious that more needs to be done. The constituting of an active peer group of learners is important for the quality of learning in graduate divinity programs.

TABLE 2:
Comparisons of Total Enrollment, 1978–1989
Total Number of Individuals and Their Full-time Equivalents

Year	Total Persons (HC)	% Change	FTE Enrollment	% Change	FTE % of Total Person Enrollment (HC)
1978	46,460		36,219		78.0%
1979	48,433	+4.2%	36,795	+1.6%	76.0%
1980	49,611	+2.4%	37,245	+1.2%	75.1%
1981	50,559	+1.9%	37,254	+0.02%	73.7%
1982	52,620	+4.1%	37,705	+1.2%	71.7%
1983	55,112	+4.7%	38,923	+3.3%	70.6%
1984	56,466	+2.5%	39,414	+1.3%	69.8%
1985	56,377	−0.16%	38,841	−1.5%	68.9%
1986	56,328	−0.09%	38,286	−1.4%	68.0%
1987	55,766	−1.0%	38,329	+0.1%	68.7%
1988	55,405	−0.6%	37,073	−3.3%	66.9%
1989	56,082	+1.2%	36,431	−1.7%	65.0%

Table 3 reports the ratio of women seminary students for each year since 1972 when collection of data was begun. Seventeen years ago women constituted only 10.2% of the total student group. This year they constituted 29% of the student group. Although growth during the past year was only 0.1%, average growth for the past five years was 2.9%. The representation of women on administrative staff is close to that in the student body. Representation on the faculty, however, is somewhat lower because change and turnover of full-time faculty members is slower.

TABLE 3: Women Theological Students

	Number of Women	% Annual Increase	% Total Enrollment
1972	3,358		10.2%
1973	4,021	+19.7%	11.8%
1974	5,255	+30.7%	14.3%
1975	6,505	+23.8%	15.9%
1976	7,349	+13.0%	17.1%
1977	8,371	+13.9%	18.5%
1978	8,972	+ 7.2%	19.3%
1979	10,204	+13.7%	21.1%
1980	10,830	+ 6.1%	21.8%
1981	11,683	+ 7.9%	23.1%
1982	12,473	+ 6.8%	23.7%
1983	13,451	+ 7.8%	24.4%
1984	14,142	+ 5.1%	25.0%
1985	14,572	+ 3.0%	25.8%
1986	14,864	+ 2.0%	26.4%
1987	15,310	+ 3.0%	27.0%
1988	16,258	+ 6.2%	29.3%
1989	16,270	+ 0.1%	29.0%

Data on black student population in theological schools has been gathered since 1970. Total enrollment has grown from 1987 to 1989 by 435 students (12.9%). There is a steady increase which has averaged 5.5% per year for the past five years. The percentage of blacks in the total student population has grown to 6.8% from 4.2% a decade ago. There is reason for encouragement in these statistics.

TABLE 4: Black Student Enrollment

	Number of Black Students	% Annual Increase	% Total Enrollment
1970	808		2.6%
1971	908	+12.4%	2.8%
1972	1,061	+16.9%	3.2%
1973	1,210	+14.0%	3.6%
1974	1,246	+ 3.0%	3.4%
1975	1,365	+ 9.6%	3.3%
1976	1,524	+11.6%	3.5%
1977	1,759	+15.4%	3.9%
1978	1,919	+ 9.1%	4.1%
1979	2,043	+ 6.5%	4.2%
1980	2,205	+ 7.9%	4.4%
1981	2,371	+ 7.5%	4.7%
1982	2,576	+ 8.6%	4.9%
1983	2,881	+11.8%	5.2%
1984	2,917	+ 1.2%	5.2%
1985	3,046	+ 4.4%	5.4%
1986	3,277	+ 7.6%	5.8%
1987	3,379	+ 3.1%	6.0%
1988	3,658	+ 8.3%	6.6%
1989	3,814	+ 4.3%	6.8%

Table 5 provides data on the enrollment of Hispanics in schools of theology. The increase in enrollment of 2.8% is slow. Total growth for the past five years has been only 12.9%. Continuing efforts of denominations to reach out to this group will be a challenge to the existing programs of theological schools. With this increase in numbers the proportion of Hispanics in the total student body grew to 2.6%.

TABLE 5: Hispanic Student Enrollment

	Number of Hispanic Students	% Annual Increase	% Total Enrollment
1972	264		0.8%
1973	387	+46.8%	1.1%
1974	448	+15.8%	1.2%
1975	524	+17.0%	1.3%
1976	541	+ 3.2%	1.3%
1977	601	+11.1%	1.3%
1978	681	+13.3%	1.5%
1979	822	+20.7%	1.7%
1980	894	+ 8.8%	1.8%
1981	955	+ 6.8%	1.9%
1982	1,180	+23.6%	2.2%
1983	1,381	+17.0%	2.5%
1984	1,314	− 4.9%	2.3%
1985	1,454	+10.6%	2.6%
1986	1,297	−10.8%	2.3%
1987	1,385	+ 6.8%	2.5%
1988	1,443	+ 4.2%	2.6%
1989	1,483	+ 2.8%	2.6%

Table 6 provides data on the enrollment of persons of Pacific/Asian American ancestry. Though the numbers are quite small, they are already greater than those of Hispanic students. The growth this year of 4.9% is lower than in recent years. With this advance, Pacific/Asian Americans now constitute 3.7% of the total student body.The determination of this group to provide an educated ministry is obvious in these statistics.

TABLE 6: Pacific/Asian American Students

	Number of Students	% Annual Increase	% Total Enrollment
1977	494		1.1%
1978	499	+ 1.0%	1.1%
1979	577	+15.6%	1.2%
1980	602	+ 4.3%	1.2%
1981	716	+18.9%	1.4%
1982	707	− 1.3%	1.3%
1983	779	+10.2%	1.4%
1984	1,130	+45.1%	2.0%
1985	1,195	+ 5.8%	2.1%
1986	1,393	+16.6%	2.5%
1987	1,645	+18.0%	2.9%
1988	1,961	+19.2%	3.5%
1989	2,058	+ 4.9%	3.7%

4. SURVEYS OF RELIGION IN AMERICAN LIFE

RETURN OF THE BABY BOOMERS
TO ORGANIZED RELIGION

Wade Clark Roof
J. F. Rowny Professor of Religion and Society
University of California, Santa Barbara

The "baby boomers" are once again in the news. The oldest of them now in their forties and approaching mid-life, influence is omnipresent on the contemporary American landscape. Seventy-five million strong—roughly one-third of the American population—they shape the nation's lifestyles and consumer culture; the nation's "lead cohort," they set trends in moral values and political attitudes, family styles and career patterns.

By their sheer numbers, the largest cohort of youth ever in our nation's history, baby boomers have impacted American society at every point of passage in their journey from infancy to middle age. All the major institutions have felt this generation's influence: the post-war expansion of higher education occurred as a response to their growing numbers; the radical politics of the late sixties vented the youthful frustrations and disillusionments during the civil rights and Vietnam years; they were at the epicenter of the cultural upheavals of the sixties, a generation whose experiences and life-events would set them apart from those before and those after them.

The influence applies as well, of course, to religion. In the 1950s, the swelling number of school-age children prompted the suburban expansion of the churches and synagogues. Religious membership increased as parents sought out an affinity between religion and family values, and sought religious instruction for their children. Symbolism of religion, family, and country was pervasive, buttressed no doubt by rising affluence and the cold-war ideology of the times.

Then in the late 1960s, when large numbers of this generation were in their adolescence and youth, they altered the religious climate of the country significantly. Trauma surrounding the civil rights movement and later the Vietnam War, plus the changing moral, sexual and familial values of the countercultural years, all combined to produce a youthful defection from the religious establishment. New religious and spiritual movements flourished, as did human potential movements and "alternative lifestyles." Trends persisted into the 1970s although social activism dissipated and the countercultural values of the "new morality" turned in an individualistic "drop out and turn on" (to drugs, sex, self, etc.) direction. And throughout this period many youth did just that—drop out of the religious institutions (see Roof and McKinney, 1987).

And now, once again, we are at a critical phase in the life of this generation—the time of their "second coming," as Annie Gottlieb (1987) puts it. To the extent there is a dominant direction to changes within the post-war generation in the 1980s it is into family formation and parenting, mid-life career concerns, and some reassessment of value commitments, the latter often in a more "conservative" direction. There are widespread spiritual yearnings and a burgeoning self-help movement catering to the search for meaning and purpose in life. Spirituality often seems to be more a concern than religion, although the two blend together in ways that make them difficult to sort out. "Multi-layered" meaning systems are commonplace—that is, beliefs and practices drawing off a variety of sources, both religious and quasi-religious—including Eastern meditation, Native American religion, psychotherapy, ecology, feminism, as well as more traditional Judeo-Christian elements.

There is also evidence that many within this generation are returning to active involvement in churches and synagogues (Roozen and McKinney, forthcoming). The NORC General Social Surveys show that worship attendance has increased from the early 1970s to the early 1980s, and remained at elevated levels through the 1980s, for both older and younger boomers. Return to more active involvement appears, however, to be on different terms than for previous generations. While previous generations generally took their religious commitments and participation for granted, it appears that baby boomers approach these more as a calculated choice, one which consciously involves discriminating decisions between various religious alternatives, including of course the option of no participation in organized religion at all. Choice in matters of faith and practice is as much taken for granted for this generation as were expectations of religious involvement for previous generations.

The purpose of this paper is to explore one aspect of the religious changes—the return to organized religion. Who among them are returning? What accounts for the return? The findings are descriptive, drawn from a recent Lilly-funded survey of 536 baby boomers in four states (California, Massachusetts, North Carolina, and Ohio).

Cohort Experiences

Age is a major division among baby boomers: those born at the front end of the generation in the late forties are different from those born at the very back in the early sixties. Fifteen years apart, the two constituencies have had quite differing cohort experiences. Older baby boomers remember freedom marches and the assassination of President Kennedy; they came of age in a period of counter-cultural and political turmoil, and were deeply affected by the Vietnam War. People now in their late thirties and early forties experienced the sixties head-on, and were the most transformed by that momentous decade.

In contrast, younger baby boomers are more likely to remember gas lines in the seventies, Three Mile Island, and Chernoble; they came of age in a quieter time marked less by social protests than by

scarcity and a return to greater inwardness; generally they have achieved an easier blend of pragmatism and idealism than their elders. That each generation receives a distinctive imprint from the social and political events of its youth is an old idea, most often associated with the name of Karl Mannheim (Mannheim, 1928) and the role of events during the late adolescent and early adulthood years in shaping social experience.

As shown in Table 1, roughly two-thirds of all boomers have dropped out for a period of two years or more; of these, 43 percent of the older and 38 percent of the younger have returned to active involvement. Older baby boomers are returning to organized religion, but they are not necessarily the most religious in others ways. Younger boomers are more religious in matters of personal faith and practice: they consider themselves more religious and affirm traditional Judeo-Christian beliefs and practices more so than do older member of the generation. This appears to be the case across a wide spectrum of issues including belief in the Devil and conflict between religion and science. Interestingly also, they are more inclined to say they would call upon religious institutions for "rites of passage" for themselves or for family members—for baptisms, weddings, and funerals. To say this does not of course mean that they will necessarily participate in such rites, but it does suggest a higher level of normative religious expectations. Their greater religious traditionalism goes hand in hand with a more conservative stance generally. Younger boomers voted for Bush in 1988 in greater numbers, view themselves more as political conservatives, and hold to more conventional views on moral issues than older boomers.

If the seventies and eighties are imprinted on the younger, more traditional boomers, the anti-establishment ethos of the sixties shows up with the older members of the generation. The latter are more likely to endorse alternative religious beliefs and practices: they tend more to believe in reincarnation, to practice meditation, and to view all religions as equally true and good. The sixties live on insofar as the spirituality and practices of the period continue to influence the lives of this segment of the population.

Family Cycle

A second important factor is the family cycle. From the discussion already, one might conclude that the increased religious involvement on the part of the older boomers can be explained by the simple fact that more of them are married and have children. There is indeed considerable evidence in the research literature to support the argument (Carroll and Roozen, 1979; Schroeder, 1975; Roozen and McKinney, forthcoming). Married persons typically are more settled than unmarried, and the presence of children is a stabilizing influence. Frequently it has been observed that young adults return to active religious participation once they begin to raise their own children.

the evidence from this study is unambiguous: family cycle and family situation are potent factors affecting the contemporary religious styles of baby boomers (see Table 2). First it is clear that married persons with children are far more likely to be loyalists, that is not to have dropped out of church or synagogue at any time, and even more significantly, to have returned to active religious participation if they have dropped out. Forty-one percent of married people with children are loyalists and fifty percent of all who have dropped out are returnees—much higher than for any of the other constituencies. It is also clear that married people are more religious of the several constituencies on a wide array of indicators, ranging from personal beliefs, experiences and practices to attitudes toward organized religion. Data not shown here also reveal them to have had less exposure to countercultural influence—46 percent say they have smoked marijuana whereas considerably more than half have done so in all the other constituencies. They hold far more conservative values on moral issues such as abortion, unmarried couples living together, the legalization of marijuana, respect for authority, and calling for a return to stricter moral standards.

In contrast, married people without children are the mirror opposite. Only 16 percent of those who have dropped out in this category are returnees, considerably lower than for the divorced/separated or even the singles. They rank lower than singles on all the religious items, on some items considerably lower, which is counter to our expectations. What this suggests is a changing subculture for married couples who have postponed having children, many of whom have dual careers. Their lower levels of religiosity fit with their very liberal views—even more liberal than singles—on such matters as the legalization of marijuana, legal abortion regardless of reason, unmarried couples living together, and acceptance of different lifestyles. Again age as a factor interacts with family cycle considerations: married persons without children generally are older than singles, and as we saw earlier are less conservative than the younger wave of baby boomers on moral, political, and religious values.

The divorced/separated constitute a changing profile group. Past research has often described the divorced/separated as having very low rates of participation presumably because they did not feel accepted in many congregations. The present data show them to have the highest numbers who have left organized religion, yet are returning at levels higher than for either married persons without children or singles. That they may be returning in greater numbers is no doubt explained by the large proportion of them who have children—that is, the fact that they are single parents. As the number of single parents have increased in this generation, patterns of religious participation have changed.

Educational Differences

Babyboomers are the most educated of all generations in American history. Eighty-five percent of the baby boomer sample finished high school, and 36 percent graduated from college. However, because of their unprecedented opportunities for education, they are a generation deeply divided by their degree of education. Baby boomers share nearly a universal high-school education, but there is a clear division between those who sent on to college and pursued degrees in higher education and those who did not.

Generally we found the split between college graduate and those pursuing post-graduate study of more importance than whether one had completed some college or not. The college educated were far more exposed to countercultural influences (e.g., smoking marijuana and attending rock concerts); they were more likely to have participated in a demonstration or march and to have opposed the Vietnam War. Similar differences as would be expected are observed on a wide range of attitudes—gender equality, environmental concerns, racial attitudes, and the like. However, the most pronounced gap often was that between the college educated and post-graduates and professionals. Post-graduates and professionals are very egalitarian in their view especially with respect to civil liberties, favor government spending on welfare, express low levels of confidence in the government, and hold permissive views on sex and morality, considerably more so than college graduates. This constellation of values and attitudes is often associated with the so-called "new class" and suggests the emergence of its own distinctive ideology.

The expansion of higher education has had, of course, an enormous influence on religion. As Wuthnow (1988) has recently argued, education has contributed significantly to the deepening division between religious liberals and religious conservatives. In the period in which baby boomers have grown up—the 1960s and 1970s—this split has greatly intensified. Levels of traditional belief and of religious participation have declined considerably among the better educated during this period. On matters as varied as belief in God, interpretations of the Bible, Sabbath observance, prayer, and church and Sunday School attendance, there have been precipitous declines. And of course the better educated have come to constitute a more significant proportion of the population, thus contributing as Wuthnow says to an "education gap" in religious commitment.

The Lilly study offers further support of an education gap in religion, though again, there is no simple linear pattern with level of education (see Table 3). Levels of dropping out are fairly high across all educational levels—the lowest being college graduates, contrary to expectations. Forty-three percent of college graduates are Loyalist, which is at least ten points higher than for any other educational level. Why this should be so is not altogether obvious. One interpretation would be that the declines in religious participation which occurred most precipitously among the better educated in the 1960s and 1970s had by the 1980s become widespread throughout the young adult culture. This would point toward a general levelling of differences over time as more liberated norms pertaining to religious involvement became accepted, although such explanation would not account for why college graduates have a higher, rather than a lower rate of commitment.

The influence of education shows up among the defectors: fewer college graduates and post-graduates return to active involvement. Among those dropping out, seventy percent of postgraduates and 62 percent of college graduates remain dropouts, as compared with 57 percent of high school or less and 53 percent of those with some college experience. Once having broken ties with the institution, the chances of returning to church or synagogue are simply less among the educated.

In matters of belief and practice, patterns are fairly predictable. Traditional Judeo-Christian beliefs are more common among the lesser educated. The gap separating liberals and conservatives in style and substance of belief varies directly with level of education. Even beliefs in reincarnation and in astrology are more prevalent for the lesser educated. With religious practices, there are important differences: prayer and saying grace are more common among the lesser educated; meditation and attending spiritual growth seminars among the better educated.

One of the most important consequences of education is what we are calling "religious individualism," or the tendency to appropriate religious beliefs and values for oneself and to place greater emphasis on personal choice and conscience than on institutional authority. As level of education increases, so does greater religious individualism. This is true across all major religious traditions—Protestant, Catholic, Jewish. On a variety of measures tapping sentiments toward organized religion, the better educated are consistently more inclined to express a more personal, privatized view. Religious individualism encourages personal autonomy and responsibility in religious matters, but is a corrosive influence upon institutional loyalties.

Conclusion

It should be noted that the results reported here by age cohort, family type, and education are all based on preliminary analysis. Inferences about trends or causal factors should be interpreted cautiously. Multivariate analysis of the data are obviously necessary in order to specify more clearly the, interrelationships. also no attention has been given here to mainline Protestant versus conservative Protestant, Catholic, or Jewish comparisons.

Two concluding comments: One is that because many who were dropouts are now returning to organized religion, we need to explore further who are returning and why. We really don't know very much about who the returnees are in terms of their spiritual quests and what it is about religious institutions they like and dislike. A second is that we need to explore further the unexpected findings as reported here: for example, the younger boomers and their higher levels of religiosity, and also, that married persons without children are the least religiously involved of any of the family types. the former suggests an important change in religious climate for those coming into adulthood in the 1970s, and possibly an even greater return to religion of these boomers once they are into parenting, and the second suggests an emerging distinct boomer subculture, shaped by dual careers and postponement of having children—and presumably postponement of religious re-affiliation. Further attention to both is essential if we are to grasp the changes now underway in the changing shape of boomer religiosity. And of course, we must specify more exactly what is meant by returning to organized religion. Returning to active involvement does not necessarily mean "joining" religious institutions. It is said that many boomers are returning as visitors, and that permanent ties to organizations are unlikely. If so, we need to arrive at new measures of such involvement and exposure to religion and what the meaning and implications of such involvement are for religious institutions.

TABLE 1: Religious Characteristics of Older and Younger Baby Boomer Cohorts

	Older (N = 293)	Younger (N = 243)
Institutional Involvement		
Percent Loyalist	35%	32%
Percent Dropping Out	65	68
Of these:		
Percent Returnee	43	38
Percent Dropout	57	62
Personal Beliefs and Practices		
Consider to be religious	83	89
Say grace at meals	36	39
Believe in Eternal Life	80	83
Believe in Devil	61	67
Born Again	43	45
View religion and science in conflict	53	63
Attitudes toward Organized Religion		
Consider church membership important	67	60
Would expect to call upon church for		
rites for self or family: Baptism	71	82
Wedding	74	86
Funeral	85	90
Alternative Beliefs and Practices		
Believe in Reincarnation	30	25
Practice Meditation	17	11
Agree that all religions are equally		
good and true	51	43

TABLE 2: Religious Characteristics by Boomer Family Type

	Single (N=93)	Married without children (N=56)	Married with children (N=289	Divorced/ Separated (N=92)
Institutional Involvement				
Percent Loyalists	29%	34%	41%	14%
Percent Dropping Out	71	66	59	86
Of these:				
Percent Returnees	29	16	50	36
Percent Dropouts	71	84	50	64
Personal Beliefs and Practices				
Consider to be religious	78	78	91	82
Say grace at meals	24	21	46	32
Born Again	39	21	50	40
Definitely Believe in God	77	64	83	82
Believe in Devil	60	50	69	59
Religion "very important" in life	34	29	53	44
Attitudes Toward Organized Religion				
Agree it is important to attend church/synagogue as a family	42	32	67	40
Consider church membership as important	59	48	68	66
Would expect to call upon institution for rites for self or family:				
Baptism	72	58	82	72
Wedding	82	66	85	68
Funeral	85	82	91	81

TABLE 3. Religious Characteristics of Boomers by Education

	High School or less (N = 209)	Some College (N = 124)	College Grad. (N = 111)	Post-Grad. (N = 91)
Institutional Involvement				
Loyalist	31%	33%	43%	39%
Percent Dropping Out	69	67	57	71
Of These:				
Returnees	43	47	38	30
Dropouts	57	53	62	70
Beliefs				
Definitely believe in God	86	80	81	64
Believe in Devil	71	69	63	42
Say Bible is to be taken literally	56	38	23	15
Believe religion prepares for afterlife	59	44	28	23
Believe a child is born guilty of sin	35	26	20	15
Believe in reincarnation	31	28	29	20
Believe in astrology	35	27	14	19
Practices				
Pray daily	59	54	50	45
Say grace	35	44	40	29
Practice meditation	9	11	16	29
Attend spiritual growth seminars	19	21	24	31
Religious Individualism				
Agree that one should follow conscience, even if it means going against organized religion	74	75	86	89
Say people have God within them so churches aren't necessary	29	31	32	37
Say more important to be alone and meditate than worship with others	45	53	63	60
Prefer to explore many teachings than stick to a particular faith	52	63	66	69

Bibliography

Carroll, Jackson W. and David A. Roozen
1975 *Religious Participation in American Society: An Analysis of Social and Religious Trends and their Interaction.* Hartford, Ct.: Hartford Seminary Foundation.

Gottlieb, Annie
1987 *Do you Believe in Magic? The Second Coming of the 60s Generation.* New York: Times Books

Manheim, Karl
1928 "The Problem of Generations." Pp. 276-322 in *Essays on the Sociology of Knowledge,* by Karl Mannheim. London: Routledge and Kegan Paul.

Roof, Wade Clark and William McKinney
1987 *American Mainline Religion.* New Brunswick: Rutgers University Press.

Roozen, David A.
1980 "Church Dropouts: Changing Patterns of Disengagement and Re-Entry," *Review of Religious Research* 21 (Supplement), 427-450.

Roozen, David A. and William McKinney
1990 "The 'Big Chill' Generation Warms to Worship: Family Cycle and Political Orientation Effects on Increases in Worship Attendance from the 1970s to the 1980s among the Baby Boom Generation," *Review of Religious Research,* forthcoming.

Schroeder, Widick
1975 "Age Cohorts, the Family Life Cycle, and Participation in the Voluntary Church in America: Implications for Memberhsip Patterns, 1950-2000," *Chicago Theological Seminary Register* 65: 13-28.

Walrath, Douglas A.
1987 *Frameworks: Patterns for Living and Believing Today.* New York: Pilgrim Press.

Wuthnow, Robert
1988 *The Restructuring of American Religion.* Princeton: Princeton University Press.

CHURCH ATTENDANCE AND OTHER POLLS

"Young adults often are conspicuously absent at worship services in the average week. The pews are more likely to be filled by the very young, their middle aged parents, and their grandparents" according to data released by The Gallup Organization, Princeton, NJ (*PRRC emerging trends,* Vol. 12, No. 1, Jan. 1990).

"Teen-agers set a modern attendance record in 1989 when 57% participated in worship services during the average week at a church or synagogue. The previous high mark of attendance was 54% of the teens reached in both 1986 and 1981," Gallup notes.

WORSHIP SERVICE ATTENDANCE IN PAST SEVEN DAYS

	Adults	Teens
1989	43%	57%
1988	42	51
1987	40	52
1986	40	54
1985	42	52
1984	40	52
1983	40	53
1982	41	50
1981	41	54
1980	41	50
1972	40	*
1967	43	
1962	46	
1958	49	
1954	46	
1950	39	
1940	37	
1939	41	

*Teen attendance figures unavailable for earlier years.

"Overall attendance in 1989 by adults, ages 18 or older, averaged 43% in a typical week. This represents only a one percentage point increase over 1988, but it is the first time since 1967 that this level of attendance has been achieved. The record high attendance for adults in America is 59%, accomplished in both 1959 and 1955."

The data in the above table on adult and teen attendance "mask a drop in formal worship practices among older teens and young adults," Gallup notes. "Attendance is highest among young teens, ages 13 to 15, with 62 percent reporting they went to church or synagogue the previous week in 1989. Among those who are 16 to 17 years of age, attendance drops to 50 percent. Lowest attendance by any age group is found among young adults, 18 to 29 with only one in three (32%) going to religious services in 1989. Attendance then advances as people mature, with 4 in 10 (40%) of those who are 30 to 49, and over half (52%) of those who are 50 and older, reporting attendance in an average week."

Gallup notes that the above findings "strongly suggest that worship service attendance for children and teens may be enforced rather than voluntary." For instance in an 1988 Gallup Organization study of *Teen-age Attitudes and Behavior Concerning Religion,* "one teen in three reports attending church only because 'my parents wanted me to go' (24%) [and] . . . 'my parents told me to go (12%).' "

Gallup notes that: "Geographically, attendance by teens is particularly high in the South where two teens in three (67%) went to worship services in 1989. Attendance was fairly high in the Midwest (55%), but comparatively fewer teens attended religious services in the East (52%) and the West (45%). Adult residents of the South (47%), East (43%), and Midwest (43%) also are more likely to be church goers than are those who live in the West (34%).

"Adult women are more likely than men to have attended services in 1989, by a margin of

48% to 38%. A similar disparity in attendance is found among teens, with young women outnumbering young men at places of worship by 61% to 52%. Teen attendance also peaks among non-whites (62%) and those who come from white-collar households (60%).

"The adult church attendance figures are based on 3,251 interviews conducted by the Gallup Organization nationwide throughout 1989 and have a sampling variance of plus or minus 3 percentage points. The findings for teen-agers are based on telephone interviews with a representative national cross section of 1,003 teen-agers, 13 to 17, conducted by The Gallup Youth Survey, throughout 1989, and have a sampling variance of plus or minus 4 percentage points."

Denominational Preferences of Teen-agers

"Protestants currently outnumber Catholics among the adult U.S. population by over two to one, with approximately 56% of adults on recent Gallup Polls stating a preference for one of the Protestant denominations and 25% saying they are Catholics," according to *PRRC emerging trends*, Vol. 12, No. 1, Jan. 1990.

"The ranks of Roman Catholics, however, would appear to be growing faster among the young. In surveys taken by the Gallup Youth Survey in 1989, fewer teens than adults identify themselves as Protestants, while more say they are Catholics. Currently, slightly over half of the teens (52%) cite preference for one of the Protestant denominations, while one in three (32%) is a Catholic by preference.

"Very few Catholic teens (18%) are found in the South where 72% of the young people claim allegiance to the Protestant faith. Protestants also outnumber Catholics in the Midwest, by a margin of 49% to 40%. In the East there is a slight plurality of Catholics (42%) over Protestants (40%), but in the West the edge goes to the Protestants, 36% to 33%.

RELIGIOUS PREFERENCE OF TEENS

	Protestant	Catholic
National	53%	32%
Sex		
Male	48	33
Female	55	31
Age		
Ages 13 to 15	54	30
Ages 16 to 17	54	30
Race		
Whites	49	33
Non-Whites	64	28
Family		
White-collar family background	48	35
Blue-collar family background	56	30
Region		
East	40	42
Midwest	49	40
South	72	18
West	36	33
Urbanization		
Central cities	49	36
Suburbs	49	32
Non-metropolitan areas	60	27

"Young Catholics most often are found in large cities (36%) and in the suburbs (32%) but in small towns and rural areas are outnumbered by Protestants by two to one (60% to 27%).

"In a bygone era Catholics were largely viewed as recent immigrants with trade, labor or service occupations, but today there are more Catholic teens who come from white-collar households (35%) than are found in blue-collar families (30%). By contrast, the majority of Protestant teens now come from blue-collar family backgrounds (56%) rather than from white-collar households (48%).

Gallup says that: "The findings are based on telephone interviews with a representative national cross section of 1,003 teen-agers, ages 13 to 17, conducted throughout 1989. For results based on a sample of this size, one can say with 95% confidence that the error attributable to sampling and other random effects is plus or minus three percentage points."

VALUE OF NEW CONSTRUCTION OF RELIGIOUS BUILDINGS IN CURRENT AND CONSTANT 1982 DOLLARS
(In Millions of Dollars)

Year	Current Dollars	1982 Dollars	Year	Current Dollars	1982 Dollars
1964	$ 992	$3,605	1977	$1,046	$1,659
1965	1,201	4,220	1978	1,248	1,779
1966	1,145	3,869	1979	1,548	1,996
1967	1,063	3,491	1980	1,637	1,884
1968	1,079	3,336	1981	1,665	1,746
1969	989	2,827	1982	1,543	1,541
1970	929	2,488	1983	1,780	1,712
1971	813	2,004	1984	2,132	1,968
1972	845	1,947	1985	2,409	2,161
1973	814	1,734	1986	2,702	2,365
1974	918	1,707	1987	2,753	2,340
1975	867	1,543	1988	2,822	2,359
1976	956	1,631			

Source: U. S. Department of Commerce, *Bureau of the Census, Value of New Construction Put in Place in the United States:* "Current Construction Reports, C-30, Value of New Construction Put in Place," Table 1.

In constant 1982 dollars, the peak year for the value of new construction of religious buildings was 1965, when the value in real terms was 1.8 times that of 1988. The amount expended in 1986, however, was higher than for any year since 1970.

5. MAIN DEPOSITORIES OF CHURCH HISTORY MATERIAL AND SOURCES

Many denominations have established central archival-manuscript depositories and, in addition, are dealing with regional, diocesan, synodical, or provincial subdivisions. Communions functioning through this type of structure especially are the Roman Catholic, Episcopal, Baptist, Lutheran, and Methodist.

Some denominations with headquarters in the United States also have churches in Canada. Historical material on Canadian sections of these denominations will occasionally be found at the various locations cited below. The reader is also referred to the section "In Canada," which follows.

IN THE UNITED STATES

Adventist:

Adventual Library, Aurora College, Aurora, IL 60507 (Advent Christian Church)

Dr. Linden J. Carter Library, Berkshire Christian College, Lenox, MA 01240

Andrews University, Berrien Springs, MI 49104

General Conference of Seventh-day Adventists, 6840 Eastern Ave. NW, Washington, DC 20012

Baptist:

American Baptist Historical Society (including Samuel Colgate Baptist Historical Collection), 1100 South Goodman St., Rochester, NY 14620

Andover Newton Theological School (including Backus Historical Society), Newton Centre, MA 02159

Bethel Seminary (Swedish Baptist material), 3949 Bethel Dr., St. Paul, MN 55112

Historical Commission, Southern Baptist Convention, 901 Commerce St., Suite 400, Nashville TN 37203

Seventh Day Baptist Historical Society, 3120 Kennedy Rd., P.O. Box 1678, Janesville, WI 53547

Primitive Baptist Archives, Elon College, Elon, NC 27244

Brethren in Christ Church:

Archives of the Brethren in Christ Church, Messiah College, Grantham, PA 17027

Church of the Brethren:

Bethany Theological Seminary, Butterfield and Meyers Roads, Oak Brook, IL 60521

Brethren Historical Library and Archives, 1451 Dundee Ave., Elgin, IL 60120

Juniata College, Huntingdon, PA 16652

Churches of Christ:

Abilene Christian University Library, Abilene, TX 79699

Harding Graduate School of Religion Library, 1000 Cherry Rd., Memphis, TN 38117

Pepperline University Library, Malibu, CA 90265

Churches of God, General Conference:

Archives/Museum of the Churches of God, General Conference, 700 E. Melrose Ave., P.O. Box 926, Findlay, OH 45839

Congregationalist: (See United Church of Christ)

Disciples:

The Disciples of Christ Historical Society, 1101 Nineteenth Ave., S., Nashville, TN 37212

Christian Theological Seminary, Indianapolis, IN 46208

Lexington Theological Seminary, Lexington, KY 40508

The Disciples Divinity House, University of Chicago, Chicago, IL 60637

Texas Christian University, Fort Worth, TX 76219

Culver-Stockton College, Canton, MO 63435

Episcopalian:

National Council, Protestant Episcopal Church, 815 2nd Ave., New York, NY 10017

Library and Archives of the Church Historical Society, 606 Rathervue Pl., Austin, TX 78767

Berkeley Divinity School at Yale, New Haven, CT 06510

General Theological Seminary, 175 Ninth Ave., New York, NY 10011

Evangelical United Brethren:

(see United Methodist Church)

Evangelical Congregational Church:

Historical Society of the Evangelical Congregational Church, 121 S. College St., Myerstown, PA 17067

Friends:

Friends' Historical Library, Swarthmore College, Swarthmore, PA 19081

Haverford College, Quaker Collection, Magill Library, Haverford, PA 19041

Jewish:

American Jewish Archives, 3101 Clifton Ave., Cincinnati, OH 45220

Yiddish Scientific Institute—YIVO, 1048 Fifth Ave., New York, NY 10028

American Jewish Historical Society, 2 Thornton Rd., Waltham, MA 02154

Latter Day Saints:

Historian's Office, Church Archives, Historical Department, 50 East North Temple St., Salt Lake City, UT 84150

The Genealogical Society, 50 E. North Temple, Salt Lake City, UT 84150

Lutheran:

Concordia Historical Institute, Dept. of Archives and History. The Lutheran Church-Missouri Synod, Historical Library, Archives and Museum on Lutheranism, 801 De Mun Ave., St. Louis, MO 63105.

Archives of American Lutheran Church, Wartburg Theological Seminary, 333 Wartburg Place, Dubuque, IA 52001

Archives of the Lutheran Church in America, Lutheran School of Theology at Chicago, 1100 East 55th St., Chicago, IL 60615

Luther College, Decorah, IA 52101

Lutheran Archives Center at Philadelphia, 7301 Germantown Ave., Philadelphia, PA 19119

Lutheran Theological Seminary, Gettysburg, PA 17325
Concordia Theological Seminary, St. Louis, MO 63105
Finnish-American Historical Archives, Hancock, MI 49930
St. Olaf College (Norwegian), Northfield, MN 55057
Archives of Cooperative Lutheranism, Office of the Secretary, Evangelical Lutheran Church in America, 8765 West Higgins Rd., Chicago, IL 60631
Lutheran Theological Southern Seminary, 4201 N. Main St., Columbia, SC 29203

Mennonite:

Bethel College, Historical Library, N. Newton, KS 67117
Centre for MB Studies, 4824 E. Butler, Fresno, CA 93727
The Archives of the Mennonite Church, 1700 South Main, Goshen, IN 46526
Menno Simons Historical Library and Archives, Eastern Mennonite College, Harrisonburg, VA 22801
Mennonite Historical Library, Bluffton College, Bluffton, OH 45817

Methodist:

Archives and Historical Library, The Wesleyan Church, P. O. Box 50434, Indianapolis, IN 46520. Daniel L. Burnett, Dir.
B. L. Fisher Library, Asbury Theological Seminary, Wilmore, KY 40390; David W. Faupel, Dir.
Bridwell Library Center for Methodist Studies, Perkins School of Theology, Southern Methodist University, Dallas, TX 75275. Dr. Richard P. Heitzenrater, Dir.
Center for Evangelical United Brethren Studies, United Theological Seminary, 1810 Harvard Blvd., Dayton, OH 45406. Elmer J. O'Brien, Lib.
Drew University Library, Madison, NJ 07940, Kenneth E. Rowe, Methodist Lib.
Duke Divinity School Library, Duke University, Durham, NC 27706. Harriet V. Leonard, Ref. Lib.
General Commission on Archives and History, The United Methodist Church, PO. Box 127, Madison, NJ 07940. Arthur W. Swarthout, Asst. Gen. Sec.
Indiana United Methodist Archives, Roy O. West Library, DePauw University, Greencastle, IN 46135
Interdenominational Theological Center Library, 671 Beckwith Street, S.W., Atlanta, GA 30314. (black Methodism)
Marston Memorial Historical Center, Free Methodist World Headquarters, Winona Lake, IN 46590.Evelyn Mottweiler, Lib.
New England Methodist Historical Society Library, Boston University School of Theology, 745 Commonwealth Ave., Boston, MA 02215.William Zimpfer, Lib.
Nippert Memorial Library, German Methodist Collection, Cincinnati Historical Society, Eden Park, Cincinnati, OH 45402
Pitts Theology Library, Candler School of Theology, Emory University, Atlanta, GA 30322.Channing Jeschke, Lib.
The United Library, (Garrett-Evangelical and Seabury Western Theological Seminaries) 2121 Sheridan Road, Evanston, IL 60201. David K. Himrod, Ref. Lib.
United Methodist Historical Library, Beeghley Library, Ohio Wesleyan University, Delaware, OH 43015
United Methodist Publishing House Library, Room 122, 201 Eighth Ave., South, Nashville, TN 37202. Rosalyn Lewis, Librarian

The Upper Room Library, 1908 Grand Avenue, Nashville, TN 37203
World Methodist Council Library, P.O. Box 518, Lake Junaluska, NC 28745. Evelyn Sutton, Lib.

Moravian:

The Archives of the Moravian Church, 41 W. Locust St., Bethlehem, PA 18018
Moravian Archives, Southern Province of the Moravian Church, Drawer M., Salem Station, Winston-Salem, NC 27108

Nazarene:

Nazarene Theological Seminary, 1700 East Meyer Blvd., Kansas City, MO 64131. William C. Miller, Librarian

Pentecostal:

Oral Roberts University Library, 7777 South Lewis, Tulsa, OK 74105
Assemblies of God Archives, 1445 Boonville Ave., Springfield, MO 65802. Dir., Wayne Warner
Pentecostal Research Center, Church of God (Cleveland, Tenn.), P. O. Box 3448, Cleveland, TN 37320. Dir., Joseph Byrd

Polish National Catholic:

Commission on History and Archives, Polish National Catholic Church, 1031 Cedar Ave., Scranton, PA 18505. Chmn., Joseph Wielczerzak

Presbyterian:

Presbyterian Historical Association and Department of History, Presbyterian Church (USA), 425 Lombard St., Philadelphia, PA 19147
Historical Foundation Montreat, NC 28757
Princeton Theological Seminary, Speer Library, Princeton, NJ 08540
McCormack Theological Seminary, 800 West Belden Ave., Chicago, IL 60614
Presbyterian Church in America, Historical Center, 12330 Conway Rd., St. Louis, MO 63141

Reformed:

Calvin College, Grand Rapids, MI 49056 (Christian Reformed)
Commission on History, Reformed Church in America, New Brunswick Theological Seminary, New Brunswick, NJ 08901
Evangelical and Reformed Historical Society, Lancaster Theological Seminary, Lancaster, PA 17603. (Reformed in the U.S., Evangelical and Reformed)

Roman Catholic:

Archives of the American Catholic Historical Society of Philadelphia, St. Charles Boromeo Seminary, Overbrook, Philadelphia, PA 19151
Department of Archives and Manuscripts, Catholic University of America, Washington, DC 20017
University of Notre Dame Archives, Box 513, Notre Dame, IN 46556
St. Mary's Sem. & Univ., Roland Park, Baltimore, MD 21210
Georgetown University, Washington, DC 20007
St. Louis University, St. Louis, MO 63103

Salvation Army:

The Salvation Army Archives and Research Center, 120 W. 14th St., New York, NY 10011

Schwenkfelder:

Schwenkfelder Library, Seminary Ave., Pennsburg, PA 18073

Shaker:

Western Reserve Historical Society, Cleveland, OH 44106

Ohio Historical Society, Division of Archives & Manuscripts, Columbus, OH 43211

Swendenborgian:

Academy of the New Church Library, Bryn Athyn, PA 19009

Unitarian and Universalist:

Harvard Divinity School Library, 45 Francis Ave., Cambridge, MA 02138

Rhode Island Historical Society, Providence, RI

Meadville Theological School, 5701 S. Woodlawn Ave., Chicago, IL 60637

Archives of the Unitarian-Universalist Association, 25 Beacon St., Boston, MA 02108

The United Church of Christ:

Archives of the United Church of Christ, 555 W. James St., Lancaster, PA 17603

Congregational Library, 14 Beacon St., Boston, MA 02108

Chicago Theological Seminary, 5757 University Ave., Chicago, IL 60637

Divinity Library, and University Library, Yale University, New Haven, CT 06520

Library of Hartford Theological Seminary, Hartford, CT 06105

Harvard Divinity School Library, Cambridge, MA 02138

Eden Archives, 475 E. Lockwood Ave., Webster Groves, MO 63119. (Evangelical and Reformed)

STANDARD GUIDES TO CHURCH ARCHIVES

William Henry Allison, **Inventory of Unpublished Material for American Religious History in Protestant Church Archives and other Depositories** (Washington, D. C., Carnegie Institution of Washington, 1910, 254 pp.).

John Graves Barrow, **A Bibliography of Bibliographies in Religion** (Ann Arbor, Mich., 1955), pp. 185-198.

Edmund L. Binsfield, "Church Archives in the United States and Canada: a Bibliography," in **American Archivist,** V. 21, No. 3 (July 1958) pp. 311-332, 219 entries.

Nelson R. Burr, "Sources for the Study of American Church History in the Library of Congress," 1953. 13 pp. Reprinted from **Church History,** Vol. XXII, No. 3 (Sept. 1953).

Homer L. Calkin, **Catalog of Methodist Archival and Manuscript Collections.** Mont Alto, PA: World Methodist Historical Society, 1982—(4 vols. to date)

Church Records Symposium, **American Archivist,** Vol. 24, October 1961, pp. 387-456.

Mable Deutrich, "Supplement to Church Archives in the United States and Canada, a Bibliography," Washington, DC: 1964.

Andrea Hinding, ed. **Women's History Sources: A Guide to Archives and Manuscript Collections in the U.S.** New York: Bowker, 1979. 2 vols.

E. Kay Kirkham, **A Survey of American Church Records, for the Period Before The Civil War, East of the Mississippi River** (Salt Lake City, 1959-60, 2 vols.). Includes the depositories and bibliographies.

Peter G. Mode, **Source Book and Bibliographical Guide for American Church History** (Menasha, Wisc., George Banta Publishing Co., 1921, 735 pp.).

Society of American Archivists. **American Archivist,** 1936/37 (continuing). Has articles on church records and depositories.

Aug. R. Suelflow, **A Preliminary Guide to Church Records Repositories,** Society of American Archivists, Church Archives Committee, 1969. Lists more than 500 historical-archival depositories with denominational and religious history in America.

U. S. National Historical Publications and Records Commission, **Directory of Archives and Manuscript Repositories in the United States.** Washington: NHPRC, 1978

United States, Library of Congress, Division of Manuscripts, **Manuscripts in Public and Private Collections in the United States** (Washington, D.C., 1924).

U. S. Library of Congress, Washington, D. C.: **The National Union Catalog of Manuscript Collections,** A59—22 vols., 1959-1986. Based on reports from American repositories of manuscripts.

Contains many entries for collections of church archives. This series is continuing. Extremely valuable collection. Researchers must consult the cumulative indexes.

Notes

The Libraries of the University of Chicago, Chicago; Union Theological Seminary, New York; and Yale Divinity School, New Haven, have large collections.

Day Missions Library, Yale Divinity School, 409 Prospect St., New Haven, CT 06510

The Archives of the National Council of the Churches of Christ in the U.S.A., and predecessor agencies, are located in the Presbyterian Historical Association, 425 Lombard St., Philadelphia, PA 19147. Tel. (215)627-1852.

The Missionary Research Library Collection of the Union Theological Seminary Library, 3041 Broadway, New York, NY 10027, has a large collection of interdenominational material.

The Library of the American Bible Society, Broadway at 61st St., New York, NY 10023, has material on the history of transmission of the Bible text, Bible translation, etc.

The Archives of the Billy Graham Center, Wheaton College, Wheaton, IL 60187, Tel. (312)260-5910, has a large collection of North American nondenominational missions and evangelism materials.

Zion Research Library, Boston University, 771 Commonwealth Ave., Boston, MA 02215 has a noteworthy archival collection.

"Specialized Research Libraries in Missions" are described by Frank W. Price in **Library Trends,** Oct, 1960, V. 9, No 2, University of Illinois Graduate School of Library Science, Urbana, IL 61801.

IN CANADA

The list of depositories of church history material which follows was reviewed recently by Dr. Neil Semple, Senior Archivist—Manuscripts, The United Church of Canada, to whom the editor is grateful.

A few small Canadian religious bodies have headquarters in the United States, and therefore the reader is advised to consult "Main Depositories of Church History Material and Sources in the United States," which immediately precedes this section for possible sources of information on Canadian religious groups. Another source: *Directory of Canadian Archives,* edited by Marcel Caya.

The use of the term "main" depositories in this section implies that there are some smaller communions with archival collections not listed below and also that practically every judicatory of large religious bodies (e.g., diocese, presbytery, conference) has archives excluded from this listing. For information on these collections, write directly to the denominational headquarters or to the judicatory involved.

The major libraries in the United States listed above under "Notes" contain material relating to Canadian Church history. Most American Protestant denominational archives have important primary and secondary source material relating to missionary work in Canada during the pioneer era.

Anglican:

General Synod Archives, 600 Jarvis St., Toronto, Ontario M4Y 2J6. Archivist: Mrs. Terry Thompson. Also Archives.

Baptist:

Canadian Baptist Archives, McMaster Divinity College, Hamilton, Ontario L8S 4K1. Librarian: Judith Colwell

Evangelical Baptist Historical Library, 3034 Bayview Ave., Willowdale, Ontario M2N 6J5

Baptist Historical Collection, Vaughan Memorial library, Acadia University, Wolfville, Nova Scotia BOP 1XO. Archivist: Mrs. Pat Thompson

Disciples of Christ:

Canadian Disciples Archives, 39 Arkell Rd., R.R. 2, Guelph, Ontario N1H 6H8. Archivist: James A. Whitehead

Reuben Butchart Collection, Victoria University, Toronto, Ontario M5S1K7

Jewish:

Jewish Historical Society of Western Canada, 404-365 Hargrave St., Winnipeg, Manitoba R3B 2K3. Archivist: Dorothy Hershfield

Canadian Jewish Congress (Central Region) Archives, 4600 Bathurst St., Toronto, Ontario M5T 1Y6. Archivist: Stephen A. Speisman

Lutheran:

Lutheran Council in Canada, 500-365 Hargrave St., Winnipeg, Manitoba R3B 2K3. Archivist: Rev. N. J. Threinen

Evangelical Lutheran Church in Canada, 1512 St. James St., Winnipeg, Manitoba R3H 0L2. Archivist: Rev. Leon C. Gilbertson (incorporating archives of the Evangelical Lutheran Church of Canada, the Lutheran Church in America—Canada Section's Central Synod Archives and those of the Western Canada Synod) The Eastern Synod Archives are housed at Wilfrid Laurier University, Waterloo, Ontario N2L 3C5. Archivist: Rev. E.R.W. Schultz.

Lutheran Church—Canada, Ontario District, 149 Queen St., S., Kitchener, Ontario N2H 1W2. Archivist: Rev. W. W. Wentzlaff; Manitoba-Saskatchewan District, 411 Leighton Ave., Winnipeg, Monitoba R2K 0J8. Archivist Mr. Harry Laudin.

Concordia College, Edmonton, Alberta T5B 4E4. Archivist: Mrs. Hilda Robinson.

Mennonite:

Conrad Grebel College, Archives Centre, Waterloo, Ontario N2L 3G6. Archivist: Sam Steiner

Mennonite Brethren Bible College, Center for Mennonite Brethren Studies in Canada, 1-169 Riverton Ave., Winnipeg, Manitoba R2L 2E5. Archivist: Kenneth Reddig

Mennonite Heritage Centre. Archives of the General Conference of Mennonites in Canada, 600 Shaftesbury Blvd., Winnipeg, Manitoba R3P 0M4. Tel (204) 888-6781. Historian-archivist: Lawrence Klippenstein

Free Methodist:

4315 Village Centre Ct., Mississauga, Ontario L4Z 1S2

Pentecostal:

The Pentecostal Assemblies of Canada, 10 Overlea Blvd., Toronto Ontario M4H 1A5.

Presbyterian:

Presbyterian Archives, Knox College, University of Toronto, 59 St. George St., Toronto, Ontario M5S 2E6. Archivist: Rev. T. M. Bailey; Deputy Archivist, Mrs. Kim Moir

Roman Catholic:

For guides to many Canadian Catholic diocesan religious community, and institutional archives, write: Rev. Pierre Hurtubise, O.M.I., Dir. of the Research Center in Religious History in Canada, St. Paul Univ., 223 Main St., Ottawa, Ontario K1S 1C4.

Salvation Army:

The George Scott Railton Heritage Centre, 2130 Bayview Ave., Toronto, Ontario M4N 3K6. Contact: Catherine Sequin.

The United Church of Canada:

Central Archives, Victoria University, Toronto, Ontario M5S 1K7. Archivist-Historian: Miss Jean Dryden. (Methodist, Presbyterian, Congregational, Evangelical United Brethren.) Also Regional Conference Archives.

Note: The archives of the Canadian Council of Churches and related organizations have been deposited in the Public Archives of Canada, 395 Wellington, Ottawa, Ontario K1A 0N3. Some remain at the Canadian Council of Churches located at 40 St. Clair Ave. E., Toronto, Ontario M4T 1M9. The Public Archives of Canada also contains a large number of records and personal papers related to the various churches.

IV: INDEX

Greek Orthodox Archdiocese of North and South America, 72
Holy Ukrainian Autocephalic Orthodox Church in Exile, 73
Orthodox Church in America, The, 86
Romanian Orthodox Church in America, 104
Romanian Orthodox Episcopate of America, The, 104
Russian Orthodox Church in the U.S.A., Patriarchal Parishes of the, 104
Russian Orthodox Church Outside of Russia, The, 105
Serbian Orthodox Church in the U.S.A. and Canada, 106
Syrian Orthodox Church of Antioch (Archdiocese of the U.S.A. and Canada), 111
True (Old Calendar) Orthodox Church of Greece (Synod of Metropolitan Cyprian), American Exarchate, 111
Ukrainian Orthodox Church in America (Ecumenical Patriarchate), 112
Ukrainian Orthodox Church of the U.S.A., 112
Eastern Orthodox Churches, 165
Ecumenical Agencies, 177-202
Ecumenical Agencies, Canada, 203-4
Elim Fellowship, 56
Elim Fellowship of Evangelical Churches and Ministers, 136
Elizabeth Fry Society of Toronto, 244
Enrollment in Seminaries, 1980-89, U.S. and Canada, 281-83
Episcopal Church, The, 56
Estonian Evangelical Lutheran Church, The, 59
Estonian Evangelical Lutheran Church, The (Canada), 136
Ethical Culture Movement, 59
Ethical Union, American, 59
Evangelical Baptist Churches in Canada, The Fellowship of, 137
Evangelical Bible Churches, Fellowship of, 65
Evangelical Bible Churches, Fellowship of, Canada, 155
Evangelical Church Alliance, The, 8
Evangelical Church in Canada, The, 137
Evangelical Church, The, 59
Evangelical Congregational Church, 60
Evangelical Council for Financial Accountability, 240
Evangelical Covenant Church, The, 60
Evangelical Covenant Church of Canada, The, 137
Evangelical Fellowship of Canada, 18
Evangelical Free Church of America, The, 61
Evangelical Free Church of Canada, 137
Evangelical Friends Alliance, 61
Evangelical Lutheran Church in America, 61
Evangelical Lutheran Church in Canada, 138
Evangelical Lutheran Synod, 64
Evangelical Mennonite Church, Inc., 64
Evangelical Mennonite Conference (Canada), 138
Evangelical Mennonite Mission Conference (Canada), 138
Evangelical Methodist Church, 64
Evangelical Presbyterian Church, 64
Evangelical Press Association, 9
Evangelical Theological Society of Canada, 244
Evangelistic Associations (U.S.)
  Apostolic Christian Church (Nazarean), 28
  Apostolic Christian Churches of America, 28
  Apostolic Faith Mission of Portland, Oregon, 28
  Christian Congregation, Inc., The, 41
  Church of Daniel's Band, 43

Fellowship of Evangelical Baptist Churches in Canada, The, 137
Fellowship of Evangelical Bible Churches, 65
Fellowship of Evangelical Bible Churches, Canada, 155
Fellowship of Fundamental Bible Churches, 66
Fellowship of Reconciliation, The, 240
Finances, Church, 265-70
Fire-Baptized Holiness Church (Wesleyan), The, 66
Foreign Policy Association, 240
Foursquare Gospel Church of Canada, 139
Free Christian Zion Church of Christ, 66

Free Lutheran Congregations, The Association of, 66
Free Methodist Church in Canada, The, 139
Free Methodist Church of North America, 67
Free Will Baptists, 67
Free Will Baptists (Canada), 139
French Baptist Union (Canada), 133
Friends (U.S.)
  Evangelical Friends Alliance, 61
  Friends General Conference, 68
  Friends United Meeting, 68
  Religious Society of Friends (Conservative), 97
  Religious Society of Friends (Unaffiliated Meetings), 97
Friends Committee on National Legislation, 240
Friends General Conference, 68
Friends United Meeting, 68
Friends World Committee for Consultation, Section of the Americas, 164
Frontiers Foundation/Operation Beaver, 244
Full Gospel Assemblies, International, 69
Full Gospel Fellowship of Churches and Ministers, International, 69
Fundamental Methodist Church, Inc., 69

GATT-Fly, 244
General Association of Regular Baptist Churches, 70
General Baptists, General Association of, 70
General Church of the New Jerusalem, 70
General Church of the New Jerusalem (Canada), 140
General Conference of Mennonite Brethren Churches, 70
General Conference of the Evangelical Baptist Church, Inc., 71
General Convention The Swedenborgian Church, 71
General Federation of Women's Clubs, 240
General Six-Principle Baptists, 71
Gideons International in Canada, 244
Girl Guides of Canada—Guides du Canada, 244
Girl Scouts of the U.S.A., 240
Giving, per Capita, Effects of Inflation on, 1961-1988, 270
Glenmary Research Center, 241
Gospel Missionary Association, The (Canada), 140
Grace Brethren Churches, Fellowship of, 71
Grace Gospel Fellowship, 72
Greek Orthodox Archdiocese of North and South America, 72
Greek Orthodox Diocese of Toronto, 140
Guide for the User of Church Statistics, ix

Heads of Orthodox Churches, 165
Health League of Canada, The, 244
Hierarchy of the Roman Catholic Church, 165
Higher Education Ministries Team, 9
Holiness Church of God, Inc., The, 73
Holy Ukrainian Autocephalic Orthodox Church in Exile, 73
House of God, Which Is the Church of the Living God, the Pillar and Ground of the Truth, Inc., 73
Hungarian Reformed Church in America, 73
Hutterian Brethren, 73
Hutterian Brethren (Canada), 155

Inclusive Membership 1890-1988, 264
Independent Assemblies of God—Canada, 140
Independent Fundamental Churches of America, 73
Independent Holiness Church (Canada), 140
Inflation, Effects of on Per Capita Giving, 1961-1988, 270
Institute for Christian Studies, 244
Institute of International Education, 241
Institutes of Religion and Health, 241
Inter-Church Committee for Refugees, 245
Interchurch Committee for World Development Education, 245
Inter-Church Committee on Human Rights in Latin America, 245
Inter-Church Communications, 245
Inter-Church Fund for International Development (Canada), 245
Interdenominational International Agencies, 157-73
Interfaith Action for Economic Justice, 9
Interfaith Forum on Religion, Art and Architecture, 241
International Agencies, Confessional Interdenominational Cooperative, 157-73
International Bible Society, 166

303